Checklist of Fuchsias
2002 – 2009

A Compilation of Cultivars
of the Genus Fuchsia

Compiled by Rick Stevens

In conjunction with and published by

Published in 2011 by
The British Fuchsia Society
P.O. Box 8177
Reading
RG6 9PH
and
Rick Stevens

ISBN 978-0-901774-63-7

email rick@findthatfuchsia.info

CONTENTS:

A Ma Fille. Upright. Single. COROLLA: Half flared; opens & matures dark reddish purple (59A); 10mm (3/8") long x 16mm (5/8") wide. SEPALS: half up, tips reflexed up; rose (61D) upper surface; light rose (58D) lower surface; 26mm (1") long x 7mm (1/4") wide. TUBE: rose (61D); medium length & thickness; 17mm (5/8") long x 7mm (1/4") wide. FOLIAGE is dark green (137A) upper surface; medium green (137C) lower surface. PARENTAGE: 'Roesse Lupus' x 'Lye's Unique'. Decoster 2007 BE AFS6624.

A Team. Upright. Single. COROLLA opens purple, matures slightly lighter; corolla is half flared. SEPALS pale pink on the upper surface, pink on lower surface; sepals are half up with recurved tips. TUBE pink. PARENTAGE Crosby Soroptimist x Unknown Seedling. Proven to be hardy in Merseyside, for 3 years. Norcross 2008 UK BFS0062.

A Tout Jamais. Upright/Trailer. Single. COROLLA: Three quarter flared; opens dark reddish purple (70A); matures magenta (71C); 18mm (11/16") long x 19mm (3/4") wide. SEPALS: fully up, tips recurved; dark rose (58C) upper surface; light rose (63D) lower surface; 21mm (13/16") long x 7mm (1/4") wide. TUBE: dark rose (58C); short & thick; 6mm (1/4") long x 6mm (1/4") wide. FOLIAGE is dark green (137A) upper surface; medium green (137C) lower surface. PARENTAGE: 'Dereu Sigrid' x 'Vancuyck Isabeau'. Decoster 2007 BE AFS6622.

Aalters Glorie. Upright. Double. COROLLA: half flared, turned under smooth petal margins; opens dark reddish purple (61A), matures reddish purple (59B); 25mm (1") long x 17mm (11/16") wide. PETALOIDS: same colour as corolla; 15mm (9/16") long x 17mm (11/16") wide. SEPALS: half down; tips recurved; magenta (59C), red (53C) base, upper surface; dark red (53A), red (53C) base, lower surface; 26mm (1") long x 12mm (1/2") wide. TUBE: red (53C); medium length & thickness; 22mm (7/8") long x 9mm (3/8") wide. STAMENS: extend 3mm (1/8") below the corolla; magenta (63A) filaments, purple (71A) anthers. PISTIL extends 11mm (7/16") below the corolla; magenta (67B) style, rose (63C) stigma. BUD: ovate. FOLIAGE: dark green (137A) upper surface, medium green (138B) lower surface. Leaves are 58mm (2 5/16") long x 26mm (1") wide, elliptic shaped, serrulated edges, acute tips and rounded bases. Veins are dark reddish

purple (187D), stems are dark reddish purple (187B), branches dark red (185A). PARENTAGE: 'WALZ Harp' x 'Rohees New Millennium'. Medium upright. Makes good upright. Prefers full sun. Best bloom and foliage colour in bright light. Tested 3 years in Itegem, Belgium. NBFK certificate at Meise. Distinguished by bloom shape. Geerts L 2003 BE AFS5088.

Aan De Linge. Upright/Trailer. Double. COROLLA is three quarter flared with turned under wavy petal margins; opens white (155B), purple (82B) base; matures white (155B), dark purple (78A) base; 34mm (1 5&Mac218;16") long x 31mm (1 1&Mac218;4") wide. PETALOIDS: Same colour as corolla; 14mm (9&Mac218;16") long x 11mm (7&Mac218;16") wide. SEPALS are horizontal, tips recurved; white (155B), light green (145D) base, tipped yellowish green (145A) upper surface; pale pink (56C), white (155B) base, tipped yellowish green (145A) lower surface; 49mm (1 15&Mac218;16") long x 18mm (11&Mac218;16") wide. TUBE is light green (145D); medium length & thickness; 19mm (3&Mac218;4") long x 8mm (5&Mac218;16") wide. FOLIAGE: dark green (137A) upper surface; medium green (138B) lower surface. Leaves are 57mm (2 1&Mac218;4") long x 46mm (1 13&Mac218;16") wide, cordate shaped. PARENTAGE: 'Snow Burner' x 'Tilla Dohmen'. Meis 3-7-04. Distinguished by very large flowers. Ector 2005 BE AFS5665.

Aarschotse Parel. Upright/Trailer. Single. COROLLA is quarter flared with turned under smooth petal margins; opens light purple (78B), matures dark purple (78A); 19mm (3/4") long x 14mm (9/16") wide. SEPALS are horizontal, tips recurved; rose (55B) upper surface, dark rose (54B) lower surface; 33mm (1 5/16") long x 10mm (3/8") wide. TUBE is light pink (65B), medium length and thickness; 14mm (9/16") long x 5mm (3/16") wide. STAMENS extend 7mm (1/4") beyond the corolla; reddish purple (61B) filaments, magenta (71C) anthers. PISTIL extends 10mm (3/8") below the corolla; rose (68C) style, pale yellow (18D) stigma. BUD is ovate. FOLIAGE is dark green (136A) upper surface, medium green (139C) lower surface. Leaves are 47mm (1 7/8") long x 25mm (1") wide, ovate shaped, serrulated edges, acute tips and rounded bases. Veins are plum (183B), stems are yellowish green (144B), branches are light green (143C). PARENTAGE: "Found" seedling. Lax upright

1

or stiff trailer. Self branching. Makes good upright. Prefers full sun. Best bloom and foliage colour in bright light. Tested three years in Rillaar, Belgium. Certificate N.B.F.K. at Meise. Distinguished by stalked petals when mature.
Willems 2002 BE AFS4890.

Aart. Upright. Single. COROLLA: quarter flared; opens purple (77A); matures magenta (71C); 17mm (5/8") long x 23mm (7/8") wide. SEPALS: half up, tips recurved up; pale yellow (8D) upper surface; light pink (65C) lower surface; 24mm (15/16") long x 10mm (3/8") wide. TUBE: light yellow (10D); 14mm (9/16") long x 6mm (1/4") wide. FOLIAGE is dark green (147A) upper surface; yellowish green (146B) lower surface. PARENTAGE: seedling of 'Wormerveer' x 'Minirose'.
Krom 2008 NL AFS6941.

Aart Verschoor. Upright/Trailer. Double. COROLLA is three quarter flared with smooth petal margins; opens purple (83A); matures purple (77A); 22mm (7/8") long x 23mm (15/16") wide. SEPALS are horizontal, tips recurved; dark reddish purple (60A) upper and lower surfaces; 27mm (1 1/16") long x 16mm (5/8") wide. TUBE is dark reddish purple (60A); medium length and thickness; 10mm (3/8") long x 7mm (1/4") thick. STAMENS extend 17mm (11/16") beyond the corolla; reddish purple (59B) filaments, dark reddish purple (59A) anthers. PISTIL extends 29mm (1 1/8") beyond the corolla; magenta (58B) style, dark reddish purple (60C) stigma. BUD is ovate, pointed. FOLIAGE is dark green (137A) upper surface, medium green (138A) lower surface. Leaves are 64mm (2 1/2") long x 37mm (1 7/16") wide, ovate shaped, serrated edges, acute tips and obtuse bases. Veins, stems and branches are green. PARENTAGE: 'Rohees Mintaka' x 'Gilian Althea'. Lax upright or stiff trailer. Makes good stiff trailer. Prefers overhead filtered light and cool climate. Best bloom colour in filtered light. Tested four years in Duizel, The Netherlands. Distinguished by bloom colour.
Tamerus 2002 NL AFS4982.

Achilles Tops. Trailer. Double. COROLLA is half flared with turned under smooth petal margins; opens dark purple (79B), dark reddish purple (64A) base; matures dark reddish purple (59A); 21mm (13/16") long x 18mm (11/16") wide. PETALOIDS: Same colour as corolla; 13mm (1/2") long x 18mm (11/16") wide. SEPALS are half down, tips recurved; dark reddish purple (61A) tipped

medium green (139C) upper surface; magenta (63A) tipped medium green (139C) lower surface; 35mm (1 3/8") long x 12mm (1/2") wide. TUBE is reddish purple (58A); medium length & thickness; 19mm (3/4") long x 5mm (3/16") wide. FOLIAGE: dark green (136B) upper surface; medium green (138B) lower surface. Leaves are 86mm (3 3/8") long x 46mm (1 13/16") wide, ovate shaped. PARENTAGE: 'Roesse Blacky' x 'Erika Frohman'. Meise 8-14-04. Distinguished by flower colour combination.
Michiels 2005 BE AFS5736.

Ad Van Heijst. Upright/Trailer. Double. COROLLA is three quarter flared with smooth petal margins; opens dark reddish purple (72A), matures magenta (71C); 19mm (3/4") long x 20mm (13/16") wide. SEPALS are half up, tips reflexed up; pink (62A) upper surface; dark rose (64C) lower surface; 26mm (1") long x 17mm (11/16") wide. TUBE is pale yellow (2D); medium length and thin; 21mm (13/16") long x 5mm (3/16") thick. STAMENS extend 14mm (9/16") beyond the corolla; light reddish purple (72C) filaments and anthers. PISTIL extends 22mm (7/8") beyond the corolla; light rose (73C) style, light yellow (2C) stigma. BUD is globular, pointed. FOLIAGE is dark green (139A) upper surface, medium green (138A) lower surface. Leaves are 70mm (2 3/4") long x 43mm (1 11/16") wide, cordate shaped, serrulated edges, acute tips and obtuse bases. Veins are green, stems and branches are red. PARENTAGE: [('Bon Accord' x 'Bicentennial') x ('Vobeglo' x 'Dancing Flame') x 'Rohees Alrami'] x ('Annabel' x 'Annabel'). Lax upright or stiff trailer. Makes good stiff trailer. Prefers overhead filtered light and cool climate. Best bloom colour in filtered light. Tested four years in Duizel, The Netherlands. Distinguished by bloom and foliage combination.
Tamerus 2002 NL AFS4999.

Adalbert Bogner. Upright/Trailer. Double. COROLLA: Fully flared; opens dark purple (79B) spotted dark reddish purple (72A); matures dark reddish purple (61A); 40mm (1 9/16") long x 65mm (2 9/16") wide. SEPALS: horizontal, tips recurved; dark reddish purple (61A) upper & lower surfaces; 44mm (1 3/4") long x 24mm (15/16") wide. TUBE: reddish purple (61B); long medium thickness; 30mm (1 3/16") long x 7mm (1/4") wide. FOLIAGE is dark green (137A) upper surface; medium green (137C) lower surface. PARENTAGE: 'Rohees King' x 'Southgate'.

Burkhart 2007 BE AFS6492.

Adriana Van Heijst. Upright. Double. COROLLA is three quarter flared with smooth petal margins; opens purple (77A), matures dark reddish purple (64A); 18mm (11/16") long x 18mm (11/16") wide. SEPALS are half up, tips recurved up; light pink (62B) upper surface; dark rose (67C) lower surface; 27mm (1 1/16") long x 12mm (1/2") wide. TUBE is light pink (62B); medium length and thickness; 10mm (3/8") long x 7mm (1/4") thick. STAMENS extend 12mm (1/2") beyond the corolla; magenta (63B) filaments and anthers. PISTIL extends 24mm (15/16") beyond the corolla; magenta (63B) style, light yellow (3C) stigma. BUD is globular, pointed. FOLIAGE is dark green (137A) upper surface, medium green (138B) lower surface. Leaves are 70mm (2 3/4") long x 37mm (1 7/16") wide, ovate shaped, serrated edges, acute tips and obtuse bases. Veins, stems and branches are green. PARENTAGE: [('Bon Accord' x 'Bicentennial') x ('Vobeglo' x 'Dancing Flame') x 'Rohees Alrami'] x ('Annabel' x 'Annabel'). Small upright. Makes good standard. Prefers overhead filtered light and cool climate. Best bloom colour in filtered light. Tested four years in Duizel, The Netherlands. Distinguished by bloom colour. Tamerus 2002 NL AFS5000.

Adrienne. Trailer. Double. COROLLA is three quarter flared with smooth petal margins; opens purple (88B) and matures purple (82B); 32mm (1 1/4") long x 51mm (2") wide. PETALOIDS are same colour as corolla, flecked rose at base; 19mm (3/4") long x 12mm (1/2") wide. SEPALS are horizontal, tips recurved; magenta (58B) tipped green upper surface and magenta (58B) lower surface; 44mm (1 3/4) long x 19mm (3/4") wide. TUBE is magenta (58B), medium length and thickness; 15mm (5/8") long x 7mm (1/4") wide. STAMENS extend 2mm (1/16") below the corolla; rose (68B) filaments and orangish brown (174A) anthers. PISTIL extends 25mm (1") below the corolla; rose (68B) style and cream (158C) stigma. BUD is lantern shaped, pointed. FOLIAGE is medium green (137B) upper surface and medium green (137C) lower surface. Leaves are 44mm (1 3/4") long x 25mm (1") wide, elliptic shaped, serrulated edges, acute tips and rounded bases. Veins are rose, stems are green shaded rose and branches are brown. PARENTAGE: 'Lancashire Lad' x 'Fancy Free'. Natural trailer. Self branching. Makes good basket.

Prefers overhead filtered light. Best bloom colour in filtered light. Tested four years in Ormskirk, Lancashire, England. Distinguished by earliness and quantity of flowers. Sinton 2002 UK AFS4825.

Aferdita Ajasllari. Upright. Single. COROLLA: half flared, cup shaped, turned under petal margins; opens red (46C) edged red (53B); matures red (53B); 22mm (7/8") long 24mm (15/16") wide. SEPALS: horizontal; tips recurved; gloss red (46C) upper & lower surfaces; 35mm (1 3/8") long x 12mm (1/2") wide. TUBE: gloss red (46C); medium length & thickness; pipe shaped; 15mm (9/16") long x 6mm (1/4") wide. STAMENS: extend 12mm (1/2") below corolla; red (50A) filaments; red (53B) anthers. PISTIL: extends 29mm (1 1/8") below the corolla; red (50A) style; grayish yellow (161B) stigma. BUD: long, round. FOLIAGE: dark green (137A) upper surface; medium green (137C) lower surface. Leaves are 95mm (3 3/4") long x 43mm (1 11/16") wide, ovate shaped, smooth edges, acute tips and rounded bases. Reddish brown veins, stems & branches. PARENTAGE: 'Pink Bon Accord' x unknown. Tall upright. Self branching. Makes good upright, standard, pyramid or pillar. Prefers overhead filtered light, warm climate. Best bloom and foliage colour in bright light. Tested 3 years in Leens, The Netherlands. Distinguished by blossom shape similar to Chinese rice cups. van der Made 2004 NL AFS5581.

Agar Minella. Upright. Double. COROLLA: half flared, turned under petal margins; opens dark reddish purple (64A) & reddish purple (70B); matures magenta (61C); 24 mm (15/16") long x 17mm (5/8") wide. PETALOIDS: dark reddish purple (64A); 14mm (9/16") long x 12mm (7/16") wide. SEPALS are horizontal, tips reflexed; light pink (55D), tipped light apple green (145C) upper surface; rose (52C), tipped light apple green (145C) lower surface; 41mm (1 5/8") long x 16mm (5/8") wide. TUBE is pale pink (56A); long & thin; 27mm (1 1/16") long x 6mm (1/4") wide. STAMENS extend 18mm (11/16") beyond the corolla; magenta (58B) filaments; reddish purple (67A) anthers. PISTIL extends 29mm (1 1/8") beyond the corolla; rose (61D) style; yellowish white (4D) stigma. BUD is globular. FOLIAGE is medium green (137B) upper surface; medium green (138B) lower surface. Leaves are 64mm (2 1/2") long x 33mm (1 5/16") wide, ovate shaped, serrulate edges, acute tips, obtuse

3

bases. Veins are yellowish green (145A), stems are light apple green (145B) & branches are light green (138D). PARENTAGE: 'Manfried Kleinau' x 'Berba's Coronation'. Lax upright or stiff trailer; self branching. Makes good basket or upright. Prefers overhead filtered light, cool climate. Best bloom & foliage in filtered light. Tested 3 years in Koningshooikt, Belgium. Waanrode 8/9/08. Distinguished by bloom colour. Michiels 2009 BE AFS7139.

Ahehee. Trailer. Double. COROLLA is three quarter flared with turned under smooth petal margins; opens reddish purple (61B) edged dark reddish purple (70A), dark rose (58C) at base; matures dark reddish purple (64A); 26mm (1") long x 39mm (1 9/16") wide. PETALOIDS: Two per sepal, same colour as corolla; 18mm (11/16") x 12mm (1/2"). SEPALS are half up, tips recurved up; magenta (58B) upper surface, rose (50B) lower surface; 40mm (1 9/16") long x 19mm (3/4") wide. TUBE is magenta (58B), long with medium thickness; 50mm (2") long x 7mm (1/4") wide. STAMENS extend 8mm (5/16") beyond the corolla; light rose (58D) filaments, orangy brown (163B) anthers. PISTIL extends 10mm (3/8") below the corolla; dark rose (58C) style, light yellow (5C) stigma. BUD is ovate. FOLIAGE is dark green (139A) upper surface, medium green (137C) lower surface. Leaves are 104mm (4 1/8") long x 73mm (2 7/8") wide, cordate shaped, serrulated edges, acute tips and cordate bases. Veins, stems and branches are very dark purple (187A). PARENTAGE: 'Justine Heymans' x unknown. Natural trailer. Makes good basket. Prefers overhead filtered light. Best bloom and foliage colour in filtered light. Tested three years in Rummen, Belgium. Certificate N.B.F.K. at Meise. Distinguished by bloom colour and long Tube. Ector 2002 BE AFS4891.

Aimee Hueber. Upright. Single. COROLLA is unflared with smooth petal margins; opens and matures orangy red (39A); 17mm (11/16") long x 11mm (7/16") wide. SEPALS are half down, tips recurved; light orange (39C) tipped yellowish green upper and lower surfaces; 20mm (13/16") long x 6mm (1/4") wide. TUBE is light orange (39C); medium length and thickness; 29mm (1 1/8") long x 6mm (1/4") thick. STAMENS extend 0 to 3mm (1/8") beyond the corolla; pink (48D) filaments, light yellow (4C) anthers. PISTIL extends 16mm (5/8") beyond the corolla; pink (48D) style, light yellow (4C) stigma.

BUD is long, ovate. FOLIAGE is dark green (137A) upper surface, medium green (147B) lower surface. Leaves are 100mm (3 15/16") long x 85mm (3 3/8") wide, ovate shaped, serrated edges, acute tips and rounded bases. Veins and stems are yellowish green, branches are yellowish green and light brown. PARENTAGE: 'Porte Océane' x 'Speciosa'. Small upright. Makes good upright. Prefers overhead filtered light and cool climate. Best bloom colour in filtered light. Tested three years in Pornic, France. Distinguished by bloom colour and blooming in terminal clusters. Masse 2002 FR AFS5007.

Airel Bolero. Trailer. Double. COROLLA: three quarter flared, petticoat shape; opens violet (76B); matures light violet (84C) veined pink; 20mm (3/4") long x 22mm (7/8") wide. SEPALS: fully up, tips recurved; rose (54C) tipped green upper surface; light pink (49C) edged pink (54D) lower surface; 29mm (1 1/8") long x 24mm (15/16") wide. TUBE: very pale orange (19D);19 mm (3/4") long x 7mm (1/4") wide. FOLIAGE is dark green (147A) upper surface; medium green (147B) lower surface. PARENTAGE: 'Corneille' x unknown. Richard L 2008 AFS6837.

Airel Cocktail. Upright/Trailer. Semi Double. COROLLA: three quarter flared, petticoat shape; opens reddish purple (64B) veined rose (55B); matures reddish purple (61B); 28mm (1 1/8") long x 27mm (1 1/16") wide. PETALOIDS: reddish purple (64B); 15mm (9/16") long x 18mm (11/16") wide. SEPALS: horizontal, tips recurved; rose (55B) veined white, tipped green upper surface; pale pink (56D) lower surface; 45mm (1 3/4") long x 14mm (9/16") wide. TUBE: light pink (49C);18 mm (11/16") long x 7mm (1/4") wide. FOLIAGE is dark green (137A) upper surface; medium green (147B) lower surface. PARENTAGE: 'Bicentennial' x unknown. Richard L 2008 AFS6835.

Airel Concerto. Trailer. Semi Double. COROLLA: half flared, petticoat shape; opens dark rose (55A) & purple (89C); matures rose (63C) & purple (83B); 27mm (1 1/16") long x 24mm (1 15/16") wide. PETALOIDS: purple (80A), rose (61D) & light rose (68D); 21mm (13/16") long x 19mm (3/4") wide. SEPALS: half down, tips reflexed; rose (61D) tipped medium green (132C) upper surface; magenta (58B) lower surface; 38mm (1 1/2") long x 19mm (3/4") wide. TUBE: magenta (58B); 15mm (9/16") long x 6mm (1/4") wide.

4

FOLIAGE is dark green (137A) upper surface; medium green (137C) lower surface. PARENTAGE: 'Aveler Land' x unknown. Richards L 2008 AFS6839.

Airel Helico. Trailer. Semi Double. COROLLA: half flared, turned under smooth petal margins, triangle shape; opens pale pink (56D) veined red purple; matures pale pink (56C) veined red purple; 30mm (1 3/16") long x 30mm (1 3/16") wide. PETALOIDS: rose (55B); 21mm (13/16") long x 11mm (7/16") wide. SEPALS: horizontal, tips recurved, twisted at maturity; dark rose (54A) tipped green upper surface; magenta (61C) lower surface; 48mm (1 7/8") long x 13mm (1/2") wide. TUBE: rose (52B); short & thin; 12mm (7/16") long x 7mm (1/4") wide. STAMENS extend 40mm (1 9/16") beyond the corolla; reddish purple (67A) filaments; reddish purple (58A) anthers. PISTIL extends 68mm (2 11/16") beyond the corolla; dark rose (67C) style; pale yellow (1D) stigma. BUD: ovate. FOLIAGE: medium green (137B) upper surface; yellowish green (146B) lower surface. Leaves are 68mm (2 11/16") long x 33mm (1 5/16") wide; ovate shaped, smooth edges, acute tips, acute bases. Veins & stems are green, branches are red. PARENTAGE: 'Lucinda' x unknown. Natural trailer. Self branching. Makes good basket. Prefers overhead filtered light. Heat tolerant if shaded. Cold weather hardy to 1° C (34° F). Best bloom & foliage colour in filtered light. Tested 7 years in Aywaille, Belgium. Distinguished by long Tube & Sepals. Leonard R. 2009 BE AFS7242.

Airel Majestic. Upright/Trailer. Single. COROLLA: unflared, square shape; opens dark rose (71D); matures reddish purple (74B); 22mm (7/8") long x 25mm (1") wide. SEPALS: full down, tips reflexed; pink (49A) tipped green upper surface; pale pink (49D) lower surface; 36mm (1 7/16") long x 12mm (7/16") wide. TUBE: light rose (58D) veined pale pink (62D); 26 mm (1") long x 9mm (5/16") wide. FOLIAGE is dark green (147A) upper surface; olive green (148A) lower surface. PARENTAGE: 'WALZ Fagot' x unknown. Richard L. 2008 AFS6836.

Airel Medusine. Upright/Trailer. Single. COROLLA: three quarter flared, turned under smooth petal margins, petticoat shape; opens violet (83B); matures violet (87A), pink base; 15mm (9/16") long x 15mm (9/16") wide. PETALOIDS: Same colour as corolla; 5mm (3/16") long x 7mm (1/4") wide.

SEPALS: fully up, tips recurved; light magenta (57D) upper surface; dark rose (58C) lower surface; 24mm (15/16") long x 9mm (5/16") wide. TUBE: magenta (58B); short & thin; 12mm (7/16") long x 5mm (3/16") wide. STAMENS extend 42mm (1 5/8") beyond the corolla; light reddish purple (66C) filaments; dark reddish purple (72A) anthers. PISTIL extends 62mm (2 7/16") beyond the corolla; magenta (67B) style; light reddish purple (66C) stigma. BUD: ovate. FOLIAGE: dark green (137A) upper surface; medium green (147B) lower surface. Leaves are 49mm (1 15/16") long x 25mm (1") wide; lanceolate shaped, serrulate edges, acute tips, acute bases. Veins are green, stems & branches are red. PARENTAGE: 'Shelley Lynn' x unknown. Lax upright or stiff trailer. Self branching. Makes good basket. Prefers overhead filtered light. Heat tolerant if shaded. Cold weather hardy to 2° C (36° F). Best bloom & foliage colour in filtered light. Tested 6 years in Aywaille, Belgium. Distinguished by flower colour combination and long flowering period. Leonard R. 2009 BE AFS7241.

Airel Melodie. Trailer. Single. COROLLA is unflared, square shaped; opens dark rose (71D); matures reddish purple (70B); 16mm (5/8") long x 15mm (9/16") wide. SEPALS are full down, tips reflexed; pink (43D) tipped yellowish green (145A) upper surface; pink (52D) lower surface; 22mm (7/8") long x 8mm (5/16") wide. TUBE is very pale orange (159B); 41mm (1 5/8") long x 4mm (1/8") wide. FOLIAGE: dark green (147A) upper surface; medium green (147B) lower surface. PARENTAGE: 'WALZ Fagot' x unknown. Distinguished by early flowering, ornamental appearance & bloom colour. Leonard R. 2006 BE AFS6059.

Airel Opaline. Upright/Trailer. Semi Double. COROLLA: half flared, petticoat shape; opens dark rose (55A) & dark violet (87A); matures dark rose (55A) & dark purple (78A); 29mm (1 1/8") long x 32mm (1 1/4") wide. PETALOIDS: dark rose (58C) veined violet (75A); 21mm (13/16") long x 12mm (7/16") wide. SEPALS: horizontal, tips recurved; dark rose (55A) tipped green upper surface; dark rose (55A) veined rose (55B) lower surface; 36mm (1 7/16") long x 17mm (5/8") wide. TUBE: rose (52C); 18 mm (11/16") long x 6mm (5/16") wide. FOLIAGE is dark green (137A) upper surface; medium green (138A) lower surface. PARENTAGE: 'Corneille' x unknown. Richard L. 2008 AFS6838.

5

Airel Prelude. Upright. Double. COROLLA is three quarter flared, petticoat shaped; opens light pink (62B) & pale lavender (69B); matures light rose (68D) & pale purple (75D); 30mm (1 3/16") long x 27mm (1 1/16") wide. PETALOIDS: pale pink (62D); 25mm (1") long x 11mm (7/16") wide. SEPALS are half up, tips recurved up; pale pink (62D) tipped light green (145D) upper surface; pale lavender (65D) lower surface; 35mm (1 3/8") long x 16mm (5/8") wide. TUBE is pale yellow (158B); 10mm (3/8") long x 7mm (1/4") wide. FOLIAGE: dark green (137A) upper surface; medium green (137C) lower surface. PARENTAGE: 'Corneille' x unknown. Distinguished by bloom colour combination & profuse blooms.
Leonard R. 2006 BE AFS6056.

Airel Rapsodie. Upright/Trailer. Double. COROLLA is fully flared, petticoat shaped; opens light purple (86C); matures dark violet (87A); 34mm (1 3/8") long x 29mm (1 1/8") wide. PETALOIDS: violet (83D); 17mm (5/8") long x 14mm (9/16") wide. SEPALS are fully up, tips recurved; magenta (58B) upper surface; rose (52B) lower surface; 35mm (1 3/8") long x 14mm (9/16") wide. TUBE is magenta (58B); 9mm (5/16") long x 8mm (5/16") wide. FOLIAGE: dark green (137A) upper surface; medium green (137C) lower surface. PARENTAGE: 'Coxeen' x unknown. Distinguished by ornamental appearance & bloom colour.
Leonard R. 2006 BE AFS6058.

Airel Sonate. Upright. Semi Double. COROLLA is three quarter flared, petticoat shaped; opens violet (85B); matures violet (85A); 26mm (1") long x 25mm (1") wide. PETALOIDS: violet (85A), pink (55C) base; 18mm (11/16") long x 10mm (3/8") wide. SEPALS are horizontal, tips recurved; pink (55C) tipped light apple green (145C) upper surface; rose (54C) lower surface; 39mm (1 1/2") long x 17mm (5/8") wide. TUBE is light pink (49C); 15mm (9/16") long x 8mm (5/16") wide. FOLIAGE: dark green (147A) upper surface; medium green (137C) lower surface. PARENTAGE: 'Corneille' x unknown. Distinguished by bloom colour.
Leonard R 2006 BE AFS6061.

Airel Symphonie. Upright. Single. COROLLA is quarter flared, square shaped; opens reddish purple (67A); matures red (53D); 16mm (5/8") long x 12mm (1/2") wide. SEPALS are horizontal, tips recurved; light orange (41C) tipped light green (143B) upper surface; coral (39B) tipped light green (143B)

lower surface; 29mm (1 1/8") long x 10mm (3/8") wide. TUBE is rose (48B) veined dark rose (48A); 51mm (2") long x 9mm (5/16") wide. FOLIAGE: dark green (137A) upper surface; medium green (138B) lower surface. PARENTAGE: 'WALZ Fagot' x unknown. Distinguished by bloom colour combination.
Leonard R. 2006 BE AFS6062.

Airelle. Upright/Trailer. Single. COROLLA is unflared, square shaped; opens red (45B); matures red (45C); 14mm (9/16") long x 15mm (9/16") wide. SEPALS are half down, tips recurved; red (52A) tipped green upper surface; orange (41B) lower surface; 18mm (11/16") long x 9mm (5/16") wide. TUBE is pink (52D); 28mm (1 1/8") long x 8mm (5/16") wide. FOLIAGE: dark green (137A) upper surface; medium green (137C) lower surface. PARENTAGE: 'WALZ Fagot' x unknown. Distinguished by bloom colour combination.
Leonard R. 2006 BE AFS6055.

Albertien Kremer. Upright. Single. COROLLA is unflared, erect; opens & matures light purple (74C), light rose (73C) base; 12mm (7/16") long x 8mm (5/16") wide. SEPALS are horizontal, tips recurved; light rose (73C) tipped green upper surface; light rose (73B) lower surface; 24mm (15/16") long x 6mm (1/4") wide. TUBE is pale tan (159A) striped light rose (73C); 12mm (1/2") long x 6mm (1/4") wide. FOLIAGE: dark green (137A) upper surface; medium green (139B) lower surface. PARENTAGE: 'Andrew Hadfield' x 'Prince Syray'. Distinguished by flower colour & erect growth in racemes along branches.
Koerts T. 2006 NL AFS6288.

Albertus Lokhorst. Upright. Single. COROLLA is half flared with smooth petal margins; opens & matures violet (80C), pale pink (56C) at base, edged reddish purple (80B); 14mm (9/16") long x 18mm (11/16") wide. SEPALS are fully up, tips recurved; pale pink (56C), blushed rose (52B), tipped green upper surface; rose (52B) tipped green lower surface; 24mm (15/16") long x 8mm (5/16") wide. TUBE is orange (179B); short & thick; 3mm (1/8") long x 3mm (1/8") wide. FOLIAGE: dark green (137A) upper surface; medium green (138B) lower surface. Leaves are 52mm (2 1/16") long x 32mm (1 1/4") wide, cordate shaped. PARENTAGE: 'Gerharda's Panache' x 'Wendy Van Wanten'. Distinguished by colour; clusters of erect flowers.
Koerts T. 2005 NL AFS5779.

6

Albert-Wiske. Upright. Semi Double. COROLLA is quarter flared with turned under wavy petal margins; opens magenta (63B), light rose (58D) base; matures rose (63C); 17mm (11/16") long x 14mm (9/16") wide. SEPALS are half down, tips recurved; magenta (58B) upper surface; dark rose (58C) lower surface; 28mm (1 1/8") long x 8mm (5/16") wide. TUBE is dark rose (55A); long, medium thickness; 26mm (1") long x 6mm (1/4") wide. FOLIAGE: medium green (139C) upper surface; medium green (138B) lower surface. Leaves are 78mm (3 1/16") long x 47mm (1 7/8") wide, ovate shaped. PARENTAGE: 'Triphylla Hybrid' x 'Annabel'. Meise 9-18-04. Distinguished by flower colour.
van den Bussche 2005 BE AFS5858.

Alderford. Single. SEPALS white with green tips. COROLLA blue.
Clitheroe 2002 UK.

Alexandr Balyasnikov. Upright. Double. COROLLA: full flared, turned under petal margins; opens purple (77A) striped reddish purple (71B); matures dark reddish purple (70A) & dark reddish purple (72A); 28 mm (1 1/8") long x 22mm (7/8") wide. PETALOIDS: purple (77A); 21mm (13/16") long x 8mm (5/16") wide. SEPALS are half up, tips recurved up, twisted left to right; magenta (61C) & rose (63C) upper surface; magenta (63B) lower surface; 52mm (2 1/16") long x 17mm (5/8") wide. TUBE is light rose (58D); long & medium thickness; 30mm (1 3/16") long x 6mm (1/4") wide. STAMENS extend 20mm (3/4") beyond the corolla; violet (77B) filaments; purple (77A) anthers. PISTIL extends 35mm (1 3/8") beyond the corolla; reddish purple (72B) style; yellowish white (4D) stigma. BUD is elongated. FOLIAGE is dark green (137A) upper surface; medium green (138B) lower surface. Leaves are 88mm (3 1/2") long x 49mm (1 15/16") wide, ovate shaped, serrate edges, acute tips, rounded bases. Veins are red purple (N186D), stems are plum (185C) & branches are light red purple (185D) & medium green (138B). PARENTAGE: 'Eurofuchsia Denmark 2007' x 'Bert Beekman'. Lax upright or stiff trailer, self branching. Makes good basket or upright. Prefers overhead filtered light, cool climate. Best bloom & foliage in filtered light. Tested 3 years in Koningshooikt, Belgium. Waanrode 7/5/08, Outstanding. Distinguished by unique bloom colour combination.
Michiels 2009 BE AFS7140.

Alfred Fuhrmann. Trailer. Double. COROLLA: three quarter flared; opens white (155C) and light purple (75B); matures violet (76A); 29mm (1 1/8") long x 21mm (13/16") wide. PETALOIDS: pale purple (76C); 12mm (7/16") long x 9mm (5/16") wide. SEPALS are horizontal, tips reflexed; white (155C) & light pink (65C) tipped light yellowish green (150C) upper surface & pale lavender (69C) tipped light yellowish green (150C) lower surface; 54mm (2 1/8") long x 17mm (5/8") wide. TUBE is white (155C) & light apple green (145B); medium length & thickness; 12mm (7/16") long x 6mm (1/4") wide. FOLIAGE is dark green (136A) upper surface; medium green (138B) lower surface. PARENTAGE: 'Vreni Schleeweiss' x 'Futura'.
Michiels 2007 BE AFS6548.

Alice Harper. Upright. Single. COROLLA is half flared with smooth petal margins; opens dark purple (79A); matures dark reddish purple (59A); 9mm (3/8") long x 7mm (1/4") wide. SEPALS are horizontal, tips recurved; yellowish green (144A) upper and lower surfaces; 15mm (9/16") long x 7mm (1/4") wide. TUBE is magenta (59D), medium length and thickness; 23mm (7/8") long x 8mm (5/16") wide. STAMENS extend 3mm (1/8") beyond the corolla; magenta (59C) filaments, very light olive green (153D) anthers. PISTIL extends 7mm (1/4") beyond the corolla; magenta (59C) style; yellowish green (146C) stigma. BUD is constricted near base, pointed. FOLIAGE is medium green (137C) upper surface, medium green (138B) lower surface. Leaves are 50mm (2") long x 28mm (1 1/8") wide, ovate shaped, serrulated edges, acute tips and rounded bases. Veins are pale green, stems are pale magenta, branches are pale green. PARENTAGE: 'F. splendens' x 'F. colensoi'. Small upright. Makes good compact shrub with early pinching. Prefers full sun and cool climate. Best bloom colour in bright light. Tested six years in Coos Bay, Oregon and Eureka, California, USA. Distinguished by blossom colour combination.
Joyce 2002 USA AFS4934.

Alie Oosterveen. Trailer. Double. COROLLA: three quarter flared, smooth petal margins; opens purple (83B); matures reddish purple (71B); 24mm (15/16") long x 20mm (13/16") wide. SEPALS: fully up; tips recurved; light reddish purple (73A) upper surface; dark rose (67C) lower surface; 26mm (1") long x 12mm (1/2") wide. TUBE: dark rose (67C); medium length & thickness; 14mm (9/16")

long x 8mm (5/16") wide. STAMENS: extend 19mm (3/4") below corolla; light reddish purple (72C) filaments; dark reddish purple (72A) anthers. PISTIL: extends 34mm (1 5/16") below the corolla; light reddish purple (72C) style; pale pink (62D) stigma. BUD: cordate. FOLIAGE: medium green (138A) upper surface; medium green (138B) lower surface. Leaves are 63mm (2 1/2") long x 32mm (1 1/4") wide, lanceolate shaped, serrated edges, acute tips and cordate bases. Veins & branches are green, stems are red. PARENTAGE: 'Sofie Michiels' x 'Rohees Mintaka'. Natural trailer. Makes good basket. Prefers overhead filtered light and cool climate. Best bloom and foliage colour in filtered light. Tested 4 years in Duizel, The Netherlands. Distinguished by bloom colour & profuse flowering.
Tamerus 2003 NL AFS5305.

All Aglow. Upright. Single. COROLLA: quarter flared, bell shaped, smooth petal margins; opens purple (82A); matures reddish purple (72B); 25mm (1") long 28mm (1 1/8") wide. SEPALS: half down; tips recurved; light pink (55D), tipped light green (145D), upper surface; rose (55B), tipped light green (145D), lower surface; 40mm (1 9/16") long x 15mm (9/16") wide. TUBE: rose (55B); medium length & thickness; 10mm (3/8") long x 6mm (1/4") wide. STAMENS: extend 18mm (11/16") below corolla; dark rose (67C) filaments; dark reddish purple (70A) anthers. PISTIL: extends 32mm (1 1/4") below the corolla; pink (55C) style; light yellow (18C) stigma. BUD: oval, pointed. FOLIAGE: medium green (137C) upper surface; medium green (137C) lower surface. Leaves are 65mm (2 9/16") long x 33mm (1 5/16") wide, ovate shaped, serrated edges, acute tips and rounded bases. Gray green (195C) veins; dark red (185A) stems; brown (199B) branches. PARENTAGE: 'Richita' x seedling of 'Blue Ice' x 'Norah Henderson'. Medium upright. Makes good standard or bush. Prefers full sun, cool climate. Best bloom and foliage colour in bright light. Tested 3 years in N.E. England. Distinguished by "glow" appearance of blossom colours.
Hall 2004 UK AFS5580.

Allen Jackson. SEPALS pink, underside orange.
Evans 2007 UK.

Alysha. Upright. Double. COROLLA: half flared, turned under smooth petal margins; opens violet (85B); matures violet (75A);

21mm (13/16") long, 25mm (1") wide. PETALOIDS: purple (82B); 12mm (1/2") long x 11mm (7/16") wide. SEPALS: horizontal; tips reflexed; white (155B), striped light pink (49C), tipped light yellowish green (150C) upper surface; white (155D), tipped light yellowish green (150C) lower surface; 26mm (1") long x 14mm (9/16") wide. TUBE: light pink (49C); short, thick; 9mm (3/8") long x 6mm (1/4") wide. STAMENS: extend 8mm (5/16") below corolla; magenta (68A) filaments; reddish purple (71B) anthers. PISTIL: extends 22mm (7/8") below the corolla; pale rose (73D) style; pale yellow (1D) stigma. BUD: bulbous. FOLIAGE: medium green (139B) upper surface; medium green (139C) lower surface. Leaves are 35mm (1 3/8") long x 19mm (3/4") wide, ovate shaped, serrulated edges, acute tips and rounded bases. Pale purple (186D) veins; light red purple (185D) stems; plum (185C) branches. PARENTAGE: 'La Campanella' x unknown. Tall upright. Makes good upright or standard. Prefers overhead filtered light. Best bloom and foliage colour in bright light. Tested 3 years in Lommel, Belgium. Award, Meise, 9/20/03. Distinguished by bloom colour.
Jansen 2004 BE AFS5614.

Amanda Storey. Upright. Single. COROLLA: unflared, bell shaped; smooth petal margins; opens purple (81A); matures purple (80A); 7mm (1/4") long x 7mm (1/4") wide. SEPALS: half down, tips reflexed; red (46C) upper surface; red (46C) lower surface; 11mm (7/16") long x 3mm (1/8") wide. TUBE: red (46B); short, medium thickness; 2mm (1/16") long x 2mm (1") wide. STAMENS extend 5mm (3/16") beyond the corolla; orangy red (44B) filaments; red (46B) anthers. PISTIL extends 7mm (1/4") beyond the corolla; orangy red (44B) style; red (46B) stigma. BUD is round, oblong. FOLIAGE is dark green (137A) upper surface; medium green (137C) lower surface. Leaves are 22mm (7/8") long x 10mm (3/8") wide; cordate shaped, smooth edges, acute tips, obtuse bases. Veins, stems & branches are green. PARENTAGE: ('Estelle Marie' x 'Pink Fantasia') x F. *lyciodes*. Small upright. Self branching. Makes good upright, miniature or bonsai. Prefers full sun. Cold weather hardy to -3°C (26° F). Best bloom & foliage colour in bright light. Tested 9 years in East Yorkshire, England. Distinguished by small flowers held horizontal to erect.
Storey 2009 UK AFS7011.

8

Amaranth. Upright. Single. COROLLA is half flared, bell shaped, with turned up petal margins; opens & matures orange (31B); 7mm (1/4") long x 4mm (3/16") wide. SEPALS are horizontal, tips reflexed; reddish orange (43C) upper surface; light grayish yellow (160C) lower surface; 10mm (3/8") long x 3mm (1/8") wide. TUBE is reddish orange (43B); medium length & thickness; 16mm (5/8") long x 3mm (1/8") wide. FOLIAGE: dark green (147A) upper surface; medium green (146A) lower surface. Leaves are 65mm (2 9/16") long x 34mm (1 5/16") wide, ovate shaped. PARENTAGE: [('F. michoacanensis' x 'F. obconica') x 'Ashley'] x 'F. splendens'. Nomination by N.K.V.F. as recommendable cultivar. Distinguished by small, bright, free hanging flowers. Dijkstra 2005 NL AFS5787.

Amata. Upright. Single. COROLLA: three quarter flared, saucer shape; opens light purple (75B); matures violet (75A); 14mm (9/16") long x 10mm (3/8") wide. SEPALS: horizontal, tips reflexed; reddish purple (61B) tipped olive green (152A) upper surface; magenta (67B) lower surface; 10mm (3/8") long x 5mm (3/16") wide. TUBE: reddish purple (61B); 22mm (7/8") long x 52mm (2 1/16") wide. FOLIAGE is dark green (147A) upper surface; medium green (147B) lower surface. PARENTAGE: 'F. *paniculata*' (tetraploid) x 'Gerhard's Panache'. Nomination by NKVF as Recommendable Cultivar. Dijkstra 2008 NL AFS6801.

Amazing Grace 2006. Upright. Double. COROLLA: three quarter flared, smooth petal margins; opens dark purple (N79B) blushed reddish purple (61B); matures purple (N79C); 22mm (7/8") long x 40mm (1 9/16") wide. SEPALS: fully up, tips recurved; red (53B) upper & lower surfaces; 33mm (1 5/16") long x 13mm (1/2") wide. TUBE: red (53B); medium length & thickness; 20mm (3/4") long x 6mm (1/4") wide. STAMENS extend 11mm (7/16") beyond the corolla; reddish purple (N66A) filaments; reddish purple (N79C) anthers. PISTIL extends 32mm (1 1/4") beyond the corolla; reddish purple (N66A) style; rose (67A) stigma. BUD: elongated. FOLIAGE: dark green (137B) upper surface; medium green (138B) lower surface. Leaves are 105mm (4 3/16") long x 58mm (2 5/16") wide; elliptic shaped, serrate edges, acute tips, rounded bases. Veins & stems are red, branches are brown. PARENTAGE: 'König Manasse' x 'Mantilla'. Medium upright. Self branching. Makes good basket or upright. Prefers full sun, warm climate. Heat tolerant if shaded. Best bloom & foliage colour in bright light. Tested 4 years in Bavaria, Southern Germany. Distinguished by bloom colour combination. Burkhart 2009 DE AFS7101.

Amita. Upright/Trailer. Single. COROLLA: quarter flared; smooth petal margins; opens orange (30B); matures dark orange (41A); 7mm (1/4") long x 5mm (3/16") wide. SEPALS: half down, tips reflexed; orange (33C) tipped red (46A) upper surface; orange (33C) edged & tipped red (46A) lower surface; 16mm (5/8") long x 8mm (5/16") wide. TUBE: orange (33C) striped & blushed reddish orange (42A); short & thick; 25mm (1") long x 9mm (5/16") wide. STAMENS extend 2mm (1/16") beyond the corolla; light pink (36B) filaments; light yellowish orange (19C) anthers. PISTIL extends 7mm (1/4") beyond the corolla; coral (37A) style; pink (36A) stigma. BUD: pegtop shape. FOLIAGE: dark green (147A) upper surface; medium green (138B) lower surface. Leaves are 65mm (2 9/16") long x 44mm (1 3/4") wide; cordate shaped, serrulate edges, acute tips, acute bases. Veins & stems are light green, branches are medium green (147B). PARENTAGE: 'Thalia' (Turner) x 'Happy Reneé'. Lax upright or stiff trailer. Self branching. Makes good basket or upright. Prefers full sun. Best bloom & foliage colour in bright light. Tested 3 years in Stadskanaal, The Netherlands. Distinguished by flower shape & colour. Koerts T 2009 NL AFS7046.

Amy. Single. COROLLA lilac edged deep rose. SEPALS white flushed pink. Parkes 2004 UK.

Amy Jade Whitehouse. Trailer. Single. COROLLA opens magenta; corolla is quarter flared and is 20mm long x 15mm wide. SEPALS white, lightly flushed pink, tipped green on the upper surface, slightly darker on the lower surface; sepals are half down with recurved tips and are 30mm long x 10mm wide. TUBE white, lightly flushed pink and is 10mm long x 5mm wide. PARENTAGE Anita x Unknown. This cultivar is named after the raisers grand-daughter, makes a very nice standard, which has won several positions in local shows. Asson 2006 UK BFS0026.

Amy Yates. Upright/Trailer. Double. COROLLA is three quarter flared with turned up petal margins; opens purple (71A)

9

splashed peach (33D), matures magenta (71C) splashed pink (36A); 18mm (11/16") long x 41mm (1 5/8") wide. SEPALS are half up, tips recurved up; pale pink (62D) tipped green upper surface, pink (62A) lower surface; 32mm (1 1/4") long x 18mm (11/16") wide. TUBE is white (155A) striped green, medium length and thickness; 14mm (9/16") long x 7mm (1/4") wide. STAMENS extend 16mm (5/8") below the corolla; magenta (63B) filaments, rose (63C) anthers. PISTIL extends 22mm (7/8") below the corolla; light rose (63D) style, light gray (156D) stigma. BUD is ovate. FOLIAGE is dark green (137A) upper surface, medium green (137D) lower surface. Leaves are 54mm (2 1/8") long x 31mm (1 1/4") wide, lanceolate shaped, serrulated edges, acute tips and rounded bases. Veins, stems and branches are green. PARENTAGE: 'Branksome Belle' x 'Ruth Graham'. Lax upright or stiff trailer. Self branching. Makes good basket. Prefers overhead filtered light and cool climate. Best bloom colour in filtered light. Tested three years in Stockbridge, Hampshire, England. Distinguished by blossom colour. Graham 2002 UK AFS4871.

Amy's Imp. Upright. Single. COROLLA: half flared; opens reddish purple (74B); matures reddish purple (74A); 34mm (1 5/16") long x 6mm (1/4") wide. SEPALS: horizontal; tips recurved; pale purple (74D) upper surface; light magenta (57D) lower surface; 3mm(1/8") long x 4mm (3/16") wide. TUBE: reddish purple (74A); long & thin; 6mm (3/8") long x 3mm (1/8") wide. STAMENS: do not extend below corolla; white (155D) filaments & anthers. PISTIL: extends 4mm (3/16") below the corolla, pale lavender (69D) style & stigma. BUD: lanceolate shaped. FOLIAGE: dark green (137A) & bronze upper surface; medium green (137D) lower surface. Leaves are 14mm (9/16") long x 10mm (3/8") wide, ovate shaped, serrated edges, obtuse tips and bases. Veins are dark green & bronze, stems are bronze; branches are light brown. PARENTAGE: found seedling. Small upright. Self branching. Makes good upright, mini-standard or bonsai. Prefers full sun. Heat tolerant if shaded. Cold weather hardy to 30° F. Best bloom colour in bright light. Tested 3 years in Enfield, London, England. Distinguished by bloom shape. Nutt 2003 UK AFS5158.

Andre Eyletten. Trailer. Single. COROLLA is quarter flared with smooth petal margins; opens dark reddish purple (59A); matures purple (71A); 20mm (13/16") long x 24 mm (15/16") wide. SEPALS are horizontal, tips recurved; pale lavender (65D) upper surface; light pink (65B) lower surface; 41mm (1 5/8") long x 15mm (9/16") wide. TUBE is rose (68C), medium length & thickness; 14mm (9/16") long x 6mm (1/4") wide. FOLIAGE: medium green (137B) upper surface; medium green (137D) lower surface. Leaves are 58mm (2 5/16") long x 32mm (1 1/4") wide, ovate shaped. PARENTAGE: 'Orange Blossom' x 'Judy Salome'. Distinguished by bloom colour.
van Bree 2005 NL AFS5645.

André Ramm. Upright. Semi Double. COROLLA: unflared, smooth petal margins; opens dark purple (N79A); matures dark reddish purple (61A); 20mm (3/4") long x 16mm (5/8") wide. SEPALS: horizontal, tips recurved; dark reddish purple (60B) upper surface; reddish purple (59B) lower surface; 38mm (1 1/2") long x 10mm (3/8") wide. TUBE: reddish purple (59B); long, medium thickness; 17mm (5/8") long x 6mm (1/4") wide. STAMENS extend 22mm (7/8") beyond the corolla; purple (N79C) filaments; dark purple (N79B) anthers. PISTIL extends 42mm (1 5/8") beyond the corolla; purple (N79C) style; cream (11D) stigma. BUD: elongated. FOLIAGE: dark green (137A) upper surface; medium green (137C) lower surface. Leaves are 90mm (3 9/16") long x 60mm (2 3/8") wide; ovate shaped, serrulate edges, acute tips, rounded bases. Veins are light green, stems are red, branches are reddish brown. PARENTAGE: 'Delta's Night' x ('Gimli von Moria' x F. *regia* ssp. *serrae* hoya. Small upright. Makes good upright or standard. Prefers full sun, warm climate. Heat tolerant if shaded. Best bloom & foliage colour in filtered light. Tested 4 years in Bavaria, Southern Germany. Distinguished by bloom colour & shape.
Burkhart 2009 DE AFS7104.

Andre Renaerts. Upright. Double. COROLLA: three-quarter flared; opens purple (77A) & matures purple (71A); 20mm (3/4") long x 24mm (15/16") wide. SEPALS are horizontal, tips recurved; rose (65A) upper surface & magenta (68A) lower surface; 30mm (1 3/16") long x 20mm (3/4") wide. TUBE is light pink (65C); 19mm (3/4") long x 10mm (3/8") wide. FOLIAGE is dark green (137A) upper surface & medium green (137C) lower surface. PARENTAGE: 'Deco Inoubliable' x 'Caesar'.
Decoster 2008 BE AFS6873.

Andries Ophof. Upright. Single. COROLLA: Quarter flared, bell shaped; opens light purple (78C), light rose (73C) base; matures light rose (73C); 14mm (9/16") long x 16mm (5/8") wide. SEPALS: half down, tips reflexed; white (158A), light rose (73C) at base, tipped yellowish green (144B) upper surface; light rose (73C) lower surface; 22mm (7/8") long x 8mm (5/16") wide. TUBE: red (45B); short, medium thickness; 7mm (1/4") long x 11mm (7/16") wide. FOLIAGE is dark green (147A) upper surface; yellowish green (146B) lower surface. PARENTAGE: 'Audrey Hatfield' x 'Prince Syray'. Koerts T. 2007 NL AFS6451.

Anelore Van Vaerenbergh. Upright/Trailer. Double. COROLLA: three quarter flared, turned under smooth petal margins; opens dark purple (78A) veined reddish purple (66B); matures purple (80A); 31mm (1 1/4") long x 22mm (7/8") wide. PETALOIDS: two per sepal; dark purple (78A); 19mm (3/4") long x 11mm (7/16") wide. SEPALS: horizontal; tips reflexed; reddish purple (61B) upper surface; magenta (58B) lower surface; 30mm (1 3/16") long x 12mm (1/2") wide. TUBE: dark rose (58C); medium length & thickness; 17mm (11/16") long x 6mm (1/4") wide. STAMENS: extend 16mm (5/8") below the corolla; light reddish purple (66C) filaments, light yellow (11C) anthers. PISTIL extends 30mm (1 3/16") below the corolla; reddish purple (66A) style, light yellow (11B) stigma. BUD: long, ovate, pointed. FOLIAGE: medium green (139B) upper surface; medium green (138B) lower surface. Leaves are 48mm (1 7/8") long x 25mm (1") wide, ovate shaped, serrulated edges, acute tips and rounded bases. Veins are plum (185B), stems are dark red (185A), branches are plum (184B). PARENTAGE: 'Rohees New Millennium' x 'Pinto de Blue'. Lax upright or stiff trailer. Self branching. Makes good basket. Prefers overhead filtered light. Best bloom and foliage colour in filtered light. Tested 3 years in Koningshooikt, Belgium. NBFK certificate at Meise. Distinguished by bloom colour. Michiels 2003 BE AFS5098.

Angela Dawn. Upright. Single. COROLLA opens and matures to white; corolla is quarter flared and is 12mm long x 16mm wide. SEPALS are pale pink, tipped green on the upper and lower surfaces; sepals are horizontally held with recurved tips and are 20mm long x 7mm wide. TUBE pale pink and is 5mm long x 5mm wide. PARENTAGE Barbara Windsor x Katrina Thompsen. This

cultivar is capable of producing an excellent show plant.
Riley 2005 UK BFS0015.

Angela's Wedding. Upright. Double. COROLLA white. SEPALS light pink. Ainsworth 2006 UK.

Angelika Fuhrmann. Upright/Trailer. Double. COROLLA is three quarter flared with turned under wavy petal margins; opens dark purple (79B), reddish purple (71B) base; matures purple (77A), dark reddish purple (60B) base; 24mm (15/16") long x 18mm (11/16") wide. PETALOIDS: purple (77A), reddish purple (61B) base; 14mm (9/16") long x 8mm (3/16") wide. SEPALS are turned left, horizontal, tips recurved; dark reddish purple (64A) upper surface; reddish purple (61B) lower surface; 47mm (1 7/8") long x 15mm (9/16") wide. TUBE is dark reddish purple (60B); medium length & thickness; 13mm (1/2") long x 6mm (1/4") wide. FOLIAGE: dark green (137A) upper surface; medium green (137C) lower surface. Leaves are 71mm (2 13/16") long x 33mm (1 5/16") wide, ovate shaped. PARENTAGE: 'Roesse Blacky' x 'Bella Rosella'. Meise 9-18-04, Outstanding. Distinguished by flower colour. Michiels 2005 BE AFS5845.

Angélique. Upright/Trailer. Single. COROLLA: half flared; toothed margins; opens & matures violet (75A); 15mm (9/16") long x 15mm (9/16") wide. SEPALS: horizontal to half down, tips recurved; light pink (38D) tipped yellowish white upper & lower surfaces; 25mm (1") long x 4mm (1/8") wide. TUBE: light pink (38D); long & thin; 25mm (1") long x 3mm (1/8") wide. STAMENS extend 5mm (3/16") beyond the corolla; light pink (49C) filaments; light tan (161C) anthers. PISTIL extends 19mm (3/4") beyond the corolla; light pink (49B) style; pink (49A) stigma. BUD is ovate. FOLIAGE is yellowish green (146B) upper surface; yellowish green (146C) lower surface. Leaves are 35mm (1 3/8") long x 27mm (1 1/16") wide; ovate shaped, serrulate edges, acute tips, rounded bases. Veins & stems are yellowish green, branches are yellowish green & light brown. PARENTAGE: 'Philippe Boënnec' x 'Celia Smedley'. Lax upright or stiff trailer. Makes good basket or upright. Prefers overhead filtered light & cool climate. Tested 3 years in Pornic, France. Distinguished by bloom form & colour. Masse 2009 FR AFS6985.

Angels Teardrop. Upright. Single. COROLLA opens purple; corolla has no flared and is 14mm long x 7mm wide. SEPALS red on the upper surface, red on the lower surface; sepals are half down with recurved tips and are 32mm long x 7mm wide. TUBE red and is 16mm long x 5mm wide. PARENTAGE found seedling. This cultivar is a free flowering, self branching large upright. Williams S. 2007 UK BFS0050.

Angel's Tears. Upright. Double. COROLLA cerise. SEPALS white. Ainsworth 2006 UK.

Angel's Wings. Upright. Single. COROLLA cerise. SEPALS pink. Ainsworth 2002 UK.

Anita Comperen. Upright. Semi Double. COROLLA: three quarter flared, smooth petal margins; opens purple (71A); matures dark reddish purple (60C); 17mm (11/16") long x 21mm (13/16") wide. SEPALS: half up; tips reflexed up; dark red (46A) upper surface; red (45A) lower surface; 20mm (13/16") long x 10mm (3/8") wide. TUBE: dark red (46A); medium length & thickness; 9mm (3/8") long x 7mm (1/4") wide. STAMENS: extend 15mm (9/16") below corolla; red (45B) filaments; dark red (46A) anthers. PISTIL: extends 32mm (1 1/4") below the corolla; red (45B) style, light rose (63D) stigma. BUD: ovate. FOLIAGE: dark green (137A) upper surface; medium green (138A) lower surface. Leaves are 60mm (2 3/8") long x 42mm (1 5/8") wide, ovate shaped, serrulated edges, acute tips and rounded bases. Veins, stems & branches are green. PARENTAGE: 'Dorothy Oosting' x 'Maxima'. Medium upright. Makes good standard. Prefers overhead filtered light and cool climate. Best bloom and foliage colour in filtered light. Tested 4 years in Diessen, The Netherlands. Distinguished by bloom colour. Comperen 2003 NL AFS5270.

Anja Van Ossel. Upright/Trailer. Double. COROLLA is three quarter flared with turned under smooth petal margins; opens dark purple (79B), light rose (59D) base; matures purple (71A); 20mm (13/16") long x 18mm (11/16") wide. PETALOIDS: same colour as corolla; 14mm (9/16") long x 12mm (1/2") wide. SEPALS are half up, tips recurved up; magenta (59C) upper surface; reddish purple (64B) lower surface; 28mm (1 1/8") long x 12mm (1/2") wide. TUBE is magenta (59C); medium length & thickness; 15mm (9/16") long x 6mm (1/4") wide. FOLIAGE: dark

green (137A) upper surface; medium green (138B) lower surface. Leaves are 71mm (2 13/16") long x 27mm (1 1/16") wide, elliptic shaped. PARENTAGE: 'Roesse Blacky' x 'Breevis Anactus'. Meise 9-18-04. Distinguished by very dark flower colour. Michiels 2005 BE AFS5848.

Ann Paul. Upright. Single. COROLLA: quarter flared, wavy petal margins; opens violet (82C); matures pale purple (80D); 22mm (7/8") long x 22mm (7/8") wide. SEPALS: half up; tips recurved up; light rose (68D) upper surface; rose (68C) lower surface; tipped green; 38mm (1 1/2") long x 8mm (5/16") wide. TUBE: medium green (143A); medium length, thin; 8mm (5/16") long x 3mm (1/8") wide. STAMENS: extend 9-12mm (3/8-1/2") below corolla; white (155A) filaments; brown (200A) anthers. PISTIL: extends 19mm (3/4") below the corolla; white (155A) style; yellowish white (155A) stigma. BUD: ovate, long, chubby. FOLIAGE: medium green (137B) upper surface, medium green (141C) lower surface. Leaves are 44mm (1 3/4") long x 25mm (1") wide, lanceolate shaped, serrulated edges, acute tips and rounded bases. medium green (141C) veins & stems; medium green (143A) branches. PARENTAGE: 'Estelle Marie' x 'Love's Reward'. Small upright. Makes good upright or standard. Prefers overhead filtered light. Cold weather hardy to 45⁰ F. Best bloom and foliage colour in filtered light. Tested 4 years in West Yorkshire, England. Distinguished by colour combination. Preston 2004 UK AFS5442.

Ann T. Upright. Double. COROLLA opens and matures purple with red base and veining; corolla is three quarter flared and is 30mm long x 47mm wide. SEPALS are red on the upper and lower surfaces; sepals are horizontally held with recurved tips and are 40mm long x 15mm wide. TUBE is red and is 22mm long x 8mm wide. PARENTAGE Alice Hoffman x Unknown. This cultivars flower is approximately 15% larger than "Dollar Princess" both in size and number of petals. This plant seems to be hardy and resistant to rust but leaves do turn blue in the cold weather. Metcalf 2004 UK BFS0004.

Ann G. Trailer. Double. COROLLA: three quarter flared, turned under petal margins; opens rose (48B) & rose (68B) & matures pink (48D) & light purple (70C); 24 mm (15/16") long x 17mm (5/8") wide. PETALOIDS: rose (48B) & rose (68B); 17mm

12

(5/8") long x 9mm (5/16") wide. SEPALS are half up, tips recurved up, twisted left to right; pale pink (69A), tipped light yellowish green (150C) upper surface; pink (48C), tipped light yellowish green (150C) lower surface; 34mm (1 3/8") long x 13mm (1/2") wide. TUBE is pale lavender (69D); short & thick; 13mm (1/2") long x 6mm (1/4") wide. STAMENS extend 15mm (9/16") beyond the corolla; dark rose (54B) filaments; dark reddish purple (61A) anthers. PISTIL extends 28mm (1 1/8") beyond the corolla; rose (52C) style; pale yellow (2D) stigma. BUD is globular square. FOLIAGE is medium green (138A) upper surface; light green (139D) lower surface. Leaves are 62mm (2 7/16") long x 41mm (1 5/8") wide, ovate shaped, serrate edges, acute tips, rounded bases. Veins are plum (185B), stems are very dark reddish purple (186A) & branches are plum (184B) & medium green (138B). PARENTAGE: 'Manfried Kleinau' x 'First Lord'. Natural trailer; self branching. Makes good basket. Prefers overhead filtered light, cool climate. Best bloom & foliage in filtered light. Tested 3 years in Koningshooikt, Belgium. Waanrode 8/9/08. Distinguished by unique bloom colour.
Michiels 2009 BE AFS7141.

Anna Eyley. Upright. Double. COROLLA opens deep lavender fading to rose with white at base, matures to rose; corolla is quarter flared. SEPALS are pale cream with pink veining, maturing slightly lighter on the upper and lower surfaces; Sepals are fully up with a slight twist and recurved tips. TUBE cream. PARENTAGE Carmel Blue x Unknown.
Chatfield 2009 UK BFS0102

Anna Louise. Upright. Single. COROLLA light blue. SEPALS white tipped green.
Wilkinson 2004 UK.

Annalisa Perna. Upright. Single. COROLLA: quarter flared, bell shape; opens & matures dark reddish purple (61A); 17mm (5/8") long x 10mm (3/8") wide. SEPALS: full down, tips recurved; magenta (57A) tipped green upper & lower surfaces; 32mm (1 1/4") long x 5mm (3/16") wide. TUBE: magenta (57A); 16mm (5/8") long x 5mm (3/16") wide. FOLIAGE is dark green (147A) upper surface; medium green (146A) lower surface. PARENTAGE: 'Zulu King' x 'Oranje van Os.
Ianne 2008 IT AFS6949.

Anne De Bretagne. Upright. Single. COROLLA: unflared, smooth petal margins;

opens & matures reddish purple (80B), clearer at base; 20mm (13/16") long x 10mm (3/8") wide. SEPALS: half down; tips recurved; pale rose (73D) upper surface; light rose (73B) lower surface; 21mm (13/16") long x 7mm (1/4") wide. TUBE: pale rose (73D); medium length & thickness; 15mm (9/16") long x 3.5mm (1/8") wide. STAMENS: extend 6-9mm (1/4-3/8") below corolla; pink (62C) filaments; plum (184C) anthers. PISTIL: extends 12mm (1/2") below the corolla; pale pink (62D) style; light yellow (4B) stigma. BUD: ovate. FOLIAGE: dark green (147A) upper surface, medium green (147B) lower surface. Leaves are 80mm (3 3/16") long x 26mm (1") wide, ovate shaped, serrulated edges, acute tips and rounded bases. Light yellowish green veins & stems; Light yellowish green & light brown branches. PARENTAGE: 'Prince of Orange' x 'Mantilla'. Medium upright. Makes good upright. Prefers overhead filtered light and cool climate. Best bloom and foliage colour in filtered light. Tested 3 years in Pornic, France. Distinguished by profuse blooming.
Masse 2004 FR AFS5445.

Anne Hoogedam. Trailer. Single. COROLLA: bell shape, half flared, smooth petal margins; opens white (155D), rose (64D) base & veins; matures white (155D); 33 mm (1 5/16") long x 25mm (1") wide. SEPALS are fully up, tips recurved; white (155B) veined red, tipped yellowish green (145A) upper surface; light pink (62B) to white lower surface; 33mm (1 5/16") long x 8mm (5/16") wide. TUBE is light pink (62C); medium length & thin; 26mm (1") long x 7mm (1/4") wide. STAMENS extend 17mm (5/8") beyond the corolla; dark reddish purple (72A) filaments & anthers. PISTIL extends 20mm (3/4") beyond the corolla; light purple (75B) style; light pink (62B) stigma. BUD is ovate. FOLIAGE is medium green (138A) upper surface; medium green (138B) lower surface. Leaves are 65mm (2 9/16") long x 23mm (7/8") wide, lanceolate shaped, serrate edges, acute tips & bases. Veins are medium green, stems & branches are reddish. PARENTAGE: 'de Groot's Prinses' x 'Herjan de Groot'. Natural trailer. Makes good basket. Prefers overhead filtered light. Best bloom & foliage in bright light. Tested 11 years in Elburg, The Netherlands. Distinguished by flower shape and colour.
de Groot 2009 NL AFS6980.

Anne Tamerus. Upright/Trailer. COROLLA is quarter flared with smooth petal margins; opens light pink (62B); matures pale pink

(62D); 17mm (11/16") long x 22mm (7/8") wide. SEPALS are half up, tips reflexed up; light pink (62B) upper and lower surfaces; 24mm (15/16") long x 7mm (1/4") wide. TUBE is rose (63C); short and thick; 6mm (1/4") long x 6mm (1/4") thick. STAMENS extend 7mm (1/4") beyond the corolla; magenta (63B) filaments and anthers. PISTIL extends 15mm (5/8") beyond the corolla; light pink (62B) style, light yellow (4B) stigma. BUD is elliptic, pointed. FOLIAGE is dark green (137A) upper surface, medium green (137C) lower surface. Leaves are 58mm (2 5/16") long x 36mm (1 7/16") wide, ovate shaped, serrated edges, acute tips and rounded bases. Veins, stems and branches are red. PARENTAGE: ('Bon Accord' x 'Vobeglo') x 'Delta's Bride'. Lax upright or stiff trailer. Makes good stiff trailer. Prefers overhead filtered light and cool climate. Best bloom colour in filtered light. Tested four years in Knegsel, The Netherlands. Distinguished by bloom and foliage combination.
Roes 2002 NL AFS5044.

Anneke Janssens. Upright. Double. COROLLA: three quarter flared, turned under petal margins; opens dark purple (79B), blotched reddish purple (61B); matures dark reddish purple (64A), blotched magenta (63A); 29 mm (1 1/8") long x 25mm (1") wide. PETALOIDS: dark purple (79B), blotched reddish purple (61B); 16mm (5/8") long x 11mm (7/16") wide. SEPALS are horizontal, tips recurved, twisted left to right; pale pink (56A), tipped light yellow green (150B) upper surface; magenta (63B), tipped light yellow green (150B) lower surface; 39mm (1 1/2") long x 14mm (9/16") wide. TUBE is light pink (39D); short & medium thickness; 9mm (5/16") long x 5mm (3/16") wide. STAMENS extend 19mm (3/4") beyond the corolla; dark reddish purple (64A) filaments; reddish purple (72B) anthers. PISTIL extends 27mm (1 1/16") beyond the corolla; magenta (71C) style; pale yellow (8D) stigma. BUD is elongated. FOLIAGE is medium green (137B) upper surface; medium green (138B) lower surface. Leaves are 56mm (2 1/4") long x 24mm (15/16") wide, elliptic shaped, serrulate edges, acute tips, rounded bases. Veins are olive green (152D), stems are medium green (138B), dark rose (180D), branches are medium green (138B) & light grayish rose (181D). PARENTAGE: 'Manfried Kleinau' x 'Beauty of Meise'. Lax upright or stiff trailer; self branching. Makes good basket or upright. Prefers overhead filtered light, cool climate. Best bloom & foliage in

filtered light. Tested 3 years in Koningshooikt, Belgium. Waanrode 7/5/08. Distinguished by bloom colour and shape. Michiels 2009 BE AFS7142.

Anneke Saluyts. Trailer. Single. COROLLA is half flared with turned under wavy petal margins; opens light reddish purple (66C), matures magenta (61C); 12mm (1/2") long x 15 mm (5/8") wide. SEPALS are horizontal, tips reflexed; rose (52C) upper surface, rose (52B) lower surface; 26mm (1") long x 15mm (5/8") wide. TUBE is light pink (36C), medium length and thickness; 25mm (1") long x 6mm (1/4") wide. STAMENS do not extend beyond the corolla; light magenta (57D) filaments, magenta (57C) anthers. PISTIL do not extend beyond the corolla; rose (65A) style; pale yellow (8D) stigma. BUD is round, pointed. FOLIAGE is dark green (137A) upper surface, medium green (137C) lower surface. Leaves are 65mm (2 9/16") long x 38mm (1 1/2") wide, ovate shaped, serrated edges, acute tips and rounded bases. Veins are apple green (144C), stems are dark rose (59C), branches are plum (184C). PARENTAGE: 'WALZ Harp' x 'Blue Veil'. Natural trailer. Makes good basket. Prefers overhead filtered light and cool climate. Best bloom and foliage colour in filtered light. Tested three years in Itegem, Belgium. Certificate N.B.F.K. at Meise. Distinguished by profuse blooms and bloom shape.
Geerts L. 2002 BE AFS4922.

Annelies Marcus. Upright. Single. COROLLA is quarter flared, bell shaped; opens violet (75A); matures pale lavender (65D); 14mm (9/16") long x 15mm (9/16") wide. SEPALS are fully up, tips recurved; light pink (65C) upper surface; pale lavender (65D) lower surface; 21mm (13/16") long x 20mm (3/4") wide. TUBE is rose (65A); 12mm (7/16") long x 4mm (1/8") wide. FOLIAGE: dark green (147A) upper surface; gray green (194A) lower surface. PARENTAGE: ('Straat Futami' x 'Straat Futami') x [('F. procumbens' x 'F. paniculata') x ('F. apetala')]. Distinguished by profuse flowering & flower shape.
de Boer J. 2006 NL AFS6277.

Annelin Goris. Trailer. Single. COROLLA: quarter flared; opens purple (71A); matures reddish purple (71B); 15mm (9/16") long x 17mm (5/8") wide. SEPALS are horizontal, tips reflexed; dark reddish purple (60A) upper surface; dark reddish purple (64A) lower surface; 30mm (1 3/16") long x 11mm (7/16") wide. TUBE is dark reddish purple

14

(60C); 25mm (1") long x 5mm (3/16") wide. FOLIAGE is medium green (137B) upper surface; medium green (138B) lower surface. PARENTAGE: 'Walter Rosa' x 'Wilma Versloot'. Geerts L. 2008 BE AFS6727.

Ann-Elisabeth Fuhrmann. Upright/Trailer. Double. COROLLA: 3 quarter flared; opens light purple (N78B) blotched light reddish purple (73A); matures dark rose (71D); 18mm (11/16") long x 14mm (9/16") wide. PETALOIDS: same colour as corolla; 14mm (9/16") long x 8mm (5/16") wide. SEPALS: half down, tips recurved; white (155C) tipped yellowish green (144B) upper surface; pale lavender (69D) tipped yellowish green (144B) lower surface; 32mm (1 1/4") long x 19mm (3/4") wide. TUBE: white (155C) striped medium green (138B); short & thick; 10mm (3/8") long x 8mm (5/16") wide. FOLIAGE is dark green (136A) upper surface; medium green (138A) lower surface. PARENTAGE: 'Vreni Schleeweiss' x 'Kiss'. Michiels 2007 BE AFS6367.

Annemarie. Upright. Single. COROLLA: quarter flared; opens orange (41B) & reddish purple (72B); matures light orange (41C) & reddish purple (58A); 26mm (1") long x 26mm (1") wide. PETALOIDS: light orange (41C) & reddish purple (72B); 17mm (5/8") long x 9mm (5/16") wide. SEPALS: half up, tips recurved up; pink (54D) upper surface; rose (54C) lower surface; 36mm (1 7/16") long x 14mm (9/16") wide. TUBE: light pink (36C); 25mm (1") long x 7mm (1/4") wide. FOLIAGE is medium green (146A) upper surface; yellowish green (146B) lower surface. PARENTAGE: 'Klaas' x unknown. Krom 2008 NL AFS6942.

Anne-Valentine. Upright/Trailer. Single. COROLLA: quarter flared; turned up petal margins; opens white (155A), rose veins & base; matures white (155B) , rose veins & base; 35mm (1 3/8") long x 32mm (1 1/4") wide. SEPALS: horizontal, tips recurved; magenta (68A) striped white upper surface; rose (68B), white base lower surface; 57mm (2 1/4") long x 15mm (9/16") wide. TUBE: magenta (68A); medium length & thickness; 18mm (11/16") long x 7mm (1/4") wide. STAMENS extend 15mm (9/16") beyond the corolla; magenta (68A) filaments; dark reddish purple (64A) anthers. PISTIL extends 35mm (1 3/8") beyond the corolla; white (155B) style; light rose (73C) stigma. BUD: long. FOLIAGE: dark green (137A) upper surface; medium green (139C) lower surface.

Leaves are 68mm (2 11/16") long x 40mm (1 9/16") wide; ovate shaped, serrate edges, acute tips, acute bases. Veins are light green, stems are dark red, branches are red. PARENTAGE: ('Nouvelle Republique' x 'Annabel') x 'Nellie Nuttall'. Lax upright or stiff trailer. Makes good basket. Prefers overhead filtered light, cool climate. Cold weather hardy to -3° C (27° F). Best bloom colour in filtered light. Best foliage colour in bright light. Tested 4 years in Central France. Distinguished by contrast of flowers with foliage & fluorescent appearing flower colours. Gaucher 2009 FR AFS7055.

Annie Geurts. Upright/Trailer. Single. COROLLA: Fully flared; one split petal divided with stems; opens & matures purple (83B); 10mm (3/8") long x 10mm (3/8") wide. SEPALS are half up, tips recurved up; dark rose (54B) upper surface, and rose (52B) lower surface; 38mm (1 1/2") long x 9mm (5/16") wide. TUBE is rose (54C); medium length and thickness; 27mm (1 1/16") long x 4mm (1/8") wide. FOLIAGE is medium green (146A) upper surface; yellowish green (146B) lower surface. PARENTAGE: [(Carlotta Fiore' x 'F. brevilobis') x 'Miss California'] x 'F. brevilobis'. Nomination by NKVF as Recommendable Cultivar. Geurts 2007 NL AFS6428.

Annie M G Schmidt. Trailer. Single. COROLLA: quarter flared; opens pale purple (75D) & magenta (57A); matures pale purple (75D); 23mm (7/8") long x 15mm (9/16") wide. SEPALS: horizontal, tips recurved; magenta (57A) upper & lower surfaces; 34mm (1 3/8") long x 8mm (5/16") wide. TUBE: magenta (57A); 15mm (9/16") long x 6mm (1/4") wide. FOLIAGE is dark green (147A) upper surface; medium green (147B) lower surface. PARENTAGE: 'Insa' x unknown. AWARDS: VKC Aalsmeer 17 Aug, 1996; Floriade Keurings 25 July, 2002. Krom 2008 NL AFS6943.

Annik Dewispelaere. Trailer. Double. COROLLA: three quarter flared, turned under petal margins; opens dark rose (71D); matures magenta (63B); 25 mm (1") long x 23mm (7/8") wide. PETALOIDS: light purple (70C) & reddish purple (71B); 20mm (3/4") long x 14mm (9/16") wide. SEPALS are half up, tips recurved up, twisted left to right; white (155C), tipped apple green (144C) upper surface; white (155B) & pale purple (70D), tipped apple green (144C) lower surface; 43mm (1 11/16") long x 18mm

(11/16") wide. TUBE is white (155C); short & thin; 12mm (7/16") long x 5mm (3/16") wide. STAMENS extend 16mm (5/8") beyond the corolla; dark rose (67C) filaments; reddish purple (71B) anthers. PISTIL extends 28mm (1 1/8") beyond the corolla; light rose (68D) style; pale yellow (2D) stigma. BUD is bulbous. FOLIAGE is dark green (136B) upper surface; medium green (138B) lower surface. Leaves are 78mm (3 1/8") long x 41mm (1 5/8") wide, ovate shaped, serrate edges, acute tips, rounded bases. Veins are plum (185C), stems are light plum (184D) & branches are plum (183C). PARENTAGE: 'Manfried Kleinau' x 'Jan Vander Kuylen'. Natural trailer; self branching. Makes good basket. Prefers overhead filtered light, cool climate. Best bloom & foliage in filtered light. Tested 3 years in Koningshooikt, Belgium. Waanrode 5/7/08. Distinguished by bloom colour.
Michiels 2009 BE AFS7143.

Annmarie Batty. Upright. Single. COROLLA: quarter flared, smooth petal margins, open bell shaped; opens dark reddish purple (61A); matures reddish purple (64B); 22mm (7/8 ") long x 22mm (7/8 ") wide. SEPALS: half up, tips recurved up; reddish purple (66A) upper surface; magenta (67B) lower surface; 23mm (7/8") long x 11mm (7/16") wide. TUBE: reddish purple (66A); short, medium thickness; 6mm (1/4") long x 7mm (1/4") wide. STAMENS extend 13mm (1/2") beyond the corolla; magenta (57B) filaments; reddish purple (59B) anthers. PISTIL extends 25mm (1") beyond the corolla; magenta (57B) style; magenta (59C) stigma. BUD: square, short, stubby. FOLIAGE: dark green (139A) upper surface; medium green (139C) lower surface. Leaves are 41mm (1 5/8") long x 24mm (15/16") wide; cordate shaped, serrulate edges, acute tips, rounded bases. Veins, stems & branches are green. PARENTAGE: ('Estelle Marie' x 'Pink Fantasia') x 'Fuchsiade 88'. Small upright. Self branching. Makes good upright. Prefers full sun. Cold weather hardy to -3° C (26° F). Best bloom & foliage colour in bright light. Tested 8 years in Gainsborough, Lincolnshire & Burstwick, East Yorkshire, England. Distinguished by very dark bloom colour & erect blooms.
Storey 2009 UK AFS7137.

Another Little Cracker. COROLLA light blue ageing to light mauve. SEPALS light pink. TUBE light pink.
Reynolds G. 2006 UK.

Anouchka De Weirdt. Trailer. Semi Double. COROLLA: half flared; opens reddish purple (72B), rose (68C) base; matures reddish purple (67A); 28mm (1 1/8") long x 26mm (1") wide. PETALOIDS: same colour as corolla; 15mm (9/16") long x 12mm (7/16") wide. SEPALS: half down, tips recurved; pale pink (69A) tipped apple green (144C) upper surface; rose (68C) tipped apple green (144C) lower surface; 39mm (1 1/2") long x 12mm (7/16") wide. TUBE: white (155C); long, medium thickness; 24mm (15/16") long x 6mm (1/4") wide. FOLIAGE is dark green (136A) upper surface; medium green (138A) lower surface. PARENTAGE: 'Rune Peeters' x 'Illusion'.
Michiels 2007 BE AFS6368.

Ans. Upright. Single. COROLLA is quarter flared; opens rose (47D) matures rose (47C); 16mm (5/8") long x 17mm (5/8") wide. SEPALS are horizontal, tips recurved; rose (55B) upper surface; pink (55C) lower surface; 27mm (1 1/16") long x 10mm (3/8") wide. TUBE is rose (55B); 25mm (1") long x 7mm (1/4") wide. FOLIAGE: dark to medium green (147A-147B) upper surface; medium green (147B) lower surface. PARENTAGE: 'F fulgens speciosa' x unknown. Distinguished by bloom shape & colour.
Krom 2006 NL AFS6267.

Antoine De Saint Exupery. Upright/Trailer. Single. COROLLA: quarter flared, smooth petal margins; opens & matures magenta (63A) & light rose (63D); 21mm (13/16") long x 12mm (1/2") wide. SEPALS: half down; tips recurved; peach (38B) tipped yellowish green (146C) upper surface; light rose (73C) lower surface; 27mm (1 1/16") long x 6mm (1/4") wide. TUBE: peach (38B); medium length & thickness; 29mm (1 1/8") long x 6mm (1/4") wide. STAMENS: extend 11-14mm (7/16-9/16") below corolla; light rose (58D) filaments, magenta (63B) anthers. PISTIL: extends 15mm (9/16") below the corolla, light rose (63D) style, yellowish white (4D) stigma. BUD: ovate. FOLIAGE: medium green (146A) upper surface; yellowish green (146B) lower surface. Leaves are 62mm (2 7/16") long x 32mm (1 1/4") wide, ovate shaped, serrulated edges, acute tips and rounded bases. Veins, stems & branches are yellowish green. PARENTAGE: 'Philippe Boennec' x 'Mirobolant'. Lax upright or stiff trailer. Makes good basket or upright. Prefers overhead filtered light and cool climate. Best bloom and foliage colour in filtered light. Tested 4 years in Pornic, France.

16

Distinguished by corolla colour for a single corolla.
Masse 2003 FR AFS5230.

Anton Pieck. Upright/Trailer. Semi Double. COROLLA is half flared; opens & matures pale pink (56D); 28mm (1 1/8") long x 30mm (1 3/16") wide. SEPALS are fully up, tips reflexed; pink (55C) upper surface; rose (55B) lower surface; 40mm (1 9/16") long x 14mm (9/16") wide. TUBE is pink (54D); 16mm (5/8") long x 6mm (1/4") wide. FOLIAGE: dark green (147A) upper surface; medium green (147B) lower surface. PARENTAGE: 'Southgate' x 'Greg Walker'. Distinguished by bloom shape & colour.
Krom 2006 NL AFS6275.

Antonie Van Heijst. Upright. Semi Double. COROLLA is three quarter flared with smooth petal margins; opens purple (77A), matures dark reddish purple (64A); 18mm (11/16") long x 26mm (1") wide. SEPALS are half up, tips recurved up; light pink (62B) upper surface; magenta (68A) lower surface; 22mm (7/8") long x 12mm (1/2") wide. TUBE is light pink (62B); medium length and thickness; 7mm (1/4") long x 6mm (1/4") thick. STAMENS extend 26mm (1") beyond the corolla; magenta (63B) filaments, dark reddish purple (64B) anthers. PISTIL extends 18mm (11/16") beyond the corolla; rose (63C) style, light yellow (2C) stigma. BUD is elliptic, pointed. FOLIAGE is dark green (137A) upper surface, medium green (137C) lower surface. Leaves are 72mm (2 13/16") long x 45mm (1 3/4") wide, ovate shaped, serrated edges, acute tips and obtuse bases. Veins, stems and branches are green. PARENTAGE: [('Bon Accord' x 'Bicentennial') x ('Vobeglo' x 'Dancing Flame') x 'Rohees Alrami'] x ('Annabel' x 'Annabel'). Small upright. Makes good standard. Prefers overhead filtered light and cool climate. Best bloom colour in filtered light. Tested four years in Duizel, The Netherlands. Distinguished by bloom colour.
Tamerus 2002 NL AFS5001.

Antonius Eusebius. Upright. Single. COROLLA: half flared, turned under wavy petal margins; opens reddish purple (64B); matures red (53C) & magenta (71C); 13mm (1/2") long x 12mm (7/16") wide. SEPALS: half down, tips recurved; red (53B) upper surface; red (53C) lower surface; 16mm (5/8") long x 7mm (1/4") wide. TUBE: dark rose (51A); short & thick; 6mm (1/4") long x 6mm (1/4") wide. STAMENS extend 15mm (9/16") beyond the corolla; magenta (63B)

filaments; purple (71A) anthers. PISTIL extends 15mm (9/16") beyond the corolla; magenta (63A) style; light rose (58D) stigma. BUD: globular. FOLIAGE: dark green (136B) upper surface; medium green (138B) lower surface. Leaves are 33mm (1 5/16") long x 22mm (7/8") wide; ovate shaped, serrate edges, obtuse tips, rounded bases. Veins are light reddish purple (185D), stems are reddish purple (186B), branches are dark reddish purple (186D). PARENTAGE: 'Pink La Campanella' x 'Roesse Mimas'. Small upright. Self branching. Makes good upright. Prefers overhead filtered light, cool climate. Best bloom & foliage colour in filtered light. Tested 3 years in Opglabbeek, Belgium. Waanrode 9/20/08. Distinguished by bloom colour.
Cuppens 2009 BE AFS7061.

Anya Jane Yates. Upright. Single. COROLLA bright orange. SEPALS cream.
Porter J. 2002 UK.

Apolonia. Trailer. Double. COROLLA is three quarter flared with wavy petal margins; opens and matures white (155D) flamed pale pink (56D); 47mm (1 7/8") long x 41mm (1 5/8") wide. SEPALS are half up, tips recurved up, twisted ±45°; white (155C) tipped green upper surface, white (155D) tipped green lower surface; 60mm (2 3/8") long x 24mm (15/16") wide. TUBE is cream (158D); long, medium thickness; 26mm (1") long x 8mm (5/16") wide. STAMENS extend 20mm (13/16") beyond the corolla; rose (55B) filaments, light pink (55D) anthers. PISTIL extends 57mm (2 1/4") beyond the corolla; white (155D) to pale pink (56D) style, cream (158B) stigma. BUD is ovate, pointed. FOLIAGE is dark green (147A) upper surface, light olive green (148B) lower surface. Leaves are 88mm (3 1/2") long x 46mm (1 13/16") wide, ovate shaped, serrated edges, acute tips and rounded bases. Veins, stems and branches are reddish. PARENTAGE: Seedling of unknown Parentage. Natural trailer. Self branching. Makes good basket. Prefers overhead filtered light and cool climate. Best bloom and foliage colour in filtered light. Tested four years in Wognum, The Netherlands. Distinguished by blossom colour and large profuse blossoms.
Dekker 2002 NL AFS4947.

Aramis. Upright. Single. COROLLA: quarter flared; smooth margins; opens & matures light reddish purple (73A), lighter base; 18mm (11/16") long x 15mm (9/16") wide. SEPALS: half down, tips recurved; white

17

(155A) tipped yellowish white (4C) upper surface; white (155B) lower surface; 28mm (1 1/8") long x 7mm (1/4") wide. TUBE: white (155A), cream (158D) base; medium length & thickness; 12mm (7/16") long x 6mm (1/4") wide. STAMENS extend 3-6mm (1/8-1/4") beyond the corolla; light pink (49B) filaments; pink (49A) anthers. PISTIL extends 24mm (15/16") beyond the corolla; light pink (49C) style; light yellow (4C) stigma. BUD is ovate. FOLIAGE is medium green (146A) upper surface; light olive green (147C) lower surface. Leaves are 67mm (2 5/8") long x 31mm (1 1/4") wide; ovate shaped, serrulate edges, acute tips, rounded bases. Veins, stems & branches are yellowish green. PARENTAGE: 'Porte Océane' x 'Papy René'. Small upright. Makes good upright. Prefers overhead filtered light & cool climate. Tested 3 years in Pornic, France. Distinguished by pretty colour contrast.
Masse 2009 FR AFS6986.

Archangel Michael. Upright. Single. COROLLA orange. SEPALS pale orange.
Ainsworth 2003 UK.

Arels Arjen. Upright/Trailer. Single. COROLLA is quarter flared with turned under petal margins; opens dark reddish purple (68A); matures dark reddish purple (61A); 33mm (1 5/16") long x 29mm (1 1/8") wide. SEPALS are fully up, tips recurved; reddish purple (65B) upper surface; rose (65A) lower surface; 41mm (1 5/8") long x 10mm (3/8") wide. TUBE is light pink (65C); medium length & thickness; 27mm (1 1/16") long x 7mm (1/4") wide. FOLIAGE: dark green (147A) upper surface; medium green (147B) lower surface. Leaves are 57mm (2 1/4") long x 27mm (1 1/16") wide, ovate shaped. PARENTAGE: 'Arek Avondzon' x 'Zellertal'. Distinguished by profuse flowers & long blooming period.
Elsman 2005 NL AFS5794.

Arles Nadia. Upright/Trailer. Single. COROLLA is quarter flared with turned under wavy petal margins; opens & matures red (50A); 23mm (15/16") long x 22mm (7/8") wide. SEPALS are half down, tips reflexed; light pink (49C) upper surface; light pink (49B) lower surface; 25mm (1") long x 9mm (3/8") wide. TUBE is pale pink (49D); long, medium thickness; 35mm (1 3/8") long x 5mm (3/16") wide. FOLIAGE: dark green (147A) upper surface; medium green (147B) lower surface. Leaves are 60mm (2 3/8") long x 34mm (1 5/16") wide, ovate shaped. PARENTAGE: 'Whirlaway' x 'WALZ Harp'.

Nomination by N.K.V.F. as recommendable cultivar. Distinguished by long Tube & bright red corolla..
Elsman 2005 NL AFS5795.

Arianne Fuhrmann. Upright/Trailer. Double. COROLLA: 3 quarter flared; opens dark purple (N78A), pale pink (69A) base; matures reddish purple (72B), pale lavender (69D) base; 23mm (7/8") long x 18mm (11/16") wide. PETALOIDS: pale purple (N87D), pale pink (69A) base; 15mm (9/16") long x 9mm (5/16") wide. SEPALS: half down, tips recurved; pale lavender (69D) tipped apple green (144C) upper surface; pale pink (69A) tipped apple green (144C) lower surface; 41mm (1 5/8") long x 6mm (1/4") wide. TUBE: reddish purple (61D) striped pale lavender (69D); medium length & thickness; 28mm (1 1/8") long x 6mm (1/4") wide. FOLIAGE is dark green (139A) upper surface; medium green (137B) lower surface. PARENTAGE: 'Waanrode Silver Star' x 'Ine Frazer'.
Michiels 2007 BE AFS6369.

Arie Tamerus. Trailer. Single. COROLLA is quarter flared with smooth petal margins; opens purple (71A); matures dark reddish purple (61A); 30mm (1 3/16") long x 24mm (15/16") wide. SEPALS are half up, tips reflexed up; reddish purple (67A) upper and lower surfaces; 40mm (1 9/16") long x 14mm (9/16") wide. TUBE is reddish purple (67A); medium length and thickness; 34mm (1 3/8") long x 7mm (1/4") thick. STAMENS extend 27mm (1 1/16") beyond the corolla; purple (71A) filaments, magenta (61C) anthers. PISTIL extends 32mm (1 1/4") beyond the corolla; magenta (61C) style, yellowish white (4D) stigma. BUD is ovate, pointed. FOLIAGE is dark green (137A) upper surface, medium green (138B) lower surface. Leaves are 52mm (2 1/16") long x 27mm (1 1/16") wide, ovate shaped, serrated edges, acute tips and rounded bases. Veins, stems and branches are red. PARENTAGE: 'Rohees King' x 'Anta'. Natural trailer. Makes good basket. Prefers overhead filtered light and cool climate. Best bloom colour in filtered light. Tested four years in Duizel, The Netherlands. Distinguished by bloom colour.
Tamerus 2002 NL AFS4992.

Aristo. Upright/Trailer. Single. COROLLA: quarter flared; opens & matures dark rose (71D), whitish base; 18mm (11/16") long x 17mm (5/8") wide. SEPALS: half down, tips reflexed; pure white tipped light green (145D) upper & lower surfaces; 25mm (1") long x

18

9mm (5/16") wide. TUBE: pure white; medium length & thickness; 11mm (7/16") long x 5mm (3/16") wide. STAMENS extend 12-16mm (7/16-5/8") beyond the corolla; light pink (49B) filaments; light yellow (4C) anthers. PISTIL extends 26mm (1") beyond the corolla; pale pink (49D) style; light yellow (4C) stigma. BUD is ovate. FOLIAGE is medium green (146A) upper surface; yellowish green (146B) lower surface. Leaves are 54mm (2 1/8") long x 27mm (1 1/16") wide; ovate shaped, serrulate edges, acute tips, rounded bases. Veins & stems are yellowish green, branches are yellowish green & light brown. PARENTAGE: 'Philippe Boënnec' x 'Kathleen Muncaster'. Lax upright or stiff trailer. Makes good upright. Prefers overhead filtered light & cool climate. Tested 3 years in Pornic, France. Distinguished by colour contrast & pure white Sepals. Masse 2009 FR AFS6987.

Arjan Spoelstra. Trailer. Double. COROLLA: three quarter flared, smooth petal margins; opens violet blue (92A); matures purple (81B); 17mm (11/16") long 19mm (3/4") wide. SEPALS: half up; tips recurved up; magenta (63B) upper surface; magenta (63A) lower surface; 33mm (1 5/16") long x 14mm (9/16") wide. TUBE: magenta (63B); medium length & thickness; 10mm (3/8") long x 5mm (3/16") wide. STAMENS: extend 9mm (3/8") below corolla; magenta (63B) filaments; light pink (65B) anthers. PISTIL: extends 17mm (11/16") below the corolla; rose (63C) style; magenta (63B) stigma. BUD: small, round, pointed. FOLIAGE: dark green (137A) upper surface; medium green (137C) lower surface. Leaves are 55mm (2 3/16") long x 28mm (1 1/8") wide, lanceolate shaped, serrulated edges, acute tips and obtuse bases. Red veins, stems & branches. PARENTAGE: ('Cameron Ryle' x 'Parasol') x 'Shangri-La'. Natural trailer. Self branching. Makes good basket. Prefers overhead filtered light and cool climate. Best bloom and foliage colour in filtered light. Tested 4 years in Knegsel, The Netherlands. Distinguished by bloom colour. Roes 2004 NL AFS5466.

Arkie. Upright. Single. COROLLA pale pink veined rose pink. SEPALS white flushed pale pink. TUBE white. Kirby 2009 UK.

Armbro Campbell. Upright. Double. COROLLA: half flared, turned under petal margins; opens rose (61D) & red purple (N77B); matures red (53D) & magenta (59D); 30 mm (1 3/16") long x 21mm (13/16") wide.

PETALOIDS: light reddish purple (73A) & violet (77B); 21mm (13/16") long x 14mm (9/16") wide. SEPALS are horizontal, tips recurved; pink (62B), tipped light olive green (153D) upper surface; rose (52B), tipped light olive green (153D) lower surface; 47mm (1 7/8") long x 16mm (5/8") wide. TUBE is rose (61D); medium length & thickness; 15mm (9/16") long x 8mm (5/16") wide. STAMENS extend 13mm (1/2") beyond the corolla; rose (61D) filaments; dark reddish purple (72A) anthers. PISTIL extends 31mm (1 1/4") beyond the corolla; dark rose (64C) style; light pink (62C) stigma. BUD is elongated. FOLIAGE is dark green (136A) upper surface; medium green (137D) lower surface. Leaves are 42mm (1 5/8") long x 26mm (1") wide, ovate shaped, serrulate edges, acute tips, rounded bases. Veins are plum (184C), stems are plum (185C) & branches are very dark reddish purple (186A). PARENTAGE: 'Manfried Kleinau' x 'Frans Vander Kuylen'. Lax upright or stiff trailer, self branching. Makes good basket or upright. Prefers overhead filtered light, cool climate. Best bloom & foliage in filtered light. Tested 3 years in Koningshooikt, Belgium. Waanrode 9/8/08. Distinguished by bloom colour combination. Michiels 2009 BE AFS7144.

Armo Van Bree. Upright. Single. COROLLA: quarter flared; opens red (44A); matures reddish orange (43B); 12mm (7/16") long x 10mm (3/8") wide. SEPALS: half up, tips reflexed up; orange (40C) upper surface; light orange (40D) lower surface; 24mm (15/16") long x 7mm (1/4") wide. TUBE: orange (40C); 16mm (5/8") long x 8mm (5/16") wide. FOLIAGE is dark green (137A) upper surface; medium green (137C) lower surface. PARENTAGE: 'Roesse Lupus' x 'Lye's Unique'. van Bree 2008 NL AFS6888.

Arno Spin. Trailer. Double. COROLLA: half flared; opens dark reddish purple (59A); matures dark reddish purple (60C); 12mm (7/16") long x 14mm (9/16") wide. SEPALS: horizontal; tips reflexed; light pink (65B) upper surface; rose (65A) lower surface; 31mm (1 1/4") long x 14mm (9/16") wide. TUBE: light pink (65C); long & thin; 42mm (1 5/8") long x 4mm (1/8") wide. FOLIAGE is medium green (137C) upper surface; medium green (137D) lower surface. PARENTAGE: 'Roesse Lupus' x 'Roesse Rhea'. Roes 2007 NL AFS6309.

Aronst Hoeck. Trailer. Single. COROLLA: half flared, turned under smooth petal margins; opens dark purple (79B), magenta (67B) at base; matures purple (71A), dark reddish purple (64A) at base; 19mm (3/4") long x 25mm (1") wide. SEPALS: half up; tips reflexed up; reddish purple (61B) upper surface; reddish purple (64B) lower surface; 25mm (1") long x 13mm (1/2") wide. TUBE: magenta (63A); short & thick; 9mm (3/8") long x 9mm (3/8") wide. STAMENS: extend 25mm (1") below the corolla; dark reddish purple (61A) filaments, violet (77B) anthers. PISTIL extends 31mm (1 1/4") below the corolla; magenta (67B) style, rose (61D) stigma. BUD: ovate, pointed. FOLIAGE: dark green (137A) upper surface; medium green (137C) lower surface. Leaves are 46mm (1 13/16") long x 27mm (1 1/16") wide, ovate shaped, serrulated edges, acute tips and rounded bases. Veins are medium green (141D), stems & branches are reddish purple (186B). PARENTAGE: 'Dommelgalm' x unknown. Natural trailer. Self branching. Makes good basket. Prefers overhead filtered light. Best bloom and foliage colour in filtered light. Tested 3 years in Rummen, Belgium. NBFK certificate at Meise. Distinguished by bloom shape and colour.
Ector 2003 BE AFS5108.

Arthur Phillips. Single. COROLLA deep rose. SEPALS creamy white. TUBE creamy white. Reynolds G. 2009 UK.

Artosa. Trailer. Double. COROLLA: half flared; opens red purple (N78C), light pink (65B) base; matures reddish purple (71B); 18mm (11/16") long x 16mm (5/8") wide. PETALOIDS: light red purple (N78D), light pink (65B) base; 10mm (3/8") long x 7mm (1/4") wide. SEPALS: horizontal, tips reflexed; pale pink (62D) tipped light yellowish green (150C) upper surface; light pink (65B) tipped light yellowish green (150C) lower surface; 19mm (3/4") long x 12mm (7/16") wide. TUBE: light green (145D); long, medium thickness; 19mm (3/4") long x 5mm (3/16") wide. FOLIAGE is dark green (139A) upper surface; medium green (138B) lower surface. PARENTAGE: 'Rune Peeters' x 'Illusion'.
Michiels 2007 BE AFS6362.

Ashley Vander Loo. Upright. Double. COROLLA is three quarter flared with smooth petal margins; opens purple (71A); matures magenta (71C); 28mm (1 1/8") long x 30mm (13/16") wide. SEPALS are half up, tips recurved up; pale lavender (65D) upper

surface; pink (62A) lower surface; 27mm (1 1/16") long x 14mm (9/16") wide. TUBE is pale yellow (1D); medium length and thickness; 12mm (1/2") long x 7mm (1/4") thick. STAMENS extend 40mm (1 9/16") beyond the corolla; rose (68B) filaments, purple (71A) anthers. PISTIL extends 52mm (2 1/16") beyond the corolla; rose (68B) style, light yellow (3D) stigma. BUD is elliptic. FOLIAGE is medium green (137B) upper surface, medium green (138B) lower surface. Leaves are 78mm (3 1/16") long x 31mm (1 1/4") wide, lanceolate shaped, serrated edges, acute tips and obtuse bases. Veins, stems and branches are green. PARENTAGE: {[('Bon Accord' x 'Bicentennial') x ('Vobeglo' x 'Dancing Flame)] x Rohees Alrami'} x 'Annabel' x 'Annabel'. Small upright. Makes good standard. Prefers overhead filtered light and cool climate. Best bloom colour in filtered light. Tested four years in Duizel, The Netherlands. Distinguished by bloom colour.
Tamerus 2002 NL AFS4983.

Assendelft. Upright. Single. COROLLA is half flared; opens & matures red (46B); 16mm (5/8") long x 8mm (5/16") wide. SEPALS are full down, tips recurved; pink (55C) upper surface; dark rose (55A) lower surface; 22mm (7/8") long x 5mm (3/16") wide. TUBE is pale pink (56A); 48mm (1 7/8") long x 3-6mm (1/8-1/4") wide. FOLIAGE: light green (137C) upper surface; yellowish green (146B) lower surface. PARENTAGE: 'WALZ Polka' x 'Pink Cornet'. Distinguished by flowers in racemes & large leaves.
Krom 2006 NL AFS6266.

Astrid Oudenaar. Upright. Double. COROLLA: three quarter flared, turned under petal margins; opens light rose (73C) & light purple (N78C); matures magenta (61C) & reddish purple (67A); 27 mm (1 1/16") long x 24mm (15/16") wide. PETALOIDS: light rose (73C) & light purple (N78C); 19mm (3/4") long x 16mm (5/8") wide. SEPALS are half down, tips recurved; pale pink (56B) upper surface; rose (55B) lower surface; 32mm (1 1/4") long x 17mm (5/8") wide. TUBE is pale pink (56C); medium length & thickness; 15mm (9/16") long x 8mm (5/16") wide. STAMENS extend 12mm (7/16") beyond the corolla; reddish purple (70B) filaments; light reddish purple (73A) anthers. PISTIL extends 26mm (1") beyond the corolla; rose (68C) style; pale yellow (1D) stigma. BUD is bulbous. FOLIAGE is dark green (136B) upper surface; medium green (138B) lower surface. Leaves

20

are 52mm (2 1/16") long x 30mm (1 3/16") wide, ovate shaped, entire edges, obtuse tips, rounded bases. Veins are very dark purple (187A), stems are dark red purple (N186D) & branches are dark red (185A). PARENTAGE: 'Manfried Kleinau' x 'Bianca'. Lax upright or stiff trailer, self branching. Makes good basket. Prefers cool climate. Best bloom & foliage in filtered light. Tested 3 years in Koningshooikt, Belgium. Waanrode 9/8/08. Distinguished by bloom colour. Michiels 2009 BE AFS7145.

Astrid Van Vliet. Trailer. Double. COROLLA: three quarter flared, turned under petal margins; opens dark rose (55A) & light reddish purple (72C); matures magenta (63B) & magenta (67B); 22mm (7/8") long x 20mm (3/4") wide. PETALOIDS: dark rose (53A) & light reddish purple (72C); 16mm (5/8") long x 12mm (7/16") wide. SEPALS are horizontal, tips recurved; light pink (62C), tipped pale yellowish green (154D) upper surface; dark rose (58C), tipped pale yellowish green (154D) lower surface; 33mm (1 5/16") long x 17mm (5/8") wide. TUBE is pale pink (62D); medium length & thickness; 14mm (9/16") long x 7mm (1/4") wide. STAMENS extend 14mm (9/16") beyond the corolla; light rose (63D) filaments; rose (68C) anthers. PISTIL extends 31mm (1 1/4") beyond the corolla; pink (55C) style; pale yellow (1D) stigma. BUD is bulbous. FOLIAGE is dark green (137A) upper surface; medium green (138B) lower surface. Leaves are 47mm (1 7/8") long x 32mm (1 1/4") wide, ovate shaped, serrate edges, acute tips, rounded bases. Veins are dark red (185A), stems are plum (185B) & branches are plum (185C) & light green (139D). PARENTAGE: 'Manfried Kleinau' x 'Panhoven'. Natural trailer, self branching. Makes good basket. Prefers overhead filtered light, cool climate. Best bloom & foliage in filtered light. Tested 3 years in Koningshooikt, Belgium. Waanrode 9/8/08. Distinguished by bloom colour combination. Michiels 2009 BE AFS7146.

Astrolaya. Upright. Single. COROLLA magenta rose. SEPALS light pink. PARENTAGE WALZ Gitaar x WALZ Harp. Geerts L. 2003 BE AFS5089.

Auenland. Trailer. Double. COROLLA: quarter flared, smooth petal margins; opens purple (N79C); matures dark reddish purple (61A) & reddish purple (61B); 30mm (1 3/16") long x 34mm (1 3/8") wide. SEPALS: horizontal, tips recurved; dark reddish

purple (60B) upper & lower surfaces; 34mm (1 3/8") long x 16mm (5/8") wide. TUBE: magenta (58B); long & thin; 25mm (1") long x 5mm (3/16") wide. STAMENS extend 7mm (1/4") beyond the corolla; dark reddish purple (60B) filaments; dark purple (N79B) anthers. PISTIL extends 24mm (15/16") beyond the corolla; dark reddish purple (60B) style; pink (62C) stigma. BUD: globular. FOLIAGE: dark green (137A) upper surface; medium green (137C) lower surface. Leaves are 82mm (3 1/4") long x 44mm (1 3/4") wide; ovate shaped, serrulate edges, acute tips, rounded bases. Veins & stems are red, branches are reddish brown. PARENTAGE: 'George Gloßner' x 'Katrien Michiels'. Natural trailer. Self branching. Makes good basket or upright (with support). Prefers warm climate. Heat tolerant if shaded. Best bloom & foliage colour in bright light. Tested 4 years in Bavaria, Southern Germany. Distinguished by bloom colour combination. Burkhart 2009 DE AFS7100.

Aunt Hilda. Upright. Single. COROLLA: quarter flared, bell shaped, held horizontal, smooth petal margins; opens & matures white (155D) veined red in throat; 21mm (13/16") long x 18mm (11/16") wide. SEPALS: horizontal, tips recurved; magenta (57A) upper surface; magenta (57B) lower surface; 27mm (1 1/16") long x 8mm (5/16") wide. TUBE: magenta (57A); short, medium thickness; 7mm (1/4") long x 6mm (1/4") wide. STAMENS extend 16mm (5/8") beyond the corolla; reddish orange (43B) filaments; red (45A) anthers. PISTIL extends 27mm (1 1/16") beyond the corolla; reddish orange (43B) style; dark red (46A) stigma. BUD: round, pointed, twisted. FOLIAGE: dark green (139A) upper surface; medium green (138B) lower surface. Leaves are 35mm (1 3/8") long x 22mm (7/8") wide; cordate shaped, serrulate edges, acute tips, rounded bases. Veins, stems & branches are green. PARENTAGE: 'Estelle Marie' x 'Pink Fantasia'. Small upright. Self branching. Makes good upright. Prefers full sun. Cold weather hardy to -3° C (26° F). Best bloom & foliage colour in bright light. Tested 10 years in Burstwick, East Yorkshire, England. Distinguished by horizontally erect flowers. Storey 2009 UK AFS7130.

Authentique. Upright/Trailer. Single. COROLLA: unflared; opens & matures reddish orange (43C); 19mm (3/4") long x 10mm (3/8") wide. SEPALS: horizontal, tips recurved; white (155B) tipped light yellow (4C) upper surface; white (155B) lower

surface; 32mm (1/4") long x 6mm (1/4") wide. TUBE: white (155B); longish & thinnish; 24mm (15/16") long x 5mm (3/16") wide. STAMENS extend 5-9mm (3/16-5/16") beyond the corolla; pink (43D) filaments; light pink (36B) anthers. PISTIL extends 30mm (1 1/4") beyond the corolla; pale orange (29D) style; light yellow (4C) stigma. BUD is long, ovate. FOLIAGE is dark green (147A) upper surface; medium green (147B) lower surface. Leaves are 76mm (3") long x 33mm (1 5/16") wide; ovate shaped, serrulate edges, acute tips, rounded bases. Veins & stems are yellowish green, branches are yellowish green & light brown. PARENTAGE: 'Nancy Lou' x 'Annabel'. Lax upright or stiff trailer. Self branching. Makes good upright. Prefers overhead filtered light & cool climate. Tested 3 years in Pornic, France. Distinguished by colour contrast & profuse flowers.
Masse 2009 FR AFS6988.

Averbode Boven. Trailer. Single. COROLLA: quarter flared; opens dark rose (51A); matures rose (52B); 29mm (1 1/8") long x 23mm (7/8") wide. SEPALS are half down, tips reflexed; pink (49A) tipped light apple green (145B) upper surface; pink (48C) tipped light apple green (145B) lower surface; 35mm (1 3/8") long x 8mm (5/16") wide. TUBE is dark rose (54B); 87mm (3 7/16") long x 5mm (3/16") wide. FOLIAGE is medium green (138A) upper surface; medium green (138B) lower surface. PARENTAGE: 'Big Slim' x 'Tanja's Favourite'. Waanrode Outstanding 7/7/2007.
Geerts L. 2008 BE AFS6726.

Aylish Rowan. Upright. Single. COROLLA opens reddish purple; corolla is half flared and is 4mm long x 9mm wide. SEPALS red on the upper surface, red on the lower surface; sepals are half down with reflexed tips and are 6mm long x 4mm wide. TUBE red and is 8mm long x 4mm wide. PARENTAGE Seedling Jap van Erp. This cultivar is an encliandra and has been tested 3yrs and found to be hardy in Derbyshire, UK.
Parkes T. 2007 UK BFS0040.

Baby Jingles. Upright. Semi Double. COROLLA is quarter flared, bell shaped; opens and matures white (155B) veined red; 10mm (3/8") long x 13mm (1/2") wide. SEPALS are half down, tips recurved; dark red (46A) upper surface, red (46B) lower surface; 13mm (1/2") long x 5 - 6mm (3/16" - 1/4") wide. TUBE is dark red (46A), short

and thick; 6mm (1/4") long. STAMENS extend 6 - 8mm (1/4" - 5/16") below the corolla; magenta (58B) filaments and reddish purple (59B) anthers. PISTIL extends 13 - 16mm (1/2" - 5/8") below the corolla; dark rose (58C) style, reddish purple (59B) stigma. BUD is erect, heart shaped. FOLIAGE is dark green (139A) on upper surface and medium green (146A) on lower surface. Leaves are 38 - 44mm (1 1/2" - 1 3/4") long x 13 - 16mm (1/2" - 5/8") wide, ovate shaped, smooth edges, acute tips and rounded bases. Veins are red, stems green with reddish line and branches are light brown. PARENTAGE: Jingle Bells x unknown. Small upright. Makes good miniature or bonsai. Prefers full sun. Cold weather hardy to 0° F. Best bloom colour in bright light. Tested three years in Portland, Oregon area. Distinguished by small and profuse flowers.
Peter 2003 USA AFS5060.

Baby Van Eijk. Upright. Double. COROLLA is three quarter flared with smooth petal margins; opens & matures pale pink (62D); 25mm (1") long x 29mm (1 1/8") wide. SEPALS are horizontal, tips recurved; light rose (68D) upper surface; rose (68C) lower surface; 32mm (1 1/4") long x 12mm (1/2") wide. TUBE is light rose (68D); medium length & thickness; 11mm (7/16") long x 6mm (1/4") wide. FOLIAGE: medium green (137B) upper surface; medium green (138B) lower surface. Leaves are 70mm (2 3/4") long x 32mm (1 1/4") wide, lanceolate shaped. PARENTAGE: 'Sofie Michiels' x 'Flament Rose'. Distinguished by bloom & foliage combination.
van Eijk 2005 NL AFS5902.

Ballerena Dancer. Upright. Semi Double. COROLLA: half flared, turned up petal margins; opens white (155A); matures white (155B); 20mm (3/4") long x 20mm (3/4") wide. PETALOIDS: light green (143B); 30mm (1 3/16") long. SEPALS: half up, tips recurved up; pink (69A) tipped green upper surface; pink (62C) lower surface; 25mm (1") long x 15mm (9/16") wide. TUBE: pale pink (69A); short, thin; 15mm (9/16") long x 5mm (3/16") wide. STAMENS extend 15mm (9/16") beyond the corolla; pink (62C) filaments; pale pink (69A) anthers. PISTIL extends 30mm (1 3/16") beyond the corolla; pale pink (69A) style; white (155A) stigma. BUD: ovate. FOLIAGE: medium green (137D) upper surface; medium green (137D) lower surface. Leaves are 40mm (1 9/16") long x 20mm (3/4") wide; lanceolate shaped, serrulate edges, acute tips, acute bases.

Veins & branches are light green stems are light brown. PARENTAGE: 'Swingtime' x 'Diana Princess of Wales'. Small upright. Self branching. Makes good upright or standard. Prefers overhead filtered light. Best bloom colour in filtered light. Tested 3 years in Rayleigh, Essex, England. Distinguished by blossom colour & shape.
Smith R. 2009 UK AFS7123.

Barachiel. Upright. Double. COROLLA pale lavender. SEPALS white flushed pink.
Ainsworth 2002 UK.

Barbara Meier. Upright. Double. COROLLA: quarter flared, smooth petal margins; opens dark purple (79A); matures dark reddish purple (61A); 22mm (7/8") long x 20mm (3/4") wide. SEPALS: half up, tips recurved up; dark reddish purple (60B) upper & lower surfaces; 30mm (1 3/16") long x 9mm (5/16") wide. TUBE: dark reddish purple (60B); medium length & thickness; 10mm (3/8") long x 6mm (1/4") wide. STAMENS extend 15mm (9/16") beyond the corolla; dark reddish purple (60B) filaments; dark purple (N79B) anthers. PISTIL extends 38mm (1 1/2") beyond the corolla; dark reddish purple (60B) style; reddish purple (59B) stigma. FOLIAGE: grayish green (189A) upper surface; medium green (147B) lower surface. Leaves are 85mm (3 3/8") long x 40mm (1 9/16") wide; elliptic shaped, serrate edges, acute tips, rounded bases. Veins & stems are red, branches are reddish maturing to light brown. PARENTAGE: [(F. *glaziovana* x 'Daniel Pfaller') x 'Düsterwald] x ('Naaldwijk 800' x Gimli von Moria'). Medium upright. Self branching. Makes good upright, standard or pyramid – can be trained in many forms. Prefers full sun, warm climate. Heat tolerant. Best bloom & foliage colour in bright light. Tested 3 years in Bavaria, Southern Germany. Distinguished by corolla colour & shape; very heat tolerant.
Burkhart 2009 DE AFS7112.

Barbara Norton. Upright. Single. COROLLA: quarter flared, turned under petal margins; opens light purple (88C); matures violet (77B); 19mm (3/4") long x 25mm (1") wide. SEPALS: half down; tips recurved; light rose (58D) tipped green upper & lower surfaces; 32mm (1 1/4") long x 12mm (1/2") wide. TUBE: light rose (58D) striped darker pink; medium length & thickness; 12mm (1/2") long x 7mm (1/4") wide. STAMENS: extend 19mm (3/4") below corolla; magenta (68A) filaments & anthers. PISTIL: extends 25mm

(1") below the corolla; magenta (68A) style; rose (68C) stigma. BUD: pointed. FOLIAGE: yellowish green (144B) variegated greenish yellow (151B) upper & lower surfaces. Leaves are 57mm (2 1/4") long x 32mm (1 1/4") wide, elliptic shaped, smooth edges, acute tips and rounded bases. Pale purple veins & stems; brown branches. PARENTAGE: sport of 'Breeder's Delight'. Small upright. Self branching. Makes good upright, standard or decorative. Prefers overhead filtered light. Best bloom and foliage colour in filtered light. Tested 4 years in Ormskirk, Lancashire, England. Distinguished by foliage variegation and prolific flowering combination.
Sinton 2004 UK AFS5456.

Barbara Reynolds. Upright. Single. COROLLA white. SEPALS white flushed pink tipped green.
Reynolds G. 2005 UK.

Barnara Van Kooperen. Upright. Single. COROLLA is half flared with turned up wavy petal margins; opens light rose (73C); matures light purple (75B); 24mm (15/16") long x 24mm (15/16") wide. SEPALS are horizontal, tips recurved; white (155D), magenta (67B) at base, upper surface; white (155D), magenta (58B) at base, lower surface; 32mm (1 1/4") long x 10mm (3/8") wide. TUBE is white (155D); medium length & thickness; 18mm (11/16") long x 7mm (1/4") wide. FOLIAGE: medium green (146A) upper surface; yellowish green (146B) lower surface. Leaves are 66mm (2 5/8") long x 42mm (1 5/8") wide, ovate shaped. PARENTAGE: 'Delta's Wonder' x 'Montalba'. Distinguished by shape & bright colour.
Elsman 2005 BE AFS5793.

Barbara's Beauty. Upright/Trailer. Single. COROLLA: unflared, turned under smooth petal margins; opens light purple (74C) fused light purple (75B); matures reddish purple (74A) fused light purple (75B); 23mm (15/16") long x 18mm (11/16") wide. SEPALS: half up; tips recurved up; pale pink (62D) tipped green upper & lower surfaces; 35mm (1 3/8") long x 11mm (7/16") wide. TUBE: light yellow (10D); medium length & thickness; 23mm(15/16") long x 13mm (1/2") wide. STAMENS: extend 23mm (15/16") below corolla; dark rose (54A) filaments, purple (77A) anthers. PISTIL: extends 33mm (1 5/16") below the corolla, pink (62C) style, yellowish white (158A) stigma. BUD: elongated. FOLIAGE: yellowish green (144A) upper surface; light olive green (147C) lower surface. Leaves are 65mm (2

23

9/16") long x 35mm (1 3/8") wide, lanceolate shaped, serrated edges, acute tips and rounded bases. Veins are green, stems are red; branches are brown. PARENTAGE: 'Rose of Denmark' x 'Carla Johnson'. Lax upright or stiff trailer. Self branching. Makes good basket or standard. Prefers overhead filtered light. Heat tolerant if shaded. Cold weather hardy to 32° F. Best bloom and foliage colour in filtered light. Tested 3 years in Walthamstow, London, England. Distinguished by bloom colour combination. Allsop J. 2003 UK AFS5211.

Barnet Belle. Single. COROLLA shades of red. SEPALS shades of red. TUBE shades of red.
Allsop M. 2008 UK.

Baron Van Homeck. Upright. Double. COROLLA: half flared; opens dark rose (64C); matures magenta (63A); 17mm (5/8") long x 17mm (5/8") wide. SEPALS: horizontal, tips recurved; white (155C) & dark rose (51A) tipped yellowish green (145A) upper surface; rose (55B) tipped yellowish green (145A) lower surface; 23mm (7/8") long x 8mm (5/16") wide. TUBE: rose (52C); 14mm (9/16") long x 8mm (5/16") wide. FOLIAGE is medium green (137B) upper surface; light green (138C) lower surface. PARENTAGE: 'Pink La Campanella' x unknown.
Cuppens 2009 BE AFS6752.

Baroncelli. Trailer. Double. COROLLA: half flared; opens light purple (N78C) edged reddish purple (71B) & matures magenta (71C) edged reddish purple (67A); 21mm (13/16") long x 19mm (3/4") wide. PETALOIDS: light purple (N78C) edged reddish purple (71B); 12mm (7/16") long x 8mm (5/16") wide. SEPALS are half down, tips reflexed; pale pink (62D) tipped light apple green (145C) upper surface & rose (65A) tipped light apple green (145C) lower surface; 24mm (15/16") long x 12mm (7/16") wide. TUBE is white (155D); medium length & thickness; 16mm (5/8") long x 6mm (1/4") wide. FOLIAGE is dark green (137A) upper surface; medium green (138B) lower surface. PARENTAGE: 'Rune Peeters' x 'Collingwood'. Michiels 2007 BE AFS6549.

Baronin Süsskind. Upright. Double. COROLLA is three quarter flared; opens dark purple (61A); matures reddish purple (61B); 30mm (1 3/16") long x 40mm (1 9/16") wide. SEPALS are fully up, tips reflexed; rose (52C) upper & lower surfaces; 33mm (1 5/16") long x 16mm (5/8") wide. TUBE is rose (52C);

18mm (11/16") long x 10mm (3/8") wide. FOLIAGE: dark green (137A) upper surface; medium green (137C) lower surface. PARENTAGE: 'Danny Kaye' x 'Daniel Pfaller'. Distinguished by bloom colour & heat tolerance.
Burkhart 2006 DE AFS6049.

Bart-Els. Trailer. Double. COROLLA: half flared; opens white (155B) striped magenta (63B); matures pale pink (49D); 18mm (11/16") long x 16mm (5/8") wide. PETALOIDS: same colour as corolla; 15mm (9/16") long x 7mm (1/4") wide. SEPALS: horizontal, tips reflexed; white (155C) tipped light apple green (145B) upper surface; white (155B) tipped light apple green (145B) lower surface; 27mm (1 1/16") long x 12mm (7/16") wide. TUBE: white (155C) striped magenta (63B); long & thin; 18mm (11/16") long x 4mm (1/8") wide. FOLIAGE is dark green (136A) upper surface; medium green (137B) lower surface. PARENTAGE: 'Vreni Schleeweiss' x 'Kiss'.
Michiels 2007 BE AFS6361.

Basseveldse Ezels. Upright. Double. COROLLA: half flared, turned under petal margins; opens dark reddish purple (64A); matures dark reddish purple (61A); 25 mm (1") long x 20mm (3/4") wide. PETALOIDS: dark reddish purple (64A); 16mm (5/8") long x 13mm (1/2") wide. SEPALS are half down, tips recurved; rose (63C) upper surface; magenta (63B) lower surface; 30mm (13/16") long x 16mm (5/8") wide. TUBE is pink (62B); medium length & thickness; 14mm (9/16") long x 7mm (1/4") wide. STAMENS extend 13mm (1/2") beyond the corolla; magenta (63A) filaments; purple (83A) anthers. PISTIL extends 21mm (13/16") beyond the corolla; dark rose (64C) style; yellowish white (4D) stigma. BUD is globular. FOLIAGE is dark green (136B) upper surface; medium green (138B) lower surface. Leaves are 55mm (2 3/16") long x 34mm (1 3/8") wide, ovate shaped, entire edges, acute tips, rounded bases. Veins are yellowish green (144A), stems are yellowish green (144A) & plum (184D) & branches are light green (138C). PARENTAGE: 'Manfried Kleinau' x 'Impala'. Lax upright or stiff trailer, self branching. Makes good upright. Prefers overhead filtered light, cool climate. Best bloom & foliage in filtered light. Tested 3 years in Koningshooikt, Belgium. Waanrode 9/8/08. Distinguished by unique bloom colour combination.
Michiels 2009 BE AFS7147.

24

Be My Love. Upright. Semi Double. COROLLA: quarter flared; opens cream (158C); matures greenish white (157A); 25mm (1") long x 15mm (9/16") wide. SEPALS: fully up, tips reflexed; white (155B), streaked pink, tipped green upper surface; white (155C), streaked pink, tipped green lower surface; 25mm (1") long x 14mm (9/16") wide. TUBE: greenish white (157A); 20mm (3/4") long x 10mm (3/8") wide. FOLIAGE is dark green (137A) upper surface; medium green (137C) lower surface. PARENTAGE: 'Snowbird' x 'Dana Samantha'. Smith R. 2008 UK AFS6818.

Beamish. Upright. Single. COROLLA: unflared, smooth petal margins; opens & matures coral (37A); 35mm (1 3/8") long x 21mm (13/16") wide. PETALOIDS: same colour as corolla; 5mm (3/16") long x 3mm (1/8") wide. SEPALS: full down; tips reflexed; coral (37A) upper & lower surfaces; 30mm(1 3/16") long x 11mm (7/16") wide. TUBE: coral (37A); short & thin; 11mm (7/16") long x 5mm (3/16") wide. STAMENS: do not extend below corolla; cream (11D) filaments; pink (37E) anthers. PISTIL: does not extend below the corolla; pink (52D) style & stigma. BUD: sharp point. FOLIAGE: medium green (138A) upper surface; medium green (138B) lower surface. Leaves are 50mm (2") long x 45mm (1 3/4") wide, cordate shaped, wavy edges, acute tips and rounded bases. Veins, stems & branches are red. PARENTAGE: 'Coralle' x unknown. Small upright. Self branching. Makes good upright. Prefers overhead filtered light. Best bloom and foliage colour in bright light. Tested 3 years in Stoke-on-Trent, England. Distinguished by profuse flowers on the end of stems. Rowell 2003 UK AFS5134.

Beansweyr. Upright/Trailer. Double. COROLLA is half flared with turned under wavy petal margins; opens light purple (82D), pale violet (76D) base; matures pale purple (81D); 29mm (1 1/8") long x 19mm (3/4") wide. PETALOIDS: same colour as corolla; 19mm (3/4") long x 11mm (7/16") wide. SEPALS are twisted clockwise; half up, tips recurved up; light pink (62B), tipped pale yellow green (150D) upper surface; rose (63C), tipped pale yellow green (150D) lower surface; 48mm (1 7/8") long x 13mm (1/2") wide. TUBE is white (155B); medium length & thickness; 17mm (11/16") long x 7mm (1/4") wide. FOLIAGE: dark green (139A) upper surface; medium green (138B) lower surface. Leaves are 74mm (2 15/16") long x 31mm (1 1/4") wide, elliptic shaped.

PARENTAGE: 'Sofie Michiels' x 'Weleveld'. Meise 8-14-04, Outstanding. Distinguished by flower colour. Michiels 2005 BE AFS5751.

Beauty Of Ann. Upright. Single. COROLLA: quarter flared, turned under smooth petal margins; opens magenta (71C); matures reddish purple (71B); 12mm (1/2") long x 9mm (3/8") wide. SEPALS: half down; tips reflexed; magenta (59C) upper surface; magenta (58B) lower surface; 13mm(1/2") long x 6mm (1/4") wide. TUBE: reddish purple (58A); medium length & thickness; 25mm (1") long x 7mm (1/4") wide. STAMENS: do not extend below corolla; magenta (63B) filaments; magenta (63A) anthers. PISTIL extends 3mm (1/8") below the corolla; rose (63C) style, magenta (63B) stigma. BUD: ovate. FOLIAGE: dark green (139A) upper surface; medium green (139B) lower surface. Leaves are 46mm (1 13/16") long x 24mm (15/16") wide, ovate shaped, serrulated edges, acute tips and rounded bases. Veins are dark grayish purple (184A), stems are plum (183C), branches are plum (184C). PARENTAGE: found seedling. Medium upright. Self branching. Makes good upright. Prefers overhead filtered light. Best bloom and foliage colour in filtered light. Tested 3 years in Voerendaal, The Netherlands. NBFK Certificate at Meise. Distinguished by bloom shape. Dewez 2003 NL AFS5132.

Beauty Of Everbeur. Upright/Trailer. Double. COROLLA is three quarter flared; opens light rose (78B), light purple (68D) base; matures reddish purple (66A); 35mm (1 3/8") long x 24mm (15/16") wide. PETALOIDS: violet (77B), light rose (68D) base; 15mm (9/16") long x 11mm (7/16") wide. SEPALS are half down, tips recurved; pale pink (62D) tipped yellowish green (145A) upper surface; light rose (68D) tipped yellowish green (145A) lower surface; 44mm (1 3/4") long x 16mm (5/8") wide. TUBE is white (155D); 16mm (5/8") long x 6mm (1/4") wide. FOLIAGE: dark green (136A) upper surface; medium green (138B) lower surface. PARENTAGE: 'Sofie Michiels' x 'Annabelle Stubbs'. Meise 9/17/05. Distinguished by bloom colour combination. Michiels 2006 BE AFS6070.

Beauty Of Meise. Upright. Double. COROLLA: half flared; opens violet (75A) base pale purple (75C) edged violet (85A); matures light reddish purple (73A) & violet (76B); 20mm (3/4") long x 16mm (5/8") wide.

25

PETALOIDS: violet (75A) edged violet (85A); 11mm (7/16") long x 10mm (3/8") wide. SEPALS are half down, tips reflexed; pale lavender (69C) tipped light greenish yellow (151C) upper surface and pale purple (75C) tipped light greenish yellow (151C) lower surface; 38mm (1 1/2") long x 15mm (9/16") wide. TUBE is pale pink (62D); long & thin; 20mm (3/4") long x 5mm (3/16") wide. FOLIAGE is dark green (139A) upper surface; medium green (137C) lower surface. PARENTAGE: 'Jef vander Kuylen' x 'Hilda'. Michiels 2007 BE AFS6550.

Bébé Futé. Upright/Trailer. Single. COROLLA: unflared, smooth petal margins; opens purple (71A); matures reddish purple (71B); 20mm (13/16") long x 9mm (3/8") wide. SEPALS: horizontal; tips recurved; pink (48C) upper surface; rose (48B) lower surface; 35mm (1 3/8") long x 7mm (1/4") wide. TUBE: rose (48B); short, medium thickness; 10mm (3/8") long x 2.5-4mm (1/8-3/16") wide. STAMENS: extend 12-15mm (1/2-9/16") below corolla; pink (48D) filaments; rose (48B) anthers. PISTIL: extends 34mm (1 3/8") below the corolla; rose (48B) style; dark rose (48A) stigma. BUD: ovate. FOLIAGE: dark green (147A) upper surface, medium green (147B) lower surface. Leaves are 90mm (3 9/16") long x 28mm (1 1/8") wide, lanceolate shaped, serrulated edges, acute tips and acute bases. Yellowish green veins & stems; yellowish green & light brown branches. PARENTAGE: 'Porte Océane' x 'Loveliness'. Lax upright or stiff trailer. Self branching. Makes good upright or standard. Prefers overhead filtered light and cool climate. Best bloom and foliage colour in filtered light. Tested 3 years in Pornic, France. Distinguished by profuse blooming and flower/foliage contrast. Masse 2004 FR AFS5446.

Becci Van Rensberg. Upright/Trailer. Double. Upright/Trailer. COROLLA: half flared, turned up petal margins; opens violet (86D) lightly splashed pink (62A); matures light purple (74C); 26mm (1") long x 34mm (1 5/16") wide. SEPALS: fully up; tips recurved; light rose (63D) tipped green upper surface; pink (62A) lower surface; 32mm(1 1/4") long x 15mm (9/16") wide. TUBE: white (155D) striped green; medium length & thickness; 18mm (11/16") long x 6mm (1/4") wide. STAMENS: extend 16mm (5/8") below corolla; light purple (70C) filaments; reddish purple (58A) anthers. PISTIL: extends 24mm (15/16") below the corolla, light rose (73C) style; cream (158D) stigma. BUD: obtuse.

FOLIAGE: dark green (139A) upper surface; medium green (138A) lower surface. Leaves are 55mm (2 3/16") long x 24mm (15/16") wide, lanceolate shaped, serrulated edges, acute tips and rounded bases. Veins, stems & branches are green. PARENTAGE: 'Branksome Beauty' x 'Devonshire Dumpling'. Lax upright or stiff trailer. Makes good basket. Prefers overhead filtered light and cool climate. Best bloom and foliage colour in filtered light. Tested 3 years in Stockbridge, Hampshire, England. Distinguished by colour combination. Graham 2003 UK AFS5142.

Bel Anne. Upright/Trailer. Single. COROLLA: quarter flared, bell shape; opens dark reddish purple (60C); matures red (46B); 19mm (3/4") long x 22mm (7/8") wide. SEPALS: horizontal, tips recurved; red (46D) upper surface; dark red (47A) lower surface; 27mm (1 1/16") long x 15mm (9/16") wide. TUBE: magenta (58B); 21mm (13/16") long x 9mm (5/16") wide. FOLIAGE is dark green (147A) upper surface; light olive green (148B) lower surface. PARENTAGE: 'Marinka' x 'Kwintet'. Tourneur 2008 AFS6851.

Bel Valérie. Upright/Trailer. Double. COROLLA: three quarter flared, petticoat shape; opens violet (90C); matures light purple (88C) veined pink (62A); 21mm (1 13/16") long x 28mm (1 1/8") wide. SEPALS: horizontal, tips recurved; rose (65A) veined white, tipped green upper surface; light pink (65C) lower surface; 24mm (15/16") long x 16mm (5/8") wide. TUBE: pink (36A); 18mm (11/16") long x 14mm (9/16") wide. FOLIAGE is dark green (147A) upper surface; medium green (147B) lower surface. PARENTAGE: 'La Campanella' x unknown. Tourneur 2008 AFS6850.

Belize. Trailer. Double. COROLLA: three quarter flared, turned under petal margins; opens magenta (59D) & red purple (N79C); matures dark reddish purple (61A) & purple (71A); 38mm (1 1/2") long x 27mm (1 1/16") wide. PETALOIDS: magenta (59D) & dark purple (79B); 14mm (9/16") long x 11mm (7/16") wide. SEPALS are horizontal, tips recurved, twisted left to right; magenta (61C), tipped yellowish green (144B) upper surface; magenta (59D), tipped yellowish green (144B) lower surface; 63mm (2 1/2") long x 27mm (1 1/16") wide. TUBE is magenta (61C), striped light green (143C); medium length & thickness; 18mm (11/16") long x 7mm (1/4") wide. STAMENS extend 18mm (11/16")

26

beyond the corolla; reddish purple (71B) filaments; dark purple (79A) anthers. PISTIL extends 44mm (1 3/4") beyond the corolla; purple (71A) style; red purple (N79C) stigma. BUD is bulbous. FOLIAGE is dark green (137A) upper surface; medium green (138B) lower surface. Leaves are 82mm (3 9/16") long x 39mm (1 1/2") wide, elliptic shaped, serrulate edges, acute tips, rounded bases. Veins are magenta (59C), stems are very dark reddish purple (186A) & branches are reddish purple (186B) & medium green (138B). PARENTAGE: 'Coen Bakker' x 'Comperen Lutea'. Lax upright or stiff trailer, self branching. Makes good basket. Prefers overhead filtered light, cool climate. Best bloom & foliage in filtered light. Tested 3 years in Koningshooikt, Belgium. Waanrode 5/7/08, Outstanding. Distinguished by combination of dark bloom colours. Michiels 2009 BE AFS7148.

Bella Bella. Upright. Single. COROLLA is half flared, bell shaped, with smooth turned under petal margins; opens light purple (88C), matures reddish purple (80B); lightly veined pink, flushed white at base; 23mm (15/16") long x 32mm (1 1/4") wide. SEPALS are horizontal, tips recurved; light pink (55D) tipped yellowish green upper surface, pink (55C) striped pale pink along center lower surface; 33mm (1 5/16") long x 12mm (1/2") wide. TUBE is light pink (55D), short with medium thickness; 8mm (5/16") long x 8mm (5/16") wide. STAMENS extend 25mm (1") beyond the corolla; light pink (55D) filaments and dark reddish purple (60C) anthers. PISTIL extends 38mm (1 1/2") below the corolla; pale pink (55C) style, light apple green (145C) stigma. BUD is narrow, pointed. FOLIAGE is dark green (137A) upper surface, medium green (137C) lower surface. Leaves are 38mm (1 1/2") long x 34mm (1 5/16") wide, ovate shaped, serrulated edges, acute tips and rounded bases. Veins are light purple (186C), stems are plum (185C), branches are light brown (200D). PARENTAGE: 'Blue Ice' x 'Mayfield'. Medium upright. Makes good upright, standard, bush or shrub. Prefers full sun and cool climate. Best bloom colour in bright light. Tested four years in Northumberland, England. Distinguished by profuse blossoms and contrasting vibrant blossom colours. Hall M. 2002 UK AFS4887.

Bella Harris. Upright. Semi Double. COROLLA mauve. SEPALS pink. Harris 2002 UK.

Belle De Prefailles. Upright/Trailer. Single. COROLLA is quarter flared with smooth petal margins; opens and matures red (53C); 19mm (3/4") long x 21mm (13/16") wide. SEPALS are half down, tips recurved; pink (48D) tipped yellowish green (146C) upper and lower surfaces; 30mm (1 3/16") long x 8mm (5/16") wide. TUBE is pink (48D), medium length and thickness; 29mm (1 1/8") long x 8mm (5/16") wide. STAMENS extend up to 2mm (1/16") below the corolla; light pink (55D) filaments and light yellow (4C) anthers. PISTIL extends 20mm (13/16") below the corolla; light pink (36C) style; light yellow (4C) stigma. BUD is long, ovate. FOLIAGE is dark green (147A) upper surface, medium green (147B) lower surface. Leaves are 85mm (3 3/8") long x 65mm (2 9/16") wide, cordate shaped, serrated edges, acute tips and rounded bases. Veins are light yellowish green, stems and branches are light yellowish green and pale brown. PARENTAGE: 'Speciosa' x 'Mrs. W. Rundle'. Lax upright or stiff trailer. Makes good basket or upright. Prefers overhead filtered light and cool climate. Best bloom colour in filtered light. Tested four years in Prefailles, France. Distinguished by bloom colour and profuse blooms. Boquien 2002 FR AFS4865.

Beloved Brian. Upright/Trailer. Single. COROLLA is quarter flared, bell shaped, with turned under smooth petal margins; opens red (50A), dark orange (41A) near Tube; matures rose (50B), orange (41B) near Tube; 10mm (3/8") long x 15mm (9/16") wide. SEPALS are horizontal, tips recurved; light pink (49C) upper surface; pale pink (49D) lower surface; 30mm (1 3/16") long x 9mm (3/8") wide. TUBE is light orange (27A); medium length & thickness; 12mm (1/2") long x 5mm (3/16") wide. FOLIAGE: dark green (147A) upper surface; medium green (147B) lower surface. Leaves are 50mm (2") long x 30mm (1 3/16") wide, cordate shaped. PARENTAGE: 'Coachman' x 'Hawaiian Sunset'. Distinguished by profuse blooms and corolla/sepal colour combination. Allsop M.R. 2005 UK AFS5689.

Bendtes Bonzai. Upright. Single. COROLLA: quarter flared, turned under smooth petal margins; opens rose (52B); matures red (53D); 4mm (3/16") long x 3mm (1/8") wide. SEPALS: horizontal; tips reflexed; light rose (58D) tipped yellowish green (145A) upper surface; rose (52C) tipped yellowish green (145A) lower surface; 7mm (1/4") long x 3mm (1/8") wide. TUBE: light rose (58D);

short & thin; 4mm(3/16") long x 2mm (1/16") wide. STAMENS: do not extend below corolla; pale yellow (1D) filaments, light yellow (1C) anthers. PISTIL: extends 3mm (1/8") below the corolla, light pink (49C) style, light pink (49B) stigma. BUD: elongated. FOLIAGE: medium green (137B) upper surface; medium green (138B) lower surface. Leaves are 30mm (1 3/16") long x 18mm (11/16") wide, lanceolate shaped, serrulated edges, acute tips and rounded bases. Veins are medium green (137D), stems & branches are medium green (137D) & light grayish rose (181D & 181C). PARENTAGE: 'Rosea' x 'F. *fulgens* var. *michocan*'. Small upright. Self branching. Makes good upright or bonsai. Prefers full sun. Best bloom and foliage colour in bright light. Tested 3 years in Nakskov, Denmark. NBFK Certificate at Meise. Distinguished by blossom shape.
Struck 2003 DE AFS5191.

Beninkust. Upright. Single. COROLLA is quarter flared, bell shaped; opens reddish purple (61B); matures magenta (58B); 7mm (1/4") long x 4mm (3/16") wide. SEPALS are half down, tips reflexed; rose (51B) upper surface; rose (52B) lower surface; 15mm (9/16") long x 3mm (1/8") wide. TUBE is dark rose (51A); 10mm (3/8") long x 2mm (1/16") wide. FOLIAGE: dark green (147A) upper surface; grayish green (191A) lower surface. PARENTAGE: 'Hinnerike' x ('F. vulcanica' x 'F. magellanica'). Distinguished by shape & colour.
de Boer J. 2006 NL AFS5986.

Berke En Lizet. Trailer. Single. COROLLA is unflared; opens purple (71A); matures magenta (71C); 19mm (3/4") long x 11mm (7/16") wide. SEPALS are fully up, tips recurved; reddish purple (71B) upper surface; dark reddish purple (72A) lower surface; 28mm (1 1/8") long x 7mm (1/4") wide. TUBE is reddish purple (71B); 13mm (1/2") long x 5mm (3/16") wide. FOLIAGE: dark green (136B) upper surface; medium green (138A) lower surface. PARENTAGE: 'Rosea' x 'Katrien Michiels'. Meise 9/17/05. Distinguished by dark bloom colour.
Michiels 2006 BE AFS6067.

Berke 'T Compostmenneke. Upright. Single. COROLLA: half flared, turned under wavy petal margins; opens purple (82A), magenta (63B) at base; matures reddish purple (80B); 20mm (13/16") long x 24mm (15/16") wide. SEPALS: horizontal; tips recurved; red (46B) upper surface; dark rose (51A) lower surface; 29mm(1 1/8") long x 11mm (7/16") wide. TUBE: red (46B); long & thick; 30mm (1 3/16") long x 5mm (3/16") wide, 10mm (3/8") at base, bent. STAMENS: extend 9mm (3/8") below the corolla; magenta (58B) filaments, light tan (162B) anthers. PISTIL extends 5mm (3/16") below the corolla; dark rose (58C) style, yellowish (17A) stigma. BUD: ovate. FOLIAGE: dark green (137A) upper surface; medium green (138A) lower surface. Leaves are 76mm (3") long x 38mm (1 1/2") wide, ovate shaped, serrulated edges, acute tips and rounded bases. Veins, stems & branches are dark red (178A). PARENTAGE: 'Alda Alders' x 'Wingrove's Mammoth'. Tall upright. Makes good standard. Prefers overhead filtered light and warm climate. Best bloom and foliage colour in bright light. Tested 4 years in Leopoldsburg, Belgium. NBFK Certificate at Meise. Distinguished by long Tube, bloom shape.
Busschodts 2003 BE AFS5125.

Bert Beekman. Upright/Trailer. Double. COROLLA is half flared with smooth petal margins; opens purple (79C), matures dark reddish purple (72A); 24mm (15/16") long x 28 mm (1 1/8") wide. SEPALS are horizontal, tips recurved; magenta (71C) upper surface; dark rose (64C) lower surface; 52mm (2 1/16") long x 20mm (13/16") wide. TUBE is magenta (71C), medium length and thickness; 17mm (11/16") long x 8mm (5/16") wide. STAMENS extend 12mm (1/2") beyond the corolla; dark reddish purple (70A) filaments & anthers. PISTIL extends 27mm (1 1/16") below the corolla; dark rose (71D) style; light yellow (4C) stigma. BUD is ovate, pointed. FOLIAGE is dark green (137A) upper surface, medium green (138B) lower surface. Leaves are 80mm (3 1/8") long x 46mm (1 13/16") wide, ovate shaped, serrulated edges, acute tips and obtuse bases. Veins, stems & branches are red. PARENTAGE: 'Bicentennial' x ('Rohees King' x 'Miniskirt'). Lax upright or stiff trailer. Makes good stiff trailer. Prefers overhead filtered light & cool climate. Best bloom and foliage colour in filtered light. Tested four years in Knegsel, The Netherlands. Distinguished by bloom colour.
van Bree 2004 NL AFS5358.

Bert Comperen. Upright. Semi Double. COROLLA: three quarter flared, smooth petal margins; opens dark purple (79B); matures purple (71A); 17mm (11/16") long x 19mm (3/4") wide. SEPALS: horizontal; tips recurved; rose (63C) upper surface; magenta

28

(63B) lower surface; 27mm (1 1/16") long x 10mm (3/8") wide. TUBE: magenta (63A); medium length & thickness; 12mm (1/2") long x 7mm (1/4") wide. STAMENS: extend 20mm (13/16") below corolla; purple (71A) filaments & anthers. PISTIL: extends 44mm (1 3/4") below the corolla; magenta (71C) style, light yellow (11D) stigma. BUD: ovate. FOLIAGE: dark green (137A) upper surface; medium green (138B) lower surface. Leaves are 55mm (2 3/16") long x 20mm (13/16") wide, lanceolate shaped, serrulated edges, acute tips and obtuse bases. Veins, stems & branches are green. PARENTAGE: 'Maxima' x 'Belle de Spa'. Medium upright. Makes good upright or standard. Prefers overhead filtered light and cool climate. Best bloom and foliage colour in filtered light. Tested 4 years in Diessen, The Netherlands. Distinguished by bloom colour.
Comperen 2003 NL AFS5264.

Bert's Jante. Upright. Single. COROLLA is quarter flared, bell shaped, with turned under smooth petal margins; opens and matures magenta (57A); 29mm (1 1/8") long x 38mm (1 1/2") wide. SEPALS are half up, tips reflexed up; yellowish white (158A) upper surface; white (155A) lower surface; 35mm (1 3/8") long x 14mm (9/16") wide. TUBE is pale yellow (158B); medium length and thin; 15mm (5/8") long x 9mm (3/8") thick. STAMENS extend 36mm (1 7/16") beyond the corolla; light pink (72B) filaments, rose (63C) anthers. PISTIL extends 51mm (2") beyond the corolla; white (155D) style, white (155A) stigma. BUD is elliptic. FOLIAGE is medium green (139B) upper surface, light green (139C) lower surface. Leaves are 73mm (2 7/8") long x 46mm (1 13/16") wide, cordate shaped, serrated edges, acute tips and cordate bases. Veins are green, branches and stems are yellow green. PARENTAGE: 'Voodoo' x unknown. Small upright. Makes good basket. Prefers full sun. Best bloom and foliage colour in bright light. Tested four years in Edegem, Belgium. Approved by the Belgium Fuchsia Judging Commission. Distinguished by corolla/sepal colour combination.
Pelgrims 2002 BE AFS5056.

Beryl Clark. Upright. Single. COROLLA lilac. SEPALS vivid pink. TUBE vivid pink. PARENTAGE sport of Daniela.
Bielby/Oxtoby 2009 UK.

Bery's Elizabeth. Trailer. Single. COROLLA: unflared, barrel shaped, smooth petal margins; opens violet (86B) edged dark

purple (86A); matures light purple (78B); 19mm (3/4") long x 12mm (1/2") wide. SEPALS: horizontal; tips recurved; pale pink (56B) veined magenta (58B) upper surface; magenta (58B) tipped green lower surface; 32mm (1 1/4") long x 7mm (1/4") wide. TUBE: pale pink (56D) with darker stripes; medium length & thickness; 19mm(3/4") long x 7mm (1/4") wide. STAMENS: 25mm (1") below corolla; magenta (57C) filaments, white (155D) anthers. PISTIL: extends 38mm (1 1/2") below the corolla, light rose (58D) style, white (155D) stigma. BUD: ovate. FOLIAGE: yellowish green (145A) upper surface; apple green (144C) lower surface. Leaves are 25mm (1") long x 12mm (1/2") wide, elliptic shaped, serrulated edges, acute tips and obtuse bases. Veins, stems & branches are red. PARENTAGE: 'Genni' x 'Jenny Sorenson'. Natural trailer. Makes good basket or miniature. Prefers overhead filtered light. Best bloom and foliage colour in bright light. Tested 4 years in Birmingham, England. Distinguished by golden foliage and flower colour combination.
Greenway L. 2003 UK AFS5207.

Beth Alana. Upright. Single. COROLLA is quarter flared, bell shaped, with smooth petal margins; opens & matures pink (51D); 11mm (7/16") long x 19mm (3/4") wide. SEPALS are half up, tips recurved up; rose (52B) light pink (36C) base, tipped greenish yellow upper surface; rose (52C) lower surface; 32mm (1 1/4") long x 10mm (3/8") wide. TUBE is rose (52B); medium length & thickness; 13mm (1/2") long x 7mm (1/4") wide. FOLIAGE: yellowish green (146B) upper surface; yellowish green (146C) lower surface. Leaves are 55mm (2 3/16") long x 25mm (1") wide, ovate shaped. PARENTAGE: 'Forward Look' x ('Mieke Meursing' x 'Iceburg'). Distinguished by profuse blooms.
Jackson 2005 UK AFS5692.

Bets Tamerus. Upright. Double. COROLLA is three quarter flared with smooth petal margins; opens purple (83B); matures dark reddish purple (72A); 26mm (1") long x 24mm (15/16") wide. SEPALS are half up, tips recurved up; red(52A) upper and lower surfaces; 30mm (1 3/16") long x 15mm (5/8") wide. TUBE is red (52A); medium length and thickness; 12mm (1/2") long x 6mm (1/4") thick. STAMENS extend 15mm (5/8") beyond the corolla; dark rose (51A) filaments, dark rose (54A) anthers. PISTIL extends 32mm (1 1/4") beyond the corolla; red (50A) style, pale orange (23D) stigma. BUD is round, pointed. FOLIAGE is dark

29

green (137A) upper surface, medium green (138B) lower surface. Leaves are 74mm (2 15/16") long x 42mm (1 11/16") wide, ovate shaped, serrated edges, acute tips and rounded bases. Veins are green, stems and branches are red. PARENTAGE: 'Rohees Mintaka' x 'Gilian Althea'. Medium upright. Makes good standard. Prefers overhead filtered light and cool climate. Best bloom colour in filtered light. Tested four years in Duizel, The Netherlands. Distinguished by bloom colour.
Tamerus 2002 NL AFS4993.

Betsy Huuskes. Upright. Single. COROLLA is three quarter flared; opens reddish orange (42A); matures light reddish orange (42D); 12mm (1/2") long x 21mm (13/16") wide. SEPALS are fully up, tips recurved; light orange (39C) tipped green upper surface; coral (39B) tipped green lower surface; 21mm (13/16") long x 15mm (9/16") wide. TUBE is light orange (39C); 10mm (3/8") long x 10mm (3/8") wide. FOLIAGE: dark green (137A) upper surface; medium green (138A) lower surface. PARENTAGE: 'Roesse Carme' x ('Swanley Gem' x 'Eisvogel'). Distinguished by bloom colour & shape.
Roes 2006 NL AFS5983.

Bettini Stubi. Upright/Trailer. Single. COROLLA: three quarter flared, turned under smooth petal margins; opens dark reddish purple (70A), white (155B) at base; matures magenta (63A), dark reddish purple (64A) at base; 19mm (3/4") long x 26mm (1") wide. PETALOIDS: one per sepal; same colour as corolla, 10mm (3/8") long x 7mm (1/4") wide. SEPALS: half down; tips reflexed; dark rose (58C) upper surface; rose (52C) lower surface; 27mm (1 1/16") long x 13mm (1/2") wide. TUBE: white (155A); medium length & thickness; 12mm (1/2") long x 8mm (5/16") wide. STAMENS: extend 7mm (1/4") below the corolla; dark rose (58C) filaments, light yellow (2C) anthers. PISTIL extends 22mm (7/8") below the corolla; dark rose (58C) style, dark yellowish orange (14A) stigma. BUD: ovate. FOLIAGE: dark green (137A) upper surface; medium green (138B) lower surface. Leaves are 57mm (2 1/4") long x 31mm (1 1/4") wide, ovate shaped, serrulated edges, acute tips and rounded bases. Veins & stems are light green (138C), branches are light brown (199B). PARENTAGE: 'WALZ Fagot' x unknown. Lax upright or stiff trailer. Self branching. Makes good basket. Prefers overhead filtered light. Best bloom and foliage colour in filtered light. Tested 3 years in Rummen, Belgium. NBFK

certificate at Meise. Distinguished by bloom colour.
Ector 2003 BE AFS5109.

Betty Swennen. Upright/Trailer. Double. COROLLA is three quarter flared with turned under smooth petal margins; opens violet (76B); matures pale purple (75D); 25mm (1") long x 46mm (1 13/16") wide. SEPALS are horizontal, tips recurved; rose (50B), white (155C) tipped light yellowish green (149B) upper surface; white (155D) lower surface; 39mm (1 9/16") long x 18mm (11/16") wide. TUBE is white (155C) striped light pink (62B); medium length and thickness; 24mm (15/16") long x 8mm (5/16") wide. STAMENS extend 8mm (5/16") beyond the corolla; light pink (65B) filaments, tan (162A) anthers. PISTIL extends 10 (3/8") beyond the corolla; white (155A) style, pale yellow (2D) stigma. BUD is round, pointed. FOLIAGE is medium green (138A) upper surface, medium green (138B) lower surface. Leaves are 62mm (2 7/16") long x 37mm (1 7/16") wide, ovate to cordate shaped, serrated edges, acute tips and rounded to cordate bases. Veins and stems are tan (166C), branches are medium green (138A). PARENTAGE: 'Rhees Beauty' x 'Fey'. Lax upright or stiff trailer. Self branching. Makes good upright. Prefers overhead filtered light. Best bloom and foliage colour in filtered light. Tested four years in Leopoldsburg, Belgium. Certificate N.B.F.K. at Meise. Distinguished by delicate bloom colour.
Busschodts 2002 BE AFS4978.

Beverley Sisters. Upright/Trailer. Double. COROLLA is unflared, plum shaped, with turned up smooth petal margins; opens light purple (74C) shaded dark rose (58C) red (50A) at base; matures strawberry rose (50B); 35mm (1 3/8") long x 30mm (1 3/16") wide. SEPALS are fully up, tips recurved; red (45B) tipped green upper surface, red(45B) lower surface; 48mm (1 7/8") long x 15mm (5/8) wide. TUBE is red (45B) medium length and thickness; 19mm (3/4") long x 6mm (1/4") wide. STAMENS extend 15mm (5/8") below the corolla; dark rose (48A) filaments and anthers. PISTIL extends 45mm (1 3/4") below the corolla; pink (48C) style and pale pink (49D) stigma. BUD is pear shaped, thin, pointed. FOLIAGE is dark green (137A) upper surface, medium green (138B) lower surface. Leaves are 60mm (2 3/8") long x 25mm (1") wide, lanceolate shaped, serrulated edges, acute tips and rounded bases. Veins are green, stems are light green and branches are red. PARENTAGE: 'Elsie Mitchell' x

30

'Seventh Heaven'. Lax upright or stiff trailer. Makes good basket or standard. Prefers cool climate. Heat tolerant if shaded. Best bloom colour in filtered light. Tested five years in Gloucester, England. Distinguished by bloom colour.
Hickman 2002 UK AFS4860.

Biance Fuhrmann. Upright. Double. COROLLA: three quarter flared; opens rose (48B) & violet (76A); matures light pink (49B), rose (51B) & light purple (75B); 30mm (1 3/16") long x 26mm (1") wide. PETALOIDS: rose (48B) & violet (76A); 22mm (7/8") long x 18mm (11/16") wide. SEPALS are horizontal, tips recurved, twisted left to right; white (155C); light pink (62C) tipped light green (143C) upper surface; pink (52D) tipped light green (143C) lower surface; 27mm (1 1/16") long x 11mm (7/16") wide. TUBE is white (155C) striped light green (143B); 9mm (5/16") long x 7mm (1/4") wide. FOLIAGE is dark green (139A) upper surface; medium green (138B) lower surface. PARENTAGE: 'Vendelzwaaier' x 'Hampshire Treasure'. Waanrode 7/7/2007.
Michiels 2008 BE AFS6720.

Big David. Upright/Trailer. Double. COROLLA: Three quarter flared; opens light purple (N78C) striped magenta (63A); matures light purple (N80C) striped dark rose (67C); 26mm (1") long x 21mm (13/16") wide. PETALOIDS: violet (77B) striped magenta (63A); 23mm (7/8") long x 14mm (9/16") wide. SEPALS: horizontal, tips recurved; magenta (63B) tipped pale pink (62D) upper surface; light reddish purple (N66C) lower surface; 44mm (1 3/4") long x 18mm (11/16") wide. TUBE: magenta (61C); short & thick; 11mm (7/16") long x 7mm (1/4") wide. FOLIAGE is dark green (137A) upper surface; medium green (137C) lower surface. PARENTAGE: 'Allison Reynolds' x 'Onbekend'.
Willems 2007 BE AFS6599.

Big White. Trailer. Double. COROLLA: quarter flared, turned under wavy petal margins; opens white (155C), rose (68C) base; matures white (155B), light pink (65B) base; 24mm (15/16") long x 16mm (5/8") wide. PETALOIDS: Same colour as corolla; 14mm (9/16") long x 5mm (3/16") wide. SEPALS: half down, tips reflexed; white (155C) & rose (68C) tipped pale yellowish green (154D) upper surface; white (155B) & rose (68C) tipped pale yellowish green (154D) lower surface; 56mm (3 1/4") long x 16mm (5/8") wide. TUBE: white (155C); long & thin;

24mm (15/16") long x 5mm (3/16") wide. STAMENS extend 14mm (9/16") beyond the corolla; rose (65A) filaments; light rose (73C) anthers. PISTIL extends 19mm (3/4") beyond the corolla; white (155B) style; pale yellow (2D) stigma. BUD: oblong. FOLIAGE: dark green (139A) upper surface; medium green (137C) lower surface. Leaves are 68mm (2 11/16") long x 32mm (1 1/4") wide; ovate shaped, serrate edges, acute tips, rounded bases. Veins are light green (138C), stems are medium green (138B), branches are very dark reddish purple (186A) & medium green (138B). PARENTAGE: 'Pink Panther' x unknown. Natural trailer. Self branching. Makes good basket. Prefers overhead filtered light. Tested 3 years in Rillaar, Belgium. Waanrode 8/9/08, Awarded Outstanding. Distinguished by white & pink variegation on sepal.
Willems 2009 BE AFS7076.

Bilberry Sorbet. Upright/Trailer. Semi Double. COROLLA: half flared, turned under wavy petal margins; opens purple (71A); matures dark reddish purple (59A); 26mm (1") long x 18mm (11/16") wide. PETALOIDS: purple (71A); 21mm (13/16") long x 14mm (9/16") wide. SEPALS: horizontal; tips recurved; reddish purple (64B) upper surface; reddish purple (61B) lower surface; 37mm (1 7/16") long x 11mm (7/16") wide. TUBE: reddish purple (61B); long, medium thickness; 35mm (1 3/8") long x 6mm (1/4") wide. STAMENS: extend 17mm (11/16") below the corolla; reddish purple (67A) filaments, dark reddish purple (59A) anthers. PISTIL extends 28mm (1 1/8") below the corolla; reddish purple (67A) style, dark reddish purple (61A) stigma. BUD: ovate. FOLIAGE: medium green (138B) upper surface; light green (138C) lower surface. Leaves are 70mm (2 3/4") long x 31mm (1 1/4") wide, lanceolate shaped, serrulated edges, acute tips and rounded bases. Veins & stems are dark red (185A), branches are dark red purple (187D). PARENTAGE: 'WALZ Mandoline' x 'Rohees Mintaka'. Lax upright or stiff trailer. Self branching. Makes good basket. Prefers overhead filtered light. Best bloom and foliage colour in filtered light. Tested 3 years in Koningshooikt, Belgium. NBFK certificate at Meise. Distinguished by bloom colour.
Michiels 2003 BE AFS5099.

Birgit Verstoep. Trailer. Double. COROLLA: three quarter flared, turned under petal margins; opens rose (68B) & purple (N78C); matures magenta (67B) & reddish purple

(72B); 21mm (13/16") long x 19mm (3/4") wide. PETALOIDS: rose (68B) & purple (N78C); 14mm (9/16") long x 9mm (5/16") wide. SEPALS are horizontal, tips reflexed; pale lavender (69D), tipped light yellow green (150B) upper surface; pale lavender (69B), tipped light yellow green (150B) lower surface; 34mm (1 3/8") long x 17mm (5/8") wide. TUBE is white (155C); medium length & thickness; 13mm (1/2") long x 6mm (1/4") wide. STAMENS extend 8mm (5/16") beyond the corolla; magenta (63B) filaments; light reddish purple (73A) anthers. PISTIL extends 15mm (9/16") beyond the corolla; light pink (62C) style; yellowish white (4D) stigma. BUD is bulbous. FOLIAGE is dark green (136A) upper surface; medium green (137C) lower surface. Leaves are 69mm (2 3/4") long x 37mm (1 7/16") wide, ovate shaped, serrulate edges, acute tips, rounded bases. Veins are greenish yellow (151A), stems are very dark reddish purple (186A) & branches are plum (184C) & light green (138C). PARENTAGE: 'Manfried Kleinau' x 'Laura Biolcati-Rinaldi'. Natural trailer, self branching. Makes good basket. Prefers overhead filtered light, cool climate. Best bloom & foliage in filtered light. Tested 3 years in Koningshooikt, Belgium. Waanrode 9/8/08. Distinguished by bloom colour combination.
Michiels 2009 BE AFS7149.

Black Country 21. Single. COROLLA dark violet to aubergine. SEPALS deep pink. TUBE deep pink.
Reynolds G. 2007 UK.

Blauwe Geschelpte Montauban. Upright. Double. COROLLA is half flared with turned under smooth petal margins; opens violet (84A), rose (52B) at base; matures dark reddish purple (61A), light pink (62B) at base; 17mm (11/16") long x 26 mm (1") wide. SEPALS are fully up, tips recurved; red (50A) tipped light green (142A) upper surface, rose (52C) lower surface; 26mm (1") long x 11mm (7/16") wide. TUBE is rose (50B), short with medium thickness; 9mm (3/8") long x 4mm (3/16") wide. STAMENS extend 20mm (13/16") beyond the corolla; rose (65A) filaments, dark reddish purple (61A) anthers. PISTIL extends 31mm (1 1/4") below the corolla; rose (65A), white (155A) at base style; reddish purple (58A) stigma. BUD is round, pointed. FOLIAGE is dark green (137A) upper surface, medium green (137C) lower surface. Leaves are 75mm (2 15/16") long x 31mm (1 1/4") wide, lanceolate shaped, serrulated edges, acute tips and acute bases. Veins,

stems and branches are light green (138B). PARENTAGE: 'Areler Land' x 'Christel Stumpf. Medium upright. Self branching. Makes good upright. Prefers overhead filtered light. Best bloom and foliage colour in bright to filtered light. Tested three years in Hoeselt, Belgium. Certificate N.B.F.K. at Meise. Distinguished by bloom colour and shape.
Wagemans 2002 BE AFS4900.

Blober. Upright. Single. COROLLA: Quarter flared; opens magenta (58B) & rose (52C); matures reddish purple (61B); 28mm (1 1/8") long x 26mm (1") wide. SEPALS: half down, tips reflexed; rose (52C) tipped light apple green (145B) upper surface; light orange (41C) tipped light apple green (145B) lower surface; 37mm (1 7/16") long x 15mm (9/16") wide. TUBE: rose (54C); long & thin; 48mm (1 7/8") long x 7mm (1/4") wide. FOLIAGE is dark green (139A) upper surface; medium green (138B) lower surface. PARENTAGE: 'WALZ Harp' x 'Ting-a-Ling'. Small upright. Self branching.
Geerts L 2007 BE AFS6382.

Bloemen-Jetje. Trailer. Double. COROLLA is half flared; opens white (155A); matures white (155D); 17mm (5/8") long x 16mm (5/8") wide. PETALOIDS are white (155C); 10mm (3/8") long x 8mm (5/16") wide. SEPALS are horizontal, tips reflexed; white (155C), tipped light green (142B) upper surface; white (155B), tipped light green (142B) lower surface; 38mm (1 1/2") long x 15mm (9/16") wide. TUBE is white (155B); 13mm (1/2") long x 5mm (3/16") wide. FOLIAGE is dark green (137A) upper surface; medium green (138B) lower surface. PARENTAGE: 'Sofie Michiels' x 'White Queen'. Meise 8/13/05: "Outstanding". Distinguished by bloom colour.
Michiels 2006 BE AFS6022.

Bloemfontein. Trailer. Single. COROLLA: quarter flared, square shape; opens dark rose (55A); matures magenta (68A); 15mm (9/16") long x 14mm (9/16") wide. SEPALS: half down, tips reflexed; pink (49A) upper & lower surfaces; 32mm (1 1/4") long x 9mm (5/16") wide. TUBE: pink (49A); 30mm (1 3/16") long x 8mm (5/16") wide. FOLIAGE is medium green (146A) upper surface; light olive green (147C) lower surface. PARENTAGE: ('Sparkling Whisper' x 'F. boliviana') x 'Alaska'.
de Boer 2008 NL AFS6853.

Blue Dancer. Upright/Trailer. Single. COROLLA is half to three quarter flared with

32

smooth petal margins; opens violet blue to violet (92A-92C), matures light purple (88C); 25-35mm (1 - 1 3/8") long x 30mm (1 3/16") wide. SEPALS are twisted horizontal, tips recurved; white tipped light apple green (145B) upper & lower surfaces; creped lower surface; 45-50mm (1 3/4 - 2") long x 14mm (9/16") wide. TUBE is white striped light green (145D), medium length and thickness; 15mm (9/16") long x 7mm (1/4") wide. STAMENS extend 23mm (15/16") beyond the corolla; pale pink (62D) filaments; light pink (62B) anthers. PISTIL extends 23mm (15/16") below the corolla; white style & stigma. BUD is oval, elongated. FOLIAGE is medium green (146A) upper surface, yellowish green (146B) lower surface. Leaves are 85mm (3 3/8") long x 36mm (1 7/16") wide, ovate shaped, serrated edges, acute tips and rounded bases. Veins are light olive green (147C), stems are light yellowish green (146D) & branches are reddish purple. PARENTAGE: 'Ting-A-Ling' x 'Quasar'. Lax upright or stiff trailer. Makes good basket, standard, pillar or trellis. Prefers overhead filtered light. Heat tolerant if shaded. Best bloom colour in bright light. Tested eight years in Napa, CA, USA. Distinguished by bloom colour combination
McGowan R. 2004 USA AFS5363.

Blumenfreunden.   Upright.   Single.
COROLLA: quarter flared, turned under smooth petal margins; opens purple (83A), reddish purple (64B) base; matures purple (77A); 18mm (11/16") long x 22mm (7/8") wide. PETALOIDS: Same colour as corolla; 15mm (9/16") long x 12mm (1/2") wide. SEPALS: half up; tips recurved up; reddish purple (64B) upper surface; reddish purple (67A) lower surface; 35mm (1 3/8") long x 13mm (1/2") wide. TUBE: dark reddish purple (64A); medium length & thickness; 12mm(1/2") long x 6mm (1/4") wide. STAMENS: extend 19mm (3/4") below corolla; dark reddish purple (61A) filaments, dark purple (79A) anthers. PISTIL: extends 41mm (1 5/8") below the corolla, dark rose (64C) style, yellow (10A) stigma. BUD: elongated. FOLIAGE: medium green (137B) upper surface; medium green (138B) lower surface. Leaves are 58mm (2 5/16") long x 31mm (1 1/4") wide, ovate shaped, serrulated edges, acute tips and rounded bases. Veins are light plum (184D), stems are plum (184C), branches are plum (185B). PARENTAGE: 'Rohees New Millennium' x 'Frank Saunders'. Medium upright. Self branching. Makes good upright. Prefers overhead filtered light. Best bloom and

foliage colour in filtered light. Tested 3 years in Koningshooikt, Belgium. NBFK Certificate at Meise. Distinguished by bloom colour.
Michiels 2003 BE AFS5195.

Blush   Queen.   Upright/Trailer.   Single.
COROLLA is quarter flared; opens rose (52C), matures rose (55B); 10mm (3/8") long x 7mm (1/4") wide. SEPALS are half down, tips reflexed; pale pink (56C) upper and lower surfaces; 10mm (3/8") long x 4mm (3/16") wide. TUBE is pale pink (56B) with dark base, long and thin; 29mm (1 1/8") long x 5mm (3/16") wide.   STAMENS are 2mm (1/16") inside the corolla; pale pink (56B) filaments and greenish white (157A) anthers. PISTIL extends 2mm (1/16") below the corolla; pale pink (56B) style, light pink (65B) stigma. BUD is long Tubed, ovate. FOLIAGE is dark green (147A) upper surface, medium green (146A) lower surface. Leaves are 42mm (1 11/16") long x 27mm (1 1/16") wide, ovate shaped, serrulated edges, obtuse tips and obtuse bases. Veins and stems are yellow green, branches are reddish yellow green. PARENTAGE: 'Panache' x 'F. venusta'. Lax upright or stiff trailer. Self branching. Makes good basket or upright. Prefers overhead filtered light. Heat tolerant if shaded. Best bloom and foliage colour in filtered light. Tested five years in Lisse, Holland. Distinguished by flowers on racemes (a shoot bearing clusters of flowers on short stalks) of unique colour and shape.
de Graaff 2002 NL AFS4884.

Bob Bartrum. Trailer. Single. COROLLA purple turning to rose. SEPALS pale pink tipped darker pink. TUBE pale pink.
Chatters 2006 UK.

Bobby Juliana. Upright. Single. COROLLA: Quarter flared; opens light reddish purple (72D) spotted reddish purple (61B); matures light reddish purple (72C); 21mm (13/16") long x 23mm (7/8") wide. SEPALS: fully up, tips recurved; light rose (68D) upper & lower surfaces; 30mm (1 3/16") long x 11mm (7/16") wide. TUBE: light magenta (N57A); short & thick; 12mm (7/16") long x 10mm (3/8") wide. FOLIAGE is dark green (137A) upper surface; medium green (137C) lower surface. PARENTAGE: 'Maria Landy' x 'Danny Kaye'.Burkhart 2007 DE AFS6494.

Bobonne Alice Berger. Upright. Single. COROLLA: unflared, turned under wavy petal margins; opens & matures rose (65A) edged magenta (68A); 12mm (1/2") long x 11mm (7/16") wide. SEPALS: half down; tips

reflexed; dark rose (58C) tipped light yellow (11B) upper surface; dark rose (58C) lower surface; 20mm (13/16") long x 7mm (1/4") wide. TUBE: dark rose (58C); long, medium thickness; 33mm (1 5/16") long x 7mm (1/4") wide. STAMENS: extend 4mm (3/16") below the corolla; magenta (58B) filaments, tan (162A) anthers. PISTIL extends 19mm (3/4") below the corolla; dark rose (58C) style, dark tan (164B) stigma. BUD: ovate. FOLIAGE: dark green (137A) upper surface, medium green (138A) lower surface. Leaves are 82mm (3 1/4") long x 38mm (1 1/2") wide, lanceolate shaped, serrated edges, acute tips and acute bases. Veins are medium green (139C), stems & branches are dark grayish purple (184A). PARENTAGE: 'Roger de Cooker' x unknown. Medium upright. Self branching. Makes good upright or standard. Prefers overhead filtered light and cool climate. Best bloom and foliage colour in filtered light. Tested 3 years Vreren, Belgium. NBFK certificate at Meise. Distinguished by profuse blooms and corolla colour combination.
Mathoul 2003 BE AFS5084.

Boer Louis. Trailer. Single. COROLLA is quarter flared with turned under wavy petal margins; opens dark purple (89A) veined magenta (57A), magenta (57B) at base; matures purple (89B) veined reddish purple (60D), magenta (58B) at base; 17mm (11/16") long x 15mm (5/8") wide. PETALOIDS are dark purple (89A), magenta (57C) at base; 13mm (1/2") long x 8mm (5/16") wide. SEPALS are horizontal, tips reflexed; magenta (57B) upper surface, dark rose (58C) lower surface; 24mm (15/16") long x 12mm (1/2") wide. TUBE is magenta (57B); medium length and thickness; 11mm (7/16") long x 6mm (1/4") wide. STAMENS extend 8mm (5/16") beyond the corolla; light magenta (57D) filaments, rose (61D) anthers. PISTIL extends 30mm (13/16") beyond the corolla; magenta (57B) style, light yellowish orange (19B) stigma. BUD is ovate, pointed. FOLIAGE is dark green (139A) upper surface, medium green (138B) lower surface. Leaves are 51mm (2") long x 20mm (13/16") wide, elliptic shaped, serrulated edges, acute tips and acute bases. Veins and branches are plum (184C), stems are dark red (185A). PARENTAGE: 'Rohees New Millennium' x 'Mystery'. Natural trailer. Self branching. Makes good basket. Prefers overhead filtered light. Best bloom and foliage colour in filtered light. Tested three years in Koningshooikt, Belgium. Certificate N.B.F.K. at Meise. Distinguished by bloom colour.

Michiels 2002 BE AFS4965.

Boke. Upright/Trailer. Single. COROLLA is quarter flared with turned under wavy petal margins; opens purple (80A); matures purple (81B); 16mm (5/8") long x 18 mm (11/16") wide. PETALOIDS: Same colour as corolla; 15mm (5/8") x 10mm (3/8"). SEPALS are horizontal, tips recurved; light reddish purple (66C) upper surface; dark rose (67C) lower surface; 33mm (1 5/16") long x 11mm (7/16") wide. TUBE is red (52A), long and thin; 34mm (1 3/8") long x 5mm (3/16") wide. STAMENS do not extend beyond the corolla; reddish purple (74B) filaments, purple (71A) anthers. PISTIL extends 10mm (3/8") below the corolla; magenta (71C) style; pink (50D) stigma. BUD is ovate, long, pointed. FOLIAGE is dark green (147A) upper surface, medium green (143A) lower surface. Leaves are 60mm (2 3/8") long x 32mm (1 1/4") wide, elliptic shaped, serrulated edges, acute tips and rounded bases. Veins are light plum (184D), stems are plum (184C), branches are grayish red (181A). PARENTAGE: 'WALZ Harp' x 'Rohees New Millennium'. Lax upright or stiff trailer, dwarf growth. Self branching. Makes good basket. Prefers overhead filtered light. Best bloom and foliage colour in filtered light. Tested three years in Berlaar, Belgium. Certificate N.B.F.K. at Meise. Distinguished by corolla shape.
Geerts J. 2002 BE AFS4917.

Bolleke De Beer. Upright. Single. COROLLA: quarter flared; opens pink (49A) & dark rose (51A); matures rose (51B); 12mm (7/16") long x 10mm (3/8") wide. SEPALS are half down, tips reflexed; rose (52C) tipped light greenish yellow (151D) upper surface; rose (47D) tipped light greenish yellow (151D) lower surface; 18mm (11/16") long x 7mm (1/4") wide. TUBE is rose (51B); 54mm (2 1/8") long x 8mm (5/16") wide. FOLIAGE is dark green (137A) upper surface; medium green (138B) lower surface. PARENTAGE: 'WALZ Harp' x 'Big Slim'. Waanrode 8/11//2007.
Geerts L. 2008 BE AFS6733.

Bon Roi René. Upright. Single. COROLLA: quarter flared, smooth petal margins; opens & matures purple (77A); 18mm (11/16") long x 14mm (9/16") wide. SEPALS: horizontal; tips recurved; red (46D) upper & lower surfaces; 38mm (1 1/2") long x 10mm (3/8") wide. TUBE: red (46D); short, medium thickness; 9mm (3/8") long x 4mm (3/16") wide. STAMENS: extend 2-5mm (1/16-3/16")

below corolla; light rose (73B) filaments; light tan (161C) anthers. PISTIL: extends 32mm (1 1/4") below the corolla; light purple (74C) style; plum (185B) stigma. BUD: ovate. FOLIAGE: medium green (146A) upper surface, yellowish green (146B) lower surface. Leaves are 65mm (2 9/16") long x 32mm (1 1/4") wide, ovate shaped, serrulated edges, acute tips and rounded bases. Yellowish green/light brown veins; light brown stems & branches. PARENTAGE: 'Henri Verdeur' x 'Speciosa'. Tall upright. Self branching. Makes good upright or standard. Prefers overhead filtered light and cool climate. Cold weather hardy to -8º C. Best bloom and foliage colour in filtered light. Tested 3 years in Pornic, France. Distinguished by hardiness and flower/foliage contrast.
Masse 2004 FR AFS5447.

Boneput. Trailer. Double. COROLLA: half flared, turned under petal margins; opens light reddish purple (73A) & light rose (N74C); matures rose (68B); 22mm (7/8") long x 18mm (11/16") wide. PETALOIDS: magenta (67B); 16mm (5/8") long x 11mm (7/16") wide. SEPALS are horizontal, tips recurved; pale lavender (69C), tipped light apple green (145B) upper surface; pink (55C), tipped light apple green (145B) lower surface; 37mm (1 7/16") long x 14mm (9/16") wide. TUBE is pale lavender (65D); medium length & thickness; 15mm (9/16") long x 7mm (1/4") wide. STAMENS extend 16mm (5/8") beyond the corolla; reddish purple (67A) filaments; purple (71A) anthers. PISTIL extends 29mm (1 1/8") beyond the corolla; rose rose (73D) style; pale yellow (2D) stigma. BUD is elongated, square. FOLIAGE is dark green (136B) upper surface; medium green (138B) lower surface. Leaves are 55mm (1 13/16") long x 33mm (1 5/16") wide, ovate shaped, serrulate edges, acute tips, rounded bases. Veins are light grayish red (182D), stems are light grayish rose (181D) & branches are light red purple (185D) & light green (139D). PARENTAGE: 'Manfried Kleinau' x 'Joergen Hahn'. Natural trailer, self branching. Makes good basket. Prefers cool climate. Best bloom & foliage in filtered light. Tested 3 years in Koningshooikt, Belgium. Waanrode 5/7/08. Distinguished by bloom colour combination & profuse flowering.
Michiels 2009 BE AFS7150.

Bonjour Claude. Upright/Trailer. Single. COROLLA is quarter flared with smooth petal margins; opens dark reddish purple (64A);

matures reddish purple (64B); 28mm (1 1/8") long x 27mm (1 1/16") wide. SEPALS are horizontal, tips recurved; pale pink (62D) splashed pink (62A), tipped light yellow (4C) upper surface; pink (62C) splashed pink (62A) lower surface; 43mm (1 11/16") long x 12mm (1/2") wide. TUBE is yellowish white (4D) streaked pale lavender (69C); medium length and thick; 20mm (13/16") long x 9mm (3/8") thick. STAMENS extend 15 to 20mm (5/8 – 13/16") beyond the corolla; dark rose (64C) filaments, reddish purple (64B) anthers. PISTIL extends 35mm (1 3/8") beyond the corolla; pale pink (62D) style, light yellow (4C) stigma. BUD is ovate. FOLIAGE is dark green (147A) upper surface, medium green (147B) lower surface. Leaves are 83mm (3 1/4") long x 48mm (1 7/8") wide, ovate shaped, serrulated edges, acute tips and rounded bases. Veins, stems and branches are yellowish green and light brown. PARENTAGE: 'Joan Gilbert' x 'Subliem'. Lax upright or stiff trailer. Makes good basket or upright. Prefers overhead filtered light and cool climate. Best bloom colour in filtered light. Tested four years in Pornic, France. Distinguished by bloom colour combination.
Masse 2002 FR AFS5008.

Bonjour Diane. Upright. Double. COROLLA: three quarter flared, smooth petal margins; opens dark purple (78A); matures light purple (78B); 15mm (9/16") long x 25mm (1") wide. SEPALS: horizontal; tips recurved; cream (159D) tipped yellowish green (146C) upper & lower surfaces; 24mm (15/16") long x 14mm (9/16") wide. TUBE: cream (159D); short, medium thickness; 13mm (1/2") long x 6mm (1/4") wide. STAMENS: extend 6-9mm (1/4-3/8") below corolla; dark rose (64C) filaments, light purple (78B) anthers. PISTIL: extends 34mm (1 5/16") below the corolla, white (155C) style, yellowish white (4D) stigma. BUD: ovate. FOLIAGE: dark green (147A) upper surface; medium green (147B) lower surface. Leaves are 37mm (1 7/16") long x 37mm (1 7/16") wide, cordate shaped, smooth to serrulated edges, acute tips and cordate bases. Veins, stems & branches are yellowish green. PARENTAGE: 'La Campanella' x 'Papy René'. Medium upright. Makes good upright. Prefers overhead filtered light and cool climate. Best bloom and foliage colour in filtered light. Tested 3 years in Pornic, France. Distinguished by bloom colour contrast.
Masse 2003 FR AFS5229.

Bonzai Overijsel. Upright. Single. COROLLA is three quarter flared; opens dark reddish purple (59A); matures reddish purple (59B); 14mm (9/16") long x 19mm (3/4") wide. SEPALS are horizontal, tips recurved; reddish purple (64B) upper surface; dark reddish purple (64A) lower surface; 17mm (5/8") long x 7mm (1/4") wide. TUBE is reddish purple (64B); 9mm (3/8") long x 6mm (1/4") wide. FOLIAGE: medium green (138A) upper surface; light green (138D) lower surface. PARENTAGE: 'Roesse Carme' x 'Roesse Vega'. Distinguished by erect blooms.
Roes 2006 NL AFS6136.

Boscastle. Upright/Trailer. Single. COROLLA is half flared, bell shaped, with turned under slightly toothed petal margins; opens purple (82A); matures purple (82B); 32mm (1 1/4") long x 23mm (15/16") wide. SEPALS are twisted counterclockwise, fully up, tips recurved; light violet (84C) upper surface; light purple (78D) lower surface; thin light reddish purple (73A) line in center of each sepal; 45mm (1 3/4") long x 12mm (1/2") wide. TUBE is dark rose (64C); medium length & thin; 10mm (3/8") long x 5mm (3/16") wide. FOLIAGE: dark green (137A) upper surface; medium green (137D) lower surface. Leaves are 56mm (2 3/16") long x 30mm (1 3/16") wide, lanceolate shaped. PARENTAGE: 'Orange Mirage' x unnamed seedling. Distinguished by large bell shape. Sepals appear to be woven into foliage.
Negus 2005 UK AFS5980.

Boschhook. Trailer. Double. . COROLLA: half flared, turned under petal margins; opens magenta (63A), blotched light purple (70C); matures magenta (61C), blotched rose (68C); 26 mm (1") long x 21mm (13/16") wide. PETALOIDS: magenta (63A), blotched light purple (70C); 11mm (7/16") long x 9mm (5/16") wide. SEPALS are half up, tips recurved up, twisted left to right; pink (55C), tipped pale yellow green (150D) upper surface; pink (62A), tipped pale yellow green (150D) lower surface; 39mm (1 1/2") long x 18mm (11/16") wide. TUBE is pale pink (56B); medium length & thickness; 15mm (9/16") long x 6mm (1/4") wide. STAMENS extend 7mm (1/4") beyond the corolla; rose (64D) filaments; reddish purple (71B) anthers. PISTIL extends 11mm (7/16") beyond the corolla; rose (67D) style; pale yellow (2D) stigma. BUD is globular. FOLIAGE is dark green (137A) upper surface; medium green (138B) lower surface. Leaves are 62mm (2 7/16") long x 33mm (1 5/16")

wide, elliptic shaped, entire edges, acute tips, rounded bases. Veins are light red purple (185D), stems are very dark reddish purple (186A) & branches are plum (184C) & light green (139D). PARENTAGE: 'Manfried Kleinau' x 'Laura Biolcati-Rinaldi'. Natural trailer, self branching. Makes good basket. Prefers overhead filtered light, cool climate. Best bloom & foliage in filtered light. Tested 3 years in Koningshooikt, Belgium. Waanrode 9/8/08. Distinguished by bloom colour combination.
Michiels 2009 BE AFS7151.

Bourguignon. Upright/Trailer. Single. COROLLA is quarter flared with wavy margins; opens dark reddish purple (64A), matures dark reddish purple (61A); 21mm (13/16") long x 14mm (9/16") wide. SEPALS are horizontal, tips recurved; rose (65A) tipped yellowish green (149A) upper surface, pink (62A) lower surface; 33mm (1 5/16") long x 7mm (1/4") wide. TUBE is pink (62C), long with medium thickness; 27mm (1 1/16") long x 10mm (3/8") wide. STAMENS extend 16mm (5/8") beyond the corolla; reddish purple (64B) filaments and dark purple (79A) anthers. PISTIL extends 37mm (1 7/16") below the corolla; light pink (62B-62C) style, pale yellow (158B) stigma. BUD is long Tubed with tear drop shape. FOLIAGE is dark green (147A) upper surface, medium green (146A) lower surface. Leaves are 41mm (1 5/8") long x 23mm (15/16") wide, ovate shaped, serrated edges, acute tips and rounded bases. Veins, stems and branches are light yellow green. PARENTAGE: 'Petit Four' x 'Orange Flare'. Lax upright or stiff trailer. Self branching. Makes good basket. Prefers overhead filtered light. Heat tolerant if shaded. Best bloom and foliage colour in filtered light. Tested eight years in Lisse, Holland. Distinguished by unique shape and colour combination.
de Graaff 2003 NL AFS4880.

Boy Comperen. Upright/Trailer. Semi Double. COROLLA: half flared, smooth petal margins; opens purple (71A); matures dark reddish purple (64A); 24mm (15/16") long x 22mm (7/8") wide. SEPALS: half up; tips recurved up; reddish purple (64B) upper surface; reddish purple (67A) lower surface; 29mm (1 1/8") long x 14mm (9/16") wide. TUBE: reddish purple (64B); medium length & thickness; 11mm (7/16") long x 6mm (1/4") wide. STAMENS: extend 12mm (1/2") below corolla; purple (71A) filaments; dark rose (71D) anthers. PISTIL: extends 22mm (7/8") below the corolla; dark rose (67C)

style; light yellow (11C) stigma. BUD: ovate. FOLIAGE: medium green (137B) upper surface; medium green (138B) lower surface. Leaves are 82mm (3 1/4") long x 34mm (1 5/16") wide, lanceolate shaped, serrulated edges, acute tips and obtuse bases. Veins, stems & branches are green. PARENTAGE: 'Bicentennial' x ['Bicentennial' x ('Rohees King' x 'Miniskirt')]. Lax upright or stiff trailer. Makes good stiff trailer. Prefers overhead filtered light and cool climate. Best bloom and foliage colour in filtered light. Tested 4 years in Diessen, The Netherlands. Distinguished by bloom colour.
Comperen 2003 NL AFS5283.

Bram Verdonk. Trailer. Double. COROLLA: 3 quarter flared; opens reddish purple (72B), dark rose (58C) base; matures reddish purple (70B); 26mm (1") long x 22mm (7/8") wide. PETALOIDS: same colour as corolla; 20mm (3/4") long x 12mm (7/16") wide. SEPALS: horizontal, tips recurved; rose (65A) tipped apple green (145C) upper surface; dark rose (58C) tipped apple green (145C) lower surface; 38mm (1 1/2") long x 12mm (7/16") wide. TUBE: white (155B); long & thin; 29mm (1 1/8") long x 6mm (1/4") wide. FOLIAGE is dark green (136A) upper surface; medium green (138B) lower surface. PARENTAGE: 'Rune Peeters' x 'Illusion'.
Michiels 2007 BE AFS6370.

Brancaster. Upright. Single. COROLLA blue mauve. SEPALS pale pink.
Clitheroe 2003 UK.

Branksome Blaze. Upright/Trailer. Single. COROLLA: unflared, bell shaped, smooth petal margins; opens red (45B); matures red (46B); 17mm (11/16") long x 15mm (9/16") wide. SEPALS: half down; tips recurved; red (46D) upper surface; reddish orange (43C) lower surface; 35mm(1 3/8") long x 11mm (7/16") wide. TUBE: rose (52C); medium length & thickness; 15mm (9/16") long x 5mm (3/16") wide. STAMENS: extend 22mm (7/8") below corolla; rose (47D) filaments; pink (49A) anthers. PISTIL: extends 27mm (1 1/16") below the corolla, pink (48D) style; pale yellow (18D) stigma. BUD: blunt-ended. FOLIAGE: medium green (147B) upper surface; medium green (137C) lower surface. Leaves are 34mm (1 5/16") long x 20mm (13/16") wide, lanceolate shaped, serrulated edges, acute tips and rounded bases. Veins, stems & branches are red. PARENTAGE: 'Ruth Graham' x 'Branksome Beauty'. Lax upright or stiff trailer. Makes good basket. Prefers warm climate. Heat tolerant if

shaded. Best bloom and foliage colour in filtered light. Tested 3 years in Stockbridge, Hampshire, England. Distinguished by continual flowering.
Graham 2003 UK AFS5139.

Branksom Emma. Trailer. Semi Double. . COROLLA: unflared, bell shaped, smooth petal margins; opens dark purple (78A), heavily veined & flushed magenta (57B); matures violet (77B) flushed magenta (57A); 21mm (13/16") long x 21mm (13/16") wide. SEPALS: fully up; tips recurved; light magenta (66D) tipped green upper surface; dark rose (58C) lower surface; 27mm(1 1/16") long x 11mm (7/16") wide. TUBE: white (155D) striped pink; medium length & thickness; 15mm (9/16") long x 5mm (3/16") wide. STAMENS: extend 12mm (1/2") below corolla; light magenta (57D) filaments; magenta (57A) anthers. PISTIL: extends 22mm (7/8") below the corolla, pink (62A) style; white (155B) stigma. BUD: obtuse. FOLIAGE: dark green (137A) upper surface; medium green (137D) lower surface. Leaves are 28mm (1 1/8") long x 16mm (5/8") wide, lanceolate shaped, serrulated edges, acute tips and rounded bases. Veins, stems & branches are red. PARENTAGE: 'Ruth Graham' x 'Branksome Beauty'. Natural trailer. Makes good basket. Prefers overhead filtered light and cool climate. Best bloom and foliage colour in filtered light. Tested 3 years in Stockbridge, Hampshire, England. Distinguished by profuse blooms and compact growth
Graham 2003 UK AFS5140.

Branksome Flossie. Upright. Single. COROLLA is half flared with smooth petal margins; opens purple (83C) veined light rose (58D), matures violet (84A), pink (62A) at, veined light rose (58D); 22mm (7/8") long x 27mm (1 1/16") wide. SEPALS are horizontal, tips recurved; magenta (58B) upper surface, dark rose (58C) lower surface; 50mm (2") long x 11mm (7/16") wide. TUBE is light rose (58D), medium length and thickness; 15mm (5/8") long x 8mm (5/16") wide. STAMENS extend 17mm (11/16") below the corolla; reddish purple (64B) filaments, dark rose (64C) anthers. PISTIL extends 28mm (1 1/8") below the corolla; dark rose (64C) style, rose (65A) stigma. BUD is lanceolate. FOLIAGE is dark green (137A) upper surface, medium green (138A) lower surface. Leaves are 57mm (2 1/4") long x 32mm (1 1/4") wide, lanceolate shaped, serrulated edges, acute tips and rounded bases. Veins, stems and branches are red.

PARENTAGE: 'Aintree' x 'Mrs. Popple'. Small upright. Makes good upright. Prefers overhead filtered light and cool climate. Best bloom colour in filtered light. Tested five years in Stockbridge, Hampshire, England. Distinguished by long Sepals blossom colour. Graham 2002 UK AFS4872.

Branksome Lucy. Upright/Trailer. Double. COROLLA: half flared, wavy petal margins; opens purple (82A), pink (62C) at base; matures reddish purple (74B), pale pink (62D) at base; 18mm (11/16") long x 26mm (1"") wide. SEPALS: fully up; tips recurved; dark rose (55A) flushed green upper surface; dark rose (55A) lower surface; 29mm(1 1/8") long x 12mm (1/2") wide. TUBE: pink (55C) striped green; short, medium thickness; 7mm (1/4") long x 6mm (1/4") wide. STAMENS: extend 12mm (1/2") below corolla; rose (68B) filaments; dark reddish purple (60B) anthers. PISTIL: extends 27mm (1 1/16") below the corolla, light pink (65C) style; white (155D) stigma. BUD: obtuse. FOLIAGE: dark green (137A) upper surface; medium green (138B) lower surface. Leaves are 42mm (2 5/8") long x 28mm (1 1/16") wide, lanceolate shaped, serrulated edges, acute tips and rounded bases. Veins are green, stems & branches are red. PARENTAGE: 'Carla Johnson' x 'Ruth graham'. Lax upright or stiff trailer. Makes good basket or upright. Prefers overhead filtered light. Heat tolerant if shaded. Best bloom and foliage colour in filtered light. Tested 3 years in Stockbridge, Hampshire, England. Distinguished by bright colour combination. Graham 2003 UK AFS5141.

Branksome Redhead. Upright/Trailer. Single. COROLLA is unflared, square shaped, with smooth petal margins; opens dark purple (78A), matures dark purple (78B); 17mm (11/16") long x 15mm (5/8") wide. SEPALS are full down, tips recurved; red (46C) upper surface, red (47B) lower surface; 31mm (1 1/4") long x 14mm (9/16") wide. TUBE is dark red (46A), long and thin; 52mm (2 1/16") long x 4mm (3/16") wide. STAMENS do not extend below the corolla; pale pink (69A) filaments, dark reddish purple (70A) anthers. PISTIL extends 21mm (13/16") beyond the corolla; magenta (68A) style, light pink (65B) stigma. BUD is oblate. FOLIAGE is medium green (137C) upper surface, medium green (138B) lower surface. Leaves are 52mm (2 1/16") long x 26mm (1") wide, lanceolate shaped, serrulated edges, acute tips and rounded bases. Veins are

green, stems and branches are red. PARENTAGE: 'WALZ Harp' x 'Penelope'. Lax upright or stiff trailer. Makes good basket. Prefers cool climate. Heat tolerant if shaded. Best bloom colour in filtered light. Tested three years in Stockbridge, Hampshire, England. Distinguished by long thin Tube and square corolla. Graham 2002 UK AFS4873.

Bravo Christine. Upright/Trailer. Single. COROLLA: quarter flared; opens & matures light purple (75B) veined rose to light reddish purple; 25mm (1") long x 19mm (3/4") wide. SEPALS: fully up, tips recurved; dark rose (54A) upper & lower surfaces; 36mm (1 7/16") long x 11mm (7/16") wide. TUBE: dark rose (54A) streaked darker; 10 mm (3/8") long x 4mm (1/8") wide. FOLIAGE is medium green (146A) upper surface; yellowish green (146B) lower surface. PARENTAGE: 'String of Pearls' x 'Brigitte Harnisch'. Masse 2008 FR AFS6830.

BreeVis Adonia. Upright. Single. COROLLA is half flared with smooth petal margins; opens purple (71A); matures dark reddish purple (64A); 19mm (3/4") long x 32mm (1 1/4") wide. SEPALS are half up, tips reflexed up; magenta (61C) upper surface; purple (77A) lower surface; 29mm (1 1/8") long x 14mm (9/16") wide. TUBE is magenta (57A); short & thick; 14mm (9/16") long x 10mm (3/8") wide. FOLIAGE: dark green (137A) upper surface; medium green (137D) lower surface. Leaves are 61mm (2 3/8") long x 36mm (1 7/16") wide, ovate shaped. PARENTAGE: 'Roesse Carme' x 'Leon Pauwels'. Distinguished by bloom & foliage combination. van Bree 2005 NL AFS5878.

BreeVis Anactus. Trailer. Double. Trailer. COROLLA is full flared with smooth petal margins; opens purple (89C); matures dark purple (78A); 28mm (1 1/8") long x 30mm (1 3/16") wide. SEPALS are fully up, tips recurved; magenta (58B) upper and lower surfaces; 34mm (1 3/8") long x 15mm (5/8") wide. TUBE is magenta (58B); short and thick; 10mm (3/8") long x 8mm (5/16") wide. STAMENS extend 34mm (1 3/8") beyond the corolla; magenta (58B) filaments, magenta (59C) anthers. PISTIL extends 46mm (1 13/16") beyond the corolla; light rose (58D) style and stigma. BUD is globular, pointed. FOLIAGE is medium green (137B) upper surface, medium green (138B) lower surface. Leaves are 59mm (2 5/16") long x 32mm (1

1/4") wide, lanceolate shaped, smooth edges, acute tips and rounded bases. Veins are green, stems and branches are red. PARENTAGE: 'Rohees Queen' x 'Cecile'. Natural trailer. Makes good basket. Prefers overhead filtered light and cool climate. Best bloom colour in filtered light. Tested four years in Knegsel, The Netherlands. Distinguished by bloom and foliage combination.
van Bree 2002 NL AFS4962.

BreeVis Arion. Upright/Trailer. Double. COROLLA is three quarter flared; opens violet (84A); matures reddish purple (80B); 22mm (7/8") long x 19mm (3/4") wide. SEPALS are fully up, tips reflexed; rose (68C) upper surface; pink (62A) lower surface; 33mm (1 5/16") long x 22mm (7/8") wide. TUBE is rose (68C); 22mm (7/8") long x 9mm (3/8") wide. FOLIAGE: dark green (137A) upper surface; medium green (137D) lower surface. PARENTAGE: 'Luuk van Riet' x 'BreeVis Evelien'. Distinguished by bloom colour.
van Bree 2006 NL AFS6090.

BreeVis Atlas. Trailer. Single. COROLLA: quarter flared, smooth petal margins; opens violet (92A); matures light violet (84B); 24mm (15/16") long 22mm (7/8") wide. SEPALS: horizontal; tips recurved; pale pink (62D), tipped green, upper surface; pink (62C), tipped green, lower surface; 56mm (2 3/16") long x 14mm (9/16") wide. TUBE: pale pink (62D); medium length & thickness; 9mm (3/8) long x 6mm (1/4") wide. STAMENS: extend 13mm (1/2") below corolla; dark rose (71D) filaments; magenta (63A) anthers. PISTIL: extends 24mm (15/16") below the corolla; pale lavender (69D) style; light yellow (4C) stigma. BUD: ovate, long, pointed. FOLIAGE: dark green (137A) upper surface; medium green (138A) lower surface. Leaves are 54mm (2 1/8") long x 24mm (15/16") wide, lanceolate shaped, serrated edges, acute tips and rounded bases. Red veins, stems & branches. PARENTAGE: ('Cameron Ryle' x 'Parasol') x 'Sleigh Bells'. Natural trailer. Makes good basket. Prefers overhead filtered light and cool climate. Best bloom and foliage colour in filtered light. Tested 4 years in Knegsel, The Netherlands. Distinguished by bloom colour.
van Bree 2004 NL AFS5505.

BreeVis Bibles. Trailer. Single. COROLLA: Half flared; opens reddish purple (72B); matures reddish purple (70B); 16mm (5/8") long x 27mm (1 1/16") wide. SEPALS: half

up, tips reflexed up; light rose (58D) upper surface; dark rose (58C) lower surface; 29mm (1 1/8") long x 12mm (7/16") wide. TUBE: light rose (58D); medium length & thickness; 9mm (5/16") long x 8mm (5/16") wide. FOLIAGE is medium green (137B) upper surface; medium green (137D) lower surface. PARENTAGE: 'Roesse Lupus' x 'BreeVis Paradoxa'.
van Bree 2007 NL AFS6637.

BreeVis Bolina. Upright/Trailer. Double. COROLLA is half flared; opens violet (86B); matures light purple (86C); 14mm (9/16") long x 19mm (3/4") wide. SEPALS are fully up, tips reflexed; magenta (63A) upper & lower surfaces; 34mm (1 3/8") long x 16mm (5/8") wide. TUBE is magenta (63A); 11mm (7/16") long x 6mm (1/4") wide. FOLIAGE: medium green (137B) upper surface; medium green (138B) lower surface. PARENTAGE: 'Roesse Elara' x 'BreeVis Evelien'. Distinguished by bloom colour.
van Bree 2006 NL AFS6092.

BreeVis Caja. Upright/Trailer. Semi Double. COROLLA: half flared, smooth petal margins; opens violet (77C); matures light purple (78B); 27mm (1 1/16") long 22mm (7/8") wide. SEPALS: horizontal; tips recurved; pale pink (62D), tipped green, upper surface; pink (62A) lower surface; 47mm (1 7/8") long x 14mm (9/16") wide. TUBE: pale pink (62D); medium length & thickness; 11mm (7/16) long x 7mm (1/4") wide. STAMENS: extend 26mm (1") below corolla; magenta (63B) filaments; light rose (58D) anthers. PISTIL: extends 24mm (15/16") below the corolla; pink (62C) style; pale yellow (1D) stigma. BUD: ovate, pointed. FOLIAGE: medium green (137B) upper surface; medium green (138B) lower surface. Leaves are 62mm (2 7/16") long x 41mm (1 5/8") wide, ovate shaped, serrulated edges, acute tips and rounded bases. Green veins, stems & branches. PARENTAGE: ('Cameron Ryle' x 'Parasol') x 'Sleigh Bells'. Lax upright or stiff trailer. Makes good stiff trailer. Prefers overhead filtered light and cool climate. Best bloom and foliage colour in filtered light. Tested 4 years in Knegsel, The Netherlands. Distinguished by bloom and foliage combination.
van Bree 2004 NL AFS5507.

BreeVis Calliste. Upright/Trailer. Single. COROLLA: Half flared; opens dark reddish purple (70A); matures magenta (63A); 26mm (1") long x 24mm (15/16") wide. SEPALS: half up, tips recurved up; red (50A) upper surface; red (52A) lower surface; 33mm (1 5/16") long x 11mm (7/16") wide. TUBE: red (50A); medium length & thickness; 15mm (9/16") long x 12mm (7/16") wide. FOLIAGE is dark green (137A) upper surface; medium green (137C) lower surface. PARENTAGE: 'Roesse Lupus' x 'Jacques Wijnen'. van Bree 2007 NL AFS6633.

BreeVis Camilla. Upright/Trailer. Double. COROLLA is half flared; opens purple (82B); matures dark reddish purple (70A); 21mm (13/16") long x 28mm (1 1/8") wide. SEPALS are fully up, tips recurved; magenta (57B) upper surface; magenta (57B) lower surface; 31mm (1 1/4") long x 16mm (5/8") wide. TUBE is dark reddish purple (72A); 22mm (7/8") long x 8mm (5/16") wide. FOLIAGE: dark green (137A) upper surface; medium green (137C) lower surface. PARENTAGE: 'Roesse Elara' x 'BreeVis Evelien'. Distinguished by bloom & foliage combination.
van Bree 2006 NL AFS6094.

BreeVis Cleone. Upright/Trailer. Single. COROLLA: Three quarter flared; opens purple (83B); matures dark reddish purple (61A); 27mm (1 1/16") long x 31mm (1 1/4") wide. SEPALS: half up, tips reflexed up; dark reddish purple (60B) upper & lower surfaces; 31mm (1 1/4") long x 24mm (15/16") wide. TUBE: dark reddish purple (60B); medium length & thickness; 12mm (7/16") long x 6mm (1/4") wide. FOLIAGE is dark green (137A) upper surface; medium green (137D) lower surface. PARENTAGE: 'Maxima's Baby' x 'Reg Gubler'.
van Bree 2007 NL AFS6638.

BreeVis Clorinde. Upright. Single. COROLLA is full flared with smooth petal margins; opens purple (83B); matures reddish purple (72B); 22mm (7/8") long x 32mm (1 1/4") wide. SEPALS are fully up, tips recurved; red (46B) upper surface; dark red (47A) lower surface; 24mm (15/16") long x 12mm (1/2") wide. TUBE is red (46B); medium length & thickness; 11mm (7/16") long x 6mm (1/4") wide. FOLIAGE: dark green (137A) upper surface; medium green (138A) lower surface. Leaves are 71mm (2 13/16") long x 37mm (1 7/16") wide, ovate shaped. PARENTAGE: 'Swanley Gem' x 'Roesse Apus'. Distinguished by bloom colour & shape.
van Bree 2005 NL AFS5890.

BreeVis Coon. Upright. Semi Double. COROLLA: Three quarter flared; opens dark purple (79B); matures dark reddish purple

(64A); 17mm (5/8") long x 17mm (5/8") wide. SEPALS: fully up, tips reflexed; reddish purple (61B) upper surface; dark reddish purple (61A) lower surface; 21mm (13/16") long x 12mm (7/16") wide. TUBE: reddish purple (61B); short & thick; 12mm (7/16") long x 12mm (7/16") wide. FOLIAGE is dark green (137A) upper surface; medium green (137C) lower surface. PARENTAGE: 'Roesse Carme' x 'BreeVis Homerus'.
van Bree 2007 NL AFS6634.

BreeVis Core. Trailer. Single. COROLLA is half flared; opens magenta (68A); matures rose (68B); 22mm (7/8") long x 24mm (15/16") wide. SEPALS are half up, tips recurved up; magenta (58B) upper & lower surfaces; 28mm (1 1/8") long x 11mm (7/16") wide. TUBE is magenta (58B); 14mm (9/16") long x 8mm (5/16") wide. FOLIAGE: dark green (137A) upper surface; medium green (137C) lower surface. PARENTAGE: 'Roesse Carme' x 'Regent Gubler'. Distinguished by bloom & foliage combination.
van Bree 2006 NL AFS6100.

BreeVis Cossus. Upright. Single. COROLLA: Three quarter flared; opens purple (83B); matures reddish purple (67A); 24mm (15/16") long x 26mm (1") wide. SEPALS: half up, tips reflexed up; magenta (61C) upper surface; reddish purple (61B) lower surface; 27mm (1 1/16") long x 7mm (1/4") wide. TUBE: magenta (61C); medium length & thickness; 13mm (1/2") long x 8mm (5/16") wide. FOLIAGE is dark green (137A) upper surface; medium green (137B) lower surface. PARENTAGE: 'Maxima's Baby' x 'Reg Gubler'.
van Bree 2007 NL AFS6630.

BreeVis Cressida. Trailer. Double. COROLLA: half flared, smooth petal margins; opens magenta (63B); matures rose (63C); 19mm (3/4") long x 21mm (13/16") wide. SEPALS: half down, tips reflexed; magenta (67B) upper surface; magenta (58B) lower surface; 24mm (15/16") long x 16mm (5/8") wide. TUBE: magenta (67B); short & thick; 10mm (3/8") long x 9mm (5/16") wide. STAMENS extend 4mm (1/8") beyond the corolla; magenta (63B) filaments; dark reddish purple (60A) anthers. PISTIL extends 4mm (1/8") beyond the corolla; magenta (63B) style; white (155D) stigma. BUD: ovate. FOLIAGE: dark green (137A) upper surface; medium green (138A) lower surface. Leaves are 63mm (2 1/2") long x 34mm (1 3/8") wide; ovate shaped, serrulate edges, acute

tips, obtuse bases. Veins & stems are red, branches are green. PARENTAGE: 'Luuk van Riet' x 'Roesse Parel'. Natural trailer. Makes good basket. Prefers overhead filtered light. Best bloom colour in filtered light. Tested 3 years in Knegsel, The Netherlands. Distinguished by bloom colour & foliage combination.
van Bree 2009 NL AFS7248.

BreeVis Cypris. Upright/Trailer. Double. . COROLLA is half flared; opens dark reddish purple (70A); matures magenta (67B); 22mm (7/8") long x 31mm (1 1/4") wide. SEPALS are half down, tips reflexed; rose (68C) upper surface; pink (62A) lower surface; 26mm (1") long x 18mm (11/16") wide. TUBE is light rose (68D); 22mm (7/8") long x 6mm (1/4") wide. FOLIAGE: dark green (137A) upper surface; medium green (138A) lower surface. PARENTAGE: 'Luuk van Riet' x 'BreeVis Evelien'. Distinguished by bloom colour.
van Bree 2006 NL AFS6089.

BreeVis Danis. Upright. Semi Double. COROLLA: half flared, smooth petal margins; opens purple (83C); matures dark purple (78A); 24mm (1 15/16") long 26mm (1") wide. SEPALS: fully up; tips recurved; pale pink (62D) upper surface; pink (62C) lower surface; 43mm (1 11/16") long x 12mm (1/2") wide. TUBE: pale pink (62D); medium length & thickness; 10mm (3/8") long x 8mm (5/16") wide. STAMENS: extend 16mm (5/8") below corolla; light reddish purple (72C) filaments; dark reddish purple (60C) anthers. PISTIL: extends 35mm (1 3/8") below the corolla; pale pink (62D) style; pale yellow (1D) stigma. BUD: ovate. FOLIAGE: dark green (137A) upper surface; medium green (137C) lower surface. Leaves are 62mm (2 7/16") long x 31mm (1 1/4") wide, elliptic shaped, smooth edges, acute tips and cordate bases. Green veins, stems & branches. PARENTAGE: ('Cameron Ryle' x 'Parasol') x 'Sleigh Bells'. Medium upright. Makes good upright or standard. Prefers overhead filtered light and cool climate. Best bloom and foliage colour in filtered light. Tested 4 years in Knegsel, The Netherlands. Distinguished by bloom colour.
van Bree 2004 NL AFS5508.

BreeVis Daphne. Upright/Trailer. Semi Double. COROLLA: half flared, smooth petal margins; opens purple (89C); matures purple (77A); 18mm (11/16") long 26mm (1") wide. SEPALS: fully up; tips recurved; dark rose (51A) upper & lower surfaces; 26mm (1") long x 13mm (1/2") wide. TUBE: dark rose (51A);

medium length & thickness; 15mm (9/16") long x 5mm (3/16") wide. STAMENS: extend 22mm (7/8") below corolla; dark rose (51A) filaments; dark red (53A) anthers. PISTIL: extends 37mm (1 7/16") below the corolla; dark rose (54B) style & stigma. BUD: round, pointed. FOLIAGE: medium green (137C) upper surface; medium green (137D) lower surface. Leaves are 56mm (2 3/16") long x 31mm (1 1/4") wide, ovate shaped, serrulated edges, acute tips and obtuse bases. Red veins, stems & branches. PARENTAGE: 'Bicentennial' x 'Swanley Gem'. Lax upright or stiff trailer. Makes good stiff trailer. Prefers overhead filtered light and cool climate. Best bloom and foliage colour in filtered light. Tested 4 years in Knegsel, The Netherlands. Distinguished by bloom and foliage combination.
van Bree 2004 NL AFS5509.

BreeVis Dero. Upright/Trailer. Single. COROLLA: half flared, smooth petal margins; opens & matures light reddish purple (73A); 15mm (9/16") long 20mm (13/16") wide. SEPALS: fully up; tips reflexed; pale pink (62D), tipped green, upper & lower surfaces; 17mm (11/16") long x 7mm (1/4") wide. TUBE: pale pink (62D); medium length & thickness; 9mm (3/8") long x 6mm (1/4") wide. STAMENS: extend 12mm (1/2") below corolla; light pink (62B) filaments; dark reddish purple (60B) anthers. PISTIL: extends 21mm (13/16") below the corolla; pale pink (62D) style; pink (37D) stigma. BUD: round. FOLIAGE: dark green (137A) upper surface; medium green (137C) lower surface. Leaves are 51mm (2") long x 30mm (1 3/16") wide, ovate shaped, smooth edges, acute tips and obtuse bases. Green veins, stems & branches. PARENTAGE: 'Roesse Carme' x 'Cameron Ryle'. Lax upright or stiff trailer. Makes good stiff trailer. Prefers overhead filtered light and cool climate. Best bloom and foliage colour in filtered light. Tested 4 years in Knegsel, The Netherlands. Distinguished by bloom and foliage combination.
van Bree 2004 NL AFS5511.

BreeVis Dia. Upright. Single. COROLLA: full flared, smooth petal margins; opens light pink (65B); matures light pink (65C); 20mm (13/16") long 28mm (1 1/8") wide. SEPALS: fully up; tips reflexed; rose (68B), tipped green, upper surface; rose (68C) lower surface; 22mm (7/8") long x 11mm (7/16") wide. TUBE: rose (68B); short & thick; 8mm (5/16") long x 8mm (5/16") wide. STAMENS: extend 16mm (5/8") below corolla; magenta

(63B) filaments; reddish purple (60D) anthers. PISTIL: extends 24mm (15/16") below the corolla; rose (65A) style; yellowish white (4D) stigma. BUD: round. FOLIAGE: dark green (139A) upper surface; medium green (138A) lower surface. Leaves are 64mm (2 1/2") long x 42mm (1 5/8") wide, ovate shaped, serrated edges, acute tips and rounded bases. Green veins, stems & branches. PARENTAGE: 'Roesse Carme' x 'Cameron Ryle'. Medium upright. Makes good upright or standard. Prefers overhead filtered light and cool climate. Best bloom and foliage colour in filtered light. Tested 4 years in Knegsel, The Netherlands. Distinguished by erect bloom.
van Bree 2004 NL AFS5512.

BreeVis Dirtea. Upright/Trailer. Double. COROLLA is half flared; opens reddish purple (67A); matures light reddish purple (66C); 24mm (15/16") long x 27mm (1 1/16") wide. SEPALS are fully up, tips reflexed; pink (62C) upper surface; pink (62A) lower surface; 38mm (1 1/2") long x 16mm (5/8") wide. TUBE is pink (62C); 16mm (5/8") long x 7mm (1/4") wide. FOLIAGE: dark green (139A) upper surface; medium green (137C) lower surface. PARENTAGE: 'Roesse Elara' x 'BreeVis Evelien'. Distinguished by bloom colour.
van Bree 2006 NL AFS6097.

BreeVis Dispar. Trailer. Double. COROLLA is three quarter flared; opens purple (77A); matures reddish purple (67A); 17mm (5/8") long x 28mm (1 1/8") wide. SEPALS are fully up, tips recurved; magenta (61C) upper & lower surfaces; 21mm (13/16") long x 15mm (9/16") wide. TUBE is magenta (61C); 9mm (3/8") long x 6mm (1/4") wide. FOLIAGE: medium green (137B) upper surface; medium green (137C) lower surface. PARENTAGE: ('Roesse Apus' x 'Roesse Apus') x 'Centenary'. Distinguished by bloom & foliage combination.
van Bree 2006 NL AFS6101.

BreeVis Egina. Upright. Single. COROLLA: quarter flared, smooth petal margins; opens violet (84A); matures light purple (78B); 14mm (9/16") long 24mm (15/16") wide. SEPALS: fully up; tips recurved; magenta (58B), tipped green, upper surface; dark rose (58C) lower surface; 21mm (13/16") long x 11mm (7/16") wide. TUBE: magenta (58B); short & thick; 12mm (1/2") long x 12mm (1/2") wide. STAMENS: extend 22mm (7/8") below corolla; magenta (63B) filaments; reddish purple (59B) anthers. PISTIL:

extends 28mm (1 1/8") below the corolla; pink (62A) style; light rose (68D) stigma. BUD: round. FOLIAGE: dark green (137A) upper surface; medium green (137C) lower surface. Leaves are 78mm (3 1/16") long x 32mm (1 1/4") wide, lanceolate shaped, serrulated edges, acute tips and acute bases. Green veins, stems & branches. PARENTAGE: 'Roesse Carme' x 'Cameron Ryle'. Medium upright. Makes good upright or standard. Prefers overhead filtered light and cool climate. Best bloom and foliage colour in filtered light. Tested 4 years in Knegsel, The Netherlands. Distinguished by bloom and foliage combination.
van Bree 2004 NL AFS5513.

BreeVis Electo. Upright. Semi Double. COROLLA is half flared with smooth petal margins; opens purple (77A); matures purple (71A); 19mm (3/4") long x 26mm (1") wide. SEPALS are fully up, tips recurved; rose (68C) upper surface; magenta (68A) lower surface; 24mm (15/16") long x 16mm (5/8") wide. TUBE is light rose (68D); short & thick; 7mm (1/4") long x 9mm (3/8") wide. FOLIAGE: dark green (139A) upper surface; medium green (137B) lower surface. Leaves are 55mm (2 3/16") long x 36mm (1 7/16") wide, ovate shaped. PARENTAGE: ('Roesse Apus' x 'Roesse Apus') x 'Bert Beckman'. Distinguished by bloom shape & colour.
van Bree 2005 NL AFS5888.

BreeVis Erato. Upright/Trailer. Double. Upright/Trailer. COROLLA: three quarter flared, smooth petal margins; opens purple (83B); matures purple (71A); 32mm (1 1/4") long x 28mm (1 1/8") wide. SEPALS: fully up; tips recurved; dark rose (64C) upper surface; reddish purple (67A) lower surface; 42mm (1 11/16") long x 18mm (11/16") wide. TUBE: pink (62A); medium length & thickness; 17mm (11/16") long x 7mm (1/4") wide. STAMENS: extend 23mm (15/16") below corolla; dark reddish purple (70A) filaments, light purple (70C) anthers. PISTIL: extends 39mm (1 9/16") below the corolla, pale purple (70D) style, light yellow (4C) stigma. BUD: spherical. FOLIAGE: dark green (137A) upper surface; medium green (137D) lower surface. Leaves are 84mm (3 5/16") long x 37mm (1 7/16") wide, lanceolate shaped, serrulated edges, acute tips and obtuse bases. Veins, stems & branches are red. PARENTAGE: 'Bicentennial' x ('Rohees King' x 'Miniskirt'). Natural trailer. Makes good stiff trailer. Prefers overhead filtered light and cool climate. Best bloom and foliage colour in

filtered light. Tested 4 years in Knegsel, The Netherlands. Distinguished by blossom colour.
van Bree 2003 NL AFS5235.

BreeVis Eupale. Trailer. Single. COROLLA: Half flared; opens & matures red (46B); 17mm (5/8") long x 26mm (1") wide. SEPALS: horizontal, tips recurved; pink (50B) upper surface; red (50A) lower surface; 26mm (1") long x 11mm (7/16") wide. TUBE: pink (50B); medium length & thickness; 17mm (5/8") long x 6mm (1/4") wide. FOLIAGE is medium green (137C) upper surface; medium green (137D) lower surface. PARENTAGE: 'Roesse Lupus' x 'BreeVis Homerus'.
van Bree 2007 NL AFS6635.

BreeVis Fagi. Upright/Trailer. Semi Double. COROLLA is half flared with smooth petal margins; opens magenta (63A); matures magenta (58B); 22mm (7/8") long x 26mm (1") wide. SEPALS are fully up, tips recurved; pink (62A) upper surface; light rose (63D) lower surface; 24mm (15/16") long x 11mm (7/16") wide. TUBE is pink (62A); short & thick; 11mm (7/16") long x 10mm (3/8") wide. FOLIAGE: medium green (137B) upper surface; medium green (137D) lower surface. Leaves are 61mm (2 3/8") long x 33mm (1 5/16") wide, ovate shaped. PARENTAGE: 'Roesse Carme' x 'Bert Beckman'. Distinguished by bloom & foliage combination.
van Bree 2005 NL AFS5886.

BreeVis Forella. Upright. Single. COROLLA: quarter flared, smooth petal margins; opens purple (71A); matures magenta (61C); 24mm (15/16") long 20mm (13/16") wide. SEPALS: fully up; tips recurved; rose (61D), tipped green, upper & lower surfaces; 21mm (13/16") long x 11mm (7/16") wide. TUBE: rose (61D); short & thick; 7mm (1/4") long x 7mm (1/4") wide. STAMENS: extend 18mm (11/16") below corolla; rose (61D) filaments; magenta (59D) anthers. PISTIL: extends 31mm (1 1/4") below the corolla; pale pink (62D) style; light yellow (1C) stigma. BUD: ovate. FOLIAGE: dark green (137A) upper surface; medium green (138A) lower surface. Leaves are 66mm (2 5/8") long x 41mm (1 5/8") wide, ovate shaped, serrulated edges, acute tips and obtuse bases. Green veins, stems & branches. PARENTAGE: 'Roesse Carme' x 'Cameron Ryle'. Medium upright. Makes good upright or standard. Prefers overhead filtered light and cool climate. Best bloom and foliage colour in filtered light.

Tested 4 years in Knegsel, The Netherlands. Distinguished by bloom and foliage combination.
van Bree 2004 NL AFS5514.

BreeVis Hageni. Upright/Trailer. Single. COROLLA: half flared, smooth petal margins; opens dark purple (78A); matures reddish purple (74B); 20mm (13/16") long 27mm (1 1/16") wide. SEPALS: horizontal; tips recurved; magenta (63C); tipped green, upper & lower surfaces; 26mm (1") long x 12mm (1/2") wide. TUBE: magenta (63C); short & thick; 10mm (3/8") long x 10mm (3/8") wide. STAMENS: extend 10mm (3/8") below corolla; magenta (63A) filaments; peach (38B) anthers. PISTIL: extends 21mm (13/16") below the corolla; pink (62A) style; peach (38B) stigma. BUD: round, pointed. FOLIAGE: dark green (137A) upper surface; medium green (138B) lower surface. Leaves are 48mm (1 7/8") long x 34mm (1 5/16") wide, ovate shaped, serrulated edges, acute tips and rounded bases. Green veins, stems & branches. PARENTAGE: 'Roesse Carme' x 'Cameron Ryle'. Lax upright or stiff trailer. Makes good stiff trailer. Prefers overhead filtered light and cool climate. Best bloom and foliage colour in filtered light. Tested 4 years in Knegsel, The Netherlands. Distinguished by erect blooms.
van Bree 2004 NL AFS5515.

BreeVis Hector. Trailer. Double. COROLLA is three quarter flared; opens violet (84A); matures magenta (68A); 30mm (1 3/16") long x 27mm (1 1/16") wide. SEPALS are fully up, tips reflexed; rose (65A) upper surface; rose (64D) lower surface; 39mm (1 1/2") long x 21mm (13/16") wide. TUBE is rose (65A); 29mm (1 1/8") long x 7mm (1/4") wide. FOLIAGE: dark green (137A) upper surface; medium green (137D) lower surface. PARENTAGE: 'Roesse Elara' x 'BreeVis Evelien'. Distinguished by bloom colour.
van Bree 2006 NL AFS6098.

BreeVis Hesperus. Upright/Trailer. Single. COROLLA: three quarter flared, smooth petal margins; opens red (46B); matures red (46C); 27mm (1 1/16") long x 24mm (15/16") wide. SEPALS: fully up, tips reflexed; magenta (68A) upper & lower surfaces; 50mm (2") long x 14mm (9/16") wide. TUBE: magenta (68A); medium length & thickness; 21mm (13/16") long x 12mm (7/16") wide. STAMENS extend 19mm (3/4") beyond the corolla; rose (51C) filaments & anthers. PISTIL extends 32mm (1 1/4") beyond the corolla; rose (51B) style; rose (52B) stigma. BUD: ovate, curved, thin.

43

FOLIAGE: dark green (137A) upper surface; medium green (138A) lower surface. Leaves are 67mm (2 5/8") long x 56mm (2 1/4") wide; cordate shaped, serrulate edges, acute tips, cordate bases. Veins, stems & branches are red. PARENTAGE: 'Roesse Lupus' x 'Texas Star'. Lax upright or stiff trailer. Makes good upright or stiff trailer. Prefers overhead filtered light. Best bloom colour in filtered light. Tested 3 years in Knegsel, The Netherlands. Distinguished by bloom colour & shape.
van Bree 2009 NL AFS7253.

BreeVis Homerus. Trailer. Double. COROLLA is full flared with smooth petal margins; opens purple (83A); matures dark reddish purple (72A); 20mm (13/16") long x 25mm (1") wide. SEPALS are fully up, tips reflexed; dark reddish purple (70A) upper surface; reddish purple (70A) lower surface; 24mm (15/16") long x 13mm (1/2") wide. TUBE is dark reddish purple (70A); medium length and thickness; 11mm (7/16") long x 6mm (1/4") wide. STAMENS extend 23mm (15/16") beyond the corolla; dark reddish purple (72A) filaments and anthers. PISTIL extends 48mm (1 7/8") beyond the corolla; reddish purple (71B) style, magenta (68A) stigma. BUD is globular, pointed. FOLIAGE is medium green (137C) upper surface, medium green (138B) lower surface. Leaves are 56mm (2 3/16") long x 32mm (1 1/4") wide, ovate shaped, smooth edges, acute tips and rounded bases. Veins, stems and branches are green. PARENTAGE: 'Rohees Queen' x 'Cecile'. Natural trailer. Self branching. Makes good basket. Prefers overhead filtered light and cool climate. Best bloom colour in filtered light. Tested four years in Knegsel, The Netherlands. Distinguished by bloom colour.
van Bree 2002 NL AFS4961.

BreeVis Horta. Trailer. Double. COROLLA is three quarter flared with smooth petal margins; opens purple (83A); matures reddish purple (72B); 25mm (1") long x 24mm (15/16") wide. SEPALS are fully up, tips recurved; pale pink (62D) upper, light pink (62B) lower surface; 36mm (1 7/16") long x 14mm (9/16") wide. TUBE is pale pink (62D); medium length and thickness; 14mm (9/16") long x 7mm (1/4") wide. STAMENS extend 24mm (15/16") beyond the corolla; violet (83D) filaments, violet (75A) anthers. PISTIL extends 53mm (2 1/8") beyond the corolla; light reddish purple (73A) style, pale lavender (65D) stigma. BUD is ovate, pointed. FOLIAGE is medium green (137C)

upper surface, medium green (138B) lower surface. Leaves are 59mm (2 5/16") long x 36mm (1 7/16") wide, ovate shaped, serrated edges, acute tips and rounded bases. Veins, stems and branches are green. PARENTAGE: 'Rohees Queen' x 'Cecile'. Natural trailer. Self branching. Makes good basket. Prefers overhead filtered light and cool climate. Best bloom colour in filtered light. Tested four years in Knegsel, The Netherlands. Distinguished by bloom colour.
van Bree 2002 NL AFS4963.

BreeVis Hova. Trailer. Single. COROLLA: Half flared; opens reddish purple (71B); matures magenta (71C); 20mm (3/4") long x 24mm (15/16") wide. SEPALS: fully up, tips reflexed; rose (52B) upper surface; red (52A) lower surface; 31mm (1 1/4") long x 13mm (1/2") wide. TUBE: rose (52B); medium length & thickness; 16mm (5/8") long x 6mm (1/4") wide. FOLIAGE is dark green (137A) upper surface; medium green (137C) lower surface. PARENTAGE: 'Roesse Lupus' x 'BreeVis Mitch'.
van Bree 2007 NL AFS6631.

BreeVis Hyale. Upright/Trailer. Single. COROLLA: Fully flared; opens reddish purple (59B); matures reddish purple (60D); 25mm (1") long x 31mm (1 1/4") wide. SEPALS: fully up, tips recurved; magenta (63B) upper surface; dark reddish purple (59A) lower surface; 32mm (1 1/4") long x 15mm (9/16") wide. TUBE: magenta (61C); short & thick; 7mm (1/4") long x 7mm (1/4") wide. FOLIAGE is dark green (137A) upper surface; medium green (138A) lower surface. PARENTAGE: 'Roesse Lupus' x 'BreeVis Homerus'.
van Bree 2007 NL AFS6636.

BreeVis Ilia. Upright/Trailer. Double. COROLLA: three quarter flared, smooth petal margins; opens magenta (63A); matures magenta (63B); 24mm (15/16") long x 22mm (7/8") wide. SEPALS: horizontal; tips recurved; light pink (65B) upper surface; rose (65A) lower surface; 32mm (1 1/4") long x 24mm (15/16") wide. TUBE: light pink (65B); long & thin; 36mm (1 7/16") long x 6mm (1/4") wide. STAMENS: extend 16mm (5/8") below corolla; rose (63C) filaments; reddish purple (61B) anthers. PISTIL: extends 42mm (1 5/8") below the corolla, pink (62C) style, light rose (68D) stigma. BUD: spherical. FOLIAGE: medium green (137C) upper surface; medium green (138B) lower surface. Leaves are 72mm (2 13/16") long x 28mm (1 1/8") wide, lanceolate shaped, serrulated

44

edges, acute tips and acute bases. Veins, stems & branches are green. PARENTAGE: 'Bicentennial' x 'Allure'. Lax upright or stiff trailer. Makes good stiff trailer. Prefers overhead filtered light and cool climate. Best bloom and foliage colour in filtered light. Tested 4 years in Knegsel, The Netherlands. Distinguished by bloom & foliage combination.

van Bree 2003 NL AFS5240.

BreeVis Julia. Upright/Trailer. Double. COROLLA: half flared, smooth petal margins; opens purple (77A); matures reddish purple (60D); 26mm (1") long 17mm (11/16") wide. SEPALS: half down; tips recurved; dark rose (64C) upper surface; magenta (63A) lower surface; 62mm (2 7/16") long x 17mm (11/16") wide. TUBE: dark rose (64C); medium length & thickness; 18mm (11/16") long x 7mm (1/4") wide. STAMENS: extend 22mm (7/8") below corolla; magenta (63A) filaments; dark reddish purple (59A) anthers. PISTIL: extends 51mm (2") below the corolla; magenta (63A) style; pale yellow (5D) stigma. BUD: cordate, pointed. FOLIAGE: dark green (137A) upper surface; medium green (137C) lower surface. Leaves are 71mm (2 7/16") long x 41mm (1 5/8") wide, ovate shaped, serrulated edges, acute tips and obtuse bases. Red veins, stems & branches. PARENTAGE: 'Bicentennial' x 'Rohees Miram'. Lax upright or stiff trailer. Makes good stiff trailer. Prefers overhead filtered light and cool climate. Best bloom and foliage colour in filtered light. Tested 4 years in Knegsel, The Netherlands. Distinguished by bloom colour.

van Bree 2004 NL AFS5519.

BreeVis Leda. Trailer. Double. COROLLA is half flared; opens violet (85B); matures light violet (84C); 22mm (7/8") long x 14mm (9/16") wide. SEPALS are half up, tips recurved up; light pink (65C) upper surface; rose (65A) lower surface; 38mm (1 1/2") long x 16mm (5/8") wide. TUBE is light pink (65C); 23mm (7/8") long x 8mm (5/16") wide. FOLIAGE: dark green (137A) upper surface; medium green (138B) lower surface. PARENTAGE: 'Luuk van Riet' x 'BreeVis Evelien'. Distinguished by bloom colour.

van Bree 2006 NL AFS6091.

BreeVis Lucina. Upright/Trailer. Semi Double. COROLLA is three quarter flared with smooth petal margins; opens dark reddish purple (64A); matures magenta (63A); 16mm (5/8") long x 19mm (3/4") wide. SEPALS are fully up, tips reflexed; light apple

green (145B) upper & lower surfaces; 27mm (1 1/16") long x 11mm (7/16") wide. TUBE is light green (145D); medium length & thickness; 12mm (1/2") long x 6mm (1/4") wide. FOLIAGE: dark green (137A) upper surface; medium green (138A) lower surface. Leaves are 69mm (2 3/4") long x 36mm (1 7/16") wide, ovate shaped. PARENTAGE: 'Roesse Carme' x 'Leon Pauwels'. Distinguished by bloom & foliage combination.

van Bree 2005 NL AFS5881.

BreeVis Luna. Upright/Trailer. Double. COROLLA is three quarter flared with smooth petal margins; opens dark purple (79A); matures reddish purple (59B); 32mm (1 1/4") long x 37mm (1 7/16") wide. SEPALS are half up, tips reflexed up; dark reddish purple (64A) upper surface; magenta (63A) lower surface; 42mm (1 11/16") long x 18mm (11/16") wide. TUBE is dark reddish purple (64A); medium length and thickness; 17mm (11/16") long x 6mm (1/4") wide. STAMENS extend 37mm (1 7/16") beyond the corolla; reddish purple (71B) filaments, purple (71A) anthers. PISTIL extends 45mm (1 3/4") beyond the corolla; reddish purple (71B) style, light pink (65B) stigma. BUD is tear drop shaped. FOLIAGE is dark green (137A) upper surface, medium green (138A) lower surface. Leaves are 87mm (3 7/16") long x 42mm (1 11/16") wide, ovate shaped, serrated edges, acute tips and obtuse bases. Veins are green, stems and branches are red. PARENTAGE: 'Breevis Evelien' x 'Rohees King'. Lax upright or stiff trailer. Makes good stiff trailer. Prefers overhead filtered light and cool climate. Best bloom colour in filtered light. Tested four years in Knegsel, The Netherlands. Distinguished by blossom colour.

van Bree 2002 NL AFS4956.

BreeVis Medusa. Trailer. Single. COROLLA: Half flared; opens dark reddish purple (72A); matures reddish purple (71B); 21mm (13/16") long x 20mm (3/4") wide. SEPALS: fully up, tips recurved; dark rose (64C) upper surface; reddish purple (64B) lower surface; 31mm (1 1/4") long x 5mm (3/16") wide. TUBE: dark rose (64C); medium length & thickness; 17mm (5/8") long x 6mm (1/4") wide. FOLIAGE is dark green (137A) upper surface; medium green (137C) lower surface. PARENTAGE: 'Roesse Lupus' x 'BreeVis Mitch'.

van Bree 2007 NL AFS6632.

BreeVis Megaera. Upright/Trailer. Double. COROLLA: Half flared; opens & matures light rose (63D); 14mm (9/16") long x 21mm (13/16") wide. SEPALS: fully up, tips reflexed; red (45A) upper & lower surfaces; 27mm (1 1/16") long x 9mm (5/16") wide. TUBE: red (45A); medium length & thickness; 17mm (5/8") long x 6mm (1/4") wide. FOLIAGE is dark green (137A) upper surface; medium green (137C) lower surface. PARENTAGE: 'Roesse Scutum' x ('Roesse Elara' x 'Magda Vanbets'). van Bree 2007 NL AFS6629.

BreeVis Mi. Trailer. Single. COROLLA: three quarter flared, smooth petal margins; opens purple (77A); matures dark reddish purple (64A); 17mm (11/16") long 14mm (9/16") wide. SEPALS: fully up; tips reflexed; pale lavender (69C) upper surface; pale pink (69A) lower surface; 31mm (1 1/4") long x 7mm (1/4") wide. TUBE: pale lavender (69C); medium length & thickness; 16mm (5/8") long x 5mm (3/16") wide. STAMENS: extend 15mm (9/16") below corolla; reddish purple (64B) filaments; light pink (62B) anthers. PISTIL: extends 40mm (1 9/16") below the corolla; light pink (65C) style; pale yellow (2D) stigma. BUD: ovate, pointed. FOLIAGE: yellowish green (146B) upper surface; yellowish green (146C) lower surface. Leaves are 71mm (2 13/16") long x 36mm (1 7/16") wide, ovate shaped, serrated edges, acute tips and obtuse bases. Green veins, stems & branches. PARENTAGE: 'Orangeblossom' x 'Judy Salome'. Natural trailer. Makes good basket. Prefers overhead filtered light and cool climate. Best bloom and foliage colour in filtered light. Tested 4 years in Knegsel, The Netherlands. Distinguished by bloom colour. van Bree 2004 NL AFS5517.

BreeVis Minimus. Upright/Trailer. Single. COROLLA: quarter flared, smooth petal margins; opens purple (71A); matures reddish purple (64B); 25mm (1") long 23mm (15/16") wide. SEPALS: fully up; tips reflexed; pale yellow (158B) upper surface; cream (158D) lower surface; 31mm (1 1/4") long x 9mm (3/8") wide. TUBE: pale yellow (158B); medium length & thickness; 21mm (13/16") long x 12mm (1/2") wide. STAMENS: extend 20mm (13/16") below corolla; reddish purple (64B) filaments; purple (71A) anthers. PISTIL: extends 41mm (1 5/8") below the corolla; rose (68B) style; pale yellow (5D) stigma. BUD: cordate, pointed. FOLIAGE: dark green (137A) upper surface; medium green (137D) lower surface. Leaves are 62mm (2 7/16") long x 37mm (1

7/16") wide, ovate shaped, serrated edges, acute tips and obtuse bases. Green veins, stems & branches. PARENTAGE: 'Orangeblossom' x 'Judy Salome'. Lax upright or stiff trailer. Makes good stiff trailer. Prefers overhead filtered light and cool climate. Best bloom and foliage colour in filtered light. Tested 4 years in Knegsel, The Netherlands. Distinguished by bloom colour. van Bree 2004 NL AFS5518.

BreeVis Mittrei. Trailer. Single. COROLLA: three quarter flared, smooth petal margins; opens dark reddish purple (61A); matures dark reddish purple (60C); 32mm (1 1/4") long x 24mm (15/16") wide. SEPALS: fully up, tips reflexed; reddish purple (59B) upper & lower surfaces; 36mm (1 7/16") long x 10mm (3/8") wide. TUBE: reddish purple (59B); medium length & thickness; 14mm (9/16") long x 6mm (1/4") wide. STAMENS extend 20mm (3/4") beyond the corolla; magenta (68A) filaments & anthers. PISTIL extends 34mm (1 3/8") beyond the corolla; dark reddish purple (61A) style; white (155A) stigma. BUD: ovate, thin. FOLIAGE: dark green (137C) upper surface; medium green (138B) lower surface. Leaves are 46mm (1 13/16") long x 30mm (1 3/16") wide; cordate shaped, serrulate edges, acute tips, obtuse bases. Veins, stems & branches are red. PARENTAGE: 'Roesse Lupus' x 'Texas Star'. Natural trailer. Makes good basket. Prefers overhead filtered light. Best bloom colour in filtered light. Tested 3 years in Knegsel, The Netherlands. Distinguished by bloom colour. van Bree 2009 NL AFS7252.

BreeVis Mori. Upright/Trailer. Double. COROLLA: three quarter flared, smooth petal margins; opens purple (71A); matures reddish purple (67A); 22mm (7/8") long x 28mm (1 1/8") wide. SEPALS: horizontal; tips reflexed; red (52A) upper & lower surfaces; 28mm (1 1/8") long x 19mm (3/4") wide. TUBE: red (52A); medium length & thickness; 16mm (5/8") long x 6mm (1/4") wide. STAMENS: extend 20mm (13/16") below corolla; dark rose (64C) filaments; dark reddish purple (64A) anthers. PISTIL: extends 27mm (1 1/16") below the corolla, rose (61D) style, pale pink (62D) stigma. BUD: spherical. FOLIAGE: dark green (137A) upper surface; medium green (138A) lower surface. Leaves are 60mm (2 3/8") long x 28mm (1 1/8") wide, lanceolate shaped, serrulated edges, acute tips and rounded bases. Veins, stems & branches are red. PARENTAGE: 'Bicentennial' x ('Rohees King' x 'Miniskirt'). Lax upright or stiff trailer.

Makes good stiff trailer. Prefers overhead filtered light and cool climate. Best bloom and foliage colour in filtered light. Tested 4 years in Knegsel, The Netherlands. Distinguished by bloom colour.
van Bree 2003 NL AFS5239.

BreeVis Mylitta. Upright/Trailer. Double. COROLLA is half flared with smooth petal margins; opens dark purple (78A); matures dark reddish purple (61A); 29mm (1 1/8") long x 24mm (15/16") wide. SEPALS are fully up, tips reflexed; rose (65A) upper surface; magenta (63B) lower surface; 36mm (1 7/16") long x 16mm (5/8") wide. TUBE is rose (65A); short & thick; 10mm (3/8") long x 9mm (3/8") wide. FOLIAGE: dark green (137A) upper surface; medium green (138B) lower surface. Leaves are 56mm (2 3/16") long x 34mm (1 5/16") wide, ovate shaped. PARENTAGE: 'Roesse Carme' x 'Leon Pauwels'. Distinguished by bloom & foliage combination.
van Bree 2005 NL AFS5879.

BreeVis Mysis. Trailer. Double. COROLLA: Half flared; opens light reddish purple (73A); matures light rose (73B); 19mm (3/4") long x 14mm (9/16") wide. SEPALS: half down, tips recurved; magenta (57B) tipped green upper surface; magenta (57B) lower surface; 26mm (1") long x 9mm (5/16") wide. TUBE: pale lavender (65D); long, thin; 31mm (1 1/4") long x 4mm (1/8") wide. FOLIAGE is dark green (137A) upper surface; medium green (138A) lower surface. PARENTAGE: 'Roesse Scutum' x ('Roesse Elara' x 'Magda Vanbets).
van Bree 2007 NL AFS6627.

BreeVis Natalica. Upright/Trailer. Double. COROLLA is three quarter flared with smooth petal margins; opens dark purple (79B); matures dark reddish purple (61A); 24mm (15/16") long x 24mm (15/16") wide. SEPALS are half up, tips reflexed up; reddish purple (67A) upper surface; magenta (67B) lower surface; 42mm (1 11/16") long x 21mm (13/16") wide. TUBE is reddish purple (67A); medium length and thickness; 20mm (13/16") long x 10mm (3/8") wide. STAMENS extend 28mm (1 1/8") beyond the corolla; reddish purple (61B) filaments, dark purple (79A) anthers. PISTIL extends 44mm (1 3/4") beyond the corolla; dark rose (67C) style, light yellow (2C) stigma. BUD is ovate, pointed. FOLIAGE is dark green (137A) upper surface, medium green (138B) lower surface. Leaves are 84mm (3 5/16") long x 52mm (2 1/16") wide, ovate shaped, serrated edges, acute tips and obtuse bases. Veins are green,

stems and branches are red. PARENTAGE: 'Rohees New Millennium' x 'Breevis Evelien'. Lax upright or stiff trailer. Makes good stiff trailer. Prefers overhead filtered light and cool climate. Best bloom colour in filtered light. Tested four years in Knegsel, The Netherlands. Distinguished by blossom colour.
van Bree 2002 NL AFS4957.

BreeVis Nero. Trailer. Single. COROLLA: half flared, smooth petal margins; opens purple (71A); matures dark reddish purple (60A); 20mm (13/16") long 14mm (9/16") wide. SEPALS: half up; tips recurved up; pink (62C) upper surface; light pink (62B) lower surface; 26mm (1") long x 7mm (1/4") wide. TUBE: pale pink (62D); medium length & thickness; 20mm (13/16") long x 5mm (3/16") wide. STAMENS: extend 17mm (11/16") below corolla; dark reddish purple (70A) filaments; dark reddish purple (60A) anthers. PISTIL: extends 29mm (1 1/8") below the corolla; magenta (68A) style; pale yellow (1D) stigma. BUD: ovate, pointed. FOLIAGE: medium green (137B) upper surface; medium green (137C) lower surface. Leaves are 45mm (1 3/4") long x 27mm (1 1/16") wide, ovate shaped, serrulated edges, acute tips and obtuse bases. Green veins, stems & branches. PARENTAGE: 'Orangeblossom' x 'Judy Salome'. Natural trailer. Makes good basket. Prefers overhead filtered light and cool climate. Best bloom and foliage colour in filtered light. Tested 4 years in Knegsel, The Netherlands. Distinguished by bloom and foliage combination.
van Bree 2004 NL AFS5516.

BreeVis Ninus. Trailer. Double. COROLLA: three quarter flared, smooth petal margins; opens violet (90D); matures dark purple (78A); 20mm (13/16") long 26mm (1") wide. SEPALS: horizontal; tips recurved; light rose (68D) upper surface; rose (68B) lower surface; 42mm (1 5/8") long x 14mm (9/16") wide. TUBE: light rose (68D); medium length & thickness; 14mm (9/16") long x 7mm (1/4") wide. STAMENS: extend 17mm (11/16") below corolla; magenta (63B) filaments; pink (62A) anthers. PISTIL: extends 22mm (7/8") below the corolla; magenta (63B) style; light yellow (3D) stigma. BUD: cordate, pointed. FOLIAGE: medium green (137C) upper surface; medium green (138A) lower surface. Leaves are 58mm (2 5/16") long x 40mm (1 9/16") wide, ovate shaped, serrulated edges, acute tips and rounded bases. Green veins, stems &

branches. PARENTAGE: 'Sofie Michiels' x 'Audrey Tamerus'. Natural trailer. Makes good basket. Prefers overhead filtered light and cool climate. Best bloom and foliage colour in filtered light. Tested 4 years in Knegsel, The Netherlands. Distinguished by bloom colour.
van Bree 2004 NL AFS5520.

BreeVis Nobilis. Trailer. Double. COROLLA is three quarter flared with smooth petal margins; opens purple (83B); matures reddish purple (71B); 24mm (15/16") long x 18mm (11/16") wide. SEPALS are horizontal, tips recurved; magenta (57C) upper surface; magenta (57A) lower surface; 24mm (15/16") long x 14mm (9/16") wide. TUBE is magenta (57C); medium length and thickness; 12mm (1/2") long x 7mm (1/4") wide. STAMENS extend 18mm (11/16") beyond the corolla; magenta (58B) filaments, reddish purple (58A) anthers. PISTIL extends 32mm (1 1/4") beyond the corolla; dark rose (58C) style, rose (63C) stigma. BUD is ovate, pointed. FOLIAGE is dark green (137A) upper surface, medium green (138A) lower surface. Leaves are 57mm (2 1/4") long x 27mm (1 1/16") wide, lanceolate shaped, smooth edges, acute tips and rounded bases. Veins, stems and branches are green. PARENTAGE: 'Rohees King' x 'Cecile'. Natural trailer. Self branching. Makes good basket. Prefers overhead filtered light and cool climate. Best bloom colour in filtered light. Tested four years in Knegsel, The Netherlands. Distinguished by bloom and foliage combination.
van Bree 2002 NL AFS4958.

BreeVis Nox. Trailer. Semi Double. COROLLA: half flared, wavy petal margins; opens violet blue (91A); matures violet (75A); 22mm (7/8") long 24mm (15/16") wide. SEPALS: horizontal; tips recurved; magenta (58B) upper & lower surfaces; 42mm (1 5/8") long x 16mm (5/8") wide. TUBE: magenta (58B); medium length & thickness; 16mm (5/8") long x 6mm (1/4") wide. STAMENS: extend 12mm (1/2") below corolla; magenta (58B) filaments; light rose (58D) anthers. PISTIL: extends 34mm (1 5/16") below the corolla; light rose (58D) style; light yellow (4C) stigma. BUD: ovate, pointed. FOLIAGE: dark green (137A) upper surface; medium green (138B) lower surface. Leaves are 52mm (2 1/16") long x 29mm (1 1/8") wide, lanceolate shaped, serrulated edges, acute tips and rounded bases. Red veins, stems & branches. PARENTAGE: 'Sofie Michiels' x 'Audrey Tamerus'. Natural trailer. Makes

good basket. Prefers overhead filtered light and cool climate. Best bloom and foliage colour in filtered light. Tested 4 years in Knegsel, The Netherlands. Distinguished by bloom colour.
van Bree 2004 NL AFS5521.

BreeVis Nupta. Trailer. Double. COROLLA is half flared; opens violet (76A); matures magenta (68A); 19mm (3/4") long x 21mm (13/16") wide. SEPALS are half down, tips reflexed; light pink (65C) upper surface; rose (68C) lower surface; 18mm (11/16") long x 13mm (1/2") wide. TUBE is light pink (65C); 19mm (3/4") long x 6mm (1/4") wide. FOLIAGE: dark green (137A) upper surface; medium green (137C) lower surface. PARENTAGE: 'Roesse Elara' x 'BreeVis Evelien'. Distinguished by bloom colour.
van Bree 2006 NL AFS6095.

BreeVis Orion. Upright/Trailer. Double. COROLLA: three quarter flared, smooth petal margins; opens purple (79C); matures purple (71A); 22mm (7/8") long x 24mm (15/16") wide. SEPALS: horizontal; tips recurved; reddish purple (64B) upper & lower surfaces; 35mm (1 3/8") long x 16mm (5/8") wide. TUBE: light yellow (10D); medium length & thickness; 40mm (1 9/16") long x 17mm (11/16") wide. STAMENS: extend 12mm (1/2") below corolla; purple (71A) filaments; dark rose (71D) anthers. PISTIL: extends 26mm (1") below the corolla, reddish purple (71B) style, yellowish white (4D) stigma. BUD: ovate. FOLIAGE: dark green (137A) upper surface; medium green (138B) lower surface. Leaves are 76mm (3") long x 32mm (1 1/4") wide, lanceolate shaped, serrulated edges, acute tips and rounded bases. Veins, stems & branches are red. PARENTAGE: 'Bicentennial' x ('Rohees King' x 'Miniskirt'). Lax upright or stiff trailer. Makes good stiff trailer. Prefers overhead filtered light and cool climate. Best bloom and foliage colour in filtered light. Tested 4 years in Knegsel, The Netherlands. Distinguished by bloom & foliage combination.
van Bree 2003 NL AFS5238.

BreeVis Palamades. Trailer. Double. COROLLA is full flared with smooth petal margins; opens purple (71A); matures dark reddish purple (61A); 18mm (11/16") long x 20mm (13/16") wide. SEPALS are horizontal, tips recurved; magenta (71C) upper surface; reddish purple (67A) lower surface; 46mm (1 13/16") long x 13mm (1/2") wide. TUBE is magenta (71C); medium length and thickness; 14mm (9/16") long x 9mm (3/8")

wide. STAMENS extend 28mm (1 1/8")
beyond the corolla; dark reddish purple (61A)
filaments, magenta (61C) anthers. PISTIL
extends 52mm (2 1/16") beyond the corolla;
magenta (61C) style, rose (63C) stigma. BUD
is ovate, pointed. FOLIAGE is dark green
(137A) upper surface, medium green (137C)
lower surface. Leaves are 74mm (2 15/16")
long x 35mm (1 3/8") wide, lanceolate
shaped, smooth edges, acute tips and acute
bases. Veins are green, stems and branches
are red. PARENTAGE: 'Rohees King' x
'Cecile'. Natural trailer. Makes good basket.
Prefers overhead filtered light and cool
climate. Best bloom colour in filtered light.
Tested four years in Knegsel, The
Netherlands. Distinguished by bloom and
foliage combination.
van Bree 2002 NL AFS4959.

BreeVis Pandione. Upright. Double.
COROLLA is half flared with smooth petal
margins; opens dark purple (79B); matures
dark purple (79A); 14mm (9/16") long x
21mm (13/16") wide. SEPALS are half up,
tips reflexed up; reddish purple (61B) upper
& lower surfaces; 21mm (13/16") long x
12mm (1/2") wide. TUBE is reddish purple
(61B); medium length & thickness; 16mm
(5/8") long x 8mm (3/16") wide. FOLIAGE:
dark green (137A) upper surface; medium
green (137D) lower surface. Leaves are 46mm
(1 13/16") long x 32mm (1 1/4") wide, ovate
shaped. PARENTAGE: 'Roesse Carme' x
'Roesse Rana'. Distinguished by bloom
colour.
van Bree 2005 NL AFS5889.

BreeVis Paphia. Trailer. Single. COROLLA:
Three quarter flared; opens dark reddish
purple (61A); matures magenta (63A); 20mm
(3/4") long x 22mm (7/8") wide. SEPALS:
horizontal, tips recurved; rose (63C) upper &
lower surfaces; 56mm (2 1/4") long x 14mm
(9/16") wide. TUBE: rose (63C); medium
length & thickness; 22mm (7/8") long x 7mm
(1/4") wide. FOLIAGE is dark green (137A)
upper surface; medium green (137C) lower
surface. PARENTAGE: 'Roesse Lupus' x
'BreeVis Mitch'.
van Bree 2007 NL AFS6628.

BreeVis Paradoxa. Trailer. Double.
COROLLA is full flared with smooth petal
margins; opens purple (89C); matures violet
(87B); 20mm (13/16") long x 24mm (15/16")
wide. SEPALS are fully up, tips reflexed;
magenta (63B) upper surface; pink (62A)
lower surface; 22mm (7/8") long x 14mm
(9/16") wide. TUBE is magenta (63B);

medium length and thickness; 14mm (9/16")
long x 6mm (1/4") wide. STAMENS extend
26mm (1") beyond the corolla; light purple
(74C) filaments, pale purple (74D) anthers.
PISTIL extends 46mm (1 13/16") beyond the
corolla; pale purple (74D) style, cream (11D)
stigma. BUD is globular, pointed. FOLIAGE
is medium green (137C) upper surface,
medium green (137D) lower surface. Leaves
are 56mm (2 3/16") long x 32mm (1 1/4")
wide, ovate shaped, smooth edges, acute tips
and obtuse bases. Veins, stems and
branches are green. PARENTAGE: 'Rohees
Queen' x 'Cecile'. Natural trailer. Makes good
basket. Prefers overhead filtered light and
cool climate. Best bloom colour in filtered
light. Tested four years in Knegsel, The
Netherlands. Distinguished by bloom and
foliage combination.
van Bree 2002 NL AFS4960.

BreeVis Patilla. Trailer. Semi Double.
COROLLA: half flared, smooth petal margins;
opens dark reddish purple (59A); matures
magenta (59C); 21mm (13/16") long x 19mm
(3/4") wide. SEPALS: half up, tips reflexed
up; rose (68C) upper surface; magenta (68A)
lower surface; 27mm (1 1/16") long x 14mm
(9/16") wide. TUBE: rose (68C); medium
length & thickness; 12mm (7/16") long x
7mm (1/4") wide. STAMENS extend 4mm
(1/8") beyond the corolla; dark rose (64C)
filaments & anthers. PISTIL extends 7mm
(1/4") beyond the corolla; dark rose (64C)
style; white (155D) stigma. BUD: cordate.
FOLIAGE: dark green (137A) upper surface;
medium green (137C) lower surface. Leaves
are 69mm (2 3/4") long x 40mm (1 9/16")
wide; ovate shaped, serrulate edges, acute
tips, obtuse bases. Veins, stems & branches
are green. PARENTAGE: 'Roesse Lupus' x
'Roesse Bootes'. Natural trailer. Makes good
basket. Prefers overhead filtered light. Best
bloom colour in filtered light. Tested 3 years
in Knegsel, The Netherlands. Distinguished
by bloom colour.
van Bree 2009 NL AFS7251.

BreeVis Polytes. Trailer. Semi Double.
COROLLA is three quarter flared with
smooth petal margins; opens purple (83A);
matures dark purple (78A); 20mm (13/16")
long x 24mm (15/16") wide. SEPALS are half
up, tips reflexed up; rose (50B) upper
surface, red (50A) lower surface; 24mm
(15/16") long x 13mm (1/2") wide. TUBE is
rose (50B), medium length and thickness;
17mm (11/16") long x 7mm (1/4") wide.
STAMENS extend 35mm (1 3/8") beyond the
corolla; light reddish purple (66C) filaments,

light yellow (6D) anthers. PISTIL extends 61mm (2 7/16") beyond the corolla; light magenta (66D) style, light yellow (6D) stigma. BUD is round, pointed. FOLIAGE is medium green (138A) upper surface, medium green (138B) lower surface. Leaves are 61mm (2 7/16") long x 33mm (1 5/16") wide, ovate shaped, serrated edges, acute tips and rounded bases. Veins are green, stems and branches are red. PARENTAGE: 'Rohees King' x 'Cecile'. Natural trailer. Self branching. Makes good basket. Prefers overhead filtered light and cool climate. Best bloom colour in filtered light. Tested four years in Knegsel, The Netherlands. Distinguished by bloom and foliage combination.
van Bree 2002 NL AFS4937.

BreeVis Pomona. Trailer. Double. COROLLA is half flared; opens reddish purple (72B); matures magenta (61C); 27mm (1 1/16") long x 32mm (1 1/4") wide. SEPALS are half down, tips recurved; red (45B) upper surface; red (46C) lower surface; 39mm (1 1/2") long x 15mm (9/16") wide. TUBE is red (45B); 31mm (1 1/4") long x 4mm (1/8") wide. FOLIAGE: medium green (137C) upper surface; medium green (138B) lower surface. PARENTAGE: 'Roesse Elara' x 'BreeVis Evelien'. Distinguished by bloom shape & colour.
van Bree 2006 NL AFS6096.

BreeVis Rashti. Upright. Double. COROLLA is half flared with smooth petal margins; opens dark reddish purple (60A); matures magenta (61C); 16mm (5/8") long x 21mm (13/16") wide. SEPALS are horizontal, tips recurved; rose (63C) upper surface; magenta (63B) lower surface; 21mm (13/16") long x 13mm (1/2") wide. TUBE is magenta (63B); medium length & thickness; 12mm (1/2") long x 6mm (1/4") wide. FOLIAGE: dark green (137A) upper surface; medium green (137C) lower surface. Leaves are 45mm (1 3/4") long x 36mm (1 7/16") wide, ovate shaped. PARENTAGE: 'Roesse Carme' x 'Leon Pauwels'. Distinguished by bloom & foliage combination.
van Bree 2005 NL AFS5880.

BreeVis Rubi. Trailer. Semi Double. COROLLA is half flared with smooth petal margins; opens dark red (46A); matures red (47B); 22mm (7/8") long x 24mm (15/16") wide. SEPALS are fully up, tips recurved; magenta (61C) upper surface; orange (35B) lower surface; 26mm (1") long x 14mm (9/16") wide. TUBE is magenta (61C);

medium length & thickness; 16mm (5/8") long x 7mm (1/4") wide. FOLIAGE: dark green (137A) upper surface; medium green (138B) lower surface. Leaves are 62mm (2 7/16") long x 32mm (1 1/4") wide, ovate shaped. PARENTAGE: 'Swanley Gem' x 'Delta's Wonder'. Distinguished by bloom colour..
van Bree 2005 NL AFS5885.

BreeVis Sannio. Upright. Single. COROLLA: Half flared; opens purple (90B); matures light violet (84B); 21mm (13/16") long x 26mm (1") wide. SEPALS: half up, tips recurved up; magenta (63B) upper & lower surfaces; 34mm (1 3/8") long x 8mm (5/16") wide. TUBE: magenta (63B); short, medium thickness; 7mm (1/4") long x 6mm (1/4") wide. FOLIAGE is dark green (137A) upper surface; medium green (138A) lower surface. PARENTAGE: 'Reg Gubler' x ('Roesse Elara' x 'Magda Vanbets).
van Bree 2007 NL AFS6626.

BreeVis Sara. Upright/Trailer. Double. COROLLA: quarter flared, smooth petal margins; opens purple (71A); matures reddish purple (70B); 16mm (5/8") long x 21mm (13/16") wide. SEPALS: half up; tips recurved up; pink (62A) upper surface; dark rose (58C) lower surface; 35mm (1 3/8") long x 15mm (9/16") wide. TUBE: reddish purple (58A); medium length & thickness; 16mm (5/8") long x 5mm (3/16") wide. STAMENS: extend 17mm (11/16") below corolla; pale purple (70D) filaments; dark reddish purple (59A) anthers. PISTIL: extends 27mm (1 1/16") below the corolla, light rose (63D) style, yellowish white (4D) stigma. BUD: spherical. FOLIAGE: dark green (137A) upper surface; medium green (138A) lower surface. Leaves are 72mm (2 13/16") long x 46mm (1 13/16") wide, cordate shaped, serrulated edges, acute tips and obtuse bases. Veins & stems are red, branches are green. PARENTAGE: 'Bicentennial' x 'Allure'. Lax upright or stiff trailer. Makes good stiff trailer. Prefers overhead filtered light and cool climate. Best bloom and foliage colour in filtered light. Tested 4 years in Knegsel, The Netherlands. Distinguished by blossom colour.
van Bree 2003 NL AFS5236.

BreeVis Scylla. Upright/Trailer. Double. COROLLA: half flared, smooth petal margins; opens purple (88A); matures violet (77C); 16mm (5/8") long 21mm (13/16") wide. SEPALS: fully up; tips recurved; greenish yellow (1B), tipped green, upper surface; light

yellow (1C), tipped green, lower surface; 36mm (1 7/16") long x 16mm (5/8") wide. TUBE: magenta (58B); medium length & thickness; 11mm (7/16) long x 6mm (1/4") wide. STAMENS: extend 12mm (1/2") below corolla; rose (68C) filaments; pale lavender (65D) anthers. PISTIL: extends 16mm (5/8") below the corolla; light rose (68D) style; light yellow (4C) stigma. BUD: elliptic, long. FOLIAGE: dark green (137A) upper surface; medium green (138B) lower surface. Leaves are 46mm (1 13/16") long x 30mm (1 3/16") wide, ovate shaped, serrulated edges, acute tips and obtuse bases. Green veins, stems & branches. PARENTAGE: ('Cameron Ryle' x 'Parasol') x 'Sleigh Bells'. Lax upright or stiff trailer. Makes good stiff trailer. Prefers overhead filtered light and cool climate. Best bloom and foliage colour in filtered light. Tested 4 years in Knegsel, The Netherlands. Distinguished by bloom colour.
van Bree 2004 NL AFS5506.

BreeVis Selene. Trailer. Double. COROLLA is three quarter flared with smooth petal margins; opens dark purple (79B); matures dark reddish purple (59A); 24mm (15/16") long x 24mm (15/16") wide. SEPALS are horizontal, tips recurved; dark reddish purple (64A) upper surface; rose (64D) lower surface; 36mm (1 7/16") long x 16mm (5/8") wide. TUBE is dark reddish purple (64A); medium length and thickness; 14mm (9/16") long x 8mm (5/16") wide. STAMENS extend 17mm (11/16") beyond the corolla; dark purple (79B) filaments, reddish purple (72B) anthers. PISTIL extends 30mm (1 3/16") beyond the corolla; reddish purple (71B) style, pale lavender (65D) stigma. BUD is tear drop shaped. FOLIAGE is dark green (137A) upper surface, medium green (138A) lower surface. Leaves are 74mm (2 15/16") long x 30mm (1 3/16") wide, lanceolate shaped, serrated edges, acute tips and obtuse bases. Veins, stems and branches are red. PARENTAGE: 'Rohees King' x 'Cecile'. Natural trailer. Self branching. Makes good basket. Prefers overhead filtered light and cool climate. Best bloom colour in filtered light. Tested four years in Knegsel, The Netherlands. Distinguished by blossom colour.
van Bree 2002 NL AFS4955.

BreeVis Sexta. Trailer. Single. COROLLA: half flared, smooth petal margins; opens reddish purple (59B); matures dark reddish purple (60A); 21mm (13/16") long x 32mm (1 1/4") wide. SEPALS: fully up, tips recurved; light pink (65A) upper surface; magenta

(58B) lower surface; 37mm (1 7/16") long x 16mm (5/8") wide. TUBE: pale pink (69A); long & thin; 52mm (2 1/16") long x 4mm (1/8") wide. STAMENS extend 24mm (15/16") beyond the corolla; reddish purple (60D) filaments; pale pink (62D) anthers. PISTIL extends 19mm (3/4") beyond the corolla; pink (62A) style; white (155B) stigma. BUD: ovate, elongated. FOLIAGE: dark green (137A) upper surface; medium green (137D) lower surface. Leaves are 50mm (2") long x 29mm (1 1/8") wide; cordate shaped, serrulate edges, acute tips, obtuse bases. Veins, stems & branches are red. PARENTAGE: 'Roesse Lupus' x 'Rob Knapen'. Natural trailer. Makes good basket. Prefers overhead filtered light. Best bloom colour in filtered light. Tested 3 years in Knegsel, The Netherlands. Distinguished by bloom colour.
van Bree 2009 NL AFS7249.

BreeVis Simla. Upright/Trailer. Double. COROLLA: quarter flared, smooth petal margins; opens reddish purple (71B); matures dark rose (71D); 30mm (1 3/16") long x 22mm (7/8") wide. SEPALS: half up; tips recurved up; pink (62A) upper surface; magenta (63B) lower surface; 35mm (1 3/8") long x 16mm (5/8") wide. TUBE: light yellow (10D); medium length & thickness; 16mm (5/8") long x 7mm (1/4") wide. STAMENS: extend 12mm (1/2") below corolla; magenta (68A) filaments; dark reddish purple (59A) anthers. PISTIL: extends 26mm (1") below the corolla, pale lavender (65D) style, yellowish white (4D) stigma. BUD: ovate. FOLIAGE: medium green (137B) upper surface; medium green (137D) lower surface. Leaves are 66mm (2 5/8") long x 38mm (1 1/2") wide, ovate shaped, serrated edges, acute tips and rounded bases. Veins, stems & branches are green. PARENTAGE: 'Bicentennial' x 'Allure'. Lax upright or stiff trailer. Makes good stiff trailer. Prefers overhead filtered light and cool climate. Best bloom and foliage colour in filtered light. Tested 4 years in Knegsel, The Netherlands. Distinguished by bloom & foliage combination.
van Bree 2003 NL AFS5237.

BreeVis Sorana. Upright. Double. COROLLA is three quarter flared with smooth petal margins; opens purple (71A); matures dark reddish purple (61A); 20mm (13/16") long x 24mm (15/16") wide. SEPALS are fully up, tips recurved; light rose (58D) tipped green upper surface; dark rose (58C) tipped green lower surface; 24mm (13/16") long x 13mm (1/2") wide. TUBE is light rose (58D); short &

thick; 7mm (1/4") long x 9mm (3/8") wide.
FOLIAGE: dark green (139A) upper surface;
medium green (137C) lower surface. Leaves
are 56mm (2 3/16") long x 34mm (1 5/16")
wide, ovate shaped. PARENTAGE: 'Roesse
Carme' x 'Leon Pauwels'. Distinguished by
bloom colour.
van Bree 2005 NL AFS5884.

BreeVis Spini. Trailer. Double. COROLLA:
half flared, smooth petal margins; opens
purple (77A); matures reddish purple (71B);
22mm (7/8") long x 24mm (15/16") wide.
SEPALS: horizontal; tips recurved; dark rose
(64C) upper surface; reddish purple (64B)
lower surface; 34mm (1 5/16") long x 15mm
(9/16") wide. TUBE: dark rose (64C);
medium length & thickness; 22mm (7/8")
long x 7mm (1/4") wide. STAMENS: extend
17mm (11/16") below corolla; reddish purple
(64B) filaments; dark reddish purple (72A)
anthers. PISTIL: extends 42mm (1 5/8")
below the corolla; magenta (68A) style, light
rose (63D) stigma. BUD: ovate, pointed.
FOLIAGE: dark green (137A) upper surface;
medium green (137C) lower surface. Leaves
are 68mm (2 11/16") long x 24mm (15/16")
wide, lanceolate shaped, serrulated edges,
acute tips and acute bases. Veins, stems &
branches are green. PARENTAGE:
'Bicentennial' x ('Rohees King' x 'Miniskirt').
Natural trailer. Makes good basket. Prefers
overhead filtered light and cool climate. Best
bloom and foliage colour in filtered light.
Tested 4 years in Knegsel, The Netherlands.
Distinguished by bloom colour.
van Bree 2003 NL AFS5242.

BreeVis Sylvata. Upright/Trailer. Single.
COROLLA: half flared, smooth petal margins;
opens reddish purple (67A); matures dark
rose (67C); 19mm (3/4") long 25mm (1")
wide. SEPALS: half up; tips recurved up;
light pink (65C), tipped green, upper surface;
rose (65A) lower surface; 28mm (1 1/8") long
x 10mm (3/8") wide. TUBE: light pink (65C);
short & thick; 9mm (3/8") long x 8mm
(5/16") wide. STAMENS: extend 14mm
(9/16") below corolla; pink (62A) filaments;
peach (37B) anthers. PISTIL: extends 12mm
(1/2") below the corolla; pink (62A) style;
peach (37B) stigma. BUD: elliptic, curved,
pointed. FOLIAGE: dark green (137A) upper
surface; medium green (137D) lower surface.
Leaves are 62mm (2 7/16") long x 24mm
(15/16") wide, ovate shaped, serrulated
edges, acute tips and obtuse bases. Green
veins, stems & branches. PARENTAGE:
'Roesse Carme' x 'Cameron Ryle'. Lax upright
or stiff trailer. Makes good stiff trailer.

Prefers overhead filtered light and cool
climate. Best bloom and foliage colour in
filtered light. Tested 4 years in Knegsel, The
Netherlands. Distinguished by bloom and
foliage combination.
van Bree 2004 NL AFS5510.

BreeVis Tages. Upright. Semi Double.
COROLLA: three quarter flared, smooth petal
margins; opens red (46B); matures red (46C);
26mm (1") long x 27mm (1 1/16") wide.
SEPALS: half up, tips reflexed up; red (46D)
upper surface; red (45D) lower surface;
24mm (15/16") long x 14mm (9/16") wide.
TUBE: red (46D); medium length &
thickness; 21mm (13/16") long x 8mm
(5/16") wide. STAMENS extend 16mm (5/8")
beyond the corolla; red (52A) filaments; dark
reddish purple (61A) anthers. PISTIL extends
24mm (15/16") beyond the corolla; magenta
(58B) style; reddish purple (67A) stigma.
BUD: elliptic, elongated. FOLIAGE: dark
green (137A) upper surface; medium green
(137C) lower surface. Leaves are 74mm (2
15/16") long x 41mm (1 5/8") wide; ovate
shaped, serrate edges, acute tips, obtuse
bases. Veins, stems & branches are red.
PARENTAGE: 'Roesse Lupus' x 'Roesse
Mason'. Small upright. Makes good upright.
Prefers overhead filtered light. Best bloom
colour in filtered light. Tested 3 years in
Knegsel, The Netherlands. Distinguished by
bloom & foliage combination.
van Bree 2009 NL AFS7250.

BreeVis Terra. Upright/Trailer. Double.
COROLLA: Three quarter flared; opens &
matures light rose (68D); 22mm (7/8") long x
26mm (1") wide. SEPALS: fully up, tips
recurved; magenta (58B) upper & lower
surfaces; 36mm (1 7/16") long x 14mm
(9/16") wide. TUBE: magenta (58B); medium
length, thick; 16mm (5/8") long x 4mm
(1/8") wide. FOLIAGE is dark green (137A)
upper surface; medium green (137C) lower
surface. PARENTAGE: 'Roesse Scutum' x
('Roesse Elara' x 'Magda Vanbets').
van Bree 2007 NL AFS6625.

BreeVis Varuna. Upright/Trailer. Double.
COROLLA is half flared with smooth petal
margins; opens purple (71A); matures
reddish purple (59B); 18mm (11/16") long x
16mm (5/8") wide. SEPALS are half up, tips
recurved up; dark reddish purple (64A)
tipped green upper & lower surfaces; 24mm
(15/16") long x 7mm (1/4") wide. TUBE is
dark reddish purple (64A); medium length &
thickness; 11mm (7/16") long x 6mm (1/4")
wide. FOLIAGE: dark green (137A) upper

52

surface; medium green (138B) lower surface. Leaves are 60mm (2 3/8") long x 29mm (1 1/8") wide, ovate shaped. PARENTAGE: ('Roesse Apus' x 'Roesse Apus') x ('Rohees Queen' x 'Sofie Michiels'). Distinguished by bloom colour.
van Bree 2005 NL AFS5891.

BreeVis Vinula. Upright/Trailer. Double. COROLLA is full flared with smooth petal margins; opens purple (77A); matures magenta (63A); 19mm (3/4") long x 32mm (1 1/4") wide. SEPALS are half up, tips reflexed up; magenta (58B) upper & lower surfaces; 22mm (7/8") long x 12mm (1/2") wide. TUBE is magenta (58B); medium length & thickness; 9mm (3/8") long x 6mm (1/4") wide. FOLIAGE: dark green (137A) upper surface; medium green (138A) lower surface. Leaves are 68mm (2 11/16") long x 40mm (1 9/16") wide, ovate shaped. PARENTAGE: ('Roesse Apus' x 'Roesse Apus') x 'Centenary'. Distinguished by bloom & foliage combination.
van Bree 2005 NL AFS5882

BreeVis Zetes. Upright/Trailer. Double. COROLLA is three quarter flared with smooth petal margins; opens dark purple (86A); matures dark purple (78A); 18mm (11/16") long x 22mm (7/8") wide. SEPALS are half down, tips reflexed; rose (68B) upper and lower surfaces; 27mm (1 1/16") long x 14mm (9/16") wide. TUBE is rose (68B); short, medium thickness; 9mm (3/8") long x 14mm (9/16") wide. STAMENS extend 12mm (1/2") beyond the corolla; rose (68B) filaments, pink (62C) anthers. PISTIL extends 34mm (1 3/8") beyond the corolla; rose (68B) style, pale pink (62D) stigma. BUD is ovate, pointed. FOLIAGE is dark green (137A) upper surface, medium green (138B) lower surface. Leaves are 67mm (2 5/8") long x 29mm (1 1/8") wide, ovate shaped, serrated edges, acute tips and cordate bases. Veins, stems and branches are green. PARENTAGE: 'Rohees King' x 'Cecile'. Lax upright or stiff trailer. Makes good stiff trailer. Prefers overhead filtered light and cool climate. Best bloom colour in filtered light. Tested four years in Knegsel, The Netherlands. Distinguished by bloom and foliage combination.
van Bree 2002 NL AFS4964.

BreeVis Zodiaca. Upright. Double. COROLLA is three quarter flared with smooth petal margins; opens dark purple (78A); matures dark reddish purple (61A); 21mm (13/16") long x 24mm (15/16") wide.

SEPALS are fully up, tips recurved; dark reddish purple (60A) upper surface; magenta (63B) lower surface; 29mm (1 1/8") long x 14mm (9/16") wide. TUBE is dark reddish purple (60A); short & thick; 9mm (3/8") long x 8mm (3/16") wide. FOLIAGE: dark green (137A) upper surface; medium green (138B) lower surface. Leaves are 67mm (2 5/8") long x 47mm (1 7/8") wide, cordate shaped. PARENTAGE: ('Roesse Apus' x 'Roesse Apus') x 'Centenary'. Distinguished by bloom & foliage combination.
van Bree 2005 NL AFS5883.

Brenda Krekels. Upright/Trailer. Double. COROLLA: half flared, smooth petal margins; opens dark reddish purple (70A); matures magenta (63A); 26mm (1") long x 24mm (15/16") wide. SEPALS: half up; tips reflexed up; pink (52D) upper surface; light rose (50C) lower surface;46mm (1 13/16") long x 15mm (9/16") wide. TUBE: pink (52D); medium length & thickness; 22mm (7/8") long x 6mm (1/4") wide. STAMENS: extend 12mm (1/2") below corolla; rose (61D) filaments & anthers. PISTIL: extends 26mm (1") below the corolla; rose (61D) style, yellowish white (4D) stigma. BUD: cordate. FOLIAGE: dark green (137A) upper surface; medium green (138B) lower surface. Leaves are 42mm (1 5/8") long x 35mm (1 3/8") wide, cordate shaped, serrulated edges, acute tips and rounded bases. Veins, stems & branches are red. PARENTAGE: 'Bicentennial' x 'Parasol'. Lax upright or stiff trailer. Makes good stiff trailer. Prefers overhead filtered light and cool climate. Best bloom and foliage colour in filtered light. Tested 4 years in Reusel, The Netherlands. Distinguished by bloom & foliage combination.
van Eijk 2003 NL AFS5252.

Brenda Welton. Upright. Semi Double. COROLLA opens dark purple at edges fading to nearly white at the veins, with red veining, purple fades on maturity; corolla is three quarter flared and is 30mm long x 27mm wide. SEPALS are red on the upper and lower surfaces; sepals are half up with recurved tips and are 40mm long x 15mm wide. TUBE is red and is 20mm long x 8mm wide. PARENTAGE Alice Hoffman x Unknown. This cultivar has very attractive blooms which have a strong purple colouring. The corolla's four main petals are held in a fairly tight tube, while the petaloids flare outwards, the corolla also flares with age.
Metcalfe 2004 UK BFS0007.

53

Brentano. Trailer. Semi Double. COROLLA: half flared; opens pale purple (76C) striped pink (62C); matures violet (76B); 27mm (1 1/16") long x 22mm (7/8") wide. PETALOIDS: pale lavender (69B) striped pink (62C); 13mm (1/2") long x 7mm (1/4") wide. SEPALS are half up, tips recurved up, twisted to the left; pale lavender (69D) tipped yellowish green (144B) upper surface & pale lavender (69C) tipped yellowish green (144B) lower surface; 38mm (1 1/2") long x 12mm (7/16") wide. TUBE is white (155D); medium length & thickness; 17mm (5/8") long x 6mm (1/4") wide. FOLIAGE is dark green (137A) upper surface; medium green (138B) lower surface. PARENTAGE: 'Vendelzwaaier' x 'Jackie Bull'.
Michiels 2007 BE AFS6534.

Brey. Trailer. Double. COROLLA: half flared, turned under petal margins; opens dark rose (58C) & violet (77B); matures rose (51B) & dark rose (64C); 27mm (1 1/16") long x 24mm (15/16") wide. PETALOIDS: light orange (41C) & reddish purple (61B); 21mm (13/16") long x 10mm (3/8") wide. SEPALS are horizontal, tips recurved; white (155B) & pink (55C), tipped light apple green (144D) upper surface; pink (49A), tipped light apple green (144D) lower surface; 32mm (1 1/4") long x 13mm (1/2") wide. TUBE is light pink (49C) and pink (54D); medium length & thickness; 16mm (5/8") long x 5mm (3/16") wide. STAMENS extend 14mm (9/16") beyond the corolla; pink (62B) filaments; magenta (63B) anthers. PISTIL extends 17mm (5/8") beyond the corolla; light pink (65B) style; light yellow (1C) stigma. BUD is globular. FOLIAGE is dark green (137A) upper surface; medium green (138B) lower surface. Leaves are 54mm (2 1/8") long x 36mm (1 7/16") wide, ovate shaped, serrate edges, acute tips, rounded bases. Veins are reddish purple (67A), stems are purple (71A) & branches are very dark reddish purple (186A). PARENTAGE: 'Manfried Kleinau' x 'Corsage'. Natural trailer. Self branching. Makes good basket. Prefers overhead light, cool climate. Best bloom & foliage in filtered light. Tested 3 years in Koningshooikt, Belgium. Waanrode 5/7/2008. Distinguished by bloom colour combination.
Michiels 2009 BE AFS7152.

Brian Hilton. Single. COROLLA deep violet maturing mauve. SEPALS rose pink.
Evans 2002 UK.

Brian Mcfetridge. Upright. Semi Double. COROLLA opens purple, matures to reddish purple; corolla is quarter flared. SEPALS light reddish purple on the upper surface, magenta on the lower surface; Sepals are half up with recurved tips. TUBE light reddish purple. PARENTAGE Sophie Louise x seedling from London 2000 x (Dorothy Handley x Voodoo).
Swaby 2009 UK BFS0124.

Bright And Beautiful. Upright. Single. COROLLA: quarter flared; opens & matures pale lavender (65D); 18mm (11/16") long x 18mm (11/16") wide. SEPALS: horizontal, tips reflexed; light pink (55D) tipped green upper & lower surfaces; 15mm (9/16") long x 10mm (3/8") wide. TUBE: light green (129A) & pink (55C); 8mm (5/16") long x 8mm (5/16") wide. FOLIAGE is dark green (139A) upper surface; medium green (139B) lower surface. PARENTAGE: 'Lovely Charlotte' x 'Alison Patricia'.
Smith R. 2008 UK AFS6814.

Bright Lights. Upright. Single. COROLLA mid red. SEPALS white tipped green.
Chatters 2004 UK.

Brigitta Vaan Verm. Trailer. Single. COROLLA: quarter flared, turned under smooth petal margins; opens red (53C), matures magenta (58B); 21mm (13/16") long x 19mm (3/4") wide. SEPALS: horizontal; tips reflexed; pink (55C), light apple green (145B) at base, upper surface; rose (47D), light apple green (145B) at base, lower surface; 29mm (1 1/8") long x 12mm (1/2") wide. TUBE: pink (55C), long & thin; 37mm (1 7/16") long x 5mm (3/16") wide. STAMENS: do not extend below the corolla; light rose (58D) filaments, brown (177C) anthers. PISTIL extends 17mm (11/16") below the corolla; pink (54D) style, light yellow (2C) stigma. BUD: cordate. FOLIAGE: dark green (136A) upper surface, medium green (138B) lower surface. Leaves are 58mm (2 5/16") long x 27mm (1 1/16") wide, elliptic shaped, serrulated edges, acute tips and rounded bases. Veins are plum (185B), stems are dark red (185A), branches are plum (185C). PARENTAGE: 'WALZ Harp' x 'La Bergère'. Natural trailer. Self branching. Makes good basket. Prefers overhead filtered light. Best bloom and foliage colour in filtered light. Tested 3 years Hoeselt, Belgium. NBFK certificate at Meise. Distinguished by bloom shape.
Wagemans 2003 BE AFS5083.

Brigitte-Andreas. Trailer. Single. COROLLA: full flared, turned under smooth petal margins; opens & matures white (155D), dark rose (51A) at base; 19mm (3/4") long x 59mm (2 5/16") wide. PETALOIDS: two per sepal; same colour as corolla, 22mm (7/8") long x 13mm (1/2") wide. SEPALS: half up; tips reflexed up; dark rose (51A) upper surface; rose (51B) lower surface; 35mm (1 3/8") long x 28mm (1 1/8") wide. TUBE: dark rose (48A); short, medium thickness; 8mm (5/16") long x 6mm (1/4") wide. STAMENS: extend 23mm (15/16") below the corolla; dark rose (55A) filaments, light yellow (2B) anthers. PISTIL extends 37mm (1 7/16") below the corolla; pink (55C) style, yellowish white (4D) stigma. BUD: bulbous, pointed. FOLIAGE: dark green (137A) upper surface; medium green (137D) lower surface. Leaves are 62mm (2 7/16") long x 32mm (1 1/4") wide, elliptic shaped, serrulated edges, acute tips and rounded bases. Veins are light green (138D) stems & branches are tan (163B). PARENTAGE: 'Joanne' x unknown. Natural trailer. Self branching. Makes good basket. Prefers overhead filtered light. Best bloom and foliage colour in filtered light. Tested 3 years in Rummen, Belgium. NBFK certificate at Meise. Distinguished by bloom shape. Ector 2003 BE AFS5110.

Brilliant Star. Upright. Single. COROLLA: half flared; trumpet shaped; smooth petal margins; opens & matures orange red (35A); 6mm (1/4") long x 5mm (3/16") wide. SEPALS: half down; tips recurved; light reddish orange (42D) upper surface; light rose (35D) tipped light green lower surface; 10mm(3/8") long x 4mm (3/16") wide. TUBE: red orange (42B), dark base; long, medium thickness; 19mm (3/4") long x 4mm (3/16") wide. STAMENS: extend 5mm (3/16) below corolla; pale pink (36D) filaments, light yellow (11C) anthers. PISTIL: extends 7mm (1/4") below the corolla; reddish orange (43C) style, light yellowish orange (19B) stigma. BUD: cylindrical, cordate tip. FOLIAGE: dark green (147A) upper surface; medium green (147C) lower surface. Leaves are 96mm (3 13/16") long x 39mm (1 9/16") wide, ovate shaped, serrulated edges, acute tips and rounded bases. Veins, stems & branches are green. PARENTAGE: 'Göttingen' x {'F. splendens' x [(F. paniculata' x F. splendens') x 'F. magdalenae]}. Small dwarf upright. Makes good basket or miniature. Prefers overhead filtered light and cool or warm climate. Heat tolerant if shaded. Best bloom and foliage colour in filtered light. Tested 5 years in Lisse, Holland. Distinguished by small, erect flowers held in terminal racemes. de Graaff 2003 NL AFS5163.

Brise Marine. Upright/Trailer. Single. COROLLA is unflared with smooth petal margins; opens and matures dark rose (48A); 10mm (3/8") long x 11mm (7/16") wide. SEPALS are horizontal, tips recurved; pale pink (62D), waxy, upper surface; pink (62C) lower surface; 22mm (7/8") long x 6mm (1/4") wide. TUBE is pale pink (62D), waxy, tipped yellowish white (4D); medium length and thickness; 22mm (7/8") long x 6mm (1/4") thick. STAMENS extend 2 to 4mm (1/16 - 3/16") beyond the corolla; light pink (49B) filaments and anthers. PISTIL extends 18mm (11/16") beyond the corolla; light pink (49C) style, light yellow (4C) stigma. BUD is ovate. FOLIAGE is medium green (146A) upper surface, medium green (147B) lower surface. Leaves are 60mm (2 3/8") long x 43mm (1 11/16") wide, ovate shaped, serrulated edges, acute tips and rounded bases. Veins and stems are yellowish green, branches are yellowish green and light brown. PARENTAGE: 'Prince of Orange' x 'Mantilla'. Lax upright or stiff trailer. Makes good basket or upright. Prefers overhead filtered light and cool climate. Best bloom colour in filtered light. Tested three years in Pornic, France. Distinguished by short corolla and profuse blooms. Masse 2002 FR AFS5009.

Broederke Valentijn. Upright/Trailer. Single. COROLLA is quarter flared with turned under wavy petal margins; opens reddish purple (74B), matures dark reddish purple (64A); 17mm (11/16") long x 19 mm (3/4") wide. SEPALS are half down, tips recurved; pink (55C) upper surface, pink (51D) lower surface; 35mm (1 3/8") long x 15mm (5/8") wide. TUBE is light rose (73C), long and thin; 60mm (2 3/8") long x 5mm (3/16") wide. STAMENS do not extend beyond the corolla; cream (159D) filaments, very pale orange (159B) anthers. PISTIL do not extend beyond the corolla; light greenish white (157D) style; pink (55C) stigma. BUD is ovate, pointed. FOLIAGE is dark green (135A) upper surface, medium green (139C) lower surface. Leaves are 60mm (2 3/8") long x 30mm (1 3/16") wide, ovate shaped, serrulated edges, acute tips and rounded bases. Veins are medium green (137C), stems are grayish red (181B), branches are dark grayish purple (184A). PARENTAGE: 'Big Slim' x 'Annabel'. Lax upright or stiff trailer. Makes good upright. Prefers overhead filtered light and full sun. Best bloom and foliage colour in bright light. Tested three years in Itegem, Belgium. Certificate N.B.F.K.

at Meise. Distinguished by long Tube and bloom shape. Geerts L. 2002 BE AFS4923.

Broer De Simppele. Upright/Trailer. Double. COROLLA: three quarter flared; opens orange red (35A) & light reddish violet (180A); matures orange red (35B) & light reddish violet (180B); 21mm (7/8") long x 17mm (5/8") wide. SEPALS: half up, tips recurved up; pink (52D) tipped green upper & lower surfaces; 31mm (1 1/4") long x 14mm (9/16") wide. TUBE: pink (52D); 14mm (9/16") long x 7mm (1/4") wide. FOLIAGE is dark green (137A) upper surface; medium green (138A) lower surface. PARENTAGE: 'Roesse Lupus' x 'Het Mauwerke'. Roes 2008 NL AFS6894.

Bromley Beauty. Lax Upright. Single to Semi Double. COROLLA rose red on the upper and lower surfaces; SEPALS are horizontally held with recurved tips. Sepals rose red on the upper and lower surfaces; Sepals are horizontally held with recurved tips. TUBE rose red. PARENTAGE Bernies Big Un x Texas Longhorn. Allen 2009 UK BFS0108.

Brouckmanshof. Upright/Trailer. Single. COROLLA is quarter flared with turned under smooth petal margins; opens dark purple (79B); matures dark reddish purple (64A); 20mm (13/16") long x 15 mm (5/8") wide. SEPALS are half up, tips recurved up; magenta (63A) upper surface, reddish purple (67A) lower surface; 38mm (1 1/2") long x 9mm (3/8") wide. TUBE is magenta (63A), medium length and thickness; 16mm (5/8") long x 5mm (3/16") wide. STAMENS extend 19mm (3/4") beyond the corolla; magenta (63A) filaments, tan (162A) anthers. PISTIL extends 37mm (1 7/16") below the corolla; reddish purple (64B) style, dark reddish purple (61A) stigma. BUD is long, pointed. FOLIAGE is dark green (137A) upper surface, medium green (137C) lower surface. Leaves are 44mm (1 3/4") long x 26mm (1") wide, ovate shaped, serrulated edges, acute tips and rounded bases. Veins are medium green (137C), stems and branches are reddish purple (186B). PARENTAGE: 'Areler Land' x 'Christel Stumpf'. Lax upright or stiff trailer. Self branching. Makes good upright. Prefers overhead filtered light and full sun. Best bloom and foliage colour in bright to filtered light. Tested three years in Hoeselt, Belgium. Certificate N.B.F.K. at Meise. Distinguished by bloom colour. Wagemans 2002 BE AFS4899.

Bruchtal. Upright. Semi Double. COROLLA is three quarter flared with wavy petal margins; opens dark purple (N78A) spotted reddish purple (N66B); matures dark reddish purple (72A); 33mm (1 5/16") long x 40mm (1 9/16") wide. SEPALS are fully up, tips recurved; reddish purple (N66A) upper & lower surfaces; 55mm (2 3/16") long x 15mm (9/16") wide. TUBE is pale rose (73D) striped reddish purple (N66B); medium length & thickness; 20mm (13/16") long x 8mm (5/16") wide. FOLIAGE: dark green (137A) upper surface; medium green (137C) lower surface. Leaves are 90mm (3 9/16") long x 48mm (1 7/8") wide, elliptic shaped. PARENTAGE: 'Orange King' x 'Rohees Queen'. Distinguished by bloom shape & colour. Burkhart 2005 DE AFS5694.

Buchnesia. Upright/Trailer. Double. COROLLA: half flared, smooth petal margins; opens dark reddish purple (72A); matures reddish purple (67A); 35mm (1 3/8") long x 38mm (1 1/2") wide. SEPALS: fully up, tips recurved; magenta (68A) upper surface; rose (68B) lower surface; 52mm (2 1/16") long x 16mm (5/8") wide. TUBE: rose (68B); long, medium thickness; 30mm (1 3/16") long x 7mm (1/4") wide. STAMENS extend 25mm (1") beyond the corolla; reddish purple (N66A) filaments; dark reddish purple (72A) anthers. PISTIL extends 48mm (1 7/8") beyond the corolla; reddish purple (N66A) style; pale lavender (65D) stigma. BUD: elongated. FOLIAGE: dark green (137A) upper surface; medium green (137C) lower surface. Leaves are 95mm (3 3/4") long x 60mm (2 3/8") wide; ovate shaped, serrate edges, acute tips, obtuse bases. Veins & stems are red, branches are brown. PARENTAGE: 'Danny Kaye' x 'Wade'. Lax upright or stiff trailer. Makes good basket, upright or standard. Prefers warm climate. Heat tolerant if shaded. Best bloom & foliage colour in bright light. Tested 7 years in Bavaria, Southern Germany. Distinguished by flower colour & shape. Burkhart 2009 DE AFS7094.

Bunty Milton. Upright/Trailer. Double. COROLLA: Half flared; opens light purple (93C) flushed white at base; matures violet (84A) flushed white at base; 20mm (3/4") long x 30mm (1 3/16") wide. PETALOIDS: same colour as corolla; 12mm (7/16") long x 15mm (9/16") wide. SEPALS: horizontal, tips recurved; white (155D) faintly flushed pink upper & lower surfaces; 30mm (1 3/16") long x 15mm (9/16") wide. TUBE: pale pink (36D)

slightly flushed darker pink; medium length & thickness; 12mm (7/16") long x 8mm (5/16") wide. FOLIAGE is dark green (139A) upper surface; medium green (146B) lower surface. PARENTAGE: 'Patio Princess' x 'Powder Blue'.
(Note: Cultivar is named after Mrs. Bunty Milton, founder of the Western Cape Fuchsia Society in South Africa). Registered with the BFS in 2006.
Breytenbach. 2007 AFS6553 BFS0039.

Burg. Upright. Double. COROLLA: half flared, turned under petal margins; opens dark rose (64C) & dark reddish purple (70C); matures reddish purple (64B); 22 mm (7/8") long x 14mm (9/16") wide. PETALOIDS: dark rose (64C) & dark reddish purple (70A); 18mm (11/16") long x 10mm (3/8") wide. SEPALS are half up, tips recurved up; rose (64D) upper surface; magenta (63B) lower surface; 34mm (1 3/8") long x 12mm (7/16") wide. TUBE is pale lavender (65D); short & thick; 8mm (5/16") long x 5mm (3/16") wide. STAMENS extend 9mm (5/16") beyond the corolla; light rose (73C) filaments; purple (83B) anthers. PISTIL extends 12mm (7/16") beyond the corolla; magenta (71C) style; pale lavender 69D) stigma. BUD is elongated. FOLIAGE is medium green (137B) upper surface; medium green (138B) lower surface. Leaves are 51mm (2") long x 29mm (1 1/8") wide, ovate shaped, entire edges, acute tips, rounded bases. Veins are plum (184D), stems are plum (184C) & branches are plum (184C) & light green (138C). PARENTAGE: 'Manfried Kleinau' x 'Britelite'. Lax upright or stiff trailer. Makes good basket or upright. Prefers overhead filtered light, cool climate. Best bloom & foliage in filtered light. Tested 3 years in Koningshooikt, Belgium. Waanrode 9/8/2008. Distinguished by bloom colour.
Michiels 2009 BE AFS7153.

Burgi's Hanna. Upright/Trailer. Single. COROLLA: Half flared, bell shaped; opens dark purple (78A); matures light purple (78B); 20mm (3/4") long x 20mm (3/4") wide. SEPALS: half up, tips recurved up; dark rose (58C) upper & lower surfaces; 30mm (1 3/16") long x 13mm (1/2") wide. TUBE: dark rose (58C); short, medium thickness; 10mm (3/8") long x 7mm (1/4") wide. FOLIAGE is medium green (137B) upper surface; medium green (147B) lower surface. PARENTAGE: 'Alison Ewart' x unknown.
Klemm 2007 AT AFS6469.

Burgi's Heidi. Lax Upright. Single. COROLLA light burgundy (71b); corolla is

half flared. SEPALS rhodamine purple (65c) on the upper and lower surfaces; SEPALS are half down with reflexed tips. TUBE light amaranth rose (65b). PARENTAGE Braamt's Glorie x Fiery Spider.
Klemm 2009 AT BFS0126.

Burg's Ingrid. Upright. Single. COROLLA: Unflared, bell shaped; opens white (155D) & light pink (62C); matures white (155D) & pink (62A); 25mm (1") long x 20mm (3/4") wide. SEPALS: fully up, tips recurved; pink (62A) upper & lower surfaces; 30mm (1 3/16") long x 10mm (3/8") wide. TUBE: pale yellow (158B); medium length & thickness; 15mm (9/16") long x 7mm (1/4") wide. FOLIAGE is dark green (139A) upper surface; medium green (138B) lower surface. PARENTAGE: 'Cliff's Own' x unknown.
Klemm 2007 AT AFS6470.

Burg's Jakob. Upright/Trailer. Semi Double. COROLLA: Half flared, bell shaped; opens white (155D) & dark rose (55A); matures white (155A); 35mm (1 3/8") long x 30mm (1 3/16") wide. SEPALS: full down, tips recurved; rose (55B) to dark rose (55A) upper surface; dark rose (55A) lower surface; 55mm (2 3/16") long x 13mm (1/2") wide. TUBE: dark rose (55A) to rose (55B); medium length & thickness; 16mm (5/8") long x 5mm (3/16") wide. FOLIAGE is medium green (137B) upper surface; medium green (138B) lower surface. PARENTAGE: 'Sweet Darling' x unknown.
Klemm 2007 AT AFS6467.

Burgi's Jana. Trailer. Single. COROLLA: 3 quarter flared; opens & matures pale pink (69A); 20mm (3/4") long x 25mm (1") wide. SEPALS: horizontal, tips recurved; pale pink (56B) upper surface; pink (55C) lower surface; 35mm (1 3/8") long x 17mm (5/8") wide. TUBE: pale pink (56C); medium length & thickness; 18mm (11/16") long x 6mm (1/4") wide. FOLIAGE is dark green (147A) upper surface; medium green (147B) lower surface. PARENTAGE: 'Cliff's Own' x unknown.
Klemm 2007 AT AFS6465.

Burgi's Jonas. Upright/Trailer. Semi Double. COROLLA: 3 quarter flared, globate shaped; opens purple (83A); matures purple (83C); 20mm (3/4") long x 35mm (1 3/8") wide. PETALOIDS: rose (52B)& purple (83A); 10mm (3/8") long x 5mm (3/16") wide. SEPALS: half up, tips reflexed up; rose (52B) upper & lower surfaces; 25mm (1") long x 16mm (5/8") wide. TUBE: rose (52B); short,

medium thickness; 11mm (7/16") long x 4mm (1/8") wide. FOLIAGE is medium green (137B) upper surface; medium green (147B) lower surface. PARENTAGE: 'Cliff's Own' x unknown.
Klemm 2007 AT AFS6468.

Burgi's Kerstin. Upright/Trailer. Semi Double. COROLLA: Half flared, bell shape, wavy petal margins; opens purple (88A); matures purple (88B); 20mm (3/4") long x 28mm (1 1/8") wide. SEPALS: half up, tips recurved up; greenish white (157C) upper surface; pale lavender (69C) lower surface; 40mm (1 9/16") long x 12mm (7/16") wide. TUBE: greenish white (157B); medium length & thickness; 17mm (5/8") long x 4mm (1/8") wide. FOLIAGE is medium green (137B) upper surface; medium green (147B) lower surface. PARENTAGE: 'Sweet Darling' x unknown.
Klemm 2007 AT AFS6463.

Burgi's Kurti. Upright. Single. COROLLA purple (89c); corolla is quarter flared. SEPALS china rose (58d) tipped green on the upper and lower surfaces; SEPALS are half up with reflexed tips. TUBE rose red (58b), veined china rose (58d). PARENTAGE Cheltenham x Cliff's Own.
Klemm 2009 AT BFS0127.

Burgi's Leonie. Upright. Semi Double. COROLLA: Half flared, bell shaped; opens pale lavender (69D); matures pale pink (56C); 24mm (15/16") long x 20mm (3/4") wide. SEPALS: horizontal, tips recurved; dark rose (54A) upper surface; rose (54C) lower surface; 38mm (1 1/2") long x 11mm (3/8") wide. TUBE: dark rose (54A); short, medium thickness; 8mm (5/16") long x 5mm (3/16") wide. FOLIAGE is medium green (147B) upper surface; light olive green (148B) lower surface. PARENTAGE: 'Alison Ewart' x unknown.
Klemm 2007 AT AFS6471.

Burgi's LIse. Upright. Double. COROLLA lavender, with pink marbling at base; corolla is fully flared. SEPALS white tipped green on the upper and lower surfaces; sepals are fully up with recurved tips. TUBE greenish white. PARENTAGE Hans Schnedl x Brian Morrison.
Klemm 2008 AT BFS0077.

Burgi's Luca. Upright. Semi Double. COROLLA: 3 quarter flared, bell shaped; opens dark purple (79A) & dark reddish purple (59A); matures dark purple (79B);

20mm (3/4") long x 50mm (2") wide. SEPALS: fully up, tips reflexed; red (45A) upper surface; red (45B) lower surface; 30mm (1 3/16") long x 13mm (1/2") wide. TUBE: dark reddish purple (59A); short, medium thickness; 13mm (1/2") long x 17mm (5/8") wide. FOLIAGE is medium green (137B) upper surface; medium green (147B) lower surface. PARENTAGE: 'Display' x unknown.
Klemm 2007 AT AFS6462.

Burgi's Sonja. Upright. Single. COROLLA red purple (57a); corolla is quarter flared and is 12mm long x 10mm wide. SEPALS red purple (57b); sepals are horizontally held with recurved tips and are 28mm long x 10mm wide. TUBE red purple (57b) and is 18mm long x 8mm wide. PARENTAGE WALZ Gitaar x WALZ Banjo. Free flowering.
Klemm 2008 AT BFS0057.

Burgi's Tilda. Trailer. Semi Double. COROLLA: Fully flared; opens dark purple (79A); matures dark reddish purple (59A); 20mm (3/4") long x 30mm (1 3/16") wide. SEPALS: fully up, tips reflexed; dark reddish purple (59A) upper surface; reddish purple (59B) lower surface; 35mm (1 3/8") long x 10mm (3/8") wide. TUBE: dark reddish purple (60A); medium length & thickness; 15mm (9/16") long x 6mm (1/4") wide. FOLIAGE is medium green (138A) upper surface; medium green (138B) lower surface. PARENTAGE: 'Zulu Queen' x unknown.
Klemm 2007 AT AFS6464.

Burgi's Waltrud. Upright. Double. COROLLA: 3 quarter flared, bell shaped; opens & matures white (155D); 22mm (7/8") long x 40mm (1 9/16") wide. PETALOIDS: white (155A), pink base; 20mm (3/4") long x 7mm (1/4") wide. SEPALS: half down, tips reflexed; pale lavender (65D) upper surface; light pink (65C) lower surface; 50mm (2") long x 17mm (5/8") wide. TUBE: greenish white (157B); medium length & thickness; 17mm (5/8") long x 16mm (5/8") wide. FOLIAGE is medium green (137B) upper surface; medium green (147B) lower surface. PARENTAGE: 'Sweet Darling' x unknown.
Klemm 2007 AT AFS6461.

Burgi's Willa. Upright. Single. . COROLLA: Quarter flared, bell shaped; opens violet (76A); matures violet (76B); 20mm (3/4") long x 15mm (9/16") wide. SEPALS: half down, tips recurved; light coral (38A) upper surface; pink (62A) lower surface; 30mm (1 3/16") long x 10mm (3/8") wide. TUBE:

peach (37B); medium length & thickness; 15mm (9/16") long x 6mm (1/4") wide. FOLIAGE is medium green (146A) upper surface; yellowish green (146B) lower surface. PARENTAGE: 'Cliff's Own' x unknown.
Klemm 2007 AT AFS6466.

Burgundy Velvet. Upright/Trailer. Single. COROLLA is quarter flared with smooth petal margins; opens dark purple (N79A); matures dark reddish purple (60B); 17mm (11/16") long x 17 mm (11/16") wide. SEPALS are horizontal, tips recurved; pink (62A) upper surface; magenta (58B) lower surface; 25mm (1") long x 10mm (3/8") wide. TUBE is rose (63C); medium length & thickness; 12mm (1/2") long x 5mm (3/16") wide. FOLIAGE: medium green (138A) upper surface; medium green (137C) lower surface. Leaves are 50mm (2") long x 37 mm (1 1/2") wide, ovate shaped. PARENTAGE: 'Arcadia Aubergine' x 'Orange Crush'. Distinguished by sepal & corolla colour combination. Also registered with the BFS.
Swaby 2005 UK AFS5653 BFS0021.

Burnt Hill. Single. COROLLA aubergine to violet. SEPALS light aubergine.
Horsham 2002 UK.

Buster. Upright/Trailer. Single. COROLLA is half flared with turned under wavy petal margins; opens violet (75A), light pink (65C) base; matures light magenta (66D), light pink (65C) base; 29mm (1 1/16") long x 36mm (1 7/16") wide. PETALOIDS: pale purple (74D), light pink (65C) base; 11mm (7/16") long x 4mm (3/16") wide. SEPALS are half up, tips recurved up; pale pink (56B), tipped light green (145D) upper surface; rose (55B), tipped light green (145D) lower surface; 42mm (1 5/8") long x 11mm (7/16") wide. TUBE is white (155B); medium length, thick; 14mm (9/16") long x 7mm (1/4") wide. FOLIAGE: dark green (137A) upper surface; medium green (138B) lower surface. Leaves are 75mm (2 15/16") long x 43mm (1 11/16") wide, ovate shaped. PARENTAGE: 'Sofie Michiels' x 'Weleveld'. Meise 8-14-04. Distinguished by flower colour & shape.
Michiels 2005 BE AFS5753.

Camillius Maria. Upright/Trailer. Semi Double. COROLLA is three quarter flared with turned under wavy petal margins; opens dark reddish purple (72A); matures light reddish purple (72C); 21mm (13/16") long x 22mm (7/8") wide. PETALOIDS: reddish purple (60D), blotched dark reddish purple

(72A); 21mm (13/16") long x 9mm (3/8") wide. SEPALS are horizontal, tips reflexed; dark reddish purple (60C) upper surface; reddish purple (60D) lower surface; 36mm (1 7/16") long x 17mm (11/16") wide. TUBE is dark reddish purple (60C); medium length & thickness; 16mm (5/8") long x 7mm (1/4") wide. FOLIAGE: dark green (139A) upper surface; medium green (139C) lower surface. Leaves are 68mm (2 11/16") long x 41mm (1 5/8") wide, ovate shaped. PARENTAGE: 'Roesse Blacky' x 'Danny Kaye'. Meis 3-7-04. Distinguished by colour combination.
Michiels 2005 BE AFS5675.

Cannington Decade. Upright. Single. COROLLA is unflared, bell shaped, smooth petal margins; opens red (45C) overlaid dark reddish purple (70A), matures red (45C) overlaid reddish purple (70B); 15mm (9/16") long x 13mm (1/2") wide. SEPALS are half down; tips recurved; red (45D) tipped yellow upper surface, red (45C) tipped yellow lower surface; 22mm (7/8") long x 6mm (1/4") wide. TUBE red (45D), medium length & thin; 12mm (1/2") long x 4mm (3/16") wide. STAMENS extend 12mm (1/2") below the corolla; dark rose (51A) filaments & anthers. PISTIL extends 24mm (15/16") below the corolla; rose (51A) style, cream stigma. BUD is ovate. FOLIAGE is dark green (147A) upper surface, lighter green lower surface. Leaves are 62mm (2 7/16") long x 30mm (1 3/16") wide, lanceolate shaped, serrated edges, acute tips and rounded bases. Veins and stems are light green, branches are dull red. PARENTAGE: 'Anita' x 'Edie Lester'. Small upright. Self branching. Makes good upright, standard, pyramid, pillar or bedding. Prefers full sun. Best bloom colour in bright light. Tested 4 years in Edenbridge, Kent, England. Distinguished by blossom colour and shape.
Holmes 2003 UK AFS5069.

Carla Knapen. Upright/Trailer. Double COROLLA is three quarter flared with smooth petal margins; opens & matures white (155D); 22mm (7/8") long x 22mm (7/8") wide. SEPALS are half up, tips reflexed up; white (155A) upper surface; white (155D) lower surface; 27mm (1 1/16") long x 15mm (9/16") wide. TUBE is white (155A); medium length & thickness; 10mm (3/8") long x 5mm (3/16") wide. FOLIAGE: dark green (137A) upper surface; medium green (138A) lower surface. Leaves are 79mm (3 1/8") long x 36mm (1 7/16") wide, lanceolate shaped. PARENTAGE: 'Sofie Michiels' x 'Sofie

Michiels'. Distinguished by bloom & foliage combination.
Roes 2005 NL AFS5971.

Carlos. Trailer. Double. COROLLA: half flared; opens dark purple (79A); matures dark reddish purple (70A); 19mm (3/4") long x 11mm (7/16") wide. SEPALS are half up, tips reflexed up; pale lavender (69C) upper surface; light purple (70C) lower surface; 21mm (13/16") long x 12mm (7/16") wide. TUBE is pale lavender (69C); 19mm (3/4") long x 4mm (1/8") wide. FOLIAGE is medium green (137B) upper surface & medium green (138B) lower surface. PARENTAGE: 'Roesse Charon' x 'Roesse Ophelia'.
Spoelstra 2008 NL AFS6876.

Carlotta. Upright/Trailer. Double. COROLLA: half flared; opens flat, matures bell shaped, smooth petal margins; opens violet blue (91A); matures violet (85B); 50mm (2") long x 30mm (1 3/16") wide. SEPALS: fully up; tips recurved; white (155C) flushed pink upper surface; pink (62C) lower surface; 68mm (2 11/16") long x 20mm (13/16") wide. TUBE: white (155C); medium length & thickness; 20mm(13/16") long x 8mm (5/16") wide. STAMENS: extend 22mm (7/8") below corolla; dark rose (55A) filaments, magenta (57B) anthers. PISTIL: extends 36mm (1 7/16") below the corolla, white (155C) style, white (155A) stigma. BUD: long small. FOLIAGE: medium green (139C) upper surface; dark green (147A) lower surface. Leaves are 84mm (3 5/16") long x 46mm (1 13/16") wide, elliptic shaped, serrulated edges, acute tips and rounded bases. Veins are light green (147D), stems are medium green (147B), branches are medium green (137D). PARENTAGE: 'Miss California' x 'Nepean'. Lax upright or stiff trailer. Self branching. Makes good basket or weeping tree. Prefers overhead filtered light. Best bloom and foliage colour in filtered light. Tested 3 years in Tegelen, The Netherlands. Award of Merit, VKC/KMTP, The Netherlands. Distinguished by flower colour combination, shape and form.
Geurts 2003 NL AFS5181.

Carmine Tacchio. Upright/Trailer. Single. COROLLA: Half flared; opens red (45B) striped pink (43D); matures magenta (58B) striped red (45C); 22mm (7/8") long x 19mm (3/4") wide. PETALOIDS: Same colour as corolla; 12mm (7/16") long x 9mm (5/16") wide. SEPALS: horizontal, tips recurved; pink (49A) tipped light apple green (145C) upper surface; orange (44D) tipped light apple

green (145C) lower surface; 23mm (7/8") long x 11mm (7/16") wide. TUBE: light pink (49B) striped yellowish green (144A); short & thick; 11mm (7/16") long x 9mm (5/16") wide. FOLIAGE is dark green (136A) upper surface; medium green (138B) lower surface. PARENTAGE: ('F. magdalenae' x 'F. fulgens var. rubra grandiflora') x 'Danny Kaye'.
Ianne 2008 IT AFS6590.

Carojan. Upright/Trailer. Single. COROLLA: three quarter flared, turned under smooth petal margins; opens violet blue (91A) veined red (46B) at base, matures violet (85A) veined dark red (46A) at base; 17mm (11/16") long x 30mm (1 3/16") wide. SEPALS: half up; tips recurved up; dark rose (58C) tipped light green (142A) upper surface, rose (52B) lower surface; 23mm (15/16") long x 10mm (3/8") wide. TUBE: dark rose (58C) flushed green, medium length & thickness; 9mm (3/8") long x 6mm (1/4") wide. STAMENS: extend 14mm (9/16") below the corolla; dark rose (58C) filaments, light yellow (2C) anthers. PISTIL extends 27mm (1 1/16") below the corolla; light rose (58D) style, light coral (38A) stigma. BUD: ovate. FOLIAGE: dark green (137A) upper surface, medium green (138A) lower surface. Leaves are 64mm (2 1/2") long x 45mm (1 3/4") wide, ovate shaped, serrulated edges, acute tips and rounded bases. Veins & stems are reddish purple (58A), branches are brown (200D). PARENTAGE: 'Anniek Geerlings' x unknown. Lax upright or stiff trailer. Self branching. Makes good upright or basket. Prefers full sun. Best bloom and foliage colour in bright light. Tested 3 years St. Lenaarts, Belgium. NBFK certificate at Meise. Distinguished by bloom colour and strong growth.
Snels 2003 BE AFS5082.

Carole Hipkin. Single. COROLLA blue purple maturing deep rose. SEPALS white maturing pink. TUBE short pink.
Chatters 2007 UK.

Caroline Bell. Upright. Single. COROLLA: half flared, square shape; opens & matures reddish purple (66A); 23mm (7/8") long x 35mm (1 3/8") wide. SEPALS: half up, tips recurved up; white (155D) upper surface; white (155D) striped rose (68C) lower surface; 42mm (1 5/8") long x 11mm (7/16") wide. TUBE: white (155D) flushed rose (68C); 23 mm (7/8") long x 10mm (3/8") wide. FOLIAGE is medium green (138B) upper surface; light green (138D) lower surface. PARENTAGE: 'Swingtime' x 'Millennium'.
Bell 2008 UK AFS6827.

Carrie Van Rensberg. Upright/Trailer. Double. COROLLA: unflared, bell shaped, smooth petal margins; opens reddish purple (74C) flushed magenta (68A); matures violet (82C) flushed rose (68C); 24mm (15/16") long x 31mm (1 1/4") wide. SEPALS: full down; tips recurved; pink (62C) tipped white upper surface; pink (62C) lower surface; 33mm(1 5/16") long x 16mm (5/8") wide. TUBE: pale pink (62D) striped green; medium length & thickness; 16mm (5/8") long x 7mm (1/4") wide. STAMENS: extend 25mm (1") below corolla; light purple (74C) filaments; pale yellow (18D) anthers. PISTIL: extends 37mm (1 7/16") below the corolla, light purple (74C) style; light yellowish orange (19B) stigma. BUD: obtuse. FOLIAGE: medium green (138A) upper surface; medium green (138B) lower surface. Leaves are 43mm (1 11/16") long x 25mm (1") wide, lanceolate shaped, serrulated edges, acute tips and rounded bases. Veins are green, stems & branches are red. PARENTAGE: 'Branksome Beauty' x 'Ruth Graham'. Lax upright or stiff trailer. Makes good basket. Prefers overhead filtered light and cool climate. Best bloom and foliage colour in filtered light. Tested 3 years in Stockbridge, Hampshire, England. Distinguished by bloom colour.
Graham 2003 UK AFS5143.

Castello. Upright. Semi Double. COROLLA: quarter flared, turned under smooth petal margins; opens dark reddish purple (61A), magenta (58B) at base; matures reddish purple (64B), magenta (59C) at base; 16mm (5/8") long x 14mm (9/16") wide. PETALOIDS: reddish purple (61B), magenta (58B) at base; 14mm (9/16") long x 12mm (1/2") wide. SEPALS: horizontal; tips recurved; magenta (58B) upper surface; dark rose (51A) lower surface; 26mm(1") long x 9mm (3/8") wide. TUBE: magenta (58B); long, medium thickness; 34mm (1 5/16") long x 5mm (3/16") wide. STAMENS: extend 11mm (7/16") below the corolla; dark rose (58C) filaments, brown (177D) anthers. PISTIL extends 18mm (11/16") below the corolla; magenta (58B) style, magenta (59C) stigma. BUD: elongated. FOLIAGE: dark green (137A) upper surface; medium green (138B) lower surface. Leaves are 60mm (2 3/8") long x 32mm (1 1/4") wide, ovate shaped, serrulated edges, acute tips and rounded bases. Veins are light plum (184D); stems are plum (184C), branches are plum (184B). PARENTAGE: 'WALZ Harp' x 'Rohees New Millennium'. Medium upright. Makes good upright. Prefers full sun. Best bloom and foliage colour in bright light. Tested 3

years in Berlaar, Belgium. NBFK certificate at Meise. Distinguished by bloom shape, profuse blooms.
Geerts J. 2003 BE AFS5118.

Castricum. Upright/Trailer. Single. COROLLA: half flared; opens pale pink (56C); matures pale pink (56A); 20mm (3/4") long x 20mm (3/4") wide. SEPALS: horizontal, tips recurved; red (45A) upper surface; magenta (63A) lower surface; 22mm (7/8") long x 11mm (7/16") wide. TUBE: red (45A); short, thin; 4mm (1/8") long x 4mm (1/8") wide. STAMENS extend 30mm (1 3/16") beyond the corolla; magenta (63B) filaments; dark reddish purple (64A) anthers. PISTIL extends 38mm (1 1/2") beyond the corolla; magenta (63B) style; rose (64D) stigma. BUD: ovate. FOLIAGE: dark green (147A) upper surface; medium green (147B) lower surface. Leaves are 30mm (1 3/16") long x 19mm (3/4") wide; cordate shaped, serrulate edges, acute tips, rounded bases. Veins are dark green (147A), stems are dark reddish purple (59A) & green, branches are dark reddish purple (59A). PARENTAGE: 'Sunangels Cheerio' x unknown. Lax upright or stiff trailer. Makes good standard. Prefers full sun. Best bloom colour in filtered light. Tested 4 years in Amsterdam, The Netherlands. Distinguished by flower colour & shape.
Krom 2009 NL AFS7058.

Catharina Kwint. Upright/Trailer. Double. COROLLA is three quarter flared with smooth petal margins; opens purple (77A), matures reddish purple (67A); 27mm (1 1/16") long x 24mm (15/16") wide. SEPALS are full up, tips recurved; reddish purple (64B) upper surface, reddish purple (61B) lower surface; 44mm (1 3/4") long x 17mm (11/16") wide. TUBE is reddish purple (64B), proportionately medium length and thickness; 12mm (1/2") long x 8mm (5/16") wide. STAMENS extend 32mm (1 1/4") below the corolla; reddish purple (61B) filaments and anthers. PISTIL extends 38mm (1 1/2") below the corolla; reddish purple (61B) style and pink (62C) stigma. BUD is long, thin and pointed. FOLIAGE is dark green (137A) on upper surface and medium green (138B) on lower surface. Leaves are 74mm (2 15/16") long x 41mm (1 5/8") wide, ovate shaped, serrated edges, acute tips and rounded bases. Veins, stems and branches are green. PARENTAGE: ('Annabel' x 'Annabel') x 'Rohees King'. Lax upright or stiff trailer. Makes good stiff trailer. Prefers overhead filtered light and cool climate. Best bloom colour in filtered light. Tested four years in

61

Knegsel, The Netherlands. Distinguished by bloom and foliage combination.
Roes 2002 NL AFS4790.

Cece B. Upright. Single. COROLLA: quarter flared, smooth petal margins, bell shaped; opens purple (88B); matures reddish purple (80B); 18mm (11/16") long x 16mm (5/8") wide. SEPALS: half down, tips reflexed; light pink (65B) tipped green upper surface; light pink (65C) tipped green lower surface; 24mm (15/16") long x 9mm (5/16") wide. TUBE: light reddish purple (66C); short & thin; 10mm (3/8") long x 5mm (3/16") wide. STAMENS extend 7mm (1/4") beyond the corolla; light magenta (66D) filaments; reddish purple (67A) anthers. PISTIL extends 20mm (3/4") beyond the corolla; rose (68C) style; magenta (68A) stigma. BUD is ovate. FOLIAGE is medium green (137C) upper surface; medium green (138B) lower surface. Leaves are 30mm (1 3/16") long x 25mm (1") wide; ovate shaped, serrulate edges, acute tips, rounded bases. Veins & stems are medium green (138B); branches are medium green (139D). PARENTAGE: found seedling. Medium upright. Makes good upright. Prefers full sun. Cold weather hardy to -7° C (20° F). Best bloom colour in bright light. Tested 8 years in Puget Sound, Washington, USA. Distinguished by colour combination.
Gibbs 2009 UK AFS6954.

Cee-Jay-En. Upright. Single. COROLLA opens violet, matures paler; corolla is quarter flared and is 26mm long x 21mm wide. SEPALS cerise on the upper and lower surfaces; sepals are half up with recurved tips and are 44mm long x 14mm wide. TUBE cerise and is 11mm long x 6mm wide. PARENTAGE ((Helen Nicholls x Katrina Thompsen Seedling) x Sophie Louise) x Sophie Louise.
Nicholls A. 2007 UK BFS0053.

Centaurus. Trailer. Single. COROLLA orange. SEPALS pale pink.
Unknown 2006.

Cercle Horticole Herstal. Upright. Single. COROLLA: quarter flared, petticoat shape; opens purple (89C), pink base; matures purple (81A); 20mm (3/4") long x 22mm (7/8") wide. PETALOIDS: same colour as corolla; 16mm (5/8") long x 13mm (1/2") wide. SEPALS: horizontal, tips recurved; red (53D) upper surface; red (53C) lower surface; 31mm (1 1/4") long x 10mm (3/8") wide. TUBE: red (53C); 10mm (3/8") long x 7mm (1/4") wide. FOLIAGE is dark green (139A)

upper surface; light green (138A) lower surface. PARENTAGE: 'Fey' x unknown.
Ricard 2008 BE AFS6845.

C'est Mon Choix. Upright. Single. COROLLA is unflared; opens reddish purple (58A); matures reddish purple (61B); 19mm (3/4") long x 10mm (3/8") wide. SEPALS are half down, tips recurved; pink (52D) upper surface; rose (52B) lower surface; 40mm (1 9/16") long x 7mm (1/4") wide. TUBE is pink (52D); 12mm (7/16") long x 4mm (1/8") wide. FOLIAGE: dark green (147A) upper surface; medium green (147B) lower surface. PARENTAGE: 'Henri Massé' x 'Subliem'. Distinguished by bloom colour.
Masse 2006 FR AFS6235.

Chantel Lavrijsen. Trailer. Double. COROLLA: half flared; opens purple (N80A), rose (68B) base; matures purple (N79C), pale purple (70D) base; 20mm (3/4") long x 15mm (9/16") wide. PETALOIDS: same colour as corolla; 16mm (5/8") long x 10mm (3/8") wide. SEPALS: half down, tips reflexed; rose (68C) tipped light apple green (144D) upper surface; rose (68B) tipped light apple green (144D) lower surface; 31mm (1 1/4") long x 14mm (9/16") wide. TUBE: light rose (73C); medium length & thickness; 15mm (9/16") long x 7mm (1/4") wide. FOLIAGE is medium green (137B) upper surface; medium green (138B) lower surface. PARENTAGE: 'Mathy' x 'Guidewell Quest'.
Michiels 2007 BE AFS6371.

Chantelle Garcia. Upright. Double. COROLLA opens deep lavender, matures to mauve; corolla is three quarter flared. SEPALS very pale pink, tipped green on the upper and lower surfaces; SEPALS are half up with -recurved tips. TUBE very pale pink. PARENTAGE Lillian Annetts x Grandad Hobbs.
Garcia 2009 UK BFS0116.

Charelke Dop. Upright. Semi Double. COROLLA: half flared, turned under wavy petal margins; opens dark reddish purple (64A), dark purple (79B) base; matures reddish purple (70B), dark purple (79A) base; 11mm (7/16") long x 9mm (3/8") wide. PETALOIDS: dark purple (79B); 12mm (1/2") long x 7mm (1/4") wide. SEPALS: half down; tips recurved; rose (55B) tipped yellowish green (145A) upper surface; magenta (57C) tipped yellowish green (145A) lower surface; 34mm (1 5/16") long x 10mm (3/8") wide. TUBE: light pink (49C); short & thin; 14mm (9/16") long x 7mm (1/4") wide. FOLIAGE:

dark green (137A) upper surface, medium green (138B) lower surface. Leaves are 54mm (2 1/8") long x 29mm (1 1/8") wide, ovate shaped. PARENTAGE: 'Danny Kaye' x 'Rohees Queen'. Award at Meise, 9/8/03. Distinguished by bloom colour and shape. Wagemans 2004 BE AFS5416.

Charles Welch. Upright. Single. COROLLA: half flared, smooth petal margins; opens dark purple (79A); matures dark reddish purple (79A); 16mm (11/16") long, 13mm (1/2") wide. SEPALS: half up; tips reflexed up; dark rose (67C) tipped lime green upper surface; reddish purple (67A), tipped white lower surface; 20mm (13/16") long x 7mm (1/4") wide. TUBE: magenta (68A); medium length, thin; 12mm (1/2") long x 5mm (3/16") wide. STAMENS: extend 4mm (3/16")below corolla; dark rose (67C) filaments; light violet (84A) anthers. PISTIL: extends 14mm (9/16") below the corolla; dark rose (67C) style; light yellow (5C) stigma. BUD: long, conical. FOLIAGE: medium green (137B) upper surface; medium green (137D) lower surface. Leaves are 37mm (1 7/16") long x 25mm (1") wide, ovate shaped, smooth edges, acute tips and rounded bases. Pale green veins, stems & branches. PARENTAGE: 'Ben Jammin' x 'Ben Jammin'. Small upright. Self branching. Makes good upright, pyramid or pillar. Heat tolerant if shaded. Cold weather hardy to 32⁰ F. Best bloom and foliage colour in bright light. Tested 3 years in Cambridge, England. Distinguished by profuse blooms; retains colour with age.
Chapman 2004 UK AFS5623.

Charles Wesley. Upright. Semi Double. COROLLA pink edged darker pink. SEPALS pale green.
Ainsworth 2003 UK.

Charlie Boy. Upright/Trailer. Semi Double. COROLLA: half flared, bell shaped, turned under smooth petal margins; opens violet (87B), fades to light pink (65C) at base; matures purple (81B), fades to light pink (65C) at base; 40mm (1 9/16") long x 35mm (1 3/8") wide. PETALOIDS: same colour as corolla; 30mm (1 3/16") long x 15mm (9/16") wide. SEPALS: fully up; tips reflexed; half twist counterclockwise; white (155A) tipped green upper & lower surfaces; 55mm(2 3/16") long x 16mm (5/8") wide. TUBE: yellowish white (158A) striped green; medium length , thick; 20mm (13/16") long x 8mm (5/16") wide. STAMENS: extend 10mm (3/8") below corolla; light pink (62B) filaments; light

rose (73C) anthers. PISTIL: extends 15mm (9/16") below the corolla, white (155C) style; yellowish white (158A) stigma. BUD: large, elongated. FOLIAGE: dark green (147A) upper surface; yellowish green (146B) lower surface. Leaves are 70mm (2 3/4") long x 40mm (1 9/16") wide, cordate shaped, serrated edges, acute tips and rounded bases. Veins are green, stems are brown, branches are red. PARENTAGE: 'Loveable Rascal' x 'Quasar'. Lax upright or stiff trailer. Self branching. Makes good basket or hanging pot. Heat tolerant if shaded. Prefers warm climate. Cold weather hardy to 32° F. Tested 3 years in Walthamstow, London, England. Distinguished by bloom colour combination.
Allsop M.R. 2003 UK AFS5147.

Charlie's Angels. Upright/Trailer. COROLLA: half flared; opens white (155A) veined pink; matures white (155B) veined pink; 25mm (1") long x 25mm (1") wide. SEPALS: half up, tips recurved up; pale pink (62A) tipped green upper surface; pink (62B) lower surface; 30mm (1 3/16") long x 15mm (9/16") wide. TUBE: pale pink (62A); 20mm (3/4") long x 10mm (3/8") wide. FOLIAGE is dark green (139A) upper surface; medium green (138B) lower surface. PARENTAGE: 'Swingtime' x 'Diana Princess of Wales'.
Smith R. 2008 UK AFS6812.

Charlie's Beauty. Trailer. Semi Double. COROLLA: half flared, smooth petal margins; opens purple (90B) streaked pink; matures violet (90C) streaked pink; 20mm (3/4") long x 18mm (11/16") wide. SEPALS: half up, tips recurved up; cream (158C) streaked pink, tipped green upper surface; cream (158D) streaked pink, tipped green lower surface; 30mm (1 3/16") long x 10mm (3/8") wide. TUBE: magenta (63B); medium length, thin; 20mm (3/4") long x 8mm (5/16") wide. STAMENS extend 20mm (3/4") beyond the corolla; light pink (62B) filaments; magenta (63B) anthers. PISTIL extends 40mm (1 9/16") beyond the corolla; light pink (62B) style; white (155A) stigma. BUD: ovate. FOLIAGE: medium green (137B) upper surface; medium green (139C) lower surface. Leaves are 30mm (1 3/16") long x 18mm (11/16") wide; elliptic shaped, serrulate edges, acute tips, obtuse bases. Veins are green, stems are light brown, branches are light green. PARENTAGE: 'Special Angel' x 'Diana Princess of Wales'. Natural trailer. Makes good standard. Heat tolerant if shaded. Best bloom colour in filtered light.

Tested 3 years in Rayleigh, Essex, England. Distinguished by blossom colour & shape. Smith R. 2009 UK AFS7127.

Charm Of Chelmsford. Trailer. Double. COROLLA salmon with a darker touch of plum. SEPALS white flushed pink. TUBE waxy white. Goulding 2004 UK.

Charme D'antan. Upright. Single. COROLLA: half flared, smooth petal margins; opens & matures light violet (84C) veined pink; 16mm (5/8") long x 16mm (5/8") wide. SEPALS: fully up; tips recurved; red (45B) upper surface; dark rose (51A) lower surface; 26mm (1") long x 8mm (5/8") wide. TUBE: bright red (45B); short, medium thickness; 9mm (3/8") long x 6mm (1/4") wide. STAMENS: extend 12-14mm (1/2-9/16") below corolla; rose (54C) filaments; dark rose (54A) anthers. PISTIL: extends 25mm (1") below the corolla; rose (54C) style; dark rose (54A) stigma. BUD: ovate. FOLIAGE: medium to dark green (147A/B) upper surface, medium green (147B) lower surface. Leaves are 62mm (2 7/16") long x 26mm (1") wide, ovate/lanceolate shaped, serrulated edges, acute tips and rounded bases. Yellowish green veins, stems & branches. PARENTAGE: 'Pornic Junior' x 'Annick Boquien'. Medium upright. Self branching. Makes good upright or standard. Prefers overhead filtered light and cool climate. Best bloom and foliage colour in filtered light. Tested 3 years in Pornic, France. Distinguished by bloom colour combination and flower/foliage contrast. Masse 2004 FR AFS5448.

Charmeur. Upright. Single. COROLLA is quarter flared with smooth petal margins; opens violet (77B), lighter base; matures violet (77B); 20mm (13/16") long x 13mm (1/2") wide. SEPALS are fully up, tips recurved in a circle; rose (51B) tipped darker rose upper surface; rose (51B) lower surface; 26mm (1") long x 6mm (1/4") wide. TUBE is rose (51B); short, medium thickness; 6mm (1/4") long x 4mm (3/16") wide. FOLIAGE: dark green (147A) upper surface; medium green (147B) lower surface. Leaves are 50mm (2") long x 25mm (1") wide, ovate shaped. PARENTAGE: ('String of Pearls' x F. regia reitzii 4574') x 'Papy René. Distinguished by bloom/foliage contrast. Masse 2005 FR AFS5833.

Charming Anne Adamson. Upright. Single. COROLLA opens purple, matures to reddish purple, cerise at base; corolla is quarter flared and is 23mm long x 25mm wide. SEPALS are carmine on the upper and lower surfaces; sepals are fully up with recurved tips and are 43mm long x 12mm wide. TUBE is carmine and is 20mm long x 7mm wide. PARENTAGE sport of Charming. Adamson 2005 UK BFS0013.

Chateau D'ars'. Upright. Semi Double. COROLLA: unflared, smooth petal margins; opens red (46B), lighter at base; matures red (46A); 24mm (15/16") long x 22mm (7/8") wide. SEPALS: half up; tips recurved up; coral (39B) upper surface; orangy red (39A) lower surface; 35mm (1 3/8") long x 12mm (1/2") wide. TUBE: peach (37B); short & thick; 15mm(9/16") long x 7mm (1/4") wide. STAMENS: extend 23mm (15/16") below corolla; red (46B) filaments, red (46A) anthers. PISTIL: extends 36mm (1 7/16") below the corolla, coral (38B) style, light orange (39C) stigma. BUD: Long. FOLIAGE: medium green (137B) upper surface; medium green (137D) lower surface. Leaves are 70mm (2 3/4") long x 43mm (1 11/16") wide, ovate shaped, serrated edges, acute tips and rounded bases. Veins are light green (138E), stems are light green (138C); branches are medium green (138B). PARENTAGE: 'Condor' x 'Orange Crush'. Lax upright. Makes good upright or standard. Prefers overhead filtered light and warm climate. Cold weather hardy to -2° C. Best bloom colour in bright light. Best foliage colour in filtered light. Tested 3 years in Central France. Distinguished by bright bloom colour combination. Gaucher 2003 FR AFS5216.

Chatts Delight. Trailer. Single. COROLLA medium purple fading to rose purple. SEPALS white flushed faint pink. TUBE white flushed faint pink. Chatters 2005 UK.

Chaz. Upright. Single. COROLLA pure white; corolla is quarter flared. SEPALS candy pink on the upper and lower surfaces; SEPALS are horizontally held with recurved tips. TUBE candy pink. PARENTAGE June Marie Shaw x Tancred. Riley 2009 UK BFS0121.

Cheeky Girl. Upright. Single. COROLLA: full flared; opens dark violet (87A), pink (62A) at base; matures violet (87B); 20mm (3/4") long x 13mm (1/2") wide. SEPALS: horizontal, tips recurved; dark rose (58C) tipped green upper surface; light rose (58D) lower surface; 25mm (1") long x 7mm (1/4") wide. TUBE:

dark rose (58C); 7mm (1/4") long x 7mm (1/4") wide. FOLIAGE is dark green (137A) upper surface; medium green (137C) lower surface. PARENTAGE: 'Julie Ann Goodwin' x 'Paloma'. Small upright.
Goodwin 2008 UK AFS6939.

Cheerfulness. Upright/Trailer. Single. COROLLA: quarter flared, bell shape, toothed petal margins; opens & matures pale purple (76C); 7mm (1/4") long, 5mm (3/16") wide. SEPALS: horizontal; tips recurved; light violet (84C), tipped apple green (144C) upper & lower surfaces; 11mm (7/16") long x 4mm (3/16") wide. TUBE: light violet (84C); medium length & thickness; 13mm (1/2") long x 5mm (3/16") wide. STAMENS: extend 3mm (1/8") below corolla; pale purple (75D) filaments; olive green (152D) anthers. PISTIL: extends 5mm (3/16") below the corolla; pale purple (75D) style; light yellow green (154C) stigma. BUD: short triphylla type. FOLIAGE: dark green (147A) upper surface; medium green (147B) lower surface. Leaves are 72mm (2 13/16") long x 31mm (1 1/4") wide, elliptic shaped, serrulated edges, acute tips and obtuse bases. Reddish veins; red stems & branches. PARENTAGE: 'Gerharda's Panache' x 'F. *splendens*'. Lax upright or stiff trailer. Self branching. Makes good basket. Prefers overhead filtered light. Heat tolerant if shaded. Best bloom and foliage colour in filtered light. Tested 4 years in Lisse, The Netherlands. Distinguished by small light violet flowers held in multiple racemes.
de Graaff 2004 NL AFS5611.

Chelsea Louise. Upright. Single. COROLLA: Quarter flared, compact, bell shaped; opens purple (77A); matures reddish purple (80B); 15mm (9/16") long x 20mm (3/4") wide. SEPALS: horizontal, tips reflexed; pink (62A) upper & lower surface; 26mm (1") long x 10mm (3/8") wide. TUBE: pale lavender (65D); medium length & thick; 10mm (3/8") long x 8mm (5/16") wide. FOLIAGE is dark green (137A) upper surface; medium green (147B) lower surface. PARENTAGE: 'Nikki's Findling' x un-named.
Chapman 2007 UK AFS6715.

Cherry Pop. COROLLA red. SEPALS red.
Robson 2002 UK.

Chiara Anne. Upright. Single. three quarter flared; trumpet shaped; wavy petal margins; opens light purple (75B); matures rose (68B); 6mm (1/4") long x 7mm (1/4") wide. SEPALS: horizontal; tips reflexed; rose (55B)

tipped red; light pink (62B) tipped red lower surface; 9mm(3/8") long x 4mm (3/16") wide. TUBE: rose (55B); long, medium thickness; 22mm (7/8") long x 5mm (3/16") wide. STAMENS: extend 1mm (1/16") below corolla; dark rose (55A) filaments, pale yellow (158B) anthers. PISTIL: extends 5mm (3/16") below the corolla, light pink (62B) style, pink (62C) stigma. BUD: triphylla shaped. FOLIAGE: dark green (147A) upper surface; medium green (147B) lower surface. Leaves are 82mm (3 1/4") long x 35mm (1 3/8") wide, elliptic shaped, serrulated edges, acute tips and acute bases. Veins are light yellow green, stems & branches are red. PARENTAGE: 'Gerharda's Panache' x 'Gerharda's Panache'. Medium upright. Makes good basket. Prefers overhead filtered light and cool climate. Heat tolerant if shaded. Best bloom and foliage colour in filtered light. Tested 4 years in Lisse, Holland. Distinguished by small, long TUBEd flowers held in small multiple racemes.
de Graaff 2003 NL AFS5162.

Chosebuz. Upright/Trailer. Single. COROLLA: three quarter flared, smooth petal margins; opens & matures magenta (67B); 25mm (1") long, 35mm (1 3/8") wide. SEPALS: half up; tips reflexed up; rose (68B) upper surface; magenta (68A) lower surface; 40mm (1 9/16") long x 12mm (1/2") wide. TUBE: white (155B); medium length & thickness; 12mm (1/2") long x 4mm (3/16") wide. STAMENS: extend 10mm (3/8") below corolla; magenta (67B) filaments; magenta (59C) anthers. PISTIL: extends 15mm (11/16") below the corolla; light pink (65A) style; yellow (6A) stigma. BUD: tubular shaped. FOLIAGE: medium green (139B) upper surface; medium green (139C) lower surface. Leaves are 55mm (2 3/16") long x 30mm (1 3/16") wide, ovate shaped, serrulated edges, acute tips and rounded bases. Green veins & branches; light brown stems. PARENTAGE: 'Gitana' x ('Schneckerl' x 'Shy Lady'). Lax upright or stiff trailer. Makes good basket or standard. Prefers full sun. Best bloom and foliage colour in bright light. Tested 5 years in Göttingen, Germany. Bronze Medal, BUGA Cottbus 1995. Distinguished by free, long lasting flowers.
Strümper 2004 DE AFS5625.

Chris Bright. Upright. Single. COROLLA opens light powder pink; corolla is half flared and is 22mm long x 18mm wide. SEPALS pink on the upper and lower surfaces; sepals are horizontally held with recurved tips and are 24mm long x 7mm wide. TUBE pink and

is 5mm long x 5mm wide. PARENTAGE Winters Touch x Diva Areatha. This cultivar this cultivar has already proven to be a winner on the show bench. Runner up to best in show at Cumbria.
Flemming J. 2007 UK BFS0052.

Chris Joiner. Upright. Single. COROLLA opens coral pink; corolla is half flared and is 16mm long x 18mm wide. SEPALS pale pink on the upper surface, pink on the lower surface; sepals are horizontally held with recurved tips and are 29mm long x 10mm wide. TUBE pale pink and is 13mm long x 7mm wide. PARENTAGE London 2000 x Unknown.
Joiner 2006 UK BFS0037.

Chris Lohner. Upright/Trailer. Double. COROLLA is full flared with smooth petal margins; opens purple (80A); matures light purple (80C); 23mm (15/16") long x 50mm (2") wide. SEPALS are fully up, tips reflexed; dark red (46A) upper surface, red (46C) creped lower surface; 30mm (1 3/16") long x 20mm (13/16") wide. TUBE is dark red (46A); short and thick; 11mm (7/16") long x 9mm (3/8") thick. STAMENS extend 20mm (13/16") beyond the corolla; magenta (63B) filaments, grayish red (181A) anthers. PISTIL extends 40mm (1 9/16") beyond the corolla; magenta (63B) style, grayish red (181B) stigma. BUD is globular. FOLIAGE is medium green (137B) upper surface, medium green (137C) lower surface. Leaves are 50mm (2") long x 33mm (1 5/16") wide, ovate shaped, serrated edges, acute tips and rounded bases. Veins are green, stems and branches are gray-brown. PARENTAGE: 'Heron' x unknown. Lax upright or stiff trailer. Self branching. Makes good upright or standard. Prefers overhead filtered light. Best bloom colour in filtered light. Tested five years in Amstetten, Austria. Distinguished by large, compact flower in this colour.
Gindl 2002 AT AFS5048.

Chris Tarrant. Upright. Double. COROLLA opens violet blue, matures to violet with pink tinge then to white ; corolla is three quarter flared. SEPALS white flushed pink, matures from flush pink to white on the upper and lower surfaces; sepals are half up with recurved tips. TUBE white flushed pink. PARENTAGE Maria Landy x Lillian Annettes. This cultivar is free flowering.
Welch 2009 UK BFS0100.

Chris Yendell. Upright. Double. COROLLA: half flared, turned under petal margins;

opens magenta (58B), pink (62A) & purple (N82A); matures red (53C) & dark reddish purple (72A); 26 mm (1") long x 18mm (11/16") wide. PETALOIDS: magenta (58B), pink (62A) & purple (N82A); 16mm (5/8") long x 8mm (5/16") wide. SEPALS are half down, tips reflexed; dark rose (58C) upper surface; dark rose (55A) lower surface; 52mm (2 1/16") long x 14mm (9/16") wide. TUBE is rose (55B); long & medium thickness; 27mm (1 1/16") long x 6mm (1/4") wide. STAMENS extend 13mm (1/2") beyond the corolla; red (53B) filaments; purple (71A) anthers. PISTIL extends 23mm (7/8") beyond the corolla; dark rose (58C) style; light rose (73C) stigma. BUD is elongated. FOLIAGE is dark green (136B) upper surface; medium green (137C) lower surface. Leaves are 67mm (2 5/8") long x 32mm (1 1/4") wide, ovate shaped, serrate edges, acute tips, rounded bases. Veins are very dark reddish purple (186A), stems are light red purple (185D) & branches are red purple (N186D). PARENTAGE: 'Coen Bakker' x 'First Lord'. Lax upright or stiff trailer, self branching. Makes good basket. Prefers overhead filtered light, cool climate. Best bloom & foliage in filtered light. Tested 3 years in Koningshooikt, Belgium. Waanrode 9/8/2008. Distinguished by bloom colour combination & profuse blooms.
Michiels 2009 BE AFS7154.

Christa Lehmeier. Trailer. Single. COROLLA: half flared; opens reddish purple (N74A), pale pink (69A) base; matures reddish purple (N74B); 32mm (1 1/4") long x 35mm (1 3/8") wide. SEPALS: half down, tips recurved; rose (68C) upper surface; pink (62A) lower surface; 48mm (1 7/8") long x 15mm (9/16") wide. TUBE: pale lavender (69B); long & thick; 24mm (15/16") long x 8mm (5/16") wide. FOLIAGE is dark green (139A) upper surface; medium green (139C) lower surface. PARENTAGE: 'Rune Peeters' x 'Illusion'.
Michiels 2007 BE AFS6372.

Christel Dardenne. Trailer. Double. COROLLA is three quarter flared with turned under wavy petal margins; opens violet (76B), pale pink (36D) base; matures light purple (75B), light pink (65B) base; 33mm (1 5/16") long x 24mm (15/16") wide. SEPALS are horizontal, tips recurved; white (155C), pale pink (36D) base, tipped light apple green (145B) upper surface; white (155C), light pink (65B) base, tipped light apple green (145B) lower surface; 54mm (2 1/8") long x 16mm (5/8") wide. TUBE is pale pink (36D); medium length & thickness; 19mm (3/4")

long x 6mm (1/4") wide. FOLIAGE: dark green (137A) upper surface; medium green (138B) lower surface. Leaves are 68mm (2 11/16") long x 38mm (1 1/2") wide, ovate shaped. PARENTAGE: 'Sofie Michiels' x 'Weleveld'. Meise 9-18-04. Distinguished by flower colour combination.
Michiels 2005 BE AFS5851.

Christel Poelmans. Trailer. Single. COROLLA: 3 quarter flared; opens purple (79C), magenta (67B) base; matures purple (83B); 26mm (1") long x 17mm (5/8") wide. PETALOIDS: same colour as corolla; 16mm (5/8") long x 7mm (1/4") wide. SEPALS: horizontal, tips recurved; rose (68C) tipped light apple green (145B) upper surface; magenta (67B) tipped light apple green (145B) lower surface; 36mm (1 7/16") long x 11mm (7/16") wide. TUBE: magenta (61C); medium length & thickness; 14mm (9/16") long x 6mm (1/4") wide. FOLIAGE is dark green (137A) upper surface; medium green (138B) lower surface. PARENTAGE: 'Leon Pauwels' x 'Monique Sleiderink'.
Michiels 2007 BE AFS6535.

Christelle Leonard. Trailer. Single. COROLLA is quarter flared, little petticoat shaped; opens reddish purple (80B); matures reddish purple (72B); 32mm (1 1/4") long x 28mm (1 1/8") wide. SEPALS are twisted, half down, tips recurved; rose (55B) tipped light green (143C) upper surface; pink (55C) lower surface; 48mm (1 7/8") long x 12mm (1/2") wide. TUBE is pale pink (49D); 40mm (1 9/16") long x 9mm (5/16") wide. FOLIAGE: medium green (146A) upper surface; yellowish green (146B) lower surface. PARENTAGE: 'Alda Alders' x unknown. Natural trailer. Self branching. Makes good basket or decorative. Distinguished by bloom colour & shape.
Leonard 2006 BE AFS6054.

Christine Rogers. Upright. Single. COROLLA: unflared, bell shaped, smooth petal margins; opens purple (71A); matures light purple (74B); 17mm (5/8") long x 20mm (3/4") wide. SEPALS: full down, tips reflexed; magenta (57B) tipped green upper surface; dark rose (67C) tipped green lower surface; 15mm (9/16") long x 9mm (5/16") wide. TUBE: light reddish purple (66C) mottled white, green stripe; medium length & thickness; 5mm (3/16") long x 9mm (1/4") wide. STAMENS extend 14mm (9/16") beyond the corolla; magenta (63B) filaments; dark reddish purple (64A) anthers. PISTIL extends 27mm (1 1/16") beyond the corolla;

magenta (63B) style; pale lavender (65D) stigma. BUD: almost square, pointed. FOLIAGE: dark green (137A) upper surface; medium green (137D) lower surface. Leaves are 42mm (1 5/8") long x 23mm (7/8") wide; cordate shaped, serrulate edges, acute tips, rounded bases. Veins, stems & branches are green. PARENTAGE: F. *coccinea* x 'Eileen Storey'. Small upright. Self branching. Makes good upright. Prefers full sun. Cold weather hardy to -3° C (26° F). Best bloom & foliage colour in bright light. Tested 5 years in Burstwick, East Yorkshire, England. Distinguished by 3/4 erect corolla with SEPALS down.
Storey 2009 UK AFS7129.

Chirwito. Upright/Trailer. Single. COROLLA is quarter flared; opens reddish purple (59B); matures magenta (59C); 20mm (3/4") long x 23mm (7/8") wide. SEPALS are horizontal, tips recurved; reddish purple (61B) upper surface, and magenta (59C) lower surface; 34mm (1 3/8") long x 10mm (3/8") wide. TUBE is magenta (59D); medium length and thicknesss; 24mm (15/16") long x 5mm (3/16") wide. FOLIAGE is dark green (137A) upper surface; medium green (138B) lower surface. PARENTAGE: 'Rohees New Millenium' x 'Onbekend'.
Willems 2007 BE AFS6424.

Ciske De Rat. Upright. Single. COROLLA: unflared; opens dark purple (79A); matures dark purple (79B); 14mm (9/16") long x 10mm (3/8") wide. SEPALS: fully up, tips recurved; dark red (53A) upper; magenta (63A) lower surface; 20mm (3/4") long x 5mm (3/16") wide. TUBE: dark red (53A); 6mm (1/4") long x 4mm (1/8") wide. FOLIAGE is dark green (147A) upper surface; medium green (146A) lower surface. PARENTAGE: seedling of 'Insa'.
Krom 2008 NL AFS6944.

City Lights. Upright. Single. COROLLA violet. SEPALS cream. TUBE cream.
Weston 2006 UK.

Clara Agnes. Upright/Trailer. Single. . COROLLA: half flared, smooth petal margins; opens magenta (57C); matures light magenta (57D); 20mm (13/16") long 23mm (15/16") wide. SEPALS: half down; tips recurved; light rose (58D) upper surface; dark rose (58C) lower surface; 40mm (1 9/16") long x 15mm (9/16") wide. TUBE: pale pink (62D); medium length & thickness; 18mm (11/16") long x 9mm (3/8") wide. STAMENS: extend 25mm (1") below corolla; dark rose (54B) filaments;

purple (77A) anthers. PISTIL: extends 40mm (1 9/16") below the corolla; pale pink (62D) style; pale yellow (158B) stigma. BUD: long, elongated. FOLIAGE: medium green (138A) upper surface; medium green (138B) lower surface. Leaves are 70mm (2 3/4") long x 40mm (1 9/16") wide, lanceolate shaped, serrated edges, acute tips and rounded bases. Green veins; green/red stems & brown/green branches. PARENTAGE: 'Pink Jade' x 'Display'. Lax upright or stiff trailer. Self branching. Makes good basket or half basket. Prefers overhead filtered light. Heat tolerant if shaded. Cold weather hardy to 32⁰ F. Best bloom and foliage colour in bright light. Tested 3 years in Walthamstow, London, England. Distinguished by early and profuse blossoms.
Allsop J. 2004 UK AFS5572.

Clara Visser. Upright. Double. COROLLA: three quarter flared, smooth petal margins; opens dark reddish purple (62B); matures red (45A); 27mm (1 1/16") long x 25mm (1") wide. SEPALS: fully up, tips recurved; pink (62C) tipped green upper & lower surfaces; 37mm (1 7/16") long x 14mm (9/16") wide. TUBE: pink (62C); medium length & thickness; 22mm (7/8") long x 6mm (1/4") wide. STAMENS extend 6mm (1/4") beyond the corolla; rose (63C) filaments & anthers. PISTIL extends 24mm (15/16") beyond the corolla; light rose (63D) style; pale yellow (158B) stigma. BUD is round, long TUBE. FOLIAGE is medium green (137C) upper surface; medium green (138B) lower surface. Leaves are 70mm (2 3/4") long x 42mm (1 5/8") wide; cordate shaped, serrulate edges, acute tips, obtuse bases. Veins & branches are green, stems are red. PARENTAGE: 'Roesse Lupus' x 'HeRi Chessa'. Small upright. Makes good upright or standard. Prefers overhead filtered light, cool climate. Best bloom colour in filtered light. Tested 3 years in Veldhoven, The Netherlands. Distinguished by bloom & foliage combination.
Buiting 2009 NL AFS6936.

Claudia Denter. Upright. Semi Double. COROLLA: half flared, smooth petal margins, bell shaped; opens magenta (67B); matures rose (67D); 18mm (11/16") long x 25mm (1") wide. SEPALS: fully up, tips recurved; pale pink (56A) upper surface; pale pink (56B) lower surface; 20mm (3/4") long x 8mm (5/16") wide. TUBE: pink (62C); medium length & thickness; 12mm (7/16") long x 7mm (1/4") wide. STAMENS extend 12mm (7/16") beyond the corolla; light rose (58D)

filaments; brownish orange (175B) anthers. PISTIL extends 25mm (1") beyond the corolla; light gray (156C) style; brownish orange (175B) stigma. BUD: ovate. FOLIAGE: dark green (137A) upper surface; medium green (137C) lower surface. Leaves are 50mm (2") long x 35mm (1 3/8") wide; ovate shaped, serrate edges, acute tips, rounded bases. Veins are bright green, stems are green & red, branches are green. PARENTAGE: 'Ms Mumm 50' x 'Waldis Isabel'. Medium upright. Makes good upright or standard. Heat tolerant if shaded. Best bloom & foliage colour in bright light. Tested 3 years in South Germany. Distinguished by bloom shape & colour. Also registered with the BFS. Dietrich 2009 DE AFS7117 BFS0066 (2008).

Clement Ader. Upright/Trailer. Single. COROLLA: quarter flared, smooth petal margins; opens dark reddish purple (70A); matures reddish purple (70B); 18mm (11/16") long x 13mm (1/2") wide. SEPALS: half down; tips reflexed; pale pink (36D) tipped yellowish green (144B) upper surface; light pink (36B) lower surface; 30mm (1 3/16") long x 9mm (3/8") wide. TUBE: pale pink (36D); medium length & thickness; 18mm (11/16") long x 6mm (1/4") wide. STAMENS: extend 15-17mm (9/16-11/16") below corolla; light rose (73B) filaments, grayish red (182B) anthers. PISTIL: extends 22mm (7/8") below the corolla, pale rose (73D) style, pale yellow (158B) stigma. BUD: ovate. FOLIAGE: dark green (147A) upper surface; medium green (147B) lower surface. Leaves are 47mm (1 7/8") long x 32mm (1 1/4") wide, ovate shaped, serrulated edges, acute tips and rounded bases. Veins, stems & branches are yellowish green. PARENTAGE: 'String of Pearls' x 'Clair de Lune'. Lax upright or stiff trailer. Self branching. Makes good basket or upright. Prefers overhead filtered light and cool climate. Best bloom and foliage colour in filtered light. Tested 10 years in Pornic, France. Distinguished by bloom colour contrast.
Masse 2003 FR AFS5228.

Clement Duault-Seveno. Upright. Single. COROLLA: Quarter flared; opens purple (83B), light reddish purple (72D) base; matures purple (83B); 22mm (7/8") long x 19mm (3/4") wide. SEPALS: half down, tips recurved; red (45C) upper & lower surfaces; 34mm (1 3/8") long x 6mm (1/4") wide. TUBE: red (45C); short, medium thickness; 8mm (5/16") long x 5-6mm (3/16"-1/4") wide. FOLIAGE is dark green (147A) upper

68

surface; medium green (147B) lower surface. PARENTAGE: 'String of Pearls' x 'F. regia reitzii 4574'. Masse 2007 FR AFS6477.

Clovis. Upright/Trailer. Single. COROLLA: Quarter flared; opens & matures magenta (63A), lighter base; 24mm (15/16") long x 6mm (1/4") wide. SEPALS: horizontal, tips recurved; white (155D) tipped light yellowish green (149C) upper surface; white (155D) lower surface; 36mm (1 7/16") long x 6mm (1/4") wide. TUBE: yellowish white (4D); medium length & thickness; 13mm (1/2") long x 4-5mm (1/8"-3/16") wide. FOLIAGE is medium green (146A) upper surface; medium green (147B) lower surface. PARENTAGE: 'Porte Océane' x 'Subliem'. Masse 2007 FR AFS6478.

Club Nordcoast. Upright. Single. COROLLA is quarter flared with turned under wavy petal margins; opens orange (40C); matures light orange (41C); 12mm (1/2") long x 10mm (3/8") wide. SEPALS are horizontal, tips recurved; pale orange (22C), light orange (41C) base upper surface; coral (37A) lower surface; 15mm (9/16") long x 5mm (3/16") wide. TUBE is reddish purple (61B); long & thin; 48mm (1 7/8") long x 4mm (3/16") wide. FOLIAGE: dark green (139A) upper surface; medium green (138B) lower surface. Leaves are 127mm (5") long x 71mm (2 13/16") wide, ovate shaped. PARENTAGE: 'Insulinde' x 'F. fulgens var gesnariana'. Meise 8-14-04. Distinguished by small groups of flowers. Michiels 2005 BE AFS5733.

Coby Van Made. Upright/Trailer. Single. COROLLA: quarter flared; opens & matures magenta (58B); 10mm (3/8") long x 14mm (9/16") wide. SEPALS: horizontal, tips reflexed; magenta (58B) upper surface; rose (52B) tipped yellowish green (149A) lower surface; 19 mm (3/4") long x 9mm (5/16") wide. TUBE: dark rose (55A) flushed magenta (57B); 11mm (7/16") long x 14mm (9/16") wide. FOLIAGE is very dark green (131A) upper surface; medium green (146A) lower surface. PARENTAGE: 'Candy Bob' x 'Loxhore Mazurka'. van der Made 2008 NL AFS6783.

Codex. Upright/Trailer. Double. COROLLA is three quarter flared with turned under wavy petal margins; opens reddish purple (80B), rose (51C) base; matures light purple (78B); 23mm (15/16") long x 13mm (1/2") wide. PETALOIDS: light purple (80C), rose (51C)

base; 10mm (3/8") long x 8mm (5/16") wide. SEPALS are fully up, tips recurved; white (155C), tipped light apple green (145C) upper surface; pale pink (55C), tipped light apple green (145C) lower surface; 36mm (1 7/16") long x 10mm (3/8") wide. TUBE is white (155C); medium length & thickness; 14mm (9/16") long x 5mm (3/16") wide. FOLIAGE: dark green (139A) upper surface; medium green (138A) lower surface. Leaves are 68mm (2 11/16") long x 27mm (1 1/16") wide, ovate shaped. PARENTAGE: 'Sofie Michiels' x 'Weleveld'. Meise 8-14-04. Distinguished by flower shape. Michiels 2005 BE AFS5756.

Coen Bakker. Trailer. Double. COROLLA: half flared; opens violet (85A) striped rose (68B) and matures magenta (68A) striped rose (65A); 21mm (3/4") long x 14mm (9/16") wide. PETALOIDS: light violet (84B); 7mm (1/4") long x 4mm (1/8") wide. SEPALS are half up, tips recurved up, twisted left; white (155C) tipped light yellowish green (150C) upper surface & pale lavender (69B) tipped light yellowish green (150C) lower surface; 37mm (1 7/16") long x 11mm (7/16") wide. TUBE is white (155B); medium length & thickness; 18mm (11/16") long x 6mm (1/4") wide. FOLIAGE is dark green (137A) upper surface; medium green (138B) lower surface. PARENTAGE: 'Vreni Schleeweiss' x 'Kiss'. Michiels 2007 BE AFS6537.

Colette Kelly. Upright. Single. Norcross 2007 UK.

Comperen Acari. Upright/Trailer. Double. COROLLA: half flared, smooth petal margins; opens reddish purple (80B); matures light purple (78C); 22mm (7/8") long x29mm (1 1/8") wide. SEPALS: horizontal; tips recurved; reddish purple (61B) upper surface; reddish purple (67A) lower surface; 39mm (1 9/16") long x 12mm (1/2") wide. TUBE: reddish purple (61B); medium length & thickness; 17mm (11/16") long x 5mm (3/16") wide. STAMENS: extend 12mm (1/2") below corolla; magenta (68A) filaments; dark reddish purple (70A) anthers. PISTIL: extends 44mm (1 3/4") below the corolla; reddish purple (67A) style, light rose (63D) stigma. BUD: ovate. FOLIAGE: medium green (137B) upper surface; medium green (138A) lower surface. Leaves are 70mm (2 3/4") long x 48mm (1 7/8") wide, ovate shaped, serrated edges, acute tips and rounded bases. Veins, stems & branches are red. PARENTAGE: ('Sofie Michiels' x 'Rohees Metallah') x 'Veenlust'. Lax upright or stiff

trailer. Makes good stiff trailer. Prefers overhead filtered light and cool climate. Best bloom and foliage colour in filtered light. Tested 4 years in Diessen, The Netherlands. Distinguished by bloom colour.
Comperen 2003 NL AFS5263.

Comperen Alba. Upright/Trailer. Single. COROLLA: quarter flared, smooth petal margins; opens purple (71A); matures dark reddish purple (60A); 21mm (13/16") long 23mm (15/16") wide. SEPALS: half up; tips recurved up; magenta (63A) upper surface; dark reddish purple (60B) lower surface; 36mm (1 7/16") long x 11mm (7/16") wide. TUBE: magenta (63A); medium length & thickness; 11mm (7/16") long x 6mm (1/4") wide. STAMENS: extend 2mm (1/16") below corolla; magenta (63A) filaments; dark reddish purple (59A) anthers. PISTIL: extends 24mm (15/16") below the corolla; magenta (63A) style; light yellow (4C) stigma. BUD: ovate, curved, pointed. FOLIAGE: medium green (137B) upper surface; medium green (138B) lower surface. Leaves are 47mm (1 7/8") long x 26mm (1") wide, ovate shaped, serrulated edges, acute tips and rounded bases. Green veins, stems & branches. PARENTAGE: ('Sofie Michiels' x 'Rohees Metallah') x 'Willy Tamerus'. Lax upright or stiff trailer. Makes good stiff trailer. Prefers overhead filtered light and cool climate. Best bloom and foliage colour in filtered light. Tested 4 years in Diessen, The Netherlands. Distinguished by bloom colour.
Comperen 2004 NL AFS5538.

Comperen Alk. Upright. Single. COROLLA is half flared; opens & matures rose (65A); 20mm (3/4") long x 26mm (1") wide. SEPALS are half up, tips reflexed up; magenta (58B) upper surface; red (45A) lower surface; 26mm (1") long x 12mm (7/16") wide. TUBE is magenta (58B); 9mm (3/8") long x 8mm (5/16") wide. FOLIAGE: dark green (137A) upper surface; medium green (138A) lower surface. PARENTAGE: 'Roesse Carme' x 'Regent Gubler'. Distinguished by bloom colour.
Comperen 2006 AFS6202.

Comeperen Aluca. Upright. Semi Double. COROLLA: unflared, smooth petal margins; opens & matures light rose (73C) delicately veined light rose (73B); 28mm (1 1/8") long x 12mm (1/2") wide. SEPALS: full down; tips recurved; magenta (58B) upper surface; dark rose (58C) lower surface; 39mm (1 9/16") long x 8mm (5/16") wide, joined on 40% of its length. TUBE: dark rose (58C); short,

medium thickness; 6mm (1/4") long x 5mm (3/16") wide. STAMENS: extend 9-12mm (3/8–1/2") below corolla; light reddish purple (73A) filaments; reddish purple (70B) anthers. PISTIL: extends 33mm (1 5/16") below the corolla, light reddish purple (73A) style; reddish purple (64B) stigma. BUD: ovate. FOLIAGE: dark green (147A) upper surface; medium green (147B) lower surface. Leaves are 54mm (2 1/8") long x 32mm (1 1/4") wide, ovate shaped, serrulated edges, acute tips and rounded bases. Veins, stems & branches are yellowish green. PARENTAGE: ('String of Pearls' x unknown) x 'Caroline'. Small upright. Self branching. Makes good upright. Prefers overhead filtered light and cool climate. Best bloom and foliage colour in filtered light. Tested 5 years in Pornic, France. Distinguished by bloom form.
Comperen 2004 AFS5226.

Comperen Applevink. Upright. Double. COROLLA is half flared; opens dark reddish purple (64A); matures magenta (63A); 24mm (15/16") long x 26mm (1") wide. SEPALS are fully up, tips reflexed; pink (62C) upper surface; pink (62A) lower surface; 33mm (1 5/16) long x 12mm (7/16") wide. TUBE is pink (62C); 10mm (3/8") long x 5mm (3/16") wide. FOLIAGE: dark green (137A) upper surface; medium green (137C) lower surface. PARENTAGE: ['Indy van Roovert' x ('Roesse Apus' x 'Roesse Apus')] x 'Sam'. Distinguished by bloom colour.
Comperen 2006 NL AFS6209.

Comperen Arend. Upright/Trailer. Double. COROLLA: Half flared; opens light purple (86C) & rose (68B); matures light violet (84B) & rose (68B); 21mm (13/16") long x 16mm (5/8") wide. SEPALS: horizontal, tips recurved; rose (68C) upper surface; rose (68B) lower surface; 24mm (15/16") long x 10mm (3/8") wide. TUBE: rose (68C); medium length & thickness; 21mm (13/16") long x 4mm (1/8") wide. FOLIAGE is dark green (137A) upper surface; medium green (138B) lower surface. PARENTAGE: 'Roesse Elara' x 'Roesse Parel'.
Comperen 2007 NL AFS6602.

Comperen Atrata. Trailer. Single. COROLLA: quarter flared, smooth petal margins; opens dark red (46A); matures red (46C); 16mm (5/8") long 19mm (3/4") wide. SEPALS: fully up; tips recurved; rose (52B) upper & lower surfaces; 49mm (1 15/16") long x 10mm (3/8") wide. TUBE: light pink (38C); medium length & thickness; 16mm (5/8") long x 5mm (3/16") wide. STAMENS: extend 17mm

(11/16") below corolla; pink (48C) filaments; red (53B) anthers. PISTIL: extends 3mm (1/8") below the corolla; pink (48C) style; light yellow (4C) stigma. BUD: ovate, curved, pointed. FOLIAGE: medium green (137B) upper surface; medium green (138B) lower surface. Leaves are 64mm (2 1/2") long x 40mm (1 9/16") wide, ovate shaped, serrated edges, acute tips and cordate bases. Red veins, stems & branches. PARENTAGE: 'Roesse Apus' x 'Willy Tamerus'. Natural trailer. Makes good basket. Prefers overhead filtered light and cool climate. Best bloom and foliage colour in filtered light. Tested 4 years in Diessen, The Netherlands. Distinguished by bloom colour.
Comperen 2004 NL AFS5537.

Comperen Azurea. Upright/Trailer. Single. COROLLA: half flared, smooth petal margins; opens purple (81A); matures dark purple (78A); 20mm (13/16") long 27mm (1 1/16") wide. SEPALS: half up; tips recurved up; reddish purple (66B) upper surface; reddish purple (67A) lower surface; 31mm (1 1/4") long x 11mm (7/16") wide. TUBE: reddish purple (66B); medium length & thickness; 14mm (9/16") long x 8mm (5/16") wide. STAMENS: extend 5mm (3/16") below corolla; reddish purple (74A) filaments; pale purple (74D) anthers. PISTIL: extends 17mm (11/16") below the corolla; reddish purple (74A) style; light yellow (4C) stigma. BUD: ovate, curved, pointed. FOLIAGE: dark green (137A) upper surface; medium green (138B) lower surface. Leaves are 45mm (1 3/4") long x 24mm (15/16") wide, ovate shaped, serrulated edges, acute tips and obtuse bases. Green veins, stems & branches. PARENTAGE: 'Roesse Carme' x 'Madalyn Drago'. Lax upright or stiff trailer. Makes good stiff trailer. Prefers overhead filtered light and cool climate. Best bloom and foliage colour in filtered light. Tested 4 years in Diessen, The Netherlands. Distinguished by bloom colour.

Comperen Beflijster. Upright. Single. COROLLA is quarter flared with smooth petal margins; opens magenta (58B); matures dark rose (58C); 15mm (9/16") long x 19mm (3/4") wide. SEPALS are half up, tips reflexed up; dark rose (58C) upper & lower surfaces; 21mm (13/16") long x 11mm (7/16") wide. TUBE is dark rose (58C); short & thick; 14mm (9/16") long x 12mm (1/2") wide. FOLIAGE: dark green (137A) upper surface; medium green (138A) lower surface. Leaves are 49mm (1 15/16") long x 33mm (1 5/16") wide, ovate shaped. PARENTAGE: 'Roesse

Carme' x 'Lye's Unique'. Distinguished by bloom colour.
Comperen 2005 NL AFS5913.

Comperen Bergfluiter. Upright. Single. COROLLA is half flared; opens purple (83B); matures dark reddish purple (61A); 24mm (15/16") long x 29mm (1 1/8") wide. SEPALS are fully up, tips recurved; light rose (58D) upper surface; magenta (58B) lower surface; 26mm (1") long x 12mm (7/16") wide. TUBE is light rose (58D); 8mm (5/16") long x 7mm (1/4") wide. FOLIAGE: medium green (137B) upper surface; medium green (137C) lower surface. PARENTAGE: 'Roesse Carme' x 'Leon Pauwels'. Distinguished by bloom & foliage combination.
Comperen 2006 NL AFS6207.

Comperen Blauwborst. Upright. Single. COROLLA is three quarter flared with smooth petal margins; opens purple (77A); matures reddish purple (67A); 21mm (13/16") long x 29mm (1 1/8") wide. SEPALS are half up, tips recurved up; dark rose (51A) upper surface; red (52A) lower surface; 31mm (1 1/4") long x 12mm (1/2") wide. TUBE is dark rose (51A); medium length & thickness; 15mm (9/16") long x 7mm (1/4") wide. FOLIAGE: medium green (137B) upper surface; medium green (138B) lower surface. Leaves are 67mm (2 5/8") long x 37mm (1 7/16") wide, ovate shaped. PARENTAGE: 'Roesse Apus' x 'Marielle Comperen'. Distinguished by bloom shape.
Comperen 2005 NL AFS5916.

Comperen Borneo. Upright. Single. COROLLA: half flared, smooth petal margins; opens reddish purple (61B); matures dark reddish purple (60C); 21mm (13/16") long x 22mm (7/8") wide. SEPALS: horizontal; tips recurved; dark rose (58C) upper surface; magenta (58B) lower surface; 17mm (11/16") long x 11mm (7/16") wide. TUBE: dark rose (58C); medium length & thickness; 10mm (3/8") long x 7mm (1/4") wide. STAMENS: extend 9mm (3/8") below corolla; dark reddish purple (60B) filaments; dark reddish purple (60A) anthers. PISTIL: extends 20mm (13/16") below the corolla; pink (62A) style; rose (67D) stigma. BUD: round. FOLIAGE: dark green (137A) upper surface; medium green (138B) lower surface. Leaves are 64mm (2 1/2") long x 44mm (1 3/4") wide, ovate shaped, serrated edges, acute tips and rounded bases. Red veins, stems & branches. PARENTAGE: 'Roesse Carme' x 'Cameron Ryle'. Medium upright. Makes good upright or standard. Prefers overhead filtered light and cool climate. Best bloom and foliage colour in filtered light. Tested 4 years in Diessen, The Netherlands. Distinguished by bloom and foliage combination. Comperen 2004 NL AFS5551.

Comperen Buizerd. Upright. Single. COROLLA is quarter flared with smooth petal margins; opens rose (50B); matures red (52A); 14mm (9/16") long x 19mm (3/4") wide. SEPALS are half up, tips reflexed up; magenta (58B) upper & lower surfaces; 22mm (7/8") long x 9mm (3/8") wide. TUBE is magenta (58B); short & thick; 12mm (1/2") long x 9mm (3/8") wide. FOLIAGE: dark green (137A) upper surface; medium green (138B) lower surface. Leaves are 60mm (2 3/8") long x 34mm (1 5/16") wide, ovate shaped. PARENTAGE: 'Roesse Carme' x 'Lye's Unique'. Distinguished by bloom shape. Comperen 2005 NL AFS5912.

Comperen Cana. Upright/Trailer. Semi Double. COROLLA: three quarter flared, smooth petal margins; opens purple (77A); matures reddish purple (72B); 24mm (15/16") long 40mm (1 9/16") wide. SEPALS: fully up; tips recurved; red (53B) upper surface; red (45C) lower surface; 34mm (1 5/16") long x 13mm (1/2") wide. TUBE: red (53B); short & thick; 9mm (3/8") long x 9mm (3/8") wide. STAMENS: extend 24mm (15/16") below corolla; red (45C) filaments; reddish purple (59B) anthers. PISTIL: extends 46mm (1 13/16") below the corolla; red (45C) style & stigma. BUD: ovate, pointed. FOLIAGE: dark green (137A) upper surface; medium green (138B) lower surface. Leaves are 60mm (2 3/8") long x 32mm (1 1/4") wide, ovate shaped, serrated edges, acute tips and rounded bases. Red veins, stems & branches. PARENTAGE: 'Roesse Apus' x 'Maxima'. Lax upright or stiff trailer. Makes good stiff trailer. Prefers overhead filtered light and cool climate. Best bloom and foliage colour in filtered light. Tested 4 years in Diessen, The Netherlands. Distinguished by bloom shape. Comperen 2004 NL AFS5554.

Comperen Casarca. Upright. Single. COROLLA is half flared with smooth petal margins; opens & matures rose (68B); 19mm (3/4") long x 15mm (9/16") wide. SEPALS are horizontal, tips recurved; magenta (58B) upper & lower surfaces; 26mm (1") long x 8mm (5/16") wide. TUBE is magenta (58B); short & thick; 9mm (3/8") long x 7mm (1/4") wide. FOLIAGE: dark green (137A) upper surface; medium green (138B) lower surface.

Leaves are 36mm (1 7/16") long x 21mm (13/16") wide, cordate shaped. PARENTAGE: 'Roesse Carme' x 'Roesse Mondi'. Distinguished by erect bloom. Comperen 2005 NL AFS5915.

Comperen Duizendpoot. Upright/Trailer. Single. COROLLA: half flared, smooth petal margins; opens purple (82A); matures purple (81A); 24mm (15/16") long x 22mm (7/8") wide. SEPALS: horizontal; tips recurved; dark rose (54A) upper surface; dark rose (51A) lower surface; 32mm (1 1/4") long x 12mm (1/2") wide. TUBE: dark rose (54A); medium length & thickness; 12mm (1/2") long x 8mm (5/16") wide. STAMENS: extend 12mm (1/2") below corolla; dark rose (54B) filaments; red (53C) anthers. PISTIL: extends 32mm (1 1/4") below the corolla; dark rose (54B) style, dark rose (54A) stigma. BUD: tear drop. FOLIAGE: medium green (137B) upper surface; medium green (138B) lower surface. Leaves are 60mm (2 3/8") long x 30mm (1 3/16") wide, ovate shaped, serrulated edges, acute tips and rounded bases. Veins, stems & branches are green. PARENTAGE: 'Maxima' x 'Billy Green'. Lax upright or stiff trailer. Makes good upright or standard. Prefers overhead filtered light and cool climate. Best bloom and foliage colour in filtered light. Tested 4 years in Diessen, The Netherlands. Distinguished by bloom & foliage combination. Comperen 2003 NL AFS5273.

Comperen Dwergarend. Upright. Semi Double. COROLLA is half flared; opens purple (80A); matures light purple (80C); 16mm (5/8") long x 21mm (13/16") wide. SEPALS are half up, tips recurved up; light green (139D) upper surface; light rose (73C) lower surface; 16mm (5/8) long x 7mm (1/4") wide. TUBE is light green (139D); 7mm (1/4") long x 7mm (1/4") wide. FOLIAGE: dark green (139A) upper surface; medium green (137B) lower surface. PARENTAGE: 'Roesse Carme' x 'Wentworth'. Distinguished by bloom & foliage combination. Comperen 2006 NL AFS6214.

Comperen Elegans. Upright. Single. COROLLA: three quarter flared, smooth petal margins; opens & matures white (155D); 18mm (11/16") long 21mm (13/16") wide. SEPALS: fully up; tips reflexed; pale pink (62D) upper surface; light pink (62B) lower surface; 42mm (1 5/8") long x 14mm (9/16") wide. TUBE: pale pink (62D); medium length & thickness; 15mm (9/16") long x 6mm (1/4") wide. STAMENS: extend 11mm (7/16")

below corolla; rose (68C) filaments; reddish purple (61B) anthers. PISTIL: extends 29mm (1 1/8") below the corolla; light rose (68D) style; white (155D) stigma. BUD: ovate, long, pointed. FOLIAGE: dark green (137A) upper surface; medium green (138B) lower surface. Leaves are 47mm (1 7/8") long x 21mm (13/16") wide, lanceolate shaped, serrulated edges, acute tips and rounded bases. Green veins, stems & branches. PARENTAGE: 'Katrien Michiels' x 'Delta's Wonder'. Medium upright. Makes good upright or standard. Prefers overhead filtered light and cool climate. Best bloom and foliage colour in filtered light. Tested 4 years in Diessen, The Netherlands. Distinguished by bloom and foliage combination.
Comperen 2004 NL AFS5562.

Comperen Fitis. Upright. Single. COROLLA is three quarter flared with smooth petal margins; opens rose (68B); matures rose (68C); 20mm (13/16") long x 20mm (13/16") wide. SEPALS are fully up, tips reflexed; white (155C) tipped green upper & lower surfaces; 24mm (15/16") long x 7mm (1/4") wide. TUBE is magenta (63B); short & thick; 7mm (1/4") long x 7mm (1/4") wide. FOLIAGE: medium green (137C) upper surface; medium green (138A) lower surface. Leaves are 42mm (1 11/16") long x 29mm (1 1/8") wide, cordate shaped. PARENTAGE: 'Roesse Carme' x 'Impala'. Distinguished by bloom colour.
Comperen 2005 NL AFS5921.

Comperen Flamingo. Upright. Single. COROLLA is half flared with smooth petal margins; opens & matures magenta (58B); 14mm (9/16") long x 18mm (11/16") wide. SEPALS are horizontal, tips recurved; magenta (63A) tipped green upper surface; dark rose (58C) lower surface; 19mm (3/4") long x 11mm (7/16") wide. TUBE is magenta (63A); short & thick; 9mm (3/8") long x 9mm (3/8") wide. FOLIAGE: dark green (137A) upper surface; medium green (138A) lower surface. Leaves are 54mm (2 1/8") long x 34mm (1 5/16") wide, cordate shaped. PARENTAGE: 'Roesse Carme' x 'Comperen Pluvier'. Distinguished by bloom & foliage combination.
Comperen 2005 NL AFS5920.

Comperen Goudbuikje. Upright. Double. COROLLA: half flared, smooth petal margins; opens purple (77A) & magenta (63B); matures purple (71A) & magenta (63B); 16mm (5/8") long 12mm (1/2") wide. SEPALS: horizontal; tips recurved; light rose

(63D), tipped green, upper surface; reddish purple (64B), tipped green, lower surface; 24mm (15/16") long x 16mm (5/8") wide. TUBE: light rose (63D); medium length & thickness; 25mm (1") long x 6mm (1/4") wide. STAMENS: extend 6mm (1/4") below corolla; dark reddish purple (72A) filaments & anthers. PISTIL: extends 19mm (3/4") below the corolla; light reddish purple (72C) style; light yellow (4C) stigma. BUD: round. FOLIAGE: medium green (137D) upper surface; medium green (138B) lower surface. Leaves are 70mm (2 3/4") long x 38mm (1 1/2") wide, ovate shaped, serrulated edges, acute tips and rounded bases. Green veins, stems & branches. PARENTAGE: 'Swanley Gem' x 'WALZ Piano'. Medium upright. Makes good upright or standard. Prefers overhead filtered light and cool climate. Best bloom and foliage colour in filtered light. Tested 4 years in Diessen, The Netherlands. Distinguished by bloom colour.
Comperen 2004 NL AFS5549.

Comperen Goudvink. Upright/Trailer. Semi Double. COROLLA is half flared with smooth petal margins; opens & matures magenta (68A); 19mm (3/4") long x 21mm (13/16") wide. SEPALS are half up, tips recurved up; pink (62A) upper surface; light rose (58D) lower surface; 23mm (15/16") long x 9mm (3/8") wide. TUBE is pink (62A); medium length & thickness; 14mm (9/16") long x 7mm (1/4") wide. FOLIAGE: dark green (137A) upper surface; medium green (138A) lower surface. Leaves are 68mm (2 11/16") long x 31mm (1 1/4") wide, cordate shaped. PARENTAGE: 'Roesse Carme' x 'Comperen Stepera'. Distinguished by bloom & foliage combination.
Comperen 2005 NL AFS5917.

Comperen Groenling. Upright. Single. COROLLA is quarter flared; opens & matures magenta (63B); 17mm (5/8") long x 20mm (3/4") wide. SEPALS are horizontal, tips recurved; light rose (68D) upper & lower surfaces; 24mm (15/16) long x 8mm (5/16") wide. TUBE is light rose (68D); 12mm (7/16") long x 8mm (5/16") wide. FOLIAGE: dark green (137A) upper surface; medium green (138A) lower surface. PARENTAGE: ('Sofie Michiels' x 'Venus Victrix') x 'Lye's Unique'. Distinguished by bloom colour.
Comperen 2006 NL AFS6208.

Comperen Grutto. Upright. Single. COROLLA: quarter flared, smooth petal margins; opens very dark reddish purple (186A); matures plum (185C); 14mm (9/16")

long 21mm (13/16") wide. SEPALS: horizontal; tips recurved; dark rose (51A), tipped green upper surface; reddish orange (42A) lower surface; 24mm (15/16") long x 11mm (7/16") wide. TUBE: dark rose (51A); medium length & thickness; 19mm (3/4") long x 6mm (1/4") wide. STAMENS: extend 14mm (9/16") below corolla; magenta (68A) filaments; rose (68C) anthers. PISTIL: extends 38mm (1 1/2") below the corolla; magenta (63B) style; light yellow (4C) stigma. BUD: elliptic, pointed. FOLIAGE: dark green (137A) upper surface; medium green (138A) lower surface. Leaves are 67mm (2 5/8") long x 41mm (1 5/8") wide, ovate shaped, serrulated edges, acute tips and rounded bases. Green veins, stems & branches. PARENTAGE: 'Roesse Apus' x 'Willy Tamerus'. Tall upright. Makes good upright or standard. Prefers overhead filtered light and cool climate. Best bloom and foliage colour in filtered light. Tested 4 years in Diessen, The Netherlands. Distinguished by bloom colour.
Comperen 2004 NL AFS5556.

Comperen Gularis. Upright/Trailer. Single. COROLLA: half flared, smooth petal margins; opens magenta (63A); matures magenta (63B); 16mm (5/8") long 13mm (1/2") wide. SEPALS: horizontal; tips recurved; pale pink (62D) upper surface; pink (62C) lower surface; 32mm (1 1/4") long x 12mm (1/2") wide. TUBE: pale pink (62D); medium length & thickness; 12mm (1/2") long x 6mm (1/4") wide. STAMENS: extend 12mm (1/2") below corolla; pink (62A) filaments; dark reddish purple (59A) anthers. PISTIL: extends 36mm (1 7/16") below the corolla; pink (62C) style; light yellow (4C) stigma. BUD: ovate, pointed. FOLIAGE: medium green (137C) upper surface; medium green (138B) lower surface. Leaves are 57mm (2 1/4") long x 26mm (1") wide, lanceolate shaped, serrulated edges, acute tips and rounded bases. Green veins, stems & branches. PARENTAGE: 'Orangeblossom' x 'Judy Salome'. Lax upright or stiff trailer. Makes good stiff trailer. Prefers overhead filtered light and cool climate. Best bloom and foliage colour in filtered light. Tested 4 years in Diessen, The Netherlands. Distinguished by bloom and foliage combination.
Comperen 2004 NL AFS5563.

Comperen Guttata. Upright. Single. COROLLA: half flared, smooth petal margins; opens rose (68B); matures light rose (73B); 20mm (13/16") long 21mm (13/16") wide. SEPALS: half up; tips reflexed up; red (52A)

upper & lower surfaces; 21mm (13/16") long x 11mm (7/16") wide. TUBE: red (52A); medium length & thickness; 11mm (7/16") long x 7mm (1/4") wide. STAMENS: extend 8mm (5/16") below corolla; rose (65A) filaments; dark reddish purple (60C) anthers. PISTIL: extends 14mm (9/16") below the corolla; magenta (63B) style; very pale orange (27D) stigma. BUD: elliptic, pointed. FOLIAGE: medium green (137B) upper surface; medium green (138B) lower surface. Leaves are 49mm (1 15/16") long x 27mm (1 1/16") wide, ovate shaped, serrulated edges, acute tips and rounded bases. Green veins, stems & branches. PARENTAGE: 'Katrien Michiels' x 'Delta's Wonder'. Medium upright. Makes good upright or standard. Prefers overhead filtered light and cool climate. Best bloom and foliage colour in filtered light. Tested 4 years in Diessen, The Netherlands. Distinguished by bloom colour.
Comperen 2004 NL AFS5546.

Comperen Havik. Upright. Double. COROLLA is half flared; opens purple (83B); matures reddish purple (72B); 30mm (1 3/16") long x 38mm (1 1/2") wide. SEPALS are half up, tips recurved up; light rose (63D) upper surface; magenta (63B) lower surface; 42mm (1 5/8") long x 16mm (5/8") wide. TUBE is light rose (63D); 15mm (9/16") long x 7mm (1/4") wide. FOLIAGE: dark green (137A) upper surface; medium green (138B) lower surface. PARENTAGE: 'Sofie Michiels' x 'Mission Bells'. Distinguished by bloom & foliage combination.
Comperen 2006 NL AFS6205.

Comperen Hop. Upright. Single. COROLLA is half flared; opens light reddish purple (73A); matures light rose (73B); 20mm (3/4") long x 25mm (1") wide. SEPALS are fully up, tips recurved; light rose (73B) upper & lower surfaces; 22mm (7/8) long x 10mm (3/8") wide. TUBE is light rose (73B); 10mm (3/8") long x 7mm (1/4") wide. FOLIAGE: dark green (137A) upper surface; medium green (138A) lower surface. PARENTAGE: 'Roesse Carme' x 'Centenary'. Distinguished by bloom & foliage combination.
Comperen 2006 NL AFS6213.

Comperen Ijsvogel. Upright. Double. COROLLA is three quarter flared; opens purple (77A); matures purple (80A); 24mm (15/16") long x 34mm (1 3/8") wide. SEPALS are half up, tips recurved up; magenta (58B) upper & lower surfaces; 29mm (1 1/16") long x 16mm (5/8") wide. TUBE is magenta (58B); 5mm (3/16") long x 5mm (3/16") wide.

74

FOLIAGE: dark green (137A) upper surface; medium green (137C) lower surface. PARENTAGE: 'Sofie Michiels' x 'Mission Bells'. Distinguished by bloom & foliage combination.
Comperen 2006 NL AFS6204.

Comperen Jager. Trailer. Semi Double. COROLLA: half flared; opens purple (77A); matures purple (82A); 27mm (1 1/16") long x 24mm (15/16") wide. SEPALS: fully up, tips recurved; pale purple (75C) upper surface; magenta (71C) lower surface; 49mm (1 15/16") long x 14mm (9/16") wide. TUBE: pale purple (75C); 10mm (3/8") long x 7mm (1/4") wide. FOLIAGE is dark green (137A) upper surface; medium green (137C) lower surface. PARENTAGE: 'Fenne Comperen' x 'Miet van Eijk'.
Comperen 2008 NL AFS6884.

Comperen Kanoek. Upright. Semi Double. COROLLA: Half flared; opens violet (75A); matures light purple (75B); 24mm (15/16") long x 31mm (1 1/4") wide. SEPALS: fully up, tips recurved; light apple green (145C) upper surface; rose (68B) tipped green lower surface; 24mm (15/16") long x 9mm (5/16") wide. TUBE: light apple green (145C); medium length & thickness; 17mm (5/8") long x 7mm (1/4") wide. FOLIAGE is dark green (137A) upper surface; medium green (137C) lower surface. PARENTAGE: 'Roesse Carme' x 'Silver Dawn'.
Comperen 2007 NL AFS6607.

Comperen Karekiet. Upright. Single. COROLLA is half flared; opens reddish purple (72B); matures light reddish purple (72C); 25mm (1") long x 27mm (1 1/16") wide. SEPALS are fully up, tips reflexed; red (45A) upper surface; red (45B) lower surface; 26mm (1) long x 11mm (7/16") wide. TUBE is red (45A); 8mm (5/16") long x 8mm (5/16") wide. FOLIAGE: dark green (137A) upper surface; medium green (138B) lower surface. PARENTAGE: 'Roesse Carme' x 'Swanley Gem'. Distinguished by bloom colour.
Comperen 2006 NL AFS6212.

Comperen Kemphaan. Upright. Semi Double. COROLLA: quarter flared, smooth petal margins; opens dark reddish purple (60A); matures magenta (58B); 15mm (9/16") long 21mm (13/16") wide. SEPALS: half up; tips recurved up; rose (61D) upper surface; magenta (58B) lower surface; 24mm (15/16") long x 11mm (7/16") wide. TUBE: rose (61D); long & thin; 31mm (1 1/4") long x 4mm

(3/16") wide. STAMENS: extend 7mm (1/4") below corolla; dark rose (58C) filaments; reddish purple (59B) anthers. PISTIL: extends 31mm (1 1/4") below the corolla; magenta (58B) style; light yellow (4C) stigma. BUD: round, long TUBE. FOLIAGE: dark green (137A) upper surface; medium green (138A) lower surface. Leaves are 54mm (2 1/8") long x 32mm (1 1/4") wide, ovate shaped, serrated edges, acute tips and rounded bases. Red veins, stems & branches. PARENTAGE: 'Roesse Carme' x 'Impala'. Medium upright. Makes good upright or standard. Prefers overhead filtered light and cool climate. Best bloom and foliage colour in filtered light. Tested 4 years in Diessen, The Netherlands. Distinguished by bloom and foliage combination.
Comperen 2004 NL AFS5531.

Comperen Kerkuil. Upright/Trailer. Double. COROLLA is half flared; opens purple (83A); matures purple (71A); 26mm (1") long x 21mm (13/16") wide. SEPALS are half down, tips recurved; reddish purple (61B) upper surface; magenta (61C) lower surface; 51mm (2) long x 16mm (5/8") wide. TUBE is reddish purple (61B); 23mm (7/8") long x 6mm (1/4") wide. FOLIAGE: medium green (137C) upper surface; medium green (138B) lower surface. PARENTAGE: 'Sailor' x 'Boy Comperen'. Distinguished by bloom colour.
Comperen 2006 NL AFS6217.

Comperen Kievit. Trailer. Single. COROLLA: Half flared; opens dark reddish purple (70A); matures reddish purple (58B); 20mm (3/4") long x 21mm (13/16") wide. SEPALS: fully up, tips recurved; pale lavender (65D) tipped green upper surface; light pink (65B) lower surface; 29mm (1 1/8") long x 8mm (5/16") wide. TUBE: pale lavender (65D); medium length & thickness; 12mm (7/16") long x 5mm (3/16") wide. FOLIAGE is dark green (137A) upper surface; medium green (138A) lower surface. PARENTAGE: 'Roesse Lupus' x 'Comperen Millitaris'.
Comperen 2007 NL AFS6603.

Comperen Kluut. Upright. Single. COROLLA is three quarter flared with smooth petal margins; opens purple (71A); matures dark reddish purple (61A); 25mm (1") long x 27mm (1 1/16") wide. SEPALS are half up, tips recurved up; pink (62A) upper surface; magenta (68A) lower surface; 24mm (15/16") long x 11mm (7/16") wide. TUBE is pink (62A); medium length & thickness; 19mm (3/4") long x 8mm (5/16") wide. FOLIAGE:

dark green (137A) upper surface; medium green (138B) lower surface. Leaves are 66mm (2 5/8") long x 35mm (1 3/8") wide, cordate shaped. PARENTAGE: 'Roesse Carme' x ('Roesse Apus' x 'Northway'. Distinguished by bloom colour. Comperen 2005 NL AFS5926.

Comperen Knopsprietje. Upright/Trailer. Semi Double. COROLLA: half flared, smooth petal margins; opens purple (71A); matures reddish purple (59B); 17mm (11/16") long x 17mm (11/16") wide. SEPALS: half up; tips recurved up; magenta (63A) upper surface; reddish purple (64B) lower surface; 22mm (7/8") long x 7mm (1/4") wide. TUBE: magenta (63A); medium length & thickness; 12mm (1/2") long x 7mm (1/4") wide. STAMENS: extend 17mm (11/16") below corolla; dark reddish purple (61A) filaments & anthers. PISTIL: extends 32mm (1 1/4") below the corolla; reddish purple (64B) style, white (155B) stigma. BUD: ovate. FOLIAGE: medium green (137B) upper surface; medium green (138B) lower surface. Leaves are 48mm (1 7/8") long x 28mm (1 1/8") wide, ovate shaped, serrulated edges, acute tips and obtuse bases. Veins, stems & branches are red. PARENTAGE: 'Dorothy Oosting' x 'Maxima'. Lax upright or stiff trailer. Makes good stiff trailer. Prefers overhead filtered light and cool climate. Best bloom and foliage colour in filtered light. Tested 4 years in Diessen, The Netherlands. Distinguished by bloom colour. Comperen 2003 NL AFS5262.

Comperen Korhoen. Trailer. Double. COROLLA is half flared; opens purple (83B); matures reddish purple (72B); 26mm (1") long x 22mm (7/8") wide. SEPALS are horizontal, tips recurved; pale yellow (2D) upper surface; pale lavender (69D) lower surface; 29mm (1 1/8") long x 16mm (5/8") wide. TUBE is pale yellow (2D); 10mm (3/8") long x 6mm (1/4") wide. FOLIAGE: dark green (137A) upper surface; medium green (138A) lower surface. PARENTAGE: 'Roesse Carme' x 'Cameron Ryle'. Distinguished by bloom colour. Comperen 2006 NL AFS6206.

Comperen Krekel. Upright/Trailer. Semi Double. COROLLA: half flared, smooth petal margins; opens dark purple (79B); matures dark reddish purple (59A); 22mm (7/8") long x 20mm (13/16") wide. SEPALS: fully up; tips recurved; rose (64D) upper surface; reddish purple (64B) lower surface; 26mm

(1") long x 7mm (1/4") wide. TUBE: dark rose (64C); medium length & thickness; 10mm (3/8") long x 5mm (3/16") wide. STAMENS: extend 17mm (11/16") below corolla; dark reddish purple (61A) filaments & anthers. PISTIL: extends 17mm (11/16") below the corolla; light reddish purple (72C) style, light rose (73C) stigma. BUD: ovate. FOLIAGE: dark green (137A) upper surface; medium green (138B) lower surface. Leaves are 70mm (2 3/4") long x 41mm (1 5/8") wide, ovate shaped, serrulated edges, acute tips and rounded bases. Veins, stems & branches are red. PARENTAGE: 'Hertogin van Brabant' x 'Phenomenal'. Lax upright or stiff trailer. Makes good stiff trailer. Prefers overhead filtered light and cool climate. Best bloom and foliage colour in filtered light. Tested 4 years in Diessen, The Netherlands. Distinguished by bloom colour. Comperen 2003 NL AFS5274.

Comperen Kruisbek. Upright. Double. COROLLA is three quarter flared; opens purple (77A); matures dark reddish purple (64A); 19mm (3/4") long x 26mm (1") wide. SEPALS are fully up, tips reflexed; reddish purple (60D) upper surface; dark reddish purple (60B) lower surface; 22mm (7/8) long x 12mm (7/16") wide. TUBE is reddish purple (60D); 8mm (5/16") long x 6mm (1/4") wide. FOLIAGE: dark green (137A) upper surface; medium green (137C) lower surface. PARENTAGE: ['Indy van Roovert' x ('Roesse Apus' x 'Roesse Apus')] x ('Swanley Gem' x 'Monique Sleiderink'). Distinguished by bloom & foliage combination. Comperen 2006 NL AFS6210.

Comperen Kwikstaart. Trailer. Single. COROLLA: three quarter flared, smooth petal margins; opens & matures reddish purple (64B); 14mm (9/16") long 10mm (3/8") wide. SEPALS: horizontal; tips recurved; pale pink (62D) upper surface; light pink (62B) lower surface; 29mm (1 1/8") long x 9mm (3/8") wide. TUBE: pink (62A); long & thin; 27mm (1 1/16") long x 4mm (3/16") wide. STAMENS: extend 17mm (11/16") below corolla; magenta (58B) filaments; reddish purple (58A) anthers. PISTIL: extends 47mm (1 7/8") below the corolla; magenta (58B) style; light yellow (4C) stigma. BUD: ovate, pointed. FOLIAGE: medium green (138A) upper surface; medium green (138B) lower surface. Leaves are 44mm (1 3/4") long x 22mm (7/8") wide, ovate shaped, serrulated edges, acute tips and rounded bases. Green veins, stems & branches. PARENTAGE: 'Orangeblossom' x 'Judy Salome'. Natural

76

trailer. Makes good basket. Prefers overhead filtered light and cool climate. Best bloom and foliage colour in filtered light. Tested 4 years in Diessen, The Netherlands. Distinguished by bloom colour.
Comperen 2004 NL AFS5543.

Comperen Lepelaar. Upright. Single.
COROLLA is three quarter flared; opens dark reddish purple (70A); matures reddish purple (70B); 21mm (13/16") long x 29mm (1 1/16") wide. SEPALS are fully up, tips reflexed; light rose (58D) upper surface; reddish purple (58A) lower surface; 24mm (15/16) long x 14mm (9/16") wide. TUBE is magenta (58B); 11mm (7/16") long x 11mm (7/16") wide. FOLIAGE: medium green (137B) upper surface; medium green (138B) lower surface. PARENTAGE: 'Roesse Carme' x ('Madalyn Drago' x 'Roesse Blacky'). Distinguished by bloom shape & colour.
Comperen 2006 NL AFS6215

Comperen Libel. Upright. Double.
COROLLA: three quarter flared, smooth petal margins; opens dark reddish purple (60A); matures dark reddish purple (60C); 17mm (11/16") long x 14mm (9/16") wide. SEPALS: fully up; tips recurved; light rose (63D) upper surface; magenta (63A) lower surface; 21mm (13/16") long x 11mm (7/16") wide. TUBE: magenta (63A); medium length & thickness; 14mm (9/16") long x 7mm (1/4") wide. STAMENS: extend 21mm (13/16") below corolla; magenta (61C) filaments; dark reddish purple (60A) anthers. PISTIL: extends 34mm (1 5/16") below the corolla; magenta (61C) style, pale pink (62D) stigma. BUD: ovate. FOLIAGE: dark green (137A) upper surface; medium green (138B) lower surface. Leaves are 72mm (2 13/16") long x 35mm (1 3/8") wide, ovate shaped, serrulated edges, acute tips and rounded bases. Veins, stems & branches are green. PARENTAGE: {[('Bon Accord' x 'Bicentennial') x ('Vobeglo' x 'Dancing Flame')] x 'Rohees Alrami'} x 'Veenlust'. Medium upright. Makes good upright or standard. Prefers overhead filtered light and cool climate. Best bloom and foliage colour in filtered light. Tested 4 years in Diessen, The Netherlands. Distinguished by bloom colour.
Comperen 2003 NL AFS5276.

Comperen Lijster. Upright. Double.
COROLLA is three quarter flared; opens dark reddish purple (64A); matures red (45C); 21mm (13/16") long x 22mm (7/8") wide. SEPALS are horizontal, tips recurved; magenta (58B) upper surface; dark rose

(58C) lower surface; 28mm (1 1/8) long x 11mm (7/16") wide. TUBE is magenta (58B); 10mm (3/8") long x 9mm (3/8") wide. FOLIAGE: dark green (137A) upper surface; medium green (138B) lower surface. PARENTAGE: 'Sofie Michiels' x 'Roesse Parel'. Distinguished by bloom colour.
Comperen 2006 NL AFS6216.

Comperen Limosa. Upright. Semi Double.
COROLLA: quarter flared, smooth petal margins; opens dark reddish purple (59A); matures magenta (59C); 14mm (9/16") long 24mm (15/16") wide. SEPALS: full down; tips recurved; dark reddish purple (60A) upper & lower surfaces; 22mm (7/8") long x 10mm (3/8") wide. TUBE: dark reddish purple (60A); medium length & thickness; 20mm (13/16") long x 5mm (3/16") wide. STAMENS: extend 10mm (3/8") below corolla; rose (61D) filaments; dark reddish purple (59A) anthers. PISTIL: does not extend below the corolla; rose (61D) style; light yellow (4C) stigma. BUD: round. FOLIAGE: dark green (137A) upper surface; medium green (138A) lower surface. Leaves are 63mm (2 1/2") long x 34mm (1 5/16") wide, ovate shaped, serrulated edges, acute tips and rounded bases. Green veins, stems & branches. PARENTAGE: 'Roesse Apus' x 'Willy Tamerus'. Medium upright. Makes good upright or standard. Prefers overhead filtered light and cool climate. Best bloom and foliage colour in filtered light. Tested 4 years in Diessen, The Netherlands. Distinguished by bloom colour.
Comperen 2004 NL AFS5557.

Comperen Lineola. Trailer. Semi Double.
COROLLA: quarter flared, smooth petal margins; opens & matures white (155D); 22mm (7/8") long 31mm (1 1/4") wide. SEPALS: horizontal; tips recurved; white (155D) upper surface; pale lavender (69D) lower surface; 43mm (1 11/16") long x 17mm (11/16") wide. TUBE: white (155D); short, medium thickness; 7mm (1/4") long x 6mm (1/4") wide. STAMENS: extend 9mm (3/8") below corolla; pale purple (70D) filaments; magenta (63A) anthers. PISTIL: extends 9mm (3/8") below the corolla; white (155D) style; light yellow (4C) stigma. BUD: elliptic, curved, pointed. FOLIAGE: dark green (137A) upper surface; medium green (138A) lower surface. Leaves are 82mm (3 1/4") long x 32mm (1 1/4") wide, lanceolate shaped, serrated edges, acute tips and obtuse bases. Green veins, stems & branches. PARENTAGE: 'Sofie Michiels' x 'Martinus'. Natural trailer. Self branching.

Makes good basket. Prefers overhead filtered light and cool climate. Best bloom and foliage colour in filtered light. Tested 4 years in Diessen, The Netherlands. Distinguished by bloom and foliage combination.
Comperen 2004 NL AFS5525.

Comperen Lory. Upright. Double. SEPALS COROLLA: half flared, smooth petal margins; opens dark reddish purple (60A); matures dark reddish purple (60B); 19mm (3/4") long 17mm (11/16") wide. SEPALS: half up; tips reflexed up; magenta (63B) upper surface; magenta (63A) lower surface; 17mm (11/16") long x 9mm (3/8") wide. TUBE: magenta (63B); medium length & thickness; 10mm (3/8") long x 6mm (1/4") wide. STAMENS: extend 2mm (1/16") below corolla; magenta (63B) filaments; reddish purple (59B) anthers. PISTIL: extends 19mm (3/4") below the corolla; magenta (63B) style; magenta (59D) stigma. BUD: ovate, pointed. FOLIAGE: dark green (137A) upper surface; medium green (138B) lower surface. Leaves are 73mm (2 7/8") long x 46mm (1 13/16") wide, ovate shaped, serrulated edges, acute tips and rounded bases. Red veins, stems & branches. PARENTAGE: 'Roesse Apus' x 'Joman'. Medium upright. Makes good upright or standard. Prefers overhead filtered light and cool climate. Best bloom and foliage colour in filtered light. Tested 4 years in Diessen, The Netherlands. Distinguished by bloom colour.
Comperen 2004 NL AFS5547.

Comperen Lutea. Upright/Trailer. Double. COROLLA: three quarter flared, smooth petal margins; opens & matures white (155D); 24mm (15/16") long 21mm (13/16") wide. SEPALS: fully up; tips recurved; white (155D) upper & lower surfaces; 46mm (1 13/16") long x 16mm (5/8") wide. TUBE: white (155D); medium length & thickness; 12mm (1/2") long x 7mm (1/4") wide. STAMENS: extend 12mm (1/2") below corolla; rose (51C) filaments & anthers. PISTIL: extends 39mm (1 9/16") below the corolla; white (155D) style & stigma. BUD: ovate, curved, pointed. FOLIAGE: dark green (137A) upper surface; medium green (138A) lower surface. Leaves are 74mm (2 15/16") long x 35mm (1 3/8") wide, lanceolate shaped, serrated edges, acute tips and obtuse bases. Red veins, stems & branches. PARENTAGE: 'Sofie Michiels' x 'Martinus'. Lax upright or stiff trailer. Makes good stiff trailer. Prefers overhead filtered light and cool climate. Best bloom and foliage colour in filtered light. Tested 4 years in Diessen, The Netherlands.

Distinguished by bloom and foliage combination.
Comperen 2004 NL AFS5524.

Comperen Major. Upright/Trailer. Single. COROLLA: quarter flared, smooth petal margins; opens light pink (65B); matures pink (62C); 17mm (11/16") long 14mm (9/16") wide. SEPALS: half up; tips reflexed up; pale lavender (65D) upper & lower surfaces; 21mm (13/16") long x 7mm (1/4") wide. TUBE: pale lavender (65D); medium length & thickness; 12mm (1/2") long x 6mm (1/4") wide. STAMENS: extend 8mm (5/16") below corolla; pink (62C) filaments; very pale orange (27C) anthers. PISTIL: extends 19mm (3/4") below the corolla; pale pink (62D) style; very pale orange (27C) stigma. BUD: ovate, pointed. FOLIAGE: dark green (137A) upper surface; medium green (138B) lower surface. Leaves are 47mm (1 7/8") long x 29mm (1 1/8") wide, ovate shaped, serrated edges, acute tips and rounded bases. Green veins, stems & branches. PARENTAGE: 'Sofie Michiels' x 'Judy Salome'. Lax upright or stiff trailer. Makes good stiff trailer. Prefers overhead filtered light and cool climate. Best bloom and foliage colour in filtered light. Tested 4 years in Diessen, The Netherlands. Distinguished by bloom and foliage combination.
Comperen 2004 NL AFS5541.

Comperen Melba. Upright. Double. COROLLA: three quarter flared, smooth petal margins; opens magenta (67B); matures rose (67D); 16mm (5/8") long 24mm (15/16") wide. SEPALS: half up; tips reflexed up; rose (68C) upper surface; dark rose (58C) lower surface; 20mm (13/16") long x 13mm (1/2") wide. TUBE: rose (68C); short & thick; 11mm (7/16") long x 10mm (3/8") wide. STAMENS: extend 8mm (5/16") below corolla; rose (68C) filaments; reddish purple (59B) anthers. PISTIL: does not extend below the corolla; rose (68C) style; light yellow (4C) stigma. BUD: round. FOLIAGE: dark green (139A) upper surface; medium green (137C) lower surface. Leaves are 50mm (2") long x 37mm (1 7/16") wide, ovate shaped, serrulated edges, acute tips and cordate bases. Green veins, stems & branches. PARENTAGE: 'Roesse Carme' x 'Cameron Ryle'. Medium upright. Makes good upright or stsndard. Prefers overhead filtered light and cool climate. Best bloom and foliage colour in filtered light. Tested 4 years in Diessen, The Netherlands. Distinguished by bloom and foliage combination.
Comperen 2004 NL AFS5553.

Comperen Merula. Upright. Single. COROLLA: quarter flared, smooth petal margins; opens dark reddish purple (60A); matures magenta (58B); 20mm (13/16") long 18mm (11/16") wide. SEPALS: half up; tips recurved up; rose (63A) upper surface; magenta (58B) lower surface; 22mm (7/8") long x 11mm (7/16") wide. TUBE: rose (65A); short & thick; 8mm (5/16") long x 8mm (5/16") wide. STAMENS: extend 9mm (3/8") below corolla; magenta (63A) filaments; magenta(59C) anthers. PISTIL: extends 31mm (1 1/4") below the corolla; pink (62A) style & stigma. BUD: elliptic. FOLIAGE: medium green (137B) upper surface; medium green (138B) lower surface. Leaves are 67mm (2 5/8") long x 43mm (1 11/16") wide, ovate shaped, serrulated edges, acute tips and rounded bases. Green veins, stems & branches. PARENTAGE: 'Roesse Carme' x 'Impala'. Medium upright. Makes good upright or standard. Prefers overhead filtered light and cool climate. Best bloom and foliage colour in filtered light. Tested 4 years in Diessen, The Netherlands. Distinguished by bloom and foliage combination. Comperen 2004 NL AFS5532.

Comperen Millitaris. Upright. Semi Double. COROLLA: three quarter flared, smooth petal margins; opens light pink (62B); matures pink (62C); 32mm (1 1/4") long 26mm (1") wide. SEPALS: half down; tips recurved; light rose (73C) upper surface; rose (68B) lower surface; 36mm (1 7/16") long x 15mm (9/16") wide. TUBE: light rose (73B); medium length & thickness; 16mm (5/8") long x 8mm (5/16") wide. STAMENS: extend 22mm (7/8") below corolla; magenta (63B) filaments; pale pink (62D) anthers. PISTIL: extends 31mm (1 1/4") below the corolla; rose (63C) style; pale pink (62D) stigma. BUD: ovate, curved, pointed. FOLIAGE: dark green (137A) upper surface; medium green (138B) lower surface. Leaves are 74mm (2 15/16") long x 36mm (1 7/16") wide, ovate shaped, serrulated edges, acute tips and rounded bases. Green veins, stems & branches. PARENTAGE: 'Indy van Roovert' x 'Delta's Wonder'. Medium upright. Makes good upright or standard. Prefers overhead filtered light and cool climate. Best bloom and foliage colour in filtered light. Tested 4 years in Diessen, The Netherlands. Distinguished by bloom colour. Comperen 2004 NL AFS5535.

Comperen Milvis. Upright/Trailer. Semi Double. COROLLA: three quarter flared, smooth petal margins; opens pink (62A); matures rose (65A); 23mm (15/16") long 21mm (13/16") wide. SEPALS: fully up; tips recurved; rose (63C) upper surface; dark rose (58C) lower surface; 27mm (1 1/16") long x 12mm (1/2") wide. TUBE: rose (63C); short & thick; 10mm (3/8") long x 10mm (3/8") wide. STAMENS: extend 4mm (3/16") below corolla; magenta (68A) filaments; dark reddish purple (59A) anthers. PISTIL: extends 22mm (7/8") below the corolla; magenta (68A) style; light rose (58D) stigma. BUD: elliptic, pointed. FOLIAGE: medium green (137B) upper surface; medium green (137D) lower surface. Leaves are 61mm (2 3/8") long x 42mm (1 5/8") wide, ovate shaped, serrated edges, obtuse tips and rounded bases. Green veins, stems & branches. PARENTAGE: 'Roesse Carme' x 'Madalyn Drago'. Lax upright or stiff trailer. Makes good stiff trailer. Prefers overhead filtered light and cool climate. Best bloom and foliage colour in filtered light. Tested 4 years in Diessen, The Netherlands. Distinguished by bloom colour. Comperen 2004 NL AFS5533.

Comperen Minor. Trailer. Double. SEPALS COROLLA: three quarter flared, smooth petal margins; opens violet (75A); matures light rose (73C); 20mm (13/16") long 23mm (15/16") wide. SEPALS: horizontal; tips reflexed; light pink (62B) upper surface; pink (62A) lower surface; 37mm (1 7/16") long x 14mm (9/16") wide. TUBE: light pink (62B); short & thick; 9mm (3/8") long x 8mm (5/16") wide. STAMENS: extend 10mm (3/8") below corolla; light rose (73C) filaments; magenta (63A) anthers. PISTIL: extends 33mm (1 5/16") below the corolla; pale rose (73D) style; light yellow (4C) stigma. BUD: ovate, pointed. FOLIAGE: dark green (137A) upper surface; medium green (138A) lower surface. Leaves are 50mm (2") long x 29mm (1 1/8") wide, ovate shaped, serrulated edges, acute tips and rounded bases. Green veins, stems & branches. PARENTAGE: 'Sofie Michiels' x 'Judy Salome'. Lax upright or stiff trailer. Makes good stiff trailer. Prefers overhead filtered light and cool climate. Best bloom and foliage colour in filtered light. Tested 4 years in Diessen, The Netherlands. Distinguished by bloom colour. Comperen 2004 NL AFS5560.

Comperen Nachtegaal. Upright. Single. COROLLA is quarter flared with smooth petal margins; opens violet (76A); matures light violet (84B); 19mm (3/4") long x 21mm (13/16") wide. SEPALS are horizontal, tips recurved; light rose (73C) upper surface; dark rose (58C) lower surface; 27mm (1

1/16") long x 8mm (5/16") wide. TUBE is light rose (73C); medium length & thickness; 9mm (3/8") long x 7mm (1/4") wide. FOLIAGE: medium green (137C) upper surface; medium green (137D) lower surface. Leaves are 56mm (2 3/16") long x 30mm (1 3/16") wide, ovate shaped. PARENTAGE: 'Roesse Carme' x 'Comperen Stepera'. Distinguished by bloom colour.
Comperen 2005 NL AFS5918.

Comperen Nana. Upright. Double. COROLLA: full flared, smooth petal margins; opens purple (77A); matures reddish purple (72B); 24mm (15/16") long 26mm (1") wide. SEPALS: fully up; tips recurved; dark rose (58C) upper surface; magenta (58B) lower surface; 20mm (13/16") long x 14mm (9/16") wide. TUBE: dark rose (58C); short & thick; 6mm (1/4") long x 6mm (1/4") wide. STAMENS: extend 21mm (13/16") below corolla; magenta (58B) filaments; reddish purple (58A) anthers. PISTIL: extends 44mm (1 3/4") below the corolla; magenta (58B) style; light rose (58D) stigma. BUD: round, pointed. FOLIAGE: dark green (137A) upper surface; medium green (137B) lower surface. Leaves are 66mm (2 5/8") long x 43mm (1 11/16") wide, ovate shaped, serrulated edges, acute tips and rounded bases. Green veins, stems & branches. PARENTAGE: 'Roesse Apus' x 'Maxima'. Medium upright. Makes good upright or standard. Prefers overhead filtered light and cool climate. Best bloom and foliage colour in filtered light. Tested 4 years in Diessen, The Netherlands. Distinguished by bloom and foliage combination.
Comperen 2004 NL AFS5558.

Comperen Nivalis. Upright/Trailer. Single. COROLLA: three quarter flared, smooth petal margins; opens magenta (63A); matures magenta (63B); 22mm (7/8") long 26mm (1") wide. SEPALS: half up; tips recurved up; dark rose (54A) upper surface; red (47B) lower surface; 26mm (1") long x 13mm (1/2") wide. TUBE: dark rose (54A); short & thick; 7mm (1/4") long x 9mm (3/8") wide. STAMENS: extend 20mm (13/16") below corolla; dark red (47A) filaments; red (50A) anthers. PISTIL: extends 41mm (1 5/8") below the corolla; pink (49A) style; light yellow (4C) stigma. BUD: ovate, pointed. FOLIAGE: dark green (137A) upper surface; medium green (138A) lower surface. Leaves are 42mm (1 5/8") long x 31mm (1 1/4") wide, ovate shaped, serrulated edges, acute tips and rounded bases. Green veins, stems & branches. PARENTAGE: 'Roesse Carme' x

'Cameron Ryle'. Lax upright or stiff trailer. Makes good stiff trailer. Prefers overhead filtered light and cool climate. Best bloom and foliage colour in filtered light. Tested 4 years in Diessen, The Netherlands. Distinguished by bloom and foliage combination.
Comperen 2004 NL AFS5542.

Comperen Ornatus. Upright. Semi Double. COROLLA: three quarter flared, smooth petal margins; opens dark purple (78A); matures magenta (67B); 19mm (3/4") long 24mm (15/16") wide. SEPALS: horizontal; tips recurved; rose (52B) upper surface; rose (51B) lower surface; 24mm (15/16") long x 11mm (7/16") wide. TUBE: rose (52B); short & thick; 12mm (1/2") long x 9mm (3/8") wide. STAMENS: extend 10mm (3/8") below corolla; dark rose (58C) filaments; magenta (58B) anthers. PISTIL: extends 31mm (1 1/4") below the corolla; dark rose (58C) style & stigma. BUD: ovate, pointed. FOLIAGE: dark green (137A) upper surface; medium green (138B) lower surface. Leaves are 54mm (2 1/8") long x 39mm (1 9/16") wide, ovate shaped, serrulated edges, acute tips and rounded bases. Green veins, stems & branches. PARENTAGE: 'Roesse Carme' x 'Madalyn Drago'. Medium upright. Makes good upright or standard. Prefers overhead filtered light and cool climate. Best bloom and foliage colour in filtered light. Tested 4 years in Diessen, The Netherlands. Distinguished by bloom colour.
Comperen 2004 NL AFS5540.

Comperen Paapje. Upright/Trailer. Single. COROLLA: Half flared; opens reddish purple (64B); matures magenta (58B); 22mm (7/8") long x 26mm (1") wide. SEPALS: half up, tips reflexed up; pale purple (75D) upper surface; rose (65A) lower surface; 32mm (1 1/4") long x 10mm (3/8") wide. TUBE: pale purple (75D); medium length & thickness; 19mm (3/4") long x 7mm (1/4") wide. FOLIAGE is dark green (137A) upper surface; medium green (137C) lower surface. PARENTAGE: 'Roesse Lupus' x 'Anna Pauline'.
Comperen 2007 NL AFS6601.

Comperen Patagonis. Upright/Trailer. Single. COROLLA: half flared, smooth petal margins; opens purple (77A); matures reddish purple (74A); 21mm (13/16") long 17mm (11/16") wide. SEPALS: horizontal; tips recurved; light rose (73C) upper surface; light reddish purple (73A) lower surface; 32mm (1 1/4") long x 11mm (7/16") wide. TUBE: pale rose (73D); medium length &

thickness; 14mm (9/16") long x 8mm (5/16") wide. STAMENS: extend 7mm (1/4") below corolla; rose (68B) filaments; dark reddish purple (59A) anthers. PISTIL: extends 26mm (1") below the corolla; rose (68B) style; light yellow (4C) stigma. BUD: ovate, curved, pointed. FOLIAGE: medium green (137B) upper surface; medium green (138B) lower surface. Leaves are 53mm (2 1/16") long x 42mm (1 5/8") wide, ovate shaped, serrated edges, obtuse tips and rounded bases. Green veins, stems & branches. PARENTAGE: 'Orangeblossom' x 'Judy Salome'. Lax upright or stiff trailer. Makes good stiff trailer. Prefers overhead filtered light and cool climate. Best bloom and foliage colour in filtered light. Tested 4 years in Diessen, The Netherlands. Distinguished by bloom colour. Comperen 2004 NL AFS5552.

Comperen Pica. Upright. Semi Double. COROLLA: half flared, smooth petal margins; opens dark purple (78A); matures magenta (67B); 14mm (9/16") long 21mm (13/16") wide. SEPALS: half up; tips recurved up; rose (67D) upper surface; magenta (58B) lower surface; 19mm (3/4") long x 11mm (7/16") wide. TUBE: rose (67D); short & thick; 8mm (5/16") long x 8mm (5/16") wide. STAMENS: extend 9mm (3/8") below corolla; rose (61D) filaments; reddish purple (59B) anthers. PISTIL: extends 14mm (9/16") below the corolla; magenta (61C) style; light yellow (4C) stigma. BUD: cordate. FOLIAGE: medium green (137B) upper surface; medium green (138B) lower surface. Leaves are 42mm (1 11/16") long x 32mm (1 1/4") wide, ovate shaped, serrulated edges, acute tips and rounded bases. Red veins, stems & branches. PARENTAGE: 'Roesse Carme' x 'Corrie Spoelstra'. Medium upright. Makes good upright or standard. Prefers overhead filtered light and cool climate. Best bloom and foliage colour in filtered light. Tested 4 years in Diessen, The Netherlands. Distinguished by bloom colour. Comperen 2004 NL AFS5529.

Comperen Plevier. Upright/Trailer. Double. COROLLA: three quarter flared, smooth petal margins; opens violet (75A); matures magenta (68A); 21mm (13/16") long 22mm (7/8") wide. SEPALS: half up; tips recurved up; rose (65A) upper surface; rose (63C) lower surface; 18mm (11/16") long x 14mm (9/16") wide. TUBE: rose (65A); medium length & thickness; 12mm (1/2") long x 8mm (5/16") wide. STAMENS: extend 12mm (1/2") below corolla; magenta (63B) filaments; magenta (63A) anthers. PISTIL: extends

29mm (1 1/8") below the corolla; light rose (63D) style; light yellow (5C) stigma. BUD: cordate. FOLIAGE: dark green (137A) upper surface; medium green (138A) lower surface. Leaves are 67mm (2 5/8") long x 37mm (1 7/16") wide, ovate shaped, serrated edges, acute tips and rounded bases. Green veins, stems & branches. PARENTAGE: 'Roesse Carme' x 'Corrie Spoelstra'. Lax upright or stiff trailer. Makes good stiff trailer. Prefers overhead filtered light and cool climate. Best bloom and foliage colour in filtered light. Tested 4 years in Diessen, The Netherlands. Distinguished by bloom colour. Comperen 2004 NL AFS5528.

Comperen Prachtkever. Upright/Trailer. Double. COROLLA: half flared, smooth petal margins; opens dark purple (79A); matures dark reddish purple (60A); 20mm (13/16") long x 22mm (7/8") wide. SEPALS: fully up; tips recurved; reddish purple (61B) upper surface; dark reddish purple (60B) lower surface; 17mm (11/16") long x 10mm (3/8") wide. TUBE: reddish purple (61B); medium length & thickness; 12mm (1/2") long x 7mm (1/4") wide. STAMENS: extend 12mm (1/2") below corolla; purple (71A) filaments; dark purple (79A) anthers. PISTIL: extends 34mm (1 5/16") below the corolla; reddish purple (74B) style, light rose (63D) stigma. BUD: ovate. FOLIAGE: dark green (137A) upper surface; medium green (138B) lower surface. Leaves are 62mm (2 7/16") long x 33mm (1 5/16") wide, ovate shaped, serrulated edges, acute tips and rounded bases. Veins, stems & branches are green. PARENTAGE: {[('Bon Accord' x 'Bicentennial') x ('Vobeglo' x 'Dancing Flame')] x 'Rohees Alrami'} x 'Maxima'. Lax upright or stiff trailer. Makes good stiff trailer. Prefers overhead filtered light and cool climate. Best bloom and foliage colour in filtered light. Tested 4 years in Diessen, The Netherlands. Distinguished by bloom colour. Comperen 2003 NL AFS5266.

Comperen Prasina. Upright. Single. COROLLA: half flared, smooth petal margins; opens dark rose (58C); matures light rose (58D); 20mm (13/16") long 16mm (5/8") wide. SEPALS: half up; tips recurved up; dark rose (58C) upper & lower surface; 26mm (1") long x 14mm (9/16") wide. TUBE: light rose (58D); medium length & thickness; 12mm (1/2") long x 8mm (5/16") wide. STAMENS: extend 10mm (3/8") below corolla; pink (62C) filaments; reddish purple (59B) anthers. PISTIL: extends 21mm (13/16") below the corolla; pink (62C) style;

light pink (65C) stigma. BUD: cordate, pointed. FOLIAGE: dark green (137A) upper surface; medium green (138A) lower surface. Leaves are 61mm (2 3/8") long x 40mm (19/16") wide, ovate shaped, serrulated edges, acute tips and rounded bases. Green veins, stems & branches. PARENTAGE: 'Roesse Carme' x 'Delta's Wonder'. Medium upright. Makes good upright or standard. Prefers overhead filtered light and cool climate. Best bloom and foliage colour in filtered light. Tested 4 years in Diessen, The Netherlands. Distinguished by bloom colour. Comperen 2004 NL AFS5534.

Comperen Pullaria. Upright. Single. COROLLA: half flared, smooth petal margins; opens magenta (67B) & rose (47C); matures dark rose (67C) & rose (47C); 21mm (13/16") long 23mm (15/16") wide. SEPALS: half up; tips recurved up; dark rose (54A) upper surface; red (53C) lower surface; 39mm (1 9/16") long x 13mm (1/2") wide. TUBE: dark rose (54A); medium length & thickness; 12mm (1/2") long x 6mm (1/4") wide. STAMENS: extend 12mm (1/2") below corolla; magenta (63A) filaments & anthers. PISTIL: extends 36mm (1 7/16") below the corolla; magenta (58B) style; light yellow (4C) stigma. BUD: ovate, pointed. FOLIAGE: medium green (137B) upper surface; light green (138C) lower surface. Leaves are 55mm (2 3/16") long x 39mm (1 9/16") wide, ovate shaped, serrulated edges, acute tips and cordate bases. Green veins, stems & branches. PARENTAGE: 'Swanley Gem' x 'WALZ Piano'. Medium upright. Makes good upright or standard. Prefers overhead filtered light and cool climate. Best bloom and foliage colour in filtered light. Tested 4 years in Diessen, The Netherlands. Distinguished by bloom and foliage combination. Comperen 2004 NL AFS5555.

Comperen Putter. Upright. Single. COROLLA: three quarter flared, smooth petal margins; opens purple (71A); matures dark reddish purple (60A); 23mm (15/16") long 24mm (15/16") wide. SEPALS: half up; tips recurved up; red (53C) upper surface; rose (68B) lower surface; 24mm (15/16") long x 9mm (3/8") wide. TUBE: red (53C); medium length & thickness; 13mm (1/2") long x 5mm (3/16") wide. STAMENS: extend 17mm (11/16") below corolla; magenta (63B) filaments; reddish purple (64B) anthers. PISTIL: extends 26mm (1") below the corolla; magenta (63B) style; pale lavender (65D) stigma. BUD: ovate, curved, pointed. FOLIAGE: medium green (137C) upper

surface; medium green (138B) lower surface. Leaves are 54mm (2 1/8") long x 26mm (1") wide, lanceolate shaped, serrulated edges, acute tips and obtuse bases. Green veins, stems & branches. PARENTAGE: 'Roesse Apus' x 'Wentworth'. Medium upright. Makes good upright or standard. Prefers overhead filtered light and cool climate. Best bloom and foliage colour in filtered light. Tested 4 years in Diessen, The Netherlands. Distinguished by bloom colour. Comperen 2004 NL AFS5539.

Comperen Rietgans. Upright. Double. COROLLA is three quarter flared with smooth petal margins; opens dark reddish purple (64A); matures reddish purple (61B); 14mm (9/16") long x 19mm (3/4") wide. SEPALS are horizontal, tips recurved; light rose (58D) upper surface; dark rose (58C) lower surface; 19mm (3/4") long x 9mm (3/8") wide. TUBE is light rose (58D); medium length & thickness; 14mm (9/16") long x 6mm (1/4") wide. FOLIAGE: medium green (137C) upper surface; medium green (138B) lower surface. Leaves are 43mm (1 11/16") long x 32mm (1 1/4") wide, ovate shaped. PARENTAGE: 'La Campanella' x 'Marcel Michiels'. Distinguished by bloom & foliage combination. Comperen 2005 NL AFS5919.

Comperen Roek. Upright. Semi Double. COROLLA: Three quarter flared; opens light violet (84B); matures light purple (80C); 22mm (7/8") long x 25mm (1") wide. SEPALS: fully up, tips recurved; pale pink (62D) upper & lower surfaces; 25mm (1") long x 9mm (5/16") wide. TUBE: pale pink (62D); medium length & thickness; 19mm (3/4") long x 7mm (1/4") wide. FOLIAGE is dark green (137A) upper surface; medium green (137C) lower surface. PARENTAGE: 'Comperen Korhoen' x 'Comperen Lutea'. Comperen 2007 NL AFS6604.

Comperen Roodborst. Upright. Single. COROLLA is quarter flared with smooth petal margins; opens purple (79C); matures dark reddish purple (70A); 14mm (9/16") long x 18mm (11/16") wide. SEPALS are horizontal, tips recurved; magenta (58B) upper & lower surfaces; 17mm (11/16") long x 11mm (7/16") wide. TUBE is magenta (58B); short, medium thickness; 7mm (1/4") long x 5mm (3/16") wide. FOLIAGE: medium green (137B) upper surface; medium green (138B) lower surface. Leaves are 58mm (2 5/16") long x 32mm (1 1/4") wide, ovate shaped. PARENTAGE: 'Roesse Carme' x [('Roesse

Apus' x 'Roesse Apus') x 'Maxima's Baby'].
Distinguished by bloom & foliage combination.
Comperen 2005 NL AFS5924.

Comperen Roodmuis. Upright. Single.
COROLLA: half flared; opens dark purple (79A); matures purple (71A); 9mm (5/16") long x 12mm (7/16") wide. SEPALS: fully up, tips reflexed; dark reddish purple (61A) upper & lower surfaces; 24mm (15/16") long x 8mm (5/16") wide. TUBE: dark reddish purple (61A); 12mm (7/16") long x 5mm (3/16") wide. FOLIAGE is dark green (137A) upper surface; medium green (138A) lower surface. PARENTAGE: 'Roesse Blacky' x 'Rosea'.
Comperen 2008 NL AFS6886.

Comperen Severa. Upright. Double.
COROLLA: three quarter flared, smooth petal margins; opens & matures white (155D); 25mm (1") long 21mm (13/16") wide. SEPALS: horizontal; tips recurved; white (155D), tipped green, upper surface; white (155D) lower surface; 46mm (1 13/16") long x 11mm (7/16") wide. TUBE: white (155D); medium length & thickness; 12mm (1/2") long x 6mm (1/4") wide. STAMENS: extend 7mm (1/4") below corolla; light pink (65C) filaments; magenta (61C) anthers. PISTIL: extends 36mm (1 7/16") below the corolla; white (155D) style & stigma. BUD: elliptic. FOLIAGE: dark green (137A) upper surface; medium green (138B) lower surface. Leaves are 87mm (3 7/16") long x 37mm (1 7/16") wide, lanceolate shaped, serrated edges, acute tips and acute bases. Green veins, stems & branches. PARENTAGE: 'Sofie Michiels' x 'Martinus'. Medium upright. Makes good upright or standard. Prefers overhead filtered light and cool climate. Best bloom and foliage colour in filtered light. Tested 4 years in Diessen, The Netherlands. Distinguished by bloom and foliage combination.
Comperen 2004 NL AFS5530.

Comperen Snip. Upright. Single. COROLLA: Three quarter flared; opens purple (83C); matures light purple (80C); 14mm (9/16") long x 19mm (3/4") wide. SEPALS: horizontal, tips recurved; light rose (58D) tipped green upper surface; light rose (58D) lower surface; 17mm (5/8") long x 7mm (1/4") wide. TUBE: light rose (58D); short & thick; 12mm (7/16") long x 7mm (1/4") wide. FOLIAGE is dark green (137A) upper surface; medium green (137C) lower surface.

PARENTAGE: 'Comperen Korhoen' x 'Doris Deaves'.
Comperen 2007 NL AFS6605.

Comperen Specht. Upright. Single.
COROLLA is half flared with turned up petal margins; opens dark reddish purple (61A); matures magenta (61C); 20mm (13/16") long x 14mm (9/16") wide. SEPALS are horizontal, tips recurved; red (52A) upper & lower surfaces; 24mm (15/16") long x 8mm (3/16") wide. TUBE is red (52A); medium length & thickness; 9mm (3/8") long x 6mm (1/4") wide. FOLIAGE: dark green (137A) upper surface; medium green (138B) lower surface. Leaves are 54mm (2 1/8") long x 36mm (1 7/16") wide, lanceolate shaped. PARENTAGE: 'Roesse Carme' x 'Centenary'. Distinguished by bloom colour.
Comperen 2005 NL AFS5922.

Comperen Sperwer. Trailer. Double.
COROLLA: half flared, smooth petal margins; opens light pink (62B); matures pale lavender (65D); 21mm (13/16") long 17mm (11/16") wide. SEPALS: horizontal; tips recurved; light pink (65C) upper surface; light pink (65B) lower surface; 26mm (1") long x 14mm (9/16") wide. TUBE: light pink (65C); medium length & thickness; 14mm (9/16") long x 7mm (1/4") wide. STAMENS: extend 10mm (3/8") below corolla; pink (62A) filaments & anthers. PISTIL: extends 19mm (3/4") below the corolla; pink (62C) style; light yellow (4C) stigma. BUD: round, pointed. FOLIAGE: dark green (137A) upper surface; medium green (138A) lower surface. Leaves are 81mm (3 3/16") long x 34mm (1 5/16") wide, lanceolate shaped, serrated edges, acute tips and rounded bases. Green veins, stems & branches. PARENTAGE: 'Sofie Michiels' x 'Guurtje'. Natural trailer. Makes good basket. Prefers overhead filtered light and cool climate. Best bloom and foliage colour in filtered light. Tested 4 years in Diessen, The Netherlands. Distinguished by bloom colour.
Comperen 2004 NL AFS5559.

Comperen Staartmees. Trailer. Double.
COROLLA: three quarter flared; opens & matures white (155D); 20mm (3/4") long x 24mm (15/16") wide. SEPALS: fully up, tips reflexed; pale purple (75D) upper surface; light pink (65B) lower surface; 35mm (1 3/8") long x 17mm (5/8") wide. TUBE: pale purple (75D); 17mm (5/8") long x 8mm (5/16") wide. FOLIAGE is dark green (139A) upper surface; medium green (137B) lower surface.

PARENTAGE: 'Fenne Comperen' x 'Comperen Lutea'.
Comperen 2008 NL AFS6883.

Comperen Steenuil. Trailer. Double. COROLLA: three quarter flared; opens purple (77A); matures purple (82A); 26mm (1") long x 26mm (1") wide. SEPALS: fully up, tips reflexed; pale rose (73D) upper surface; light reddish purple (73A) lower surface; 32mm (1 1/4") long x 17mm (5/8") wide. TUBE: pale rose (73D); 12mm (7/16") long x 8mm (5/16") wide. FOLIAGE is dark green (137A) upper surface; medium green (137C) lower surface. PARENTAGE: 'Fenne Comperen' x 'Boy Comperen'.
Comperen 2008 NL AFS6885.

Comperen Stepera. Upright/Trailer. Single. COROLLA: half flared, smooth petal margins; opens & matures white (155D); 19mm (3/4") long 19mm (3/4") wide. SEPALS: horizontal; tips reflexed; pale lavender (69D) upper & lower surfaces; 27mm (1 1/16") long x 7mm (1/4") wide. TUBE: pale pink (69A); medium length & thickness; 12mm (1/2") long x 6mm (1/4") wide. STAMENS: extend 12mm (1/2") below corolla; magenta (68A) filaments; pale lavender (69C) anthers. PISTIL: extends 37mm (1 7/16") below the corolla; light rose (68D) style; pale lavender (69C) stigma. BUD: ovate, pointed. FOLIAGE: dark green (137A) upper surface; medium green (138B) lower surface. Leaves are 61mm (2 3/8") long x 37mm (1 7/16") wide, ovate shaped, serrated edges, acute tips and rounded bases. Green veins & branches; red stems. PARENTAGE: 'Indy van Roovert' x 'Delta's Wonder'. Lax upright or stiff trailer. Makes good stiff trailer. Prefers overhead filtered light and cool climate. Best bloom and foliage colour in filtered light. Tested 4 years in Diessen, The Netherlands. Distinguished by bloom and foliage combination.
Comperen 2004 NL AFS5548.

Comperen Sultanea. Upright. Semi Double. COROLLA: half flared, smooth petal margins; opens pale purple (75C); matures pale purple (75D); 25mm (1") long 26mm (1") wide. SEPALS: horizontal; tips recurved; pale lavender (69C) upper surface; pale pink (69A) lower surface; 41mm (1 5/8") long x 17mm (11/16") wide. TUBE: rose (68C); medium length & thickness; 19mm (3/4") long x 7mm (1/4") wide. STAMENS: extend 6mm (1/4") below corolla; magenta (68A) filaments; dark reddish purple (64A) anthers. PISTIL: extends 31mm (1 1/4") below the corolla; light rose (68D) style; light yellow (4C)

stigma. BUD: ovate, pointed. FOLIAGE: dark green (137A) upper surface; medium green (138B) lower surface. Leaves are 61mm (2 3/8") long x 36mm (1 7/16") wide, ovate shaped, serrated edges, acute tips and rounded bases. Green veins, stems & branches. PARENTAGE: 'Katrien Michiels' x 'Delta's Wonder'. Medium upright. Makes good upright or standard. Prefers overhead filtered light and cool climate. Best bloom and foliage colour in filtered light. Tested 4 years in Diessen, The Netherlands. Distinguished by bloom colour.
Comperen 2004 NL AFS5561.

Comperen Taranta. Upright/Trailer. Single. COROLLA: half flared, smooth petal margins; opens violet (76A); matures pale purple (75C); 32mm (1 1/4") long 34mm (1 5/16") wide. SEPALS: horizontal; tips recurved; pale lavender (69D) upper & lower surfaces; 44mm (1 3/4") long x 12mm (1/2") wide. TUBE: pale lavender (69D); medium length & thickness; 14mm (9/16") long x 6mm (1/4") wide. STAMENS: extend 10mm (3/8") below corolla; violet (75A) filaments & anthers. PISTIL: extends 36mm (1 7/16") below the corolla; pale purple (75D) style; light yellow (4C) stigma. BUD: ovate, pointed. FOLIAGE: medium green (137C) upper surface; medium green (138B) lower surface. Leaves are 72mm (2 13/16") long x 37mm (1 7/16") wide, cordate shaped, serrulated edges, acute tips and rounded bases. Green veins, stems & branches. PARENTAGE: 'Katrien Michiels' x 'Delta's Wonder'. Lax upright or stiff trailer. Makes good stiff trailer. Prefers overhead filtered light and cool climate. Best bloom and foliage colour in filtered light. Tested 4 years in Diessen, The Netherlands. Distinguished by bloom colour.
Comperen 2004 NL AFS5545.

Comperen Torenvalk. Upright. Single. COROLLA is quarter flared with smooth petal margins; opens purple (83A); matures purple (77A); 9mm (3/8") long x 19mm (3/4") wide. SEPALS are half up, tips reflexed up; magenta (63A) upper & lower surfaces; 16mm (5/8") long x 10mm (3/8") wide. TUBE is magenta (63A); short & thick; 4mm (3/16") long x 6mm (1/4") wide. FOLIAGE: dark green (137A) upper surface; medium green (138A) lower surface. Leaves are 58mm (2 5/16") long x 46mm (1 13/16") wide, cordate shaped. PARENTAGE: 'Roesse Carme' x [('Roesse Apus' x 'Roesse Apus') x 'Maxima's Baby']. Distinguished by erect blooms.
Comperen 2005 NL AFS5923.

Comperen Tortel. Upright/Trailer. Single. COROLLA: unflared; opens violet (83D); matures dark purple (78A); 15mm (9/16") long x 10mm (3/8") wide. SEPALS: fully up, tips recurved; magenta (67B) upper & lower surfaces; 24mm (15/16") long x 7mm (1/4") wide. TUBE: magenta (67B); 10mm (3/8") long x 5mm (3/16") wide. FOLIAGE is dark green (137A) upper surface; medium green (137C) lower surface. PARENTAGE: 'Rosea' x 'Fenne Comperen'.
Comperen 2008 NL AFS6887.

Comperen Trichora. Upright. Single. COROLLA: three quarter flared, smooth petal margins; opens dark reddish purple (61A); matures reddish purple (61B); 21mm (13/16") long 17mm (11/16") wide. SEPALS: fully up; tips reflexed; dark rose (51A) upper surface; red (52A) lower surface; 29mm (1 1/8") long x 12mm (1/2") wide. TUBE: dark rose (51A); medium length & thickness; 10mm (3/8") long x 6mm (1/4") wide. STAMENS: extend 8mm (5/16") below corolla; dark rose (51A) filaments; dark red (46A) anthers. PISTIL: extends 22mm (7/8") below the corolla; dark rose (51A) style; pink (51D) stigma. BUD: ovate, pointed. FOLIAGE: medium green (137C) upper surface; medium green (138A) lower surface. Leaves are 57mm (2 1/4") long x 31mm (1 1/4") wide, ovate shaped, serrulated edges, acute tips and rounded bases. Green veins, stems & branches. PARENTAGE: 'Sofie Michiels' x ('Roesse Apus' x 'Maxima'). Medium upright. Makes good upright or standard. Prefers overhead filtered light and cool climate. Best bloom and foliage colour in filtered light. Tested 4 years in Diessen, The Netherlands. Distinguished by bloom colour.
Comperen 2004 NL AFS5536.

Comperen Trontalis. Trailer. Semi Double. COROLLA: quarter flared, smooth petal margins; opens dark purple (79B); matures purple (71A); 21mm (13/16") long 24mm (15/16") wide. SEPALS: half up; tips recurved up; dark reddish purple (61A) upper & lower surfaces; 26mm (1") long x 10mm (3/8") wide. TUBE: dark reddish purple (61A); medium length & thickness; 8mm (5/16") long x 4mm (3/16") wide. STAMENS: extend 12mm (1/2") below corolla; purple (71A) filaments; dark reddish purple (59A) anthers. PISTIL: extends 26mm (1") below the corolla; dark reddish purple (64A) style; light rose (68D) stigma. BUD: elliptic, curved, pointed. FOLIAGE: dark green (137A) upper surface; medium green (138B) lower surface. Leaves are 62mm (2

7/16") long x 31mm (1 1/4") wide, lanceolate shaped, serrated edges, acute tips and rounded bases. Green veins, stems & branches. PARENTAGE: ('Sofie Michiels' x 'Rohees Metallah') x 'Anne Pauline'. Natural trailer. Makes good basket. Prefers overhead filtered light and cool climate. Best bloom and foliage colour in filtered light. Tested 4 years in Diessen, The Netherlands. Distinguished by bloom colour.
Comperen 2004 NL AFS5527.

Comperen Tureluur. Upright. Semi Double. COROLLA is half flared with smooth petal margins; opens red (45A); matures red (45C); 14mm (9/16") long x 12mm (1/2") wide. SEPALS are fully up, tips reflexed; magenta (62A) upper & lower surfaces; 19mm (3/4") long x 10mm (3/8") wide. TUBE is magenta (58B); short & thick; 16mm (5/8") long x 6mm (1/4") wide. FOLIAGE: medium green (138A) upper surface; medium green (138B) lower surface. Leaves are 58mm (2 5/16") long x 37mm (1 7/16") wide, cordate shaped. PARENTAGE: 'Roesse Carme' x 'Lye's Unique'. Distinguished by bloom shape.
Comperen 2005 NL AFS5911.

Comperen Vernalis. Upright. Semi Double. COROLLA: half flared, smooth petal margins; opens reddish purple (61B); matures magenta (61C); 17mm (11/16") long 12mm (1/2") wide. SEPALS: fully up; tips recurved; red (53B) upper surface; red (45C) lower surface; 29mm (1 1/8") long x 11mm (7/16") wide. TUBE: red (53B); medium length & thickness; 14mm (9/16") long x 8mm (5/16") wide. STAMENS: extend 10mm (3/8") below corolla; magenta (61C) filaments & anthers. PISTIL: extends 26mm (1") below the corolla; magenta (58B) style; light rose (58D) stigma. BUD: elliptic, pointed. FOLIAGE: dark green (137A) upper surface; medium green (137D) lower surface. Leaves are 57mm (2 1/4") long x 30mm (1 3/16") wide, lanceolate shaped, serrulated edges, acute tips and rounded bases. Red veins, stems & branches. PARENTAGE: 'Roesse Apus' x 'Willie Tamerus'. Medium upright. Makes good upright or standard. Prefers overhead filtered light and cool climate. Best bloom and foliage colour in filtered light. Tested 4 years in Diessen, The Netherlands. Distinguished by erect blooms.
Comperen 2004 NL AFS5523.

Comperen Vulgaris. Upright. Double. COROLLA: half flared, smooth petal margins; opens purple (71A); matures dark reddish purple (60B); 17mm (11/16") long 23mm

(15/16") wide. SEPALS: half up; tips recurved up; magenta (58B) upper surface; red (52A) lower surface; 28mm (1 1/8") long x 14mm (9/16") wide. TUBE: magenta (58B); medium length & thickness; 7mm (1/4") long x 6mm (1/4") wide. STAMENS: extend 12mm (1/2") below corolla; dark reddish purple (60C) filaments; dark reddish purple (60A) anthers. PISTIL: extends 26mm (1") below the corolla; dark reddish purple (60C) style; light rose (58D) stigma. BUD: ovate, pointed. FOLIAGE: dark green (137A) upper surface; medium green (138B) lower surface. Leaves are 76mm (3") long x 41mm (1 5/8") wide, ovate shaped, serrulated edges, acute tips and rounded bases. Green veins, stems & branches. PARENTAGE: 'Sofie Michiels' x ('Roesse Apus' x 'Maxima'). Medium upright. Makes good upright or standard. Prefers overhead filtered light and cool climate. Best bloom and foliage colour in filtered light. Tested 4 years in Diessen, The Netherlands. Distinguished by bloom and foliage combination.
Comperen 2004 NL AFS5564.

Comperen Vuurvinkje. Upright. Semi Double. COROLLA: half flared, smooth petal margins; opens & matures pink (52A); 12mm (1/2") long 18mm (11/16") wide. SEPALS: fully up; tips reflexed; red (52A), tipped green, upper surface; reddish orange (42A) lower surface; 17mm (11/16") long x 12mm (1/2") wide. TUBE: red (52A); short & thick; 7mm (1/4") long x 8mm (5/16") wide. STAMENS: extend 8mm (5/16") below corolla; rose (63C) filaments; light rose (73B) anthers. PISTIL: extends 16mm (5/8") below the corolla; rose (63C) style; light pink (62B) stigma. BUD: round. FOLIAGE: medium green (137B) upper surface; medium green (138B) lower surface. Leaves are 61mm (2 3/8") long x 41mm (1 5/8") wide, cordate shaped, serrulated edges, obtuse tips and rounded bases. Green veins, stems & branches. PARENTAGE: 'Roesse Carme' x 'Roesse Apus'. Medium upright. Makes good upright or standard. Prefers overhead filtered light and cool climate. Best bloom and foliage colour in filtered light. Tested 4 years in Diessen, The Netherlands. Distinguished by bloom and foliage combination.
Comperen 2004 NL AFS5522.

Comperen Wats. Upright. Double. COROLLA: three quarter flared, smooth petal margins; opens purple (71A); matures dark reddish purple (61A); 24mm (15/16") long x 27mm (1 1/16") wide. SEPALS: half up; tips recurved up; reddish purple (64B) upper surface; magenta (63B) lower surface; 22mm (7/8") long x 14mm (9/16") wide. TUBE: dark rose (64C); medium length & thickness; 12mm (1/2") long x 6mm (1/4") wide. STAMENS: extend 14mm (9/16") below corolla; reddish purple (61B) filaments; dark reddish purple (61A) anthers. PISTIL: extends 42mm (1 11/16") below the corolla; magenta (61C) style, white (155B) stigma. BUD: spherical. FOLIAGE: dark green (137A) upper surface; medium green (138A) lower surface. Leaves are 76mm (3") long x 52mm (2 1/16") wide, cordate shaped, serrated edges, acute tips and cordate bases. Veins, stems & branches are green. PARENTAGE: {[('Bon Accord' x 'Bicentennial') x ('Vobeglo' x 'Dancing Flame')] x 'Rohees Alrami'} x 'Veenlust'. Medium upright. Makes good upright. Prefers overhead filtered light and cool climate. Best bloom and foliage colour in filtered light. Tested 4 years in Diessen, The Netherlands. Distinguished by bloom colour.
Comperen 2003 NL AFS5271.

Comperen Wiek. Trailer. Semi Double. COROLLA: Half flared; opens purple (77A); matures magenta (71C); 19mm (3/4") long x 16mm (5/8") wide. SEPALS: fully up, tips recurved; dark rose (51A) upper & lower surfaces; 34mm (1 3/8") long x 10mm (3/8") wide. TUBE: dark rose (51A); medium length & thickness; 10mm (3/8") long x 4mm (1/8") wide. FOLIAGE is dark green (137A) upper surface; medium green (138A) lower surface. PARENTAGE: 'Rosea' x 'Comperen Lutea'.
Comperen 2007 NL AFS6606.

Comperen Wielewaal. Upright. Single. COROLLA is half flared; opens purple (88A); matures dark violet (87A); 21mm (13/16") long x 26mm (1") wide. SEPALS are half up, tips recurved up; red (45C) upper & lower surfaces; 26mm (1") long x 11mm (7/16") wide. TUBE is red (45C); 11mm (7/16") long x 6mm (1/4") wide. FOLIAGE: dark green (137A) upper surface; medium green (138B) lower surface. PARENTAGE: 'Luuk van Riet' x 'Swanley Gem'. Distinguished by bloom & foliage combination.
Comperen 2006 NL AFS6203.

Comperen Wulp. Upright. Single. COROLLA is three quarter flared with smooth petal margins; opens light pink (65B); matures light pink (65C); 22mm (7/8") long x 34mm (1 5/16") wide. SEPALS are half up, tips reflexed up; rose (68C) upper surface; rose (68B) lower surface; 31mm (1 1/4") long x 16mm (5/8") wide. TUBE is rose (68C); short & thick; 4mm (3/16") long x 4mm (3/16")

wide. FOLIAGE: dark green (137A) upper surface; medium green (138B) lower surface. Leaves are 54mm (2 1/8") long x 36mm (1 7/16") wide, ovate shaped. PARENTAGE: 'Roesse Apus' x 'Silvia van Heyst'. Distinguished by bloom colour.
Comperen 2005 NL AFS5914.

Comperen Zilvervisje. Upright/Trailer. Double. COROLLA: three quarter flared, smooth petal margins; opens violet (86B); matures dark purple (78A); 22mm (7/8") long x 22mm (7/8") wide. SEPALS: half up; tips recurved up; white (155B) upper surface; pale purple (75D) lower surface; 26mm (1") long x 12mm (1/2") wide. TUBE: white (155A); medium length & thickness; 8mm (5/16") long x 6mm (1/4") wide. STAMENS: extend 12mm (1/2") below corolla; light rose (73C) filaments & anthers. PISTIL: extends 38mm (1 1/2") below the corolla; pale rose (73D) style, light yellow (11C) stigma. BUD: ovate. FOLIAGE: dark green (137A) upper surface; medium green (137D) lower surface. Leaves are 64mm (2 1/2") long x 28mm (1 1/8") wide, ovate shaped, serrated edges, acute tips and obtuse bases. Veins, stems & branches are green. PARENTAGE: 'Sofie Michiels' x 'Cameron Ryle'. Lax upright or stiff trailer. Makes good stiff trailer. Prefers overhead filtered light and cool climate. Best bloom and foliage colour in filtered light. Tested 4 years in Diessen, The Netherlands. Distinguished by bloom colour.
Comperen 2003 NL AFS5261.

Comperen Zwartkop. Upright. Single. COROLLA is half flared; opens dark purple (79A); matures purple (71A); 19mm (3/4") long x 29mm (1 1/8") wide. SEPALS are fully up, tips reflexed; reddish purple (60D) upper surface; dark reddish purple (60C) lower surface; 19mm (3/4) long x 11mm (7/16") wide. TUBE is reddish purple (60D); 8mm (5/16") long x 8mm (5/16") wide. FOLIAGE: medium green (137B) upper surface; medium green (138B) lower surface. PARENTAGE: ('Roesse Carme' x 'Roesse Apus') x 'Maxima's Baby'. Distinguished by bloom colour & erect blooms.
Comperen 2006 NL AFS6211.

Cons Marjorette. Trailer. Semi Double. COROLLA: unflared, bell shaped, turned under petal margins; opens dark reddish purple (71A); matures dark reddish purple (70A); 31mm (1 1/4") long x 22mm (7/8") wide. SEPALS: fully up; tips recurved; magenta (57B) upper & lower surfaces; 55mm (2 3/16") long x 24mm (15/16") wide.

TUBE: magenta (57B); long, medium thickness; 23mm (15/16") long x 6mm (1/4") wide. STAMENS: extend 14mm (9/16") below corolla; reddish purple (66A) filaments & anthers. PISTIL: extends 30mm (1 1/8") below the corolla; reddish purple (66A) style & stigma. BUD: very long. FOLIAGE: spring green (134C) upper surface, darker green (134B) lower surface. Leaves are 74mm (2 15/16") long x 40mm (1 9/16") wide, elliptic shaped, serrulated edges, acute tips and rounded bases. Dark reddish purple (61A) veins, stems & branches. PARENTAGE: 'Taffeta Bow' x 'Bicentennial'. Natural trailer. Makes good basket. Heat tolerant if shaded. Best bloom and foliage colour in filtered light. Tested 6 years in Berchem, Belgium. Distinguished by long stems and sepal/corolla colour combination.
Janssens 2004 BE AFS5435.

Constantinus Virginius. Upright. Single. COROLLA is half flared with turned under smooth petal margins; opens purple (77A); matures dark reddish purple (72A); 26mm (1") long x 18mm (11/16") wide. SEPALS are horizontal, tips reflexed; dark reddish purple (60B) upper surface; reddish purple (61B) lower surface; 34mm (1 5/16") long x 14mm (9/16") wide. TUBE is dark reddish purple (60B); medium length & thickness; 34mm (1 5/16") long x 13mm (1/2") wide. FOLIAGE: dark green (137A) upper surface; medium green (137C) lower surface. Leaves are 70mm (2 3/4") long x 34mm (1 5/16") wide, elliptic shaped. PARENTAGE: 'Roesse Blacky' x 'Blue Boy'. Meis 3-7-04. Distinguished by purple flower shape.
Michiels 2005 BE AFS5674.

Consuelo. Trailer. Double. COROLLA: 3 quarter flared; opens pale purple (76C), pale lavender (69B) base; matures violet (77B); 28mm (1 1/8") long x 24mm (15/16") wide. PETALOIDS: same colour as corolla; 17mm (5/8") long x 7mm (1/4") wide. SEPALS: horizontal, tips recurved; pale lavender (69D) tipped light apple green (145B) upper surface; pale lavender (69B) tipped light apple green (145B) lower surface; 43 mm (1 11/16") long x 15mm (9/16") wide. TUBE: white (155B); medium length & thickness; 22mm (7/8") long x 7mm (1/4") wide. FOLIAGE is dark green (136A) upper surface; medium green (138A) lower surface. PARENTAGE: 'Vreeni Schleeweiss' x 'Kiss'.
Michiels 2007 BE AFS6351.

Convention 2004. Upright/Trailer. Double. COROLLA: fully flared, wavy petal margins;

opens reddish purple (64B); matures magenta (71C); 38mm (1 1/2") long x 79mm (3 1/8 ") wide. SEPALS: horizontal; tips recurved; white (155A) upper surface; white (155B) lower surface; 63mm(2 1/2") long x 25mm (1") wide. TUBE: white (155B); medium length & thick; 51mm (2") long. STAMENS: extend 32mm (1 1/4") below corolla; light reddish purple (66C) filaments; reddish purple (67A) anthers. PISTIL: extends 51mm (2") below the corolla, light pink (62B) style; pale pink (49D) stigma. BUD: heart shaped, four ribs. FOLIAGE: dark green (137A) upper surface. Leaves are 89-140mm (3 1/2"–5 1/2") long x 38-51mm (1 1/2"-2") wide, lanceoate shaped, serrulated edges, acute tips and rounded bases. Veins are pale red to light green; branches & stems are magenta. PARENTAGE: 'Ovation' x 'Ice Maiden'. Lax upright or stiff trailer. Makes good upright. Prefers overhead filtered light. Best bloom colour in bright light. Tested 3 years in Crescent City area, CA, USA. Distinguished by very large blossoms, white, shaded smoky magenta blossom colour.
Helsel 2004 USA AFS5376.

Cor Bruÿn. Upright. Single. COROLLA is three quarter flared with smooth petal margins; opens violet (86D); matures light purple (78B); 22mm (7/8") long x 26mm (1") wide. SEPALS are half up, tips recurved up; white (155A) upper surface; light pink (65B) lower surface; 30mm (1 3/16") long x 9mm (3/8") wide. TUBE is light purple (73B); short & thin; 9mm (3/8") long x 6mm (1/4") wide. FOLIAGE: dark green (147A) upper surface; medium green (147B) lower surface. Leaves are 40mm (1 9/16") long x 20mm (13/16") wide, ovate shaped. PARENTAGE: 'Thamar' x unknown. Distinguished by flower shape & colour.
Krom 2005 NL AFS5837.

Cor Leeuwestijn. Trailer. Double. COROLLA: half flared; opens violet (75A) striped magenta (67B); matures reddish purple (67A); 18mm (11/16") long x 13mm (1/2") wide. PETALOIDS: violet (77C); 13mm (1/2") long x 7mm (1/4") wide. SEPALS are half up, tips recurved up, twisted left & right; white (155C) tipped light green (138C) upper & lower surfaces; 35mm (1 3/8") long x 8mm (5/16") wide. TUBE is white (155B) & light green (138C); medium length & thickness; 14mm (9/16") long x 5mm (3/16") wide. FOLIAGE is dark green (136B) upper surface; medium green (138B) lower surface. PARENTAGE: 'Vreni Schleeweiss' x 'Kiss'.

Michiels 2007 BE AFS6536.

Corneel Cornelis. Trailer. Double. COROLLA: 3 quarter flared; opens light purple (N80C) edged purple (N81A); matures magenta (61A); 31mm (1 1/4") long x 13mm (1/2") wide. PETALOIDS: same colour as corolla; 13mm (1/2") long x 13mm (1/2") wide. SEPALS: horizontal, tips reflexed; white (155C) tipped medium green (139C) upper surface; pale lavender (69D) tipped medium green (139C) lower surface; 33mm (1 5/16") long x 14mm (9/16") wide. TUBE: light green (139C); medium length & thickness; 14mm (9/16") long x 6mm (1/4") wide. FOLIAGE is dark green (139A) upper surface; medium green (139B) lower surface. PARENTAGE: 'Vreni Schleeweiss' x 'Kiss'.
Michiels 2007 BE AFS6373.

Cornish Beauty. Upright. Semi Double. COROLLA is unflared with smooth petal margins; opens purple (81B), light pink (65C) in center of petal, edged violet; matures light rpurple (80C); 17mm (11/16") long x 15mm (9/16") wide. SEPALS are horizontal, tips recurved; magenta (67B) tipped light yellowish green (154C) upper surface; pale rose (73D) tipped light yellowish green (154C) lower surface; 25mm (1") long x 10mm (3/8") wide. TUBE is magenta (67B); medium length & thickness; 12mm (1/2") long x 5mm (3/16") wide. FOLIAGE: very dark green (131A) upper & lower surfaces. Leaves are 50mm (2") long x 30mm (1 3/16") wide, lanceolate shaped. PARENTAGE: Found seedling. Distinguished by colour combination.
Negus 2005 UL AFS5977.

Cornish Dancer. Upright/Trailer. Double. COROLLA: Fully flared; opens & matures white (155D), top petals tinged pink (52D); 55mm (2 3/16") long x 55mm (2 3/16") wide. SEPALS: horizontal, tips recurved; light rose (73B) tipped light green (138C) upper surface; light rose (73B) lower surface; 33mm (1 5/16") long x 14mm (9/16") wide. TUBE: pale rose (73D); long, medium thickness, bent at blossom end; 33mm (1 5/16") long x 4-7mm (1/8"-1/4) wide. FOLIAGE is medium green (147B) upper surface; light yellowish green (149A) lower surface. PARENTAGE: 'Carol Brown' x found seedling.
Negus 2007 UK AFS6501.

Cornish Display. Upright. Single. COROLLA is full flared with smooth petal margins; opens and matures dark rose (51A); 25mm (1") long x 50mm (2") wide. SEPALS are fully up, tips recurved; magenta (71C) upper surface, red (50A) lower surface; 25mm (1") long x 17mm (11/16") wide. TUBE is dark rose (51A); medium length and thickness; 15mm (5/8") long x 5mm (3/16) thick. STAMENS extend 18mm (11/16") beyond the corolla; red (50A) filaments, dark reddish purple (60B) anthers. PISTIL extends 38mm (1 1/2") beyond the corolla; red (50A) style, white (155A) stigma. BUD is cordate. FOLIAGE is dark green (139A) upper surface, grayish green (191A) lower surface. Leaves are 55mm (2 3/16") long x 30mm (1 3/16") wide, lanceolate shaped, serrulated edges, acute tips and rounded bases. Veins are dark grayish red (182A), stems are brown (199B) and branches are light brown (199C). PARENTAGE: unknown. Small upright. Makes good upright, standard or decorative. Prefers cool climate. Heat tolerant if shaded. Best bloom colour in filtered light. Tested six years in Cornwall, England. Distinguished by single, wide corolla and profuse flowers. Negus 2005 UK AFS5047.

Cornish Man. Upright/Trailer. Double. COROLLA: full flared, turned up petal margins; opens purple (77A), rose (52B) base; matures reddish purple (74B); 25mm (1") long, 60mm (2 3/8") wide. PETALOIDS: purple (77A); 8mm (5/16") long x 8mm (5/16") wide. SEPALS: fully up; tips recurved; red (52A) upper surface; rose (52B) lower surface; 32mm (1/4") long x 10mm (3/8") wide. TUBE: purple (77A); short, medium thickness; 15mm (9/16") long x 6mm (1/4") wide. STAMENS: extend 24mm (15/16") below corolla; purple (77A) filaments & anthers. PISTIL: extends 40mm (1 9/16") below the corolla; purple (77A) style; pink (36A) stigma. BUD: lanceolate. FOLIAGE: dark green (137A) upper surface; medium green (138B) lower surface. Leaves are 90mm (3 9/16") long x 60mm (2 3/8") wide, lanceolate shaped, serrated edges, obtuse tips and obtuse bases. Grayish red (181A) veins & stems; gray green (194B) branches. PARENTAGE: 'Bealings' x 'Heidi Ann'. Lax upright or stiff trailer. Makes good upright or standard. Prefers overhead filtered light. Heat tolerant if shaded. Best bloom and foliage colour in filtered light. Tested 7 years in West Cornwall, England. Distinguished by bloom shape & colour. Negus 2004 UK AFS 5632.

Cornish Pixie. Upright. Single. COROLLA is unflared with smooth petal margins; opens purple (77A); matures dark purple (78A); 14mm (9/16") long x 8mm (5/16") wide.

SEPALS are horizontal, tips recurved; light reddish purple (73A) fading to pale pink (69A) upper surface, light reddish purple (73A) lower surface; 25mm (1") long x 5mm (3/16") wide. TUBE is light reddish purple (73A); medium length and thin; 12mm (1/2") long x 5mm (3/16) thick. STAMENS extend 12mm (1/2") beyond the corolla; light reddish purple (73A) filaments, dark purple (78A) anthers. PISTIL extends 19mm (3/4") beyond the corolla; light reddish purple (73A) style, cream (159D) stigma. BUD is lanceolate. FOLIAGE is medium green (143A) upper surface, medium green (147B) lower surface. Leaves are 53mm (2 1/8") long x 27mm (1 1/16") wide, lanceolate shaped, serrulated edges, acute tips and rounded bases. Veins are dark grayish red (182A), stems are light olive green (147C) and branches are gray green (194B). PARENTAGE: 'Fuchsia 88' x 'Katrina Thompson'. Small upright. Makes good standard. Prefers overhead filtered light. Heat tolerant if shaded. Best bloom colour in filtered light. Tested three years in West Cornwall, England. Distinguished by small and profuse flowers. Negus 2002 UK AFS5046.

Cornish Sea Shells. Upright. Single. COROLLA: Quarter flared, bell shaped; opens & matures dark rose (67C); 35mm (1 3/8") long x 22mm (7/8") wide. SEPALS: half down, tips recurved; pink (36A) upper surface; pink (48D) lower surface; 25mm (1") long x 8mm (5/16") wide. TUBE: pink (36A); medium length & thickness; 8mm (5/16") long x 4mm (1/8") wide. FOLIAGE is dark green (137A) upper surface; medium green (147B) lower surface. PARENTAGE: found seedling x found seedling. Negus 2007 UK AFS6499.

Cornish Sunset. Upright/Trailer. Double. COROLLA: Quarter flared; opens reddish purple (71B) tinged pink; matures rose (53C), red (68B) top; 50mm (2") long x 40mm (9/16") wide. SEPALS: half down, tips recurved; red (52A) upper surface; rose (52B) lower surface; 29mm (1 1/8") long x 12mm (7/16") wide. TUBE: red (52A); medium length & thickness; 25mm (1") long x 5mm (3/16") wide. FOLIAGE is dark green (141A) upper surface; light olive green (147C) lower surface. PARENTAGE: 'Michelle Louise' x 'David Negus'. Negus 2007 UK AFS6500.

Corrie Barten. Upright. Double. COROLLA is three quarter flared with smooth petal

89

margins; opens & matures rose (68C); 16mm (5/8") long x 21mm (13/16") wide. SEPALS are horizontal, tips recurved; light rose (68D) tipped green upper surface; rose (68B) tipped green lower surface; 20mm (13/16") long x 12mm (1/2") wide. TUBE is light rose (68D); short & thick; 6mm (1/4") long x 8mm (5/16") wide. FOLIAGE: medium green (137B) upper surface; medium green (138B) lower surface. Leaves are 66mm (2 5/8") long x 36mm (1 7/16") wide, ovate shaped. PARENTAGE: 'Roesse Carme' x 'Cameron Ryle'. Distinguished by bloom & foliage combination.
van Eijk 2005 NL AFS5900.

Corrie Comperen. Upright. Double. COROLLA: three quarter flared, smooth petal margins; opens dark reddish purple (60A); matures dark reddish purple (60B); 20mm (13/16") long x 22mm (7/8") wide. SEPALS: half up; tips recurved up; rose (65A) upper & lower surfaces; 26mm (1") long x 14mm (9/16") wide. TUBE: light reddish purple (66C); short & thick; 11mm (7/16") long x 10mm (3/8") wide. STAMENS: extend 20mm (13/16") below corolla; magenta (63B) filaments; dark reddish purple (60A) anthers. PISTIL: extends 39mm (1 9/16") below the corolla; magenta (61C) style; light yellow (11C) stigma. BUD: round. FOLIAGE: dark green (137A) upper surface; medium green (137C) lower surface. Leaves are 89mm (3 1/2") long x 42mm (1 5/8") wide, ovate shaped, serrated edges, acute tips and rounded bases. Veins, stems & branches are green. PARENTAGE: {[('Bon Accord' x 'Bicentennial') x ('Vobeglo' x 'Dancing Flame')] x 'Rohees Alrami'} x 'Veenlust'. Medium upright. Makes good standard. Prefers overhead filtered light and cool climate. Best bloom and foliage colour in filtered light. Tested 4 years in Diessen, The Netherlands. Distinguished by bloom colour.
Comperen 2003 NL AFS5281.

Corrie Dillen. Upright/Trailer. Double. COROLLA is three quarter flared; opens dark reddish purple (61A); matures dark reddish purple (60C); 31mm (1 1/4") long x 28mm (1 1/8") wide. SEPALS are half up, tips reflexed up; pink (62A) upper surface; rose (63C) lower surface; 46mm (1 13/16") long x 16mm (5/8") wide. TUBE is pale pink (62D); 19mm (3/4") long x 7mm (1/4") wide. FOLIAGE: medium green (137B) upper surface; medium green (138B) lower surface. PARENTAGE: 'Denna Krekels' x 'Leon Pauwels'. Distinguished by bloom & foliage combination.

Buiting 2006 NL AFS6122.

Corrie Spoelstra. Upright/Trailer. Double. COROLLA is three quarter flared, smooth petal margins; opens purple (89C); matures dark purple (78A); 24mm (15/16") long x 22mm (7/8") wide. SEPALS are fully up, tips reflexed; pink (62C) upper surface; pink (62A) lower surface; 24mm (15/16") long x 16mm (5/8") wide. TUBE is pink (62C); short & thick; 10mm (3/8") long x 8mm (5/16") wide. STAMENS extend 32mm (1 1/4") beyond the corolla; magenta (68A) filaments; light rose (68D) anthers. PISTIL extends 38mm (1 1/2") below the corolla; pink (62C) style; cream (11D) stigma. BUD is round, pointed. FOLIAGE is dark green (137A) upper surface, medium green (138A) lower surface. Leaves are 60mm (2 3/8") long x 36mm (1 7/16") wide, ovate shaped, serrulated edges, acute tips and cordate bases. Veins, stems & branches are green. PARENTAGE: 'Sofie Michiels' x 'Thea Kroesse'. Lax upright or stiff trailer. Makes good stiff trailer. Prefers overhead filtered light & cool climate. Best bloom colour in filtered light. Tested four years in Knegsel, The Netherlands. Distinguished by bloom colour.
Roes 2004 NL AFS5371.

Cotopaxi. Triphylla. SEPALS red (45a) on the upper and lower surfaces; SEPALS are horizontally held with recurved tips. corolla red (45a); corolla is half flared. TUBE red (45a).. PARENTAGE Eruption x F. magdalenae.
Lamb 2009 UK BFS0147.

Courtisan. Upright/Trailer. Single. COROLLA: unflared; smooth petal margins; opens purple (77A); matures violet (77B); 31mm (1 1/4") long x 11mm (7/16") wide. SEPALS: fully up, tips recurved, twisted; red (52A) upper & lower surfaces; 44mm (1 3/4") long x 8mm (5/16") wide. TUBE: red (52A); long, medium thickness; 26mm (1") long x 5mm (3/16") wide. STAMENS extend 25-30mm (1-1 3/16") beyond the corolla; dark rose (54B) filaments; dark red (53A) anthers. PISTIL extends 46mm (1 13/16") beyond the corolla; dark rose (54B) style; dark red (53A) stigma. BUD is long, ovate. FOLIAGE is medium green (146A) upper surface; yellowish green (146B) lower surface. Leaves are 82mm (3 1/4") long x 38mm (1 1/2") wide; ovate shaped, serrulate edges, acute tips, rounded to acute bases. Veins are yellowish green, stems are light reddish brown, branches are light brown. PARENTAGE: 'Belgique' x unknown. Lax upright or stiff trailer. Makes good upright or basket. Prefers overhead filtered light & cool climate. Tested 4 years in Pornic, France. Distinguished by long & twisted SEPALS. Massé 2009 FR AFS6989.

Creiler Azure. Upright. Single. COROLLA: unflared, square shape; opens violet (85B); matures violet (75A); 19mm (3/4") long x 18mm (11/16") wide. SEPALS: half up, tips recurved up; white (155A) upper surface; pale pink (69A) lower surface; 40 mm (1 9/16") long x 10mm (3/8") wide. TUBE: white (155A); 9mm (5/16") long x 5mm (3/16") wide. FOLIAGE is medium green (137B) upper surface; medium green (138A) lower surface. PARENTAGE: 'Delicate White' x 'Azure Sky'. Nomination by NKVF as Recommendable Cultivar.
van Kranenburg 2008 NL AFS6792.

Creiler Bellefleur. Upright. Double. COROLLA: quarter flared, filled rose shape; opens pink (43D); matures rose (51B); 10mm (3/8") long x 11mm (7/16") wide. PETALOIDS: peach (38B) spotted light orange pink; 10mm (3/8") long x 15mm (9/16") wide. SEPALS: horizontal, tips recurved; light rose (58D) tipped light apple green (145B) upper surface; light rose (58D) lower surface; 20 mm (3/4") long x 10mm (3/8") wide. TUBE: pink (62A); 23mm (7/8") long x 5mm (3/16") wide. FOLIAGE is dark green (139A) upper surface; medium green (139D) lower surface. PARENTAGE: 'Creiler Flora' x 'Sundial'. Nomination by NKVF as Recommendable Cultivar.
van Kranenburg 2008 NL AFS6793.

Creiler Flora. Upright/Trailer. Single. COROLLA is half flared, bell shaped; opens & matures orangy red (39A); 18mm (5/8") long x 9mm (3/8") wide. SEPALS are horizontal, tips recurved; orangy red (39A) upper surface; coral (39B) lower surface; 31mm (1 1/4") long x 8mm (5/16") wide. TUBE is pink (48C); 45mm (1 3/4") long x 8mm (5/16") wide. FOLIAGE: dark green (147A) upper surface; medium green (147B) lower surface. PARENTAGE: 'Hidden Treasure' x 'Loxhore Mazurka'. Nominated by NKVF as recommendable cultivar. Distinguished by bright flowers and sun tolerance.
van Kranenburg 2006 NL AFS6283.

Creiler Lord. Upright. Single. COROLLA: unflared, bell shape; opens & matures orange (31B); 14mm (9/16") long x 11mm (7/16") wide. SEPALS: full down, tips recurved; rose (52C) tipped light greenish

yellow (151C) upper surface; light orange (41D) lower surface; 37mm (1 7/16") long x 10mm (3/8") wide. TUBE: light pink (36C); 32mm (1 1/4") long x 7mm (1/4") wide. FOLIAGE is medium green (138A) upper surface; medium green (138B) lower surface. PARENTAGE: 'Creiler Flora' x 'Lord Lonsdale'. Nomination by NKVF as Recommendable Cultivar.
van Kranenburg 2008 NL AFS6794.

Creiler Sprinter. Trailer. Single. COROLLA: unflared, bell shape; opens dark purple (79B); matures reddish purple (64A); 17mm (5/8") long x 14mm (9/16") wide. SEPALS: horizontal, tips recurved; reddish purple (64B) upper surface; magenta (67B) lower surface; 33 mm (1 5/16") long x 6mm (1/4") wide. TUBE: magenta (63A); 22mm (7/8") long x 4mm (1/8") wide. FOLIAGE is dark green (137A) upper surface; medium green (138B) lower surface. PARENTAGE: 'Delicate White' x 'Zulu King'. Nomination by NKVF as Recommendable Cultivar.
van Kranenburg 2008 NL AFS6791.

Crilou. Trailer. Single. COROLLA: quarter flared, turned under wavy petal margins, square shape; opens violet (83D), pale purple (80D) base; matures purple (80A), pale purple (80D) base; 20mm (3/4") long x 21mm (13/16") wide. SEPALS: half down, tips reflexed; rose (55B) tipped green upper surface; rose (54C) lower surface; 35mm (1 3/8") long x 13mm (1/2") wide. TUBE: pale orange (27B); long, medium thickness, curved shape; 35mm (1 3/8") long x 11mm (7/16") wide. STAMENS extend 40mm (1 9/16") beyond the corolla; light gray (156D) filaments; yellowish white (158A) anthers. PISTIL extends 63mm (2 1/2") beyond the corolla; pale pink (62D) style; pale yellowish orange (20C) stigma. BUD: ovate. FOLIAGE: dark green (147A) upper surface; medium green (147B) lower surface. Leaves are 66mm (2 5/8") long x 40mm (1 9/16") wide; cordate shaped, serrate edges, acute tips, rounded bases. Veins are green stems & branches are red. PARENTAGE: 'Alda Alders' x unknown. Natural trailer. Self branching. Makes good basket. Prefers overhead filtered light. Heat tolerant if shaded. Cold weather hardy to 2° C (36° F). Best bloom & foliage colour in filtered light. Tested 4 years in Aywaille, Belgium. Distinguished by curved TUBE & flower colour combination.
Leonard R. 2009 BE AFS7243.

Cristien van Tilburg. Upright. Single. Upright. COROLLA: quarter flared, smooth

petal margins; opens magenta (68A); matures rose (68B); 20mm (13/16") long x 22mm (7/8") wide. SEPALS: horizontal; tips recurved; very pale orange (19D) tipped green upper surface; pale lavender (69D) tipped green lower surface; 32mm (1 1/4") long x 10mm (3/8") wide. TUBE: light yellowish orange (19C); medium length & thickness; 16mm (5/8") long x 6mm (1/4") wide. STAMENS: extend 19mm (3/4") below corolla; rose (61D) filaments; reddish orange (42A) anthers. PISTIL: extends 42mm (1 5/8") below the corolla; rose (61D) style, yellow (10C) stigma. BUD: ovate. FOLIAGE: dark green (137A) upper surface; medium green (138B) lower surface. Leaves are 64mm (2 1/2") long x 46mm (1 13/16") wide, ovate shaped, serrulated edges, acute tips and obtuse bases. Veins, stems & branches are green. PARENTAGE: found seedling. Medium upright. Makes good standard. Prefers overhead filtered light and cool climate. Best bloom and foliage colour in filtered light. Tested 4 years in Leende, The Netherlands. Distinguished by bloom colour.
Liebregts 2003 NL AFS5245.

Curious Casey. Trailer. Double. COROLLA: three quarter flared, turned under smooth petal margins; opens & matures white (155D); 30mm (1 3/16") long x 20mm (13/16") wide. PETALOIDS: same colour as corolla; 15mm (9/16") long x 10mm (3/8") wide. SEPALS: fully up; tips recurved; half twist counterclockwise; white (155D), light pink (49C) near TUBE upper surface; white (155D) lower surface; 40mm(1 9/16") long x 14mm (9/16") wide. TUBE: light pink (49C); long & thin; 20mm (13/16") long x 6mm (1/4") wide. STAMENS: extend 25mm (1") below corolla; pink (62C) filaments; rose (63C) anthers. PISTIL: extends 30mm (1 3/16") below the corolla, white (155D) style; yellowish white (158A) stigma. BUD: medium, pointed. FOLIAGE: medium green (146A) upper surface, yellowish green (146B) lower surface. Leaves are 55mm (2 3/16") long x 35mm (1 3/8") wide, cordate shaped, serrated edges, acute tips and rounded bases. Veins are red; branches are red; stems are brown. PARENTAGE: 'Loveable Rascal' x 'Heavenly Hayley'. Natural trailer. Self branching. Makes good basket or standard. Prefers overhead filtered light and warm climate. Heat tolerant if shaded. Cold weather hardy to 32⁰ F. Best bloom colour in bright light. Tested 3 years in Walthamstow, London, England. Distinguished by pure white colour & colour retention.
Allsop M. 2004 UK AFS5378.

Cyrano. Upright/Trailer. Single. COROLLA is quarter flared with smooth petal margins; opens and matures dark rose (51A); 16mm (5/8") long x 16mm (5/8") wide. SEPALS are half down, tips recurved; pink (48C) upper surface; rose (48B) - pink (48C) lower surface; 26mm (1") long x 16mm (1/4") wide. TUBE is pink (48C); long and thin; 52mm (2 1/16") long x 5mm (3/16") thick. STAMENS do not extend beyond the corolla; pink (50D) filaments, yellowish white (4D) anthers. PISTIL extends 17mm (11/16") beyond the corolla; rose (48B) style, light pink (49C) stigma. BUD is long, ovate. FOLIAGE is medium green (146A) and bronze upper surface, medium green (147B) and bronze lower surface. Leaves are 80mm (3 1/8") long x 39mm (1 9/16") wide, ovate shaped, serrulated edges, acute tips and acute bases. Veins, stems and branches are light brown. PARENTAGE: 'Gartenmeister Bonstedt' x unknown. Lax upright or stiff trailer. Self branching. Makes good basket or upright. Prefers overhead filtered light and cool climate. Best bloom colour in filtered light. Tested three years in Pornic & Luçon, France. Distinguished by long TUBE.
Massé 2002 FR AFS5010.

D.D.F.G.G. Trailer. Double. COROLLA: three quarter flared, turned under petal margins; opens reddish purple (61B) & dark rose (64C); matures dark reddish purple (61A); 29mm (1 1/8") long x 24mm (15/16") wide. PETALOIDS: reddish purple (61B) & dark rose (64C; 14mm (9/16") long x 11mm (7/16") wide. SEPALS are horizontal, tips recurved; light pink (62C), tipped light yellowish green (150C) upper surface; dark rose (N57C), tipped light yellowish green (150C) lower surface; 39mm (1 1/2") long x 18mm (11/16") wide. TUBE is pale pink (62D); medium length & thickness; 19mm (3/4") long x 6mm (1/4") wide. STAMENS extend 16mm (5/8") beyond the corolla; dark reddish purple (70A) filaments; purple (83A) anthers. PISTIL extends 21mm (13/16") beyond the corolla; reddish purple (70B) style; pale lavender (65D) stigma. BUD is elongated, square. FOLIAGE is dark green (136A) upper surface; medium green (137D) lower surface. Leaves are 75mm (3") long x 43mm (1 11/16") wide, ovate shaped, serrate edges, acute tips, rounded bases. Veins are dark reddish purple (187C), stems are light red purple (185D) & branches are plum (185C) & light green (139D). PARENTAGE: 'Manfried Kleinau' x 'Joergen Hahn'. Natural trailer, self branching. Makes good basket. Prefers overhead filtered light, cool climate.

Best bloom & foliage in filtered light. Tested 3 years in Koningshooikt, Belgium. Waanrode 9/8/2008. Distinguished by bloom colour combination.
Michiels 2009 BE AFS7155.

Daan Bakker. Upright. Single. COROLLA is quarter flared, saucer shaped; opens & matures pink (50D) edged pink (52D); 20mm (3/4") long x 15mm (9/16") wide. SEPALS are half up, tips reflexed up; dark red (46A) tipped green upper surface; dark red (46A), edged pink (52D), tipped green lower surface; 24mm (15/16") long x 8mm (5/16") wide. TUBE is dark red (46A); 20mm (3/4") long x 4mm (1/8") wide. FOLIAGE: dark green (147A) upper surface; medium green (146A) lower surface. PARENTAGE: 'Andrew Hadfield' x 'Prince Syray'. Distinguished by flower fluorescent colour & erect growth.
Koerts T. 2006 NL AFS6289.

Daluna. Upright/Trailer. Double. COROLLA: half flared; turned up petal margins; opens purple (77A); matures reddish purple (71B); 23mm (7/8") long x 21mm (3/4") wide inner petals; 12mm (7/16") long x 10mm (3/8") wide, outer petals. SEPALS: half down, tips recurved; pale yellowish green (149D) blushed red upper surface; pale yellowish green (150D) lower surface; 16mm (5/8") long x 4mm (1/8") wide. TUBE: pale yellowish green (149D); medium length & thickness; 15mm (9/16") long x 4mm (1/8") wide. STAMENS extend 4mm (1/8") beyond the corolla; pink (62A) filaments; pale yellow (1D) anthers. PISTIL extends 12mm (7/16") beyond the corolla; pink (62A) style; light gray (156C) stigma. FOLIAGE is medium green (137B) upper surface; yellowish green (146C) lower surface. Leaves are 64mm (2 1/2") long x 32mm (1 1/4") wide; cordate shaped, wavy edges, rounded tips, rounded bases. Veins, stems & branches are reddish brown. PARENTAGE: Sport of 'Mood Indigo'. Lax upright. Makes good basket. Prefers overhead filtered light. Best bloom & foliage colour in filtered light. Tested 3 years in Hoogezand, The Netherlands. Nominated by NKvF as recommendable cultivar. Distinguished by leaf colour.
Scheper 2009 NL AFS7016.

Damien Guillet. Upright. Single. COROLLA is unflared with smooth petal margins; opens & matures dark reddish purple (61A); 15mm (9/16") long x 10mm (3/8") wide. SEPALS are half down, tips recurved; bright red (45A) upper & lower surfaces; 30mm (1 3/16") long x 6mm (1/4") wide. TUBE is bright red (45A);

long, medium thickness; 22mm (7/8") long x 3mm (1/8") wide. FOLIAGE: dark green (147A) upper surface; medium green (147B) lower surface. Leaves are 90mm (3 9/16") long x 34mm (1 5/16") wide, lanceolate shaped. PARENTAGE: 'Whiteknight's Pearl' x 'F. regia ssp reitzii". Distinguished by long & thin flowers, tall growth.
Massé 2005 FR AFS5702.

D'amon Nos-ôtes. Upright/Trailer. Semi Double. COROLLA: unflared; opens red (53C) veined coral (37A); matures red (53D) veined light coral (38A); 29mm (1 1/8") long x 25mm (1") wide. SEPALS: half up, tips recurved up; pink (62A), veined cream (158C), tipped light green (138C) upper surface; light pink (62C) lower surface; 49mm (1 15/16") long x 10mm (3/8") wide. TUBE: pale pink (49D); 19mm (3/4") long x 6mm (1/4") wide. FOLIAGE is dark green (147A) upper surface; olive green (148A) lower surface. PARENTAGE: 'Bicentennial' x unknown.
Richard L 2008 AFS6840.

Dana Jolie. Trailer. Single. COROLLA: three quarter flared, trumpet shape, toothed petal margins; opens light purple (75B); matures violet to light purple (75A/75B); 14mm (9/16") long, 10mm (3/8") wide. SEPALS: horizontal; tips recurved; magenta (61C) upper surface; rose (64D) lower surface; 16mm (5/8") long x 4.5mm (3/16") wide. TUBE: reddish purple (61B); medium length, thin; 16mm (5/8") long x 3mm (1/8") wide. STAMENS: extend 6mm (1/4") below corolla; violet (75A) filaments; light tan (161C) anthers. PISTIL: does not extend below the corolla; violet (75A) style; magenta (61C) stigma. BUD: oblong. FOLIAGE: dark green (147A) upper surface; olive green (148A) lower surface. Leaves are 42mm (1 11/16") long x 22mm (7/8") wide, ovate shaped, serrulated edges, acute tips and rounded bases. Red veins, stems & branches. PARENTAGE: 'Gerharda's Panache' x ('Gerharda's Panache' x 'Loeky'). Natural trailer. Self branching. Makes good basket. Prefers overhead filtered light, cool climate. Best bloom and foliage colour in filtered light. Tested 4 years in Lisse, The Netherlands. Distinguished by flower shape & colour; flowers in small terminal clusters.
de Graaff 2004 NL AFS5606.

Dana Samantha. Upright. Single. COROLLA: Quarter flared, rounded; opens violet (85B); matures pale purple (87D); 17mm (5/8") long x 20mm (3/4") wide. SEPALS: fully up, tips reflexed; white (155B) tipped green upper surface; pale purple (75D) lower surface; 27mm (1 1/16") long x 10mm (3/8") wide. TUBE: cream (158D); medium length & thickness; 10mm (3/8") long x 5mm (3/16") wide. FOLIAGE is medium green (146A) upper surface; yellowish green (144A) lower surface. PARENTAGE: 'Katie Rogers' x unnamed.

Chapman 2007 UK AFS6717.

Dancing Earrings. Upright/Trailer. Semi Double. Upright/Trailer. COROLLA: quarter flared; opens & matures violet (86D) veined red; 20mm (3/4") long x 20mm (3/4") wide. SEPALS: half up, tips recurved up; red (46C) upper & lower surfaces; 30mm (1 3/16") long x 15mm (9/16") wide. TUBE: red (46C); 18 mm (11/16") long x 10mm (3/8") wide. FOLIAGE is medium green (138A) upper surface; medium green (138B) lower surface. PARENTAGE: 'Checkerboard' x 'Ann Howard Tripp'.

Smith R 2008 UK AFS6824.

Dancing Elves. Upright/Trailer. Semi Double. COROLLA: half flared, turned under smooth petal margins; opens magenta (59D); matures magenta (59C); 11mm (7/16") long x 16mm (5/8") wide. PETALOIDS: same colour as corolla; 12mm (1/2") long x 8mm (5/16") wide. SEPALS: horizontal; tips reflexed; rose (55B) tipped light yellow (1C) upper surface; rose (52C) tipped light yellow (1C) lower surface; 31mm (1 1/4") long x 9mm (3/8") wide. TUBE: pink (55C); long, thin; 63mm (2 1/2") long x 4mm (3/16") wide. STAMENS: do not extend below the corolla; rose (68B) filaments, dark reddish purple (59A) anthers. PISTIL does not extend below the corolla; magenta (68A) style, yellowish white (4D) stigma. BUD: elongated. FOLIAGE: dark green (139A) upper surface; medium green (138B) lower surface. Leaves are 58mm (2 5/16") long x 26mm (1") wide, ovate shaped, serrulated edges, acute tips and rounded bases. Veins are light grayish red (182C), stems are grayish red (182B), branches are grayish red (182B) & medium green (138B). PARENTAGE: 'WALZ Harp' x 'La Bergère'. Lax upright or stiff trailer. Self branching. Makes good basket. Prefers overhead filtered light. Best bloom and foliage colour in filtered light. Tested 3 years in Koningshooikt, Belgium. NBFK certificate at Meise. Distinguished by bloom colour and shape.

Michiels 2003 BE AFS5100.

Daniel Pfaller. Upright/Trailer. Double. COROLLA: three quarter flared, smooth petal

margins; opens dark purple (N79B); matures dark reddish purple (59A); 25mm (1") long x 45mm (1 3/4") wide. SEPALS: fully up; tips recurved; red (52A) upper & lower surfaces; 35mm (1 3/8") long x 15mm (9/16") wide. TUBE: red (52A); medium length & thickness; 18mm (11/16") long x 8mm (5/16") wide. STAMENS: extend 30mm (1 3/16") below corolla; dark rose (51A) filaments; dark reddish purple (61A) anthers. PISTIL: extends 50mm (2") below the corolla; dark rose (51A) style; pale yellow (158B) blushed light red stigma. BUD: oblong, pointed. FOLIAGE: medium green (146A) upper surface, yellowish green (146B) lower surface. Leaves are 70mm (2 3/4") long x 40mm (1 9/16") wide, elliptic shaped, serrulated edges, acute tips and rounded bases. Red veins; dark red stems & light brown branches. PARENTAGE: 'Orange King' x 'Rohees Queen'. Lax upright or stiff trailer. Makes good basket or standard. Prefers warm climate. Heat tolerant if shaded. Best bloom and foliage colour in bright light. Tested 3 years in Southern Germany & Belgium. Distinguished by blossom colour and prolific flowering throughout the summer.

Burkhart 2004 DE AFS5455.

Daniel Reynolds. Single. COROLLA lavender blue. SEPALS white.

Reynolds G 2005 UK

Daniel Walton. COROLLA lilac blue. SEPALS white veined light pink.

Norcross 2007 UK.

Danielle Hine. Upright. Single. COROLLA: Unflared; opens violet (90D); matures light purple (78B); 20mm (3/4") long x 15mm (9/16") wide. SEPALS: half up, tips recurved up; dark rose (58C) tipped yellowish green (144B) upper & lower surfaces; 17mm (5/8") long x 8mm (5/16") wide. TUBE: pink (37C); medium length & thickness; 15mm (9/16") long x 5mm (3/16") wide. FOLIAGE is medium green (137B) upper surface; medium green (137C) lower surface. PARENTAGE: 'Shelford' x 'F. magellanica'.

Bell 2007 UK AFS6399.

Danique Lankhuizen. Upright. Semi Double. COROLLA: three quarter flared, turned under petal margins; opens reddish purple (71B) & red purple (N79C); matures dark reddish purple (61A); 24mm (15/16") long x 19mm (3/4") wide. SEPALS are half up, tips recurved up; rose (65A), tipped light apple green (145C) upper surface; magenta (63B),

94

tipped light apple green (145C) lower surface; 38mm (1 1/2") long x 16mm (5/8") wide. TUBE is light pink (65B); short and thick; 9mm (5/16") long x 8mm (5/16") wide. STAMENS extend 15mm (9/16") beyond the corolla; reddish purple (61B) filaments; purple (83A) anthers. PISTIL extends 36mm (1 7/16") beyond the corolla; dark rose (64C) style; pale yellow (2D) stigma. BUD is globular. FOLIAGE is dark green (136B) upper surface; medium green (137D) lower surface. Leaves are 54mm (2 1/8") long x 36mm (1 7/16") wide, ovate shaped, serrate edges, acute tips, rounded bases. Veins are grayish red (181C), stems are light grayish red (182C) & branches are light grayish red (182C) & light green (138C). PARENTAGE: 'Manfried Kleinau' x 'Cameron Ryle'. Lax upright or stiff trailer, self branching. Makes good basket or upright. Prefers overhead light, cool climate. Best bloom & foliage in filtered light. Tested 3 years in Koningshooikt, Belgium. Waanrode 9/8/2008. Distinguished by bloom colour. Michiels 2009 BE AFS7156.

Danny en Marina. Upright. Double. COROLLA: half flared, turned under petal margins; opens reddish purple (71B), edged purple (77A); matures reddish purple (64B); 28mm (1 1/8") long x 28mm (1 1/8") wide. PETALOIDS: reddish purple (71B), edged purple (77A); 16mm (5/8") long x 14mm (9/16") wide. SEPALS are horizontal, tips recurved, twisted left to right; white (155A) & pale lavender (65D), tipped yellowish green (144B) upper surface; magenta (68A), tipped yellowish green (144B) lower surface; 35mm (1 3/8") long x 15mm (9/16") wide. TUBE is white (155A); medium length & thickness; 15mm (9/16") long x 7mm (1/4") wide. STAMENS extend 15mm (9/16") beyond the corolla; dark reddish purple (70A) filaments; dark purple (79A) anthers. PISTIL extends 24mm (15/16") beyond the corolla; reddish purple (72B) style; yellowish white (4D) stigma. BUD is bulbous. FOLIAGE is medium green (N138B) upper surface; medium green (138B) lower surface. Leaves are 52mm (2 1/16") long x 32mm (1 1/4") wide, ovate shaped, serrulate edges, acute tips, rounded bases. Veins are light green (145D), stems are plum (184B) & branches are plum (184B) & medium green (138B). PARENTAGE: 'Manfried Kleinau' x 'Dal's Conquest'. Lax upright or stiff trailer, self branching. Makes good basket or upright. Prefers overhead filtered light, cool climate. Best bloom & foliage in filtered light. Tested 3 years in Koningshooikt, Belgium. Waanrode

5/7/2008. Distinguished by bloom colour combination.
Michiels 2009 BE AFS7157.

David Attenborough. Upright/Trailer. Double. COROLLA is full flared, square shaped, with wavy petal margins and folded outer petals; opens violet (87B), light purple (87C) marbling, white (155) at base; matures light purple (74C); 45mm (1 3/4") long x 95mm (3 3/4") wide. SEPALS are horizontal, tips reflexed; white (155) tipped green upper surface, white (155) creped lower surface; 45mm (1 3/4") long x 22mm (7/8) wide. TUBE is white (155C); short with medium thickness; 17mm (11/16") long x 10mm (3/8") wide. STAMENS extend 22mm (7/8") below the corolla; magenta (58B) filaments and anthers. PISTIL extends 30mm (1 3/16") below the corolla; white (155) style, white (155C) stigma. BUD is globular, pointed. FOLIAGE is medium green (137B) upper surface, medium green (138B) lower surface. Leaves are 95mm (3 3/4") long x 56mm (2 3/16") wide, ovate shaped, serrulated edges, obtuse tips and rounded bases. Veins are medium green, stems are pale green, branches are red. PARENTAGE: 'Malibu Mist' x 'Roy Castle'. Lax upright or stiff trailer. Makes good basket, upright or standard. Prefers cool climate. Heat tolerant if shaded. Best bloom colour in filtered light. Tested five years in Gloucester, England. Distinguished by unusual shape of central petals on corolla.
Hickman 2002 UK AFS4863.

David Burn. Upright. Double. COROLLA: three quarter flared, smooth petal margins; opens light purple (80C); matures reddish purple (64B); 25mm (1") long x 22mm (7/8") wide. SEPALS: horizontal; tips recurved; rose (47D) tipped green upper & lower surfaces; 35mm(1 3/8") long x 12mm (1/2") wide. TUBE: pale yellow green (150D); short & thin; 12mm (1/2") long x 8mm (5/16") wide. STAMENS: extend 20mm (13/16") below corolla; light rose (73C) filaments; rose (68B) anthers. PISTIL: extends 25mm (1") below the corolla; very pale orange (19D) style, rose (68B) stigma. BUD: pointed. FOLIAGE: medium green (138A) upper surface; medium green (138B) lower surface. Leaves are 45mm (1 3/4") long x 30mm (1 3/16") wide, cordate shaped, serrated edges, acute tips and cordate bases. Veins are pink, stems & branches are red. PARENTAGE: 'Jenny Sorenson' x unknown. Small upright. Self branching. Makes good upright. Prefers overhead filtered light. Best bloom and

foliage colour in filtered light. Tested 4 years in Stoke-on-Trent, England. Distinguished by colour combination.
Rowell 2003 UK AFS5135.

David Jason. Upright. Single. COROLLA is three quarter flared, bell shaped, with smooth petal margins; opens purple (88A) veined red (45A) at base; matures violet (87A); 27mm (1 1/16") long x 38mm (1 1/2") wide. SEPALS are half up, tips recurved up; vivid red (45A) upper surface, red (45A) creped lower surface; 30mm (1 3/16") long x 17mm (11/16) wide. TUBE is vivid red (45A); short with medium thickness; 6mm (13/16") long x 4mm (1/8") wide. STAMENS extend 15mm (5/8") below the corolla; red (45A) filaments; red (45B) anthers. PISTIL extends 33mm (1 5/16") below the corolla; red (45B) style and stigma. BUD is round. FOLIAGE is dark green (137A) upper surface, medium green (138A) lower surface. Leaves are 67mm (2 5/8") long x 36mm (1 7/16") wide, ovate shaped, smooth edges, acute tips and cordate bases. Veins are green, stems and branches are red. PARENTAGE: 'Dark Eyes' x 'Swanley Gem'. Upright. Self branching. Makes good upright, standard or pillar. Prefers cool climate. Heat tolerant if shaded. Best bloom colour in filtered light. Tested six years in Gloucester, England. Distinguished by short jointed growth, bloom colour and shape.
Hickman 2002 UK AFS4855.

David Preston. Upright/Trailer. Single. COROLLA is quarter flared, square shaped on bottom, with wavy petal margins; opens light purple (78B); matures reddish purple (74A); 18mm (11/16") long x 12mm (1/2") wide. SEPALS are half up, tips recurved up; pale pink (56D) upper surface, pink (48D) tipped green lower surface; 25mm (1") long x 8mm (5/16") wide. TUBE is pale pink (56D), medium length and thickness; 12mm (1/2") long x 6mm (1/4") wide. STAMENS extend 12mm (1/2") beyond the corolla; magenta (58B) filaments, light rose (58D) anthers. PISTIL extends 22mm (7/8") beyond the corolla; light pink (65B) style; pale yellow (2D) stigma. BUD is oval, tapering to a point. FOLIAGE is dark green (137A) upper surface, medium green (138B) lower surface. Leaves are 45mm (1 3/4") long x 25mm (1") wide, cordate shaped, serrulated edges, acute tips and rounded bases. Veins and stems are green, branches are dark pink tipped green. PARENTAGE: 'Marilyn Olsen' x 'Bealings'. Lax upright or stiff trailer. Makes good upright, standard or bonsai. Prefers

overhead filtered light and cool climate. Best bloom and foliage colour in filtered light. Tested three years in West Yorkshire, England. Distinguished by corolla shape.
Preston 2002 UK AFS4935.

David Savage. Upright. Semi Double. COROLLA is quarter flared, bell shaped, with smooth petal margins; opens pale lavender (69C) veined dark rose (58C), matures pale lavender (69D) veined pink; 28mm (1 1/8") long x 28mm (1 1/8") wide. PETALOIDS are same colour as corolla; 16mm (5/8") long x 14mm (9/16") wide. SEPALS are half up, tips recurved up; magenta (58B) upper surface, dark rose (58C) lower surface; 38mm (1 1/2") long x 13mm (1/2") wide. TUBE is magenta (58B), medium length and thickness; 12mm (1/2") long x 6mm (1/4") wide. STAMENS extend 18mm (11/16") below the corolla; magenta (63B) filaments, magenta (63A) anthers. PISTIL extends 30mm (1 3/16") below the corolla; rose (65A) style and stigma. BUD is ovate. FOLIAGE is dark green (139A) upper surface, medium green (137C) lower surface. Leaves are 50mm (2") long x 22mm (7/8") wide, lanceolate shaped, serrated edges, acute tips and rounded bases. Veins are dark green (139C), stems are plum (183D) and branches are plum (183C). PARENTAGE: "Found" seedling. Small upright. Makes good upright. Prefers overhead filtered light. Heat tolerant if shaded. Best bloom colour in filtered light. Tested three years in Worthing, Sussex, England. Distinguished by vigorous growth and long lasting blooms.
Hobbs 2002 UK AFS4842.

Dawn's Dream. Upright/Trailer. Semi Double. COROLLA: half flared, turned under toothed petal margins; opens violet (62B), white (155C) base, edged reddish purple (80B); matures reddish purple (72B), rose (65A) base, edged light purple (80C); 25mm (1") long x 13mm (1/2") wide. PETALOIDS: light pink (62B), white (155C) base, edged reddish purple (71B); 16mm (5/8") long x 10mm (3/8") wide. SEPALS: half down; tips reflexed; light pink (49C), white (155C) base, tipped apple green (144C) upper surface; rose (51C), white (155C) base, tipped apple green (144C) lower surface; 29mm (1 1/8") long x 16mm (5/8") wide. TUBE: white (155C); short, medium thickness; 13mm (1/2") long x 5mm (3/16") wide. STAMENS: extend 13mm (1/2") below the corolla; rose (63C) filaments, brown (176C) anthers. PISTIL extends 22mm (7/8") below the corolla; pale pink (62D) style, pale yellow

(1D) stigma. BUD: ovate. FOLIAGE: very dark green (131A) upper surface; medium green (136C) lower surface. Leaves are 71mm (2 13/16") long x 39mm (1 9/16") wide, ovate shaped, serrulated edges, acute tips and rounded bases. Veins are dark reddish purple (187D), stems are dark reddish purple (187C), branches are dark reddish purple (187B). PARENTAGE: 'Moonshot' x unknown. Lax upright or stiff trailer. Makes good basket. Prefers overhead filtered light. Best bloom and foliage colour in filtered light. Tested 3 years in Rillaar, Belgium. NBFK certificate at Meise. Distinguished by bloom shape and colour combination.
Willems 2003 BE AFS5095.

De Achterhoek. Upright/Trailer. Single. COROLLA is quarter flared with smooth petal margins; opens red (53C); matures red (53D); 24mm (15/16") long x 26mm (1") wide. SEPALS are half up, tips recurved up; light pink (49B) upper surface; light pink (49C) lower surface; 45mm (1 3/4") long x 12mm (1/2") wide. TUBE is pink (37D); long, medium thickness; 70mm (2 3/4") long x 6mm (1/4") wide. FOLIAGE: dark green (137A) upper surface; medium green (138B) lower surface. Leaves are 90mm (3 9/16") long x 50mm (2") wide, ovate shaped. PARENTAGE: 'WALZ Harp' x 'Lye's Excelsior'. VKC Award of Merit, The Netherlands. Distinguished by long white TUBE.
Braam 2005 NL AFS5804.

De Bellefroid Poswick. Trailer. Semi Double. COROLLA: half flared, turned under smooth petal margins; opens dark reddish purple (64A); matures magenta (59C); 25mm (1") long x 17mm (11/16") wide. SEPALS: horizontal; tips recurved; dark reddish purple (61A) upper surface; reddish purple (64B) lower surface; 32mm (1 1/4") long x 8mm (5/16") wide. TUBE: reddish purple (61B); long, medium thickness; 44mm (1 3/4") long x 7mm(1/4") wide. STAMENS: extend 3mm (1/8") below corolla; light reddish purple (72C) filaments; dark purple (79B) anthers. PISTIL: extends 8mm (5/16") below the corolla; reddish purple (72B) style; purple (77A) stigma. BUD: oblong. FOLIAGE: dark green (137A) upper surface, medium green (138B) lower surface. Leaves are 47mm (1 7/8") long x 23mm (7/8") wide, elliptic shaped, serrulated edges, acute tips and rounded bases. Veins are plum (185C); stems are plum (185C); branches are plum (184C). PARENTAGE: 'WALZ Harp' x 'Rohees New Millenium'. Natural trailer. Makes good basket. Prefers overhead filtered light and

cool climate. Best bloom and foliage colour in filtered light. Tested 3 years in Itegem, Belgium. Award at Meise, 5/7/03. Distinguished by bloom shape.
Geerts L. 2004 BE AFS5410.

De Bellekens Hemiksem. Upright. Single. COROLLA: quarter flared, turned under wavy petal margins; opens red (47B); matures red (46C) & reddish purple (61B); 18mm (11/16") long x 14mm (9/16") wide. SEPALS: half down, tips reflexed; rose (54C) tipped light green (145D) upper surface; dark rose (54A) tipped light green (145D) lower surface; 29mm (1 1/8") long x 7mm (1/4") wide. TUBE: pale pink (56A); long & thin; 45mm (1 3/4") long x 5mm (3/16") wide. STAMENS do not extend beyond the corolla; pale pink (49D) filaments; yellowish white (4D) anthers. PISTIL extends 12mm (7/16") beyond the corolla; pink (48D) style; pale yellow (1D) stigma. BUD: elongated. FOLIAGE: dark green (139A) upper surface; medium green (138B) lower surface. Leaves are 89mm (3 1/2") long x 46mm (1 13/16") wide; ovate shaped, serrulate edges, acute tips, rounded bases. Veins are dark red (185A), stems are plum (184C), branches are plum (184C) & light green (139D). PARENTAGE: 'WALZ Harp' x 'Ernest Claes'. Small upright. Makes good upright. Prefers overhead filtered light or full sun, cool climate. Best bloom & foliage colour in bright light. Tested 3 years in Itegem, Belgium. Waanrode 8/9/08. Distinguished by bloom colour.
Geerts L. 2009 BE AFS7071.

De Boerenkrijg. Trailer. Semi Double, COROLLA: half flared; opens light reddish purple (72D), light rose (58D) base; matures light reddish purple (72C); 22mm (7/8") long x 18mm (11/16") wide. PETALOIDS: same colour as corolla; 18mm (11/16") long x 8mm (5/16") wide. SEPALS: half down, tips recurved; rose (54C) tipped pale yellow green (150D) upper surface; light pink (55D) & light apple green (145C) tipped light apple green (145B) lower surface; 30mm (1 3/16") long x 11mm (7/16") wide. TUBE: pink (52D) striped rose (52B); long; 45mm (1 3/4") long x 6mm (1/4") wide. FOLIAGE is dark green (137A) upper surface; medium green (138B) lower surface. PARENTAGE: 'Lechlade Rocket' x 'Tubingen 2001'.
Vandenbussche 2008 BE AFS6741.

De Boerin. Trailer. Double. COROLLA is half to three quarter flared with turned under smooth petal margins; opens dark purple

(79A), purple (80A) at base; matures dark purple (79B), dark purple (79A) at base; 25mm (1") long x 20mm (13/16") wide. PETALOIDS are dark purple (79B); 14mm (9/16") long x 12mm (1/2") wide. SEPALS are horizontal, tips recurved; red (53D) upper surface, magenta (61C) lower surface; 38mm (1 1/2") long x 15mm (5/8") wide. TUBE is magenta (58B); short, medium thickness; 10mm (3/8") long x 8mm (5/16") wide. STAMENS do not extend beyond the corolla; reddish purple (61B) filaments, pale yellowish orange (20C) anthers. PISTIL extends 21mm (13/16") beyond the corolla; reddish purple (67A) style, reddish purple (70B) stigma. BUD is ovate, pointed. FOLIAGE is medium green (138A) upper surface, medium green (138B) lower surface. Leaves are 40mm (1 9/16") long x 18mm (11/16") wide, elliptic shaped, serrulated edges, acute tips and rounded bases. Veins are dark red purple (187D), branches are dark red purple (187B), stems are plum (183C). PARENTAGE: 'Rohees New Millennium' x 'Pinto De Blue'. Natural trailer. Self branching. Makes good basket. Prefers overhead filtered light. Best bloom and foliage colour in filtered light. Tested three years in Koningshooikt, Belgium. Certificate N.B.F.K. at Meise. Distinguished by bloom colour.
Michiels 2002 BE AFS4966.

De Brommel. Upright. Double. COROLLA is three quarter flared with turned under smooth petal margins; opens magenta (57A), white (155C) base; matures magenta (58B), white (155C) base; 29mm (1 1/8") long x 26mm (1") wide. PETALOIDS: same colour as corolla; 22mm (7/8") long x 12mm (1/2") wide. SEPALS are half down, tips recurved; white (155C), tipped light apple green (145C) upper surface; dark rose (58C), white (155C) base, tipped light apple green (145C) lower surface; 37mm (1 7/16") long x 19mm (3/4") wide. TUBE is white (155B); medium length & thickness; 13mm (1/2") long x 5mm (3/16") wide. FOLIAGE: dark green (137A) upper surface; medium green (138B) lower surface. Leaves are 79mm (3 1/8") long x 41mm (1 5/8") wide, ovate shaped. PARENTAGE: 'Sofie Michiels' x 'Diana Wills'. Meise 8-14-04. Distinguished by flower colour.
Michiels 2005 BE AFS5747.

De Gieter. Trailer. Double. COROLLA: half flared; opens reddish purple (N80B), base pale pink (69A); matures light purple (N78B), base pale lavender (69B); 25mm (1") long x

20mm (3/4") wide. PETALOIDS: violet (76A), base pale pink (69A); 17mm (5/8") long x 8mm (5/16") wide. SEPALS are fully up, tips recurved; pale lavender (69D) tipped light yellowish green (149C) upper surface and pale pink (69A) tipped light yellowish green (149C) lower surface; 45mm (1 3/4") long x 14mm (9/16") wide. TUBE is white (155C); medium length & thickness; 17mm (5/8") long x 6mm (1/4") wide. FOLIAGE is dark green (136B) upper surface; medium green (138B) lower surface. PARENTAGE: 'Waanrodes Silver Star' x 'Ine Frazer'.
Michiels 2007 BE AFS6538.

De Glansmerel. Upright. Single. COROLLA is half flared with turned under smooth petal margins; opens reddish purple (74A), matures dark purple (78A); 27mm (1 1/16") long x 16 mm (5/8") wide. SEPALS are half down, tips reflexed; light purple (58D) upper surface, rose (52B) lower surface; 35mm (1 3/8") long x 14mm (9/16") wide. TUBE is pale lavender (65D), medium length and thickness; 32mm (1 1/4") long x 6mm (1/4") wide. STAMENS do not extend beyond the corolla; dark rose (58C) filaments, dark tan (164B) anthers. PISTIL extends 7mm (1/4") beyond the corolla; magenta (58B) style; reddish purple (61B) stigma. BUD is long, pointed. FOLIAGE is dark green (139A) upper surface, medium green (138B) lower surface. Leaves are 64mm (2 1/2") long x 32mm (1 1/4") wide, elliptic shaped, serrulated edges, acute tips and rounded bases. Veins are light green (139D), stems are light apple green (145B), branches are yellowish green (144A). PARENTAGE: 'WALZ Harp' x 'Annabel'. Small upright. Makes good upright. Prefers overhead filtered light and full sun. Best bloom and foliage colour in bright light. Tested three years in Itegem, Belgium. Certificate N.B.F.K. at Meise. Distinguished by profuse blooms and bloom shape.
Geerts L. 2002 BE AFS4924.

De Groot's Balloon. Trailer. Single. COROLLA is half flared, very rounded; opens dark rose (54B); matures dark rose (54A); 33mm (1 5/16") long x 33mm (1 5/16") wide. SEPALS are half down, tips reflexed; pale pink (56D) upper surface; pale pink (56D), white in the middle, lower surface; 54mm (2 1/8") long x 25mm (1") wide. TUBE is pale pink (56D); 22mm 7/8") long x 9mm (5/16") wide. FOLIAGE is dark green (147A) upper surface; medium green (147B) lower surface. PARENTAGE: 'Galadriel' x 'unknown'. Nomination by NKVF as Recommendable

Cultivar. Distinguished by bloom colour & large round flowers".
de Groot 2006 BE AFS6259.

De Groot's Floriant. Upright. Single. COROLLA: 3 quarter flared; opens & matures orange (33B); 13mm (1/2") long x 9mm (5/16") wide. SEPALS: horizontal, tips reflexed; red (52A) upper surface; light orange (41D) lower surface; 15mm (9/16") long x 6mm (1/4") wide. TUBE: red (52A); medium length & thickness; 30mm (1 3/16") long x 6mm (1/4") wide. FOLIAGE is medium green (138A) upper surface; medium green (138B) lower surface. PARENTAGE: 'Fuji-san' x 'F. *andrei*'. Nomination by NKvF as recommendable cultivar.
de Groot J. 2007 BE AFS6457.

De Groot's Kattensnor. Upright. Single. COROLLA: Unflared; opens reddish purple (67A); matures reddish purple (58A); 24mm (15/16") long x 17mm (5/8") wide. SEPALS: full down, tips recurved; magenta (67B) upper surface; reddish purple (67A) lower surface; 45mm (1 3/4") long x 9mm (5/16") wide. TUBE: magenta (61C); medium length & thickness; 10mm (3/8") long x 5mm (3/16") wide. FOLIAGE is dark green (147A) upper surface; medium green (146A) lower surface. PARENTAGE: 'de Groot's Dream' x unknown . Nomination by NKvF as recommendable cultivar.
de Groot J. 2007 BE AFS6456.

De Groot's Parasol. Trailer. Single. COROLLA is unflared with turned under petal margins; opens dark rose (58C); matures magenta (57B); 24mm (15/16") long x 14mm (9/16") wide. SEPALS are full down, tips recurved; pale pink (36D) upper surface; pink (50D), tipped apple green (144C) lower surface; 32mm (1 1/4") long x 8mm (5/16") wide. TUBE is dark rose (51A); medium length & thickness; 7mm (1/4") long x 6mm (1/4") wide. FOLIAGE: dark green (147A) upper surface; medium green (147B) lower surface. Leaves are 70mm (2 3/4") long x 35mm (1 . 3/8") wide, ovate shaped. PARENTAGE: 'Alfred de Groot' x 'F. brevilobis'. Nomination by N.K.V.F. as recommendable cultivar. Distinguished by spreading growth.
de Groot J. 2005 BE AFS5782.

De Kempenbende. Upright/Trailer. Double. COROLLA: Half flared; opens dark purple (79A) & magenta (63B); matures dark purple (79C) & magenta (63B); 20mm (3/4") long x 18mm (11/16") wide. SEPALS: fully up, tips recurved; magenta (58B) upper & lower surfaces; 31mm (1 1/4") long x 17mm (5/8") wide. TUBE: magenta (58B); medium length & thickness; 10mm (3/8") long x 6mm (1/4") wide. FOLIAGE is medium green (137B) upper surface; medium green (138A) lower surface. PARENTAGE: 'Roesse Lupus' x 'HeRi Mochara'.
Buiting 2007 NL AFS6664.

De Klooster Rebellen. Upright. Single. COROLLA is quarter flared; opens dark purple (79B) with dark reddish purple (59A) base; matures reddish purple (59B); 19mm (3/4") long x 17mm (5/8") wide. SEPALS are horizontal, tips reflexed; reddish purple (59B) upper surface; dark reddish purple (61A) lower surface; 28mm (1 1/8") long x 9mm (5/16") wide. TUBE is magenta (59C); 12mm (7/16") long x 5mm (3/16") wide. FOLIAGE is medium green (137B) upper surface; medium green (138B) lower surface. PARENTAGE: 'Rosea' x 'Rohees New Millennium'. Meise 8/13/05. Distinguished by bloom colour.
Michiels 2006 BE AFS6036.

De Kluisberg. Upright/Trailer. Single. COROLLA is three quarter flared with turned under wavy petal margins; opens purple (93A), reddish purple (64B) at base; matures dark reddish purple (64A), reddish purple (64B) at base; 23mm (15/16") long x 22mm (7/8") wide. SEPALS are half down, tips reflexed; dark reddish purple (61A) tipped light apple green (145B) upper surface, reddish purple (61B) tipped light apple green (145B) lower surface; 28mm (1 1/8") long x 15mm (5/8") wide. TUBE is dark reddish purple (61A); medium length and thin; 12mm (1/2") long x 5mm (3/16") wide. STAMENS extend 11mm (7/16") beyond the corolla; reddish purple (74A) filaments, dark reddish purple (72A) anthers. PISTIL extends 29mm (1 1/8") beyond the corolla; reddish purple (74B) style, yellow (10C) stigma. BUD is ovate, pointed. FOLIAGE is dark green (139A) upper surface, medium green (138B) lower surface. Leaves are 42mm (1 11/16") long x 23mm (15/16") wide, ovate shaped, smooth edges, acute tips and rounded bases. Veins are grayish red (181C), stems are plum (184B) branches are dark red purple (187B). PARENTAGE: 'Rohees New Millennium' x 'Tanya'. Lax upright or stiff trailer. Self branching. Makes good basket. Prefers overhead filtered light. Best bloom and foliage colour in filtered light. Tested three years in Koningshooikt, Belgium. Certificate N.B.F.K. at Meise. Distinguished by bloom colour and profuse blooms.

Michiels 2002 BE AFS4967.

'De Koningsvelden. Trailer. Semi Double. COROLLA: three quarter flared; opens dark reddish purple (72A) and reddish purple (67A) & matures dark reddish purple (70A) & reddish purple (67A); 16mm (5/8") long x 15mm (9/16") wide. PETALOIDS: dark reddish purple (72A) & dark rose (67C); 10mm (3/8") long x 9mm (5/16") wide. SEPALS are horizontal, tips reflexed; rose (61D) upper surface & dark rose (58C) lower surface; 26mm (1") long x 15mm (9/16") wide. TUBE is light rose (58D); medium length & thickness; 11mm (7/16") long x 5mm (3/16") wide. FOLIAGE is dark green (139A) upper surface; medium green (137B) lower surface. PARENTAGE: 'Mathy' x 'Guidewell Quest'.
Michiels 2007 BE AFS6539.

De Lemmentjes. Trailer. Double. COROLLA is half flared; opens light pink (65B); matures light pink (65C); 12mm (7/16") long x 21mm (13/16") wide. SEPALS are half up, tips reflexed up; magenta (58B) upper & lower surfaces; 27mm (1 1/16") long x 25mm (1") wide. TUBE is white (155C); 22mm (7/8") long x 3mm (1/8") wide. FOLIAGE: dark green (137A) upper surface; medium green (138B) lower surface. PARENTAGE: 'Luuk van Riet' x 'Roesse Betelgeuze'. Distinguished by bloom colour & shape.
Roes 2006 NL AFS6177.

De Mijnlamp. Upright/Trailer. Double. COROLLA is quarter flared; opens dark purple (79A), striped reddish purple (71B); matures dark reddish purple (72A); 16mm (5/8") long x 7mm (1/4") wide. PETALOIDS: dark purple (79A); 10mm (3/8") long x 4mm (1/8") wide. SEPALS are horizontal, tips reflexed; dark reddish purple (72A) upper surface; reddish purple (71B) lower surface; 30mm (1 3/16") long x 7mm (1/4") wide. TUBE is reddish purple (71B); 32mm (1 1/4") long x 3mm (1/8") wide. FOLIAGE: dark green (137A) upper surface; medium green (138B) lower surface. PARENTAGE: 'Rosea' x 'Katrien Michiels'. Meise 9/17/05. Distinguished by dark bloom colour.
Michiels 2006 BE AFS6074.

De Nachtwacht. Trailer. Single. COROLLA: Quarter flared; opens dark purple (79A); matures reddish purple (58A); 21mm (13/16") long x 21mm (13/16") wide. SEPALS: half up, tips reflexed up; dark reddish purple (61A) upper surface; reddish purple (61B) lower surface; 28mm (1 1/8") long x 14mm (9/16") wide. TUBE: dark reddish purple (61A); short, medium thickness; 12mm (7/16") long x 8mm (5/16") wide. FOLIAGE is medium green (146A) upper surface; yellowish green (146B) lower surface. PARENTAGE: 'Keteltje' x unknown.
Krom 2007 NL AFS6556.

De Neer Hofvrienden. Upright. Double. COROLLA: one quarter flared, turned under petal margins; opens reddish purple (71B) & dark reddish purple (72A); matures purple (71A); 25mm (1") long x 18mm (11/16") wide. PETALOIDS: dark reddish purple (70A); 16mm (5/8") long x 11mm (7/16") wide. SEPALS are horizontal, tips recurved; light pink (65C), tipped pale yellow green (150D) upper surface; light reddish purple (N66C), tipped pale yellow green (150D) lower surface; 37mm (1 7/16") long x 15mm (9/16") wide. TUBE is rose (68B); medium length & thickness; 15mm (9/16") long x 6mm (1/4") wide. STAMENS extend 12mm (7/16") beyond the corolla; light reddish purple (72C) filaments; purple (83B) anthers. PISTIL extends 21mm (13/16") beyond the corolla; light rose (73B) style; pale yellow (2D) stigma. BUD is globular. FOLIAGE is dark green (137A) upper surface; medium green (138B) lower surface. Leaves are 52mm (2 1/16") long x 30mm (1 3/16") wide, ovate shaped, serrulate edges, acute tips, rounded bases. Veins are reddish purple (186B), stems are very dark reddish purple (186A) & branches are plum (183B) & very dark reddish purple (186A). PARENTAGE: 'Manfried Kleinau' x 'Tef Vander Kuylen'. Lax upright or stiff trailer, self branching. Makes good basket or upright. Prefers overhead filtered light, cool climate. Best bloom & foliage in filtered light. Tested 3 years in Koningshooikt, Belgium. Waanrode 5/7/2008, Outstanding. Distinguished by unique bloom colour combination.
Michiels 2009 BE AFS7158.

De Niro. Trailer. Double. COROLLA: quarter flared; opens white (155C) striped light rose (63D) and matures white (155D) striped light pink (65B); 15mm (9/16") long x 14mm (9/16") wide. PETALOIDS: white (155C) striped light rose (63D); 10mm (3/8") long x 7mm (1/4") wide. SEPALS are horizontal, tips recurved; white (155C) & pale lavender (69D) tipped pale yellow green (150D) upper surface & pale lavender (69C) tipped pale yellow green (150D) lower surface; 38mm (1 1/2") long x 12mm (7/16") wide. TUBE is white (155C); medium length & thin; 20mm (3/4") long x 5mm (3/16") wide. FOLIAGE is

100

dark green (137A) upper surface; medium green (138B) lower surface. PARENTAGE: 'Lavender Heaven' x 'Delta's Trick'. Michiels 2007 BE AFS6540.

De Oelewappers. Trailer. Single. COROLLA is half flared; opens magenta (63A); matures magenta (58B); 20mm (3/4") long x 24 (15/16wide. SEPALS are half up, tips recurved up; rose (55B) tipped yellowish green (144A) upper surface, and dark rose (55A) tipped yellowish green (144A), lower surface; 26mm (1") long x 8mm (5/16") wide. TUBE is light pink (55D); 15mm (9/16") long x 6mm (1/4") wide. FOLIAGE is dark green (139A) upper surface; medium green (137B) lower surface. PARENTAGE: 'Tresco' x 'Danny Kay'. Meise 8/13/05. Distinguished by bloom colour, shape. Michiels 2006 BE AFS6041.

De Schalm. Upright/Trailer. Single. COROLLA: three quarter flared, turned under wavy petal margins; opens and matures pink (62A) edged violet (84A); 13mm (1/2") long x 22mm (7/8") wide. SEPALS: horizontal; tips reflexed; magenta (63A), tipped yellowish green (149A) upper surface; light orange (41D) lower surface; 29mm(1 1/8") long x 14mm (9/16") wide. TUBE: pale lavender (65D) striped light pink (65B); long, medium thickness; 40mm (1 9/16") long x 14mm (9/16") wide. STAMENS: do not extend below corolla; no filaments; yellow (6B) anthers. PISTIL extends 25mm (1") below the corolla; light rose (58D) style, light yellow (2C) stigma. BUD: ovate, long TUBE. FOLIAGE: dark green (137A) upper surface; medium green (138B) lower surface. Leaves are 74mm (2 15/16") long x 55mm (2 3/16") wide, cordate shaped, serrated edges, acute tips and cordate bases. Veins, stems & branches are dark grayish purple (184A). PARENTAGE: 'Alda Alders' x 'Wingrove's Mammoth'. Lax upright or stiff trailer. Self branching. Makes good basket. Prefers overhead filtered light. Best bloom and foliage colour in filtered light. Tested 4 years in Leopoldsburg, Belgium. NBFK Certificate at Meise. Distinguished by bloom shape. Busschodts 2003 BE AFS5130.

De Schommel. Upright/Trailer. Single. COROLLA is half flared; opens light rose (73B); matures light purple (74C); 20mm (13/16") long x 16mm (5/8") wide. SEPALS are half up, tips recurved up; light pink (62B), tipped light apple green (145B) upper surface; pink (62A), tipped light apple green (145B) lower surface; 28mm (1 1/8") long x

7mm (1/4") wide. TUBE is pink (62C); 12mm (1/2") long x 5mm (3/16") wide. FOLIAGE: dark green (139A) upper surface; medium green (138A) lower surface. PARENTAGE: 'Query' x 'Onbekend'. Meise 8/13/05. Distinguished by unique bloom colour. Willems 2006 BE AFS5997.

De Spasbink. Upright. Single. COROLLA is half flared with turned under smooth petal margins; opens dark purple (79B), dark reddish purple (60A) base; matures reddish purple (59B); 21mm (13/16") long x 18mm (11/16") wide. SEPALS are horizontal, tips reflexed; reddish purple (59B) upper surface; dark reddish purple (60A) lower surface; 29mm (1 1/8") long x 11mm (7/16") wide. TUBE is reddish purple (59B); short & thick; 19mm (3/4") long x 10mm (3/8") wide. FOLIAGE: dark green (139A) upper surface; medium green (138A) lower surface. Leaves are 68mm (2 11/16") long x 35mm (1 3/8") wide, ovate shaped. PARENTAGE: 'Roesse Blacky' x 'California'. Meis 3-7-04. Distinguished by colour fade from brown to aubergine. Michiels 2005 BE AFS5677.

De Steeg. Trailer. Single. COROLLA: quarter flared, turned under smooth petal margins; opens pale pink (56C), reddish purple (80B) base; matures purple (80A); 22mm (7/8") long x 22mm (7/8") wide. SEPALS: horizontal; tips reflexed; pale pink (56C) tipped light apple green (145B) upper surface; pale pink (56D) tipped light apple green (145B) lower surface; 39mm (1 9/16") long x 11mm (7/16") wide. TUBE: pale pink (56C); long & thin; 25mm (1") long x 5mm (3/16") wide. STAMENS: extend 6mm (1/4") below corolla; magenta (67B) filaments; purple (77A) anthers. PISTIL: extends 13mm (1/2") below the corolla; rose (63C) style; pale pink (62D) stigma. BUD: oblong. FOLIAGE: medium green (139B) upper surface, medium green (138B) lower surface. Leaves are 54mm (2 1/8") long x 26mm (1") wide, elliptic shaped, serrulated edges, acute tips and rounded bases. Medium green (138B) veins; medium green (138B) & grayish red (182B) stems; medium green (138B) & plum (184C) branches. PARENTAGE: 'Checkerboard' x 'Bert's Whisky'. Natural trailer. Self branching. Makes good basket. Prefers overhead filtered light and cool climate. Best bloom and foliage colour in filtered light. Tested 3 years in Werm, Belgium. Award at Meise, 5/7/03. Distinguished by bloom shape. Wagemans 2004 BE AFS5413.

De Vuurdoorn. Upright. Single. COROLLA: unflared, turned under wavy petal margins; opens & matures magenta (68A); 8mm (5/16") long x 15mm (5/8") wide. SEPALS: half up; tips recurved up; magenta (58B) upper & lower surfaces; 37mm(1 7/16") long x 11mm (7/16") wide. TUBE: white (155B); medium length & thickness; 17mm (11/16") long x 6mm (1/4") wide. STAMENS: do not extend below the corolla; reddish purple (58A) filaments, yellow (4A) anthers. PISTIL extends 15mm (5/8") below the corolla; dark rose (58C) style, yellow orange (23C) stigma. BUD: rectangular, pointed. FOLIAGE: dark green (137A) upper surface; medium green (138A) lower surface. Leaves are 65mm (2 9/16") long x 42mm (1 5/8") wide, ovate shaped, serrulated edges, acute tips and rounded bases. Veins, stems & branches are reddish purple (58A). PARENTAGE: 'Leverküsen' x 'WALZ Toorts'. Medium upright. Makes good upright. Prefers overhead filtered light. Best bloom and foliage colour in filtered light. Tested 5 years in Leopoldsburg, Belgium. NBFK Certificate of Merit at Meise. Distinguished by profuse blooms, bloom shape.
Busschodts 2003 BE AFS5126.

De Weekkrant. Upright/Trailer. Single. COROLLA is quarter flared with turned under wavy petal margins; opens dark violet (87A), rose (51B) at base; matures light reddish purple (72C); 26mm (1") long x 28 mm (1 1/8") wide. SEPALS are horizontal, tips recurved; rose (51B) tipped yellowish green (145A) upper surface; rose (52B) lower surface; 32mm (1 1/4") long x 16mm (5/8") wide. TUBE is white (155B) striped pink (55C), long with medium thickness; 40mm (1 9/16") long x 8mm (5/16") wide. STAMENS do not extend beyond the corolla; pink (62C) filaments, yellowish white (4D) anthers. PISTIL extends 25mm (1") below the corolla; pink (62A) style; yellow (11A) stigma. BUD is ovate, long TUBEd. FOLIAGE is dark green (139A) upper surface, medium green (138A) lower surface. Leaves are 94mm (3 11/16") long x 49mm (1 15/16") wide, elliptic shaped, serrulated edges, acute tips and rounded bases. Veins and stems are brown (166A); branches are yellowish green (144A). PARENTAGE: 'Alda Alders' x 'Party Frock'. Lax upright or stiff trailer. Self branching. Makes good upright or basket. Prefers overhead filtered light and cool climate. Best bloom and foliage colour in filtered light. Tested three years in Leopoldsburg, Belgium. Certificate N.B.F.K. at Meise. Distinguished

by long TUBE, colour combination and profuse blooms.
Busschodts 2002 BE AFS4909.

De Zaager. Upright. Single. COROLLA is three quarter flared; opens purple (90A); matures reddish purple (72B); 24mm (15/16") long x 29mm (1 1/8") wide. SEPALS are horizontal, tips recurved; magenta (57A) upper & lower surfaces; 26mm (1") long x 16mm (5/8") wide. TUBE is magenta (57A); 6mm (1/4") long x 6mm (1/4") wide. FOLIAGE: dark green (137A) upper surface; medium green (137C) lower surface. PARENTAGE: 'Maxima's Baby' x 'Reg Gubler'. Distinguished by bloom shape & colour.
Roes 2006 NL AFS6182.

De Zeveraar. Upright/Trailer. Double. COROLLA is three quarter flared; opens violet (86B); matures purple (81B); 17mm (5/8") long x 24mm (15/16") wide. SEPALS are half down, tips reflexed; pale lavender (69C) upper surface; pale lavender (69B) lower surface; 22mm (7/8") long x 15mm (9/16") wide. TUBE is white (155A); 24mm (15/16") long x 3mm (1/8") wide. FOLIAGE: dark green (137A) upper surface; medium green (137C) lower surface. PARENTAGE: 'Roesse Apus' x 'Magda van Bets'. Distinguished by bloom & foliage combination.
Roes 2006 NL AFS6174.

Deborah Jane. Upright. Single. COROLLA pale lilac. SEPALS white veined light pink. TUBE pale pink.
Wilkinson 2008 UK.

DebRons Austin Allan. Upright. Double. COROLLA: quarter flared; smooth margins; opens very dark purple (187A), veined dark reddish purple (187D); matures dark reddish purple (187D); 24mm (15/16") long x 23mm (7/8") wide. PETALOIDS: Same colour as corolla; 17mm (5/8") long x 11mm (7/16") wide. SEPALS: half up, tips recurved up, curled back to TUBE; magenta (63A) upper & lower surfaces; 30mm (1 3/16") long x 12mm (7/16") wide. TUBE: magenta (59D); short, medium thickness; 11mm (7/16") long x 7mm (1/4") wide. STAMENS extend 22mm (7/8") beyond the corolla; dark reddish purple (187C) filaments; dark purple (79A) anthers. PISTIL extends 40mm (1 9/16") beyond the corolla; dark reddish purple (187D) style; dark reddish purple (61A) stigma. BUD is lanceolate. FOLIAGE is dark green (137A) upper surface; medium green (138B) lower surface. Leaves are 45mm (1

3/4") long x 30mm (1 3/16") wide; lanceolate shaped, serrulate edges, acute tips, rounded bases. Veins are reddish purple (59B), stems & branches are dark reddish purple (59A). PARENTAGE: 'Angelique' x 'Rohees New Millennium'. Small upright. Self branching. Makes good upright. Prefers overhead filtered light. Best bloom colour in bright light. Tested 3 years in Woodburn, Oregon, USA. Distinguished by intense blossom colour & shape, profuse blooms.
Monnier 2009 USA AFS6960.

DebRons Beau Dean Richard. Upright. Double. COROLLA: quarter flared; smooth turned under margins; opens dark purple (79A); matures dark reddish purple (61A); 26mm (1") long x 24mm (15/16") wide. SEPALS: horizontal, tips recurved; magenta (61C) upper surface; magenta (63A) lower surface; 41mm (1 5/8") long x 17mm (5/8") wide. TUBE: red (53D); short, medium thickness; 14mm (9/16") long x 10mm (3/8") wide. STAMENS extend 20mm (3/4") beyond the corolla; magenta (63A) filaments; dark purple (79A) anthers. PISTIL extends 50mm (2") beyond the corolla; magenta (63A) style; light magenta (66D) stigma. BUD is oblong. FOLIAGE is medium green (137C) upper surface; medium green (138B) lower surface. Leaves are 47mm (1 7/8") long x 30mm (1 3/16") wide; cordate shaped, serrulate edges, acute tips, rounded bases. Veins are plum (183D), stems & branches are dark grayish purple (183A). PARENTAGE: 'Hermiena' x 'Rohees New Millennium'. Small upright. Self branching. Makes good upright. Prefers overhead filtered light. Best bloom & foliage colour in filtered light. Tested 3 years in Woodburn, Oregon, USA. Distinguished by blossom colour & shape, profuse blooms.
Monnier 2009 USA AFS6981.

DebRons Kaite Belle. Upright/Trailer. Single. COROLLA: unflared; smooth turned under margins; opens white (155D); matures white (155D) veined pink (62A); 25mm (1") long x 21mm (13/16") wide. SEPALS: half up, tips recurved up; pale pink (62D) veined dark rose (58C) upper surface; pink (62C) tipped light apple green (145B) lower surface; 37mm (1 7/16") long x 13mm (1/2") wide. TUBE: light rose (58D) veined dark rose (58C); medium length & thickness; 12mm (7/16") long x 6mm (1/4") wide. STAMENS extend 18mm (11/16") beyond the corolla; light pink (62B) filaments; magenta (63A) anthers. PISTIL extends 50mm (2") beyond the corolla; pink (62A) style; yellowish white (158A) stigma. BUD is ovate/lanceolate.

FOLIAGE is dark green (137A) upper surface; medium green (138B) lower surface. Leaves are 48mm (1 7/8") long x 30mm (1 3/16") wide; ovate shaped, serrulate edges, acute tips, rounded bases. Veins are medium green (138B), stems are dark red (46A), branches are dark red (53A). PARENTAGE: 'Heston Blue' x 'Brookwood Belle'. Lax upright or stiff trailer. Self branching. Makes good basket or upright. Prefers overhead filtered light. Best bloom & foliage colour in bright light. Tested 3 years in Woodburn, Oregon, USA. Distinguished by profuse/continuous blooms.
Monnier 2009 USA AFS6983.

DebRons Madison Mae. Trailer. Double. COROLLA: quarter flared; opens light purple (78C), reddish purple (74B) edges & veins; matures light magenta (57D), reddish purple (74B) edges & veins; 28mm (1 1/8") long x 30mm (1 3/16") wide. SEPALS: half up, tips recurved up; curled back tips touch TUBE; white (155D) tipped light apple green (145C) upper surface; pink (62B) tipped light apple green (145C) lower surface; 48mm (1 7/8") long x 18mm (11/16") wide. TUBE: cream (158C); medium length & thickness; 14mm (9/16") long x 10mm (3/8") wide. STAMENS extend 20mm (3/4") beyond the corolla; magenta (63B) filaments; reddish purple (61B) anthers. PISTIL extends 32mm (1 1/4") beyond the corolla; white (155B) style; pale yellow (18D) stigma. BUD is fusiform (oval). FOLIAGE is medium green (137C) upper surface; medium green (138B) lower surface. Leaves are 50mm (2") long x 30mm (1 3/16") wide; lanceolate shaped, serrate edges, acute tips, rounded bases. Veins are medium green (138B), stems are plum (183C), branches are light green (145D). PARENTAGE: 'Celebration' x 'Drama Girl'. Natural trailer. Self branching. Makes good basket. Prefers overhead filtered light. Best bloom & foliage colour in bright light. Tested 3 years in Woodburn, Oregon, USA. Distinguished by blossom colour, early blooming, profuse blossoms.
Monnier 2009 USA AFS6958.

DebRons Party Girls. Upright. Single. COROLLA: three quarter flared; flared shape, wavy margins; opens purple (83A), veined light rose (58D); matures reddish purple (74A), veined light rose (58D); 25mm (1") long x 30mm (1 3/16") wide. SEPALS: fully up, tips recurved; light rose (58D) tipped light yellowish green (149B) upper & lower surfaces; 45mm (1 3/4") long x 14mm (9/16") wide. TUBE: light rose (58D); short, medium thickness; 10mm (3/8") long x 7mm (1/4") wide. STAMENS extend 30mm (1 3/16") beyond the corolla; dark rose (58C) filaments; magenta (57A) anthers. PISTIL extends 45mm (1 3/4") beyond the corolla; light magenta (57D) style; peach (179D) stigma. BUD is lanceolate. FOLIAGE is yellowish green (146B) upper surface; reddish purple (59B) lower surface. Leaves are 65mm (2 9/16") long x 28mm (1 1/8") wide; lanceolate shaped, smooth edges, acute tips, rounded bases. Veins, stems & branches are dark reddish purple (59A). PARENTAGE: 'Ting-a-Ling' x 'Maxima'. Small upright. Makes good upright or decorative. Prefers overhead filtered light. Best bloom & foliage colour in filtered light. Tested 3 years in Woodburn, Oregon, USA. Distinguished by intense blossom & foliage colour. Monnier 2009 USA AFS6959.

DebRons Tonii Nicole. Trailer. Double. COROLLA: half flared; smooth turned under margins; opens & matures light violet (84C) splashed pink (54D); 27mm (1 1/16") long x 23mm (7/8") wide. PETALOIDS: Same colour as corolla; 17mm (5/8") long x 12mm (7/16") wide. SEPALS: fully up, tips recurved; white (155B) tipped apple green (145B) upper surface; pink (54D) lower surface; 40mm (1 9/16") long x 16mm (5/8") wide. TUBE: yellowish white (158A); medium length & thickness; 12mm (7/16") long x 8mm (5/16") wide. STAMENS extend 18mm (11/16") beyond the corolla; pink (55C) filaments; dark red (46A) anthers. PISTIL extends 12mm (7/16") beyond the corolla; white (155B) style; pale yellow (158B) stigma. BUD is ovate. FOLIAGE is medium green (137C) upper surface; medium green (139C) lower surface. Leaves are 52mm (2 1/16") long x 32mm (1 1/4") wide; cordate shaped, serrate edges, acute tips, cordate bases. Veins are medium green (139C), stems are light green (142B), branches are light apple green (145B). PARENTAGE: 'Celebration' x 'Drama Girl'. Natural trailer. Self branching. Makes good basket. Prefers overhead filtered light. Best bloom & foliage colour in bright light. Tested 3 years in Woodburn, Oregon, USA. Distinguished by early bloom, blossom colour & shape, profuse blooms. Monnier 2009 USA AFS6982.

Deco Aime Moi. Upright/Trailer. Double. COROLLA: three-quarter flared; opens violet (77B) & matures reddish purple (74A); 24mm (15/16") long x 21mm (13/16") wide. SEPALS are fully up, tips reflexed; rose (65A) upper & lower surfaces; 44mm (1 3/4") long x 19mm

(3/4") wide. TUBE is light pink (65C); 26mm (1") long x 9mm (5/16") wide. FOLIAGE is dark green (137A) upper surface; medium green (138A) lower surface. PARENTAGE: 'Roesse Franklin' x 'Bree Vis Evelien'. Decoster 2008 BE AFS6869.

Deco Amour Perdu. Upright. Double. COROLLA: three quarter flared, smooth petal margins; opens violet (85A) & matures light purple (81C); 27mm (1 1/16") long x 27mm (1 1/16") wide. SEPALS are fully up, tips recurved; light rose (68D) upper surface; rose (68C) lower surface; 33mm (1 3/16") long x 16mm (5/8") wide. TUBE is light rose (68D); medium length & thickness; 11mm (7/16") long x 17mm (5/8") wide. STAMENS extend 12mm (7/16") beyond the corolla; violet (85A) filaments; dark reddish purple (61A) anthers. PISTIL extends 32mm (1 1/4") beyond the corolla; rose (68B) style; white (155D) stigma. BUD is ovate. FOLIAGE is dark green (137A) upper surface; medium green (138A) lower surface. Leaves are 67mm (2 5/8") long x 35mm (1 3/8") wide, cordate shaped, serrulate edges, acute tips, rounded bases. Veins, stems & branches are green. PARENTAGE: 'Gerard Domingos' x 'Baby van Eijk'. Lax upright or stiff trailer. Makes good upright or stiff trailer. Prefers overhead filtered light. Best bloom in filtered light. Tested 3 years in Lubbeek, Belgium. Distinguished by bloom colour. Decoster 2009 BE AFS7258.

Deco Formidable. Upright/Trailer. Double. COROLLA: full flare; opens dark reddish purple (70A); matures magenta (67B); 27mm (1 1/16") long x 29mm (1 1/8") wide. SEPALS are fully up, tips reflexed; pink (62A) upper surface; dark rose (58C) lower surface; 45mm (1 3/4") long x 21mm (13/16") wide. TUBE is pale pink (62D); 25mm (1") long x 8mm (5/16") wide. FOLIAGE is dark green (137A) upper surface; medium green (138B) lower surface. PARENTAGE: 'Deco Inoubliable' x 'Caesar'. Decoster 2008 BE AFS6872.

Deco Indespensable. Trailer. Single. COROLLA: full flare; opens dark reddish purple (70A); matures magenta (67B); 27mm (1 1/16") long x 29mm (1 1/8") wide. SEPALS are fully up, tips reflexed; pink (62A) upper surface; dark rose (58C) lower surface; 45mm (1 3/4") long x 21mm (13/16") wide. TUBE is pale pink (62D); 25mm (1") long x 8mm (5/16") wide. FOLIAGE is dark green (137A) upper surface; medium green (138B) lower surface. PARENTAGE: 'Deco Inoubliable' x 'Caesar'. Decoster 2008 BE AFS6872.

Deco Inoubliable. Upright. Double. COROLLA: Three quarter flared; opens dark reddish purple (59A); matures reddish purple (59B); 16mm (5/8") long x 18mm (11/16") wide. SEPALS: half up, tips recurved up; light rose (63D) upper surface; reddish purple (64B) lower surface; 16mm (5/8") long x 14mm (9/16") wide. TUBE: magenta (63A); medium length & thickness; 15mm (9/16") long x 7mm (1/4") wide. FOLIAGE is dark green (137A) upper surface; medium green (138A) lower surface. PARENTAGE: 'Roesse Lupus' x 'Roesse Circinus'. Decoster 2007 BE AFS6621.

Deco Intoxiqué. Upright/Trailer. Double. COROLLA: three-quarter flared; opens dark (83A); matures reddish purple (61B); 19mm (3/4") long x 21mm (13/16") wide. SEPALS are fully up, tips reflexed; rose (68C) upper surface & pink (62A) lower surface; 42mm (1 5/8") long x 21mm (13/16") wide. TUBE is light rose (68D); 32mm (1 1/4") long x 10mm (3/8") wide. FOLIAGE is medium green (137D) upper & lower surfaces. PARENTAGE: 'Deco Inoubliable' x 'Caesar'. Decoster 2008 BE AFS6871.

Deco Le Toreador. Upright. Double. COROLLA: three quarter flared, smooth petal margins; opens light purple (75B) & matures reddish purple (70B); 34mm (1 3/8") long x 4mm (1/8") wide. SEPALS are fully up, tips recurved; pale lavender (65D) upper surface; rose (65A) lower surface; 42mm (1 5/8") long x 12mm (7/16") wide. TUBE is rose (63C); medium length & thickness; 15mm (9/16") long x 7mm (1/4") wide. STAMENS extend 10mm (3/8") beyond the corolla; light rose (73B) filaments; dark reddish purple (61A) anthers. PISTIL extends 41mm (1 5/8") beyond the corolla; rose (65A) style; magenta (63B) stigma. BUD is ovate. FOLIAGE is dark green (137A) upper surface; medium green (138B) lower surface. Leaves are 92mm (3 5/8") long x 44mm (1 3/4") wide, cordate shaped, serrulate edges, acute tips, acute bases. Veins, stems & branches are green. PARENTAGE: 'Gerard Domingos' x 'Baby van Eijk'. Lax upright or stiff trailer. Makes good upright or stiff trailer. Prefers overhead filtered light. Best bloom in filtered light. Tested 3 years in Lubbeek, Belgium. Distinguished by bloom & foliage colour combinations. Decoster 2009 AFS7257.

Deco Ma Biche. Upright/Trailer. Double. COROLLA: three-quarter flared; opens dark purple (79A); matures purple (71A); 21mm (13/16") long x 20mm (3/4") wide. SEPALS are horizontal, tips recurved; light pink (65C) upper surface; light pink (65B) lower surface; 49mm (1 15/16") long x 18mm (11/16") wide. TUBE is light pink (65C); 20mm (3/4") long x 7mm (1/4") wide. FOLIAGE is medium green (137B) upper surface; medium green (138B) lower surface. PARENTAGE: 'Roesse Franklin' x 'BreeVis Evelien'. Decoster 2008 BE AFS6867.

Deco Paradis Perdu. Upright. Double. COROLLA: three quarter flared, smooth petal margins; opens pale pink (69A) & matures pale lavender (69C); 22mm (7/8") long x 22mm (7/8") wide. SEPALS are half up, tips reflexed up; light rose (68D) upper surface; rose (68C) lower surface; 41mm (1 5/8") long x 17mm (5/8") wide. TUBE is light rose (68D); medium length & thickness; 10mm (3/8") long x 7mm (1/4") wide. STAMENS extend 11mm (7/16") beyond the corolla; magenta (68A) filaments; dark reddish purple (64A) anthers. PISTIL extends 39mm (1 1/2") beyond the corolla; rose (68C) style; white (155D) stigma. BUD is ovate. FOLIAGE is dark green (139A) upper surface; medium green (138A) lower surface. Leaves are 81mm (3 1/4") long x 49mm (1 15/16") wide, cordate shaped, serrulate edges, acute tips, rounded bases. Veins, stems & branches are green. PARENTAGE: 'Gerard Domingos' x 'Baby van Eijk'. Lax upright or stiff trailer. Makes good stiff trailer. Prefers overhead filtered light. Best bloom in filtered light. Tested 3 years in Lubbeek, Belgium. Distinguished by bloom & foliage colour combinations. Decoster 2009 BE AFS7255.

Deco Plein Délire. Upright/Trailer. Semi Double. COROLLA: Half flared; opens purple (77A); matures dark purple (78A); 11mm (7/16") long x 14mm (9/16") wide. SEPALS: half up, tips reflexed up; light rose (68D) upper surface; rose (68C) lower surface; 24mm (15/16") long x 12mm (7/16") wide. TUBE: light rose (68D); medium length & thickness; 12mm (7/16") long x 6mm (1/4") wide. FOLIAGE is dark green (137A) upper surface; medium green (137C) lower surface. PARENTAGE: 'Roesse Lupus' x 'Roesse Circinus'. Decoster 2007 BE AFS6623.

Deco Prenier Pas. Upright. Double. COROLLA: half flared, smooth petal margins;

opens & matures light rose (68D); 27mm (1 1/16") long x 12mm (7/16") wide. SEPALS are fully up, tips recurved; pink (62B) upper & lower surfaces; 24mm (15/16") long x 16mm (5/8") wide. TUBE is pink (62B); medium length & thickness; 29mm (1 1/8") long x 6mm (1/4") wide. STAMENS extend 12mm (7/16") beyond the corolla; rose (68B) filaments; magenta (63A) anthers. PISTIL extends 30mm (1 3/16") beyond the corolla; light rose (68D) style & stigma. BUD is globular. FOLIAGE is medium green (137B) upper surface; medium green (138B) lower surface. Leaves are 62mm (2 7/16") long x 26mm (1") wide, lanceolate shaped, serrulate edges, acute tips, rounded bases. Veins, stems & branches are red. PARENTAGE: 'Carla Knapen' x 'Baby van Eijk'. Lax upright or stiff trailer. Makes good stiff trailer. Prefers overhead filtered light. Best bloom in filtered light. Tested 3 years in Lubbeek, Belgium. Distinguished by bloom & foliage colour combinations.
Decoster 2009 BE AFS7254.

Deco Sans Limite. Trailer. Double. COROLLA: three-quarter flared; opens & matures pale rose (73D); 20mm (3/4") long x 21mm (13/16") wide. SEPALS are half up, tips reflexed up; red (52A) upper & lower surfaces; 36mm (1 7/16") long x 16mm (5/8") wide. TUBE is red (52A); 24mm (15/16") long x 6mm (1/4") wide. FOLIAGE is dark green (137A) upper surface; medium green (138B) lower surface. PARENTAGE: ('Cameron Ryle' x 'Parasol') x 'Luuk van Riet'.
Decoster 2008 BE AFS6866.

Deco Tant Attendu. Trailer. Single. COROLLA: three quarter flared, smooth petal margins; opens violet (82C) & matures light purple (82D); 22mm (7/8") long x 24mm (15/16") wide. SEPALS are fully up, tips recurved; light apple green (145C) upper surface; rose (68C) lower surface; 28mm (1 1/8") long x 12mm (7/16") wide. TUBE is light apple green (145C); medium length & thickness; 17mm (5/8") long x 7mm (1/4") wide. STAMENS extend 5mm (3/16") beyond the corolla; rose (68B) filaments; rose (65A) anthers. PISTIL extends 21mm (13/16") beyond the corolla; light pink (65C) style; white (155D) stigma. BUD is ovate. FOLIAGE is dark green (137A) upper surface; medium green (138B) lower surface. Leaves are 76mm (3") long x 46mm (1 13/16") wide, cordate shaped, serrulate edges, acute tips, rounded bases. Veins & stems are red; branches are green. PARENTAGE: 'Rohees Dubhe' x 'A Tout Jamais'. Natural trailer. Makes good

basket. Prefers overhead filtered light. Best bloom in filtered light. Tested 3 years in Lubbeek, Belgium. Distinguished by bloom colour.
Decoster 2009 BE AFS7256.

Deco Tendre Almé. Upright/Trailer. Single. COROLLA: three-quarter flared; opens dark red (46A) & matures red (46B); 17mm (5/8") long x 24mm (15/16") wide. SEPALS are half up, tips recurved up; rose (51C) upper surface; rose (50B) lower surface; 32mm (1 1/4") long x 12mm (7/16") wide. TUBE is rose (51C); 14mm (9/16") long x 8mm (5/16") wide. FOLIAGE is medium green (137C) upper surface; medium green (138B) lower surface. PARENTAGE: 'Roesse Carme' x 'Lye's Unique'.
Decoster 2008 BE AFS6868.

Decoster Edith. Upright. Single. COROLLA is half flared; opens dark reddish purple (59A); matures reddish purple (59B); 12mm (1/2") long x 15mm (9/16") wide. SEPALS are half up, tips reflexed up; magenta (58B) upper surface; magenta (59D) lower surface; 18mm (11/16") long x 8mm (5/16") wide. TUBE is magenta (58B); 20mm (3/4") long x 6mm (1/4") wide. FOLIAGE: medium green (137C) upper surface; medium green (137D) lower surface. PARENTAGE: 'Roesse Lupus' x 'Lye's Unique'. Distinguished by bloom colour.
Decoster 2006 BE AFS6083.

Delia Smith. Upright. Double. COROLLA white, tinged pink, pink at base, matures to pure white; corolla is half flared SEPALS white flushed pink on the upper and lower surfaces; sepals are half up with recurved tips. TUBE white flushed pink. PARENTAGE Star Wars x Bill Welch. This cultivar self branching and free flowering.
Welch 2009 UK BFS0099.

Demerklokje. Upright/Trailer. Single. COROLLA: quarter flared, turned under wavy petal margins; opens reddish purple (64B); matures dark reddish purple (64A); 15mm (9/16") long x 13mm (1/2") wide. SEPALS: half up; tips reflexed up; white (155A) tipped pale yellow green (150D) upper surface; pink (55C) tipped pale yellow green (150D) lower surface; 21mm (13/16") long x 7mm (1/4") wide. TUBE: white (155A); medium length & thickness; 15mm (9/16") long x 5mm (3/16") wide. STAMENS: extend 3mm (1/8") below corolla; magenta (67B) filaments; purple (79D) anthers. PISTIL: extends 23mm (15/16") below the corolla; rose (67D) style;

106

dark purple (79B) stigma. BUD: oblong. FOLIAGE: medium green (139B) upper surface, medium green (138B) lower surface. Leaves are 64mm (2 1/2") long x 31mm (1 1/4") wide, ovate shaped, serrulated edges, acute tips and rounded bases. Light red purple (185D) veins; plum (185B) stems; plum (185D) branches. PARENTAGE: unknown. Lax upright or stiff trailer. Self branching. Makes good basket. Prefers overhead filtered light. Best bloom and foliage colour in filtered light. Tested 3 years in Rillaar, Belgium. Award at Meise, 9/8/03. Distinguished by bloom colour.
Willems 2004 BE AFS5425.

Demerona.   Upright/Trailer.   Single. COROLLA: quarter flared; opens violet (76B) & violet (84A), light pink (62C) base; matures violet (77B); 26mm (1") long x 23mm (7/8") wide. SEPALS: horizontal, tips recurved; pale pink (56D) tipped light apple green (145C) upper surface; light pink (62C) tipped light apple green (145C) lower surface; 38mm (1 1/2") long x 13mm (1/2") wide. TUBE: white (155B); 15mm (9/16") long x 7mm (1/4") wide. FOLIAGE is dark green (137A) upper surface; medium green (138B) lower surface. PARENTAGE: found seedling.
Willems 2008 BE AFS6745.

Demi. Upright. Single. COROLLA is half flared with turned under wavy petal margins; opens red (53D), pink (48C) base; matures red (50A); 28mm (1 1/8") long x 24mm (15/16") wide. SEPALS are half down, tips recurved; pink (43D) upper surface; orange (44D) lower surface; 41mm (1 5/8") long x 13mm (1/2") wide. TUBE is pale pink (36D); medium length & thickness; 16mm (5/8") long x 6mm (1/4") wide. FOLIAGE: dark green (137A) upper surface; medium green (138B) lower surface. Leaves are 72mm (2 13/16") long x 36mm (1 7/16") wide, ovate shaped. PARENTAGE: 'Roesse Blacky' x 'WALZ Harp'. Meis 3-7-04. Distinguished by flower shape & red orange colour.
Michiels 2005 BE AFS5680.

Den Dweep. Upright/Trailer. Semi Double. COROLLA: half flared, turned under smooth petal margins; opens dark reddish purple (61A), reddish purple (61B) at base; matures magenta (61C); 23mm (15/16") long x 14mm (9/16") wide. PETALOIDS: same colour as corolla; 12mm (1/2") long x 9mm (3/8") wide. SEPALS: horizontal; tips reflexed; magenta (63B) upper surface; dark rose (64C) lower surface; 30mm(1 3/16") long x 14mm (9/16") wide. TUBE: magenta (63B); long, medium

thickness; 34mm (1 5/16") long x 6mm (1/4") wide. STAMENS: do not extend below the corolla; magenta (61C) filaments, dark reddish purple (187B) anthers. PISTIL extends 6mm (1/4") below the corolla; magenta (61C) style, very dark purple (187A) stigma. BUD: ovate. FOLIAGE: dark green (147A) upper surface; medium green (137C) lower surface. Leaves are 72mm (2 13/16") long x 28mm (1 1/8") wide, elliptic shaped, serrulated edges, acute tips and rounded bases. Veins are plum (185C); stems are very dark reddish purple (186A), branches are dark red purple (187D). PARENTAGE: 'WALZ Harp' x 'Rohees New Millennium'. Lax upright or stiff trailer. Makes good basket. Prefers overhead filtered light. Best bloom and foliage colour in filtered light. Tested 3 years in Berlaar, Belgium. NBFK certificate at Meise. Distinguished by bloom colour, long TUBE.
Geerts J 2003 BE AFS5119.

Deneb. Upright. Double. COROLLA light plum. SEPALS pink.
Ainsworth 2005 UK.

Denise Courcier. Upright. Single. COROLLA: Half flared; opens & matures dark rose (54A), orange (40C) base; 25mm (1") long x 23mm (7/8") wide. SEPALS: half up, tips reflexed up; pink (49A) upper surface; rose (55B) lower surface; 40mm (1 9/16") long x 10mm (3/8") wide. TUBE: peach (38B); medium length, thick; 20mm (3/4") long x 18mm (11/16") wide. FOLIAGE is medium green (137C) upper surface; medium green (137D) lower surface. PARENTAGE: ('Earl of Beaconsfield' x 'Golden Dawn') x 'Bella Mia'.
Gaucher 2007 FR AFS6439.

Dennis Townsend. Upright/Trailer. Single. COROLLA is unflared, bell shaped; opens & matures reddish purple (64B), red (53D) at base; 17mm (11/16") long x 12mm (1/2") wide. SEPALS are full down, tips recurved; red (53D) tipped light green upper & lower surfaces; 24mm (15/16") long x 6mm (1/4") wide. TUBE is red (53D); 20mm (13/16") long x 5mm (3/16") wide. FOLIAGE: dark green (147A) upper surface; medium green (147B) lower surface. PARENTAGE: 'Anita' x 'Charles Lester'. Distinguished by blossom shape & colour.
Holmes 2006 UK AFS5990.

Depardieu. Trailer. Double. COROLLA: half flared; opens violet (85B) striped light rose (73B) and matures violet (75A) striped pale rose (73D); 21mm (13/16") long x 17mm

(5/8") wide. PETALOIDS: violet (85B) striped light rose (73B); 13mm (1/2") long x 10mm (3/8") wide. SEPALS are half up, tips recurved up, twisted to the left; pale lavender (69D) tipped light apple green (145C) upper surface & light pink (65C) tipped light apple green (145C) lower surface; 43mm (1 11/16") long x 14mm (9/16") wide. TUBE is white (155A); medium length & thickness; 13mm (1/2") long x 5mm (3/16") wide. FOLIAGE is dark green (137A) upper surface; medium green (137D) lower surface. PARENTAGE: 'Vreni Schleeweiss' x 'Futura'. Michiels 2007 BE AFS6541.

Dereu Sigrid. Upright/Trailer. Double. COROLLA is three quarter flared; opens violet (90C); matures reddish purple (70B); 23mm (7/8") long x 26mm (1") wide. SEPALS are horizontal, tips recurved; dark rose (58C) upper surface; magenta (58B) lower surface; 24mm (15/16") long x 11mm (7/16") wide. TUBE is dark rose (58C); 12mm (1/2") long x 7mm (1/4") wide. FOLIAGE: medium green (137B) upper surface; medium green (138B) lower surface. PARENTAGE: 'Regent Gubler' x 'Thea Kroese'. Distinguished by bloom colour.
Decoster 2006 BE AFS6086.

Dermine W. Upright/Trailer. Single. COROLLA: Quarter flareds; opens reddish purple (61B); matures magenta (61C); 6mm (1/4") long x 4mm (1/8") wide. SEPALS: half up, tips recurved up; magenta (58B) upper & lower surfaces; 12mm (7/16") long x 2mm (1/16") wide. TUBE: magenta (58B); short & thin; 6mm (1/4") long x 2mm (1/16") wide. FOLIAGE is dark green (137A) upper surface; medium green (138A) lower surface. PARENTAGE: 'Rosea' x 'Venus Victrix'.
Roes 2007 NL AFS6701.

Desmond. Upright. Single. COROLLA: quarter flared, wavy petal margins; opens rose (52B) flushed orange (40C); matures rose (52A) flushed orange (40C); 17mm (11/16") long x 18mm (11/16") wide. SEPALS: half up; tips recurved up; pale pink (62D) upper surface; white (155D) tipped green lower surface; 10mm (3/8") long x 6mm (1/4") wide. TUBE: pale pink (62D); medium length & thickness; 25mm(1") long x 6mm (1/4") wide. STAMENS: extend 5mm (3/16") below corolla; dark rose (55A) filaments, magenta (63B) anthers. PISTIL: extends 6mm (1/4") below the corolla, rose (55B) style, yellowish white (158A) stigma. BUD: Long, oval. FOLIAGE: dark green (141B) upper surface; yellowish green (144A)

lower surface. Leaves are 82mm (3 1/4") long x 65mm (2 9/16") wide, cordate shaped, serrulated edges, acute tips and rounded bases. Veins are light green, stems are pale green; branches are brown. PARENTAGE: 'F. speciosa' x 'Amy Lye'. Medium upright. Self branching. Makes good upright. Prefers full sun and warm climate. Heat tolerant if shaded. Cold weather hardy to 32° F. Best bloom colour in filtered light. Tested 3 years in Barkingside, Ilford, Essex, England. Distinguished by bloom colour combination. Tibbatts 2003 UK AFS5214.

Deta Bechtel. Trailer. Double. COROLLA deep rose flushed orange; corolla is quarter flared. SEPALS rose flushed orange on the upper and lower surfaces; SEPALS are half to fully up with recurved tips. TUBE rose flushed orange. PARENTAGE 'Margaret Tebbit' x 'Johanna Rosenbach'.
Strümper 2009 DE BFS0143.

Devin Lankhuizen. Upright/Trailer. Double. COROLLA: half flared, turned under wavy petal margins; opens purple (N82B) bloched pale purple (75C); matures dark reddish purple (72A) bloched pale purple (75D); 24mm (15/16 ") long x 21mm (13/16 ") wide. PETALOIDS: Same colour as corolla; 12mm (7/16") long x 10mm (3/8") wide. SEPALS: half down, tips recurved; white (155C) tipped pale yellow green (150D) upper surface; pale lavender (69D) tipped pale yellow green (150D) lower surface; 39mm (1 1/2") long x 14mm (9/16") wide. TUBE: white (155B); medium length & thickness; 18mm (11/16") long x 6mm (1/4") wide. STAMENS extend 13mm (1/2") beyond the corolla; light rose (68D) filaments; dark red purple (N79A) anthers. PISTIL extends 28mm (1 11/8") beyond the corolla; white (155B) style; yellowish white (4D) stigma. BUD: elongated. FOLIAGE: dark green (137A) upper surface; medium green (137C) lower surface. Leaves are 70mm (2 3/4") long x 42mm (1 5/8") wide; ovate shaped, serrate edges, acute tips, rounded bases. Veins are plum (185C), stems are light red purple (185D), branches are plum (184C) & light green (138C). PARENTAGE: 'Coen Bakker' x 'Lut'. Lax upright or stiff trailer. Self branching. Makes good basket or upright. Prefers overhead filtered light, cool climate. Best bloom & foliage colour in filtered light. Tested 3 years in Koningshooikt, Belgium. Waanrode 8/9/08. Distinguished by bloom colour combination.
Michiels 2009 BE AFS7159.

108

Dian van Heijst. Upright/Trailer. Double. COROLLA is three quarter flared with smooth petal margins; opens purple (83A), matures dark reddish purple (72A); 22mm (7/8") long x 22mm (7/8") wide. SEPALS are half up, tips reflexed up; red (46B) upper surface; red (45C) lower surface; 29mm (1 1/8") long x 12mm (1/2") wide. TUBE is red (46B); medium length and thickness; 16mm (5/8") long x 5mm (3/16") thick. STAMENS extend 20mm (13/16") beyond the corolla; red (45C) filaments, pale orange (23D) anthers. PISTIL extends 29mm (1 1/8") beyond the corolla; red (45C) style, dark rose (58C) stigma. BUD is elliptic, pointed. FOLIAGE is dark green (139A) upper surface, medium green (137B) lower surface. Leaves are 52mm (2 1/16") long x 31mm (1 1/4") wide, ovate shaped, serrated edges, acute tips and obtuse bases. Veins, stems and branches are red. PARENTAGE: 'Rohees Mintaka' x 'Gilian Althea'. Lax upright or stiff trailer. Makes good stiff trailer. Prefers overhead filtered light and cool climate. Best bloom colour in filtered light. Tested four years in Duizel, The Netherlands. Distinguished by bloom and foliage combination.
Tamerus 2002 NL AFS5002.

Diana, Princess of Wales. Upright. Single. COROLLA is unflared with wavy petal margins; opens violet blue (91A); matures pale violet (91C), lighter base; 18mm (11/16") long x 18mm (11/16") wide. SEPALS are horizontal, tips recurved; pale pink (36D) tipped green upper surface; light pink (49B) lower surface; 25mm (1") long x 12mm (1/2") wide. TUBE is pale pink (36D); medium length & thickness; 11mm (7/16") long x 5mm (3/16") wide. FOLIAGE: medium green (146A) upper surface; yellowish green (146B) lower surface. Leaves are 50mm (2") long x 25mm (1") wide, lanceolate shaped. PARENTAGE: 'Shelford' x 'Chelsea Louise'. Distinguished by unique petals & bloom shape.
Smith R. 2005 UK AFS5770.

Diane Marie. Single. COROLLA pinky lavender. SEPALS bright pink.
Wilkinson 2002 UK.

Diane Massebeuf. Upright/Trailer. Single. COROLLA is unflared with smooth petal margins; opens purple (83A); matures reddish purple (58A); 20mm (13/16") long x 11mm (7/16") wide. SEPALS are horizontal, tips recurved; red (45C) upper and lower surfaces; 38mm (1 1/2") long x 7mm (1/4")

wide. TUBE is red (45C); short, medium thickness; 10mm (3/8") long x 4.5mm (3/16") thick. STAMENS extend 20 – 26mm (13/16 – 1") beyond the corolla; magenta (58B) filaments, magenta (63A) anthers. PISTIL extends 40mm (1 9/16") beyond the corolla; red (45C) style, dark red (46A) stigma. BUD is long, ovate. FOLIAGE is dark green (137A) upper surface, medium green (147B) lower surface. Leaves are 88mm (3 1/2") long x 38mm (1 1/2") wide, lanceolate shaped, serrulated to smooth edges, acute tips and rounded bases. Veins are yellowish green, stems are dark red (185A) and branches are plum (185B). PARENTAGE: 'Woodnook' x 'F. regia' ssp 'reitzii' No. 4574. Lax upright or stiff trailer. Makes good upright or standard. Prefers cool climate. Heat tolerant if shaded. Cold weather hardy to -10° C. Best bloom colour in filtered light. Tested five years in Pornic, France. Distinguished by hardiness and profuse blooms.
Massé 2002 FR AFS5011.

Diane Stephens. COROLLA glowing pink edged picotee. SEPALS white. TUBE white.
Hewitson B. 2006 UK.

Dick Laan. Upright. Single. COROLLA is quarter flared, round, with smooth petal margins; opens magenta (67B); matures reddish purple (67A); 12mm (1/2") long x 18mm (11/16") wide. SEPALS are horizontal, tips recurved; pink (62A) upper surface; rose (65A) lower surface; 22mm (7/8") long x 8mm (5/16") wide. TUBE is light pink (65C); medium length & thickness; 12mm (1/2") long x 5mm (3/16") wide. FOLIAGE: medium green (146A) upper surface; medium green (147B) lower surface. Leaves are 37mm (1 7/16") long x 23mm (15/16") wide, ovate shaped. PARENTAGE: 'Wormerveer' x 'Minirose'. Distinguished by profuse blooms & compact growth.
Krom 2005 NL AFS5797.

Dick Sadler. Upright. Single. COROLLA: quarter flared; opens & matures violet (77B), light pink (62C) base; 17mm (5/8") long x 16mm (5/8") wide. SEPALS: horizontal, tips recurved; light pink (62C) tipped light green (143C) upper & lower surfaces; 17mm (5/8") long x 7mm (1/4") wide. TUBE: light pink (62C) overlaid & striped light reddish purple (66C); medium length & thickness; 15mm (9/16") long x 5mm (3/16") wide. FOLIAGE is dark green (147A) upper surface; medium green (147B) lower surface. PARENTAGE: 'Dot Woodage' x 'Karen Marie'.

Holmes 2007 UK AFS6314.

Didgeridoo. Trailer. Double. COROLLA: half flared; opens magenta (71C) edged violet (75A) & matures magenta (68A); 18mm (11/16") long x 14mm (9/16") wide. PETALOIDS: magenta (71C) edged violet (75A); 12mm (7/16") long x 9mm (5/16") wide. SEPALS are horizontal; tips recurved; white (155C) tipped light apple green (145B) upper surface & pale pink (69A) tipped light apple green (145B) lower surface; 36mm (1 7/16") long x 12mm (7/16") wide. TUBE is white (155C) & light apple green (144D); long & thin; 26mm (1") long x 5mm (3/16") wide. FOLIAGE is dark green (136B) upper surface; medium green (137B) lower surface. PARENTAGE: 'Leen vander Kuylen' x 'Charlotte Martens'.
Michiels 2007 BE AFS6544.

Die Schone Pinzgauerin. Upright. Double. COROLLA violet (82a) flamed with pale rose purple (62c); corolla is fully flared. SEPALS light amaranth rose (65b) on the upper and lower surfaces; SEPALS are half up with recurved tips. TUBE white, veined light rhodamine purple (65d). PARENTAGE 'Turandot' x 'Bert's Whisky'. Lax upright.
Klemm 2009 AT BFS0128.

Dien Frenken. Trailer. Double. COROLLA is half flared; opens purple (90B); matures dark purple (78A); 21mm (13/16") long x 19mm (3/4") wide. SEPALS are horizontal, tips recurved; dark reddish purple (72A) upper surface; magenta (58B) lower surface; 32mm (1 1/4") long x 17mm (5/8") wide. TUBE is dark reddish purple (72A); 24mm (15/16") long x 7mm (1/4") wide. FOLIAGE: dark green (137A) upper surface; medium green (138B) lower surface. PARENTAGE: 'Roesse Elara' x 'BreeVis Evelien'. Distinguished by bloom colour.
van Bree 2006 NL AFS6093.

Dijk van Tuin. Trailer. Double. COROLLA: half flared; opens violet (85B) blotched violet (75A), base white (155C) and matures light purple (N78C), base white (155C); 23mm (7/8") long x 21mm (13/16") wide. PETALOIDS: violet (85B) blotched violet (75A), base white (155C); 11mm (7/16") long x 7mm (1/4") wide. SEPALS are half up, tips recurved up, twisted to the left; white (155C) tipped light apple green (145C) upper surface & light pink (65C) tipped light apple green (145C) lower surface; 34mm (1 3/8") long x 13mm (1/2") wide. TUBE is white (155C); medium length & thickness; 16mm (5/8")

long x 6mm (1/4") wide. FOLIAGE is dark green (136B) upper surface; medium green (138B) lower surface. PARENTAGE: 'Vreni Schleeweiss' x 'Futura'.
Michiels 2007 BE AFS6542.

Dirk van Megen. Upright/Trailer. Semi Double. COROLLA: three quarter flared, turned under wavy petal margins; opens purple (71A) striped dark rose (64C); matures magenta (71C); 32mm (1 1/4 ") long x 24mm (15/16 ") wide. PETALOIDS: Same colour as corolla; 23mm (7/8") long x 14mm (9/16") wide. SEPALS: horizontal, tips recurved, twisted left to right; light pink (62C) tipped light apple green (144D) upper surface; magenta 63B) tipped light apple green (144D) lower surface; 48mm (1 7/8") long x 13mm (1/2") wide. TUBE: pale pink (162D); medium length & thickness; 18mm (11/16") long x 6mm (1/4") wide. STAMENS extend 16mm (5/8") beyond the corolla; dark reddish purple (64A) filaments; dark red purple (79A) anthers. PISTIL extends 22mm (7/8") beyond the corolla; light reddish purple (72D) style; pale yellow (1D) stigma. BUD: oblong. FOLIAGE: dark green (136B) upper surface; medium green (137D) lower surface. Leaves are 68mm (2 11/16") long x 32mm (1 1/4") wide; elliptic shaped, serrulate edges, acute tips, rounded bases. Veins are plum (185C), stems are plum (185B), branches are light red purple (185D) & light green (138C). PARENTAGE: 'Manfried Kleinau' x 'Joergen Hahn'. Lax upright or stiff trailer. Self branching. Makes good basket. Prefers overhead filtered light, cool climate. Best bloom & foliage colour in filtered light. Tested 3 years in Koningshooikt, Belgium. Waanrode 8/9/08. Distinguished by bloom colour combination.
Michiels 2009 BE AFS7160.

Doerak. Upright. Double. COROLLA is three quarter flared; opens purple (71A); matures reddish purple (59B); 19mm (3/4") long x 29mm (1 1/8") wide. SEPALS are horizontal, tips recurved; magenta (63A) upper & lower surfaces; 29mm (1 1/8") long x 11mm (7/16") wide. TUBE is magenta (63A); 15mm (9/16") long x 8mm (5/16") wide. FOLIAGE: medium green (137B) upper surface; medium green (137D) lower surface. PARENTAGE: 'Roesse Apus' x 'Luuk van Riet'. Distinguished by bloom colour.
Buiting 2006 NL AFS6128.

Doffie. Upright. Single. COROLLA: quarter flared, smooth petal margins; opens dark purple (79B) suffusing to purple (77A) at

base; matures magenta (71C); 19mm (3/4")
long x 19mm (3/4") wide. SEPALS: half up,
tips recurved up; reddish purple (61B) upper
surface; dark reddish purple (67A) lower
surface; 19mm (3/4") long x 9mm (5/16")
wide. TUBE: reddish purple (61B); medium
length & thickness; 13mm (1/2") long x 6mm
(1/4") wide. STAMENS extend 19mm (3/4")
beyond the corolla; magenta (61C) filaments;
dark reddish purple (61A) anthers. PISTIL
extends 28mm (1 1/8") beyond the corolla;
dark reddish purple (60C) style; rose (64D)
stigma. BUD: ovate, pointed. FOLIAGE:
medium green (137C) maturing to dark green
(137A) upper surface; medium green (138B)
lower surface. Leaves are 50mm (2") long x
25mm (1") wide; cordate shaped, serrulate
edges, acute tips, rounded bases. Veins,
stems & branches are light olive green.
PARENTAGE: ('Baby Bright' x 'Zulu King') x
'Shirley'. Small upright. Makes good upright
or standard. Prefers overhead filtered light.
Cold weather hardy to 0° C (32° F). Best
bloom colour in filtered light. Tested 3 years
in Leeds & Manchester, England.
Distinguished by display of various shades of
bloom colour, maturing from dark purple to
magenta. Registered with the BFS in 2008.
Swaby 2009 UK AFS7118 BFS0092.

Domein Vrijbroek. Trailer. Double.
COROLLA: unflared, turned under smooth
petal margins; opens dark reddish purple
(72A); matures purple (71A); 25mm (1") long
x 22mm (7/8") wide. PETALOIDS: two per
sepal; dark reddish purple (72A), reddish
purple (71B) at base; 19mm (3/4") long x
15mm (9/16") wide. SEPALS: full down; tips
reflexed; reddish purple (61B) upper surface;
magenta (61C) lower surface; 38mm (1 1/2")
long x 17mm (11/16") wide. TUBE: reddish
purple (61B); medium length & thickness;
16mm (5/8") long x 7mm (1/4") wide.
STAMENS: extend 16mm (5/8") below the
corolla; reddish purple (67A) filaments, dark
tan (164B) anthers. PISTIL extends 18mm
(11/16") below the corolla; magenta (67B)
style, orangish brown (172B) stigma. BUD:
long, ovate, pointed. FOLIAGE: medium
green (139B) upper surface; medium green
(138B) lower surface. Leaves are 70mm (2
3/4") long x 32mm (1 1/4") wide, elliptic
shaped, serrulated edges, acute tips and
rounded bases. Veins are reddish purple
(186B), stems are very dark reddish purple
(186A), branches are plum (185B).
PARENTAGE: 'Rohees New Millennium' x
'Pinto de Blue'. Natural trailer. Self
branching. Makes good basket. Prefers
overhead filtered light. Best bloom and

foliage colour in filtered light. Tested 3 years
in Koningshooikt, Belgium. NBFK certificate
at Meise. Distinguished by dark bloom
colour.
Michiels 2003 BE AFS5101.

Domitiaan.   Upright/Trailer.   Single.
COROLLA is quarter flared with turned
under wavy petal margins; opens purple
(77A), dark rose (58C) veins and base;
matures dark rose (58C) veins and base; dark rose
(58C) veins and base; 27mm (1 1/16") long x
24 mm (15/16") wide. SEPALS are half down,
tips recurved; magenta (58B) upper surface,
dark rose (51A) lower surface; 33mm (1
5/16") long x 9mm (3/8") wide. TUBE is
magenta (58B), medium length and
thickness; 14mm (9/16") long x 7mm (1/4")
wide. STAMENS extend 6mm (1/4") beyond
the corolla; dark rose (58C) filaments,
grayish yellow (160A) anthers. PISTIL does
not extend below the corolla; light rose (58D);
rose (68C) stigma. BUD is ovate. FOLIAGE is
dark green (137A) upper surface, medium
green (138B) lower surface. Leaves are 64mm
(2 1/2") long x 45mm (1 3/4") wide, cordate
shaped, serrated edges, acute tips and
cordate bases. Veins are light green (142B),
stems and branches are orangy brown
(176A). PARENTAGE: 'Red Spider' x
unknown. Lax upright or stiff trailer. Self
branching. Makes good basket. Prefers
overhead filtered light and full sun. Best
bloom and foliage colour in filtered light.
Tested three years in Hoeselt, Belgium.
Certificate N.B.F.K. at Meise. Distinguished
by strong growth and bloom colour.
Wagemans 2002 BE AFS4901.

Domme Tielko. Upright. Double. COROLLA:
three quarter flared; opens purple (83A);
matures dark reddish purple (59A); 20mm
(3/4") long x 22mm (7/8") wide. SEPALS:
fully up, tips recurved; rose (67D) upper
surface; dark rose (67C) lower surface;
25mm (1") long x 12mm (7/16") wide. TUBE:
rose (67D); 25mm (1") long x 4mm (1/8")
wide. FOLIAGE is dark green (137A) upper
surface; medium green (137C) lower surface.
PARENTAGE: 'Roesse Lupus' x 'Roesse
Apus'.
Roes 2008 NL AFS6896.

Donicetto. Single. COROLLA smoky violet.
SEPALS white. TUBE white.
Clitheroe 2004 UK.

Doretteke. Upright. Single. COROLLA is half
flared; opens light reddish purple (72D);
matures light purple (70C); 16mm (5/8") long

x 24mm (15/16") wide. SEPALS are horizontal, tips reflexed; magenta (59D) upper surface; reddish purple (60D) lower surface; 28mm (1 1/8") long x 12mm (1/2") wide. TUBE is rose (61D); 10mm (3/8") long x 8mm (5/16") wide. FOLIAGE: dark green (137A) upper surface; medium green (138B) lower surface. PARENTAGE: 'Onbekend' x 'Onbekend'. Meise 8/13/05. Distinguished by unique bloom colour.
Willems 2006 BE AFS5996.

Dorothy Clive. Upright. Single. COROLLA: quarter flared, smooth petal margins; opens purple (83A); matures dark reddish purple (61A); 25mm (1") long x 20mm (7/8") wide. SEPALS: half up, tips recurved up; reddish purple (61B) upper & lower surfaces; 39mm (1 1/2") long x 12mm (7/16") wide. TUBE: reddish purple (61B); medium length & thickness; 13mm (1/2") long x 10mm (3/8") wide. STAMENS extend 7mm (1/4") beyond the corolla; dark reddish purple (61A) filaments & anthers. PISTIL extends 20mm (3/4") beyond the corolla; reddish purple (61B) style; light pink (65C) stigma. BUD: pointed. FOLIAGE: medium green (138A) upper surface; medium green (138B) lower surface. Leaves are 50mm (2") long x 25mm (1") wide; elliptic shaped, serrulate edges, acute tips, rounded bases. Veins are light rose, stems are rosy purple branches are brown. PARENTAGE: 'Dorothy Hanley' x 'Blaze Away'. Small upright. Self branching. Makes good upright, standard or garden border. Prefers overhead filtered light, cool climate. Best bloom colour in filtered light. Tested 8 years in Ormskirk, Lancashire, England. Distinguished by flower shape & colour, long bloom period.
Sinton 2009 UK AFS7089.

Dorothy Oosting. Trailer. Double. COROLLA is three quarter flared with smooth petal margins; opens purple (71A), matures reddish purple (70B); 22mm (7/8") long x 27mm (1 1/16") wide. SEPALS are full up, tips reflexed; light reddish purple (72C) upper and lower surfaces; 30mm (1 3/16") long x 17mm (11/16") wide. TUBE is light rose (73C), proportionately medium length and thickness; 16mm (5/8") long x 5mm (3/16") wide. STAMENS extend 18mm (11/16") below the corolla; light reddish purple (72D) filaments; purple (71A) anthers. PISTIL extends 37mm (1 7/16") below the corolla; light reddish purple (72D) style and cream (11D) stigma. BUD is ovate. FOLIAGE is dark green (137A) on upper surface and medium green (138A) on lower surface.

Leaves are 91mm (3 9/16") long x 35mm (1 3/8") wide, lanceolate shaped, serrated edges, acute tips and obtuse bases. Veins, stems and branches are red. PARENTAGE: 'Rohees King' x 'Miniskirt'. Natural trailer. Makes good basket. Prefers overhead filtered light and cool climate. Tested four years in Knegsel, The Netherlands. Distinguished by bloom colour.
Roes 2003 NL AFS5057.

Dorothy Wright. Upright. Single. COROLLA: quarter flared; opens dark purple (79A); matures dark purple (79B); 17mm (5/8") long x 17mm (5/8") wide. SEPALS: half up, tips recurved up; dark reddish purple (60B) upper & lower surfaces; 27mm (1 1/16") long x 8mm (5/16") wide. TUBE: magenta (58B); 15 mm (9/16") long x 5mm (3/16") wide. FOLIAGE is dark green (137A) upper surface; medium green (137C) lower surface. PARENTAGE: 'F. magellanica alba' x 'Autumnale'.
Bell 2008 UK AFS6826.

Doublet Grande. Upright. Single. COROLLA is unflared; opens reddish purple (67A), red (52A) base; matures reddish purple (67A); 24mm (15/16") long x 10mm (3/8") wide. SEPALS are full down, tips reflexed; rose (63C), dark rose (58C) base, tipped green upper surface; rose (63C), tipped green lower surface; 32mm (1 1/4") long x 9mm (3/8") wide. TUBE is pale purple (70D), striped reddish purple (63A); 50mm (2") long x 6mm (1/4") wide. FOLIAGE: dark green (137A) upper surface; medium green (138B) lower surface. PARENTAGE: 'WALZ Trompet' x 'Gerharda's Panache'. Distinguished by bloom shape & colour; growth in racemes along and on ends of branches.
Koerts T. 2006 NL AFS6300.

Doublet Orange. Upright/Trailer. Single. COROLLA: full flared, smooth petal margins; opens & matures red (52A), dark rose (67C) base; 19mm (3/4") long 12mm (1/2") wide. SEPALS: horizontal; tips reflexed; pink (62A), tipped green upper surface; light pink (62B) lower surface; 21mm (13/16") long x 11mm (7/16") wide. TUBE: pink (62A); medium length & thickness; 29mm (1 1/8") long x 8mm (5/16") wide. STAMENS: extend 10mm (3/8") below corolla; magenta (63B) filaments; light yellowish orange (19B) anthers. PISTIL: extends 15mm (9/16") below the corolla; magenta (63B) style; grayish yellow (161B) stigma. BUD: long TUBE & ball shape. FOLIAGE: dark green (137A) upper surface; medium green (147B)

lower surface. Leaves are 90mm (3 9/16") long x 50mm (2") wide, cordate shaped, serrated edges, acute tips and rounded bases. Medium green (147B) veins; reddish purple (59A) stems & branches. PARENTAGE: 'Gerharda's Panache' x 'Lord Lonsdale'. Lax upright or stiff trailer. Makes good basket, upright or standard. Prefers overhead filtered light, warm climate. Best bloom and foliage colour in bright light. Tested 3 years in Stadskanaal, The Netherlands. Distinguished by blossoms in flat panicles and blossom colour.
Koerts T. 2004 NL AFS5582.

Doublet Orange White. Upright/Trailer. Single. COROLLA: quarter flared, bell shaped, smooth petal margins; opens red (52A) edged reddish purple (58A); matures red (52A) edged reddish purple (58A), spotted orange (30A); 20mm (13/16") long 18mm (11/16") wide. SEPALS: horizontal; tips reflexed; pale pink (36D) upper surface; light pink (38C) lower surface; 20mm (13/16") long x 9mm (3/8") wide. TUBE: pale pink (36D); medium length, thick; 13mm (1/2") long x 7mm (1/4") wide. STAMENS: extend 8mm (5/16") below corolla; cream (158C) filaments; reddish purple (58A) anthers. PISTIL: extends 6mm (1/4") below the corolla; light pink (65C) style; grayish yellow (160B) stigma. BUD: ball shape. FOLIAGE: dark green (147A) upper surface; light olive green (147C) lower surface. Leaves are 60mm (2 3/8") long x 40mm (1 9/16") wide, cordate shaped, smooth edges, acute tips and rounded bases. Light green (147C) veins, stems & branches. PARENTAGE: 'Eleanor Leythem' x 'Prince Syray'. Lax upright or stiff trailer. Self branching. Makes good basket, upright or standard. Prefers full sun, warm climate. Best bloom and foliage colour in bright light. Tested 3 years in Stadskanaal, The Netherlands. Distinguished by blossoms in spreading panicles and blossom colour.
Koerts T. 2004 NL AFS5583.

Doublet Red. Upright/Trailer. Single. COROLLA: Unflared, bell shaped; opens & matures reddish purple (61B); 18mm (11/16") long x 12mm (7/16") wide. SEPALS: half down, tips reflexed; dark rose (51A) upper surface; red (50A) lower surface; 27mm (1 1/16") long x 12mm (7/16") wide. TUBE: red (52A); short, medium thickness; 12mm (7/16") long x 6mm (1/4") wide. FOLIAGE is medium green (146A) upper surface; yellowish green (146B) lower surface. PARENTAGE: 'Cambridge Louie' x 'Prince Syray'.

Koerts T. 2007 NL AFS6449.

Doublet Rose. Upright/Trailer. Single. COROLLA: quarter flared, bell shaped, smooth petal margins; opens violet (77C) veined violet (77B); matures light purple (78C); 20mm (13/16") long 18mm (11/16") wide. SEPALS: horizontal; tips reflexed; light rose (73C), tipped cream (158C) upper surface; light rose (73C) lower surface; 11mm (7/16") long x 4mm (3/16") wide. TUBE: light rose (73C) spotted light reddish purple (73A); short, medium thickness; 13mm (1/2") long x 5mm (3/16") wide. STAMENS: extend 4mm (3/16") below corolla; light purple (78C) filaments; yellow (10C) anthers. PISTIL: extends 15mm (9/16") below the corolla; light purple (78C) style; light gray (156C) stigma. BUD: long & small. FOLIAGE: dark green (137A) upper surface; yellow green (146C) lower surface. Leaves are 62mm (2 7/16") long x 32mm (1 1/4") wide, elliptic shaped, serrated edges, acute tips and rounded bases. Light green veins & stems; grayish red (179A) branches. PARENTAGE: 'Gerharda's Panache' x 'Prince Syray'. Lax upright or stiff trailer. Self branching. Makes good basket or upright. Prefers overhead filtered light, warm climate. Best bloom and foliage colour in filtered light. Tested 3 years in Stadskanaal, The Netherlands. Distinguished by blossoms in flat panicles and blossom colour.
Koerts T. 2004 NL AFS5584.

Dr. Bart Vander Kuylen. Trailer. Semi Double. COROLLA is half flared with turned under smooth petal margins; opens dark purple (79B), reddish purple (64B) base; matures dark reddish purple (59A); 19mm (3/4") long x 21mm (13/16") wide. SEPALS are horizontal, tips recurved; dark reddish purple (60C) upper surface; reddish purple (61B) lower surface; 29mm (1 1/8") long x 11mm (7/16") wide. TUBE is reddish purple (61B); medium length & thickness; 10mm (3/8") long x 5mm (3/16") wide. FOLIAGE: dark green (139A) upper surface; medium green (138B) lower surface. Leaves are 44mm (1 3/4") long x 23mm (15/16") wide, ovate shaped. PARENTAGE: 'Roesse Blacky' x 'Rohees Reda'. Meise 8-14-04. Distinguished by unique colour play.
Michiels 2005 BE AFS5738.

Dr. Dominique Cottron. Upright. Single. COROLLA: quarter flared, smooth petal margins; opens & matures magenta (63B); 18mm (11/16") long x 11mm (7/16") wide. SEPALS: half up; tips recurved up in a circle;

red (47B) tipped yellowish green upper surface; rose (47C) lower surface; 27mm (1 1/16") long x 5mm (3/16") wide. TUBE: red (47B); medium length & thickness; 17mm (11/16") long x 4.5mm (3/16") wide. STAMENS: extend 5mm (3/16") below corolla; rose (68B) filaments; red (180B) anthers. PISTIL: extends 35mm (1 3/8") below the corolla; reddish purple (66B) style; magenta (63A) stigma. BUD: ovate, long. FOLIAGE: dark green (147A) upper surface, medium green (147B) lower surface. Leaves are 83mm (3 1/4") long x 36mm (1 7/16") wide, ovate/lanceolate shaped, serrulated edges, acute tips and rounded bases. Yellowish green veins; light brown stems & branches. PARENTAGE: 'Willie Tamerus' x unknown. Tall upright. Self branching. Makes good standard. Prefers overhead filtered light and cool climate. Cold weather hardy to –8⁰ C. Best bloom and foliage colour in filtered light. Tested 3 years in Pornic, France. Distinguished by profuse blooms along the stems.
Massé 2004 FR AFS5449.

Dr. Gustaaf R. Möhlmann. Upright. Double. COROLLA is three quarter flared, star shaped, 4 petals, with smooth petal margins; opens magenta (63B) edged light reddish purple (66C); matures dark reddish purple (72A) edged reddish purple (66B); 21mm (13/16") long x 13mm (1/2") wide. PETALOIDS: reddish purple (66A); 12mm (1/2") long x 5mm (3/16") wide. SEPALS are half up, tips reflexed up; light pink (62B), tipped yellow green upper surface; light pink (62B), edged magenta (63A) lower surface; 22mm (7/8") long x 9mm (3/8") wide. TUBE is pink (62A); short, medium thickness; 3mm (1/8") long x 6mm (1/4") wide. FOLIAGE: medium green (143A) upper surface; yellowish green (145A) lower surface. Leaves are 60mm (2 3/8") long x 42mm (1 11/16") wide, cordate shaped. PARENTAGE: 'Summerdaffodil' x 'Prince Syray'. Distinguished by star shaped flowers & foliage/flower colour combination.
Koerts T. 2005 NL AFS5816.

Dr. Maria Dobner. Upright. Single. COROLLA: quarter flared; opens light reddish purple (73A); matures light rose (73B); 21mm (13/16") long x 25mm (1") wide. SEPALS: horizontal, tips recurved; pink (62A) upper & lower surfaces; 24mm (15/16") long x 12mm (7/16") wide. TUBE: pink (62A); 9mm (5/16") long x 7mm (1/4") wide. FOLIAGE is dark green (137A) upper surface; medium green (138B) lower surface.

PARENTAGE: 'Bobby Juliana' x 'Carla Johnston'.
Burkhart 2008 DE AFS6858.

Dr. Xavier Papillon. Upright/Trailer. Single. COROLLA: unflared; opens purple (83A), rose base: matures purple (71A); 31mm (1 1/4") long x 10mm (3/8") wide. SEPALS: half up, tips recurved up; bright dark red (47A) upper & lower surfaces; 36mm (1 7/16") long x 9mm (5/16") wide. TUBE: bright dark red (47A); 5 mm (3/16") long x 6mm (1/4") wide. FOLIAGE is dark green (147A) upper surface; medium green (147B) lower surface. PARENTAGE: 'Swingtime' x 'Bicentennial'.
Massé 2008 FR AFS6831.

Dr. Philippe Hémery. Upright. Single. COROLLA: unflared, smooth petal margins; opens purple (83C); matures reddish purple (80B); 13mm (1/2") long x 7mm (1/4") wide. SEPALS: horizontal; tips recurved; red (45C) upper surface; red (45D) lower surface; 29mm (1 1/8") long x 6mm (1/4") wide. TUBE: red (45C); very short, medium thickness; 3mm (1/8") long x 3mm (1/8") wide. STAMENS: extend 9-13mm (3/8-1/2") below corolla; pink (62C) filaments; magenta (61C) anthers. PISTIL: extends 35mm (1 3/8") below the corolla; reddish purple (66B) style; dark reddish purple (61A) stigma. BUD: ovate. FOLIAGE: medium green (147B) upper surface, light olive green (148B) lower surface. Leaves are 62mm (2 7/16") long x 24mm (15/16") wide, ovate/lanceolate shaped, serrulated edges, acute tips and rounded bases. Yellowish green/light brown veins; light brown stems & branches. PARENTAGE: ('String of Pearls' x 'F. regia subsp. reitzii') x Papy René. Medium upright. Self branching. Makes good upright, standard or pillar. Prefers overhead filtered light and cool climate. Cold weather hardy to –7⁰ C. Best bloom and foliage colour in filtered light. Tested 3 years in Pornic, France. Distinguished by long pistil, hardiness, bloom/foliage contrast.
Massé 2004 FR AFS5450.

Dragon Bird. Upright/Trailer. Double. COROLLA is quarter flared, bell shaped; opens light purple (87C), edged dark violet (87A), splashed white; matures pale purple (87D), edged dark violet (87A), splashed white; 24mm (15/16") long x 36mm (1 7/16") wide. PETALOIDS: light purple (87C), light rose (73B) base; 12mm (7/16") long x 10mm (3/8") wide. SEPALS are fully up, tips recurved; white (155D) upper & lower surfaces; 42mm (1 5/8") long x 12mm

(7/16") wide. TUBE is white (155D); 30mm (1 3/16") long x 6mm (1/4") wide. FOLIAGE: yellowish green (144A) upper surface; yellowish green (145A) lower surface. PARENTAGE: 'Gingham Girl' x 'Wendy van Wanten'. Distinguished by combination of flower & foliage colours.
Koerts T. 2006 NL AFS6304.

Dragon Fang. Upright. Single. COROLLA is quarter flared with turned under petal margins; opens & matures reddish orange (43B) on stems; 8mm (5/16") long x 4mm (3/16") wide. SEPALS are half down, tips recurved; rose (52C) upper surface; reddish orange (43B) lower surface; 26mm (1") long x 8mm (5/16") wide. TUBE is rose (52C); long, medium thickness; 26mm (1") long x 5mm (3/16") wide at top, 8mm (5/16") wide at SEPALS. FOLIAGE: dark green (139A) upper surface; light olive green (148B) edged brownish lower surface. Leaves are 68mm (2 11/16") long x 48mm (1 7/8") wide, cordate shaped. PARENTAGE: 'Thalia' (Turner) x 'Albert H.'. Distinguished by clusters of triphylla type reflexed red flowers.
Koerts T. 2005 NL AFS5812.

Dragon Fire. Upright. Single. COROLLA is quarter flared, square shaped, with smooth petal margins; opens reddish purple (71B), red (46D) base; matures reddish purple (67A), red (46D) base; 13mm (1/2") long x 12mm (1/2") wide. SEPALS are horizontal, tips recurved; pink (37C) blushed red (46D) upper surface; red (46D) lower surface; 19mm (3/4") long x 6mm (1/4") wide. TUBE is pink (37C) blushed dark rose (51A); medium length & thin; 14mm (9/16") long x 4mm (3/16") wide. FOLIAGE: dark green (147A) upper surface; medium green (147B) lower surface. Leaves are 62mm (2 7/16") long x 32mm (1 1/4") wide, cordate shape. PARENTAGE: 'Rosea' x 'Gerharda's Panache'. Distinguished by clusters of flowers & colour combination.
Koerts T. 2005 NL AFS5813.

Dragon Knight. Upright. Single. COROLLA is unflared, bell shaped, with smooth petal margins; opens & matures dark reddish purple (64A), rose (65A) base; 14mm (9/16") long x 7mm (1/4") wide. SEPALS are half down, tips reflexed; magenta (61C) upper surface; dark reddish purple (60B) lower surface; 17mm (11/16") long x 3mm (1/8") wide. TUBE is dark reddish purple (60B); short & thin; 8mm (5/16") long x 2mm (1/16") wide. FOLIAGE: medium green (146A) upper surface; light olive green (148B) lower surface. Leaves are 52mm (2 1/16") long x 38mm (1 1/2") wide, cordate shaped. PARENTAGE: 'Rosea' x 'Gerharda's Panache'. Distinguished by flower shape & colour.
Koerts T. 2005 NL AFS5814.

Dragon Moon. Upright/Trailer. Double. COROLLA is half flared; opens & matures violet (76A) edged violet (86B); 19mm (3/4") long x 26mm (1") wide. PETALOIDS: violet (76A); 14mm (9/16") long x 14mm (9/16") wide. SEPALS are horizontal, tips recurved; light pink (65C) edged light reddish purple (66C) upper surface; pink (62C) lower surface; 54mm (2 1/8") long x 16mm (5/8") wide. TUBE is white (155C) striped green; 14mm (9/16") long x 6mm (1/4") wide. FOLIAGE: dark green (147A) upper surface; olive green (148A) lower surface. PARENTAGE: 'Gingham Girl' x 'Quasar'. Distinguished by velvety appearance of flower & flower colour.
Koerts T. 2006 NL AFS6286.

Dragon Quest. Upright. Single. COROLLA: quarter flared, bell shaped; smooth petal margins; opens orangy red (44B); matures red (43A); 10mm (3/8") long x 12mm (7/16") wide. SEPALS: full down, tips reflexed; light rose (48C) upper & lower surfaces; 24mm (15/16") long x 7mm (1/4") wide. TUBE: light rose (48C) blushed light rose (50C); long & thin; 70mm (2 3/4") long x 7mm (1/4") wide. STAMENS do not extend beyond the corolla; pale pink (49D) filaments; light yellow (11B) anthers. PISTIL extends 8mm (5/16") beyond the corolla; pink (43D) style; yellow (11A) stigma. BUD: long, triphylla type. FOLIAGE: dark green (137A) upper surface; medium green (137D) lower surface. Leaves are 80mm (3 3/16") long x 55mm (2 3/16") wide; cordate shaped, wavy edges, acute tips, cordate bases. Veins, stems & branches are grayish red (181A). PARENTAGE: 'Thalia' (Turner) x 'Kelly Stableford'. Tall upright. Makes good upright or standard. Prefers full sun, warm climate. Best bloom & foliage colour in bright light. Tested 3 years in Stadskanaal, The Netherlands. Distinguished by flower colour and very long TUBE.
Koerts 2009 NL AFS7050.

Dragon Rolls. Upright/Trailer. Double. COROLLA is quarter flared; opens magenta (57C) edged purple (82A); matures reddish purple (67C); 32mm (1 1/4") long x 34mm (1 3/8") wide. PETALOIDS: purple (82A), magenta (57C) base; 14mm (9/16") long x 10mm (3/8") wide. SEPALS are rolled up twice to TUBE; white (155D), splashed pink

at tips, upper & lower surfaces; 60mm (2 3/8") long x 18mm (11/16") wide. TUBE is white (155D); 60mm (2 3/8") long x 6mm (1/4") wide. FOLIAGE: dark green (147A) upper surface; light olive green (147C) lower surface. PARENTAGE: 'Lynn Phipp' x 'Bella Rosella'. Distinguished by curled SEPALS & flower colour.
Koerts 2006 NL AFS6303.

Drücki Marlies. Trailer. Double. COROLLA is half flared with turned under smooth petal margins; opens and matures light pink (65B), veins and base magenta (58B); matures pink (62C), veins and base magenta (58B); 19mm (3/4") long x 31mm (1 1/4") wide. SEPALS are fully up, tips recurved; red (53C) upper surface, red (53D) lower surface; 32mm (1 1/4") long x 15mm (5/8") wide. TUBE is red (45A), long with medium thickness; 31mm (1 1/4") long x 4mm (3/16") wide, 6mm (1/4") at base. STAMENS extend 13mm (1/2") beyond the corolla; magenta (58B) filaments, orangy brown (163B) anthers. PISTIL extends 20mm (13/16") below the corolla; magenta (58B) style, dark rose (58C) stigma. BUD is ovate. FOLIAGE is dark green (137A) upper surface, medium green (138C) lower surface. Leaves are 91mm (3 9/16") long x 49mm (1 15/16") wide, ovate shaped, serrated edges, acute tips and rounded bases. Veins, stems and branches are dark grayish red (182A). PARENTAGE: 'WALZ Triangel' x unknown. Natural trailer. Makes good basket. Prefers overhead filtered light. Best bloom and foliage color in filtered light. Tested three years in Rummen, Belgium. Certificate N.B.F.K. at Meise. Distinguished by unique bloom color and long TUBE.
Ector 2002 BE AFS4892.

Dunkler Herrscher. Upright/Trailer. Double. COROLLA is three quarter flared; opens dark purple (79A); matures dark reddish purple (N79C); 30mm (1 3/16") long x 42mm (1 5/8") wide. SEPALS are fully up, tips recurved; reddish purple (61B) upper surface; magenta (61C) lower surface; 40mm (1 9/16") long x 16mm (5/8") wide. TUBE is magenta (61C); 15mm (9/16") long x 6mm (1/4") wide. FOLIAGE: dark green (137A) upper surface; medium green (137C) lower surface. PARENTAGE: 'Georg Glossner' x 'Rohees Queen'. Distinguished by bloom colour.
Burkhart 2006 DE AFS6048.

Düsterwald. Upright. Single. COROLLA: unflared; opens dark purple (79A); matures

dark purple (N79B); 15mm (9/16") long x 12mm (7/16") wide. SEPALS: horizontal, tips recurved; dark reddish purple (60B) upper & lower surfaces; 30mm (1 3/16") long x 10mm (3/8") wide. TUBE: dark reddish purple (60B); 15mm (9/16") long x 8mm (5/16") wide. FOLIAGE is medium green (137B) upper surface; yellowish green (146B) lower surface. PARENTAGE: 'Rohees King' x 'F. regia ssp serrae Hoya.
Burkhart 2008 DE AFS6860.

Duveltje. Upright/Trailer. Double. COROLLA: quarter flared, turned under smooth petal margins; opens dark reddish purple (64A), reddish purple (58A) base; matures reddish purple (64B); 17mm (11/16") long x 15mm (9/16") wide. SEPALS: horizontal; tips reflexed; red (53B) upper surface; red (46B) lower surface; 29mm (1 1/8") long x 12mm (1/2") wide. TUBE: magenta (61C); long & thin; 37mm(1 7/16") long x 4mm (3/16") wide. STAMENS: do not extend below corolla; magenta (61C) filaments, dark rose (64C) anthers. PISTIL: extends 3mm (1/8") below the corolla, reddish purple (61B) style, rose (61D) stigma. BUD: elongated. FOLIAGE: dark green (136A) upper surface; medium green (137D) lower surface. Leaves are 72mm (2 13/16") long x 32mm (1 1/4") wide, elliptic shaped, serrulated edges, acute tips and rounded bases. Veins are dark red (185A), stems are dark reddish purple (187C), branches are dark reddish purple (187B). PARENTAGE: 'WALZ Gitaar' x 'Rohees New Millennium'. Lax upright or stiff trailer. Makes good basket. Prefers overhead filtered light. Best bloom and foliage color in filtered light. Tested 3 years in Berlaar, Belgium. NBFK Certificate at Meise. Distinguished by bloom color and shape.
Geerts J. 2003 BE AFS5196.

Dwerg Bloosje. Upright/Trailer. Single. COROLLA: Half flared; opens purple (71A); matures dark reddish purple (70A); 10mm (3/8") long x 17mm (5/8") wide. SEPALS: fully up, tips recurved; rose (64D) upper surface; rose (64D) lower surface; 20mm (3/4") long x 9mm (5/16") wide. TUBE: rose (64D); short & thin; 5mm (3/16") long x 3mm (1/8") wide. FOLIAGE is dark green (137A) upper surface; medium green (137C) lower surface. PARENTAGE: 'Roesse Lupus' x ('Reg Gubler' x 'Maxima's Baby').
Roes 2007 NL AFS6709.

Dwerg Dommel. Upright. Single. COROLLA: Quarter flared; opens dark reddish purple

(42A); matures red orange (42C); 18mm (11/16") long x 7mm (1/4") wide. SEPALS: half up, tips reflexed up; magenta (58B) upper & lower surfaces; 22mm (7/8") long x 5mm (3/16") wide. TUBE: magenta (58B); medium length & thickness; 16mm (5/8") long x 4mm (1/8") wide. FOLIAGE is dark green (137A) upper surface; medium green (137C) lower surface. PARENTAGE: 'Rosea' x 'Oranje van Os'.
Roes 2007 NL AFS6707.

Dwerg Giechel. Upright/Trailer. Single. COROLLA: Quarter flared; opens purple (83A); matures purple (80A); 14mm (9/16") long x 11mm (7/16") wide. SEPALS: half up, tips recurved up; red (53C) upper surface; red (53B) lower surface; 21mm (13/16") long x 8mm (5/16") wide. TUBE: red (53C); medium length & thickness; 10mm (3/8") long x 4mm (1/8") wide. FOLIAGE is dark green (137A) upper surface; medium green (138B) lower surface. PARENTAGE: 'Roesse Lupus' x ('Reg Gubler' x 'Maxima's Baby').
Roes 2007 NL AFS6704.

Dwerg Grumpy. Upright/Trailer. Single. COROLLA: Quarter flared; opens & matures pale rose (73D); 12mm (7/16") long x 14mm (9/16") wide. SEPALS: horizontal, tips recurved; light rose (58D) upper surface; dark rose (58C) lower surface; 24mm (15/16") long x 7mm (1/4") wide. TUBE: light rose (58D); medium length & thickness; 9mm (5/16") long x 4mm (1/8") wide. FOLIAGE is dark green (137A) upper surface; medium green (138A) lower surface. PARENTAGE: 'Roesse Duck' x 'Maxima'.
Roes 2007 NL AFS6706.

Dwerg Niezel. Trailer. Single. COROLLA: Quarter flared; opens purple (83A); matures purple (77A); 7mm (1/4") long x 8mm (5/16") wide. SEPALS: fully up, tips recurved; reddish purple (72B) upper surface; light reddish purple (72C) lower surface; 15mm (9/16") long x 4mm (1/8") wide. TUBE: reddish purple (72B); short & thin; 4mm (1/8") long x 2mm (1/16") wide. FOLIAGE is dark green (137A) upper surface; medium green (137C) lower surface. PARENTAGE: 'Roesse Lupus' x ('Reg Gubler' x 'Maxima's Baby').
Roes 2007 NL AFS6710.

Dwerg Stoetel. Upright/Trailer. Single. COROLLA: Quarter flared; opens dark purple (78A); matures violet (77B); 17mm (5/8") long x 12mm (7/16") wide. SEPALS: half up, tips recurved up; magenta (58B) upper &

lower surfaces; 26mm (1") long x 6mm (1/4") wide. TUBE: magenta (58B); short & thin; 5mm (3/16") long x 4mm (1/8") wide. FOLIAGE is dark green (137A) upper surface; medium green (138A) lower surface. PARENTAGE: 'Roesse Lupus' x ('Reg Gubler' x 'Maxima's Baby').
Roes 2007 NL AFS6708.

Dyonne Lankhuizen. Upright/Trailer. Double. COROLLA: three quarter flared, turned under wavy petal margins; opens white (155C), dark rose (67C) & dark rose (71D); matures white (155B), magenta (68A) & light reddish purple (71D); 35mm (1 3/8") long x 21mm (13/16 ") wide. PETALOIDS: white (155C) striped rose (55B); 28mm (1 1/8") long x 11mm (7/16") wide. SEPALS: horizontal, tips recurved, twisted left to right; white (155C) tipped light apple green (145B) upper surface; white (155C) & magenta (61C) tipped light apple green (145B) lower surface; 48mm (1 7/8") long x 14mm (9/16") wide. TUBE: white (155B) & medium green (139C); medium length & thickness; 18mm (11/16") long x 6mm (1/4") wide. STAMENS extend 5mm (3/16") beyond the corolla; light rose (63D) filaments; pale rose (73D) anthers. PISTIL does not extend beyond the corolla; white (155B) style; rose (68C) stigma. BUD: elongated. FOLIAGE: dark green (137A) upper surface; medium green (138B) lower surface. Leaves are 78mm (3 1/8") long x 47mm (1 7/8") wide; ovate shaped, serrate edges, acute tips, rounded bases. Veins are light purple (186C), stems are reddish purple (186B), branches are light red purple (185D) & light green (139D). PARENTAGE: 'Eurofuchsia Denmark 2007' x 'Cor Leeuwestyn'. Lax upright or stiff trailer. Self branching. Makes good basket. Prefers overhead filtered light, cool climate. Best bloom & foliage colour in filtered light. Tested 3 years in Koningshooikt, Belgium. Waanrode 8/9/08. Distinguished by bloom colour pattern.
Michiels 2009 BE AFS7161.

Ector's Ilse Cora. Upright/Trailer. Double. COROLLA: half flared, turned under smooth petal margins; opens violet (85A), light purple (75B) at base; matures violet (84A), white (155B) at base; 28mm (1 1/8") long x 37mm (1 7/16") wide. PETALOIDS: 1per sepal; rose (65A) edged violet (85A), 25mm (1") long x 16mm (5/8") wide. SEPALS: horizontal; tips recurved; white (155B) edged pink (62A) tipped light yellow green (150A) upper surface; white (155B) flushed pink (62A) lower surface; 42mm (2 11/16") long x

17mm (11/16") wide. TUBE: white (155B); medium length & thickness; 16mm (5/8") long x 7mm (1/4") wide. STAMENS: extend 17mm (11/16") below the corolla; pink (62A) filaments, orangy brown (164A) anthers. PISTIL extends 23mm (15/16") below the corolla; white (155B) style, yellowish white (4D) stigma. BUD: ovate. FOLIAGE: dark green (138A) upper surface; yellowish green (144A) lower surface. Leaves are 43mm (1 11/16") long x 30mm (1 3/16") wide, ovate shaped, serrulated edges, acute tips and rounded bases. Veins are yellowish green (144A), stems & branches are dark grayish red (182A). PARENTAGE: 'Blue Mist' x unknown. Lax upright or stiff trailer. Self branching. Makes good upright. Prefers overhead filtered light. Best bloom and foliage color in filtered light. Tested 3 years in Rummen, Belgium. NBFK certificate at Meise. Distinguished by bloom shape and color.
Ector 2003 BE AFS5111.

Ed Salome. Upright. Double. COROLLA is three quarter flared with smooth petal margins; opens purple (71A), matures reddish purple (72B); 31mm (1 1/4") long x 34mm (1 5/16") wide. SEPALS are half up, tips recurved up; dark rose (67C) upper surface and reddish purple (67A) lower surface; 32mm (1 1/4") long x 17mm (11/16") wide. TUBE is dark rose (67C), medium length and thickness; 8mm (5/16") long x 6mm (1/4") wide. STAMENS extend 20mm (13/16) below the corolla; reddish purple (71B) filaments, dark purple (79A) anthers. PISTIL extends 37mm (1 7/16") below the corolla; reddish purple (71B) style, light rose (68D) stigma. BUD is ovate, pointed. FOLIAGE is medium green (137C) upper surface and medium green (138B) lower surface. Leaves are 74mm (2 15/16") long x 36mm (1 7/16") wide, lanceolate shaped, serrated edges, acute tips and obtuse bases. Veins, stems and branches are red. PARENTAGE: [('Bon Accord' x 'Bicentennial') x ('Vobeglo' x Dancing Flame)] x 'Rohees Alrami'. Small upright. Makes good standard. Prefers overhead filtered light and cool climate. Best bloom colour in filtered light. Tested four years in Knegsel, The Netherlands. Distinguished by bloom colour.
Roes 2007 NL AFS4833.

Eddie Gasaway. Upright. Single. COROLLA is quarter flared with smooth petal margins; opens dark purple (79B), matures dark reddish purple (64A); 12mm (1/2") long x 12mm (1/2") wide. SEPALS are horizontal,

tips recurved; magenta (63A) upper surface and magenta (63B) lower surface; 21mm (13/16") long x 8mm (5/16") wide. TUBE is magenta (63A), thick and short; 6mm (1/4") long x 7mm (1/4") wide. STAMENS extend 9mm (3/8) below the corolla; reddish purple (72B) filaments and anthers. PISTIL extends 12mm (1/2") below the corolla; reddish purple (72B) style and light rose (73B) stigma. BUD is ovate, pointed. FOLIAGE is medium green (137B) upper surface and medium green (138A) lower surface. Leaves are 50mm (2") long x 27mm (1 1/16") wide, ovate shaped, serrated edges, acute tips and obtuse bases. Veins, stems and branches are green. PARENTAGE: {['Vobeglo' x ('Foline' x 'Dancing Flame')] x 'Roesse Eslie'} x 'Gruss aus dem Bodethal'. Small upright. Makes good standard. Prefers overhead filtered light and cool climate. Best bloom colour in filtered light. Tested four years in Knegsel, The Netherlands. Distinguished by bloom and foliage combination.
Roes 2002 NL AFS4830.

Ede Staal. Upright. Single. COROLLA: half flared, turned up petal margins; opens & matures rose (65A) edged magenta (58B); 15mm (9/16") long 22mm (7/8") wide. SEPALS: horizontal; tips recurved; yellowish white (158A) blushed rose (55B) upper surface; dark rose (58C) tipped reddish purple (61B) lower surface; 22mm (7/8") long x 12mm (1/2") wide. TUBE: yellowish white (158A) blushed rose (50B); long, medium thickness; 24mm (15/16") long x 8mm (5/16") wide. STAMENS: extend 2mm (1/16") below corolla; light pink (65B) filaments; light yellow (12C) anthers. PISTIL: extends 18mm (11/16") below the corolla; yellowish white (158A) style; yellow (20B) stigma. BUD: long & small, pointed. FOLIAGE: dark green (147A) upper surface; light olive green (148B) lower surface. Leaves are 86mm (3 3/8") long x 52mm (2 1/16") wide, ovate shaped, serrated edges, acute tips and rounded bases. Light green (137C) veins; light green (148C) stems; plum (184B) branches. PARENTAGE: 'Gerharda's Panache' x 'Lord Lonsdale'. Medium upright. Makes good upright, standard or decorative. Prefers overhead filtered light, warm climate. Best bloom and foliage colour in bright light. Tested 3 years in Stadskanaal, The Netherlands. Distinguished by flowering in long racemes and blossom colour combination.
Koerts T. 2004 NL AFS5585.

Edeltraud Goßner. Upright. Double. COROLLA: quarter flared, smooth petal margins; opens dark purple (79A) blushed dark rose (55A); matures dark purple (79C) blushed dark rose (55A); 22mm (7/8") long x 30mm (1 3/16") wide. SEPALS: horizontal, tips recurved; dark rose (55A) upper & lower surfaces; 33mm (1 5/16") long x 15mm (9/16") wide. TUBE: dark rose (55A); medium length & thickness; 13mm (1/2") long x 6mm (1/4") wide. STAMENS extend 20mm (3/4") beyond the corolla; rose (55B) filaments; dark red (47A) anthers. PISTIL extends 30mm (1 3/16") beyond the corolla; dark rose (55A) style; pale pink (49D) stigma. BUD: globular. FOLIAGE: dark green (137A) upper surface; medium green (138A) lower surface. Leaves are 72mm (2 7/8") long x 39mm (1 1/2") wide; ovate shaped, serrate edges, acute tips, rounded bases. Veins are red, stems are red maturing to light green, branches are reddish light brown. PARENTAGE: 'Georg Goßner' x ('Orange King' x 'Düsterwald'). Lax upright or stiff trailer. Self branching. Makes good basket, upright or standard. Prefers full sun, warm climate. Heat tolerant. Best bloom & foliage colour in bright light. Tested 3 years in Bavaria, Southern Germany. Distinguished by beautiful bloom colour combination.
Burkhart 2009 DE AFS7113.

Eden Leonard. Trailer. Double. COROLLA is three quarter flared, petticoat shaped; opens magenta (59C) veined red (51C); matures magenta (57A); 22mm (7/8") long x 27mm (1 1/16") wide. PETALOIDS: coral (39B) veined white (155A); 21mm (13/16") long x 18mm (11/16") wide. SEPALS are half up, tips reflexed up; pale pink (56C) upper surface; pale pink (56D) lower surface; 40mm (1 9/16") long x 17mm (5/8") wide. TUBE is yellowish white (158A); 12mm (1/2") long x 8mm (5/16") wide. FOLIAGE: dark green (137A) upper surface; medium green (146A) lower surface. PARENTAGE: 'Corneille' x unknown. Distinguished by bloom colour combination & profuse blooms.
Leonard 2006 BE AFS6053.

Edith Annie. Upright. Single. COROLLA is quarter flared, bell shaped; opens violet (76A) veined red at base; matures violet (77C); 15mm (9/16") long x 20mm (13/16") wide. SEPALS are half up, tips recurved up; red (53D) upper and lower surfaces, creped lower surface; 20mm (13/16") long x 9mm (3/8") wide. TUBE is red (53D), short and thick; 7mm (1/4") long x 5mm (3/16") wide. STAMENS extend 10mm (3/8") below the corolla; red (53D) filaments and anthers. PISTIL extends 15mm (9/16") below the corolla; red (53D) style and stigma. BUD is cordate shaped. FOLIAGE is dark green (147A) on upper surface and lower surfaces. Leaves are 52mm (2 1/6") long x 22mm (7/8") wide, lanceolate shaped, serrated edges, acute tips and rounded bases. Veins are light green, stems and branches are dull red. PARENTAGE: Kellyjo x Paul Pini. Small upright.Self branching. Makes good upright, standard, pillar, miniature or bonsai. Prefers full sun. Best bloom colour in bright light. Tested four years in Edenbridge, Kent and Southern England area. Distinguished by colour and profuse flowers.
Holmes 2003 UK AFS5061.

Edith Moik. Upright. Single. COROLLA: unflared, rolling shape, smooth petal margins; opens purple (82B); matures reddish purple (72B); 22mm (7/8") long 18mm (11/16") wide. PETALOIDS: same colour as corolla; 24mm (15/16") long x 20mm (13/16") wide. SEPALS: twisted; fully up; tips recurved; pink (49D), tipped green, upper surface; pink (62A) lower surface; 25mm (1") long x 7mm (1/4") wide. TUBE: pink (49D); medium length & thickness; 13mm (1/2") long x 5mm (3/16") wide. STAMENS: extend 12mm (1/2") below corolla; magenta (68A) filaments; dark red (46A) anthers. PISTIL: extends 37mm (1 7/16") below the corolla; rose (63C) style; light yellow (11B) stigma. BUD: oblong. FOLIAGE: dark green (147A) upper surface; olive green (147C) lower surface. Leaves are 76mm (3") long x 38mm (1 1/2") wide, lanceolate shaped, serrated edges, acute tips and rounded bases. Medium green (138B) veins; reddish stems & branches. PARENTAGE: 'Seventy Stars' x 'Love's Reward'. Tall upright. Makes good upright or decorative. Prefers overhead filtered light. Best bloom and foliage colour in bright light. Tested 3 years in Austria. Distinguished by long pistil, compact growth and continuous blossoms.
Haubenhofer 2004 AT AFS5570.

Edith Piaf. Trailer. Single. COROLLA: quarter flared, smooth petal margins; opens dark purple (79A); matures purple (71A); 20mm (13/16") long x 12mm (1/2") wide. SEPALS: horizontal; tips recurved; bright dark red (53A) upper surface; red (53B) lower surface; 24mm (15/16") long x 6mm (1/4") wide. TUBE: bright dark red (53A); medium length & thickness; 14mm (9/16) long x 7mm (1/4") wide. STAMENS: extend 14-

119

16mm (9/16–5/8") below corolla; dark reddish purple (64A) filaments, magenta (68A) anthers. PISTIL: extends 29mm (1 1/8") below the corolla, reddish purple (64B) style, dark reddish purple (60A) stigma. BUD: ovate. FOLIAGE: dark green (147A) upper surface; olive green (148A) lower surface. Leaves are 51mm (2") long x 19mm (3/4") wide, lanceolate shaped, serrulated edges, acute tips and rounded bases. Veins, stems & branches are light brown. PARENTAGE: 'Zulu King' x unknown. Natural trailer. Makes good basket. Prefers overhead filtered light and cool climate. Best bloom and foliage colour in filtered light. Tested 3 years in Pornic, France. Distinguished by profuse blooms of two axial blooms at tips of branches.
Massé 2003 FR AFS5221.

Edith van Kessel. Trailer. Double. COROLLA: three quarter flared, smooth petal margins; opens reddish purple (72B); matures reddish purple (61B); 27mm (1 1/16") long x 16mm (5/8") wide. SEPALS: horizontal; tips recurved; rose (68C) upper surface; dark rose (58C) lower surface; 42mm (1 5/8") long x 16mm (5/8") wide. TUBE: rose (68C); medium length & thickness; 22mm (7/8") long x 7mm (1/4") wide. STAMENS: extend 12mm (1/2") below corolla; magenta (63B) filaments; reddish purple (58B) anthers. PISTIL: extends 23mm (15/16") below the corolla, light rose (68D) style, yellowish white (4D) stigma. BUD: ovate, pointed. FOLIAGE: medium green (137B) upper surface; medium green (138B) lower surface. Leaves are 68mm (2 11/16") long x 32mm (1 1/4") wide, lanceolate shaped, serrulated edges, acute tips and rounded bases. Veins & stems are red, branches are green. PARENTAGE: 'Bicentennial' x ('Rohees King' x 'Miniskirt').Natural trailer. Makes good basket. Prefers overhead filtered light and cool climate. Best bloom and foliage colour in filtered light. Tested 4 years in Knegsel, The Netherlands. Distinguished by bloom & foliage combination.
van Bree 2003 NL AFS5241.

Edoardo Salarin Fassetta. Upright. Single. COROLLA: quarter flared, triphylla type, wavy & toothed petal margins; opens rose (55B); matures light orange (40D) edged reddish purple (66B); 10mm (3/8") long, 15mm (9/16") wide. SEPALS: full down; tips recurved; dark rose (55A), edged red (53C), tipped green upper surface; rose (55B) lower surface; 23mm (15/16") long x 8mm (5/16")

wide. TUBE: dark rose (55A) flushed rose (54C); long, thick; 65mm (2 9/16") long x 8mm (5/16") wide. STAMENS: do not extend below corolla; light pink (49C) filaments; pale yellow (2D) anthers. PISTIL: extends 20mm (13/16") below the corolla; pink (48D) style; light yellow (11B) stigma. BUD: ovate. FOLIAGE: dark green (147A) upper surface; (reddish) medium green (146A) lower surface. Leaves are 90mm (3 9/16") long x 50mm (2") wide, ovate shaped, wavy edges, acute tips and cordate bases. Reddish veins & stems; brown branches. PARENTAGE: 'Gartenmeister Bonstedt' x unknown. Medium upright. Makes good upright. Prefers warm climate. Heat tolerant if shaded. Best bloom colour in bright light. Best foliage colour in filtered light. Tested 3 years in Vicenza, Italy. Distinguished by striking contrast of colours in corolla and SEPALS.
Ianne 2004 IT AFS5635.

Edward Comperen. Upright/Trailer. Double. COROLLA: half flared, smooth petal margins; opens violet (90C); matures dark purple (78A); 24mm (15/16") long x 27mm (1 1/16") wide. SEPALS: fully up; tips reflexed; magenta (63A) upper surface; magenta (58B) lower surface; 27mm (1 1/16") long x 15mm (9/16") wide. TUBE: magenta (63A); medium length & thickness; 7mm (1/4") long x 5mm (3/16") wide. STAMENS: extend 12mm (1/2") below corolla; reddish purple (67A) filaments, rose (68C) anthers. PISTIL: does not extend below the corolla; rose (68C) style, light yellow (11C) stigma. BUD: ovate. FOLIAGE: dark green (137A) upper surface; medium green (138A) lower surface. Leaves are 47mm (1 7/8") long x 23mm (15/16") wide, lanceolate shaped, serrulated edges, acute tips and rounded bases. Veins, stems & branches are red. PARENTAGE: 'Sofie Michiels' x 'Die Fledermaus'. Lax upright or stiff trailer. Makes good stiff trailer. Prefers overhead filtered light and cool climate. Best bloom and foliage colour in filtered light. Tested 4 years in Diessen, The Netherlands. Distinguished by bloom & foliage combination.
Comperen 2003 NL AFS5260.

Edwin J. Jones. Trailer. Single. COROLLA: half flared, turned under smooth petal margins; opens reddish purple (74B), lighter near TUBE, veined light pink (62B); matures reddish purple (66B) veined red; 20mm (13/16") long x 30mm (1 3/16") wide. PETALOIDS: reddish purple (66B); 12mm (1/2") long x 10mm (3/8") wide. SEPALS: half up; tips recurved up; pale tan (159A)

tipped green upper surface; light pink (49C) tipped green lower surface; 30mm(1 3/16") long x 9mm (3/8") wide. TUBE: yellowish white (158A); medium length & thickness; 10mm (3/8") long x 6mm (1/4") wide. STAMENS: extend 15mm (9/16") below corolla; rose (55B) filaments; dark rose (55A) anthers. PISTIL: extends 25mm (1") below the corolla, white (155A) style; grayish yellow (160A) stigma. BUD: medium, elongated. FOLIAGE: medium green (146A) upper surface, yellowish green (146B) lower surface. Leaves are 55mm (2 3/16") long x 35mm (1 3/8") wide, cordate shaped, serrulated edges, acute tips and rounded bases. Veins & stems are green; branches are brown. PARENTAGE: 'Pink La Campanella' x 'Loveable Rascal'. Natural trailer. Self branching. Makes good basket or standard. Prefers overhead filtered light and warm climate. Heat tolerant if shaded. Cold weather hardy to 32⁰ F. Best bloom colour in bright light. Tested 3 years in Walthamstow, London, England. Distinguished by profuse, continuous blooms.
Allsop M. 2004 UK AFS5383.

Edwin van Stenis. Upright/Trailer. Double. COROLLA: Half flared; opens violet (90C) edged purple (90B); matures purple (81B); 18mm (11/16") long x 30mm (1 3/16") wide. PETALOIDS: purple (90B), heart shaped; 8mm (5/16") long x 6mm (1/4") wide. SEPALS: fully up, tips reflexed; rose (68C) upper surface; rose (68B) lower surface; 28mm (1 1/8") long x 12mm (7/16") wide. TUBE: pale yellow (158B); short & thin; 6mm (1/4") long x 4mm (1/8") wide. FOLIAGE is dark green (139A) upper surface; medium green (138B) lower surface. PARENTAGE: 'Benjamin' x 'Quasar'.
Koerts T. 2007 NL AFS6453.

Edwin's Choice. Upright/Trailer. Single. COROLLA is three quarter flared, square shaped; opens violet (77C); matures violet (75A); 22mm (7/8") long x 12mm (7/16") wide. SEPALS are horizontal, tips recurved; magenta (63B) upper surface; rose (65A) lower surface; 19mm (3/4") long x 7mm (1/4") wide. TUBE is rose (63D), darker base; 12mm (7/16") long x 6mm (1/4") wide. FOLIAGE: medium green (147B) upper surface; light olive green (147C) lower surface. PARENTAGE: 'Gerharda's Panache' x 'Summerdaffodil'. Distinguished by flowers in terminal racemes; separated petals.
de Graaff H. 2006 NL AFS6250.

Eerste Cyclist. Upright. Semi Double. COROLLA is half flared with turned under smooth petal margins; opens purple (79C), reddish purple (72B) base; matures magenta (71C); 23mm (15/16") long x 24mm (15/16") wide. PETALOIDS: same colour as corolla; 12mm (1/2") long x 15mm (9/16") wide. SEPALS are half down, tips reflexed; reddish purple (64B) upper surface; magenta (61C) lower surface; 37mm (1 7/16") long x 15mm (9/16") wide. TUBE is magenta (57C); medium length & thickness; 18mm (11/16") long x 8mm (5/16") wide. FOLIAGE: medium green (137B) upper surface; medium green (138B) lower surface. Leaves are 72mm (2 13/16") long x 33mm (1 5/16") wide, ovate shaped. PARENTAGE: 'Roesse Blacky' x 'Sofie Michiels'. Meis 3-7-04. Distinguished by colour combination.
Michiels 2005 BE AFS5678.

Efant d'Jibloux. Upright/Trailer. Single. COROLLA: quarter flared, square shape, turned under smooth petal margins; opens purple (80A); matures reddish purple (80B); 21mm (13/16") long x 22mm (7/8") wide. SEPALS: horizontal, tips recurved; pink (49A) veined red (50D) tipped green upper surface; light pink (49C) lower surface; 21mm (13/16") long x 9mm (5/16") wide. TUBE: pale yellowish orange (20C); medium length & thickness; 19mm (3/4") long x 6mm (1/4") wide. STAMENS extend 39mm (1 1/2") beyond the corolla; rose (68B) filaments; magenta (71C) anthers. PISTIL extends 53mm (2 1/8") beyond the corolla; light pink (49C) style; cream (11D) stigma. BUD: ovate. FOLIAGE: medium green (146A) upper surface; light olive green (147B) lower surface. Leaves are 52mm (2 1/16") long x 34mm (1 3/8") wide; cordate shaped, serrulate edges, acute tips, rounded bases. Veins & stems are green, branches are red. PARENTAGE: found seedling. Lax upright or stiff trailer. Self branching. Makes good basket. Prefers full sun. Cold weather hardy. Best bloom & foliage colour in bright light. Tested 15 years in Gembloux, Belgium. Distinguished by blossom colour combination & profuse, continuous blooms.
Tourneur 2009 BE AFS7120.

Eggetingen. Trailer. Single. COROLLA: quarter flared; opens dark rose (55A); matures rose (51C); 15mm (9/16") long x 14mm (9/16") wide. SEPALS: half down, tips reflexed; pink (43D) tipped light yellowish green (145A) upper surface; light coral (38A) tipped light yellowish green (145A) lower surface; 36mm (1 7/16") long x 12mm

(7/16") wide. TUBE: pink (49A); square shaped; 53mm (2 1/8") long x 7mm (1/4") wide. FOLIAGE is dark green (139A) upper surface; medium green (137C) lower surface. PARENTAGE: 'WALZ Harp' x 'Wentworth'. Awarded Outstanding, Waanrode 7-7-2007. Wagemans 2008 BE 6744.

Eileen Drew. Upright. Single. COROLLA deep lilac blue. SEPALS deep rose. Drew 2003 UK.

Eiram. Upright/Trailer. Double. COROLLA is three quarter flared with turned under wavy petal margins; opens purple (71A); matures dark reddish purple (61A); 18mm (11/16") long x 16mm (5/8") wide. SEPALS are horizontal, tips reflexed; reddish purple (58A) upper surface; dark reddish purple (60B) lower surface; 30mm (1 3/16") long x 12mm (1/2") wide. TUBE is magenta (59C); long, medium thickness; 33mm (1 5/16") long x 6mm (1/4") wide. FOLIAGE: dark green (139A) upper surface; medium green (139C) lower surface. Leaves are 74mm (2 15/16") long x 27mm (1 1/16") wide, elliptic shaped. PARENTAGE: 'WALZ Harp' x 'Rohees New Millenium'. Meise 9-18-04. Distinguished by flower colour. Geerts L 2005 BE AFS5857.

Ejner Andersen. Upright/Trailer. Single. COROLLA is half flared with turned under smooth petal margins; opens rose (52C); matures rose (48B); 10mm (3/8") long x 7mm (1/4") wide. SEPALS are horizontal, tips reflexed; rose (55B) upper surface; dark rose (55A) lower surface; 15mm (9/16") long x 4mm (3/16") wide. TUBE is rose (55B); medium length & thickness; 14mm (9/16") long x 4mm (3/16") wide. FOLIAGE: dark green (137A) upper surface; medium green (136C) lower surface. Leaves are 41mm (1 5/8") long x 22mm (7/8") wide, ovate shaped. PARENTAGE: 'Rosea' x 'F. fulgens gesneriana'. Meis 3-7-04. Distinguished by small flower and rich blooming period. Struck 2005 DK AFS5668.

Elaine Taylor. Upright. Double. COROLLA purple striped pink & white. SEPALS white tipped green. Allen 2004 UK.

Elburg's Blauwtje. Upright/Trailer. Single. COROLLA is quarter flared with turned under petal margins; opens purple (89C); matures purple (77A); 24mm (15/16") long x 24mm (15/16") wide. PETALOIDS: same colour as corolla; 18mm (11/16") long x

12mm (1/2") wide. SEPALS are fully up, tips recurved; light pink (65C) upper surface; rose (55B) lower surface; 37mm (1 7/16") long x 12mm (1/2") wide. TUBE is white (155A); medium length & thickness; 14mm (9/16") long x 7mm (1/4") wide. FOLIAGE: medium green (146A) upper surface; yellowish green (146B) lower surface. Leaves are 63mm (2 1/2") long x 24mm (15/16") wide, lanceolate shaped. PARENTAGE: {'Maori Pipes' x [('Rogier de Groot' x 'Herjan de Groot) x ('Geertje Sheffel' x 'Herjan de Groot')]} x ('Herjan de Groot' x 'Janna Roddenhof'). Distinguished by very blue colour, retained almost to end of bloom. de Groot J. 2005 NL AFS5784.

Elburg's Bloemfontein. Upright. Single. COROLLA: closed shape, unflared, smooth petal margins; opens & matures purple (80A); 22 mm (7/8") long x 20mm (3/4") wide. SEPALS are half up, tips recurved up; reddish purple (61B) tipped greenish yellow (151A) upper surface; reddish purple (61B) lower surface; 35mm (1 3/8") long x 8mm (5/16") wide. TUBE is reddish purple (61B); medium length & thickness; 16mm (5/8") long x 5mm (3/16") wide. STAMENS extend 20mm (3/4") beyond the corolla; reddish purple (59B) filaments; purple (71A) anthers. PISTIL extends 35mm (1 3/8") beyond the corolla; dark reddish purple (59A) style & stigma. BUD is ovate. FOLIAGE is dark green (137A) upper surface; medium green (137C) lower surface. Leaves are 55mm (2 3/16") long x 22mm (7/8") wide, lanceolate shaped, serrulate edges, acute tips & bases. Veins are reddish, stems & branches are red. PARENTAGE: F. coccinia x 'Ampie Bouw'. Lax upright or stiff trailer; self branching. Makes good basket. Prefers full sun or overhead filtered light. Best bloom & foliage in filtered light. Tested 9 years in Elburg, The Netherlands. Distinguished by flower shape. de Groot J. 2009 NL AFS6978.

Elburg's Lampion. Upright/Trailer. Single. COROLLA is unflared, slender and closed, with turned under petal margins; opens rose (64D); matures dark rose (64C); 21mm (13/16") long x 14mm (9/16") wide. SEPALS are half down, tips recurved; pale pink (66A); light pink (55D) lower surface; 34mm (1 5/16") long x 7mm (1/4") wide. TUBE is white (155B) blushed rose; medium length & thin; 20mm (13/16") long x 5mm (3/16") wide. FOLIAGE: dark green (147A) upper surface; medium green (147B) lower surface. Leaves are 52mm (2 1/16") long x 26mm (1") wide, elliptic shaped. PARENTAGE: ('De

Groot's Prinses' x 'Herjan de Groot') x 'F. fulgens var. miniata'. Distinguished by colour; four to five buds on each leaf axil. de Groot J. 2005 NL AFS5781.

Elburg's Minibel. Upright. Single. COROLLA: saucer shape, full flared, smooth petal margins; opens white (155B) & matures dark red (53A); 1 mm (1/16") long x 1mm (1/16") wide. SEPALS are fully up, tips recurved; white (155A) maturing dark red (53A) upper & lower surfaces; 3mm (1/8") long x 1mm (1/16") wide. TUBE is white (155A), maturing dark red (53A); short & thin; 1mm (1/16") long x 1mm (1/16") wide. STAMENS do not extend beyond the corolla; white (155A), maturing dark red (53A) filaments & anthers. PISTIL extends 5mm (3/16") beyond the corolla; white (155A), maturing dark red (53A) pistil & stigma. BUD is long. FOLIAGE is yellowish green (145A) upper surface; light green (147D) lower surface. Leaves are 61mm (2 7/16") long x 30mm (1 3/16") wide, lanceolate shaped, entire edges, acute tips & bases. Veins are light green, stems are light green & branches are light green. PARENTAGE: found seedling. Tall upright; self branching. Makes good upright or pyramid. Prefers overhead filtered light. Best bloom & foliage in bright light. Tested 2 years in Elburg, The Netherlands. Distinguished by extremely small flower & maturing colour change. de Groot J. 2009 NL AFS6979.

Elburg's Mirakel. Upright. Single. COROLLA is quarter flared, round; opens light rose (68D); matures magenta (68A); 22mm (7/8") long x 23mm (7/8") wide. SEPALS are horizontal, tips recurved; rose (63C) upper surface, and pink (52D) lower surface; 33mm (1 5/16") long x 10mm (3/8") wide. TUBE is white (155A); 23mm (7/8") long x 8mm (5/16") wide. FOLIAGE is dark green (137A) upper surface; medium green (137C) lower surface. PARENTAGE: ('De Groot's Prinses' x 'Herjan de Groot') x 'F. fulgens var. miniata'. Distinguished by bloom colour. de Groot J. 2006 NL AFS6261.

Elburg's Rebel. Upright/Trailer. Single. COROLLA: Quarter flared; opens magenta (68A); matures light purple (78C); 27mm (1 1/16") long x 26mm (1") wide. SEPALS: fully up, tips recurved, twisted left, turned right; pale pink (49D) upper surface; rose (55B) lower surface; 34mm (1 3/8") long x 10mm (3/8") wide. TUBE: white (155A); medium length & thickness; 20mm (3/4") long x 6mm (1/4") wide. FOLIAGE is dark green (147A)

upper surface; medium green (147B) lower surface. PARENTAGE: ('de Groot's Prinses' x 'Herjan de Groot') x 'de Groot's Robbedoes'. de Groot J. 2007 NL AFS6455.

Elburg's Roodkapje. Trailer. Single. COROLLA is quarter flared with turned up petal margins; opens magenta (61C); matures dark red (47A); 30mm (1 3/16") long x 17mm (11/16") wide. SEPALS are half up, tips recurved up; red (45C) upper & lower surfaces; 30mm (1 3/16") long x 9mm (3/8") wide. TUBE is red (45C); medium length & thickness; 10mm (3/8") long x 4mm (3/16") wide. FOLIAGE: dark green (147A) upper surface; medium green (147B) lower surface. Leaves are 53mm (2 1/8") long x 31mm (1 1/4") wide, ovate shaped. PARENTAGE: [('Rogier de Groot' x 'Herjan de Groot') x ('Herjan de Groot' x 'Janna Roddenhof')] x 'F. regia var. typica'. Distinguished by very bright colour and very leathery leaves. de Groot J. 2005 NL AFS5783.

Elburg's Trompet. Upright. Single. COROLLA: bell shape, quarter flared, smooth petal margins; opens & matures orange (32A); 12 mm (7/16") long x 9mm (5/16") wide. SEPALS are half down, tips reflexed; yellow to apple green (144C), orange base upper surface; yellowish white (4D) to light green (143C) lower surface; 17mm (5/8") long x 6mm (1/4") wide. TUBE is orange (35B); long & thin; 55mm (2 3/16") long x 5mm (3/16") wide. STAMENS do not extend beyond the corolla; light coral (38A) filaments; yellow (7A) anthers. PISTIL extends 6mm (1/4") beyond the corolla; pink (36A) style; yellowish green (145A) stigma. BUD is triphylla shape. FOLIAGE is dark green (137A) upper surface; medium green (137C) lower surface. Leaves are 100mm (4") long x 65mm (2 9/16") wide, ovate shaped, entire edges, acute tips, rounded bases. Veins are red, stems & branches are reddish. PARENTAGE: 'Martin's Choice Improved' x F. fulgens var. miniata. Tall upright; self branching. Makes good upright or standard. Prefers full sun. Best bloom in filtered light; best foliage in filtered light. Tested 3 years in Elburg, The Netherlands. Distinguished by flower shape & colour. de Groot J. 2009 NL AFS6977.

Eleanor Jones. Upright. Single. COROLLA is quarter flared with smooth petal margins; opens magenta (57B), light at base; matures magenta (58B), light at base; 19mm (3/4") long x 16 mm (5/8") wide. SEPALS are half down, tips recurved; orangish white (159C)

123

upper surface; orangish white (159C), tipped red, lower surface; 25mm (1") long x 8mm (5/16") wide. TUBE is orangish white (159C), medium length and thickness; 22mm (7/8") long x 9mm (3/8") wide. FOLIAGE: medium green (138A) upper surface; light olive green (148B) lower surface. Leaves are 50mm (2") long x 30mm (1 3/16") wide, cordate shaped. PARENTAGE: 'Loveliness' x 'Alyce Larson'. Distinguished by bloom colour.
Gibson 2005 UK AFS5638.

Elegant Rose. Upright/Trailer. Single. COROLLA is quarter flared; opens & matures rose (52B); 16mm (5/8") long x 12mm (1/2") wide. SEPALS are fully up, tips recurved; dark rose (55A) upper & lower surfaces; 34mm (1 5/16") long x 7mm (1/4") wide. TUBE is ight coral (38A); 5mm (3/16") long x 20mm (13/16") wide. FOLIAGE: dark green (147A) upper surface; light olive green (148A) lower surface. PARENTAGE: 'Campo Victor' x 'Other Fellow. Distinguished by mite resistance, blossom shape & colour.
Cooke 2006 USA AFS5988.

Eleonore Brunner. Upright. Double. COROLLA: three quarter flared, smooth petal margins, square shape; opens & matures purple (81A); 30mm (1 3/16") long x 30mm (1 3/16") wide. SEPALS: half up, tips recurved up; reddish purple (61B) upper & lower surfaces; 27mm (1 1/16") long x 12mm (7/16") wide. TUBE: reddish purple (61B); medium length & thickness; 17mm (5/8") long x 12mm (7/16") wide. STAMENS extend 15mm (9/16") beyond the corolla; magenta (63B) filaments; grayish yellow (160B) anthers. PISTIL extends 18mm (11/16") beyond the corolla; magenta (63B) style; grayish yellow (160C) stigma. BUD: drop shape, yellow tip. FOLIAGE: medium green (139B) upper surface; medium green (139C) lower surface. Leaves are 100mm (4") long x 45mm (1 3/4") wide; cordate shaped, serrulate edges, acute tips, rounded bases. Veins & branches are gray brown, stems are darker gray brown. PARENTAGE: 'Santa Cruz' x 'Blue Veil'. Medium upright. Makes good upright. Prefers overhead filtered light, cool climate. Best bloom colour in filtered light. Tested 4 years in Dorf Haag, Austria. Distinguished by flower shape & colour.
Gindl 2009 AT AFS7088.

Eline Brantz. Upright/Trailer. Semi Double to Double. COROLLA is half flared with turned under petal margins; opens reddish purple (74B), dark rose (67C) at base; matures reddish purple (74B), light reddish purple (66C) at base; 27mm (15/16") long x 29mm (1 1/8") wide. SEPALS are half down, tips recurved; rose (55B), tipped light green (138C) upper surface; pink (48C) tipped rose (50B) lower surface; 32mm (1 1/4") long x 11mm (7/16") wide. TUBE is pale pink (56B); long, medium thickness; 29mm (1 1/8") long x 7mm (1/4") wide. STAMENS do not extend beyond the corolla; pink (62A) filaments, pale yellow (8D) anthers. PISTIL does not extend beyond the corolla; rose (61D) style, cream (11D) stigma. BUD is square, pointed. FOLIAGE is dark green (137A) upper surface, light green (137D) lower surface. Leaves are 60mm (2 3/8") long x 23mm (15/16") wide, ovate shaped, serrulated edges, acute tips and obtuse bases. Veins are reddish purple (186B), stems and branches are plum (185C). PARENTAGE: 'Alda Alders' x 'Wingrove's Mammoth'. Lax upright or stiff trailer. Self branching. Makes good basket or upright. Prefers overhead filtered light. Best bloom and foliage colour in filtered light. Tested three years in Leopoldsburg, Belgium. Certificate N.B.F.K. at Meise. Distinguished by bloom shape.
Busschodts 2002 BE AFS4979.

Elizabeth Haverkamp. Upright. Single. COROLLA deep red splashed aubergine. SEPALS dark red. TUBE dark red.
Beije 2004 NL.

Elize-Catharina. Upright. Single. COROLLA is quarter flared, bell shaped; opens & matures rose (68C); 18mm (11/16") long x 19mm (3/4") wide. SEPALS are half down, tips reflexed; pink (52D) upper surface; pink (49A) lower surface; 17mm (5/8") long x 19mm (3/4") wide. TUBE is pink (52D); 46mm (1 13/16") long x 8mm (5/16") wide. FOLIAGE: medium green (138A) upper surface; gray green (191B) lower surface. PARENTAGE: ('F. procumbens' x 'F. paniculata') x 'F. apetala'. Distinguished by profuse flowering & flower shape.
de Boer 2006 NL AFS6278.

Elke Pardon. Upright/Trailer. Double. COROLLA: half flared, turned under wavy petal margins; opens pink (48C) & light reddish purple (72C); matures pink (43D) & magenta (63B); 22mm (7/8 ") long x 19mm (3/4 ") wide. PETALOIDS: same colour as corolla; 12mm (7/16") long x 10mm (3/8") wide. SEPALS: horizontal, tips reflexed; pale pink (56D) tipped light yellow green (150B) upper surface; rose (52C) tipped light yellow green (150B) lower surface; 29mm (1 1/8") long x 14mm (9/16") wide. TUBE: pale pink

(56C); short & thick; 11mm (7/16") long x 6mm (1/4") wide. STAMENS extend 14mm (9/16") beyond the corolla; magenta (58B) filaments; magenta (63A) anthers. PISTIL extends 18mm (11/16") beyond the corolla; dark rose (58C) style; pale pink (49D) stigma. BUD: bulbous. FOLIAGE: dark green (136B) upper surface; medium green (137D) lower surface. Leaves are 82mm (3 1/4") long x 45mm (1 3/4") wide; ovate shaped, serrulate edges, acute tips, rounded bases. Veins are light grayish red (182D), stems are light grayish red (182D) & light green (138D), branches are dark rose (180D) & light green (139D). PARENTAGE: 'Manfried Kleinau' x 'First Lord'. Lax upright or stiff trailer. Self branching. Makes good upright. Prefers overhead filtered light, cool climate. Best bloom & foliage colour in filtered light. Tested 3 years in Koningshooikt, Belgium. Waanrode 8/9/08. Distinguished by bloom colour combination.
Michiels 2009 BE AFS7162.

Ellen Joiner. Upright. Single. COROLLA opens white, pink flush near base; corolla is quarter flared and is 15mm long x 20mm wide. SEPALS rose pink on the upper and lower surfaces; sepals are horizontally held with recurved tips and are 20mm long x 8mm wide. TUBE rose pink and is 12mm long x 8mm wide. PARENTAGE Sweet Linda x Brookwood Belle
Joiner C. 2007 UK BFS0044.

Ellen Sophia Wilson. Upright. Single. COROLLA is quarter flared, cone shaped; opens & matures dark orange (40B); 12mm (1/2") long x 15mm (9/16") wide. PETALOIDS: Same colour as corolla; 16mm (5/8") long x 12mm (1/2") wide. SEPALS are half down, tips reflexed; light coral (38A) to white, tipped green upper & lower surfaces; 12mm (1/2") long x 7mm (1/4") wide. TUBE is light coral (38A); medium length & thickness; 22mm (7/8") long x 7mm (1/4") wide. FOLIAGE: dark green (137A) upper surface; medium green (147B) lower surface. Leaves are 95mm (3 3/4") long x 57mm (2 1/4") wide, cordate shaped. PARENTAGE: 'F. splendens' x 'F. magellanica alba'. Distinguished by bloom colour.
Weber 2005 CA AFS5693.

Ellen Spoelstra. Trailer. Single. COROLLA: quarter flared, turned under petal margins; opens purple (90A) & light rose (73B); matures violet (84A) & light rose (73C); 15mm (9/16") long 21mm (13/16") wide. SEPALS: fully up; tips recurved; magenta

(58B) upper surface; rose (61D) lower surface; 18mm (11/16") long x 12mm (1/2") wide. TUBE: magenta (58B); medium length & thickness; 5mm (3/16") long x 5mm (3/16") wide. STAMENS: extend 22mm (7/8") below corolla; reddish purple (60D) filaments; dark reddish purple (60A) anthers. PISTIL: extends 22mm (7/8") below the corolla; magenta (61C) style; rose (67D) stigma. BUD: round, pointed. FOLIAGE: medium green (137B) upper surface; medium green (138B) lower surface. Leaves are 47mm (1 7/8") long x 29mm (1 1/8") wide, cordate shaped, serrulated edges, acute tips and rounded bases. Red veins, stems & branches. PARENTAGE: 'Swanley Gem' x 'Monique Sleiderink'. Natural trailer. Self branching. Makes good basket. Prefers overhead filtered light and cool climate. Best bloom and foliage colour in filtered light. Tested 4 years in Knegsel, The Netherlands. Distinguished by bloom colour.
Roes 2004 NL AFS5465.

Elvee. Upright. COROLLA violet. SEPALS red. PARENTAGE Janice Ann x Glazioviana.
Evans 2008 UK.

Elly. Upright/Trailer. Single to Semi Double. COROLLA: half flared; opens pale purple (88D); matures purple (81B); 47mm (1 7/8") long x 33mm (1 5/16") wide. SEPALS: horizontal, tips recurved; pale pink (56D) upper & lower surfaces; 48mm (1 7/8") long x 16mm (5/8") wide. TUBE: pale pink (56D); long, medium thickness; 42mm (1 5/8") long x 5mm (3/16") wide. STAMENS extend 50mm (2") beyond the corolla; light reddish purple (73A) filaments; dark tan (164B) anthers. PISTIL extends 70mm (2 3/4") beyond the corolla; light rose (73C) style; pale rose (73D) stigma. BUD: ovate. FOLIAGE: yellowish green (144A) upper surface; light olive green (147C) lower surface. Leaves are 88mm (3 1/2") long x 48mm (1 7/8") wide; cordate shaped, serrulate edges, acute tips, rounded bases. Veins & branches are dark reddish purple (59A), stems are dark reddish purple (59A) & green. PARENTAGE: 'Gladoor' x 'Riant'. Lax upright or stiff trailer. Makes good basket. Prefers overhead filtered light, cool climate. Best bloom colour in filtered light. Tested 12 years in Amsterdam, The Netherlands. V.K.C Aalsmeer 8/16/2003. Distinguished by flower colour & shape.
Krom 2009 NL AFS7057.

Elsy De Pauw. Trailer. Double. COROLLA: 3 quarter flared; opens white (155C), light rose

(58D) base; matures white (155A), rose (63C) base; 26mm (1") long x 20mm (3/4") wide. PETALOIDS: same colour as corolla; 18mm (11/16") long x 9mm (5/16") wide. SEPALS: horizontal, tips recurved; white (155C) tipped light apple green (144D) upper surface; pale lavender (69D) tipped light apple green (144D) lower surface; 35mm (1 3/8") long x 17mm (5/8") wide. TUBE: white (155C); long & thin; 16mm (5/8") long x 5mm (3/16") wide. FOLIAGE is dark green (136A) upper surface; medium green (138B) lower surface. PARENTAGE: 'Godelieve Elli' x 'Jessie Pearson'.
Michiels 2007 BE AFS6374.

Elza's Jommeke. Upright/Trailer. Semi Double. COROLLA: quarter flared, turned under smooth petal margins; opens light purple (78B), pink (52D) base; matures purple (80A); 21mm (13/16") long x 15mm (9/16") wide. PETALOIDS: pink (52D), violet (77B) base; 15mm (9/16") long x 8mm (5/16"0 wide. SEPALS: horizontal; tips recurved; pale pink (56A) tipped light apple green (145C) upper surface; pink (52D) tipped light apple green (145C) lower surface; 37mm (1 7/16") long x 12mm (1/2") wide. TUBE: pink (55C), white base (155B); long & thin; 30mm (1 3/16") long x 4mm (3/16") wide. STAMENS: extend 7mm (1/4") below corolla; magenta (63B) filaments; dark reddish purple (61A) anthers. PISTIL: extends 20mm (13/16") below the corolla; pink (62C) style; pale lavender (65D) stigma. BUD: oblong. FOLIAGE: dark green (136B) upper surface, medium green (138B) lower surface. Leaves are 51mm (2") long x 14mm (9/16") wide, ovate shaped, serrulated edges, acute tips and rounded bases. Veins & branches are medium green (138B); stems are medium green (139C). PARENTAGE: 'Checkerboard' x 'Bert's Whisky. Lax upright or stiff trailer. Self branching. Makes good basket or upright. Prefers overhead filtered light and cool climate. Best bloom and foliage colour in filtered light. Tested 3 years in Werm, Belgium. Award at Meise, 5/7/03. Distinguished by bloom colour.
Wagemans 2004 BE AFS5412.

Emily Armstrong. Trailer. Single. COROLLA: quarter flared, smooth petal margins; opens reddish purple (67A), reddish purple (66B) at base; matures reddish purple (61B), dark rose (58C) at base; 23mm (15/16") long x 30mm (1 3/16") wide. SEPALS: half down; tips recurved; magenta (57C), dark rose (55A) near TUBE, upper surface; dark rose (54A) tipped greenish white (157B) lower surface;

48mm (1 7/8") long x 12mm (1/2") wide. TUBE: dark rose (55A) striped magenta (57C); medium length & thick; 20mm(13/16") long x 8mm (5/16") wide. STAMENS: extend 15mm (9/16) below corolla; dark rose (55A) filaments & anthers. PISTIL: extends 35mm (1 3/8") below the corolla, rose (55B) style, pale yellow (158B) stigma. BUD: ovate. FOLIAGE: dark green (137A) upper surface; medium green (147B) lower surface. Leaves are 80mm (3 1/8") long x 40mm (1 9/16") wide, cordate shaped, serrated edges, acute tips and rounded bases. Veins are green, stems are red; branches are brown. PARENTAGE: 'Cascade' x 'Jack Shahan'. Natural trailer. Self branching. Makes good basket or half basket. Prefers overhead filtered light. Best bloom and foliage colour in filtered light. Tested 4 years in Walthamstow, London, England. Distinguished by bloom shape and colour.
Allsop J. 2003 UK AFS5209.

Emma Margaret. Upright. Single. COROLLA violet purple. SEPALS pinkish white.
Waving 2003 UK.

Emmakins. Upright/Trailer. Double. COROLLA: Half flared broad inverted triangle shape; opens & matures light pink (65C); 15mm (9/16") long x 20mm (3/4") wide. SEPALS: fully up, tips reflexed; light apple green (145C) tipped light apple green (145B) upper surface; light green (36B) tipped light apple green (145B) lower surface; 13mm (1/2") long x 8mm (5/16") wide. TUBE: light apple green (145C); short & thick; 5mm (3/16") long x 5mm (3/16") wide. FOLIAGE is dark green (137A) upper surface; medium green (137D) lower surface. PARENTAGE: 'La Campanella' x 'Helen Nicholls'.
Broughton 2007 UK AFS6496.

Emma's Gold. Upright. Single. COROLLA: quarter flared; opens violet (82C) veined rose (68C); matures purple (81B); 16mm (5/8") long x 12mm (1/2") wide. SEPALS: horizontal; tips recurved; white (155D) tipped pale green (142D) upper surface; white (155C) tinged pale pink (69A) lower surface; 22mm(7/8") long x 12mm (1/2") wide. TUBE: white (155D); medium length & thickness; 10mm (3/8") long x 8mm (5/16") wide. STAMENS: extend 10mm (3/8") below corolla; magenta (68A) filaments & anthers. PISTIL: extends 15mm (9/16") below the corolla, pale lavender (69D) style; white (155D) stigma. BUD: spear shaped. FOLIAGE: yellowish green (144B) edged light

126

yellowish green (154C) upper surface; yellowish green (144A) edged yellowish green (154B) lower surface. Leaves are 35mm (1 3/8") long x 17mm (11/16") wide, lanceolate shaped, serrulated edges, acute tips and rounded bases. Veins & stems are light green; branches are light brown. PARENTAGE: sport of 'Frank Saunders'. Small upright. Self branching. Makes good upright, standard or decorative. Prefers overhead filtered light or full sun. Cold weather hardy to 30° F. Best bloom and foliage colour in filtered light. Tested 3 years in Enfield, London, England. Distinguished by bloom shape and variegated foliage. Nutt 2003 UK AFS5157.

Emmenez Moi. Upright/Trailer. Semi Double. COROLLA: half flared; opens dark reddish purple (60A); matures dark reddish purple (60C); 30mm (1 3/16") long x 29mm (1 1/8") wide. SEPALS are fully up, tips reflexed; light pink (65B) upper surface; rose (65A) lower surface; 40mm (1 9/16") long x 16mm (5/8") wide. TUBE is light pink (65B); 25mm (1") long x 9mm (5/16") wide. FOLIAGE is medium green (137B) upper surface & medium green (138B) lower surface. PARENTAGE: 'Roesse Lupus' x 'Roesse Cressida'. Decoster 2008 BE AFS6874.

Emotion. Upright/Trailer. Single. COROLLA: quarter flared, bell shape, wavy petal margins; opens & matures reddish purple (74B); 16mm (5/8") long, 11mm (7/16") wide. SEPALS: horizontal; tips recurved; pale purple (75C), tipped pale yellowish green (154D), upper surface; light purple (80C), tipped pale yellowish green (154D) lower surface; 22mm (7/8") long x 5mm (3/16") wide. TUBE: pale purple (70D); long, medium thickness; 22mm (7/8") long x 5mm (3/16") wide. STAMENS: extend 5mm (3/16") below corolla; purple (77A) filaments; dark reddish purple (187C) anthers. PISTIL: extends 12mm (1/2") below the corolla; reddish purple (74A) style; grayish yellow (160A) stigma. BUD: long TUBE, elliptic, pointed. FOLIAGE: yellowish green (146B) upper surface; yellow green (146C) lower surface. Leaves are 51mm (2") long x 29mm (1 1/8") wide, ovate shaped, serrulated edges, acute tips and rounded bases. Light yellow green veins, stems & branches. PARENTAGE: 'Gerharda's Panache' x 'Bourguignon'. Lax upright or stiff trailer. Self branching. Makes good basket. Prefers overhead filtered light. Heat tolerant if shaded. Best bloom and foliage colour in filtered light. Tested 4 years

in Lisse, The Netherlands. Distinguished by flower & foliage colour combination. de Graaff 2004 NL AFS5609.

Encelados. Upright. Single. COROLLA red. SEPALS red. Ainsworth 2003 UK.

Enchanting Emma. Upright/Trailer. Double. COROLLA: three quarter flared, turned under smooth petal margins; opens purple (82A), splashed light rose (73C); matures light purple (78B) splashed pale rose (73D); 35mm (1 3/8") long x 55mm (2 3/16") wide. PETALOIDS: Same colour as corolla; 22mm (7/8") long x 12mm (1/2") wide. SEPALS: fully up; tips reflexed; pale tan (159A), rose (55B) near TUBE, upper surface; orangish white (159C), rose (55B) near TUBE, lower surface; 35mm(1 3/8") long x 17mm (11/16") wide. TUBE: pale tan (159A); medium length & thick; 12mm (1/2") long x 8mm (5/16") wide. STAMENS: extend 20mm (13/16") below corolla; dark rose (55A) filaments; rose (55B) anthers. PISTIL: extends 25mm (1") below the corolla, pale pink (36D) style; yellowish white (158A) stigma. BUD: medium, rounded. FOLIAGE: medium green (146A) upper surface, yellowish green (146B) lower surface. Leaves are 70mm (2 3/4") long x 40mm (1 9/16") wide, cordate shaped, serrated edges, acute tips and rounded bases. Veins are green, red through center, stems are red; branches are brown. PARENTAGE: 'Loveable Rascal' x 'Heavenly Hayley'. Lax upright or stiff trailer. Self branching. Makes good basket or standard. Prefers overhead filtered light and warm climate. Heat tolerant if shaded. Cold weather hardy to 32° F. Best bloom colour in bright light. Tested 4 years in Walthamstow, London, England. Distinguished by colour combination. Allsop M. 2004 UK AFS5381.

Entente Florale Européenne. Upright. Single. COROLLA is unflared; opens reddish purple (61B); matures magenta (58B); 18mm (11/16") long x 12mm (7/16") wide. SEPALS are horizontal, tips recurved; pink to rose (54C-D) upper & lower surfaces; 25mm (1") long x 7mm (1/4") wide. TUBE is pink to dark rose (54B-C-D); 16mm (5/8") long x 6mm (1/4") wide. FOLIAGE: medium green (146A) upper surface; medium green (147B) lower surface. PARENTAGE: 'Rosea' x 'Lye's Unique'. Distinguished by bloom/foliage contrast. Massé 2006 FR AFS6236.

Ephsieny.　Upright/Trailer.　Double. COROLLA: half flared, turned under wavy petal margins; opens purple (N78C); matures light reddish purple (72C); 28mm (1 1/8") long x 24mm (15/16") wide. PETALOIDS: pink (49A) & violet (77B); 18mm (11/16") long x 14mm (9/16") wide. SEPALS: horizontal, tips recurved; rose (55B) tipped yellowish green (144B) upper surface; pink (62A) tipped yellowish green (144B) lower surface; 28mm (1 1/8") long x 15mm (9/16") wide. TUBE: white (155C); medium length & thickness; 11mm (7/16") long x 5mm (3/16") wide. STAMENS extend 14mm (9/16") beyond the corolla; rose (63C) filaments; reddish purple (60D) anthers. PISTIL extends 16mm (5/8") beyond the corolla; rose (65A) style; pale yellow (2D) stigma. BUD: bulbous. FOLIAGE: dark green (136A) upper surface; medium green (138A) lower surface. Leaves are 69mm (2 3/4") long x 36mm (1 7/16") wide; ovate shaped, serrate edges, acute tips, rounded bases. Veins are dark grayish purple (183A), stems are plum (183C), branches are plum (184B) & medium green (138B). PARENTAGE: 'Moonschot' x unknown. Lax upright or stiff trailer. Self branching. Makes good basket. Prefers overhead filtered light, cool climate. Tested 3 years in Rillaar, Belgium. Waanrode 7/5/08. Distinguished by pink & violet variegation on petaloid.
Willems 2009 BE AFS7077.

Eric Stanlick.　Trailer.　Semi Double. COROLLA: half flared, smooth petal margins; opens reddish purple (N80B) flushed light rose (73B); matures light purple (N80C) flushed (light rose (73B); 25mm (1") long 20mm (13/16") wide. SEPALS: 1 1/2 full twists; half up; tips recurved up; white (155D), tipped green, upper & lower surfaces; 40mm (1 9/16") long x 15mm (9/16") wide. TUBE: white (155D) striped green; medium length & thickness; 25mm (1") long x 12mm (1/2") wide. STAMENS: extend 20mm (13/16") below corolla; dark rose (54A) filaments; rose (47C) anthers. PISTIL: extends 25mm (1") below the corolla; white (155C) style; yellowish white (158A) stigma. BUD: medium, elongated. FOLIAGE: yellowish green (144A) upper surface; apple green (144C) lower surface. Leaves are 50mm (2") long x 30mm (1 3/16") wide, lanceolate shaped, serrulated edges, acute tips and rounded bases. Green veins; green/red stems & brown branches. PARENTAGE: 'Blue Veil' x 'Marcus Graham'. Natural trailer. Self branching. Makes good basket. Prefers overhead filtered light. Heat tolerant if shaded. Cold weather hardy to 32⁰ F. Best bloom and foliage colour in filtered light. Tested 3 years in Walthamstow, London, England. Distinguished by blossom colour and twisted SEPALS.
Allsop J. 2004 UK AFS5571.

Erik.　Upright.　Single.　COROLLA　rose. SEPALS pale coral rose. TUBE pale coral rose.
BRUNNERT 2004 UK.

Erika's Freude.　Trailer.　Single.　COROLLA: Fully flared, bell shaped; opens purple (83B), red (45B) base; matures dark purple (78A), red (45B) base; 65mm (2 9/16") long x 25mm (1") wide. SEPALS: fully up, tips recurved; red (45B) upper surface; red (45C) lower surface; 40mm (1 9/16") long x 12mm (7/16") wide. TUBE: red (45B); short & thin; 6mm (1/4") long x 4mm (1/8") wide. FOLIAGE is medium green (146A) upper surface; medium green (147B) lower surface. PARENTAGE: 'Mission Bells' x Mrs. Lovelle Swisher'.
Klemm 2007 AT AFS6474.

Erna van den Brink.　Upright.　Double. COROLLA: Quarter flared, bell shaped; opens purple (83A); matures purple (71A); 34mm (1 3/8") long x 27mm (1 1/16") wide. SEPALS: half up, tips recurved up, twisted; reddish purple (64B) upper & lower surfaces; 44mm (1 3/4") long x 15mm (9/16") wide. TUBE: magenta (57A); medium length & thickness; 27mm (1 1/16") long x 9mm (5/16") wide. FOLIAGE is medium green (146A) upper surface; yellowish green (146B) lower surface. PARENTAGE: 'Voodoo' x unknown. Award of Merit, VKC Aalsmeer, 2000.
van den Brink 2007 NL AFS6444.

Ernie Wise.　Upright/Trailer.　Double. COROLLA is fully flared with smooth petal margins; opens violet (77B) feathered light magenta (66D), light reddish purple (66C) at base; matures violet (77C), light magenta (66D) at base; 38mm (1 1/2") long x 80mm (3 1/8") wide. SEPALS are fully up, tips recurved; pale violet (76D) upper surface, pale violet (77D) flushed violet (76B) lower surface; 46mm (1 13/16") long x 8mm (5/16") wide. TUBE is pale violet (76D) striped violet (76B); medium length and thickness; 16mm (5/8") long x 9mm (3/8") wide. STAMENS extend 30mm (1 3/16") below the corolla; rose (65A) filaments and anthers. PISTIL extends 35mm (1 3/8") below the corolla; white (155B) style and stigma. BUD is pear shaped. FOLIAGE is

128

medium green (137A) upper surface, medium green (138B) lower surface. Leaves are 57mm (2 1/4") long x 25mm (1") wide, ovate shaped, serrated edges, acute tips and rounded bases. Veins are dark green, stems are pale green, branches are red. PARENTAGE: 'Roy Castle' x 'Quasar'. Lax upright or stiff trailer. Self branching. Makes good basket, upright, standard, pyramid, decorative or trellis. Prefers cool climate. Heat tolerant if shaded. Best bloom colour in filtered light. Tested six years in Gloucester, England. Distinguished by bloom shape and colour.
Hickman 2002 UK AFS4851.

Ernst Scharf. Upright. Semi Double. COROLLA is quarter flared with smooth petal margins; opens dark reddish purple (59A); matures dark reddish purple (61A); 24mm (15/16") long x 26mm (1") wide. SEPALS are fully up, tips recurved; rose (67D) upper surface; dark rose (67C) lower surface; 31mm (1 1/4") long x 12mm (1/2") wide. TUBE is rose (67D); short & thick; 10mm (3/8) long x 9mm (3/8") wide. FOLIAGE: medium green (137B) upper surface; medium green (138B) lower surface. Leaves are 81mm (3 3/16") long x 42mm (1 5/8") wide, ovate shaped. PARENTAGE: 'Roesse Carme' x 'Beekman'. Distinguished by bloom colour.
van Eijk 2005 NL AFS5906.

Errington. Upright/Trailer. Single. COROLLA opens purple, matures to paler purple; corolla is none flared. SEPALS pink on the upper and lower surfaces; SEPALS are horizontally held with recurved tips. TUBE pink. PARENTAGE 'Daisy Belle' x 'Emily'.
Norcross 2009 UK BFS0106.

Eruption. Upright/Trailer. Single. COROLLA is half flared, trumpet shaped, with toothed petal margins; opens rose (52C), matures dark rose (55A); 9mm (3/8") long x 7mm (1/4") wide. SEPALS are half down, tips reflexed; light magenta (57D) upper surface, rose (63C) lower surface; 14mm (9/16") long x 5mm (3/16") wide. TUBE is light magenta (57D) with dark base, long and thin; 33mm (1 5/16") long x 6mm (1/4") wide. STAMENS extend 1mm (1/16") beyond the corolla; light magenta (57D) filaments and pale yellow (158B) anthers. PISTIL extends 5mm (3/16") below the corolla; rose (63C) style, dark rose (55B) stigma. BUD is long TUBEd, ovate. FOLIAGE is dark green (147A) shaded purple upper surface, medium green (147B) shaded purple lower surface. Leaves are 81mm (3 3/16") long x 23mm (15/16") wide, elliptic

shaped, serrulated edges, acute tips and acute bases. Veins are dark red purple, stems and branches are red purple. PARENTAGE: 'Panache' x 'Panache'. Lax upright or stiff trailer. Self branching. Makes good basket. Prefers full sun. Heat tolerant if shaded. Best bloom and foliage colour in bright light. Tested four years in Lisse, Holland. Distinguished by panicles of profuse long flowers and dark shaded reddish purple leaves.
de Graaff 2002 NL AFS4886.

Esther Jansen. Upright. Double. COROLLA: half flared, smooth petal margins; opens purple (71A); matures reddish purple (71B); 24mm (15/16") long x 27mm (1 1/16") wide. SEPALS: fully up; tips recurved; magenta (61C) upper surface; reddish purple (61B) lower surface; 27mm (1 1/16") long x 11mm (7/16") wide. TUBE: magenta (61C); medium length & thickness; 12mm (1/2") long x 6mm (1/4") wide. STAMENS: extend 17mm (11/16") below corolla; magenta (71C) filaments; purple (71A) anthers. PISTIL: extends 32mm (1 1/4") below the corolla; magenta (71C) style; light pink (36C) stigma. BUD: round. FOLIAGE: dark green (137A) upper surface; medium green (138B) lower surface. Leaves are 67mm (2 5/8") long x 35mm (1 3/8") wide, cordate shaped, serrated edges, acute tips and cordate bases. Veins, stems & branches are red. PARENTAGE: {[('Bon Accord' x 'Bicentennial') x ('Vobeglo' x 'Dancing Flame')] x 'Rohees Alrami'} x ('Sofie Michiels' x 'Lechlade Rocket'). Medium upright. Makes good upright or standard. Prefers overhead filtered light and cool climate. Best bloom and foliage colour in filtered light. Tested 4 years in Duizel, The Netherlands. Distinguished by bloom colour & profuse flowers.
Tamerus 2003 NL AFS5294.

Ethel Lester. Upright. Double. COROLLA is three quarter flared, frilly with smooth margins; opens violet (86B), pink (55C) veined red (52A) at base; matures reddish purple (74A), pink (55C) veined red (52A) at base; 20mm (13/16") long x 35mm (1 3/8") wide. SEPALS are half up, tips recurved up; red (52A) upper and lower surfaces, creped lower surface; 29mm (1 1/8") long x 12mm (1/2") wide. TUBE is red (52A), short, medium thickness; 12mm (1/2") long x 6mm (1/4") wide. STAMENS extend 15mm (9/16") below the corolla; red (52A) filaments and anthers. PISTIL extends 35mm (1 3/8") below the corolla; red (52A) style and stigma. BUD is ovate shaped. FOLIAGE is medium

green (137B) on upper and lower surfaces. Leaves are 35mm (1 3/8") long x 25mm (1") wide, ovate shaped, serrated edges, acute tips and rounded bases. Veins are light green, stems and branches are dull red. PARENTAGE: 'Poppet' x 'Doris Yvonne'. Small upright.Self branching. Makes good upright, standard, pillaror bedding plant. Prefers full sun. Best bloom colour in bright light. Tested three years in Edenbridge, Kent and Southern England area. Distinguished by frilly flared corolla.
Holmes 2003 UK AFS5062.

Ethel May. Upright. Semi Double. COROLLA deep rose. SEPALS white flushed rose pink. This is the same name as the 1940 Evans & Reeves USA.
Kirby 2003 UK.

Etoile Du Matin. Upright. Double. COROLLA: three quarter flared, petticoat shape; opens pale pink (56D); matures pale pink (56C); 22mm (7/8") long x 26mm (1") wide. PETALOIDS: same colour as corolla; 19mm (3/4") long x 23mm (7/8") wide. SEPALS: horizontal, tips recurved; pale pink (56D), pink base, upper surface; white (155D), pink base, lower surface; 29mm (1 1/8") long x 15mm (9/16") wide. TUBE: pale pink (49D); 11mm (7/16") long x 7mm (1/4") wide. FOLIAGE is medium green (137B) upper surface; medium green (137D) lower surface. PARENTAGE: 'Showtime' x unknown.
Simon 2008 AFS6843.

Étoiles Filantes. Upright. Single. COROLLA: unflared, smooth petal margins; opens & matures reddish purple (72B); 18mm (11/16") long x 7mm (1/4") wide. SEPALS: horizontal; tips recurved; rose (52B) tipped light yellowish green (146D) upper surface; rose (52C) lower surface; 35mm (1 3/8") long x 3mm (1/8") wide. TUBE: red (45C); long, very thin; 22mm (7/8") long x 2mm (1/16") wide. STAMENS: extend 12mm (1/2") below corolla; dark rose (51A) filaments; dark red (47A) anthers. PISTIL: extends 30mm (1 3/16") below the corolla; dark rose (51A) style; brown (166A) stigma. BUD: lanceolate. FOLIAGE: medium green (146A) upper surface, yellowish green (146B/C) lower surface. Leaves are 62mm (2 7/16") long x 30mm (1 3/16") wide, ovate shaped, serrulated edges, acute tips and rounded bases. Light yellowish green veins; light brown stems & branches. PARENTAGE: 'Philippe Boënnec' x 'Mirobolant'. Tall upright. Self branching. Makes good standard. Prefers overhead filtered light and cool climate. Best bloom colour in filtered light. Best foliage colour in bright light. Tested 3 years in Pornic, France. Distinguished by very profuse blooms throughout the stems.
Massé 2004 FR AFS5451.

Eurofuchsia 2007 Denmark. Trailer. Double. COROLLA: half flared; opens violet (77C) striped pale rose (73D) & matures reddish purple (70B); 17mm (5/8") long x 15mm (9/16") wide. PETALOIDS: violet (77B) striped pale rose (73D); 12mm (7/16") long x 6mm (1/4") wide. SEPALS are fully up, tips recurved; pale lavender (69C) tipped light apple green (144D) upper surface & pale purple (70D) tipped light apple green (144D) lower surface; 38mm (1 1/2") long x 10mm (3/8") wide. TUBE is white (155C) striped light green (143C); medium length & thickness; 19mm (3/4") long x 6mm (1/4") wide. FOLIAGE is dark green (136A) upper surface; medium green (138A) lower surface. PARENTAGE: 'Vreni Schleeweiss' x 'Kiss'.
Michiels 2007 BE AFS6543.

Evelyn Harris. Upright. Single. COROLLA: Unflared; opens dark purple (79A); matures reddish purple (59A); 15mm (9/16") long x 10mm (3/8") wide. SEPALS: half up, tips recurved up; reddish purple (61B) upper & lower surfaces; 27mm (1 1/16") long x 6mm (1/4") wide. TUBE: reddish purple (61B); medium length, thin; 13mm (1/2") long x 4mm (1/8") wide. FOLIAGE is medium green (137B) upper surface; medium green (137C) lower surface. PARENTAGE: 'F. magellanica alba' x 'Autumnale'.
Bell 2007 UK AFS6401.

Evenstar. Trailer. Single. COROLLA is quarter flared, bell shaped; opens violet (77B); matures reddish purple (72B); 18mm (11/16") long x 12mm (7/16") wide. SEPALS are horizontal; pink (62C) upper surface; light pink (65B) lower surface; 22mm (7/8") long x 4mm (1/8") wide. TUBE is pale pink (62D); 23mm (7/8") long x 3mm (1/8") wide. FOLIAGE: dark green (147A) upper surface; medium green (147B) lower surface. PARENTAGE: 'Gerharda's Panache' x 'Gerharda's Panache'. Distinguished by panicles of flowers; shape & colour.
de Graaff H. 2006 NL AFS6248.

Everbeur. Upright. Semi Double. COROLLA is half flared; opens reddish purple (61B), reddish orange (43C) at base; matures reddish purple (67A), reddish orange (43C) at base; 22mm (7/8") long x 25mm (1") wide. SEPALS are horizontal, tips reflexed; rose (48B) tipped light yellowish green (150C) upper surface; reddish orange (43C) tipped light yellowish green (150C) lower surface; 32mm (1 1/4") long x 13mm (1/2") wide. TUBE is light pink (49B); 48mm (1 7/8") long x 9mm (3/8") wide. FOLIAGE: dark green (139A) upper surface; medium green (138B) lower surface. PARENTAGE: 'WALZ Harp' x 'Ting-A-Ling'. Meise 8/13/05. Distinguished by unique bloom colour combination. Geerts L. 2006 BE AFS5995.

Everlasting Love. Upright. Single. COROLLA: unflared; opens & matures white (155B), striped veins; 25mm (1") long x 25mm (1") wide. SEPALS: horizontal, tips reflexed; red (45C) upper & lower surfaces; 25mm (1") long x 13mm (1/2") wide. TUBE: yellowish green (144B); short & thin; 8mm (5/16") long x 4mm (1/8") wide. FOLIAGE is medium green (138A) upper surface; medium green (138B) lower surface. PARENTAGE: 'Nice N Easy' x 'Aloha'. Smith R. 2007 UK AFS6719.

Faimmie James. Upright/Trailer. Semi Double. COROLLA: full flared, ruffled, turned under smooth petal margins; opens pale purple (87D) splashed pink (62A); matures light purple (82D) light pink (62B); 20mm (13/16") long x 40mm (1 9/16") wide. PETALOIDS: same colour as corolla; 10mm (3/8") long x 6mm (1/4") wide. SEPALS: fully up; tips reflexed; dark rose (58C) upper surface; rose (67D) lower surface; 30mm(1 3/16") long x 9mm (3/8") wide. TUBE: dark rose (58C); long, medium thickness; 35mm (1 3/8") long x 10mm (3/8") wide. STAMENS: extend 20mm (13/16") below corolla; magenta (63B) filaments; magenta (67B) anthers. PISTIL: extends 35mm (1 3/8") below the corolla, magenta (63B) style; pale tan (159A) stigma. BUD: medium, round. FOLIAGE: medium green (146A) upper surface; light yellowish green (146D) lower surface. Leaves are 65mm (2 9/16") long x 35mm (1 3/8") wide, cordate shaped, serrulated edges, acute tips and rounded bases. Veins & branches are red, stems are brown. PARENTAGE: 'Loveable Rascal' x 'R.A.F.'. Lax upright or stiff trailer. Self branching. Makes good basket or standard. Heat tolerant if shaded. Prefers warm climate. Cold weather hardy to 32° F. Tested 3 years in Walthamstow, London, England. Distinguished by splashed pink blooms. Allsop M.R. 2003 UK AFS5145.

Falco. Upright/Trailer. Double. COROLLA is full flared with turned under smooth petal margins; opens dark purple (79B), reddish purple (64B) base; matures dark reddish purple (72A), red (52A) base; 18mm (11/16") long x 23mm (15/16") wide. SEPALS are horizontal, tips recurved; magenta (58B) upper surface; dark rose (51A) lower surface; 22mm (7/8") long x 14mm (9/16") wide. TUBE is magenta (58B); short & thick; 11mm (7/16") long x 7mm (1/4") wide. FOLIAGE: dark green (137A) upper surface; medium green (138B) lower surface. Leaves are 69mm (2 3/4") long x 38mm (1 1/2") wide, ovate shaped. PARENTAGE: 'Roesse Blacky' x 'Domein Vrijbroek'. Meise 8-14-04. Distinguished by unique colour play. Michiels 2005 BE AFS5739.

Falko. Trailer. Double. COROLLA: 3 quarter flared; opens dark purple (86A); matures light reddish purple (73A); 20mm (3/4") long x 11mm (7/16") wide. SEPALS: half up, tips reflexed up; pale pink (69A) upper surface; pink (62A) lower surface; 30mm (1 3/16") long x 18mm (11/16") wide. TUBE: pale pink (69A); medium length, thick; 17mm (5/8") long x 10mm (3/8") wide. FOLIAGE is dark green (137A) upper surface; medium green (138A) lower surface. PARENTAGE: 'Rose Bradwardine' x 'Pinto The Blue'. Scharf 2007 NL AFS6571.

Farfadet. Upright/Trailer. Single. COROLLA: quarter flared; smooth petal margins; opens & matures light pink (62B); 25mm (1") long x 16mm (5/8") wide. SEPALS: horizontal, tips recurved; light pink (62C) upper surface; light pink (62B) lower surface; 46mm (1 13/16") long x 10mm (3/8") wide. TUBE: light pink (62B); medium length & thickness; 20mm (3/4") long x 7mm (1/4") wide. STAMENS extend 2-6mm (1/16-1/4") beyond the corolla; light pink (62B) filaments; dark red (178A) anthers. PISTIL extends 33mm (1 5/16") beyond the corolla; light pink (62C) style; light yellow (4C) stigma. BUD is ovate. FOLIAGE is medium green (146A) upper surface; light olive green (148B) lower surface. Leaves are 79mm (3 1/8") long x 43mm (1 11/16") wide; ovate shaped, serrulate edges, acute tips, rounded base. Veins & stems are yellowish green, branches are yellowish green & light brown. PARENTAGE: 'Nancy Lou' x 'Annabel'. Lax upright or stiff trailer. Self branching. Makes good upright. Prefers overhead filtered light & cool climate. Tested 3 years in Pornic, France. Distinguished by unicolour rose blossom.

Massé 2009 FR AFS6990.

Fascinating Double. Upright. Double. COROLLA: quarter flared; opens violet blue (91A); matures reddish purple (70B); 20mm (3/4") long x 15mm (9/16") wide. SEPALS: half up, tips recurved up; magenta (57B) upper & lower surfaces; 25mm (1") long x 15mm (9/16") wide. TUBE: light orange (32C); 18mm (11/16") long x 8mm (5/16") wide. FOLIAGE is dark green (139A) upper surface; medium green (139C) lower surface. PARENTAGE: 'Aloha' x 'Brookwood Belle'. Smith R. 2008 UK AFS6816.

Fata Morgana. Trailer. Double. COROLLA is three quarter flared with turned under wavy petal margins; opens reddish purple (67A), rose (54C) base; matures reddish purple (64B); 20mm (13/16") long x 29mm (1 1/8") wide. PETALOIDS: dark reddish purple (70A), magenta (59D) base; 16mm (5/8") long x 8mm (5/16") wide. SEPALS are horizontal, tips recurved; white (155C), tipped yellowish green (145A) upper surface; white (155C), light rose (58D) base, tipped yellowish green (145A) lower surface; 34mm (1 5/16") long x 14mm (9/16") wide. TUBE is white (155D); medium length & thickness; 12mm (1/2") long x 5mm (3/16") wide. FOLIAGE: dark green (136B) upper surface; medium green (138B) lower surface. Leaves are 65mm (2 9/16") long x 31mm (1 1/4") wide, ovate shaped. PARENTAGE: 'Sofie Michiels' x 'Annabelle Stubbs'. Meise 8-14-04, Outstanding. Distinguished by flower colour combination.
Michiels 2005 BE AFS5749.

Feeke. Upright/Trailer. Semi Double. COROLLA: half flared, turned under wavy petal margins; opens reddish purple (71B), matures light reddish purple (72C); 28mm (1 1/8") long x 21mm (13/16") wide. PETALOIDS: magenta (71C); 12mm (1/2") long x 9mm (3/8") wide. SEPALS: half down; tips reflexed; reddish purple (61B) upper surface; magenta (58B) lower surface; 39mm (1 9/16") long x 14mm (9/16") wide. TUBE: dark reddish purple (61B); medium length & thickness; 24mm (15/16") long x 8mm (5/16") wide. STAMENS: extend 13mm (1/2") below the corolla; dark rose (67C) filaments, reddish purple (67A) anthers. PISTIL extends 24mm (15/16") below the corolla; magenta (63B) style, reddish purple (61B) stigma. BUD: ovate. FOLIAGE: dark green (139A) upper surface, medium green (137B) lower surface. Leaves are 47mm (1 7/8") long x 32mm (1 1/4") wide, ovate shaped,

serrulated edges, acute tips and rounded bases. Veins are dark reddish purple (187D), stems are are dark reddish purple (187B), branches dark grayish purple (183A). PARENTAGE: 'WALZ Harp' x 'Regal Robe'. Lax upright or stiff trailer. Self branching. Makes good upright. Prefers overhead filtered light. Best bloom and foliage colour in filtered light. Tested 3 years Scherpenheuvel, Belgium. NBFK certificate at Meise. Distinguished by bloom shape.
Antoon 2005 BE AFS5086.

Feichtbergmädl. Upright/Trailer. Single. COROLLA is half flared with smooth petal margins; opens and matures light violet (77D); 20mm (13/16") long x 22mm (7/8") wide. SEPALS are fully up, tips recurved; rose (55B) tipped green upper surface, dark rose (55A) tipped green lower surface; 24mm (15/16") long x 10mm (3/8") wide. TUBE is rose (55B), medium length and thickness; 8mm (5/16") long x 7mm (1/2") wide. STAMENS do not extend beyond the corolla; rose (55B) filaments, dark tan (164B) anthers. PISTIL does not extend beyond the corolla; pink (55C) style, cream (158C) stigma. BUD is longish with green tip. FOLIAGE is dark green (147A) upper surface, light olive green (147C) lower surface. Leaves are 50mm (2") long x 28mm (1 1/8") wide, ovate shaped, serrated edges, acute tips and rounded bases. Veins are green, stems are brown (199A), branches are light brown (199C). PARENTAGE: 'La Campanella' x 'Leineperle'. Lax upright or stiff trailer. Self branching. Makes good basket. Prefers overhead filtered light. Heat tolerant if shaded. Best bloom colour in filtered light. Gold medal at the BUGA 2001 in Potsdam, Germany. Tested four years in Plettenberg, Germany. Distinguished by blossom colour.
Strümper 2002 DE AFS4944.

Felicity Kendal. Upright/Trailer. Double. COROLLA is three quarter flared, square shaped, with smooth turned under petal margins; opens light pink (65B) darker at base, veined pink (62A); matures pink (62C); 40mm (1 9/16") long x 70mm (2 3/4") wide. SEPALS are fully up, tips recurved; rose (65A) upper surface, pink (62A) creped lower surface; 49mm (1 15/16") long x 22mm (7/8") wide. TUBE is light pink (65B) striped pink (62A); medium length and thickness; 20mm (13/16") long x 8mm (5/16") wide. STAMENS extend 26mm (1") below the corolla; light pink (62B) filaments; magenta (63A) anthers. PISTIL extends 40mm (1 9/16") below the corolla; light pink (65B)

style; white (155D) stigma. BUD is round, pointed. FOLIAGE is dark green (137A) upper surface, medium green (138B) lower surface. Leaves are 63mm (2 1/2") long x 40mm (1 9/16") wide, cordate shaped, smooth edges, acute tips and cordate bases. Veins, stems, branches are red. PARENTAGE: 'White King' x 'Miss Vallejo'. Lax upright or stiff trailer. Makes good basket or standard. Prefers cool climate. Heat tolerant if shaded. Best bloom colour in filtered light. Tested five years in Gloucester, England. Distinguished by bloom colour and shape.
Hickman 2002 UK AFS4854.

Félieke. Upright. Single. COROLLA is three quarter flared with turned under wavy petal margins; opens reddish purple (64B), matures reddish purple (61B); 20mm (13/16") long x 18 mm (11/16") wide. SEPALS are half up, tips recurved up; rose (52B) upper surface, red (52A) lower surface; 28mm (1 1/8") long x 17mm (11/16") wide. TUBE is rose (52B), medium length and thickness; 20mm (13/16") long x 9mm (3/8") wide. STAMENS extend 8mm (5/16") beyond the corolla; reddish purple (66B) filaments, reddish purple (70B) anthers. PISTIL extends 22mm (7/8") below the corolla; pink (62A) style; pale yellow (8D) stigma. BUD is round, pointed. FOLIAGE is dark green (147A) upper surface, medium green (138B) lower surface. Leaves are 68mm (2 11/16") long x 36mm (1 7/16") wide, ovate shaped, serrated edges, acute tips and rounded bases. Veins are light green (139D), stems are light grayish red (182D), branches are light grayish red (182C). PARENTAGE: 'Die Fledermaus' x 'Roesse Ben'. Small upright. Makes good upright. Prefers overhead filtered light. Best bloom and foliage colour in filtered light. Tested three years in Berlaar, Belgium. Certificate N.B.F.K. at Meise. Distinguished by bloom colour.
Geerts J. 2002 BE AFS4918.

Felley. Upright. Single. corolla purple (83b), matures to dark rosy purple (80a); corolla is fully flared. SEPALS dark magenta rose (57a) on the upper and lower surfaces; SEPALS are half up with recurved tips. TUBE dark magenta rose (57a). PARENTAGE 'F. regia' x 'Belle de Limburg'.
Lamb 2009 UK BFS0148.

Femke Comperen. Upright/Trailer. Single. COROLLA: half flared, smooth petal margins; opens dark purple (86A); matures purple (77A); 25mm (1") long x 28mm (1 1/8") wide. SEPALS: fully up; tips recurved; peach (37B)

upper surface; magenta (68A) lower surface; 43mm (1 11/16") long x 12mm (1/2") wide. TUBE: peach (37B); medium length & thickness; 9mm (3/8") long x 7mm (1/4") wide. STAMENS: extend 15mm (9/16") below corolla; dark reddish purple (72A) filaments; purple (77A) anthers. PISTIL: extends 42mm (1 11/16") below the corolla; reddish purple (72B) style, yellow (11C) stigma. BUD: ovate. FOLIAGE: medium green (137B) upper surface; medium green (138A) lower surface. Leaves are 67mm (2 5/8") long x 42mm (1 5/8") wide, ovate shaped, serrulated edges, acute tips and rounded bases. Veins, stems & branches are red. PARENTAGE: 'Dorothy Oosting' x 'Parasol'. Lax upright or stiff trailer. Makes good upright. Prefers overhead filtered light and cool climate. Best bloom and foliage colour in filtered light. Tested 4 years in Diessen, The Netherlands. Distinguished by bloom colour.
Comperen 2003 NL AFS5269.

Femke Lemmen. Upright/Trailer. Single. COROLLA is full flared with smooth petal margins; opens magenta (68A); matures rose (68B); 25mm (1") long x 25mm (1") wide. SEPALS are half up, tips recurved up; pale lavender (65D) upper surface; light pink (65C) lower surface; 26mm (1") long x 12mm (1/2") wide. TUBE is pale lavender (65D); short & thick; 10mm (3/8") long x 11mm (7/16") wide. FOLIAGE: dark green (139A) upper surface; medium green (138A) lower surface. Leaves are 62mm (2 7/16") long x 42mm (1 5/8") wide, ovate shaped. PARENTAGE: 'Roesse Carme' x 'Impala'. Distinguished by bloom & foliage combination.
Roes 2005 NL AFS5975.

Femke Senne Mesens. Upright. Single. COROLLA: half flared, turned under wavy petal margins; opens rose (N74C) edged magenta (71C); matures light reddish purple (72D) edged dark rose (58C); 19mm (3/4") long x 17mm (5/8") wide. SEPALS: horizontal, tips recurved; pale pink (56C) tipped light greenish yellow (151D) upper surface; light pink (65B) tipped light greenish yellow (151D) lower surface; 30mm (1 3/16") long x 10mm (3/8") wide. TUBE: pale pink (56D); short & thick; 14mm (9/16") long x 9mm (5/16") wide. STAMENS extend 21mm (13/16") beyond the corolla; reddish purple (61B) filaments; magenta (71C) anthers. PISTIL extends 34mm (1 3/8") beyond the corolla; pale rose (73D) style; light yellow (2C) stigma. BUD: oblong. FOLIAGE: dark green (136B) upper surface; medium green (137D)

lower surface. Leaves are 63mm (2 1/2") long x 39mm (1 1/2") wide; ovate shaped, serrate edges, acute tips, rounded bases. Veins are grayish red (181A), stems are grayish red (181A) & yellowish green (146C), branches are light grayish red (182C) & yellowish green (146D). PARENTAGE: found seedling. Small upright. Self branching. Makes good upright or standard. Prefers full sun, warm climate. Best bloom & foliage colour in bright light. Tested 4 years in Rillaar, Belgium. Waanrode 7/5/08. Distinguished by bloom colour.
Willems 2009 BE AFS7078.

Fenne Comperen. Trailer. Double, COROLLA: Three quarter flared; opens rose (65A); matures light pink (65B); 25mm (1") long x 27mm (1 1/16") wide. SEPALS: fully up, tips recurved; pale lavender (65D) upper & lower surfaces; 34mm (1 3/8") long x 14mm (9/16") wide. TUBE: pale lavender (65D); medium length & thickness; 10mm (3/8") long x 7mm (1/4") wide. FOLIAGE is dark green (137A) upper surface; medium green (137C) lower surface. PARENTAGE: 'Comperen Korhoen' x 'Comperen Lutea'.
Comperen 2007 NL AFS6608.

Fennechien Lokhorst Lanting. Upright. Single. COROLLA is quarter flared with smooth petal margins; opens & matures fluorescent red (52A); 18mm (11/16") long x 18mm (11/16") wide. SEPALS are half down, tips reflexed; rose (50B) tipped green upper & lower surfaces; 25mm (1") long x 14mm (9/16") wide. TUBE is red (50B); long & thick; 50mm (2") long x 10mm (9/16") wide, triphylla shaped. FOLIAGE: dark green (147A) upper surface; medium green (147B) lower surface. Leaves are 91mm (3 9/16") long x 42mm (1 11/16") wide, lanceolate shaped. PARENTAGE: 'Pipers Vale' x ('F. magdalenae' x 'F. fulgens rubra grandiflora'). Distinguished by fire red clusters of blooms.
Koerts T. 2005 NL AFS5811.

Ferre Peeters. Trailer. Double. COROLLA: half flared; opens purple (83B), magenta (71C) base; matures purple (77A); 20mm (3/4") long x 14mm (9/16") wide. PETALOIDS: same colour as corolla; 14mm (9/16") long x 8mm (5/16") wide. SEPALS: horizontal, tips recurved; reddish purple (70B) tipped apple green (144C) upper surface; magenta (71C) tipped apple green (144C) lower surface; 35 mm (1 3/8") long x 13mm (1/2") wide. TUBE: rose (63C); short, medium thickness; 6mm (1/4") long x 4mm (1/8") wide. FOLIAGE is dark green (136B) upper surface; medium green (138B) lower

surface. PARENTAGE: 'Stad Genk' x 'Rocket Fire'.
Michiels 2007 BE AFS6352.

Ffion. Trailer. Single. COROLLA: quarter flared; opens reddish purple (64B); matures dark rose (64C); 25mm (1") long x 20mm (13/16") wide. SEPALS: half up; tips recurved up; pale lavender (69B) upper & lower surfaces; 43mm(1 11/16") long x 12mm (1/2") wide. TUBE: pale lavender (69C); medium length & thickness; 20mm (13/16") long x 8mm (5/16") wide. STAMENS: extend 15mm (9/16") below corolla; rose (63C) filaments, pale lavender (69C) anthers. PISTIL: extends 28mm (1 1/8") below the corolla, rose (63C) style; orangish white (159C) stigma. BUD: pointed. FOLIAGE: dark green (137A) upper surface; medium green (138B) lower surface. Leaves are 50mm (2") long x 30mm (1 1/16") wide, ovate shaped, serrulated edges, rounded tips and rounded bases. Veins & stems are dark reddish purple (64A); branches are light grayish red (182C). PARENTAGE: 'Atlantic Crossing' x 'Bill Welch'. Natural trailer. Makes good basket or standard. Prefers full sun. Cold weather hardy to 34° F. Best bloom colour in bright light. Tested 3 years in Walthamstow, Carbrooke, Norfolk, England. Distinguished by bloom shape and colour.
Welch 2003 UK AFS5156.

Fiesta Gitana. Upright. Single. COROLLA: unflared; opens & matures rose (52B) sometimes veined & variegated light pink (49B/C); 30mm (1 3/16") long x 20mm (3/4") wide. SEPALS: half up, tips recurved up; cream (158C) tipped pale yellowish green (149D) upper surface; cream (158C) lower surface; 42mm (1 5/8") long x 9mm (5/16") wide. TUBE: cream (158C); medium length & thickness; 16mm (5/8") long x 5mm (3/16") wide. FOLIAGE is medium green (147B) upper surface; light olive green (148C) lower surface. PARENTAGE: Found seedling.
Massé 2007 FR AFS6479.

Fina Creten. Upright/Trailer. Single. COROLLA is quarter flared with turned under wavy petal margins; opens dark purple (78A) edged purple (82A), rose (61D) at base; matures reddish purple (67A); 26mm (1") long x 28 mm (1 1/8") wide. SEPALS are horizontal, tips reflexed; magenta (58B) upper surface; red (52A) lower surface; 32mm (1 1/4") long x 17mm (11/16") wide. TUBE is magenta (58B), long with medium thickness; 40mm (1 9/16") long x 4mm

(3/16") wide, 8mm (5/16") at base. STAMENS do not extend beyond the corolla; rose (55B) filaments, dark yellowish orange (14A) anthers. PISTIL extends 15mm (5/8") below the corolla; red (52A) style; light yellow (8C) stigma. BUD is round. FOLIAGE is dark green (147A) upper surface, light yellowish green (146D) lower surface; young leaves flushed dark grayish red (182A). Leaves are 115mm (4 9/16") long x 47mm (1 7/8") wide, elliptic shaped, serrulated edges, acute tips and rounded bases. Veins, stems and branches are dark reddish purple (59A). PARENTAGE: 'Alda Alders' x 'Wingrove's Mammoth'. Lax upright or stiff trailer. Self branching. Makes good upright, basket or standard. Prefers overhead filtered light and warm climate. Best bloom and foliage colour in filtered light. Tested three years in Leopoldsburg, Belgium. Certificate N.B.F.K. at Meise. Distinguished by long TUBE, bronze leaves when young. Busschodts 2002 BE AFS4910.

Fiona Graham. Upright/Trailer. Semi Double. COROLLA is unflared, bell shaped with smooth margins; opens light purple (87C) flushed white and pink, matures reddish purple (80B); 28mm (1 1/8") long x 21mm (13/16") wide. SEPALS are half up, tips recurved up; white (155B) striped pale green upper surface, white (155D) streaked with pink (62A) lower surface; 33mm (1 5/16") long x 12mm (1/2") wide. TUBE is white (155D) striped pale green, short with medium thickness; 12mm (1/2") long x 7mm (1/4") wide. STAMENS extend 11mm (7/16") below the corolla; reddish purple (66B) filaments, light magenta (66D) anthers. PISTIL extends 17mm (11/16") below the corolla; pale lavender (65D) style, white (155D) stigma. BUD is lanceolate. FOLIAGE is dark green (137A) upper surface, medium green (138B) lower surface. Leaves are 51mm (2") long x 26mm (1") wide, lanceolate shaped, serrulated edges, acute tips and rounded bases. Veins are green, stems and branches are red. PARENTAGE: 'Annabel' x 'Ruth Graham'. Lax upright or stiff trailer. Self branching. Makes good basket. Prefers overhead filtered light and cool climate. Best bloom colour in filtered light. Tested three years in Stockbridge, Hampshire, England. Distinguished by profuse blooms and colour combination. Graham 2002 UK AFS4874.

Firey Gem. Upright. Single. COROLLA: quarter flared, bell shaped, smooth petal margins; opens purple (83A) splashed dark rose (58C); matures purple (80A) splashed dark rose (58C); 16mm (5/8") long 19mm (3/4") wide. SEPALS: half up; tips recurved up; rose (50B) upper & lower surface; 19mm (3/4") long x 7mm (1/4") wide. TUBE: light rose (50C); medium length & thickness; 3mm (1/8") long x 3mm (1/8") wide. STAMENS: do not extend below corolla; pink (62A) filaments; rose (61D) anthers. PISTIL: does not extend below the corolla; cream (158D) style & stigma. BUD: oval, pointed. FOLIAGE: dark green (139A) upper surface; medium green (138A) lower surface. Leaves are 44mm (1 3/4") long x 32mm (1 1/4") wide, cordate shaped, serrulated edges, acute tips and rounded bases. Green veins, stems & branches. PARENTAGE: 'Bon Accord' x 'Pink Cross'. Small upright. Self branching. Makes good upright or miniature. Prefers overhead filtered light, cool climate. Best bloom and foliage colour in filtered light. Tested 3 years in Stoke-On-Trent, England. Distinguished by erect blossoms and blossom colour combination. Goodwin 2004 UK AFS5573.

Fiorelli Flowers. Upright. Double. COROLLA: half flared, turned under wavy petal margins; opens dark reddish purple (59A); matures dark reddish purple/reddish purple (61A/61B); 20mm (13/16") long, 18mm (11/16") wide. PETALOIDS: dark reddish purple (59A); 11mm (7/16") long x 12mm (1/2") wide. SEPALS: horizontal; tips reflexed; dark reddish purple (61A) upper surface; reddish purple (71B) lower surface; 29mm (1 1/8") long x 15mm (9/16") wide. TUBE: reddish purple (61B); long, medium thickness; 37mm (1 7/16") long x 7mm (1/4") wide. STAMENS: extend 10mm (3/8") below corolla; reddish purple (64B) filaments; white (155C) anthers. PISTIL: extends 16mm (5/8") below the corolla; reddish purple (61B) style; white (155A) stigma. BUD: cordate. FOLIAGE: dark green (137A) upper surface; medium green (138B) lower surface. Leaves are 95mm (3 3/4") long x 53mm (2 1/16") wide, ovate shaped, serrulated edges, acute tips and rounded bases. Grayish red/medium green (182B/139C) veins; grayish red/medium green (182A/138B) stems; grayish red/medium green (182A/138A) branches. PARENTAGE: 'WALZ Harp' x 'Rohees New Millenium'. Small upright. Makes good upright. Prefers full sun. Best bloom and foliage colour in bright light. Tested 3 years in Itegem, Belgium. Award, Meise, 9/8/03. Distinguished by bloom shape & colour. Geerts L. 2004 BE AFS5613.

Flamme von Gera. Upright/Trailer. Double. COROLLA: three quarter flared, smooth petal margins; opens dark reddish purple (61A) blushed orange (41B); matures reddish purple (61B) blushed light orange (41C); 25mm (1") long x 48mm (1 7/8") wide. SEPALS: horizontal, tips recurved; reddish orange (43C) upper & lower surfaces; 40mm (1 9/16") long x 15mm (9/16") wide. TUBE: reddish orange (43C) striped medium green (138A); short, medium thickness; 9mm (5/16") long x 7mm (1/4") wide. STAMENS extend 16mm (5/8") beyond the corolla; reddish orange (43C) filaments; red (53B) anthers. PISTIL extends 35mm (1 3/8") beyond the corolla; reddish orange (43C) style; cream (11D) stigma. BUD: globular. FOLIAGE: dark green (137A) upper surface; medium green (147B) lower surface. Leaves are 80mm (3 3/16") long x 50mm (2") wide; ovate shaped, serrulate edges, acute tips, rounded bases. Veins & stems are red, branches are reddish maturing to light brown. PARENTAGE: 'Danny Kaye' x ('Düsterwald' x 'Bicentennial'). Lax upright or stiff trailer. Makes good basket, upright or standard. Prefers full sun, warm climate. Heat tolerant if shaded. Best bloom & foliage colour in bright light. Tested 3 years in Bavaria, Southern Germany. Distinguished by corolla colour combination.
Burkhart 2009 DE AFS7107.

Flockske. Upright/Trailer. Single. COROLLA is half flared with turned under toothed petal margins; opens dark reddish purple (72A), matures reddish purple (74A); 28mm (1 1/8") long x 22 mm (7/8") wide. SEPALS are horizontal, tips recurved; red (52A) upper surface, red (45B) lower surface; 36mm (1 7/16") long x 15mm (5/8") wide. TUBE is red (45C), medium length and thickness; 14mm (9/16") long x 8mm (5/16") wide. STAMENS extend 4mm (3/16") beyond the corolla; red (52A) filaments, reddish purple (61B) anthers. PISTIL extends 9mm (3/8") below the corolla; dark rose (54B) style; dark reddish purple (60A) stigma. BUD is ovate, pointed. FOLIAGE is dark green (137A) upper surface, medium green (139C) lower surface. Leaves are 62mm (2 7/16") long x 28mm (1 1/8") wide, lanceolate shaped, serrulated edges, acute tips and rounded bases. Veins are plum (184C), stems are plum (185B), branches are dark reddish purple (187C). PARENTAGE: 'WALZ Harp' x 'Rohees New Millennium'. Lax upright or stiff trailer, dwarf growth. Makes good basket. Prefers overhead filtered light. Best bloom and foliage colour in filtered light. Tested three years in Berlaar,

Belgium. Certificate N.B.F.K. at Meise. Distinguished by profuse blooms, stalked petals.
Geerts J. 2002 BE AFS4919.

Floere Het Fluwijn. Upright/Trailer. Double. COROLLA: half flared, turned under wavy petal margins; opens purple (71A); matures dark reddish purple (72A); 17mm (11/16") long x 21mm (13/16") wide. SEPALS: half down; tips reflexed; reddish purple (59B) upper surface; dark reddish purple (60B) lower surface; 26mm (1") long x 12mm (1/2") wide. TUBE: magenta (59C); long, medium thickness; 23mm(15/16") long x 5mm (3/16") wide. STAMENS: below 18mm (11/16") below corolla; magenta (67B) filaments, dark reddish purple (72A) anthers. PISTIL: extends 24mm (15/16") below the corolla, reddish purple (67A) style, dark purple (79B) stigma. BUD: cordate. FOLIAGE: dark green (136A) upper surface; medium green (136C) lower surface. Leaves are 70mm (2 3/4") long x 32mm (1 1/4") wide, elliptic shaped, serrulated edges, acute tips and rounded bases. Veins are dark red purple (187D), stems are dark reddish purple (187B), branches are plum (184C). PARENTAGE: 'WALZ Gitaar' x 'Rohees New Millennium'. Lax upright or stiff trailer. Makes good basket. Prefers overhead filtered light. Best bloom and foliage colour in filtered light. Tested 3 years in Berlaar, Belgium. NBFK Certificate at Meise. Distinguished by bloom colour, profuse blooms.
Geerts J. 2003 BE AFS5197.

Floren Kennes. Trailer. Double. COROLLA: half flared; white (155C) & pale violet (84D) edged violet (85B) & matures light violet (84C) & violet (77C); 18mm (11/16") long x 15mm (9/16") wide. PETALOIDS: white (155C) & pale violet (84D); 11mm (7/16") long x 7mm (1/4") wide. SEPALS are horizontal, tips recurved; white (155D) tipped light apple green (144D) upper surface & pale lavender (69D) tipped light apple green (144D) lower surface; 28mm (1 1/8") long x 10mm (3/8") wide. TUBE is white (155D) striped light green (141D); medium length & thickness; 11mm (7/16") long x 5mm (3/16") wide. FOLIAGE is dark green (137A) upper surface; medium green (137C) lower surface. PARENTAGE: 'Waanrodes Silver Star' x 'Ine Frazer'.
Michiels 2007 BE AFS6546.

Florence May Joiner. Upright. Single. COROLLA opens bluish pink, matures to deep pink; corolla is quarter flared and is

16mm long x 12mm wide. SEPALS light pink light pink; sepals are horizontally held with recurved tips and are 22mm long x 7mm wide.. TUBE light pink and is 6mm long x 5mm wide. PARENTAGE 'Sophie Louise' x 'Maria Landy'.
Joiner 2006 UK BFS0031.

Florencio. Trailer. Semi Double. COROLLA: half flared; opens violet (85A); matures light purple (N78B) & violet (86D); 15mm (9/16") long x 16mm (5/8") wide. PETALOIDS: violet (85A); 11mm (7/16") long x 11mm (7/16") wide. SEPALS are horizontal, tips recurved; rose (65A) tipped light yellowish green (150C) upper surface and pink (62A) tipped light yellowish green (150C) lower surface; 29mm (1 1/8") long x 11mm (7/16") wide. TUBE is pale pink (56A); medium length & thickness; 14mm (9/16") long x 6mm (1/4") wide. FOLIAGE is medium green (137C) upper surface; medium green (138B) lower surface. PARENTAGE: 'Jef Vander Kuylen' x 'Hilda'.
Michiels 2007 BE AFS6545.

Florama. Upright. Double. COROLLA is fully flared with turned under smooth petal margins; opens pale violet (76D), white (155C) base; matures pale purple (75D), white (155C) base; 26mm (1") long x 22mm (7/8") wide. PETALOIDS: same colour as corolla; 19mm (3/4") long x 12mm (1/2") wide. SEPALS are fully up, tips reflexed; rose (65A), white (155C) base, tipped light apple green (145C) upper surface; rose (68C), white (155B) base, tipped light apple green (145C) lower surface; 57mm (2 1/4") long x 20mm (13/16") wide. TUBE is rose (65A), white (155C) base; medium length & thickness; 21mm (13/16") long x 6mm (1/4") wide. FOLIAGE: dark green (139A) upper surface; medium green (138B) lower surface. Leaves are 97mm (3 13/16") long x 50mm (2") wide, ovate shaped. PARENTAGE: 'Sofie Michiels' x 'Annabelle Stubbs'. Meis 3-7-04. Distinguished by beautiful colour combination.
Michiels 2005 BE AFS5672.

Fokko's Katrientje. Upright. Single. COROLLA: quarter flared, turned under petal margins; opens light pink (55D) striped & splashed red (46B); matures pink (55C) striped & splashed red (46B); 26mm (1") long x 36mm (1 7/16") wide. SEPALS: half up; tips reflexed up; light pink (55D) striped red (46B) upper surface; pink (55C) striped red (46B) lower surface; 35mm (1 3/8") long x 12mm (1/2") wide. TUBE: light pink (55D) striped red (46B); medium length &

thickness; 16mm(5/8") long x 8mm (5/16") wide. STAMENS: extend 44mm (1 3/4") below corolla; light pink (55D) filaments & anthers. PISTIL: extends 24mm (15/16") below the corolla, light pink (55D) style, red (46B) stigma. BUD: long, medium. FOLIAGE: medium green (147B) upper surface; dark green (147A) lower surface. Leaves are 85mm (3 3/8") long x 48mm (1 7/8") wide, elliptic shaped, serrulated edges, acute tips and rounded bases. Veins, stems & branches are light green. PARENTAGE: Sport of 'Beacon Rosa'. Tall upright. Self branching. Makes good upright, standard, pyramid or trellis. Prefers overhead filtered light and cool climate. Best bloom and foliage colour in filtered light. Tested 5 years in Oude Pekela, The Netherlands. Award of Merit, VKC/KMTP, The Netherlands. Distinguished by stripes and splashes on corolla and SEPALS.
Martena 2003 NL AFS5182.

Fonske. Trailer. Single. COROLLA is quarter flared with turned under wavy petal margins; opens light reddish purple (66C), reddish purple (67A) at base; matures reddish purple (74B), reddish purple (66A) at base; 9mm (3/8") long x 8mm (5/16") wide. SEPALS are half down, tips reflexed; red (53D), red (53C) at base, tipped gray green (194A) upper surface; red (52A), rose (52B) at base, tipped grayish green (191A) lower surface; 26mm (1") long x 12mm (1/2") wide. TUBE is magenta (58B); long and thin; 28mm (1 1/8") long x 4mm (3/16") wide. STAMENS do not extend beyond the corolla; reddish purple (66A) filaments, yellow (8B) anthers. PISTIL extends 5mm (3/16") beyond the corolla; reddish purple (66B) style, dark rose (64C) stigma. BUD is ovate, pointed. FOLIAGE is medium green (137B) upper surface, medium green (139C) lower surface. Leaves are 52mm (2 1/16") long x 25mm (1") wide, elliptic shaped, serrulated edges, acute tips and rounded bases. Veins are grayish red (181B), stems are plum (184B), branches are dark red purple (187C). PARENTAGE: 'WALZ Harp' x 'Rohees New Millennium'. Natural trailer. Self branching. Makes good basket. Prefers overhead filtered light. Best bloom and foliage colour in filtered light. Tested three years in Koningshooikt, Belgium. Certificate N.B.F.K. at Meise. Distinguished by bloom shape and bronze leaf colour.
Michiels 2002 BE AFS4968.

Fonzy Flower. Trailer. Single. COROLLA: unflared; opens & matures red (46D); 19mm (3/4") long x 15mm (9/16") wide. SEPALS:

half down, tips reflexed; rose (48B) upper surface; coral (39B) lower surface; 31mm (1 1/4") long x 8mm (5/16") wide. TUBE: rose (54C); 29mm (1 1/8") long x 6mm (1/4") wide. FOLIAGE is dark green (136A) & dark red (185A) upper surface; medium green (137C) & plum (185B) lower surface. PARENTAGE: 'Ernest Claes' x unknown. Willems 2008 BE AFS6748.

For Fun. Upright/Trailer. Single. COROLLA: half flared, turned under smooth petal margins; opens rose (64D), reddish purple (64B) base; matures dark reddish purple (64A); 22mm (7/8") long x 22mm (7/8") wide. SEPALS: horizontal; tips recurved; rose (61D) & white (155D) tipped light yellow green (150B) upper surface; pale pink (56A) tipped light yellow green (150B) lower surface; 29mm (1 1/8") long x 11mm (7/16") wide. TUBE: rose (61D); medium length & thickness; 20mm (13/16") long x 7mm (1/4") wide. STAMENS: extend 7mm (1/4") below corolla; pale lavender (65D) filaments; dark reddish purple (187C) anthers. PISTIL: extends 24mm (15/16") below the corolla; dark rose (64C) style; light yellow (11B) stigma. BUD: oblong. FOLIAGE: medium green (137B) upper surface, medium green (138B) lower surface. Leaves are 49mm (1 15/16") long x 28mm (1 1/8") wide, ovate shaped, serrulated edges, acute tips and cordate bases. Light green (138C) veins; light green (138C) & grayish red (182B) stems & branches. PARENTAGE: 'Checkerboard' x 'Lassie'. Lax upright or trailer. Makes good basket. Prefers overhead filtered light and warm climate. Best bloom and foliage colour in filtered light. Tested 3 years in Werm, Belgium. Award at Meise, 5/7/03. Distinguished by bloom colour.
Wagemans 2004 BE AFS5414.

Forever My Love. Upright. Semi Double. COROLLA: quarter flared; opens & matures purple (77A); 20mm (3/4") long x 20mm (3/4") wide. SEPALS: horizontal, tips reflexed; reddish purple (66A) upper & lower surfaces; 30mm (3/16") long x 15mm (9/16") wide. TUBE: medium green (143A); 5mm (3/16") long x 10mm (3/8") wide. FOLIAGE is medium green (139B) upper surface; medium green (139C) lower surface. PARENTAGE: 'Diana Princess of Wales' x 'Prince Charming'.
Smith R. 2008 UK AFS6822.

Fort Royal. Upright. Double. COROLLA: three quarter flared, smooth petal margins; opens purple (83B); matures dark reddish

purple (72A); 25mm (1") long x 51mm (2") wide. SEPALS: fully up; tips recurved; magenta (58B) upper & lower surfaces; 38mm (1 1/2") long x 12mm (1/2") wide. TUBE: magenta (58B); medium length & thickness; 12mm (1/2") long x 8mm (5/16") wide. STAMENS: extend 12mm (1/2") below corolla; magenta (61C) filaments; dark reddish purple (61A) anthers. PISTIL: extends 25mm (1") below the corolla; magenta (61D) style; light pink (62B) stigma. BUD: pointed. FOLIAGE: medium green (137B) upper surface; medium green (137D) lower surface. Leaves are 57mm (2 1/4") long x 25mm (1") wide, ovate shaped, smooth edges, acute tips and rounded bases. Light rose to green veins; purple stems; brown branches. PARENTAGE: 'Madeleine Sweeney' x 'Purple Patch'. Small upright. Makes good upright or standard. Prefers overhead filtered light. Heat tolerant if shaded. Best bloom and foliage colour in filtered light. Tested 4 years in Ormskirk, Lancashire, England. Distinguished by bright, vibrant flower colour.
Sinton 2004 UK AFS5458.

Fortuna Gem. Upright. Double. COROLLA is quarter flared with wavy petal margins; opens & matures red (53B) streaked reddish orange (43C); 22mm (7/8") long x 29mm (1 1/8") wide. PETALOIDS: Same colour as corolla (looks fluorescent); 19mm (3/4") long x 11mm (7/16") wide. SEPALS are half down, tips reflexed; pink (43D) upper surface, dark rose (48A) lower surface; 44mm (1 3/4") long x 12mm (1/2") wide. TUBE is pale orange (27B) veined light orange (24B), medium length & thickness; 10mm (3/8") long x 19mm (3/4") wide. STAMENS do not extend beyond the corolla; rose (47C) filaments; light pink (49B) anthers. PISTIL extends 22mm (7/8") below the corolla; rose (47C) style; light tan (162A) stigma. BUD is long, medium full. FOLIAGE is dark green (137A) upper surface, medium green (138B) lower surface. Leaves are 35mm (1 1/2") long x 29mm (1 1/8") wide, ovate shaped, serrated edges, acute tips and rounded bases. Veins, stems & branches are medium green (139C). PARENTAGE: ('Feather Duster' x 'San Francisco') x 'Rose of Castile'. Medium upright. Self branching. Makes good upright, decorative or trellis. Prefers overhead filtered light & cool climate. Cold weather hardy to 32⁰ F. Best bloom & foliage colour in bright or filtered light. Tested five years in Fortuna, CA, USA. Distinguished by prolific blooms & long blooming period.
McLaughlin 2004 USA AFS5367.

Francine Russier. Upright/Trailer. Single. COROLLA is half to three quarter flared; opens and matures pink (55B) to rose (55A); 17mm (11/16") long x 26mm (1") wide. SEPALS fully up, tips recurved; light green (145D) tipped light apple green (145B) upper and lower surfaces; 35mm (1 3/8") long x 9mm (3/8") wide. TUBE is light apple green (145C), long with medium thickness; 30mm (1 3/16") long x 6 - 8mm (1/4" - 5/16") wide. STAMENS extend 3 - 5mm (1/8" – 3/16") below the corolla; light pink (55D) filaments and light yellow (4C) anthers. PISTIL extends 35mm (1 3/8") below the corolla; pale pink (36D) style; light yellow (4C) stigma. BUD is long, ovate. FOLIAGE is dark green (147A) upper surface, light olive green (147C) lower surface. Leaves are 93mm (3 11/16") long x 69mm (2 3/4") wide, cordate shaped, serrated edges, acute tips and rounded bases. Veins are light yellowish green, stems and branches are light yellowish green and light brown. PARENTAGE: 'Speciosa' x 'Mrs. W. Rundle'. Lax upright or stiff trailer. Makes good basket or upright. Prefers overhead filtered light and cool climate. Best bloom and foliage colour in filtered light. Tested four years in Prefailles, France. Distinguished by bloom colour and shape. Boquien 2002 FR AFS4866.

Françoise Bichon. Upright/Trailer. Single. COROLLA: unflared; opens & matures purple (77A); 16mm (5/8") long x 6mm (1/4") wide. SEPALS: half up, tips recurved up; red (47B) upper & lower surfaces; 35mm (1 3/8") long x 5mm (3/16") wide. TUBE: red (47B); 11 mm (7/16") long x 3mm (1/8") wide. FOLIAGE is dark green (147A) upper surface; medium green (147B) lower surface. PARENTAGE: 'Jules Verne' x unknown. Massé 2008 FR AFS6832.

Frankfurt 2006. Upright. Single. COROLLA: quarter flared, smooth petal margins; opens dark purple (N79A); matures dark reddish purple (61A); 22mm (7/8") long x 16mm (5/8") wide. SEPALS: half up, tips recurved up; reddish purple (67A) upper & lower surfaces; 43mm (1 11/16") long x 10mm (3/8") wide. TUBE: reddish purple (67A); medium length & thickness; 14mm (9/16") long x 7mm (1/4") wide. STAMENS extend 24mm (15/16") beyond the corolla; reddish purple (67A) filaments; dark purple (N79B) anthers. PISTIL extends 45mm (1 3/4") beyond the corolla; reddish purple (N66A) style; reddish purple (N66B) stigma. BUD: elongated. FOLIAGE: dark green (137A) upper surface; medium green (138B) lower

surface. Leaves are 118mm (4 11/16") long x 41mm (1 5/8") wide; lanceolate shaped, serrate edges, acute tips, rounded bases. Veins are red, stems are dark red, branches are reddish brown. PARENTAGE: F. *alpestris* x 'Jens Weißflog'. Medium upright. Makes good upright or standard. Prefers full sun. Heat tolerant if shaded. Best bloom & foliage colour in bright light. Tested 4 years in Bavaria, Southern Germany. Distinguished by bloom colour & & foliage similar to species seed parent. Burkhart 2009 DE AFS7106.

Frank-Marlyse. Upright/Trailer. Double. COROLLA: half flared; opens magenta (71C) & dark purple (N78A), light rose (73B) base; matures dark reddish purple (72A), pale rose (73D) base; 31mm (1 1/4") long x 28mm (1 1/8") wide. SEPALS: horizontal, tips recurved; pale pink (62D) tipped apple green (144C) upper surface; rose (63C) tipped apple green (144C) lower surface; 46 mm (1 13/16") long x 18mm (11/16") wide. TUBE: white (155B); medium length & thickness; 27mm (1 1/16") long x 8mm (5/16") wide. FOLIAGE is dark green (136A) upper surface; medium green (137C) lower surface. PARENTAGE: 'Rune Peeters' x 'Illusion'. Michiels 2007 BE AFS6353.

Frans van Otterdijk. Upright/Trailer. Double. COROLLA: three quarter flared, smooth petal margins; opens purple (71A); matures reddish purple (61B); 17mm (11/16") long x 15mm (9/16") wide. SEPALS: fully up; tips recurved; very pale orange (19D) upper surface; pale pink (62D) lower surface; 20mm (13/16") long x 8mm (5/16") wide. TUBE: very pale orange (19D); medium length & thickness; 9mm (3/8") long x 5mm (3/16") wide. STAMENS: extend 20mm (13/16") below corolla; magenta (63B) filaments & anthers. PISTIL: extends 36mm (1 7/16") below the corolla; rose (63C) style; pale pink (62D) stigma. BUD: round. FOLIAGE: dark green (137A) upper surface; medium green (138B) lower surface. Leaves are 44mm (1 3/4") long x 29mm (1 1/8") wide, cordate shaped, smooth edges, acute tips and cordate bases. Veins, stems & branches are green. PARENTAGE: {[('Bon Accord' x 'Bicentennial')] x ('Vobeglo' x 'Dancing Flame')] x 'Rohees Alrami'} x ('Sofie Michiels' x 'Lechlade Rocket'). Lax upright or stiff trailer. Makes good stiff trailer. Prefers overhead filtered light and cool climate. Best bloom and foliage colour in filtered light. Tested 4 years in Duizel, The Netherlands.

Distinguished by bloom & foliage combination. Tamerus 2003 NL AFS5307.

Frans Vandenbremt. Upright/Trailer. Double. COROLLA: half flared, turned under wavy petal margins; opens dark reddish purple (64A) & purple (77A); matures reddish purple (64B); 23mm (7/8 ") long x 19mm (3/4 ") wide. PETALOIDS: same colour as corolla; 10mm (3/8") long x 8mm (5/16") wide. SEPALS: half up, tips recurved up & horizontal, tips recurved; white (155C) & pale lavender (69D) tipped light apple green (145B) upper surface; light rose (63D) tipped light apple green (145B) lower surface; 36mm (1 7/16") long x 13mm (1/2") wide. TUBE: white (155C) & pale lavender (69D); medium length & thickness; 17mm (5/8") long x 7mm (1/4") wide. STAMENS extend 4mm (1/8") beyond the corolla; reddish purple (72B) filaments; violet (77B) anthers. PISTIL extends 16mm (5/8") beyond the corolla; reddish purple (70B) style; pale yellow (2D) stigma. BUD: elongated. FOLIAGE: medium green (137B) upper surface; medium green (138B) lower surface. Leaves are 55mm (2 3/16") long x 26mm (1") wide; elliptic shaped, serrulate edges, acute tips, rounded bases. Veins are plum (184C), stems are plum (185C), branches are plum (185C) & medium green (138C). PARENTAGE: 'Manfried Kleinau' x 'Jeff Vander Kuylen'. Lax upright or stiff trailer. Self branching. Makes good basket or upright. Prefers overhead filtered light, cool climate. Best bloom & foliage colour in filtered light. Tested 3 years in Koningshooikt, Belgium. Waanrode 5/7/08. Distinguished by bloom colour combination. Michiels 2009 BE AFS7163.

Frans Vander Kuylen. Upright. Double. COROLLA is three quarter flared with turned under smooth petal margins; opens reddish purple (64B), dark rose (51A) base; matures magenta (57C), red (53D) base; 20mm (13/16") long x 18mm (11/16") wide. SEPALS are half up, tips reflexed up; pink (55C), pale pink (49D) base, tipped yellowish green (145B) upper surface; rose (52C), tipped yellowish green (145B) lower surface; 33mm (1 5/16") long x 14mm (9/16") wide. TUBE is pale pink (49D); medium length & thickness; 21mm (13/16") long x 6mm (1/4") wide. FOLIAGE: dark green (137A) upper surface; medium green (138B) lower surface. Leaves are 83mm (3 1/4") long x 51mm (2") wide, ovate shaped. PARENTAGE: 'Sofie Michiels' x 'Annabelle Stubbs'. Meise 8-14-

04, Outstanding. Distinguished by flower colour. Michiels 2005 BE AFS5743.

Frau Bettina Heinz. Upright. Single. COROLLA is quarter flared with turned under wavy petal margins; opens light reddish purple (73A), pale pink (49D) base; matures light purple (74C); 12mm (1/2") long x 8mm (5/16") wide. SEPALS are half down, tips recurved; pink (54D), pale pink (49D) base, tipped light yellow green (150A) upper surface; pink (55C), pale pink (49D) base, tipped light yellow green (150A) lower surface; 26mm (1") long x 9mm (3/8") wide. TUBE is pale pink (49D); medium length & thickness; 16mm (5/8") long x 5mm (3/16") wide. FOLIAGE: dark green (136A) upper surface; medium green (137D) lower surface. Leaves are 67mm (2 5/8") long x 33mm (1 5/16") wide, ovate shaped. PARENTAGE: 'Querry' x unknown. Meise 8-14-04. Distinguished by bloom shape. Willems 2005 BE AFS5721.

Frau Traude Beren. Upright. Single. COROLLA opens violet, light pink veins and base, matures to deep mallow purple; corolla is three quarter flared. SEPALS light pink on the upper and lower surfaces; sepals are half up with recurved tips. TUBE light pink. PARENTAGE ('Cliff's Own' x 'Delta's Parade') x ('Delta's Parade' x 'Cliff's Own'). Klemm 2008 AT BFS0075.

Fred Bleijs. Upright. Double. COROLLA is half flared with smooth petal margins; opens magenta (63B); matures magenta (61C); 19mm (3/4") long x 16mm (5/8") wide. SEPALS are fully up, tips recurved; light pink (65B) tipped green upper & lower surfaces; 23mm (15/16") long x 10mm (3/8") wide. TUBE is light pink (65B); medium length & thickness; 17mm (11/16) long x 8mm (5/16") wide. FOLIAGE: dark green (137A) upper surface; medium green (138B) lower surface. Leaves are 57mm (2 1/4") long x 37mm (1 7/16") wide, cordate shaped. PARENTAGE: 'Roesse Carme' x 'Leon Pauwels'. Distinguished by bloom & foliage combination. van Eijk 2005 NL AFS5908.

Freddy De Fluiter. Upright/Trailer. Double. COROLLA is half flared with turned under smooth petal margins; opens purple (80A), pink (62A) at base; matures dark purple (78A), dark rose (54B) at base; 30mm (1 3/16") long x 44mm (1 3/4") wide. SEPALS are horizontal, tips recurved; magenta (58B)

140

tipped yellowish green (145A) upper surface, dark rose (51A) lower surface; 38mm (1 1/2") long x 20mm (13/16") wide. TUBE is dark rose (58C), short with medium thickness; 9mm (3/8") long x 4mm (3/16") wide. STAMENS extend 8mm (5/16") beyond the corolla; reddish purple (67A) filaments, dark rose (58C) anthers. PISTIL extends 15mm (5/8") below the corolla; magenta (68A) style, grayish yellow (161A) stigma. BUD is ovate. FOLIAGE is dark green (139A) upper surface, medium green (137C) lower surface. Leaves are 95mm (3 3/4") long x 61mm (2 7/16") wide, ovate shaped, serrulated edges, acute tips and rounded bases. Veins and stems are very dark reddish purple, branches are dark reddish purple (184A). PARENTAGE: 'Bora-Bora' x unknown. Lax upright or stiff trailer. Self branching. Makes good upright. Prefers overhead filtered light. Best bloom and foliage colour in filtered light. Tested three years in Rummen, Belgium. Certificate N.B.F.K. at Meise. Distinguished by bloom colour and shape.
Ector 2002 BE AFS4893.

Freddy Fuhrmann. Upright/Trailer. Double. COROLLA: half flared, turned under wavy petal margins; opens magenta (68A) & light reddish purple (72C); matures magenta (63A) & light purple (70C); 26mm (1 ") long x 21mm (13/16 ") wide. PETALOIDS: same colour as corolla; 17mm (5/8") long x 10mm (3/8") wide. SEPALS: horizontal, tips recurved; pink (55C) tipped light green (145D) upper surface; dark rose (54B) tipped light green (145D) lower surface; 33mm (1 5/16") long x 14mm (9/16") wide. TUBE: rose (55B); medium length & thickness; 13mm (1/2") long x 6mm (1/4") wide. STAMENS extend 13mm (1/2") beyond the corolla; magenta (61C) filaments; magenta (63A) anthers. PISTIL extends 16mm (5/8") beyond the corolla; pink (62A) style; pale yellow (8D) stigma. BUD: oblong. FOLIAGE: dark green (137A) upper surface; medium green (137D) lower surface. Leaves are 76mm (3") long x 35mm (1 3/8") wide; ovate shaped, serrate edges, acute tips, rounded bases. Veins are light red purple (185D), stems are light plum (184D), branches are plum (184C). PARENTAGE: 'Manfried Kleinau' x 'Lenny Erwin'. Lax upright or stiff trailer. Self branching. Makes good basket or upright. Prefers overhead filtered light, cool climate. Best bloom & foliage colour in filtered light. Tested 3 years in Koningshooikt, Belgium. Waanrode 9/8/08. Distinguished by bloom colour combination & profuse blooms.

Michiels 2009 BE AFS7164.

Frédéric Baudon. Upright. Single. COROLLA is unflared with smooth petal margins; opens purple (71A); matures reddish purple (71B); 22mm (7/8") long x 11mm (7/16") wide. SEPALS are half down, tips recurved; reddish purple (60D) upper & lower surfaces; 35mm (1 3/8") long x 4mm (3/16") wide. TUBE is reddish purple (60D); long, medium thickness; 23mm (15/16") long x 5mm (3/16") wide. FOLIAGE: yellowish green (144A) upper surface; yellowish green (146C) lower surface. Leaves are 84mm (3 5/16") long x 34mm (1 5/16") wide, ovate to lanceolate shaped. PARENTAGE: 'Porte Océane' x 'Zulu King'. Distinguished by aubergine colour.
Massé 2005 FR AFS5701.

Frédéric Harnisch. Upright/Trailer. Semi Double. COROLLA: quarter flared; opens & matures purple (93A), rose (65A) on exterior petals; 25mm (1") long x 21mm (13/16") wide. SEPALS: half down, tips recurved; red (47B) upper & lower surfaces; 33mm (1 5/16") long x 11mm (7/16") wide. TUBE: red (47B); medium length & thickness; 10mm (3/8") long x 6mm (1/4") wide. STAMENS extend 9-13mm (5/16-1/2") beyond the corolla; rose (47C) filaments; dark red (53A) anthers. PISTIL extends 36mm (1 3/8") beyond the corolla; rose (47C) style; dark red (185A) stigma. BUD is ovate. FOLIAGE is dark green (147A) upper surface; medium green (147B) lower surface. Leaves are 62mm (2 7/16") long x 27mm (1 1/16") wide; ovate to lanceolate shaped, serrulate edges, acute tips, rounded bases. Veins are yellowish green, stems are yellowish green & light brown, branches are light brown. PARENTAGE: found seedling. Lax upright or stiff trailer. Makes good basket or upright. Prefers overhead filtered light & cool climate. Cold weather hardy to -7° C (19° F). Tested 12 years in Pornic, France. Distinguished by corolla colour combination.
Massé 2009 FR AFS6991.

Frederick Woodward. Upright. Single. COROLLA is quarter flared, fluted, with smooth petal margins; opens red (52A); matures rose (52B); 19mm (3/4") long x 12mm (1/2") wide. SEPALS are horizontal, tips recurved; dark reddish purple (60A) tipped light yellowish green (149C) upper surface; white (155D) flushed dark reddish purple (187B) lower surface; 28mm (1 1/8") long x 10mm (3/8") wide. TUBE is white (155D) flushed rose (55B); long, medium

141

thickness; 82mm (3 1/4") long x 6mm (1/4") wide. FOLIAGE: dark green (137A) upper surface; medium green (137C) lower surface. Leaves are 108mm (4 1/4") long x 70mm (2 3/4") wide, ovate shaped. PARENTAGE: 'Thalia' x 'Kolding Perle'. Distinguished by colour and long TUBEd flowers.
Kimberley 2005 UK AFS5688.

Freunden Tanzer. Trailer. Double. COROLLA: half flared; opens light violet (84C) striped light reddish purple (72D) & matures violet(75A); 28mm (1 1/8") long x 22mm (7/8") wide. PETALOIDS: light violet (84B); 15mm (9/16") long x 8mm (5/16") wide. SEPALS are horizontal, tips recurved, twisted to the left; white (155C) tipped yellowish green (144B) upper surface & pale lavender (69D) tipped yellowish green (144B) lower surface; 42mm (1 5/8") long x 11mm (7/16") wide. TUBE is white (155C) striped light green (141D); long & thin; 29mm (1 1/8") long x 5mm (3/16") wide. FOLIAGE is dark green (139A) upper surface; medium green (138A) lower surface. PARENTAGE: 'Leen vander Kuylen' x 'Kiss'.
Michiels 2007 BE AFS6547.

Frida Cox. Upright. Double. COROLLA is half flared with smooth petal margins; opens dark purple (79B); matures purple (77A); 17mm (11/16") long x 22mm (7/8") wide. SEPALS are half up, tips recurved up; pale pink (62D) upper surface; pink (62A) lower surface; 25mm (1") long x 10mm (3/8") wide. TUBE is pale pink (62D); medium length & thickness; 10mm (3/8") long x 8mm (5/16") wide. FOLIAGE: dark green (137A) upper surface; medium green (138B) lower surface. Leaves are 75mm (2 15/16") long x 45mm (1 3/4") wide, ovate shaped. PARENTAGE: ('Roesse Apus' x 'Roesse Apus') x 'Yvette Klessens'. Distinguished by bloom.
Buiting 2005 NL AFS5873.

Fuchsienfreunden Rhein-Ruhr. Trailer. Double. COROLLA: 3 quarter flared; opens light purple (N87C) blotched rose (63C); matures light purple (N78B); 21mm (13/16") long x 14mm (9/16") wide. PETALOIDS: same colour as corolla; 16mm (5/8") long x 13mm (1/2") wide. SEPALS: horizontal, tips reflexed; pale lavender (69D) tipped light apple green (144D) upper surface; pale purple (75D) tipped light apple green (144D) lower surface; 33mm (1 5/16") long x 14mm (9/16") wide. TUBE: white (155C); medium length & thickness; 11mm (7/16") long x 5mm (3/16") wide. FOLIAGE is dark green (138A) upper surface; medium green (139C)

lower surface. PARENTAGE: 'Mieke' x 'Dorset Delight'.
Michiels 2007 BE AFS6375.

Fuchsi's Hobby. Trailer. Semi Double. COROLLA: unflared, longish; opens reddish purple (71B); matures purple (71A); 30mm (1 3/16") long x 20mm (3/4") wide. SEPALS: half up, tips recurved up; magenta (61C) tipped green upper surface; rose (61D) tipped green lower surface; 40mm (1 9/16") long x 12mm (7/16") wide. TUBE: dark rose (54B); long & thin; 28mm (1 1/8") long x 7mm (1/4") wide. FOLIAGE is dark green (139A) upper surface; medium green (139C) lower surface. PARENTAGE: 'Land Van Beveren' x 'Zellertal'.
Gindl 2007 AT AFS6711.

Fulvia Boreal. Upright. Single. COROLLA: quarter flared, smooth petal margins; opens dark reddish purple (70A), matures dark reddish purple (61A); 15mm (9/16") long x 10mm (3/8") wide. SEPALS: half down; tips recurved; dark rose (55A) upper & lower surfaces; 23mm (15/16") long x 5mm (3/16") wide. TUBE: red (52A), medium length & thickness; 15mm (9/16") long x 6mm (1/4") wide. STAMENS: extend 16mm (5/8") below the corolla; dark rose (51A) filaments, pale tan (159A) anthers. PISTIL extends 20mm (13/16") below the corolla; light rose (50C) style, pale tan (159A) stigma. BUD: ovate. FOLIAGE: dark green (147A) upper surface, medium green (147B) lower surface. Leaves are 61mm (2 3/8") long x 33mm (1 5/16") wide, lanceolate shaped, serrated edges, acute tips and rounded bases. Veins & stems are reddish, branches are brown. PARENTAGE: 'Phyllis' x 'F. fulgens'. Medium upright. Makes good upright. Prefers full sun and warm climate. Best bloom and foliage colour in bright light. Tested 3 years in Como, Italy. Distinguished by bright colour and long pedicels.
Ianne 2003 AT AFS5076.

Gabriel. Upright. Double. COROLLA white veined pink. SEPALS cerise red.
Ainsworth 2002 UK.

Gabriele Breitmayer. Upright/Trailer. Double. COROLLA: half flared, turned under wavy petal margins; opens orange (44D) & reddish purple (186B); matures rose (52B) & light red purple (185D); 25mm (1") long x 18mm (11/16 ") wide. PETALOIDS: same colour as corolla; 16mm (5/8") long x 14mm (9/16") wide. SEPALS: horizontal, tips recurved; pink (55C) tipped light green

142

(145D) upper surface; dark rose (54B) tipped light green (145D) lower surface; 33mm (1 5/16") long x 14mm (9/16") wide. TUBE: rose (55B); medium length & thickness; 13mm (1/2") long x 6mm (1/4") wide. STAMENS extend 13mm (1/2") beyond the corolla; magenta (61C) filaments; magenta (63A) anthers. PISTIL extends 16mm (5/8") beyond the corolla; pink (62A) style; pale yellow (8D) stigma. BUD: oblong. FOLIAGE: dark green (137A) upper surface; medium green (137D) lower surface. Leaves are 76mm (3") long x 35mm (1 3/8") wide; ovate shaped, serrate edges, acute tips, rounded bases. Veins are light red purple (185D), stems are light plum (184D), branches are plum (184C). PARENTAGE: 'Manfried Kleinau' x 'Lenny Erwin'. Lax upright or stiff trailer. Self branching. Makes good basket or upright. Prefers overhead filtered light, cool climate. Best bloom & foliage colour in filtered light. Tested 3 years in Koningshooikt, Belgium. Waanrode 9/8/08. Distinguished by bloom colour combination & profuse blooms.
Michiels 2009 BE AFS7165.

Gamin de Paris. Upright. Single. COROLLA: unflared; opens purple (83A); matures reddish purple (71B); 15mm (9/16") long x 6mm (1/4") wide. SEPALS: horizontal, tips recurved up in a full circle; red (47B) upper & lower surfaces; 32mm (1 1/4") long x 4mm (1/8") wide. TUBE: red (47B); long, very thin; 17mm (5/8") long x 3mm (1/8") wide. FOLIAGE is dark green (147A) upper surface; medium green (147B) lower surface. PARENTAGE: Found seedling.
Massé 2007 FR AFS6480.

Gänseliesel. Upright/Trailer. Single. COROLLA: three quarter flared, smooth petal margins; opens reddish purple (67A); matures magenta (57B); 20mm (13/16") long, 24mm (15/16") wide. SEPALS: horizontal; tips recurved; white (155B), flushed rose (63C), tipped green upper & lower surfaces; 30mm (1 3/16") long x 10mm (3/8") wide. TUBE: white (155B) striped pink; medium length & thickness; 15mm (9/16") long x 3mm (1/8") wide. STAMENS: extend 5mm (3/16") below corolla; pink (62A) filaments; magenta (59D) anthers. PISTIL: extends 28mm (1 1/8") below the corolla; pale pink (62D) style; light yellow (4B) stigma. BUD: slender. FOLIAGE: medium green (138B) upper surface; medium green (138C) lower surface. Leaves are 60mm (2 3/8") long x 40mm (1 9/16") wide, ovate shaped, serrated edges, acute tips and

rounded bases. Green veins & branches; tan stems. PARENTAGE: 'Leonora' x Deutche Perle'. Lax upright or stiff trailer. Makes good basket or standard. Prefers full sun. Best bloom and foliage colour in bright light. Tested 3 years in Göttingen, Germany. Gold Medal, BUGA Magdeburg 2001 & IGA Rostock 2003. Distinguished by free, long lasting flowers.
Strümper 2004 DE AFS5626.

Garoeda. Upright/Trailer. Single. COROLLA: quarter flared; separate petals; turned up wavy petal margins; opens dark orange (33A) edged orangy red (39A); matures coral (39B) edged orangy red; 18mm (11/16") long x 15mm (9/16") wide. SEPALS: horizontal; coral (39B) tipped green upper surface; orange (35B) tipped green lower surface; 31mm(1 1/4") long x 10mm (3/8") wide. TUBE: orange (41B), dark base; long & thick; 37mm (1 7/16") long x 11mm (7/16") wide. STAMENS: extend 11mm (7/16) below corolla; orangy red (39A) filaments, pale tan (159A) anthers. PISTIL: extends 18mm (11/16") below the corolla, orangy red (39A) style, yellow (2D) stigma. BUD: cylindrical, cordate tip. FOLIAGE: medium green (147B) upper surface; yellowish green (146B) lower surface. Leaves are 81mm (3 3/16") long x 51mm (2") wide, ovate shaped, serrulated edges, obtuse tips and rounded bases. Veins & stems are light green; branches are light green blushed red. PARENTAGE: 'Insulinde' x 'Smoky'. Lax upright or stiff trailer. Makes good basket. Prefers overhead filtered light and cool or warm climate. Heat tolerant if shaded. Best bloom and foliage colour in filtered light. Tested 6 years in Lisse, Holland. Distinguished by erect, wax-like flowers held in terminal clusters.
de Graaff 2003 NL AFS5164.

Gartenbauverein Eupen. Trailer. Double. COROLLA: half flared; opens light pink (65B); matures pale pink (62D); 23mm (7/8") long x 17mm (5/8") wide. SEPALS: horizontal, tips reflexed; pale lavender (69B) tipped apple green (144C) upper surface; pale purple (75D) tipped apple green (144C) lower surface; 39 mm (1 1/2") long x 15mm (9/16") wide. TUBE: white (155C); medium length & thickness; 18mm (11/16") long x 7mm (1/4") wide. FOLIAGE is dark green (136B) upper surface; medium green (138B) lower surface. PARENTAGE: 'Vreni Schleeweiss' x 'Futura'.
Michiels 2007 BE AFS6354.

Gartenfreunden Eupen. Trailer. Double. COROLLA: 3 quarter flared; opens purple (N80B), light violet (77D) base; matures purple (N80A); 24mm (15/16") long x 23mm (7/8") wide. PETALOIDS: same colour as corolla; 12mm (7/16") long x 7mm (1/4") wide. SEPALS: horizontal, tips reflexed; pale purple (76C) tipped light apple green (144D) upper surface; light violet (77D) tipped light apple green (144D) lower surface; 29 mm (1 1/8") long x 12mm (7/16") wide. TUBE: pale violet (76D); medium length & thickness; 13mm (1/2") long x 5mm (3/16") wide. FOLIAGE is dark green (137A) upper surface; medium green (138B) lower surface. PARENTAGE: 'Stad Genk' x 'Shooting Star'. Michiels 2007 BE AFS6355.

Gärtenmeister Gloßner. Upright. Single. COROLLA: unflared, compact, smooth petal margins; opens dark purple (79A); matures dark purple (79B); 22mm (7/8") long x 15mm (9/16") wide. SEPALS: half up, tips recurved up; dark reddish purple (60A) upper & lower surfaces; 36mm (1 7/16") long x 12mm (7/16") wide. TUBE: dark reddish purple (60A); medium length & thickness; 15mm (9/16") long x 7mm (1/4") wide. STAMENS extend 25mm (1") beyond the corolla; dark reddish purple (60A) filaments; dark reddish purple (61A) anthers. PISTIL extends 33mm (1 5/16") beyond the corolla; dark reddish purple (60A) style & stigma. BUD: elongated. FOLIAGE: dark green (147A) upper surface; yellowish green (147B) lower surface. Leaves are 78mm (3 1/8") long x 42mm (1 5/8") wide; elliptic shaped, serrate edges, acute tips, rounded bases. Veins & stems are red, branches are brown. PARENTAGE: 'Rohees King' x F. regia ssp. serrae hoya. Medium upright. Makes good upright or standard. Prefers full sun, warm climate. Heat tolerant if shaded. Cold weather hardy to -15° C (6° F). Best bloom & foliage colour in bright light. Tested 6 years in Bavaria, Southern Germany. Distinguished by flower colour & shape.
Burkhart 2009 DE AFS7097.

Gary Peters. Upright. Single. COROLLA: quarter flared, smooth petal margins, bell shaped; opens dark reddish purple (N79C); matures purple (71A); 13mm (1/2") long x 13mm (1/2") wide. SEPALS: full down, tips recurved; red (52A) upper surface; rose (50B) lower surface; 38mm (1 1/2") long x 16mm (5/8") wide. TUBE: magenta (57C); medium length & thickness; 38mm (1 1/2") long. STAMENS extend 13mm (1/2") beyond the corolla; magenta (58B) filaments; magenta

(57A) anthers. PISTIL extends 32mm (1 1/4") beyond the corolla; magenta (63B) style; rose (64D) stigma. BUD is oval. FOLIAGE is dark green (141A) upper surface; yellowish green (144A) lower surface. Leaves are 51mm (2") long x 32mm (1 1/4") wide; ovate shaped, serrulate edges, acute tips, rounded bases. Veins & stems are green; branches are purple. PARENTAGE: found seedling. Small upright. Makes good upright. Prefers overhead filtered light. Cold weather hardy to -7° C (20° F). Best bloom colour in filtered light. Tested 3 years in Telford, Shropshire, UK. Distinguished by bloom colour & shape. Peters 2009 UK AFS6957.

Gary Rhodes. Upright/Trailer. Double. COROLLA is half flared and rounded with smooth petal margins; opens dark purple (79A), matures dark reddish purple (59A), 30mm(1 3/16") long x 60mm (2 3/8") wide. SEPALS are half up, tips recurved up; magenta (59D) upper surface, magenta (59D) creped lower surface; 40mm (1 5/8") long x 20mm (13/16") wide. TUBE is magenta (59D) short with medium thickness; 15mm(5/8") long x 6mm (1/4") wide. STAMENS extend 30mm (1 3/16") below the corolla; magenta (59D) filaments and anthers. PISTIL extends 40mm(1 9/16") below the corolla; magenta (61C) style and stigma. BUD is pear shaped. FOLIAGE is dark green (137A) upper surface, medium green (137C) lower surface. Leaves are 94mm (3 11/16") long x 45mm(1 3/4") wide, ovate shaped serrulated edges, acute tips and rounded bases. Veins are pale aubergine, stems and branches are aubergine. PARENTAGE: 'Sunset Boulevard' x 'Gerharda's Aubergine'. Lax upright or stiff trailer. Makes a good upright, standard or decorative. Prefers cool climate. Heat tolerant if shaded. Best bloom colour in filtered light. Tested for 3 years in Gloucester England. Distinguished by bloom shape and very dark aubergine bloom colour.
Hickman 2002 UK AFS4861.

Gaston-Hilda 50. Upright/Trailer. Double. COROLLA: half flared, turned under wavy petal margins; opens red (53D) & purple (83B); matures magenta (71C) & purple (77A); 26mm (1 ") long x 25mm (1 ") wide. PETALOIDS: same colour as corolla; 17mm (5/8") long x 14mm (9/16") wide. SEPALS: horizontal, tips recurved; red (53C) tipped medium green (139C) upper surface; red (53C) & reddish purple (61B) lower surface; 37mm (1 7/16") long x 18mm (11/16") wide. TUBE: red (53B); medium length & thickness; 15mm (9/16") long x 6mm (1/4")

wide. STAMENS extend 13mm (1/2") beyond the corolla; purple (71A) filaments; purple (77A) anthers. PISTIL extends 32mm (1 1/4") beyond the corolla; magenta (63A) style; pale rose (73D) stigma. BUD: bulbous. FOLIAGE: dark green (136B) upper surface; medium green (138B) lower surface. Leaves are 78mm (3 1/8") long x 35mm (1 3/8") wide; ovate shaped, serrulate edges, acute tips, rounded bases. Veins are dark purple (79B), stems are dark purple (79A), branches are dark purple (N79B). PARENTAGE: 'Niagara Falls' x 'Fleurjoux'. Lax upright or stiff trailer. Self branching. Makes good upright. Prefers overhead filtered light, cool climate. Best bloom & foliage colour in filtered light. Tested 3 years in Koningshooikt, Belgium. Waanrode 5/7/08. Distinguished by bloom colour combination.
Michiels 2009 BE AFS7166.

Gaulois Futé. Upright. Single. COROLLA is unflared with smooth petal margins; opens purple (77A); matures violet (77B); 17mm (11/16") long x 8mm (5/16") wide. SEPALS are horizontal, tips recurved; red (52A) tipped lighter upper surface; rose (52B) lower surface; 30mm (1 3/16") long x 10mm (3/8") wide. TUBE is red (52A); very short, medium thickness; 7mm (1/4") long x 7mm (1/4") wide. FOLIAGE: dark green (147A) upper surface; medium green (147B) lower surface. Leaves are 78mm (3 1/16") long x 31mm (1 1/4") wide, ovate to lanceolate shaped. PARENTAGE: ('String of Pearls' x F. regia reitzii 4574') x 'F. boliviana alba'. Distinguished by profuse blooms.
Massé 2005 FR AFS5835.

Geerharda's Debutante. Trailer. Single. COROLLA is quarter flared, bell shaped; opens dark reddish purple (59A); matures reddish purple (59B); 11mm (7/16") long x 10mm (3/8") wide. SEPALS are horizontal, tips recurved; dark reddish purple (70A) upper surface; dark reddish purple (64A) lower surface; 28mm (1 1/8") long x 5mm (3/16") wide. TUBE is reddish purple (71B); long, 26mm (1") long x 5mm (3/16") wide. FOLIAGE: dark green (147A) upper surface; olive green (148A) lower surface. PARENTAGE: 'Eruption' x 'Zulu King'. Distinguished by aubergine coloured flowers in terminal sub racemes.
de Graaff H. 2006 NL AFS6245.

Generous Jean. Upright/Trailer. Double. COROLLA is three quarter flared, ruffled with smooth turned under petal margins; opens purple (81B) splashed white (155D) near

TUBE; matures light purple (80C) splashed white (155D) near TUBE; 30mm (1 3/16") long x 50mm (2") wide. PETALOIDS are same colour as corolla; 20mm (13/16") long x 12mm (1/2") wide. SEPALS are half twisted counterclockwise, fully up, tips reflexed; white (155D) upper surface, white (155D) w/slight hint of pale purple (75C) lower surface; 45mm (1 3/4") long x 12mm (1/2") wide. TUBE is light greenish white (157C), medium length and width; 15mm (5/8") long x 6mm (1/4") wide. STAMENS extend 10mm (3/8") below the corolla; dark rose (67C) filaments and yellowish white (158A) anthers. PISTIL extends 15mm (5/8") below the corolla; white (155D) style and yellowish white (158A) stigma. BUD is large, elongated. FOLIAGE is dark green (147A) on upper surface and medium green (147B) on lower surface. Leaves are 90mm (3 9/16") long x 45mm (1 3/4") wide, cordate shaped, serrulated edges, acute tips and rounded bases. Veins are green; stems brown; branches are green. PARENTAGE: 'Loveable Rascal' x 'Grandma Rose'. Lax upright or stiff trailer. Self branching. Makes good basket or standard. Prefers overhead filtered light and warm climate. Heat tolerant if shaded. Hardy to 32°F. Best bloom colour in bright light. Tested three years in Walthamstow, London, England. Distinguished by profuse blooms and dense growth.
Allsop 2002 UK AFS4813.

Geoff Oak. Upright. Single. COROLLA porcelain blue. SEPALS creamy white.
Reynolds G. 2003 UK.

Geoffrey Wickham. Upright. Single. COROLLA opens violet, white at base, matures to a darker violet, white blushed violet at base; corolla is quarter flared and is 25mm long x 28mm wide. SEPALS are white with a slight pink blush on the upper and lower surfaces with slight green tips, matures a deeper pink blush; sepals are fully recurved with recurved tips and are 30mm long x 10mm wide. TUBE. is white with a slight pink blush and is 7mm long x 5mm wide. PARENTAGE 'Lady Isobel Barnett' x 'Eden Lady'. This cultivar is named after the late Geoffrey Wickham, chairman of the Thanet Fuchsia Group, where it took 1st prize at their Show. Capable of making a large full standard.
Pownceby 2005 UK BFS0018.

Georg Glossner. Upright/Trailer. Double. COROLLA: half flared, smooth petal margins; opens reddish purple (71B); matures reddish purple (67A); 25-30mm (1-1 3/16") long x 35mm (1 3/8") wide. SEPALS: half up; tips recurved up; dark rose (55A) upper surface; rose (55B) lower surface; 30-35mm (1 3/16-1 3/8") long x 15mm (9/16") wide. TUBE: white (155C), touch of pink; short & thick; 15mm(9/16") long x 6mm (1/4") wide. STAMENS: extend 35mm (1 3/8") below corolla; magenta (57D) filaments, magenta (63A) anthers. PISTIL: extends 50mm (2") below the corolla, pale lavender (69B) style, cream (159D) stigma. BUD: short, round. FOLIAGE: dark green (147A) upper surface; medium green (147B) lower surface. Leaves are 70mm (2 3/4") long x 40mm (1 9/16") wide, elliptic shaped, serrated edges, acute tips and obtuse bases. Veins are light green, stems are dark red, branches are light brown. PARENTAGE: 'Danny Kaye' x 'Southgate'. Lax upright or stiff trailer. Self branching. Makes good basket, standard or pyramid. Prefers cool climate. Heat tolerant if shaded. Best bloom and foliage colour in bright light. Tested 3 years in Bavaria, southern Germany. Distinguished by blossom shape and colour. Burkhart 2003 DE AFS5189.

Georg von Peuerbach. Upright. Double. COROLLA: Three quarter flared; opens & matures violet (77B); 20mm (3/4") long x 40mm (1 9/16") wide. SEPALS: half up, tips recurved up; purple (70C) tipped green upper surface; reddish purple (70B) lower surface; 25mm (1") long x 15mm (9/16") wide. TUBE: reddish purple (70C); short & thick; 15mm (9/16") long x 10mm (3/8") wide. FOLIAGE is dark green (139A) upper surface; medium green (139B) lower surface. PARENTAGE: 'Gründlsee' x 'Chris Lohner'. Gindl 2007 AT AFS6712.

Georges Guynemer. Upright. Single. COROLLA: quarter flared, smooth petal margins; opens violet (84A) veined pale rose (73D); matures reddish purple (70B); 30mm (1 3/16") long x 20mm (13/16") wide. SEPALS: horizontal; tips recurved; rose (52B) tipped yellowish green (145A) upper surface; rose (52B) lower surface; 45mm (1 3/4") long x 12mm (1/2") wide. TUBE: dark rose (48A); very short, medium thickness; 7mm (1/4") long x 5-7mm (3/16-1/4") wide, diamond shaped. STAMENS: extend 9-11mm (3/8– 7/16") below corolla; pink (62A) filaments, dark red (47A) anthers. PISTIL: extends 28mm (1 1/8") below the corolla, light pink (62B) style, grayish orange (179B) stigma. BUD: ovate. FOLIAGE: medium green (146A) upper surface; yellowish green (146B) lower

surface. Leaves are 84mm (3 5/16") long x 53mm (2 1/16") wide, ovate shaped, serrulated edges, acute tips and rounded bases. Veins & stems are yellowish green, branches are light brown. PARENTAGE: 'Philippe Boennec' x 'Mirobolant'. Small upright. Makes good upright or standard. Prefers overhead filtered light and cool climate. Best bloom and foliage colour in filtered light. Tested 4 years in Pornic, France. Distinguished by diamond TUBE shape and bloom colour. Massé 2003 FR AFS5223.

Gera. Upright. Semi Double. COROLLA white veined red. SEPALS cherry red. Rijkers 2004 NL.

Geranette Joco. Upright/Trailer. Semi Double. COROLLA is half flared with turned under smooth petal margins; opens dark purple (78A), orangy red (39A) base; matures reddish purple (70B), orangy red (39A) base; 31mm (1 1/4") long x 29 mm (1 1/8") wide. SEPALS are half down, tips recurved; white (155C) upper surface flushed pink (52D) tipped light green (142A); pink (52D) lower surface; 42mm (1 11/16") long x 15mm (5/8") wide. TUBE is white (155A), medium length and thickness; 25mm (1") long x 4mm (3/16") wide. STAMENS extend 9mm (3/8") beyond the corolla; magenta (63B) filaments, reddish purple (58A) anthers. PISTIL extends 19mm (3/4") below the corolla;dark rose (58C); light yellow (2B) stigma. BUD is ovate. FOLIAGE is dark green (139A) upper surface, medium green (137C) lower surface. Leaves are 88mm (3 1/2") long x 39mm (1 9/16") wide, elliptic shaped, serrated edges, acute tips and acute bases. Veins are light green (138C), stems and branches are orangish brown (174A). PARENTAGE: 'Red Spider' x 'Onbekend'. Lax upright or stiff trailer. Self branching. Makes good basket. Prefers overhead filtered light and full sun. Best bloom and foliage colour in bright to filtered light. Tested three years in Hoeselt, Belgium. Certificate N.B.F.K. at Meise. Distinguished by bloom colour and shape. Wagemans 2002 BE AFS4902.

Gerard Domingos. Upright/Trailer. Double. COROLLA: Three quarter flared; opens dark reddish purple (72A); matures reddish purple (64B); 26mm (1") long x 34mm (1 3/8") wide. SEPALS: half up, tips recurved up; magenta (61C) upper & lower surfaces; 41mm (1 5/8") long x 16mm (5/8") wide. TUBE: magenta (61C); medium length & thickness; 10mm (3/8") long x 6mm (1/4") wide. FOLIAGE is dark green (137A) upper surface; medium green (137C) lower surface. PARENTAGE: 'Roesse Lupus' x 'Roesse Octans'. Decoster 2007 BE AFS6620.

Gerard Verbocht. Upright. Single. COROLLA: quarter flared, turned under smooth petal margins; opens rose (65A); matures light pink (65B); 22mm (7/8") long x 17mm (11/16") wide. SEPALS: fully up; tips recurved; red (46B) striped yellowish green (144A), tipped yellowish green (144B) upper surface; red (45A) lower surface; 22mm (7/8") long x 9mm (3/8") wide. TUBE: red (45B), striped yellowish green (144B); medium length, thin; 15mm (9/16") long x 4mm (3/16") wide. STAMENS: do not extend below corolla; no filaments; light yellow (1C) anthers. PISTIL: extends 2mm (1/16") below the corolla; red (45A) style; rose (50B) stigma. BUD: ovate. FOLIAGE: dark green (139A) upper surface, medium green (138A) lower surface. Leaves are 90mm (3 9/16") long x 40mm (1 9/16") wide, elliptic shaped, serrated edges, acute tips and acute bases. Medium green (138B) veins & stems; light brown (199B) branches. PARENTAGE: 'Leverkusen' x 'WALZ Toorts'. Medium upright. Self branching. Makes good upright or standard. Prefers warm climate. Heat tolerant if shaded. Best bloom and foliage colour in filtered light. Tested 4 years in Leopoldsburg & Helchteren, Belgium. Distinguished by colour combination and no filaments.
Busschodts 2004 BE AFS5439.

Gerd Pardon. Upright/Trailer. Double. COROLLA: three quarter flared, turned under wavy petal margins; opens light purple (71C) & dark reddish purple (60B); matures dark rose (71D) & dark reddish purple (60C); 30mm (1 3/16 ") long x 25mm (1 ") wide. PETALOIDS: dark reddish purple (61A) & dark reddish purple (59A); 19mm (3/4") long x 17mm (5/8") wide. SEPALS: horizontal, tips recurved; reddish purple (58A) tipped light apple green (144D) upper surface; dark rose (54A) tipped light apple green (144D) lower surface; 35mm (1 3/8") long x 16mm (5/8") wide. TUBE: pale pink (56D) & light rose (58D); short & thick; 10mm (3/8") long x 7mm (1/4") wide. STAMENS extend 18mm (11/16") beyond the corolla; rose (67D) filaments; brownish orange (174D) anthers. PISTIL extends 27mm (1 1/16") beyond the corolla; dark reddish purple (70A) style; grayish orange (179C) stigma. BUD: oblong. FOLIAGE: dark green (139A) upper surface; medium green (137D) lower surface. Leaves

are 58mm (2 5/16") long x 42mm (1 5/8") wide; ovate shaped, serrulate edges, obtuse tips, rounded bases. Veins are light grayish red (182C), stems are plum (185C), branches are light green (138D). PARENTAGE: 'Manfried Kleinau' x 'Imperial Fantasy'. Lax upright or stiff trailer. Self branching. Makes good basket. Prefers overhead filtered light, cool climate. Best bloom & foliage colour in filtered light. Tested 3 years in Koningshooikt, Belgium. Waanrode 8/9/08. Distinguished by bloom colour.
Michiels 2009 BE AFS7167.

Gerda Valgaerts. Upright. Single. COROLLA: quarter flared, turned under smooth petal margins; opens dark purple (78A); matures reddish purple (74A); 19mm (3/4") long x 16mm (5/8") wide. SEPALS: fully up; tips recurved; white (155B) tipped light green (142A) upper surface; white (155D) flushed rose (65A) lower surface; 29mm(1 1/8") long x 10mm (3/8") wide. TUBE: white (155B); long, medium thickness; 40mm (1 9/16") long x 6mm (1/4") wide. STAMENS: extend 1mm (1/16") below the corolla; light pink (62B) filaments, greenish yellow (1B) anthers. PISTIL extends 1mm (1/16") below the corolla; white (155D) style, yellow (2A) stigma. BUD: ovate, long TUBE. FOLIAGE: dark green (137A) upper surface; medium green (138B) lower surface. Leaves are 110mm (4 5/16") long x 55mm (2 3/16") wide, elliptic shaped, serrated edges, acute tips and rounded bases. Veins & stems are brown (166A), branches are light green (138D). PARENTAGE: 'Alda Alders' x 'Evy Penders'. Tall upright. Self branching. Makes good upright or standard. Prefers overhead filtered light. Best bloom and foliage colour in filtered light. Tested 4 years in Leopoldsburg, Belgium. NBFK Certificate at Meise. Distinguished by long TUBE, profuse blooms. Busschodts 2003 BE AFS5127.

Gerharda's Katja. Upright/Trailer. Single. COROLLA is half flared, trumpet shaped, with toothed margins; opens light purple (78D), matures violet (75A); 9mm (3/8") long x 7mm (1/4") wide. SEPALS are horizontal, tips recurved; rose (68C) tipped light yellowish green (149C) upper surface, pale pink (69A) tipped pale yellowish green (149D) lower surface; 14mm (9/16") long x 4mm (3/16") wide. TUBE is rose (68B), long with medium thickness; 20mm (13/16") long x 5mm (3/16") wide. STAMENS are 2mm (1/16") inside the corolla; light rose (68D) filaments and yellowish white (158A) anthers. PISTIL extends 9mm (3/8") below

the corolla; light rose (68D) style, very pale orange (159B) stigma. BUD is long, pointed. FOLIAGE is dark green (147A) upper surface, medium green (147B) lower surface. Leaves are 109mm (4 5/16") long x 35mm (1 3/8") wide, lanceolate shaped, serrulated edges, acute tips and acute bases. Veins are light yellowish green, stems and branches are reddish. PARENTAGE: ('F. *splendens*' x 'F. *lycioides*') x 'Panache'. Lax upright or stiff trailer. Self branching. Makes good basket or upright. Prefers overhead filtered light. Heat tolerant if shaded. Best bloom and foliage colour in filtered light. Tested five years in Lisse, Holland. Distinguished by blossom colour and flowering in branched flat panicles.
de Graaff 2002 NL AFS4878.

Gerharda's Panache. Upright. Single. COROLLA: half flared; trumpet shaped; turned up toothed petal margins; opens pale purple (74D); matures rose (68A); 9mm (3/8") long x 10mm (3/8") wide. SEPALS: horizontal; tips reflexed; rose (68C),darker tips, upper surface; light rose (73B), darker tips, lower surface; 17mm(11/16") long x 5mm (3/16") wide. TUBE: rose (68C), darker at base; long & thin; 31mm (1 1/4") long x 5mm (3/16") wide. STAMENS: extend 5mm (3/16) below corolla; rose (68B) filaments, light yellow (10D) anthers. PISTIL: extends 6mm (1/4") below the corolla, light rose (73B) style, rose (68C) stigma. BUD: long, thin, cylindrical, cordate tip. FOLIAGE: medium green (147B) upper surface; yellowish green (146B) lower surface. Leaves are 97mm (3 13/16") long x 44mm (1 3/4") wide, elliptic shaped, serrulated edges, acute tips and acute bases. Veins are reddish light green; stems & branches are red. PARENTAGE: 'Small Pipes' x 'Pan'. Medium upright. Makes good upright. Prefers overhead filtered light and cool or warm climate. Heat tolerant if shaded. Best bloom and foliage colour in filtered light. Tested 10 years in Lisse, Holland. Award of Merit, VKC, Aalsmeer. Distinguished by long TUBEd flowers carried in multiple racemes.
de Graaff 2003 NL AFS5168.

Gerhards Waldhof. Upright. Semi Double. COROLLA opens violet blue (94b), matures to dark violet purple (90a); corolla is half flared. SEPALS white, tipped green on the upper and lower surfaces; SEPALS are half down with recurved tips. TUBE white, with green veins. PARENTAGE 'Cliff's Own' x seedling of ('Cliff's Own' x 'Delta's Parade').
Klemm 2009 AT BFS0129.

Gerrien's Super. Upright. Single. COROLLA is three quarter flared with turned up petal margins; opens & matures white (155D); 14mm (9/16") long x 14mm (9/16") wide. SEPALS are horizontal, tips recurved; dark rose (55A) upper surface; pink (55C) lower surface; 22mm (7/8") long x 8mm (5/16") wide. TUBE is rose (55B); medium length & thickness; 7mm (1/4") long x 5mm (3/16") wide. FOLIAGE: medium green (147A) edged white upper & lower surfaces. Leaves are 58mm (2 5/16") long x 37mm (1 7/16") wide, ovate shaped. PARENTAGE: Sport of 'Supernova'. Nomination by N.K.V.F. as recommendable cultivar. Distinguished by silvery appearance form white edged leaves and erect pink-white flowers.
van de Steen 2005 NL AFS5799.

Gerrit de Jong. Upright. Double. COROLLA is half flared; opens & matures purple (83A); 20mm (3/4") long x 20mm (3/4") wide. SEPALS are half down, tips recurved; dark reddish purple (61A) upper surface; reddish purple (61B) lower surface; 29mm (1 1/8") long x 11mm (7/16") wide. TUBE is dark reddish purple (60A); 11mm (7/16") long x 6mm (1/4") wide. FOLIAGE: dark green (147A) upper surface; medium green (147B) lower surface. PARENTAGE: 'Sunangels Cheerio' x 'Hertogin van Brabant'. Distinguished by bloom shape & colour.
Krom 2006 NL AFS6272.

Gerrit Hasselerharm. Upright/Trailer. Semi Double. COROLLA is half flared with smooth petal margins; opens dark purple (78A), matures reddish purple (80B); 22mm (7/8") long x 25 mm (1") wide. SEPALS are fully up, tips recurved; rose (68B) upper surface; reddish purple (64B) lower surface; 68mm (2 11/16") long x 15mm (9/16") wide. TUBE is rose (68B), medium length and thickness; 10mm (3/8") long x 6mm (1/4") wide. STAMENS extend 16mm (5/8") beyond the corolla; reddish purple (71B) filaments; purple (71A) anthers. PISTIL extends 34mm (1 5/16") below the corolla; magenta (68A) style; light rose (68D) stigma. BUD is ovate, pointed. FOLIAGE is medium green (137B) upper surface, medium green (138B) lower surface. Leaves are 76mm (3") long x 38mm (1 1/2") wide, lanceolate shaped, serrulated edges, acute tips and acute bases. Veins, stems & branches are red. PARENTAGE: 'Bicentennial' x 'Maxima'. Lax upright or stiff trailer. Makes good stiff trailer. Prefers overhead filtered light & cool climate. Best bloom and foliage colour in filtered light.

Tested four years in Knegsel, The Netherlands. Distinguished by bloom colour. van Bree 2004 NL AFS5359.

Gerrit Tamerus. Trailer. Semi Double. COROLLA is quarter flared with smooth petal margins; opens purple (77A); matures dark reddish purple (61A); 26mm (1") long x 20mm (13/16") wide. SEPALS are half up, tips recurved up; reddish purple (61B) upper and lower surfaces; 34mm (1 3/8") long x 12mm (1/2") wide. TUBE is dark reddish purple (61B); medium length and thickness; 21mm (13/16") long x 7mm (1/4") thick. STAMENS extend 20mm (13/16") beyond the corolla; reddish purple (64B) filaments, purple (71A) anthers. PISTIL extends 41mm (1 5/8") beyond the corolla; reddish purple (64B) style, pale pink (62D) stigma. BUD is ovate, pointed. FOLIAGE is dark green (137A) upper surface, medium green (138B) lower surface. Leaves are 57mm (2 1/4") long x 32mm (1 1/4") wide, ovate shaped, serrated edges, acute tips and rounded bases. Veins, stems and branches are red. PARENTAGE: 'Rohees King' x 'Anta'. Natural trailer. Makes good basket. Prefers overhead filtered light and cool climate. Best bloom colour in filtered light. Tested four years in Duizel, The Netherlands. Distinguished by bloom colour. Tamerus 2002 NL AFS4995.

Gerrit van den Brink. Upright. Double. COROLLA: unflared, compact shape; opens violet (87B); matures reddish purple (80B); 29mm (1 1/8") long x 25mm (1") wide. PETALOIDS: violet (87B) veined dark pink; 27mm (1 1/16") long x 25mm (1") wide. SEPALS: fully up, tips recurved; reddish purple (64B) upper surface; reddish purple (61B) lower surface; 40 mm (1 9/16") long x 13mm (1/2") wide. TUBE: magenta (58B); 20mm (3/4") long x 18mm (11/16") wide. FOLIAGE is medium green (146A) upper surface; yellowish green (146C) lower surface. PARENTAGE: 'Gerwin van den Brink' x 'White King'. Nomination by NKVF as Recommendable Cultivar. van den Brink 2008 NL AFS6790.

Gerrit vanden Huevel. Upright. Semi Double. COROLLA: half flared, smooth petal margins; opens light reddish purple (73A); matures light rose (73B); 22mm (7/8") long 24mm (15/16") wide. SEPALS: half down; tips reflexed; pale pink (62D) upper & lower surface; 44mm (1 3/4") long x 11mm (7/16") wide. TUBE: pale pink (62D); medium length & thickness; 17mm (11/16) long x 7mm (1/4") wide. STAMENS: extend 10mm (3/8")

below corolla; dark rose (64C) filaments & anthers. PISTIL: extends 21mm (13/16") below the corolla; light pink (65C) style; light yellow (4C) stigma. BUD: elliptic, long. FOLIAGE: dark green (137A) upper surface; medium green (138B) lower surface. Leaves are 56mm (2 3/16") long x 34mm (1 5/16") wide, ovate shaped, serrulated edges, acute tips and rounded bases. Green veins, stems & branches. PARENTAGE: 'Sofie Michiels' x 'Judy Salome'. Medium upright. Makes good upright or stsndard. Prefers overhead filtered light and cool climate. Best bloom and foliage colour in filtered light. Tested 4 years in Reusel, The Netherlands. Distinguished by bloom colour. van Eijk 2004 NL AFS5504.

Gerwin van den Brink. Upright. Single. COROLLA: Quarter flared, bell shaped; opens & matures purple (83A); 30mm (1 3/16") long x 28mm (1 1/8") wide. PETALOIDS: same colour as corolla; 26mm (1") long x 20mm (3/4") wide. SEPALS: half up, tips recurved up; reddish purple (67A) upper & lower surfaces; 52mm (2 1/16") long x 7mm (1/4") wide. TUBE: magenta (57A); medium length & thickness; 26mm (1") long x 6mm (1/4") wide. FOLIAGE is medium green (146A) upper surface; yellowish green (146B) lower surface. PARENTAGE: 'Voodoo' x unknown. Award of Merit, VKC Aalsmeer, 2001. van den Brink 2007 NL AFS6443.

Geurts Bella. Upright. Single. COROLLA: quarter flared, bell shaped; smooth petal margins; opens & matures light pink (36D); 21mm (13/16") long x 20mm (3/4") wide. SEPALS: half up, tips recurved up; light pink (36D) tipped light green (145D) upper surface; light pink (36D) lower surface; 26mm (1") long x 6mm (1/4") wide. TUBE: pink (37D); medium length & thickness; 22mm (7/8") long x 5mm (3/16") wide. STAMENS extend .5mm (1/16") beyond the corolla; pink (49A) filaments; cream (19D) anthers. PISTIL does not extend beyond the corolla; white style; very pale orange (19D) stigma. BUD: long. FOLIAGE: dark green (137A) upper surface; medium green (137D) lower surface. Leaves are 47mm (1 7/8") long x 36mm (1 7/16") wide; elliptic shaped, serrate edges, acute tips, rounded bases. Veins, stems & branches are light green. PARENTAGE: 'Waternymph' x F. *fulgens goselli*. Medium upright. Makes good upright. Prefers overhead filtered light. Best bloom colour in filtered light. Tested 4 years in Steyl, The Netherlands. Nominated by NKvF

as recommendable cultivar. Distinguished by flower combination & flowering in clusters year-round.
Geurts 2009 NL AFS7037.

Geurts Orange. Upright/Trailer. Single. COROLLA: quarter flared, bell shaped; wavy petal margins; opens pink (43D); matures red (47B); 26mm (1") long x 20mm (3/4") wide. SEPALS: horizontal, tips recurved; pink (49A) tipped light apple green (145C) upper surface; pink (49A) lower surface; 45mm (1 3/4") long x 11mm (7/16") wide. TUBE: pink (49A); medium length, thick; 12mm (7/16") long x 5mm (3/16") wide. STAMENS extend 10mm (3/8") beyond the corolla; pink (48C) filaments; reddish purple (59B) anthers. PISTIL extends 30mm (3/16") beyond the corolla; pink (48C) style; pale yellow (4D) stigma. BUD: long. FOLIAGE: medium green (137B) upper surface; medium green (137D) lower surface. Leaves are 79mm (3 1/8") long x 38mm (1 1/2") wide; elliptic shaped, serrulate edges, acute tips, rounded bases. Veins, stems & branches are light green. PARENTAGE: 'Danny Kaye' x 'Golden Glow'. Lax upright or stiff trailer. Makes good upright. Prefers overhead filtered light. Best bloom & foliage colour in limited light. Tested 4 years in Steyl, The Netherlands. Nominated by NKvF as recommendable cultivar. Distinguished by bright flower colours.
Geurts 2009 NL AFS7036.

Ghrete K. Olsen. Trailer. Semi Double. COROLLA: half flared, turned under wavy petal margins; opens rose (48B) & reddish purple (61B); matures reddish purple (70B) & light purple (70C); 31mm (1 1/4 ") long x 28mm (1 1/8 ") wide. PETALOIDS: Same colour as corolla; 22mm (7/8") long x 14mm (9/16") wide. SEPALS: horizontal, tips recurved; pale pink (56A) tipped pale pink (56D) upper surface; rose (52C) tipped pale pink (56D) lower surface; 44mm (1 3/4") long x 19mm (3/4") wide. TUBE: pale pink (56D); medium length & thickness; 17mm (5/8") long x 7mm (1/4") wide. STAMENS extend 16mm (5/8") beyond the corolla; light purple (70C) filaments; purple (71A) anthers. PISTIL extends 19mm (3/4") beyond the corolla; rose (68C) style; pale yellow (1D) stigma. BUD: bulbous. FOLIAGE: dark green (136B) upper surface; medium green (137D) lower surface. Leaves are 81mm (3 1/4") long x 48mm (1 7/8") wide; ovate shaped, serrulate edges, acute tips, rounded bases. Veins are greenish yellow (151A), stems are greenish yellow (151A) & light red purple (185D), branches are plum (184B) & light

green (139D). PARENTAGE: 'Manfried Kleinau' x 'Corsage'. Natural trailer. Self branching. Makes good basket. Prefers overhead filtered light, cool climate. Best bloom & foliage colour in filtered light. Tested 3 years in Koningshooikt, Belgium. Waanrode 8/9/08. Distinguished by bloom colour combination & profuse blooming.
Michiels 2009 BE AFS7168.

Gigi. Upright. Single. COROLLA: half flared, smooth petal margins; opens rose (50B); matures light rose (50C); 22mm (7/8") long x 30mm (1 3/16") wide. SEPALS: half up; tips recurved up; orangy red (39A) tipped green upper surface; coral (39B) lower surface; 40mm (1 9/16") long x 15mm (9/16") wide. TUBE: white (155A) striped coral (39B); medium length & thickness; 15mm(9/16") long x 6mm (1/4") wide. STAMENS: extend 10mm (3/8") below corolla; coral (39B) filaments, light brown (199D) anthers. PISTIL: extends 35mm (1 3/8") below the corolla, light orange (39C) style, pale pink (49D) stigma. BUD: ovate. FOLIAGE: medium green (138A) upper surface; medium olive green (138B) lower surface. Leaves are 85mm (3 3/8") long x 55mm (2 3/16") wide, ovate shaped, serrated edges, acute tips and rounded bases. Veins & branches are green, stems are green-brown. PARENTAGE: {[('Tousendschön' x 'Baby Pink') x 'Liebes' x 'Träume] x 'Isarperle'} x ('Baby Pink' x 'Brookwood Joy'). Tall upright. Self branching. Makes good standard. Prefers full sun. Heat tolerant if shaded. Best bloom and foliage colour in bright light. Tested 3 years in München, Germany. Distinguished by shining orange SEPALS and compact flowers.
Dietrich 2003 DE AFS5188.

Gigis Montserrat. Upright. Double. COROLLA opens pink; corolla is three quarter flared. SEPALS neyron neyron rose striped rose on the upper surface, neyron rose on the lower surface; sepals are half down to horizontal with recurved tips. TUBE rose. PARENTAGE 'Gigis Perone' x 'Gigis Perone'.
Durr 2008 DE BFS0072.

Gigis Norma. Upright. Semi Double. COROLLA opens magenta rose, veined crimson; corolla is half flared. SEPALS carmine rose on the upper surface, crimson on the lower surface; sepals are fully up with light green recurved tips. TUBE light pink. PARENTAGE 'Gigis Annina' x 'Gigis Annina'.
Durr 2008 DE BFS0071.

150

Gilbert Roelandt. Trailer. Double. COROLLA is three quarter flared with turned under smooth petal margins; opens purple (83A), magenta (58B) at base, matures violet (76A), dark rose (58C) at base; 23mm (15/16") long x 22mm (7/8") wide. SEPALS are half down, tips reflexed; pink (62A) tipped grayish yellow (160A), light pink (49B) at base, upper surface; rose (52B), pink (62C) at base, lower surface; 33mm (1 5/16") long x 18mm (11/16") wide. TUBE is light pink (49B); medium length and thickness; 20mm (13/16") long x 6mm (1/4") thick. STAMENS extend 4mm (3/16") beyond the corolla; magenta (58B) filaments, dark purple (79B) anthers. PISTIL extends 6mm (1/4") beyond the corolla; rose (65A) style, light rose (58D) stigma. BUD is round. FOLIAGE is medium green (146A) upper surface, dark green (147B) lower surface. Leaves are 37mm (1 7/16") long x 28mm (1 1/8") wide, cordate shaped, serrulated edges, acute tips and cordate bases. Veins are grayish red (181C), stems and branches are dark grayish red (182A). PARENTAGE: 'Topscore' x unknown. Natural trailer. Makes good basket. Prefers overhead filtered light. Best bloom and foliage colour in filtered light. Tested three years in Rummen, Belgium. Certificate N.B.F.K. at Meise. Distinguished by bloom shape and stalked petals.
Ector 2002 BE AFS5004.

Gillian's Gem. Trailer. Double. COROLLA: quarter flared, turned under smooth petal margins; opens reddish purple (61B) fused pink (49A); matures magenta (57A) fused pink (49A); 25mm (1") long x 30mm (1 3/16") wide. PETALOIDS: Same colour as corolla; 15mm (9/16") long x 8mm (5/16") wide. SEPALS: half down; tips recurved; pink (62C) tipped green upper surface; light rose (58D) tipped green lower surface; 30mm (1 3/16") long x 14mm (9/16") wide. TUBE: very pale orange (27C) veined light orange (27A); medium length & thin; 12mm(1/2") long x 6mm (1/4") wide. STAMENS: extend 20mm (13/16") below corolla; dark rose (54A) filaments & anthers. PISTIL: extends 40mm (1 9/16") below the corolla, pink (54D) style, yellowish white (158A) stigma. BUD: oval. FOLIAGE: dark green (137A) upper surface; medium green (146A) lower surface. Leaves are 70mm (2 3/4") long x 37mm (1 7/16") wide, lanceolate shaped, serrated edges, acute tips and rounded bases. Veins are red/green, stems are red; branches are brown. PARENTAGE: 'Beth Robley' x 'Welsh Dragon'. Natural trailer. Self branching. Makes good basket. Prefers overhead filtered

light. Heat tolerant if shaded. Cold weather hardy to 32° F. Best bloom and foliage colour in filtered light. Tested 3 years in Walthamstow, London, England. Distinguished by distinctive petaloids and flaring of inner petals when mature.
Allsop J. 2003 UK AFS5213.

Gimli von Moria. Upright/Trailer. Double. COROLLA is three quarter flared; opens dark purple (79B); matures purple (71A); 29mm (1 1/8") long x 40mm (1 9/16") wide. SEPALS are half down, tips recurved; reddish purple (61B) upper & lower surface; 36mm (1 7/16") long x 15mm (9/16") wide. TUBE is reddish purple (61B); 12mm (1/2") long x 9mm (3/8") wide. FOLIAGE: medium green (137B) upper surface; medium green (137C) lower surface. PARENTAGE: 'Georg Glossner' x 'Rohees Queen'. Distinguished by bloom shape & colour.
Burkhart 2006 DE AFS6046.

Gina. Single. COROLLA rich bright purple. SEPALS red.
Chambers 2004 UK.

Gina Bouwman. Trailer. Double. COROLLA: three quarter flared, turned under wavy petal margins; opens white (155C); matures white (155B); 38mm (1 1/2") long x 24mm (15/16") wide. PETALOIDS: Same colour as corolla; 27mm (1 1/16") long x 15mm (9/16") wide. SEPALS: horizontal, tips recurved, twisted left to right; white (155C) tipped light apple green (145B) upper surface; pink (55C) tipped light apple green (145B) lower surface; 52mm (2 1/16") long x 18mm (11/16") wide. TUBE: white (155B) dk pink (54D); medium length & thickness; 19mm (3/4") long x 7mm (1/4") wide. STAMENS extend 20mm (3/4") beyond the corolla; pink (55C) filaments; light rose (73B) anthers. PISTIL extends 33mm (1 5/16") beyond the corolla; white (155C) style; pale pink (69A) stigma. BUD: globular. FOLIAGE: dark green (136B) upper surface; medium green (138B) lower surface. Leaves are 67mm (2 5/8") long x 38mm (1 1/2") wide; ovate shaped, serrate edges, acute tips, rounded bases. Veins are light olive green (153D) & dark rose (54A), stems are dark rose (54A), branches are dark reddish purple (187B). PARENTAGE: 'Nestor-Berthe Menten' x 'Jessie Pearson'. Natural trailer. Self branching. Makes good basket. Prefers overhead filtered light, cool climate. Best bloom & foliage colour in filtered light. Tested 3 years in Koningshooikt, Belgium. Waanrode 7/5/08. Distinguished by bloom colour.

Michiels 2009 BE AFS7169.

Gitte Struck. Upright/Trailer. Single. COROLLA is quarter flared with turned under wavy petal margins; opens reddish purple (71B); matures reddish purple (70B); 11mm (7/16") long x 9mm (3/8") wide. SEPALS are horizontal, tips recurved; magenta (61C) tipped yellowish green (145A) upper surface; magenta (58B) lower surface; 18mm (11/16") long x 4mm (3/16") wide. TUBE is magenta (61C); long & thin; 16mm (5/8") long x 2mm (1/16") wide. FOLIAGE: dark green (139A) upper surface; medium green (138B) lower surface. Leaves are 71mm (2 13/16") long x 32mm (1 1/4") wide, elliptic shaped. PARENTAGE: 'Rosea' x 'White Knight's Pearl'. Distinguished by colour combination.
Struck 2005 DK AFS5806.

Glabonzer Perlen. Upright/Trailer. Double. COROLLA: half flared, turned under wavy petal margins; opens purple (N80B); matures reddish purple (N78A); 19mm (3/4") long x 17mm (5/8") wide. PETALOIDS: purple (N81B); 16mm (5/8") long x 14mm (9/16") wide. SEPALS: horizontal, tips reflexed; rose (54C) & pale pink (56D) tipped light yellowish green (149D) upper surface; pink (62B) tipped light yellowish green (149D) lower surface; 44mm (1 3/4") long x 18mm (11/16") wide. TUBE: pale pink (56D) striped rose (54C); medium length & thickness; 26mm (1") long x 10mm (3/8") wide. STAMENS extend 2mm (1/16") beyond the corolla; rose (68B) filaments; pale purple (70D) anthers. PISTIL extends 27mm (1 1/16") beyond the corolla; light rose (73C) style; pale yellow (1D) stigma. BUD: cylindrical. FOLIAGE: dark green (136A) upper surface; medium green (138A) lower surface. Leaves are 78mm (3 1/8") long x 42mm (1 5/8") wide; ovate shaped, serrate edges, acute tips, rounded bases. Veins are dark rose (180D), stems are light red purple (185D), branches are light red purple (185D) & medium green (138B). PARENTAGE: 'Alison Reynolds' x unknown. Lax upright or stiff trailer. Self branching. Makes good basket. Prefers overhead filtered light, cool climate. Best bloom & foliage colour in filtered light. Tested 5 years in Rillaar, Belgium. Waanrode 7/5/08. Distinguished by bloom colour.
Willems 2009 BE AFS7079.

Glad B. Upright. Single. COROLLA opens white; corolla is quarter flared and is 17mm long x 18mm wide. SEPALS pink, tipped green on the upper and lower surfaces; sepals are half up with recurved tips and are 30mm long x 8mm wide. TUBE pink and is 7mm long x 7mm wide. PARENTAGE 'Sophie Louise' x 'Baby Bright'.
Joiner 2006 UK BFS0038.

Glorious Glosters. Trailer. Double. COROLLA is full flared with smooth petal margins; opens purple (93A), pale lavender (69C) patches at base; matures purple (93B); 50mm (2") long x 75mm (2 15/16") wide. SEPALS are half up, tips reflexed up; white (155A) tipped green upper surface, white (155A) creped lower surface; 55mm (2 3/16") long x 24mm (15/16) wide. TUBE is pale yellowish green (149D); short with medium thickness; 20mm (13/16") long x 10mm (3/8) wide. STAMENS extend 30mm (1 3/16") below the corolla; pale lavender (69D) filaments; cream (158D) anthers. PISTIL extends 40mm (1 9/16") below the corolla; white (155A) style and white (155A) stigma. BUD is round. FOLIAGE is yellowish green (144A) edged yellow upper surface, yellowish green (144A) lower surface. Leaves are 83mm (3 1/4") long x 43mm (1 11/16") wide, ovate shaped, serrulated edges, acute tips and cordate bases. Veins are green, stems and branches are red. PARENTAGE: Sport of 'Golden Anniversary'. Natural trailer. Self branching. Makes good basket or decorative. Prefers overhead filtered light. Best bloom and foliage colour in filtered light. Tested three years in Gloucester, England. Distinguished by foliage variegation.
Hickman 2002 UK AFS4857.

Glorious Star. Upright. Double. COROLLA mauve with a slash of lilac. SEPALS white flushed pink.
Ainsworth 2004 UK.

Godelieve Elli. Upright/Trailer. Double. COROLLA is full flared with turned under wavy petal margins; opens white (155B), pink (62C) base; matures white (155B), light rose (73D) base; 23mm (15/16") long x 26mm (1") wide. PETALOIDS: white (155B), pale pink (62D) base; 12mm (1/2") long x 10mm (3/8") wide. SEPALS are half up, tips recurved up; white (155C) tipped yellowish green (150D) upper surface; pale pink (62D) tipped yellowish green (150D) lower surface; 34mm (1 5/16") long x 19mm (3/4") wide. TUBE is white (155A); medium length & thickness; 27mm (1 1/16") long x 5mm (3/16") wide. FOLIAGE: dark green (139A) upper surface; medium green (138A) lower surface. Leaves are 79mm (3 1/8") long x 42mm (1 5/8") wide, ovate shaped. PARENTAGE: 'Sofie Michiels' x 'Diana Wills'. Meise 8-14-04. Distinguished by flower colour & shape. Michiels 2005 BE AFS5761.

Godelieve van Romain. Upright. Single. COROLLA: half flared, turned under smooth petal margins; opens light reddish purple (72C), rose (55B) base; matures reddish purple (72B); 22mm (7/8") long x 17mm (11/16") wide. PETALOIDS: light reddish purple (72C); 9mm (3/8") long x 8mm (5/16") wide. SEPALS: horizontal; tips recurved; rose (55B) tipped light apple green (145B) upper surface; light rose (55B) tipped light apple green (145B) lower surface; 27mm (1 1/16") long x 8mm (5/16") wide. TUBE: rose (54C); medium length & thickness; 17mm (11/16") long x 6mm (1/4") wide. STAMENS: extend 6mm (1/4") below corolla; dark rose (67C) filaments; dark reddish purple (59A) anthers. PISTIL: extends 24mm (15/16") below the corolla; pale pink (62D) style; light yellow (1C) stigma. BUD: oblong. FOLIAGE: dark green (139A) upper surface, medium green (138B) lower surface. Leaves are 46mm (1 13/16") long x 16mm (5/8") wide, lanceolate shaped, serrulated edges, acute tips and rounded bases. Light green (138C) veins; medium green (139C) stems; medium green (138B) branches. PARENTAGE: 'Salmon Glow' x unknown. Small upright. Self branching. Makes good upright. Prefers full sun and warmclimate. Best bloom and foliage colour in bright light. Tested 3 years in Wellen, Belgium. Award at Meise, 5/7/03. Distinguished by bloom colour & shape. Van Walleghem 2004 BE AFS5417.

Godelieve Vandenbussche. Upright/Trailer. Single. COROLLA is quarter flared with turned under wavy petal margins; opens magenta (57C); matures dark rose (55A); 17mm (11/16") long x 14mm (9/16") wide. SEPALS are half down, tips reflexed; rose (54C) tipped light apple green (145B) upper surface; dark rose (54B) tipped light apple green (145B) lower surface; 24mm (15/16") long x 8mm (5/16") wide. TUBE is rose (54C); long & thick; 32mm (1 1/4") long x 8mm (5/16") wide. FOLIAGE: dark green (139A) upper surface; medium green (137C) lower surface. Leaves are 61mm (2 3/8") long x 29mm (1 1/8") wide, elliptic shaped. PARENTAGE: 'WALZ Orgelpijp' x 'Annabel'. Meise 8-14-04. Distinguished by flower shape & colour. Vandenbussche 2005 BE AFS5729.

Goke Sol. Upright/Trailer. Double. COROLLA: three quarter flared, smooth petal margins; opens dark purple (79A); matures dark reddish purple (59A); 29mm (1 1/8") long x 26mm (1") wide. SEPALS: fully up; tips reflexed; dark reddish purple (61A) upper surface; reddish purple (61B) lower surface; 41mm (1 5/8") long x 21mm (13/16") wide. TUBE: dark reddish purple (61A); medium length & thickness; 12mm (1/2") long x 7mm (1/4") wide. STAMENS: extend 12mm (1/2") below corolla; dark reddish purple (61A) filaments; dark purple (79B) anthers. PISTIL: extends 23mm (15/16") below the corolla; dark reddish purple (61A) style; light reddish purple (72C) stigma. BUD: cordate. FOLIAGE: dark green (137A) upper surface; medium green (138A) lower surface. Leaves are 67mm (2 5/8") long x 32mm (1 1/4") wide, lanceolate shaped, serrulated edges, acute tips and obtuse bases. Veins, stems & branches are green. PARENTAGE: 'Sofie Michiels' x 'Rohees Mintake'. Lax upright or stiff trailer. Makes good stiff trailer. Prefers overhead filtered light and cool climate. Best bloom and foliage colour in filtered light. Tested 4 years in Duizel, The Netherlands. Distinguished by bloom colour. Tamerus 2003 NL AFS5287.

Golden Regina. Upright. Single. COROLLA: quarter flared, turned under smooth petal margins; opens light purple (70C); matures light rose (73C); 29mm (1 1/8") long x 21mm (13/16") wide. SEPALS: horizontal; tips reflexed; light pink (49C) tipped light apple green (144D) upper surface; pale pink (56A) tipped light apple green (144D) lower surface; 36mm (1 7/16") long x 13mm (1/2") wide. TUBE: light greenish white (157C); short, medium thickness; 12mm (1/2") long x 7mm (1/4") wide. STAMENS: extend 3mm (1/8") below the corolla; magenta (63A) filaments, reddish purple (64B) anthers. PISTIL extends 34mm (1 5/16") below the corolla; pale lavender (65D) style, light yellow (1C) stigma. BUD: elongated. FOLIAGE: medium green (137B) edged yellowish green (144B) upper surface; medium green (138B) edged yellowish green (144B) lower surface. Leaves are 56mm (2 3/16") long x 30mm (1 3/16") wide, ovate shaped, serrulated edges, acute tips and rounded bases. Veins are apple green (144C), stems are plum (185C), branches are plum (185B). PARENTAGE: sport of 'Johanna Regina'. Medium upright. Makes good upright. Prefers overhead filtered light. Best bloom and foliage colour in filtered light. Tested 3 years in Koningshooikt,

Belgium. NBFK certificate at Meise. Distinguished by leaf colour. Michiels 2003 BE AFS5102.

Goldy. Upright. Single. COROLLA is quarter flared, bell shaped; opens reddish purple (71B); matures dark rose (54A); 16mm (5/8") long x 13mm (1/2") wide. SEPALS are horizontal, tips recurved; white (155D) upper surface, light rose (58D) lower surface; 25mm (1") long x 6mm (1/4") wide. TUBE is white (155D); 13mm (1/2") long x 6mm (1/4") wide. FOLIAGE: apple green (144C) upper surface; light yellowish green (146D) lower surface. PARENTAGE: 'Lookout' x 'Cherry'. Distinguished by profuse blooms & golden foliage colour. Goodwin 2006 UK AFS6044.

Gonard Tamerus. Trailer. Single. COROLLA is quarter flared with smooth petal margins; opens purple (83A); matures purple (71A); 22mm (7/8") long x 17mm (11/16") wide. SEPALS are fully up, tips reflexed; dark rose (67C) upper surface; reddish purple (67A) lower surface; 30mm (13/16") long x 9mm (3/8") wide. TUBE is dark rose (67C); medium length and thickness; 22mm (7/8") long x 7mm (1/4") thick. STAMENS extend 22mm (7/8") beyond the corolla; purple (79C) filaments and anthers. PISTIL extends 37mm (1 7/16") beyond the corolla; reddish purple (72B) style, pale yellow (5D) stigma. BUD is ovate, pointed. FOLIAGE is dark green (137A) upper surface, medium green (138A) lower surface. Leaves are 66mm (2 5/8") long x 27mm (1 1/16") wide, elliptic shaped, serrated edges, acute tips and obtuse bases. Veins, stems and branches are green. PARENTAGE: 'Rohees King' x 'Anta'. Natural trailer. Makes good basket. Prefers overhead filtered light and cool climate. Best bloom colour in filtered light. Tested four years in Duizel, The Netherlands. Distinguished by bloom colour. Tamerus 2002 NL AFS4996.

Good Girl. Upright. Single. COROLLA: quarter flared, bell shaped; opens violet (86B); matures light purple (78B); 20mm (3/4") long x 13mm (1/2") wide. SEPALS: horizontal, tips recurved; light pink (62C) upper & lower surfaces; 32mm (1 1/4") long x 10mm (3/8") wide. TUBE: pink (62C); 10mm (3/8") long x 6mm (1/4") wide. FOLIAGE is greenish yellow (144A) upper surface; greenish yellow (144B) lower surface. PARENTAGE: 'Julie Ann Goodwin' x 'Shellford'. Goodwin 2008 UK AFS6937.

Gooseberry Pearl. Trailer. Single. COROLLA: unflared, bell shaped, turned up petal margins; opens light pink (65C), matures light pink (65B); 15mm (9/16") long x 11mm (7/16") wide. SEPALS: half down; tips recurved; pale pink (56D) upper & lower surfaces; 27mm (1 1/16") long x 6mm (1/4") wide. TUBE: pale pink (56D), medium length & thin; 17mm (11/16") long x 5mm (3/16") wide. STAMENS: extend 15mm (9/16") below the corolla; pale pink (56D) filaments, white (155C) anthers. PISTIL extends 22mm (7/8") below the corolla; pale pink (56D) style, white (155C) stigma. BUD: angular. FOLIAGE: medium green (138A) upper surface, medium green (138B) lower surface. Leaves are 47mm (1 7/8") long x 25mm (1") wide, ovate shaped, serrated edges, acute tips and rounded bases. Veins & stems are light green (138C), branches are medium green (138B). PARENTAGE: ('Gooseberry Hill' x 'Whiteknight's Pearl') x 'Margaret brown'. Natural trailer. Self branching. Makes good basket. Prefers overhead filtered light. Cold weather hardy to 27° F. Best bloom and foliage colour in filtered light. Tested 4 years Luton, Bedfordshire, England. Distinguished by waxy light pink colour and profuse blooms. Hutchins 2003 UK AFS5079.

Gordon Goodwin. Upright. Single. COROLLA: Quarter flared, bell shaped; opens & matures red (45B); 19mm (3/4") long x 15mm (9/16") wide. SEPALS: half down, tips reflexed; peach (37B) tipped dark green (140A) upper & lower surfaces; 16mm (5/8") long x 6mm (1/4") wide. TUBE: cream (158C); medium length, thick; 9mm (5/16") long x 6mm (1/4") wide. FOLIAGE is dark green (137A) upper surface; light olive green (148C) lower surface. PARENTAGE: [('F. magdalenae' x 'F. fulgens rubra grandiflora) x 'Wendy Van Wanten'] x 'Prince Syray'. Koerts T. 2007 NL AFS6445.

Gota. Upright. Single. COROLLA is quarter flared, bell shaped with turned under petal margins; opens dark reddish purple (64A); matures dark reddish purple (61A); 18mm (11/16") long x 21mm (13/16") wide. SEPALS are half up, tips recurved up; pale lavender (65D) upper surface; rose (63C) lower surface; 25mm (1") long x 10mm (3/8") wide. TUBE is light pink (65C); medium length & thickness; 10mm (3/8") long x 9mm (3/8") wide. FOLIAGE: dark green (147A) upper surface; medium green (147B) lower surface. Leaves are 58mm (2 5/16") long x 34mm (1 5/16") wide, ovate shaped.

PARENTAGE: 'Rohees King' x 'North Way'. Nomination by N.K.V.F. as recommendable cultivar. Distinguished by flower colour. Tamerus 2005 NL AFS5800.

Gouden Pater. Upright/Trailer. Semi Double. COROLLA is three quarter flared with turned under wavy petal margins; opens light magenta (66D), matures light purple (74C); 25mm (1") long x 35 mm (1 3/8") wide. SEPALS are half down, tips reflexed; reddish purple (61B) upper surface, magenta (63A) lower surface; 32mm (1 1/4") long x 20mm (13/16") wide. TUBE is rose (61D), medium length and thickness; 20mm (13/16") long x 7mm (1/4") wide. STAMENS extend 8mm (5/16") beyond the corolla; magenta (58B) filaments, dark reddish purple (59A) anthers. PISTIL extends 30mm (1 3/16") below the corolla; dark rose (58C) style; grayish yellow (160A) stigma. BUD is ovate, pointed. FOLIAGE is grayish green (189A) upper surface, medium green (147B) lower surface. Leaves are 56mm (2 3/16") long x 35mm (1 3/8") wide, ovate shaped, serrulated edges, acute tips and rounded bases. Veins are apple green (144C), stems are dark red (53A), branches are dark reddish purple (187C). PARENTAGE: Sport of 'Figaro'. Lax upright or stiff trailer. Makes good basket. Prefers overhead filtered light. Best bloom and foliage colour in filtered light. Tested three years in Berlaar, Belgium. Certificate N.B.F.K. at Meise. Distinguished by bloom colour, strong growth. Geerts J. 2002 BE AFS4920.

Graaf van Bamberg. Upright/Trailer. Single. COROLLA: half flared, turned under wavy petal margins; opens purple (71A); matures reddish purple (67A); 19mm (3/4") long x 16mm (5/8") wide. SEPALS: half up, tips recurved up; red (53C) upper surface; rose (52B) lower surface; 27mm (1 1/16") long x 11mm (7/16") wide. TUBE: red (53D); short, medium thickness; 9mm (5/16") long x 5mm (3/16") wide. STAMENS extend 14mm (9/16") beyond the corolla; magenta (63A) filaments; reddish purple (67A) anthers. PISTIL extends 26mm (1") beyond the corolla; magenta (61C) style; dark rose (58C) stigma. BUD: globular. FOLIAGE: dark green (137A) upper surface; medium green (138B) lower surface. Leaves are 39mm (1 1/2") long x 26mm (1") wide; ovate shaped, serrulate edges, obtuse tips, rounded bases. Veins are reddish purple (186B), stems are plum (185C), branches are plum (185C) & light green (138D). PARENTAGE: 'Pink La Campanella' x 'Maxima'. Lax upright or stiff

trailer. Self branching. Makes good upright. Prefers overhead filtered light, cool climate. Best bloom & foliage colour in filtered light. Tested 3 years in Opglabbeek, Belgium. Waanrode 9/20/08. Distinguished by bloom colour. Cuppens 2009 BE AFS7063.

Grace Bell. Single. COROLLA white splashed pink. SEPALS pink tipped green. PARENTAGE sport of 'Leonora'. Bielby/Oxtoby 2007 UK.

Grady Alice. Upright/Trailer. Double. COROLLA: three quarter flared, ruffled, turned up smooth petal margins; opens magenta (57B), veined red; matures magenta (58B) veined red; 20mm (13/16") long x 35mm (1 3/8") wide. PETALOIDS: magenta (57B) splashed pale pink (62D); 20mm (13/16") long x 10mm (3/8") wide. SEPALS: half up; tips recurved up; half twist counterclockwise; cream (159D), tipped green upper & lower surfaces; 40mm(1 9/16") long x 12mm (1/2") wide. TUBE: cream (158D); long, medium width; 20mm (13/16") long x 7mm (1/4") wide. STAMENS: extend 25mm (1") below corolla; light pink (62B) filaments; pale pink (49D) anthers. PISTIL: extends 30mm (1 3/16") below the corolla, white (155D) style; yellowish white (158A) stigma. BUD: medium, elongated. FOLIAGE: medium green (146A) upper surface, yellowish green (146B) lower surface. Leaves are 45mm (1 3/4") long x 30mm (1 3/16") wide, ovate shaped, serrated edges, acute tips and cordate bases. Veins & stems are green; branches are brown. PARENTAGE: 'Pink La Campanella' x 'Marcus Graham'. Lax upright or stiff trailer. Self branching. Makes good basket or standard. Prefers overhead filtered light and warm climate. Heat tolerant if shaded. Cold weather hardy to 32⁰ F. Best bloom colour in bright light. Tested 3 years in Walthamstow, London, England. Distinguished by magenta splashed white colour in petaloids. Allsop M. 2004 UK AFS5379.

Grand Cru. Trailer. Single. COROLLA: quarter flared, bell shape, wavy petal margins; opens orange (34C); matures orange (41B); 19mm (3/4") long, 13mm (1/2") wide. SEPALS: horizontal; tips recurved; light apple green (145C), tipped yellowish green (145A), upper & lower surfaces; 24mm (15/16") long x 9mm (3/8") wide. TUBE: light apple green (145C); long, thick; 31mm (1 1/4") long x 10mm (3/8") wide. STAMENS: extend 7mm (1/4") below

corolla; rose (52B) filaments; cream (11D) anthers. PISTIL: extends 9mm (3/8") below the corolla; light pink (49C) style; light yellow green (150C) stigma. BUD: long TUBE, ovate, pointed. FOLIAGE: medium green (146A) upper surface; yellow green (146C) lower surface. Leaves are 54mm (2 1/8") long x 36mm (1 7/16") wide, cordate shaped, serrated edges, acute tips and cordate bases. Light yellow green veins, stems & branches. PARENTAGE: 'John Maynard Scales' x ('Jülchen' x 'Smoky'). Natural trailer. Self branching. Makes good basket. Prefers overhead filtered light. Heat tolerant if shaded. Best bloom and foliage colour in filtered light. Tested 4 years in Lisse, The Netherlands. Distinguished by unique shape & colour of flower.
de Graaff 2004 NL AFS5608.

Grandad's Delightful Ribbans. Upright/Trailer. Semi Double. COROLLA is three quarter flared with smooth turned under petal margins; opens reddish purple (66A); matures magenta (57B); 20mm (13/16") long x 30mm (1 3/16") wide. PETALOIDS are same colour as corolla; 8mm (5/16") long x 4mm (3/16") wide. SEPALS are fully up, tips recurved; pink (52D) tipped green upper and lower surfaces; 35mm (1 3/8") long x 12mm (1/2") wide. TUBE is pink (52D), medium length and thick; 10mm 3/8") long x 7mm (1/4") wide. STAMENS extend 15mm (5/8") below the corolla; pink (62A) filaments and magenta (57A) anthers. PISTIL extends 30mm (1 3/16") below the corolla; rose (65A) style and yellowish white (158A) stigma. BUD is medium, elongated. FOLIAGE is medium green (146A) on upper surface and yellowish green (146B) on lower surface. Leaves are 70mm (2 3/4") long x 35mm (1 3/8") wide, cordate shaped, serrulated edges, acute tips and cordate bases. Veins are green; stems brown; branches are red. PARENTAGE: 'Pink La Campanella' x 'Marcus Graham'. Lax upright or stiff trailer. Self branching. Makes good basket or upright. Prefers overhead filtered light and warm climate. Heat tolerant if shaded. Hardy to 32°F. Best bloom colour in bright light. Tested three years in Walthamstow, London, England. Distinguished by profuse blooms and bloom colour combination.
Allsop 2002 UK AFS4814.

Gratia Dei. Upright. Semi Double. COROLLA: half flared, petticoat shape; opens reddish purple (71B); matures magenta (61C); 22mm (7/8") long x 26mm (1") wide. PETALOIDS: magenta (61C); 18mm (11/16")

long x 18mm (11/16") wide. SEPALS: horizontal, tips recurved; pale pink (49D) upper surface; very pale orange (27D) lower surface; 28mm (1 1/8") long x 14mm (9/16") wide. TUBE: pale yellow (158B); 12mm (7/16") long x 8mm (5/16") wide. FOLIAGE is medium green (146A) upper surface; medium green (138B) lower surface. PARENTAGE: 'Showtime' x unknown.
Simon 2008 AFS6842.

Gravette. Upright. Single. COROLLA: Unflared; smooth petal margins; opens purple (83B); matures dark reddish purple (60B); 27mm (1 1/16") long x 11mm (7/16") wide. SEPALS: half down, tips recurved; dark red (47A) upper surface; red (46C) lower surface; 33mm (1 5/16") long x 6mm (1/4") wide. TUBE: dark red (47A); medium length & thickness; 19mm (3/4") long x 6mm (1/4") wide. FOLIAGE is dark green (147A) upper surface; medium green (147B) lower surface. PARENTAGE: 'Henri Massé' x 'F. regia reitzii 4514'.
Massé 2007 FR AFS6481.

Greti Peeters. Trailer. Double. COROLLA is three quarter flared with turned under wavy petal margins; opens light purple (78C), edged purple (82B), pale purple (75C) base; matures light purple (78B); 34mm (1 5/16") long x 32mm (1 1/4") wide. PETALOIDS: light purple (80C), pale purple (80D) base; 13mm (1/2") long x 12mm (1/2") wide. SEPALS are half up, tips recurved up; pink (55C), tipped light yellowish green (149B) upper surface; pink (55C), tipped light yellowish green (149B) lower surface; 40mm (1 9/16") long x 16mm (5/8") wide. TUBE is white (155C); medium length & thickness; 15mm (9/16") long x 7mm (1/4") wide. FOLIAGE: dark green (139A) upper surface; medium green (138A) lower surface. Leaves are 79mm (3 1/8") long x 43mm (1 11/16") wide, ovate shaped. PARENTAGE: 'Sofie Michiels' x 'Weleveld'. Meise 8-14-04. Distinguished by flower colour combination.
Michiels 2005 BE AFS5758.

Grietus Luisman. Upright/Trailer. Semi Double. COROLLA: 3 quarter flared; opens violet (83D); matures violet (85A); 18mm (11/16") long x 24mm (15/16") wide. SEPALS: half up; tips reflexed up; magenta (58B) upper & lower surfaces; 29mm (1 1/8") long x 7mm (1/4") wide. TUBE: light green (145D); long & thin; 24mm (15/16") long x 5mm (3/16") wide. FOLIAGE is dark green (137A) upper surface; medium green (138B) lower surface. PARENTAGE: 'Roesse Tucana' x 'Roesse Parel'. Roes 2007 NL AFS6308.

Grossglockner. Upright/Trailer. Semi Double. COROLLA rhodonite red (51a); corolla is quarter flared. SEPALS geranium lake (47d) on the upper and lower surfaces; SEPALS are half up with recurved tips. TUBE geranium lake (47d). PARENTAGE 'Buttercup' x 'Checkerboard'. Klemm 2009 AT BFS0130.

Grumpy Gord. COROLLA deep cerise. SEPALS pale pink. Reynolds G. 2003 UK.

Grundlsee. Upright/Trailer. Double. COROLLA is full flared with smooth petal margins, very fluffy; opens and matures pale pink (56D) veined dark rose (55A); 20mm (13/16") long x 45mm (1 3/4") wide. PETALOIDS are dark rose (55A); 10mm (3/8") x 10mm (3/8"). SEPALS are half down, tips reflexed; rose (55B) tipped green upper surface, dark rose (55A) lower surface; 22mm (7/8") long x 16mm (5/8") wide. TUBE is rose (55B); short, medium thickness; 8mm (5/16") long x 7mm (1/4") thick. STAMENS extend 20mm (13/16") beyond the corolla; dark rose (54A) filaments, tan (166B) anthers. PISTIL extends 38mm (1 1/2") beyond the corolla; rose (54C) style, tan (166C) stigma. BUD is globular. FOLIAGE is dark green (136A) upper surface, dark green (136B) lower surface. Leaves are 55mm (2 3/16") long x 32mm (1 1/4") wide, cordate shaped, serrulated edges, acute tips and cordate bases. Veins and branches are green, stems are green-brown. PARENTAGE: 'Swingtime' x 'Dollar Princess'. Lax upright or stiff trailer. Self branching. Makes good upright. Prefers overhead filtered light. Best bloom colour in bright light. Tested six years in Amstetten, Austria. Distinguished by full, compact flower, flower/leaf colour combination. Gindl 2002 AT AFS5049.

Gudrun Kleinau. Upright/Trailer. Double. COROLLA: three quarter flared, turned under wavy petal margins; opens rose (52C) & magenta (61C); matures dark rose (58C) & reddish purple (64B); 34mm (1 3/8 ") long x 32mm (1 1/4 ") wide. PETALOIDS: coral (37A) & reddish purple (61B); 16mm (5/8") long x 11mm (7/16") wide. SEPALS: fully up, tips recurved, twisted left to right; white (155B) & rose (52C) tipped yellowish green (144B) upper surface; pink (49A) tipped

yellowish green (144B) lower surface; 45mm (1 3/4") long x 17mm (5/8") wide. TUBE: white (155B) & rose (52C); medium length & thickness; 17mm (5/8") long x 7mm (1/4") wide. STAMENS extend 8mm (5/16") beyond the corolla; rose (68C) filaments; reddish purple (59B) anthers. PISTIL extends 21mm (13/16") beyond the corolla; light coral (38A) style; pale yellow (2D) stigma. BUD: globular. FOLIAGE: dark green (137A) upper surface; medium green (138B) lower surface. Leaves are 62mm (2 7/16") long x 37mm (1 7/16") wide; ovate shaped, serrulate edges, acute tips, rounded bases. Veins are olive green (153B), stems are very dark reddish purple (186A), branches are light red purple (185D) & light green (139D). PARENTAGE: 'Manfried Kleinau' x 'First Lord'. Lax upright or stiff trailer. Self branching. Makes good basket or upright. Prefers overhead filtered light, cool climate. Best bloom & foliage colour in filtered light. Tested 3 years in Koningshooikt, Belgium. Waanrode 7/5/08. Distinguished by bloom colour combination & profuse blooms. Michiels 2009 BE AFS7170.

Gully Ridge. Upright/Trailer. Double. COROLLA: half flared, turned under wavy petal margins; opens dark reddish purple (61A); matures reddish purple (61B); 21mm (13/16 ") long x 19mm (3/4 ") wide. PETALOIDS: Same colour as corolla; 15mm (9/16") long x 12mm (7/16") wide. SEPALS: horizontal, tips recurved; pale pink (56A) tipped light green (145D) upper surface; dark rose (54A) tipped light green (145D) lower surface; 27mm (1 1/16") long x 12mm (7/16") wide. TUBE: magenta (61C); medium length & thickness; 16mm (5/8") long x 6mm (1/4") wide. STAMENS extend 16mm (5/8") beyond the corolla; reddish purple (70B) filaments; purple (77A) anthers. PISTIL extends 28mm (1 1/8") beyond the corolla; light reddish purple (72C) style; pale lavender (69D) stigma. BUD: bulbous. FOLIAGE: dark green (139A) upper surface; medium green (138B) lower surface. Leaves are 67mm (2 5/8") long x 37mm (1 7/16") wide; ovate shaped, serrate edges, acute tips, rounded bases. Veins are plum (185B), stems are very dark reddish purple (186A), branches are plum (185C) & light green (138C). PARENTAGE: 'Manfried Kleinau' x 'Berba's Coronation'. Lax upright or stiff trailer. Self branching. Makes good basket or upright. Prefers overhead filtered light, cool climate. Best bloom & foliage colour in filtered light. Tested 3 years in

Koningshooikt, Belgium. Waanrode 8/9/08. Distinguished by bloom colour. Michiels 2009 BE AFS7171.

Gunar Reich. Upright/Trailer. Double. COROLLA: half flared, turned under wavy petal margins; opens reddish purple (N80B); matures light purple (N78B); 26mm (1") long x 18mm (11/16") wide. PETALOIDS: light purple (N80C); 17mm (5/8") long x 9mm (5/16") wide. SEPALS: half up, tips recurved up; pale rose (73D) & light rose (73C) upper surface; pale lavender (69C) lower surface; 48mm (1 7/8") long x 13mm (1/2") wide. TUBE: pale rose (73D); medium length & thickness; 12mm (7/16") long x 6mm (1/4") wide. STAMENS extend 19mm (3/4") beyond the corolla; light reddish purple (73A) filaments; dark purple (79B) anthers. PISTIL extends 27mm (1 1/16") beyond the corolla; pale purple (75C) style; dark rose (64C) stigma. BUD: elongated. FOLIAGE: dark green (139A) upper surface; medium green (139C) lower surface. Leaves are 71mm (2 13/16") long x 34mm (1 3/8") wide; ovate shaped, serrulate edges, acute tips, rounded bases. Veins are plum (184C), stems are plum (185C), branches are plum (185C) & medium green (139C). PARENTAGE: 'Niagara Falls' x 'Ector's Ann Gaby'. Lax upright or stiff trailer. Self branching. Makes good basket or upright. Prefers overhead filtered light, cool climate. Best bloom & foliage colour in filtered light. Tested 3 years in Koningshooikt, Belgium. Waanrode 8/9/08. Distinguished by bloom colour combination & profuse blooms. Michiels 2009 BE AFS7172.

Guniwirt. Upright. Double. COROLLA rose red and violet; corolla is three quarter flared. SEPALS rose red on the upper and lower surfaces; sepals are –horizontally held with recurved tips. TUBE rose red. PARENTAGE 'Hanau' x 'Mission Bells'. Klemm 2008 AT BFS0074.

Gunnar Hagedorn. Trailer. Double. COROLLA: three quarter flared, turned under wavy petal margins; opens light reddish purple (73A) & purple (77A); matures reddish purple (64B) & dark reddish purple (61A); 29mm (1 1/8") long x 21mm (13/16 ") wide. PETALOIDS: Same colour as corolla; 18mm (11/16") long x 16mm (5/8") wide. SEPALS: half down, tips recurved; reddish purple (60D) upper surface; magenta (59D) lower surface; 35mm (1 3/8") long x 16mm (5/8") wide. TUBE: dark rose (54B); medium length & thickness; 23mm (7/8") long x 5mm

(3/16") wide. STAMENS extend 9mm (5/16") beyond the corolla; reddish purple (70B) filaments; dark purple (79A) anthers. PISTIL extends 9mm (5/16") beyond the corolla; magenta (71C) style; yellowish white (4D) stigma. BUD: bulbous. FOLIAGE: dark green (137A) upper surface; medium green (138B) lower surface. Leaves are 85mm (3 3/8") long x 38mm (1 1/2") wide; elliptic shaped, serrulate edges, acute tips, rounded bases. Veins are reddish purple (186B), stems are light red purple (185D), branches are plum (185C) & light green (139D). PARENTAGE: 'Manfried Kleinau' x 'Laura Biolcati-Rinaldi'. Natural trailer. Self branching. Makes good basket. Prefers overhead filtered light, cool climate. Best bloom & foliage colour in filtered light. Tested 3 years in Koningshooikt, Belgium. Waanrode 8/9/08. Distinguished by bloom colour combination. Michiels 2009 BE AFS7173.

Gustje Krekels. Upright. Single. COROLLA: quarter flared, smooth petal margins; opens violet (75A); matures light purple (75B); 24mm (15/16") long x 17mm (11/16") wide. SEPALS: half up; tips reflexed up; white (155B) upper surface; pale pink (62D) lower surface;34mm (1 5/16") long x 8mm (5/16") wide. TUBE: white (155B); medium length & thickness; 10mm (3/8") long x 6mm (1/4") wide. STAMENS: extend 12mm (1/2") below corolla; rose (68C) filaments, dark reddish purple (60A) anthers. PISTIL: extends 24mm (15/16") below the corolla; light rose (68D) style & stigma. BUD: cordate. FOLIAGE: dark green (137A) upper surface; medium green (138B) lower surface. Leaves are 66mm (2 5/8") long x 36mm (1 7/16") wide, ovate shaped, serrated edges, acute tips and obtuse bases. Veins, stems & branches are green. PARENTAGE: 'Sophie Michiels' x 'Veenlust'. Medium upright. Makes good upright or standard. Prefers overhead filtered light and cool climate. Best bloom and foliage colour in filtered light. Tested 4 years in Reusel, The Netherlands. Distinguished by bloom & foliage combination. van Eijk 2003 NL AFS5251.

Guurtje. Upright/Trailer. Double. COROLLA is three quarter flared with smooth petal margins; opens light reddish purple (73A), light rose (73B) & light purple (86C); matures light rose (73B) & dark purple (78A); 34mm (1 5/16") long x 34mm (1 5/16") wide. SEPALS are half down, tips recurved; rose (54C) & dark rose (54B) upper surface; rose (64D) lower surface; 35mm (1 3/8") long x 18mm (11/16") wide. TUBE is rose (54C) &

dark rose (54B); medium length & thickness; 15mm (9/16") long x 9mm (3/8") wide. FOLIAGE: dark green (147A) upper surface; medium green (147B) lower surface. Leaves are 60mm (2 3/8") long x 30mm (1 3/16") wide, ovate shaped. PARENTAGE: 'Southgate' x 'Greg Walker'. V.K.C. Aalsmeer, 8-19-89. Distinguished by flower colour. Krom 2005 NL AFS5821.

Gwendoline Clare. Trailer. Single. COROLLA is half flared; opens pale lavender (69C); matures pale purple (76C); 15mm (9/16") long x 15mm (9/16") wide. SEPALS are half up, tips recurved up; dark rose (54B) tipped light apple green (145B) upper surface, and rose (51C) tipped light apple green (145B) lower surface; 27mm (1 1/16") long x 7mm (1/4") wide. TUBE is rose (51C); 8mm (5/16") long x 4mm (1/8") wide. FOLIAGE is dark green (137A) upper surface; medium green (138B) lower surface. PARENTAGE: 'Rosea' x 'Berba's Inge Mariel'. Meise 8/13/05. Distinguished by bloom shape & colour. Michiels 2006 BE AFS6039.

Hage Assepoester. Upright. Single. COROLLA: unflared, closed shape; opens light purple (86C); matures violet (77B); 24mm (15/16") long x 26mm (1") wide. SEPALS: half up, tips recurved up; light pink (49C) upper surface; pink (54D) lower surface; 37mm (1 7/16") long x 11mm (7/16") wide. TUBE: light pink (36C); 10mm (3/8") long x 6mm (1/4") wide. FOLIAGE is medium green (143A) upper surface; yellowish green (146B) lower surface. PARENTAGE: 'Ria v.d. Leest' x 'Doreen Redfern'. Nomination by NKVF as Recommendable Cultivar. Rijkers 2008 NL AFS6807.

Hage Astrid. Upright. Double. COROLLA: Unflared, compact; opens red (52A); matures reddish purple (58A); 23mm (7/8") long x 25mm (1") wide. PETALOIDS: same colour as corolla; 27mm (1 1/16") long x 30mm (1 3/16") wide. SEPALS: horizontal, tips recurved; dark rose (55A) upper surface; pink (52D) lower surface; 40mm (1 9/16") long x 11mm (7/16") wide. TUBE: pink (55C); medium length & thickness; 39mm (1 1/2") long x 8mm (5/16") wide. FOLIAGE is dark green (147A) upper surface; yellowish green (146B) lower surface. PARENTAGE: 'Veenlust' x 'WALZ Harp'. Rijkers 2007 NL AFS6460.

Hage Blauwbaard. Upright/Trailer. Double. COROLLA: quarter flared, ovate shape; opens

violet (76A); matures violet (84A); 20mm (3/4") long x 23mm (7/8") wide. SEPALS: fully up, tips recurved; white (155B) tipped pale yellowish green (150D) upper surface; white (155B) lower surface; 38mm (1 1/2") long x 14mm (9/16") wide. TUBE: white (155A); 11mm (7/16") long x 6mm (1/4") wide. FOLIAGE is medium green (137B) upper surface; light green (137D) lower surface. PARENTAGE: 'Ria v.d. Leest' x 'Bianca'. Rijkers 2008 NL AFS6809.

Hage Langnek. Upright. Single. COROLLA: quarter flared; opens magenta (67B); matures reddish purple (74B); 27mm (1 1/16") long x 30mm (1 3/16") wide. SEPALS: horizontal, tips recurved; light pink (62C) tipped pale yellowish green (154D) upper surface; pink (58D) lower surface; 41mm (1 5/8") long x 13mm (1/2") wide. TUBE: pale pink (62D); 55mm (2 3/16") long x 6mm (1/4") wide. FOLIAGE is dark green (147A) upper surface; medium green (147B) lower surface. PARENTAGE: 'WALZ Harp' x unknown. Rijkers 2008 NL AFS6810.

Hage Michiel. Upright. Single. COROLLA: Half flared; opens magenta (57C); matures magenta (57A); 32mm (1 1/4") long x 35mm (1 3/8") wide. SEPALS: half up, tips reflexed up; rose (52C) upper surface; rose (47C) lower surface; 45mm (1 3/4") long x 10mm (3/8") wide. TUBE: light pink (49C); medium length & thickness; 41mm (1 5/8") long x 9mm (5/16") wide. FOLIAGE is dark green (147A) upper surface; yellowish green (146B) lower surface. PARENTAGE: 'Veenlust' x 'WALZ Harp'. Rijkers 2007 NL AFS6458.

Hage Pinkeltje. Upright. Single. COROLLA: unflared; opens light purple (81C) veined pink; matures reddish purple (80B); 20mm (3/4") long x 18mm (11/16") wide. SEPALS: horizontal, tips reflexed; reddish purple (61B) upper surface; magenta (61C) lower surface; 35mm (1 3/8") long x 10mm (3/8") wide. TUBE: dark reddish purple (60C); 16mm (5/8") long x 6mm (1/4") wide. FOLIAGE is dark green (147A) upper surface; olive green (148A) lower surface. PARENTAGE: 'Ria v.d. Leest' x 'Henkelly's Billy'. Nomination by NKVF as Recommendable Cultivar. Rijkers 2008 NL AFS6806.

Hage Pocahontas. Trailer. Single. COROLLA: quarter flared, bell shaped; wavy petal margins; opens rose (68B) edged purple

(77A); matures reddish purple (71B); 20mm (3/4") long x 20mm (3/4") wide. SEPALS: half up, tips recurved up; magenta (58B) tipped light yellowish green (149C) upper surface; magenta (58B) lower surface; 33mm (1 5/16") long x 11mm (7/16") wide. TUBE: pink (62C); medium length & thickness; 12mm (7/16") long x 5mm (3/16") wide. STAMENS extend 3mm (1/8") beyond the corolla; pink (62A) filaments; magenta (63B) anthers. PISTIL extends 16mm (5/8") beyond the corolla; magenta (63B) style; cream (159D) stigma. BUD: ovate. FOLIAGE: dark green (147A) upper surface; medium green (147B) with red glow lower surface. Leaves are 64mm (2 1/2") long x 38mm (1 1/2") wide; elliptic shaped, serrulate edges, acute tips, rounded bases. Veins are dark green, stems & branches are red. PARENTAGE: ('Ria van de Leest' x 'Paulus') x ('Ria van de Leest' x 'Paulus'). Natural trailer. Self branching. Makes good basket. Prefers overhead filtered light. Best bloom & foliage colour in bright or filtered light. Tested 3 years in Erp, The Netherlands. Nominated by NKvF as recommendable cultivar. Distinguished by corolla petal shape & large splitting pistil.
Rijkers 2009 NL AFS7039.

Hage Roodkapje. Trailer. Single. COROLLA: half flared, bell shaped; opens white (155A) veined red (53B); matures white (155A); 28mm (1 1/8") long x 28mm (1 1/8") wide. SEPALS: half up, tips recurved up; red (52A) upper & lower surfaces; 47mm (1 7/8") long x 13mm (1/2") wide. TUBE: red (52A); 11mm (7/16") long x 5mm (3/16") wide. FOLIAGE is dark green (147A) upper surface; medium green (147B) lower surface. PARENTAGE: 'Ria v.d. Leest' x 'Anna Pauline'.
Rijkers 2008 NL AFS6805.

Hage Stefan. Trailer. Double. COROLLA: Half flared, bell shaped; opens & matures pale purple (88D); 35mm (1 3/8") long x 26mm (1") wide. PETALOIDS: same colour as corolla; 23mm (7/8") long x 12mm (7/16") wide. SEPALS: half down, tips reflexed; white (155D) upper surface; light pink (65B) lower surface; 41mm (1 5/8") long x 13mm (1/2") wide. TUBE: white (155D); medium length & thickness; 27mm (1 1/16") long x 7mm (1/4") wide. FOLIAGE is medium green (147B) upper surface; light olive green (147C) lower surface. PARENTAGE: 'Ria van de Leest' x 'Bianca'. Nomination by NKvF as recommendable cultivar.
Rijkers 2007 NL AFS6459.

Hage Zwartrok. Upright/Trailer. Semi Double. COROLLA: quarter flared, bell shape; opens dark purple (79A); matures purple (79C); 16mm (5/8") long x 19mm (3/4") wide. PETALOIDS: Same colour as corolla; 14mm (9/16") long x 10mm (3/8") wide. SEPALS: horizontal, tips recurved; reddish purple (61B) upper & lower surfaces; 36mm (1 7/16") long x 11mm (7/16") wide. TUBE: magenta (63A); 17mm (5/8") long x 7mm (1/4") wide. FOLIAGE is yellowish green (144A) upper surface; medium green (147B) lower surface. PARENTAGE: 'Ria v.d. Leest' x 'Roesse Blacky'.
Rijkers 2008 NL AFS6808.

Han van Eijk. Upright. Semi Double. COROLLA is three quarter flared with smooth petal margins; opens reddish orange (42A); matures red orange (42B); 11mm (7/16") long x 19mm (3/4") wide. SEPALS are fully up, tips reflexed; rose (64D) tipped green upper surface; light orange (41C) tipped green lower surface; 16mm (5/8") long x 9mm (3/8") wide. TUBE is rose (64D); short & thick; 14mm (9/16") long x 7mm (1/4") wide. FOLIAGE: medium green (137B) upper surface; medium green (138B) lower surface. Leaves are 46mm (1 13/16") long x 31mm (1 1/4") wide, ovate shaped. PARENTAGE: 'Roesse Carme' x ('Swanley Gem' x 'Eisvogel'). Distinguished by bloom & foliage combination.
van Eijk 2005 NL AFS5897.

Hannah Rogers. Upright. Single. COROLLA white. SEPALS white.
Evans 2003 UK.

Hannah Suttner. Upright. Single. COROLLA: Quarter flared; opens violet blue (91B); matures light violet (84B); 30mm (1 3/16") long x 35mm (1 3/8") wide. SEPALS: half up, tips recurved up; light pink (65B) upper surface; white (N155C), red (N57B) base lower surface; 42mm (1 5/8") long x 16mm (5/8") wide. TUBE: white (N155C) blushed light pink; short & thick; 12mm (7/16") long x 10mm (3/8") wide. FOLIAGE is medium green (137B) upper surface; medium green (138B) lower surface. PARENTAGE: 'Lorna Swinbank' x 'Carla Johnston'.
Burkhart 2007 DE AFS6493.

Hans Larsen. Trailer. Single. COROLLA is half flared; opens dark purple (86A) with reddish purple (64B) base; matures purple (71A); 28mm (1 1/8") long x 25mm (1") wide. PETALOIDS are dark purple (86A) with reddish purple (64B) base; 19mm (3/4") long

x11mm (7/16") wide. SEPALS are horizontal, tips recurved; reddish purple (61B) upper surface; reddish purple (64B) lower surface; 39mm (1 1/2") long x 14mm (9/16") wide. TUBE is dark reddish purple (60B); 16mm (5/8") long x 6mm (1/4") wide. FOLIAGE is dark green (136A) upper surface; medium green (138B) lower surface. PARENTAGE: 'Roesse Blacky' x 'Rohees Alioth'. Meise 8/13/05. Distinguished by bloom shape & colour.
Michiels 2006 BE AFS6030.

Happy René. Upright/Trailer. Single. COROLLA is quarter flared with smooth petal margins; opens orange (32A), blushed reddish purple (67B) to dark purple (79A); matures orange (32A), blushed reddish purple (67B); 20mm (13/16") long x 8mm (5/16") wide. SEPALS are half down, tips reflexed; coral (39B) edged light coral (38A) upper surface; light orange (41C) lower surface; 25mm (1") long x 7mm (1/4") wide. TUBE is pale orange (29D); long & thin; 35mm (1 3/8") long x 4mm (3/16") wide. FOLIAGE: dark green (137A) upper surface; medium green (138B) lower surface. Leaves are 55mm (2 3/16") long x 35mm (1 3/8") wide, cordate shaped. PARENTAGE: 'Papa René' x 'Prince Syray'. Distinguished by flower colour & shape.
Koerts T. 2005 NL AFS5776.

Harbour Lites. Upright/Trailer. Single. COROLLA: quarter flared, smooth petal margins; opens & matures white (155D) veined reddish purple (66A); 25mm (1") long x 19mm (3/4") wide. SEPALS: half up; tips recurved up; reddish purple (67A) upper surface; reddish purple (66A) lower surface; 25mm (1") long x 7mm (1/4") wide. TUBE: magenta (67B); short, medium thickness; 12mm(1/2") long x 7mm (1/4") wide. STAMENS: do not extend below corolla; reddish purple (67A) filaments, purple (71A) anthers. PISTIL: extends 25mm (1") below the corolla, light magenta (66D) style, white (155D) stigma. BUD: long, elliptic. FOLIAGE: medium green (137B) upper surface; medium green (138B) lower surface. Leaves are 32mm (1 1/4") long x 12mm (1/2") wide, lanceolate shaped, smooth edges, acute tips and rounded bases. Veins & stems are green; branches are pink/green. PARENTAGE: ('Rose Fantasia' x 'Ben Jammin') x 'Caradella'. Lax upright or stiff trailer. Self branching. Makes good basket or upright. Prefers overhead filtered light and cool climate. Best bloom in filtered light. Best foliage colour in bright light. Tested 4 years

in Filey, North Yorkshire, England. Distinguished by flower colour combination.
Edmonds 2003 UK AFS5208.

Harm oet Riessen. Trailer. Double. COROLLA is three-quarter flared, rosette shaped; opens reddish purple (72B); matures reddish purple (71B); 15mm (9/16") long x 13mm (1/2") wide. PETALOIDS are reddish purple (67A); 10mm (3/8") long x 8mm (5/16") wide. SEPALS are half down, tips recurved; red (52A) upper surface, and red (52A) lower surface; 27mm (1 1/16") long x 13mm (1/2") wide. TUBE is rose (52B); 30mm (1 3/16") long x 9mm (5/16") wide. FOLIAGE is medium green (146A) upper surface; yellowish green (146B) lower surface. PARENTAGE: 'Bicentennial' x 'Henkelly's Sandro'. Nomination by NKVF as Recommendable Cultivar. Distinguished by bloom colour.
Spierings 2006 NL AFS6254.

Harry's Sunshine. Upright. Single. COROLLA is quarter flared, square shaped, with smooth turned under petal margins; opens reddish purple (71B) splashed reddish purple (61B); matures dark reddish purple (64A) splashed magenta (61C); 15mm (5/8") long x 17mm (11/16") wide. SEPALS are half down, tips reflexed; reddish purple (61B) upper and lower surfaces; 25mm (1") long x 9mm (3/8") wide. TUBE is reddish purple (61B); short and thick; 9mm (3/8") long x 7mm (1/4") wide. STAMENS extend 10mm (3/8") below the corolla; magenta (71C) filaments and purple (77A) anthers. PISTIL extends 25mm (1") below the corolla; reddish purple (67A) style and yellowish white (158A) stigma. BUD is small, pointed. FOLIAGE is medium green (146A) on upper surface and yellowish green (146B) on lower surface. Leaves are 70mm (2 3/4") long x 45mm (1 3/4") wide, cordate shaped, serrated edges, acute tips and cordate bases. Veins are green; stems brown; branches are red. PARENTAGE: 'Janneke Brinkman-Saletijn' x 'Orange Glow'. Medium upright. Self branching. Makes good upright. Prefers full sun and warm climate. Heat tolerant if shaded. Hardy to -3°F. Best bloom colour in bright light. Tested three years in Walthamstow, London, England. Distinguished by profuse blooms, compact growth.
Allsop 2002 UK AFS4818.

Harti's Phonix. Upright. Double. COROLLA robin red. SEPALS white.
Pfefferle 2002 DE.

161

Harvey's Reward. Upright. Single. COROLLA: half flared, square shaped, turned under smooth petal margins; opens reddish purple (74A) edged reddish purple (66A); matures magenta (57B) edged reddish purple (66A), pale pink (62D) near TUBE; 25mm (1") long x 20mm (13/16") wide. SEPALS: horizontal; tips recurved; white (155A) tipped green upper & lower surfaces; 30mm(1 3/16") long x 10mm (3/8") wide. TUBE: white (155A) striped green; short & thick; 10mm (3/8") long x 7mm (1/4") wide. STAMENS: extend 10mm (3/8") below corolla; rose (55B) filaments; dark rose (51A) anthers. PISTIL: extends 20mm (3/8") below the corolla, white (155C) style; yellowish white (158A) stigma. BUD: medium, elongated. FOLIAGE: dark green (147A) upper surface, medium green (147B) lower surface. Leaves are 50mm (2") long x 25mm (1") wide, cordate shaped, serrulated edges, acute tips and rounded bases. Veins & stems are green; branches are brown. PARENTAGE: 'Anita' x 'Hawaiian Sunset'. Small upright. Self branching. Makes good upright, standard or bedding plant. Prefers overhead filtered light and warm climate. Heat tolerant if shaded. Cold weather hardy to 32⁰ F. Best bloom colour in bright light. Tested 6 years in Walthamstow, London, England. Distinguished by compact growth with blooms held in terminal clusters.
Allsop M. 2004 UK AFS5384.

Hastings. Upright. Single. COROLLA opens very pale lavender, matures slightly lighter; corolla has no flare and is 14mm long x 12mm wide. SEPALS pale pink, fades to white towards tips, tipped green on the upper and lower surfaces; sepals are half up with recurved tips and are 27mm long x 7mm wide. TUBE pale pink and is 10mm long x 4mm wide. PARENTAGE 'Sophie Louise' x 'Seedling No 1012'. This cultivar will create a nice compact 5½ pot show plant.
Riley B. 2007 UK BFS0047.

Hayley Jay. Upright. Double. COROLLA opens deep lavender to mauve, matures to mauve; corolla is half flared. SEPALS rose tipped cream, matures lighter; SEPALS are horizontally held with recurved tips. TUBE rose pink. PARENTAGE 'Lillian Annetts' x 'Grandad Hobbs'.
Garcia 2009 UK BFS0115.

Hedda. Upright. Single. COROLLA opens purple (70a); corolla is quarter flared and is 29mm long x 22mm wide. SEPALS red (46b)

on the upper and lower surfaces; sepals are half down with recurved tips and are 34mm long x 10mm wide. TUBE red (46b) and is 23mm long x 7mm wide. PARENTAGE 'Checkerboard' x 'Mrs. Popple'. This cultivar has proven to be hardy in Cheshire, it's free-flowering and a self-branching vigourous cutivar which requires regular feeding and does not like to be dry; responds well to pinching out, and will produce a compact plant.
Gibson 2007 UL BFS0055.

Hedens Montana. Upright/Trailer. Semi Double. COROLLA is three quarter flared with turned under smooth petal margins; opens purple (82A) edged purple (82A), light orange (40D) at base; matures reddish purple (74A) edged purple (80A), orange (40C) at base; 21mm (13/16") long x 18mm (11/16") wide. PETALOIDS are violet (87B), light orange (40D) at base; 13mm (1/2") long x 11mm (7/16") wide. SEPALS are horizontal, tips recurved; red (53D) upper surface; rose (61D) lower surface; 26mm (1") long x 16mm (5/8") wide. TUBE is rose (61D); medium length and thickness; 14mm (9/16") long x 6mm (1/4") wide. STAMENS extend 12mm (1/2") beyond the corolla; reddish purple (66B) filaments, dark reddish purple (72A) anthers. PISTIL extends 25mm (1") beyond the corolla; reddish purple (66B) style, dark rose (54A) stigma. BUD is round, pointed. FOLIAGE is medium green (137B) upper surface, medium green (138B) lower surface. Leaves are 56mm (2 3/16") long x 30mm (1 3/16") wide, ovate shaped, serrulated edges, acute tips and rounded bases. Veins are light plum (184D), stems are plum (184B), branches are dark red purple (187C). PARENTAGE: 'Rohees New Millennium' x 'Pinto de Blue. Lax upright or stiff trailer. Self branching. Makes good basket. Prefers overhead filtered light and cool climate. Best bloom and foliage colour in filtered light. Tested three years in Koningshooikt, Belgium. Certificate N.B.F.K. at Meise. Distinguished by bloom shape and colour.
Michiels 2002 BE AFS4969.

Heidebieke. Upright. Semi Double. COROLLA: quarter flared, turned under wavy petal margins; opens magenta (63A); matures dark reddish purple (72A), magenta (63A) at base; 14mm (9/16") long x 20mm (13/16") wide. PETALOIDS: 2 per sepal, same colour as corolla; 11mm (7/16") long x 6mm (1/4") wide. SEPALS: half down; tips recurved; white (155B) edged dark rose (58C) tipped

light yellow green (150B) upper surface; dark rose (58C) lower surface; 28mm(1 1/8") long x 12mm (1/2") wide. TUBE: white (155B); medium length & thickness; 15mm (9/16") long x 4mm (3/16") wide. STAMENS: no filaments or anthers. PISTIL extends 28mm (1 1/8") below the corolla; magenta (58B) style, orange (35B) stigma. BUD: rectangular, pointed. FOLIAGE: dark green (139A) upper surface; medium green (138A) lower surface. Leaves are 63mm (2 1/2") long x 43mm (1 11/16") wide, ovate shaped, serrated edges, acute tips and rounded bases. Veins, stems & branches are medium green (139C). PARENTAGE: 'Dommelgalm' x 'WALZ Toorts'. Medium upright. Self branching. Makes good upright. Prefers overhead filtered light. Best bloom and foliage colour in filtered light. Tested 5 years in Leopoldsburg, Belgium. NBFK Certificate of Merit at Meise. Distinguished by profuse blooms, no filaments or anthers.
Busschodts 2003 BE AFS5128.

Heiko Fuhrmann. Upright/Trailer. Double. COROLLA: half flared, turned under wavy petal margins; opens reddish purple (70B) & dark purple (79A); matures reddish purple (64B) & reddish purple (59B); 23mm (7/8") long x 19mm (3/4 ") wide. PETALOIDS: same colour as corolla; 15mm (9/16") long x 12mm (7/16") wide. SEPALS: half up, tips recurved up; rose (63C) upper surface; magenta (61C) lower surface; 26mm (1") long x 12mm (7/16") wide. TUBE: light pink (61C); medium length & thickness; 12mm (7/16") long x 5mm (3/16") wide. STAMENS extend 17mm (5/8") beyond the corolla; magenta (63B) filaments; purple (71A) anthers. PISTIL extends 24mm (15/16") beyond the corolla; dark rose (64C) style; pale yellow (1D) stigma. BUD: globular. FOLIAGE: dark green (136B) upper surface; medium green (138B) lower surface. Leaves are 56mm (2 1/4") long x 26mm (1") wide; elliptic shaped, serrulate edges, acute tips, rounded bases. Veins are very dark reddish purple (186A), stems are reddish purple (186B), branches are plum (183C) & medium green (139C). PARENTAGE: 'Manfried Kleinau' x 'Bert Beekman'. Lax upright or stiff trailer. Self branching. Makes good basket or upright. Prefers overhead filtered light, cool climate. Best bloom & foliage colour in filtered light. Tested 3 years in Koningshooikt, Belgium. Waanrode 8/9/08. Distinguished by bloom colour combination.
Michiels 2009 BE AFS7174.

Helen Fahey. Upright. Single. COROLLA: quarter flared, smooth petal margins; opens purple (82A); matures dark purple (78A); 25mm (1") long x 32mm (1 1/4") wide. SEPALS: horizontal; tips recurved; red (52A) upper & lower surfaces; 32mm (1 1/4") long x 16mm (5/8") wide. TUBE: red (52A); short, medium thickness; 10mm (3/8") long x 8mm (5/16") wide. STAMENS: extend 7mm (1/4") below corolla; rose (68B) filaments; dark reddish purple (60A) anthers. PISTIL: extends 19mm (3/4") below corolla; rose (68B) style; light rose (68D) stigma. BUD: fat, round. FOLIAGE: medium green (137B) upper surface; medium green (137D) lower surface. Leaves are 51mm (2") long x 38mm (1 1/2") wide, ovate shaped, serrulated edges, obtuse tips and rounded bases. Green veins; green, shaded rose, stems; brown branches. PARENTAGE: 'Madeleine Sweeney' x 'Purple Patch'. Small upright. Makes good upright, standard or garden plant. Prefers overhead filtered light. Best bloom colour in filtered light. Tested 4 years in Ormskirk, Lancashire, England. Distinguished by compact, bushy growth.
Sinton 2004 UK AFS5457.

Helen Lang. Single. COROLLA deep red tinged purple. SEPALS bright red.
Chatters 2008 UK.

Helen McLaughlin. Upright/Trailer. Double. COROLLA is half flared, square shaped, with smooth petal margins; opens purple (90B); matures dark reddish purple (70A) & purple (82A), fades to white then yellow at the TUBE; 38mm (1 1/2") long x 25-38mm (1 – 1 1/2") wide. PETALOIDS: Same colour as corolla; 16mm (5/8") long x 7-16mm (1/4 – 5/8") wide. SEPALS are horizontal, tips reflexed; white striped pink at base tipped green upper & lower surfaces; 44mm (1 3/4") long x 22mm (7/8") wide. TUBE is white striped rose (51B); long, medium thickness; 22mm (7/8") long x 11mm (7/16") wide. STAMENS extend 12mm (1/2") to 25mm (1") beyond the corolla; light pink filaments; light brown anthers. PISTIL extends 32mm (1 1/4") below the corolla; white style; yellow (8A) stigma. BUD is ovate, blunt point. FOLIAGE is dark green (137A) upper surface, medium green (138A) lower surface. Leaves are 76mm (3") long x 41mm (1 5/8") wide, ovate shaped, serrated edges, acute tips and rounded bases. Veins are light green (142A), stems are red (46B) & branches are light green (124A). PARENTAGE: 'Deep Purple' x 'White King'. Small lax upright or stiff trailer. Makes good basket, upright, or standard.

Prefers overhead filtered light & cool climate. Cold weather hardy to 32⁰ F. Best bloom & foliage colour in bright or filtered light. Tested five years in Fortuna, CA, USA. Distinguished by large prolific blooms. McLaughlin 2004 USA AFS5368.

Helen Moore. Upright. Double. COROLLA is quarter flared with smooth petal margins; opens white, shaded pale lavender (69D), veined red (53C); matures white, shaded pale lavender (69B), veined red (53C); 20mm (13/16") long x 25 mm (1") wide. SEPALS are horizontal, tips recurved; red (53D) upper surface; dark rose (54A) lower surface; 30-32mm (1 3/16 – 1 1/4") long x 15mm (9/16") wide. TUBE is red (53D), medium length and thickness; 15mm (9/16") long x 6mm (1/4") wide. FOLIAGE opens olive green (152D), matures medium green (146A) upper surface; opens olive green (152B), matures from light yellowish green (146D) to medium green (147B) lower surface. Leaves are 77mm (3 1/16") long x 35mm (1 3/8") wide, ovate shaped. PARENTAGE: Sport of 'Conspicua'. First prize, Bush section Wellington Fuchsia Society Show 2000. Distinguished by foliage variegated colours.
Moore 2005 NZ AFS5637.

Helen Nicholls. Upright. Semi Double. COROLLA: half flared, smooth petal margins; opens & matures pale pink (50C) veined pink; 20mm (13/16") long x 20mm (13/16") wide. SEPALS: half up; tips recurved up; light pink (55D) tipped green upper & lower surfaces; 27mm (1 1/16") long x 14mm (9/16") wide. TUBE: pale pink (56D) striped pale pink (56A), medium length & thickness; 10mm (3/8") long x 8mm (5/16") wide. STAMENS: extend 14mm (9/16") below the corolla; pink (62C) filaments, magenta (63B) anthers. PISTIL extends 30mm (1 3/16") below the corolla; light rose (63D) style, cream (159D) stigma. BUD: round. FOLIAGE: dark green (137A) upper surface, medium green (138B) lower surface. Leaves are 65mm (2 9/16") long x 34mm (1 3/8") wide, ovate shaped, serrulated edges, acute tips and rounded bases. Veins & stems are medium green, branches are dark green. PARENTAGE: ('Baby Bright' x 'Alison Patricia') x 'Shelford'. Small upright. Makes good upright. Prefers overhead filtered light. Best bloom and foliage colour in filtered light. Tested 5 years in Bolsover, Chesterfield, Derbyshire, England. Distinguished by delicate pink colour.
Nicholls 2003 UK AFS5078.

Hello Charlotte. Upright/Trailer. Single. COROLLA is unflared to quarter flared; opens pale pink (36D) veined dark rose to rose (51A-B); matures pale pink (36D); 24mm (15/16") long x 14mm (9/16") wide. SEPALS are fully up, tips recurved in a complete circle; red (47B) upper surface; dark rose (54B) lower surface; 31mm (1 1/4") long x 8mm (5/16") wide. TUBE is bright dark red (47A); 6mm (1/4") long x 5mm (3/16") wide. FOLIAGE: medium green (146A) upper surface; yellowish green (146B) lower surface. PARENTAGE: 'La Campanella' x 'Dancing Flame'. Distinguished by SEPALS forming a complete vertical circle.
Massé 2006 FR AFS6237.

Hello Christine. Upright. Single. COROLLA: Quarter flared; smooth petal margins; opens purple (83B); matures purple (80A); 17mm (5/8") long x 12mm (7/16") wide. SEPALS: horizontal, tips recurved; light pink (49C) to pink (48C) if in sun upper & lower surfaces; 30mm (1 3/16") long x 4mm (1/8") wide. TUBE: cream (158C) to light pink (49C) if in sun; short, medium thickness; 3mm (1/8") long x 4mm (1/8") wide. FOLIAGE is medium green (146A) upper surface; yellowish green (146B) lower surface. PARENTAGE: 'Joy Patmore' x 'Celia Smedley'.
Massé 2007 FR AFS6482.

Hello Diane. Upright. Single. COROLLA is unflared; opens dark rose (48B), lighter base; matures dark rose (48B); 15mm (9/16") long x 9mm (3/8") wide. SEPALS are horizontal, tips recurved; cream (159D) upper & lower surfaces; 20mm (3/4") long x 5mm (3/16") wide. TUBE is white (155D); 18mm (11/16") long x 4mm (1/8") wide. FOLIAGE: dark green (147A) upper surface; medium green (147B) lower surface. PARENTAGE: 'Prince of Orange' x 'Subliem'. Distinguished by bloom colour.
Massé 2006 FR AFS6238.

Hello Frans. Upright. Single. COROLLA: quarter flared; opens & matures rose (52B); 23mm (7/8") long x 17mm (5/8") wide. SEPALS: half down, tips recurved; light pink (62B) tipped cream (158D) upper & lower surfaces; 44mm (1 3/4") long x 9mm (5/16") wide. TUBE: pale pink (69A); 23 mm (7/8") long x 7mm (1/4") wide. FOLIAGE is dark green (147A) upper surface; medium green (147B) lower surface. PARENTAGE: ('Howlett's Hardy' x 'Passionnement') x 'Checkerboard'.
Massé 2008 FR AFS6833.

Hello Marie-Jo. Upright. Single. COROLLA: Unflared; smooth petal margins; opens reddish purple (74B); matures magenta (58B); 32mm (1 1/4") long x 17mm (5/8") wide. SEPALS: half down, tips recurved; red (52A) upper & lower surfaces; 43mm (1 11/16") long x 8mm (5/16") wide. TUBE: red (52A); longish, medium thickness; 20mm (3/4") long x 6mm (1/4") wide. FOLIAGE is dark green (147A) upper surface; medium green (147B) lower surface. PARENTAGE: 'Prince of Orange' x 'Subliem'.
Massé 2007 FR AFS6483.

Helston Flora. Upright/Trailer. Semi Double. COROLLA: three quarter flared, turned up petal margins; opens light purple (88C) edged light pink (62B); matures violet (87B); 30mm (1 3/16") long, 45mm (1 3/4") wide. PETALOIDS: Light purple (88C); 10mm (3/8") long x 5mm (3/16") wide, folded. SEPALS: horizontal; tips recurved; light pink (62B), fading to pale pink (69A) towards tip, upper surface; pale lavender (69B) lower surface; 56mm (2 3/16") long x 20mm (13/16") wide. TUBE: pale pink (69A); short, thick; 9mm (3/8") long x 9mm (3/8") wide. STAMENS: extend 15mm (9/16") below corolla; reddish purple (64B) filaments; light rose (73B) anthers. PISTIL: extends 35mm (1 3/8") below the corolla; pale pink (69A) style & stigma. BUD: lanceolate. FOLIAGE: medium green (138A) upper surface; gray (195A) lower surface. Leaves are 95mm (3 3/4") long x 50mm (2") wide, lanceolate shaped, serrated edges, acute tips and acute bases. Dark reddish purple (59A) veins & stems; light brown (199D) branches. PARENTAGE: 'Jonathon Negus' x 'Sleigh Bells'. Lax upright or stiff trailer. Makes good basket or standard. Prefers overhead filtered light. Best bloom colour in filtered light. Best foliage colour in bright light. Tested 5 years in West Cornwall, England. Distinguished by large blooms & delicate bloom colours.
Negus 2004 UK AFS5630.

Hendrik Van Wassenaer. Trailer. Single. COROLLA: half flared; opens dark rose (64C); matures magenta (63A); 17mm (5/8") long x 17mm (5/8") wide. SEPALS: horizontal, tips recurved; white (155C) & dark rose (51A) tipped yellowish green (145A) upper surface; rose (55B) tipped yellowish green (145A) lower surface; 23mm (7/8") long x 8mm (5/16") wide. TUBE: rose (52C); 14mm (9/16") long x 8mm (5/16") wide. FOLIAGE is medium green (137B) upper surface; light green (138C) lower surface. PARENTAGE: 'Pink La Campanella' x unknown.

Cuppens 2008 BE AFS6752.

Hendrik Leenaerts. Upright. Semi Double. COROLLA is half flared; opens purple (79C); matures purple (71A); 19mm (3/4") long x 18mm (11/16") wide. SEPALS are half down, tips reflexed; reddish purple (59B) upper surface; dark reddish purple (60C) lower surface; 27mm (1 1/16") long x 13mm (1/2") wide. TUBE is magenta (59C); 19mm (3/4") long x 5mm (3/16") wide. FOLIAGE: dark green (136B) upper surface; medium green (138B) lower surface. PARENTAGE: 'Aalters Glorie' x 'Rohees New Millenium'. Meise 8/13/05. Distinguished by dark bloom colour.
Geerts J. 2006 BE AFS5991.

Henk Kaspers. Trailer. Double. COROLLA is three quarter flared, smooth petal margins; opens light reddish purple (77A); matures light rose (73C); 24mm (15/16") long x 27mm (1 1/16") wide. SEPALS are half up, tips recurved up; pale lavender (65D) upper & lower surfaces; 28mm (1 1/8") long x 16mm (5/8") wide. TUBE is pale lavender (65D); medium length & thickness; 7mm (1/4") long x 6mm (1/4") wide. STAMENS extend 9mm (3/8") beyond the corolla; light rose (73C) filaments; magenta (63B) anthers. PISTIL extends 21mm (13/16") below the corolla; light rose (73C) style; light yellow (4C) stigma. BUD is cordate, pointed. FOLIAGE is medium green (137C) upper surface, medium green (139C) lower surface. Leaves are 51mm (2") long x 27mm (1 1/16") wide, ovate shaped, serrulated edges, acute tips and cordate bases. Veins, stems & branches are green. PARENTAGE: 'Sofie Michiels' x 'Delta's Wonder'. Natural trailer. Makes good basket. Prefers overhead filtered light & cool climate. Best bloom colour in filtered light. Tested four years in Knegsel, The Netherlands. Distinguished by bloom colour.
Roes 2004 NL AFS5373.

Henk Takken. Upright. Single. COROLLA is quarter flared, bell shaped; opens magenta (63A); matures light reddish purple (72C); 24mm (15/16") long x 24mm (15/16") wide. SEPALS are half down, tips recurved; rose (52B) upper surface, and rose (50B) lower surface; 28mm (1 1/8") long x 9mm (5/16") wide. TUBE is red (53C); 10mm (3/8") long x 9mm (5/16") wide. FOLIAGE is dark green (147A) upper surface; medium green (147B) lower surface. PARENTAGE: 'De Groot's Passie' x 'Patricia van Mossel'. Nomination by

165

NKVF as Recommendable Cultivar. Distinguished by bloom colour. de Groot J. 2006 BE AFS6260.

Henk van de Beerekamp. Upright. Semi Double. COROLLA: quarter flared; bell shaped, smooth petal margins; opens purple (83A); matures dark reddish purple (64A); 31mm (1 1/4") long x 33mm (1 5/16") wide. PETALOIDS: violet (85B) veined red purple; 21mm (13/16") long x 13mm (1/2") wide. SEPALS: fully up, tips recurved; magenta (63A) upper & lower surfaces; 43mm (1 11/16") long x 14mm (9/16") wide. TUBE: magenta (63A); medium length & thin; 22mm (7/8") long x 4mm (1/8") wide. STAMENS extend 16mm (5/8") beyond the corolla; dark reddish purple (64A) filaments; dark purple (79A) anthers. PISTIL extends 22mm (7/8") beyond the corolla; dark reddish purple (60A) style; rose (64D) stigma. BUD: pegtop shaped. FOLIAGE: medium green (138A) upper surface; medium green (138B) lower surface. Leaves are 64mm (2 1/2") long x 29mm (1 1/8") wide; elliptic shaped, serrate edges, acute tips, rounded bases. Veins, stems & branches are red. PARENTAGE: 'Voodoo' x unknown. Tall upright. Self branching. Makes good upright or standard. Prefers overhead filtered light, warm climate. Tested 11 years in Hulshorst, The Netherlands. Nominated by NKvF as recommendable cultivar. Distinguished by winter hardiness. van den Brink 2009 NL AFS7018.

Henkelly's Anneke. Trailer. Semi Double. COROLLA is unflared with turned under petal margins; opens light magenta (57D); matures magenta (57C); 24mm (15/16") long x 24mm (15/16") wide. SEPALS are half down, tips recurved; magenta (58B) upper surface; red (52A) lower surface; 39mm (1 9/16") long x 12mm (1/2") wide. TUBE is dark rose (58C); long; medium thickness; 29mm (1 1/8") long x 6mm (1/4") wide. FOLIAGE: medium green (146A) upper surface; yellowish green (146B) lower surface. Leaves are 65mm (2 9/16") long x 34mm (1 5/16") wide, elliptic shaped. PARENTAGE: 'Henkelly's Tonnie' x 'Heidi Ann'. Distinguished by colour & long flowering period. Spierings 2005 NL AFS5792.

Henkelly's Athena. Upright/Trailer. Single. COROLLA is unflared, round, with turned under petal margins; opens reddish purple (61B); matures dark reddish purple (61A); 17mm (3/4") long x 17mm (3/4") wide.

SEPALS are half down, tips reflexed; pale pink (56A) upper surface; magenta (68A) lower surface; 23mm (15/16") long x 9mm (3/8") wide. TUBE is pale pink (56C); medium length & thickness; 11mm (7/16") long x 6mm (1/4") wide. FOLIAGE: dark green (147A) upper surface; medium green (147B) lower surface. Leaves are 50mm (2") long x 25mm (1") wide, ovate shaped. PARENTAGE: 'Ron Ewart' x 'Henkelly's Tim'. Nomination by N.K.V.F. as recommendable cultivar. Distinguished by colour & shape. Spierings 2005 NL AFS5790.

Henkelly's Bianca. Upright. Single. COROLLA: quarter flared; smooth petal margins; opens dark reddish purple (71B), white (155B) base; matures dark reddish purple (61A); 9mm (5/16") long x 10mm (3/8") wide. SEPALS: horizontal, tips recurved; white (155B) tipped medium green (146A) upper surface; pink (62A) lower surface; 24mm (15/16") long x 9mm (5/16") wide. TUBE: white (155A); short, medium thickness; 10mm (3/8") long x 6mm (1/4") wide. STAMENS extend 13mm (1/2") beyond the corolla; magenta (67B) filaments; dark purple (79A) anthers. PISTIL extends 27mm (1 1/16") beyond the corolla; pink (62C) style; light yellow (4C) stigma. BUD: long. FOLIAGE: dark green (137A) upper surface; medium green (137C) lower surface. Leaves are 62mm (2 7/16") long x 30mm (1 3/16") wide; elliptic shaped, serrate edges, acute tips, rounded bases. Veins, stems & branches are light green. PARENTAGE: 'Henkelly's Athena' x 'Prince Syray'. Small upright. Self branching. Makes good upright. Prefers overhead filtered light or full sun. Best bloom & foliage colour in bright light. Tested 4 years in Sint Michielsgestel, The Netherlands. Nominated by NKvF as recommendable cultivar. Distinguished by off-standing flowers. Spierings 2009 NL AFS7030.

Henkelly's Bettina. Upright. Single. COROLLA: quarter flared, bell-shaped; opens orange (44D) and matures rose (47D); 16mm (5/8") long x 9mm (5/16") wide. SEPALS are horizontal, tips recurved; peach (38B) upper surface and peach (37B) lower surface; 22mm (7/8") long x 7mm (1/4") wide. TUBE is pink (36A); short, medium thickness; 17mm (5/8") long x 6mm (1/4") wide. FOLIAGE is dark green (147A) upper surface; medium green (147B) lower surface. PARENTAGE: 'Loxhore Mazurka' x 'Prince

Syray'. Nomination by NKVF as Recommendable Cultivar.
Spierings 2006 NL AFS6437.

Henkelly's Boerenhof. Trailer. Semi Double.
COROLLA is unflared; opens reddish purple (59B); matures dark reddish purple (61A); 34mm (1 3/8") long x 26mm (1") wide. SEPALS are half down, tips recurved; dark reddish purple (60C) upper surface; dark reddish purple (60B) lower surface; 50mm (2") long x 13mm (1/2") wide. TUBE is red (53C); 13mm (1/2") long x 8mm (5/16") wide. FOLIAGE is dark green (147A) upper surface; medium green (146A) lower surface. PARENTAGE: 'Bicentennial' x 'Henkelly's Mysterie'. Nomination by NKVF as Recommendable Cultivar. Distinguished by bloom colour.
Spierings 2006 NL AFS6256.

Henkelly's Brabander. Trailer. Double.
COROLLA is half flared; opens reddish purple (70B); matures reddish purple (70B); 31mm (1 1/4") long x 29mm (1 1/8") wide. PETALOIDS are pale pink (49D); 27mm (1 1/16") long x 22mm (7/8") wide. SEPALS are fully up, tips recurved; pale pink (49D) upper surface; pale pink (49D) lower surface; 32mm (1 1/4") long x 17mm (5/8") wide. TUBE is white (155A); 18mm (11/16") long x 6mm (1/4") wide. FOLIAGE is medium green (146A) upper surface; yellowish green (146B) lower surface. PARENTAGE: ('Applause' x 'Seventh Heaven') x ('WALZ Harp' x 'Applause').
Spierings 2006 NL AFS6255.

Henkelly's Brabito. Upright/Trailer. Double.
COROLLA: unflared, compact shape; opens magenta (67B); matures reddish purple (70B); 22mm (7/8") long x 25mm (1") wide. PETALOIDS: magenta (67B) spotted pink (49A) & violet (75A); 25mm (1") long x 15mm (9/16") wide. SEPALS: horizontal, tips recurved; pale pink (49D) upper surface; light pink (49B) lower surface; 34mm (1 3/8") long x 16mm (5/8") wide. TUBE: white (155A); 19mm (3/4") long x 7mm (1/4") wide. FOLIAGE is dark green (139A) upper surface; medium green (137C) lower surface. PARENTAGE: 'Braampt's Glorie' x ('Bicentennial' x 'Toby Bridger'). Nomination by NKVF as Recommendable Cultivar.
Spierings 2008 NL AFS6800.

Henkelly's Cachet. Upright. Single.
COROLLA: half flared, bell-shaped; opens and matures pink (37C); 21mm (13/16") long x 15mm (9/16") wide. PETALOIDS: pink (37C); 17mm (5/8") long x 10mm (3/8") wide. SEPALS are horizontal, tips recurved; white (155A) upper surface and orangish white (159C) lower surface; 30mm (1 3/16") long x 10mm (3/8") wide. TUBE is greenish white (157A); medium length & thickness; 20mm (3/4") long x 5mm (3/16") wide. FOLIAGE is dark green (147A) upper surface; medium green (146A) lower surface. PARENTAGE: 'Braamt's Glorie' x 'Prince Syray'. Nomination by NKVF as Recommendable Cultivar.
Spierings 2007 NL AFS6436.

Henkelly's Chloris. Upright/Trailer. Single.
COROLLA: unflared, closed shape; opens purple (71A); matures reddish purple (71B); 16mm (5/8") long x 21mm (13/16") wide. SEPALS: horizontal, tips recurved; rose (68B) tipped olive green (152A) upper surface; magenta (68A) lower surface; 33mm (1 5/16") long x 11mm (7/16") wide. TUBE: pink (62C); 17mm (5/8") long x 6mm (1/4") wide. FOLIAGE is dark green (147A) upper surface; medium green (147B) lower surface. PARENTAGE: ('Drama Girl' x 'Roesse Blacky') x 'Loxhore Mazurka'.
Spierings 2008 NL AFS6796.

Henkelly's Consivia. Upright. Single.
COROLLA: quarter flared, long, bell shaped; opens rose (63C), matures magenta (63B); 26mm (1") long x 21mm (13/16") wide. SEPALS are half down, tips reflexed; light pink (65C) upper surface, rose (65A) lower surface; 37mm (1 7/16") long x 11mm (7/16") wide. TUBE is light pink (65C); long, medium thickness; 25mm (1") long x 7mm (1/4") wide. FOLIAGE is medium green (146A) upper surface; yellowish green (146B) lower surface. PARENTAGE: ('Cambridge Louie' x 'Henkelly's Billy') x [('Cambridge Louie' x 'Loxhore Mazurka') x Henkelly's Billy]. Nomination by NKVF as Recommendable Cultivar.
Spierings 2007 NL AFS6432.

Henkelly's Diana. Trailer. Single. COROLLA: half flared; opens reddish purple (59B), matures magenta (59C); 20mm (3/4") long x 15mm (9/16") wide. SEPALS are full down, tips recurved; light magenta (66D) upper & lower surface; 30mm (1 3/16") long x10mm (3/8") wide. TUBE is white (155A); medium length & thickness; 10mm (3/8") long x 5mm (3/16") wide. FOLIAGE is dark green (147A) upper surface; yellowish green (146B) lower surface. PARENTAGE: 'Henkelly's Athena' x 'Prince Syray'. Nomination by NKVF as Recommendable Cultivar.
Spierings 2007 NL AFS6433.

Henkelly's Euphemia. Upright/Trailer. Double. COROLLA: quarter flared; closed shape, wavy petal margins; opens light purple (78B); matures magenta (67B); 32mm (1 1/4") long x 31mm (1 1/4") wide. PETALOIDS: light purple (78B) spotted orange (40C); 33mm (1 5/16") long x 26mm (1") wide. SEPALS: horizontal, tips recurved; pink (48D) upper surface; rose (52C) lower surface; 43mm (1 11/16") long x 20mm (3/4") wide. TUBE: white (155A); medium length & thickness; 11mm (7/16") long x 8mm (5/16") wide. STAMENS extend 18mm (11/16") beyond the corolla; reddish purple (67A) filaments; dark reddish purple (64A) anthers. PISTIL extends 24mm (15/16") beyond the corolla; light reddish purple (73C) style; light yellow (4C) stigma. BUD: pegtop shaped. FOLIAGE: medium green (137B) upper surface; medium green (137D) lower surface. Leaves are 79mm (3 1/8") long x 44mm (1 3/4") wide; elliptic shaped, wavy edges, acute tips, rounded bases. Veins, stems & branches are red. PARENTAGE: 'Bicentennial' x 'Henkelly's Brabito'. Lax upright or stiff trailer. Self branching. Makes good basket. Prefers overhead filtered light. Best bloom & foliage colour in filtered light. Tested 5 years in Sint Michielsgestel, The Netherlands. Nominated by NKvF as recommendable cultivar. Distinguished by flower colour combination.
Spierings 2009 NL AFS7029.

Henkelly's Eureka. Upright. Semi Double. COROLLA: quarter flared; opens reddish purple (64A); matures reddish purple (67A); 14mm (9/16") long x 18mm (11/16") wide. PETALOIDS: same colour as corolla; 10mm (3/8") long x 11mm (7/16") wide. SEPALS: full down, tips recurved; pink (62A) upper surface; magenta (68A) lower surface; 17mm (5/8") long x 9mm (5/16") wide. TUBE: pale pink (62D); 9mm (5/16") long x 6mm (1/4") wide. FOLIAGE is dark green (147A) upper surface; medium green (147B) lower surface. PARENTAGE: 'Henkelly's Athena' x 'Prince Syray'. Nomination by NKVF as Recommendable Cultivar.
Spierings 2008 NL AFS6799.

Henkelly's Feronia. Upright. Single. COROLLA is three quarter flared, bell shaped; opens violet (76A); matures violet (77B); 35mm (1 3/8") long x 26mm (1") wide. PETALOIDS: violet (76A); 30mm (1 3/16") long x 17mm (5/8") wide. SEPALS are half up, tips recurved up; pink (62C) upper & lower surfaces; 46mm (1 13/16") long x 15mm (9/16") wide. TUBE is cream (159D);

16mm (5/8") long x 8mm (5/16") wide. FOLIAGE: medium green (138A) upper surface; medium green (139C) lower surface. PARENTAGE: 'Drama Girl' x 'Blush O' Dawn'. Distinguished by curly SEPALS; corolla shape & colour.
Spierings 2006 NL AFS6284.

Henkelly's Gitano. Upright. Single. COROLLA: quarter flared; wavy petal margins; opens dark reddish purple (59A); matures dark reddish purple (61A); 29mm (1 1/8") long x 30mm (1 3/16") wide. SEPALS: horizontal, tips recurved; red (53B) upper & lower surfaces; 35mm (1 3/8") long x 18mm (11/16") wide. TUBE: red (53B); medium length & thickness; 14mm (9/16") long x 15mm (9/16") wide. STAMENS extend 10mm (3/8") beyond the corolla; reddish purple (64B) filaments; dark reddish purple (64A) anthers. PISTIL extends 33mm (1 5/16") beyond the COROLLA; dark rose (64C) style; rose (64D) stigma. BUD: long. FOLIAGE: dark green (138A) upper surface; medium green (138B) lower surface. Leaves are 75mm (3") long x 43mm (1 11/16") wide; elliptic shaped, serrate edges, acute tips, rounded bases. Veins are light green, stems are bronze green & branches are red. PARENTAGE: ('Drama Girl' x 'Roesse Blacky') x 'Loxhore Mazurka'. Tall upright. Self branching. Makes good upright or standard. Prefers full sun. Best bloom & foliage colour in bright light. Tested 4 years in Sint Michielsgestel, The Netherlands. Distinguished by contrasting flower colours.
Spierings 2009 NL AFS7033.

Henkelly's Griffioen. Upright. Semi Double. COROLLA: quarter flared, ovate shaped; opens violet (77C); matures violet (77B); 25mm (1") long x 22mm (7/8") wide. PETALOIDS: light purple (75B) spotted & veined pink (62A); 20mm (3/4") long x 9mm (5/16") wide. SEPALS: horizontal, tips reflexed; rose (54C) upper surface; rose (55B) lower surface; 39mm (1 1/2") long x 11mm (7/16") wide. TUBE: rose (54C); 25mm (1") long x 6mm (1/4") wide. FOLIAGE is yellowish green (146B) upper surface; yellowish green (146C) lower surface. PARENTAGE: seedling of 'Braamt's Glorie' x 'Loxhore Mazurka'. Nomination by NKVF as Recommendable Cultivar.
Spierings 2008 NL AFS6774.

Henkelly's Iris. Upright/Trailer. Double. COROLLA: quarter flared, compact shape; opens dark purple (78A); matures purple (83B); 29mm (1 1/8") long x 29mm (1 1/8")

wide. PETALOIDS: dark purple (78A) spotted pinkish orange, veined pink; 24mm (15/16") long x 14mm (9/16") wide. SEPALS: fully up, tips recurved; red (46B) upper surface; red (46C) lower surface; 38mm (1 7/16") long x 12mm (7/16") wide. TUBE: red (45A); 20mm (3/4") long x 6mm (1/4") wide. FOLIAGE is dark green (137A) upper surface; medium green (137C) lower surface. PARENTAGE: 'Wilma Versloot' x seedling of 'Cambridge Louie'. Nomination by NKVF as Recommendable Cultivar.
Spierings 2008 NL AFS6772.

Henkelly's Isabella. Trailer. Single. COROLLA: unflared, closed shape; smooth petal margins; opens & matures purple (77A); 18mm (11/16") long x 18mm (11/16") wide. SEPALS: half up, tips recurved up, light twisting to the left; magenta (63B) tipped light green (142B) upper surface; magenta (63B) lower surface; 46mm (1 13/16") long x 7mm (1/4") wide. TUBE: magenta (63B); medium length & thickness; 18mm (11/16") long x 5mm (3/16") wide. STAMENS do not extend beyond the corolla; reddish purple (67A) filaments; purple (71A) anthers. PISTIL extends 15mm (9/16") beyond the corolla; magenta (67B) style; very pale orange (159A) stigma. BUD: long & sharp pointed. FOLIAGE: medium green (147B) upper surface; light olive green (147C) lower surface. Leaves are 65mm (2 9/16") long x 30mm (1 3/16") wide; lanceolate shaped, serrulate edges, acute tips, rounded bases. Veins, stems & branches are red. PARENTAGE: 'Cambridge Louie' x F. *glaziovana*. Natural trailer. Makes good basket. Prefers overhead filtered light or full sun, warm climate. Best bloom & foliage colour in bright light. Tested 5 years in Sint Michielsgestel, The Netherlands. Nominated by NKvF as recommendable cultivar. Distinguished by flower shape & colours.
Spierings 2009 NL AFS7034.

Henkelly's Jasmine. Upright/Trailer. Single. COROLLA: half flared, bell-shaped; opens reddish orange (43B); matures red (45B); 24mm (15/16") long x 24mm (15/16") wide. SEPALS are horizontal, tips recurved; pink (50D) upper surface and light orange (41D) lower surface; 27mm (1 1/16") long x 8mm (5/16") wide. TUBE is pale pink (56D); medium length & thickness; 30mm (1 3/16") long x 7mm (1/4") wide. FOLIAGE is dark green (147A) upper surface; medium green (146A) lower surface. PARENTAGE: 'Walz Harp' x 'Prince Syray'. Nomination by NKVF as Recommendable Cultivar.

Spierings 2007 NL AFS6435.

Henkelly's Kyra. Upright/Trailer. Double. COROLLA is half flared, bell shaped; opens purple (83C); matures reddish purple (72B); 20mm (3/4") long x 19mm (3/4") wide. PETALOIDS are purple (83C), 19 mm (3/4") long, 18 mm (11/16") wide. SEPALS are half up, tips recurved up; light purple (74C) upper surface, and reddish purple (67A) lower surface; 34mm (1 3/8") long x 13mm (1/2") wide. TUBE is white (155A); medium length and thickness; 14mm (9/16") long x 5mm (3/16") wide. FOLIAGE is dark green (137A) upper surface; medium green (147B) lower surface. PARENTAGE: 'Gerharda's Panache' x 'Henkelly'.
Spierings 2007 NL AFS6431.

Henkelly's Masha. Upright. Single. COROLLA: unflared; closed shape, wavy petal margins; opens reddish purple (72B); matures reddish purple (74B); 17mm (5/8") long x 17mm (5/8") wide. SEPALS: half down, tips reflexed; white (155A) tipped yellowish green (144A) upper surface; light pink (49B) lower surface; 24mm (15/16") long x 8mm (5/16") wide. TUBE: white (155A); short, medium thickness; 7mm (1/4") long x 7mm (1/4") wide. STAMENS extend 6mm (1/4") beyond the corolla; rose (65A) filaments; reddish purple (64B) anthers. PISTIL extends 19mm (3/4") beyond the corolla; rose (65A) style; light yellow (4C) stigma. BUD: long. FOLIAGE: medium green (137C) upper surface; medium green (137D) lower surface. Leaves are 55mm (2 3/16") long x 34mm (1 3/8") wide; elliptic shaped, smooth edges, acute tips, rounded bases. Veins, stems & branches are red. PARENTAGE: 'Henkelly's Athena' x 'Prince Syray'. Medium upright. Self branching. Makes good upright or standard. Prefers full sun. Best bloom & foliage colour in bright light. Tested 5 years in Sint Michielsgestel, The Netherlands. Distinguished by continuous seasonal flowering & off-standing flowers.
Spierings 2009 NL AFS7027.

Henkelly's Melania. Upright. Single. COROLLA: unflared, closed shape; wavy petal margins; opens magenta (71C) veined reddish purple (71B); matures purple (71A); 15mm (9/16") long x 15mm (9/16") wide. SEPALS: horizontal, tips recurved; magenta (68A) tipped yellowish white (4D) upper surface; reddish purple (67A) lower surface; 45mm (1 3/4") long x 11mm (7/16") wide. TUBE: rose (67D) striped white; medium

length & thickness; 12mm (7/16") long x 9mm (5/16") wide. STAMENS extend 11mm (7/16") beyond the corolla; dark reddish purple (64A) filaments; dark reddish purple (59A) anthers. PISTIL extends 34mm (1 3/8") beyond the corolla; dark reddish purple (64A) style; light pink (37C) stigma. BUD: long. FOLIAGE: dark green (137A) upper surface; medium green (137C) lower surface. Leaves are 71mm (2 3/16") long x 39mm (1 1/2") wide; elliptic shaped, wavy edges, acute tips, rounded bases. Veins, stems & branches are reddish. PARENTAGE: ('Drama Girl' x 'Roesse Blacky') x 'Loxhore Mazurka'. Tall upright. Self branching. Makes good upright, standard or pyramid. Prefers overhead filtered light or full sun. Best bloom colour in filtered light. Best foliage colour in bright light. Tested 4 years in Sint Michielsgestel, The Netherlands. Nominated by NKvF as recommendable cultivar. Distinguished by striking flower colour combination.
Spierings 2009 NL AFS7032.

Henkelly's Odillia. Upright/Trailer. Single/Semi Double/Double. corolla: quarter flared; closed shape, wavy petal margins; opens purple (77A); matures reddish purple (74A); 13mm (1/2") long x 14mm (9/16") wide. PETALOIDS: purple (77A) spotted light reddish purple; 15mm (9/16") long x 14mm (9/16") wide. SEPALS: horizontal, tips recurved; dark rose (67C) tipped light apple green (145B) upper surface; rose (67B) lower surface; 29mm (1 1/8") long x 11mm (7/16") wide. TUBE: pink (62A); medium length & thickness; 10mm (3/8") long x 6mm (1/4") wide. STAMENS extend 14mm (9/16") beyond the corolla; purple (71A) filaments & anthers. PISTIL extends 28mm (1 1/8") beyond the corolla; dark reddish purple (72A) style; light yellow (18C) stigma. BUD: long. FOLIAGE: dark green (137A) upper surface; medium green (137C) lower surface. Leaves are 41mm (1 5/8") long x 22mm (7/8") wide; elliptic shaped, serrate edges, acute tips, rounded bases. Veins & branches are light green, stems are red. PARENTAGE: 'Henkelly's Athena' x 'Henkelly's Diana'. Lax upright or stiff trailer. Self branching. Makes good basket or upright. Prefers overhead filtered light. Best bloom & foliage colour in filtered light. Tested 5 years in Sint Michielsgestel, The Netherlands. Distinguished by single, semi-double & double flowers on one plant.
Spierings 2009 NL AFS7028.

Henkelly's Ostara. Upright/Trailer. Single. COROLLA is half flared with turned up petal margins; opens reddish purple (70B); matures reddish purple (72B); 30mm (1 3/16") long x 23mm (15/16") wide. SEPALS are horizontal, tips recurved; pale pink (62D) upper surface; light pink (62B) lower surface; 38mm (1 1/2") long x 11mm (7/16") wide. TUBE is rose (55B); long, medium thickness; 19mm (3/4") long x 8mm (5/16") wide. FOLIAGE: medium green (146A) upper surface; yellowish green (146B) lower surface. Leaves are 72mm (2 13/16") long x 32mm (1 1/4") wide, ovate shaped. PARENTAGE: 'Svenny' x ('Applause' x 'Waternymph'). Nomination by N.K.V.F. as recommendable cultivar. Distinguished by flower & leaf colour combination.
Spierings 2005 NL AFS5791.

Henkelly's Phoenix. Upright. Double. COROLLA: quarter flared; opens violet (87B); matures reddish purple (80B); 20mm (3/4") long x 18mm (11/16") wide. PETALOIDS: same colour as corolla; 20mm (3/4") long x 15mm (9/16") wide. SEPALS: fully up, tips recurved; red (53B) tipped light green upper surface; dark rose (51A) lower surface; 31mm (1 1/4") long x 12mm (7/16") wide. TUBE: dark red (46A); 6mm (1/4") long x 6mm (1/4") wide. FOLIAGE is dark green (147A) upper surface; yellowish green (146B) lower surface. PARENTAGE: seedling of 'Cambridge Louie' x 'Henkelly's Billy'. Nomination by NKVF as Recommendable Cultivar.
Spierings 2008 NL AFS6773.

Henkelly's Plutus. Upright/Trailer. Single. COROLLA is quarter flared; opens& matures reddish purple (67A); 29mm (1 1/8") long x 28mm (1 1/8") wide. PETALOIDS: reddish purple (67A); 21mm (13/16") long x 26mm (1") wide. SEPALS are half up, tips recurved up; rose (52C) upper & lower surfaces; 48mm (1 7/8") long x 12mm (7/16") wide. TUBE is pink (62C); 42mm (1 5/8") long x 7mm (1/4") wide. FOLIAGE: medium green (137C) upper surface; medium green (137C) lower surface. PARENTAGE: 'WALZ Harp' x 'Quasar'. Distinguished by flower shape & colour.
Spierings 2006 NL AFS6285.

Henkelly's Regina. Upright/Trailer. Single. COROLLA: unflared; smooth petal margins; opens magenta (57C); matures magenta (57B); 15mm (9/16") long x 15mm (9/16") wide. SEPALS: horizontal, tips recurved; magenta (63B) tipped light apple green (145C) upper surface; rose (63C) lower surface; 21mm (13/16") long x 8mm (5/16") wide. TUBE: orangish white (159C); medium

170

length & thickness; 13mm (1/2") long x 6mm (1/4") wide. STAMENS extend 18mm (11/16") beyond the corolla; pink (62A) filaments; dark reddish purple (64A) anthers. PISTIL extends 23mm (7/8") beyond the corolla; light pink (62B) style; yellow (159C) stigma. BUD: pegtop shaped. FOLIAGE: dark green (137A) upper surface; medium green (137D) lower surface. Leaves are 50mm (2") long x 30mm (1 3/16") wide; elliptic shaped, serrate edges, acute tips, rounded bases. Veins, stems & branches are light green. PARENTAGE: 'Henkelly's Athena' x 'Prince Syray'. Lax upright or stiff trailer. Self branching. Makes good basket. Prefers full sun. Best bloom & foliage colour in bright light. Tested 5 years in Sint Michielsgestel, The Netherlands. Distinguished by flower shape & colour.
Spierings 2009 AFS7031.

Henkelly's Symmetric. Upright. Single. COROLLA: quarter flared; opens light magenta (57D) and matures magenta (57C); 20mm (3/4") long x 18mm (11/16") wide. SEPALS are half down, tips reflexed; pale pink (62D) upper surface and pink (62C) lower surface; 30mm (1 3/16") long x 10mm (3/8") wide. TUBE is white (155A); medium length & thickness; 16mm (5/8") long x 7mm (1/4") wide. FOLIAGE is medium green (146A) upper surface; medium green (147B) lower surface. PARENTAGE: ('Henkelly's Billy' x 'Cambridge Louie') x 'Loxhore Mazurka'.
Spierings 2007 NL AFS6438.

Henkelly's Truskes. Upright. Single. COROLLA: quarter flared; smooth petal margins; opens & matures rose (52C); 9mm (5/16") long x 6mm (1/4") wide. SEPALS: half down, tips reflexed; light pink (49C) tipped light green (145D) upper surface; light pink (49C) lower surface; 15mm (9/16") long x 5mm (3/16") wide. TUBE: light pink (49C); medium length & thickness; 11mm (7/16") long x 2mm (1/16") wide. STAMENS extend 5mm (3/16") beyond the corolla; light pink (62B) filaments & anthers. PISTIL extends 10mm (3/8") beyond the corolla; light pink (62B) style; cream (158C) stigma. BUD: pegtop shaped. FOLIAGE: dark green (138A) upper surface; medium green (138B) lower surface. Leaves are 42mm (1 5/8") long x 21mm (13/16") wide; elliptic shaped, serrate edges, acute tips, rounded bases. Veins, stems & branches are light green. PARENTAGE: 'Loxhore Mazurka' x unknown. Medium upright. Self branching. Makes good upright or standard. Prefers full sun. Best

bloom & foliage colour in bright light. Tested 5 years in Sint Michielsgestel, The Netherlands. Nominated by NKvF as recommendable cultivar. Distinguished by bright colours; two of the corolla petals have stems.
Spierings 2009 NL AFS7026.

Henkelly's Vanessa. Trailer. Double. COROLLA: unflared; opens reddish purple (67A); matures reddish purple (64B); 28mm (1 1/8") long x 26mm (1") wide. SEPALS: full down, tips recurved; light pink (62B) tipped pale yellowish green (149D) upper surface; pink (62A) lower surface; 32mm (1 1/4") long x 12mm (7/16") wide. TUBE: white (155B); 23mm (7/8") long x 4mm (1/8") wide. FOLIAGE is medium green (137A) upper surface; medium green (137C) lower surface. PARENTAGE: 'Drama Girl' x 'Henkelly's Billy'.
Spierings 2008 NL AFS6797.

Henkelly's Vulcanus. Upright/Trailer. Single. COROLLA: half flared; opens magenta (57C); matures magenta (61C); 15mm (9/16") long x 14mm (9/16") wide. SEPALS: half down, tips reflexed; dark rose (58C) tipped light yellow (4C) upper surface; magenta (58B) lower surface; 26mm (1") long x 7mm (1/4") wide. TUBE: magenta (58B); 20mm (3/4") long x 4mm (1/8") wide. FOLIAGE is dark green (137A) upper surface; medium green (137C) lower surface. PARENTAGE: seedling of 'Braamt's Glorie' x 'F. microphylla'. Nomination by NKVF as Recommendable Cultivar.
Spierings 2008 NL AFS6775.

Henkelly's Xanthos. Upright. Single. COROLLA: quarter flared, bell shaped; opens dark reddish purple (64A); matures magenta (58B); 14mm (9/16") long x 18mm (11/16") wide. SEPALS are half down, tips reflexed; light pink (49C) upper surface, and light rose (50C) lower surface; 21mm (13/16") long x 9mm (5/16") wide. TUBE is pink (51D); short & thick; 6mm (1/4") long x 7mm (1/4") wide. FOLIAGE is dark green (147A) upper surface; medium green (146A) lower surface. PARENTAGE: 'Henkelly's Athena' x 'Prince Syray'. Nomination by NKVF as Recommendable Cultivar.
Spierings 2007 NL AFS6430.

Hennie Bouman. Trailer. Double. COROLLA is three quarter flared with smooth petal margins; opens purple (83A), matures reddish purple (74A); 24mm (15/16") long x 19mm (3/4") wide. SEPALS are half up, tips recurved up; light purple (75B) upper surface, pale purple (74D) lower surface; 32mm (1 1/4") long x 17mm (11/16") wide. TUBE is light purple (75B), proportionately medium length and thickness; 17mm (11/16") long x 7mm (1/4") wide. STAMENS extend 21mm (13/16") below the corolla; dark reddish purple (61A) filaments and anthers. PISTIL extends 32mm (1 1/4") below the corolla; magenta (68A) style and light yellow (11C) stigma. BUD is long, thin and pointed. FOLIAGE is medium green (137B) on upper surface and medium green (138B) on lower surface. Leaves are 63mm (2 1/2") long x 38mm (1 1/2") wide, ovate shaped, serrated edges, acute tips and rounded bases. Veins, stems and branches are green. PARENTAGE: 'Rohees Queen' x ('Annabel' x 'Annabel'). Natural trailer. Makes good basket. Prefers overhead filtered light and cool climate. Best bloom colour in filtered light. Tested four years in Knegsel, The Netherlands. Distinguished by bloom colour.

Roes 2002 NL AFS4791.

Henny For You. Trailer. Semi Double. COROLLA: half flared, turned under wavy petal margins; opens rose (68B); matures light reddish purple (73A); 21mm (13/16") long, 20mm (13/16") wide. PETALOIDS: dark rose (64C); 17mm (11/16") long x 11mm (7/16") wide. SEPALS: horizontal; tips recurved; light pink (49B), tipped light apple green (145B), upper surface; rose (52C), tipped light apple green (145B), lower surface; 33mm (1 1/4") long x 12mm (1/2") wide. TUBE: pale pink (36D); medium length & thickness; 19mm (3/4") long x 4mm (3/16") wide. STAMENS: extend 14mm (9/16") below corolla; dark rose (55A) filaments; dark reddish purple (64A) anthers. PISTIL: does not extend below the corolla; light pink (55D) style; pale yellow (1D) stigma. BUD: elongated. FOLIAGE: medium green (137B) upper surface; medium green (138B) lower surface. Leaves are 41mm (1 5/8") long x 19mm (3/4") wide, elliptic shaped, serrulated edges, acute tips and rounded bases. Light green (139D) veins; medium green (139C) stems; medium green/plum (139C/185C) branches. PARENTAGE: 'WALZ Harp' x unknown. Natural trailer. Self branching. Makes good basket. Prefers overhead filtered light, cool climate, or full sun. Best bloom and foliage colour in filtered light. Tested 5 years in Averbode, Belgium. Award, Meise, 9/20/03. Distinguished by bloom shape & colour.

Fernand 2004 BE AFS5612.

Henri Guillaumet. Upright. Single. COROLLA: unflared, smooth petal margins; opens violet (77B); matures reddish purple (70B); 28mm (1 1/8") long x 19mm (3/4") wide. SEPALS: horizontal; tips recurved; pink to light pink (62C-62B) upper surface & lower surfaces; 35mm (1 3/8") long x 8mm (5/16") wide. TUBE: pink to light pink (62C-62B); medium length & thickness; 19mm (3/4") long x 6mm (1/4") wide. STAMENS: extend 8-11mm (5/16-7/16") below corolla; pink (62A) filaments, grayish red (179A) anthers. PISTIL: extends 27mm (1 1/16") below the corolla, light pink (62B) style, peach (38B) stigma. BUD: ovate. FOLIAGE: medium green (146A) upper surface; yellowish green (146B) lower surface. Leaves are 57mm (2 1/4") long x 32mm (1 1/4") wide, ovate shaped, serrulated edges, acute tips and rounded bases. Veins & stems are yellowish green, branches are light brown. PARENTAGE: 'Philippe Boennec' x 'Mirobolant'. Medium upright. Makes good upright or standard. Prefers overhead filtered light and cool climate. Best bloom and foliage colour in filtered light. Tested 4 years in Pornic, France. Distinguished by bloom/foliage contrast.

Massé 2003 FR AFS5224.

Henrieke Dimi. Trailer. Double. COROLLA: half flared; opens reddish purple (67A) & reddish purple (72B), dark rose (58C) base; matures reddish purple (64B) & reddish purple (77A); 18mm (11/16") long x 16mm (5/8") wide. PETALOIDS: same colour as corolla; 14mm (9/16") long x 13mm (1/2") wide. SEPALS: horizontal, tips reflexed; rose (68C) tipped light yellow green (150A) upper surface; dark rose (55A) tipped light yellow green (150A) lower surface; 28mm (1 1/8") long x 13mm (1/2") wide. TUBE: white (155B) striped medium green (137D); medium length & thickness; 11mm (7/16") long x 5mm (3/16") wide. FOLIAGE is dark green (139A) upper surface; medium green (138B) lower surface. PARENTAGE: 'Demi' x 'Delta's Trick'. Meise 8/12/06, Outstanding.

Michiels 2007 BE AFS6357.

Henrimarie. Upright/Trailer. Double. COROLLA is three quarter flared with turned under smooth petal margins; opens dark purple (86A), dark rose (58C) base; matures reddish purple (74A), dark rose (58C) base; 11mm (7/16") long x 29 mm (1 1/8") wide. SEPALS are horizontal, tips recurved; magenta (58B) upper and lower surfaces; 20mm (13/16") long x 9mm (3/8") wide.

172

TUBE is magenta (58B), medium length and thickness; 8mm (15/16") long x 5mm (3/16") wide. STAMENS extend 26mm (1") beyond the corolla; dark rose (58C) filaments, grayish yellow (161A) anthers. PISTIL extends 33mm (1 5/16") below the corolla; magenta (58B) style; orangy brown (164A) stigma. BUD is ovate. FOLIAGE is dark green (137A) upper surface, medium green (137C) lower surface. Leaves are 92mm (3 5/8") long x 37mm (1 7/16") wide, lanceolate shaped, serrulated edges, acute tips and acute bases. Veins and stems are dark reddish purple (59A); branches are very dark reddish purple (186A). PARENTAGE: 'Areler Land' x 'Christel Stumpf'. Lax upright or stiff trailer. Self branching. Makes good basket. Prefers overhead filtered light and full sun. Best bloom and foliage colour in filtered light. Tested three years in Hoeselt, Belgium. Certificate N.B.F.K. at Meise. Distinguished by bloom shape.
Wagemans 2002 BE AFS4903.

HeRi Alestes. Upright. Single. COROLLA: Half flared; opens light rose (58D); matures purple (82B); 23mm (7/8") long x 31mm (1 1/4") wide. SEPALS: half up, tips recurved up; magenta (58B) upper surface; red (50A) lower surface; 54mm (2 1/8") long x 11mm (7/16") wide. TUBE: magenta (58B); medium length & thickness; 6mm (1/4") long x 6mm (1/4") wide. FOLIAGE is dark green (137A) upper surface; medium green (137C) lower surface. PARENTAGE: 'Reg Gubler' x 'BreeVis Danis'.
Buiting 2007 NL AFS6644.

HeRi Alver. Upright/Trailer. Semi Double. COROLLA is half flared with smooth petal margins; opens magenta (58B); matures dark rose (58C); 17mm (11/16") long x 22mm (7/8") wide. SEPALS are half up, tips reflexed up; dark rose (58C) upper surface; magenta (58B) lower surface; 29mm (1 1/8") long x 11mm (7/16") wide. TUBE is dark rose (58C); medium length & thickness; 22mm (7/8") long x 6mm (1/4") wide. FOLIAGE: dark green (137A) upper surface; medium green (138B) lower surface. Leaves are 62mm (2 7/16") long x 42mm (1 5/8") wide, ovate shaped. PARENTAGE: 'Roesse Carme' x 'Kim Klessens'. Distinguished by bloom & foliage combination.
Buiting 2005 NL AFS5863.

HeRi Arapaima. Upright/Trailer. Single. COROLLA is half flared; opens dark purple (79A); matures dark reddish purple (72A); 20mm (3/4") long x 25mm (1") wide. SEPALS

are horizontal, tips recurved; rose (68B) upper surface; magenta (68A) lower surface; 30mm (1 3/16") long x 12mm (7/16") wide. TUBE is rose (68B); 10mm (3/8") long x 8mm (5/16") wide. FOLIAGE: medium green (137C) upper surface; medium green (138B) lower surface. PARENTAGE: 'Rohees Dubhe' x 'Leon Pauwels'. Distinguished by bloom colour.
Buiting 2006 NL AFS6124.

HeRi Arari. Upright. Single. COROLLA: half flared; opens & matures red (45C); 24mm (15/16") long x 21mm (13/16") wide. SEPALS: horizontal, tips recurved; pink (48C) upper surface; red (45D) lower surface; 30mm (1 3/16") long x 11mm (7/16") wide. TUBE: pink (48C); 16mm (5/8") long x 7mm (1/4") wide. FOLIAGE is medium green (137B) upper surface; medium green (138B) lower surface. PARENTAGE: 'Roesse Lupus' x 'Bicentennial'.
Buiting 2008 NL AFS6925.

HeRi Arowana. Upright/Trailer. Semi Double. COROLLA: Three quarter flared; opens dark reddish purple (72A); matures purple (71A); 16mm (5/8") long x 22mm (7/8") wide. SEPALS: horizontal, tips recurved; pink (62A) upper surface; magenta (58B) lower surface; 26mm (1") long x 11mm (7/16") wide. TUBE: pink (62A); short & thick; 10mm (3/8") long x 10mm (3/8") wide. FOLIAGE is dark green (137A) upper surface; medium green (137D) lower surface. PARENTAGE: 'Roesse Carme' x 'Maik Luijten'.
Buiting 2007 NL AFS6658.

HeRi Asagi. Upright. Semi Double. COROLLA: three quarter flared, smooth petal margins; opens purple (71A) & matures dark reddish purple (60B); 20mm (3/4") long x 25mm (1") wide. SEPALS are fully up, tips recurved; rose (65A) upper surface; light purple (74C) lower surface; 20mm (3/4") long x 26mm (1") wide. TUBE is white (155A); medium length & thickness; 14mm (9/16") long x 6mm (1/4") wide. STAMENS extend 16mm (5/8") beyond the corolla; reddish purple (71B) filaments; purple (71A) anthers. PISTIL extends 34mm (1 3/8") beyond the corolla; light purple (74C) style; white (155A) stigma. BUD is ovate or globular. FOLIAGE is medium green (137B) upper surface; medium green (138B) lower surface. Leaves are 47mm (1 7/8") long x 30mm (1 3/16") wide, ovate shaped, entire edges, acute tips & bases. Veins, stems & branches are red. PARENTAGE: 'Roesse Carme' x 'Maik

Luijten'. Small upright. Makes good upright. Prefers overhead filtered light, cool climate. Best bloom in filtered light. Tested 3 years in Veldhoven, The Netherlands. Distinguished by bloom colour.
Buiting 2009 NL AFS7271.

HeRi Awaka. Upright/Trailer. Double. COROLLA: Three quarter flared; opens dark red (46A); matures red orange (42B); 19mm (3/4") long x 22mm (7/8") wide. SEPALS: half up, tips recurved up; red (53C) upper & lower surfaces; 26mm (1") long x 15mm (9/16") wide. TUBE: red (53C); short & thick; 9mm (5/16") long x 11mm (7/16") wide. FOLIAGE is medium green (137B) upper surface; medium green (138B) lower surface. PARENTAGE: 'Roesse Carme' x 'Suzanne Buiting'.
Buiting 2007 NL AFS6659.

HeRi Bacu. Upright. Single. COROLLA: Half flared; opens rose (68B); matures pink (62A); 25mm (1") long x 40mm (1 9/16") wide. SEPALS: half up, tips recurved up; rose (68C) tipped green upper surface; rose (68B) tipped green lower surfaces; 27mm (1 1/16") long x 17mm (5/8") wide. TUBE: rose (68C); short & thick; 10mm (3/8") long x 10mm (3/8") wide. FOLIAGE is dark green (137A) upper surface; medium green (137D) lower surface. PARENTAGE: 'Roesse Carme' x 'Paula Liebregts'.
Buiting 2007 NL AFS6660.

HeRi Barracuda. Upright/Trailer. Double. COROLLA: half flared; opens & matures dark reddish purple (60A); 16mm (5/8") long x 21mm (13/16") wide. SEPALS: half up, tips recurved up; rose (64D) upper surface; magenta (63A) lower surface; 19mm (3/4") long x 11mm (7/16") wide. TUBE: rose (64D); 23mm (7/8") long x 5mm (3/16") wide. FOLIAGE is dark green (137A) upper surface; medium green (138B) lower surface. PARENTAGE: 'Roesse Lupus' x 'HeRi Kuhli'.
Buiting 2008 NL AFS6930.

HeRi Bekko. Upright. Single. COROLLA: quarter flared, smooth petal margins; opens dark reddish purple (60B) & light pink (62C); matures reddish purple (60D) & light rose (63D); 15mm (9/16") long x 9mm (5/16") wide. SEPALS are horizontal, tips recurved; rose (64D), tipped green upper surface; rose (65A), tipped green lower surface; 28mm (1 1/8") long x 10mm (3/8") wide. TUBE is pale yellow (158B); medium length & thickness; 12mm (7/16") long x 8mm (5/16") wide. STAMENS extend 3mm (1/8") beyond the corolla; rose (68C) filaments; white (155A) anthers. PISTIL extends 10mm (3/8") beyond the corolla; rose (68C) style; white (155A) stigma. BUD is ovate. FOLIAGE is medium green (137B) upper surface; medium green (138D) lower surface. Leaves are 45mm (1 3/4") long x 29mm (1 1/8") wide, ovate shaped, serrulate edges, acute tips, rounded bases. Veins, stems & branches are green. PARENTAGE: 'Roesse Lupus' x ('Leon Pauwels' x 'Quasar'). Lax upright or stiff trailer. Makes good stiff upright. Prefers overhead filtered light, cool climate. Best bloom in filtered light. Tested 3 years in Veldhoven, The Netherlands. Distinguished by bloom & foliage colour combinations.
Buiting 2009 NL AFS7264.

HeRi Bermpje. Upright/Trailer. Single. COROLLA: quarter flared; opens & matures light rose (58D) & light pink (62C); 20mm (3/4") long x 18mm (11/16") wide. SEPALS: horizontal, tips recurved; light apple green (145C) tipped green upper & lower surfaces; 26mm (1") long x 6mm (1/4") wide. TUBE: light apple green (145C); 12mm (7/16") long x 6mm (1/4") wide. FOLIAGE is medium green (137B) upper surface; medium green (138B) lower surface. PARENTAGE: 'HeRi Knorhaan' x 'Oranje van Os'.
Buiting 2008 NL AFS6933.

HeRi Blauwe Winde. Upright. Semi Double. COROLLA: Half flared; opens violet (76A); matures violet (77C); 21mm (13/16") long x 24mm (15/16") wide. SEPALS: half up, tips recurved up; pale violet (76D) upper surface; pale purple (76C) lower surface; 32mm (1 1/4") long x 12mm (7/16") wide. TUBE: pale violet (76D); medium length & thickness; 14mm (9/16") long x 7mm (1/4") wide. FOLIAGE is dark green (137A) upper surface; medium green (137C) lower surface. PARENTAGE: 'Sofie Michiels' x 'Maik Luijten'.
Buiting 2007 NL AFS6657.

HeRi Bonito. Upright. Double. COROLLA is half flared; opens dark reddish purple (59A); matures magenta (59C); 16mm (5/8") long x 18mm (11/16") wide. SEPALS are fully up, tips recurved; rose (65A) upper & lower surfaces; 18mm (11/16") long x 12mm (7/16") wide. TUBE is light pink (65C); 9mm (3/8") long x 9mm (3/8") wide. FOLIAGE: dark green (137A) upper surface; medium green (137D) lower surface. PARENTAGE: 'Roesse Carme' x 'Paul Schats'. Distinguished by bloom colour.
Buiting 2006 NL AFS6129.

174

HeRi Boondi. Trailer. Semi Double. COROLLA: Half flared; opens violet (85A); matures light purple (78B); 24mm (15/16") long x 26mm (1") wide. SEPALS: fully up, tips recurved; pale lavender (65D) upper surface; light pink (65B) lower surface; 33mm (1 5/16") long x 13mm (1/2") wide. TUBE: pale lavender (65D); medium length & thickness; 9mm (5/16") long x 4mm (1/8") wide. FOLIAGE is dark green (137A) upper surface; medium green (137C) lower surface. PARENTAGE: 'Roesse Tucana' x 'Yvette Klessens'.
Buiting 2007 NL AFS6646.

HeRi Calico. Upright. Semi Double. COROLLA: quarter flared, smooth petal margins; opens dark reddish purple (64A); matures reddish purple (61B); 15mm (9/16") long x 18mm (11/16") wide. SEPALS are fully up, tips recurved; light pink (62C), tipped green upper surface; rose (63C), tipped green lower surface; 29mm (1 1/8") long x 9mm (5/16") wide. TUBE is light pink (62C); medium length & thickness; 20mm (3/4") long x 6mm (1/4") wide. STAMENS extend 5mm (3/16") beyond the corolla; magenta (68A) filaments; dark reddish purple (64A) anthers. PISTIL extends 22mm (7/8") beyond the corolla; rose (68B) style; white (155A) stigma. BUD: ovate, long TUBE. FOLIAGE: dark green (137A) upper surface; medium green (138B) lower surface. Leaves are 50mm (2") long x 25mm (1") wide, ovate shaped, serrulate edges, acute tips, rounded bases. Veins & stems are green & branches are brown. PARENTAGE: 'Roesse Lupus' x 'Monique Luijten'. Lax upright or stiff trailer. Makes good stiff trailer. Prefers overhead filtered light, cool climate. Best bloom in filtered light. Tested 3 years in Veldhoven, The Netherlands. Distinguished by bloom & foliage colour combinations.
Buiting 2009 NL AFS7265.

HeRi Candiru. Upright. Single. COROLLA is full flared; opens dark purple (79A); matures dark purple (79B); 18mm (11/16") long x 23mm (7/8") wide. SEPALS are half up, tips recurved up; light purple (70C) upper & lower surfaces; 24mm (15/16") long x 9mm (3/8") wide. TUBE is light purple (70C); 9mm (3/8") long x 6mm (1/4") wide. FOLIAGE: medium green (137B) upper surface; medium green (138B) lower surface.. PARENTAGE: 'Roesse Apus' x ('Swanley Gem' x 'Monique Sleiderink'). Distinguished by erect blooms & bloom colour.
Buiting 2006 NL AFS6118.

HeRi Cascudo. Upright. Double. COROLLA: Three quarter flared; opens violet blue (92A); matures violet (75A); 26mm (1") long x 29mm (1 1/8") wide. SEPALS: half up, tips recurved up; pale violet (76D) upper surface; violet (77C) lower surface; 36mm (1 7/16") long x 12mm (7/16") wide. TUBE: pale violet (76D); medium length & thickness; 10mm (3/8") long x 6mm (1/4") wide. FOLIAGE is medium green (137C) upper surface; medium green (137C) lower surface. PARENTAGE: 'Roesse Tucana' x 'Yvette Klessens'.
Buiting 2007 NL AFS6661.

HeRi Cassava. Upright/Trailer. Double. COROLLA: three quarter flared; opens purple (83A); matures reddish purple (71B); 32mm (1 1/4") long x 24mm (15/16") wide. SEPALS: fully up, tips recurved; rose (68C) upper surface; magenta (68A) lower surface; 42mm (1 5/8") long x 16mm (5/8") wide. TUBE: rose (68C); 16mm (5/8") long x 7mm (1/4") wide. FOLIAGE is dark green (137A) upper surface; medium green (137C) lower surface. PARENTAGE: 'Leon Pauwels' x 'Leon Pauwels'.
Buiting 2008 NL AFS6926.

HeRi Chessa. Upright/Trailer. Double. COROLLA: Three quarter flared; opens dark reddish purple (72A); matures magenta (63A); 20mm (3/4") long x 39mm (1 1/2") wide. SEPALS: fully up, tips recurved; pale pink (62D) upper surface; pink (62C) lower surface; 52mm (2 1/16") long x 16mm (5/8") wide. TUBE: pale pink (62D); medium length & thickness; 17mm (5/8") long x 7mm (1/4") wide. FOLIAGE is medium green (137B) upper surface; medium green (138B) lower surface. PARENTAGE: 'Senna Krekels' x 'HeRi Mochara'.
Buiting 2007 NL AFS6643.

HeRi Cyclops. Upright. Semi Double. COROLLA: full flared, smooth petal margins; opens dark reddish purple (64A); matures reddish purple (61B); 20mm (3/4") long x 18mm (11/16") wide. SEPALS are fully up, tips recurved; magenta (57B) upper surface; magenta (58B) lower surface; 26mm (1") long x 13mm (1/2") wide. TUBE is magenta (57B); medium length & thickness; 12mm (7/16") long x 8mm (5/16") wide. STAMENS extend 27mm (1 1/16") beyond the corolla; magenta (63B) filaments & anthers. PISTIL extends 40mm (1 9/16") beyond the corolla; magenta (63B) style; white (155D) stigma. BUD: ovate, long TUBE. FOLIAGE: medium green (137C) upper surface; medium green (138B) lower surface. Leaves are 37mm (1 7/16") long x

27mm (1 1/16") wide, ovate shaped, serrulate edges, obtuse tips, rounded bases. Veins, stems & branches are red. PARENTAGE: 'Roesse Lupus' x 'Maxima's Girl'. Small upright. Makes good upright. Prefers overhead filtered light, cool climate. Best bloom in filtered light. Tested 3 years in Veldhoven, The Netherlands. Distinguished by bloom shape. Buiting 2009 NL AFS7267.

HeRi Demekin. Upright. Single. COROLLA: quarter flared, smooth petal margins; opens peach (37B) & light orange (26C); matures orange (29A) & light orange (26C); 14mm (9/16") long x 9mm (5/16") wide. SEPALS are horizontal, tips recurved; peach (37B), tipped green upper surface; pink (37C) lower surface; 22mm (7/8") long x 9mm (5/16") wide. TUBE is light pink (36B); medium length & thickness; 20mm (3/4") long x 7mm (1/4") wide. STAMENS extend 3mm (1/8") beyond the corolla; rose (68C) filaments; white (155A) anthers. PISTIL extends 7mm (1/4") beyond the corolla; rose (68C) style; white (155A) stigma. BUD is globular. FOLIAGE is dark green (137A) upper surface; medium green (137C) lower surface. Leaves are 71mm (2 13/16") long x 31mm (1 1/4") wide, lanceolate shaped, serrulate edges, acute tips, obtuse bases. Veins are green, stems are red & branches are brown. PARENTAGE: 'HeRi Knorhaan' x 'Oranje van Os'. Medium upright. Makes good upright or standard. Prefers overhead filtered light, cool climate. Best bloom in filtered light. Tested 3 years in Veldhoven, The Netherlands. Distinguished by bloom & foliage colour combinations. Buiting 2009 NL AFS7262.

HeRi Dorado. Upright. Single. COROLLA is quarter flared; opens magenta (63A); matures magenta (58B); 19mm (3/4") long x 21mm (13/16") wide. SEPALS are horizontal, tips recurved; light rose (63D) tipped green upper surface; light pink (62B) tipped green lower surface; 21mm (13/16") long x 9mm (3/8") wide. TUBE is light rose (63D); 10mm (3/8") long x 8mm (5/16") wide. FOLIAGE: dark green (137A) upper surface; medium green (137D) lower surface. PARENTAGE: 'Swanley Gem' x 'Quasar'. Distinguished by erect blooms. Buiting 2006 NL AFS6103.

HeRi Elft. Upright/Trailer. Semi Double. COROLLA is three quarter flared with smooth petal margins; opens violet (77B); matures magenta (67B); 24mm (15/16") long

x 26mm (1") wide. SEPALS are fully up, tips recurved; rose (61D) upper surface; magenta (58B) lower surface; 26mm (1") long x 11mm (7/16") wide. TUBE is rose (61D); medium length & thickness; 14mm (9/16") long x 7mm (1/4") wide. FOLIAGE: medium green (137B) upper surface; medium green (138A) lower surface. Leaves are 64mm (2 1/2") long x 40mm (1 9/16") wide, ovate shaped. PARENTAGE: 'Roesse Carme' x 'Kim Klessens'. Distinguished by bloom shape. Buiting 2005 NL AFS5864.

HeRi Elrits. Upright/Trailer. Semi Double. COROLLA is three quarter flared with smooth petal margins; opens magenta (67B); matures magenta (68A); 19mm (3/4") long x 20mm (13/16") wide. SEPALS are half up, tips reflexed up; light pink (62B) upper surface; reddish purple (58A) lower surface; 17mm (11/16") long x 9mm (3/8") wide. TUBE is pink (62C); medium length & thickness; 9mm (3/8") long x 6mm (1/4") wide. FOLIAGE: medium green (137B) upper surface; medium green (138A) lower surface. Leaves are 64mm (2 1/2") long x 44mm (1 3/4") wide, ovate shaped. PARENTAGE: 'Roesse Carme' x 'Kim Klessens'. Distinguished by bloom shape. Buiting 2005 NL AFS5865.

HeRi Fint. Upright/Trailer. Semi Double. COROLLA is half flared with smooth petal margins; opens reddish purple (70B); matures reddish purple (67A); 20mm (13/16") long x 24mm (15/16") wide. SEPALS are fully up, tips recurved; light rose (68D) upper surface; rose (68C) lower surface; 17mm (11/16") long x 11mm (7/16") wide. TUBE is light rose (68D); medium length & thickness; 12mm (1/2") long x 5mm (3/16") wide. FOLIAGE: dark green (139A) upper surface; medium green (138A) lower surface. Leaves are 50mm (2") long x 27mm (1 1/16") wide, ovate shaped. PARENTAGE: 'Sofie Michiels' x ('Roesse Apus' x 'Roesse Apus') x 'Yvette Klessens'. Distinguished by bloom & foliage combination. Buiting 2005 NL AFS5866.

HeRi Giebel. Upright. Double. COROLLA is half flared with smooth petal margins; opens magenta (58B); matures light rose (58D); 18mm (11/16") long x 29mm (1 1/8") wide. SEPALS are fully up, tips recurved; dark rose (67C) upper & lower surfaces; 18mm (11/16") long x 15mm (9/16") wide. TUBE is rose (67D); medium length & thickness; 12mm (1/2") long x 6mm (1/4") wide. FOLIAGE: medium green (137B) upper surface; medium green (138B) lower surface. Leaves are 62mm (2 7/16") long x 45mm (1 3/4") wide, ovate shaped. ['Sofie Michiels' x ('Roesse Apus' x 'Roesse Apus')] x 'Delta's Wonder'. Distinguished by bloom & foliage combination. Buiting 2005 NL AFS5868.

HeRi Goonch. Upright/Trailer. Semi Double. COROLLA: three quarter flared; opens dark purple (78A); matures reddish purple (72B); 21mm (13/16") long x 23mm (7/8") wide. SEPALS: fully up, tips recurved; light rose (68D) upper surface; rose (68B) lower surface; 21mm (13/16") long x 12mm (7/16") wide. TUBE: light rose (68D); 29mm (1 1/8") long x 7mm (1/4") wide. FOLIAGE is medium green (137C) upper surface; medium green (138B) lower surface. PARENTAGE: ('Roesse Carme' x 'Roesse Apus') x 'Maik Luijten'. Buiting 2008 NL AFS6927.

HeRi Grilse. Upright/Trailer. Single. COROLLA: Half flared; opens red (45A); matures red (45C); 22mm (7/8") long x 24mm (15/16") wide. SEPALS: horizontal, tips recurved; magenta (58B) upper surface; red (46D) lower surface; 31mm (1 1/4") long x 10mm (3/8") wide. TUBE: magenta (58B); medium length & thickness; 12mm (7/16") long x 7mm (1/4") wide. FOLIAGE is medium green (137B) upper surface; medium green (137B) lower surface. PARENTAGE: 'Roesse Lupus' x 'Luuk van Riet'. Buiting 2007 NL AFS6662.

HeRi Groper. Upright/Trailer. Double. COROLLA is three quarter flared; opens dark reddish purple (72A); matures reddish purple (67A); 25mm (1") long x 15mm (9/16") wide. SEPALS are half up, tips recurved up; white (155A) upper surface; light reddish purple (72D) lower surface; 25mm (1") long x 9mm (3/8") wide. TUBE is white (155A); 10mm (3/8") long x 4mm (1/8") wide. FOLIAGE: dark green (137A) upper surface; medium green (137D) lower surface. PARENTAGE: 'Senna Krekels' x 'Paul Schats'. Distinguished by bloom colour. Buiting 2006 NL AFS6115.

HeRi Houting. Upright. Double. COROLLA is half flared with smooth petal margins; opens magenta (71C); matures reddish purple (72B); 20mm (13/16") long x 23mm (15/16") wide. SEPALS are fully up, tips recurved; rose (51B) upper surface; dark rose (51A) lower surface; 25mm (1") long x 11mm (7/16") wide. TUBE is rose (51B); medium length & thickness; 12mm (1/2") long x 8mm

(3/16") wide. FOLIAGE: medium green (137C) upper surface; medium green (138B) lower surface. Leaves are 53mm (2 1/16") long x 28mm (1 1/8") wide, ovate shaped. PARENTAGE: 'Roesse Carme' x ('Madalyn Drago' x 'Roesse Blacky'). Distinguished by erect blooms. Buiting 2005 NL AFS5869.

HeRi Jikin. Upright. Semi Double. COROLLA: quarter flared, smooth petal margins; opens red (53C) & matures red (53D); 16mm (5/8") long x 20mm (3/4") wide. SEPALS are horizontal, tips recurved; light pink (65B) upper surface; rose (65A) lower surface; 33mm (1 5/16") long x 14mm (9/16") wide. TUBE is white (155D); medium length & thickness; 33mm 1 5/16") long x 6mm (1/4") wide. STAMENS extend 14mm (9/16") beyond the corolla; light pink (65B) filaments & anthers. PISTIL extends 24mm (15/16") beyond the corolla; rose (65A) style; white (155A) stigma. BUD is ovate. FOLIAGE is dark green (137A) upper surface; medium green (137C) lower surface. Leaves are 65mm (2 9/16") long x 40mm (1 9/16") wide, ovate shaped, serrulate edges, acute tips, rounded bases. Veins & stems are green & branches are red. PARENTAGE: 'Roesse Lupus' x 'Monique Luijten'. Small upright. Makes good upright or standard. Prefers overhead filtered light, cool climate. Best bloom in filtered light. Tested 3 years in Veldhoven, The Netherlands. Distinguished by bloom & foliage colour combinations. Buiting 2009 NL AFS7272.

HeRi Knipstaart. Upright/Trailer. Single. COROLLA: half flared; opens dark reddish purple (59A); matures dark reddish purple (60A); 20mm (3/4") long x 17mm (5/8") wide. SEPALS: half up, tips recurved up; magenta (58B) upper & lower surfaces; 29mm (1 1/8") long x 11mm (7/16") wide. TUBE: magenta (58B); 26mm (1") long x 5mm (3/16") wide. FOLIAGE is dark green (137A) upper surface; medium green (137C) lower surface. PARENTAGE: 'Roesse Lupus' x 'HeRi Mahseer'. Buiting 2008 NL AFS6932.

HeRi Knorhaan. Upright/Trailer. Single. COROLLA: Quarter flared; opens & matures red orange (40A) & light orange (40D); 14mm (9/16") long x 16mm (5/8") wide. SEPALS: horizontal, tips recurved; pink (52D) tipped green upper surface; rose (52C) tipped green lower surface; 21mm (13/16") long x 12mm (7/16") wide. TUBE: pink (52D); medium length & thickness; 14mm (9/16") long x

177

7mm (1/4") wide. FOLIAGE is medium green (137C) upper surface; medium green (138B) lower surface. PARENTAGE: 'Roesse Lupus' x 'Orange van Os'.
Buiting 2007 NL AFS6639.

HeRi Kohaku. Upright. Single. COROLLA is three quarter flared; opens purple (71A); matures dark reddish purple (70A); 17mm (5/8") long x 16mm (5/8") wide. SEPALS are fully up, tips recurved; pale pink (62D) upper surface; magenta (63B) lower surface; 27mm (1 1/16") long x 11mm (7/16") wide. TUBE is pale pink (62D); 14mm (9/16") long x 9mm (3/8") wide. FOLIAGE: medium green (137C) upper surface; light green (138C) lower surface. PARENTAGE: 'Roesse Apus' x 'Roesse Tureis'. Distinguished by bloom colour & shape.
Buiting 2006 NL AFS6113.

HeRi Koi. Upright. Double. COROLLA: Half flared; opens red (46B); matures rose (51B); 28mm (1 1/8") long x 20mm (3/4") wide. SEPALS: half up, tips recurved up; rose (52B) tipped green upper surface; red (52A) tipped green lower surface; 36mm (1 7/16") long x 14mm (9/16") wide. TUBE: rose (52B); medium length & thickness; 17mm (5/8") long x 7mm (1/4") wide. FOLIAGE is dark green (137A) upper surface; medium green (137C) lower surface. PARENTAGE: 'Roesse Lupus' x 'Maik Luijten'.
Buiing 2007 NL AFS6656.

HeRi Kuhli. Upright. Semi Double. COROLLA: Half flared; opens red (46B); matures rose (51B); 28mm (1 1/8") long x 20mm (3/4") wide. SEPALS: half up, tips recurved up; rose (52B) tipped green upper surface; red (52A) tipped green lower surface; 36mm (1 7/16") long x 14mm (9/16") wide. TUBE: rose (52B); medium length & thickness; 17mm (5/8") long x 7mm (1/4") wide. FOLIAGE is dark green (137A) upper surface; medium green (137C) lower surface. PARENTAGE: 'Roesse Lupus' x 'Maik Luijten'.
Buiting 2007 NL AFS6656.

HeRi Leng. Trailer. Single. COROLLA is three quarter flared; opens purple (89B); matures dark purple (78A); 22mm (7/8") long x 26mm (1") wide. SEPALS are fully up, tips reflexed; magenta (63A) upper & lower surfaces; 31mm (1 1/4") long x 9mm (3/8") wide. TUBE is magenta (63A); 14mm (9/16") long x 7mm (1/4") wide. FOLIAGE: dark green (137A) upper surface; medium green (138B) lower surface. PARENTAGE: 'Swanley

Gem' x 'Kim Klessens'. Distinguished by bloom & foliage.
Buiting 2006 NL AFS111.

HeRi Mahseer. Upright/Trailer. Double. COROLLA is three quarter flared; opens & matures light pink (65C); 25mm (1") long x 23mm (7/8") wide. SEPALS are half up, tips reflexed up; magenta (63A) upper & lower surfaces; 41mm (1 5/8") long x 14mm (9/16") wide. TUBE is pink (62C); 17mm (5/8") long x 6mm (1/4") wide. FOLIAGE: medium green (137C) upper surface; medium green (138B) lower surface. PARENTAGE: 'Sofie Michiels' x 'Luuk van Riet'. Distinguished by bloom & foliage combination.
Buiting 2006 NL AFS6108.

HeRi Marlijn. Upright/Trailer. Double. COROLLA is three quarter flared; opens purple (77A); matures violet (77B); 25mm (1") long x 30mm (1 3/16") wide. SEPALS are fully up, tips recurved; light rose (68D) upper surface; rose (68B) lower surface; 35mm (1 3/8") long x 15mm (9/16") wide. TUBE is light rose (68D); 10mm (3/8") long x 8mm (5/16") wide. FOLIAGE: medium green (137B) upper surface; medium green (138B) lower surface. PARENTAGE: 'Roesse Apus' x 'Yvette Klessens'. Distinguished by bloom & foliage combination.
Buiting 2006 NL AFS6123.

HeRi Matsuba. Upright. Double. COROLLA: half flared, smooth petal margins; opens violet (76B); matures light purple (75B); 27mm (1 1/16") long x 17mm (5/8") wide. SEPALS are horizontal, tips recurved; white (155D), tipped green upper & lower surfaces; 22mm (7/8") long x 6mm (1/4") wide. TUBE is white (155D); medium length & thickness; 17mm (5/8") long x 5mm (3/16") wide. STAMENS extend 4mm (1/8") beyond the corolla; white (155D) filaments; rose (65A) anthers. PISTIL extends 12mm (7/16") beyond the corolla; white (155D) style & stigma. BUD is globular. FOLIAGE is medium green (137B) upper surface; medium green (138B) lower surface. Leaves are 78mm (3 1/8") long x 45mm (1 3/4") wide, ovate shaped, serrulate edges, acute tips, rounded bases. Veins, stems & branches are green. PARENTAGE: 'Sofie Michiels' x 'Roesse Plato'. Lax upright or stiff trailer. Makes good stiff trailer. Prefers overhead filtered light, cool climate. Best bloom in filtered light. Tested 3 years in Veldhoven, The Netherlands. Distinguished by bloom & foliage colour combinations.

Buiting 2009 NL AFS7263.

HeRi Minor. Upright. Single. COROLLA: Half flared; opens & matures magenta (68A); 21mm (13/16") long x 12mm (7/16") wide. SEPALS: horizontal, tips recurved; pale pink (62D) tipped green upper & lower surfaces; 34mm (1 3/8") long x 12mm (7/16") wide. TUBE: pale pink (62D); short & thick; 10mm (3/8") long x 10mm (3/8") wide. FOLIAGE is dark green (137A) upper surface; medium green (138B) lower surface. PARENTAGE: 'Sofie Michiels' x 'Oranje van Os'. Buiting 2007 NL AFS6648.

HeRi Mochara. Trailer. Double. COROLLA is three quarter flared; opens purple (83B); matures purple (71A); 27mm (1 1/16") long x 29mm (1 1/8") wide. SEPALS are horizontal, tips recurved; light violet (84C) upper surface; light violet (84B) lower surface; 37mm (1 7/16") long x 27mm (1 1/16") wide. TUBE is light violet (84C); 15mm (9/16") long x 6mm (1/4") wide. FOLIAGE: medium green (137D) upper surface; light green (138C) lower surface. PARENTAGE: 'Leon Pauwels' x 'Quasar'. Distinguished by bloom colour. Buiting 2006 NL AFS6105.

HeRi Morwong. Upright/Trailer. Single. COROLLA: half flared; opens dark reddish purple (59A); matures magenta (59C); 19mm (3/4") long x 24mm (15/16") wide. SEPALS: fully up, tips reflexed; dark rose (51A) upper & lower surfaces; 31mm (1 1/4") long x 11mm (7/16") wide. TUBE: rose (51A); 20mm (3/4") long x 8mm (5/16") wide. FOLIAGE is dark green (137A) upper surface; light green (138C) lower surface. PARENTAGE: 'Roesse Lupus' x 'Bicentennial'. Buiting 2008 NL AFS6931.

HeRi Mowi. Upright/Trailer. Double. COROLLA: Half flared; opens & matures red (46B); 21mm (13/16") long x 26mm (1") wide. SEPALS: fully up, tips recurved; dark reddish purple (60B) upper surface; red (45B) lower surface; 23mm (7/8") long x 14mm (9/16") wide. TUBE: dark reddish purple (60B); medium length & thickness; 12mm (7/16") long x 6mm (1/4") wide. FOLIAGE is dark green (137A) upper surface; medium green (138B) lower surface. PARENTAGE: 'Roesse Lupus' x 'HeRi Arapaima'. Buiting 2007 NL AFS6641.

HeRi Mullet. Upright/Trailer. Single. COROLLA: Half flared; opens dark reddish purple (59A); matures dark reddish purple (60A); 21mm (13/16") long x 23mm (7/8")

wide. SEPALS: fully up, tips reflexed; dark rose (58C) upper & lower surfaces; 24mm (15/16") long x 12mm (7/16") wide. TUBE: light rose (58D); medium length & thickness; 20mm (3/4") long x 7mm (1/4") wide. FOLIAGE is medium green (137B) upper surface; medium green (138B) lower surface. PARENTAGE: 'Roesse Lupus' x 'Maik Luijten'. Buiting 2007 NL AFS6640.

HeRi Omber. Upright/Trailer. Double. COROLLA: half flared; opens dark purple (79B); matures purple (71A); 26mm (1") long x 27mm (1 1/16") wide. SEPALS: fully up, tips recurved; white (155D) upper & lower surfaces; 31mm (1 1/4") long x 14mm (9/16") wide. TUBE: pale lavender (65D); 25mm (1") long x 6mm (1/4") wide. FOLIAGE is dark green (137A) upper surface; medium green (137C) lower surface. PARENTAGE: 'HeRi Zeewolf' x 'Jef vander Kuylen'. Buiting 2008 NL AFS6921.

HeRi Panache. Upright. Double. COROLLA: half flared, smooth petal margins; opens violet (76A); matures violet (77C); 20mm (3/4") long x 21mm (13/16") wide. SEPALS are fully up, tips recurved; white (155C) upper surface & white (155D) lower surface; 39mm (1 1/2") long x 13mm (1/2") wide. TUBE is white (155C); medium length & thickness; 28mm (1 1/8") long x 8mm (5/16") wide. STAMENS extend 14mm (9/16") beyond the corolla; pale purple (75C) filaments; light purple (75B) anthers. PISTIL extends 35mm (1 3/8") beyond the corolla; white (155D) style; white (155A) stigma. BUD: globular, long TUBE. FOLIAGE: medium green (137B) upper surface; medium green (138B) lower surface. Leaves are 47mm (1 7/8") long x 23mm (7/8") wide, ovate shaped, serrulate edges, acute tips, rounded bases. Veins, stems & branches are green. PARENTAGE: 'Pivo' x 'HeRi Pulcher'. Lax upright or stiff trailer. Makes good upright or stiff trailer. Prefers overhead filtered light, cool climate. Best bloom in filtered light. Tested 3 years in Veldhoven, The Netherlands. Distinguished by bloom & foliage colour combinations. Buiting 2009 NL AFS7268.

HeRi Panga. Upright/Trailer. Double. COROLLA is three quarter flared; opens violet (84A); matures dark purple (78A); 22mm (7/8") long x 25mm (1") wide. SEPALS are half up, tips recurved up; white (155D) upper & lower surfaces; 34mm (1 3/8") long x 17mm (5/8") wide. TUBE is white (155D);

15mm (9/16") long x 7mm (1/4") wide. FOLIAGE: dark green (137A) upper surface; medium green (137D) lower surface. PARENTAGE: 'Quasar' x 'Sofie Michiels'. Distinguished by bloom & foliage combination.
Buiting 2006 NL AFS6121.

HeRi Parelvis. Upright/Trailer. Double. COROLLA: three quarter flared; opens purple (77A); matures dark reddish purple (61A); 26mm (1") long x 24mm (15/16") wide. SEPALS: fully up, tips recurved; dark rose (58C) upper & lower surfaces; 43mm (1 11/16") long x 14mm (9/16") wide. TUBE: dark rose (58C); 10mm (3/8") long x 7mm (1/4") wide. FOLIAGE is dark green (137A) upper surface; medium green (138B) lower surface. PARENTAGE: 'Roesse Dubhe' x 'HeRi Mochara'.
Buiting 2008 NL AFS6923.

HeRi Permit. Upright/Trailer. Double. COROLLA is three quarter flared; opens purple (83B); matures violet (77B); 16mm (5/8") long x 26mm (1") wide. SEPALS are horizontal, tips recurved; magenta (58B) upper & lower surfaces; 31mm (1 1/4") long x 14mm (9/16") wide. TUBE is magenta (58B); 11mm (7/16") long x 6mm (1/4") wide. FOLIAGE: dark green (137A) upper surface; medium green (138B) lower surface. PARENTAGE: 'Swingtime' x 'Rohees New Millennium'. Distinguished by bloom & foliage combination.
Buiting 2006 NL AFS6109.

HeRi Pollak. Upright/Trailer. Double. COROLLA is three quarter flared; opens purple (88A); matures dark purple (78A); 16mm (5/8") long x 23mm (7/8") wide. SEPALS are fully up, tips recurved; light pink (65C) upper surface; rose (65A) lower surface; 29mm (1 1/16") long x 11mm (7/16") wide. TUBE is light pink (65C); 16mm (5/8") long x 5mm (3/16") wide. FOLIAGE: medium green (137B) upper surface; medium green (138B) lower surface. PARENTAGE: 'Roesse Carme' x 'Roesse Tuteis'. Distinguished by bloom colour.
Buiting 2006 NL AFS6104.

HeRi Pcs. Upright/Trailer. Single. COROLLA is half flared with smooth petal margins; opens dark purple (78A); matures violet (77B); 24mm (15/16") long x 18mm (11/16") wide. SEPALS are horizontal, tips recurved; light magenta (66D) upper surface; rose (68C) lower surface; 30mm (1 3/16") long x 14mm (9/16") wide. TUBE is light magenta

(66D); medium length & thickness; 20mm (13/16") long x 8mm (5/16") wide. FOLIAGE: medium green (137B) upper surface; medium green (137D) lower surface. Leaves are 60mm (2 3/8") long x 35mm (1 3/8") wide, ovate shaped. PARENTAGE: 'Roesse Carme' x 'Kim Klessens'. Distinguished by bloom & foliage combination.
Buiting 2005 NL AFS5871.

HeRi Pulcher. Upright/Trailer. Double. COROLLA: Three quarter flared; opens pale violet (91C); matures pale purple (75C); 27mm (1 1/16") long x 21mm (13/16") wide. SEPALS: half up, tips recurved up; pale lavender (69D) upper surface; pale lavender (69B) lower surface; 34mm (1 3/8") long x 13mm (1/2") wide. TUBE: pale lavender (69D); medium length & thickness; 14mm (9/16") long x 6mm (1/4") wide. FOLIAGE is dark green (137A) upper surface; medium green (138A) lower surface. PARENTAGE: 'Sofie Michiels' x 'Silver Dawn'.
Buiting 2007 NL AFS6647.

HeRi Ranchu. Upright. Double. COROLLA: half flared, smooth petal margins; opens dark reddish purple (70A) & matures reddish purple (72B); 19mm (3/4") long x 22mm (7/8") wide. SEPALS are half down, tips reflexed; rose (63C) upper & lower surfaces; 30mm (1 3/16") long x 20mm (3/4") wide. TUBE is rose (63C); medium length & thickness; 13mm (1/2") long x 8mm (5/16") wide. STAMENS extend 10mm (3/8") beyond the corolla; magenta (63B) filaments & anthers. PISTIL extends 24mm (15/16") beyond the corolla; light rose (63D) style; pale pink (62D) stigma. BUD is globular. FOLIAGE is dark green (137A) upper surface; medium green (137D) lower surface. Leaves are 41mm (1 5/8") long x 30mm (1 3/16") wide, ovate shaped, entire edges, acute tips, rounded bases. Veins & stems are green & branches are red. PARENTAGE: 'Rohees Dubhe' x 'HeRi Mochara'. Small upright. Makes good upright. Prefers overhead filtered light, cool climate. Best bloom in filtered light. Tested 3 years in Veldhoven, The Netherlands. Distinguished by bloom & foliage colour combinations.
Buiting 2009 NL AFS7270.

HeRi Relojito. Upright. Single. COROLLA is half flared; opens light purple (86C); matures violet (84A); 25mm (1") long x 25mm (1") wide. SEPALS are fully up, tips recurved; light reddish purple (66C) upper & lower surfaces; 32mm (1 1/4") long x 11mm (7/16") wide. TUBE is light reddish purple

(66C); 13mm (1/2") long x 8mm (5/16") wide. FOLIAGE: medium green (137C) upper surface; light green (138C) lower surface. PARENTAGE: ('Roesse Apus' x 'Roesse Apus') x 'Yvette Klessens'. Distinguished by bloom & foliage combination.
Buiting 2006 NL AFS6126.

HeRi Rozette. Upright. Semi Double. COROLLA is three quarter flared; opens & matures rose (67D); 18mm (11/16") long x 20mm (3/4") wide. SEPALS are horizontal, tips recurved; white (155A) tipped green upper surface; light pink (65B) tipped green lower surface; 23mm (7/8") long x 9mm (3/8") wide. TUBE is white (155A); 13mm (1/2") long x 9mm (3/8") wide. FOLIAGE: medium green (137B) upper surface; light green (138C) lower surface. PARENTAGE: 'Roesse Carme' x 'Sofie Michiels'. Distinguished by erect blooms.
Buiting 2006 NL AFS6119.

HeRi Sarapo. Upright. Double. COROLLA: half flared; opens dark reddish purple (70A); matures reddish purple (71B); 20mm (3/4") long x 24mm (15/16") wide. SEPALS: half up, tips reflexed up; light lavender (65D) upper surface; light pink (65B) lower surface; 30mm (1 3/16") long x 15mm (9/16") wide. TUBE: light apple green (145B); 10mm (3/8") long x 5mm (3/16") wide. FOLIAGE is dark green (137A) upper surface; medium green (138B) lower surface. PARENTAGE: 'Roesse Apus' x 'Maik Luijten'.
Buiting 2008 NL AFS6929.

HeRi Sarasa. Upright. Single. COROLLA: unflared, smooth petal margins; opens orange red (34B) & matures pink (35C); 14mm (9/16") long x 13mm (1/2") wide. SEPALS are full down, tips recurved; pink (36A), tipped green upper & lower surfaces; 18mm (11/16") long x 9mm (5/16") wide. TUBE is pink (36-A); medium length & thickness; 8mm (5/16") long x 13mm (1/2") wide. STAMENS extend 2mm (1/16") beyond the corolla; pink (62A) filaments & anthers. PISTIL extends 8mm (5/16") beyond the corolla; pink (62A) style; white (155A) stigma. BUD is globular, long TUBE. FOLIAGE is medium green (137B) upper surface; medium green (138A) lower surface. Leaves are 39mm (1 1/2") long x 31mm (1 1/4") wide, ovate shaped, serrulate edges, acute tips, cordate bases. Veins, stems & branches are green. PARENTAGE: 'Roesse Carme' x 'Oranje van Os'. Small upright. Makes good upright or stiff trailer. Prefers overhead filtered light, cool climate. Best bloom in filtered light.

Tested 3 years in Veldhoven, The Netherlands. Distinguished by bloom colour & shape.
Buiting 2009 NL AFS7269.

HeRi Serpae. Upright. Single. COROLLA: quarter flared; opens & matures red (46B); 22mm (7/8") long x 24mm (15/16") wide. SEPALS: horizontal, tips recurved; rose (65A) upper surface; dark rose (48A) lower surface; 29mm (1 1/8") long x 12mm (7/16") wide. TUBE: rose (65A); 21mm (13/16") long x 6mm (1/4") wide. FOLIAGE is medium green (137B) upper surface; medium green (138B) lower surface. PARENTAGE: 'Roesse Lupus' x 'Sofie Michiels'.
Buiting 2008 NL AFS6928.

HeRi Serpeling. Upright/Trailer. Semi Double. COROLLA is full flared with smooth petal margins; opens purple (83B); matures purple (71A); 18mm (11/16") long x 25mm (1") wide. SEPALS are fully up, tips recurved; pale lavender (69C) tipped green upper surface; rose (68C) tipped green lower surface; 26mm (1") long x 12mm (1/2") wide. TUBE is pale lavender (69C); medium length & thickness; 10mm (3/8") long x 7mm (1/4") wide. FOLIAGE: dark green (137A) upper surface; medium green (138B) lower surface. Leaves are 65mm (2 9/16") long x 35mm (1 3/8") wide, ovate shaped. PARENTAGE: ('Roesse Apus' x 'Roesse Apus') x 'Yvette Klessens'. Distinguished by bloom colour & shape.
Buiting 2005 NL AFS5870.

HeRi Shusui. Upright/Trailer. Double. COROLLA is half flared; opens dark reddish purple (64A); matures purple (71A); 25mm (1") long x 15mm (9/16") wide. SEPALS are horizontal, tips recurved; light pink (62B) upper surface; pink (62A) lower surface; 24mm (15/16") long x 10mm (3/8") wide. TUBE is pale pink (62D); 12mm (7/16") long x 6mm (1/4") wide. FOLIAGE: medium green (137B) upper surface; medium green (137D) lower surface. PARENTAGE: 'Rohees Dubhe' x 'Leon Pauwels'. Distinguished by bloom colour.
Buiting 2006 NL AFS6114.

HeRi Snapper. Upright/Trailer. Double. COROLLA is three quarter flared; opens dark purple (79B); matures reddish purple (61B); 34mm (1 3/8") long x 35mm (1 3/8") wide. SEPALS are horizontal, tips recurved; magenta (67B) upper & lower surfaces; 40mm (1 9/16") long x 15mm (9/16") wide. TUBE is magenta (67B); 14mm (9/16") long x

181

9mm (3/8") wide. FOLIAGE: medium green (137B) upper surface; medium green (137D) lower surface. PARENTAGE: 'Rohees Dubhe' x 'Leon Pauwels'. Distinguished by bloom colour.
Buiting 2006 NL AFS6117.

HeRi Sneep. Trailer. Single. COROLLA: three quarter flared; opens dark reddish purple (60A); matures dark reddish purple (61A); 19mm (3/4") long x 23mm (7/8") wide. SEPALS: horizontal, tips recurved; rose (68C) upper surface; rose (68B) lower surface; 41mm (1 5/8") long x 14mm (9/16") wide. TUBE: rose (68C); 21mm (13/16") long x 6mm (1/4") wide. FOLIAGE is medium green (137C) upper surface; medium green (138B) lower surface. PARENTAGE: 'Roesse Lupus' x 'HeRi Mahseer'.
Buiting 2008 NL AFS6924.

HeRi Suihogan. Upright. Double. COROLLA: unflared, smooth petal margins; opens violet (76A); matures light purple (78C); 15mm (9/16") long x 18mm (11/16") wide. SEPALS are full down, tips reflexed; white (155D), tipped green upper & lower surfaces; 20mm (3/4") long x 18mm (11/16") wide. TUBE is white (155A); medium length & thickness; 35mm (1 3/8") long x 4mm (1/8") wide. STAMENS extend 8mm (5/16") beyond the corolla; pink (62B) filaments; pink (62A) anthers. PISTIL extends 18mm (11/16") beyond the corolla; light pink (62C) style; white (155A) stigma. BUD: globular, long TUBE. FOLIAGE is dark green (137A) upper surface; medium green (137C) lower surface. Leaves are 65mm (2 9/16") long x 32mm (1 1/4") wide, ovate shaped, serrulate edges, acute tips, rounded bases. Veins, stems & branches are red. PARENTAGE: 'Monique Luijten' x 'Maik Luijten'. Lax upright or stiff trailer. Makes good stiff trailer. Prefers overhead filtered light, cool climate. Best bloom in filtered light. Tested 3 years in Veldhoven, The Netherlands. Distinguished by bloom & foliage colour combinations.
Buiting 2009 NL AFS7261.

HeRi Sweep. Upright/Trailer. Double. COROLLA: Three quarter flared; opens & matures reddish purple (59B); 21mm (13/16") long x 26mm (1") wide. SEPALS: half up, tips reflexed up; rose (63C) upper surface; magenta (63B) lower surface; 26mm (1") long x 16mm (5/8") wide. TUBE: rose (63C); short & thick; 16mm (5/8") long x 9mm (5/16") wide. FOLIAGE is ark green (137A) upper surface; medium green (138B)

lower surface. PARENTAGE: 'Roesse Lupus' x 'Sofie Michiels'.
Buiting   2007   NL   AFS6653.

HeRi Talapia. Upright/Trailer. Double. COROLLA is three quarter flared; opens violet (84A); matures magenta (67B); 17mm (5/8") long x 24mm (15/16") wide. SEPALS are horizontal, tips recurved; light pink (65C) upper surface; rose (65A) lower surface; 28mm (1 1/8") long x 17mm (5/8") wide. TUBE is light pink (65C); 16mm (5/8") long x 6mm (1/4") wide. FOLIAGE: medium green (137B) upper surface; medium green (138B) lower surface. PARENTAGE: 'Roesse Apus' x 'Roesse Tureis'. Distinguished by bloom colour.
Buiting 2006 NL AFS6110.

HeRi Tarpon. Trailer. Single. COROLLA is full flared; opens dark purple (79A); matures purple (71A); 22mm (7/8") long x 24mm (15/16") wide. SEPALS are horizontal, tips recurved; dark reddish purple (64A) upper & lower surfaces; 24mm (15/16") long x 9mm (3/8") wide. TUBE is dark reddish purple (64A); 9mm (3/8") long x 6mm (1/4") wide. FOLIAGE: medium green (137B) upper surface; medium green (138B) lower surface. PARENTAGE: 'Swingtime' x 'Maxima'. Distinguished by bloom shape & colour.
Buiting 2006 NL AFS6112.

HeRi Trevally. Upright. Single. COROLLA: quarter flared; opens purple (71A); matures pink (62A); 17mm (5/8") long x 22mm (7/8") wide. SEPALS: horizontal, tips recurved; reddish purple (66A) tipped green upper & lower surfaces; 26mm (1") long x 11mm (7/16") wide. TUBE: reddish purple (66B); 11mm (7/16") long x 6mm (1/4") wide. FOLIAGE is dark green (137A) upper surface; medium green (138B) lower surface. PARENTAGE: 'Roesse Lupus' x 'Maxima's Baby'.
Buiting 2008 NL AFS6934.

HeRi Tucunare. Upright. Double. COROLLA: three quarter flared; opens purple (71A); matures magenta (71C); 24mm (15/16") long x 29mm (1 1/8") wide. SEPALS: half up, tips reflexed up; magenta (63B) upper surface; magenta (63A) lower surface; 26mm (1") long x 15mm (9/16") wide. TUBE: magenta (63B); 19mm (3/4") long x 7mm (1/4") wide. FOLIAGE is medium green (137B) upper surface; medium green (138B) lower surface. PARENTAGE: 'Roesse Apus' x 'Maik Luijten'.
Buiting 2008 NL AFS6922.

HeRi Utsuri. Upright. Double. COROLLA: three quarter flared, smooth petal margins; opens reddish purple (61B) & matures red (52A); 25mm (1") long x 32mm (1 1/4") wide. SEPALS are fully up, tips recurved; pale tan (159A), tipped green upper surface; pale lavender (65A), tipped green lower surface; 30mm (1 3/16") long x 13mm (1/2") wide. TUBE is pale tan (159A); medium length & thickness; 23mm (7/8") long x 8mm (5/16") wide. STAMENS extend 5mm (3/16") beyond the corolla; rose (68C) filaments; reddish purple (61B) anthers. PISTIL extends 19mm (3/4") beyond the corolla; rose (68B) style; white (155A) stigma. BUD is ovate. FOLIAGE is dark green (137A) upper surface; medium green (137B) lower surface. Leaves are 50mm (2") long x 33mm (1 5/16") wide, ovate shaped, serrulate edges, acute tips, rounded bases. Veins, stems & branches are green. PARENTAGE: 'Roesse Lupus' x 'HeRi Chessa'. Lax upright or stiff trailer. Makes good stiff trailer. Prefers overhead filtered light, cool climate. Best bloom in filtered light. Tested 3 years in Veldhoven, The Netherlands. Distinguished by bloom & foliage colour combinations.
Buiting 2009 NL AFS7273.

HeRi Vundu. Upright/Trailer. Double. COROLLA is three quarter flared; opens dark purple (79B); matures purple (79C); 31mm (1 1/4") long x 24mm (15/16") wide. SEPALS are fully up, tips recurved; dark rose (64C) upper & lower surfaces; 32mm (1 1/4") long x 12mm (1/2") wide. TUBE is dark rose (64C); 14mm (9/16") long x 7mm (1/4") wide. FOLIAGE: medium green (137C) upper surface; medium green (136C) lower surface. PARENTAGE: 'Quasar' x 'Maxima'. Lax upright or stiff trailer. Distinguished by bloom colour & shape.
Buiting 2006 NL AFS6102.

HeRi Vuurstaart. Upright/Trailer. Single. COROLLA: Full flared; opens dark reddish purple (64A); matures reddish purple (58A); 15mm (9/16") long x 22mm (7/8") wide. SEPALS: half up, tips reflexed up; dark rose (58C) tipped green upper surface; light rose (63D) lower surface; 24mm (15/16") long x 8mm (5/16") wide. TUBE: dark rose (58C); medium length & thickness; 15mm (9/16") long x 6mm (1/4") wide. FOLIAGE is dark green (137A) upper surface; medium green (137C) lower surface. PARENTAGE: 'Senna Krekels' x 'Leon Pauwels'.
Buiting 2007 NL AFS6655.

HeRi Wahoo. Upright/Trailer. Double. COROLLA is half flared; opens reddish purple (74B); matures magenta (61C); 33mm (1 5/16") long x 25mm (1") wide. SEPALS are horizontal, tips recurved; light pink (65B) upper surface; light purple (74C) lower surface; 40mm (1 9/16") long x 10mm (3/8") wide. TUBE is white (155A); 20mm (3/4") long x 7mm (1/4") wide. FOLIAGE: medium green (138A) upper surface; medium green (138B) lower surface. PARENTAGE: 'Senna Krekels' x 'Paul Schats'. Distinguished by bloom colour.
Buiting 2006 NL AFS6116.

HeRi Watonai. Upright. Single. COROLLA: three quarter flared, smooth petal margins; opens purple (71A); matures magenta (61C); 23mm (7/8") long x 22mm (7/8") wide. SEPALS are half up, tips recurved up; pink (62A), tipped green upper surface; rose (68B), tipped green lower surface; 35mm (1 3/8") long x 15mm (9/16") wide. TUBE is white (155D); medium length & thickness; 11mm (7/16") long x 8mm (5/16") wide. STAMENS extend 3mm (1/8") beyond the corolla; pink (62A) filaments & anthers. PISTIL extends 12mm (7/16") beyond the corolla; magenta (68A) style; white (155D) stigma. BUD: ovate. FOLIAGE: medium green (137B) upper surface; medium green (138B) lower surface. Leaves are 52mm (2 1/16") long x 26mm (1") wide, lanceolate shaped, serrulate edges, acute tips & bases. Veins, stems & branches are green. PARENTAGE: 'Roesse Lupus' x ('Leon Pauwels' x 'Quasar'). Lax upright or stiff trailer. Makes good stiff trailer. Prefers overhead filtered light, cool climate. Best bloom in filtered light. Tested 3 years in Veldhoven, The Netherlands. Distinguished by bloom shape & foliage combination.
Buiting 2009 NL AFS7266.

HeRi Wirra. Trailer. Single. COROLLA: Half flared; opens & matures reddish purple (67A); 19mm (3/4") long x 26mm (1") wide. SEPALS: fully up, tips reflexed; rose (68B) upper surface; magenta (68A) lower surface; 34mm (1 3/8") long x 9mm (5/16") wide. TUBE: rose (68C); medium length & thickness; 15mm (9/16") long x 5mm (3/16") wide. FOLIAGE is dark green (137A) upper surface; medium green (137C) lower surface. PARENTAGE: 'Roesse Lupus' x 'Roesse Tucana'.
Buiting 2007 NL AFS6651.

HeRi Zeeduivel. Upright/Trailer. Double. COROLLA: Half flared; opens reddish purple (66B); matures dark rose (67C); 26mm (1")

long x 21mm (13/16") wide. SEPALS: horizontal, tips recurved; light pink (65C) upper surface; reddish purple (67A) lower surface; 42mm (1 5/8") long x 16mm (5/8") wide. TUBE: pale lavender (65D); medium length & thickness; 15mm (9/16") long x 6mm (1/4") wide. FOLIAGE is dark green (137A) upper surface; medium green (137C) lower surface. PARENTAGE: 'Senna Krekels' x 'Leon Pauwels'.
Buiting 2007 NL AFS6654.

HeRi Zeewolf. Upright. Single. COROLLA: Half flared; opens purple (71A); matures dark reddish purple (64A); 21mm (13/16") long x 22mm (7/8") wide. SEPALS: horizontal, tips recurved; rose (63C) upper surface; magenta (63B) lower surface; 34mm (1 3/8") long x 14mm (9/16") wide. TUBE: rose (63C); medium length & thickness; 19mm (3/4") long x 9mm (5/16") wide. FOLIAGE is dark green (137A) upper surface; medium green (137D) lower surface. PARENTAGE: 'Roesse Lupus' x 'Magda Vanbets'.
Buiting 2007 NL AFS6649.

HeRi Zilverhaai. Trailer. Single. COROLLA: Half flared; opens & matures violet blue (91B); 18mm (11/16") long x 20mm (3/4") wide. SEPALS: fully up, tips reflexed; white (155B) tipped green upper surface; white (155C) lower surface; 41mm (1 5/8") long x 8mm (5/16") wide. TUBE: white (155B); medium length, thin; 8mm (5/16") long x 3mm (1/8") wide. FOLIAGE is dark green (137A) upper surface; medium green (138A) lower surface. PARENTAGE: 'Roesse Tucana' x 'Yvette Klessens'.
Buiting 2007 NL AFS6642
.
Herman De Narcist. Upright. Single. COROLLA: full flared; opens dark reddish purple (61A); matures dark reddish purple (60A); 20mm (3/4") long x 25mm (1") wide. SEPALS: fully up, tips recurved; light rose (58D) upper & lower surfaces; 22mm (7/8") long x 10mm (3/8") wide. TUBE: light rose (58D); 10mm (3/8") long x 8mm (5/16") wide. FOLIAGE is dark green (137A) upper surface; medium green (137C) lower surface. PARENTAGE: 'Roesse Lupus' x 'Maxima's Girl'.
Roes 2008 NL AFS6895.

Herman Finkers. Trailer. Single. COROLLA: half flared; opens light violet (84B), matures pale purple (81D); 10mm (3/8") long x 6mm (1/4") wide. SEPALS are horizontal, tips recurved; pale pink (62D) upper surface; light rose (58D) lower surface; 13mm (1/2")

long x 4mm (1/8") wide. TUBE: pale pink (62D); long & thin; 24mm (15/16") long x 4mm (1/8") wide. FOLIAGE is dark green (147A) upper surface; medium green (146A) lower surface. PARENTAGE: 'Gerharda's Panache' x ('Sparkling-Whisper' x 'F. *fulgens* var. rubra grandiflora'). Nomination by NKVF as Recommendable Cultivar.
Geurts 2007 NL AFS6429.

Hermann Ermel. Upright. Single. COROLLA opens violet blue rose at base, matures to violet; corolla is quarter flared. SEPALS rose on the upper surface, powder pink on the lower surface; SEPALS are fully up with recurved tips. TUBE rose. PARENTAGE 'Waldis Graefin' x 'Seedling (H92)'.
Dietrich 2009 DE BFS0114.

Hermes. Trailer. Single to Semi Double. COROLLA: half flared; opens red purple (N78B), pale lavender (65D) base; matures reddish purple (67A); 23mm (7/8") long x 14mm (9/16") wide. SEPALS: horizontal, tips reflexed; pale lavender (69C) tipped light apple green (145B) upper surface; pale lavender (65D) tipped light apple green (145B) lower surface; 29mm (1 1/8") long x 13mm (1/2") wide. TUBE: pale lavender (69D) striped pale pink (69A); medium length & thickness; 21mm (13/16") long x 8mm (5/16") wide. FOLIAGE is dark green (137A) upper surface; medium green (138A) lower surface. PARENTAGE: 'Jef Vander Kuylen' x 'Chandlerii'.
Michiels 2007 BE AFS6363.

Hermine Workel. Upright. Double. COROLLA is half flared with smooth petal margins; dark reddish purple (59A), matures reddish purple (59B); 20mm (13/16") long x 24mm (15/16") wide. SEPALS are horizontal, tips recurved; dark reddish purple (60A) upper surface, dark reddish purple (60B) lower surface; 24mm (15/16") long x 16mm (5/8") wide. TUBE is dark reddish purple (60A), proportionately short and thick; 7mm (1/4") long x 7mm (1/4") wide. STAMENS extend 14mm (9/16") below the corolla; reddish purple (59B) filaments and anthers. PISTIL extends 29mm (1 1/8") below the corolla; dark reddish purple (60A) style and stigma. BUD is ovate and pointed. FOLIAGE is dark green (137A) on upper surface and medium green (138B) on lower surface. Leaves are 58mm (2 5/16") long x 24mm (15/16") wide, ovate shaped, serrulated edges, acute tips and rounded bases. Veins, stems and branches are red. PARENTAGE: [('Bon Accord' x 'Vobeglo') x ('Cameron Ryle' x

'Parasol')] x 'Rohees Princess'. Medium upright. Makes good standard. Prefers overhead filtered light and warm climate. Best bloom colour in filtered light. Tested four years in Knegsel, The Netherlands. Distinguished by bloom colour. Roes 2002 NL AFS4792.

Herps Accordeon. Upright. Single. COROLLA is half flared with smooth petal margins; each petal is curved to outside; opens & matures magenta (58B); 15mm (9/16") long x 17 mm (11/16") wide. SEPALS are fully up, tips recurved; pink (48C) upper surface; light orange (41C) lower surface; 23mm (15/16") long x 15mm (9/16") wide. TUBE is pink (36A), medium length and thickness; 15mm (9/16") long x 6mm (1/4") wide. FOLIAGE: dark green (147A) upper surface; medium green (147B) lower surface. Leaves are 70mm (2 3/4") long x 45mm (1 3/4") wide, ovate shaped. PARENTAGE: 'WALZ Triangel' x 'Prince Syray'. Award of Merit, VKC, The Netherlands. Distinguished by corolla colour and outside curve. Waldenmaier 2005 NL AFS5639.

Herps Achtspan. Upright. Single. COROLLA: Unflared; opens magenta (63B); matures rose (61D); 15mm (9/16") long x 12mm (7/16") wide. SEPALS: half down, tips reflexed; rose (51B) tipped olive green (152B) upper surface; dark rose (51A) tipped olive green (152B) lower surface; 17mm (5/8") long x 7mm (1/4") wide. TUBE: rose (52B); medium length & thickness; 13mm (1/2") long x 4mm (1/8") wide. FOLIAGE is medium green (137B) upper surface; medium green (138B) lower surface. PARENTAGE: 'Herps Parachute' x 'Prince Syray'. Waldenmaier 2007 NL AFS6574.

Herps Altsax. Upright/Trailer. Single. COROLLA is quarter flared with turned under wavy petal margins; opens rose (63A); matures magenta (61C); 21mm (13/16") long x 25mm (1"). SEPALS are half down, tips recurved; rose (55B), light apple green (145B) upper & lower surfaces; 33mm (1 3/16") long x 9mm (3/8") wide. TUBE is rose (54C); long, medium thickness; 42mm (1 11/16") long x 7mm (1/4") wide. FOLIAGE: dark green (139A) upper surface; medium green (138B) lower surface. Leaves are 57mm (2 1/4") long x 28mm (1 1/8") wide, elliptic shaped. PARENTAGE: 'WALZ Harp x 'De Groot's Prinses'. Distinguished by rich blooming period. Waldenmaier 2007 NL AFS5840.

Herps Arco. Upright. Single. COROLLA: quarter flared, smooth petal margins; opens & matures dark orange (33A); 8mm (5/16") long x 8mm (5/16") wide. SEPALS: full down; tips reflexed; light orange (32D) upper & lower surfaces; 8mm(5/16") long x 7mm (1/4") wide. TUBE: light orange (32D); long, medium thickness; 40mm (1 9/16") long x 6mm (1/4") wide. STAMENS: do not extend below corolla; pink (62C) filaments; yellowish white (4D) anthers. PISTIL: extends 3mm (1/8") below the corolla, pink (62C) style; yellowish white (4D) stigma. BUD: oblong, long. FOLIAGE: dark green (137A) upper surface, medium green (138B) lower surface. Leaves are 90mm (3 9/16") long x 55mm (2 3/16") wide, ovate shaped, wavy edges, acute tips and rounded bases. Veins, stems & branches are green. PARENTAGE: 'WALZ Orgelpijp' x 'F. fulgens michoacan'. Tall upright. Makes good upright or standard. Prefers overhead filtered light. Best bloom colour in bright light. Best foliage colour in filtered light. Tested 5 years in Herpen, The Netherlands. Award of Merit, VKC, The Netherlands. Distinguished by large dark orange corolla and long TUBE. Waldenmaier 2004 NL AFS5393.

Herps Aulos. Upright/Trailer. Single. COROLLA: quarter flared, smooth petal margins; opens & matures pink (49A); 15mm (9/16") long x 15mm (9/16") wide. SEPALS: half down; tips reflexed; orange (32B) upper & lower surfaces; 22mm(7/8") long x 8mm(5/16") wide. TUBE: orange (32B); long, medium thickness; 44mm (1 3/4") long x 7mm(1/4") wide. STAMENS: do not extend below corolla; yellowish white (4D) filaments & anthers. PISTIL: extends 13mm (1/2") below the corolla, pink (62C) style; yellowish white (4D) stigma. BUD: oblong, pointed. FOLIAGE: dark green (137A) upper surface, medium green (137B) lower surface. Leaves are 75mm (2 15/16") long x 40mm (1 9/16") wide, ovate shaped, serrated edges, acute tips and rounded bases. Veins, stems & branches are green. PARENTAGE: ('F. magdalenae' x 'F. fulgens grandiflora') x 'Bicentennial'] x 'F. apetala'. Lax upright or stiff trailer. Makes good basket. Prefers overhead filtered light. Best bloom and foliage colour in bright light. Tested 3 years in Herpen, The Netherlands. Award of Merit, VKC, The Netherlands. Distinguished by colour combination. Waldenmaier 2004 NL AFS5395.

Herps Baljurk. Upright/Trailer. Single. COROLLA: Quarter flared; opens dark purple

(79A), reddish purple (71B) base; matures reddish purple (79C); 24mm (15/16") long x 19mm (3/4") wide. SEPALS: half up, tips recurved up, turned left & right; light reddish purple (72C) tipped apple green (144C) upper surface; magenta (71C) tipped apple green (144C) lower surface; 36mm (1 7/16") long x 11mm (7/16") wide. TUBE: dark rose (67C); medium length & thickness; 14mm (9/16") long x 6mm (1/4") wide. FOLIAGE is medium green (138A) upper surface; medium green (138B) lower surface. PARENTAGE: 'Lye's Excelsior' x 'Hertogen van Brabant'.
Waldenmaier 2007 NL AFS6575.

Herps Bazuin. Upright. Single. COROLLA: quarter flared, smooth petal margins; opens & matures dark orange (33A); 12mm (1/2") long x 13mm (1/2") wide. SEPALS: full down; tips reflexed; orange (33B) upper surface; peach (33D) lower surface; 20mm(13/16") long x 9mm (3/8") wide. TUBE: light orange (33C); long, medium thickness; 98mm (3 7/8") long x 7mm (1/4") wide. STAMENS: do not extend below corolla; light orange (31C) filaments; light yellow (4B) anthers. PISTIL: extends 5mm (3/16") below the corolla, light orange (31C) style; light yellow (4B) stigma. BUD: long TUBE, rounded end. FOLIAGE: dark green (137A) upper surface, medium green (137B) lower surface. Leaves are 170mm (6 11/16") long x 110mm (4 5/16") wide, ovate shaped, wavy edges, acute tips and rounded bases. Veins, stems & branches are red. PARENTAGE: [('F. *magdalenae*' x 'F. *fulgens grandiflora*') x ('F. *fulgens gesneriana*' x self, doubled into a tetraploid after colchicine treatment). Tall upright. Makes good upright. Prefers overhead filtered light. Best bloom colour in bright light. Tested 3 years in Herpen, The Netherlands. Award of Merit, VKC, The Netherlands. Distinguished by long TUBEd flowers in terminal racemes.
Waldenmaier 2004 NL AFS5390.

Herps Belleboom. Upright/Trailer. Single. COROLLA: quarter flared, bell shaped; wavy petal margins; opens magenta (57A), red-orange base; matures magenta (57A); 7mm (1/4") long x 7mm (1/4") wide. SEPALS: half down, tips recurved; pink (62C) upper surface; pink (62A) lower surface; 20mm (3/4") long x 6mm (1/4") wide. TUBE: pink (62C); long & thin; 23mm (7/8") long x 5mm (3/16") wide. STAMENS do not extend beyond the corolla; white (155A) filaments & anthers. PISTIL extends 15mm (9/16") beyond the corolla; white (155D) style; white (155A) stigma. BUD is small & long. FOLIAGE is medium green (137B) upper

surface; medium green (138B) lower surface. Leaves are 65mm (2 9/16") long x 50mm (2") wide; ovate shaped, wavy edges, acute tips, rounded bases. Veins, stems & branches are green. PARENTAGE: 'Herps Klephoorn' x 'Veenlust'. Lax upright or stiff trailer. Makes good basket or standard. Prefers overhead filtered light. Best bloom & foliage colour in filtered light. Tested 3 years in Herpen, The Netherlands. Distinguished by bloom shape & colour.
Waldenmaier 2009 NL AFS7007.

Herps Bolero. Upright. Single. COROLLA: Unflared; opens reddish purple (70B); matures rose (67D); 14mm (9/16") long x 11mm (7/16") wide. SEPALS: half down, tips reflexed; yellowish green (144B), yellowish green (145A) base upper surface; medium green (141C), light apple green (145C) base lower surface; 21mm (13/16") long x 7mm (1/4") wide. TUBE: yellowish green (145A); short & thick; 11mm (7/16") long x 8mm (5/16") wide. FOLIAGE is dark green (139A) upper surface; medium green (138B) lower surface. PARENTAGE: [(tetraploid 'F. *splendens*' x tetraploid 'F. *juntasensis*')' x (tetraploid 'F. *fulgens gesneriana*)] x ('WALZ Polka' x 'WALZ Blaauwkous').
Waldenmaier 2007 NL AFS6576.

Herps Bonang. Upright. Single. COROLLA: quarter flared, smooth petal margins; opens & matures magenta (67B); 12mm (1/2") long x 19mm (3/4") wide. SEPALS: half down; tips reflexed; light orange (41C) upper & lower surfaces; 18mm (11/16") long x 10mm(3/8") wide. TUBE: light pink (49C); medium length & thickness; 18mm (11/16") long x 11mm(7/16") wide. STAMENS: do not extend below corolla; pink (52D) filaments & anthers. PISTIL: extends 8mm (5/16") below the corolla, rose (52C) style; light yellow (10D) stigma. BUD: small, round, pointed. FOLIAGE: dark green (137A) upper surface, medium green (137B) lower surface. Leaves are 70mm (2 3/4") long x 45mm (1 3/4") wide, cordate shaped, serrulated edges, acute tips and rounded bases. Veins are light green; stems & branches are green. PARENTAGE: [('F. *magdalenae*' x 'F. *fulgens grandiflora*') x 'Wendy van Wanten'] x 'Prince Syray'. Medium upright. Makes good upright or standard. Prefers overhead filtered light. Best bloom and foliage colour in bright light. Tested 2 years in Herpen, The Netherlands. Award of Merit, VKC, The Netherlands. Distinguished by horizontal flowers with thick rounded TUBE.
Waldenmaier 2004 NL AFS5399.

186

Herps Bongo. Upright. Single. COROLLA is quarter flared; opens magenta (61C), rose (50B) at base; matures magenta (63B); 16mm (5/8") long x 19mm (3/4") wide. SEPALS are horizontal, tips reflexed; rose (47C) tipped yellowish green (146B) upper surface; dark rose (59A) tipped dark red (53A) lower surface; 19mm (3/4") long x 9mm (3/8") wide. TUBE is dark rose (54B); 13mm (1/2") long x 11mm (7/16") wide. FOLIAGE: dark green (139A) upper surface; medium green (138B) lower surface. PARENTAGE: [('F. magdalenae' x 'F. fulgens rubra grandiflora') x 'Wendy Van Wanten'] x 'Prince Syray'. Meise 8/13/05. Distinguished by unique bloom shape & colour. Waldenmaier 2006 NL AFS5993.

Herps Bouziki. Upright. Single. COROLLA is half flared with turned under petal margins; opens pale rose (73D) striped light rose (73C); matures pale purple (75C); 16mm (5/8") long x 19mm (3/4") wide. SEPALS are horizontal, tips reflexed; light olive green (149D), pink (62A) base, tipped yellowish green (145A) upper surface; pale rose (73D) tipped yellowish green (145A) lower surface; 27mm (1 9/16") long x 16mm (5/8") wide. TUBE is light pink (49B), pale pink (49D) base, striped medium green (138B); short & thick; 14mm (9/16") long x 8mm (5/16") wide. FOLIAGE: dark green (139A) upper surface; medium green (138B) lower surface. Leaves are 56mm (2 3/16") long x 30mm (1 3/16") wide, elliptic shaped. PARENTAGE: [('F. magdalenae' x 'F. fulgens grandiflora') x 'Wendy Van Wanten] x 'WALZ Floreat'. Meise 9-18-04, Outstanding. Distinguished by flower shape & colour. Waldenmaier 2006 NL AFS5839.

Herps Buggy. Upright. Single. COROLLA: Half flared; opens light purple (N74C); matures light reddish purple (72C); 20mm (3/4") long x 17mm (5/8") wide. SEPALS: horizontal, tips reflexed; reddish purple (67A) upper surface; magenta (67B) lower surface; 27mm (1 1/16") long x 9mm (5/16") wide. TUBE: magenta (63A); medium length & thickness; 15mm (9/16") long x 6mm (1/4") wide. FOLIAGE is dark green (136B) upper surface; medium green (138B) lower surface. PARENTAGE: 'Herps Parachute' x 'Aldham'. Waldenmaier 2007 NL AFS6577.

Herps Buikorgel. Upright. Single. COROLLA: quarter flared, smooth petal margins; opens cream (11D), large yellow tips; matures light yellow (11C); 13mm (1/2") long x 13mm (1/2") wide. SEPALS: full down; tips recurved; rose (50B) upper & lower surfaces; 30mm (1 3/16") long x 15mm(9/16") wide. TUBE: rose (50B) with yellow narrowing near the SEPALS; medium length, thin; 24mm (15/16") long x 7mm(1/4") wide. STAMENS: do not extend below corolla; pink (50D) filaments, light yellow (10D) anthers. PISTIL: extends 15mm (9/16") below the corolla, pink (50D) style & stigma. BUD: small, round, pointed. FOLIAGE: yellowish green (144A) upper surface, yellowish green (144B) lower surface. Leaves are 95mm (3 3/4") long x 55mm (2 3/16") wide, ovate shaped, serrulated edges, acute tips and acute bases. Veins, stems & branches are green. PARENTAGE: [('F. magdalenae' x 'F. fulgens grandiflora') x 'F fulgens goselli '] x 'White King'. Medium upright. Makes good upright or standard. Prefers overhead filtered light. Best bloom and foliage colour in bright light. Tested 2 years in Herpen, The Netherlands. Award of Merit, VKC, The Netherlands. Distinguished by yellow on TUBE and flower/foliage colour combination. Waldenmaier 2004 NL AFS5401.

Herps Clavecimbel. Upright. Single. COROLLA: unflared, smooth petal margins; opens & matures rose (52B), orange base; 15mm (9/16") long x 18mm (11/16") wide. SEPALS: full down; tips reflexed; dark rose (51A) upper surface; rose (52C) lower surface; 25mm(1") long x 12mm(1/2") wide. TUBE: dark rose (51A); medium length, thick; 21mm (13/16") long x 12mm(1/2") wide. STAMENS: do not extend below corolla; light pink (62B) filaments; yellowish white (4D) anthers. PISTIL: extends 15mm (9/16") below the corolla, light pink (62B) style & stigma. BUD: small, thick & round. FOLIAGE: dark green (137A) upper surface, medium green (137B) lower surface. Leaves are 75mm (2 15/16") long x 45mm (1 3/4") wide, cordate shaped, serrulated edges, acute tips and rounded bases. Veins are light red; stems & branches are green. PARENTAGE: 'Lechlade Rocket' x 'Wendy van Wanten'. Medium upright. Makes good upright or standard. Prefers overhead filtered light. Best bloom and foliage colour in bright light. Tested 2 years in Herpen, The Netherlands. Award of Merit, VKC, The Netherlands. Distinguished by thick, rounded horizontal flower. Waldenmaier 2004 NL AFS5396.

Herps C. Upright/Trailer. Double. COROLLA: three quarter flared; opens purple (71A); matures dark reddish purple (64A); 23mm (7/8") long x 19mm (3/4") wide. PETALOIDS:

dark reddish purple (61A); 12mm (7/16")
long x 10mm (3/8") wide. SEPALS:
horizontal, tips recurved; magenta (59C)
tipped medium green (139B) upper surface;
reddish purple (61B) tipped medium green
(139B) lower surface; 28mm (1 1/8") long x
11mm (7/16") wide. TUBE: magenta (59C);
32mm (1 1/4") long x 7mm (1/4") wide.
FOLIAGE is dark green (137A) upper surface;
medium green (138B) lower surface.
PARENTAGE: ('F. magdalenae' x 'F. fulgens
grandiflora') x 'Hertogin Van Brabant'.
Waldenmaier 2008 NL AFS676.

Herps Contrabas. Upright. Single.
COROLLA: half flared, turned under wavy
petal margins; opens rose (47C); matures red
(47B); 12mm (1/2") long x 9mm (3/8") wide.
SEPALS: half down; tips reflexed; rose (50B)
tipped yellowish green (144B) upper surface;
rose (47C) tipped yellowish green (144B)
lower surface; 14mm (9/16") long x 10mm
(3/8") wide. TUBE: pink (50D) striped rose
(50B); medium length & thickness; 22mm
(7/8") long x 6mm(1/4") wide. STAMENS: do
not extend below corolla; pale pink (49D)
filaments; light yellow (1C) anthers. PISTIL:
extends 4mm (3/16") below the corolla; light
pink (49B) style, light yellow (2C) stigma.
BUD: sack shaped. FOLIAGE: dark green
(133A) upper surface, medium green (137B)
lower surface. Leaves are 86mm (3 3/8") long
x 45mm (1 3/4") wide, ovate shaped,
serrulated edges, acute tips and rounded
bases. Veins are medium green (137C);
stems & branches are medium green (137C)
& orangy brown (176A). PARENTAGE:
'Lechlade Rocket' x 'Wendy van Wanten'.
Small upright. Self branching. Makes good
upright. Prefers full sun. Best bloom and
foliage colour in bright light. Tested 3 years
in Herpen, The Netherlands. Award at Meise,
9/8/03. Distinguished by bloom shape.
Waldenmaier 2004 NL AFS5408.

Herps Cornu. Upright. Single. COROLLA is
quarter flared; opens magenta (57C);
matures dark rose (64C); 11mm (7/16") long
x 9mm (3/8") wide. SEPALS are half down,
tips reflexed; rose (50B) striped pink (55C),
tipped apple green (144C) upper surface;
pink (49A) tipped apple green (144C) lower
surface; 20mm (13/16") long x 9mm (3/8")
wide. TUBE is rose (50B) striped pink (55C);
14mm (9/16") long x 11mm (7/16") wide.
FOLIAGE: light green (139D) upper surface;
medium green (138B) lower surface.
PARENTAGE: [('F. magdalenae' x 'F. fulgens
grandiflora') x 'Wendy Van Wanten'] x 'Prince

Syray'. Meise 8/13/05. Distinguished by
unique bloom shape & colour.
Waldenmaier 2006 NL AFS5992.

Herps Djembe. Upright. Single. COROLLA is
half flared with turned under wavy petal
margins; opens magenta (58B), light pink
(49B) base; matures magenta (63B), light
pink (49B) base; 12mm (1/2") long x 11mm
(7/16") wide. SEPALS are half down, tips
reflexed; light pink (38D), peach (38B) base
tipped yellowish green (145A) upper surface;
light pink (49B), tipped yellowish green
(145A) lower surface; 12mm (1/2") long x
6mm (1/4") wide. TUBE is peach (38B) &
light pink (38D); 11mm
(7/16") long x 8mm (5/16") wide. FOLIAGE:
dark green (139A) to medium green (138B)
upper surface; medium green (138B) lower
surface. Leaves are 69mm (2 3/4") long x
35mm (1 3/8") wide, ovate shaped.
PARENTAGE: [('F. magdalenae' x 'F. fulgens
grandiflora') x 'Wendy Van Wanten'] x 'Prince
Syray'. Meise 8-14-04. Distinguished by
flower colour.
Waldenmaier 2005 NL AFS5704.

Herps Draaimolen. Upright. Single.
COROLLA is half flared with turned under
wavy petal margins; opens rose (52B);
matures rose (50B); 10mm (3/8") long x
9mm (3/8") wide. SEPALS are horizontal,
tips reflexed; rose (51C) tipped apple green
(144C) upper surface; pink (48C) tipped
yellowish green (144B) lower surface; 13mm
(1/2") long x 4mm (3/16") wide. TUBE is pale
pink (56A); medium length & thickness;
16mm (5/8") long x 4mm (3/16") wide.
FOLIAGE: dark green (139A) upper surface;
medium green (137C) lower surface. Leaves
are 47mm (1 7/8") long x 30mm (1 3/16")
wide, elliptic shaped. PARENTAGE: 'Loxhore
Mazurka' x 'Loxhore Mazurka'. Distinguished
by rich growing period.
Waldenmaier 2005 NL AFS5703.

Herps Draaiorgel. Upright. Single.
COROLLA: quarter flared; smooth petal
margins; opens & matures red (52A); 12mm
(7/16") long x 16mm (5/8") wide. SEPALS:
half down, tips reflexed; dark rose (51A)
upper surface; rose (52B) lower surface;
17mm (5/8") long x 8mm (5/16") wide.
TUBE: red (50A); long, medium thickness;
45mm (1 3/4") long x 7mm (1/4") wide.
STAMENS do not extend beyond the corolla;
dark rose (51A) filaments; light yellowish
orange (19B) anthers. PISTIL does not extend
beyond the corolla; rose (52B) style; pink
stigma. BUD has long TUBE, ovate end.

188

FOLIAGE is dark green (147A) upper surface; medium green (147B) lower surface. Leaves are 120mm (4 3/4") long x 60mm (2 3/8") wide; elliptic shaped, smooth edges, acute tips, acute bases. Veins are red, stems & branches are dark red. PARENTAGE: 'Herps Parachute' x F. *magdalenae*. Tall upright. Makes good upright. Prefers overhead filtered light. Best bloom & foliage colour in filtered light. Tested 3 years in Herpen, The Netherlands. Distinguished by bloom shape & colour.
Waldenmaier 2007 NL AFS7002.

Herps   Dwarsfluit.   Upright.   Single. COROLLA: quarter flared, turned under wavy petal margins; opens rose (54C); matures magenta (61C); 4mm (3/16") long, 6mm (1/4") wide. SEPALS: half down; tips reflexed; rose (47C) & greenish white (157B) upper surface; light green (143D) lower surface; 11mm (7/16") long x 5mm (3/16") wide. TUBE: rose (47C); long, thick; 33mm (1 1/4") long x 7mm (1/4") wide. STAMENS: do not extend below corolla; pale pink (49D) filaments; pale yellow (1D) anthers. PISTIL: does not extend below the corolla; light pink (49C) style; greenish yellow (1B) stigma. BUD: elongated. FOLIAGE: dark green (133A) upper surface; medium green (138A) lower surface. Leaves are 97mm (3 13/16") long x 69mm (2 3/4") wide, ovate shaped, wavy edges, acute tips and obtuse bases. Light green (138C) veins; light green/grayish rose (181D) stems; medium green/ grayish red (138B/181C) branches. PARENTAGE: ('F. *magdalenae*' x 'F. *fulgens grandiflora*') x 'F. *fulgens gesneriana*', tetraploid. Medium upright. Makes good upright. Prefers overhead filtered light or full sun. Cold weather hardy. Best bloom and foliage colour in filtered light. Tested 3 years in Herpen, Belgium.   Award,   Meise,   9/20/03. Distinguished by foliage, bloom colour & shape.
Waldenmaier 2004 NL AFS5621.

Herps Foxtrot. Upright. Single. COROLLA: quarter flared; opens dark reddish purple (64A) & purple (71A); matures reddish purple (71B); 15mm (9/16") long x 13mm (1/2") wide. SEPALS: half down, tips recurved; white (155C) & pale lavender (69B) tipped light apple green (145B) upper surface; pale pink (69A) tipped light apple green (145B) lower surface; 28mm (1 1/8") long x 10mm (3/8") wide. TUBE: white (155C); 15mm (9/16") long x 6mm (1/4") wide. FOLIAGE is dark green (139A) upper surface; medium

green (138B) lower surface. PARENTAGE: 'WALZ Polka' x 'WALZ Blauwkous'.
Waldenmaier 2008 NL AFS6768.

Herps Gamba. Upright. Double. COROLLA: quarter flared, smooth petal margins; opens & matures reddish purple (66A), orange base; 29mm (1 1/8") long x 33mm (1 5/16") wide. SEPALS: half up; tips recurved up; red (46B) upper surface; red (45B) lower surface; 38mm(1 1/2") long x 19mm(3/4") wide. TUBE: pale lavender (69B); long & thick; 42mm (1 5/8") long x 11mm(7/16") wide. STAMENS: do not extend below corolla; red (52A) filaments; light yellow (5C) anthers. PISTIL: extends 15mm (9/16") below the corolla, rose (52C) style; pink (52D) stigma. BUD: tear drop shaped. FOLIAGE: dark green (137A) upper surface, medium green (137B) lower surface. Leaves are 100mm (3 15/16") long x 85mm (3 3/8") wide, cordate shaped, serrulated edges, acute tips and rounded bases. Veins & stems are red; branches are green. PARENTAGE: 'WALZ Harp' x 'Celebrity'. Tall upright. Makes good upright. Prefers overhead filtered light. Best bloom colour in bright light. Tested 4 years in Herpen, The Netherlands. Award of Merit, VKC, The Netherlands. Distinguished by very large double flower with long TUBE.
Waldenmaier 2004 NL AFS5397.

Herps Gendir. Upright. Single. COROLLA: quarter flared, smooth petal margins; opens & matures magenta (67B); 12mm (1/2") long x 20mm (13/16") wide. SEPALS: full down; tips recurved; rose (52B) upper surface; rose (68C) lower surface; 22mm (7/8") long x 9mm(3/8") wide. TUBE: dark red (47A); medium length & thickness; 23mm (15/16") long x 8mm(5/16") wide. STAMENS: extend 2mm (1/16") below corolla; light rose (50C) filaments, light yellow (10D) anthers. PISTIL: extends 15mm (9/16") below the corolla, light rose (50C) style & stigma. BUD: ovate, pointed. FOLIAGE: dark green (137A) upper surface, medium green (137B) lower surface. Leaves are 90mm (3 9/16") long x 45mm (1 3/4") wide, ovate shaped, serrated edges, acute tips and rounded bases. Veins, stems & branches are green. PARENTAGE: ('F. *magdalenae*' x 'F. *fulgens grandiflora*') x 'Lady Kathleen Spence'. Medium upright. Makes good upright or standard. Prefers overhead filtered light. Best bloom and foliage colour in bright light. Tested 2 years in Herpen, The Netherlands. Award of Merit, VKC, The Netherlands. Distinguished by horizontal flowers with hairy and rich flowering.
Waldenmaier 2004 NL AFS5400.

189

Herps Helicopter. Upright. Single. COROLLA: Quarter flared; opens rose (55B) edged dark rose (54A); matures pink (55C); 12mm (7/16") long x 11mm (7/16") wide. SEPALS: half down, tips reflexed; dark rose (54B) upper surface; rose (55B) lower surface; 12mm (7/16") long x 6mm (1/4") wide. TUBE: rose (54C); short & thick; 14mm (9/16") long x 8mm (5/16") wide. FOLIAGE is dark green (136B) upper surface; medium green (138A) lower surface. PARENTAGE: 'Herps Parachute' x 'Herps Draaimolen'. Waldenmaier 2007 NL AFS6578.

Herps Horlepijp. Upright. Single. COROLLA is quarter flared with turned under wavy petal margins; opens orange (40C); matures light orange (41C); 16mm (5/8") long x 14mm (9/16") wide. SEPALS are half down, tips reflexed; red orange (42C), tipped apple green (144C) upper surface; light orange (41C), tipped apple green (144C) lower surface; 19mm (3/4") long x 5mm (3/16") wide. TUBE is pink (43D); long, medium thickness; 41mm (1 5/8") long x 6mm (1/4") wide. FOLIAGE: dark green (137A) upper surface; medium green (137D) lower surface. Leaves are 82mm (3 1/4") long x 43mm (1 11/16") wide, ovate shaped. PARENTAGE: ('F. magdalenae x F. fulgens grandiflora') x 'White King'. Meise 9-18-04, Outstanding. Distinguished by flower colour. Waldenmaier 2005 NL AFS5842.

Herps Jorn. Upright. Single. COROLLA: unflared, bell shaped; smooth petal margins; opens & matures light purple (80C);20mm (3/4") long x 20mm (3/4") wide. SEPALS: fully up, tips recurved; light pink (62B) upper surface; pink (62A) lower surface; 35mm (1 3/8") long x 9mm (5/16") wide. TUBE: white (155A); medium length & thickness; 13mm (1/2") long x 5mm (3/16") wide. STAMENS extend 5mm (3/16") beyond the corolla; dark reddish purple (72C) filaments; reddish purple (72B) anthers. PISTIL extends 20mm (3/4") beyond the corolla; light reddish purple (73A) style; light rose (73C) stigma. BUD is ovate, thin. FOLIAGE is dark green (137A) upper surface; medium green (138A) lower surface. Leaves are 65mm (2 9/16") long x 40mm (1 9/16") wide; ovate shaped, wavy edges, acute tips, rounded bases. Veins, stems & branches are green. PARENTAGE: F. lycioides x 'White Galore'. Tall upright. Makes good upright. Prefers overhead filtered light. Best bloom & foliage colour in filtered light. Tested 4 years in Herpen, The Netherlands. Distinguished by bloom shape & colour.

Waldenmaier 2009 NL AFS7005.

Herps Kipkar. Upright. Single. COROLLA: half flared; opens purple (71A); matures dark reddish purple (61A); 15mm (9/16") long x 12mm (7/16") wide. SEPALS: half down, tips recurved; dark reddish purple (61A) upper surface; dark reddish purple (64A) lower surface; 31mm (1 1/4") long x 5mm (3/16") wide. TUBE: reddish purple (61B); medium length & thickness; 15mm (9/16") long x 4mm (1/8") wide. FOLIAGE is dark green (137A) upper surface; medium green (138B) lower surface. PARENTAGE: 'Herps Parachute' x 'Naaldwijk 800'. Waldenmaier 2007 NL AFS6579.

Herps Klephoorn. Upright. Single. COROLLA: quarter flared; opens light purple (N78B); matures violet (77B); 15mm (9/16") long x 12mm (7/16") wide. SEPALS: half down, tips recurved; light purple (75B) tipped light green (142C) upper surface; pale purple (75C) tipped light green (142C) lower surface; 17mm (5/8") long x 7mm (1/4") wide. TUBE: white (155C); 20mm (3/4") long x 6mm (1/4") wide. FOLIAGE is dark green (139A) upper surface; medium green (138B) lower surface. PARENTAGE: ('F. magdalenae' x 'F. juntasensis') x 'Foline'. Waldenmaier 2008 NL AFS6769.

Herps Kriskras. Upright. Semi Double. COROLLA: half flared, smooth petal margins; opens & matures rose (67D); 18mm (11/16") long x 24mm (15/16") wide. SEPALS: half down; tips reflexed; light magenta (66D) upper surface; light rose (63D) lower surface; 31mm(1 1/4") long x 12mm (1/2") wide. TUBE: light reddish purple (66C); medium length & thickness; 16mm (5/8") long x 5mm (3/16") wide. STAMENS: extend 10mm (3/8") below corolla; light pink (65C) filaments; magenta (68A) anthers. PISTIL: extends 20mm (13/16") below the corolla, rose (65A) style; magenta (68A) stigma. BUD: oblong, pointed. FOLIAGE: dark green (137A) upper surface, medium green (147B) lower surface. Leaves are 68mm (2 11/16") long x 42mm (1 11/16") wide, ovate shaped, serrulated edges, acute tips and rounded bases. Veins & stems are red; branches are brown. PARENTAGE: 'Gerharda's Panache' x unknown. Medium upright. Makes good upright or standard. Prefers overhead filtered light. Best bloom and foliage colour in bright light. Tested 2 years in Herpen, The Netherlands. Award of Merit, VKC, The Netherlands. Distinguished by panicles of F. magellanica shaped flowers.

Waldenmaier 2004 NL AFS5392.

Herps Kuiwagen. Upright. Single. COROLLA:
half flared; opens purple (71A), dark reddish
purple (60A) base; matures dark reddish
purple (59A); 22mm (7/8") long x 20mm
(3/4") wide. SEPALS: half down, tips
recurved; dark reddish purple (64A) upper
surface; dark reddish purple (61A) lower
surface; 26mm (1") long x 9mm (5/16") wide.
TUBE: reddish purple (61B); medium length
& thickness; 15mm (9/16") long x 6mm
(1/4") wide. FOLIAGE is dark green (136A)
upper surface; medium green (138B) lower
surface. PARENTAGE: 'Herps Parachute' x
'Hertogin van Brabant'.
Waldenmaier 2007 NL AFS6580.

Herps Kwikstep. Upright. Single. COROLLA:
quarter flared, smooth petal margins; opens
& matures reddish purple (61B); 13mm
(1/2") long x 16mm (5/8") wide. SEPALS:
horizontal; tips recurved; pink (62A) upper &
lower surfaces; 28mm(1 1/8") long x
10mm(3/8") wide. TUBE: pink (62A); short,
medium thickness; 9mm (3/8") long x
9mm(3/8") wide. STAMENS: extend 15mm
(9/16") below corolla; rose (52B) filaments;
rose (52C) anthers. PISTIL: extends 30mm (1
3/16") below the corolla, rose (52C) style;
yellow (10B) stigma. BUD: round, pointed.
FOLIAGE: dark green (137A) upper surface,
medium green (137B) lower surface. Leaves
are 65mm (2 9/16") long x 45mm (1 3/4")
wide, cordate shaped, wavy edges, acute tips
and rounded bases. Veins are light green;
stems & branches are green. PARENTAGE:
('WALZ Polka' x 'WALZ Blauwkous') x 'Prince
Syray'. Small upright. Makes good upright or
standard. Prefers overhead filtered light. Best
bloom colour in bright light. Tested 3 years
in Herpen, The Netherlands. Award of Merit,
VKC, The Netherlands. Distinguished by
slightly erect flowers; highly visible pistil and
stigma.
Waldenmaier 2004 NL AF5398.

Herps Lars. Upright/Trailer. Single.
COROLLA: quarter flared, bell shaped;
smooth petal margins; opens & matures
reddish purple (61B);10mm (3/8") long x
8mm (5/16") wide. SEPALS: half down, tips
reflexed; reddish purple (60B) tipped green
upper surface; light pink (62B) tipped green
lower surface; 13mm (1/2") long x 7mm
(1/4") wide. TUBE: dark reddish purple
(60B); medium length & thickness; 18mm
(11/16") long x 6mm (1/4") wide. STAMENS
extend 2mm (1/16") beyond the corolla; light
pink (62B) filaments; light yellow (4C)

anthers. PISTIL extends 15mm (9/16")
beyond the corolla; magenta (61C) style;
yellow (4A) stigma. BUD is ovate, long TUBE.
FOLIAGE is medium green (137B) upper
surface; medium green (137D) lower surface.
Leaves are 90mm (3 9/16") long x 75mm (3")
wide; cordate shaped, wavy edges, acute tips,
rounded bases. Veins, stems & branches are
green. PARENTAGE: (tetraploid 'F. *splendens*'
x F. *juntasensis*) x tetraploid F. *fulgens
gesneriana*. Lax upright or stiff trailer. Makes
good basket or upright. Prefers overhead
filtered light. Heat tolerant if shaded. Best
bloom & foliage colour in filtered light. Tested
7 years in Herpen, The Netherlands.
Distinguished by hairy TUBE & SEPALS;
bloom shape & colour.
Waldenmaier 2009 NL AFS7004.

Herps Lier. Upright. Single. COROLLA is
unflared with turned under wavy petal
margins; opens dark rose (51A); matures
rose (51B); 14mm (9/16") long x 9mm (3/8")
wide. SEPALS are full down, tips reflexed;
reddish purple (59B), tipped light green
(143B) upper surface; reddish purple (61B)
tipped light green (143B) lower surface;
21mm (13/16") long x 7mm (1/4") wide.
TUBE is reddish purple (59B); long, medium
thickness; 39mm (1 9/16") long x 6mm
(1/4") wide. FOLIAGE: dark green (139A)
upper surface; medium green (137C) lower
surface. Leaves are 112mm (4 7/16") long x
38mm (1 1/2") wide, elliptic shaped.
PARENTAGE: 'F. magdalenae x 'Pink Cornet'.
Meise 9-18-04. Distinguished by deep pink
flower.
Waldenmaier 2005 NL AFS5841.

Herps Magdapet. Upright/Trailer. Single.
COROLLA: unflared, bell shaped; smooth
petal margins; opens coral (37A); matures
light coral (38A); 13mm (1/2") long x 11mm
(7/16") wide. SEPALS: half down, tips
reflexed; orange (32A) tipped green upper
surface; orange (30C) tipped green lower
surface; 15mm (9/16") long x 7mm (1/4")
wide. TUBE: orange (32A), light brown (175C)
base; long, medium thickness; 45mm (1
3/4") long x 8mm (5/16") wide. STAMENS
extend 3mm (1/8") beyond the corolla; yellow
(10C) filaments & anthers. PISTIL extends
10mm (3/8") beyond the corolla; coral (37A)
style & stigma. BUD is ovate, long TUBE.
FOLIAGE is medium green (137A) upper
surface; medium green (137C) lower surface.
Leaves are 90mm (3 9/16") long x 40mm (1
9/16") wide; lanceolate shaped, serrate
edges, acute tips, acute bases. Veins & stems
are green, branches are light red.

PARENTAGE: (F. *magdalenae* x F. *apetala*)(hexaploid) x self. Lax upright or stiff trailer. Makes good upright. Prefers overhead filtered light. Best bloom & foliage colour in filtered light. Tested 6 years in Herpen, The Netherlands. Distinguished by bloom shape & colour. Waldenmaier 2009 NL AFS7009.

Herps Marimba. Upright. Single. COROLLA: quarter flared, smooth petal margins; opens & matures dark orange (33A); 12mm (1/2") long x 16mm (5/8") wide. SEPALS: half down; tips reflexed; orange (33C) upper & lower surfaces; 19mm(3/4") long x 10mm (3/8") wide. TUBE: orange (33C); long & thick; 34mm (1 5/16") long x 14mm (9/16") wide. STAMENS: extend 2mm (1/16") below corolla; light orange (32D) filaments; cream (11D) anthers. PISTIL: extends 20mm (13/16") below the corolla, light orange (32D) style; pale pink (36D) stigma. BUD: small, round, pointed. FOLIAGE: dark green (147A) upper surface, medium green (138B) lower surface. Leaves are 150mm (5 15/16") long x 100mm (3 15/16") wide, elliptic shaped, serrated edges, acute tips and rounded bases. Veins, stems & branches are green. PARENTAGE: ('F. *magdalenae*' x F. *fulgens grandiflora*') x 'Lord Lonsdale'. Tall upright. Makes good upright or standard. Prefers overhead filtered light. Best bloom & foliage colour in bright light. Tested 3 years in Herpen, The Netherlands. Award of Merit, VKC, The Netherlands. Distinguished by pronounced orange flower colour. Waldenmaier 2004 NL AFS5387.

Herps Martina. Upright. Single. COROLLA is quarter flared with turned under wavy petal margins; opens red orange (42C); matures reddish orange (43C); 10mm (3/8") long x 5mm (3/16") wide. SEPALS are half down, tips reflexed; red (47B) tipped medium green (141C) upper surface; red (45D) tipped medium green (141C) lower surface; 13mm (1/2") long x 5mm (3/16") wide. TUBE is white (155C) blushed rose (47B); long, medium thickness; 23mm (15/16") long x 5mm (3/16") wide. FOLIAGE: dark green (137A) upper surface; medium green (138B) lower surface. Leaves are 60mm (2 3/8") long x 25mm (1") wide, elliptic shaped. PARENTAGE: 'Wilma Van Druten' x 'Wilma Van Druten'. Meise 3-7-04. Distinguished by colour combination. Waldenmaier 2005 NL AFS5661.

Herps Mellofoon. Upright. Double. COROLLA: quarter flared; opens red (52A)

edged violet (77C); matures dark rose (54A); 15mm (9/16") long x 15mm (9/16") wide. PETALOIDS: red (52A); 10mm (3/8") long x 12mm (7/16") wide. SEPALS: fully up, tips reflexed; white (155C) & rose (54C) tipped medium green (141D) upper surface; pink (52D) tipped medium green (141D) lower surface; 21mm (13/16") long x 12mm (7/16") wide. TUBE: white (155C) & medium green (141D); 16mm (5/8") long x 8mm (5/16") wide. FOLIAGE is dark green (139A) upper surface; medium green (138B) lower surface. PARENTAGE: 'WALZ Mandoline' x 'Cecile'. Waldenmaier 2008 NL AFS6770.

Herps Mignon. Upright. Semi Double to Double. COROLLA: half flared, smooth petal margins; opens & matures pale pink (62D); 17mm (11/16") long x 15mm (9/16") wide. SEPALS: half down; tips reflexed; cream (11D) upper & lower surfaces; 20mm(13/16") long x 10mm (3/8") wide. TUBE: light greenish white (157C); medium length & thickness; 11mm (7/16") long x 5mm (3/16") wide. STAMENS: do not extend below corolla; white (155D) filaments; light yellow (4B) anthers. PISTIL: extends 5mm (3/16") below the corolla, pale pink (62D) style; yellowish white (4D) stigma. BUD: rounded. FOLIAGE: dark green (147A) upper surface, medium green (147B) lower surface. Leaves are 55mm (2 3/16") long x 35mm (1 3/8") wide, ovate shaped, serrated edges, acute tips and rounded bases. Veins, stems & branches are red. PARENTAGE: [('F. *magdalenae*' x 'F. *fulgens grandiflora*') x 'Wendy van Wanten'] x 'Gerharda's Panache'. Medium upright. Makes good upright or standard. Prefers overhead filtered light. Best bloom & foliage colour in bright light. Tested 3 years in Herpen, The Netherlands. Award of Merit, VKC, The Netherlands. Distinguished by erect flowers and delicate pink colour. Waldenmaier 2004 NL AFS5389.

Herps Mondharmonica. Upright. Single. COROLLA: half flared, smooth petal margins; opens & matures red (43A); 15mm (9/16") long x 16mm (5/8") wide. SEPALS: full down; tips recurved; orange (32B) upper & lower surfaces; 17mm(11/16") long x 8mm(5/16") wide. TUBE: red (52A); medium length, thick; 13mm (1/2") long x 8mm(5/16") wide. STAMENS: extend 5mm (3/16") below corolla; rose (52C) filaments; white (155D) anthers. PISTIL: extends 10mm (3/8") below the corolla, pink (62C) style & stigma. BUD: small, rounded. FOLIAGE: dark green (137A) upper surface, medium green (137B) lower surface. Leaves are 80mm (3 1/8") long x

65mm (2 9/16") wide, cordate shaped, wavy edges, acute tips and obtuse bases. Veins, stems & branches are green. PARENTAGE: ('F. *magdalenae*' x 'F. *fulgens grandiflora*') x 'Lady Kathleen Spence'. Medium upright. Makes good upright or standard. Prefers overhead filtered light. Best bloom and foliage colour in bright light. Tested 2 years in Herpen, The Netherlands. Award of Merit, VKC, The Netherlands. Distinguished by horizontal flower with flared corolla.
Waldenmaier 2004 NL AFS5394.

Herps Ocarina. Upright. Single. COROLLA is half flared with turned under wavy petal margins; opens reddish purple (74B), pale purple (70D) base; matures reddish purple (74A); 14mm (9/16") long x 19mm (3/4") wide. SEPALS are half down, tips recurved; white (155B) tipped light apple green (145B) upper surface; rose (68C), white (155B) base, tipped light apple green (145B) lower surface; 21mm (13/16") long x 8mm (5/16") wide. TUBE is greenish white (157A); medium length & thickness; 20mm (13/16") long x 6mm (1/4") wide. FOLIAGE: dark green (136B) upper surface; medium green (138B) lower surface. Leaves are 48mm (1 7/8") long x 38mm (1 1/2") wide, ovate shaped. PARENTAGE: [('F. magdalenae' x 'F. fulgens grandiflora') x 'Wendy Van Wanten'] x 'Gerharda's Panache'. Distinguished by colour combination.
Waldenmaier 2005 NL AFS5825.

Herps Orangist. Upright. Souble. COROLLA: half flared; opens rose (48B), rose (50B) & gray (201C); matures dark rose (54B); 21mm (13/16") long x 17mm (5/8") wide. SEPALS: half down, tips recurved; rose (52B) tipped light apple green (145C) upper surface; light orange (41D) tipped light apple green (145C) lower surface; 30mm (1 3/16") long x 14mm (9/16") wide. TUBE: pink (51D); 17mm (5/8") long x 9mm (5/16") wide. FOLIAGE is dark green (139A) upper surface; medium green (137B) lower surface. PARENTAGE: 'Bicentennial' x tetraploid 'F. *fulgens gesneriana*'.
Waldenmaier 2008 NL AFS6771.

Herps Oranjerie. Upright. Semi Double. COROLLA: Quarter flared; opens dark rose (54B); matures rose (52B); 24mm (15/16") long x 21mm (13/16") wide. SEPALS: half down, tips recurved; pink (48D) tipped light apple green (145B) upper surface; pink (48C) tipped light apple green (145B) lower surface; 28mm (1 1/8") long x 10mm (3/8") wide. TUBE: dark rose (49A); medium length &

thickness; 20mm (3/4") long x 8mm (5/16") wide. FOLIAGE is dark green (136B) upper surface; medium green (138B) lower surface. PARENTAGE: 'Danny Kaye' x tetraploid 'F. *fulgens gesneriana*'.
Waldenmaier 2007 NL AFS6581.

Herps Parachute. Upright/Trailer. Single. COROLLA is three quarter flared with turned under wavy petal margins; opens dark rose (54B); matures rose (55B); 9mm (3/8") long x 8mm (5/16") wide. SEPALS are horizontal, tips reflexed; red (53C) upper surface; rose (51B) lower surface; 14mm (9/16") long x 4mm (3/16") wide. TUBE is rose (52B); long, medium thickness; 23mm (15/16") long x 4mm (3/16") wide. FOLIAGE: dark green (137A) upper surface; medium green (138B) lower surface. Leaves are 94mm (3 11/16") long x 52mm (2 1/16") wide, ovate shaped. PARENTAGE: 'Gerharda's Panache' x 'Gerharda's Panache'. Meise 8-14-04. Distinguished by flower colour.
Waldenmaier 2005 NL AFS5708.

Herps Piccolo. Upright. Single. COROLLA: quarter flared, smooth petal margins; opens reddish purple (74A) & light rose (73B); matures reddish purple (74A); 7mm (1/4") long x 7mm (1/4") wide. SEPALS: half down; tips reflexed; white (155D) upper & lower surfaces; 16mm (5/8") long x 6mm(1/4") wide. TUBE: white (155D); long, medium thickness; 20mm (13/16") long x 7mm(1/4") wide. STAMENS: extend 2mm (1/16) below corolla; yellow (10B) filaments, light yellow (4B) anthers. PISTIL: extends 15mm (9/16") below the corolla, light pink (62B) style; light yellow (4D) stigma. BUD: long, ovate, pointed. FOLIAGE: dark green (137A) upper surface, medium green (138B) lower surface. Leaves are 60mm (2 3/8") long x 40mm (1 9/16") wide, ovate shaped, serrulated edges, acute tips and obtuse bases. Veins, stems & branches are green. PARENTAGE: 'WALZ Trompet' x 'Prince Syray'. Small upright. Makes good upright or standard. Prefers overhead filtered light. Best bloom and foliage colour in bright light. Tested 4 years in Herpen, The Netherlands. Award of Merit, VKC, The Netherlands. Distinguished by horizontal flower and colour contrast in flower.
Waldenmaier 2004 NL AFS5402.

Herps Pierement. Upright. Single. COROLLA: unflared, smooth petal margins; opens & matures magenta (63B); 13mm (1/2") long x 9mm (3/8") wide. SEPALS: half down; tips reflexed; light rose (63D) upper surface; light pink (62B) lower surface; 18mm(11/16") long x 10mm (3/8") wide. TUBE: light rose (63D); medium length & thickness; 18mm (11/16") long x 8mm (5/16") wide. STAMENS: do not extend below corolla; white (155D) filaments; cream (11D) anthers. PISTIL: extends 20mm (13/16") below the corolla, light pink (62B) style; cream (11D) stigma. BUD: round, pointed. FOLIAGE: dark green (139A) upper surface, dark green (138A) lower surface. Leaves are 60mm (2 3/8") long x 40mm (1 9/16") wide, ovate shaped, serrated edges, acute tips and rounded bases. Veins, stems & branches are red. PARENTAGE: [('F. *magdalenae*' x 'F. *fulgens grandiflora*') x 'Wendy van Wanten'] x 'Prince Syray'. Medium upright. Makes good upright or standard. Prefers overhead filtered light. Best bloom & foliage colour in bright light. Tested 3 years in Herpen, The Netherlands. Award of Merit, VKC, The Netherlands. Distinguished by horizontal flowers and fresh pink colour. Waldenmaier 2004 NL AFS5388.

Herps Postkar. Upright/Trailer. Single. COROLLA: Quarter flared; opens reddish purple (N79C); matures purple (71A); 17mm (5/8") long x 13mm (1/2") wide. SEPALS: horizontal, tips reflexed; reddish purple (64B) upper surface; reddish purple (71B) lower surface; 23mm (7/8") long x 6mm (1/4") wide. TUBE: reddish purple (61B); medium length & thickness; 18mm (11/16") long x 6mm (1/4") wide. FOLIAGE is dark green (136A) upper surface; medium green (138A) lower surface. PARENTAGE: 'Herps Parachute' x Hertogin van Brabant'. Waldenmaier 2007 NL AFS6582.

Herps Rebab. Upright. Single. COROLLA is half flared with turned under wavy petal margins; opens light purple (74C); matures reddish purple (74B); 15mm (9/16") long x 14mm (9/16") wide. SEPALS are horizontal, tips reflexed; white (155B), rose (55B) base, tipped medium green (139C) upper surface; rose (54C) tipped medium green (139C) lower surface; 22mm (7/8") long x 11mm (7/16") wide. TUBE is rose (55B); long & thin; 22mm (7/8") long x 4mm (3/16") wide. FOLIAGE: dark green (139A) upper surface; medium green (139C) lower surface. Leaves are 59mm (2 5/16") long x 26mm (1") wide, ovate shaped. PARENTAGE: [('F. magdalenae' x 'F. fulgens grandiflora') x 'Wendy Van Wanten'] x 'WALZ Floreat'. Meise 3-7-04. Distinguished by colour combination. Waldenmaier 2005 NL AFS5662.

Herps Rinkelbel. Upright/Trailer. Single. COROLLA is half flared with turned under wavy petal margins; opens rose (47C); matures rose (50B); 12mm (1/2") long x 12mm (1/2") wide. SEPALS are half down, tips recurved; peach (38B) tipped light apple green (145C) upper surface; light coral (38A), tipped light apple green (145C) lower surface; 26mm (1") long x 6mm (1/4") wide. TUBE is peach (38B); long & thin; 19mm (3/4") long x 2mm (1/16") wide. FOLIAGE: dark green (139A) upper surface; medium green (138B) lower surface. Leaves are 56mm (2 3/16") long x 33mm (1 5/16") wide, ovate shaped. PARENTAGE: 'WALZ Triangel' x 'F. fulgens grandiflora'. Meise 8-14-04. Distinguished by flower colour. Waldenmaier 2005 NL AFS5705.

Herps Samba. Upright. Single. COROLLA is half flared with turned under smooth petal margins; opens magenta (68A); matures rose (61D); 14mm (9/16") long x 13mm (1/2") wide. SEPALS are half down, tips recurved; dark rose (48A) tipped yellowish green (145A) upper surface; rose (51B), tipped light apple green (145C) lower surface; 15mm (9/16") long x 7mm (1/4") wide. TUBE is dark rose (48A); medium length, thick; 14mm (9/16") long x 7mm (1/4") wide. FOLIAGE: dark green (136A) upper surface; medium green (138B) lower surface. Leaves are 50mm (2") long x 37mm (1 7/16") wide, cordate shaped. PARENTAGE: ('F. magdalenae' x 'F. fulgens grandiflora') x 'Wendy Van Wanten'. Meise 8-14-04. Distinguished by erect flowers. Waldenmaier 2005 NL AFS5706.

Herps Sandra. Upright. Single. COROLLA is half flared with turned under wavy petal margins; opens rose (52B); matures dark rose (54B); 17mm (11/16") long x 10mm (3/8") wide. SEPALS are half down, tips recurved; dark rose (55A) tipped yellowish green (144B) upper surface; reddish purple (58A) tipped yellowish green (144B) lower surface; 25mm (1") long x 6mm (1/4") wide. TUBE is dark rose (55A); long, medium thickness; 31mm (1 1/4") long x 5mm (3/16") wide. FOLIAGE: dark green (139A) upper surface; medium green (138B) lower surface. Leaves are 108mm (4 1/4") long x 33mm (1 5/16") wide, lanceolate shaped. PARENTAGE: 'Wilma Van Druten' x 'Wilma Van Druten'. Meise 8-14-04. Distinguished by flower colour. Waldenmaier 2005 NL AFS5709.

Herps Schalmei. Upright. Single. COROLLA: Unflared; opens dark rose (55A); matures

rose (52C); 16mm (5/8") long x 13mm (1/2") wide. SEPALS: half down, tips reflexed; rose (55B) & light apple green (145C) tipped yellowish green (144B) upper surface; pink (54D) & pale yellow green (150D) tipped yellowish green (144B) lower surface; 22mm (7/8") long x 6mm (1/4") wide. TUBE: rose (55B); long & thin; 24mm (15/16") long x 5mm (3/16") wide. FOLIAGE is dark green (136A) upper surface; medium green (138A) lower surface. PARENTAGE: [('F. *magdalenae*' x 'F. *fulgens grandiflora*') x tetraploid 'F. *fulgens gesneriana*'] x 'WALZ Floreat'.
Waldenmaier 2007 NL AFS6583.

Herps Schotel. Upright. Semi Double. COROLLA: Quarter flared; opens dark purple (79B) striped magenta (58B); matures purple (71A) striped magenta (61C); 22mm (7/8") long x 24mm (15/16") wide. SEPALS: horizontal, tips reflexed; reddish purple (61B) upper surface; magenta (58B) lower surface; 29mm (1 1/8") long x 15mm (9/16") wide. TUBE: magenta (58B); medium length & thickness; 11mm (7/16") long x 7mm (1/4") wide. FOLIAGE is dark green (136B) upper surface; medium green (138A) lower surface. PARENTAGE: 'Lady Boothy' x 'Citation'.
Waldenmaier 2007 NL AFS6584.

Herps Sleetje. Upright/Trailer. Single. COROLLA: quarter flared, bell shaped; smooth petal margins; opens rose (68B), edged orange-red; matures rose (68B); 14mm (9/16") long x 12mm (7/16") wide. SEPALS: horizontal, tips reflexed; magenta (57B) upper surface; rose (61D) lower surface; 15mm (9/16") long x 6mm (1/4") wide. TUBE: magenta (57B); medium length & thickness;15mm (9/16") long x 6mm (1/4") wide. STAMENS extend 2mm (1/16") beyond the corolla; rose (61D) filaments; very pale orange (27C) anthers. PISTIL extends 9mm (5/16") beyond the corolla; rose (61D) style; pale pink (62D) stigma. BUD is ovate. FOLIAGE is dark green (147A) upper surface; medium green (147B) lower surface. Leaves are 40mm (1 9/16") long x 30mm (1 3/16") wide; cordate shaped, serrate edges, obtuse tips, rounded bases. Veins are green, stems & branches are red. PARENTAGE: 'Herps Parachute' x 'Herps Draaimolen'. Lax upright or stiff trailer. Makes good basket. Prefers overhead filtered light. Best bloom colour in bright light. Best foliage colour in filtered light. Tested 4 years in Herpen, The Netherlands. Distinguished by bloom shape.
Waldenmaier 2009 NL AFS7010.

Herps Snorfiets. Upright/Trailer. Single. COROLLA: Quarter flared; opens rose (55B) edged rose (52B); matures pink (55C) edged rose (54C); 13mm (1/2") long x 12mm (7/16") wide. SEPALS: horizontal, tips reflexed; pink (54D) tipped light yellowish green (146D) upper surface; light pink (55D) tipped light yellowish green (146D) lower surface; 18mm (11/16") long x 6mm (1/4") wide. TUBE: rose (55B); long, medium thickness; 17mm (5/8") long x 5mm (3/16") wide. FOLIAGE is dark green (137A) upper surface; medium green (138A) lower surface. PARENTAGE: 'Herps Parachute' x 'Herps Parachute'.
Waldenmaier 2007 NL AFS6585.

Herps Spencer. Upright. Double. COROLLA: three quarter flared, bell shaped; smooth petal margins; opens dark reddish purple (59A); matures reddish purple (58A); 25mm (1") long x 25mm (1") wide. SEPALS: half up, tips recurved up; magenta (63A) upper surface; magenta (61C) lower surface; 37mm (1 7/16") long x16mm (5/8") wide. TUBE: pink (62A); medium length & thickness; 18mm (11/16") long x 8mm (5/16") wide. STAMENS extend 9mm (5/16") beyond the corolla; dark reddish purple (61A) filaments; purple (77A) anthers. PISTIL extends 30mm (1 3/16") beyond the corolla; reddish purple (58A) style; light pink (65B) stigma. BUD is ovate. FOLIAGE is dark green (137A) upper surface; medium green (138A) lower surface. Leaves are 80mm (3 3/16") long x 45mm (1 3/4") wide; ovate shaped, wavy edges, acute tips, obtuse bases. Veins & branches are green, stems are red. PARENTAGE: 'Schimpen's Glorie' x 'Danny Kaye'. Medium upright. Makes good basket or upright. Prefers overhead filtered light. Best bloom & foliage colour in filtered light. Tested 4 years in Herpen, The Netherlands. Distinguished by bloom colour.
Waldenmaier 2009 NL AFS7003.

Herps Steekkar. Upright. Single. COROLLA: Quarter flared; opens light purple (N78C), pale purple (76C) base; matures violet (76A); 14mm (9/16") long x 12mm (7/16") wide. SEPALS: horizontal, tips reflexed; magenta (67B) tipped olive green (152B) upper surface; magenta (71C) tipped olive green (152B) lower surface; 17mm (5/8") long x 9mm (5/16") wide. TUBE: reddish purple (67A); medium length, thick; 13mm (1/2") long x 7mm (1/4") wide. FOLIAGE is dark green (136A) upper surface; medium green (138A) lower surface. PARENTAGE: 'Herps Parachute' x 'Apart'.

195

Waldenmaier 2007 NL AFS6586.

Herps Strijkstok. Upright. Single. COROLLA is quarter flared with turned under wavy petal margins; opens orange (41B); matures light orange (41D); 4mm (3/16") long x 6mm (1/4") wide. SEPALS are half down, tips reflexed; red (53D), light pink (49B) base, tipped light green (139D) upper surface; dark red (53A), white (155C) base, tipped light green (139D) lower surface; 18mm (11/16") long x 7mm (1/4") wide. TUBE is light pink (49B); medium length, thick; 17mm (11/16") long x 9mm (3/8") wide. FOLIAGE: dark green (147A) upper surface; medium green (138B) lower surface. Leaves are 69mm (2 3/4") long x 38mm (1 1/2") wide, ovate shaped. PARENTAGE: [('F. magdalenae' x 'F. fulgens grandiflora') x 'Wendy Van Wanten'] x 'Prince Syray'. Meise 8-14-04. Distinguished by flower colour.
Waldenmaier 2005 NL AFS5707.

Herps Tamboerijn. Upright. Single. COROLLA: quarter flared, smooth petal margins; opens & matures pale pink (69A); 17mm (11/16") long x 15mm (9/16") wide. SEPALS: horizontal; tips recurved; magenta (58B) upper surface; dark rose (58C) lower surface; 26mm(1") long x 10mm (3/8") wide. TUBE: magenta (63B); medium length & thickness; 27mm (1 1/16") long x 9mm (3/8") wide. STAMENS: extend 10mm (3/8") below corolla; pale lavender (65D) filaments; light yellow (4C) anthers. PISTIL: extends 25mm (1") below the corolla, rose (65A) style; pale lavender (65D) stigma. BUD: ovate. FOLIAGE: dark green (139A) upper surface, medium green (137C) lower surface. Leaves are 90mm (3 9/16") long x 45mm (1 3/4") wide, elliptic shaped, serrated edges, acute tips and acute bases. Veins, stems & branches are red. PARENTAGE: ('F. magdalenae' x 'F. fulgens grandiflora') x 'Impudence'. Medium upright. Makes good upright or standard. Prefers overhead filtered light. Best bloom and foliage colour in bright light. Tested 3 years in Herpen, The Netherlands. Award of Merit, VKC, The Netherlands. Distinguished by horizontal flowers with pronounced visible Stamens.
Waldenmaier 2004 NL AFS5391.

Herps Tiktiri. Upright/Trailer. Single. COROLLA: unflared, cordate shaped; wavy petal margins; opens & matures magenta (63B); 15mm (9/16") long x 10mm (3/8") wide. SEPALS: full down, tips recurved; dark rose (58C) upper & lower surfaces; 16mm (5/8") long x 4mm (1/8") wide. TUBE: cream

(158D); long & thin; 22mm (7/8") long x 4mm (1/8") wide. STAMENS extend 5mm (3/16") beyond the corolla; very pale orange (19D) filaments; magenta (63A) anthers. PISTIL extends 10mm (3/8") beyond the corolla; very pale orange (19D) style; light yellow (3D) stigma. BUD is small & long. FOLIAGE is medium green (137B) upper surface; medium green (138B) lower surface. Leaves are 55mm (2 3/16") long x 40mm (1 9/16") wide; ovate shaped, wavy edges, acute tips, rounded bases. Veins, stems & branches are green. PARENTAGE: 'Herps Klephoorn' x 'Veenlust'. Lax upright or stiff trailer. Makes good basket or standard. Prefers overhead filtered light. Best bloom & foliage colour in filtered light. Tested 3 years in Herpen, The Netherlands. Distinguished by bloom shape & colour; rich flowering.
Waldenmaier 2009 NL AFS7006.

Herps Trailer. Trailer. Single. COROLLA is quarter flared; opens purple (71A); matures dark purple (79A); 18mm (11/16") long x 13mm (1/2") wide. SEPALS are horizontal, tips reflexed; reddish purple (59B) upper surface; dark reddish purple (64A) lower surface; 24mm (15/16") long x 6mm (1/4") wide. TUBE is dark reddish purple (61A); medium length & thickness; 18mm (11/16") long x 5mm (3/16") wide. FOLIAGE is dark green (136A) upper surface; medium green (137C) lower surface. PARENTAGE: 'Herps Parachute' x 'Naaldwijk 800'.
Waldenmaier 2007 NL AFS6419.

Herps Tuimelkar. Upright. Single. COROLLA: Half flared; opens violet (75A); matures light reddish purple (72D); 16mm (5/8") long x 12mm (7/16") wide. SEPALS: half down, tips recurved; magenta (63B) tipped light yellowish green (146D) upper surface; dark rose (67C) tipped light yellowish green (146D) lower surface; 24mm (15/16") long x 7mm (1/4") wide. TUBE: magenta (61C); medium length & thickness; 12mm (7/16") long x 5mm (3/16") wide. FOLIAGE is dark green (136A) upper surface; medium green (138B) lower surface. PARENTAGE: 'Herps Parachute' x 'Citation'.
Waldenmaier 2007 NL AFS6587.

Herps Tweespan. Upright. Single. COROLLA: Three quarter flared; opens light reddish purple (N66C) edged magenta (63B); matures rose (68B); 12mm (7/16") long x 14mm (9/16") wide. SEPALS: horizontal, tips reflexed; rose (51C) tipped yellowish green (144B) upper surface; rose (54C) tipped yellowish green (144B) lower surface; 17mm

(5/8") long x 8mm (5/16") wide. TUBE: light rose (50C); medium length & thickness; 13mm (1/2") long x 5mm (3/16") wide. FOLIAGE is dark green (136A) upper surface; medium green (137D) lower surface. PARENTAGE: 'Herps Parachute' x 'Prince Syray'.
Waldenmaier 2007 NL AFS6588.

Herps Udu. Upright. Single. COROLLA: unflared, circular shaped; smooth petal margins; opens purple (71A); matures reddish purple (71B); 14mm (9/16") long x 14mm (9/16") wide. SEPALS: full down, tips reflexed; magenta (66D) tipped yellow upper surface; reddish purple (64B) tipped yellow lower surface; 15mm (9/16") long x 5mm (3/16") wide. TUBE: light magenta (66D); medium length, thick; 16mm (5/8") long x 8mm (5/16") wide. STAMENS do not extend beyond the corolla; reddish purple (74B) filaments; white (155A) anthers. PISTIL extends 10mm (3/8") beyond the corolla; reddish purple (74B) style; light pink (49B) stigma. BUD is elliptic. FOLIAGE is medium green (137A) upper surface; medium green (138A) lower surface. Leaves are 50mm (2") long x 30mm (1 3/16") wide; ovate shaped, smooth edges, acute tips, rounded bases. Veins, stems & branches are green. PARENTAGE: 'Herps Klephoorn' x 'Northway'. Medium upright. Makes good upright or standard. Prefers overhead filtered light. Best bloom & foliage colour in filtered light. Tested 3 years in Herpen, The Netherlands. Distinguished by bloom shape & colour.
Waldenmaier 2009 NL AFS7008.

Herps Vierspan. Upright. Single. COROLLA: Quarter flared; opens dark rose (54A); matures magenta (58B); 17mm (5/8") long x 14mm (9/16") wide. SEPALS: horizontal, tips reflexed; rose (51B) tipped light olive green (147C) upper surface; light rose (58D) tipped light olive green (147C) lower surface; 19mm (3/4") long x 6mm (1/4") wide. TUBE: rose (54C); medium length & thickness; 13mm (1/2") long x 5mm (3/16") wide. FOLIAGE is dark green (136A) upper surface; medium green (138B) lower surface. PARENTAGE: 'Herps Parachute' x 'Prince Syray'.
Waldenmaier 2007 NL AFS6589.

Het Dansmarieke. Upright/Trailer. Double. COROLLA is half flared with turned under wavy petal margins; opens dark purple (72B), reddish purple (61B) base; matures purple (71A); 26mm (1") long x 28mm (1 1/8") wide. SEPALS are half up, tips recurved up; dark reddish purple (60B) upper surface; reddish

purple (61B) lower surface; 37mm (1 7/16") long x 12mm (1/2") wide. TUBE is dark reddish purple (60C); medium length & thickness; 18mm (11/16") long x 6mm (1/4") wide. FOLIAGE: dark green (139A) upper surface; medium green (138B) lower surface. Leaves are 64mm (2 1/2") long x 38mm (1 1/2") wide, ovate shaped. PARENTAGE: 'Roesse Blacky' x 'Erika Frohman'. Meise 8-14-04. Distinguished by flower & foliage colour combination.
Mihiels 2005 BE AFS5735.

Het Mauwerke. Upright/Trailer. Single. COROLLA is full flared; opens purple (82A); matures purple (83B); 17mm (5/8") long x 24mm (15/16") wide. SEPALS are fully up, tips recurved; dark rose (67C) upper surface; magenta (67B) lower surface; 31mm (1 1/4") long x 14mm (9/16") wide. TUBE is dark rose (67C); 9mm (3/8") long x 6mm (1/4") wide. FOLIAGE: medium green (137C) upper surface; medium green (138B) lower surface. PARENTAGE: 'Sofie Michiels' x 'Maxima'. Distinguished by bloom & foliage combination.
Roes 2006 NL AFS6158.

Het Museum. Upright/Trailer. Semi Double. COROLLA is half flared with smooth petal margins; opens purple (83B); matures dark reddish purple (72A); 22mm (7/8") long x 29 mm (1 1/8") wide. SEPALS are fully up, tips recurved; light rose (73B) upper & lower surfaces; 27mm (1 1/16") long x 16mm (5/8") wide. TUBE is light rose (73B), medium length & thickness; 17mm (11/16") long x 10mm (3/8") wide. FOLIAGE: medium green (137B) upper surface; medium green (138B) lower surface. Leaves are 72mm (2 13/16") long x 42mm (1 11/16") wide, ovate shaped. PARENTAGE: [('Roesse Apus' x 'Rohees Princess') x 'Roesse Apus'] x 'Allure'. Distinguished by bloom colour.
van Eijk 2005 NL AFS5646.

Het Wijnmenneke. Upright/Trailer. Double. COROLLA is full flared with turned under wavy petal margins; opens dark rose (67C) turning to light purple (74C) at edge, orange (44D) base; matures magenta (63B); 22mm (7/8") long x 20mm (13/16") wide. PETALOIDS: magenta (58B) turning to light reddish purple (66C), orange (44D) base; 16mm (5/8") long x 8mm (5/16") wide. SEPALS are half up, tips recurved up; pale pink (56A) tipped light yellowish green (150C) upper surface; rose (51C) tipped light yellowish green (150C) lower surface; 30mm (1 3/16") long x 13mm (1/2") wide. TUBE is

197

pale pink (56B); medium length & thickness; 18mm (11/16") long x 5mm (3/16") wide. FOLIAGE: dark green (136A) upper surface; medium green (138B) lower surface. Leaves are 71mm (2 13/16") long x 38mm (1 1/2") wide, ovate shaped. PARENTAGE: 'Sofie Michiels' x 'Annabelle Stubbs'. Meise 8-14-04. Distinguished by unique colour combination.
Michiels 2005 BE AFS5830.

Heytina Lokhorst. Upright. Single. COROLLA: Quarter flared; opens & matures dark orange red (34A); 5mm (3/16") long x 9mm (5/16") wide. SEPALS: full down, tips reflexed; light apple green (144D) tipped yellow green (144A) upper surface; dark orange (33A) lower surface; 16mm (5/8") long x 6mm (1/4") wide. TUBE: dark orange (33A); long, medium thickness; 58mm (2 5/16") long x 8mm (5/16") wide, square shaped. FOLIAGE is dark green (137A) upper surface; medium green (138A) lower surface. PARENTAGE: 'Jan De Vos' x 'F. magdalenae'.
de Keyzer 2007 NL AFS6442.

Hie Zenne Kik. Upright. Single. COROLLA is unflared with turned under smooth petal margins; opens red (43A), edged red (46C); matures red orange (43B), edged red (46B); 15mm (5/8") long x 15mm (5/8") wide. SEPALS are half down, tips recurved; orange (44D) tipped light green (143C) upper surface; orange (44D) tipped light green (143D) lower surface; 25mm (1") long x 9mm (3/8") wide. TUBE is rose (51C); medium length and thickness; 30mm (1 3/16") long x 9mm (3/8") wide. STAMENS extend 3mm (1/8") beyond the corolla; magenta (57B) filaments, light yellow (11B) anthers. PISTIL extends 5mm (3/16") beyond the corolla; rose (52C) style, tan (166B) stigma. BUD is elliptic. FOLIAGE is dark green (139A) upper surface, medium green (139C) lower surface. Leaves are 75mm (2 15/16") long x 42mm (1 11/16") wide, cordate shaped, serrulated edges, acute tips and cordate bases. Veins are plum (185B), stems are plum (184B), branches are grayish red (182B). PARENTAGE: 'WALZ Harp' x 'WALZ Harp'. Medium upright. Makes good upright. Prefers overhead filtered light or full sun. Best bloom and foliage colour in bright light. Tested three years in Itegem, Belgium. Certificate N.B.F.K. at Meise. Distinguished by bloom colour.
Geerts L. 2002 BE AFS4975.

High Five. Upright/Trailer. Single. COROLLA is half flared, bell shaped; opens

purple (71A); matures dark reddish purple (61A); 18mm (11/16") long x 14mm (9/16") wide. SEPALS are horizontal, tips recurved; magenta (67B) upper surface; reddish purple (67A) lower surface; 26mm (1") long x 7mm (1/4") wide. TUBE is reddish purple (67A) to magenta (67B); 14mm (9/16") long x 7mm (1/4") wide. FOLIAGE: medium green (146A) upper surface; yellowish green (146C) lower surface. PARENTAGE: 'Gerharda's Panache' x 'Bourguignon'. Distinguished by aubergine coloured flowers in terminal sub racemes.
de Graaff H. 2006 NL AFS6265.

Hilbri. Trailer. Single. COROLLA opens mottled lilac with darker edges; corolla is quarter flared and is 10mm long x 10mm wide. SEPALS are rose on the upper and lower surfaces and tipped green; sepals are half recurved with recurved tips and are 58mm long x 10mm wide. TUBE rose and is 11mm long x 9mm wide. PARENTAGE 'Katrina Thompsen' x 'Alisha Jade'.
Dodman 2005 UK BFS0020.

Hilda Stummer. Trailer. Single. COROLLA opens purplish red, matures to reddish pink; corolla is quarter flared. SEPALS light reddish pink on the upper and lower surfaces; SEPALS are half up with recurved tips. TUBE white. PARENTAGE 'Bella Rosella' x 'Double Otto'.
Nicola 2008 AT BFS0118.

Hilda von Semriach. Upright/Trailer. Single. COROLLA: 3 quarter flared; opens white (155C) & red (52A); matures white (155B) & rose (52B); 22mm (7/8") long x 25mm (1") wide. SEPALS: half up, tips recurved up; red (52A) upper surface; rose (52B) lower surface; 40mm (1 9/16") long x 13mm (1/2") wide. TUBE: red (52A) & rose (52B); medium length & thickness; 18mm (11/16") long x 5mm (3/16") wide. FOLIAGE is medium green (137B) upper surface; medium green (138B) lower surface. PARENTAGE: 'Cliff's Own' x unknown.
Klemm 2007 AT AFS6473.

Hilde-Jo. Trailer. Semi Doublt to Double. COROLLA: half flared; opens light reddish purple (N66C); matures light reddish purple (N66D); 22mm (7/8") long x 15mm (9/16") wide. SEPALS: horizontal, tips recurved; pink (62C) tipped light apple green (N144D) upper surface; light pink (65B) tipped light apple green (N144D) lower surface; 31mm (1 1/4") long x 17mm (5/8") wide. TUBE: pale pink (62D); medium length & thickness; 19mm (3/4") long x 5mm (3/16") wide. FOLIAGE is dark green (136B) upper surface; medium green (138B) lower surface. PARENTAGE: 'Vendelzwaaier' x 'Jackie Bull'. Michiels 2007 BE AFS6350.

Hof van Twente. Trailer. Single. COROLLA: quarter flared, bell shaped; opens reddish purple (74A); matures darker reddish purple (74A); 25mm (1") long x 32mm (1 1/4") wide. SEPALS: half down, tips reflexed q; reddish purple (71B) upper surface; magenta (71C) lower surface; 34mm (1 3/8") long x 12mm (7/16") wide. TUBE: reddish purple (71B); 31mm (1 1/4") long x 8mm (5/16") wide. FOLIAGE is medium green (137B) upper surface; medium green (137D) lower surface. PARENTAGE: 'WALZ Harp' x 'Henkelly's Misterie'. Nomination by NKVF as Recommendable Cultivar. Spierings 2008 NL AFS6798.

Homemade Pride. Trailer. Single. COROLLA: three quarter flared, square shape; opens dark purple (86A) veined dark purple (78A), light pink (65C) base; matures dark purple (78A); 35mm (1 3/8") long x 65mm (2 9/16") wide. SEPALS: fully up, tips recurved, twisted; pale pink (49D) flushed & tipped light yellowish green (149C) upper surface; rose (51C) striped cream (11D) in middle of lower surface; 58mm (2 5/16") long x 16mm (5/8") wide. TUBE: rose (68C) striped light brown (199D); 18mm (11/16") long x 7mm (1/4") wide. FOLIAGE is dark green (137A) upper surface; yellowish green (146B) lower surface. PARENTAGE: 'Pink Bon Accord' x unknown. van der Made 2008 NL AFS6780.

Homemade Saucier. Upright/Trailer. Semi Double. COROLLA: three quarter flared; opens & matures purple (77A) splashed red (52A), red (52A) base; 25mm (1") long x 38mm (1 1/2") wide. SEPALS: half up, tips recurved up; red (52A) upper & lower surfaces; 34 mm (1 3/8") long x 11mm (7/16") wide. TUBE: red (52A); 7mm (1/4") long x 15mm (9/16") wide. FOLIAGE is medium green (137B) upper surface; medium green (139B) lower surface. PARENTAGE: 'Pink Bon Accord' x unknown. van der Made 2008 NL AFS6782.

Homemade Silver Bells. Trailer. Semi Double. COROLLA: quarter flared, bell shape; opens & matures pale violet (76D), spotted & edged violet (76A), veined light reddish purple (72D); 30mm (1 3/16") long x 30mm (1 3/16") wide. SEPALS: fully up, tips recurved, curved one time to left; yellowish

white (4D), edged light pink (65B), tipped apple green (144C) upper & lower surfaces; 65 mm (2 9/16") long x 13mm (1/2") wide. TUBE: yellowish white (4D), flushed light pink (65B), striped green; 11mm (7/16") long x 7mm (1/4") wide. FOLIAGE is medium green (137C) upper surface; light olive green (147C) lower surface. PARENTAGE: 'Carla Johnson' x unknown. van der Made 2008 NL AFS6781

Hooiktenaar. Upright/Trailer. Double. COROLLA: three quarter flared, turned under wavy petal margins; opens dark rose (67C) & dark reddish purple (72A); matures reddish purple (67B); 32mm (1 1/4") long x 21mm (13/16 ") wide. PETALOIDS: Same colour as corolla; 13mm (1/2") long x 13mm (1/2") wide. SEPALS: half up, tips recurved up; rose (63C) tipped greenish yellow (151B) upper surface; magenta (61C) tipped greenish yellow (151B) lower surface; 29mm (1 1/8") long x 16mm (5/8") wide. TUBE: light rose (58D); medium length & thickness; 19mm (3/4") long x 7mm (1/4") wide. STAMENS extend 14mm (9/16") beyond the corolla; magenta (63B) filaments; purple (77A) anthers. PISTIL extends 17mm (5/8") beyond the corolla; dark rose (64C) style; pale yellow (2D) stigma. BUD: globular. FOLIAGE: dark green (137A) upper surface; medium green (138B) lower surface. Leaves are 82mm (3 1/4") long x 44mm (1 3/4") wide; ovate shaped, serrate edges, acute tips, rounded bases. Veins are dark grayish purple (184A), stems are plum (183D), branches are grayish red (182B) & light green (138C). PARENTAGE: 'Manfried Kleinau' x 'Corsage'. Lax upright or stiff trailer. Makes good basket or upright. Prefers overhead filtered light, cool climate. Best bloom & foliage colour in filtered light. Tested 3 years in Koningshooikt, Belgium. Waanrode 8/9/08. Distinguished by bloom colour combination. Michiels 2009 BE AFS7175.

Horsforth Dream. Upright/Trailer. Single. COROLLA: quarter flared, smooth petal margins; opens & matures rose (52B) suffusing to reddish orange (43C) at base; 19mm (3/4") long x 19mm (3/4") wide. SEPALS: horizontal, tips recurved; rose (61D) tipped pale green upper & lower surfaces; 28mm (1 1/8") long x 13mm (1/2") wide. TUBE: light pink (49C); medium length & thickness; 16mm (5/8") long x 6mm (1/4") wide. STAMENS extend 9mm (5/16") beyond the corolla; rose (61D) filaments; light rose (68D) anthers. PISTIL extends 25mm (1")

199

beyond the corolla; rose (61D) style; yellowish white (158A) stigma. BUD: ovate, pointed. FOLIAGE: medium green (137C) upper surface; light olive green (148C) lower surface. Leaves are 38mm (1 1/2") long x 22mm (7/8") wide; cordate shaped, serrate edges, acute tips, rounded bases. Veins are light olive green, stems are grayish red, branches are light brown. PARENTAGE: 'London 2000' x 'Waternymph'. Lax upright or stiff trailer. Makes good basket, upright or standard. Prefers overhead filtered light. Cold weather hardy to 0° C (32° F). Best bloom colour in filtered light. Tested 4 years in Leeds & Manchester, England. Distinguished by striking shades of red & orange in the flower. Also registered with the BFS in 2008. Swaby 2009 UK AFS7119 BFS0091 (2008).

Howard Hebdon. Upright. Single. COROLLA: unflared, tubular shaped, smooth petal margins; opens & matures magenta (57B); 20mm (13/16") long x 15mm (9/16") wide. SEPALS: half up; tips recurved up; light rose (50C) upper & lower surfaces; 25mm(1") long x 10mm (3/8") wide. TUBE: light rose (50C); short & thick; 12mm (1/2") long x 8mm (5/16") wide. STAMENS: extend 5mm (3/16") below corolla; dark rose (58C) filaments; light coral (38A) anthers. PISTIL: extends 30mm (1 3/16") below the corolla, light coral (38A) style; white stigma. BUD: ovate, pointed. FOLIAGE: dark green (147A) upper surface, light olive green (147C) lower surface. Leaves are 40mm (1 9/16") long x 25mm (1") wide, ovate shaped, smooth edges, acute tips and rounded bases. Veins are green; stems & branches are reddish green. PARENTAGE: 'Eva Dayes' x 'Antigon'. Small upright. Self branching. Makes good basket, upright, standard or decorative. Prefers overhead filtered light and warm climate. Heat tolerant if shaded. Cold weather hardy to 32⁰ F. Best bloom colour in bright light. Tested 7 years in East Yorkshire, England. Distinguished by bright magenta colour and profuse flowers that do not fade.
Bielby/Oxtoby 2004 UK AFS5386.

Hubert Glombitza. Upright/Trailer. Double. COROLLA: half flared; opens dark purple (N79B); matures reddish purple (59B); 22mm (7/8") long x 40mm (1 9/16") wide. SEPALS: fully up, tips reflexed; dark reddish purple (60B) upper & lower surfaces; 30mm (1 3/16") long x 15mm (9/16") wide. TUBE: dark reddish purple (60B); 22mm (7/8") long x 8mm (5/16") wide. FOLIAGE is dark green (137A) upper surface; medium green (137C)

lower surface. PARENTAGE: 'Georg Gloßner' x 'Rohees Queen'.
Burkhart 2008 DE AFS6864.

Huet's Agaat. Upright. Single. COROLLA is half flared with smooth petal margins; opens & matures reddish orange (43C); 13mm (1/2") long x 17mm (11/16") wide. SEPALS are fully up, tips reflexed; light coral (38A) upper surface; light orange (41C) lower surface; 17mm (11/16") long x 11mm (7/16") wide. TUBE is medium length & thickness; 8mm (5/16") long x 4mm (3/16") wide. FOLIAGE: dark green (139A) upper surface; medium green (147B) lower surface. Leaves are 50mm (2") long x 35mm (1 3/8") wide, elliptic shaped. PARENTAGE: 'Braamt's Glorie' x 'Rosella'. VKC Award of Merit, The Netherlands. Distinguished by very rich flowering.
Braam 2005 NL AFS5805.

Huet's Akabar. Upright. Single. COROLLA is half flared with turned under wavy petal margins; opens purple (77A), reddish purple (61B) base; matures reddish purple (72B); 15mm (9/16") long x 15mm (9/16") wide. SEPALS are horizontal, tips reflexed; reddish purple (58A) tipped yellowish green (145A) upper surface; reddish purple (61B) lower surface; 17mm (11/16") long x 9mm (3/8") wide. TUBE is dark rose (58C); short & thick; 7mm (1/4") long x 6mm (1/4") wide. FOLIAGE: dark green (136A) upper surface; medium green (138B) lower surface. Leaves are 47mm (1 7/8") long x 35mm (1 3/8") wide, cordate shaped. PARENTAGE: 'Zelhem 1200' x 'Sacramento Bells'. Meise 8-14-04. Distinguished by rich blooming period.
Braam 2005 NL AFS5711.

Huet's Akosi. Upright. Double. COROLLA is three quarter flared with turned under wavy petal margins; opens light reddish purple (72C), light magenta (57D) base; matures light reddish purple (73A); 20mm (13/16") long x 10mm (3/8") wide. PETALOIDS: magenta (57C), magenta (58B) base; 15mm (9/16") long x 11mm (7/16") wide. SEPALS are half up, tips recurved up; red (53C) upper surface; magenta (58B) lower surface; 22mm (7/8") long x 8mm (5/16") wide. TUBE is light pink (49C); long & thin; 19mm (3/4") long x 4mm (3/16") wide. FOLIAGE: dark green (135A) upper surface; medium green (138B) lower surface. Leaves are 51mm (2") long x 26mm (1") wide, ovate shaped. PARENTAGE: 'Kiwi' x 'Quasar' x 'Sacramento Bells' x 'Quasar'. Meise 8-14-04,

Outstanding. Distinguished by thin TUBE & flower shape.
Braam 2005 NL AFS5717.

Huet's Alabanda. Upright. Single. COROLLA is quarter flared with turned under smooth petal margins; opens purple (77A), dark reddish purple (60B) base; matures reddish purple (72B); 13mm (1/2") long x 12mm (1/2") wide. SEPALS are horizontal, tips reflexed; dark reddish purple (60C) upper surface; dark reddish purple (60B) lower surface; 17mm (11/16") long x 8mm (5/16") wide. TUBE is reddish purple (60D); short & thick; 9mm (3/8") long x 6mm (1/4") wide. FOLIAGE: dark green (137A) upper surface; medium green (138B) lower surface. Leaves are 62mm (2 7/16") long x 34mm (1 5/16") wide, ovate shaped. PARENTAGE: 'Zelhem 1200' x 'Sacramento Bells'. Meise 3-7-04. Distinguished by compact flower shape.
Braam 2005 NL AFS5660.

Huet's Albiet. Upright. Double. COROLLA is three quarter flared; opens reddish purple (71B) with rose (52C) base; matures dark rose (67C); 20mm (3/4") long x 22mm (7/8") wide. PETALOIDS are reddish purple (71B) with rose (52C) base; 14mm (9/16") long and wide. SEPALS are horizontal, tips reflexed; rose (65A), tipped yellowish green (144A) upper surface; rose (52C), tipped yellowish green (144A); 34mm (1 3/8") long x 19mm (3/4") wide. TUBE is dark rose (54B); 14mm (9/16") long x 10mm (3/8") wide. FOLIAGE is dark green (136A) upper surface; medium green (138A) lower surface. PARENTAGE: ('WALZ Harp' x 'Quasar') x 'Kleine Gaertnerin'. Meise 8/13/05. Distinguished by large leaves.
Braam 2006 NL AFS6007.

Huet's Almandien. Trailer. Single. COROLLA is quarter flared with turned under wavy petal margins; opens magenta (61C); matures magenta (63A); 34mm (1 3/8") long x 18mm (11/16") wide. SEPALS are half down, tips reflexed; red (46B) upper surface; red (47B) lower surface; 42mm (1 11/16") long x 9mm (3/8") wide. TUBE is red (46D); long, medium thickness; 40mm (1 9/16") long x 6mm (1/4") wide. FOLIAGE: medium green (137B) upper surface; medium green (138B) lower surface. Leaves are 87mm (3 7/16") long x 36mm (1 7/16") wide, ovate shaped. PARENTAGE: 'Wilma Versloot' x 'Pink Galore'. Meise 3-7-04. Distinguished by long flower shape.
Braam 2005 NL AFS5659.

Huet's Alpaca. Trailer. Double. COROLLA: half flared; opens pale purple (75D) & violet (84A); matures pale purple (N71A); 28mm (1 1/8") long x 26mm (1") wide. PETALOIDS: same colour as corolla; 20mm (3/4") long x 12mm (7/16") wide. SEPALS: horizontal, tips recurved, twisted left to right; light pink (65C) tipped apple green (144C) upper surface; rose (65A) tipped apple green (144C) lower surface; 43mm (1 11/16") long x 10mm (3/8") wide. TUBE: pale pink (62D); 15mm (9/16") long x 7mm (1/4") wide. FOLIAGE is medium green (137B) upper surface; medium green (138B) lower surface. PARENTAGE: 'WALZ Blaukous' x 'WALZ Floriat'.
Braam 2008 NL AFS6763.

Huet's Amaril. Upright. Double. COROLLA: Half flared; opens red (45B) striped pink (43D); matures magenta (58B) striped red (45C); 22mm (7/8") long x 19mm (3/4") wide. PETALOIDS: Same colour as corolla; 12mm (7/16") long x 9mm (5/16") wide. SEPALS: horizontal, tips recurved; pink (49A) tipped light apple green (145C) upper surface; orange (44D) tipped light apple green (145C) lower surface; 23mm (7/8") long x 11mm (7/16") wide. TUBE: light pink (49B) striped yellowish green (144A); short & thick; 11mm (7/16") long x 9mm (5/16") wide. FOLIAGE is dark green (136A) upper surface; medium green (138B) lower surface. PARENTAGE: ('F. *magdalenae*' x 'F. *fulgens* var. rubra grandiflora') x 'Danny Kaye'.
Braam 2007 NL AFS6590.

Huet's Amazoniet. Upright. Single. COROLLA: Quarter flared; opens violet (76B); matures violet (77C); 21mm (13/16") long x 14mm (9/16") wide. SEPALS: horizontal, tips recurved; reddish purple (61B) tipped yellowish green (144B) upper surface; magenta (58B) tipped yellowish green (144B) lower surface; 22mm (7/8") long x 7mm (1/4") wide. TUBE: magenta (61C); short & thick; 5mm (3/16") long x 4mm (1/8") wide. FOLIAGE is dark green (137A) upper surface; medium green (138B) lower surface. PARENTAGE: 'Bernisser Hardy' x 'Jenny Sorensen'.
Braam 2007 NL AFS6385.

Huet's Amber. Upright. Single. COROLLA: unflared, turned under wavy petal margins; opens dark rose (58C); matures magenta (58B); 13mm (1/2") long, 7mm (1/4") wide. SEPALS: horizontal; tips reflexed; pink (55C), striped dark rose (55A), tipped light apple green (145C) upper surface; pink (54B) lower surface; 24mm (15/16") long x 7mm (1/4") wide. TUBE: pink (55C), striped dark rose (55A); medium length & thickness; 16mm (5/8") long x 7mm (1/4") wide. STAMENS: extend 3mm (1/8") below corolla; magenta (67B) filaments; light yellow (1C) anthers. PISTIL: extends 8mm (5/16") below the corolla; rose (68C) style; pale yellow (1D) stigma. BUD: drop shaped. FOLIAGE: dark green (136A) upper surface; medium green (138B) lower surface. Leaves are 58mm (2 5/16") long x 31mm (1 1/4") wide, ovate shaped, serrulated edges, acute tips and rounded bases. Light green (138C) veins; light green/grayish rose (181D) stems; medium green/ grayish red (138B/181C) branches. PARENTAGE: 'WALZ Drum' x unknown. Small upright. Self branching. Makes good upright or standard. Prefers full sun, warm climate. Best bloom and foliage colour in bright light. Tested 3 years in Doetinchem, Belgium. Award, Meise, 9/20/03. Distinguished by small bush, bloom colour & shape, best colour in sun. Braam 2004 NL AFS5620.

Huet's Amethist. Trailer. Double. COROLLA is half flared; opens light magenta (66D) with light reddish purple (73A) edge; matures light reddish purple (66C); 29mm (1 1/8") long x 32mm (1 1/4") wide. SEPALS are horizontal, tips recurved; dark rose (58C), tipped apple green (144C) upper surface; red (53D), tipped apple green (144C); 42mm (1 5/8") long x 14mm (9/16") wide. TUBE is white (155C), striped dark rose (58C); 15mm (9/16") long x 9mm (5/16") wide. FOLIAGE is dark green (136B) upper surface; medium green (139C) lower surface. PARENTAGE: 'Kiwi' x 'Enid Carter'. Meise 8/13/05. Distinguished by TUBE colour. Braam 2006 NL AFS6005.

Huet's Ametrien. Upright. Single. COROLLA is quarter flared; opens purple (81A), reddish purple (61B) base; matures dark reddish purple (72A); 23mm (7/8") long x 19mm (3/4") wide. SEPALS are horizontal, tips recurved; dark reddish purple (60B), tipped light olive green (144C) upper surface; reddish purple (61B), tipped light olive green (144C); 30mm (1 3/16") long x 8mm (5/16") wide. TUBE is reddish purple (58A); 12mm (7/16") long x 6mm (1/4") wide. FOLIAGE is dark green (136B) upper surface; medium green (139C) lower surface. PARENTAGE: 'Naald Wyk 800' x 'Little Witch'. Meise 8/13/05. Distinguished by bloom colour. Braam 2006 NL AFS6003.

Huet's Andalusiet. Upright. Double. COROLLA is three quarter flared; opens light purple (74C); matures light reddish purple (72D); 17mm (5/8") long x 22mm (7/8") wide. SEPALS are fully up, tips reflexed; magenta (61C), tipped yellowish green (145A) upper surface; magenta (58B), tipped yellowish green (145A); 18mm (11/16") long x 10mm (3/8") wide. TUBE is magenta (61C); 6mm (1/4") long x 5mm (3/16") wide. FOLIAGE is dark green (136A) upper surface; medium green (137B) lower surface. PARENTAGE: ('Wendy Van Wanten' x 'Centenary') x 'Amigo'. Meise 8/13/05. Distinguished by bloom colour. Braam 2006 NL AFS6009.

Huet's Angeliet. Upright. Single. COROLLA: full flared, turned up wavy petal margins; opens dark rose (64C); matures reddish purple (64B); 7mm (1/4") long, 8mm (5/16") wide. SEPALS: fully up; tips recurved; light pink (62B) upper surface; pink (62A) lower surface; 6mm (1/4") long x 3mm (1/8") wide. TUBE: pale pink (56C); medium length & thickness; 7mm (1/4") long x 3mm (1/8") wide. STAMENS: extend 2mm (1/16") below corolla; light pink (55D) filaments; light yellow (11C) anthers. PISTIL: extends 4mm (3/16") below the corolla; pink (55C) style; pink (62A) stigma. BUD: globular. FOLIAGE: dark green (136B) upper surface; medium green (139B) lower surface. Leaves are 49mm (1 15/16") long x 23mm (15/16") wide, elliptic shaped, wavy edges, acute tips and acute bases. Light green (139D) veins; light green/grayish red (181B) stems; light grayish red (182C) branches. PARENTAGE: 'Lechlade Tinkerbell' x 'Obcilin'. Small upright. Self branching. Makes good upright. Prefers overhead filtered light, cool climate. Best bloom and foliage colour in filtered light. Tested 3 years in Doetinchem, Belgium. Award, Meise, 9/20/03. Distinguished by small bush, bloom colour & shape. Braam 2004 NL AFS5619.

Huet's Atlantis. Upright. Single. COROLLA: Quarter flared; opens light reddish purple (N66C); matures rose (64D); 19mm (3/4") long x 24mm (15/16") wide. SEPALS: horizontal, tips reflexed; pink (55C) tipped light greenish yellow (151C) upper surface; pink (62C) tipped light greenish yellow (151C) lower surface; 23mm (7/8") long x 11mm (7/16") wide. TUBE: reddish purple (61B); medium length & thickness; 14mm (9/16") long x 6mm (1/4") wide. FOLIAGE is dark green (136A) upper surface; medium

202

green (137C) lower surface. PARENTAGE: 'WALZ Fagot' x 'Huet's Zoisiet'. Braam 2007 NL AFS6386.

Huet's Aventurijn. Upright/Trailer. Single. COROLLA: quarter flared, turned under smooth petal margins; opens red (53C); matures red (53B); 24mm (15/16") long x 21mm (13/16") wide. SEPALS: half up; tips recurved up; rose (51C), light pink (49B) base, tipped light green (142B) upper surface; pink (49A) tipped light green (142B) lower surface; 32mm (1 1/4") long x 6mm (1/4") wide. TUBE: light rose (51C) striped rose (51B); long & thin; 44mm (1 3/4") long x 5mm (3/16") wide. STAMENS: extend 6mm (1/4") below corolla; rose (51B) filaments; brown (176C) anthers. PISTIL: extends 15mm (9/16") below the corolla; pink (50D) style; pale yellow (1D) stigma. BUD: very long. FOLIAGE: dark green (137A) upper surface, medium green (138B) lower surface. Leaves are 82mm (3 1/4") long x 43mm (1 11/16") wide, ovate shaped, serrulated edges, acute tips and rounded bases. Purple (71A) veins; light plum (184D) & medium green (137D) stems & branches. PARENTAGE: 'WALZ Harp' x 'WALZ Mandoline'. Lax upright or stiff trailer. Self branching. Makes good basket or standard. Prefers full sun. Best bloom and foliage colour in bright light. Tested 4 years in Doetinchem, The Netherlands. Award at Meise, 9/8/03. Distinguished by bloom colour and shape. Braam 2004 NL AFS5434.

Huet's Azuriet. Upright. Double. COROLLA is half flared with turned under wavy petal margins; opens light rose (73B), white (155C) base, edged violet (76A); matures light rose (73C), edged violet (76B); 29mm (1 1/8") long x 20mm (13/16") wide. PETALOIDS: light rose (73B), white (155C) base, edged violet (75A); 22mm (7/8") long x 7mm (1/4") wide. SEPALS are half up, tips recurved up; twisted clockwise; light pink (55D), white (155C) base, tipped light apple green (145B) upper surface; pink (55C), white (155C) base, tipped light apple green (145B) lower surface; 31mm (1 1/4") long x 9mm (3/8") wide. TUBE is white (155C); medium length & thickness; 10mm (3/8") long x 4mm (3/16") wide. FOLIAGE: dark green (139A) upper surface; medium green (138A) lower surface. Leaves are 52mm (2 1/16") long x 31mm (1 1/4") wide, ovate shaped. PARENTAGE: 'Jenny Sorensen' x 'Heston Blue'. Meise 8-14-04. Distinguished by colour combination. Braam 2005 NL AFS5714.

Huet's Baraketh. Upright/Trailer. Single. COROLLA: Quarter flared; opens dark reddish purple (N79C); matures purple (71A); 22mm (7/8") long x 20mm (3/4") wide. SEPALS: horizontal, tips recurved; reddish purple (71B) tipped light yellowish green (150C) upper surface; reddish purple (64B) tipped light yellowish green (150C) lower surface; 27mm (1 1/16") long x 9mm (5/16") wide. TUBE: magenta (59C); medium length & thickness; 18mm (11/16") long x 4mm (1/8") wide. FOLIAGE is dark green (136A) upper surface; medium green (138A) lower surface. PARENTAGE: 'Loxhore Mazurka' x 'Hertogen Van Brabant'. Lax upright or stiff trailer. Braam 2007 NL AFS6387.

Huet's Beryl. Trailer. Double. COROLLA is three quarter flared with turned under wavy petal margins; opens magenta (57C), white (155C) base; matures light reddish purple (66C), white (155C) base; 38mm (1 1/2") long x 27mm (1 1/16") wide. PETALOIDS: magenta (61C) blotched, white (155C) base; 30mm (1 3/16") long x 14mm (9/16") wide. SEPALS are horizontal, tips recurved, twisted at base; rose (64D), white (155C) base, tipped light green (143D) upper surface; rose (65A), white (155D) base, tipped light green (143D) lower surface; 58mm (2 5/16") long x 18mm (11/16") wide. TUBE is white (155A), medium length & thickness; 18mm (3/4") long x 8mm (5/16") wide. FOLIAGE: dark green (135A) upper surface; medium green (138B) lower surface. Leaves are 51mm (2") long x 25mm (1") wide, elliptic shaped. PARENTAGE: 'Enid Carter' x 'Imperial Fantasy'. Natural trailer. Self branching. Makes good basket. Approved with excellence at Meise, 3-7-04. Distinguished by beautiful colour and long bloom period. Braam 2005 NL AFS5655.

Huet's Bixbiet. Trailer. Double. COROLLA: Half flared; opens magenta (63A) striped rose (51C); matures rose (61D); 30mm (1 3/16") long x 23mm (7/8") wide. PETALOIDS: magenta (63A) blotched rose (51C); 26mm (1") long x 10mm (3/8") wide. SEPALS: half up, tips recurved up, turned to the right; pale pink (62D) tipped light yellowish green (154C) upper surface; pink (62A) tipped light yellowish green (154C) lower surface; 43mm (1 11/16") long x 14mm (9/16") wide. TUBE: white (155B); medium length & thickness; 18mm (11/16") long x 5mm (3/16") wide. FOLIAGE is dark green (136A) upper surface; medium green (137C) lower surface.

PARENTAGE: 'Huet's Adventuryn' x 'Huet's Koraal'. Braam 2007 NL AFS6591.

Huet's Brenkiet. Upright. Single. COROLLA: flared shape, fully flared, turned up petal margins; opens violet blue (91B); matures violet (75A); 30 mm (1 3/16") long x 35mm (1 3/8") wide. PETALOIDS: light violet (84B); 20mm (3/4") long x 25mm (1") wide. SEPALS are half up, tips recurved up; pale pink (69D) upper surface; pink (62A) lower surface; 27mm (1 1/16") long x 14mm (9/16") wide. TUBE is pink (62C); medium length & thickness; 15mm (9/16") long x 7mm (1/4") wide. STAMENS extend 30mm (1 3/16") beyond the corolla; reddish purple (74B) filaments; reddish purple (74A) anthers. PISTIL extends 50mm (2") beyond the corolla; pale pink (69A) style; white (155D) stigma. BUD is round. FOLIAGE is dark green (137A) upper surface; medium green (137C) lower surface. Leaves are 55mm (2 3/16") long x 28mm (1 1/8") wide, cordate shaped, serrulate edges, acute tips, rounded bases. Veins are light green, stems & branches are green. PARENTAGE: 'WALZ Floreat' x 'Huet's Akosi'. Lax upright or stiff trailer; self branching. Makes good upright or pyramid or pillar. Prefers overhead filtered light; heat tolerant if shaded. Best bloom & foliage in limited light. Tested 4 years in Doetinchem, The Netherlands. Fuchsia Nieuwigheden Certificering. Distinguished by bloom colour & shape. Braam 2009 NL AFS6974.

Huet's Bronziet. Upright/Trailer. Double. COROLLA: Half flared; opens purple (79C) striped magenta (71C); matures purple (71A); 22mm (7/8") long x 17mm (5/8") wide. PETALOIDS: Same colour as corolla; 13mm (1/2") long x 9mm (5/16") wide. SEPALS: fully up, tips recurved, turned to the right; reddish purple (71B) upper surface; magenta (71C) lower surface; 48mm (1 7/8") long x 12mm (7/16") wide. TUBE: reddish purple (67A); medium length & thickness; 16mm (5/8") long x 7mm (1/4") wide. FOLIAGE is dark green (136B) upper surface; medium green (138B) lower surface. PARENTAGE: ('Hertogin van Brabant' x 'Guurtje') x ('Hertogin van Brabant' x 'Fey'). Braam 2007 NL AFS6592.

Huet's Calamijn. Upright/Trailer. Double. COROLLA is three quarter flared; opens light purple (78C); matures light purple (78D); 29mm (1 1/8") long x 26mm (1") wide. PETALOIDS: light purple (78B); 10mm (3/8")

long x 8mm (5/16") wide. SEPALS are horizontal, tips recurved; light pink (62B) tipped light yellowish green (150C) upper surface; pink (62A) tipped yellowish green (150C) lower surface; 42mm (1 5/8") long x 14mm (9/16") wide. TUBE is pink (62C); 12mm (1/2") long x 6mm (1/4") wide. FOLIAGE: dark green (137A) upper surface; medium green (138B) lower surface. PARENTAGE: 'Hesset Festival' x 'Zaailing van Cancan'. Meise 9/17/05. Distinguished by bloom colour. Braam 2006 NL AFS6077.

Huet's Calciet. Trailer. Single. COROLLA: flared, half flared, smooth petal margins; opens magenta (57A); matures magenta (57B); 28 mm (1 1/8") long x 24mm (15/16") wide. SEPALS are horizontal, tips recurved; magenta (58B) upper surface; dark rose (58C) lower surface; 35mm (1 3/8") long x 8mm (5/16") wide. TUBE is pink (62C); medium length & thickness; 20mm (3/4") long x 5mm (3/16") wide. STAMENS extend 20mm (3/4") beyond the corolla; dark rose (58C) filaments; cream (158C) anthers. PISTIL extends 35mm (1 3/8") beyond the corolla; pink (62C) style; dark rose (58C) stigma. BUD is round. FOLIAGE is dark green (137A) upper surface; medium green (137C) lower surface. Leaves are 75mm (3") long x 35mm (1 3/8") wide, cordate shaped, wavy edges, acute tips, rounded bases. Veins are green, stems are green & branches are green. PARENTAGE: 'Herps Parachute' x 'WALZ Harp'. Natural trailer; self branching. Makes good basket. Prefers full sun, warm climate. Best bloom & foliage in limited light. Tested 3 years in Doetinchem, The Netherlands. Fuchsia Nieuwigheden Certificering. Distinguished by bloom shape. Braam 2009 NL AFS6966.

Huet's Carneool. Upright. Single to Semi Double. COROLLA: quarter flared, turned under wavy petal margins; opens reddish purple (64B); matures dark reddish purple (64A); 14mm (9/16") long x 19mm (3/4") wide. SEPALS: horizontal; tips reflexed; rose (51C), light pink (49C) base, tipped light yellowish green (149B) upper surface; rose (52C) tipped light yellowish green (149B) lower surface; 17mm (11/16") long x 9mm (3/8") wide. TUBE: light pink (49C); long & thin; 30mm (1 3/16") long x 5mm (3/16") wide. STAMENS: extend 2mm (1/16") below corolla; magenta (67B) filaments; light yellow (11B) anthers. PISTIL: extends 2mm (1/16") below the corolla; rose (68C) style; pale lavender (69C) stigma. BUD: rounded.

FOLIAGE: dark green (137A) upper surface, medium green (138B) lower surface. Leaves are 68mm (2 11/16") long x 43mm (1 11/16") wide, ovate shaped, serrated edges, acute tips and rounded bases. Light Green (139D) veins; grayish red (181A) & medium green (138B) stems; grayish red (181C) & medium green (138B) branches. PARENTAGE: 'WALZ Harp' x 'WALZ Saxofoon'. Small upright. Makes good upright or standard. Prefers full sun. Best bloom and foliage colour in bright light. Tested 4 years in Doetinchem, The Netherlands. Award at Meise, 9/8/03. Distinguished by bloom colour.
Braam 2004 NL AFS5432.

Huet's Celestiet. Upright. Single. COROLLA: bell shaped, unflared, smooth petal margins; opens dark purple (79A); matures dark purple (79B); 15 mm (9/16") long x 15mm (9/16") wide. SEPALS are half up, tips recurved up; dark reddish purple (61A) upper surface; reddish purple (61B) lower surface; 30mm (1 3/16") long x 18mm (11/16") wide. TUBE is reddish purple (61B); long & thin; 20mm (3/4") long x 2mm (1/16") wide. STAMENS extend 5mm (3/16") beyond the corolla; purple (71A) filaments; purple (77A) anthers. PISTIL extends 25mm (1") beyond the corolla; purple (71A) style & stigma. BUD is long, round. FOLIAGE is dark green (137A) upper surface; medium green (137C) lower surface. Leaves are 55mm (2 3/16") long x 20mm (3/4") wide, lanceolate shaped, serrulate edges, acute tips & bases. Veins are green, stems are green & branches are green. PARENTAGE: 'Rosea' x 'Huet's Ametrien'. Tall upright; self branching. Makes good upright or pillar. Prefers overhead filtered light or full sun, warm climate. Best bloom & foliage in filtered light. Tested 3 years in Doetinchem, The Netherlands. Fuchsia Nieuwigheden Certificering. Distinguished by bloom shape & colour.
Braam 2009 NL AFS6964.

Huet's Chaoriet. Upright. Single. COROLLA is half flared with turned under wavy petal margins; opens red (46C); matures magenta (58B); 18mm (11/16") long x 24mm (15/16") wide. SEPALS are half down, tips recurved; pale pink (36D), light pink (36C) base, tipped pale yellowish green (149D) upper surface; light pink (49C), light pink (49B) base, tipped pale yellowish green (149D) lower surface; 24mm (15/16") long x 8mm (5/16") wide. TUBE is light pink (36C); medium length, thick; 30mm (1 3/16") long x 9mm (3/8")

wide. FOLIAGE: medium green (138A) upper surface; medium green (138B) lower surface. Leaves are 67mm (2 5/8") long x 48mm (1 7/8") wide, cordate shaped. PARENTAGE: 'WALZ Mandoline' x 'WALZ Harp'. Meise 8-14-04. Distinguished by bloom colour & shape.
Braam 2005 NL AFS5826.

Huet's Chrysoliet. Upright. Single. COROLLA: Half flared; opens light purple (75B) edged reddish purple (N80B); matures violet (75A); 21mm (13/16") long x 26mm (1") wide. SEPALS: fully up, tips recurved; light rose (63D) tipped light apple green (145C) upper surface; rose (68C) tipped light apple green (145C) lower surface; 29mm (1 1/8") long x 14mm (9/16") wide. TUBE: pale pink (62D); short & thick; 9mm (5/16") long x 9mm (5/16") wide. FOLIAGE is dark green (136A) upper surface; medium green (138B) lower surface. PARENTAGE: ('Huet's Agaat' x 'Huet's Uvardiet') x 'Hidcote Beauty'.
Braam 2007 NL AFS6593.

Huet's Cinnabar. Upright. Single to Semi Double. COROLLA: Quarter flared; opens dark rose (64C); matures dark rose (67C); 22mm (7/8") long x 19mm (3/4") wide. PETALOIDS: Magenta (63B); 15mm (9/16") long x 12mm (7/16") wide. SEPALS: half down, tips reflexed; magenta (63A) tipped apple green (144C) upper surface; magenta (58B) tipped apple green (144C) lower surface; 21mm (13/16") long x 9mm (5/16") wide. TUBE: magenta (58B); medium length & thickness; 8mm (5/16") long x 4mm (1/8") wide. FOLIAGE is dark green (136A) upper surface; medium green (137C) lower surface. PARENTAGE: 'Bernisser Hardy' x 'Jenny Sorensen'.
Braam 2007 NL AFS6388.

Huet's Citrien. Upright/Trailer. Semi Double. COROLLA: Quarter flared; opens pale pink (62D); matures light rose (63D); 12mm (7/16") long x 10mm (3/8") wide. SEPALS: horizontal, tips reflexed; pale pink (56D) tipped light apple green (145B) upper surface; pale pink (49D) tipped light apple green (145B) lower surface; 27mm (1 1/16") long x 9mm (5/16") wide. TUBE: pale pink (56D); medium length & thickness; 22mm (7/8") long x 6mm (1/4") wide. FOLIAGE is dark green (136A) upper surface; medium green (138B) lower surface. PARENTAGE: 'WALZ Klavier' x 'WALZ Triangel'.
Braam 2007 NL AFS6389.

Huet's Cupriet. Trailer. Single. COROLLA: quarter flared; opens reddish purple (64B) & dark reddish purple (72A); matures purple (71A); 17mm (5/8") long x 17mm (5/8") wide. SEPALS: half down, tips recurved; reddish purple (61B) tipped pale yellow green (150D) upper surface; reddish purple (64B) tipped pale yellow green (150D) lower surface; 28mm (1 1/8") long x 9mm (5/16") wide. TUBE: dark reddish purple (60B); 11mm (7/16") long x 8mm (5/16") wide. FOLIAGE is dark green (139A) upper surface; medium green (137C) lower surface. PARENTAGE: 'Huet's Akabar' x 'Lye's Excelsior'. Braam 2008 NL AFS6762.

Huet's Cymafoon. Upright/Trailer. Single. COROLLA: Quarter flared; opens red (52A); matures rose (52B); 22mm (7/8") long x 17mm (5/8") wide. SEPALS: half down, tips reflexed; rose (52C) tipped apple green (N144D) upper surface; pink (49A) tipped apple green (N144D) lower surface; 32mm (1 1/4") long x 9mm (5/16") wide. TUBE: pink (48D); medium length & thickness; 26mm (1") long x 7mm (1/4") wide. FOLIAGE is dark green (136A) upper surface; medium green (138B) lower surface. PARENTAGE: 'WALZ Harp' x 'Louise Emershaw'. Braam 2008 NL AFS6390.

Huet's Diopsied. Upright. Single. COROLLA is half flared with turned under wavy petal margins; opens reddish purple (74A), rose (51B) base; matures light magenta (66D); 15mm (9/16") long x 13mm (1/2") wide. SEPALS are horizontal, tips recurved; rose (52C), tipped light yellow green (150B) upper surface; dark rose (54A) lower surface; 25mm (1") long x 10mm (3/8") wide. TUBE is rose (52C); long & thin; 27mm (1 1/16") long x 5mm (3/16") wide. FOLIAGE: medium green (138A) upper surface; light green (138C) lower surface. Leaves are 56mm (2 3/16") long x 26mm (1") wide, elliptic shaped. PARENTAGE: 'WALZ Harp' x 'Ghislaine'. Meise 8-14-04. Distinguished by colour combination. Braam 2005 NL AFS5715.

Huet's Draviet. Trailer. Single. COROLLA: Half flared; opens violet (77B), dark reddish purple (60B) base; matures magenta (67B), violet (77C) base; 24mm (15/16") long x 16mm (5/8") wide. SEPALS: horizontal, tips reflexed; dark reddish purple (60B) tipped light apple green (145B) upper surface; reddish purple (64B) tipped light apple green (145B) lower surface; 30mm (1 3/16") long x 13mm (1/2") wide. TUBE: dark reddish

purple (60B) striped white (155B); short & thick; 11mm (7/16") long x 7mm (1/4") wide. FOLIAGE is dark green (136A) upper surface; medium green (137C) lower surface. PARENTAGE: 'Danny Kaye' x 'Mary Fairclo'. Braam 2007 NL AFS6391.

Huet's Fluoriet. Upright. Semi Double. COROLLA: flared, half-flared, smooth petal margins; opens violet (76A); matures light rose (73B); 20 mm (3/4") long x 12mm (7/16") wide. PETALOIDS: dark rose (55A); 10mm (3/8") long x 6mm (1/4") wide. SEPALS are half down, tips reflexed; red (46C), tipped green upper surface; red (46D) tipped green lower surface; 25mm (1") long x 12mm (7/16") wide. TUBE is dark orange (40B) and medium green (138B); long & thin; 24mm (15/16") long x 4mm (1/8") wide. STAMENS extend 2mm (1/16") beyond the corolla; dark rose (55A) filaments; dark rose (54A) anthers. PISTIL extends 5mm (3/16") beyond the corolla; dark rose (54A) style; red (50A) stigma. BUD is round. FOLIAGE is medium green (138A) upper surface; medium green (139C) lower surface. Leaves are 60mm (2 3/8") long x 40mm (1 9/16") wide, cordate shaped, wavy edges, acute tips, rounded bases. Veins are light green, stems are green & branches are green. PARENTAGE: 'Huet's Akosi' x 'WALZ Floreat'. Medium upright; self branching. Makes good upright or pyramid. Prefers overhead filtered light, cool climate. Best bloom & foliage in filtered light. Tested 3 years in Doetinchem, The Netherlands. Fuchsia Nieuwigheden Certificering. Distinguished by bloom colour. Braam 2009 NL AFS6962.

Huet's Galeniet. Upright. Double. COROLLA: square, three-quarter flared, wavy petal margins; opens reddish purple (70B), base rose (51A); matures magenta (68A); 40 mm (1 9/16") long x 25mm (1") wide. PETALOIDS: dark rose (55A); 20mm (3/4") long x 8mm (5/16") wide. SEPALS are horizontal, tips reflexed; rose (68C) upper surface; dark rose (55A) lower surface; 55mm (2 3/16") long x 20mm (3/4") wide. TUBE is very pale orange (27D); medium length & thickness; 20mm (3/4") long x 9mm (5/16") wide. STAMENS extend 10mm (3/8") beyond the corolla; reddish purple (67A) filaments; magenta (63A) anthers. PISTIL extends 25mm (1") beyond the COROLLA; magenta (63B) style; pale yellowish orange (20C) stigma. BUD is round, thick. FOLIAGE is medium green (137C) upper surface; medium green (139C) lower surface. Leaves are 90mm (3 9/16") long x 55mm (2 3/16") wide,

206

cordate shaped, serrulate edges, acute tips, cordate bases. Veins are green, stems are reddish green & branches are green. PARENTAGE: ('WALZ Harp' x 'Quasar') x 'Laurie'. Lax upright or stiff trailer; self branching. Makes good basket or upright. Heat tolerant if shaded; prefers cool climate. Best bloom & foliage in filtered light. Tested 5 years in Doetinchem, The Netherlands. Fuchsia Nieuwigheden Certificering. Distinguished by bloom shape & colour.
Braam 2009 NL AFS6968.

Huet's Girasol. Upright. Single to Semi Double. COROLLA: flared, half flared, turned under petal margins; opens light pink (65B); matures rose (65A); 15 mm (9/16") long x 20mm (3/4") wide. SEPALS are half up, tips recurved up; light pink (55D) tipped green upper surface; rose (55B) tipped green lower surface; 26mm (1") long x 12mm (7/16") wide. TUBE is pink (55C); long & medium thickness; 34mm (1 3/8") long x 8mm (5/16") wide. STAMENS do not extend beyond the corolla; dark rose (55A) filaments; light pink (55D) anthers. PISTIL extends 10mm (3/8") beyond the corolla; rose (55B) style; very pale orange (27C) stigma. BUD is long, round. FOLIAGE is dark green (139A) upper surface; light green (139C) lower surface. Leaves are 60mm (2 3/8") long x 40mm (1 9/16") wide, cordate shaped, wavy edges, acute tips, rounded bases. Veins are light green, stems are red brown & branches are green. PARENTAGE: 'De Acht Zagigheden' x 'Hidcote Beauty'. Tall upright; self branching. Makes good upright or pillar. Prefers full sun, warm climate. Best bloom & foliage in filtered light. Tested 3 years in Doetinchem, The Netherlands. Fuchsia Nieuwigheden Certificering. Distinguished by bloom shape & colour.
Braam 2009 NL AFS6971.

Huet's Granaat. Upright/Trailer. Semi Double. COROLLA: three quarter flared, turned under wavy petal margins; opens light reddish purple (73A), dark reddish purple (72A) base; matures purple (77A); 18mm (11/16") long x 21mm (13/16") wide. PETALOIDS: light reddish purple (73A), reddish purple (70B) base; 13mm (1/2") long x 10mm (3/8") wide. SEPALS: half up; tips reflexed up; rose (68B) tipped light apple green (145B) upper surface; magenta (68A) tipped light apple green (145B) lower surface; 21mm (13/16") long x 11mm (7/16") wide. TUBE: rose (68B); short & thick; 11mm (7/16") long x 7mm (1/4") wide. STAMENS: extend 14mm (9/16") below corolla; reddish

purple (72B) filaments; dark purple (79B) anthers. PISTIL: extends 16mm (5/8") below the corolla; light reddish purple (72C) style; white (155B) stigma. BUD: cordate shaped. FOLIAGE: dark green (137A) upper surface, medium green (138B) lower surface. Leaves are 55mm (2 3/16") long x 29mm (1 1/8") wide, elliptic shaped, serrulated edges, acute tips and rounded bases. Light grayish red (182D) veins; Light grayish red (182D) & medium green (138B) stems; light grayish red (182B) & light green (139D) branches. PARENTAGE: 'Braamt's Glorie' x 'Schimpen's Glorie'. Lax upright or stiff trailer. Self branching. Makes good upright or standard. Prefers overhead filtered light or full sun. Best bloom and foliage colour in limited light. Tested 4 years in Doetinchem, The Netherlands. Award at Meise, 9/8/03. Distinguished by bloom shape.
Braam 2004 NL AFS5433.

Huet's Heliodor. Upright/Trailer. Single. COROLLA is half flared with turned under wavy petal margins; opens reddish purple (61B); matures magenta (58B); 16mm (5/8") long x 12mm (1/2") wide. SEPALS are horizontal, tips recurved; rose (51C), tipped light apple green (145B) upper surface; dark rose (51A) tipped light apple green (145B) lower surface; 23mm (15/16") long x 8mm (5/16") wide. TUBE is light pink (49CC); long & thin; 19mm (3/4") long x 4mm (3/16") wide. FOLIAGE: medium green (138A) upper surface; medium green (138B) lower surface. Leaves are 69mm (2 3/4") long x 38mm (1 1/2") wide, ovate shaped. PARENTAGE: 'WALZ Harp' x 'Lye's Excelsior'. Meise 8-14-04, Outstanding. Distinguished by colour combination.
Braam 2005 NL AFS5716.

Huet's Heliotroop. Upright/Trailer. Double. COROLLA: Three quarter flared; opens violet (77C), reddish purple (70B) base; matures light purple (N78C); 27mm (1 1/16") long x 24mm (15/16") wide. PETALOIDS: same colour as corolla; 19mm (3/4") long x 12mm (7/16") wide. SEPALS: horizontal, tips recurved; pink (62A) tipped light apple green (145B) upper surface; rose (63C) tipped light apple green (145B) lower surface; 38mm (1 1/2") long x 16mm (5/8") wide. TUBE: pale pink (56C); short & thick; 11mm (7/16") long x 8mm (5/16") wide. FOLIAGE is dark green (136A) upper surface; medium green (138B) lower surface. PARENTAGE: 'Hesset Festival' x ('Gay Parasol' x 'Meadowlark').
Braam 2007 NL AFS6594.

Huet's Hematiet. Upright. Single. COROLLA is half flared with turned under wavy petal margins; opens red (50A); matures rose (51B); 16mm (5/8") long x 20mm (13/16") wide. SEPALS are half down, tips recurved; red (52A) tipped light yellowish green (149B) upper surface; dark rose (51A) tipped light yellowish green (149B) lower surface; 23mm (15/16") long x 7mm (1/4") wide. TUBE is red (52A); medium length, thick; 27mm (1 1/16") long x 8mm (5/16") wide. FOLIAGE: dark green (139A) upper surface; medium green (138A) lower surface. Leaves are 50mm (2") long x 31mm (1 1/4") wide, ovate shaped. PARENTAGE: 'WALZ Trompet' x 'Lechlade Rocket'. Meise 8-14-04. Distinguished by unique colour combination. Braam 2005 NL AFS5713.

Huet's Hercyniet. Upright. Single. COROLLA: square, quarter flared, wavy petal margins; opens reddish purple (66A), purple (82A) flames; matures reddish purple (67A); 20 mm (13/16") long x 10mm (3/8") wide. SEPALS are half down, tips reflexed; red (46C) upper surface; dark rose (54A) lower surface; 50mm (2") long x 15mm (9/16") wide. TUBE is red (46B); long & medium thickness; 45mm (1 3/4") long x 5mm (3/16") wide. STAMENS extend 2mm (1/16") beyond the corolla; magenta (57A) filaments; pale yellow (158B) anthers. PISTIL extends 10mm (3/8") beyond the corolla; magenta (57A) style; magenta (63B) stigma. BUD is long, thick. FOLIAGE is dark green (137A) upper surface; medium green (138B) lower surface. Leaves are 90mm (3 9/16") long x 45mm (1 3/4") wide, cordate shaped, wavy edges, acute tips, rounded bases. Veins are reddish green, stems are red & branches are red. PARENTAGE: 'WALZ Harp' x 'Quasar'. Lax upright or stiff trailer; self branching. Makes good basket or upright. Prefers full sun, warm climate. Best bloom & foliage in bright light. Tested 6 years in Doetinchem, The Netherlands. Fuchsia Nieuwigheden Certificering. Distinguished by bloom shape. Braam 2009 NL AFS6961.

Huet's Hessoniet. Upright. Single. COROLLA: quarter flared; opens purple (N82A); matures dark reddish purple (N72A); 21mm (13/16") long x 14mm (9/16") wide. SEPALS: half up, tips recurved up; reddish purple (71B) & pale lavender (69D) tipped apple green (144C) upper surface; light rose (73B) tipped apple green (144C) lower surface; 15mm (9/16") long x 9mm (5/16") wide. TUBE: reddish purple (71B) & pale lavender (69D); 12mm (7/16") long x 7mm

(1/4") wide. FOLIAGE is dark green (137A) upper surface; medium green (137D) lower surface. PARENTAGE: 'Huet's Ametrien' x 'Huet's Kunziet'. Braam 2008 NL AFS6755.

Huet's Indigoliet. Upright/Trailer. Double. COROLLA: Half flared; opens violet (85A), dark rose (58C) base; matures violet (77B), dark rose (58C) base; 22mm (7/8") long x 16mm (5/8") wide. PETALOIDS: same colour as corolla; 10mm (3/8") long x 8mm (5/16") wide. SEPALS: half up, tips recurved up; rose (63C) tipped apple green (144C) upper surface; dark rose (58C) tipped apple green (144C) lower surface; 28mm (1 1/8") long x 12mm (7/16") wide. TUBE: magenta (N57C); short & thick; 8mm (5/16") long x 4mm (1/8") wide. FOLIAGE is dark green (136B) upper surface; medium green (137C) lower surface. PARENTAGE: 'Huet's Azuriet' x 'Huet's Alabanda'. Braam 2007 NL AFS6392.

Huet's Jaspis. Upright. Semi Double. COROLLA: quarter flared, turned under wavy petal margins; opens pale yellowish green (150D); matures light yellowish green (150C); 6mm (1/4") long, 8mm (5/16") wide. SEPALS: half down; tips reflexed; red (53B) upper surface; red (53C) lower surface; 21mm (13/16") long x 10mm (3/8") wide. TUBE: red (53B); medium length, thick; 18mm (11/16") long x 9mm (3/8") wide. STAMENS: extend 5mm (3/16") below corolla; light magenta (57D) filaments; light pink (65C) anthers. PISTIL: extends 13mm (1/2") below the corolla; magenta (58B) style; light pink (62B) stigma. BUD: oblong. FOLIAGE: medium green (139B) upper surface; medium green (138B) lower surface. Leaves are 61mm (2 3/8") long x 42mm (1 11/16") wide, ovate shaped, serrulated edges, acute tips and rounded bases. Plum (183D) veins; plum (183B) stems; plum/medium green (183B/138B) branches. PARENTAGE: 'WALZ Saxofoon' x unknown. Tall upright. Makes good upright or standard. Prefers overhead filtered light, warm climate. Best bloom and foliage colour in bright light. Tested 3 years in Doetinchem, Belgium. Award, Meise, 9/20/03. Distinguished by bloom shape & colour. Braam 2004 NL AFS5616.

Huet's Katchalong. Upright/Trailer. Double. COROLLA: Half flared; opens purple (83A), purple (71A) base; matures reddish purple (71B); 14mm (9/16") long x 11mm (7/16") wide. PETALOIDS: same colour as corolla;

8mm (5/16") long x 6mm (1/4") wide. SEPALS: horizontal, tips recurved; dark reddish purple (61A) upper surface; reddish purple (64B) lower surface; 17mm (5/8") long x 10mm (3/8") wide. TUBE: dark reddish purple (61A); short & thick; 8mm (5/16") long x 5mm (3/16") wide. FOLIAGE is dark green (137A) upper surface; medium green (138B) lower surface. PARENTAGE: 'Rosea' x 'Huet's Ametrien'.
Braam 2007 NL AFS6393.

Huet's Kimberliet. Upright. Single. COROLLA: bell shape, quarter flared, turned up petal margins; opens light pink (38D) & matures peach (38B); 20 mm (3/4") long x 15mm (9/16") wide. SEPALS are horizontal, tips recurved; white (155B) upper surface; light pink (36B) lower surface; 25mm (1") long x 15mm (9/16") wide. TUBE is white (155B); medium length & thickness; 15mm (9/16") long x 8mm (5/16") wide. STAMENS extend 12mm (7/16") beyond the corolla; light pink (36A) filaments; light coral (38A) anthers. PISTIL extends 20mm (3/4") beyond the corolla; light pink (36C) style; white (155B) stigma. BUD is round. FOLIAGE is medium green (137C) upper surface; medium green (138B) lower surface. Leaves are 60mm (2 3/8") long x 35mm (1 3/8") wide, cordate shaped, wavy edges, acute tips, cordate bases. Veins & branches are green, stems are dark red. PARENTAGE: ('WALZ Harp' x 'Quasar') x 'Fey'. Lax upright or stiff trailer; self branching. Makes good upright or pillar. Prefers overhead filtered light, warm climate. Best bloom & foliage in limited light. Tested 5 years in Doetinchem, The Netherlands. Fuchsia Nieuwigheden Certificering. Distinguished by bloom colour & shape.
Braam 2009 NL AFS6973.

Huet's Koraal. Trailer. Single. COROLLA is half flared with turned under smooth petal margins; opens magenta (58B); matures magenta (63B); 38mm (1 1/2") long x 22mm (7/8") wide. PETALOIDS: red (53C); 23mm (7/8") long x 18mm (11/16") wide. SEPALS are half up, tips recurved up; rose (52B) tipped light apple green (145B) upper surface; rose (48B) tipped light apple green (145B) lower surface; 50mm (2") long x 12mm (1/2") wide. TUBE. FOLIAGE: medium green (137B) upper surface; light green (138C) lower surface. Leaves are 75mm (2 15/16") long x 50mm (2") wide, ovate shaped. PARENTAGE: 'Danny Kaye' x 'Laurie'. Meise, 3-7-04. Distinguished by beautiful colour combination.
Braam 2005 NL AFS5656.

Huet's Kunziet. Upright. Single. COROLLA is quarter flared; opens reddish purple (71B), magenta (68A) base, dark reddish purple (72A) edge; matures dark reddish purple (72A), rose (65A) base; 20mm (3/4") long x 17mm (5/8") wide. SEPALS are horizontal, tips recurved; pale lavender (69B) upper surface, white (155B) base, tipped light yellow green (150B); light pink (65B) lower surface, white (155B) base, tipped light yellow green (150B); 24mm (15/16") long x 9mm (5/16") wide. TUBE is pale lavender (69B), white base (155B); 18mm (11/16") long x 6mm (1/4") wide. FOLIAGE is dark green (136B) upper surface; medium green (138B) lower surface. PARENTAGE: 'Checkerboard' x 'Ghislaine'. Meise 8/13/05. Distinguished by bloom colour.
Braam 2006 NL AFS6000.

Huet's Kwarts. Upright. Single. COROLLA is half flared; opens purple (83A) with dark reddish purple (60B) base; matures purple (79D); 14mm (9/16") long x 15mm (9/16") wide. SEPALS are horizontal, tips reflexed; magenta (59C), tipped yellowish green (146B) upper surface; reddish purple (61B), tipped yellowish green (146B); 18mm (11/16") long x 8mm (5/16") wide. TUBE is dark reddish purple (60B); 7mm (1/4") long x 6mm (1/4") wide. FOLIAGE is dark green (136B) upper surface; medium green (138B) lower surface. PARENTAGE: ('Braamt's Glorie' x 'Rohees New Millenium') x 'Sacramento Bells'. Meise 8/13/05. Distinguished by bloom colour and long blooming period.
Braam 2006 NL AFS6008.

Huet's Labradoriet. Upright/Trailer. Double. COROLLA is three quarter flared; opens purple (83A); matures purple (83C); 18mm (11/16") long x 14mm (9/16") wide. PETALOIDS: dark purple (86A); 11mm (7/16") long x 12mm (1/2") wide. SEPALS are horizontal, tips recurved; light reddish purple (66C) tipped yellowish green (144A) upper surface; magenta (71C) tipped yellowish green (144A) lower surface; 24mm (15/16") long x 13mm (1/2") wide. TUBE is light magenta (66D); 11mm (7/16") long x 7mm (1/4") wide. FOLIAGE: dark green (136A) upper surface; medium green (137B) lower surface. PARENTAGE: ('Naaldwijk800' x 'Little Witch') x ('Hertogin van Brabant' x 'Guurtje'). Meise 9/17/05. Distinguished by bloom colour combination.
Braam 2006 NL AFS6076.

Huet's Lapis. Upright. Double. COROLLA: flared, quarter flared, wavy petal margins;

opens dark purple (89A), light rose (73B) flames & matures purple (82A); 30 mm (1 3/16") long x 20mm (3/4") wide. SEPALS are half down, tips reflexed; white (155B), tipped green upper surface; pale purple (75C) tipped yellow lower surface; 45mm (1 3/4") long x 15mm (9/16") wide. TUBE is white (155B); medium length & thickness; 15mm (9/16") long x 8mm (5/16") wide. STAMENS extend 20mm (3/4") beyond the corolla; reddish purple (80B) filaments; purple (77A) anthers. PISTIL extends 33mm (1 5/16") beyond the corolla; light rose (73C) style; white (155A) stigma. BUD is round. FOLIAGE is medium green (139B) upper surface; medium green (139C) lower surface. Leaves are 55mm (2 3/16") long x 40mm (1 9/16") wide, ovate shaped, serrate edges, acute tips, rounded bases. Veins are light green, stems are green & branches are green. PARENTAGE: ['Huet's Amethist' x ('Gay Parasol x 'Meadowlark')]' x ('WALZ Floreat' x 'Tamerus Koerol'). Lax upright or stiff trailer; self branching. Makes good upright or pillar. Prefers overhead filtered light, cool climate. Best bloom & foliage in filtered or limited light. Tested 3 years in Doetinchem, The Netherlands. Fuchsia Nieuwigheden Certificering. Distinguished by bloom colour and shape. Braam 2009 NL AFS6965.

Huet's Larimar. Upright/Trailer. Double. COROLLA: Three quarter flared; opens dark purple (N78A); matures reddish purple (72B); 32mm (1 1/4") long x 23mm (7/8") wide. PETALOIDS: same colour as corolla; 19mm (3/4") long x 13mm (1/2") wide. SEPALS: half up, tips recurved up; white (155C) tipped pale yellowish green (149D) upper surface; pale lavender (69D) tipped pale yellowish green (149D) lower surface; 40mm (1 9/16") long x 11mm (7/16") wide. TUBE: light green (145D); medium length & thickness; 17mm (5/8") long x 5mm (3/16") wide. FOLIAGE is dark green (137A) upper surface; medium green (138B) lower surface. PARENTAGE: 'Schimpens Glorie' x 'Gay Parasol'. Lax upright or stiff trailer. Braam 2007 NL AFS6595.

Huet's Markasiet. Upright/Trailer. Single. COROLLA: Half flared; opens magenta (58B), magenta (68A) base; matures magenta (63A) & pink (62A); 36mm (1 7/16") long x 23mm (7/8") wide. SEPALS: horizontal, tips recurved; light pink (65C) tipped light yellowish green (150C) upper surface; pink (62A) tipped light yellowish green (150C) lower surface; 30mm (1 3/16") long x 9mm (5/16") wide. TUBE: white (155D); long &

thick; 21mm (13/16") long x 9mm (5/16") wide. FOLIAGE is dark green (136B) upper surface; medium green (138B) lower surface. PARENTAGE: 'WALZ Klavier' x 'Hidcote Beauty'. Braam 2007 NL AFS6394.

Huet's Nefriet. Upright/Trailer. Single. COROLLA: quarter flared; opens violet (77B); matures light reddish purple (72C); 10mm (3/8") long x 7mm (1/4") wide. SEPALS: half down, tips recurved; dark rose (55A) tipped apple green (144C) upper surface; rose (61D) tipped apple green (144C) lower surface; 36mm (1 7/16") long x 12mm (7/16") wide. TUBE: pink (55C); 8mm (5/16") long x 6mm (1/4") wide. FOLIAGE is medium green (137B) upper surface; medium green (138B) lower surface. PARENTAGE: 'Sacramento Bells' x 'Huet's Andalusiet'. Braam 2008 NL AFS6756.

Huet's Olivijn. Trailer. Single. COROLLA: square shape, half flared, wavy petal margins; opens dark violet (87A); matures reddish purple (66B); 40 mm (1 9/16") long x 18mm (11/16") wide. PETALOIDS: magenta (58B); 25mm (1") long x 10mm (3/8") wide. SEPALS are horizontal, tips recurved; pink (62A) upper surface; magenta (58B) lower surface; 60mm (2 3/8") long x 15mm (9/16") wide. TUBE is pale pink (62D); medium length & thickness; 20mm (3/4") long x 7mm (1/4") wide. STAMENS extend 10mm (3/8") beyond the corolla; reddish purple (66B) filaments; light reddish purple (66C) anthers. PISTIL extends 20mm (3/4") beyond the corolla; reddish purple (66B) style; dark rose (58C) stigma. BUD is round. FOLIAGE is medium green (138A) upper surface; medium green (138B) lower surface. Leaves are 45mm (1 3/4") long x 30mm (1 3/16") wide, cordate shaped, wavy edges, acute tips, rounded bases. Veins are light green, stems are red & branches are green. PARENTAGE: ('WALZ Harp' x 'Quasar') x 'Laurie'. Natural trailer; self branching. Makes good basket. Prefers full sun, warm climate. Best bloom & foliage in bright light. Tested 4 years in Doetinchem, The Netherlands. Fuchsia Nieuwigheden Certificering. Distinguished by bloom colour & shape. Braam 2009 NL AFS6975.

Huet's Onyx. Upright/Trailer. Single. COROLLA: quarter flared; opens dark purple (79A); matures purple (71A); 22mm (7/8") long x 17mm (5/8") wide. SEPALS: half up, tips recurved up; dark reddish purple (60A) upper surface; dark reddish purple (60B)

lower surface; 34mm (1 3/8") long x 8mm (5/16") wide. TUBE: reddish purple (59B); 12mm (7/16") long x 6mm (1/4") wide. FOLIAGE is dark green (137A) upper surface; medium green (138B) lower surface. PARENTAGE: 'De Groot's Regenboog' x 'Huet's Baraketh'.
Braam 2008 NL AFS6757.

Huet's Opaal. Upright. Single. COROLLA: quarter flared, turned under wavy petal margins; opens magenta (67B); matures reddish purple (64B); 13mm (1/2") long x 9mm (3/8") wide. SEPALS: horizontal; tips recurved; rose (55B), rose (55C) base, tipped light yellowish green (150C) upper surface; rose (68B) lower surface; 19mm (3/4") long x 6mm (1/4") wide. TUBE: rose (54C); medium length & thickness; 15mm (9/16") long x 3mm (1/8") wide. STAMENS: extend 2mm (1/16") below corolla; pale purple (75D) filaments; pale yellowish green (149D) anthers. PISTIL: extends 6mm (1/4") below the corolla; pale purple (75C) style; pale yellow green (150D) stigma. BUD: cordate shaped. FOLIAGE: medium green (137B) upper surface, medium green (138B) lower surface. Leaves are 46mm (1 13/16") long x 28mm (1 1/8") wide, ovate shaped, serrulated edges, acute tips and rounded bases. Medium Green (138B) veins; dark reddish purple (187D) & medium green (138B) stems; dark reddish purple (187D) & medium green (139C) branches. PARENTAGE: 'WALZ Trumpet' x 'Mrs. W.P. Wood'. Small upright. Self branching. Makes good upright or standard. Prefers full sun. Best bloom and foliage colour in bright light. Tested 4 years in Doetinchem, The Netherlands. Award at Meise, 9/8/03. Distinguished by bloom colour.
Braam 2008 NL AFS5431.

Huet's Parel. Upright. Single. COROLLA is quarter flared with turned under wavy petal margins; opens light reddish purple (73A); matures magenta (68A); 13mm (1/2") long x 12mm (1/2") wide. SEPALS are half up, tips recurved up; pink (62C), yellowish white (158A) base, tipped yellowish green (145A) upper surface; light rose (68D) tipped yellowish green (145C) lower surface; 18mm (11/16") long x 10mm (3/8") wide. TUBE is yellowish white (158A); short & thick; 6mm (1/4") long x 4mm (3/16") wide. FOLIAGE: dark green (139A) upper surface; medium green (138B) lower surface. Leaves are 32mm (1 1/4") long x 25mm (1") wide, cordate shaped. PARENTAGE: 'Braamt's Glorie' x

'Rosella'. Meise 8-14-04. Distinguished by flower form.
Braam 2005 NL AFS5710.

Huet's Parelmoer. Trailer. Double. COROLLA: Half flared; opens purple (N78C), light pink (62B) base; matures light reddish purple (72C); 33mm (1 5/16") long x 22mm (7/8") wide. SEPALS: horizontal, tips recurved; pink (55C) upper surface; light pink (62B) lower surface; 39mm (1 1/2") long x 16mm (5/8") wide. TUBE: white (155B); medium length & thickness; 19mm (3/4") long x 7mm (1/4") wide. FOLIAGE is dark green (136B) upper surface; medium green (138B) lower surface. PARENTAGE: 'WALZ Floreat' x ('Sacramento Bells' x 'Quasar').
Braam 2007 NL AFS6395.

Huet's Peridot. Upright. Single. COROLLA is half flared; opens rose (68B); matures light magenta (66D); 24mm (15/16") long x 21mm (13/16") wide. SEPALS are fully up, tips reflexed; rose (55B), tipped yellowish green (145A) upper surface; dark rose (54B), tipped yellowish green (145A); 30mm (1 3/16") long x 11mm (7/16") wide. TUBE is pale pink (56B); 12mm (7/16") long x 7mm (1/4") wide. FOLIAGE is dark green (136A) upper surface; medium green (138B) lower surface. PARENTAGE: 'Huet's Agaat' x [('Braamt's Glorie' x 'Sneewitchen') x 'Rosella']. Meise 8/13/05, Outstanding. Distinguished by bloom colour.
Braam 2006 NL AFS6010.

Huet's Petaliet. Upright. Single. COROLLA is half flared; opens reddish purple (61B); matures dark rose (64C); 20mm (3/4") long x 14mm (9/16") wide. SEPALS are horizontal, tips recurved; pale pink (56A) upper surface, white (155C) base, tipped light yellowish green (149C); pink (49A) lower surface, white (155C) base, tipped light yellowish green (149C); 43mm (1 11/16") long x 11mm (7/16") wide. TUBE is white (155C); 18mm (11/16") long x 6mm (1/4") wide. FOLIAGE is dark green (137A) upper surface; medium green (138B) lower surface. PARENTAGE: 'Kiwi' x 'Zellertal'. Meise 8/13/05. Distinguished by bloom colour.
Braam 2006 NL AFS6001.

Huet's Pyriet. Upright. Single. COROLLA: quarter flared; opens dark rose (54B) edged red (52A); matures rose (55B); 13mm (1/2") long x 12mm (7/16") wide. SEPALS: half down, tips reflexed; magenta (53C) tipped greenish yellow (151B) upper surface; rose (64D) tipped greenish yellow (151B) lower surface;15mm (9/16") long x 4mm (1/8") wide. TUBE: magenta (61C); 14mm (9/16") long x 6mm (1/4") wide. FOLIAGE is dark green (137A) upper surface; medium green (138B) lower surface. PARENTAGE: 'Loxhore Mazurka' x 'Huet's Agaat'. Braam 2008 NL AFS6758.

Huet's Pyroop. Upright. Single. COROLLA: unflared; opens dark rose (54A) edged dark rose (51A); matures rose (52B); 11mm (7/16") long x 8mm (5/16") wide. SEPALS: half down, tips reflexed; dark rose (54A) tipped light olive green (153D) upper surface; dark rose (58C) tipped light olive green (153D) lower surface;14mm (9/16") long x 7mm (1/4") wide. TUBE: rose (55B); 12mm (7/16") long x 6mm (1/4") wide. FOLIAGE is medium green (138A) upper surface; medium green (138B) lower surface. PARENTAGE: 'Loxhore Mazurka' x 'Huet's Parel'. Braam 2008 NL AFS6759.

Huet's Realgaar. Upright. Double. COROLLA: bell shaped, quarter flared, smooth petal margins; opens & matures red (45B), dark orange red (34A) base; 25 mm (1") long x 15mm (9/16") wide. SEPALS are half up, tips recurved up; coral (39B) tipped light pink (36B) upper surface; dark orange (41A) tipped (light pink (36B) ; 30mm (1 3/16") long x 10mm (3/8") wide. TUBE is orangish white (159C); long & medium thickness; 30mm (1 3/16") long x 4mm (1/8") wide. STAMENS do not extend beyond the corolla; white (155B) filaments; white (155A) anthers. PISTIL extends 20mm (3/4") beyond the corolla; pale pink (56D) style; very pale orange (19D) stigma. BUD is long. FOLIAGE is medium green (137C) upper surface; medium green (138B) lower surface. Leaves are 90mm (3 9/16") long x 38mm (1 1/2") wide, lanceolate shaped, serrate edges, acute tips, cordate bases. Veins are red, stems are red & branches are red. PARENTAGE: 'WALZ Harp' x 'Arels Avondzon'. Lax upright or stiff trailer; self branching. Makes basket. Prefers full sun. Best bloom & foliage in bright light. Tested 5 years in Doetinchem, The Netherlands. Fuchsia Nieuwigheden Certificering. Distinguished by bloom shape & colour. Braam 2009 NL AFS6967.

Huet's Rhodoniet. Upright/Trailer. Semi Double. COROLLA: half flared, turned under wavy petal margins; opens light reddish purple (73A); matures light purple (74C); 20mm (13/16") long, 18mm (11/16") wide. SEPALS: half down; tips reflexed up; rose (68C), tipped light apple green (145C), upper surface; rose (65A), tipped light apple green (145C), lower surface; 21mm (13/16") long x 9mm (3/8") wide. TUBE: rose (68C); medium length & thickness; 27mm (1 1/16") long x 8mm (5/16") wide. STAMENS: extend 6mm (1/4") below corolla; light rose (68D) filaments; light yellow (11C) anthers. PISTIL: extends 28mm (1 1/8") below the corolla; rose (67D) style; pale yellow (1D) stigma. BUD: oblong. FOLIAGE: dark green (136A) upper surface; medium green (137C) lower surface. Leaves are 52mm (2 1/16") long x 21mm (13/16") wide, elliptic shaped, serrulated edges, acute tips and rounded bases. Medium green (138B) veins; dark grayish red (182A) stems; plum(184B) branches. PARENTAGE: 'WALZ Klavier' x 'Impala'. Lax upright or stiff trailer. Self branching. Makes good upright or standard. Prefers overhead filtered light. Best bloom and foliage colour in filtered light. Tested 3 years in Doetinchem, Belgium. Award, Meise, 9/20/03. Distinguished by bloom shape. Braam 2004 NL AFS5618.

Huet's Robyn. Trailer. Semi Double. COROLLA: half flared, turned under wavy petal margins; opens dark rose (48A), dark rose (64C) base; matures reddish purple (64B); 21mm (13/16") long, 19mm (3/4") wide. SEPALS: half down; tips recurved; pink (49A), tipped light yellowish green (150C) upper surface; dark orange (41A) lower surface; 18mm (11/16") long x 11mm (7/16") wide. TUBE: light pink (65B); long, thin; 60mm (2 3/8") long x 4mm (3/16") wide. STAMENS: do not extend below corolla; pale pink (62D) filaments; reddish purple (71B) anthers. PISTIL: does not extend below the corolla; light pink (49B) style; pale yellow (1D) stigma. BUD: elongated. FOLIAGE: dark green (136B) upper surface; medium green (138A) lower surface. Leaves are 65mm (2 9/16") long x 32mm (1 1/4") wide, ovate shaped, serrulated edges, acute tips and rounded bases. Medium green (139C) veins; medium green/ grayish red (138B/182B) stems; medium green/light grayish red (138B/182C) branches. PARENTAGE: 'WALZ Harp' x 'Lye's Favorite'. Natural trailer. Self branching. Makes good basket. Prefers full sun. Best bloom and foliage colour in bright light. Tested 3 years in Doetinchem, Belgium. Award, Meise, 9/20/03. Distinguished by bloom colour combination. Braam 2004 NL AFS5617.

Huet's Rosaniet. Upright. Double. COROLLA: half flared, wavy petal margins;

opens magenta (63A), light orange (27A) base; matures dark rose (64C); 30 mm (1 3/16") long x 18mm (11/16") wide. SEPALS are fully up, tips recurved; pink (36A) upper surface; light coral (38A) lower surface; 25mm (1") long x 15mm (9/16") wide. TUBE is light orange (27A); long & thick; 30mm (1 3/16") long x 14mm (9/16") wide. STAMENS do not extend beyond the corolla; white (155B) filaments; white (155A) anthers. PISTIL extends 10mm (3/8") beyond the corolla; light coral (38A) style; white (155D) stigma. BUD is round. FOLIAGE is dark green (138A) upper surface; medium green (137C) lower surface. Leaves are 70mm (2 3/4") long x 45mm (1 3/4") wide, cordate shaped, serrate edges, acute tips, rounded bases. Veins are light green, stems are red & branches are green. PARENTAGE: 'WALZ Bekken' x 'WALZ Saxofoon'. Lax upright or stiff trailer; self branching. Makes good upright or pillar. Prefers overhead filtered light. Best bloom & foliage in filtered light. Tested 4 years in Doetinchem, The Netherlands. Fuchsia Nieuwigheden Certificering. Distinguished by bloom shape & thick TUBE.
Braam 2009 NL AFS6969.

Huet's Rubeliet. Upright. Double. COROLLA: half flared; opens rose (51C) & dark rose (64C); matures dark rose (67C); 27mm (1 1/16") long x 19mm (3/4") wide. PETALOIDS: same colour as corolla; 12mm (7/16") long x 10mm (3/8") wide. SEPALS: horizontal, tips reflexed; magenta (61C) upper surface; dark rose (58C) lower surface; 27mm (1 1/16") long x 15mm (9/16") wide. TUBE: magenta (63A); 9mm (5/16") long x 6mm (1/4") wide. FOLIAGE is dark green (136B) upper surface; medium green (138A) lower surface. PARENTAGE: 'Braamt's Glorie' x 'Jan Lammertink'.
Braam 2008 NL AFS6760.

Huet's Saffier. Upright/Trailer. Double. COROLLA: three quarter flareds; opens reddish purple (71B) & purple (83A); matures purple (71A); 26mm (1") long x 25mm (1") wide. PETALOIDS:same colour as corolla; 18mm (11/16") long x 11mm (7/16") wide. SEPALS: half up, tips recurved up, twisted left to right; reddish purple (71B) tipped pale yellow green (150D) upper surface; reddish purple (67A) tipped pale yellow green (150D) lower surface; 37mm (1 7/16") long x 14mm (9/16") wide. TUBE: dark reddish purple (60C); 18mm (11/16") long x 6mm (1/4") wide. FOLIAGE is medium green (137B) upper surface; medium green (138B) lower

surface. PARENTAGE: 'Moonraker' x 'Hertogen van Brabant'.
Braam 2008 NL AFS6761.

Huet's Sardonix. Upright/Trailer. Double. COROLLA is three quarter flared with turned under smooth petal margins; opens light reddish purple (73A), light rose (73C) base, edged reddish purple (74B); matures light purple (74C), light rose (73C) base; 20mm (13/16") long x 20mm (13/16") wide. SEPALS are half down, tips recurved; rose (52B) upper surface; dark rose (58C) lower surface; 25mm (1") long x 12mm (1/2") wide. TUBE is rose (52C); short & thick; 6mm (1/4") long x 6mm (1/4") wide. FOLIAGE: dark green (139A) upper surface; medium green (138B) lower surface. Leaves are 67mm (2 5/8") long x 27mm (1 1/16") wide, lanceolate shaped. PARENTAGE: ('WALZ Triangel' x 'Lye's Excelsior') x ('WALZ Harp' x 'Quasar'). Meise 8-14-04. Distinguished by unique colour.
Braam 2005 NL AFS5712.

Huet's Schorliet. Trailer. Single. COROLLA is quarter flared; opens dark reddish purple (64A), dark reddish purple (60C) base; matures reddish purple (61B); 24mm (15/16") long x 14mm (9/16") wide. SEPALS are half up, tips recurved up; dark reddish purple (60C) upper and lower surfaces; 36mm (1 7/16") long x 8mm (5/16") wide. TUBE is magenta (59C); 15mm (9/16") long x 6mm (1/4") wide. FOLIAGE is dark green (139A) upper surface; medium green (138A) lower surface. PARENTAGE: 'De Groots Dreumes' x 'Zulu King'. Meise, 8/13/05. Distinguished by bloom colour.
Braam 2006 NL AFS6002.

Huet's Siberiet. Trailer. Double. COROLLA is quarter flared; opens light reddish purple (73A); matures magenta (67B); 19mm (3/4") long x 19mm (3/4") wide. PETALOIDS: light reddish purple (72C); 15mm (9/16") long x 7mm (1/4") wide. SEPALS are horizontal, tips recurved; rose (54C) tipped light apple green (144D) upper surface; dark rose (55A) tipped light apple green (144D) lower surface; 33mm (1 5/16") long x 13mm (1/2") wide. TUBE is pale pink (56C); 19mm (3/4") long x 6mm (1/4") wide. FOLIAGE: dark green (139A) upper surface; medium green (137C) lower surface. PARENTAGE: 'Kiwi' x 'WALZ Harp'. Meise 8/13/05. Distinguished by bloom colour & leaf shape.
Braam 2006 NL AFS6015.

Huet's Spinel. Upright. Single. COROLLA is fully flared with turned up smooth petal margins; opens dark rose (54B); matures dark rose (58C); 8mm (5/16") long x 6mm (1/4") wide. SEPALS are half up, tips recurved up; rose (54C) upper surface; dark rose (54B) lower surface; 5mm (3/16") long x 3mm (1/8") wide. TUBE is rose (54C), medium length & thickness; 10mm (3/8") long x 3mm (1/8") wide. FOLIAGE: dark green (136A) upper surface; medium green (138B) lower surface. Leaves are 42mm (1 11/16") long x 22mm (7/8") wide, ovate shaped. PARENTAGE: ('Tiny Van de Sande' x 'F. encliandra') x 'Obcilin'. Meise 3-7-04. Distinguished by bloom shape & colour. Braam 2005 NL AFS5657.

Huet's Stephaniet. Upright. Single. COROLLA: bell shaped, half flared, smooth petal margins; opens light purple (186C); matures pale purple (186D); 25 mm (1") long x 20mm (3/4") wide. PETALOIDS: rose (55B); 20mm (3/4") long x 4mm (1/8") wide. SEPALS are horizontal, tips recurved; light purple (186C) tipped green upper surface; reddish purple (186B) lower surface; 25mm (1") long x 10mm (3/8") wide. TUBE is pale pink (56B); medium length and thickness; 22mm (7/8") long x 4mm (1/8") wide. STAMENS extend 15mm (9/16") beyond the corolla; dark rose (54A) filaments; pale pink (56D) anthers. PISTIL extends 32mm (1 1/4") beyond the corolla; pale pink (56B) style; white (155A) stigma. BUD is long, round. FOLIAGE is dark green (137A) upper surface; medium green (138A) lower surface. Leaves are 55mm (2 3/16") long x 35mm (1 3/8") wide, cordate shaped, serrate edges, acute tips, rounded bases. Veins are green, stems are green & branches are green. PARENTAGE: 'Huet's Akosi' x 'WALZ Floreat'. Lax upright or stiff trailer; self branching. Makes good upright or standard. Prefers overhead filtered light, cool climate. Best bloom & foliage in filtered light. Tested 3 years in Doetinchem, The Netherlands. Fuchsia Nieuwigheden Certificering. Distinguished by bloom shape & colour. Braam 2009 NL AFS6970.

Huet's Topaas. Trailer. Single. COROLLA is half flared; opens magenta (63A); matures magenta (61C); 28mm (1 1/8") long x 26mm (1") wide. SEPALS are half down, tips recurved; dark rose (51A) upper surface; rose (47C) lower surface; 30mm (1 3/16") long x 12mm (1/2") wide. TUBE is pink (48C) striped yellowish green (144B); 28mm (1 1/8") long x 8mm (5/16") wide. FOLIAGE is

dark green (139A) upper surface; medium green (138A) lower surface. PARENTAGE: 'Walz Klavier' x 'Impala'. Meise 8/13/05. Distinguished by TUBE colour combination. Braam 2006 NL AFS5999.

Huet's Turkoois. Trailer. Single. COROLLA: Quarter flared; opens purple (71A); matures light reddish purple (72C); 18mm (11/16") long x 12mm (7/16") wide. SEPALS: horizontal, tips recurved; dark rose (71D) upper surface; magenta (67B) lower surface; 36mm (1 7/16") long x 7mm (1/4") wide. TUBE: reddish purple (70B) striped pale pink (62D); medium length & thickness; 17mm (5/8") long x 5mm (3/16") wide. FOLIAGE is dark green (136B) upper surface; medium green (138B) lower surface. PARENTAGE: 'Naaldwijk 800' x 'Delta's Paljas'. Braam 2007 NL AFS6396.

Huet's Ulexiet. Upright/Trailer. Double. COROLLA: Quarter flared; opens light reddish purple (73A); matures rose (68B); 19mm (3/4") long x 16mm (5/8") wide. SEPALS: half down, tips recurved; rose (54C) tipped yellowish green (145A) upper surface; rose (55B) tipped light apple green (145B) lower surface; 29mm (1 1/8") long x 9mm (5/16") wide. TUBE: light pink (55D); long, medium thickness; 26mm (1") long x 8mm (5/16") wide. FOLIAGE is medium green (137B) upper surface; medium green (138B) lower surface. PARENTAGE: ('F. magdalenae' x 'F. fulgens rubra grandiflora') x 'Fey'. Braam 2007 NL AFS6596.

Huet's Uvardiet. Upright. Double. COROLLA is three quarter flared; opens purple (82B) with pale pink (56D) base; matures light reddish purple (74B); 15mm (9/16") long x 16mm (5/8") wide. SEPALS are horizontal, tips recurved; light pink (62B), tipped pale yellowish green (149D) upper surface; rose (65A), tipped pale yellowish green (149D); 34mm (1 3/8") long x 14mm (9/16") wide. TUBE is pale pink (56D); 13mm (1/2") long x 5mm (3/16") wide. FOLIAGE is dark green (136B) upper surface; medium green (138B) lower surface. PARENTAGE: 'Sacramento Bells' x 'Quasar'. Meise 8/13/05. Distinguished by bloom colour and easy flowering. Braam 2006 NL AFS6006.

Huet's Waveliet. Upright. Single. COROLLA: square, quarter flared, wavy petal margins; opens reddish purple (74A), dark blue (102A) flames; matures reddish purple (74B); 21 mm (3/4") long x 12mm (7/16") wide.

SEPALS are horizontal, tips recurved; reddish purple (66A) tipped green upper surface; reddish purple (67A) lower surface; 30mm (1 3/16") long x 10mm (3/8") wide. TUBE is reddish purple (66B); long & medium thickness; 30mm (1 3/16") long x 6mm (1/4") wide. STAMENS extend 18mm (11/16") beyond the corolla; dark reddish purple (64A) filaments; rose (64D) anthers. PISTIL extends 30mm (1 3/16") beyond the corolla; reddish purple (64B) style; rose (68C) stigma. BUD is long, round. FOLIAGE is dark green (139A) upper surface; medium green (139C) lower surface. Leaves are 65mm (2 9/16") long x 40mm (1 9/16") wide, cordate shaped, serrate edges, acute tips, acute bases. Veins are light brown red, stems are red & branches are red green. PARENTAGE: 'De Acht Zagigheden' x 'La Rosita'. Lax upright or stiff trailer; self branching. Makes good basket or standard. Prefers full sun, warm climate. Best bloom & foliage in limited light. Tested 3 years in Doetinchem, The Netherlands. Fuchsia Nieuwigheden Certificering. Distinguished by corolla colour pattern.
Braam 2009 NL AFS6972.

Huet's Wulveniet. Upright. Double. COROLLA: bell shaped, half flared, wavy petal margins; opens magenta (67B); matures reddish purple (66A); 25 mm (1") long x 25mm (1") wide. PETALOIDS: reddish purple (67A), orange (30B) flame;10mm (3/8") long x 8mm (5/16") wide. SEPALS are fully up, tips reflexed; rose (54C) upper surface; dark rose (54B) lower surface; 25mm (1") long x 13mm (1/2") wide. TUBE is light pink (55D); medium length & thickness; 12mm (7/16") long x 8mm (5/16") wide. STAMENS extend 12mm (7/16") beyond the corolla; reddish purple (67A) filaments; magenta (67B) anthers. PISTIL extends 22mm (7/8") beyond the corolla; rose (68C) style; very pale orange (27C) stigma. BUD is round. FOLIAGE is dark green (137A) upper surface; medium green (139D) lower surface. Leaves are 70mm (2 3/4") long x 40mm (1 9/16") wide, cordate shaped, serrulate edges, acute tips, rounded bases. Veins are green, stems are red & branches are green. PARENTAGE: 'Huet's Labradoriet' x ('Braamt's Glorie' x 'Sacramento Bells'). Lax upright or stiff trailer; self branching. Makes good basket or standard. Heat tolerant if shaded. Best bloom & foliage in filtered light. Tested 3 years in Doetinchem, The Netherlands. Fuchsia Nieuwigheden Certificering. Distinguished by bloom colour.
Braam 2009 NL AFS6963.

Huet's Zirkoon. Trailer. Single. COROLLA is quarter flared with turned under smooth petal margins; opens magenta (61C); matures light reddish purple (66C); 26mm (1") long x 12mm (1/2") wide. SEPALS are horizontal, tips recurved; rose (55B) tipped light apple green (145C) upper surface; light pink (62B) tipped light apple green (145C) lower surface; 42mm (1 11/16") long x 6mm (1/4") wide. TUBE is rose (55B), medium length & thickness; 22mm (7/8") long x 5mm (3/16") wide. FOLIAGE: medium green (138A) upper surface; medium green (139C) lower surface. Leaves are 52mm (2 1/16") long x 30mm (1 3/16") wide, ovate shaped. PARENTAGE: 'Wilma Versloot' x 'Pink Galore'. Meise 3-7-04. Distinguished by free long lasting flowers.
Braam 2005 NL AFS5658.

Huet's Zoisiet. Upright. Double. COROLLA is three quarter flared; opens dark purple (78A), light pink (62B) base; matures dark reddish purple (72A); 23mm (7/8") long x 15mm (9/16") wide. SEPALS are fully up, tips recurved; pale pink (62D) upper surface; light pink (62B); 34mm (1 3/8") long x 15mm (9/16") wide. TUBE is pale pink (56D); 15mm (9/16") long x 6mm (1/4") wide. FOLIAGE is dark green (136A) upper surface; medium green (138A) lower surface. PARENTAGE: 'Schimpens Glorie' x 'Brechtje'. Meise 8/13/05. Distinguished by bloom colour.
Braam 2006 NL AFS6004.

Hugo Buts. Upright/Trailer. Single. COROLLA is unflared with turned under smooth petal margins; opens pale pink (56D) edged light reddish purple (72C); matures pale pink (56C) edged light reddish purple (73A); 19mm (3/4") long x 17mm (11/16") wide. SEPALS are horizontal, tips reflexed; rose (51C) tipped light olive green (147C) upper surface; rose (50B) tipped light olive green (148C) lower surface; 23mm (15/16") long x 12mm (1/2") wide. TUBE is pale pink (56C); medium length and thickness; 28mm (1 1/8") long x 6mm (1/4") wide. STAMENS extend 7mm (1/4") beyond the corolla; light magenta (66D) filaments, light yellow (18B) anthers. PISTIL extends 9mm (3/8") beyond the corolla; light rose (68D) style, tan (166C) stigma. BUD is round, pointed. FOLIAGE is dark green (136B) upper surface, medium green (137C) lower surface. Leaves are 51mm (2") long x 27mm (1 1/16") wide, elliptic shaped, serrulated edges, acute tips and rounded bases. Veins are light red purple (185D), stems are plum (185C), branches are dark grayish red (182A). PARENTAGE: 'WALZ

Harp' x 'Annabel'.Lax upright or stiff trailer. Makes good basket. Prefers overhead filtered light or full sun. Best bloom and foliage colour in bright light. Tested three years in Itegem, Belgium. Certificate N.B.F.K. at Meise. Distinguished by bloom colour and shape.
Geerts L. 2002 BE AFS4976.

Hulshorst Bloei. Upright. Double. COROLLA: unflared; opens light purple (78B); matures reddish purple (80B); 27mm (1 1/16") long x 22mm (7/8") wide. PETALOIDS: same colour as corolla; 24mm (15/16") long x 27mm (1 1/16") wide. SEPALS: half up, tips recurved up, light twist to the left; light reddish purple (72D) upper surface; light reddish purple (72C) tipped yellowish green (144A) lower surface; 41mm (1 5/8") long x 13mm (1/2") wide. TUBE: light rose (58D) blushed pink; 18mm (11/16") long x 7mm (1/4") wide. FOLIAGE is medium green (137B) upper surface; medium green (137D) lower surface. PARENTAGE: 'Gerwin van den Brink' x 'Kelly Stableford'. Nomination by NKVF as Recommendable Cultivar.
van den Brink 2008 NL AFS6778.

Huub Jetten. Upright/Trailer. Double. COROLLA: half flared, turned under wavy petal margins; opens reddish purple (72B) & light reddish purple (72C); matures magenta (71C); 22mm (7/8") long x 20mm (3/4") wide. PETALOIDS: reddish purple (72B) & light reddish purple (72D); 13mm (1/2") long x 10mm (3/8") wide. SEPALS: horizontal, tips recurved; pale lavender (69D) tipped pale yellow green (150D) upper surface; pale pink (56D) tipped pale yellow green (150D) lower surface; 28mm (1 1/8") long x 9mm (5/16") wide. TUBE: white (155B) striped pink (62B); medium length & thickness; 15mm (9/16") long x 5mm (3/16") wide. STAMENS extend 14mm (9/16") beyond the corolla; magenta (63B) filaments; reddish purple (70B) anthers. PISTIL extends 26mm (1") beyond the corolla; pale pink (62D) style; pale yellow (1D) stigma. BUD: bulbous. FOLIAGE: dark green (137A) upper surface; medium green (138B) lower surface. Leaves are 82mm (3 1/4") long x 48mm (1 7/8") wide; ovate shaped, serrate edges, acute tips, rounded bases. Veins are light yellowish green (146D), stems are light yellowish green (146D) & light plum (184D), branches are light apple green (145B) & light grayish red (182D). PARENTAGE: 'Ons Mariaklokje' x 'Veenlust'. Lax upright or stiff trailer. Self branching. Makes good basket or upright. Prefers

overhead filtered light, cool climate. Best bloom & foliage colour in filtered light. Tested 4 years in Werm-Hoeselt, Belgium. Waanrode 7/5/08. Distinguished by bloom colour.
Wagemans 2009 BE AFS7085.

Huygen Ireen. Trailer. Double. COROLLA: half flared; opens dark rose (64C) and violet (75A) and matures magenta (68A); 26mm (1") long x 18mm (11/16") wide. PETALOIDS: light violet (77B) base light rose (58D); 15mm (9/16") long x 12mm (7/16") wide. SEPALS are horizontal, tips reflexed; white (155C) tipped light apple green (145B) upper surface; and pale rose (73D) tipped light apple green (145B) lower surface; 35mm (1 3/8") long x 16mm (5/8") wide. TUBE is white (155C); medium length & thickness; 19mm (3/4") long x 6mm (1/4") wide. FOLIAGE is dark green (139A) upper surface; medium green (137C) lower surface. PARENTAGE: 'Vreeni Schleeweiss' x 'Kiss'.
Michiels 2007 BE AFS6529.

Hyancinthe Dumaine. Upright/Trailer. Single. COROLLA is unflared with smooth petal margins; opens and matures red (53C), base clearer; 19mm (3/4") long x 14mm (9/16") wide. SEPALS are horizontal, tips recurved; yellowish white (4D) tipped yellowish green (144B)) upper surface; pale pink (36D) lower surface; 34mm (1 3/8") long x 6mm (1/4") wide. TUBE is yellowish white (4D); medium length and thickness; 16mm (5/8") long x 6mm (1/4") thick. STAMENS extend 11 – 15mm (7/16 – 5/8") beyond the corolla; pink (62B) filaments, pale yellow (158B) anthers. PISTIL extends 26mm (1") beyond the corolla; light pink (62C) style, yellowish white (4D) stigma. BUD is ovate. FOLIAGE is dark green (137A) upper surface, medium green (147B) lower surface. Leaves are 65mm (2 9/16") long x 44mm (1 3/4") wide, ovate shaped, serrulated to quasi-smooth edges, acute tips and rounded bases. Veins and stems are yellowish green, branches are light brown. PARENTAGE: 'Porte Océane' x 'Chang'. Lax upright or stiff trailer. Makes good upright or standard. Prefers overhead filtered light and cool climate. Best bloom colour in filtered light. Tested three years in Pornic & Luçon, France. Distinguished by corolla/TUBE contrast.
Massé 2002 FR AFS5012.

I Love Antwerp. Upright/Trailer. Single. COROLLA is half flared; opens rose (61D) & reddish purple (67A), matures reddish purple (64B); 28mm (1 1/8") long x 27mm (1 1/16")

wide. SEPALS: half down, tips recurved; rose (50B) tipped light yellowish green (150C) upper surface; coral (39B) tipped light yellowish green (150C) lower surface; 38mm (1 1/2") long x 13mm (1/2") wide. TUBE: pink (52D); long, medium thickness; 33mm (1 5/16") long x 8mm (5/16") wide. FOLIAGE is dark green (139A) upper surface; medium green (137C) lower surface. PARENTAGE: 'WALZ Harp' x 'Ting-a-Ling'.
Geerts L. 2007 BE AFS6317.

Ian Storey. Upright. Single. COROLLA is unflared, bell shaped, with smooth petal margins; opens dark purple (79A); matures purple (79C); 20mm (13/16") long x 17mm (11/16") wide. SEPALS are half down, tips recurved; dark reddish purple (60A) upper surface; dark reddish purple (60B) lower surface; 31mm (1 1/4") long x 9mm (3/8") wide. TUBE is dark reddish purple (60A); short, medium thickness; 12mm (1/2") long x 7mm (1/4") wide. FOLIAGE: dark green (135A) upper surface; medium green (137C) lower surface. Leaves are 72mm (2 13/16") long x 28mm (1 1/8") wide, lanceolate shaped. PARENTAGE: 'Susan Storey' x 'Susan Storey'. Distinguished by colour & long blooming period (March – December).
Storey 2005 UK AFS5686.

Ida van Mameren. Upright/Trailer. Double. COROLLA: Half flared; opens & matures white (155D); 29mm (1 1/8") long x 24mm (15/16") wide. SEPALS: fully up, tips reflexed; pink (62A) tipped green upper surface; light pink (62B) lower surface; 39mm (1 1/2") long x 16mm (5/8") wide. TUBE: pink (62A); medium length & thickness; 14mm (9/16") long x 5mm (3/16") wide. FOLIAGE is yellowish green (144A) upper surface; yellowish green (146C) lower surface. PARENTAGE: 'Annabel' x unknown.
Liebregts 2007 NL AFS6610.

Ien Van Adrichem. Upright/Trailer. Double. COROLLA: half flared; opens light reddish purple (72C); matures magenta (71C); 18mm (11/16") long x 18mm (11/16") wide. PETALOIDS: light reddish purple (72D); 10mm (3/8") long x 7mm (1/4") wide. SEPALS: horizontal, tips reflexed; rose (62A) tipped light apple green (144D) upper surface; dark rose (55A) tipped light apple green (144D) lower surface; 36mm (1 7/16") long x 19mm (5/8") wide. TUBE: white (155B); long & thin; 28mm (1 1/8") long x 5mm (3/16") wide. FOLIAGE is dark green (136A) upper surface; medium green (138A)

lower surface. PARENTAGE: 'Rune Peeters' x 'Collingwood'.
Michiels 2007 BE AFS6345.

Ieva Valioniene. Trailer. Double. COROLLA: 3 quarter flared; opens reddish purple (64B), dark rose (55A) base; matures magenta (71C); 26mm (1") long x 24mm (15/16") wide. PETALOIDS: same colour as corolla; 16mm (5/8") long x 12mm (7/16") wide. SEPALS: half down, tips recurved; light rose (58D) tipped light green (139D) upper surface; dark rose (55A) tipped light green (139D) lower surface; 34mm (1 3/8") long x 18mm (11/16") wide. TUBE: white (155C) striped medium green (138B); medium length & thickness; 20mm (3/4") long x 8mm (5/16") wide. FOLIAGE is dark green (136A) upper surface; medium green (138A) lower surface. PARENTAGE: 'Rune Peeters' x 'Illusion'.
Michiels 2007 BE AFS6376.

Ignace Carpentier. Upright. Single. COROLLA is quarter flared with turned under smooth petal margins; opens rose (68B); matures magenta (68A); 10mm (3/8") long x 13 mm (1/2") wide. SEPALS are horizontal, tips reflexed; red (45A) tipped yellowish green (149A) upper surface; dark red (47A) lower surface; 21mm (13/16") long x 10mm (3/8") wide. TUBE is red (45A), long and thin; 23mm (15/16") long x 3mm (1/8") wide. STAMENS do not extend beyond the corolla; dark rose (58C) filaments, light tan (163B) anthers. PISTIL extends 16mm (5/8") below the corolla; light rose (58D) style; pale tan (159A) stigma. BUD is round. FOLIAGE is dark green (139A) upper surface, medium green (138A) lower surface. Leaves are 51mm (2") long x 26mm (1") wide, elliptic shaped, serrulated edges, acute tips and obtuse bases. Veins are light green (138D), stems and branches are brown (173A). PARENTAGE: 'Leverküsen' x 'WALZ Toorts'. Small upright. Self branching. Makes good upright. Prefers overhead filtered light, full sun and warm climate. Best bloom and foliage colour in filtered light. Tested four years in Leopoldsburg, Belgium. Certificate N.B.F.K. at Meise. Distinguished by bloom shape and dwarf growth.
Busschodts 2002 BE AFS4911.

Imca Marina. Upright/Trailer. Double. COROLLA is half flared; opens purple (80A), veined reddish purple (67A); matures reddish purple (67A), edged purple (80A); 35mm (1 3/8") long x 52mm (2 1/16") wide. PETALOIDS: purple (80A), white (155A) base; 16mm (5/8") long x 6mm (1/4") wide.

217

SEPALS are fully up, tips recurved, & twisted; white (155A) flushed pink (62C), tipped green upper surface; white (155A) flushed pink (62C) lower surface; 60mm (2 3/8") long x 15mm (9/16") wide. TUBE is white (155A), striped green; 35mm (1 3/8") long x 8mm (5/16") wide. FOLIAGE: dark green (147A) upper surface; light olive green (147C) lower surface. PARENTAGE: 'Gingham Girl' x 'Bella Rosella'. Koerts T. 2006 NL AFS6299.

Imhotep. Upright. Single. COROLLA is quarter flared; opens reddish purple (61B), rose (61D) base; matures magenta (61C); 26mm (1") long x 15mm (9/16") wide. SEPALS are half down, tips recurved; pale pink (56B) tipped light yellowish green (146A) upper surface; pink (55B) lower surface; 40mm (1 9/16") long x 5.5mm (3/16") wide. TUBE is white (155A); 15mm (9/16") long x 7mm (1/4") wide. FOLIAGE: medium green (146A) upper surface; yellowish green (146B) lower surface. PARENTAGE: 'Checkerboard' x 'Speciosa'. Distinguished by bloom & foliage contrast. Massé 2006 FR AFS6239.

Imogen Crystal Seet. Single. COROLLA ruby red. SEPALS pale carmine rose. Porter 2002 UK.

In The Pink. Upright/Trailer. Single. COROLLA is quarter flared with smooth petal margins; opens dark rose (67C); matures reddish purple (66B); 32mm (1 1/4") long x 26mm (1") wide. SEPALS are fully up; tips recurved; white (155B) upper and lower surfaces; 44mm (1 3/4") long x 10mm (3/8") wide. TUBE is white (155B), medium length and thickness; 19mm (3/4") long x 6mm (1/4") wide. STAMENS extend 19mm (3/4") below the corolla; rose (65A) filaments reddish purple (66B) anthers. PISTIL extends 52mm (2") below the corolla; light pink (65C) style and light pink (65B) stigma. BUD is long and slender. FOLIAGE is yellowish green (144A) on upper and light olive green (148C) on lower surface. Leaves are 64mm (2 1/2") long x 44mm (1 3/4") wide, ovate shaped, serrated edges, acute tips and rounded bases. Veins are light olive green (148C), stems are plum (185C) and branches are light brown. PARENTAGE: 'Rasberry Punch' x 'Moonglow'. Lax upright or stiff trailer. Makes good upright. Prefers overhead filtered light. Best bloom colour in bright light. Tested 6 years in Kent, Washington, USA. Distinguished by unique shade of pink blooms.

Pearson 2003 USA AFS5064.

Indy van Roovert. Trailer. Double. COROLLA is half flared with smooth petal margins; opens purple (88A); matures light purple (78B); 30mm (1 3/16") long x 24mm (15/16") wide. SEPALS are half up, tips recurved up; pale pink (62D) upper surface, rose (63C) lower surface; 27mm (1 1/16") long x 12mm (1/2") wide. TUBE is pink (62C); medium length and thickness; 21mm (13/16") long x 6mm (1/4") thick. STAMENS extend 20mm (13/16") beyond the corolla; magenta (63B) filaments, magenta (63A) anthers. PISTIL extends 37mm (1 7/16") beyond the corolla; light rose (68D) style, pale lavender (65D) stigma. BUD is ovate, pointed. FOLIAGE is medium green (137B) upper surface, medium green (137D) lower surface. Leaves are 57mm (2 1/4") long x 32mm (1 1/4") wide, ovate shaped, serrated edges, acute tips and obtuse bases. Veins and branches are green, stems are red. PARENTAGE: ('Annabel' x 'Annabel') x [('Gruss Aus dem Bodethal') x ('Bicentennial x Delta's Wonder')]. Natural trailer. Makes good basket. Prefers overhead filtered light and cool climate. Best bloom colour in filtered light. Tested four years in Knegsel, The Netherlands. Distinguished by bloom colour.
Roes 2002 NL AFS5043.

Ine Fox. Upright/Trailer. Single. COROLLA is half flared, smooth petal margins; opens purple (77A); matures violet (77B); 16mm (5/8") long x 14mm (9/16") wide. SEPALS are half up, tips recurved up; light pink (65B) upper surface; light reddish purple (66C) lower surface; 27mm (1 1/16") long x 14mm (9/16") wide. TUBE is light pink (65B); medium length & thickness; 12mm (1/2") long x 7mm (1/4") wide. STAMENS extend 8mm (5/16") beyond the corolla; dark reddish purple (64A) filaments & anthers. PISTIL extends 16mm (5/8") below the corolla; reddish purple (64B) style; cream (11D) stigma. BUD is ovate, pointed. FOLIAGE is dark green (137A) upper surface, medium green (137C) lower surface. Leaves are 76mm (3") long x 34mm (1 5/16") wide, lanceolate shaped, serrated edges, acute tips and rounded bases. Veins, stems & branches are red. PARENTAGE: 'Roesse Apus' x 'Delta's Bride'. Lax upright or stiff trailer. Makes good stiff trailer. Prefers overhead filtered light & cool climate. Best bloom colour in filtered light. Tested four years in Knegsel, The Netherlands. Distinguished by bloom & foliage combination.

Roes 2004 NL AFS5372.

Ine van den Haak. Upright. Single.
COROLLA: unflared; smooth petal margins;
opens rose (68B); matures magenta (68A);
21mm (13/16") long x 22mm (7/8") wide.
SEPALS: horizontal, tips recurved; pale pink
(62D) tipped yellowish green (145A) upper
surface; light pink (62B) lower surface;
33mm (1 5/16") long x 11mm (7/16") wide.
TUBE: pale pink (62D); medium length &
thickness; 15mm (9/16") long x 9mm (5/16")
wide. STAMENS extend 13mm (1/2") beyond
the corolla; pink (62A) filaments; olive green
(162A) anthers. PISTIL extends 23mm (7/8")
beyond the corolla; light pink (62B) style;
olive green (152A) stigma. BUD: long.
FOLIAGE: medium green (146A) upper
surface; yellowish green (146B) lower
surface. Leaves are 73mm (2 7/8") long x
40mm (1 9/16") wide; cordate shaped,
serrulate edges, acute tips, rounded bases.
Veins are yellow green, stems & branches are
red. PARENTAGE: ('Cambridge Louie' x
'Henkelly's Billy') x 'Loxhore Mazurka'. Tall
upright. Makes good upright or standard.
Prefers full sun. Best bloom & foliage colour
in bright light. Tested 4 years in Sint
Michielsgestel, The Netherlands. Nominated
by NKvF as recommendable cultivar.
Distinguished by bright flower colours that
contrast against the leaves.
Spierings 2009 NL AFS7035.

Ingrid Rempfer. Upright/Trailer. Semi
Double to Double. COROLLA: three quarter
flared, turned under wavy petal margins;
opens purple (N79B); matures reddish purple
(59B); 28mm (1 1/8") long x 22mm (7/8")
wide. SEPALS: fully up, tips recurved;
reddish purple (61B) upper surface; dark
reddish purple (60C) lower surface; 44mm (1
3/4") long x 17mm (5/8") wide. TUBE:
magenta (59C); medium length & thickness;
17mm (5/8") long x 7mm (1/4") wide.
STAMENS extend 16mm (5/8") beyond the
corolla; reddish purple (71B) filaments;
purple (71A) anthers. PISTIL extends 44mm
(1 3/4") beyond the corolla; dark rose (67C)
style; light rose (73C) stigma. BUD: acorn
shape. FOLIAGE: dark green (137A) upper
surface; medium green (138B) lower surface.
Leaves are 66mm (2 5/8") long x 31mm (1
1/4") wide; elliptic shaped, serrate edges,
acute tips, rounded bases. Veins are olive
green (152D), stems are plum (185C),
branches are dark reddish purple (N186D).
PARENTAGE: 'Manfried Kleinau' x
'Centerpiece'. Lax upright or stiff trailer. Self
branching. Makes good basket. Prefers

overhead filtered light, cool climate. Best
bloom & foliage colour in filtered light. Tested
3 years in Koningshooikt, Belgium.
Waanrode 7/5/08. Distinguished by bloom
colour combination.
Michiels 2009 BE AFS7176.

Ingrid Schaak. Trailer. Double. COROLLA is
three quarter flared with smooth petal
margins; opens purple (83B); matures dark
reddish purple (72A); 28mm (1 1/8") long x
12mm (1/2") wide. SEPALS are horizontal,
tips reflexed; dark rose (58C) upper surface;
red (47B) lower surface; 28mm (1 1/8") long
x 12mm (1/2") wide. TUBE is dark rose
(58C); medium length & thickness; 12mm
(1/2") long x 6mm (1/4") thick. STAMENS
extend 12mm (1/2") beyond the corolla;
magenta (58B) filaments, light rose (58D)
anthers. PISTIL extends 32mm (1 1/4")
beyond the corolla; magenta (58B) style, light
rose (58D) stigma. BUD is ovate, pointed.
FOLIAGE is medium green (137C) upper
surface, medium green (138B) lower surface.
Leaves are 52mm (2 1/16") long x 32mm (1
1/4") wide, ovate shaped, serrated edges,
acute tips and rounded bases. Veins, stems
and branches are red. PARENTAGE: 'Rohees
Mintaka' x 'Gilian Althea'. Natural trailer.
Makes good basket. Prefers overhead filtered
light and cool climate. Best bloom colour in
filtered light. Tested four years in Duizel, The
Netherlands. Distinguished by bloom and
foliage combination.
Tamerus 2002 NL AFS4986.

Ingrid van Eijk. Upright/Trailer. Double.
COROLLA: three quarter flared, smooth petal
margins; opens dark purple (79A); matures
dark reddish purple (72A); 30mm (1 3/16")
long x 27mm (1 1/16") wide. SEPALS: fully
up; tips recurved; dark reddish purple (70A)
upper & lower surfaces; 44mm (1 3/4") long
x 16mm (5/8") wide. TUBE: dark reddish
purple (70A); medium length & thickness;
15mm (9/16") long x 7mm (1/4") wide.
STAMENS: extend 25mm (1") below corolla;
dark reddish purple (60A) filaments, purple
(71A) anthers. PISTIL: extends 31mm (1
1/4") below the corolla; dark reddish purple
(60A) style, magenta (61C) stigma. BUD:
ovate. FOLIAGE: medium green (137B) upper
surface; medium green (138B) lower surface.
Leaves are 57mm (2 1/4") long x 27mm (1
1/16") wide, ovate shaped, serrulated edges,
acute tips and rounded bases. Veins, stems
& branches are red. PARENTAGE:
'Bicentennial' x 'Rohees Queen'. Lax upright
or stiff trailer. Makes good stiff trailer.
Prefers overhead filtered light and cool

climate. Best bloom and foliage colour in filtered light. Tested 4 years in Reusel, The Netherlands. Distinguished by bloom colour. van Eijk 2003 NL AFS5247.

Inekris. Upright/Trailer. Single. COROLLA: quarter flared; opens orangy red (39A); matures light orange (41D); 11mm (7/16") long x 9mm (5/16") wide. SEPALS: half down, tips reflexed; pink (43D) tipped light apple green (145C) upper surface; orange (44D) tipped light apple green (145C) lower surface; 30mm (1 3/16") long x 7mm (1/4") wide. TUBE: pink (48D); 32mm (1 1/4") long x 5mm (3/16") wide. FOLIAGE is dark green (139A) upper surface; medium green (138B) lower surface. PARENTAGE: 'WALZ Harp' x 'Wentworth'.
Wagemans 2008 BE AFS6743.

Irisina. Upright/Trailer. Double. COROLLA: half flared, turned under wavy petal margins; opens magenta (58B); matures dark rose (54A); 29mm (1 1/8") long x 24mm (15/16") wide. SEPALS: half down, tips recurved; red (53C) upper surface; magenta (58B) lower surface; 41mm (1 5/8") long x 15mm (9/16") wide. TUBE: dark rose (51A); long & thin; 42mm (1 5/8") long x 6mm (1/4") wide. STAMENS do not extend beyond the corolla; light pink (55D) filaments; pale yellowish orange (20C) anthers. PISTIL extends 18mm (11/16") beyond the corolla; dark rose (54B) style; pale pink (49D) stigma. BUD: elongated square. FOLIAGE: dark green (136B) upper surface; medium green (137C) lower surface. Leaves are 98mm (3 7/8") long x 54mm (2 1/8") wide; ovate shaped, serrulate edges, acute tips, rounded bases. Veins are dark reddish purple (187B), stems are dark red purple (187D), branches are dark grayish purple (184A). PARENTAGE: 'WALZ Harp' x unknown. Lax upright or stiff trailer. Makes good basket. Prefers overhead filtered light, cool climate. Best bloom & foliage colour in filtered light. Tested 4 years in Scherpenheuuel-Zichem, Belgium. Waanrode 8/9/08. Distinguished by bloom colour.
Saenen 2009 BE AFS7084.

Irmgard Krikke. Upright. Semi Double. COROLLA: half flared, smooth petal margins; opens dark purple (86A); matures violet (86D); 14mm (9/16") long 21mm (13/16") wide. SEPALS: half down; tips recurved; light rose (58D) upper surface; dark rose (58C) lower surface; 24mm (15/16") long x 14mm (9/16") wide. TUBE: light rose (58D); medium length & thickness; 10mm (3/8") long x 5mm (3/16") wide. STAMENS: extend 7mm (1/4")

below corolla; magenta (63A) filaments; magenta (68A) anthers. PISTIL: extends 16mm (5/8") below the corolla; magenta (63A) style & stigma. BUD: round, pointed. FOLIAGE: yellowish green (145A) upper surface; light apple green (145C) lower surface. Leaves are 44mm (1 3/4") long x 24mm (15/16") wide, ovate shaped, serrulated edges, acute tips and rounded bases. Red veins, stems & branches. PARENTAGE: ('Cameron Ryle' x 'Parasol') x 'Loeky'. Small upright. Makes good upright or standard. Prefers overhead filtered light and cool climate. Best bloom and foliage colour in filtered light. Tested 4 years in Knegsel, The Netherlands. Distinguished by bloom and foliage combination.
Roes 2004 NL AFS5464.

Isabel Baker. Trailer. Single. COROLLA: unflared, bell shaped, smooth petal margins; opens purple (83B) edged & veined red; matures violet (83D) edged & veined red; 26mm (1") long x 21mm (13/16") wide. SEPALS: half up; tips recurved up; pink (62C) upper surface; rose (63C) lower surface; 32mm(1 1/4") long x 14mm (9/16") wide. TUBE: light yellowish green (149C) striped pink; short, medium thickness; 12mm (1/2") long x 8mm (5/16") wide. STAMENS: extend 15mm (9/16") below corolla; light reddish purple (66C) filaments; magenta (63B) anthers. PISTIL: extends 22mm (7/8") below the corolla, light pink (62B) style; cream (158D) stigma. BUD: obtuse. FOLIAGE: dark green (147A) upper surface; light olive green (147C) lower surface. Leaves are 44mm (1 3/4") long x 28mm (1 1/8") wide, lanceolate shaped, serrulated edges, acute tips and rounded bases. Veins are green, stems & branches are red. PARENTAGE: 'Branksome Belle' x 'Ruth Graham'. Natural trailer. Makes good basket. Heat tolerant if shaded. Prefers cool climate. Best bloom and foliage colour in filtered light. Tested 3 years in Stockbridge, Hampshire, England. Distinguished by bloom colour combination.
Graham 2003 UK AFS5144.

Isabel Erdkamp. Upright/Trailer. Semi Double. COROLLA is half flared with turned under smooth petal margins; opens magenta (68A) edged reddish purple (66A), rose (68C) at base; matures magenta (58B) edged magenta (61C), light pink (65B) at base; 31mm (1 1/4") long x 20mm (13/16") wide. PETALOIDS: magenta (68A) edged magenta (67B), rose (68C) at base;23mm (15/16") x 16mm (5/8"). SEPALS are horizontal, tips recurved; grayish yellow (160A) tipped yellowish green (145A), pink (62A) at base, upper surface; yellowish gray (160D), pink (62A) at base, lower surface; 33mm (1 5/16") long x 13mm (1/2") wide. TUBE is pink (48D); medium length and thickness; 15mm (5/8") long x 7mm (1/4") thick. STAMENS extend 4mm (3/16") beyond the corolla; light reddish purple (66C) filaments, magenta (63A) anthers. PISTIL extends 11mm (7/16") beyond the corolla; orangish white (159C) style, yellowish gray (160D) stigma. BUD is ovate, pointed. FOLIAGE is dark green (136A) upper surface, medium green (137C) lower surface. Leaves are 42mm (1 11/16") long x 26mm (1") wide, elliptic shaped, serrated edges, acute tips and obtuse bases. Veins are light olive green (148D), stems are plum (184B), branches are yellowish green (146C). PARENTAGE: 'Diana' x unknown. Lax upright or stiff trailer. Self branching. Makes good basket. Prefers overhead filtered light. Best bloom and foliage colour in filtered light. Tested three years in Rummen, Belgium. Certificate N.B.F.K. at Meise. Distinguished by bloom colour and profuse blooms. Ector 2002 BE AFS5005.

Isabell Reim. Upright. Single. COROLLA: quarter flared; opens & matures reddish orange (42A); 20mm (3/4") long x 18mm (11/16") wide. SEPALS: horizontal, tips recurved; orange (41B) upper surface; light orange (41D) lower surface; 30mm (1 3/16") long x 11mm (7/16") wide. TUBE: light orange (41D); 11mm (7/16") long x 8mm (5/16") wide. FOLIAGE is dark green (147A) upper surface; medium green (137C) lower surface. PARENTAGE: 'Galadriel' x 'Danny Kaye'.
Burkhart 2008 DE AFS6863.

Iseut. Upright/Trailer. Single. COROLLA: half flared; smooth petal margins; opens dark reddish purple (61A); matures reddish purple (61B); 20mm (3/4") long x 27mm (1 1/16") wide. SEPALS: half up, tips recurved up to horizontal, tips recurved; pink (62C) upper & lower surfaces; 33mm (1 5/16") long x 8mm (5/16") wide. TUBE: pink (62C); short, medium to thick; 10mm (3/8") long x 9mm (5/16") wide. STAMENS extend 13-16mm (1/2-5/8") beyond the corolla; light rose (73C) filaments; magenta (61C) anthers. PISTIL extends 33mm (1 5/16") beyond the corolla; pale pink (69A) style; light yellow (4C) stigma. BUD is ovate. FOLIAGE is dark green (147A) upper surface; medium green (147B) lower surface. Leaves are 50mm (2") long x 33mm (1 5/16") wide; ovate shaped,

serrulate edges, acute tips, rounded bases. Veins are yellowish green, stems are yellowish green & light brown, branches are light brown. PARENTAGE: 'La Campanella' x 'Annabel'. Small, lax upright or stiff trailer. Makes good upright. Prefers overhead filtered light & cool climate. Tested 3 years in Pornic, France. Distinguished by colour combination.
Massé 2009 FR AFS6992.

It's A Beauty. Upright. Double. COROLLA: full flared; opens violet blue (92A); matures purple (82B); 25mm (1") long x 25mm (1") wide. SEPALS: horizontal, tips recurved; light rose (55B), streaked white (155A), tipped green upper surface; light rose (55B) lower surface; 40mm (1 9/16") long x 20mm (3/4") wide. TUBE: pale pink (62D); 20mm (3/4") long x 10mm (3/8") wide. FOLIAGE is dark green (139A) upper surface; medium green (138A) lower surface. PARENTAGE: 'Lovely Charlotte' x 'Snowbird'.
Smith R. 2008 UK AFS6811.

Jachthuis Rullingen. Upright/Trailer. Single. COROLLA: quarter flared, turned under smooth petal margins; opens dark rose (51A), dark orange (41A) at base; matures dark orange (41A), edged reddish purple (67A); 15mm (9/16") long x 16mm (5/8") wide. SEPALS: half up; tips recurved up; coral (39B), tipped light yellowish green (150A) upper surface; orange red (35A), lower surface; 23mm (15/16") long x 8mm (5/16") wide. TUBE: light coral (38A); long, medium thickness; 45mm (1 3/4") long x 5mm (3/16") wide, 7mm (1/4") at base. STAMENS: extend 9mm (3/8") below the corolla; light pink (49B) filaments, light yellow (4B) anthers. PISTIL extends 20mm (13/16") below the corolla; light rose (50C) style, yellow (17A) stigma. BUD: ovate, long TUBE. FOLIAGE: dark green (139A) upper surface, medium green (138A) lower surface. Leaves are 52mm (2") long x 46mm (1 13/16") wide, cordate shaped, serrulated edges, acute tips and cordate bases. Veins are brown (176D), stems & branches are orangy brown (176A). PARENTAGE: 'WALZ Harp' x unknown. Lax upright or stiff trailer. Self branching. Makes good upright. Prefers full sun. Best bloom and foliage colour in bright light. Tested 3 years in Wellen, Belgium. NBFK certificate at Meise. Distinguished by long TUBE.
Vanwalleghem 2003 BE AFS5090.

Jack. Upright/Trailer. Single. COROLLA: unflared, square shape; opens violet (77B); matures light purple (80C); 25mm (1") long x

20mm (3/4") wide. SEPALS: horizontal, tips recurved; pale pink (56A) tipped green upper surface; pale pink (36D) lower surface; 36mm (1 7/16") long x 12mm (7/16") wide. TUBE: very pale orange (19D); 20mm (3/4") long x 8mm (5/16") wide. FOLIAGE is medium green (146A) upper surface; yellowish green (146B) lower surface. PARENTAGE: 'Belle de Spa' x unknown. Ricard 2008 BE AFS6849.

Jack The Lad. Upright. Single. COROLLA: quarter flared, turned under smooth petal margins; opens dark reddish purple (72A) fused magenta (58B); matures reddish purple (71B) fused magenta (58B); 15mm (9/16") long x 16mm (5/8") wide. SEPALS: half down; tips reflexed; reddish purple (58A), upper surface; magenta (58B) lower surface; 23mm (15/16") long x 7mm (1/4") wide. TUBE: reddish purple (58A); medium length & thickness; 13mm(1/2") long x 5mm (3/16") wide. STAMENS: extend 22mm (7/8) below corolla; dark rose (55A) filaments, magenta (63A) anthers. PISTIL: extends 37mm (1 7/16") below the corolla, rose (55B) style, pink (55C) stigma. BUD: small, ovate. FOLIAGE: dark green (137A) upper surface; dark green (147A) lower surface. Leaves are 38mm (1 1/2") long x 22mm (7/8") wide, lanceolate shaped, serrated edges, acute tips and rounded bases. Veins are green, stems are red; branches are brown. PARENTAGE: 'Son of Thumb' x 'Doctor Foster'. Small upright. Self branching. Makes good upright, miniature or rockery fuchsia. Prefers overhead filtered light. Heat tolerant if shaded. Cold weather hardy to 28° F. Best bloom and foliage colour in filtered light. Tested 3 years in Walthamstow, London, England. Distinguished by bloom colour combination.
Allsop J. 2003 UK AFS521.

Jacob de Vries. Upright. Single. COROLLA: half flared, smooth petal margins; opens & matures dark rose (55A) striped cream (158D); 18mm (11/16") long 22mm (7/8") wide. SEPALS: half down; tips reflexed; cream (11D), tipped green, upper & lower surfaces; 27mm (1 1/16") long x 8mm (5/16") wide. TUBE: pale yellow (12D); short, thick; 10mm (3/8") long x 8mm (5/16") wide. STAMENS: extend 9mm (3/8") below corolla; orangish white (159C) filaments; rose (55B) anthers. PISTIL: extends 20mm (13/16") below the corolla; orangish white (159C) style; grayish yellow (160A) stigma. BUD: round. FOLIAGE: medium green (146A) upper surface; yellowish green (146B) lower

surface. Leaves are 60mm (2 3/8") long x 40mm (1 9/16") wide, ovate shaped, serrulated edges, acute tips and rounded bases. Light green (146C) veins & stems; light green (146B) branches. PARENTAGE: 'Bobby Shaftoe' x 'Prince Syray'. Medium upright. Self branching. Makes good upright, standard or pyramid. Prefers overhead filtered light, warm climate. Best bloom and foliage colour in bright light. Tested 3 years in Stadskanaal, The Netherlands. Distinguished by flowering in clusters and blossom colour combination.
Koerts T. 2004 NL AFS5586.

Jacq Puts. Upright/Trailer. Single. COROLLA: 3 quarter flared; opens dark violet (N87A) striped light reddish purple (N66C); matures light purple (N78B) striped dark rose (58C); 25mm (1") long x 22mm (7/8") wide. SEPALS: fully up, tips recurved; light reddish purple (N66C) tipped apple green (144C) upper surface; dark rose (58C) tipped apple green (144C) lower surface; 35mm (1 3/8") long x 22mm (7/16") wide. TUBE: light reddish purple (N66C); short & thick; 8mm (5/16") long x 6mm (1/4") wide. FOLIAGE is dark green (136A) upper surface; medium green (138B) lower surface. PARENTAGE: 'Lavender Heaven' x 'Delta's Trick'. Meise 7/1/06, Outstanding.
Michiels 2007 BE AFS6377.

Jacques Wijne. Upright/Trailer. Single. COROLLA is quarter flared with smooth petal margins; opens purple (90A); matures purple (81B); 26mm (1") long x 30 mm (1 3/16") wide. SEPALS are fully up, tips recurved; magenta (58B) upper surface; dark rose (58C) lower surface; 52mm (1 1/16") long x 11mm (7/16") wide. TUBE is magenta (58B), medium length & thickness; 13mm (1/2") long x 7mm (1/4") wide. FOLIAGE: medium green (137B) upper surface; medium green (137C) lower surface. Leaves are 46mm (1 13/16") long x 41mm (1 5/8") wide, cordate shaped. PARENTAGE: 'Madalyn Drago' x 'Roesse Blacky'. Distinguished by bloom and foliage combination.
van Bree 2005 NL AFS5644.

JaDi Barbus Ticto. Trailer. Single. COROLLA: quarter flared; opens dark reddish purple (64A); matures magenta (61C); 20mm (3/4") long x 22mm (7/8") wide. SEPALS: half up, tips reflexed up; light pink (65B) upper & lower surfaces; 34mm (1 3/8") long x 7mm (1/4") wide. TUBE: light pink (65B); 17mm (5/8") long x 5mm (3/16") wide. FOLIAGE is dark green (137A) upper surface;

medium green (137C) lower surface. PARENTAGE: 'Roesse Lupus' x 'Petra van Bergen'. Geenen 2008 NL AFS6915.

JaDi Belontia Signata. Upright. Single. COROLLA: half flared; opens reddish purple (59B); matures dark reddish purple (60B); 17mm (5/8") long x 16mm (5/8") wide. SEPALS: horizontal, tips recurved; reddish purple (58B) upper & lower surfaces; 27mm (1 1/16") long x 12mm (7/16") wide. TUBE: reddish purple (58B); 29mm (1 1/8") long x 6mm (1/4") wide. FOLIAGE is dark green (137A) upper surface; medium green (138A) lower surface. PARENTAGE: 'Kristel vanden Velden' x 'Oranje van Os'. Geenen 2008 NL AFS6916.

JaDi Betta Splendens. Trailer. Double. COROLLA: three quarter flared; opens dark reddish purple (61A); matures magenta (61C); 31mm (1 1/4") long x 30mm (1 3/16") wide. SEPALS: fully up, tips recurved; white (155D) upper & lower surfaces; 34mm (1 3/8") long x 10mm (3/8") wide. TUBE: white (155D); 16mm (5/8") long x 5mm (3/16") wide. FOLIAGE is dark green (137A) upper surface; medium green (137D) lower surface. PARENTAGE: 'Sofie Michiels' x 'Veenlust'. Geenen 2008 NL AFS6913.

JaDi Callistusminor. Upright/Trailer. Double. COROLLA: Three quarter flared; opens violet (92A); matures violet (77C); 22mm (7/8") long x 15mm (9/16") wide. SEPALS: horizontal, tips recurved; white (155D) upper & lower surfaces; 27mm (1 1/16") long x 12mm (7/16") wide. TUBE: white (155D); medium length & thickness; 20mm (3/4") long x 5mm (3/16") wide. FOLIAGE is dark green (137A) upper surface; medium green (137C) lower surface. PARENTAGE: 'Sofie Michiels' x 'Silver Dawn'. Geenen 2007 NL AFS6616.

JaDi Celebes. Trailer. Single. COROLLA: Half flared; opens violet blue (91A); matures violet (87B); 26mm (1") long x 17mm (5/8") wide. SEPALS: fully up, tips reflexed; magenta (63A) upper & lower surfaces; 31mm (1 1/4") long x 11mm (7/16") wide. TUBE: magenta (63A); medium length & thickness; 12mm (7/16") long x 6mm (1/4") wide. FOLIAGE is dark green (137A) upper surface; medium green (137D) lower surface. PARENTAGE: 'Reg Gubler' x 'Roesse Parel'. Geenen 2007 NL AFS6617.

JaDi Citroentetra. Upright. Single. COROLLA is half flared; opens red (46B); matures red (45B); 12mm (7/16") long x 16mm (5/8") wide. SEPALS are half up, tips reflexed up; rose (47C) tipped green upper surface; rose (47C) lower surface; 20mm (3/4) long x 8mm (5/16") wide. TUBE is rose (47C); 19mm (3/4") long x 7mm (1/4") wide. FOLIAGE: dark green (137A) upper surface; medium green (138A) lower surface. PARENTAGE: 'Roesse Lupus' x 'Lye's Unique'. Distinguished by bloom & foliage combination. Geenen 2006 NL AFS6218.

JaDi Colisa Chuna. Upright/Trailer. Single. COROLLA: half flared; opens reddish purple (61B); matures dark reddish purple (60C); 16mm (5/8") long x 22mm (7/8") wide. SEPALS: horizontal, tips recurved; white (155D) tipped green upper & lower surfaces; 31mm (1 1/4") long x 10mm (3/8") wide. TUBE: pale yellow (2D); 17mm (5/8") long x 7mm (1/4") wide. FOLIAGE is dark green (137A) upper surface; medium green (137C) lower surface. PARENTAGE: 'Roesse Carme' x 'Roesse Parel'. Geenen 2008 NL AFS6917.

JaDi Discus. Trailer. Single. COROLLA: Half flared; opens dark reddish purple (61A); matures dark reddish purple (60C); 16mm (5/8") long x 20mm (3/4") wide. SEPALS: fully up, tips reflexed; magenta (58B) upper surface; reddish purple (58A) lower surface; 30mm (1 3/16") long x 8mm (5/16") wide. TUBE: magenta (58B); long & thin; 21mm (13/16") long x 4mm (1/8") wide. FOLIAGE is dark green (137A) upper surface; medium green (137C) lower surface. PARENTAGE: 'Roesse Lupus' x ('Roesse Lupus' x 'Lyes Unique'). Geenen 2007 NL AFS6613.

JaDi Femke. Upright/Trailer. Semi Double. COROLLA is three quarter flared; opens pink (62A); matures light pink (62B); 26mm (1") long x 29mm (1 1/8") wide. SEPALS are half up, tips recurved up; light rose (68D) upper surface; pale lavender (68B) lower surface; 19mm (3/4) long x 8mm (5/16") wide. TUBE is light rose (68D); 12mm (7/16") long x 9mm (3/8") wide. FOLIAGE: medium green (137B) upper surface; medium green (138B) lower surface. PARENTAGE: 'Roesse Carme' x 'Cameron Ryle'. Distinguished by bloom colour & leaf shape. Geenen 2006 NL AFS6225.

JaDi Fleur. Upright. Single. COROLLA is half flared; opens reddish purple (72B); matures magenta (71C); 15mm (9/16") long x 21mm (13/16") wide. SEPALS are half down, tips recurved; pale purple (70D) tipped green upper surface; light purple (70C) tipped green lower surface; 20mm (3/4) long x 10mm (3/8") wide. TUBE is pale purple (70D); 19mm (3/4") long x 7mm (1/4") wide. FOLIAGE: dark green (137A) upper surface; medium green (138A) lower surface. PARENTAGE: ('Parasol' x 'Cameron Ryle') x 'Mission Bells'. Distinguished by bloom & foliage combination.
Geenen 2006 NL AFS6223.

JaDi Gevlekte Acara. Upright/Trailer. Single. COROLLA is half flared; opens reddish orange (42A); matures red (43A); 17mm (5/8") long x 20mm (3/4") wide. SEPALS are half up, tips recurved up; light orange (39C) upper & lower surfaces; 19mm (3/4) long x 6mm (1/4") wide. TUBE is light orange (39C); 19mm (3/4") long x 7mm (1/4") wide. FOLIAGE: dark green (137A) upper surface; medium green (137D) lower surface. PARENTAGE: 'Roesse Lupus' x 'Lye's Unique'. Distinguished by bloom colour.
Geenen 2006 NL AFS6222.

JaDi Goudvlekrio. Trailer. Single. COROLLA: Half flared; opens violet (85A); matures light purple (87C); 20mm (3/4") long x 22mm (7/8") wide. SEPALS: horizontal, tips recurved; pink (62C) upper & lower surfaces; 24mm (15/16") long x 13mm (1/2") wide. TUBE: pink (62C); medium length & thickness; 15mm (9/16") long x 6mm (1/4") wide. FOLIAGE is dark green (137A) upper surface; medium green (137D) lower surface. PARENTAGE: 'Sofie Michiels' x ('Reg Gubler' x 'Maxima').
Geenen 2007 NL AFS6615.

JaDi Jack Dempsey. Upright. Single. COROLLA is three quarter flared; opens purple (71A); matures magenta (58B); 16mm (5/8") long x 22mm (7/8") wide. SEPALS are fully up, tips recurved; magenta (58B) upper & lower surfaces; 24mm (15/16) long x 11mm (7/16") wide. TUBE is magenta (58B); 10mm (3/8") long x 10mm (3/8") wide. FOLIAGE: dark green (137A) upper surface; medium green (138A) lower surface. PARENTAGE: 'Roesse Carme' x 'Monique Sleiderink'. Distinguished by bloom & foliage combination.
Geenen 2006 NL AFS6228.

JaDi Kaap Lopez. Upright. Single. COROLLA is half flared; opens red (45A); matures red (45B); 24mm (15/16") long x 27mm (1 1/16") wide. SEPALS are half up, tips recurved up; pink (62C) upper surface; pink (62A) lower surface; 22mm (7/8) long x 11mm (7/16") wide. TUBE is pink (62C); 16mm (5/8") long x 7mm (1/4") wide. FOLIAGE: dark green (137A) upper surface; medium green (138B) lower surface. PARENTAGE: 'Roesse Lupus' x 'Roesse Rhea'. Distinguished by bloom colour.
Geenen 2006 NL AFS6227.

JaDi Kardinaaltetra. Trailer. Single. COROLLA is full flared; opens purple (83C); matures light reddish purple (72D); 24mm (15/16") long x 34mm (1 3/8") wide. SEPALS are fully up, tips recurved; light rose (58D) upper surface; magenta (58B) lower surface; 24mm (15/16) long x 16mm (5/8") wide. TUBE is light rose (58D); 14mm (9/16") long x 7mm (1/4") wide. FOLIAGE: dark green (137A) upper surface; medium green (138A) lower surface. PARENTAGE: ('Regent Gubler' x 'Maxima') x ('Swanley Gem' x 'Monique Sleiderink'). Distinguished by bloom colour & shape.
Geenen 2006 NL AFS6224.

JaDi Labeo Bicolour. Upright. Single. COROLLA: half flared; opens rose (68B); matures light rose (68D); 20mm (3/4") long x 22mm (7/8") wide. SEPALS: fully up, tips recurved; dark reddish purple (60C) upper surface; reddish purple (60D) lower surface; 22mm (7/8") long x 14mm (9/16") wide. TUBE: dark reddish purple (60C); 9mm (5/16") long x 10mm (3/8") wide. FOLIAGE is dark green (137A) upper surface; medium green (137C) lower surface. PARENTAGE: 'Roesse Carme' x 'Cameron Ryle'.
Geenen 2008 NL AFS6914.

JaDi Messingtetra. Upright. Trailer. Single. COROLLA: Full flared; opens violet (90C); matures dark purple (78A); 20mm (3/4") long x 26mm (1") wide. SEPALS: half up, tips recurved up; white (155D) tipped green upper & lower surfaces; 22mm (7/8") long x 12mm (7/16") wide. TUBE: white (155D); medium length & thickness; 8mm (5/16") long x 5mm (3/16") wide. FOLIAGE is dark green (137A) upper surface; medium green (137C) lower surface. PARENTAGE: ('Parasol' x 'Cameron Ryle') x 'Delta's Bride'.
Geenen 2007 NL AFS6618.

JaDi Neontetra. Upright. Single. COROLLA: Three quarter flared; opens reddish purple

(74A); matures reddish purple (74B); 22mm (7/8") long x 20mm (3/4") wide. SEPALS: half up, tips recurved up; rose (68B) tipped green upper & lower surfaces; 24mm (15/16") long x 8mm (5/16") wide. TUBE: rose (68B); medium length & thickness; 11mm (7/16") long x 6mm (1/4") wide. FOLIAGE is dark green (137A) upper surface; medium green (138B) lower surface. PARENTAGE: 'Roesse Carme' x 'Cameron Ryle'.
Geenen 2007 NL AFS6611.

JaDi Netbotia. Upright/Trailer. Single. COROLLA is full flared; opens purple (80A); matures reddish purple (64B); 22mm (7/8") long x 27mm (1 1/16") wide. SEPALS are half up, tips recurved up; dark rose (58C) upper & lower surfaces; 21mm (13/16) long x 7mm (1/4") wide. TUBE is dark rose (58C); 13mm (1/2") long x 5mm (3/16") wide. FOLIAGE: dark green (137A) upper surface; medium green (138B) lower surface. PARENTAGE: ('Regent Gubler' x 'Maxima') x ('Swanley Gem' x 'Monique Sleiderink'). Distinguished by bloom shape.
Geenen 2006 NL AFS6231.

JaDi Piranha. Upright. Single. COROLLA is quarter flared; opens orangy red (39A); matures coral (39B); 8mm (5/16") long x 14mm (9/16") wide. SEPALS are horizontal, tips recurved; cream (11D) upper & lower surfaces; 17mm (5/8) long x 18mm (11/16") wide. TUBE is rose (47C); 15mm (9/16") long x 7mm (1/4") wide. FOLIAGE: dark green (137A) upper surface; medium green (137D) lower surface. PARENTAGE: ('Parasol' x 'Cameron Ryle') x 'Delta's Bride'. Distinguished by bloom colour & shape.
Geenen 2006 NL AFS6226.

JaDi Purperkop. Upright/Trailer. Single. COROLLA is full flared; opens purple (83B); matures reddish purple (80B); 26mm (1") long x 30mm (1 3/16") wide. SEPALS are fully up, tips recurved; light rose (68D) upper surface; rose (68C) lower surface; 26mm (1) long x 16mm (5/8") wide. TUBE is light rose (68D); 12mm (7/16") long x 7mm (1/4") wide. FOLIAGE: dark green (137A) upper surface; medium green (138B) lower surface. PARENTAGE: ('Parasol' x 'Cameron Ryle') x 'Mission Bells'. Distinguished by bloom shape.
Geenen 2006 NL AFS6230.

JaDi Rasbora Tornieri. Upright. Double. COROLLA: three quarter flared; opens violet (84A); matures light purple (78B); 22mm

(7/8") long x 17mm (5/8") wide. SEPALS: half up, tips recurved up; white (155D) upper & lower surfaces; 36mm (1 7/16") long x 17mm (5/8") wide. TUBE: light rose (63D); 20mm (3/4") long x 5mm (3/16") wide. FOLIAGE is dark green (137A) upper surface; medium green (137C) lower surface. PARENTAGE: 'Sofie Michiels' x 'Veenlust'.
Geenen 2008 NL AFS6919.

JaDi Rode Acara. Upright/Trailer. Single. COROLLA is half flared; opens dark red (53A); matures red (53B); 14mm (9/16") long x 16mm (5/8") wide. SEPALS are half down, tips recurved; pale lavender (65D) upper & lower surfaces; 39mm (1 1/2) long x 6mm (1/4") wide. TUBE is pale lavender (65D); 30mm (1 3/16") long x 6mm (1/4") wide. FOLIAGE: dark green (137A) upper surface; medium green (137D) lower surface. PARENTAGE: 'Roesse Lupus' x 'Lye's Unique'. Distinguished by bloom colour.
Geenen 2006 NL AFS6219.

JaDi Rode Badis. Upright. Single. COROLLA is three quarter flared; opens purple (71A); matures dark reddish purple (61A); 20mm (3/4") long x 27mm (1 1/16") wide. SEPALS are fully up, tips recurved; rose (68B) upper & lower surfaces; 17mm (5/8) long x 8mm (5/16") wide. TUBE is rose (68B); 17mm (5/8") long x 6mm (1/4") wide. FOLIAGE: dark green (137A) upper surface; medium green (138B) lower surface. PARENTAGE: 'Roesse Carme' x 'Monique Sleiderink'. Distinguished by bloom & foliage combination.
Geenen 2006 NL AFS6229.

JaDi Rode Rio. Upright. Single. COROLLA is half flared; opens reddish orange (42A); matures red orange (42B); 15mm (9/16") long x 21mm (13/16") wide. SEPALS are horizontal, tips recurved; rose (51C) upper surface; dark rose (51A) lower surface; 24mm (15/16) long x 7mm (1/4") wide. TUBE is rose (51C); 20mm (3/4") long x 5mm (3/16") wide. FOLIAGE: dark green (137A) upper surface; medium green (137D) lower surface. PARENTAGE: 'Roesse Carme' x ('Swanley Gem' x 'Eisvogel'). Distinguished by bloom & foliage combination.
Geenen 2006 NL AFS6221.

JaDi Sumatraan. Trailer. Single. COROLLA is three quarter flared; opens violet (86B); matures reddish purple (72B); 30mm (1 3/16") long x 26mm (1") wide. SEPALS are fully up, tips recurved; magenta (63A) upper & lower surfaces; 34mm (1 3/8) long x

17mm (5/8") wide. TUBE is magenta (63A); 7mm (1/4") long x 4mm (1/8") wide. FOLIAGE: dark green (137A) upper surface; medium green (138A) lower surface. PARENTAGE: 'Regent Gubler' x 'Roesse Rhea'. Distinguished by bloom shape & colour. Geenen 2006 NL AFS6220.

JaDi Tilapia Dolloi. Trailer. Double. COROLLA: three quarter flared; opens purple (83A); matures purple (71A); 25mm (1") long x 21mm (13/16") wide. SEPALS: fully up, tips recurved; light pink (61B) upper & lower surfaces; 26mm (1") long x 14mm (9/16") wide. TUBE: magenta (61C); 12mm (7/16") long x 5mm (3/16") wide. FOLIAGE is dark green (137A) upper surface; medium green (138A) lower surface. PARENTAGE: 'Roesse Apus' x 'Corrie Spoelstra'. Geenen 2008 NL AFS6918.

JaDi Zilverzalm. Upright. Single. COROLLA: Three quarter flared; opens reddish purple (67A); matures magenta (58B); 12mm (7/16") long x 12mm (7/16") wide. SEPALS: fully up, tips reflexed; pale pink (62D) upper & lower surfaces; 15mm (9/16") long x 6mm (1/4") wide. TUBE: pale pink (62D); medium length & thickness; 9mm (3/8") long x 6mm (1/4") wide. FOLIAGE is dark green (137A) upper surface; medium green (137C) lower surface. PARENTAGE: 'Roesse Apus' x 'Diva-Cel'. Geenen 2007 NL AFS6612.

Jako van Steenberghe. Upright/Trailer. Double. COROLLA: half flared, turned under wavy petal margins; opens purple (77A) striped dark reddish purple (61A); matures dark reddish purple (60B) striped magenta (61C); 22mm (7/8") long x 19mm (3/4") wide. PETALOIDS: Same colour as corolla; 14mm (9/16") long x 8mm (5/16") wide. SEPALS: half up, tips recurved up; magenta (58B) upper surface; dark rose (54A) lower surface; 33mm (1 5/16") long x 13mm (1/2") wide. TUBE: white (155B); short & thick; 8mm (5/16") long x 7mm (1/4") wide. STAMENS extend 16mm (5/8") beyond the corolla; dark reddish purple (64A) filaments; dark purple (79A) anthers. PISTIL extends 22mm (7/8") beyond the corolla; magenta (63B) style; light rose (73C) stigma. BUD: bulbous. FOLIAGE: dark green (136B) upper surface; medium green (137D) lower surface. Leaves are 68mm (2 11/16") long x 40mm (1 9/16") wide; ovate shaped, serrulate edges, acute tips, rounded bases. Veins are light grayish red (182D) & olive green (152D), stems are light grayish red (182D), branches are light green (139D).

PARENTAGE: 'Manfried Kleinau' x 'De Boerin'. Lax upright or stiff trailer. Self branching. Makes good basket or upright. Prefers overhead filtered light, cool climate. Best bloom & foliage colour in filtered light. Tested 3 years in Koningshooikt, Belgium. Waanrode 8/9/08. Distinguished by bloom colour combination. Michiels 2009 BE AFS7177.

James Savage. Trailer. Single. COROLLA is quarter flared with smooth petal margins; opens purple 80A) lightly veined magenta (63A) at base, matures dark purple (78A); 24mm (15/16") long x 30mm (1 3/16") wide. SEPALS are horizontal, tips recurved; dark rose (58C) tipped green upper and lower surfaces; 30mm (1 3/16") long x 10mm (3/8") wide. TUBE is dark rose (58C), long and thin; 12mm (1/2") long x 5mm (3/16") wide. STAMENS extend 15mm (5/8") below the corolla; dark rose (58C) filaments, reddish purple (58A) anthers. PISTIL extends 20mm (13/16") below the corolla; rose (63C) style, light pink (65C) stigma. BUD is ovate. FOLIAGE is medium green (137B) upper surface, medium green (138B) lower surface. Leaves are 45mm (1 3/4") long x 30mm (1 3/16") wide, cordate shaped, smooth edges, acute tips and rounded bases. Veins are light green (138C), stems and branches are plum (184C). PARENTAGE: "Found" seedling. Natural trailer. Self branching. Makes good basket. Prefers overhead filtered light. Heat tolerant if shaded. Best bloom colour in filtered light. Tested three years in Worthing, Sussex, England. Distinguished by profuse, self cleaning, blooms. Hobbs 2002 UK AFS4843.

Jan Breydel. Upright/Trailer. Double. COROLLA: half flared, turned under wavy petal margins; opens white (155C) & pale rose (73D); matures white (155B) & pale purple (75D); 28mm (1 1/8") long x 23mm (7/8") wide. PETALOIDS: same colour as corolla; 17mm (5/8") long x 14mm (9/16") wide. SEPALS: horizontal, tips recurved, twisted left & right; white (155B) tipped yellowish green (144B) upper surface; white (155B) tipped yellowish green (144D) lower surface; 32mm (1 1/4") long x 11mm (7/16") wide. TUBE: white (155A) & yellowish green (145A); medium length & thickness; 12mm (7/16") long x 6mm (1/4") wide. STAMENS extend 12mm (7/16") beyond the corolla; light rose (68D) filaments; pink (36A) anthers. PISTIL extends 18mm (11/16") beyond the corolla; white (155C) style; pale pink (62D) stigma. BUD: oblong. FOLIAGE:

medium green (137C) upper surface; light green (138B) lower surface. Leaves are 52mm (1 1/16") long x 23mm (7/8") wide; elliptic shaped, serrulate edges, acute tips, rounded bases. Veins are dark reddish purple (64A), stems are reddish purple (64B), branches are dark grayish red (182A) & medium green (138B). PARENTAGE: 'Sofie Michiels' x 'Pink Marshmallow'. Lax upright or stiff trailer. Self branching. Makes good basket. Prefers overhead filtered light or full sun, cool climate. Best bloom & foliage colour in filtered light. Tested 3 years in Londerzeel, Belgium. Waanrode 8/9/08. Distinguished by white/rose bloom colour combination.
Vandenbussche 2009 BE AFS7081.

Jan L'Espoir. Upright. Single. COROLLA: 3 quarter flared; opens dark rose (67C), white (155C) base; matures reddish purple (70B); 25mm (1") long x 22mm (7/8") wide. SEPALS: fully up, tips reflexed; light pink (55D) tipped light apple green (145B) upper surface; rose (55B) tipped light apple green (145D) lower surface; 31mm (1 1/4") long x 12mm (7/16") wide. TUBE: white (155C); short & thick; 11mm (7/16") long x 8mm (5/16") wide. FOLIAGE is dark green (136A) upper surface; medium green (137B) lower surface. PARENTAGE: 'Rune Peeters' x 'Illusion'.
Michiels 2007 BE AFS6346.

Jan Lokhorst. Upright. Single. COROLLA: quarter flared, smooth petal margins; opens magenta (57C), magenta (58B) base; matures magenta (57B); 15mm (9/16") long 17mm (11/16") wide. SEPALS: half down; tips recurved; pink (51D) upper surface; rose (55B) lower surface; 25mm (1") long x 9mm (3/8") wide. TUBE: rose (51D) striped rose (51B); long, medium thickness; 40mm (1 9/16") long x 7mm (1/4") wide. STAMENS: do not extend below corolla; dark rose (51A) filaments; light yellow (11B) anthers. PISTIL: extends 23mm (15/16") below the corolla; red (52A) style; light pink (38C) stigma. BUD: small, light brown. FOLIAGE: dark green (147A) upper surface; medium green (137C) lower surface. Leaves are 52mm (2 1/16") long x 32mm (1 1/4") wide, ovate shaped, wavy edges, obtuse tips and rounded bases. Light green (146C) veins & stems; light green (146B) branches. PARENTAGE: 'Piper's Vale' x 'Jess'. Tall upright. Self branching. Makes good upright, standard, pyramid or pillar. Prefers overhead filtered light, warm climate. Best bloom colour in filtered light. Best foliage colour in bright light. Tested 3 years in Stadskanaal, The Netherlands. Award of

Merit, VKC-KMTP Aalsmeer, 1996. Distinguished by easy growth and profuse blossoms.
Koerts T. 2004 NL AFS5587.

Jan Meijer. Upright. Double. COROLLA is three quarter flared with smooth petal margins; opens dark rose (71D); matures light purple (74C); 22mm (7/8") long x 16 mm (5/8") wide. SEPALS are horizontal, tips recurved; red (46B) upper surface; red (46C) lower surface; 24mm (15/16") long x 6mm (1/4") wide. TUBE is red (46B), medium length & thickness; 18mm (11/16") long x 8mm (5/16") wide. FOLIAGE: dark green (137A) upper surface; medium green (138B) lower surface. Leaves are 50mm (2") long x 36mm (1 7/16") wide, ovate shaped. PARENTAGE: 'Roesse Carme' x 'Delta's Wonder'. Distinguished by bloom colour.
Comperen 2005 NL AFS5643.

Jan Murray. Upright. Single. COROLLA opens violet (n87a) with rose bengal veining, matures to a lighter violet (bishop's violet n51b); corolla is none flared as is 28mm long x 21mm wide. SEPALS are rose bengal (n57b) on the upper and lower surfaces; sepals are horizontally held with recurved tips, also have a twist and are 45mm long x 15mm wide. TUBE is rose bengal (n57b) and is 12mm long x 6mm wide. PARENTAGE 'Ashtede' x 'Kenny Walking' x 'Frank Lawrence'.
Waving P. 2004 BFS0002.

Jan Pelleboer. Upright. Single. COROLLA is quarter flared with turned up smooth petal margins; opens magenta (63B), edged reddish purple (71B); matures magenta (57B); 12mm (1/2") long x 14mm (9/16") wide. SEPALS are full down, tips recurved; red (52A) tipped green upper surface; red (46D) lower surface; 22mm (7/8") long x 10mm (3/8") wide. TUBE is red (52A); medium length & thick; 10mm (3/8") long x 20mm (13/16") wide. FOLIAGE: dark green (147A) upper surface; yellowish green (146B) lower surface. Leaves are 70mm (2 3/4") long x 50mm (2") wide, ovate shaped. PARENTAGE: 'WALZ Trompet' x 'Gerharda's Panache'. Distinguished by erect triphylla type flowers in racemes at the end of branches.
Koerts T. 2005 NL AFS5778.

Jan Rekers. Upright. Single. COROLLA: unflared; square shaped, smooth petal margins; opens peach (39B) cream (158D) base; matures cream (158C); 12mm (7/16")

227

long x 16mm (5/8") wide. SEPALS: half down, tips reflexed; cream (158C) tipped light green (145D) upper surface; cream (158C) lower surface; 15mm (9/16") long x 6mm (1/4") wide. TUBE: cream (158C); medium length & thickness; 11mm (7/16") long x 6mm (1/4") wide. STAMENS extend 5mm (3/16") beyond the corolla; white (155A) filaments; pale yellow (158B) anthers. PISTIL extends 17mm (5/8") beyond the corolla; cream (158C) style; yellowish white (158A) stigma. BUD: pegtop shape. FOLIAGE: dark green (137A) upper surface; medium green (137C) lower surface. Leaves are 50mm (2") long x 40mm (1 9/16") wide; elliptic shaped, serrulate edges, acute tips, rounded bases. Veins, stems & branches are red. PARENTAGE: 'Eleanor Leytham' x 'Mrs. Lovell Swisher'. Medium upright. Makes good upright or standard. Prefers overhead filtered light. Best bloom & foliage colour in filtered light. Tested 6 years in Hulshorst, The Netherlands. Nominated by NKvF as recommendable cultivar. Distinguished by flower colour, rich flowering.
van den Brink 2009 NL AFS7022.

Jan Tomat. Upright. Double. COROLLA: three quarter flared, turned under smooth petal margins; opens reddish purple (64B), dark rose (54A) base, matures dark reddish purple (64A), dark rose (54B) base; 24mm (15/16") long x 26mm (1") wide. PETALOIDS: Dark rose (64C), dark rose (54A) base; 16mm (5/8") long x 11mm (7/16") wide. SEPALS: half up; tips recurved up; red (53B) upper surface, red (52A) lower surface; 34mm (1 5/16") long x 16mm (5/8") wide. TUBE: red (53C), short & thick; 14mm (9/16") long x 8mm (5/16") wide. STAMENS: extend 23mm (15/16") below the corolla; dark rose (58C) filaments, red (180B) anthers. PISTIL extends 38mm (1 1/2") below the corolla; magenta (58B) style, pale pink (56C) stigma. BUD: round. FOLIAGE: dark green (139A) upper surface, medium green (137C) lower surface. Leaves are 60mm (2 3/8") long x 32mm (1 1/4") wide, ovate shaped, serrulated edges, acute tips and rounded bases. Veins & branches are plum (185B), stems are plum (184C). PARENTAGE: 'Danny Kay' x 'Rohees Queen'. Medium upright. Makes good upright. Prefers overhead filtered light. Best bloom and foliage colour in filtered light. Tested 3 years Itegem, Belgium. Distinguished by bloom colour and shape.
Verret 2003 BE AFS5081.

Jan van Brakel. Upright/Trailer. Single. COROLLA is quarter flared with smooth petal

margins; opens magenta (68A); matures rose (68C); 16mm (5/8") long x 12mm (1/2") wide. SEPALS are horizontal, tips recurved; rose (65A) upper surface, pink (62A) lower surface; 29mm (1 1/8") long x 7mm (1/4") wide. TUBE is pale lavender (65D), medium length and thickness; 16mm (5/8") long x 8mm (5/16") wide. STAMENS extend 14mm (9/16") beyond the corolla; dark rose (58C) filaments, light rose (58D) anthers. PISTIL extends 26mm (1") beyond the corolla; pale pink (62D) style, cream (11D) stigma. BUD is tear drop shaped. FOLIAGE is medium green (137B) upper surface, medium green (137D) lower surface. Leaves are 52mm (2 1/16") long x 26mm (1") wide, ovate shaped, serrated edges, acute tips and obtuse bases. Veins, stems and branches are green. PARENTAGE: 'Lisi' x 'Willy Tamerus'. Lax upright or stiff trailer. Makes good stiff trailer. Prefers overhead filtered light and cool climate. Best bloom colour in filtered light. Tested four years in Göttingen, Germany. Distinguished by bloom and foliage combination.
Strümper 2002 DE AFS4941.

Jan van Bylandt. Upright/Trailer. Single. COROLLA: half flared, turned under wavy petal margins; opens red purple (N79B); matures purple (71A); 14mm (9/16") long x 16mm (5/8") wide. SEPALS: half up, tips recurved up; dark reddish purple (60C) tipped olive green (152D) upper surface; reddish purple (61B) tipped olive green (152D) lower surface; 20mm (3/4") long x 7mm (1/4") wide. TUBE: red (53C); short & thick; 7mm (1/4") long x 5mm (3/16") wide. STAMENS extend 10mm (3/8") beyond the corolla; reddish purple (59B) filaments; dark reddish purple (59A) anthers. PISTIL extends 18mm (11/16") beyond the corolla; dark reddish purple (64A) style; pale purple (70D) stigma. BUD: elongated. FOLIAGE: medium green (137B) upper surface; medium green (138B) lower surface. Leaves are 47mm (1 7/8") long x 22mm (7/8") wide; elliptic shaped, serrate edges, acute tips, rounded bases. Veins are very dark reddish purple (186A), stems are reddish purple (186B), branches are light purple (186C) & medium green (138B). PARENTAGE: 'Pink La Campanella' x 'Maxima'. Lax upright or stiff trailer. Self branching. Makes good upright. Prefers overhead filtered light, cool climate. Best bloom & foliage colour in filtered light. Tested 3 years in Opglabbeek, Belgium. Waanrode 9/20/08. Distinguished by bloom colour.
Cuppens 2009 BE AFS7064.

Jan van Eynatten. Upright/Trailer. Single. COROLLA: half flared, turned under wavy petal margins; opens purple (71A); matures dark reddish purple (61A); 14mm (9/16") long x 17mm (5/8") wide. SEPALS: horizontal, tips reflexed; dark reddish purple (61A) upper surface; magenta (59D) lower surface; 18mm (11/16") long x 8mm (5/16") wide. TUBE: dark reddish purple (60B); short & thick; 9mm (5/16") long x 9mm (5/16") wide. STAMENS extend 11mm (7/16") beyond the corolla; dark reddish purple (61A) filaments; dark purple (79A) anthers. PISTIL extends 25mm (1") beyond the corolla; dark reddish purple (64A) style; light rose (68D) stigma. BUD: bulbous. FOLIAGE: dark green (137A) upper surface; medium green (138B) lower surface. Leaves are 62mm (2 7/16") long x 36mm (1 7/16") wide; ovate shaped, serrulate edges, acute tips, rounded bases. Veins are very dark reddish purple (186A), stems are plum (185C), branches are light plum (184D). PARENTAGE: 'Pink La Campanella' x 'Maxima'. Lax upright or stiff trailer. Self branching. Makes good upright. Prefers overhead filtered light, cool climate. Best bloom & foliage colour in filtered light. Tested 3 years in Opglabbeek, Belgium. Waanrode 9/20/08. Distinguished by bloom colour.
Cuppens 2009 BE AFS7065.

Jan van Goor. Trailer. Single. COROLLA: quarter flared, turned under smooth petal margins; opens magenta (58B); matures magenta (63A); 23mm (7/8") long x 21mm (13/16") wide. SEPALS: horizontal, tips recurved; rose (55B) tipped apple green (144C) upper surface; light rose (58D) tipped light apple green (144C) lower surface; 32mm (1 1/4") long x 12mm (7/16") wide. TUBE: pink (52D); medium length & thickness; 15mm (9/16") long x 7mm (1/4") wide. STAMENS extend 7mm (1/4") beyond the corolla; pink (62A) filaments; dark rose (64C) anthers. PISTIL extends 11mm (7/16") beyond the corolla; rose (65A) style; pale yellow (2D) stigma. BUD: globular. FOLIAGE: dark green (137A) upper surface; medium green (138B) lower surface. Leaves are 39mm (1 1/2") long x 27mm (1 1/16") wide; ovate shaped, serrate edges, acute tips, rounded bases. Veins are grayish red (181C), stems are light grayish red (182C), branches are light grayish red (182C) & medium green (138B). PARENTAGE: 'Pink La Campanella' x 'Amapola'. Natural trailer. Makes good basket. Prefers overhead filtered light, cool climate. Best bloom & foliage colour in filtered light. Tested 4 years in Opglabbeek,

Belgium. Waanrode 5/7/08. Distinguished by bloom colour.
Cuppens 2009 BE AFS7066.

Jan van Heinsberg. Upright/Trailer. Single. COROLLA: half flared, turned under wavy petal margins; opens red (53C); matures red (53C) & dark rose (51A); 21mm (13/16") long x 20mm (3/4") wide. SEPALS: half up, tips recurved up; red (53C) upper surface; red (46D) lower surface; 32mm (1 1/4") long x 9mm (5/16") wide. TUBE: red (53B); medium length & thickness; 20mm (3/4") long x 7mm (1/4") wide. STAMENS extend 13mm (1/2") beyond the corolla; rose (51C) filaments; dark reddish purple (59A) anthers. PISTIL extends 24mm (15/16") beyond the corolla; rose (52B) style; rose (50B) stigma. BUD: elongated. FOLIAGE: dark green (137A) upper surface; medium green (137C) lower surface. Leaves are 64mm (2 1/2") long x 38mm (1 1/2") wide; ovate shaped, serrate edges, acute tips, rounded bases. Veins are greenish yellow (151A), stems are dark purple (N186D), branches are dark red purple (N186C) & light green (138C). PARENTAGE: 'Pink La Campanella' x 'Ben's Ruby'. Lax upright or stiff trailer. Self branching. Makes good basket. Prefers overhead filtered light, cool climate. Best bloom & foliage colour in filtered light. Tested 3 years in Opglabbeek, Belgium. Waanrode 8/9/08. Distinguished by bloom colour.
Cuppens 2009 BE AFS7067.

Jan Vander Kuylen. Upright/Trailer. Double. COROLLA is half flared with turned under wavy petal margins; opens reddish purple (74B), light pink (49C) base; matures reddish purple (61B), light pink (49C) base, edged pale purple (74D); 23mm (15/16") long x 18mm (11/16") wide. SEPALS are horizontal, tips recurved; rose (50B), pale pink (49D) edge & base, tipped light apple green (145C) upper surface; pale pink (49D), rose (50B) edge & base, tipped light apple green (145C) lower surface; 38mm (1 1/2") long x 15mm (9/16") wide. TUBE is light pink (49C); medium length & thickness; 22mm (7/8") long x 6mm (1/4") wide. FOLIAGE: dark green (136A) upper surface; medium green (138B) lower surface. Leaves are 79mm (3 1/8") long x 43mm (1 11/16") wide, ovate shaped. PARENTAGE: 'Sofie Michiels' x 'Diana Wills'. Meise 9-18-04. Distinguished by flower colour.
Michiels 2005 BE AFS5850.

Jan Vandervelpen. Upright/Trailer. Double. COROLLA: half flared, turned under wavy

petal margins; opens magenta (61C) & dark reddish purple (70A) striped light pink (65B); matures dark rose (67C) & reddish purple (71B) striped rose (68B); 20mm (3/4") long x 11mm (7/16") wide. PETALOIDS: dark reddish purple (70A); 9mm (5/16") long x 7mm (1/4") wide. SEPALS: horizontal, tips recurved; white (155B) tipped light apple green (145B) upper surface; white (155B) & rose (68B) tipped light apple green (145B) lower surface; 33mm (1 5/16") long x 12mm (7/16") wide. TUBE: white (155C); medium length & thickness; 12mm (7/16") long x 6mm (1/4") wide. STAMENS extend 9mm (5/16") beyond the corolla; light reddish purple (71C) filaments; purple (71A) anthers. PISTIL extends 16mm (5/8") beyond the corolla; light rose (73C) style; pale yellow (1D) stigma. BUD: elongated. FOLIAGE: dark green (137A) upper surface; medium green (138B) lower surface. Leaves are 46mm (1 13/16") long x 21mm (13/16") wide; ovate shaped, serrulate edges, acute tips, rounded bases. Veins are light apple green (144D), stems are plum (184B), branches are light green (139D) & plum (184B). PARENTAGE: 'Manfried Kleinau' x 'Ann-Elisabeth Fuhrmann'. Lax upright or stiff trailer, small. Makes good upright. Prefers overhead filtered light, cool climate. Best bloom & foliage colour in filtered light. Tested 3 years in Koningshooikt, Belgium. Waanrode 7/5/08, Outstanding. Distinguished by bloom colour combination.
Michiels 2009 BE AFS7178.

Janina Breitmayer. Trailer. Double. COROLLA: full flared, turned up wavy petal margins; opens purple (N80B); matures magenta (71C); 26mm (1") long x 22mm (7/8") wide. PETALOIDS: Same colour as corolla; 17mm (5/8") long x 12mm (7/16") wide. SEPALS: half up, tips recurved up; pale lavender (69D) tipped light apple green (145B) upper surface; pale lavender (69C) tipped light apple green (145B) lower surface; 48mm (1 7/8") long x 20mm (3/4") wide. TUBE: light apple green (144D) striped magenta (59C); short & thick; 10mm (3/8") long x 8mm (5/16") wide. STAMENS extend 30mm (1 3/16") beyond the corolla; rose (61D) filaments; dark reddish purple (70A) anthers. PISTIL extends 55mm (2 3/16") beyond the corolla; pale violet (76D) style; pale purple (75D) stigma. BUD: oblong. FOLIAGE: dark green (137A) upper surface; medium green (138B) lower surface. Leaves are 55mm (2 3/16") long x 32mm (1 1/4") wide; ovate shaped, serrulate edges, acute tips, rounded bases. Veins are greenish

yellow (151A), stems are pale purple (186D), branches are pale purple (186D) & medium green (138B). PARENTAGE: 'Nestor-Berthe Menten' x 'Impulse'. Natural trailer. Self branching. Makes good basket. Prefers overhead filtered light, cool climate. Best bloom & foliage colour in filtered light. Tested 3 years in Koningshooikt, Belgium. Waanrode 7/5/08. Distinguished by bloom colour combination.
Michiels 2009 BE AFS7179.

Janine. Upright/Trailer. Semi Double. COROLLA is half flared; opens white (155D); matures white (155A); 18mm (11/16") long x 23mm (7/8") wide. SEPALS are half down, tips recurved; white (155D), dark rose (55A) base upper surface; white (155A), dark rose (55A) base lower surface; 25mm (1") long x 10mm (3/8") wide. TUBE is dark rose (55A), pink (55C) base; 17mm (5/8") long x 8mm (5/16") wide. FOLIAGE: dark green (147A) upper surface; medium green (147B) lower surface. PARENTAGE: seedling of 'La Campanella'. Distinguished by bloom shape & colour.
Krom 2006 NL AFS6270.

Janine. Upright. Single. COROLLA: unflared, smooth petal margins; opens & matures dark rose (64C); 12mm (1/2") long, 7mm (1/4") wide. SEPALS: horizontal; tips reflexed; white (155D) upper & lower surfaces; 20mm (13/16") long x 5mm (3/16") wide. TUBE: cream (158D); medium length, thin; 13mm (1/2") long x 3mm (1/8") wide. STAMENS: extend 7mm (1/4") below corolla; white (155D) filaments; dark rose (64C) anthers. PISTIL: extends 19mm (3/4") below the corolla; white (155D) style & stigma. BUD: lanceolate. FOLIAGE: medium green (137B) upper surface; medium green (147B) lower surface. Leaves are 60mm (2 3/8") long x 60mm (2 3/8") wide, lanceolate shaped, serrulated edges, acute tips and rounded bases. Medium green (147B) veins; light brown (199C) stems & branches. PARENTAGE: 'Mrs. Lovell Swisher' x 'Northway'. Small upright. Self branching. Makes good standard or miniature. Prefers overhead filtered light. Heat tolerant if shaded. Best bloom and foliage colour in filtered light. Tested 5 years in West Cornwall, England. Distinguished by bloom colour combination.
Negus 2004 UK AFS5633.

Janjopiet Driessen. Upright. Single. COROLLA: half flared, turned under smooth petal margins; opens purple (83A); matures reddish purple (72B) edged purple (83B); 19mm (3/4") long x 29mm (1 1/8") wide. SEPALS: fully up; tips recurved; magenta (71C) tipped light yellow green (150B) upper surface; reddish purple (64B) lower surface; 37mm (1 7/16") long x 13mm (1/2") wide. TUBE: magenta (58B); short & thick; 11mm (7/16") long x 8mm (5/16") wide. STAMENS: extend 18mm (11/16") below the corolla; reddish purple (59B) filaments & anthers. PISTIL extends 35mm (1 3/8") below the corolla; dark reddish purple (61A) style, rose (61D) stigma. BUD: ovate. FOLIAGE: medium green (137B) upper surface; medium green (138B) lower surface. Leaves are 55mm (2 3/16") long x 28mm (1 1/8") wide, elliptic shaped, serrulated edges, acute tips and rounded bases. Veins are light green (138C), stems & branches are orangish brown (174A). PARENTAGE: 'Ampie Bouw' x unknown. Medium upright. Self branching. Makes good upright. Prefers overhead filtered light. Best bloom and foliage colour in filtered light. Tested 3 years in Rummen, Belgium. NBFK certificate at Meise. Distinguished by profuse blooms and bloom shape. Ector 2003 BE AFS5113.

Janne den Breejen. Upright. Single. COROLLA: quarter flared; bell shaped; petal margins; opens rose (52B); matures red (52A); 26mm (1") long x 29mm (1 1/8") wide. SEPALS: horizontal, tips recurved, lightly twisted clockwise; white (155B) blushed rose (61D) upper surface; white (155B) lower surface; 42mm (1 5/8") long x 11mm (7/16") wide. TUBE: white (155A); short & thick; 11mm (7/16") long x 8mm (5/16") wide. STAMENS extend 23mm (7/8") beyond the corolla; pink (62A) filaments; purple (71A) anthers. PISTIL extends 36mm (1 7/16") beyond the corolla; pale pink (63D) style; yellow (10C) stigma. BUD: long. FOLIAGE: dark green (147A) upper surface; medium green (147B) lower surface. Leaves are 47mm (1 7/8") long x 35mm (1 3/8") wide; elliptic shaped, serrate edges, acute tips, rounded bases. Veins, stems & branches are light green. PARENTAGE: 'Estelle Marie' x unknown. Medium upright. Self branching. Makes good upright. Prefers overhead filtered light. Best bloom colour in filtered light. Best foliage colour in bright light. Tested 6 years in Hulshorst, The Netherlands. Distinguished by flower shape & profuse flowers. van den Brink 2009 NL AFS7019.

Janne van Eijk. Upright. Single. COROLLA: 3 quarter flared; opens dark rose (51A); matures rose (51C); 19mm (3/4") long x

21mm (13/16") wide. SEPALS: fully up, tips reflexed; pink (37D) upper surface; rose (51C) lower surface; 21mm (13/16") long x 15mm (9/16") wide. TUBE: peach (37B); short & thick; 10mm (3/8") long x 14mm (9/16") wide. FOLIAGE is dark green (137A) upper surface; medium green (137D) lower surface. PARENTAGE: 'Roesse Carme' x 'Oranje van Os'. van Eijk 2007 NL AFS6568.

Jannie-Adriana. Upright/Trailer. Double. COROLLA is full flared with turned under petal margins; opens & matures pale pink (56D); 35mm (1 3/8") long x 34mm (1 5/16") wide. PETALOIDS: same colour as corolla; 20mm (13/16") long x 22mm (7/8") wide. SEPALS are half up, tips recurved up; pink (52D) upper & lower surfaces; 40mm (1 9/16") long x 19mm (3/4") wide. TUBE is dark rose (54B); medium length & thickness; 22mm (7/8") long x 9mm (3/8") wide. FOLIAGE: dark green (147A) upper surface; medium green (147B) lower surface. Leaves are 55mm (2 3/16") long x 34mm (1 5/16") wide, cordate shaped. PARENTAGE: 'Pink Marshmallow' x 'Guurtje'. Distinguished by flower shape & colour. Krom 2005 NL AFS5838.

Janske Vermeulen. Trailer. Single. COROLLA is quarter flared, bell shaped; opens red (43A); matures red (43A); 21mm (13/16") long x 10mm (3/8") wide. SEPALS are full down, tips recurved; red (46D) upper surface; light orange (41C) lower surface; 26mm (1") long x 8mm (5/16") wide. TUBE is red (46D); 50mm (2") long x 7mm (1/4") wide. FOLIAGE is dark green (147A) upper surface; medium green (147B) lower surface. PARENTAGE: 'Thalia' (Turner) x 'Jaspers Zuurstok'. Nomination by NKVF as Recommendable Cultivar. Distinguished by bloom colour. van Aspert 2006 NL AFS6252.

Jara Cimrman. Upright/Trailer. Double. COROLLA: half flared, turned under wavy petal margins; opens pink (62A) & reddish purple (64B); matures light rose (58D) & reddish purple (61B); 32mm (1 1/4") long x 24mm (15/16") wide. PETALOIDS: Same colour as corolla; 22mm (7/8") long x 14mm (9/16") wide. SEPALS: half up, tips recurved up & horizontal, tips recurved; rose (55B) tipped light apple green (145C) upper surface; rose (52C) tipped light apple green (145C) lower surface; 52mm (2 1/16") long x 16mm (5/8") wide. TUBE: pink (55C); medium length & thickness; 16mm (5/8")

long x 6mm (1/4") wide. STAMENS extend 14mm (9/16") beyond the corolla; dark rose (64C) filaments; pale purple (75C) anthers. PISTIL extends 26mm (1") beyond the corolla; light pink (65B) style; pale yellow (2D) stigma. BUD: elongated. FOLIAGE: dark green (136B) upper surface; medium green (138B) lower surface. Leaves are 73mm (2 7/8") long x 38mm (1 1/2") wide; ovate shaped, serrate edges, acute tips, rounded bases. Veins are pale purple (N186D), stems are dark reddish purple (187B), branches are dark grayish purple (184A) & light green (139D). PARENTAGE: 'Coen Bakker' x 'Rusty Olympic'. Lax upright or stiff trailer. Self branching. Makes good upright. Prefers overhead filtered light, cool climate. Best bloom & foliage colour in filtered light. Tested 3 years in Koningshooikt, Belgium. Waanrode 8/9/08. Distinguished by bloom colour.
Michiels 2009 BE AFS7180.

Jardins Familliaux Liége. Upright. Single. COROLLA: quarter flared; opens purple (80A), pink (62A) base; matures dark purple (78A); 17mm (5/8") long x 19mm (3/4") wide. SEPALS: half up, tips recurved up; dark rose (58C) upper surface; magenta (58B) lower surface; 32mm (1 1/4") long x 9mm (5/16") wide. TUBE: magenta (58B); short, medium thickness; 10mm (3/8") long x 7mm (1/4") wide. FOLIAGE is medium green (146A) upper surface; yellowish green (146C) lower surface. PARENTAGE: 'Jean-Marie Ricard' x unknown.
Ricard 2007 BE AFS6313.

Jarno Vangeneugden. Upright/Trailer. Semi Double. COROLLA is half flared with turned under wavy petal margins; opens purple (82B), rose (51C) base; matures reddish purple (74B); 18mm (11/16") long x 15mm (9/16") wide. PETALOIDS: same colour as corolla; 10mm (3/8") long x 8mm (5/16") wide. SEPALS are horizontal, tips recurved; rose (55B), white (155C) base, tipped pale yellow green (150D) upper & lower surfaces; 29mm (1 1/8") long x 12mm (1/2") wide. TUBE is pink (55C), white (155C) base; long, medium thickness; 27mm (1 1/16") long x 6mm (1/4") wide. FOLIAGE: dark green (135A) upper surface; medium green (138B) lower surface. Leaves are 81mm (3 3/16") long x 35mm (1 3/8") wide, elliptic shaped. PARENTAGE: 'WALZ Harp' x 'Rohees New Millenium'. Meise 8-14-04. Distinguished by flower colour combination.
Geerts L. 2005 BE AFS5727.

Järvsöfäks. Upright/Trailer. Double. COROLLA: half flared, turned under wavy petal margins; opens purple (77A) striped magenta (71C); matures dark reddish purple (64A) striped reddish purple (67A); 28mm (1 1/8") long x 19mm (3/4") wide. PETALOIDS: Same colour as corolla; 15mm (9/16") long x 12mm (7/16") wide. SEPALS: half up, tips recurved up; pink (62B) upper surface; magenta (68A) lower surface; 33mm (1 5/16") long x 13mm (1/2") wide. TUBE: light pink (62C); medium length & thickness; 16mm (5/8") long x 7mm (1/4") wide. STAMENS extend 13mm (1/2") beyond the corolla; purple (71A) filaments; dark purple (79A) anthers. PISTIL extends 19mm (3/4") beyond the corolla; reddish purple (70B) style; pale yellow (1D) stigma. BUD: globular. FOLIAGE: dark green (137A) upper surface; medium green (137D) lower surface. Leaves are 48mm (1 7/8") long x 27mm (1 1/16") wide; ovate shaped, serrate edges, acute tips, rounded bases. Veins are yellowish green (144B), stems are apple green (144C) & light grayish red (182C), branches are light grayish red (182C) & light green (139D). PARENTAGE: 'Manfried Kleinau' x 'Drama Girl'. Lax upright or stiff trailer. Self branching. Makes good basket. Prefers overhead filtered light, cool climate. Best bloom & foliage colour in filtered light. Tested 3 years in Koningshooikt, Belgium. Waanrode 8/9/08. Distinguished by bloom colour & shape.
Michiels 2009 BE AFS7181.

Jasmine. Trailer. Single to Semi Double. COROLLA: half flared, turned under smooth petal margins; opens reddish purple (64B), orange red (35A) at base; matures dark rose (51A); 22mm (7/8") long x 33mm (1 5/16") wide. PETALOIDS: 2 per sepal; same colour as corolla, 20mm (13/16") long x 13mm (1/2") wide. SEPALS: horizontal; tips reflexed; pink (52D) tipped light apple green (145B) upper surface; light orange (41C) lower surface; 29mm (1 1/8") long x 14mm (9/16") wide. TUBE: pale pink (62D) striped pink (62A); medium length & thickness; 25mm (1") long x 7mm (1/4") wide. STAMENS: extend 23mm (15/16") below the corolla; magenta (63A) filaments, dark reddish purple (64A) anthers. PISTIL extends 34mm (1 5/16") below the corolla; dark rose (58C) style, yellow (4A) stigma. BUD: ovate. FOLIAGE: dark green (137A) upper surface; medium green (137D) lower surface. Leaves are 62mm (2 7/16") long x 31mm (1 1/4") wide, elliptic shaped, serrulated edges, acute tips and rounded bases. Veins, stems &

branches are dark reddish purple (59A). PARENTAGE: 'Becky Logan' x unknown. Natural trailer. Self branching. Makes good basket. Prefers full sun. Best bloom and foliage colour in bright light. Tested 3 years in Rummen, Belgium. NBFK certificate at Meise. Distinguished by bloom colour. Ector 2003 BE AFS5112.

Jasper Marnix. Upright. Single. COROLLA: unflared, bell shape; opens & matures dark reddish purple (187B); 8m m (5/16") long x 4mm (1/8") wide. SEPALS: fully up, tips recurved; dark reddish purple (187B) upper & lower surfaces; 16mm (5/8") long x 4mm (1/8") wide. TUBE: plum (185B); 8mm (5/16") long x 4mm (1/8") wide. FOLIAGE is yellowish green (144A) upper surface; light olive green (148B) lower surface. PARENTAGE: ('F. *perscandens*' x 'F. *procumbens*') x ''Lechlade Chinaman' x 'F. *splendens*'). de Boer 2008 NL AFS6854.

Jaspers Druppeltje. Upright. Single. COROLLA: unflared, ovate shape; opens & matures rose (48B); 3mm (1/8") long x 2mm (1/16") wide. SEPALS: full down, tips reflexed; red (45B) upper & lower surfaces; 9 mm (5/16") long x 4mm (1/8") wide. TUBE: red (45B); 16mm (5/8") long x 5mm (3/16") wide. FOLIAGE is medium green (139B) upper surface; medium green (138A) lower surface. PARENTAGE: 'Göttingen' x 'Whiteknight's Pearl'. VKC Aalsmeer, 1995. van Aspert 2008 NL AFS6785.

Jasper's Jeroen. Upright. Single. COROLLA is half flared, bell shaped; opens purple (79C); matures dark reddish purple (60C); 11mm (7/16") long x 11mm (7/16") wide. SEPALS are horizontal, tips recurved; dark reddish purple (60A) upper surface; dark reddish purple (60B) lower surface; 19mm (3/4") long x 8mm (5/16") wide. TUBE is dark reddish purple (60A); 11mm (7/16") long x 9mm (5/16") wide. FOLIAGE is dark green (147A) upper surface; medium green (147B) lower surface. PARENTAGE: ('Toos'' x 'Whiteknight's Amethyst') x 'Prince Syray'. Nomination by NKVF as Recommendable Cultivar. Distinguished by little dark red flowers. van Aspert 2006 NL AFS6251.

Jaspers Ria. Upright. Single. COROLLA: quarter flared, bell shaped; smooth petal margins; opens reddish orange (43C) edged dark rose (64C); matures dark rose (64C); 13mm (1/2") long x 7mm (1/4") wide.

SEPALS: horizontal, tips recurved; pale pink (62D) tipped yellowish green (145A) upper surface; pale pink (62C) lower surface; 16mm (5/8") long x 4mm (1/8") wide. TUBE: pale pink (62D); long, medium thickness; 17mm (5/8") long x 5mm (3/16") wide. STAMENS extend 5mm (3/16") beyond the corolla; light pink (62B) filaments; light yellow (2C) anthers. PISTIL extends 19mm (3/4") beyond the corolla; light pink (62B) style; yellowish white (4D) stigma. BUD: long. FOLIAGE: medium green (137D) upper surface; medium green (137C) lower surface. Leaves are 63mm (2 1/2") long x 35mm (1 3/8") wide; elliptic shaped, wavy edges, acute tips, rounded bases. Veins, stems & branches are light green. PARENTAGE: 'Gerharda's Panache' x 'Pappy Reneé'. Medium upright. Self branching. Makes good upright or standard. Prefers overhead filtered light or full sun. Best bloom colour in bright light. Tested 8 years in Arnhem, The Netherlands. Distinguished by profuse flowers & flower colour combination. van Aspert 2009 NL AFS7038.

Jaspers Triphywhite. Upright. Single. COROLLA: unflared; opens & matures pale pink (49D); 5mm (3/16") long x 4mm (1/8") wide. SEPALS: full down, tips reflexed; light pink (49B) tipped yellow green upper & lower surfaces; 8 mm (5/16") long x 4mm (1/8") wide. TUBE: light pink (49B); 12mm (7/16") long x 7mm (1/4") wide. FOLIAGE is dark green (147A) upper surface; medium green (147B) lower surface. PARENTAGE: 'Göttingen' x unknown. Nomination by NKVF as Recommendable Cultivar. van Aspert 2008 NL AFS6787.

Jaspers Triphyred. Upright. Single. COROLLA: quarter flared, bell shaped; opens & matures orange (40C); 7mm (1/4") long x 9mm (5/16") wide. SEPALS: half down, tips reflexed; red (46D) upper surface; orange (33C) lower surface; 16 mm (5/8") long x 9mm (5/16") wide. TUBE: dark reddish purple (61A) to reddish orange (42A); 45mm (1 3/4") long x 12mm (7/16") wide. FOLIAGE is dark green (147A) upper surface; medium green (147B) lower surface. PARENTAGE: 'Göttingen' x unknown. Medium upright. Nomination by NKVF as Recommendable Cultivar. van Aspert 2008 NL AFS6788.

Jaspers Vlammetje. Upright. Single. COROLLA: quarter flared; opens & matures pink (49A); 4mm (1/8") long x 3mm (1/8") wide. SEPALS: full down, tips reflexed; pink

(48C) upper surface; pale pink (36D) lower surface; 8 mm (5/16") long x 5mm (3/16") wide. TUBE: rose (47D); 18mm (11/16") long x 7mm (1/4") wide. FOLIAGE is dark green (147A) upper surface; medium green (146A) lower surface. PARENTAGE: 'Göttingen' x 'F. *fulgens variegata'*. VKC Aalsmeer, 2001. van Aspert 2008 NL AFS6784.

Jean Canton. Upright/Trailer. Double. COROLLA is fully flared with turned under smooth petal margins; opens reddish purple (66B), pale pink (62D) near TUBE, marbled light pink (62B); matures dark rose (58C) marbled pale rose (73D); 25mm (1") long x 40mm (1 9/16") wide. PETALOIDS: dark rose (58C) marbled pale rose (73D). 20mm (13/16") long x 12mm (1/2") wide. SEPALS are half up, tips recurved up; pale pink (36D) tipped green upper surface; light pink (36C) lower surface; 35mm (1 3/8") long x 12mm (1/2") wide. TUBE is white (155D); long & thin; 20mm (13/16") long x 6mm (1/4") wide. FOLIAGE: medium green (146A) upper surface; yellowish green (146B) lower surface. Leaves are 60mm (2 3/8") long x 35mm (1 3/8") wide, cordate shaped. PARENTAGE: 'Loveable Rascal' x 'Heavenly Hayley'. Distinguished by flared blooms & marbled colour combination. Allsop M. 2005 UK AFS5690.

Jean de Fakteur. Upright. Double. COROLLA is half flared; opens purple (83A), dark rose (67C) base; matures purple (79D); 22mm (7/8") long x 18mm (11/16") wide. PETALOIDS: same colour as corolla; 15mm (9/16") long x 14mm (9/16") wide. SEPALS are horizontal, tips reflexed; reddish purple (67A) upper surface; dark rose (67C) lower surface; 30mm (1 3/16") long x 13mm (1/2") wide. TUBE is reddish purple (67A); 13mm (1/2") long x 7mm (1/4") wide. FOLIAGE: dark green (136B) upper surface; medium green (137B) lower surface. PARENTAGE: 'Roesse Blacky' x 'Cosmopolitan'. Meise 9/17/05. Distinguished by bloom colour combination. Michiels 2006 BE AFS6075.

Jean Mermoz. Upright. Single. COROLLA: unflared, smooth petal margins; opens violet (86B); matures dark purple (78A); 29mm (1 1/8") long x 9mm (3/8") wide. SEPALS: horizontal; tips recurved in a circle, jointed tips; red (45C) upper surface; red (45D) lower surface; 52mm (2 1/16") long x 7mm (1/4") wide. TUBE: red (45C); medium length & thin; 18mm (11/16") long x 4mm (3/16") wide. STAMENS: extend 30-36mm (1 3/16–1

7/16") below corolla; dark rose (64C) filaments, dark reddish purple (64A) anthers. PISTIL: extends 50mm (2") below the corolla, dark rose (64C) style, dark reddish purple (64A) stigma. BUD: lanceolate. FOLIAGE: dark green (147A) upper surface; medium green (147B) lower surface. Leaves are 90mm (3 9/16") long x 45mm (1 3/4") wide, ovate to lanceolate shaped, serrulated edges, acute tips and rounded to acute bases. Veins are light yellowish green & light brown, stems & branches are light brown. PARENTAGE: 'Jules Verne' x unknown. Tall upright. Self branching. Makes good standard. Prefers overhead filtered light and cool climate. Cold weather hardy to -7° C. Best bloom and foliage colour in filtered light. Tested 3 years in Pornic, France. Distinguished by long pistil and flowers; corolla colour. Massé 2003 FR AFS5225.

Jean Taylor. Upright. Double. COROLLA: half flared, smooth petal margins; opens & matures violet (76A) shaded rose at base; 32mm (1 1/4") long x 32mm (1 1/4") wide. PETALOIDS: light purple (80C); 16mm (5/8") long x 13mm (1/2") wide. SEPALS: half up, tips reflexed up; dark rose (54B) upper surface; dark rose (54A) lower surface; 45mm (1 3/4") long x 20mm (3/4") wide. TUBE: dark rose (54B); short & thick; 7mm (1/4") long x 7mm (1/4") wide. STAMENS extend 13mm (1/2") beyond the corolla; dark rose (54A) filaments; dark red (53A) anthers. PISTIL extends 25mm (1") beyond the corolla; dark rose (54A) style; pale yellowish orange (20C) stigma. BUD: oval, pointed. FOLIAGE: medium green (147B) upper surface; light olive green (147C) lower surface. Leaves are 56mm (2 1/4") long x 32mm (1 1/4") wide; elliptic shaped, serrulate edges, acute tips, rounded bases. Veins & stems are red, branches are brown. PARENTAGE: 'Rachael Sinton' x 'Cliantha'. Medium upright. Self branching. Makes good basket, standard or decorative. Prefers overhead filtered light, cool climate. Best bloom & foliage colour in filtered light. Tested 4 years in Ormskirk, Lancashire, England. Distinguished by flower & foliage colour & shape. Sinton 2009 UK AFS7091.

Jean vander Loo. Upright. Single. COROLLA is half flared with smooth petal margins; opens dark reddish purple (61A); matures reddish purple (67A); 17mm (11/16") long x 20mm (13/16") wide. SEPALS are half up, tips reflexed up; pale pink (62D) upper surface; light pink (62B) lower surface; 18mm (11/16") long x 6mm (1/4") wide.

TUBE is yellowish white (4D); medium length and thickness; 11mm (7/16") long x 6mm (1/4") thick. STAMENS extend 17mm (11/16") beyond the corolla; pink (62A) filaments, dark reddish purple (60B) anthers. PISTIL extends 20mm (13/16") beyond the corolla; pale pink (62D) style and stigma. BUD is ovate, pointed. FOLIAGE is dark green (137A) upper surface, medium green (138B) lower surface. Leaves are 57mm (2 1/4") long x 27mm (1 1/16") wide, lanceolate shaped, smooth edges, acute tips and obtuse bases. Veins, stems and branches are red. PARENTAGE: {[('Bon Accord' x 'Bicentennial') x ('Vobeglo' x 'Dancing Flame)] x Rohees Alrami'} x 'Annabel' x 'Annabel'. Small upright. Makes good standard. Prefers overhead filtered light and cool climate. Best bloom colour in filtered light. Tested four years in Duizel, The Netherlands. Distinguished by bloom and foliage combination. Tamerus 2002 NL AFS4984.

Jean-Jacques Arrayet. Upright. Single. COROLLA: quarter flared; opens purple (77A); matures reddish purple (71B); 23mm (7/8") long x 20mm (3/4") wide. SEPALS: horizontal, tips recurved; red (46C) upper & lower surfaces; 46mm (1 13/16") long x 6mm (1/4") wide. TUBE: red (46C); 10 mm (3/8") long x 5mm (3/16") wide. FOLIAGE is dark green (147A) upper surface; medium green (147B) lower surface. PARENTAGE: 'String of Pearls' x 'F. regia reitzii 4514'. Massé 2008 FR AFS6834.

Jean-Marc Huot. Upright. Single. COROLLA is quarter flared with smooth petal margins; opens and matures dark rose (51A);13mm (1/2") long x 13mm (1/2") wide. SEPALS are half down, tips recurved; dark rose (51A) tipped yellowish green (145D)) upper surface; dark rose (51A) lower surface; 19mm (3/4") long x 3.5mm (1/8") wide. TUBE is dark rose (51A); long and thin; 44mm (1 3/4") long x 4mm (3/16") thick. STAMENS extend 0 – 2mm (1/16") beyond the corolla; pink (48D) filaments, yellowish white (4D) anthers. PISTIL extends 6mm (1/4") beyond the corolla; pink (48D) style, yellowish white (4D) stigma. BUD is very long, ovate. FOLIAGE is dark green (147A) upper surface, medium green (147B) lower surface; bronze when young. Leaves are 63mm (2 1/2") long x 40mm (1 9/16") wide, ovate shaped, serrulated edges, acute tips and rounded bases. Veins, stems and branches are light brown. PARENTAGE: 'Checkerboard' x 'Willie Tamerus'. Small upright. Self branching.

Makes good upright. Prefers overhead filtered light and cool climate. Best bloom colour in filtered light. Tested three years in Pornic, France. Distinguished by very long flowers and unique coloured foliage. Massé 2002 FR AFS5013.

Jean-Marie. Upright/Trailer. Semi Double. COROLLA is quarter flared; opens purple (77A); matures dark reddish purple (72A); 21mm (13/16") long x 18mm (11/16") wide. PETALOIDS: purple (77A); 16mm (5/8") long x 10mm (3/8") wide. SEPALS are horizontal, tips recurved; purple (71A) upper surface; dark reddish purple (72A) lower surface; 37mm (1 7/16") long x 8mm (5/16") wide. TUBE is purple (71A); 15mm (9/16") long x 7mm (1/4") wide. FOLIAGE: dark green (136B) upper surface; medium green (138B) lower surface. PARENTAGE: 'Rosea' x 'Katrien Michiels'. Meise 9/17/05. Distinguished by dark bloom colour. Michiels 2006 BE AFS6071.

Jeannine de Koek. Trailer. Double. COROLLA: half flared; opens magenta (63B) & light reddish purple (72C) & matures light reddish purple (73A); 24mm (15/16") long x 22mm (7/8") wide. PETALOIDS: magenta (63B) & light reddish purple (72C); 13mm (1/2") long x 9mm (5/16") wide. SEPALS are half down, tips recurved, twisted; white (155C) tipped pale yellowish green (149D) upper surface & white (155D) tipped pale yellowish green (149D) lower surface; 35mm (1 3/8") long x 14mm (9/16") wide. TUBE is white (155C); medium length & thickness; 14mm (9/16") long x 6mm (1/4") wide. FOLIAGE is dark green (136A) upper surface; medium green (138B) lower surface. PARENTAGE: 'Sam' x 'Monte Rosa'. Michiels 2007 BE AFS6551.

Jef Vander Kuylen. Upright/Trailer. Double. COROLLA is three quarter flared with turned under wavy petal margins; opens & matures white (155C), light pink (65C) base; 14mm (9/16") long x 16mm (5/8") wide. PETALOIDS: same colour as corolla; 18mm (11/16") long x 13mm (1/2") wide. SEPALS are half up, tips recurved up; white (155C) upper & lower surfaces; 37mm (1 9/16") long x 14mm (9/16") wide. TUBE is white (155C); medium length & thickness; 14mm (9/16") long x 6mm (1/4") wide. FOLIAGE: dark green (139A) upper surface; medium green (137D) lower surface. Leaves are 68mm (2 11/16") long x 31mm (1 1/4") wide, ovate shaped. PARENTAGE: 'Sofie Michiels' x

'White Queen'. Meise 9-18-04. Distinguished by white shaded pink flower colour. Michiels 2005 BE AFS5847.

Jegudiel. Upright. Double. COROLLA pale lilac veined red. SEPALS red. Ainsworth 2002 UK.

Jelle Veeman. Upright. Single. COROLLA is quarter flared with smooth petal margins; opens magenta (68A); matures rose (68B); 14mm (9/16") long x 13mm (1/2") wide. SEPALS are horizontal, tips recurved; light pink (65C) tipped green upper & lower surfaces; 19mm (3/4") long x 8mm (3/16") wide. TUBE is light pink (65C); short & thick; 7mm (1/4") long x 7mm (1/4") wide. FOLIAGE: dark green (137A) upper surface; medium green (138A) lower surface. Leaves are 62mm (2 7/16") long x 37mm (1 7/16") wide, ovate shaped. PARENTAGE: 'Roesse Carme' x ('Swanley Gem' x 'Eisvogel'). Distinguished by bloom & foliage combination. Roes 2005 NL AFS5972.

Jennifer Ann Porter. Upright. Single. COROLLA white. SEPALS pink. Reynolds G. 2005 UK.

Jennifer Anne. Single. COROLLA orange. SEPALS cream. Sinton 2005 UK.

Jens Paszehr. Upright/Trailer. Double. COROLLA: three quarter flared, turned under wavy petal margins; opens rose (63C) & reddish purple (72B); matures rose (63B) & reddish purple (71B); 25mm (1") long x 22mm (7/8") wide. PETALOIDS: rose (50B) & dark reddish purple (70A); 14mm (9/16") long x 11mm (7/16") wide. SEPALS: half up, tips recurved up; light pink (65C) tipped apple green (144C) upper surface; pink (62A) tipped apple green (144C) lower surface; 28mm (1 1/8") long x 17mm (5/8") wide. TUBE: light pink (65B); short & thick; 9mm (5/16") long x 6mm (1/4") wide. STAMENS extend 15mm (9/16") beyond the corolla; dark rose (67C) filaments; purple (71A) anthers. PISTIL extends 21mm (13/16") beyond the corolla; rose (68C) style; pale yellow (2D) stigma. BUD: bulbous. FOLIAGE: dark green (137A) upper surface; medium green (137D) lower surface. Leaves are 54mm (2 1/8") long x 32mm (1 1/4") wide; ovate shaped, serrate edges, acute tips, rounded bases. Veins are dark rose (54A), stems are dark rose (54B), branches are very dark reddish purple (186A). PARENTAGE:

'Manfried Kleinau' x 'Carla Knapen'. Lax upright or stiff trailer. Self branching. Makes good basket or upright. Prefers overhead filtered light, cool climate. Best bloom & foliage colour in filtered light. Tested 3 years in Koningshooikt, Belgium. Waanrode 8/9/08. Distinguished by bloom colour combination. Michiels 2009 BE AFS7182.

Jens Weißflog. Upright. Semi Double. COROLLA: three quarter flared; opens purple (77A); matures violet (N77B); 30mm (1 3/16") long x 36mm (1 1/2") wide. SEPALS: horizontal, tips recurved; reddish purple (61B) upper & lower surfaces; 42mm (1 5/8") long x 11mm (7/16") wide. TUBE: dark red (53A); 12mm (7/16") long x 10mm (3/8") wide. FOLIAGE is medium green (137C) upper surface; medium green (138B) lower surface. PARENTAGE: 'Baronin Süsskind' x 'Rohees New Millenium'. Burkhart 2008 DE AFS6862.

Jenthe Peeters. Upright. Double. COROLLA is three quarter flared with turned under wavy petal margins; opens magenta (58B), magenta (51C) base; matures magenta (63B); 24mm (15/16") long x 25mm (1") wide. PETALOIDS: magenta (67B), reddish purple (64B) base; 9mm (3/8") long x 5mm (3/16") wide. SEPALS are horizontal, tips recurved; white (155C), tipped light apple green (145B) upper surface; pale pink (56C), tipped light apple green (145B) lower surface; 33mm (1 5/16") long x 14mm (9/16") wide. TUBE is white (155C); medium length & thickness; 17mm (11/16") long x 6mm (1/4") wide. FOLIAGE: dark green (137A) upper surface; medium green (138A) lower surface. Leaves are 76mm (3") long x 43mm (1 11/16") wide, ovate shaped. PARENTAGE: 'Sofie Michiels' x 'Diana Wills'. Meise 8-14-04. Distinguished by flower colour combination. Michiels 2005 BE AFS5750.

Jeremiel. Upright. Double. COROLLA lavender splashed light pink. SEPALS carmine pink. Ainsworth 2002 UK.

Jesse. Upright. Double. COROLLA: half flared; smooth petal margins; opens & matures white (155A) veined magenta (68A); 20mm (3/4") long x 26mm (1") wide. PETALOIDS: same colour as corolla; 12mm (7/16") long x 10mm (3/8") wide. SEPALS: fully up, tips recurved, tips are lightly twisted; white (155A), pink (62A) base, tipped light green (145D) upper surface; white

(155A), pink (62A) base, lower surface; 36mm (1 7/16") long x 16mm (5/8") wide. TUBE: white (155A) striped green; long, medium thickness; 13mm (1/2") long x 7mm (1/4") wide. STAMENS extend 15mm (9/16") beyond the corolla; light purple (75B) filaments; reddish purple (58A) anthers. PISTIL extends 41mm (1 5/8") beyond the corolla; white (155A) style; light yellow (2C) stigma. BUD: pegtop shape. FOLIAGE: dark green (147A) upper surface; medium green (147B) lower surface. Leaves are 53mm (2 1/8") long x 33mm (1 5/16") wide; elliptic shaped, wavy edges, acute tips, rounded bases. Veins, stems & branches are light green. PARENTAGE: ('Lyn Philip' x 'Bicentennial') x 'Shelly Lynn'. Medium upright. Self branching. Makes good upright. Prefers overhead filtered light. Best bloom & foliage colour in filtered light. Tested 3 years in Stadskanaal, The Netherlands. Distinguished by subtle lilac coloured veining in the corolla.
Koerts T. 2009 NL AFS7053.

Jesse Kennes. Trailer. Double. COROLLA: half flared; opens light purple (N80C) striped white (155C) and matures reddish purple (72B) striped pale lavender (69C); 22mm (7/8") long x 20mm (3/4") wide. PETALOIDS: light purple (N78C) striped white (155C); 13mm (1/2") long x 11mm (7/16") wide. SEPALS are horizontal, tips reflexed; white (155C) tipped light yellowish green (150C) upper surface & pale violet (76D) tipped light yellowish green (150C) lower surface; 36mm (1 7/16") long x 15mm (9/16") wide. TUBE is white (155C); medium length & thickness; 19mm (3/4") long x 8mm (5/16") wide. FOLIAGE is dark green (136B) upper surface; medium green (138B) lower surface. PARENTAGE: 'Vreeni Schleeweiss' x 'Kiss'.
Michiels 2007 BE AFS6530.

Jim Lewark. Upright/Trailer. Single. COROLLA is unflared; opens reddish purple (N74B) splashed white; matures light purple (N74C) splashed white; 19mm (3/4") long x 12mm (1/2") wide. SEPALS are half down, tips reflexed; white (155D) tipped green upper surface; pale purple (76C) lower surface; 22mm (7/8") long x 9mm (3/8") wide. TUBE is white (155D); 19mm (3/4") long x 5mm (3/16") wide. FOLIAGE: medium green (146A) upper surface; yellowish green (146C) lower surface, rosy base. PARENTAGE: 'Campo Victor' x 'Other Fellow'. Distinguished by bright blossoms with variegated petals.
Cooke 2006 USA AFS5989.

Jim Watts. Upright. Single. COROLLA: unflared, bell shaped, smooth petal margins; opens & matures pale pink (62D); 15mm (9/16") long x 12mm (1/2") wide. SEPALS: horizontal; tips recurved; pale pink (62D) upper & lower surfaces; 25mm (1") long x 7mm (1/4") wide. TUBE: pale pink (62D), short & thin; 14mm (9/16") long x 5mm (3/16") wide. STAMENS: extend 15mm (9/16") below the corolla; pale pink (62D) filaments, white (155C) anthers. PISTIL extends 22mm (7/8") below the corolla; pale pink (62D) style, white (155C) stigma. BUD: angular. FOLIAGE: medium green (137D) upper surface, medium green (138B) lower surface. Leaves are 55mm (2 3/16") long x 30mm (1 3/16") wide; ovate shaped, serrulated edges, acute tips and rounded bases. Veins & stems are light green (138C), branches are medium green (138B). PARENTAGE: ('Gooseberry Hill' x 'Whiteknight's Pearl') x 'Margaret brown'. Small upright. Self branching. Makes good upright or pillar. Prefers overhead filtered light. Cold weather hardy to 27° F. Best bloom and foliage colour in filtered light. Tested 4 years Luton, Bedfordshire, England. Distinguished by colour and shape.
Hutchins 2003 UK AFS5080.

Jisp. Trailer. Single. COROLLA is quarter flared; opens & matures dark reddish purple (64A); 15mm (9/16") long x 16mm (5/8") wide. SEPALS are half up, tips reflexed up; dark rose (55A), light pink (55D) base, tipped yellowish green (145A) upper surface; pink (55C) tipped light apple green (145B) lower surface; 17mm (5/8") long x 6mm (1/4") wide. TUBE is light pink (65C), rose (65A) base; 11mm (7/16") long x 7mm (1/4") wide. FOLIAGE: medium green (146A) upper surface; medium green (147B) lower surface. PARENTAGE: seedling of 'Insa'. Distinguished by bloom shape & colour.
Krom 2006 NL AFS6268.

Jizerske Ticho. Upright/Trailer. Double. COROLLA: three quarter flared, turned under wavy petal margins; opens white (155C) striped rose (68B); matures pale lavender (69D) striped rose (67D); 32mm (1 1/4") long x 32mm (1 1/4") wide. PETALOIDS: Same colour as corolla; 22mm (7/8") long x 13mm (1/2") wide. SEPALS: horizontal, tips recurved, twisted left to right; white (155C) tipped apple green (144C) upper surface; pink (55C) tipped apple green (144C) lower surface; 53mm (2 1/8") long x 16mm (5/8") wide. TUBE: white (155C) striped dark rose (55A); short & thick; 13mm (1/2") long x

237

9mm (5/16") wide. STAMENS extend 16mm (5/8") beyond the corolla; light pink (62C) filaments; light reddish purple (73A) anthers. PISTIL extends 43mm (1 11/16") beyond the corolla; light pink (65C) style; pale yellow (1D) stigma. BUD: elongated. FOLIAGE: medium green (137B) upper surface; medium green (137D) lower surface. Leaves are 57mm (2 1/4") long x 32mm (1 1/4") wide; ovate shaped, serrate edges, acute tips, rounded bases. Veins are dark reddish purple (187C), stems are dark red purple (187D), branches are light red purple (185D) & light green (139D). PARENTAGE: 'Coen Bakker' x 'Cotta Fairy'. Lax upright or stiff trailer. Self branching. Makes good basket. Prefers overhead filtered light, cool climate. Best bloom & foliage colour in filtered light. Tested 3 years in Koningshooikt, Belgium. Waanrode 8/9/08. Distinguished by bloom colour combination. Michiels 2009 BE AFS7183.

JJ Roberts. Upright. Single. COROLLA pale mauve. SEPALS pale pink. Reynolds G. 2006 UK.

Jo Kolsters. Upright. Single. COROLLA: half flared, smooth petal margins; opens purple (77A); matures reddish purple (59B); 19mm (3/4") long 18mm (11/16") wide. SEPALS: half down; tips reflexed; light pink (62B) upper surface; pink (62A) lower surface; 27mm (1 1/16") long x 11mm (7/16") wide. TUBE: light pink (62D); medium length & thickness; 17mm (11/16") long x 7mm (1/4") wide. STAMENS: extend 9mm (3/8") below corolla; magenta (59C) filaments; dark reddish purple (59A) anthers. PISTIL: extends 31mm (1 1/4") below the corolla; magenta (59C) style; light yellow (4C) stigma. BUD: elliptic. FOLIAGE: medium green (137C) upper surface; medium green (138B) lower surface. Leaves are 54mm (2 1/8") long x 35mm (1 3/8") wide, ovate shaped, serrulated edges, acute tips and obtuse bases. Green veins, stems & branches. PARENTAGE: 'Orangeblossom' x 'Judy Salome'. Medium upright. Makes good upright or standard. Prefers overhead filtered light and cool climate. Best bloom and foliage colour in filtered light. Tested 4 years in Diessen, The Netherlands. Distinguished by bloom colour. Comperen 2004 NL AFS5565.

Jo Lemaire. Trailer. Double. COROLLA: three quarter flared, petticoat shape; opens violet (87B); matures rose (68B), pale purple

(87D) base; 17mm (5/8") long x 21mm (13/16") wide. PETALOIDS: light purple (78B); 17mm (5/8") long x 15mm (9/16") wide. SEPALS: half down, tips reflexed; rose (68C) tipped green upper surface; pale pink (62D) lower surface; 21mm (13/16") long x 12mm (7/16") wide. TUBE: pink (62A); 25mm (1") long x 12mm (7/16") wide. FOLIAGE is dark green (147A) upper surface; medium green (147B) lower surface. PARENTAGE: 'Lisa' x 'La Campanella'. Tourneur 2008 AFS6852.

Jo Siekman. Upright/Trailer. Semi Double. COROLLA: three quarter flared, SEPALS & petaloids stand out; smooth petal margins; opens dark purple (78A) veined purple (77A), rose (65A) base; matures light purple (78C) base; 18mm (11/16") long x 18mm (11/16") wide. PETALOIDS: dark purple (78A); 18mm (11/16") long x 6mm (1/4") wide. SEPALS: half up, tips recurved up, twisted to the right; magenta (57A) upper & lower surfaces; 35mm (1 3/8") long x 12mm (7/16") wide. TUBE: magenta (57A); medium length & thickness; 15mm (9/16") long x 8mm (5/16") wide. STAMENS extend 14mm (9/16") beyond the corolla; reddish purple (66A) filaments; red (46B) anthers. PISTIL extends 42mm (1 5/8") beyond the corolla; reddish purple (66A) style; red (46B) stigma. BUD: pegtop shape. FOLIAGE: dark green (147A) upper surface; medium green (147B) lower surface. Leaves are 58mm (2 5/16") long x 34mm (1 3/8") wide; cordate shaped, serrate edges, acute tips, rounded bases. Veins, stems & branches are medium green (147B). PARENTAGE: 'Götz-vier' x 'Rita Annie'. Lax upright or stiff trailer. Self branching. Makes good basket. Prefers overhead filtered light. Best bloom colour in filtered light. Tested 3 years in Stadskanaal, The Netherlands. Distinguished by twisted long SEPALS & out-standing growth of SEPALS & petaloids. Koerts T. 2009 NL AFS7045.

Jo Tamerus. Trailer. Semi Double. COROLLA is half flared with smooth petal margins; opens purple (89C); matures purple (80A); 28mm (1 1/8") long x 40mm (1 9/16") wide. SEPALS are half up, tips recurved up; dark red (47A) upper surface, red (47B) lower surface; 37mm (1 7/16") long x 16mm (5/8") wide. TUBE is dark red (47A), long and thin; 20mm (13/16") long x 5mm (3/16") wide. STAMENS extend 20mm (13/16") below the corolla; red (45A) filaments and light pink (62B) anthers. PISTIL extends 34mm (1 3/8") below the corolla; magenta (57B) style and light pink (62B) stigma. BUD is ovate.

FOLIAGE is medium green (137B) on upper surface and medium green (138B) on lower surface. Leaves are 57mm (2 1/4") long x 38mm (1 1/2") wide, ovate shaped, serrated edges, acute tips and rounded bases. Veins, stems and branches are green. PARENTAGE: 'Rohees Mintake' x 'Gillian Althea'. Natural trailer. Self branching. Makes good basket. Prefers overhead filtered light and cool climate. Best bloom colour in filtered light. Tested four years in Duizel, The Netherlands. Distinguished by bloom and foliage combination.
Tamerus 2002 NL AFS4821.

Jo vander Hamsvoord. Upright/Trailer. Semi Double. COROLLA: half flared, smooth petal margins; opens purple (83A); matures purple (77A); 29mm (1 1/8") long x 33mm (1 5/16") wide. SEPALS: fully up; tips recurved; reddish purple (70B) upper surface; dark reddish purple (70A) lower surface; 43mm (1 11/16") long x 10mm (3/8") wide. TUBE: reddish purple (70B); medium length & thickness; 10mm (3/8") long x 7mm (1/4") wide. STAMENS: extend 26mm (1") below corolla; magenta (71C) filaments; purple (71A) anthers. PISTIL: extends 52mm (2 1/16") below the corolla; dark rose (71D) style, light yellow (11C) stigma. BUD: ovate, pointed. FOLIAGE: dark green (137A) upper surface; medium green (137C) lower surface. Leaves are 70mm (2 3/4") long x 38mm (1 1/2") wide, ovate shaped, serrated edges, acute tips and rounded bases. Veins, stems & branches are green. PARENTAGE: 'Dorothy Oosting' x 'Parasol'. Lax upright or stiff trailer. Makes good stiff trailer. Prefers overhead filtered light and cool climate. Best bloom and foliage colour in filtered light. Tested 4 years in Diessen, The Netherlands. Distinguished by bloom & foliage combination.
Comperen 2003 NL AFS5275.

Joan Bell. Upright/Trailer. Single. COROLLA: Unflared; opens dark purple (79A); matures dark purple (79B); 20mm (3/4") long x 17mm (5/8") wide. SEPALS: horizontal, tips recurved; dark reddish purple (59A) upper surface; dark reddish purple (60A) lower surface; 28mm (1 1/8") long x 10mm (3/8") wide. TUBE: dark reddish purple (59A); medium length & thickness; 13mm (1/2") long x 5mm (3/16") wide. FOLIAGE is medium green (137B) upper surface; medium green (137C) lower surface. PARENTAGE: 'F. magellanica alba' x 'Autumnale'.
Bell 2007 UK AFS6397.

Joan Butland. Upright. Semi Double. COROLLA is half flared, bell shaped with smooth petal margins; opens and matures reddish purple (80B), peach (38B) at base; 19mm (3/4") long x 27mm (1 1/16") wide. PETALOIDS are same colour as corolla; 13 mm (1/2") long x 9 mm (3/8") wide. SEPALS are half up, tips recurved up; peach (38B) upper surface, peach (38B) creped lower surface; 19mm (3/4") long x 27mm (1 1/16") wide. TUBE is peach (38B), short with medium thickness; 6mm (1/4") long x 8mm (5/16") wide. STAMENS extend 6mm (1/4") below the corolla; rose (61D) filaments and magenta (68A) anthers. PISTIL extends 25mm (1") below the corolla; rose (68C) style and stigma. BUD is round. FOLIAGE is dark green (137A) on upper surface and yellowish green (144B) on lower surface. Leaves are 35mm (1 3/8") long x 22mm (7/8") wide, cordate shaped, serrulated edges, acute tips and obtuse bases. Veins are yellowish green (144B); stems are yellowish green (144A); branches are redish purple (70B). PARENTAGE: 'Empress of Prussia' x 'Army Nurse'. Small upright. Self branching. Makes good upright or standard. Prefers full sun and warm climate. Best bloom colour in bright light. Tested three years in East Sussex, England. Distinguished by compact blooms, growing clear of foliage.
Lorimer 2002 UK AFS4810.

Joan Jones. Upright. Semi Double. COROLLA opens white with rich pink veining; corolla is three quarter flared and is 26mm long x 40mm wide. SEPALS rich pink on the upper and lower surfaces; sepals are horizontally held with recurved tips and are 36mm long x 13mm wide. TUBE rich pink and is 11mm long x 7mm wide. PARENTAGE 'Mieke Meursing' x 'Shelford'.
Joiner 2006 UK BFS0032.

Joanie. Upright. Semi Double. COROLLA: unflared, smooth petal margins, long with pointed tip; opens purple (90B); matures purple (80A); 24mm (15/16") long x 24mm (15/16") wide. PETALOIDS: Same colour as corolla; 15mm (9/16") long x 10mm (3/8") wide. SEPALS: horizontal, tips recurved; rose (61D) upper & lower surfaces; 30mm (1 3/16") long x 10mm (3/8") wide. TUBE: pink (62A); medium length & thickness; 12mm (7/16") long x 10mm (3/8") wide. STAMENS extend 13mm (1/2") beyond the corolla; reddish purple (66A) filaments; reddish purple (67A) anthers. PISTIL extends 30mm (1 3/16") beyond the corolla; magenta (68A) style; dark rose (67C) stigma. BUD is long.

FOLIAGE is dark green (137A) upper surface; medium green (137D) lower surface. Leaves are 45mm (1 3/4") long x 24mm (15/16") wide; ovate shaped, smooth edges, acute tips, rounded bases. Veins are reddish purple (61B) & light green (139D); stems & branches are dark reddish purple (61A). PARENTAGE: 'Carla Johnson' x 'Margaret Roe'. Small upright. Self branching. Makes good upright. Prefers full sun. Cold weather hardy to -7° C (20° F). Best bloom colour in bright light. Tested 5 years in Puget Sound, Washington, USA. Distinguished by colour combination.
Roach 2009 USA AFS6953.

Joanne McDonald. Upright. Single. COROLLA: half flared, smooth petal margins; opens violet (87B), white throat; matures light purple (78C), white throat; 22mm (7/8") long x 25mm (1") wide. SEPALS: fully up, tips recurved; light apple green (145B)(50%) to light pink (49C)(50%) upper surface; yellowish green (144A)(25%) to light pink (49C)(75%) lower surface; 15mm (9/16") long x 6mm (1/4") wide. TUBE: yellowish green (144A), blushed pink; short, medium thickness; 4mm (1/8") long x 4mm (1/8") wide. STAMENS extend 10mm (3/8") beyond the corolla; pink (49A) filaments; rose (48B) anthers. PISTIL extends 25mm (1") beyond the corolla; light pink (49C) style; white (155A) stigma. BUD: globular. FOLIAGE: dark green (139A) upper surface; medium green (138A) lower surface. Leaves are 37mm (1 7/16") long x 30mm (1 3/16") wide; lanceolate shaped, serrulate edges, acute tips, rounded bases. Veins, stems & branches are green. PARENTAGE: 'Eileen Storey' x 'Estelle Marie'. Small upright. Makes good upright. Prefers overhead filtered light. Cold weather hardy to -3° C (26° F). Best bloom & foliage colour in filtered light. Tested 5 years in Gainsborough, Lincolnshire & Burstwick, East Yorkshire, England. Distinguished by bloom colour, horizontally erect flowers.
Storey 2009 UK AFS7134.

Joan's Flower. Upright. Double. COROLLA: quarter flared; opens violet (85A), pale violet (85D) base; matures pale purple (75C) & light purple (N78C); 27mm (1 1/16") long x 25mm (1") wide. PETALOIDS: pink (62B) base, light violet (84C) & violet (85A); 18mm (1 1/16") long x 11mm (7/16") wide. SEPALS are horizontal, tips recurved, twisted left to right; white (155D) tipped pale yellow green (150D) upper surface; white (155D) & light pink (62C) tipped pale yellow green (150D) lower

surface; 52mm (2 1/16") long x 17mm (5/8") wide. TUBE is white (155D) striped light pink (62C); 17mm (5/8") long x 7mm (1/4") wide. FOLIAGE is dark green (139A) upper surface; medium green (138B) lower surface. PARENTAGE: 'Vreni Schleeweiss' x 'Futura'. Waanrode 8/11/2007.
Geerts L. 2008 BE AFS6730.

Joep Luijten. Upright. Single. COROLLA: half flared, smooth petal margins; opens orange (41B); matures red orange (42B); 15mm (9/16") long x 22mm (7/8") wide. SEPALS are horizontal, tips recurved; light orange (27A) upper surface; pink (37C) lower surface; 24mm (15/16") long x 10mm (3/8") wide. TUBE is light orange (27A); medium length & thickness; 13mm (1/2") long x 10mm (3/8") wide. STAMENS extend 9mm (5/16") beyond the corolla; pink (62B) filaments; pink (62A) anthers. PISTIL extends 24mm (15/16") beyond the corolla; light pink (62C) style; white (155A) stigma. BUD is elongated. FOLIAGE is dark green (137A) upper surface; medium green (138B) lower surface. Leaves are 48mm (1 7/8") long x 32mm (1 1/4") wide, ovate shaped, serrulate edges, acute tips, cordate bases. Veins & stems are green & branches are brown. PARENTAGE: 'Roesse Carme' x 'Oranje van Os'. Medium upright. Makes good upright or standard. Prefers overhead filtered light, cool climate. Best bloom in filtered light. Tested 3 years in Veldhoven, The Netherlands. Distinguished by bloom & foliage colour combinations.
Buiting 2009 NL AFS7260.

Joergen Hahn. Trailer. Double. COROLLA is half flared with turned under wavy petal margins; opens violet (82C), light purple (82D) base; matures violet (75A); 23mm (7/8") long x 19mm (3/4") wide. PETALOIDS: light purple (82D); 16mm (5/8") long x 11mm (7/16") wide. SEPALS are half down, tips recurved; white (155C), tipped light yellowish green (149B) upper surface; white (155C), reddish purple (74A) base, tipped light yellowish green (149B) lower surface; 50mm (2") long x 16mm (5/8") wide. TUBE is white (155C); medium length & thickness; 21mm (13/16") long x 8mm (5/16") wide. FOLIAGE: dark green (136A) upper surface; medium green (138B) lower surface. Leaves are 81mm (3 3/16") long x 48mm (1 7/8") wide, ovate shaped. PARENTAGE: 'Sofie Michiels' x 'Diana Wills'. Meis 3-7-04. Distinguished by colour combination .
Michiels 2005 BE AFS5683.

240

Johan Comperen. Upright/Trailer. Double. COROLLA: three quarter flared, smooth petal margins; opens dark purple (79A); matures dark reddish purple (61A); 20mm (13/16") long x 22mm (7/8") wide. SEPALS: fully up; tips recurved; dark rose (64C) upper surface; reddish purple (64B) lower surface; 26mm (1") long x 10mm (3/8") wide. TUBE: dark rose (64C); medium length & thickness; 7mm (1/4") long x 5mm (3/16") wide. STAMENS: extend 24mm (15/16") below corolla; purple (71A) filaments & anthers. PISTIL: extends 46mm (1 13/16") below the corolla; dark rose (71D) style, light yellow (11C) stigma. BUD: ovate. pointed. FOLIAGE: medium green (137C) upper surface; medium green (137D) lower surface. Leaves are 72mm (2 13/16") long x 35mm (1 3/8") wide, ovate shaped, serrulated edges, acute tips and rounded bases. Veins, stems & branches are green. PARENTAGE: 'Dorothy Oosting' x 'Parasol". Lax upright or stiff trailer. Makes good trailer. Prefers overhead filtered light and cool climate. Best bloom and foliage colour in filtered light. Tested 4 years in Diessen, The Netherlands. Distinguished by bloom colour. Comperen 2003 NL AFS5277.

Johan Raits van Wentz. Upright/Trailer. Single. COROLLA: half flared; opens pale pink (56B) striped dark rose (54B); matures pale pink (56C) striped pink (55C); 21mm (13/16") long x 17mm (5/8") wide. SEPALS: half up, tips recurved up; white (155B) tipped light apple green (145B) upper surface; dark rose (54B) & white (155C) tipped light apple green (145B) lower surface; 28mm (1 1/8") long x 13mm (1/2") wide. TUBE: dark rose (54B) & white (155B); short & thick; 8mm (5/16") long x 7mm (1/4") wide. STAMENS extend 8mm (5/16") beyond the corolla; rose (61D) filaments; rose (64D) anthers. PISTIL extends 22mm (7/8") beyond the corolla; pink (62C) style; light yellow (1C) stigma. BUD: elongated. FOLIAGE: dark green (136B) upper surface; medium green (137D) lower surface. Leaves are 43mm (1 11/16") long x 25mm (1") wide; ovate shaped, serrate edges, acute tips, rounded bases. Veins are dark grayish purple (184A), stems & branches are plum (184C). PARENTAGE: 'Pink La Campanella' x 'Yvette Klessens'. Lax upright or stiff trailer. Self branching. Makes good basket. Prefers overhead filtered light, cool climate. Best bloom & foliage colour in filtered light. Tested 3 years in Opglabbeek, Belgium. Waanrode 9/20/08. Distinguished by bloom colour. Cuppens 2009 BE AFS7068.

Johann Brunner. Upright. Double. COROLLA beetroot purple; corolla is three quarter flared. SEPALS magenta tipped yellowish green on the upper and lower surfaces; sepals are half up with recurved tips. TUBE magenta. PARENTAGE 'Birgit Heinke' x 'Maxima'. Klemm 2008 AT BFS0076.

Johann leprich. Upright. Single. COROLLA beetroot purple; corolla is fully flared. SEPALS dark reddish purple on the upper and lower surfaces; sepals are horizontally held with recurved tips. TUBE dark reddish purple. PARENTAGE 'Schwarzer Stern' x 'Lord Byron'. Klemm 2008 AT BFS0084.

John Bartlett. Single. COROLLA white veined red. SEPALS rose pink. TUBE rose pink. Humphries 2002 UK.

John Green. Upright. Single. COROLLA purple. SEPALS bright red. Wilkinson 2004 UK.

John Quirk. Upright/Trailer. Semi Double. COROLLA is three quarter flared with smooth turned under petal margins; opens purple (81A) splashed light rose (71C); matures light purple (81C) splashed pale rose (73D); 30mm (1 3/16") long x 25mm (1") wide. PETALOIDS are same colour as corolla; 20mm (13/16") long x 8mm (5/16") wide. SEPALS are half twisted counterclockwise, fully up, tips reflexed; rose (55B) tipped green upper surface, dark rose (55A) tipped green lower surface; 50mm (2") long x 14mm (9/16") wide. TUBE is light coral (38A), medium length and thickness; 15mm (5/8") long x 6mm (1/4") wide. STAMENS extend 15mm (5/8") below the corolla; magenta (57A) filaments and pink (36A) anthers. PISTIL extends 30mm (1 3/16") below the corolla; light rose (73B) style and rose (52B) stigma. BUD is large, elongated. FOLIAGE is medium green (146A) on upper surface and yellowish green (146B) on lower surface. Leaves are 65mm (2 9/16") long x 35mm (1 3/8") wide, cordate shaped, serrated edges, acute tips and rounded bases. Veins are green; stems brown; branches are red. PARENTAGE: 'Loveable Rascal' x 'R.A.F.'. Lax upright or stiff trailer. Self branching. Makes good basket or standard. Prefers overhead filtered light and warm climate. Heat tolerant if shaded. Hardy to 32°F. Best bloom colour in bright light. Tested three years in Walthamstow, London, England.

Distinguished by bloom splashed colour contrast.
Allsop 2002 UK AFS4820.

John van Bree. Upright. Double. COROLLA: half flared; opens dark reddish purple (61A); matures dark reddish purple (60A); 20mm (3/4") long x 21mm (13/16") wide. SEPALS: half up, tips recurved up; red (45A) upper & lower surfaces; 20mm (3/4") long x 11mm (7/16") wide. TUBE: red (45A); 10mm (3/8") long x 9mm (5/16") wide. FOLIAGE is dark green (137A) upper surface; medium green (137D) lower surface. PARENTAGE: 'Roesse Carme' x 'Maxima's Baby'.
van Bree 2008 NL AFS6889.

John Wesley. Upright. Double. COROLLA lilac splashed pink. SEPALS light pink.
Ainsworth 2007 UK.

Joke Koek. Upright/Trailer. Double. COROLLA: three quarter flared, wavy petal margins; opens light purple (88C); matures light violet (84B); 26mm (1") long, 18mm (11/16") wide. PETALOIDS: rose (67D); 11mm (7/16") long x 1mm (1/16") wide. SEPALS: twisted, horizontal; tips recurved; rose (55B), tipped yellowish white upper & lower surfaces; 93mm (3 11/16") long x 10mm (3/8") wide. TUBE: pale pink (56D); medium length, thin; 18mm (11/16") long x 5mm (3/16") wide. STAMENS: extend 23mm (15/16") below corolla; dark rose (54B) filaments; rose (51C) anthers. PISTIL: extends 35mm(1 3/8") below the corolla; rose (55B) style; light pink (49C) stigma. BUD: medium TUBE, ovate, pointed. FOLIAGE: yellowish green (146B) upper surface; olive green (148C) lower surface. Leaves are 69mm (2 3/4") long x 31mm (1 1/4") wide, elliptic shaped, serrulated edges, acute tips and rounded bases. Red to light yellow green veins; red stems & branches. PARENTAGE: found seedling. Lax upright or stiff trailer. Self branching. Makes good basket. Prefers overhead filtered light. Best bloom and foliage colour in filtered light. Tested 14 years in Noordwykerhout, The Netherlands. Distinguished by corolla shape and colour.
Franck 2004 NL AFS5603.

Joke vande Pol. Trailer. Double. COROLLA: Three quarter flared; opens violet (84A); matures light violet (84B); 20mm (3/4") long x 22mm (7/8") wide. SEPALS: fully up, tips recurved; pale lavender (65D) upper surface; light pink (65B) lower surface; 26mm (1") long x 11mm (7/16") wide. TUBE: pale lavender (65D); short & thick; 10mm (3/8")

long x 10mm (3/8") wide. FOLIAGE is dark green (137B) upper surface; medium green (138A) lower surface. PARENTAGE: 'Comperen Korhoen' x 'Comperen Lutea'.
Comperen 2007 NL AFS6609.

Jolie Frimousse. Upright. Single. COROLLA: unflared, smooth petal margins; opens purple (71A); matures reddish purple (71B); 17mm (11/16") long x 6mm (1/4") wide. SEPALS: half up; tips recurved up; red (47B) tipped light yellowish green (146D) upper surface; red (47B) lower surface; 28mm (1 1/8") long x 4.5mm (3/16") wide. TUBE: red (47B); medium length, thin; 13mm (1/2") long x 3.5mm (1/8") wide. STAMENS: extend 2-5mm (1/16-3/16") below corolla; pink (48C) filaments; light yellow (12C) anthers. PISTIL: extends 17mm (11/16") below the corolla; dark rose (48A) style; dark red (185A) stigma. BUD: lanceolate. FOLIAGE: medium green (146A) upper surface, yellowish green (146B) lower surface. Leaves are 45mm (1 3/4") long x 17mm (11/16") wide, ovate/lanceolate shaped, serrulated edges, acute tips and rounded bases. Yellowish green veins; yellowish green/light brown stems & branches. PARENTAGE: 'Philippe Boënnec' x 'Mirobolant'. Small upright. Self branching. Makes good upright. Prefers overhead filtered light and cool climate. Best bloom and foliage colour in filtered light. Tested 3 years in Pornic, France. Distinguished by very profuse blooms and sepal colour.
Massé 2004 FR AFS5452.

Jomi Hemschoote. Upright/Trailer. Double. COROLLA: three quarter flared, turned under wavy petal margins; opens reddish purple (59B) striped reddish purple (61B); matures dark rose (59C); 31mm (1 1/4") long x 29mm (1 1/8") wide. PETALOIDS: Same colour as corolla; 22mm (7/8") long x 14mm (9/16") wide. SEPALS: half down, tips recurved; dark reddish purple (60C) upper surface; reddish purple (61B) lower surface; 44mm (1 3/4") long x 18mm (11/16") wide. TUBE: magenta (59D); short & thick; 10mm (3/8") long x 8mm (5/16") wide. STAMENS extend 25mm (1") beyond the corolla; reddish purple (61B) filaments; dark purple (N79A) anthers. PISTIL extends 42mm (1 5/8") beyond the corolla; reddish purple (60D) style; pink (62B) stigma. BUD: elongated. FOLIAGE: dark green (137A) upper surface; medium green (138B) lower surface. Leaves are 64mm (2 1/2") long x 28mm (1 1/8") wide; elliptic shaped, serrate edges, acute tips, rounded bases. Veins are dark red

(185A), stems are plum (185B), branches are plum (184C). PARENTAGE: 'Manfried Kleinau' x 'Jubie-Lin'. Lax upright or stiff trailer. Self branching. Makes good basket. Prefers overhead filtered light, cool climate. Best bloom & foliage colour in filtered light. Tested 3 years in Koningshooikt, Belgium. Waanrode 8/9/08. Distinguished by bloom colour combination.
Michiels 2009 BE AFS7184.

Jon Vincent. Upright/Trailer. Double. COROLLA is three quarter flared, ruffled, with smooth turned under petal margins; opens magenta (58B); matures dark rose (58C), light pink (65B) near TUBE; 20mm (13/16") long x 40mm (2 9/16") wide. PETALOIDS are same colour as corolla; 12mm (1/2") long x 14mm (9/16") wide. SEPALS are half up, tips recurved up; light pink (55D) tipped green upper surface, pink (48D) lower surface; 35mm (1 3/8") long x 12mm (1/2") wide. TUBE is pale pink (36D), medium length and width; 15mm (5/8") long x 6mm (1/4") wide. STAMENS extend 15mm (5/8") below the corolla; rose (55B) filaments and pale tan (159A) anthers. PISTIL extends 35mm (1 3/8") below the corolla; pale pink (56D) style and yellowish white (158A) stigma. BUD is medium, elongated. FOLIAGE is medium green (146A) on upper surface and yellowish green (146B) on lower surface. Leaves are 65mm (2 9/16") long x 40mm (1 9/16") wide, cordate shaped, serrulated edges, acute tips and rounded bases. Veins are green; stems brown; branches are green. PARENTAGE: 'Tantalizing Tracy' x 'Coachman'. Lax upright or stiff trailer. Self branching. Makes good basket or standard. Prefers overhead filtered light and warm climate. Heat tolerant if shaded. Hardy to 32°F. Best bloom colour in bright light. Tested four years in Walthamstow, London, England. Distinguished by profuse blooms and bloom colour.
Allsop 2002 UK AFS4816.

Jonne Comperen. Upright/Trailer. Single. COROLLA: half flared, smooth petal margins; opens dark purple (79A); matures dark reddish purple (59A); 17mm (11/16") long x 17mm (11/16") wide. SEPALS: fully up; tips reflexed; reddish purple (64B) upper surface; reddish purple (61B) lower surface; 24mm (15/16") long x 8mm (5/16") wide. TUBE: reddish purple (64B); medium length & thickness; 17mm (11/16") long x 7mm (1/4") wide. STAMENS: extend 14mm (9/16") below corolla; dark purple (79B) filaments; dark purple (79A) anthers. PISTIL: extends 37mm

(1 7/16") below the corolla; reddish purple (74A) style, cream (11D) stigma. BUD: ovate. FOLIAGE: medium green (137C) upper surface; medium green (138B) lower surface. Leaves are 50mm (2") long x 35mm (1 3/8") wide, cordate shaped, serrulated edges, acute tips and rounded bases. Veins & branches are green, stems are red. PARENTAGE: 'Rohees Metalla' x 'Belle de Spa'. Lax upright or stiff trailer. Makes good stiff trailer. Prefers overhead filtered light and cool climate. Best bloom and foliage colour in filtered light. Tested 4 years in Diessen, The Netherlands. Distinguished by bloom colour.
Comperen 2003 NL AFS5273.

Joop Post. Upright. Semi Double. COROLLA: three quarter flared, saucer flare shape; opens reddish purple (61B); matures magenta (61C); 15mm (9/16") long x 12mm (7/16") wide. PETALOIDS: same colour as corolla; 15mm (9/16") long x 12mm (7/16") wide. SEPALS: half down, tips reflexed; rose (61D) tipped yellowish green (145A) upper surface; rose (61D) lower surface; 19mm (3/4") long x 4mm (1/8") wide. TUBE: white (155A); 9mm (5/16") long x 7mm (1/4") wide. FOLIAGE is dark green (137A) upper surface; medium green (137C) lower surface. PARENTAGE: ('Toos' x 'Whiteknight's Amethyst') x 'Prince Syray'.
van Aspert 2006 NL AFS6795.

Jopie Tamerus. Trailer. Double. COROLLA is three quarter flared with smooth petal margins; opens and matures light pink (65B) veined reddish purple (70B); 27mm (1 1/16") long x 21mm (13/16") wide. SEPALS are half up, tips recurved up; reddish purple (64B) upper surface; reddish purple (67A) lower surface; 47mm (1 7/8") long x 11mm (7/16") wide. TUBE is rose (67D); medium length and thickness; 22mm (7/8") long x 5mm (3/16") thick. STAMENS extend 17mm (11/16") beyond the corolla; purple (83A) filaments, pale purple (75C) anthers. PISTIL extends 40mm (1 9/16") beyond the corolla; reddish purple (74B) style, yellowish white (4D) stigma. BUD is ovate, pointed. FOLIAGE is dark green (137A) upper surface, medium green (138B) lower surface. Leaves are 62mm (2 7/16") long x 37mm (1 7/16") wide, cordate shaped, serrated edges, acute tips and obtuse bases. Veins, stems and branches are green. PARENTAGE: ('Annabel' x 'Annabel') x 'Rohees Metallah'. Natural trailer. Makes good basket. Prefers overhead filtered light and cool climate. Best bloom colour in filtered light. Tested four years in

243

Knegsel, The Netherlands. Distinguished by bloom colour.
Tamerus 2002 NL AFS4994.

Jorge. Upright/Trailer. Double. COROLLA: quarter flared; rosette shaped, smooth petal margins; opens purple (80A); matures reddish purple (72B); 32mm (1 1/4") long x 25mm (1") wide. PETALOIDS: pale purple (81D) spotted light reddish purple (72D); 30mm (1 3/16") long x 24mm (15/16") wide. SEPALS: horizontal, tips recurved, lightly twisted to left & right; magenta (68A) tipped yellowish white (4D) upper surface; magenta (67B) lower surface; 47mm (1 7/8") long x 17mm (5/8") wide. TUBE: pink (62C); medium length & thickness; 27mm (1 1/16") long x 7mm (1/4") wide. STAMENS extend 28mm (1 1/8") beyond the corolla; reddish purple (70B) filaments; dark reddish purple (72A) anthers. PISTIL extends 22mm (7/8") beyond the corolla; magenta (68A) style; pale yellow (2D) stigma. BUD: long. FOLIAGE: dark green (137A) upper surface; medium green (137D) lower surface. Leaves are 60mm (2 3/8") long x 30mm (1 3/16") wide; elliptic shaped, serrate edges, acute tips, rounded bases. Veins, stems & branches are red. PARENTAGE: 'Gerwin van den Brink' x 'White King'. Lax upright or stiff trailer. Makes good basket. Prefers overhead filtered light. Best bloom & foliage colour in bright light. Tested 6 years in Hulshorst, The Netherlands. Nominated by NKvF as recommendable cultivar. Distinguished by large flowers & winter hardiness.
van den Brink 2009 NL AFS7021.

Jorma van Eijk. Upright. Double. COROLLA: half flared, smooth petal margins; opens magenta (63A); matures dark rose (68C); 24mm (15/16") long x 26mm (1") wide. SEPALS: fully up; tips recurved; white (155B) upper & lower surfaces;36mm (1 7/16") long x 20mm (13/16") wide. TUBE: pale yellowish green (149D); medium length & thickness; 10mm (3/8") long x 6mm (1/4") wide. STAMENS: extend 14mm (9/16") below corolla; light pink (65C) filaments, dark rose (58C) anthers. PISTIL: extends 32mm (1 1/4") below the corolla; white (155A) style, light yellow (4C) stigma. BUD: cordate. FOLIAGE: dark green (137A) upper surface; medium green (138B) lower surface. Leaves are 57mm (2 1/4") long x 42mm (1 5/8") wide, ovate shaped, serrated edges, acute tips and rounded bases. Veins, stems & branches are green. PARENTAGE: 'Sofie Michiels' x 'Veenlust'. Medium upright. Makes good standard. Prefers overhead

filtered light and cool climate. Best bloom and foliage colour in filtered light. Tested 4 years in Reusel, The Netherlands. Distinguished by bloom & foliage combination.
van Eijk 2003 NL AFS5258.

Jos De Smedt. Upright/Trailer. Single. COROLLA is quarter flared with turned under wavy petal margins; opens reddish purple (61B), matures dark reddish purple (64A); 18mm (11/16") long x 12 mm (1/2") wide. SEPALS are half down, tips reflexed; red (53B) upper surface, red (50A) lower surface; 17mm (11/16") long x 15mm (5/8") wide. TUBE is red (46C), medium length and thin; 12mm (1/2") long x 3mm (1/8") wide. STAMENS do not extend beyond the corolla; magenta (57B) filaments, brown (176B) anthers. PISTIL does not extend beyond the corolla; magenta (58B) style; pale yellow green (150D) stigma. BUD is round, pointed. FOLIAGE is dark green (139A) upper surface, medium green (137C) lower surface. Leaves are 32mm (1 1/4") long x 18mm (11/16") wide, ovate shaped, serrulated edges, acute tips and rounded bases. Veins are light reddish violet (180A), stems dark red purple (187D), branches are dark grayish purple (183A). PARENTAGE: 'WALZ Harp' x 'Boxberger'. Lax upright or stiff trailer, dwarf growth. Self branching. Makes good upright. Prefers overhead filtered light. Best bloom and foliage colour in filtered light. Tested three years in Koningshooikt and Hoeselt, Belgium. Certificate N.B.F.K. at Meise. Distinguished by bloom shape and dwarf growth.
Michiels 2002 BE AFS4929.

Jos Schilders. Upright. Double. COROLLA: three quarter flared, smooth petal margins; opens purple (77A); matures dark reddish purple (72A); 17mm (11/16") long x 20mm (13/16") wide. SEPALS: fully up; tips recurved; pale pink (62D) upper surface; pink (62A) lower surface; 24mm (15/16") long x 9mm (3/8") wide. TUBE: pale yellow (8D); long & thin; 34mm (1 5/16") long x 5mm (3/16") wide. STAMENS: extend 14mm (9/16") below corolla; light rose (73C) filaments; dark reddish purple (64A) anthers. PISTIL: extends 32mm (1 1/4") below the corolla; pale lavender (65D) style; pale yellow (5D) stigma. BUD: round, pointed. FOLIAGE: dark green (137A) upper surface; medium green (138B) lower surface. Leaves are 64mm (2 1/2") long x 31mm (1 1/4") wide, cordate shaped, serrated edges, acute tips and rounded bases. Veins, stems & branches are red. PARENTAGE: {[('Bon Accord' x 'Bicentennial') x ('Vobeglo' x 'Dancing Flame')] x 'Rohees Alrami'} x 'Allure'. Medium upright. Makes good upright or standard. Prefers overhead filtered light and cool climate. Best bloom and foliage colour in filtered light. Tested 4 years in Duizel, The Netherlands. Distinguished by bloom & foliage combination. Tamerus 2003 NL AFS5308.

Jos-Corn Knevels. Trailer. Double. COROLLA: unflared, opens reddish purple (66A); matures reddish purple (66B); 20mm (13/16") long x 23mm (15/16") wide. SEPALS: half up; tips reflexed up; dark rose (58C) tipped pale yellowish green (149D) upper surface; rose (52B) lower surface; 27mm (1 1/16") long x 14mm (9/16") wide. TUBE: orangish white (159C) striped pink (62A); short, medium thickness; 11mm (7/16") long x 4mm (3/16") wide. STAMENS: extend 6mm (1/4") below corolla; reddish purple (66B) filaments & anthers. PISTIL: extends 10mm (3/8") below the corolla; reddish purple (66B) style & stigma. BUD: rounded. FOLIAGE: medium green (143A) upper surface, light green (143C) lower surface. Leaves are 43mm (1 11/16") long x 29mm (1 1/8") wide, ovate shaped, serrated edges, acute tips and obtuse bases. Light green (143D) veins & stems; Light green (143C) branches. PARENTAGE: 'Kiwi' x 'Danny Kay'. Natural trailer. Self branching. Makes good basket. Heat tolerant if shaded. Best bloom and foliage colour in filtered light. Tested 3 years in Berchem, Belgium. Distinguished by flowers similar to a rose. Janssens 2004 BE AFS5436.

José Tamerus. Upright/Trailer. Double. COROLLA is half flared with smooth petal margins; opens and matures white (155A) with magenta (67B) flame; 22mm (7/8") long x 16mm (5/8") wide. SEPALS are fully up, tips recurved; magenta (67B) upper surface, reddish purple (66B) lower surface; 26mm (1 1/16) long x 12mm (1/2") wide. TUBE is light apple green (145C), medium length and thickness; 14mm (9/16") long x 6mm (1/4") wide. STAMENS extend 12mm (1/2") below the corolla; magenta (67B) filaments and purple (71A) anthers. PISTIL extends 26mm (1 1/16") below the corolla; magenta (67B) style and pink (62A) stigma. BUD is ovate. FOLIAGE is dark green (137A) on upper surface and medium green (137D) on lower surface. Leaves are 78mm (3 1/16") long x 36mm (1 7/16") wide, elliptic shaped, serrated edges, acute tips and obtuse bases.

Veins, stems and branches are green. PARENTAGE: ('Annabel' x 'Annabel') x 'Rohees Metallah'. Lax upright or stiff trailer. Makes good stiff trailer. Prefers overhead filtered light and cool climate. Best bloom colour in filtered light. Tested four years in Duizel, The Netherlands. Distinguished by bloom colour. Tamerus 2002 NL AFS4822.

Joseph Gindl. Upright. Semi Double. COROLLA is quarter flared, globular shaped, with smooth petal margins; opens purple (83B), matures reddish purple (80B); 25mm (1") long x 40mm (1 9/16") wide. SEPALS are half down, tips reflexed; red (45C) upper surface; red (45D) lower surface; 25mm (1") long x 15mm (5/8") wide. TUBE is red (45C); medium length and thickness; 14mm (9/16") long x 9mm (3/8") thick. STAMENS do not extend beyond the corolla; red (45D) filaments, red (45A) anthers. PISTIL extends 10mm (3/8") beyond the corolla; red (45D) style, yellowish orange (22A) stigma. BUD is globular. FOLIAGE is dark green (132A) upper surface, medium green (132C) lower surface. Leaves are 45mm (1 3/4") long x 30mm (1 3/16") wide, ovate shaped, serrated edges, acute tips and rounded bases. Veins and branches are reddish, stems are reddish brown. PARENTAGE: 'Dollar Princess' x 'Red Spider'. Tall upright. Makes good upright. Best bloom colour in bright light. Tested fourteen years in Amstetten, Austria. Distinguished by flower and foliage combination. Gindl 2002 AT AFS5053.

Josephine Margaretha. Upright. Single. COROLLA is quarter flared with turned under petal margins; opens purple (71A); matures reddish purple (61B); 25mm (1") long x 25mm (1") wide. SEPALS are horizontal, tips recurved; dark reddish purple (60A) upper & lower surfaces; 35mm (1 3/8") long x 10mm (3/8") wide. TUBE is dark reddish purple (60A); short, medium thickness; 13mm (1/2") long x 9mm (3/8") wide. FOLIAGE: medium green (146A) & dark green (147A) upper surface; medium green (146A) lower surface. Leaves are 70mm (2 3/4") long x 40mm (1 9/16") wide, ovate shaped. PARENTAGE: seedling of 'Insa' x unknown. Distinguished by foliage colour. Krom 2005 NL AFS5823.

Josie Riley. Upright. Single. COROLLA opens pale lavender blue, matures to pink-lilac; corolla is quarter flared and is 15mm long x 10mm wide SEPALS are pale pink, tipped green on the upper and lower surfaces, matures to a deeper pink; sepals are horizontally held with recurved tips and are 27mm long x 8mm wide. TUBE is pale pink and is 8mm long x 6mm wide. PARENTAGE 'Barbara Windsor' x 'Katrina Thompsen'. This cultivar is capable of producing an excellent show plant. Riley 2005 UK BFS0014.

Joske. Trailer. Semi Double to Double. COROLLA: half flared; opens purple (83B) striped reddish purple (64B), base dark rose (58C) & matures purple (77A) & light reddish purple (72C); 29mm (1 1/8") long x 28mm (1 1/8") wide. PETALOIDS purple (83B) striped reddish purple (64B), base dark rose (58C); 19mm (3/4") long x 15mm (9/16") wide. SEPALS are fully up, tips recurved; rose (61D) upper surface & dark rose (58C) lower surface; 49mm (1 15/16") long x 15mm (9/16") wide. TUBE is rose (54C); medium length & thickness; 15mm (9/16") long x 5mm (3/16") wide. FOLIAGE is dark green (137A) upper surface; medium green (138B) lower surface. PARENTAGE: 'Falco' x 'Illusion'. Michiels 2007 BE AFS6531.

Jo vander Hamsvoord. Upright/Trailer. Semi Double. COROLLA: half flared, smooth petal margins; opens purple (83A); matures purple (77A); 29mm (1 1/8") long x 33mm (1 5/16") wide. SEPALS: fully up; tips recurved; reddish purple (70B) upper surface; dark reddish purple (70A) lower surface; 43mm (1 11/16") long x 10mm (3/8") wide. TUBE: reddish purple (70B); medium length & thickness; 10mm (3/8") long x 7mm (1/4") wide. STAMENS: extend 26mm (1") below corolla; magenta (71C) filaments; purple (71A) anthers. PISTIL: extends 52mm (2 1/16") below the corolla; dark rose (71D) style, light yellow (11C) stigma. BUD: ovate, pointed. FOLIAGE: dark green (137A) upper surface; medium green (137C) lower surface. Leaves are 70mm (2 3/4") long x 38mm (1 1/2") wide, ovate shaped, serrulated edges, acute tips and rounded bases. Veins, stems & branches are green. PARENTAGE: 'Dorothy Oosting' x 'Parasol'. Lax upright or stiff trailer. Makes good stiff trailer. Prefers overhead filtered light and cool climate. Best bloom and foliage colour in filtered light. Tested 4 years in Diessen, The Netherlands. Distinguished by bloom & foliage combination. Comperen 2003 NL AFS5275.

Joyce van Heijst. Upright/Trailer. Single. COROLLA: quarter flared, smooth petal

margins; opens purple (83A); matures dark reddish purple (61A); 21mm (13/16") long x 24mm (15/16") wide. SEPALS: half up; tips reflexed up; reddish purple (71B) upper surface; magenta (63A) lower surface; 39mm (1 9/16") long x 12mm (1/2") wide. TUBE: reddish purple (71B); medium length & thickness; 17mm (11/16") long x 6mm (1/4") wide. STAMENS: extend 21mm (13/16") below corolla; purple (83A) filaments; purple (83C) anthers. PISTIL: extends 41mm (1 5/8") below the corolla; dark reddish purple (72A) style; light reddish purple (72D) stigma. BUD: ovate, pointed. FOLIAGE: medium green (137B) upper surface; medium green (138A) lower surface. Leaves are 61mm (2 7/16") long x 36mm (1 7/16") wide, cordate shaped, serrated edges, acute tips and rounded bases. Veins, stems & branches are red. PARENTAGE: ('Sofie Michiels' x 'Rohees Metallah') x 'Madalyn Drago'. Lax upright or stiff trailer. Makes good stiff trailer. Prefers overhead filtered light and cool climate. Best bloom and foliage colour in filtered light. Tested 4 years in Duizel, The Netherlands. Distinguished by bloom colour. Tamerus 2003 NL AFS5304.

Jubileum Lokhorst. Upright. Double. COROLLA: three quarter flared; smooth petal margins; opens red orange (42C), edged & blushed violet (77B); matures magenta (58B); 18mm (11/16") long x 34mm (1 3/8") wide. PETALOIDS: orange (40C), edged & blushed violet (77B); 19mm (3/4") long x 9mm (5/16") wide. SEPALS: half up, tips recurved up; white (155A) blushed pale green upper surface; white (155D) blushed pink lower surface; 28mm (1 1/8") long x 14mm (9/16") wide. TUBE: white (155D) upper surface; white (155C) lower surface, blushed pink; medium length & thickness; 12mm (7/16") long x 6mm (1/4") wide. STAMENS extend 6mm (1/4") beyond the corolla; light pink (65C) filaments; brownish orange (175A) anthers. PISTIL extends 25mm (1") beyond the corolla; white (155D) style; yellow (11A) stigma. BUD: round. FOLIAGE: dark green (137A) upper surface; light green (138C) lower surface. Leaves are 78mm (3 1/8") long x 40mm (1 9/16") wide; cordate shaped, wavy edges, acute tips, rounded bases. Veins & stems are light green, branches are light brown. PARENTAGE: 'Lyn Philip' x 'Bicentennial'. Tall upright. Self branching. Makes good upright, standard, pyramid or pillar. Prefers full sun. Heat tolerant if shaded. Best bloom & foliage colour in filtered light. Tested 3 years in Stadskanaal,

246

The Netherlands. Distinguished by flower colour combination.
Koerts T. 2009 NL AFS7052.

Judy Salome. Upright/Trailer. Double. COROLLA is three quarter flared with smooth petal margins; opens purple (83B), matures dark reddish purple (72A); 28mm (1 1/8") long x 30mm (1 3/16") wide. SEPALS are fully up, tips reflexed; pale pink (62D) upper and lower surfaces; 27mm (1 1/16") long x 14mm (9/16") wide. TUBE is magenta (63B), medium length and thickness; 6mm (1/4") long x 5mm (3/16") wide. STAMENS extend 21mm (13/16) below the corolla; pink (62A) filaments, magenta (63B) anthers. PISTIL extends 26mm (1") below the corolla; magenta (63B) style, greenish yellow (1B) stigma. BUD is ovate, pointed. FOLIAGE is medium green (137B) upper surface and medium green (137D) lower surface. Leaves are 56mm (2 3/16") long x 39mm (1 9/16") wide, cordate shaped, serrulated edges, acute tips and rounded bases. Veins, stems and branches are green. PARENTAGE: 'Rohees Queen' x ('Annabel' x 'Annabel'). Lax upright or stiff trailer. Makes good stiff trailer. Prefers overhead filtered light and cool climate. Best bloom colour in filtered light. Tested four years in Knegsel, The Netherlands. Distinguished by bloom and foliage combination.
Roes 2002 NL AFS4834.

Juella. Upright/Trailer. Single. COROLLA: quarter flared, square shaped, smooth petal margins; opens purple (77A); matures reddish purple (74A); 19mm (3/4") long x 25mm (1") wide. SEPALS: horizontal; tips reflexed; shiney red (45A) upper surface; red (46C) lower surface; 38mm (1 1/2") long x 12mm (1/2") wide. TUBE: red (45B); medium length & thickness; 12mm(1/2") long x 7mm (1/4") wide. STAMENS: 19mm (3/4") below corolla; magenta (57B) filaments, magenta (63A) anthers. PISTIL: extends 12mm (1/2") below the corolla, reddish purple (66A) style, pale pink (36D) stigma. BUD: ovate. FOLIAGE: light olive green (153C) upper surface; olive green (153D) lower surface. Leaves are 50mm (2") long x 32mm (1 1/4") wide, cordate shaped, serrated edges, acute tips and cordate bases. Veins are green, stems are red & branches are dark red. PARENTAGE: found seedling. Lax upright or stiff trailer. Self branching. Makes good upright. Prefers full sun. Cold weather hardy to 32° F. Best bloom and foliage colour in bright light. Tested 5 years in Birmingham,

England. Distinguished by bright golden leaf; hardy.
Bentley 2003 UK AFS5205.

Jules Linders. Upright/Trailer. Single. COROLLA: half flared, bell shape, wavy petal margins; opens magenta (61C); matures magenta (57C); 27mm (1 1/16") long, 30mm (1 3/16") wide. SEPALS: half up; tips recurved up; pink (48D) tipped greenish yellow (151A) upper surface; light rose (50C), tipped yellowish green (145A) lower surface; 29mm (1 1/8") long x 10mm (3/8") wide. TUBE: light pink (49C), light yellowish green base; long, medium thickness; 39mm (1 9/16") long x 8mm (5/16") wide. STAMENS: extend 2mm (1/16") below corolla; light rose (58D) filaments; pale yellow (13D) anthers. PISTIL: extends 27mm(1 1/16") below the corolla; light rose (58D) style; pale yellowish green (154D) stigma. BUD: long TUBE, ovate, pointed. FOLIAGE: dark green (147A) upper surface; medium green (147B) lower surface. Leaves are 54mm (2 1/8") long x 41mm (1 5/8") wide, ovate shaped, serrulated edges, acute tips and rounded bases. Light yellowish green veins, stems & branches. PARENTAGE: 'Dutch Kingsize' x unknown. Lax upright or stiff trailer. Makes good upright. Prefers overhead filtered light. Heat tolerant if shaded. Best bloom and foliage colour in filtered light. Tested 9 years in Noordwÿkerhout, The Netherlands. Distinguished by flower shape and colour.
Franck 2004 NL AFS5602.

Julia Busschodts. Trailer. Single. COROLLA is quarter flared with turned under wavy petal margins; opens and matures pink (62A) edged violet (75A); 17mm (11/16") long x 14 mm (9/16") wide. SEPALS are half down, tips recurved; light rose (58D) tipped yellowish green (149A) upper surface; rose (52C) lower surface; 36mm (1 7/16") long x 12mm (1/2") wide. TUBE is light pink (65C) striped rose (65A), long with medium thickness; 33mm (1 5/16") long x 6mm (1/4") wide. STAMENS extend 12mm (1/2") beyond the corolla; light rose (58D) filaments, dark tan (164B) anthers. PISTIL extends 7mm (1/4") below the corolla; light rose (58D) style; yellow (11A) stigma. BUD is ovate. FOLIAGE is dark green (137A) upper surface, medium green (138B) lower surface. Leaves are 78mm (3 1/16") long x 38mm (1 1/2") wide, elliptic shaped, serrated edges, acute tips and rounded bases. Veins, stems and branches are orangish brown (174A). PARENTAGE: 'Alda Alders' x 'Wingrove's Mammoth'. Natural trailer. Self branching. Makes good

basket. Prefers overhead filtered light, full sun and cool climate. Best bloom and foliage colour in filtered light. Tested three years in Leopoldsburg, Belgium. Certificate N.B.F.K. at Meise. Distinguished by bloom colour and long TUBE.
Busschodts 2002 BE AFS4912.

Julia de Smedt. Trailer. Double. COROLLA: half flared, turned under wavy petal margins; opens light rose (73B) & purple (N80A); matures light purple (70C) & reddish purple (71B); 26mm (1") long x 17mm (5/8") wide. PETALOIDS: Same colour as corolla; 14mm (9/16") long x 10mm (3/8") wide. SEPALS: half up, tips recurved up; pink (62B) tipped light apple green (145C) upper surface; pale pink (56D) tipped light apple green (145C) lower surface; 38mm (1 1/2") long x 16mm (5/8") wide. TUBE: white (155B); medium length & thickness; 16mm (5/8") long x 6mm (1/4") wide. STAMENS extend 11mm (7/16") beyond the corolla; magenta (63B) filaments; dark reddish purple (64A) anthers. PISTIL extends 24mm (15/16") beyond the corolla; rose (61D) style; pale yellow (1D) stigma. BUD: bulbous. FOLIAGE: dark green (137A) upper surface; medium green (138B) lower surface. Leaves are 57mm (2 1/4") long x 31mm (1 1/4") wide; ovate shaped, serrulate edges, acute tips, rounded bases. Veins are plum (184B), stems are light plum (184D), branches are light green (139D). PARENTAGE: 'Manfried Kleinau' x 'Annabel'. Natural trailer. Self branching. Makes good basket. Prefers overhead filtered light, cool climate. Best bloom & foliage colour in filtered light. Tested 3 years in Koningshooikt, Belgium. Waanrode 8/9/08. Distinguished by bloom colour combination.
Michiels 2009 BE AFS7185.

Julies Gem. Upright. Single. COROLLA: full flared, smooth petal margins; opens violet (94C) & white; matures light purple (81C); 16mm (5/8") long x 13mm (1/2") wide. SEPALS: horizontal, tips recurved; light pink (49C) upper surface; pink (49A) lower surface; 16mm (5/8") long x 7mm (1/4") wide. TUBE: light pink (49C); medium length & thickness; 7mm (1/4") long x 5mm (3/16") wide. STAMENS extend 20mm (3/4") beyond the corolla; rose (52C) filaments; white anthers. PISTIL extends 25mm (1") beyond the corolla; white style; pink (62A) stigma. BUD: ovate. FOLIAGE: medium green (138A) upper surface; medium green (138B) lower surface. Leaves are 38mm (1 1/2") long x 20mm (3/4") wide; ovate shaped, smooth edges, acute tips, rounded bases. Veins,

stems & branches are green. PARENTAGE: 'Julie Ann Goodwin' x 'Julies Jewel'. Small upright. Makes good upright. Prefers overhead filtered light. Best bloom colour in filtered light. Tested 3 years in Stoke-On-Trent, Staffordshire, England. Distinguished by small pale pink & blue flowers in abundance.
Goodwin 2009 UK AFS7244.

Julie's Joy. Upright. Single. COROLLA is fully flared; opens light purple (78B); matures dark rose (67C); 22mm (7/8") long x 27mm (1 1/16") wide. SEPALS are horizontal, tips recurved; light greenish white (157C) upper & lower surface; 22mm (7/8") long x 10mm (3/8") wide. TUBE is light greenish white (157C); 6mm (1/4") long x 6mm (1/4") wide. FOLIAGE: medium green (138A) upper surface; medium green (138B) lower surface. PARENTAGE: 'Julie Ann Goodwin' x 'Nellie Nuttall'. Distinguished by profuse, erect blooms & bloom colour.
Goodwin 2006 UK AFS6045.

June Marie Shaw. Upright. Single. COROLLA opens white; corolla has no flare and is 22mm long x 18mm wide. SEPALS pale pink fades to white at tips on the upper and lower surfaces; sepals are half down with reflexed tips and are 36mm long x 10mm wide. TUBE pale pink and is 7mm long x 5mm wide. PARENTAGE 'Anna Louise' x 'Emma Margaret'. This cultivar one the show bench, nice combination of bloom and leaf colour.
Riley 2007 UK BFS0046.

Jürgen Lerch. Upright. Double. COROLLA: half flared, smooth petal margins; opens purple (71A) blushed red (52A); matures reddish purple (67A); 22mm (7/8") long x 36mm (1 1/2") wide. SEPALS: half up, tips recurved up; red (52A) upper & lower surfaces; 32mm (1 1/4") long x 19mm (3/4") wide. TUBE: red (52A); short, medium thickness; 12mm (7/16") long x 8mm (5/16") wide. STAMENS extend 16mm (3/8") beyond the corolla; red (52A) filaments; red (53B) anthers. PISTIL extends 28mm (1 1/8") beyond the corolla; red (52A) style; pink (52D) stigma. BUD: globular. FOLIAGE: dark green (137A) upper surface; medium green (138B) lower surface. Leaves are 110mm (4 3/8") long x 60mm (2 3/8") wide; elliptic shaped, serrate edges, acute tips, rounded bases. Veins & stems are red, branches are reddish brown. PARENTAGE: 'Rohees Rana' x 'Oscar Lehmeier'. Medium upright. Makes good upright or standard. Prefers full sun, warm climate. Heat tolerant if shaded. Best bloom & foliage colour in bright light. Tested 3 years in Bavaria, Southern Germany. Distinguished by corolla colour & shape. Burkhart 2009 DE AFS7109.

Jurre Comperen. Upright/Trailer. Double. COROLLA: three quarter flared, smooth petal margins; opens purple (83A); matures purple (77A); 27mm (1 1/16") long x 22mm (7/8") wide. SEPALS: half down; tips recurved; reddish purple (61B) upper surface; dark reddish purple (61A) lower surface; 32mm (1 1/4") long x 20mm (13/16") wide. TUBE: reddish purple (61B); medium length & thickness; 10mm (3/8") long x 6mm (1/4") wide. STAMENS: extend 28mm (1 1/8") below corolla; dark reddish purple (72A) filaments; dark purple (79A) anthers. PISTIL: extends 38mm (1 1/2") below the corolla; reddish purple (71B) style; magenta (59D) stigma. BUD: ovate. FOLIAGE: dark green (137A) upper surface; medium green (138B) lower surface. Leaves are 52mm (2 1/16") long x 26mm (1") wide, lanceolate shaped, serrulated edges, acute tips and rounded bases. Veins, stems & branches are red. PARENTAGE: 'Maxima' x 'Die Fledermaus'. Lax upright or stiff trailer. Makes good upright or stiff trailer. Prefers overhead filtered light and cool climate. Best bloom and foliage colour in filtered light. Tested 4 years in Diessen, The Netherlands. Distinguished by bloom colour. Comperen 2003 NL AFS5286.

Jus For You. Upright. Single. COROLLA violet blue, white at base fading pale rose purple. SEPALS white tipped green. TUBE white flushed rose pink. Kirby 2007 UK.

Just Pilk. Single. COROLLA dusky pink. SEPALS creamy white. Reynolds 2009 UK.

K.B.O.F. Upright/Trailer. Double. COROLLA is quarter flared with turned under wavy petal margins; opens magenta (67B); matures rose (64D); 26mm (1 1/16") long x 22mm (7/8") wide. SEPALS are half down, tips reflexed; dark rose (55A), pink (51D) base, upper surface; dark rose (55A) lower surface; 37mm (1 7/16") long x 13mm (1/2") wide. TUBE is pink (51D); long, medium thickness; 24mm (15/16") long x 6mm (1/4") wide. FOLIAGE: dark green (139A) upper surface; medium green (138B) lower surface. Leaves are 69mm (2 3/4") long x 32mm (1 1/4") wide, elliptic shaped. PARENTAGE:

'WALZ Harp' x 'Ting-a-Ling'. Meise 9-18-04. Distinguished by flower colour & shape. Geerts L. 2005 BE AFS5853.

Kaj Nielsen. Trailer. Double. COROLLA is half flared; opens red (52A) with rose (50B) base; matures red (53C); 24mm (15/16") long x 17mm (5/8") wide. PETALOIDS are red (52A) with rose (50B) base; 16mm (5/8") long x 12mm (7/16") wide. SEPALS are horizontal, tips reflexed; rose (55B) tipped apple green (144C) upper surface, and dark rose (54B) tipped apple green (144C) lower surface; 28mm (1 1/8") long x 11mm (7/16") wide. TUBE is light pink (55D); 14mm (9/16") long x 8mm (5/16") wide. FOLIAGE is medium green (138A) upper surface; medium green (138B) lower surface. PARENTAGE: 'Tresco' x 'Danny Kay'. Meise 8/13/05. Distinguished by bloom colour. Michiels 2006 BE AFS6038.

Kaley Jackson. Upright. Single. COROLLA opens dark blue violet (89a), matures to dark pink violet (77a); corolla is quarter flared. SEPALS dark pink red (53c) on the upper and lower surfaces; SEPALS are horizontally held with recurved tips. TUBE dark pink red. PARENTAGE ('Andrew Hadfield' x 'Kobold') x 'Sophie Louise'. Wilkinson 2009 UK BFS0139.

Kalien Kerkhofs. Upright/Trailer. Semi Double. COROLLA is half flared; opens reddish purple (71B), blotched magenta (59C); matures light reddish purple (72C); 29mm (1 1/8") long x 24mm (15/16") wide. PETALOIDS: purple (71A) blotched magenta (59C); 18mm (11/16") long x 16mm (5/8") wide. SEPALS are horizontal, tips reflexed; dark reddish purple (61A) upper surface; reddish purple (61B) lower surface; 19mm (3/4") long x 13mm (1/2") wide. TUBE is magenta (59C); 13mm (1/2") long x 6mm (1/4") wide. FOLIAGE: dark green (139A) upper surface; medium green (137B) lower surface. PARENTAGE: 'Ben's Ruby' x 'Onbekend'. Meise 8/13/05. Distinguished by bloom colour. Baeten 2006 BE AFS6011.

Kandersteg. Upright/Trailer. Double. COROLLA: three quarter flared, turned under wavy petal margins; opens dark reddish purple (72A) & purple (83B); matures dark reddish purple (70A); 26mm (1") long x 22mm (7/8") wide. PETALOIDS: Same colour as corolla; 19mm (3/4") long x 15mm (9/16") wide. SEPALS: half up, tips recurved up & horizontal, tips recurved; light reddish purple

(72D) tipped light apple green (144D) upper surface; light reddish purple (73A) tipped light apple green (144D) lower surface; 31mm (1 1/4") long x 19mm (3/4") wide. TUBE: white (155C) & light rose (73B); medium length & thickness; 23mm (7/8") long x 6mm (1/4") wide. STAMENS extend 14mm (9/16") beyond the corolla; dark reddish purple (64A) filaments; dark purple (79A) anthers. PISTIL extends 23mm (7/8") beyond the corolla; violet (77C) style; pale purple (75D) stigma. BUD: bulbous. FOLIAGE: dark green (136B) upper surface; medium green (138B) lower surface. Leaves are 93mm (3 11/16") long x 44mm (1 3/4") wide; ovate shaped, serrulate edges, acute tips, rounded bases. Veins are dark grayish purple (184A), stems are very dark reddish purple (186A), branches are plum (185C). PARENTAGE: 'Manfried Kleinau' x 'Blue Ice'. Lax upright or stiff trailer. Self branching. Makes good basket. Prefers overhead filtered light, cool climate. Best bloom & foliage colour in filtered light. Tested 3 years in Koningshooikt, Belgium. Waanrode 7/5/08, Outstanding. Distinguished by bloom colour combination.
Michiels 2009 BE AFS7186.

Kapsalon Nancy. Trailer. Semi Double. COROLLA is half flared with turned under smooth petal margins; opens violet (77B) edged light purple (78B); matures reddish purple (70B) edged dark purple (78A); 19mm (3/4") long x 34 mm (1 3/8") wide. PETALOIDS: Two per sepal, same colour as corolla; 12mm (1/2") x 4mm (3/16"). SEPALS are half up, tips reflexed up; light rose (58D) tipped light green (142A) upper surface; rose (51B) lower surface; 25mm (1") long x 14mm (9/16") wide. TUBE is dark rose (58C), medium length and thickness; 10mm (3/8") long x 6mm (1/4") wide. STAMENS extend 7mm (1/4") beyond the corolla; rose (61D) filaments, light pink (62B) anthers. PISTIL extends 22mm (7/8") below the corolla; rose (63C) style; light yellow (4B) stigma. BUD is round. FOLIAGE is dark green (137A) upper surface, medium green (137D) lower surface. Leaves are 65mm (2 9/16") long x 35mm (1 3/8") wide, ovate shaped, serrated edges, acute tips and cordate bases. Veins are medium green (138A); stems and branches are dark grayish purple (184A). PARENTAGE: 'De Brouwer' x 'Bacchusgilde'. Natural trailer. Self branching. Makes good basket. Prefers overhead filtered light and cool climate. Best bloom and foliage colour in filtered light. Tested four years in Leopoldsburg, Belgium. Certificate N.B.F.K.

at Meise. Distinguished by profuse blooms, bloom colour and shape.
Busschodts 2002 BE AFS4913.

Kara Faye. Trailer. Single. COROLLA is dark red; corolla is quarter flared and is 21mm long x 14mm wide. SEPALS are rosy red on the upper and lower surface; sepals are half down with recurved tips and are 35mm long x 7mm wide. TUBE is rosy red and is 18mm long x 5mm wide. PARENTAGE 'Coachman' x 'Unknown'. This cultivar is a very vigorous self-branching grower early in the season, and requires plenty of root space, found to be hardy in Derbyshire, looks nice over hanging a retaining wall.
Parkes T. 2005 UK BFS0012.

Kareeloven. Upright. Double. COROLLA: half flared; opens light reddish purple (72D) & light purple (N78D); matures dark rose (71D); 25mm (1") long x 22mm (7/8") wide. PETALOIDS: light reddish purple (72D) & light purple (N78C); 10mm (3/8") long x 6mm (1/4") wide. SEPALS: horizontal, tips reflexed; pale rose (73D) tipped apple green (144C) upper surface; rose (63C) tipped apple green (144C) lower surface; 27mm (1 1/16") long x 13mm (1/2") wide. TUBE: white (155C); medium length & thickness; 17mm (5/8") long x 5mm (3/16") wide. FOLIAGE is dark green (136A) upper surface; medium green (138B) lower surface. PARENTAGE: 'Leen Vander Kuylen' x 'Charlotte Martens'.
Michiels 2007 BE AFS6347.

Karen. Upright/Trailer. Single. COROLLA: three quarter flared; opens & matures magenta (57C); 32mm (1 1/4") long x 24mm (15/16") wide. SEPALS: fully up; tips recurved; white (155A) upper & lower surfaces; 40mm(1 9/16") long x 7mm (1/4") wide. TUBE: white (155A); medium length & thickness; 18mm (11/16") long x 7mm (1/4") wide. STAMENS: extend 15mm (9/16) below corolla; dark grayish purple (184A) filaments & anthers. PISTIL: extends 37mm (1 7/16") below the corolla, white (155A) style, yellow (2A) stigma. BUD: ovate. FOLIAGE: medium green (138A) upper surface; medium green (138B) lower surface. Leaves are 63mm (2 1/2") long x 40mm (1 9/16") wide, ovate shaped, serrated edges, acute tips and rounded bases. Veins & branches are green; stems are green & brown. PARENTAGE: 'Pia' x 'Maresi'. Lax upright or stiff trailer. Makes good basket. Prefers overhead filtered light. Heat tolerant if shaded. Best bloom and foliage colour in bright light. Tested 5 years in Göttingen, Germany. Distinguished by magenta corolla and pure white SEPALS colour combination. Strümper 2003 DE AFS5159.

Kärnten. Upright. Double. COROLLA opens purple, matures to rich purple; corolla is three quarter flared. SEPALS rhodamine pink on the upper and lower surfaces; sepals are horizontally held with recurved tips. TUBE rhodamine pink. PARENTAGE 'Föhnhimmel' x 'Cheltenham'. Klemm 2008 AT BFS0081.

Kari and Knut Lerstoel. Trailer. Double. COROLLA: three quarter flared, turned under wavy petal margins; opens purple (77A); matures reddish purple (67A); 24mm (15/16") long x 17mm (5/8") wide. PETALOIDS: Same colour as corolla; 14mm (9/16") long x 10mm (3/8") wide. SEPALS: half up, tips recurved up & horizontal, tips recurved; pale pink (56C) tipped light yellowish green (150C) upper surface; rose (N57C) tipped light yellowish green (150C) lower surface; 36mm (1 7/16") long x 19mm (3/4") wide. TUBE: white (155C); long & thin; 22mm (7/8") long x 5mm (3/16") wide. STAMENS extend 15mm (9/16") beyond the corolla; reddish purple (70B) filaments; purple (71A) anthers. PISTIL extends 27mm (1 1/16") beyond the corolla; light purple (70C) style; pale yellow (2D) stigma. BUD: bulbous. FOLIAGE: dark green (139A) upper surface; medium green (137D) lower surface. Leaves are 74mm (2 15/16") long x 36mm (1 7/16") wide; ovate shaped, serrate edges, acute tips, rounded bases. Veins are dark purple (N79A), stems are dark purple (N79B), branches are dark grayish purple (184A) & light green (138C). PARENTAGE: 'Manfried Kleinau' x 'Corsage'. Natural trailer. Self branching. Makes good basket. Prefers overhead filtered light, cool climate. Best bloom & foliage colour in filtered light. Tested 3 years in Koningshooikt, Belgium. Waanrode 7/5/08, Outstanding. Distinguished by bloom colour combination. Michiels 2009 BE AFS7187.

Kartina. Trailer. Single. COROLLA is quarter flared; opens red purple (N79C), dark rose (51A) base; matures reddish purple (64B), magenta (71C) base; 17mm (5/8") long x 20mm (3/4") wide. SEPALS are horizontal, tips reflexed; red (53D) upper surface; dark rose (51A) lower surface; 25mm (1") long x 10mm (3/8") wide. TUBE is red (53B); medium length and thickness; 16mm (5/8") long x 6mm (1/4") wide. FOLIAGE is medium green (137B) upper surface; medium green

(138B) lower surface. PARENTAGE: 'Checkerboard' x 'Lassie'. Wagemans 2007 BE AFS6427.

Kasteel Geldrop. Upright/Trailer. Single. COROLLA: half flared, smooth petal margins; opens orangy red (39A); matures rose (47C); 15mm (9/16") long x 10mm (3/8") wide. SEPALS: half up; tips reflexed up; pink (48C) upper surface; reddish purple (43C) lower surface; 42mm (1 5/8") long x 8mm (5/16") wide. TUBE: pink (48C); medium length & thickness; 24mm (15/16") long x 10mm (3/8") wide. STAMENS: extend 20mm (13/16") below corolla; red orange (40A) filaments; peach (33D) anthers. PISTIL: extends 44mm (1 3/4") below the corolla; light orange (40D) style, light yellowish orange (19C) stigma. BUD: long, ovate. FOLIAGE: yellowish green – light apple green(144A-145B) upper surface; medium green (138B) lower surface. Leaves are 57mm (2 1/4") long x 42mm (1 5/8") wide, cordate shaped, serrated edges, acute tips and obtuse bases. Veins, stems & branches are green. PARENTAGE: Sport of 'Orange Drops'. Lax upright or stiff trailer. Makes good stiff trailer. Prefers overhead filtered light and cool climate. Best bloom and foliage colour in filtered light. Tested 4 years in Leende, The Netherlands. Distinguished by bloom & foliage combination. Liebregts 2003 NL AFS5244.

Kasteel Rullingen. Upright. Single to Semi Double. COROLLA is half flared with turned under smooth petal margins; opens dark reddish purple (187C), magenta (59D) at base; matures dark reddish purple (59A); 13mm (1/2") long x 19mm (3/4") wide. SEPALS are fully up, tips recurved; dark red (46A) upper and lower surfaces; 31mm (1 1/4") long x 14mm (9/16") wide. TUBE is dark red (46A); medium length and thickness; 15mm (5/8") long x 8mm (5/16") wide. STAMENS extend 20mm (13/16") beyond the corolla; reddish purple (58A) filaments; plum (183B) anthers. PISTIL extends 32mm (1 1/4") beyond the corolla; magenta (58B) style, light orange (29B) stigma. BUD is ovate. FOLIAGE is dark green (137A) upper surface, medium green (137C) lower surface. Leaves are 73mm (2 7/8") long x 36mm (1 7/16") wide, elliptic shaped, serrulated edges, acute tips and rounded bases. Veins and stems are medium green (138B), branches are dark grayish purple (184A). PARENTAGE: 'Rohees New Millennium' x 'Danny Boy'. Medium upright. Self branching. Makes good upright. Prefers

overhead filtered light. Best bloom and foliage colour in filtered light. Tested three years in Hoeselt, Belgium. Certificate N.B.F.K. at Meise. Distinguished by bloom colour.
Wagemans 2002 BE AFS4974.

Kasteel Ter Motten. Trailer. Single. COROLLA: quarter flared, turned under smooth petal margins; opens & matures reddish purple (59B); 14mm (9/16") long x 17mm (11/16") wide. SEPALS: half down; tips recurved; dark rose (51A) tipped light green (143B) upper surface; rose (52B) lower surface; 31mm(1 1/4") long x 10mm (3/8") wide. TUBE: dark rose (48A); medium length & thickness; 18mm (11/16") long x 4mm (3/16") wide. STAMENS: extend 4mm (3/16") below the corolla; pale pink (62D) filaments, pale yellow (1D) anthers. PISTIL extends 19mm (3/4") below the corolla; light rose (58D) style, light yellow (2B) stigma. BUD: ovate. FOLIAGE: dark green (139A) upper surface; medium green (137C) lower surface. Leaves are 53mm (2 1/16") long x 38mm (1 1/2") wide, cordate shaped, serrulated edges, acute tips and cordate bases. Veins, stems & branches are plum (183B). PARENTAGE: 'Purperklokje' x unknown. Natural trailer. Self branching. Makes good basket. Prefers overhead filtered light. Best bloom and foliage colour in filtered light. Tested 3 years in Gruitrode, Belgium. NBFK Certificate of Merit at Meise. Distinguished by profuse blooms.
Cuppens 2003 BE AFS5121.

Kasteel Van Terlaemen. Upright/Trailer. Double. COROLLA: half flared, turned under smooth petal margins; opens reddish purple (72B); matures dark reddish purple (72A); 10mm (3/8") long x 14mm (9/16") wide. PETALOIDS: reddish purple (72B); 14mm (9/16") long x 9mm (3/8") wide. SEPALS: horizontal; tips recurved; white (155D) tipped light yellowish green (149B) upper surface; white (155B) tipped light yellow green (149B) lower surface; 39mm (1 9/16") long x 14mm (9/16") wide. TUBE: rose (52B), white (155D) base; medium length & thickness; 17mm (11/16") long x 6mm (1/4") wide. STAMENS: extend 2mm (1/16") below corolla; magenta (63A) filaments; dark reddish purple (70A) anthers. PISTIL: extends 8mm (5/16") below the corolla; dark rose (64C) style; light pink (65B) stigma. BUD: oblong. FOLIAGE: medium green (137B) upper surface, medium green (138B) lower surface. Leaves are 72mm (2 13/16") long x 41mm (1 5/8") wide, ovate shaped, serrulated edges, acute tips and

rounded bases. Light green (139D) veins; medium green (141D) stems & branches. PARENTAGE: 'Checkerboard' x 'Bert's Whisky'. Lax upright or trailer. Self branching. Makes good basket or upright. Prefers overhead filtered light and cool climate. Best bloom and foliage colour in filtered light. Tested 3 years in Werm, Belgium. Award at Meise, 5/7/03. Distinguished by bloom colour.
Wagemans 2004 BE AFS5415.

Kate Taylor. Upright. Double. COROLLA: three quarter flared, smooth petal margins, petals lapped; opens purple (77A); matures purple (71A); 32mm (1 1/4") long x 38mm (1 1/2") wide. SEPALS: half up; tips recurved up; reddish purple (71B) upper & lower surfaces; 38mm (1 1/2") long x 12mm (1/2") wide. TUBE: rose (64D); medium length & thickness; 19mm(3/4") long x 7mm (1/4") wide. STAMENS: 12mm (1/2") below corolla; magenta (63A) filaments, dark purple (79A) anthers. PISTIL: extends 38mm (1 1/2") below the corolla, magenta (63A) style, orangish white (159C) stigma. BUD: ovate. FOLIAGE: dark green (147A) upper surface; yellowish green (146B) lower surface. Leaves are 76mm (3") long x 39mm (1 1/2") wide, ovate shaped, serrated edges, acute tips and rounded bases. Veins, stems & branches are green. PARENTAGE: 'President George Bartlett' x 'Brookwood Belle'. Small upright. Makes good upright or standard. Prefers overhead filtered light or full sun. Best bloom and foliage colour in bright light. Tested 4 years in Birmingham, England. Distinguished by colour combination.
Greenway 2003 UK AFS5206.

Katelijne C.J. Trailer. Double. COROLLA: three quarter flared, turned under wavy petal margins; opens dark reddish purple (60A) bloched magenta (63A); matures magenta (59C); 22mm (7/8") long x 18mm (11/16") wide. PETALOIDS: dark reddish purple (60B); 16mm (5/8") long x 11mm (7/16") wide. SEPALS: horizontal, tips recurved, twisted left; light pink (62C) upper surface; dark rose (58C) lower surface; 38mm (1 1/2") long x 18mm (11/16") wide. TUBE: light pink (65B); medium length & thickness; 21mm (13/16") long x 5mm (3/16") wide. STAMENS extend 15mm (9/16") beyond the corolla; magenta (58B) filaments; dark purple (79A) anthers. PISTIL extends 32mm (1 1/4") beyond the corolla; rose (61D) style; pale yellow (2D) stigma. BUD: globular. FOLIAGE: dark green (137A) upper surface; medium green (138B) lower surface. Leaves are 87mm

(3 7/16") long x 63mm (2 1/2") wide; cordate shaped, serrulate edges, acute tips, cordate bases. Veins are purple (71A), stems are purple (71A) & very dark reddish purple (186A), branches are dark grayish purple (184A) & light green (138C). PARENTAGE: 'Manfried Kleinau' x 'First Lord'. Lax upright or stiff trailer, small. Self branching. Makes good upright. Prefers overhead filtered light, cool climate. Best bloom & foliage colour in filtered light. Tested 3 years in Koningshooikt, Belgium. Waanrode 7/5/08. Distinguished by bloom colour.
Michiels 2009 BE AFS7188.

Kateric. Upright. Single. COROLLA opens pale violet, matures to purple pink; corolla is quarter flared. SEPALS white flushed pink at base of sepals on the upper surface, flushed pink on the lower surface; sepals are half up with recurved tips. TUBE white. PARENTAGE ('Helen Nicholls' x 'Katrina Thompsen seedling') x 'Sophie Louise'.
Nicholls 2008 UK BFS0096.

Kathleen Eva Rose Boggis. Upright/Trailer. Semi Double. COROLLA: half flared, turned under smooth petal margins; opens reddish purple (74A) splashed pink (62A); matures reddish purple (66A) splashed pink (62A); 35mm (1 3/8") long x 20mm (13/16") wide. PETALOIDS: same colour as corolla; 20mm (13/16") long x 10mm (3/8") wide. SEPALS: fully up; tips recurved, half twist counterclockwise; light pink (49C) tipped green upper surface; pink (49A) tipped green lower surface; 30mm(1 3/16") long x 10mm (3/16") wide. TUBE: light pink (49C); long & thin; 20mm (13/16") long x 6mm (1/4") wide. STAMENS: extend 15mm (9/16") below corolla; dark rose (55A) filaments, yellowish white (158A) anthers. PISTIL: extends 30mm (1 3/16") below the corolla, pink (55C) style; white (155A) stigma. BUD: medium, elongated. FOLIAGE: dark green (147A) upper surface; medium green (147B) lower surface. Leaves are 55mm (2 3/16") long x 35mm (1 3/8") wide, cordate shaped, serrated edges, acute tips and rounded bases. Veins & branches are green, stems are brown. PARENTAGE: 'Loveable Rascal' x 'Redbridge in Bloom'. Lax upright or stiff trailer. Self branching. Makes good basket or standard. Heat tolerant if shaded. Prefers warm climate. Cold weather hardy to 32° F. Best bloom colour in bright light. Tested 4 years in Walthamstow, London, England. Distinguished by burgundy splashed pink blooms.
Allsop M.R. 2003 UK AFS5153.

Katie Rogers. Upright/Trailer. Single. COROLLA: Unflared, compact; opens purple (90A); matures violet (87B); 17mm (5/8") long x 15mm (9/16") wide. SEPALS: fully up, tips recurved; light pink (65C) upper surface; rose (65A) lower surface; 34mm (1 3/8") long x 10mm (3/8") wide. TUBE: light rose (73C); short & thick; 6mm (1/4") long x 6mm (1/4") wide. FOLIAGE is medium green (137C) upper surface; medium green (138B) lower surface. PARENTAGE: 'Love's Reward' x 'Brookwood Belle'.
Chapman 2007 UK AFS6716.

Katie Susan. Upright. Single. COROLLA opens cyclamen purple (n74A), matures to lighter cyclamen purple (n74d); corolla is quarter flared and is 20mm long x 23mm wide. SEPALS are rose pink (65d) on the upper surface, rose (65a) on the lower surface; sepals are horizontally held with recurved tips and are 32mm long x 12mm wide. TUBE is rose pink with darker veining and is 10mm long x 6mm wide. PARENTAGE 'London 2000' x 'Sophie Louise'.
Waving P. 2004 UK BFS0008.

Katrientje. Upright/Trailer. Single. COROLLA is quarter flared with turned under wavy petal margins; opens dark rose (54A) edged magenta (57A), reddish orange (43C) at base; matures magenta (58B) edged dark reddish purple (60A), orangy red (44C) at base; 30mm (1 3/16") long x 25mm (1") wide. SEPALS are half down, tips reflexed; light pink (49C), pale pink (49D) at base, tipped yellowish green (145A) upper surface; pink (49A), light pink (49C) at base, tipped light apple green (145B) lower surface; 36mm (1 7/16") long x 11mm (7/16") wide. TUBE is light pink (49C); long and thin; 68mm (2 11/16") long x 3mm (1/8") wide. STAMENS do not extend beyond the corolla; rose (65A) filaments, tan (166D) anthers. PISTIL extends 32mm (1 1/4") beyond the corolla; pale pink (56A) style, pale yellow (12D) stigma. BUD is long, pointed. FOLIAGE is medium green (137B) upper surface, medium green (138B) lower surface. Leaves are 56mm (2 3/16") long x 24mm (15/16") wide, elliptic shaped, serrulated edges, acute tips and obtuse bases. Veins are light green (138C), stems are light green (139D), branches are plum (184C). PARENTAGE: 'WALZ Harp' x 't Klokske'. Lax upright or stiff trailer. Self branching. Makes good basket. Prefers overhead filtered light and cool climate. Best bloom and foliage colour in filtered light. Tested three years in Koningshooikt, Belgium. Certificate N.B.F.K. at Meise.

253

Distinguished by very long TUBE and early blooms.
Michiels 2002 BE AFS4970.

Katy Flynn. Upright. Single. COROLLA opens white with slight pink veining; corolla is none flared. SEPALS pale baby pink, darker veining with half up recurved green tips. TUBE pale baby pink, with darker veining. PARENTAGE Sport of 'Marilyn Olsen'. Makes a good show plant, been shown at London show.
Galea 2008 UK BFS0067.

Katy M. Single. COROLLA sea lavender fading to rosy mauve. SEPALS white tipped green.
Clitheroe 2002 UK.

Kayleigh Driessen. Trailer. Double. COROLLA: half flared, turned under wavy petal margins; opens reddish purple (61A) & purple (77A); matures dark reddish purple (60B); 22mm (7/8") long x 16mm (5/8") wide. PETALOIDS: reddish purple (61B) & purple (77A); 22mm (7/8") long x 16mm (5/8") wide. SEPALS: half up, tips recurved up; light pink (55D) tipped light yellowish green (150C) upper surface; magenta (68A) tipped light yellowish green (150C) lower surface; 27mm (1 1/16") long x 9mm (5/16") wide. TUBE: red (55C); long & thin; 18mm (11/16") long x 4mm (1/8") wide. STAMENS extend 11mm (7/16") beyond the corolla; reddish purple (64B) filaments; dark purple (79A) anthers. PISTIL extends 18mm (11/16") beyond the corolla; dark rose (64C) style; pale lavender (69D) stigma. BUD: globular. FOLIAGE: dark green (137A) upper surface; medium green (138B) lower surface. Leaves are 63mm (2 1/2") long x 32mm (1 1/4") wide; ovate shaped, smooth edges, acute tips, rounded bases. Veins are very dark reddish purple (186A), stems are plum (185C), branches are light plum (184D). PARENTAGE: 'Manfried Kleinau' x 'Ann-Elisabeth Fuhrmann'. Natural trailer. Self branching. Makes good basket. Prefers overhead filtered light, cool climate. Best bloom & foliage colour in filtered light. Tested 3 years in Koningshooikt, Belgium. Waanrode 7/5/08. Distinguished by bloom colour combination.
Michiels 2009 BE AFS7189.

Keech Cottage. Upright. Single. COROLLA opens coral, matures to dark pink; corolla is none flared and is 20mm long x 20mm wide. SEPALS are rose on the upper and lower surfaces; sepals are horizontally held with recurved tips and are 20mm long x 6mm

wide. TUBE is peach and is 13mm long x 5mm wide. PARENTAGE 'Rolts Bride' x 'Terry Sue'. this cultivar has been hybridised for the Children's Hospice at Luton, for the terminally ill, hopefully to raise funds for the Hospice.
Rolt G. 2004 UK BFS0001.

Kees Liebregts. Trailer. Double. COROLLA is three quarter flared; opens reddish purple (59B); matures reddish purple (58A); 21mm (13/16") long x 18mm (11/16") wide. SEPALS are horizontal, tips recurved; pink (43D) upper surface; rose (47D) lower surface; 29mm (1 1/8") long x 11mm (7/16") wide. TUBE is light pink (62B); 24mm (15/16") long x 7mm (1/4") wide. FOLIAGE: medium green (137C) upper surface; medium green (138B) lower surface. PARENTAGE: 'Bicentennial' x 'HeRi Alver'. Distinguished by bloom & foliage combination.
Buiting 2006 NL AFS6120.

Kees van Eijk. Upright. Double. COROLLA is three quarter flared with smooth petal margins; opens purple (77A); matures purple (71A); 26mm (1") long x 20mm (13/16") wide. SEPALS are half up, tips recurved up; pale pink (62D) upper surface; pink (62C) lower surface; 32mm (1 1/4") long x 12mm (1/2") wide. TUBE is pale pink (62D); medium length & thickness; 14mm (9/16") long x 7mm (1/4") wide. FOLIAGE: medium green (137B) upper surface; medium green (138B) lower surface. Leaves are 60mm (2 3/8") long x 29mm (1 1/8") wide, lanceolate shaped. PARENTAGE: 'Sofie Michiels' x 'Peerke Heylen'. Distinguished by bloom colour.
van Eijk 2005 NL AFS5899.

Keizer Inneke. Trailer. Single. COROLLA is quarter flared with turned under wavy petal margins; opens dark rose (54B), white (155C) base; matures red (52A); 12mm (1/2") long x 9mm (3/8") wide. SEPALS are half down, tips reflexed; pale pink (48D), white (155C) base, tipped pale yellow green (150D) upper surface; pale pink (49D), white (155C) base, tipped pale yellow green (150D) lower surface; 22mm (7/8") long x 6mm (1/4") wide. TUBE is white (155C); medium length & thickness; 14mm (9/16") long x 5mm (3/16") wide. FOLIAGE: dark green (139A) upper surface; medium green (138B) lower surface. Leaves are 53mm (2 1/16") long x 37mm (1 7/16") wide, cordate shaped. PARENTAGE: 'Querry' x unknown. Meise 8-14-04. Distinguished by bloom shape & colour.
Willems 2005 BE AFS5725.

Kelly Hoogeveen. Upright/Trailer. Single. COROLLA: Half flared; opens violet (76A); matures violet (75A); 30mm (1 3/16") long x 32mm (1 1/4") wide. SEPALS: horizontal, tips recurved; dark rose (67C) upper surface; magenta (58B) lower surface; 36mm (1 7/16") long x 11mm (7/16") wide. TUBE: dark rose (67C); medium length & thickness; 10mm (3/8") long x 6mm (1/4") wide. FOLIAGE is medium green (137B) upper surface; medium green (138B) lower surface. PARENTAGE: 'Reg Gubler' x 'Kim Klessens'. Buiting 2007 NL AFS6665.

Kelly Torfs. Trailer. Double. COROLLA: half flared; opens light reddish purple (72B), base rose (61D); matures magenta (67B); 16mm (5/8") long x 15mm (916") wide. PETALOIDS: reddish purple (72B), rose (61D) base; 11mm (7/16") long x 9mm (5/16") wide. SEPALS are horizontal, tips recurved; white (155C) tipped light apple green (145B) upper surface & pale lavender (69D) tipped light apple green (145B) lower surface; 34mm (1 3/8") long x 14mm (9/16") wide. TUBE is white (155C) and light green (143C); medium length & thickness; 19mm (3/4") long x 6mm (1/4") wide. FOLIAGE is dark green (137A) upper surface; medium green (137C) lower surface. PARENTAGE: 'De Brommel' x 'Bon Bon'.
Michiels 2007 BE AFS6532.

Kelsey Franck. Upright/Trailer. Double. Upright/Trailer. COROLLA: half flared; turned under smooth petal margins; opens red (52A); matures rose (52B); 25mm (1") long x 24mm (15/16") wide. SEPALS: full down; tips reflexed; rose (51C) tipped yellow green upper surface; pink (48C) lower surface; 35mm(1 3/8") long x 17mm (11/16") wide. TUBE: pink (50D); medium length & thickness; 19mm (3/4") long x 9mm (3/8") wide. STAMENS: extend 12mm (1/2") below corolla; rose (51B) filaments, dark reddish purple (70A) anthers. PISTIL: extends 34mm (1 5/16") below the corolla, pink (55C) style, yellow (10C) stigma. BUD: ovate, pointed. FOLIAGE: dark green (147A) upper surface; yellow green (146B) lower surface. Leaves are 79mm (3 1/8") long x 47mm (1 7/8") wide, ovate shaped, serrulated edges, acute tips and rounded bases. Veins are reddish to yellow green; stems & branches are reddish. PARENTAGE: found seedling. Lax upright or stiff trailer. Self branching. Makes good basket or upright. Prefers overhead filtered light and cool climate. Best bloom and foliage colour in filtered light. Tested 12 years in Noordwÿkerhout, Holland. Distinguished by flower shape and colour.
Franck 2003 NL AFS5170.

Kelsey's Kisses. Trailer. Double. COROLLA is three quarter flared, ruffled, with smooth turned under petal margins; opens violet (84A) splashed pale lavender (69C); matures violet (85A) splashed pale pink (69A); 30mm (1 3/16") long x 55mm (2 3/16") wide. PETALOIDS are same colour as corolla; 17mm (11/16") long x 14mm (9/16") wide. SEPALS are half up, tips recurved up; cream (159D) tipped green upper surface, pale pink (56B) lower surface; 40mm (1 5/8") long x 15mm (5/8") wide. TUBE is yellowish white (158A), long and thin; 20mm (13/16") long x 5mm (3/16") wide. STAMENS extend 12mm (1/2") below the corolla; magenta (57B) filaments and light pink (36B) anthers. PISTIL extends 30mm (1 3/16") below the corolla; light purple (75B) style and yellowish white (158A) stigma. BUD is medium, round. FOLIAGE is dark green (147A) on upper surface and medium green (147B) on lower surface. Leaves are 80mm (3 3/16") long x 45mm (1 3/4") wide, cordate shaped, serrated edges, acute tips and rounded bases. Veins are green; stems brown; branches are red. PARENTAGE: 'Loveable Rascal' x 'Heavenly Hayley'. Natural trailer. Self branching. Makes good basket. Prefers overhead filtered light and warm climate. Heat tolerant if shaded. Hardy to 32°F. Best bloom colour in bright light. Tested four years in Walthamstow, London, England. Distinguished by profuse blooms and violet splashed lavender colour.
Allsop 2002 UK AFS4817.

Kemiremo. Upright/Trailer. Double. COROLLA: three quarter flared, smooth petal margins; opens & matures white (155A); 20mm (13/16") long x 17mm (11/16") wide. SEPALS: half down; tips recurved; white (155A) upper & lower surfaces; 32mm (1 1/4") long x 17mm (11/16") wide. TUBE: light rose (68D); medium length & thickness; 20mm (13/16") long x 6mm (1/4") wide. STAMENS: extend 10mm (3/8") below corolla; light pink (65C) filaments, magenta (59C) anthers. PISTIL: extends 21mm (13/16") below the corolla; white (155B) style, light yellow (4C) stigma. BUD: spherical. FOLIAGE: dark green (137A) upper surface; medium green (138B) lower surface. Leaves are 67mm (2 5/8") long x 32mm (1 1/4") wide, lanceolate shaped, serrated edges, acute tips and rounded bases. Veins, stems & branches are green. PARENTAGE:

'Sophie Michiels' x 'Veenlust'. Lax upright or stiff trailer. Makes good stiff trailer. Prefers overhead filtered light and cool climate. Best bloom and foliage colour in filtered light. Tested 4 years in Reusel, The Netherlands. Distinguished by bloom colour. van Eijk 2003 NL AFS5248.

Ken Fellows. Upright. Semi Double. COROLLA: unflared, smooth petal margins; opens dark reddish purple (72A); matures reddish purple (72A); 19mm (3/4") long 19mm (3/4") wide. SEPALS: full down; tips reflexed; rose (52C) upper surface; rose (52B) lower surface; 70mm (2 3/4") long x 12mm (1/2") wide. TUBE: rose (52C); short, medium thickness; 12mm (1/2") long x 9mm (3/8") wide. STAMENS: extend 35mm (1 3/8") below corolla; rose (52C) filaments; pink (52D) anthers. PISTIL: extends 54mm (2 1/8") below the corolla; rose (52B) style; pink (55C) stigma. BUD: long & slender. FOLIAGE: medium green (146A) upper surface; light olive green (146C) lower surface. Leaves are 76mm (3") long x 51mm (2") wide, cordate shaped, serrated edges, acute tips and rounded bases. light olive green (146C) veins; plum (183B) stems; orangy brown (174B) branches. PARENTAGE: 'Seaview Sunset' x 'Double Otto'. Small upright bush. Makes good upright. Prefers full sun. Cold weather tolerant to 10⁰ F. Best bloom colour in bright light. Tested 5 years in Kent, Washington, USA. Distinguished by bloom shape and colour.
Pearson 2004 USA AFS5459.

Ken Tudor. Upright. Single. COROLLA pale mauve pink edged mauve. SEPALS cream blushed pink. TUBE cream.
Reynolds G. 2008 UK.

Kendra. Upright/Trailer. Double. COROLLA: half flared, turned under wavy petal margins; opens purple (77A); matures reddish purple (61B); 24mm (15/16") long x 21mm (13/16") wide. PETALOIDS: Same colour as corolla; 14mm (9/16") long x 12mm (7/16") wide. SEPALS: half down, tips recurved; light pink (55D) tipped light apple green (145C) upper surface; rose (N57C) tipped light apple green (145C) lower surface; 32mm (1 1/4") long x 16mm (5/8") wide. TUBE: pink (62A); medium length & thickness; 24mm (15/16") long x 7mm (1/4") wide. STAMENS extend 16mm (5/8") beyond the corolla; dark reddish purple (64A) filaments; dark purple (79A) anthers. PISTIL extends 16mm (5/8") beyond the corolla; dark rose (64C) style;

light yellow (4C) stigma. BUD: oblong. FOLIAGE: dark green (137A) upper surface; medium green (137D) lower surface. Leaves are 48mm (1 7/8") long x 29mm (1 1/8") wide; ovate shaped, serrate edges, acute tips, rounded bases. Veins are plum (185B), stems are light red purple (185D), branches are light plum (184D). PARENTAGE: 'Manfried Kleinau' x 'Joergen Hahn'. Lax upright or stiff trailer. Self branching. Makes good basket. Prefers overhead filtered light, cool climate. Best bloom & foliage colour in filtered light. Tested 3 years in Koningshooikt, Belgium. Waanrode 8/9/08. Distinguished by bloom colour.
Michiels 2009 BE AFS7190.

Kenny Walkling. Upright. Single. COROLLA: quarter flared, bell shape, wavy petal margins; opens purple (81A); matures purple (74B); 22mm (7/8") long x 20mm (13/16") wide. SEPALS: half up; tips recurved up; rose (52B) upper & lower surfaces; 22mm (7/8") long x 7mm (1/4") wide. TUBE: rose (52B); short, medium width; 8mm (5/16") long x 7mm (1/4") wide. STAMENS: extend 12mm (1/2") below corolla; light pink (62B) filaments & anthers. PISTIL: extends 20mm (13/16") below the corolla; rose (52B) style; white (155A) stigma. BUD: ovate. FOLIAGE: dark green (137A) upper surface; medium green (138A) lower surface. Leaves are 50mm (2") long x 24mm (15/16") wide, lanceolate shaped, serrulated edges, acute tips and rounded bases. Veins, stems & branches are dull red. PARENTAGE: 'Kelly Jo' x 'Janice Ann'. Medium upright. Makes good upright, standard, pyramid, pillar or decorative. Prefers overhead filtered light. Heat tolerant if shaded. Best bloom and foliage colour in filtered light. Tested 3 years in Maidstone, Kent, England. Distinguished by profuse flowering.
Waving 2003 UK AFS5356.

Kenzo. Upright/Trailer. Double. COROLLA: half flared, turned under wavy petal margins; opens reddish purple (72B); matures dark rose (64C); 28mm (1 1/8") long x 32mm (1 1/4") wide. PETALOIDS: rose (54C) & dark reddish purple (70A); 20mm (3/4") long x 16mm (5/8") wide. SEPALS: half down, tips recurved; rose (55B) tipped light yellow green (150B) upper surface; rose (52C) tipped light yellow green (150B) lower surface; 38mm (1 1/2") long x 14mm (9/16") wide. TUBE: rose (52D); medium length & thickness; 14mm (9/16") long x 6mm (1/4") wide. STAMENS extend 16mm (5/8") beyond the corolla; magenta (63B) filaments; violet (77C)

anthers. PISTIL extends 24mm (15/16")
beyond the corolla; rose (61D) style; pale
yellow (2D) stigma. BUD: globular. FOLIAGE:
dark green (139A) upper surface; medium
green (137C) lower surface. Leaves are 67mm
(2 5/8") long x 40mm (1 9/16") wide; ovate
shaped, serrulate edges, acute tips, rounded
bases. Veins are light red purple (185D),
stems are reddish purple (186B), branches
are light plum (184D) & light green (138C).
PARENTAGE: 'Manfried Kleinau' x 'Beauty of
Meise'. Lax upright or stiff trailer. Self
branching. Makes good basket. Prefers
overhead filtered light, cool climate. Best
bloom & foliage colour in filtered light. Tested
3 years in Koningshooikt, Belgium.
Waanrode 8/9/08. Distinguished by bloom
colour combination.
Michiels 2009 BE AFS7191.

Kerkveld Gotem. Trailer. Double.
COROLLA: half flared; opens purple (77A),
rose (65A) base; matures purple (N81B);
23mm (7/8") long x 18mm (11/16") wide.
PETALOIDS: same colour as corolla; 15mm
(9/16") long x 6mm (1/4") wide. SEPALS:
horizontal, tips reflexed; pale lavender (69D)
tipped light green (142B) upper surface; light
pink (65B) tipped light green (142B) lower
surface; 30mm (1 3/16") long x 12mm
(7/16") wide. TUBE: white (155C) striped
medium green (138B); medium length, thick;
11mm (7/16") long x 6mm (1/4") wide.
FOLIAGE is dark green (136B) upper surface;
medium green (138B) lower surface.
PARENTAGE: 'Leon Pauwels' x 'Oso Sweet'.
Michiels 2007 BE AFS6365.

Kerry Anne. Upright. Single. COROLLA
opens deep purple, matures to purple;
corolla is half flared. SEPALS cerise on the
upper and lower surface; sepals are half up
with recurved tips. TUBE cerise.
PARENTAGE 'Anita' x 'Roesse Blacky'.
Watts 2008 UK BFS0086.

Kerry Theresa. Upright. Single. COROLLA
white. SEPALS white edged pink. TUBE
green.
Woods 2006 UK.

Keteltje. Trailer. Single. COROLLA: unflared;
turned under petal margins; opens &
matures reddish purple (44A); 20mm (3/4")
long x 15mm (9/16") wide. SEPALS: full
down, tips recurved; dark red (53A) upper &
lower surfaces; 25mm (1") long x 13mm
(1/2") wide. TUBE: dark red (53A); medium
length, thin; 16mm (5/8") long x 9mm
(7/16") wide. STAMENS extend 20mm (3/4")

beyond the corolla; light purple (74C)
filaments; reddish purple (70B) anthers.
PISTIL extends 36mm (1 7/16") beyond the
corolla; reddish purple (64B) style; yellow
orange (16C) stigma. BUD: ovate. FOLIAGE:
medium green (147B) upper surface; light
olive green (147C) lower surface. Leaves are
46mm (1 13/16") long x 25mm (1") wide;
cordate shaped, serrulate edges, acute tips,
rounded bases. Veins, stems & branches are
dark red. PARENTAGE: seedling of 'Insa'.
Natural trailer. Makes good basket. Prefers
overhead filtered light, cool climate. Cold
weather hardy to -3° C (27° F). Best bloom
colour in filtered light. Tested 6 years in
Amsterdam, The Netherlands. V.K.C
Aalsmeer 10/1/2003. Distinguished by
flower colour & shape.
Krom 2009 NL AFS7056.

Kia Ora. Upright/Trailer. Double. COROLLA:
half flared, turned under wavy petal margins;
opens & matures dark reddish purple (72B),
magenta (63B) at base; 17mm (11/16") long
x 27mm (1 1/16") wide. SEPALS: full down;
tips recurved; red (52A) tipped yellowish
green (145A) upper surface; rose (52B) lower
surface; 32mm(1 1/4") long x 14mm (9/16")
wide. TUBE: rose (52B); medium length &
thickness; 20mm (13/16") long x 8mm
(5/16") wide. STAMENS: none. PISTIL
extends 10mm (3/8") below the corolla; dark
rose (58C) stylelight rose (58D) stigma. BUD:
ovate. FOLIAGE: dark green (137A) upper
surface; medium green (138A) lower surface.
Leaves are 51mm (2") long x 40mm (1 9/16")
wide, ovate shaped, serrulated edges, acute
tips and rounded bases. Veins, & branches
are reddish purple (58A). PARENTAGE:
'Justine Heymans' x unknown. Lax upright
or stiff trailer. Self branching. Makes good
basket. Prefers full sun. Best bloom and
foliage colour in filtered light. Tested 3 years
in Rummen, Belgium. NBFK certificate at
Meise. Distinguished by bloom colour,
profuse blooms.
Ector 2003 BE AFS5117.

Kiara Kerkhofs. Trailer. Semi Double.
COROLLA is quarter flared; opens reddish
purple (72B), dark rose (58C) base; matures
dark reddish purple (72A); 19mm (3/4") long
x 15mm (9/16") wide. SEPALS are half down,
tips recurved; magenta (58B) upper surface;
dark rose (58C) lower surface; 41mm (1 5/8")
long x 13mm (1/2") wide. TUBE is rose
(52C); 22mm (7/8") long x 6mm (1/4") wide.
FOLIAGE: dark green (137A) upper surface;
medium green (138B) lower surface.

PARENTAGE: 'Phyllis' x 'Onbekend'. Meise 8/13/05. Distinguished by bloom colour. Baeten 2006 BE AFS6012.

Kim de Groot. Upright/Trailer. Semi Double. COROLLA is three quarter flared; opens violet (76B), white (155A) at base; matures pale purple (75D); 17mm (11/16") long x 13mm (1/2") wide. PETALOIDS: same colour as corolla; 14mm (9/16") long x 6mm (1/4") wide. SEPALS are horizontal, tips recurved; light rose (63D), white (155B) at base, tipped light apple green (145B) upper surface; pink (62C), white (155A) at base, tipped light apple green (145B) lower surface; 35mm (1 3/8") long x 10mm (3/8") wide. TUBE is white (155B); 12mm (1/2") long x 7mm (1/4") wide. FOLIAGE: dark green (137A) upper surface; medium green (138B) lower surface. PARENTAGE: Sport of 'Glowing Lilac'. Meise 8/13/05. Distinguished by bloom colour. de Groot 2006 BE AFS5998.

Kim Joiner. Upright. Single. COROLLA opens cyclamen pink, matures to bluish pink; corolla is half flared and is 22mm long x 23mm wide. SEPALS light pink on the upper and lower surfaces; sepals are horizontally held with recurved tips and are 37mm long x 8mm wide. TUBE light pink and is 7mm long x 5mm wide. PARENTAGE 'Sophie Louise' x 'Baby Bright'. Joiner 2006 UK BFS0030.

Kim Klessens. Trailer. Semi Double. COROLLA: three quarter flared, wavy petal margins; opens violet blue (92A); matures light violet (84B); 19mm (3/4") long 15mm (9/16") wide. SEPALS: half up; tips reflexed up; light pink (65C) upper surface; rose (65A) lower surface; 32mm (1 1/4") long x 12mm (1/2") wide. TUBE: pale lavender (65D); medium length & thickness; 17mm (11/16") long x 4mm (3/16") wide. STAMENS: extend 16mm (5/8") below corolla; pink (62A) filaments & anthers. PISTIL: extends 37mm (1 7/16") below the corolla; pale violet (76D) style; yellowish white (4D) stigma. BUD: ovate, pointed. FOLIAGE: medium green (137B) upper surface; medium green (138A) lower surface. Leaves are 46mm (1 13/16") long x 31mm (1 1/4") wide, ovate shaped, serrulated edges, acute tips and rounded bases. Red veins, stems & branches. PARENTAGE: ('Cameron Ryle' x 'Parasol') x 'Corrie Spoelstra'. Natural trailer. Self branching. Makes good basket. Prefers overhead filtered light and cool climate. Best bloom and foliage colour in filtered light.

Tested 4 years in Knegsel, The Netherlands. Distinguished by bloom colour. Roes 2004 NL AFS5461.

Kim Nicholls. Upright. Single. COROLLA opens lavender, matures to a darker shade of lavender; corolla is quarter flared and is 20mm long x 13mm wide. SEPALS are white, pink at the base with green tips on the upper surface, pink on the lower surface; sepals are half up with recurved tips and are 27mm long x 6mm wide. TUBE white and is 8mm long x 5mm wide. PARENTAGE 'Loves Reward' x 'Katrina Thompsen'. Nicholls A. 2004 UK BFS0006.

Kimberley Hoogeveen. Upright. Single. COROLLA: Half flared; opens reddish purple (61B); matures magenta (63A); 29mm (1 1/8") long x 29mm (1 1/8") wide. SEPALS: horizontal, tips recurved; rose (68C) upper surface; rose (68C) lower surface; 42mm (1 5/8") long x 11mm (7/16") wide. TUBE: light rose (68D); medium length & thickness; 20mm (3/4") long x 12mm (7/16") wide. FOLIAGE is medium green (137B) upper surface; medium green (137D) lower surface. PARENTAGE: 'Roesse Lupus' x 'Leon Pauwels'. Buiting 2007 NL AFS6663.

Kimberly Hadfield. Trailer. Single. COROLLA: quarter flared, smooth petal margins; opens violet (76A); matures dark reddish purple (60A); 15mm (9/16") long x 15mm (9/16") wide. SEPALS: half up; tips recurved up; dark reddish purple (60B) upper & lower surfaces; 20mm(13/16") long x 7mm (1/4") wide. TUBE: dark reddish purple (60B); short, medium thickness; 10mm (3/8") long x 5mm (3/16") wide. STAMENS: extend 7mm (1/4") below corolla; magenta (58B) filaments & anthers. PISTIL extends 19mm (3/4") below the corolla; magenta (58B) style & stigma. BUD: pointed. FOLIAGE: medium green (146A) upper surface; yellowish green (146B) lower surface. Leaves are 30mm (1 3/16") long x 21mm (13/16") wide, cordate shaped, serrulated edges, acute tips and rounded bases. Veins are green, stems & branches are red. PARENTAGE: 'Purperklokje' x unknown. Natural trailer. Self branching. Makes good basket or standard. Prefers overhead filtered light, cool climate. Best bloom and foliage colour in filtered light. Tested 3 years in Stoke-on-Trent, England. Distinguished by rich colour. Rowell 2003 UK AFS5133.

Klaas. Upright. Single. COROLLA is unflared with turned under petal margins; opens & matures magenta (57B); 22mm (7/8") long x 10mm (3/8") wide. SEPALS are full down, tips recurved; light pink (65B) upper surface; rose (65A) lower surface; 34mm (1 3/8") long x 7mm (1/4") wide. TUBE is light pink (65B); medium length & thickness; 12mm (1/2") long x 6mm (1/4") wide. FOLIAGE: medium green (147B) & dark green (147A) upper surface; medium green (147B) lower surface. Leaves are 40mm (1 9/16") long x 21mm (13/16") wide, ovate shaped. PARENTAGE: 'Wormerveer' x unknown. Distinguished by graceful flowers.
Krom 2005 NL AFS5824.

Klazina Tamerus. Upright. Double. COROLLA is half flared with smooth petal margins; opens reddish purple (67A); matures dark rose (67C); 22mm (7/8") long x 17mm (11/16") wide. SEPALS are fully up, tips reflexed; rose (52B) upper surface, red (52A) lower surface; 20mm (13/16") long x 12mm (1/2") wide. TUBE is rose (52B), short and thick; 12mm (1/2") long x 12mm (1/2") wide. STAMENS extend 12mm (1/2") beyond the corolla; magenta (58B) filaments, and anthers. PISTIL extends 24mm (15/16") beyond the corolla; magenta (58B) style, yellowish white (4D) stigma. BUD is ovate, pointed. FOLIAGE is dark green (137A) upper surface, medium green (138A) lower surface. Leaves are 64mm (2 1/2") long x 37mm (1 7/16") wide, ovate shaped, serrated edges, acute tips and obtuse bases. Veins, stems and branches are green. PARENTAGE:{[('Bon Accord' x 'Bicentennial') x ('Vobeglo' x 'Dancing Flame')] x 'Rohees Alrami'} x 'Annabel' x Annabel'. Small upright. Makes good standard. Prefers overhead filtered light and cool climate. Best bloom colour in filtered light. Tested four years in Duizel, The Netherlands. Distinguished by bloom and foliage combination.
Tamerus 2002 NL AFS940.

Klooster Karmel. Upright. Semi Double. COROLLA is half flared with smooth petal margins; dark reddish purple (59A), matures reddish purple (59B); 24mm (15/16") long x 22mm (7/8") wide. SEPALS are fully up, tips recurved; reddish purple (67A) upper surface, magenta (63A) lower surface; 31mm (1 1/4") long x 12mm (1/2") wide. TUBE is reddish purple (67A), proportionately short and thick; 9mm (3/8") long x 8mm (5/16") wide. STAMENS extend 33mm (1 5/16") below the corolla; dark reddish purple (64A) filaments and dark purple (79A) anthers.

PISTIL extends 44mm (1 3/4") below the corolla; dark reddish purple (64A) style and rose (63C) stigma. BUD is ovate and pointed. FOLIAGE is medium green (137C) on upper surface and medium green (138B) on lower surface. Leaves are 52mm (2 1/16") long x 37mm (1 7/16") wide, ovate shaped, serrated edges, acute tips and rounded bases. Veins, stems and branches are red. PARENTAGE: [('Bon Accord' x 'Bicentennial') x ('Vobeglo' x 'Dancing Flame') x 'Rohees Alrami'] x 'Rohees King'. Small upright. Makes good standard. Prefers overhead filtered light and cool climate. Best bloom colour in filtered light. Tested four years in Knegsel, The Netherlands. Distinguished by bloom and foliage combination.
Roes 2002 NL AFS4793.

Knollendam. Trailer. Semi Double. COROLLA is quarter flared; opens dark red (46A); matures red (53B); 21mm (13/16") long x 30mm (1 3/16") wide. SEPALS are horizontal, tips recurved; red (45C) upper surface; red (46C) lower surface; 30mm (1 3/16") long x 13mm (1/2") wide. TUBE is red (44A); 18mm (11/16") long x 6mm (1/4") wide. FOLIAGE: dark green (147A) & yellowish green (146D) upper surface; yellowish green (146B) lower surface. PARENTAGE: 'La Campanella' x unknown. Distinguished by bloom & foliage colours.
Krom 2006 NL AFS6269.

Kobe Robinet. Trailer. Semi Double. COROLLA is half flared; opens purple (77A) with reddish purple (67A) base; matures dark reddish purple (72A); 23mm (7/8") long x 18mm (11/16") wide. SEPALS are half up, tips recurved up; dark rose (64C) upper surface, and reddish purple (67A) lower surface; 44mm (1 3/4") long x 13mm (1/2") wide. PETALOIDS are purple (77A) with reddish purple (67A) base; 12mm (7/16") long x 8mm (5/16") wide. TUBE is magenta (63B); 19mm (3/4") long x 6mm (1/4") wide. FOLIAGE is dark green (137A) upper surface; medium green (138B) lower surface. PARENTAGE: 'Roesse Blacky' x 'Diana Wills'. Meise 8/13/05. Distinguished by bloom colour and leaf shape.
Michiels 2006 BE AFS6024.

Koen Es. Trailer. Double. COROLLA is half flared; opens white (155C) striped rose (61D); matures white (155D); 24mm (15/16") long x 26mm (1") wide. PETALOIDS are white (155D) striped rose (61D); 14mm (9/16") x 16mm (5/8"). SEPALS are horizontal, tips reflexed; white (155C), tipped light yellowish green (149B) upper surface, and white (155D), tipped light yellowish green (149B) lower surface; 42mm (1 5/8") long x 21mm (13/16") wide. TUBE is white (155C); 15mm (9/16") long x 7mm (1/4") wide. FOLIAGE is dark green (136A) upper surface; medium green (138A) lower surface. PARENTAGE: 'Sofie Michiels' x 'White Queen'. Meise 8/13/05. Distinguished by bloom colour. Michiels 2006 BE AFS6021.

Koen vanden Berg. Upright. Single. COROLLA: half flared; opens dark reddish purple (59A); matures magenta (59C); 19mm (3/4") long x 20mm (3/4") wide. SEPALS: half up, tips reflexed up; magenta (61C) upper surface; magenta (63A) lower surface; 24mm (15/16") long x 12mm (7/16") wide. TUBE: magenta (61C); 12mm (7/16") long x 6mm (1/4") wide. FOLIAGE is dark green (137A) upper surface; medium green (137C) lower surface. PARENTAGE: [('Parasol' x 'Cameron Ryle') x 'Mission Bells'] x 'Roesse Apus'. Geenen 2006 NL AFS6920.

Koen Vander Werf. Upright/Trailer. Double. COROLLA: half flared; opens reddish purple (N74B); matures reddish purple (71B); 22mm (7/8") long x 24mm (15/16") wide. SEPALS: horizontal, tips reflexed; dark rose (54A) tipped yellowish green (144B) upper surface; dark rose (55A) tipped yellowish green (144B) lower surface; 27mm (1 1/16") long x 14mm (9/16") wide. TUBE: dark rose (54B); medium length & thickness; 13mm (1/2") long x 5mm (3/16") wide. FOLIAGE is dark green (137B) upper surface; medium green (138B) lower surface. PARENTAGE: 'Mieke' x 'Dorset Delight'. Michiels 2007 BE AFS6348.

König Manasse. Upright. Semi Double. COROLLA: half flared, smooth petal margins; opens purple (71A) blushed magenta (N57A); matures dark reddish purple (61A); 27mm (1 1/16") long x 30mm (1 3/16") wide. SEPALS: half up, tips recurved up; magenta (N57A) upper surface; red (53C) lower surface; 40mm (1 9/16") long x 13mm (1/2") wide. TUBE: magenta (N57A); medium length & thickness; 12mm (7/16") long x 5mm (3/16") wide. STAMENS extend 15mm (9/16") beyond the corolla; magenta (N57A) filaments; purple (71A) anthers. PISTIL extends 35mm (1 3/8") beyond the corolla; magenta (N57A) style; dark rose (58C) stigma. BUD: elongated. FOLIAGE: medium green (137B) upper surface; yellowish green (146B) lower surface. Leaves are 80mm (3

3/16") long x 48mm (1 7/8") wide; elliptic shaped, serrate edges, acute tips, rounded bases. Veins are red, branches are reddish brown. PARENTAGE: 'Danny Kaye' x 'Rohees Metallah'. Small upright. Makes good upright. Prefers full sun, warm climate. Heat tolerant if shaded. Best bloom & foliage colour in bright light. Tested 6 years in Bavaria, Southern Germany. Distinguished by flower colour & shape. Burkhart 2009 DE AFS7095.

Koningshooikt. Upright/Trailer. Single. COROLLA: half flared, turned under wavy petal margins; opens violet (76B); matures light purple (75B); 28mm (1 1/8") long x 32mm (1 1/4") wide. SEPALS: fully up, tips recurved, twisted left to right; white (155C) edged magenta (63B) tipped pale yellow green (150D) upper surface; pale pink (56C) edged rose (64D) tipped pale yellow green (150D) lower surface; 59mm (2 3/8") long x 16mm (5/8") wide. TUBE: white (155B) striped magenta (63B); short & thick; 19mm (3/4") long x 9mm (5/16") wide. STAMENS extend 14mm (9/16") beyond the corolla; dark rose (67C) filaments; magenta (63B) anthers. PISTIL extends 30mm (1 3/16") beyond the corolla; pale lavender (69C) style; pale pink (62D) stigma. BUD: elongated. FOLIAGE: dark green (137A) upper surface; medium green (137D) lower surface. Leaves are 64mm (2 1/2") long x 39mm (1 1/2") wide; ovate shaped, serrate edges, acute tips, rounded bases. Veins are dark reddish purple (61A), stems are very dark reddish purple (186A), branches are dark reddish purple (N186D). PARENTAGE: 'Coen Bakker' x 'Cotta Fairy'. Lax upright or stiff trailer. Self branching. Makes good upright. Prefers overhead filtered light, cool climate. Best bloom & foliage colour in filtered light. Tested 3 years in Koningshooikt, Belgium. Waanrode 7/5/08. Distinguished by bloom colour. Michiels 2009 BE AFS7192.

Koog Aan de Zaan. Upright. Single. COROLLA is unflared with turned under petal margins; opens orange (40C); matures orange (41B); 10mm (3/8") long x 11mm (7/16") wide. SEPALS are half down, tips reflexed; coral (37A) upper surface; orange (35B) lower surface; 14mm (9/16") long x 7mm (1/4") wide. TUBE is coral (39B); medium length & thickness; 15mm (9/16") long x 6mm (1/4") wide. FOLIAGE: dark green (147A) upper surface; medium green (147B) lower surface. Leaves are 51mm (2") long x 34mm (1 5/16") wide, ovate shaped.

PARENTAGE: 'Coachman' x unknown. Distinguished by bloom colour & shape. Krom 2005 NL AFS5810.

Kostolany. Trailer. Double. COROLLA: half flared; opens pale violet (85D); matures light violet (84C); 19mm (3/4") long x 16mm (5/8") wide. PETALOIDS: pale violet (85D); 12mm (7/16") long x 10mm (3/8") wide. SEPALS are horizontal, tips recurved; pale lavender (69D) tipped light apple green (145B) upper surface & pale pink (69A) tipped light apple green (145B) lower surface; 38mm (1 1/2") long x 14mm (9/16") wide. TUBE is white (155C); medium length & thickness; 16mm (5/8") long x 5mm (3/16") wide. FOLIAGE is dark green (137A) upper surface; medium green (138A) lower surface. PARENTAGE: 'Vreni Schleeweiss' x 'Futura'. Michiels 2007 BE AFS6533.

Kreeft. Upright/Trailer. Semi Double. COROLLA: Quarter flared; opens magenta (61C); matures dark rose (64C); 19mm (3/4") long x 24mm (15/16") wide. SEPALS: horizontal, tips reflexed; rose (52B) tipped light greenish yellow (151C) upper surface; dark rose (51A) tipped light greenish yellow (151C) lower surface; 28mm (1 1/8") long x 11mm (7/16") wide. TUBE: dark rose (54B); long & thin; 26mm (1") long x 5mm (3/16") wide. FOLIAGE is dark green (139A) upper surface; medium green (138B) lower surface. PARENTAGE: ('WALZ Harp x 'Wendy van Wanten') x 'Wendy van Wanten'. Geerts L. 2007 BE AFS6598.

Kreischberg. Upright. Single. COROLLA is half flared; opens violet (76A); matures violet (75A); 20mm (3/4") long x 25mm (1") wide. SEPALS are half up, tips recurved up; light pink (62B) upper surface; pink (62A) lower surface; 33mm (1 5/16") long x 12mm (7/16") wide. TUBE is light pink (62B); 15mm (9/16") long x 11mm (7/16") wide. FOLIAGE: dark green (137A) upper surface; medium green (137D) lower surface. PARENTAGE: 'Christina Becker' x 'Silipup'. Distinguished by bloom colour & shape. Strümper 2006 DE AFS6233.

Kristel Clerx. Upright/Trailer. Single. COROLLA: half flared, turned under wavy petal margins; opens violet (N80C) striped reddish purple (70B); matures violet (75A); 28mm (1 1/8") long x 23mm (7/8") wide. SEPALS: horizontal, tips recurved, twisted left; white (155B) & pale pink (56B) tipped light apple green (145B) upper surface; white (155B) & pink (55C) tipped light apple green

(145B) lower surface; 46mm (1 13/16") long x 12mm (7/16") wide. TUBE: white (155B); medium length & thickness ; 17mm (5/8") long x 7mm (1/4") wide. STAMENS extend 6mm (1/4") beyond the corolla; magenta (68A) filaments; light purple (70C) anthers. PISTIL extends 25mm (1") beyond the corolla; pale pink (69A) style; light yellow (2C) stigma. BUD: elongated. FOLIAGE: dark green (137A) upper surface; medium green (138B) lower surface. Leaves are 50mm (2") long x 27mm (1 1/16") wide; ovate shaped, serrulate edges, acute tips, rounded bases. Veins are light apple green (144D), stems are light apple green (144D) & light plum (184D), branches are light green (139D) & grayish red (181C). PARENTAGE: 'Coen Bakker' x 'Cotta Fairy'. Lax upright or stiff trailer. Self branching. Makes good basket or upright. Prefers overhead filtered light, cool climate. Best bloom & foliage colour in filtered light. Tested 3 years in Koningshooikt, Belgium. Waanrode 7/5/08. Distinguished by bloom colour combination. Michiels 2009 BE AFS7193.

Kristel Tans. Trailer. Semi Double. COROLLA: half flared; opens violet (85D) edged violet (85A); matures violet (N82C); 22mm (7/8") long x 19mm (3/4") wide. SEPALS: horizontal, tips reflexed; magenta (58B) tipped light green (143C) upper surface; magenta (63A) tipped light green (143C) lower surface; 30mm (1 3/16") long x 10mm (3/8") wide. TUBE: white (155B) & medium green (139C); medium length & thickness; 13mm (1/2") long x 5mm (3/16") wide. FOLIAGE is dark green (136B) upper surface; medium green (138B) lower surface. PARENTAGE: 'Lavender Heaven' x 'Delta's Trick'. Michiels 2007 BE AFS6349.

Kristel vander Velde. Upright/Trailer. Double. COROLLA: quarter flared, smooth petal margins; opens dark purple (86A); matures dark purple (78A); 30mm (1 3/16") long x 24mm (15/16") wide. SEPALS: fully up; tips reflexed; magenta (63B) upper & lower surfaces; 26mm (1") long x 14mm (9/16") wide. TUBE: pink (62C); long & thin; 28mm (1 1/8") long x 4mm (3/16") wide. STAMENS: extend 16mm (5/8") below corolla; magenta (63A) filaments; dark reddish purple (64A) anthers. PISTIL: extends 12mm (1/2") below the corolla; magenta (63A) style; rose (63C) stigma. BUD: round, long TUBE. FOLIAGE: dark green (137A) upper surface; medium green (138A) lower surface. Leaves are 52mm (2 1/16")

261

long x 30mm (1 1/4") wide, lanceolate shaped, serrulated edges, acute tips and rounded bases. Veins are green, stems & branches are red. PARENTAGE: [('Cameron Ryle' x 'Parasol') x 'Allure'] x 'Allure'. Lax upright or stiff trailer. Makes good stiff trailer. Prefers overhead filtered light and cool climate. Best bloom and foliage colour in filtered light. Tested 4 years in Knegsel, The Netherlands. Distinguished by bloom shape & colour.

Roes 2003 NL AFS5351.

Kroemekeshoef. Upright/Trailer. Single. COROLLA: quarter flared, turned under toothed petal margins; opens light purple (74C), pale purple base; matures light purple (81C); 28mm (1 1/8") long x 20mm (13/16") wide. SEPALS: half down; tips reflexed; pink (50D), pale pink (49D) base, tipped light yellow green (150A) upper surface; light pink (55C) lower surface; 48mm (1 7/8") long x 13mm (1/2") wide. TUBE: pale pink (49D); medium length & thickness; 16mm(5/8") long x 5mm (3/16") wide. STAMENS: 12mm (1/2") below corolla; reddish purple (67A) filaments, purple (71A) anthers. PISTIL: extends 34mm (1 5/16") below the corolla, light rose (68D) style, pale yellow (1D) stigma. BUD: elongated. FOLIAGE: dark green (136B) upper surface; medium green (138B) lower surface. Leaves are 53mm (2 1/16") long x 24mm (15/16") wide, ovate shaped, serrulated edges, acute tips and rounded bases. Veins are plum (183D), stems are plum (184B), branches are light red purple (185D). PARENTAGE: 'Moonshot' x unknown. Lax upright or stiff trailer. Self branching. Makes good basket. Prefers overhead filtered light. Best bloom and foliage colour in filtered light. Tested 3 years in Rillaar, Belgium. NBFK Certificate at Meise. Distinguished by bloom shape and colour.

Willems 2003 BE AFS5198.

Krommenie. Upright. Single. COROLLA is quarter flared with smooth petal margins; opens reddish purple (74A); matures reddish purple (67A); 13mm (1/2") long x 19mm (3/4") wide. SEPALS are horizontal, tips recurved; white (155D) upper & lower surfaces; 20mm (13/16") long x 9mm (3/8") wide. TUBE is white (155A); medium length & thickness; 9mm (3/8") long x 7mm (1/4") wide. FOLIAGE: dark green (147A) upper surface; medium green (147B) lower surface. Leaves are 40mm (1 9/16") long x 24mm (15/16") wide, ovate shaped. PARENTAGE: 'Wormerveer' x 'Minirose. V.K.C. Aalsmeer,

10-1-03. Distinguished by flower shape & colour.

Krom 2005 NL AFS5822.

Kuniko Atarashi. Upright/Trailer. Double. COROLLA: three quarter flared, wavy petal margins, bell shape; opens & matures light reddish purple (66C); 44mm (1 3/4") long x 69mm (2 3/4") wide. SEPALS: fully up, tips reflexed; pink (55C) tipped light apple green (145C) upper surface; dark rose (55A) tipped light apple green (145C) lower surface; 37mm (1 7/16") long x 14mm (9/16") wide. TUBE: light pink (36C); medium length & thickness; 9mm (5/16") long x 6mm (1/4") wide. STAMENS extend 25mm (1") beyond the corolla; light magenta (66D) filaments; cream (158D) anthers. PISTIL extends 32mm (1 1/4") beyond the corolla; light magenta (66D) style; cream (158D) stigma. BUD is round, pointed. FOLIAGE is medium green (138B) upper surface; light green (138C) lower surface. Leaves are 69mm (2 3/4") long x 38mm (1 1/2") wide; cordate shaped, serrulate edges, acute tips, rounded bases. Veins are light apple green (145C); stems are brown, branches are pale yellowish green (149D). PARENTAGE: 'Crinkley Bottom' x 'Dreamy Days'. Lax upright or stiff trailer. Makes good standard, decorative or trellis. Prefers overhead filtered light or full sun & warm climate. Best bloom colour in filtered light. Best foliage colour in bright light. Tested 3 years in Norfolk, England. Distinguished by fluorescent appearing colours. Also registered with the BFS in 2008.

Welch 2009 UK AFS6952 BFS0064 (2008).

L'Ami Jean-Marc. Upright. Single. COROLLA: unflared, smooth petal margins; opens & matures light rose (73C) delicately veined light rose (73B); 28mm (1 1/8") long x 12mm (1/2") wide. SEPALS: full down; tips recurved; magenta (58B) upper surface; dark rose (58C) lower surface; 39mm (1 9/16") long x 8mm (5/16") wide, joined on 40% of its length. TUBE: dark rose (58C); short, medium thickness; 6mm (1/4") long x 5mm (3/16") wide. STAMENS: extend 9-12mm (3/8–1/2") below corolla; light reddish purple (73A) filaments, reddish purple (70B) anthers. PISTIL: extends 33mm (1 5/16") below the corolla, light reddish purple (73A) style, reddish purple (64B) stigma. BUD: ovate. FOLIAGE: dark green (147A) upper surface; medium green (147B) lower surface. Leaves are 54mm (2 1/8") long x 32mm (1 1/4") wide, ovate shaped, serrulated edges, acute tips and rounded bases. Veins, stems

& branches are yellowish green. PARENTAGE: ('String of Pearls' x unknown) x 'Caroline'. Small upright. Self branching. Makes good upright. Prefers overhead filtered light and cool climate. Best bloom and foliage colour in filtered light. Tested 5 years in Pornic, France. Distinguished by bloom form. Massé 2003 FR AFS5226.

La Môme Piaf. Upright. Double COROLLA: half flared, smooth petal margins; opens & matures rose (68B); 21mm (13/16") long x 19mm (3/4") wide. SEPALS are half up, tips reflexed up; pale lavender (65D) upper surface; light pink (65B) lower surface; 31mm (1 1/4") long x 14mm (9/16") wide. TUBE is pale lavender (65D); medium length & thickness; 13mm (1/2") long x 8mm (5/16") wide. STAMENS extend 4mm (1/8") beyond the corolla; rose (65A) filaments; light pink (65B) anthers. PISTIL extends 32mm (1 1/4") beyond the corolla; light pink (65B) style; white (155A) stigma. BUD is ovate. FOLIAGE is dark green (137A) upper surface; medium green (138B) lower surface. Leaves are 62mm (2 7/16") long x 42mm (1 5/8") wide, cordate shaped, serrulate edges, acute tips, cordate bases. Veins, stems & branches are green. PARENTAGE: 'Comperen Guttata' x 'Vancuyk Lucien'. Lax upright or stiff trailer. Makes good upright or stiff trailer. Prefers overhead filtered light. Best bloom in filtered light. Tested 3 years in Lubbeek, Belgium. Distinguished by bloom colour combination.
Decoster 2009 BE AFS7259.

Lammert Krikke. Upright. Single. COROLLA is quarter flared, smooth petal margins; opens & matures red (180B); 12mm (1/2") long x 10mm (3/8") wide. SEPALS are half down, tips recurved; reddish purple (61B) tipped green upper surface; rose (61D) tipped green lower surface; 17mm (11/16") long x 8mm (5/16") wide. TUBE is magenta (59C); medium length & thickness; 10mm (3/8") long x 5mm (3/16") wide. STAMENS extend 12mm (1/2") beyond the corolla; light pink (65C) filaments & anthers. PISTIL extends 21mm (13/16") below the corolla; rose (64D) style; cream (11D) stigma. BUD is round, pointed. FOLIAGE is dark green (139A) upper surface, medium green (137B) lower surface. Leaves are 46mm (1 13/16") long x 31mm (1 1/4") wide, cordate shaped, serrated edges, acute tips and rounded bases. Veins, stems & branches are red. PARENTAGE: 'Roesse Apus' x 'Rohees Izar'. Small upright. Makes good standard. Prefers overhead filtered light & cool climate. Best bloom colour in filtered

light. Tested four years in Knegsel, The Netherlands. Distinguished by bloom & foliage combination.
Roes 2004 NL AFS5370.

Lancambe. Single. COROLLA blush violet. SEPALS rose pink.
Aldren 2002 UK.

Land Salzberg. Upright. Single. COROLLA reddish purple; corolla is three quarter flared. SEPALS indian lake on the upper and lower surfaces; sepals are horizontally held with green reflexed tips. TUBE dark indian lake. PARENTAGE 'Hanna' x 'Hanna'.
Klemm 2008 AT BFS0080.

Land Steiermark. Upright. Double. COROLLA violet blue; corolla is fully flared. SEPALS light pink veined red on the upper and lower surfaces; sepals are half down with recurved tips. TUBE light pink. PARENTAGE 'Cliff's Own' x 'Delta's Parade'.
Klemm 2008 AT BFS0082.

Lander Kennes. Upright/Trailer. Double. COROLLA: half flared; opens reddish purple (72B) base rose (55B) and matures magenta (67B) base rose (62C); 25mm (1") long x 22mm (7/8") wide. PETALOIDS: reddish purple (70B) base rose (52C); 20mm (3/4") long x 13mm (1/2") wide. SEPALS are horizontal, tips recurved; rose (55B) tipped light apple green (144D) upper surface and rose (52C) tipped light apple green (144D) lower surface; 32mm (1 1/4") long x 13mm (1/2") wide. TUBE is pale pink (56C); short & thick; 8mm (5/16") long x 5mm (3/16") wide. FOLIAGE is dark green (136B) upper surface; medium green (138B) lower surface. PARENTAGE: 'Leon Pauwels' x 'Monique Sleidernik'.
Michiels 2007 BE AFS6523.

Landeshauptstadt St. Pölten. Upright/Trailer. Double. COROLLA: Fully flared; opens dark purple (86A); matures violet (86B); 30mm (1 3/16") long x 50mm (2") wide. PETALOIDS: violet (86B) & rose (52C); 20mm (3/4") long x 18mm (11/16") wide. SEPALS: half up, tips reflexed up; red (53C) upper surface; rose (52C) lower surface; 35mm (1 3/8") long x 22mm (7/8") wide. TUBE: red (53B); medium length & thickness; 20mm (3/4") long x 6mm (1/4") wide. FOLIAGE is medium green (137B) upper surface; yellowish green (146B) lower surface. PARENTAGE: 'Lavaglüt' x unknown.
Klemm 2007 AT AFS6472.

Langsford. Upright. Single. COROLLA is unflared, bell shaped, with turned under petal margins; opens purple (77A); matures reddish purple (67A); red (53D) at base; 12mm (1/2") long x 8mm (5/16") wide. SEPALS are half down, tips recurved; red (53D) upper and lower surfaces, creped lower surface; 22mm (7/8") long x 6mm (1/4") wide. TUBE is red (53D), proportionately medium length and thin; 15mm (5/8") long x 4mm (3/16") wide. STAMENS extend 13mm (1/2") below the corolla; dark rose (54A) filaments and blushed cream anthers. PISTIL extends 28mm (1 1/8") below the corolla; dark rose (54A) style and blushed cream stigma. BUD is lanceolate shaped. FOLIAGE is dark green (147A) on upper and lighter green on lower surface. Leaves are 42mm (1 11/16") long x 25mm (1") wide, lanceolate shaped, serrated edges, acute tips and acute bases. Veins are light green, stems and branches are dark red (46A). PARENTAGE: 'F. *magellanica*' x 'Kellyjo'. Small upright. Self branching. Makes good upright, standard, pillar, decorative or bedding . Prefers full sun. Cold weather hardy to 30° F. Best bloom colour in bright light. Tested four years in Edenbridge, Kent, England. Distinguished by blossom colour
Holmes 2002 UK AFS4807.

Lanimee. Upright. Semi Double. COROLLA: quarter flared; opens magenta (61C); matures magenta (59C); 18mm (11/16") long x 7mm (1/4") wide. PETALOIDS: same colour as corolla; 15mm (9/16") long x 10mm (3/8") wide. SEPALS: half up, tips recurved up; magenta (61C) upper & lower surfaces; 40mm (1 9/16") long x 10mm (3/8") wide. TUBE: magenta (57A); 19mm (3/4") long x 9mm (5/16") wide. FOLIAGE is medium green (146A) upper surface; yellowish green (146B) lower surface. PARENTAGE: 'Gerwin van den Brink' x 'Majoor Boshardt'. Nomination by NKVF as Recommendable Cultivar.
van den Brink 2008 NL AFS6779.

Laura Biolcati-Rinaldi. Trailer. Double. COROLLA is half flared; opens light purple (81C) with white (155C) base; matures pale purple (74D); 25mm (1") long x 17mm (5/8") wide. PETALOIDS are light purple (81C) with white (155C) base; 16mm (5/8") long x11mm (7/16") wide. SEPALS are horizontal, tips reflexed; white (155C) tipped light apple green (145B) upper and lower surfaces; 44mm (1 3/4") long x 14mm (9/16") wide. TUBE is white (155C); 12mm (7/16") long x 6mm (1/4") wide. FOLIAGE is dark green (139A) upper surface; medium green (137C) lower surface. PARENTAGE: 'Sofie Michiels' x 'Breevis Lowi'. Meise 8/13/05. Distinguished by curling leaves.
Michiels 2006 BE AFS6028.

Laura Jane. Upright. Single. COROLLA is bell shaped, half flared with smooth petal margins; opens & matures dark rose (58C); 14mm (9/16") long x 12 mm (1/2") wide. SEPALS are half up, tips reflexed up; waxy white (155D) tipped green upper surface; white (155B) lower surface; 30mm (1 3/16") long x 10mm (3/8") wide. TUBE is waxy white (155D), medium length and thickness; 14mm (9/16") long x 6mm (1/4") wide. STAMENS extend 6mm (1/4") beyond the corolla; pale pink (56A) filaments & anthers. PISTIL extends 20mm (13/16") below the corolla; pale pink (56A) style; white (155B) stigma. BUD is pear shaped. FOLIAGE is medium green (137B) upper surface, medium green (137D) lower surface. Leaves are 55mm (2 3/16") long x 30mm (1 3/16") wide, lanceolate shaped, serrulated edges, acute tips and rounded bases. Veins are red (53B), stems are greenish white (157B), branches are dark red (53A). PARENTAGE: Sport of 'Anita'. Medium upright. Makes good basket or standard. Prefers warm climate. Best bloom and foliage colour in filtered light. Tested ten years in Chester, England. Best in show, six years, Chester & District Fuchsia Society. Distinguished by bloom colour.
Davies 2004 UK AFS5357.

Laura Krekels. Upright. Double. COROLLA: three quarter flared, smooth petal margins; opens violet (75A); matures light violet (75B); 24mm (15/16") long x 30mm (1 3/16") wide. SEPALS: half up; tips recurved up; pale lavender (69D) upper & lower surfaces; 42mm (1 5/8") long x 12mm (1/2") wide. TUBE: pale lavender (69D); medium length & thickness; 17mm (11/16") long x 7mm (1/4") wide. STAMENS: extend 17mm (11/16") below corolla; light rose (73C) filaments, magenta (63A) anthers. PISTIL: extends 24mm (15/16") below the corolla; pale rose (73D) style, light yellow (4C) stigma. BUD: ovate. FOLIAGE: dark green (137A) upper surface; medium green (138A) lower surface. Leaves are 70mm (2 3/4") long x 36mm (1 7/16") wide, ovate shaped, serrulated edges, acute tips and rounded bases. Veins, stems & branches are green. PARENTAGE: 'Sofie Michiels' x 'Veenlust'. Medium upright. Makes good standard. Prefers overhead filtered light and cool climate. Best bloom and foliage colour in filtered light. Tested 4

years in Reusel, The Netherlands. Distinguished by bloom colour.
van Eijk 2003 NL AFS5259.

Laure Buelens. Upright. Single. COROLLA is quarter flared with turned under smooth petal margins; opens dark purple (78A), matures light purple (78B); 12mm (1/2") long x 14 mm (9/16") wide. SEPALS are half down, tips reflexed; light rose (58D) upper surface, dark rose (58C) lower surface; 22mm (7/8") long x 14mm (9/16") wide. TUBE is light yellowish green (154C), medium length and thin; 17mm (11/16") long x 4mm (3/16") wide. STAMENS do not extend beyond the corolla; reddish purple (66B) filaments, dark reddish purple (70A) anthers. PISTIL does not extend beyond the corolla; yellowish white (4D) style; light yellow (4C) stigma. BUD is round. FOLIAGE is dark green (136A) upper surface, medium green (137C) lower surface. Leaves are 59mm (2 5/16") long x 33mm (1 5/16") wide, ovate shaped, serrulated edges, acute tips and rounded bases. Veins are plum (185B), stems dark grayish purple (183A), branches are dark reddish purple (187B). PARENTAGE: 'WALZ Harp' x 'Tanya'. Medium upright. Self branching. Makes good upright. Prefers overhead filtered light. Best bloom and foliage colour in filtered light. Tested three years in Koningshooikt and Hoeselt, Belgium. Certificate N.B.F.K. at Meise. Distinguished by bloom shape.
Michiels 2002 BE AFS4930.

Laure Peeters. Upright. Single. COROLLA is three quarter flared with turned under wavy petal margins; opens purple (77A), magenta (58B) base; matures dark reddish purple (72A); 23mm (15/16") long x 23mm (15/16") wide. SEPALS are horizontal, tips recurved; red (53C) upper surface, magenta (58B) lower surface; 25mm (1") long x 13mm (1/4") wide. TUBE is red (53B); short & thick; 25mm (1") long x 13mm (1/2") wide. FOLIAGE: dark green (136B) upper surface; medium green (138B) lower surface. Leaves are 51mm (2") long x 21mm (13/16") wide, elliptic shaped. PARENTAGE: 'Roesse Blacky' x 'Breevis Anactus'. Meise 8-14-04. Distinguished by flower colour & shape.
Michiels 2005 BE AFS5741.

Laure Verheyden. Upright/Trailer. Single. COROLLA is half flared with turned under wavy petal margins; opens reddish purple (74B), matures reddish purple (74A); 20mm (13/16") long x 18 mm (11/16") wide. PETALOIDS: reddish purple (74A); 14mm (9/16") x 12mm (1/2"). SEPALS are half down, tips reflexed; rose (52C) upper surface, rose (52B) lower surface; 35mm (1 3/8") long x 13mm (1/2") wide. TUBE is very pale orange (27D), long and thin; 35mm (1 3/8") long x 5mm (3/16") wide. STAMENS do not extend beyond the corolla; yellowish white (4D) filaments, grayish yellow (161A) anthers. PISTIL extends 10mm (3/8") beyond the corolla; pink (49A) style; light yellow (4C) stigma. BUD is ovate, pointed. FOLIAGE is dark green (137A) upper surface, medium green (138B) lower surface. Leaves are 68mm (2 11/16") long x 36mm (1 7/16") wide, ovate shaped, serrulated edges, acute tips and rounded bases. Veins are apple green (144C), stems are dark grayish purple (184A), branches are dark purple (79A). PARENTAGE: 'WALZ Harp' x 'Blue Veil'. Lax upright or stiff trailer. Makes good upright. Prefers overhead filtered light. Best bloom and foliage colour in filtered light. Tested three years in Itegem, Belgium. Certificate N.B.F.K. at Meise. Distinguished by bloom shape.
Geerts L. 2002 BE AFS4925.

Lauren Fortes. Upright/Trailer. Semi Double to Double. COROLLA: three quarter flared, turned under wavy petal margins; opens purple (71A) & dark purple (N79B); matures dark reddish purple (61A); 33mm (1 5/16") long x 27mm (1 1/16") wide. PETALOIDS: Same colour as corolla; 23mm (7/8") long x 14mm (9/16") wide. SEPALS: horizontal, tips recurved; dark reddish purple (60C) upper surface; reddish purple (58A) lower surface; 46mm (1 13/16") long x 12mm (7/16") wide. TUBE: magenta (59D); medium length & thickness; 13mm (1/2") long x 7mm (1/4") wide. STAMENS extend 17mm (5/8") beyond the corolla; purple (71A) filaments; purple (83A) anthers. PISTIL extends 31mm (1 1/4") beyond the corolla; reddish purple (71B) style; rose (61D) stigma. BUD: elongated. FOLIAGE: medium green (137C) upper surface; medium green (138B) lower surface. Leaves are 66mm (2 5/8") long x 30mm (1 3/16") wide; elliptic shaped, serrulate edges, acute tips, rounded bases. Veins are dark red (185A), stems are plum (185B), branches are plum (184B). PARENTAGE: 'Manfried Kleinau' x 'Jubie-Lin'. Lax upright or stiff trailer. Self branching. Makes good basket. Prefers overhead filtered light, cool climate. Best bloom & foliage colour in filtered light. Tested 3 years in Koningshooikt, Belgium. Waanrode 8/9/08. Distinguished by bloom colour combination.
Michiels 2009 BE AFS7194.

Laurena. Upright/Trailer. Single. COROLLA is half flared with turned under wavy petal margins; opens light reddish purple (73A), white (155A) base; matures light rose (73B); 12mm (1/2") long x 11mm (7/16") wide. SEPALS are horizontal, tips reflexed; dark rose (55A), white (155A) base, tipped yellowish green (144B) upper surface; rose (65A), white (155A) base, tipped yellowish green (144B) lower surface; 16mm (5/8") long x 6mm (1/4") wide. TUBE is white (155A); medium length & thickness; 14mm (9/16") long x 5mm (3/16") wide. FOLIAGE: dark green (139A) upper surface; medium green (139C) lower surface. Leaves are 51mm (2") long x 33mm (1 5/16") wide, ovate shaped. PARENTAGE: 'Allison Reynolds' x unknown. Meise 8-14-04. Distinguished by bloom shape & colour.
Willems 2005 BE AFS5724.

Lavender Heaven. Trailer. Double. COROLLA is half flared with turned under smooth petal margins; opens pale purple (76C); matures light violet (77D); 29mm (1 1/8") long x 25mm (1") wide. PETALOIDS: pale purple (76C), light rose (73C) base; 18mm (11/16") long x 12mm (1/2") wide. SEPALS are horizontal, tips recurved; pale rose (73D), white (155C) base, tipped light yellowish green (149B) upper surface; white (155C), light rose (73C) base, tipped light yellowish green (149B) lower surface; 48mm (1 7/8") long x 14mm (9/16") wide. TUBE is white (155C); medium length & thickness; 22mm (7/8") long x 7mm (1/4") wide. FOLIAGE: dark green (137A) upper surface; medium green (138B) lower surface. Leaves are 47mm (1 7/8") long x 24mm (15/16") wide, ovate shaped. PARENTAGE: 'Sofie Michiels' x 'Weleveld'. Meis 3-7-04. Distinguished by colour & shape combination.
Michiels 2005 BE AFS5684.

Lea Michiels. Upright/Trailer. Double. COROLLA is full flared with smooth petal margins; dark purple (79A), matures purple (71A); 24mm (15/16") long x 22mm (7/8") wide. SEPALS are half up, tips reflexed up; reddish purple (58A) upper surface, magenta (63A) lower surface; 34mm (1 3/8") long x 21mm (13/16") wide. TUBE is reddish purple (58A), proportionately medium length and thickness; 24mm (15/16") long x 9mm (3/8") wide. STAMENS extend 32mm (1 1/4") below the corolla; purple (71A) filaments and dark purple (79A) anthers. PISTIL extends 41mm (1 5/8") below the corolla; purple (71A) style and pale pink (62D) stigma. BUD is round

and pointed. FOLIAGE is dark green (137A) on upper surface and medium green (138B) on lower surface. Leaves are 67mm (2 5/8") long x 36mm (1 7/16") wide, ovate shaped, serrulated edges, acute tips and rounded bases. Veins, stems and branches are red. PARENTAGE: 'Rohees Queen' x 'Rohees Hamal'. Lax upright or stiff trailer. Makes good stiff trailer. Prefers overhead filtered light and warm climate. Best bloom colour in filtered light. Tested four years in Knegsel, The Netherlands. Distinguished by bloom colour.
Roes 2002 NL AFS4794.

Leen Vander Kuylen. Trailer. Double. COROLLA is three quarter flared with turned under smooth petal margins; opens violet (82C), light rose (63D) base; matures light purple (74C), pale rose (73D) base; 25mm (1") long x 22mm (7/8") wide. PETALOIDS: light purple (82D), light rose (63D) base; 19mm (3/4") long x 10mm (3/8") wide. SEPALS are half up, tips recurved up; pale pink (56D), tipped light apple green (145B) upper surface; light rose (63D), tipped apple green (145B) lower surface; 43mm (1 11/16") long x 15mm (9/16") wide. TUBE is white (155C); medium length & thickness; 18mm (11/16") long x 6mm (1/4") wide. FOLIAGE: dark green (136A) upper surface; medium green (138B) lower surface. Leaves are 53mm (2 1/16") long x 22mm (7/8") wide, elliptic shaped. PARENTAGE: 'Sofie Michiels' x 'Weleveld'. Meise 8-14-04. Distinguished by flower colour & shape.
Michiels 2005 BE AFS5754.

Leesa C. Struck. Upright. Single. COROLLA: quarter flared, turned under smooth petal margins; opens reddish purple (64B); matures magenta (63B); 6mm (1/4") long x 4mm (3/16") wide. SEPALS: horizontal; tips reflexed; reddish purple (61B) upper surface; magenta (61C) lower surface; 7mm (1/4") long x 3mm (1/8") wide. TUBE: reddish purple (61B); short & thin; 7mm(1/4") long x 3mm (1/8") wide. STAMENS: do not extend below corolla; pale pink (62D) filaments, dark reddish purple (60C) anthers. PISTIL: extends 3mm (1/8") below the corolla, magenta (57C) style, pink (62C) stigma. BUD: elongated. FOLIAGE: dark green (137A) upper surface; medium green (138B) lower surface. Leaves are 49mm (1 15/16") long x 23mm (15/16") wide, elliptic shaped, serrulated edges, acute tips and rounded bases. Veins are plum (184C), stems are dark grayish purple (184A), branches are plum (185C). PARENTAGE: 'Rosea' x 'F.

fulgens var. *gesneriana'*. Small upright. Self branching. Makes good upright. Prefers full sun. Best bloom and foliage colour in bright light. Tested 3 years in Nakskov, Denmark. NBFK Certificate at Meise. Distinguished by blossom shape.
Struck 2003 DK AFS5190.

Leeuw. Trailer. Single. COROLLA: quarter flared; opens white (155C) striped reddish purple (67A); matures white (155D) striped magenta (61C); 30mm (1 3/16") long x 23mm (7/8") wide. SEPALS are half down, tips recurved, twisted left; magenta (71C) upper surface; reddish purple (67A) lower surface; 57mm (2 1/4") long x 12mm (7/16") wide. TUBE is light pink (62C) striped magenta (71C); 36mm (1 7/16") long x 6mm (1/4") wide. FOLIAGE is yellowish green (144B) upper surface; light apple green (145B) lower surface. PARENTAGE: Sport of 'Trix Brouwer'. Waanrode 7/7/2007.
Geerts L. 2008 BE AFS6735.

Lena Lankman. Upright. Double. COROLLA: quarter flared; opens purple (71A); matures dark reddish purple (64A); 28mm (1 1/8") long x 24mm (15/16") wide. PETALOIDS: purple (71A), veined red (53C), spotted pink; 27mm (1 1/16") long x 24mm (15/16") wide. SEPALS: half up, tips recurved up; red (52A) tipped light yellowish green (150C) upper surface; reddish purple (66B) lower surface; 37mm (1 7/16") long x 17mm (5/8") wide. TUBE: red (52A); 27mm (1 1/16") long x 9mm (5/16") wide. FOLIAGE is medium green (137B) upper surface; light olive green (147C) lower surface. PARENTAGE: 'Gerwin van den Brink' x seedling of 'Gerwin van den Brink'. Nomination by NKVF as Recommendable Cultivar.
van den Brink 2008 NL AFS6776.

Lena-Franziska. Upright/Trailer. Semi Double. COROLLA: quarter flared; smooth petal margins; opens & matures dark reddish purple (61A); 27mm (1 1/16") long x 24mm (15/16") wide. SEPALS: horizontal, tips recurved; white (155C) upper surface; white (155C) flushed reddish purple (71B) lower surface; 45mm (1 3/4") long x 12mm (7/16") wide. TUBE: white (155C); medium length & thickness; 22mm (7/8") long x 8mm (5/16") wide. STAMENS extend 15mm (9/16") beyond the corolla; magenta (71C) filaments; tan (165B) anthers. PISTIL extends 35mm (1 3/8") beyond the corolla; magenta (71C) style; pale yellow (158B) stigma. BUD is longish, green tip. FOLIAGE is dark green (147A) upper surface; light

olive green (147C) lower surface. Leaves are 85mm (3 3/8") long x 42mm (1 5/8") wide; ovate shaped, serrate edges, acute tips, rounded bases. Veins are green, stems are grayed-orange, branches are green. PARENTAGE: 'Anita' x unknown. Lax upright or stiff trailer. Makes good basket. Prefers overhead filtered light. Heat tolerant if shaded. Best bloom colour in filtered light. Tested 4 years in Graz, Austria. Distinguished by large flowers & long SEPALS.
Strümper 2009 AT AFS7001.

Lengenfelder Dunkle. Upright. Single. COROLLA: quarter flared, smooth petal margins; opens dark reddish purple (59A); matures reddish purple (59B); 16mm (5/8") long x 18mm (11/16") wide. SEPALS: fully up, tips recurved; dark reddish purple (60B) upper & lower surfaces; 30mm (1 3/16") long x 11mm (7/16") wide. TUBE: dark reddish purple (60B); medium length & thickness; 12mm (7/16") long x 7mm (1/4") wide. STAMENS extend 20mm (3/4") beyond the corolla; dark reddish purple (60B) filaments; reddish purple (59B) anthers. PISTIL extends 40mm (1 9/16") beyond the corolla; dark reddish purple (60B) style & stigma. BUD: elongated. FOLIAGE: medium green (137B) upper surface; medium green (138B) lower surface. Leaves are 82mm (3 1/4") long x 42mm (1 5/8") wide; ovate shaped, serrate edges, acute tips, rounded bases. Veins & stems are red, branches are reddish brown. PARENTAGE: 'Rohees Rana' x 'Oscar Lehmeier'. Medium upright. Self branching. Makes good upright or standard. Prefers full sun, warm climate. Heat tolerant if shaded. Best bloom & foliage colour in bright light. Tested 3 years in Bavaria, Southern Germany. Distinguished by corolla colour & shape.
Burkhart 2009 DE AFS7110.

Lenny Erwin. Trailer. Double. COROLLA: three-quarter flared; opens reddish purple (N80B) and matures light purple (N78C); 16mm (5/8") long x 14mm (9/16") wide. PETALOIDS: violet (76A); 8mm (5/16") long x 6mm (1/4") wide. SEPALS are horizontal, tips reflexed; white (155C) tipped light apple green (144D) upper surface and pale lavender (69D) tipped light apple green (144D) lower surface; 28mm (1 1/8") long x 16mm (5/8") wide. TUBE is white (155C); medium length & thickness; 15mm (9/16") long x 6mm (1/4") wide. FOLIAGE is dark green (136B) upper surface; medium green

(138B) lower surface. PARENTAGE: 'Vreni Schleeweiss' x 'Kiss'. Michiels 2007 BE AFS6524.

Lennyben. Upright. Single. COROLLA is quarter flared with turned under wavy petal margins; opens reddish purple (74A), matures reddish purple (71B); 23mm (15/16") long x 18 mm (11/16") wide. SEPALS are half up, tips recurved up; magenta (58B) tipped yellowish green (145A) upper surface, rose (55B) tipped yellowish orange (14B) lower surface; 27mm (1 1/16") long x 10mm (3/8") wide. TUBE is dark rose (55A), medium length and thickness; 24mm (15/16") long x 6mm (1/4") wide. STAMENS extend 8mm (5/16) beyond the corolla; dark rose (55A) filaments, tan (162A) anthers. PISTIL extends 8mm (5/16) beyond the corolla; rose (55B) style; brown (165A) stigma. BUD is ovate, pointed. FOLIAGE is dark green (139A) upper surface, medium green (147B) lower surface. Leaves are 62mm (2 7/16") long x 34mm (1 3/8") wide, ovate shaped, serrulated edges, acute tips and rounded bases. Veins are light green (143D), stems are brown (176C), branches are dark grayish purple (183A). PARENTAGE: 'WALZ Harp' x 'WALZ Doedelzak'. Medium upright, dwarf growth. Self branching. Makes good upright. Prefers full sun. Best bloom and foliage colour in bright light. Tested three years in Itegem, Belgium. Certificate N.B.F.K. at Meise. Distinguished by sepal colour. Geerts L. 2002 BE AFS4926.

Leon Pauwels. Trailer. Double. COROLLA is three quarter flared with smooth petal margins; opens purple (83B), matures purple (77A); 32mm (1 1/4") long x 41 mm (1 5/8") wide. SEPALS are fully up, tips reflexed; light pink (62B) upper surface; pink (62A) lower surface; 57mm (2 1/4") long x 18mm (11/16") wide. TUBE is pink (62A), medium length and thickness; 22mm (7/8") long x 7mm (1/4") wide. STAMENS extend 10mm (3/8") beyond the corolla; reddish purple (71B) filaments; purple (71A) anthers. PISTIL extends 22mm (7/8") below the corolla; magenta (71C) style; yellowish white (4D) stigma. BUD is ovate, pointed. FOLIAGE is dark green (137A) upper surface, medium green (138B) lower surface. Leaves are 74mm (2 15/16") long x 38mm (1 1/2") wide, ovate shaped, serrulated edges, acute tips and obtuse bases. Veins are red, stems & branches are green. PARENTAGE: 'Bicentennial' x 'Allure'. Natural trailer. Makes good basket. Prefers overhead filtered light & cool climate. Best bloom and foliage

colour in filtered light. Tested four years in Knegsel, The Netherlands. Distinguished by bloom colour. van Bree 2004 NL AFS5360.

Leslie Drew. COROLLA blue to violet. SEPALS white. TUBE white. Drew 2007 UK.

Lesson Girl. Upright. Single. COROLLA is half flared with smooth petal margins; opens light reddish purple (72D) edged darker, white base; matures light rose (73B); 22mm (7/8") long x 26mm (1") wide. SEPALS are half up, tips recurved up; light pink (62B) blushed pink, tipped green upper and lower surfaces; 35mm (1 3/8") long x 12mm (1/2") wide. TUBE is white (155A) blushed pink; short and thin; 15mm (5/8") long x 12mm (1/2") wide. STAMENS extend 15mm (5/8") beyond the corolla; dark rose (54B) filaments and anthers. PISTIL extends 28mm (1 1/8") beyond the corolla; light rose (63D) style, yellowish white (158A) stigma. BUD is cylindrical, pointed. FOLIAGE is dark green (137A) upper surface, medium green (143A) lower surface. Leaves are 50mm (2") long x 32mm (1 1/4") wide, cordate shaped, serrulated edges, acute tips and rounded bases. Veins are light green, stems are red, branches are deep red. PARENTAGE: 'Carla Johnson' x 'Mr. W. Rundle'. Small upright. Self branching. Makes good upright or standard. Prefers overhead filtered light and full sun. Best bloom colour in bright or filtered light. Tested four years in Hyde, Cheshire, England. Distinguished by corolla colour combination. Gibson 2002 UK AFS4950.

Lesson Hannah. Upright/Trailer. Single. COROLLA is quarter flared, bell shaped, with turned up smooth petal margins; opens red (53B), matures red (53C); 30mm (1 3/16") long x 27mm (1 1/16") wide. SEPALS are full down, tips recurved; red (47B) tipped green upper surface, dark rose (48A) lower surface; 39mm (1 9/16") long x 13mm (1/2") wide. TUBE is white (155A) overlaid with red (52A); long and thick; 27mm (1 1/16") long x 12mm (1/2") wide. STAMENS extend 20mm (13/16") beyond the corolla; red (45C) filaments, white (155A) anthers. PISTIL extends 12mm (1/2") beyond the corolla; pink (36A) style, white (155A) stigma. BUD is cylindrical. FOLIAGE is dark green (137A) upper surface, medium green (147B) lower surface. Leaves are 60mm (2 3/8") long x 38mm (1 1/2") wide, cordate shaped, serrated edges, acute tips and rounded bases. Veins and stems are green, branches are red. PARENTAGE: 'Duchess of Albany' x 'Dollar Princess'. Lax upright or stiff trailer. Self branching. Makes good basket or standard. Prefers overhead filtered light and warm climate. Heat tolerant if shaded. Best bloom colour in bright light. Tested four years in Hyde, Cheshire, England. Distinguished by colour combination. Gibson 2002 UK AFS4949.

Lex Krekels. Upright/Trailer. Double. COROLLA: three quarter flared, smooth petal margins; opens reddish purple (72B); matures dark rose (68C); 22mm (7/8") long x 22mm (7/8") wide. SEPALS: half up; tips recurved up; magenta (58B) upper & lower surfaces;32mm (1 1/4") long x 17mm (11/16") wide. TUBE: magenta (58B); medium length & thickness; 20mm (13/16") long x 6mm (1/4") wide. STAMENS: extend 20mm (13/16") below corolla; dark rose (58C) filaments, magenta (59D) anthers. PISTIL: extends 47mm (1 7/8") below the corolla; light rose (58D) style & stigma. BUD: cordate. FOLIAGE: dark green (137A) upper surface; medium green (138B) lower surface. Leaves are 45mm (1 3/4") long x 32mm (1 1/4") wide, cordate shaped, serrulated edges, obtuse tips and obtuse bases. Veins & stems are red; branches are green. PARENTAGE: 'Bicentennial' x 'Parasol'. Lax upright or stiff trailer. Makes good stiff trailer. Prefers overhead filtered light and cool climate. Best bloom and foliage colour in filtered light. Tested 4 years in Reusel, The Netherlands. Distinguished by bloom colour. van Eijk 2003 NL AFS5253.

Lianne Venhoven. Upright/Trailer. Single. COROLLA is quarter flared with smooth petal margins; opens dark reddish purple (61A); matures dark reddish purple (60C); 21mm (13/16") long x 23mm (15/16") wide. SEPALS are fully up, tips recurved; light rose (68D) upper surface; rose (68B) lower surface; 36mm (1 7/16") long x 14mm (9/16") wide. TUBE is pale pink (36D); medium length & thickness; 36mm (1 7/16") long x 14mm (9/16") wide. FOLIAGE: medium green (137B) upper surface; medium green (138B) lower surface. Leaves are 54mm (2 1/8") long x 31mm (1 1/4") wide, ovate shaped. PARENTAGE: ('Roesse Apus' x 'Roesse Apus') x 'Yvette Klessens'. Distinguished by bloom & foliage combination. Buiting 2005 NL AFS5862.

Liberec. Upright/Trailer. Double. COROLLA: half flared, turned under wavy petal margins; opens magenta (59D) & dark reddish purple (60A); matures reddish purple (59B); 25mm (1") long x 21mm (13/16") wide. PETALOIDS: Same colour as corolla; 15mm (9/16") long x 11mm (7/16") wide. SEPALS: half down, tips recurved; light rose (58D) tipped light apple green (145C) upper surface; dark rose (58C) tipped light apple green (145C) lower surface; 29mm (1 1/8") long x 13mm (1/2") wide. TUBE: dark rose (58C); medium length & thickness; 15mm (9/16") long x 6mm (1/4") wide. STAMENS extend 14mm (9/16") beyond the corolla; reddish purple (61B) filaments; dark purple (79A) anthers. PISTIL extends 18mm (11/16") beyond the corolla; dark reddish purple (61A) style; pale lavender (65D) stigma. BUD: globular. FOLIAGE: dark green (137A) upper surface; medium green (138B) lower surface. Leaves are 50mm (2") long x 32mm (1 1/4") wide; ovate shaped, serrulate edges, acute tips, rounded bases. Veins are plum (184C), stems are plum (185B), branches are plum (184B). PARENTAGE: 'Manfried Kleinau' x 'First Lord'. Lax upright or stiff trailer. Self branching. Makes good basket or upright. Prefers overhead filtered light, cool climate. Best bloom & foliage colour in filtered light. Tested 3 years in Koningshooikt, Belgium. Waanrode 8/9/08. Distinguished by bloom colour combination. Michiels 2009 BE AFS7195.

Liebelei. Upright. Single. COROLLA Strümper. SEPALS red on the upper surface, lighter red on lower surface; sepals are fully up with recurved tips and are 20mm long x 12mm wide. TUBE red and is 5mm long x 5mm wide. PARENTAGE 'Linda Goulding' x 'Impudence'. Strümper 2008 DE BFS0060.

Lieke Comperen. Upright/Trailer. Double. COROLLA: half flared, smooth petal margins; opens dark purple (79B); matures violet (86A); 27mm (1 1/16") long x 30mm (1 3/16") wide. SEPALS: fully up; tips reflexed; magenta (63A) upper & lower surfaces; 31mm (1 1/4") long x 16mm (5/8") wide. TUBE: magenta (63A); medium length & thickness; 11mm (7/16") long x 7mm (1/4") wide. STAMENS: extend 18mm (11/16") below corolla; dark reddish purple (59A) filaments; magenta (59C) anthers. PISTIL: extends 31mm (1 1/4") below the corolla; magenta (63A) style, magenta (63B) stigma. BUD: ovate. FOLIAGE: medium green (137B) upper surface; medium green (138B) lower surface. Leaves are 67mm (2 5/8") long x 42mm (1 5/8") wide, ovate shaped, serrulated edges, acute tips and obtuse bases. Veins, stems & branches are green. PARENTAGE: 'Maxima' x 'Madalyn Drago'. Lax upright or stiff trailer. Makes good stiff trailer. Prefers overhead filtered light and cool climate. Best bloom and foliage colour in filtered light. Tested 4 years in Diessen, The Netherlands. Distinguished by bloom colour. Comperen 2003 NL AFS5267.

Lies Timmermans. Upright. Double. COROLLA is half flared with smooth petal margins; opens dark purple (79B); matures violet (83D); 21mm (13/16") long x 28mm (1 1/8") wide. SEPALS are horizontal, tips recurved; pale lavender (69C) upper surface; light rose (73C) lower surface; 26mm (1") long x 15mm (9/16") wide. TUBE is pale lavender (69D); medium length & thickness; 9mm (3/8) long x 4mm (3/16") wide. FOLIAGE: dark green (137A) upper surface; medium green (138B) lower surface. Leaves are 72mm (2 13/16") long x 40mm (1 9/16") wide, ovate shaped. PARENTAGE: 'Roesse Apus' x 'Van Eijk Triksie'. Distinguished by bloom & foliage combination. van Eijk 2005 NL AFS5907.

Liesbeth. Upright/Trailer. Semi Double. COROLLA: half flared; opens reddish purple (70B), pale lavender (65D) base; matures light reddish purple (72C); 17mm (5/8") long x 16mm (5/8") wide. SEPALS: half down, tips reflexed; pale lavender (69B) tipped light green (141D) upper surface; light rose (73B) tipped light green (141D) lower surface; 30mm (1 3/16") long x 12mm (7/16") wide. TUBE: light green (145D); medium length & thickness; 17mm (5/8") long x 4mm (1/8") wide. FOLIAGE is medium green (138A) upper surface; medium green (138B) lower surface. PARENTAGE: 'De Brommel' x 'Bon Bon'. Michiels 2007 BE AFS6364.

Lieselotje. Upright/Trailer. Single. COROLLA: quarter flared; opens rose (52B) & reddish purple (64B); matures magenta (63B); 29mm (1 1/8") long x 23mm (7/8") wide. SEPALS: half down, tips reflexed; rose (52C) upper surface; rose (52B) lower surface; 35mm (1 3/8") long x 7mm (1/4") wide. TUBE: dark rose (54B); 30mm (1 3/16") long x 5mm (3/16") wide. FOLIAGE is dark green (137A) upper surface; medium green (138B) lower surface. PARENTAGE: 'Margrit Williman' x unknown. Van Walleghem 2008 BE AFS6750.

Lieutenant Sebastien Malou. Upright. Single. COROLLA: quarter flared, smooth petal margins; opens & matures reddish orange (43B); 12mm (1/2") long x 12mm (1/2") wide. SEPALS: full down; tips recurved; pink (37C) tipped white upper surface; peach (37B) lower surface; 27mm (1 1/16") long x 5mm (3/16") wide. TUBE: pink (37C); medium length & thickness; 25mm(1") long x 5mm (3/16") wide. STAMENS: extend 13mm (1/2") below corolla; pink (43D) filaments, light reddish orange (171C) anthers. PISTIL: extends 40mm (1 9/16") below the corolla, pink (37C) style, pale pink (62D) stigma. BUD: Long, ovate. FOLIAGE: yellowish green (144A) upper surface; yellowish green (144B) lower surface. Leaves are 70mm (2 3/4") long x 50mm (2") wide, ovate shaped, serrated edges, acute tips and acute bases. Veins are light green, stems are pale green; branches are brown. PARENTAGE: 'Orange Crush' x 'Lye's Unique'. Tall upright. Makes good upright or standard. Prefers overhead filtered light and warm climate. Cold weather hardy to -3° C. Best bloom and foliage colour in filtered light. Tested 3 years in Central France. Distinguished by bright bloom colour. Gaucher 2003 FR AFS5215.

Lieutenant Violaine Gaucher. Upright. Double. COROLLA is quarter flared with wavy petal margins; opens magenta (71C) pink veins and base; matures dark rose (71D); 40mm (1 9/16") long x 35mm (1 3/8") wide. SEPALS are horizontal, tips recurved; rose (55B) upper surface; dark rose (55A) lower surface; 63mm (2 1/2") long x 16mm (5/8") wide. TUBE is rose (55B); short and thick; 14mm (9/16") long x 8mm (5/16") wide. STAMENS extend 12mm (1/2") beyond the corolla; light reddish purple (66C) filaments, dark grayish red (182A) anthers. PISTIL extends 25mm (1") beyond the corolla; rose (68C) style, yellowish white (4D) stigma. BUD is elongated. FOLIAGE is dark green (136A) upper surface, medium green (137C) lower surface. Leaves are 72mm (2 13/16") long x 40mm (1 9/16") wide, ovate shaped, acute tips and acute bases. Veins are medium green (139B), stems and branches are medium green (138B). PARENTAGE: 'Rose of Denmark' x 'Granada'. Lax upright. Makes good upright, standard, pyramid, pillar or decorative. Prefers overhead filtered light. Heat tolerant if shaded. Cold weather hardy to -3° C. Best bloom and foliage colour in bright light. Tested four years in Central France. Distinguished by form and blossom colour pattern.

270

Gaucher 2002 FR AFS4954.

Lieve En Marc. Upright/Trailer. Semi Double to Double. COROLLA: three quarter flared; opens magenta (67B), rose (51C) base; matures dark rose (64C); 24mm (15/16") long x 26mm (1") wide. PETALOIDS: rose (51C) & reddish purple (70B); 14mm (9/16") long x 8mm (5/16") wide. SEPALS: horizontal, tips reflexed; dark rose (54B) & rose (54C) tipped apple green (144C) upper surface; pink (52D) tipped apple green (144C) lower surface; 32mm (1 1/4") long x 14mm (9/16") wide. TUBE: pink (54D) striped yellowish green (144A); square shaped; 13mm (1/2") long x 8mm (5/16") wide. FOLIAGE is dark green (136A) upper surface; medium green (138B) lower surface. PARENTAGE: 'Danny Kaye' x 'Quasar'.
Van Walleghem 2008 BE AFS6749.

Lieze Brantz. Trailer. Single. COROLLA is quarter flared with turned under wavy petal margins; opens light reddish purple (72C); matures light reddish purple (72D); 13mm (1/2") long x 19mm (3/4") wide. SEPALS are half down, tips recurved; light pink (65C), tipped yellowish green (144B) upper surface; light pink (65B) lower surface; 23mm (15/16") long x 10mm (3/8") wide. TUBE is light pink (65C); long, medium thickness; 29mm (1 1/8") long x 6mm (1/4") wide. STAMENS extend 2mm (1/16") beyond the corolla; light pink (62B) filaments, orangy brown (163A) anthers. PISTIL extends 3mm (1/8") beyond the corolla; pink (62C) style, yellow (4A) stigma. BUD is ovate. FOLIAGE is dark green (139A) upper surface, medium green (137B) lower surface. Leaves are 78mm (3 1/16") long x 47mm (1 7/8") wide, cordate shaped, serrulated edges, acute tips and cordate bases. Veins and stems are dark red (178A), branches are yellowish green (144A). PARENTAGE: 'Alda Alders' x 'Wingrove's Mammoth'. Natural trailer. Self branching. Makes good basket. Prefers overhead filtered light and cool climate. Best bloom and foliage colour in filtered light. Tested three years in Leopoldsburg, Belgium. Certificate N.B.F.K. at Meise. Distinguished by delicate bloom colour and profuse blooms.
Busschodts 2002 BE AFS4980.

Lilac Tint. Upright. Single. COROLLA: quarter flared, bell shaped, smooth petal margins; opens & matures light pink (55D) edged pale purple (75C); 32mm (1 1/4") long 22mm (7/8") wide. SEPALS: half up; tips recurved up; white (155B), tipped green, upper surface; white (155D), tipped green

lower surface; 25mm (1") long x 10mm (3/8") wide. TUBE: cream (158D); medium length & thickness; 12mm (1/2") long x 7mm (1/4") wide. STAMENS: extend 12mm (1/2") below corolla; light rose (73C) filaments; cream (158D) anthers. PISTIL: extends 25mm (1") below the corolla; cream (158D) style & stigma. BUD: oval, pointed. FOLIAGE: medium green (137B) upper surface; medium green (138B) lower surface. Leaves are 57mm (2 1/4") long x 32mm (1 1/4") wide, ovate shaped, serrulated edges, acute tips and rounded bases. Green veins, stems & branches. PARENTAGE: 'Julie Ann Goodwin' x 'WALZ Jubleteen'. Small upright. Self branching. Makes good upright or pillar. Prefers overhead filtered light, warm climate. Best bloom and foliage colour in filtered light. Tested 3 years in Stoke-On-Trent, England. Distinguished by profuse blossoms and dainty blossom colour.
Goodwin 2004 UK AFS5574.

Lilian May. Upright. Single. COROLLA: Unflared; opens & matures light purple (89D); 15mm (9/16") long x 10mm (3/8") wide. SEPALS: half up, tips recurved up; pale pink (56D) tipped light apple green (145C) upper surface; dark rose (54B) lower surface; 25mm (1") long x 10mm (3/8") wide. TUBE: pale pink (56D); short & thick; 9mm (5/16") long x 6mm (1/4") wide. FOLIAGE is dark green (141B) upper surface; medium green (141C) lower surface. PARENTAGE: 'La Campanella' x ('Carla Johnston' x 'WALZ Jubelteen') seedling.
Broughton 2007 UK AFS6497.

Lily Sweety Meyers. Trailer. Single. COROLLA is quarter flared; opens dark reddish purple (59A); matures reddish purple (59B); 24mm (15/16") long x 16mm (5/8") wide. SEPALS are horizontal, tips reflexed; dark reddish purple (60B) upper surface, and magenta (59C) lower surface; 28mm (1 1/8") long x 7mm (1/4") wide. TUBE is reddish purple (61B); medium length and thickness; 18mm (11/16") long x 6mm (1/4") wide. FOLIAGE is dark green (137A) upper surface; medium green (138A) lower surface. PARENTAGE: 'Rohees New Millenium' x 'Onbekend'.
Willems 2007 BE AFS6423.

Lily Victoria. Upright. Single. COROLLA opens soft white, slight pink veining at base; corolla is quarter flared and is 24mm long x 18mm wide. SEPALS are deep pink on the upper and lower surfaces; sepals are half down with slightly recurved tips and are

271

40mm long x 11mm wide. TUBE deep pink and is 10mm long x 7mm wide. PARENTAGE found Seedling. This cultivar is capable of producing an excellent half standard, easily propagated, and has blooms which do not fade.
Pownceby 2005 UK BFS0019.

Limelight. COROLLA pale violet. SEPALS creamy white. TUBE creamy white.
Weston 2007 UK.

Limmen. Upright. Single. COROLLA: Unflared, round shape; opens red (47B); matures rose (47C); 11mm (7/16") long x 10mm (3/8") wide. SEPALS: half down, tips reflexed; very pale orange (27D) upper & lower surfaces; 20mm (3/4") long x 7mm (1/4") wide. TUBE: pale pink (36D); medium length & thickness; 18mm (11/16") long x 7mm (1/4") wide. FOLIAGE is dark green (147A) upper surface; medium green (147B) lower surface. PARENTAGE: 'Coachman' x unknown.
Krom 2007 NL AFS6554.

Limoncello. Upright. Single. COROLLA: quarter flared, bell shaped, smooth petal margins; opens purple (83A); matures light purple (78A); 17mm (11/16") long, 15mm (9/16") wide. SEPALS: half down; tips recurved; red (53C) upper surface; red (53D) lower surface; 25mm (1") long x 7mm (1/4") wide. TUBE: red (53C); short, thin; 6mm (1/4") long x 4mm (3/16") wide. STAMENS: extend 15mm (9/16") below corolla; magenta (57C) filaments; reddish purple (58A) anthers. PISTIL: extends 27mm (1 1/16") below the corolla; reddish purple (61B) style & stigma. BUD: ovate. FOLIAGE: greenish yellow (151A) upper & lower surfaces, maturing to medium green (146A) upper surface, yellowish green (146B) lower surface. Leaves are 29mm (1 1/8") long x 13mm (1/2") wide, lanceolate shaped, serrated edges, acute tips and rounded bases. Reddish veins & stems; light brown branches. PARENTAGE: 'Daniela' x unknown. Small upright. Makes good upright. Prefers overhead filtered light. Heat tolerant if shaded. Best bloom and foliage colour in bright light. Tested 3 years in Vicenza, Italy. Distinguished by foliage & leaf colour combinations.
Ianne 2004 IT AFS5636.

Lina Tamerus. Upright. Double. COROLLA is half flared with smooth petal margins; opens purple (89C) and matures reddish purple (74A); 27mm (1 1/16") long x 27mm

(1 1/16") wide. SEPALS are half down, tips reflexed; red (52A) upper and lower surfaces; 39mm (1 9/16) long x 17mm (11/16") wide. TUBE is red (52A), medium length and thickness; 15mm (5/8") long x 7mm (1/4") wide. STAMENS extend 5mm (3/16") below the corolla; red (52A) filaments and anthers. PISTIL extends 14mm (9/16") below the corolla; red (52A) style and rose (68B) stigma. BUD is round, pointed. FOLIAGE is dark green (137A) on upper surface and medium green (138B) on lower surface. Leaves are 58mm (2 5/16") long x 34mm (1 3/8") wide, ovate shaped, serrated edges, acute tips and rounded bases. Veins, stems and branches are red. PARENTAGE: 'Rohees Mintaka' x 'Gillian Althea'. Tall upright. Makes good standard. Prefers overhead filtered light and cool climate. Best bloom colour in filtered light. Tested four years in Duizel, The Netherlands. Distinguished by bloom and foliage combination.
Tamerus 2002 NL AFS4823.

Lincoln Castle. Upright. Single. COROLLA opens purple with white at base and matures rose. SEPALS white tipped green. TUBE white.
Reynolds G. 2006 UK.

Lind. Upright. Double. COROLLA opens red, orange flush at the base; corolla is fully flared and is 35mm long x 55mm wide. SEPALS cream to pink on upper surface, dark pink on the lower surface; sepals are horizontally held with recurved tips and are 30mm long x 10mm wide. TUBE cream to pink and is 10mm long x 8mm wide. PARENTAGE 'Miva' x 'Jackqueline'. Free flowering.
Strümper 2008 DE BFS0059.

Linda Dillen. Trailer. Double. COROLLA is three quarter flared; opens dark purple (79A); matures light reddish purple (72C); 25mm (1") long x 20mm (3/4") wide. SEPALS are horizontal, tips recurved; white (155D) upper surface; light magenta (66D) lower surface; 31mm (1 1/4") long x 11mm (7/16") wide. TUBE is white (155D); 15mm (9/16") long x 7mm (1/4") wide. FOLIAGE: medium green (137B) upper surface; medium green (138B) lower surface. PARENTAGE: 'Roesse Apus' x 'Kim Klessens'. Distinguished by bloom colour.
Buiting 2006 NL AFS6125.

Linda Hinchliffe. Upright. Single. COROLLA: unflared, bell shaped; smooth petal margins; opens dark purple (78A); matures reddish

purple (74A); 15mm (9/16") long x 16mm (5/8") wide. SEPALS: horizontal, tips recurved; white (155B) tipped yellowish green (145A) upper surface; white (155C) tipped light apple green (145B) lower surface; 11mm (7/16") long x 7mm (1/4") wide. TUBE: yellowish green (145A); short, medium thickness; 4mm (1/8") long x 4mm (1/8") wide. STAMENS extend 5mm (3/16") beyond the corolla; dark rose (58C) filaments; pink (62A) anthers. PISTIL extends 12mm (7/16") beyond the corolla; rose (65A) style; pale lavender (65D) stigma. BUD is slightly square, tapered to a point. FOLIAGE is dark green (139A) upper surface; medium green (139C) lower surface. Leaves are 28mm (1 1/8") long x 21mm (13/16") wide; cordate shaped, smooth edges, acute tips, cordate bases. Veins, stems & branches are green. PARENTAGE: F. *coccinia* x 'Eileen Storey'. Small upright. Self branching. Makes good upright. Prefers full sun. Cold weather hardy to -3°C (26° F). Best bloom & foliage colour in bright light. Tested 8 years in East Yorkshire, England. Distinguished by small erect flowers; contrasting corolla & sepal colours. Also registered with the BFS in 2008.
Storey 2009 UK AFS7012 BFS0098 (2008).

Linda Rosling. Upright. Double. COROLLA is half flared, uneven shape with smooth petal margins; opens white (155D) veined reddish purple (67A); matures white (155D); 24mm (15/16") long x 26mm (1") wide. PETALOIDS are mixed red & white, 16mm (5/8") long x 14mm (9/16") wide. SEPALS are half up; tips recurved up; glossy red (45C) upper surface and rose (50B) lower surface; 28mm (1 1/8") long x 16mm (5/8") wide. TUBE is glossy red (45C), short, medium thickness; 9mm (3/8") long x 6mm (1/4") wide. STAMENS extend 11mm (7/16") below the corolla; magenta (57A) filaments, dark purple (78A) anthers. PISTIL extends 22mm (7/8") below the corolla; magenta (57A) style and pink (62C) stigma. BUD is globular. FOLIAGE is medium green (146A) upper surface and yellowish green (146B) lower surface. Leaves are 45mm (1 3/4") long x 29mm (1 1/8") wide, ovate shaped, serrulated edges, acute tips and rounded bases. Veins are green, stems are dark green, branches are brown. PARENTAGE: 'Pink Fantasia' x 'Swingtime'. Small upright. Self branching. Makes good upright. Prefers full sun. Cold weather hardy to 22⁰ F. Best bloom colour in bright light. Tested 12 years in Burstwick, East Yorkshire, England. Distinguished by horizontal flowers.
Storey 2003 UK AFS5066.

Lindberg. Upright. Single. COROLLA is salmon pink; corolla is half flared and is 15mm long x 20mm wide. SEPALS light red pink, with green tips; sepals are half down with recurved tips and are 37mm long x 14mm wide. TUBE light red pink and is 15mm long x 5mm wide. PARENTAGE 'Julchen' x 'Julchen'. Free flowering.
Klemm 2008 AT BFS0056.

Linlithgow Lass. Upright/Trailer. Single. COROLLA: compact, unflared, smooth petal margins; opens violet blue (91A), white base, matures violet (86D); 30mm (1 3/16") long x 17mm (11/16") wide. SEPALS: half up; tips recurved up; pale lavender (65D) with white blends upper surface, light reddish purple (73A) lower surface; 30mm (1 3/16") long x 7mm (1/4") wide. TUBE: white (155A), medium length & thickness; 10mm (3/8") long x 5mm (3/16") wide. STAMENS: extend 8mm (5/16") below the corolla; light magenta (57D) filaments, dark reddish purple (60A) anthers. PISTIL extends 30mm (1 3/16") below the corolla; lavender (65D) style, white (155A) stigma. BUD: long, pointed. FOLIAGE: dark green (147A) upper surface, medium green (147B) lower surface. Leaves are 50mm (2") long x 28mm (1 1/8") wide, ovate shaped, serrated edges, acute tips and rounded bases. Veins are white & pale green, stems & branches are pale green. PARENTAGE: 'Norma's Glow' x 'Katrina Thompson'. Lax upright or stiff trailer. Makes good upright, standard, pillar or decorative. Prefers overhead filtered light, cool climate. Heat tolerant if shaded. Best bloom and foliage colour in filtered light. Tested 3 years in Leyland, Lancashire, England. Distinguished by colour combination and proportionately long corolla.
Reynolds 2003 UK AFS5077.

Lioba. Trailer. Semi Double. COROLLA: half flared, turned under smooth petal margins; opens reddish purple (72B); matures dark rose (71D); 15mm (9/16") long x 12mm (1/2") wide. PETALOIDS: same colour as corolla; 9mm (3/8") long x 6mm (1/4") wide. SEPALS: half down; tips reflexed; magenta (58B) tipped apple green (144C) upper surface; dark rose (58C) lower surface; 21mm (13/16") long x 10mm (3/8") wide. TUBE: dark rose (58C); medium length & thin; 15mm (9/16") long x 4mm (3/16") wide. STAMENS: extend 8mm (5/16") below corolla; dark rose (64C) filaments; dark purple (79B) anthers. PISTIL: extends 22mm (7/8") below the corolla; rose (64D) style; pale yellow (1D) stigma. BUD: rounded. FOLIAGE:

273

dark green (136A) upper surface, medium green (137C) lower surface. Leaves are 35mm (1 3/8") long x 18mm (11/16") wide, ovate shaped, serrulated edges, acute tips and cordate bases. Light red purple (185D) veins; plum (185B) stems & branches. PARENTAGE: 'Constance' x unknown. Natural trailer. Self branching. Makes good basket. Prefers overhead filtered light or full sun and warm climate. Best bloom and foliage colour in filtered light. Tested 3 years in Rillaar, Belgium. Award at Meise, 5/7/03. Distinguished by bloom colour.
Willems 2004 BE AFS5427.

Lisa Christiana Limberg. Trailer. Single to Semi Double. COROLLA: quarter flared, turned under, toothed petal margins; opens & matures dark rose (67C), rose (65A) base; 14mm (9/16") long x 15mm (9/16") wide. SEPALS: half down; tips recurved; yellowish green (154B), rose (54C) base, tipped yellowish green (144B) upper surface; coral (39B) tipped light green (143B) lower surface; 23mm (15/16") long x 10mm (3/8") wide. TUBE: white (155D); medium length & thickness; 14mm (9/16") long x 4mm (3/16") wide, 3mm (1/8") at base. STAMENS: do not extend below corolla; magenta (58B) filaments; light yellow (1C) anthers. PISTIL: extends 4mm (3/16") below the corolla; magenta (58B) style; yellow (2A) stigma. BUD: ovate rectangle. FOLIAGE: dark green (137A) upper surface, yellowish green (146B) lower surface. Leaves are 58mm (2 5/16") long x 28mm (1 1/8") wide, elliptic shaped, serrulated edges, acute tips and rounded bases. Medium green (138B) veins; brown (165A) stems & branches. PARENTAGE: 'Alda Alders' x 'Party Frock'. Natural trailer. Self branching. Makes good basket. Prefers overhead filtered light and warm climate. Best bloom and foliage colour in filtered light. Tested 4 years in Leopoldsburg & Helchteren, Belgium. Distinguished by colour combination.
Busschodts 2004 BE AFS5437.

Lisa Limberg. Upright/Trailer. Semi Double. COROLLA: quarter flared, turned up smooth petal margins; opens purple (90B) edged purple (90A), veined magenta (58B), light pink (65B) base; matures light purple (81C) edged purple (81A), white (155A) base; 35mm (1 3/8") long x 29mm (1 1/8") wide. SEPALS: fully up; tips recurved; white (155B) flushed pale pink (56B), tipped yellowish green (150C) upper surface; pale pink (56B) lower surface; 43mm (1 11/16") long x 18mm (11/16") wide. TUBE: light pink (62B);

medium length & thickness; 18mm (11/16") long x 4mm (3/16") wide. STAMENS: do not extend below corolla; pink (62A) filaments; greenish yellow (1B) anthers. PISTIL: extends 22mm (7/8") below the corolla; pink (62A) style; magenta (68A) stigma. BUD: ovate. FOLIAGE: dark green (137A) upper surface, yellowish green (146B) lower surface. Leaves are 73mm (2 7/8") long x 35mm (1 3/8") wide, elliptic shaped, serrulated edges, acute tips and obtuse bases. Yellowish green (144A) veins; brownish orange (173A) stems & branches. PARENTAGE: 'Lady in Grey' x 'Evy Penders'. Lax upright or stiff trailer. Self branching. Makes good basket. Prefers overhead filtered light and cool climate. Best bloom and foliage colour in filtered light. Tested 4 years in Leopoldsburg & Helchteren, Belgium. Distinguished by colour combination between opening & mature.
Busschodts 2004 BE AFS5440.

Lisette Fuhrmann. Upright. Double. COROLLA: half flared; opens violet (76A), magenta (61C) base; matures violet (77C), magenta (63B) base; 17mm (5/8") long x 18mm (11/16") wide. PETALOIDS: same colour as corolla; 17mm (5/8") long x 7mm (1/4") wide. SEPALS: horizontal, tips recurved; pale lavender (69C) tipped light yellowish green (150C) upper surface; light rose (73B) tipped light yellowish green (150C) lower surface; 28mm (1 1/8") long x 13mm (1/2") wide. TUBE: white (155C); medium length & thickness; 16mm (5/8") long x 5mm (3/16") wide. FOLIAGE is dark green (139A) upper surface; medium green (138B) lower surface. PARENTAGE: 'Vendelzwaaier' x 'Jackie Bull'.
Michiels 2007 BE AFS6343.

Lisette Kums. Trailer. Double. COROLLA is half flared; opens & matures white (155D); 17mm (5/8") long x 21mm (13/16") wide. SEPALS are half up, tips recurved up; reddish purple (71B) upper & lower surfaces; 27mm (1 1/16") long x 12mm (7/16") wide. TUBE is dark rose (71D); 32mm (1 1/4") long x 4mm (1/8") wide. FOLIAGE: medium green (137B) upper surface; medium green (138B) lower surface. PARENTAGE: [('Cameron Ryle' x 'Parasol') x 'Allure'] x 'Roesse Rhea'. Distinguished by bloom colour & shape.
Roes 2006 NL AFS6168.

Little Annie Gee. Upright. Single. COROLLA violet. SEPALS pale pink.
Evans 2003 UK.

274

Little Boy Blue. Upright. Double. COROLLA: Quarter flared, compact; opens purple (90A); matures purple (88A); 10mm (3/8") long x 14mm (9/16") wide. SEPALS: half down, tips recurved; magenta (58B) upper; dark rose (58C) lower surface; 19mm (3/4") long x 6mm (1/4") wide. TUBE: magenta (58B); medium length & thickness; 7mm (1/4") long x 4mm (1/8") wide. FOLIAGE is yellowish green (146B) upper surface; yellowish green (144A) lower surface. PARENTAGE: 'Bealings' x 'Phyllis'.
Chapman 2007 UK AFS6714.

Little Brook Gem. Upright. Single. COROLLA is half flared, bell shaped with turned under wavy petal margins; opens light pink (62B) edged magenta (68A), pale lavender (69B) near TUBE; matures pink (62C) edged magenta (68A), pale lavender (69C) near TUBE; 20mm (13/16") long x 30mm (1 3/16") wide. SEPALS are horizontal, tips recurved; light pink (49C) tipped green upper surface, Rose (55B) tipped green lower surface; 30mm (1 3/16") long x 12mm (1/2") wide. TUBE is light pink (49C), medium length and thin; 12mm (1/2") long x 5mm (3/16") wide. STAMENS extend 15mm (5/8") below the corolla; pink (62A) filaments and reddish purple (67A) anthers. PISTIL extends 30mm (1 3/16") below the corolla; light pink (65B) style and yellowish white (158A) stigma. BUD is medium, elongated. FOLIAGE is medium green (146A) on upper surface and yellowish green (146B) on lower surface. Leaves are 50mm (2") long x 30mm (1 3/16") wide, cordate shaped, serrulated edges, acute tips and rounded bases. Veins are green; stems brown; branches are red. PARENTAGE: unknown, found seedling. Small upright. Self branching. Makes good upright. Prefers overhead filtered light and warm climate. Heat tolerant if shaded. Hardy to 32°F. Best bloom colour in bright light. Tested five years in Ashgreen, Hampshire & London, England. Distinguished by profuse blooms and bloom colour combination.
Gubler 2002 UK AFS4812.

Little Cupido. Upright/Trailer. Semi Double. COROLLA is three quarter flared with turned under smooth petal margins; opens dark reddish purple (72A); matures magenta (71C); 14mm (9/16") long x 9mm (3/8") wide. PETALOIDS: Same colour as corolla; 10mm (3/8") long x 7mm (1/4") wide. SEPALS are horizontal, tips recurved; reddish purple (61B), tipped light green (139D) upper surface; dark reddish purple (60C) tipped

light green (139D) lower surface; 37mm (1 7/16") long x 10mm (3/8") wide. TUBE is magenta (61C); medium length & thickness; 20mm (13/16") long x 5mm (3/16") wide. FOLIAGE: dark green (135A) upper surface; medium green (138B) lower surface. Leaves are 56mm (2 3/16") long x 26mm (1") wide, elliptic shaped. PARENTAGE: 'Roesse Blacky' x 'Pretty Diana'. Meise 8-14-04. Distinguished by flower & foliage colour combination.
Michiels 2005 BE AFS5734.

Little David. Trailer. Single. COROLLA: half flared, turned under smooth petal margins; opens white (155D), rose (68B) base; matures white (155C); 23mm (15/16") long x 20mm (13/16") wide. SEPALS: horizontal; tips recurved; dark rose (54B) striped rose (68C) tipped light apple green (145B) upper surface; dark rose (58C) tipped light apple green (145B) lower surface; 37mm (1 7/16") long x 20mm (13/16") wide. TUBE: dark rose (54B); medium length & thickness; 12mm (1/2") long x 6mm (1/4") wide. STAMENS: extend 13mm (1/2") below corolla; magenta (61C) filaments; purple (83A) anthers. PISTIL: extends 20mm (13/16") below the corolla; reddish purple (61B) style; dark purple (86A) stigma. BUD: cordate shaped. FOLIAGE: medium green (138A) upper surface, medium green (138B) lower surface. Leaves are 38mm (1 1/2") long x 17mm (11/16") wide, ovate shaped, serrulated edges, acute tips and rounded bases. Magenta (67B) veins; magenta (67B) & very dark reddish purple (186A) stems; dark reddish purple (70A) & very dark reddish purple (186A) branches. PARENTAGE: 'Swingtime' x unknown. Natural trailer. Self branching. Makes good basket. Prefers overhead filtered light and cool climate. Best bloom and foliage colour in filtered light. Tested 3 years in Rillaar, Belgium. Award at Meise, 5/7/03. Distinguished by bloom colour.
Willems 2004 BE AFS5426.

Little Margaret. Upright. Single. COROLLA opens light violet (85a), veined dark pink red, matures to pink violet; corolla is half flared. SEPALS dark pink red (53c) on the upper surface, pink red (52a) on the lower surface; SEPALS are horizontally held with recurved tips. TUBE dark pink red. PARENTAGE 'Seedling' x 'Kobold'.
Edmond 2009 UK BFS0140.

Little Maud Murphy. Upright. Single. COROLLA: quarter flared, smooth petal

275

margins, bell shaped; opens light purple (87C); matures light reddish purple (73A); 20mm (3/4") long x 20mm (3/4") wide. SEPALS: half up, tips reflexed up; white & pink (55C) upper surface; light rose (63D) lower surface; 20mm (3/4") long x 10mm (3/8") wide. TUBE: dark rose (67C) & white; short, medium thickness; 7mm (1/4") long x 7mm (1/4") wide. STAMENS extend 13mm (1/2") beyond the corolla; light reddish purple (66C) filaments; reddish purple (66A) anthers. PISTIL extends 20mm (3/4") beyond the corolla; white style & stigma. BUD: ovate. FOLIAGE: medium green (143A) upper surface; light green (143C) lower surface. Leaves are 44mm (1 3/4") long x 22mm (7/8") wide; elliptic shaped, smooth edges, acute tips, rounded bases. Veins & branches are green, stems are pale green. PARENTAGE: 'Julie Ann Goodwin' x 'Paloma'. Small upright. Makes good upright. Prefers overhead filtered light, warm climate. Best bloom colour in filtered light. Tested 3 years in Stoke-On-Trent, Staffordshire, England. Distinguished by flower colour & shape. Goodwin 2009 UK AFS7093.

Little Nan. Upright/Trailer. Single. COROLLA: quarter flared, square shaped, turned under smooth petal margins; opens purple (71A); matures reddish purple (71B); 6mm (1/4") long x 9mm (3/8") wide. SEPALS: fully up; tips recurved; reddish purple (64B) tipped green upper & lower surfaces; 15mm(9/16") long x 5mm (3/16") wide. TUBE: dark reddish purple (60A); short & thick; 6mm (1/4") long x 4mm (3/16") wide. STAMENS: extend 5mm (3/16") below corolla; reddish purple (64B) filaments & anthers. PISTIL: extends 15mm (9/16") below the corolla, dark rose (64C) style; pink (49A) stigma. BUD: very small, elongated. FOLIAGE: dark green (147A) upper surface; medium green (147B) lower surface. Leaves are 40mm (1 9/16") long x 25mm (1") wide, cordate shaped, serrulated edges, acute tips and cordate bases. Veins are green, stems are brown, branches are red. PARENTAGE: 'Janneke Brinkmann-Saletijn' x 'Little Witch'. Lax upright or stiff trailer. Self branching. Makes good basket or bonsai. Heat tolerant if shaded. Prefers warm climate. Cold weather hardy to 32° F. Tested 4 years in Walthamstow, London, England. Distinguished by bloom colour retention with age. Allsop M.R. 2003 UK AFS5149.

Little Scamp. Trailer. Single. COROLLA opens pale lilac, edged dark purple, matures

to medium pink with dark pink edging; corolla is quarter flared and is 23mm long x 20mm wide. SEPALS pale pink, tipped green; sepals are held horizontally and have a slight twist with recurved tips and are 36mm long x 7mm wide. TUBE pale pink and is 7mm long x 4mm wide. PARENTAGE 'Peoples Princess' x 'Unknown'. This cultivar has caused a lot of interest at local shows, it's won best in show in 2004 & 2006 at Warminster also 1st at Wessex show 2006.
Dowell 2006 UK BFS0027.

Lizard Point. Upright. Single. COROLLA: quarter flared, bell shaped, smooth petal margins; opens dark purple (79A); matures dark reddish purple (61A); 20mm (13/16") long, 17mm (11/16") wide. SEPALS: half down; tips recurved; magenta (57B) upper surface; magenta (57C) lower surface; 27mm (1 1/16") long x 11mm (7/16") wide. TUBE: dark purple (79A); short, thin; 13mm (1/2") long x 4mm (3/16") wide. STAMENS: extend 8mm (5/16") below corolla; dark reddish purple (61A) filaments; magenta (67B) anthers. PISTIL: extends 22mm (7/8") below the corolla; magenta (67B) style; orangish white (159C) stigma. BUD: lanceolate. FOLIAGE: dark green (147A) upper surface; medium green (138A) lower surface. Leaves are 65mm (2 9/16") long x 45mm (1 3/4") wide, lanceolate shaped, serrulated edges, acute tips and acute bases. Dark reddish purple (59A) veins & stems; brown (19N/A) branches. PARENTAGE: 'Saint Ives Bay' x 'Natasha Sinton'. Medium upright. Makes good standard. Prefers overhead filtered light. Heat tolerant if shaded. Best bloom and foliage colour in filtered light. Tested 3 years in West Cornwall, England. Distinguished by leaf colour and almost black corolla.
Negus 2004 UK AFS5634.

LoCo Crinoline. Upright/Trailer. Double. COROLLA is half flared with smooth petal margins; opens purple (77A); matures magenta (71C); 17mm (11/16") long x 21mm (13/16") wide. SEPALS are half up, tips reflexed up; dark reddish purple (60C) upper & lower surfaces; 24mm (15/16") long x 12mm (1/2") wide. TUBE is dark reddish purple (60B); medium length & thickness; 17mm (11/16") long x 6mm (1/4") wide. FOLIAGE: medium green (137B) upper surface; medium green (138A) lower surface. Leaves are 57mm (2 1/4") long x 29mm (1 1/8") wide, ovate shaped. PARENTAGE: ('Roesse Apus' x 'Roesse Apus') x 'Arjan

Spoelstra'. Distinguished by bloom & foliage combination.
Spoelstra 2005 NL AFS5876.

LoCo Gerelly. Upright. Double. COROLLA is half flared; opens reddish purple (59B); matures magenta (59C); 16mm (5/8") long x 16mm (5/8") wide. SEPALS are half up, tips reflexed up; rose (63C) upper surface; dark rose (58C) lower surface; 26mm (1") long x 14mm (9/16") wide. TUBE is light rose (63D); 16mm (5/8") long x 8mm (5/16") wide. FOLIAGE: dark green (139A) upper surface; medium green (137C) lower surface. PARENTAGE: 'Roesse Lupus' x 'Corrie Spoelstra'. Distinguished by erect bloom & colour.
Spoelstra 2006 NL AFS6196.

LoCo Jewel. Upright. Semi Double. COROLLA is three quarter flared; opens pink (62A); matures light pink (62B); 14mm (9/16") long x 21mm (13/16") wide. SEPALS are fully up, tips reflexed; magenta (63B) upper surface; light rose (63D) lower surface; 29mm (1 1/8") long x 14mm (9/16") wide. TUBE is magenta (63B); 14mm (9/16") long x 11mm (7/16") wide. FOLIAGE: medium green (137B) upper surface; medium green (137D) lower surface. PARENTAGE: 'Roesse Carme' x ('Swanley Gem' x 'Eisvogel'). Distinguished by bloom shape & colour.
Spoelstra 2006 NL AFS6197.

LoCo Marelle. Trailer. Double. COROLLA is three quarter flared; opens violet blue (92A); matures dark purple (78A); 18mm (11/16") long x 22mm (7/8") wide. SEPALS are horizontal, tips recurved; light rose (58D) upper surface; dark rose (58C) lower surface; 24mm (15/16") long x 13mm (1/2") wide. TUBE is light rose (58D); 14mm (9/16") long x 12mm (7/16") wide. FOLIAGE: dark green (137A) upper surface; medium green (137D) lower surface. PARENTAGE: 'Regent Gubler' x 'Sofie Michiels'. Distinguished by bloom colour.
Spoelstra 2006 NL AFS6198.

LoCo Motion. Trailer. Single. COROLLA is half flared; opens violet (77B); matures dark rose (58C); 19mm (3/4") long x 21mm (13/16") wide. SEPALS are half up, tips recurved up; dark rose (58C) upper surface; violet (85A) lower surface; 37mm (1 7/16") long x 10mm (3/8") wide. TUBE is light magenta (58B); 9mm (3/8") long x 5mm (3/16") wide. FOLIAGE: dark green (139A) upper surface; medium green (138A) lower surface. PARENTAGE: 'Regent Gubler' x

'Roesse Pandora'. Distinguished by bloom colour.
Spoelstra 2006 NL AFS6199.

LoCo Nova. Trailer. Semi Double. COROLLA is three quarter flared; opens reddish purple (72B); matures reddish purple (70B); 14mm (9/16") long x 19mm (3/4") wide. SEPALS are half up, tips reflexed up; magenta (57C) tipped green upper surface; light rose (58D) tipped green lower surface; 19mm (3/4") long x 14mm (9/16") wide. TUBE is magenta (57C); 17mm (5/8") long x 7mm (1/4") wide. FOLIAGE: dark green (139A) upper surface; medium green (137B) lower surface. PARENTAGE: 'Roesse Carme' x 'Delta's Bride'. Distinguished by bloom colour.
Spoelstra 2006 NL AFS6200.

LoCo Silk. Trailer. Single. COROLLA is half flared with wavy petal margins; opens purple (89C); matures purple (82A); 20mm (13/16") long x 30mm (1 3/16") wide. SEPALS are fully up, tips reflexed; red (53D) upper & lower surfaces; 21mm (13/16") long x 11mm (7/16") wide. TUBE is red (53D); medium length & thickness; 15mm (9/16") long x 7mm (1/4") wide. FOLIAGE: dark green (137A) upper surface; medium green (137C) lower surface. Leaves are 61mm (2 3/8") long x 44mm (1 3/4") wide, ovate shaped. PARENTAGE: 'Swanley Gem' x 'Corrie Spoelstra'. Distinguished by bloom colour.
Spoelstra 2005 NL AFS5877.

LoCo Treasure. Upright/Trailer. Single. COROLLA is half flared; opens purple (71A); matures dark reddish purple (64A); 19mm (3/4") long x 27mm (1 1/16") wide. SEPALS are half up, tips recurved up; light pink (62B) upper surface; rose (68B) lower surface; 32mm (1 1/4") long x 8mm (5/16") wide. TUBE is light pink (62B); 16mm (5/8") long x 6mm (1/4") wide. FOLIAGE: dark green (137A) upper surface; medium green (137D) lower surface. PARENTAGE: 'Roesse Apus' x 'Jacoba Kums'. Distinguished by bloom colour.
Spoelstra 2006 NL AFS6201.

LoCo Velvet. Upright/Trailer. Semi Double. COROLLA is full flared with smooth petal margins; opens purple (83B); matures purple (71A); 15mm (9/16") long x 21mm (13/16") wide. SEPALS are fully up, tips recurved; dark rose (64C) upper surface; reddish purple (64B) lower surface; 22mm (13/16") long x 11mm (7/16") wide. TUBE is dark rose (64C); medium length & thickness; 15mm (9/16") long x 6mm (1/4") wide. FOLIAGE:

medium green (137C) upper surface; medium green (137D) lower surface. Leaves are 52mm (2 1/16") long x 37mm (1 7/16") wide, cordate shaped. PARENTAGE: ['Rohees Acrux' x ('Roesse Apus' x 'Roesse Apus')] x 'Corrie Spoelstra'. Distinguished by bloom colour.
Spoelstra 2005 NL AFS5875.

Locomotion. Upright. Single. COROLLA rosy pink, fades to white towards the base, corolla is quarter flared and is 15mm long x 15mm wide. SEPALS are white on the upper surface, white lightly flushed rose, lightly tipped green on the lower surface; sepals are horizontally held with slightly recurved tips and are 26mm long x 8mm wide. TUBE is white and is 12mm long x 5mm wide. PARENTAGE 'Anita' x 'Katrina Thompsen'. This cultivar is named after the Railway Museum at Shildon which opened in October 2004.
Porter 2005 UK BFS0010.

Lode Jordaens. Upright/Trailer. Semi Double to Double. COROLLA is three quarter flared with turned under wavy petal margins; opens reddish purple (71B), magenta (67B) base; matures dark rose (67C), dark rose (58C) base; 26mm (1 1/16") long x 21mm (13/16") wide. PETALOIDS: light reddish purple (72C), magenta (67B) base; 11mm (7/16") long x 9mm (3/8") wide. SEPALS are horizontal, tips reflexed; pink (48C) tipped pale yellowish green (154D) upper surface; light orange (41C) tipped pale yellowish green (154D) lower surface; 37mm (1 7/16") long x 10mm (3/8") wide. TUBE is rose (54C) to pink (49A); long & thick; 32mm (1 1/4") long x 9mm (3/8") wide. FOLIAGE: dark green (136A) upper surface; medium green (137C) lower surface. Leaves are 76mm (3") long x 50mm (2") wide, ovate shaped. PARENTAGE: 'WALZ Harp' x 'Ting-a-Ling'. Meise 9-18-04, Outstanding. Distinguished by flower colour & shape.
Geerts L. 2005 BE AFS5854.

Loeke's Dufky. Upright/Trailer. Single. COROLLA: half flared, turned under wavy petal margins; opens reddish purple (61B); matures magenta (63A); 31mm (1 1/4") long x 28mm (1 1/8") wide. SEPALS: horizontal, tips reflexed; rose (55B) upper surface; rose (52C) tipped magenta (59C) lower surface; 36mm (1 7/16") long x 11mm (7/16") wide. TUBE: dark rose (54B); long, medium thickness; 62mm (2 7/16") long x 8mm (5/16") wide. STAMENS extend 2mm (1/16") beyond the corolla; rose (52B) filaments; light

yellow (2C) anthers. PISTIL extends 4mm (1/8") beyond the corolla; rose (52C) style; pink (43D) stigma. BUD: elongated. FOLIAGE: dark green (139A) upper surface; medium green (137B) lower surface. Leaves are 86mm (3 7/16") long x 54mm (2 1/8") wide; ovate shaped, serrate edges, acute tips, rounded bases. Veins are grayish red (182B), stems are dark grayish purple (184A) & light green (139D), branches are dark grayish purple (183A). PARENTAGE: 'WALZ Harp' x 'Ernest Claes'. Lax upright or stiff trailer. Makes good basket or upright. Prefers full sun, cool climate. Best bloom & foliage colour in bright light. Tested 4 years in Itegem, Belgium. Waanrode 9/20/08. Distinguished by bloom colour combination & long TUBE.
Geerts L. 2009 BE AFS7072.

Loeke's Dwerg. Upright. Single. COROLLA: half flared, turned under wavy petal margins; opens dark rose (55A); matures dark rose (51A); 17mm (5/8") long x 15mm (9/16") wide. SEPALS: half down, tips reflexed; pink (52D) tipped light yellow green (150B) upper surface; rose (52C) tipped light yellow green (150B) lower surface; 21mm (13/16") long x 8mm (5/16") wide. TUBE: pale pink (49D); long & thin; 26mm (1") long x 4mm (1/8") wide. STAMENS do not extend beyond the corolla; pink (49A) filaments; yellowish white (4D) anthers. PISTIL extends 6mm (1/4") beyond the corolla; pink (48D) style; light yellow (2C) stigma. BUD: bulbous. FOLIAGE: dark green (136B) upper surface; medium green (138B) lower surface. Leaves are 52mm (2 1/16") long x 36mm (1 7/16") wide; ovate shaped, serrulate edges, acute tips, rounded bases. Veins are grayish red (181B), stems are dark grayish red (182A), branches are yellowish green (144A). PARENTAGE: 'Ronny' x 'Walteroza'. Small upright. Makes good upright. Prefers overhead filtered light or full sun, cool climate. Best bloom & foliage colour in bright or filtered light. Tested 3 years in Itegem, Belgium. Waanrode 8/9/08. Distinguished by bloom colour.
Geerts L. 2009 BE AFS7073.

Loeke's Hanger. Trailer. Single. COROLLA: quarter flared; opens red (47B); matures red (53C); 15mm (9/16") long x 11mm (7/16") wide. SEPALS are half down, tips reflexed; light rose (50C) tipped light apple green (145C) upper surface; coral (39B) tipped light apple green (145C) lower surface; 19mm (3/4") long x 8mm (5/16") wide. TUBE is pink (48D) striped rose (52C); 58mm (2 5/16") long x 8mm (5/16") wide. FOLIAGE is medium green (137C) upper surface; light green (138C) lower surface. PARENTAGE: 'Walz Harp' x 'Big Slim'. Waanrode 8/11/2007. Geerts L. 2008 BE AFS6731.

Loeke's Kromme. Trailer. Double. COROLLA: half flared, turned under wavy petal margins; opens dark reddish purple (72A); matures reddish purple (67A); 17mm (5/8") long x 12mm (7/16") wide. PETALOIDS: Same colour as corolla; 10mm (3/8") long x 6mm (1/4") wide. SEPALS: half down, tips reflexed; red (53D) upper surface; red (52A) lower surface; 28mm (1 1/8") long x 12mm (7/16") wide. TUBE: rose (51A); medium length & thickness; 22mm (7/8") long x 6mm (1/4") wide. STAMENS extend 4mm (1/8") beyond the corolla; rose (63C) filaments; pale pink (69A) anthers. PISTIL extends 10mm (3/8") beyond the corolla; rose (68B) style; light pink (62C) stigma. BUD: bulbous. FOLIAGE: dark green (137A) upper surface; medium green (138A) lower surface. Leaves are 73mm (2 7/8") long x 31mm (1 1/4") wide; elliptic shaped, serrulate edges, acute tips, rounded bases. Veins are plum (185B), stems are dark red (185A), branches are dark grayish red (182A) & light green (139D). PARENTAGE: 'WALZ Bruintje' x 'Stier'. Natural trailer. Self branching. Makes good basket. Prefers overhead filtered light or full sun, cool climate. Best bloom & foliage colour in bright or filtered light. Tested 3 years in Itegem, Belgium. Waanrode 8/9/08. Distinguished by bloom colour. Geerts L. 2009 BE AFS7074.

Loeke's Lieveling. Upright. Single. COROLLA: quarter flared, turned under wavy petal margins; opens red (52A) & dark reddish purple (60C); matures red (50A) & magenta (61C); 20mm (3/4") long x 22mm (7/8") wide. SEPALS: half down, tips recurved; pink (43D) tipped light apple green (145B) upper surface; coral (39B) tipped light apple green (145B) lower surface; 25mm (1") long x 9mm (5/16") wide. TUBE: rose (54C); long, medium thickness; 38mm (1 1/2") long x 8mm (5/16") wide. STAMENS extend 8mm (5/16") beyond the corolla; rose (52B) filaments; light rose (58D) anthers. PISTIL extends 10mm (3/8") beyond the corolla; rose (50B) style; pale yellow (2D) stigma. BUD: elongated. FOLIAGE: dark green (136A) upper surface; medium green (137D) lower surface. Leaves are 94mm (3 3/4") long x 50mm (2") wide; ovate shaped, serrate edges, acute tips, rounded bases. Veins are olive

green (153B), stems are grayish red (181C), branches are grayish red (181C) & medium green (138B). PARENTAGE: 'WALZ Harp' x 'Ernest Claes'. Small upright. Makes good upright. Prefers overhead filtered light or full sun, cool climate. Best bloom & foliage colour in bright light. Tested 3 years in Itegem, Belgium. Waanrode 8/9/08. Distinguished by bloom colour. Geerts L. 2009 BE AFS7075.

London Eye. Upright. Single. COROLLA opens purple violet, white at base, matures to cyclamen purple; corolla is quarter flared and is 13mm long x 12mm wide. SEPALS p are white, flushed baby pink on the upper surface, baby pink on the lower surface with green tips; sepals are fully up with recurved tips and are 16mm long x 7mm wide. TUBE is white, flushed pink and is 10mm long x 5mm wide. PARENTAGE 'London 2000' x 'Unknown'. Waving 2005 UK BFS0016.

London in Bloom. Upright/Trailer. Single. COROLLA: unflared, bell shaped, turned under smooth petal margins; opens purple (71A) flushed dark red (178A); matures magenta (63A) flushed dark red (178A); 25mm (1") long x 22mm (7/8") wide. SEPALS: half up; tips recurved up; half twisted as they mature; rose (52B) upper surface; red (52A) lower surface; 50mm(2") long x 11mm (7/16") wide. TUBE: rose (52B); medium length & thin; 15mm (9/16") long x 8mm (5/16") wide. STAMENS: extend 15mm (9/16") below corolla; dark rose (55A) filaments; purple (71A) anthers. PISTIL: extends 50mm (2") below the corolla, dark rose (55A) style; yellowish white (158A) stigma. BUD: long, oval. FOLIAGE: yellowish green (144A) upper surface; medium green (138A) lower surface. Leaves are 90mm (3 9/16") long x 60mm (2 3/8") wide, cordate shaped, serrated edges, acute tips and rounded bases. Veins & stems are red; branches are brown. PARENTAGE: 'Gerharda's Aubergine' x 'Welsh Dragon'. Lax upright or stiff trailer. Self branching. Makes good upright. Prefers overhead filtered light. Heat tolerant if shaded. Cold weather hardy to 32° F. Tested 3 years in Walthamstow, London, England. Distinguished by bloom colour combination & long lasting blooms. Allsop J. 2003 UK AFS5148.

Look Twice. Upright/Trailer. Single. COROLLA is full flared, saucer shaped, with smooth margins; opens purple (71A), matures dark reddish purple (64A); 18mm

(11/16") long x 21mm (13/16") wide. SEPALS are half up, tips reflexed up; dark reddish purple (60A) upper and lower surfaces; 23mm (15/16") long x 14mm (9/16") wide. TUBE is dark reddish purple (60A), short and thick; 11mm (7/16") long x 8mm (5/16") wide. STAMENS extend 22mm (7/8") beyond the corolla; dark reddish purple (60A) filaments and dark purple (79B) anthers. PISTIL extends 9mm (3/8") below the corolla; dark reddish purple (60A) style, light rose (58D) stigma. BUD is globular. FOLIAGE is medium green (146A) upper surface, medium green (138A) lower surface. Leaves are 63mm (2 1/2") long x 30mm (1 3/16") wide, ovate shaped, serrated edges, acute tips and rounded bases. Veins are red, stems and branches are reddish. PARENTAGE: 'Satchmo' x 'Art Deco'. Lax upright or stiff trailer. Self branching. Makes good basket. Heat tolerant if shaded. Best bloom colour in filtered light. Best foliage colour in bright light. Tested seven years in Lisse, Holland. Distinguished by aubergine colour and saucer shaped corolla.
de Graaff 2002 NL AFS4879.

Lord Lloyd-Webber. Upright/Trailer. Double. COROLLA is full flared, flattish, with turned under smooth petal margins; opens and matures white (155) heavily veined reddish purple (59B), darker at base; 33mm (1 5/16") long x 75mm (2 15/16") wide. SEPALS are fully up, tips reflexed; reddish purple (59B) upper surface, reddish purple (59B) creped lower surface; 34mm (1 3/8") long x 13mm (1/2) wide. TUBE is reddish purple (59B) striped magenta (59C); short with medium thickness; 13mm (1/2") long x 11mm (7/16") wide. STAMENS extend 35mm (1 3/8") below the corolla; reddish purple (59B) filaments dark reddish purple (59A) anthers. PISTIL extends 37mm (1 7/16") below the corolla; magenta (59D) style, white (155B) stigma. BUD is bulbous, pointed. FOLIAGE is dark green (139A) upper surface, medium green (137C) lower surface. Leaves are 63mm (2 1/2") long x 40mm (1 9/16") wide, cordate shaped, serrulated edges, acute tips and rounded bases. Veins, stems and branches are light green. PARENTAGE: 'Swingtime' x 'Gerharda's Aubergine'. Lax upright or stiff trailer. Makes good basket, upright, standard or decorative. Prefers cool climate. Heat tolerant if shaded. Best bloom colour in filtered light. Tested five years in Gloucester, England. Distinguished by unique bloom colour.
Hickman 2002 UK AFS4862.

Lord Loxley. Trailer. Double. COROLLA: half flared; opens reddish purple (71B) and reddish purple (72B) and matures reddish purple (67A) and reddish purple (70B); 24mm (15/16") long x 18mm 11/16") wide. PETALOIDS: purple (71A) and reddish purple (72B); 10mm (3/8") long x 9mm (5/16") wide. SEPALS are horizontal, tips reflexed; white (155C) tipped yellowish green (145A) upper surface and pale lavender (69C) tipped yellowish green (145A) lower surface; 28mm (1 1/8") long x 12mm (7/16") wide. TUBE is light apple green (145C); medium length & thickness; 14mm (9/16") long x 6mm (1/4") wide. FOLIAGE is dark green (136A) upper surface; medium green (138B) lower surface. PARENTAGE: 'Sam' x 'Monte Rosa'.
Michiels 2007 BE AFS6525.

Lord Sinclair. Trailer. Semi Double. COROLLA: half flared; opens reddish purple (71B), blotched light pink (49C) edged reddish purple (71B) and matures light reddish purple (72C) edged reddish purple (67A); 23mm (7/8") long x 21mm 15/16") wide. PETALOIDS: reddish purple (72B) blotched light pink (49C); 12mm (7/16") long x 10mm (3/8") wide. SEPALS are horizontal, tips reflexed; white (155C) tipped light apple green (144D) upper surface and pale lavender (65D) tipped light apple green (144D) lower surface; 34mm (1 3/8") long x 14mm (9/16") wide. TUBE is white (155C); medium length & thickness; 25mm (1") long x 6mm (1/4") wide. FOLIAGE is dark green (139A) upper surface; medium green (138B) lower surface. PARENTAGE: 'Rune Peeters' x 'Illusion'.
Michiels 2007 BE AFS6526.

Lore Ritscka. Upright. Semi Double. COROLLA is unflared; opens purple (71A); matures reddish purple (71B); 25mm (1") long x 30mm (1 3/16") wide. SEPALS are horizontal, tips recurved; pink (62A) tipped green upper surface; magenta (63B) lower surface; 40mm (1 9/16") long x 14mm (9/16") wide. TUBE is very pale orange (27D); 20mm (3/4") long x 9mm (3/8") wide. FOLIAGE: dark green (139A) upper surface; medium green (139B) lower surface. PARENTAGE: 'Anita' x unknown. Distinguished by bloom colour.
Strümper 2006 DE AFS6234.

Lorientje. Trailer. Single. COROLLA: half flared; opens rose (68B), white (155C) base; matures magenta (58B); 28mm (1 1/8") long x 24mm (15/16") wide. SEPALS: horizontal, tips recurved; white (155C) tipped apple

green (144C) upper surface; pale lavender (69D) tipped apple green (144C) lower surface; 43mm (1 11/16") long x 10mm (3/8") wide. TUBE: white (155C); short & thick; 18mm (11/16") long x 10mm (3/8") wide. FOLIAGE is dark green (137A) upper surface; medium green (138B) lower surface. PARENTAGE: 'Jef Vander Kuylen' x 'Chandlerii'.
Michiels 2007 BE AFS6344.

Lorna Florence. Upright. Semi Double. COROLLA opens with shades of blue to lilac with pink veining, colours slightly fading on maturity; corolla is quarter flared. SEPALS creamy white, tipped green on the upper surface, creamy white flushed slightly with pink lower surfaces; SEPALS are half up with recurved tips. TUBE creamy white striped pink. PARENTAGE 'Baby Bright' x 'Unknown'. named in memory of the hybridists Mother.
Snowden 2009 UK BFS0136.

Lotte Robinet. Upright/Trailer. Double. COROLLA: half flared; opens magenta (67B) and reddish purple (70B); matures magenta (67B); 26mm (1") long x 19mm (3/4") wide. PETALOIDS: magenta (67B) & reddish purple (70B); 16mm (5/8") long x 11mm (7/16") wide. SEPALS are half down, tips recurved, twisted left to right; white (155C) & rose (68C) tipped light apple green (144B) upper surface & white (155C) & rose (61D) tipped light apple green (144B) lower surface; 46mm (1 3/16") long x 12mm (7/16") wide. TUBE is white (155C); 12mm (7/16") long x 9mm (5/16") wide. FOLIAGE is dark green (136A) upper surface; medium green (137C) lower surface. PARENTAGE: 'Leen vander Kuylen' x 'Kiss'. Waanrode 7/7/2007.
Michiels 2008 BE AFS6723.

Lotte Vlasselaer. Trailer. Single. COROLLA: half flared; opens dark reddish purple (61A) & red (53D); matures reddish purple (71B); 20mm (3/4") long x 15mm (9/16") wide. SEPALS: horizontal, tips reflexed; magenta (58B) upper surface; red (53D) lower surface; 25mm (1") long x 13mm (1/2") wide. TUBE: reddish purple (61B); 30mm (1 3/16") long x 7mm (1/4") wide. FOLIAGE is dark green (139A) upper surface; medium green (137C) lower surface. PARENTAGE: 'WALZ Harp' x unknown.
Willems 2008 BE AFS6746.

Louis Blériot. Upright. Single. COROLLA: unflared, smooth petal margins; opens violet (83D) delicately veined light red (53B);

matures reddish purple (70B); 25mm (1") long x 8mm (5/16") wide. SEPALS: half up; tips recurved up in a circle; bright red (45A) upper surface; red (45D) lower surface; 52mm (2 1/16") long x 6mm (1/4") wide. TUBE: bright red (45A); medium length & thin; 20mm (13/16") long x 3 - 4mm (3/16") wide. STAMENS: extend 22mm (7/8") below corolla; magenta (58B) filaments, red (45A) anthers. PISTIL: extends 30mm (1 3/16") below the corolla, magenta (58B) style, red (45C) stigma. BUD: long, ovate. FOLIAGE: dark green (147A) upper surface; medium green (147B) lower surface. Leaves are 95mm (3 3/4") long x 30mm (1 3/16") wide, lanceolate shaped, serrulated edges, acute tips and rounded to acute bases. Veins, stems & branches are brown. PARENTAGE: 'Jules Verne' x unknown. Medium upright. Makes good upright or standard. Prefers cool climate. Cold weather hardy to -7° C. Best bloom and foliage colour in filtered light. Tested 3 years in Pornic, France. Distinguished by profuse and long flowers.
Massé 2003 FR AFS5227.

Louis Hasselmann. Upright. Single. COROLLA: unflared, square shaped; opens dark rose (58C); matures red (52A); 25mm (1") long x 8mm (5/16") wide. SEPALS: half up, tips recurved up; white (155B) tipped yellowish green (145A) upper surface; white (155B) lower surface; 25 mm (1") long x 8mm (5/16") wide. TUBE: light rose (58D); 19mm (3/4") long x 8mm (5/16") wide. FOLIAGE is medium green (137C) upper surface; medium green (138B) lower surface. PARENTAGE: 'Loxhore Mazurka' x 'Waterenymph'. Nomination by NKVF as Recommendable Cultivar.
Geurts 2008 NL AFS6789.

Louis Spoelstra. Upright/Trailer. Double. COROLLA is three quarter flared with smooth petal margins; opens purple (77A); matures reddish purple (61B); 26mm (1") long x 19mm (3/4") wide. SEPALS are half up, tips recurved up; dark reddish purple (60A) upper surface; magenta (58B) lower surface; 26mm (1") long x 11mm (7/16") wide. TUBE is dark reddish purple (60A); medium length & thickness; 22mm (7/8") long x 7mm (1/4") wide. FOLIAGE: dark green (137A) upper surface; medium green (138A) lower surface. Leaves are 59mm (2 5/16") long x 35mm (1 3/8") wide, ovate shaped. PARENTAGE: ('Sofie Michiels' x 'Rohees Queen') x 'Shangri-La'. Distinguished by bloom & foliage combination.
Roes 2005 NL AFS5974.

Lou's Flower. Upright. Single. COROLLA: quarter flared; opens dark rose (48A) & dark rose (54A); matures rose (52C) & magenta (58B); 22mm (7/8") long x 28mm (1 1/8") wide. SEPALS are half down, tips recurved; pink (49A) tipped light yellowish green (150C) upper surface; pink (48D) tipped light yellowish green (150C) lower surface; 27mm (1 1/16") long x 7mm (1/4") wide. TUBE is rose (51C); 54mm (2 1/8") long x 7mm (1/4") wide. FOLIAGE is dark green (139A) upper surface; medium green (138B) lower surface. PARENTAGE: 'Walz Harp' x 'Tanja's Favourite'. Waanrode 8/11//2007. Distinguished by bloom colour. Geerts L. 2008 BE AFS6729.

Love is All. Upright/Trailer. Double. COROLLA: quarter flared, bell shaped; opens purple (90B); matures violet (90C); 20mm (3/4") long x 20mm (3/4") wide. SEPALS: half up, tips reflexed up; pink (55C) & white, tipped green, upper surface; light pink (55D) streaked white, tipped green, lower surface; 20mm (3/4") long x 18mm (11/16") wide. TUBE: pinkish white; 20mm (3/4") long x 8mm (5/16") wide. FOLIAGE is medium green (139B) upper surface; medium green (138B) lower surface. PARENTAGE: 'Snowbird' x 'Dana Samantha'. Smith R. 2008 UK AFS6823

Love Me Tender. Upright. Single. COROLLA: half flared, turned up petal margins; opens violet (82C); matures light purple (82D); 13mm (1/2") long x 13mm (1/2") wide. SEPALS: half up, tips recurved up; light rose (73B) streaked white, tipped green upper surface; pale rose (73D) streaked white lower surface; 20mm (3/4") long x 5mm (3/16") wide. TUBE: light rose (73C); short & thin; 15mm (9/16") long x 5mm (3/16") wide. STAMENS extend 30mm (1 3/16") beyond the corolla; light rose (73C) filaments; reddish purple (70B) anthers. PISTIL extends 15mm (9/16") beyond the corolla; white (155A) style; white (155B) stigma. BUD: ovate. FOLIAGE: medium green (138A) upper surface; medium green (138B) lower surface. Leaves are 40mm (1 9/16") long x 25mm (1") wide; elliptic shaped, serrulate edges, acute tips, obtuse bases. Veins & branches are light green, stems are light brown. PARENTAGE: 'Snowbird' x 'Dana Samantha'. Small upright. Self branching. Makes good upright. Prefers overhead filtered light. Best bloom colour in filtered light. Tested 3 years in Rayleigh, Essex, England. Distinguished by blossom colour & shape. Smith R. 2009 UK AFS7124.

Lovely Arne. Upright/Trailer. Semi Double. COROLLA is quarter flared; opens light purple (N78B), dark rose (55A) base; matures reddish purple (N74B); 39mm (1 1/2") long x 32mm (1 1/4") wide. PETALOIDS: same colour as corolla; 21mm (13/16") long x 16mm (5/8") wide. SEPALS are half down, tips recurved; light pink (55D), tipped light green (141D) upper surface; rose (52C), tipped light green (141D) lower surface; 45mm (1 3/4") long x 23mm (7/8") wide. TUBE: pink (55C); medium length and thicknesss; 18mm (11/16") long x 5mm (3/16") wide. FOLIAGE is dark green (136A) upper surface; medium green (138B) lower surface. PARENTAGE: 'Goudenpater' x 'Rima's Jubilee'. Geerts J. 2007 BE AFS6426.

Lovely Charlotte. Upright. Semi Double. corolla is half flared, bell shaped; opens & matures violet (77B); 18mm (11/16") long x 24mm (15/16") wide. SEPALS are half up, tips recurved up; rose (68C) tipped light yellow green (150B) upper & lower surfaces; 24mm (15/16") long x 12mm (1/2") wide. TUBE is light yellow green (150B); 12mm (1/2") long x 5mm (3/16") wide. FOLIAGE: dark green (147A) upper surface; medium green (147B) lower surface. PARENTAGE: 'Gemma Fisher' x 'Annabelle Stubbs'. Distinguished by bloom colour combination. Smith R. 2006 UK AFS6063.

Lovely Corry. Upright/Trailer. Semi Double. COROLLA is half flared; opens light reddish purple (72C), dark rose (54B) at base; matures reddish purple (71B); 23mm (7/8") long x 29mm (1 1/8") wide. SEPALS are fully up, tips reflexed; rose (55B) tipped light apple green (145B) upper surface; dark rose (55A) tipped light apple green (145B) lower surface; 35mm (1 3/8") long x 15mm (9/16") wide. TUBE is rose (54C); 37mm (1 7/16") long x 5mm (3/16") wide. FOLIAGE: dark green (137A) upper surface; medium green (139C) lower surface. PARENTAGE: 'Ghislaine' x 'Wendy Van Wanten'. Meise 8/13/05. Distinguished by unique bloom shape & colour. Geerts L. 2006 BE AFS5994.

Lovely Eddy. Upright. Single. COROLLA: three quarter flared, turned under wavy petal margins; opens magenta (68A); matures light reddish purple (73A); 21mm (13/16") long, 19mm (3/4") wide. SEPALS: half up; tips recurved up; magenta (58B), tipped light green (142B), upper surface; dark rose (54B) lower surface; 35mm (1 3/8") long x 10mm

(3/8") wide. TUBE: rose (50B) striped light green (142C); medium length, thick; 11mm (7/16") long x 6mm (1/4") wide. STAMENS: extend 6mm (1/4") below corolla; light rose (55D) filaments; reddish purple (58A) anthers. PISTIL: extends 11mm (7/16") below the corolla; pale pink (56A) style; light yellow (1C) stigma. BUD: globular. FOLIAGE: medium green (138A) upper surface; medium green (138B) lower surface. Leaves are 67mm (2 5/8") long x 33mm (1 5/16") wide, ovate shaped, serrated edges, acute tips and rounded bases. Light green (139D) veins; light green /light grayish rose (139D/181D) stems; light green /light grayish red (139D/182C) branches. PARENTAGE: 'Rohees Izar' x 'Golden Dawn'. Tall upright. Makes good upright. Prefers full sun, warm climate. Best bloom and foliage colour in bright light. Tested 3 years in Berlaar, Belgium. Award, Meise, 9/20/03. Distinguished by best colour in sun. Geerts J. 2004 BE AFS5615.

Lovely Eline Hermans. Upright/Trailer. Double. COROLLA is three quarter flared with turned under wavy petal margins; opens dark purple (79B), dark reddish purple (61A) base; matures purple (79D), reddish purple (61B) base; 13mm (1/2") long x 15mm (9/16") wide. PETALOIDS: Same colour as corolla; 10mm (3/8") long x 9mm (3/8") wide. SEPALS are horizontal, tips reflexed; dark reddish purple (61A) upper surface; reddish purple (61B) lower surface; 27mm (1 1/16") long x 11mm (7/16") wide. TUBE is reddish purple (61B); long, medium thickness; 27mm (1 1/16") long x 6mm (1/4") wide. FOLIAGE: dark green (137A) upper surface; medium green (138B) lower surface. Leaves are 61mm (2 3/8") long x 39mm (1 9/16") wide, cordate shaped. PARENTAGE: 'Aalters Glory' x 'Rohees New Millenium'. Meise 8-14-04. Distinguished by flower colour & shape. Geerts J. 2005 BE AFS5732.

Lovely Fonske. Upright. Single. COROLLA is quarter flared; opens magenta (63B); matures dark rose (67C); 18mm (11/16") long x 14mm (9/16") wide. SEPALS are half down, tips reflexed; magenta (58B) upper surface; magenta (63B) lower surface; 37mm (1 7/16") long x 9mm (3/8") wide. TUBE is dark rose (58C) blotched white (155D); 26mm (1") long x 6mm (1/4") wide. FOLIAGE: dark green (136B) upper surface; medium green (138A) lower surface. PARENTAGE: 'WALZ Harp' x 'Boswinning'. Distinguished by bloom colour & blotched TUBE colour.

Geerts L. 2006 BE AFS6064.

Lovely Guy. Upright/Trailer. Single. COROLLA: half flared, turned under wavy petal margins; opens dark rose (64C), magenta 61C) base; matures reddish purple (64B), reddish purple (61B) base; 17mm (11/16") long x 17mm (11/16") wide. SEPALS: half down; tips recurved; red (53B) upper surface; red (53C) lower surface; 19mm (3/4") long x 7mm (1/4") wide. TUBE: red (53C); medium length & thickness; 16mm (5/8") long x 5mm (3/16") wide. STAMENS: extend 3mm (1/8") below corolla; rose (61D) filaments; pale pink (62D) anthers. PISTIL: extends 7mm (1/4") below the corolla; magenta (61C) style; light pink (55D) stigma. BUD: cordate shaped. FOLIAGE: dark green (136B) upper surface, medium green (137C) lower surface. Leaves are 36mm (1 7/16") long x 24mm (15/16") wide, ovate shaped, serrulated edges, acute tips and rounded bases. Light plum (184D) veins; dark reddish purple (187B) stems; dark grayish purple (183A) branches. PARENTAGE: 'Rohees Izar' x 'Twingo'. Lax upright or stiff trailer. Makes good basket. Prefers overhead filtered light. Best bloom and foliage colour in filtered light. Tested 3 years in Berlaar, Belgium. Award at Meise, 9/8/03. Distinguished by bloom shape. Geerts J. 2004 BE AFS5430.

Lovely Jenny. Upright. Double. COROLLA is three quarter flared with turned under wavy petal margins; opens reddish purple (72B) turning to purple (83B) at edge; matures reddish purple (71B); 14mm (9/16") long x 16mm (5/8") wide. PETALOIDS: reddish purple (72B); 9mm (3/8") long x 8mm (5/16") wide. SEPALS are horizontal, tips recurved; reddish purple (67A) upper surface; reddish purple (61B) lower surface; 27mm (1 1/16") long x 13mm (1/2") wide. TUBE is magenta (61C); medium length & thickness; 23mm (15/16") long x 7mm (1/4") wide. FOLIAGE: dark green (137A) upper surface; medium green (138B) lower surface. Leaves are 87mm (3 7/16") long x 46mm (1 13/16") wide, ovate shaped. PARENTAGE: 'Aalter's Glory' x 'Rohees New Millenium'. Meise 8-14-04. Distinguished by shape. Geerts J. 2005 BE AFS5828.

Lovely Jess. Upright/Trailer. Single. COROLLA: half flared, turned under wavy petal margins; opens magenta (63B), reddish purple (67A) base; matures reddish purple (71B); 26mm (1") long x 28mm (1 1/8") wide. SEPALS: half up; tips recurved up; pink

(55C) striped pale pink (56C), tipped light yellow (149C) upper surface; rose (55B) tipped light yellow green (149C) lower surface; 32mm (1 1/4") long x 11mm (7/16") wide. TUBE: pink (55C); short & thick; 10mm (3/8") long x 7mm (1/4") wide. STAMENS: extend 4mm (3/16") below corolla; magenta (68A) filaments; yellowish white (4D) anthers. PISTIL: extends 11mm (7/16") below the corolla; magenta (71C) style; pale yellow (8D) stigma. BUD: oblong. FOLIAGE: medium green (137B) upper surface, medium green (138B) lower surface. Leaves are 48mm (1 7/8") long x 32mm (1 1/4") wide, ovate shaped, serrulated edges, acute tips and rounded bases. Light red purple (185D) veins; reddish purple (186B) stems; plum (185C) & medium green (138B) branches. PARENTAGE: 'Danny Kay' x 'Twingo'. Lax upright or stiff trailer. Makes good basket. Prefers overhead filtered light and cool climate. Best bloom and foliage colour in filtered light. Tested 3 years in Berlaar, Belgium. Award at Meise, 9/8/03. Distinguished by bloom shape.
Geerts J. 2004 BE AFS5428.

Lovely Lien. Upright/Trailer. Double. COROLLA is three quarter flared with turned under wavy petal margins; opens dark reddish purple (72A), reddish purple (61B) base; matures magenta (72C), light reddish purple (61C) base; 11mm (7/16") long x 13mm (1/2") wide. PETALOIDS: Same colour as corolla; 8mm (5/16") long x 3mm (1/8") wide. SEPALS are horizontal, tips reflexed; red (53D) upper surface; red (53B) lower surface; 21mm (13/16") long x 10mm (3/8") wide. TUBE is red (53C); medium length & thickness; 24mm (15/16") long x 5mm (3/16") wide. FOLIAGE: dark green (136A) upper surface; medium green (138A) lower surface. Leaves are 53mm (2 1/16") long x 30mm (1 3/16") wide, ovate shaped. PARENTAGE: 'Aalters Glory' x 'Rohees New Millenium'. Meise 8-14-04. Distinguished by flower colour combination.
Geerts J. 2005 BE AFS5731.

Lovely Marieserge. Upright/Trailer. Single to Semi Double. COROLLA: half flared; opens magenta (63A); matures magenta (61C); 30mm (1 3/16") long x 28mm (1 1/8") wide. SEPALS: half down, tips recurved, twisted left; pink (52D) tipped light yellowish green (150C) upper surface; orange (44D) tipped light yellowish green (150C) lower surface; 37mm (1 7/16") long x 15mm (9/16") wide. TUBE: pink (50D); 44mm (1 3/4") long x 8mm (5/16") wide. FOLIAGE is dark green (137A) upper surface; medium green (138B)

lower surface. PARENTAGE: 'WALZ Harp' x 'De Acht Zaligheden'.
Geerts J. 2008 BE AFS6765.

Lovely Mitchie. Upright. Single. COROLLA: half flared, turned under smooth petal margins; opens magenta (58B); matures magenta (61C); 19mm (3/4") long x 17mm (11/16") wide. SEPALS: half up; tips recurved up; pink (55C) tipped light apple green (145C) upper surface; rose (55B) tipped light apple green (145C) lower surface; 37mm (1 7/16") long x 10mm (3/8") wide. TUBE: pale pink (56B); long & thin; 38mm (1 1/2") long x 4mm(3/16") wide. STAMENS: extend 3mm (1/8") below corolla; magenta (58B) filaments; magenta (59C) anthers. PISTIL: extends 7mm (1/4") below the corolla; pink (55C) style; light yellow (1C) stigma. BUD: oblong. FOLIAGE: dark green (139A) upper surface, medium green (139C) lower surface. Leaves are 78mm (3 1/16") long x 36mm (1 7/16") wide, lanceolate shaped, serrulated edges, acute tips and rounded bases. Veins are grayish red (181C); stems are light grayish rose (181D); branches are light grayish rose (181D) & medium green (138B). PARENTAGE: 'WALZ Harp' x 'Bleu Rebel'. Small upright. Self branching. Makes good upright. Prefers overhead filtered light and cool climate. Best bloom and foliage colour in filtered light. Tested 3 years in Itegem, Belgium. Award at Meise, 5/7/03. Distinguished by bloom shape.
Geerts L. 2004 BE AFS5409.

Lovely Patricia. Upright. Single. COROLLA: half flared; opens & matures light magenta (66C); 20mm (3/4") long x 20mm (3/4") wide. SEPALS: half down, tips recurved; dark rose (58C) upper & lower surfaces; 35mm (1 3/8") long x 20mm (3/4") wide. TUBE: light pink (55D); short & thin; 10mm (3/8") long x 5mm (3/16") wide. STAMENS extend 15mm (9/16") beyond the corolla; light pink (55D) filaments; magenta (63A) anthers. PISTIL extends 20mm (3/4") beyond the corolla; pink (55C) style; white (155A) stigma. BUD: ovate. FOLIAGE: dark green (137A) upper surface; light olive green (147C) lower surface. Leaves are 35mm (1 3/8") long x 20mm (3/4") wide; lanceolate shaped, serrulate edges, acute tips, acute bases. Veins are red, branches are light brown, stems are reddish. PARENTAGE: 'Princess Rebecca' x 'Lovely Charlotte'. Small upright. Self branching. Makes good upright. Prefers overhead filtered light. Best bloom colour in filtered light. Tested 3 years in Rayleigh,

Essex, England. Distinguished by blossom colour & shape.
Smith R. 2009 UK AFS7125.

Lovely Robin Hermans. Upright/Trailer. Single. COROLLA is three quarter flared with turned under wavy petal margins; opens reddish purple (71B); matures magenta (67B); 25mm (1") long x 27mm (1 1/16") wide. SEPALS are horizontal, tips recurved; dark rose (55A) upper surface; dark rose (51A) lower surface; 28mm (1 1/8") long x 10mm (3/8") wide. TUBE is light pink (49B); medium length & thickness; 22mm (7/8") long x 7mm (1/4") wide. FOLIAGE: dark green (137A) upper surface; medium green (139C) lower surface. Leaves are 62mm (2 7/16") long x 35mm (1 3/8") wide, ovate shaped. PARENTAGE: 'Aalters Glory' x 'Rohees New Millenium'. Meise 8-14-04. Distinguished by flower colour.
Geerts J. 2005 BE AFS5730.

Lovely Zhara. Upright/Trailer. Single to Semi Double. COROLLA: quarter flared, turned under wavy petal margins; opens purple (79C), purple (77A) base; matures dark purple (79A), dark reddish purple (64A) base; 28mm (1 1/8") long x 26mm (1") wide. PETALOIDS: purple (77A); 20mm (13/16") long x 11mm (7/16") wide. SEPALS: horizontal; tips recurved; reddish purple (67A) upper surface; reddish purple (64B) lower surface; 42mm (1 11/16") long x 12mm (1/2") wide. TUBE: magenta (67B); long & thin; 31mm (1 1/4") long x 5mm (3/16") wide. STAMENS: extend 5mm (3/16") below corolla; purple (79D) filaments; light purple (80C) anthers. PISTIL: extends 8mm (5/16") below the corolla; reddish purple (72B) style; pale purple (74D) stigma. BUD: long, sack shaped. FOLIAGE: medium green (137B) upper surface, medium green (138B) lower surface. Leaves are 71mm (2 13/16") long x 26mm (1") wide, elliptic shaped, serrulated edges, acute tips and rounded bases. Reddish purple (58A) veins; dark reddish purple (59A) stems; reddish purple (59B) branches. PARENTAGE: 'Rohees New Millenium' x 'WALZ Harp'. Lax upright or stiff trailer. Makes good basket. Prefers overhead filtered light and cool climate. Best bloom and foliage colour in filtered light. Tested 3 years in Berlaar, Belgium. Award at Meise, 9/8/03. Distinguished by bloom colour.
Geerts J. 2004 BE AFS5429.

Lovingly. Upright/Trailer. Semi Double. COROLLA: three quarter flared; opens & matures violet (75A); 20mm (3/4") long x

20mm (3/4") wide. SEPALS: half up, tips recurved up; pink (62C) tipped green upper surface; pink (62A) tipped green lower surface; 30mm (1 3/16") long x 20mm (3/4") wide. TUBE: light rose (50C); 18mm (11/16") long x 15mm (9/16") wide. FOLIAGE is dark green (137C) upper surface; medium green (138B) lower surface. PARENTAGE: 'Lovely Charlotte' x 'Princess Rebecca'.
Smith R. 2008 UK AFS6819.

Luc Lemmen. Upright/Trailer. Semi Double. COROLLA is three quarter flared with smooth petal margins; opens violet (76A); matures purple (80A); 27mm (1 1/16") long x 25mm (1") wide. SEPALS are fully up, tips recurved; red (45A) upper surface; magenta (63A) lower surface; 23mm (15/16") long x 12mm (1/2") wide. TUBE is red (45A); short & thick; 8mm (3/16") long x 6mm (1/4") wide. FOLIAGE: dark green (137A) upper surface; medium green (138A) lower surface. Leaves are 66mm (2 5/8") long x 37mm (1 7/16") wide, ovate shaped. PARENTAGE: 'Swanley Gem' x ('Roesse Carme' x 'Roesse Elara'). Distinguished by bloom & foliage combination.
Roes 2005 NL AFS5973.

Luc Noël. Trailer. Double. COROLLA: half flared; opens white (155C), pale pink (62D) base; matures white (155D); 24mm (15/16") long x 18mm (11/16") wide. PETALOIDS: same colour as corolla; 15mm (9/16") long x 9mm (5/16") wide. SEPALS: horizontal, tips reflexed; white (155C) tipped yellowish green (144B) upper & lower surfaces; 38mm (1 1/2") long x 14mm (9/16") wide. TUBE: white (155C); long & thin; 23mm (7/8") long x 5mm (3/16") wide. FOLIAGE is dark green (139A) upper surface; medium green (138B) lower surface. PARENTAGE: 'Vreni Schleeweis' x 'Kiss'.
Michiels 2007 BE AFS6342.

Luca Feilhuber. Upright/Trailer. Single. COROLLA: unflared, short & compact, smooth petal margins; opens dark purple (N78A); matures reddish purple (72B); 14mm (9/16") long x 6mm (1/4") wide. SEPALS: horizontal, tips recurved; magenta (N57B) upper & lower surfaces; 30mm (1 3/16") long x 6mm (1/4") wide. TUBE: magenta (N57B); medium length, thin; 14mm (9/16") long x 4mm (1/8") wide. STAMENS extend 19mm (3/4") beyond the corolla; dark reddish purple (61A) filaments; reddish purple (61B) anthers. PISTIL extends 34mm (1 3/8") beyond the corolla; magenta (N57B) style; light rose (73C) stigma. BUD: elongated.

285

FOLIAGE: dark green (137A) upper surface; medium green (137C) lower surface. Leaves are 75mm (3") long x 40mm (1 9/16") wide; ovate shaped, serrulate edges, acute tips, rounded bases. Veins are light green, stems are red, branches are light brown. PARENTAGE: 'Waldis Gräfin' x F. *regia ssp. serrae hoya.* Lax upright or stiff trailer. Makes good upright or standard. Prefers full sun, warm climate. Best bloom & foliage colour in bright light. Tested 5 years in Bavaria, Southern Germany. Distinguished by bloom shape & colour.
Burkhart 2009 DE AFS7099.

Luca Neggers. Upright/Trailer. Double. COROLLA: three quarter flared, turned under wavy petal margins; opens pale pink (69A) & violet (75A) striped magenta (67B); matures magenta (68A) & magenta (63B) striped rose (64D); 28mm (1 1/8") long x 25mm (1") wide. PETALOIDS: Same colour as corolla; 16mm (5/8") long x 12mm (7/16") wide. SEPALS: half down, tips recurved; pale lavender (65D) tipped light greenish yellow (151D) upper surface; dark rose (55A) tipped light greenish yellow (151D) lower surface; 38mm (1 1/2") long x 20mm (3/4") wide. TUBE: white (155B) striped pale pink (56A); short & thick; 14mm (9/16") long x 9mm (5/16") wide. STAMENS extend 12mm (7/16") beyond the corolla; magenta (63B) filaments; reddish purple (71B) anthers. PISTIL extends 21mm (13/16") beyond the corolla; light rose (58D) style; light pink (65B) stigma. BUD: bulbous. FOLIAGE: medium green (137B) upper surface; medium green (138B) lower surface. Leaves are 69mm (2 3/4") long x 43mm (1 11/16") wide; ovate shaped, serrulate edges, acute tips, rounded bases. Veins are dark grayish red (182A), stems are light plum (184D), branches are light green (139D). PARENTAGE: 'Manfried Kleinau' x 'Bianca'. Lax upright or stiff trailer. Self branching. Makes good basket. Prefers overhead filtered light, cool climate. Best bloom & foliage colour in filtered light. Tested 3 years in Koningshooikt, Belgium. Waanrode 8/9/08. Distinguished by bloom colour combination.
Michiels 2009 BE AFS7196.

Lucklaw Pink. Trailer. Single. COROLLA opens cerise; corolla is quarter flared and is 22mm long x 20mm wide. SEPALS rich pink, tipped light green on the upper and lower surfaces; sepals are horizontally held with recurved tips and are 28mm long x 12mm wide. TUBE rich pink and is 21mm long x 8mm wide. PARENTAGE 'found seedling' x

'Shelford'. This cultivar is very versatile, in the fact that it could be grown as a bush, basket, standard, and is at ease growing in a window sill.
Moscrop 2006 UK BFS0025.

Lucy Roberts. Upright. Double. COROLLA: quarter flared, bell shaped, smooth petal margins; opens violet blue (91A) & white (155D), flushed rose (55B); matures violet (77C) & white (155D), flushed dark rose (55A); 32mm (1 1/4") long 22mm (7/8") wide. SEPALS: horizontal; tips recurved; pink (55C) upper surface; dark rose (55A) lower surface; 44mm (1 3/4") long x 12mm (1/2") wide. TUBE: white (155D); medium length & thickness; 19mm (3/4") long x 7mm (1/4") wide. STAMENS: extend 12mm (1/2") below corolla; magenta (61C) filaments; reddish purple (60D) anthers. PISTIL: extends 32mm (1 1/4") below the corolla; pink (55C) style; white (155D) stigma. BUD: oval, pointed. FOLIAGE: medium green (138A) upper surface; medium green (138B) lower surface. Leaves are 57mm (2 1/4") long x 29mm (1 1/8") wide, lanceolate shaped, serrated edges, acute tips and rounded bases. Green veins; pink stems & branches. PARENTAGE: 'Andrew Hadfield' x 'Gordon's Gold'. Small upright. Self branching. Makes good upright. Prefers overhead filtered light, cool climate. Best bloom and foliage colour in filtered light. Tested 3 years in Stoke-On-Trent, England. Distinguished by profuse blossoms and blossom colour combination.
Goodwin 2004 UK AFS5575.

Lueur D'espoir. Upright/Trailer. Single. COROLLA: quarter flared; smooth petal margins; opens & matures violet (77B), lighter base; 23mm (7/8") long x 20mm (3/4") wide. SEPALS: half up, tips recurved up; pink (52D) tipped yellowish green upper & lower surfaces; 36mm (1 7/16") long x 9mm (5/16") wide. TUBE: pink (52D); short, medium thickness; 6mm (1/4") long x 6mm (1/4") wide. STAMENS extend 12-15mm (7/16-9/16") beyond the corolla; rose (48B) filaments; rose (51B) anthers. PISTIL extends 17mm (5/8") beyond the corolla; rose (48B) style; pink (48C) stigma. BUD is ovate. FOLIAGE is medium green (146A) upper surface; yellowish green (146B) lower surface. Leaves are 49mm (1 15/16") long x 34mm (1 3/8") wide; ovate shaped, serrulate edges, obtuse to acute tips, cordate bases. Veins, stems & branches are yellowish green. PARENTAGE: 'Henri Massé' x 'Leverkusen'. Lax upright or stiff trailer. Self branching. Makes good upright. Prefers overhead filtered

light & cool climate. Tested 4 years in Pornic, France. Distinguished by pastel colours of blooms.
Massé 2009 FR AFS6993.

Luigi. Upright/Trailer. Double. COROLLA opens light lilac, matures to very pale lilac; corolla is three quarter flared. SEPALS cream tipped green on the upper and lower surfaces; SEPALS are half up with recurved tips. TUBE cream flushed green. PARENTAGE 'Hans Schnedl' x 'Ulrike Scheckat'.
Strümper 2009 DE BFS0145.

Luke Bergh. Upright/Trailer. Single. COROLLA: full flared; opens dark reddish purple (59A); matures dark reddish purple (60B); 21mm (7/8") long x 20mm (3/4") wide. SEPALS: fully up, tips recurved; light rose (58D) upper surface; dark rose (58C) lower surface; 36mm (1 7/16") long x 10mm (3/8") wide. TUBE: light rose (58D); 19mm (3/4") long x 6mm (1/4") wide. FOLIAGE is dark green (137A) upper surface; medium green (138A) lower surface. PARENTAGE: 'Roesse Lupus' x 'Oranje van Os'.
Roes 2008 NL AFS6897.

Luscious Lisa. Trailer. Double. COROLLA: three quarter flared, turned under smooth petal margins; opens dark violet (87A) veined red (50A); matures light purple (81C) veined red (50A) splashed light pink (49C); 30mm (1 3/16") long x 50mm (2") wide. PETALOIDS: same colour as corolla; 12mm (1/2") long x 8mm (5/16") wide. SEPALS: fully up; tips recurved, red (50A) upper & lower surfaces; 30mm(1 3/16") long x 12mm (1/2") wide. TUBE: dark rose (55A); medium length & thickness; 12mm (1/2") long x 6mm (1/4") wide. STAMENS: extend 15mm (9/16") below corolla; red (50A) filaments, pink (49A) anthers. PISTIL: extends 25mm (1") below the corolla, pink (52D) style; grayish yellow (160A) stigma. BUD: medium, oval. FOLIAGE: medium green (146A) upper surface; yellowish green (146B) lower surface. Leaves are 65mm (2 9/16") long x 35mm (1 3/8") wide, cordate shaped, serrulated edges, acute tips and rounded bases. Veins & branches are green, stems are brown. PARENTAGE: 'Loveable Rascal' x 'R.A.F.'. Natural trailer. Self branching. Makes good basket or standard. Heat tolerant if shaded. Prefers warm climate. Cold weather hardy to 32° F. Best bloom colour in bright light. Tested 3 years in Walthamstow, London, England. Distinguished by lilac splashed pink blooms.

Allsop M.R. 2003 UK AFS5154.

Lut. Upright/Trailer. Double. COROLLA is three quarter flared with turned under wavy petal margins; opens light purple (78C), pale purple (74D) base; matures light purple (78B); 23mm (15/16") long x 20mm (13/16") wide. PETALOIDS: same colour as corolla; 15mm (9/16") long x 13mm (1/2") wide. SEPALS are horizontal, tips recurved; white (155B), tipped yellowish green (144B) upper surface; pale pink (56D), tipped yellowish green (144B) lower surface; 29mm (1 1/16") long x 12mm (1/2") wide. TUBE is white (155B); medium length & thickness; 14mm (9/16") long x 6mm (1/4") wide. FOLIAGE: dark green (139A) upper surface; medium green (138A) lower surface. Leaves are 66mm (2 5/8") long x 41mm (1 5/8") wide, ovate shaped. PARENTAGE: 'Sofie Michiels' x 'Diana Wills'. Meise 8-14-04. Distinguished by flower colour & shape.
Michiels 2005 BE AFS5755.

Luuk van Riet. Trailer. Double. COROLLA: quarter flared, smooth petal margins; opens pale lavender (65D); matures pale pink (62D); 17mm (11/16") long x 24mm (15/16") wide. SEPALS: fully up; tips reflexed; magenta (58B) upper & lower surfaces; 30mm (3/16") long x 14mm (9/16") wide. TUBE: dark rose (58C); long & thin; 32mm (1 1/4") long x 4mm (3/16") wide. STAMENS: extend 12mm (1/2") below corolla; dark rose (58C) filaments & anthers. PISTIL: extends 26mm (1") below the corolla; pale pink (62D) style & stigma. BUD: cordate. FOLIAGE: medium green (137C) upper surface; medium green (137D) lower surface. Leaves are 56mm (2 3/16") long x 29mm (1 1/8") wide, cordate shaped, serrulated edges, acute tips and rounded bases. Veins & stems are red, branches are green. PARENTAGE: [('Cameron Ryle' x 'Parasol') x 'Allure'] x'Allure'. Natural trailer. Makes good basket. Prefers overhead filtered light and cool climate. Best bloom and foliage colour in filtered light. Tested 4 years in Knegsel, The Netherlands. Distinguished by bloom & foliage combination.
Roes 2003 NL AFS5314.

Luxuriant. Upright. Single. COROLLA is unflared; opens purple (71A); matures reddish purple (71B); 17mm (5/8") long x 9mm (3/8") wide. SEPALS are fully up, tips recurved; bright red (45B) upper surface; red (45C) lower surface; 45mm (1 3/4") long x 7mm (1/4") wide. TUBE is bright red (45B); 17mm (5/8") long x 5mm (3/16") wide.

FOLIAGE: dark green (147A) upper surface; medium green (147B) lower surface. PARENTAGE: 'F. regia reitzii' x 'Zulu King'. Distinguished by long pistil & long SEPALS in complete vertical circle. Massé 2006 FR AFS6240.

Lydia. Upright. Single. COROLLA is full flared; opens light reddish purple (72C); matures reddish purple (60D); 25mm (1") long x 31mm (1 1/4") wide. SEPALS are half up, tips recurved up; white (155D) upper surface; pale pink (56D) lower surface; 38mm (1 1/2") long x 15mm (9/16") wide. TUBE is white (155A); 8mm (5/16") long x 10mm (3/8") wide. FOLIAGE is dark green (147A) upper surface; yellowish green (146B) lower surface. PARENTAGE: 'Estelle Marie' x unknown. omination by NKVF as Recommendable Cultivar. Distinguished by bloom colour. van den Brink 2006 NL AFS6258.

Lydia-Ivo. Trailer. Double. COROLLA: 3 quarter flared; opens light purple (N78B), pale purple (75D) base; matures light purple (N78C); 24mm (15/16") long x 17mm (5/8") wide. PETALOIDS: light purple (N78C), pale purple (75D) base; 16mm (5/8") long x 12mm (7/16") wide. SEPALS: horizontal, tips reflexed; white (155C) & light green (139D) tipped light green (143D) upper surface; pale purple (75D) tipped light green (143D) lower surface; 38mm (1 1/2") long x 21mm (13/16") wide. TUBE: white (155C) striped light green (139D); medium length & thickness; 22mm (7/8") long x 7mm (1/4") wide. FOLIAGE is dark green (139A) upper surface; medium green (139C) lower surface. PARENTAGE: 'Vreni Schleeweiss' x 'Kiss'. Michiels 2007 BE AFS6366.

Lynn Cunningham. Upright. Single. COROLLA: unflared, smooth petal margins, bell shaped; opens purple (89B) veined orange in throat; matures reddish purple (74A); 22mm (7/8 ") long x 20mm (3/4") wide. SEPALS: horizontal, tips reflexed; magenta (57B) upper surface; magenta (57C) lower surface; 28mm (1 1/8") long x 9mm (5/16") wide. TUBE: magenta (57B); short, medium thickness; 8mm (5/16") long x 5mm (3/16") wide. STAMENS extend 21mm (13/16") beyond the corolla; magenta (59C) filaments; reddish purple (59B) anthers. PISTIL extends 31mm (1 1/4") beyond the corolla; magenta (57A) style; reddish purple (64B) stigma. BUD: square, pointed, slight bend. FOLIAGE: medium green (137B) upper surface; light green (143B) lower surface.

Leaves are 47mm (1 7/8") long x 25mm (1") wide; cordate shaped, serrate edges, acute tips, rounded bases. Veins & branches are green stems pinkish green. PARENTAGE: F. coccinea x 'Eileen Storey'. Small upright. Self branching. Makes good upright. Prefers overhead filtered light. Cold weather hardy to -3° C (26° F). Best bloom & foliage colour in filtered light. Tested 6 years in Holderness, East Yorkshire, England. Distinguished by bloom colour & shape. Storey 2009 UK AFS7136.

Lynne Patricia. Upright. Double. COROLLA: Opens quarter flared matures full flared, saucer shaped; opens pale violet (92D) streaked magenta (58B) from base; matures pale violet (92D); 25mm (1") long x 13-19mm (1/2"-3/4") wide. SEPALS: fully up, tips recurved; dark rose (58C) at base, suffusing to white, tipped green, upper surface; dark rose (58C) lower surface; 31mm (1 1/4") long x 9mm (5/16") wide. TUBE: dark rose (58C); short & thick; 9mm (5/16") long x 6mm (1/4") wide. FOLIAGE is medium green (137C) upper surface; medium green (138B) lower surface. PARENTAGE: [('Baby Bright' x 'Zulu King' seedling') x 'Carla Johnston'] x 'Lilian Annetts' seedling. Also registered with the BFS in 2006. Swaby 2007 UK AFS6498. BFS0029.

Lynne Patricia Preston. Upright. Single. COROLLA: quarter flared, bell shaped, turned under petal margins; opens purple (82B); matures violet (82C) blending with white; 13mm (1/2") long x 19mm (3/4") wide. SEPALS: half up; tips recurved up; pale yellow green (150D) upper surface; pale yellow (8D) lower surface; 19mm(3/4") long x 8mm (5/16") wide. TUBE: pale yellow green (150D); short & thin; 3mm (1/8") long x 3mm (1/8") wide. STAMENS: extend 13mm (1/2") below corolla; very dark reddish purple (186A) filaments; light purple (186C) anthers. PISTIL: extends 25mm (1") below the corolla; white (155B) style, cream (159D) stigma. BUD: oval, short. FOLIAGE: medium green (138A) upper surface; medium green (138B) lower surface. Leaves are 32mm (1 1/4") long x 19mm (3/4") wide, cordate shaped, serrulated edges, acute tips and rounded bases. Veins are light green, stems & branches are yellow green. PARENTAGE: 'Carla Johnson' x 'Estelle Marie'. Small upright. Self branching. Makes good upright or standard. Prefers overhead filtered light & cool climate. Best bloom and foliage colour in filtered light. Tested 6 years in West

Yorkshire, England. Distinguished by colour combination.
Preston 2003 UK AFS5136.

Lysithea. Upright. Single. COROLLA light plum purple. SEPALS white flushed pink. Ainsworth 2003 UK.

Maagd. Upright/Trailer. Double. COROLLA: Quarter flared; opens light reddish purple (72C), pale pink (62D) base; matures reddish purple (71B); 18mm (11/16") long x 14mm (9/16") wide. SEPALS: half down, tips reflexed; pink (62A) tipped light apple green (145C) upper surface; dark rose (55A) tipped light apple green (145C) lower surface; 26mm (1") long x 11mm (7/16") wide. TUBE: pale pink (62D); long & thin; 27mm (1 1/16") long x 4mm (1/8") wide. FOLIAGE is dark green (136A) upper surface; medium green (138A) lower surface. PARENTAGE: 'Ghislane' x 'Rohees New Millennium'.
Geerts L. 2007 BE AFS6381.

Maartje Spoelstra. Trailer. Single. COROLLA: full flared, smooth petal margins; opens purple (77A); matures dark reddish purple (64A); 25mm (1") long 37mm (1 7/16") wide. SEPALS: fully up; tips recurved; reddish purple (71B) upper surface; reddish purple (67A) lower surface; 26mm (1") long x 17mm (11/16") wide. TUBE: reddish purple (71B); medium length & thickness; 9mm (3/8") long x 7mm (1/4") wide. STAMENS: extend 26mm (1") below corolla; dark reddish purple (61A) filaments; dark reddish purple (59A) anthers. PISTIL: extends 41mm (1 5/8") below the corolla; dark reddish purple (61A) style; pale pink (62D) stigma. BUD: round, pointed. FOLIAGE: medium green (137B) upper surface; medium green (138A) lower surface. Leaves are 52mm (2 1/16") long x 37mm (1 7/16") wide, ovate shaped, serrulated edges, acute tips and rounded bases. Red veins, stems & branches. PARENTAGE: 'Roesse Dione' x 'Delta's Bride'. Natural trailer. Self branching. Makes good basket. Prefers overhead filtered light and cool climate. Best bloom and foliage colour in filtered light. Tested 4 years in Knegsel, The Netherlands. Distinguished by bloom colour.
Roes 2004 NL AFS5463.

Madalyn Drago. Upright/Trailer. Single. COROLLA is half flared with wavy petal margins; opens violet (85A), matures light violet (77D); 28mm (1 1/8") long x 32mm (1 1/4") wide. SEPALS are horizontal, tips recurved; pink (62A) upper surface and light pink (62B) lower surface; 37mm (1 7/16)

long x 14mm (9/16") wide. TUBE is light pink (62B), medium length and thickness; 17mm (11/16") long x 8mm (5/16") wide. STAMENS extend 22mm (7/8) below the corolla; magenta (63A) filaments and anthers. PISTIL extends 28mm (1 1/8") below the corolla; magenta (63C) style and pale pink (62D) stigma. BUD is ovate. FOLIAGE is dark green (137A) upper surface and medium green (138A) lower surface. Leaves are 48mm (1 7/8") long x 34mm (1 5/16") wide, ovate shaped, serrulated edges, obtuse tips and obtuse bases. Veins, stems and branches are red. PARENTAGE: ('Parasol' x 'Cameron Ryle') x 'Rohees Queen'. Lax upright or stiff trailer. Makes good stiff trailer. Prefers overhead filtered light and cool climate. Best bloom colour in filtered light. Tested four years in Knegsel, The Netherlands. Distinguished by bloom colour.
Roes 2002 NL AFS4829.

Madleina. Trailer. Double. COROLLA: half flared, turned under smooth petal margins; opens & matures magenta (58B), light rose (58D) at base; 26mm (1") long x 32mm (1 1/4") wide. PETALOIDS: 1 per sepal; dark orange (33A) edged magenta (58B), 21mm (13/16") long x 11mm (7/16") wide. SEPALS: half down; tips reflexed; light rose (58D) tipped light yellow green (150A) upper surface; dark rose (58C) lower surface; 34mm (1 5/16") long x 18mm (11/16") wide. TUBE: white (155A); medium length & thickness; 17mm (11/16") long x 7mm (1/4") wide. STAMENS: extend 16mm (5/8") below the corolla; pink (62A) filaments, tan (162A) anthers. PISTIL extends 25mm (1") below the corolla; pink (62A) style, brown (165A) stigma. BUD: ovate. FOLIAGE: dark green (137A) upper surface; medium green (137C) lower surface. Leaves are 71mm (2 13/16") long x 42mm (1 11/16") wide, ovate shaped, serrulated edges, acute tips and rounded bases. Veins, stems & branches are dark reddish purple (59A). PARENTAGE: 'Braamt's Glorie' x unknown. Natural trailer. Self branching. Makes good basket. Prefers overhead filtered light. Best bloom and foliage colour in filtered light. Tested 3 years in Rummen, Belgium. NBFK certificate at Meise. Distinguished by bloom shape.
Ector 2003 BE AFS5114.

Magda Cerules. Upright/Trailer. Double. COROLLA is half flared with smooth petal margins; opens pale lavender (65D); matures pale pink (62D); 26mm (1") long x 21 mm (13/16") wide. SEPALS are fully up, tips reflexed; pink (62C) upper surface; light pink

(62B) lower surface; 37mm (1 7/16") long x 13mm (1/2") wide. TUBE is pink (62C), long & thin; 32mm (1 1/4") long x 4mm (3/16") wide. FOLIAGE: dark green (137A) upper surface; medium green (137C) lower surface. Leaves are 86mm (3 3/8") long x 30mm (1 3/16") wide, elliptic shaped. PARENTAGE: ('Roesse Apus' x 'Rohees Izar') x 'Allure'. Distinguished by bloom shape. Roes 2002 NL AFS5640.

Magda Vanbets. Upright/Trailer. Double. COROLLA is three quarter flared with smooth petal margins; opens white (155A), matures white (155B); 22mm (7/8") long x 20 mm (13/16") wide. SEPALS are half up, tips recurved up; white (155A) upper surface; white (155B) lower surface; 28mm (1 1/8") long x 12mm (1/2") wide. TUBE is white (155A), medium length and thickness; 22mm (7/8") long x 7mm (1/4") wide. STAMENS extend 22mm (7/8") beyond the corolla; light pink (65B) filaments; dark reddish purple (60C) anthers. PISTIL extends 42mm (1 11/16") below the corolla; light pink (65C) style; white (155B) stigma. BUD is elliptic, pointed. FOLIAGE is medium green (137B) upper surface, medium green (137C) lower surface. Leaves are 68mm (2 11/16") long x 34mm (1 3/8") wide, ovate shaped, serrulated edges, acute tips and rounded bases. Veins, stems & branches are red. PARENTAGE: 'Roesse Dione' x 'Allure'. Lax upright or stiff trailer. Makes good stiff trailer. Prefers overhead filtered light & cool climate. Best bloom and foliage colour in filtered light. Tested four years in Knegsel, The Netherlands. Distinguished by bloom & foliage combination.
Roes 2004 NL AFS5361.

Maggie Rose. Upright. Single. COROLLA opens aster violet (57a), white at base, matures to bishops violet (81b); corolla is none flared and is 20mm long x 18mm wide. SEPALS are neyron rose (58c) on the upper surface, neyron rose (53c) on the lower surface; sepals are fully up with recurved tips and are 51mm long x 12mm wide. TUBE neyron rose (53c) and is 17mm long x 7mm wide. PARENTAGE 'Breeders Delight' x 'Sophie Louise'.
Waving 2003 UK BFS0017.

Maid Marion. Single. COROLLA pale lilac. SEPALS white. TUBE pale rose.
Weston 2008 UK.

Maik Luijten. Upright/Trailer. Double. COROLLA is half flared; opens dark purple

(79A); matures purple (71A); 21mm (13/16") long x 26mm (1") wide. SEPALS are horizontal, tips recurved; light purple (75B) upper surface; magenta (68A) lower surface; 26mm (1") long x 12mm (7/16") wide. TUBE is pale purple (75D); 16mm (5/8") long x 6mm (1/4") wide. FOLIAGE: dark green (137A) upper surface; medium green (138A) lower surface. PARENTAGE: 'Maxima' x 'Roesse Tureis'. Distinguished by bloom colour.
Buiting 2006 NL AFS6107.

Majoor Bosshardt. Upright. Single. COROLLA: quarter flared; opens dark purple (79A); matures dark reddish purple (187C); 24mm (15/16") long x 24mm (15/16") wide. SEPALS: horizontal, tips recurved; dark red (46A) upper & lower surfaces; 30mm (1 3/16") long x 11mm (7/16") wide. TUBE: dark red (46A); medium length & thickness; 12mm (7/16") long x 6mm (1/4") wide. STAMENS extend 40mm (1 9/16") beyond the corolla; purple (77A) filaments; light purple (78C) anthers. PISTIL extends 45mm (1 3/4") beyond the corolla; reddish purple (74A) style; light reddish purple (73A) stigma. BUD: ovate. FOLIAGE: dark green (147A) upper surface; medium green (146A) lower surface. Leaves are 65mm (2 9/16") long x 35mm (1 3/8") wide; ovate shaped, serrulate edges, acute tips, rounded bases. Veins, stems & branches are dark reddish purple (59A). PARENTAGE: 'Casper Hauser' x seedling of 'Insa'. Tall upright. Makes good upright or standard. Prefers overhead filtered light, cool climate. Best bloom colour in filtered light. Tested 8 years in Amsterdam, The Netherlands. V.K.C Aalsmeer 8/18/2001. Distinguished by flower colour & shape.
Krom 2009 NL AFS7059.

Making Waves. Upright. Single. COROLLA white, veined deep red; corolla is three quarter flared. SEPALS aubergine to red on the upper and lower surfaces; SEPALS are half up with recurved tips. TUBE aubergine to red. PARENTAGE 'Harbour Lites' x 'Winters Touch'.
Edmond D. 2009 UK BFS0138.

Mama Lydia. Upright/Trailer. Double. COROLLA: 3 quarter flared; opens purple (71A); matures magenta (71C); 40mm (1 9/16") long x 50mm (2") wide. SEPALS: half up, tips recurved up; light rose (58D) upper surface; dark rose (58C) lower surface; 25mm (1 3/8") long x 10mm (3/8") wide. TUBE: opens light cream, matures light rose

(58D); long & thin; 28mm (1 1/8") long x 4mm (1/8") wide. FOLIAGE is dark green (137A) upper surface; medium green (137C) lower surface. PARENTAGE: 'Lord von Beveren' x 'Zellertal'.
Gindl 2007 AT AFS6503.

Mandy Marchien. Upright. Single. COROLLA is three quarter flared, bell shaped, with smooth petal margins; opens pale pink (69A); matures pale lavender (69C); 17mm (11/16") long x 22mm (7/8") wide. SEPALS are horizontal, tips recurved; pale pink (49D), edged magenta (58B), tipped green upper surface; pale pink (49D), blushed & spotted magenta (58B), tipped green lower surface; 23mm (15/16") long x 12mm (1/2") wide. TUBE is pale pink (36D), striped dark rose (51A); medium length & thickness; 22mm (7/8") long x 8mm (5/16") wide. FOLIAGE: dark green (147A) upper surface; medium green (146B) lower surface. Leaves are 64mm (2 1/2") long x 33mm (1 5/16") wide, ovate shaped. PARENTAGE: [('F. magdalenae' x 'F. fulgens rubra grandiflora') x 'Wendy van Wanten'] x 'Prince Syray'. Distinguished by erect blooms & soft pastel colours.
Koerts T. 2005 NL AFS5815.

Manfried Kleinau. Trailer. Double. COROLLA: half flared; opens purple (71A) striped light rose (58D); matures dark reddish purple (72A); 26mm (1") long x 21mm (13/16") wide. PETALOIDS: purple (71A) striped light rose (58D); 15mm (9/16") long x 9mm (5/16") wide. SEPALS are half down, tips reflexed; pale pink (62D) tipped light green (143C) upper surface and magenta (63B) tipped light green (143C) lower surface; 27mm (1 1/16") long x 14mm (9/16") wide. TUBE is pink (62A); medium length & thickness; 14mm (9/16") long x 6mm (1/4") wide. FOLIAGE is dark green (136A) upper surface; medium green (139B) lower surface. PARENTAGE: 'Leon Pauwels' x 'Oso Sweet'. Meise 9/16/2006, Outstanding.
Michiels 2007 BE AFS6527.

Manske En Stanske. Upright/Trailer. Single. COROLLA is three quarter flared with turned under smooth petal margins; opens reddish purple (74B), matures reddish purple (74A); 28mm (1 1/8") long x 15 mm (5/8") wide. SEPALS are horizontal, tips recurved; rose (55B) upper surface, dark rose (55A) lower surface; 22mm (7/8") long x 7mm (1/4") wide. TUBE is pale pink (56A), medium length and thickness; 26mm (1") long x 7mm (1/4") wide. STAMENS extend 12mm (1/2") beyond the corolla; rose (61D) filaments, light

plum (184D) anthers. PISTIL extends 22mm (7/8") below the corolla; rose (67D) style; dark tan (164B) stigma. BUD is round, pointed. FOLIAGE is dark green (139A) upper surface, medium green (138B) lower surface. Leaves are 51mm (2") long x 32mm (1 1/4") wide, ovate shaped, serrated edges, acute tips and rounded bases. Veins are light apple green (145B), stems are brownish orange (174D), branches are light green (139D). PARENTAGE: 'Quasar' x 'Twingo'. Lax upright or stiff trailer. Makes good basket. Prefers overhead filtered light. Best bloom and foliage colour in filtered light. Tested three years in Berlaar, Belgium. Certificate N.B.F.K. at Meise. Distinguished by bloom colour and shape.
Geerts J. 2002 BE AFS4921.

Manuela Fuhrmann. Upright/Trailer. Double. COROLLA: three quarter flared, turned under wavy petal margins; opens rose (54C) & magenta (67B) edged reddish purple (70B); matures magenta (63A) edged rose (64D); 22mm (7/8") long x 18mm (11/16") wide. PETALOIDS: rose (54C) & reddish purple (70B); 13mm (1/2") long x 10mm (3/8") wide. SEPALS: horizontal, tips recurved, twisted left to right; light pink (65C) tipped light apple green (145B) upper surface; rose (52B) tipped light apple green (145B) lower surface; 32mm (1 1/4") long x 15mm (9/16") wide. TUBE: light pink (62C); medium length & thickness; 14mm (9/16") long x 6mm (1/4") wide. STAMENS extend 16mm (5/8") beyond the corolla; magenta (58B) filaments; magenta (71C) anthers. PISTIL extends 22mm (7/8") beyond the corolla; light pink (62C) style; pale rose (73D) stigma. BUD: bulbous. FOLIAGE: dark green (137A) upper surface; medium green (138B) lower surface. Leaves are 60mm (2 3/8") long x 34mm (1 3/8") wide; ovate shaped, smooth edges, acute tips, rounded bases. Veins are light apple green (145B), stems are light apple green (145B) & plum (184C), branches are plum (184C) & light apple green (145B). PARENTAGE: 'Manfried Kleinau' x 'Alfred Fuhrmann'. Lax upright or stiff trailer. Self branching. Makes good basket or upright. Prefers overhead filtered light, cool climate. Best bloom & foliage colour in filtered light. Tested 3 years in Koningshooikt, Belgium. Waanrode 8/9/08. Distinguished by bloom colour combination.
Michiels 2009 BE AFS7197.

Marcel Michiels. Upright. Double. COROLLA is three quarter flared with smooth petal margins; opens dark red (53A), matures dark

red (46A); 26mm (1") long x 22mm (7/8") wide. SEPALS are fully up, tips reflexed; red (53D) upper surface; red (46B) lower surface; 26mm (1") long x 14mm (9/16") wide. TUBE is red (53D), medium length and thickness; 15mm (9/16") long x 8mm (5/16") wide. STAMENS extend 17mm (1/4") beyond the corolla; magenta (63A) filaments; dark red (53A) anthers. PISTIL extends 26mm (1") below the corolla; magenta (63A) style; pale pink (62D) stigma. BUD is round, pointed. FOLIAGE is dark green (137A) upper surface, medium green (138B) lower surface. Leaves are 52mm (2 1/16") long x 37mm (1 7/16") wide, ovate shaped, serrulated edges, acute tips and rounded bases. Veins, stems & branches are red. PARENTAGE: 'Roesse Apus' x 'Bicentennial'. Medium upright. Makes good standard. Prefers overhead filtered light & cool climate. Best bloom and foliage colour in filtered light. Tested four years in Knegsel, The Netherlands. Distinguished by bloom colour.
Roes 2004 NL AFS5362.

Marcel te Brake. Trailer. Semi Double. COROLLA: half flared, smooth petal margins; opens dark red (47A); matures rose (47D); 24mm (15/16") long x 19mm (3/4") wide. SEPALS: half up, tips reflexed up; light pink (38C) upper surface; rose (47D) lower surface; 22mm (7/8") long x 9mm (5/16") wide. TUBE: light pink (38C); medium length & thickness; 16mm (5/8") long x 6mm (1/4") wide. STAMENS extend 24mm (15/16") beyond the corolla; pink (48C) filaments & anthers. PISTIL extends 27mm (1 1/16") beyond the corolla; pink (48C) style; white (155D) stigma. BUD: ovate. FOLIAGE: dark green (137A) upper surface; medium green (138A) lower surface. Leaves are 71mm (2 13/16") long x 34mm (1 3/8") wide; ovate shaped, serrulate edges, acute tips, cordate bases. Veins, stems & branches are red. PARENTAGE: 'Roesse Lupus' x 'Magda van Bets'. Natural trailer. Makes good basket. Prefers overhead filtered light, cool climate. Best bloom colour in filtered light. Tested 3 years in Knegsel, The Netherlands. Distinguished by bloom colour.
Roes 2009 NL AFS7245.

Marchien Koerts Drayer. Upright. Single. COROLLA is quarter flared, bell shaped; opens & matures reddish orange (43C) edged red orange (40A); 12mm (7/16") long x 8mm (5/16") wide. SEPALS are horizontal, tips reflexed; dark rose (48A) tipped light green (143B) upper & lower surfaces; 15mm (9/16") long x 5mm (3/16") wide. TUBE is

light pink (49B) blushed dark rose (48A); 12mm (1/2") long x 4mm (1/8") wide. FOLIAGE: dark green (147A) upper surface; light olive green (147C) lower surface. PARENTAGE: 'Sparkling Whisper' x [('Loxhore Mazurka' x 'Papy René') x 'Lord Lonsdale']. Distinguished by flower colour & growth in racemes along branches and ends of branches.
Koerts T. 2006 NL AFS6287.

Marco Laan. Upright. Single. COROLLA is full flared with smooth petal margins; opens magenta (68A); matures rose (68C); 22mm (7/8") long x 30mm (1 3/16") wide. SEPALS are fully up, tips recurved; pink (62A) tipped green upper & lower surfaces; 24mm (15/16") long x 12mm (1/2") wide. TUBE is pink (62A); short & thick; 9mm (3/8") long x 8mm (3/16") wide. FOLIAGE: dark green (139A) upper surface; medium green (137B) lower surface. Leaves are 57mm (2 1/4") long x 37mm (1 7/16") wide, ovate shaped. PARENTAGE: 'Roesse Carme' x 'Cameron Ryle'. Distinguished by bloom shape.
van Eijk 2005 NL AFS5903.

Marcske. Trailer. Double. COROLLA is half flared; opens dark purple (79A) with reddish purple (67A) base; matures purple (79C); 18mm (11/16") long x 22mm (7/8") wide. PETALOIDS are dark purple (79A) with reddish purple (67A) base; 13mm (1/2") long x11mm (7/16") wide. SEPALS are half down, tips recurved; dark reddish purple (61A) upper surface, and reddish purple (67A) lower surface; 30mm (1 3/16") long x 14mm (9/16") wide. TUBE is reddish purple (61B); 17mm (5/8") long x 6mm (1/4") wide. FOLIAGE is dark green (136B) upper surface; medium green (138B) lower surface. PARENTAGE: 'Roesse Blacky' x 'Royal Mosaic'. Meise 8/13/05. Distinguished by bloom shape & colour.
Michiels 2006 BE AFS6029.

Maréchal Delattre de Tassigny. Upright/Trailer. Single. COROLLA is unflared with smooth petal margins; opens purple (77A) longitudinally splashed rose (62A); matures reddish purple (71B); 17mm (11/16") long x 13mm (1/2") wide. SEPALS are horizontal, tips recurved; light rose (58D) upper surface; dark rose (58C) lower surface; 39mm (1 9/16") long x 8mm (5/16") wide. TUBE is pink (62C); medium length and thickness; 20mm (13/16") long x 6mm (1/4") thick. STAMENS extend 2 – 5mm (1/16 – 3/16") beyond the corolla; light rose (73C) filaments, grayish yellow (161B) anthers.

PISTIL extends 26mm (1") beyond the corolla; light rose (73B) style, cream (158D) stigma. BUD is long, ovate. FOLIAGE is dark green (137A) upper surface, light olive green (147C) lower surface. Leaves are 64mm (2 1/2") long x 43mm (1 m11/16") wide, ovate shaped, serrated edges, acute tips and rounded bases. Veins and stems are yellowish green, branches are light brown. PARENTAGE: 'Henri Massé' x 'Subliem'. Lax upright or stiff trailer. Makes good basket or upright. Prefers overhead filtered light and cool climate. Best bloom colour in filtered light. Tested three years in Pornic, France. Distinguished by bloom colour.
Massé 2002 FR AFS5014.

Margaret Bird. Trailer. Double. COROLLA is three quarter flared, ruffled, with turned under smooth petal margins; opens light reddish purple (72C), light rose (73C) near TUBE, veined red; matures magenta (57C), pale rose (73D) near TUBE, veined red; 30mm (1 3/16") long x 50mm (2") wide. SEPALS are half up, tips recurved up; dark rose (58C) tipped green upper surface; rose (52C) lower surface; 40mm (1 9/16") long x 14mm (9/16") wide. TUBE is yellowish white (158A) striped red; medium length & thick; 20mm (13/16") long x 8mm (5/16") wide. FOLIAGE: medium green (146A) upper surface; light olive green (147C) lower surface. Leaves are 60mm (2 3/8") long x 35mm (1 3/8") wide, cordate shaped. PARENTAGE: 'Orwell' x 'Buttercup'. Distinguished by flushed & ruffled corolla.
Shaffrey 2005 UK AFS5691.

Margaret Jenkinson. Upright. Single. COROLLA white. SEPALS red.
Reynolds G. 2003 UK.

Margaret Lowis. Upright. Single. COROLLA white. SEPALS pink.
Lowis 2002.

Margaret Robinson. Trailer. Single. COROLLA violet blue. SEPALS deep pink.
Reynolds G. 2005 UK.

Margaret Woods. Upright. Single. COROLLA blue flushed white. SEPALS white. PARENTAGE 'Border Raider' x 'Sophie Louise'.
Woods 2006 UK.

Margriet Benak. Upright/Trailer. Double. COROLLA: 3 quarter flared, folded petals; opens reddish purple (66A); matures violet (87B); 25mm (1") long x 42mm (1 5/8") wide.

SEPALS: half up, tips recurved up; rose (52C) upper surface; dark rose (58C) lower surface; 40mm (1 9/16") long x 18mm (11/16") wide. TUBE: dark rose (58C); medium length & thickness; 13mm (1/2") long x 10mm (3/8") wide. FOLIAGE is dark green (137A) upper surface; medium green (139C) lower surface. PARENTAGE: 'Cutie Karin' x 'Bella Rosella'.
Koerts T. 2007 NL AFS6452.

Maria Bosch. Upright. Single. COROLLA is quarter flared, bell shaped; opens orange (33B); matures dark orange (33A); 19mm (3/4") long x 14mm (9/16") wide. SEPALS are half down, tips reflexed; light orange (41C) upper surface, and orange (33B) lower surface; 30mm (1 3/16") long x 7mm (1/4") wide. TUBE is orange (35B); 48mm (1 7/8") long x 7mm (1/4") wide. FOLIAGE is dark green (147A) upper surface; olive green (148A) lower surface. PARENTAGE: 'Christmas Gem' x 'Golden Glow'. Nomination by NKVFas Recommendable Cultivar. Distinguished by bloom colour.
Geurts 2006 NL AFS6253.

Maria Coleman. Upright. Double. COROLLA is half flared with turned up margins; opens light purple (80D) veined pink, matures light rose (73C) veined pink; 18mm (11/16") long x 31mm (11/4") wide. SEPALS are half up, tips recurved up; pink (62C) overlaid green upper surface, pink (62A) lower surface; 35mm (1 3/8") long x 14mm (9/16") wide. TUBE is white (155A) striped green, short with medium thickness; 9mm (3/8") long x 5mm (3/16") wide. STAMENS extend 11mm (7/16") below the corolla; pink (62A) filaments, pink (62C) anthers. PISTIL extends 14mm (9/16") below the corolla; pink (62C) style, white (155D) stigma. BUD is ovate. FOLIAGE is dark green (137A) upper surface, medium green (139C) lower surface. Leaves are 52mm (2 1/16") long x 28mm (1 1/8") wide, lanceolate shaped, serrulated edges, acute tips and rounded bases. Veins and branches are green, stems are red. PARENTAGE: 'Carla Johnson' seedling x 'Ruth Graham'. Small upright. Self branching. Makes good upright. Prefers overhead filtered light and cool climate. Best bloom colour in filtered light. Tested three years in Stockbridge, Hampshire, England. Distinguished by unique colour combination.
Graham 2002 UK AFS4875.

Maria Leprich. Upright. Semi Double. COROLLA dark terracotta; corolla is half flared. SEPALS baby pink on the upper surface, deeper pink on the lower surface; sepals are fully up with yellowish green recurved tips. TUBE baby pink. PARENTAGE 'WALZ Mandoline' x 'WALZ Mandoline'. Klemm 2008 AT BFS0085.

Maria Loix. Upright/Trailer. Double. COROLLA: quarter flared; turned under wavy petal margins; opens reddish purple (72B) blotched dark rose (48A) edged reddish purple (70B); matures magenta (61C) blotched light rose (50C) edged reddish purple (70B); 26mm (1") long x 17mm (5/8") wide. PETALOIDS: Same colour as corolla; 17mm (5/8") long x 7mm (1/4") wide. SEPALS: horizontal, tips recurved, twisted left to right; pale pink (56C) tipped light apple green (145B) upper surface; pink (49A) tipped light apple green (145B) lower surface; 34mm (1 3/8") long x 13mm (1/2") wide. TUBE: light pink (49B); medium length & thickness; 12mm (7/16") long x 6mm (1/4") wide. STAMENS extend 15mm (9/16") beyond the corolla; dark rose (67C) filaments; magenta (71C) anthers. PISTIL extends 34mm (1 3/8") beyond the corolla; rose (61D) style; light rose (63D) stigma. BUD: oblong. FOLIAGE: medium green (137C) upper surface; medium green (138B) lower surface. Leaves are 51mm (2") long x 36mm (1 7/16") wide; ovate shaped, serrate edges, acute tips, rounded bases. Veins are yellowish green (146C), stems are yellowish green (146C) & light grayish rose (181D), branches are light green (138C) & light grayish red (182C). PARENTAGE: 'Manfried Kleinau' x 'Panhoven'. Lax upright or stiff trailer. Self branching. Makes good basket or upright. Prefers overhead filtered light, cool climate. Best bloom & foliage colour in filtered light. Tested 3 years in Koningshooikt, Belgium. Waanrode 7/5/08. Distinguished by bloom colour combination. Michiels 2009 BE AFS7198.

Maria Paulus. Upright/Trailer. Single. COROLLA is half flared with turned under wavy petal margins; opens dark purple (79A), dark reddish purple (61A) base; matures purple (79D), reddish purple (61B) base; 21mm (7/8") long x 18mm (11/16") wide. SEPALS are horizontal, tips reflexed; dark reddish purple (60A) upper surface; dark reddish purple (60B) lower surface; 42mm (1 5/8") long x 12mm (1/2") wide. TUBE is reddish purple (61B); medium length & thickness; 15mm (9/16") long x 2mm (1/16") wide. FOLIAGE: dark green (136A) upper surface; medium green (137C) lower surface. Leaves are 64mm (2 1/2") long x 40mm (1

9/16") wide, cordate shaped. PARENTAGE: 'Roesse Blacky' x 'California'. Meis 3-7-04. Distinguished by bloom shape and colour. Michiels 2005 BE AFS5669.

Maria Van Assche. Upright/Trailer. Single. COROLLA is unflared with smooth petal margins; opens and matures magenta (67B), base clearer; 17mm (11/16") long x 15mm (5/8") wide. SEPALS are horizontal, tips recurved; pale pink (62D) tipped medium green (140B) upper surface; light pink (62B) and magenta (63B) lower surface; 34mm (1 3/8") long x 10mm (3/8") wide. TUBE is pale pink (62D) streaked pink; short, medium thickness; 10mm (3/8") long x 6mm (1/4") thick. STAMENS extend 8 – 15mm (5/16 – 5/8") beyond the corolla; pink (62A) filaments, plum (184C) anthers. PISTIL extends 25mm (1") beyond the corolla; pale pink (62D) style, rose (51B) stigma. BUD is ovate. FOLIAGE is dark green (147A) upper surface, medium green (147B) lower surface. Leaves are 97mm (3 13/16") long x 43mm (1 11/16") wide, lanceolate shaped, serrulated edges, acute tips and rounded bases. Veins and stems are yellowish green, branches are yellowish green and light brown. PARENTAGE: ('Whiteknight's Pearl' x 'Charles de Gaulle') x ('Whiteknight's Pearl' x 'Charles de Gaulle'). Lax upright or stiff trailer. Makes good upright. Prefers overhead filtered light and cool climate. Best bloom colour in filtered light. Tested four years in Pornic, France. Distinguished by bloom colours. Massé 2002 FR AFS5015.

Maria Vleugels. Upright/Trailer. Double. COROLLA: half flared; opens light purple (86C); matures violet (84A); 13mm (1/2") long x 9mm (5/16") wide. PETALOIDS: violet (76A); 7mm (1/4") long x 5mm (3/16") wide. SEPALS: horizontal, tips reflexed; pale pink (62D) tipped light green (138C) upper surface; rose (65A) tipped light green (138C) lower surface; 23mm (7/8") long x 13mm (1/2") wide. TUBE: white (155C) & light green (138D); medium length & thickness; 14mm (9/16") long x 5mm (3/16") wide. FOLIAGE is dark green (136A) upper surface; medium green (138B) lower surface. PARENTAGE: 'Mathy' x 'Guidewell Quest'. Michiels 2007 BE AFS6341.

Maria-Elisabeth Schaeffler. Upright. Double. COROLLA dark violet flushed dark pink, dark pink at base; corolla is fully flared. SEPALS cream flushed and striped rose on the upper and lower surfaces;

SEPALS are half up with recurved tips. TUBE cream flushed rose.
Gindl 2009 AT BFS0142.

Mariagaarde. Upright/Trailer. Semi Double. COROLLA: quarter flared, turned under smooth petal margins; opens dark purple (79A); matures dark reddish purple (61A); 20mm (13/16") long x 15mm (9/16") wide. PETALOIDS: 2 per sepal; same colour as corolla; 14mm (9/16") long x 7mm (1/4") wide. SEPALS: fully up; tips recurved; reddish purple (61A) upper surface; magenta (61C) lower surface; 33mm (1 5/16") long x 9mm (3/8") wide. TUBE: magenta (63A); medium length & thickness; 10mm (3/8") long x 4mm (3/16") wide. STAMENS: extend 21mm (13/16") below the corolla; dark purple (79B) filaments, dark reddish purple (64A) anthers. PISTIL extends 31mm (1 1/4") below the corolla; reddish purple (64B) style, dark rose (64C) stigma. BUD: ovate. FOLIAGE: dark green (139A) upper surface; medium green (138B) lower surface. Leaves are 64mm (2 1/2") long x 31mm (1 1/4") wide, lanceoate shaped, serrulated edges, acute tips and obtuse bases. Veins are light green (138D); stems & branches are grayish red (182B). PARENTAGE: 'Dorothy Hanley' x unknown. Lax upright or stiff trailer. Self branching. Makes good upright. Prefers overhead filtered light. Best bloom and foliage colour in filtered light. Tested 3 years in Rummen, Belgium. NBFK certificate at Meise. Distinguished by bloom colour.
Ector 2003 BE AFS5115.

Maria-Georges. Upright. Single. COROLLA: Unflared; opens dark rose (54B); matures magenta (68A); 9mm (5/16") long x 7mm (1/4") wide. SEPALS: half down, tips reflexed; rose (54C) tipped light apple green (144D) upper surface; light pink (55D) tipped light apple green (144D) lower surface; 19mm (3/4") long x 5mm (3/16") wide. TUBE: dark rose (54A); long & thick; 36mm (1 7/16") long x 7mm (1/4") wide. FOLIAGE is medium green (137B) upper surface; medium green (138B) lower surface. PARENTAGE: Triphylla Hybrida x 'Waternymph'.
Vandenbussche 2007 BE AFS6597.

Mariake Hoef. Trailer. Double. COROLLA: half flared, turned under smooth petal margins; opens dark purple (78A), pink (62A) base; matures purple (80A); 13mm (1/2") long x 16mm (5/8") wide. PETALOIDS: purple (80A) edged pink (62A); 11mm (7/16") long x 9mm (3/8") wide. SEPALS: half down;

tips reflexed; rose (61D) tipped apple green (145C) upper surface; dark rose (58C) lower surface; 18mm (11/16") long x 12mm (1/2") wide. TUBE: dark reddish purple (61D); medium length & thickness; 17mm (11/16") long x 4mm (3/16") wide. STAMENS: extend 6mm (1/4") below the corolla; magenta (68A) filaments, magenta (59C) anthers. PISTIL extends 8mm (5/16") below the corolla; light rose (68D) style, dark reddish purple (60C) stigma. BUD: round, flat. FOLIAGE: dark green (139A) upper surface; medium green (138B) lower surface. Leaves are 36mm (1 7/16") long x 21mm (13/16") wide, ovate shaped, serrulated edges, acute tips and cordate bases. Veins are reddish purple (186B), stems are very dark reddish purple (186A), branches are light purple (186C). PARENTAGE: found seedling. Natural trailer. Makes good basket. Prefers full sun. Best bloom and foliage colour in bright light. Tested 3 years in Rillaar, Belgium. NBFK certificate at Meise. Distinguished by bloom colour.
Willems 2003 BE AFS5096.

Maria-Mathilda. Trailer. Double. COROLLA is three quarter flared with turned under smooth petal margins; opens dark reddish purple (72A), reddish purple (67A) base; matures dark reddish purple (64A); 25mm (1") long x 21mm (13/16") wide. PETALOIDS: same colour as corolla; 17mm (11/16") long x 17mm (11/16") wide. SEPALS are horizontal, tips reflexed; reddish purple (64B) upper surface; reddish purple (67A) lower surface; 27mm (1 1/16") long x 15mm (9/16") wide. TUBE is dark reddish purple (61A); medium length & thickness; 14mm (9/16") long x 7mm (1/4") wide. FOLIAGE: dark green (136A) upper surface; medium green (136C) lower surface. Leaves are 65mm (2 9/16") long x 34mm (1 5/16") wide, ovate shaped. PARENTAGE: 'Roesse Blacky' x 'Heikantenaer'. Meis 3-7-04. Distinguished by compact growth.
Michiels 2005 BE AFS5671.

Marian Peters. Upright. Single. COROLLA: unflared, smooth petal margins, bell shaped; opens dark purple (N89A); matures purple (93A); 13mm (1/2") long x 19mm (3/4") wide. SEPALS: full down, tips recurved; magenta (N57A) upper surface; magenta (58B) lower surface; 38mm (1 1/2") long x 13mm (1/2") wide. TUBE: magenta (58B); medium length & thickness; 19mm (3/4") long. STAMENS extend 13mm (1/2") beyond the corolla; magenta (58B) filaments & anthers. PISTIL extends 51mm (2") beyond the corolla;

magenta (N57A) style; magenta (58B) stigma. BUD is oval. FOLIAGE is dark green (137A) upper surface; dark green (141A) lower surface. Leaves are 63mm (2 1/2") long x 32mm (1 1/4") wide; ovate shaped, serrulate edges, acute tips, rounded bases. Veins & stems are green; branches are purple. PARENTAGE: found seedling. Small upright. Makes good upright. Prefers overhead filtered light. Cold weather hardy to -7° C (20° F). Best bloom colour in filtered light. Tested 3 years in Telford, Shropshire, UK. Distinguished by early bloom, long season. Peters 2009 UK AFS6955.

Marie Perry. Upright/Trailer. Single. COROLLA is quarter flared, square shaped, turned under petal margins; opens & matures dark purple (78A); 10mm (3/8") long x 10mm (3/8") wide. SEPALS are horizontal, tips recurved; magenta (61C) upper & lower surfaces; 19mm (3/4") long x 10mm (3/8") wide. TUBE is rose (61D); medium length & thickness; 5mm (3/16") long x 3mm (1/8") wide. STAMENS extend 9mm (3/8") beyond the corolla; pink (62A) filaments; light pink (62B) anthers. PISTIL extends 25mm (1") below the corolla; pink (62A) style & stigma. BUD is tear shaped. FOLIAGE is dark green (137A) upper surface, medium green (137C) lower surface. Leaves are 44mm (1 3/4") long x 25mm (1") wide, elliptic shaped, serrulated edges, acute tips and rounded base. Veins, stems & branches are dark reddish purple. PARENTAGE: 'Army Nurse' x 'Northway'. Lax upright or stiff trailer. Self branching. Makes good basket, upright, standard or miniature. Prefers overhead filtered light & cool climate. Cold weather hardy to –3º F. Best bloom colour in filtered light. Tested nine years in Brighton, East Sussex, England. Distinguished by bloom colour & dark foliage. Lorimer 2004 UK AFS5374.

Marie van Roovert. Trailer. Double. COROLLA: 3 quarter flared; opens & matures white (155D); 19mm (3/4") long x 24mm (15/16") wide. SEPALS: horizontal; tips recurved; dark rose (58C) upper surface; magenta (58B) lower surface; 29mm (1 1/8") long x 17mm (5/8") wide. TUBE: white (155B); long & thin; 29mm (1 1/8") long x 4mm (1/8") wide. FOLIAGE is medium green (137B) upper surface; medium green (138B) lower surface. PARENTAGE: 'Luuk van Riet' x 'Roesse Betelgeuze'. omperen 2007 NL AFS6310.

Marie-France Morice. Upright. Single. COROLLA: quarter flared, smooth petal margins; opens & matures reddish orange (43B); 47mm (1 7/8") long x 19mm (3/4") wide. SEPALS: half down; tips recurved to reflexed; pink (48C), tipped yellowish green (146E), upper & lower surfaces; 35mm (1 3/8") long x 10mm (3/8") wide. TUBE: pink (48D); medium length & thickness; 28mm (1 1/8) long x 8mm (5/16") wide. STAMENS: extend 18-20mm (11/16–13/16") below corolla; dark rose (58C) filaments, light purple (186C) anthers. PISTIL: extends 22mm (7/8") below the corolla, light rose (58D) style, light yellow (4C) stigma. BUD: ovate. FOLIAGE: medium green (146A) upper surface; yellowish green (146B) lower surface. Leaves are 65mm (2 9/16") long x 45mm (1 3/4") wide, ovate shaped, serrulated edges, obtuse tips and rounded bases. Veins, stems & branches are yellowish green. PARENTAGE: 'Prince of Orange' x 'Willy Tamerus'. Medium upright. Makes good upright. Prefers overhead filtered light and cool climate. Best bloom and foliage colour in filtered light. Tested 11 years in Pornic, France. Distinguished by bloom colour combination. Massé 2003 FR AFS5220.

Marie-Hélène Mues. Upright/Trailer. Single. COROLLA is quarter flared with turned under wavy petal margins; opens violet (77C), base and veins are rose (65A); matures light reddish purple (73A), base and veins are light rose (73C); 25mm (1") long x 24 mm (15/16") wide. SEPALS are half down, tips recurved; light rose (58D) tipped light green (142B) upper surface; dark rose (58C) lower surface; 30mm (13/16") long x 15mm (5/8") wide. TUBE is white (155C) striped rose (65A), medium length and thickness; 22mm (7/8") long x 6mm (1/4") wide, 9mm (3/8") at base. STAMENS do not extend beyond the corolla; dark rose (58C) filaments, yellow (4A) anthers. PISTIL extends 8mm (5/16") below the corolla; light rose (58D) style; yellow (5A) stigma. BUD is rectangular, pointed. FOLIAGE is dark green (137A) upper surface, medium green (137D) lower surface. Leaves are 74mm (2 15/16") long x 40mm (1 9/16") wide, ovate shaped, serrated edges, acute tips and rounded bases. Veins and stems are plum (184B); branches are dark grayish green (191A). PARENTAGE: 'Alda Alders' x 'Joke's Icetea'. Lax upright or stiff trailer. Self branching. Makes good upright. Prefers overhead filtered light. Best bloom and foliage colour in filtered light. Tested three years in Leopoldsburg, Belgium. Certificate

N.B.F.K. at Meise. Distinguished by square blooms, square TUBE.
Busschodts 2003 BE AFS4914.

Marieke. Upright/Trailer. Single. COROLLA: Half flared, trumpet shaped; opens rose (63C); matures light pink (62B); 11mm (7/16") long x 10mm (3/8") wide. SEPALS: half down, tips reflexed; pink (51D) tipped pale tan (162D) upper surface; pink (49C) lower surface; 15mm (9/16") long x 6mm (1/4") wide. TUBE: pink (51D); long, medium thickness; 22mm (7/8") long x 4mm (1/8") wide. FOLIAGE is dark green (147A) upper surface; medium green (147B) lower surface. PARENTAGE: 'Gerharda's Panache' x 'Mazda'.
de Graaff 2007 NL AFS6552.

Marielle Comperen. Upright/Trailer. Double. COROLLA: half flared, smooth petal margins; opens violet (75A); matures rose (68B); 24mm (15/16") long 26mm (1") wide. SEPALS: half down; tips reflexed; light rose (58D) upper surface; magenta (58B) lower surface; 37mm (1 7/16") long x 14mm (9/16") wide. TUBE: light rose (58D); medium length & thickness; 17mm (11/16") long x 7mm (1/4") wide. STAMENS: extend 12mm (1/2") below corolla; dark rose (64C) filaments; pink (62C) anthers. PISTIL: extends 28mm (1 1/8") below the corolla; dark rose (64C) style; rose (68B) stigma. BUD: ovate, curved, pointed. FOLIAGE: medium green (137B) upper surface; medium green (138B) lower surface. Leaves are 57mm (2 1/4") long x 37mm (1 7/16") wide, ovate shaped, serrated edges, acute tips and rounded bases. Green veins, stems & branches. PARENTAGE: 'Sofie Michiels' x 'Judy Salome'. Lax upright or stiff trailer. Makes good stiff trailer. Prefers overhead filtered light and cool climate. Best bloom and foliage colour in filtered light. Tested 4 years in Diessen, The Netherlands. Distinguished by bloom colour.
Comperen 2004 NL AFS5566.

Marielle van Dommelen. Upright/Trailer. Double. COROLLA: three quarter flared, smooth petal margins; opens white (155A); matures white (155B); 22mm (7/8") long x 22mm (7/8") wide. SEPALS: fully up; tips reflexed; light yellow (3D) upper surface; white (155A) lower surface; 25mm (1") long x 11mm (7/16") wide. TUBE: light yellow (3D); medium length & thickness; 14mm (9/16") long x 5mm (3/16") wide. STAMENS: extend 24mm (15/16") below corolla; light pink (65B) filaments; rose (65A) anthers. PISTIL:

extends 24mm (15/16") below the corolla; pale lavender (65D) style, white (155C) stigma. BUD: ovate. FOLIAGE: dark green (137A) upper surface; medium green (138B) lower surface. Leaves are 60mm (2 3/8") long x 35mm (1 3/8") wide, ovate shaped, serrulated edges, acute tips and rounded bases. Veins, stems & branches are green. PARENTAGE: 'Annabel' x 'Sofie Michiels'. Lax upright or stiff trailer. Makes good stiff trailer. Prefers overhead filtered light and cool climate. Best bloom and foliage colour in filtered light. Tested 4 years in Diessen, The Netherlands. Distinguished by bloom & foliage combination.
Comperen 2003 NL AFS5268.

Marie-Louise De Wachter. Upright. Double. COROLLA is three quarter flared with turned under wavy petal margins; opens magenta (67B) turning to reddish purple (70B) at edge; matures reddish purple (61B); 18mm (11/16") long x 18mm (11/16") wide. PETALOIDS: dark purple (78A), reddish purple (58A) base; 12mm (1/2") long x 8mm (5/16") wide. SEPALS are turned left, half up, tips recurved up; light pink (55D) tipped apple green (144C) upper surface; light rose (50C) tipped apple green (144C) lower surface; 34mm (1 5/16") long x 11mm (7/16") wide. TUBE is pale pink (49D); medium length, thin; 14mm (9/16") long x 4mm (3/16") wide. FOLIAGE: dark green (136A) upper surface; medium green (138B) lower surface. Leaves are 78mm (3 1/16") long x 42mm (1 5/8") wide, ovate shaped. PARENTAGE: 'Sofie Michiels' x 'Annabelle Stubbs'. Meise 8-14-04. Distinguished by flower colour & shape.
Michiels 2005 BE AFS5831.

Marie-Louise Luyckx. Upright/Trailer. Double. COROLLA is three quarter flared with turned under smooth petal margins; opens light purple (78C), pale purple (75C) base; matures light purple (74C); 19mm (3/4") long x 15mm (9/16") wide. PETALOIDS: light purple (78C); 13mm (1/2") long x 8mm (5/16") wide. SEPALS are half up, tips recurved up; white (155C), tipped light apple green (145C) upper surface; white (155B), tipped light apple green (145C) lower surface; 37mm (1 7/16") long x 15mm (9/16") wide. TUBE is white (155C); medium length & thickness; 17mm (11/16") long x 6mm (1/4") wide. FOLIAGE: dark green (136A) upper surface; medium green (138B) lower surface. Leaves are 77mm (3 1/16") long x 32mm (1 1/4") wide, elliptic shaped. PARENTAGE: 'Sofie Michiels' x 'Diana Wills'.

Meise 8-14-04. Distinguished by flower colour combination.
Michiels 2005 BE AFS5757.

Mariken. Upright. Single. COROLLA is quarter flared with turned under smooth petal margins; opens and matures dark orange red (34A), orange (34C) at base; 16mm (5/8") long x 20mm (13/16") wide. SEPALS are horizontal, tips reflexed; dark rose (58C) upper surface, pink (48C) lower surface; 23mm (15/16") long x 12mm (1/2") wide. TUBE is dark rose (58C), medium length and thick; 19mm (3/4") long x 12mm (1/2") wide. STAMENS do not extend beyond the corolla; dark rose (48A) filaments, tan (162A) anthers. PISTIL extends 25mm (1") below the corolla; white (155C) style, grayish yellow (161A) stigma. BUD is ovate. FOLIAGE is dark green (137A) upper surface, medium green (138B) lower surface. Leaves are 70mm (2 3/4") long x 50mm (2") wide, ovate shaped, very serrulated edges, acute tips and cordate bases. Veins, stems and branches are light green (138D). PARENTAGE: 'Jan Wiggers' x unknown. Medium upright. Self branching. Makes good upright. Prefers overhead filtered light. Best bloom and foliage colour in filtered light. Tested three years in Rummen, Belgium. Certificate N.B.F.K. at Meise. Distinguished by thick TUBE, bloom form and colour.
Ector 2003 BE AFS4894.

Marilyn Jane. Upright. Single. COROLLA pink lilac. SEPALS are flushed pink and tipped green. TUBE is white.
Wilkinson 2007 UK.

Marinthe. Upright. Single. COROLLA: half flared, bell shape; opens & matures light orange (41C); 10mm (3/8") long x 7mm (1/4") wide. SEPALS: horizontal, tips recurved; red (52A) upper surface; light orange (41C) lower surface; 19mm (3/4") long x 5mm (3/16") wide. TUBE: dark rose (51A); 33mm (1 5/16") long x 4mm (1/8") wide. FOLIAGE is dark green (147A) upper surface; light olive green (147C) lower surface. PARENTAGE: {'F. *splendens*' x [('F. *michoanensis*' x 'F. *encliandra*, ssp *tetradactyla*') x 'Adenti']} x 'F. *fulgens michoacans*'. Nomination by NKVF as Recommendable Cultivar.
Dijkstra 2008 NL AFS6803.

Mario Brunner. Upright. Double. COROLLA opens violet blue with pink at base, matures to mallow purple; corolla is fully flared. SEPALS light pink on the upper surface,

deeper pink on the lower surface; sepals are fully up with recurved tips. TUBE pale pink. PARENTAGE 'Turandot' x 'Bert's Whisky'.
Klemm 2008 AT BFS0078.

Mario Fuhrmann. Upright/Trailer. Double. COROLLA: half flared, turned under wavy petal margins; opens purple (83B); matures reddish purple (71B); 27mm (1 1/16") long x 19mm (3/4") wide. PETALOIDS: Same colour as corolla; 9mm (5/16") long x 7mm (1/4") wide. SEPALS: horizontal, tips recurved; pale lavender (69D) tipped pale yellow green (150D) upper surface; magenta (68A) tipped pale yellow green (150D) lower surface; 38mm (1 1/2") long x 14mm (9/16") wide. TUBE: white (155B); medium length & thickness; 13mm (1/2") long x 6mm (1/4") wide. STAMENS extend 11mm (7/16") beyond the corolla; reddish purple (71B) filaments; purple (71A) anthers. PISTIL extends 23mm (7/8") beyond the corolla; light reddish purple (72C) style; pale rose (73D) stigma. BUD: oblong. FOLIAGE: dark green (136B) upper surface; medium green (138B) lower surface. Leaves are 72mm (2 7/8") long x 40mm (1 9/16") wide; ovate shaped, serrate edges, acute tips, rounded bases. Veins are light purple (186C), stems are light red purple (185D), branches are light red purple (185D) & light green (138C). PARENTAGE: 'Manfried Kleinau' x 'Joergen Hahn'. Lax upright or stiff trailer. Self branching. Makes good upright. Prefers overhead filtered light, cool climate. Best bloom & foliage colour in filtered light. Tested 3 years in Koningshooikt, Belgium. Waanrode 8/9/08. Distinguished by bloom colour.
Michiels 2009 BE AFS7199.

Marion Hilton. Single. COROLLA dusky pink. SEPALS rose pink.
Evans 2002 UK.

Marisca van der Kolk. Upright. Single. COROLLA: bell shape, quarter flared, wavy petal margins; opens & matures light orange (41C); 17 mm (5/8") long x 7mm (1/4") wide. SEPALS are half down, tips reflexed; red (45D), tipped olive green (152C) upper surface; dark rose (48A) lower surface; 16mm (5/8") long x 6mm (1/4") wide. TUBE is red (45D); medium length & thickness; 27mm (1 1/16") long x 6mm (1/4") wide. STAMENS do not extend beyond the corolla; orangy red (39A) filaments; yellowish white (4D) anthers. PISTIL extends 0.5mm (1/32") beyond the corolla; orangy red (39A) style; yellowish white (4D) stigma. BUD is triphylla shape.

FOLIAGE is dark green (139A) upper surface; medium green (137B) lower surface. Leaves are 90mm (3 9/16") long x 51mm (2") wide, elliptic shaped, entire edges, acute tips, rounded bases, hairy surface. Veins, stems and branches are medium green. PARENTAGE: 'Martin's Choice Improved' x F. *coccinea*. Tall upright; self branching. Makes good upright or standard. Prefers full sun. Best bloom and foliage in bright light. Tested 3 years in Elburg, The Netherlands. Nomination by N.K.vF. as recommendable cultivar. Distinguished by flat TUBE, hairy & shiny leaves.
de Groot 2009 NL AFS6976.

Mariusz J. Glebowski. Upright. Single. COROLLA is three quarter flared with turned under smooth petal margins; opens purple (71A), dark reddish purple (61A) base; matures magenta (63A); 21mm (13/16") long x 30mm (1 3/16") wide. SEPALS are horizontal, tips reflexed; reddish purple (61B) upper surface; red (53C) lower surface; 35mm (1 3/8") long x 16mm (5/8") wide. TUBE is red (53B); short, medium thickness; 13mm (1/2") long x 7mm (1/4") wide. FOLIAGE: dark green (136B) upper surface; medium green (138A) lower surface. Leaves are 54mm (2 1/8") long x 33mm (1 5/16") wide, ovate shaped. PARENTAGE: 'Roesse Blacky' x 'Beacon Baby Rose'. Meis 3-7-04. Distinguished by unique flower shape.
Michiels 2005 BE AFS5679.

Marleen Crucke. Trailer. Single. COROLLA is quarter flared, bell shaped; opens & matures dark rose (54A); 16mm (5/8") long x 13mm (1/2") wide. SEPALS are half down, tips reflexed; pink (48C) upper surface; rose (55B) lower surface; 23mm (7/8") long x 6mm (1/4") wide. TUBE is pink (48C); 18mm (11/16") long x 5mm (3/16") wide. FOLIAGE: dark green (147A) upper surface; medium green (147B) lower surface. PARENTAGE: ('Gerharda's Panache' x 'Gerharda's Panache') x [('Loxhore Mazurka' x 'Papy René') x 'Lord Lonsdale]. Nominated by NKVF as recommendable cultivar. Distinguished by bloom shape & colour.
Koerts T. 2006 NL AFS6301.

Marleen's Cyrano. Upright/Trailer. Double. COROLLA is three quarter flared with turned under smooth petal margins; opens violet (87B); matures reddish purple (74A); 18mm (11/16") long x 16mm (5/8") wide. PETALOIDS: purple (82B); 13mm (1/2") long x 13mm (1/2") wide. SEPALS are half up, tips recurved up; pink (55C), tipped light

apple green (145C) upper surface; rose (55B), tipped light apple green (145C) lower surface; 36mm (1 7/16") long x 17mm (11/16") wide. TUBE is white (155B); medium length & thickness; 14mm (9/16") long x 5mm (3/16") wide. FOLIAGE: dark green (136A) upper surface; medium green (138B) lower surface. Leaves are 80mm (3 1/8") long x 43mm (1 11/16") wide, ovate shaped. PARENTAGE: 'Sofie Michiels' x 'Weleveld'. Meise 8-14-04. Distinguished by flower colour & shape.
Michiels 2005 BE AFS5752.

Marleen's Toika. Upright/Trailer. Semi Double to Double. COROLLA is three quarter flared with turned under smooth petal margins; opens light purple (82D), violet (76B) base; matures light purple (78C); 26mm (1") long x 22mm (7/8") wide. PETALOIDS: same colour as corolla; 14mm (9/16") long x 10mm (3/8") wide. SEPALS are horizontal, tips recurved; pale pink (56C), tipped pale yellow green (150D) upper surface; pink (55C), tipped pale yellow green (150D) lower surface; 39mm (1 9/16") long x 11mm (7/16") wide. TUBE is white (155B); medium length & thickness; 16mm (5/8") long x 6mm (1/4") wide. FOLIAGE: dark green (136A) upper surface; medium green (138A) lower surface. Leaves are 67mm (2 5/8") long x 30mm (1 1/4") wide, elliptic shaped. PARENTAGE: 'Sofie Michiels' x 'Weleveld'. Meise 8-14-04. Distinguished by flower colour.
Michiels 2005 BE AFS5759.

Marlies Zeichen. Upright/Trailer. Single. COROLLA is quarter flared, bell shaped; opens rose (68B); matures magenta (68A); 25mm (1") long x 30mm (1 3/16") wide. PETALOIDS: same colour as corolla; 20mm (13/16") long x 10mm (3/8") wide. SEPALS are half up, tips reflexed up; pink (55C) tipped red upper surface, rose (55B) lower surface; 43mm (1 11/16") long x 14mm (9/16") wide. TUBE is pale pink (56C), medium length and thickness; 13mm (1/2") long x 8mm (5/16") wide. STAMENS extend 14mm (9/16") beyond the corolla; magenta (68A) filaments, red (180B) anthers. PISTIL extends 26mm (1") beyond the corolla; rose (68B) style, yellow (4A) stigma. BUD is longish. FOLIAGE is medium green (146A) upper surface, yellowish green (146C) lower surface. Leaves are 60mm (2 3/8") long x 35mm (1 3/8") wide, cordate shaped, serrated edges, acute tips and cordate bases. Veins, stems and branches are green. PARENTAGE: ('Monte Rosa' x 'Andre Le Nostre') x ('Uranus' x 'Ted Heath'). Lax

upright or stiff trailer. Self branching. Makes good stiff trailer. Prefers full sun. Best bloom colour in bright light. Difficult to root. Tested four years in Graz, Austria. Distinguished by bright colour and compact growth when mature.
Strümper 2002 AT AFS4942.

Marloes Comperen. Trailer. Semi Double. COROLLA: quarter flared, smooth petal margins; opens purple (83B); matures dark reddish purple (72A); 27mm (1 1/16") long x 22mm (7/8") wide. SEPALS: half up; tips reflexed up; reddish purple (72B) upper surface; reddish purple (71B) lower surface; 37mm (1 7/16") long x 10mm (3/8") wide. TUBE: reddish purple (72B); medium length & thickness; 11mm (7/16") long x 5mm (3/16") wide. STAMENS: extend 16mm (5/8") below corolla; dark reddish purple (72A) filaments & anthers. PISTIL: extends 37mm (1 7/16") below the corolla; reddish purple (71B) style; light yellow (11C) stigma. BUD: ovate, long. FOLIAGE: dark green (137A) upper surface; medium green (138B) lower surface. Leaves are 54mm (2 1/8") long x 26mm (1") wide, lanceolate shaped, serrulated edges, acute tips and rounded bases. Veins, stems & branches are red. PARENTAGE: 'Dorothy Oosting' x 'Parasol'. Natural trailer. Makes good basket. Prefers overhead filtered light and cool climate. Best bloom and foliage colour in filtered light. Tested 4 years in Diessen, The Netherlands. Distinguished by bloom colour.
Comperen 2003 NL AFS5284.

Mart. Upright/Trailer. Single. COROLLA is half flared, with turned up petal margins; opens & matures rose (63C); 5mm (3/16") long x 6mm (1/4") wide. SEPALS are horizontal, tips recurved; magenta (63B) upper surface; light pink (65C) lower surface; 7mm (1/4") long x 3mm (1/8") wide. TUBE is pink (65B); medium length & thickness; 11mm (7/16") long x 3mm (1/8") wide. FOLIAGE: medium green (146A) upper surface; light olive green (147C) lower surface. Leaves are 42mm (1 11/16") long x 20mm (13/16") wide, pubescent, elliptic shaped. PARENTAGE: ('F. obconica' x 'F. fulgens') x ('F. obconica' x 'F. fulgens'). Nomination by N.K.V.F. as recommendable cultivar. Distinguished by small, soft pink flowers and hairy leaves.
Dijkstra 2005 NL AFS5817.

Martha Brouwers. Upright/Trailer. Semi Double. COROLLA: three quarter flared, turned under wavy petal margins; opens pale purple (76C) striped magenta (68A); matures rose (N66D); 27mm (1 1/16") long x 25mm (1") wide. PETALOIDS: Same colour as corolla; 15mm (9/16") long x 8mm (5/16") wide. SEPALS: horizontal, tips recurved, twisted left to right; pale pink (56A) & rose (55B) tipped pale yellow green (150D) upper surface; rose (55B) tipped pale yellow green (150D) lower surface; 44mm (1 3/4") long x 16mm (5/8") wide. TUBE: pale pink (56A) striped rose (55B); medium length, thick; 21mm (13/16") long x 9mm (5/16") wide. STAMENS extend 8mm (5/16") beyond the corolla; magenta (63B) filaments; light purple (70C) anthers. PISTIL extends 22mm (7/8") beyond the corolla; rose (64D) style; pale yellow (2D) stigma. BUD: elongated. FOLIAGE: medium green (137B) upper surface; medium green (138B) lower surface. Leaves are 68mm (2 11/16") long x 48mm (1 7/8") wide; ovate shaped, serrate edges, obtuse tips, rounded bases. Veins are very dark reddish purple (186A), stems are reddish purple (186B), branches are light plum (184D) & light green (138C). PARENTAGE: 'Coen Bakker' x 'Cotta Fairy'. Lax upright or stiff trailer. Self branching. Makes good upright. Prefers overhead filtered light, cool climate. Best bloom & foliage colour in filtered light. Tested 3 years in Koningshooikt, Belgium. Waanrode 8/9/08. Distinguished by bloom colour combination.
Michiels 2009 BE AFS7200.

Martha Stegani. Upright/Trailer. Double. COROLLA: three quarter flared, turned under wavy petal margins; opens rose (68C) & dark rose (55A) edged light purple (70C); matures (68B) & dark rose (58C) edged light reddish purple (72C); 18mm (11/16") long x 16mm (5/8") wide. PETALOIDS: pink (62B) & rose (63C); 12mm (7/16") long x 11mm (7/16") wide. SEPALS: half up, tips reflexed up; dark rose (54A) tipped light apple green (145B) upper surface; rose (52C) tipped light apple green (145B) lower surface; 25mm (1") long x 14mm (9/16") wide. TUBE: rose (51C); short & thick; 13mm (1/2") long x 7mm (1/4") wide. STAMENS extend 14mm (9/16") beyond the corolla; light rose (73B) filaments; dark reddish purple (72A) anthers. PISTIL extends 22mm (7/8") beyond the corolla; rose (61D) style; light yellow (1C) stigma. BUD: bulbous. FOLIAGE: dark green (137A) upper surface; medium green (138B) lower surface. Leaves are 60mm (2 3/8") long x 32mm (1 1/4") wide; elliptic shaped, serrate edges, acute tips, rounded bases. Veins are plum (185C), stems are plum (185B), branches are plum (184C) & medium

300

green (138B). PARENTAGE: 'Manfried Kleinau' x 'First Lord'. Lax upright or stiff trailer. Self branching. Makes good basket. Prefers overhead filtered light, cool climate. Best bloom & foliage colour in filtered light. Tested 3 years in Koningshooikt, Belgium. Waanrode 8/9/08. Distinguished by bloom colour combination.
Michiels 2009 BE AFS7201.

Martien A. Soeters. Upright. Single. COROLLA is half flared, bell shaped, with smooth petal margins; opens & matures light purple (81C), edged & spotted light reddish purple (73A); 8mm (5/16") long x 12mm (1/2") wide. SEPALS are horizontal, tips reflexed; light yellow (6D), spotted magenta (63B), tipped green upper & lower surfaces; 8mm (5/16") long x 4mm (3/16") wide. TUBE is light yellow (6D); long & thin; 21mm (13/16") long x 4mm (3/16") wide. FOLIAGE: dark green (147A) upper surface; yellowish green (146B) lower surface. Leaves are 68mm (2 11/16") long x 36mm (1 7/16") wide, cordate shaped. PARENTAGE: ('Toos' x 'Prince Syray') x 'Papy René'. Distinguished by TUBE & sepal colour.
Koerts T. 2005 NL AFS5780.

Martien vande Meer. Trailer. Double. COROLLA is half flared with smooth petal margins; opens purple (83C); matures dark purple (78A); 16mm (5/8") long x 12mm (1/2") wide. SEPALS are half up, tips reflexed up; magenta (58B) upper & lower surfaces; 21mm (13/16") long x 14mm (9/16") wide. TUBE is magenta (58B); medium length & thickness; 12mm (1/2") long x 5mm (3/16") wide. FOLIAGE: dark green (137A) upper surface; medium green (137D) lower surface. Leaves are 67mm (2 5/8") long x 32mm (1 1/4") wide, ovate shaped. PARENTAGE: 'Swanley Gem' x 'Roesse Elara'. Distinguished by bloom & foliage combination.
Roes 2005 NL AFS5970.

Martin David. Upright. Single. COROLLA: half flared, wavy petal margins; opens white (155B) edged purple (82A); matures white (155B) edged purple (82B); 19mm (3/4") long x 25mm (1") wide. SEPALS: half up; tips recurved up; white (155B) upper & lower surfaces; tipped green; 22mm (7/8") long x 9mm (3/8") wide. TUBE: dark rose (58C) & white; short, medium thickness; 6mm (7/32") long x 6mm (1/4") wide. STAMENS: extend 8mm (5/8") below corolla; light rose (63D) filaments; dark brown (200B) anthers. PISTIL: extends 29mm (1 1/8") below the

corolla; white (155A) style; yellow (10C) stigma. BUD: ovate, long, chubby. FOLIAGE: medium green (146A) upper surface, medium green (146B) lower surface. Leaves are 51mm (2") long x 38mm (1 1/2") wide, cordate shaped, serrulated edges, acute tips and cordate bases. Light green (143C) veins & stems; light brown (199C) branches. PARENTAGE: 'Baby Bright' x 'Lady Isobel Barnett'. Small upright. Makes good upright or standard. Prefers overhead filtered light and warm climate. Cold weather hardy to 45⁰ F. Best bloom and foliage colour in filtered light. Tested 3 years in West Yorkshire, England. Distinguished by bright white and purple edge of corolla petals.
Preston 2004 UK AFS5443.

Martin Thiel. Upright. Double. COROLLA opens violet blue rose at base, matures to violet; corolla is half flared. SEPALS cream on the upper surface, rose on the lower surfaces; SEPALS are fully up with recurved tips. TUBE cream. PARENTAGE 'Waldis Aquamarin' x 'Gilda'.
Dietrich 2009 DE BFS0113.

Mary Malcolm. Upright/Trailer. Semi Double. COROLLA is half flared, triangular shaped, ruffled with smooth turned under petal margins; opens magenta (57A), pale pink (62D) near TUBE; matures magenta (58B), pale pink (62D) near TUBE; 20mm (13/16") long x 25mm (1") wide. SEPALS are fully up, tips recurved; dark rose (55A) tipped green upper surface, rose (52C) tipped green lower surface; 25mm (1") long x 12mm (1/2") wide. TUBE is light pink (49B), medium length and thickness; 12mm (1/2") long x 6mm (1/4") wide. STAMENS extend 25mm (1") below the corolla; pink (62A) filaments and reddish purple (71B) anthers. PISTIL extends 25mm (1") below the corolla; pink (62A) style and yellowish white (158A) stigma. BUD is small, round. FOLIAGE is medium green (146A) on upper surface and yellowish green (146B) on lower surface. Leaves are 55mm (2 3/16") long x 28mm (1 1/8") wide, cordate shaped, serrated edges, acute tips and rounded bases. Veins are green; stems brown; branches are red. PARENTAGE: 'Pink La Campanella' x 'Margaret's Mystique'. Lax upright or stiff trailer. Self branching. Makes good basket or standard. Prefers overhead filtered light and warm climate. Heat tolerant if shaded. Hardy to 32°F. Best bloom colour in bright light. Tested three years in Walthamstow, London, England. Distinguished by bloom shape and colour.

301

Allsop 2002 UK AFS4819.

Mary Rose. Upright. Single. COROLLA pink. SEPALS pink.
Ainsworth 2004 UK.

Maryse Bastié. Upright/Trailer. Single. COROLLA: quarter flared, smooth petal margins; opens purple (77A); matures reddish purple (72B); 28mm (1 1/8") long x 17mm (11/16") wide. SEPALS: horizontal; tips recurved; magenta (63B) upper surface; magenta (63A) lower surface; 42mm (1 11/16") long x 9mm (9/16") wide. TUBE: magenta (63B); short, medium thickness; 11mm (7/16") long x 7mm (1/4") wide. STAMENS: extend 22-25mm (7/8-1") below corolla; dark rose (67C) filaments, very dark reddish purple (186A) anthers. PISTIL: extends 52mm (2 1/16") below the corolla, rose (67D) style, magenta (63A) stigma. BUD: ovate. FOLIAGE: dark green (147A) upper surface; medium green (147B) lower surface. Leaves are 75mm (2 15/16") long x 26mm (1") wide, lanceolate shaped, serrulated edges, acute tips and rounded bases. Veins & stems are yellowish green, branches are yellowish green and light brown. PARENTAGE: 'Porte Océane' x 'Subliem'. Lax upright or stiff trailer. Makes good upright or standard. Prefers overhead filtered light and cool climate. Best bloom and foliage colour in filtered light. Tested 3 years in Pornic, France. Distinguished by blossom colour combination.
Massé 2003 FR AFS5232.

Mascotte. Upright/Trailer. Single. COROLLA: half flared, bell shape, toothed petal margins; opens & matures magenta (68A); 13mm (1/2") long, 8mm (5/16") wide. SEPALS: horizontal; tips recurved; light pink (62B) upper surface; pink (62A) lower surface; 16mm (5/8") long x 4mm (3/16") wide. TUBE: light pink (62B); long, thin; 24mm (15/16") long x 3mm (1/8") wide. STAMENS: extend 6mm (1/4") below corolla; pink (62C) filaments; cream (158C) anthers. PISTIL: extends 14mm (9/16") below the corolla; pale pink (62D) style & stigma. BUD: medium TUBE, ovate, pointed. FOLIAGE: medium green (146A) upper surface; yellow green (146C) lower surface. Leaves are 43mm (1 11/16") long x 25mm (1") wide, ovate shaped, serrated edges, acute tips and rounded bases. Reddish yellow green veins, stems & branches. PARENTAGE: 'Gerharda's Panache' x 'Tsjiep'. Lax upright or stiff trailer. Self branching. Makes good basket. Prefers overhead filtered light. Heat tolerant if

shaded. Best bloom and foliage colour in filtered light. Tested 4 years in Lisse, The Netherlands. Distinguished by flower shape & colour; long-TUBE flowers in small terminal clusters.
de Graaf 2004 NL AFS5607.

Master Pavlis. Upright. Double. COROLLA opens dark violet (83b), matures to red-purple (N74a); corolla is quarter to half flared. SEPALS red (N66a) on the upper and lower surfaces, matures to light red (N57a); SEPALS are fully up with recurved tips. TUBE red. PARENTAGE 'Diana Princess of Wales' x 'Black to the Fuchsia'.
Nutt 2009 UK BFS0122.

Mathy. Upright/Trailer. Double. COROLLA is three quarter flared with turned under wavy petal margins; opens dark reddish purple (64A), dark rose (51A) base; matures dark reddish purple (61A); 22mm (7/8") long x 18mm (11/16") wide. SEPALS: turned right, tips recurved – some flowers horizontal, others fully up; magenta (63A) upper surface; dark rose (51A) lower surface; 38mm (1 1/2") long x 10mm (3/8") wide. TUBE is dark rose (55A); long & thick; 35mm (1 3/8") long x 16mm (5/8") wide. FOLIAGE: medium green (137C) upper surface; light green (138C) lower surface. Leaves are 56mm (2 3/16") long x 35mm (1 3/8") wide, ovate shaped. PARENTAGE: 'Roesse Blacky' x 'Dancing Flame'. Meise 8-14-04. Distinguished by dual shaped SEPALS.
Michiels 2005 BE AFS5829.

Maxima. Upright/Trailer. Semi Double. COROLLA is three quarter flared with smooth petal margins; dark purple (79A), matures purple (79C); 22mm (7/8") long x 22mm (7/8") wide. SEPALS are fully up, tips recurved; dark reddish purple (61A) upper and lower surfaces; 44mm (1 3/4") long x 16mm (5/8") wide. TUBE is dark reddish purple (61A), proportionately medium length and thickness; 12mm (1/2") long x 6mm (1/4") wide. STAMENS extend 31mm (1 1/4") below the corolla; dark purple (79A) filaments and anthers. PISTIL extends 42mm (1 11/16") below the corolla; purple (71A) style and light reddish purple (73D) stigma. BUD is ovate and pointed. FOLIAGE is medium green (137B) on upper surface and medium green (138A) on lower surface. Leaves are 58mm (2 5/16") long x 34mm (1 5/16) wide, ovate shaped, serrulated edges, acute tips and rounded bases. Veins, stems and branches are red. PARENTAGE: 'Rohees New Millennium' x ('Rohees Alrami' x 'Stad

Elburg'). Lax upright or stiff trailer. Makes good stiff trailer. Prefers overhead filtered light and warm climate. Best bloom colour in filtered light. Tested four years in Knegsel, The Netherlands. Distinguished by bloom colour.
Roes 2002 NL AFS4795.

Maxima's Baby. Upright. Single. COROLLA: full flared, smooth petal margins; opens dark purple (78A); matures magenta (71C); 21mm (13/16") long 31mm (1 1/4") wide. SEPALS: fully up; tips recurved; reddish purple (64B) upper surface; reddish purple (61B) lower surface; 22mm (7/8") long x 12mm (1/2") wide. TUBE: reddish purple (64B); short, thick; 6mm (1/4") long x 6mm (1/4") wide. STAMENS: extend 32mm (1 1/4") below corolla; reddish purple (61B) filaments; light rose (68D) anthers. PISTIL: extends 37mm (1 7/16") below the corolla; reddish purple (61B) style; light rose (68D) stigma. BUD: round, pointed. FOLIAGE: dark green (137A) upper surface; medium green (137D) lower surface. Leaves are 56mm (2 3/16") long x 32mm (1 1/4") wide, ovate shaped, smooth edges, acute tips and rounded bases. Red veins, stems & branches. PARENTAGE: 'Swanley Gem' x 'Monique Sleiderink'. Medium upright. Makes good upright or standard. Prefers overhead filtered light and cool climate. Best bloom and foliage colour in filtered light. Tested 4 years in Knegsel, The Netherlands. Distinguished by bloom shape and colour.
Roes 2004 NL AFS5460.

Maxima's Girl. Upright/Trailer. Semi Double. COROLLA is full flared; opens purple (83A); matures dark reddish purple (61A); 22mm (7/8") long x 22mm (7/8") wide. SEPALS are horizontal, tips recurved; light pink (65C) upper surface; rose (65A) lower surface; 21mm (13/16") long x 14mm (9/16") wide. TUBE is light pink (65C); 6mm (1/4") long x 6mm (1/4") wide. FOLIAGE: medium green (137B) upper surface; medium green (138B) lower surface. PARENTAGE: 'Sofie Michiels' x 'Maxima'. Distinguished by bloom colour & shape.
Roes 2006 NL AFS6175.

May Vermeiren. Upright. Single. COROLLA is quarter flared with turned under wavy petal margins; opens dark purple (78A), rose (68B) at base; matures magenta (71C), violet (76A) at base; 29mm (1 1/8") long x 18mm (11/16") wide. SEPALS are half down, tips recurved; brilliant red (53C) upper surface; red (46B); 39mm (1 9/16") long x 8mm

(5/16") wide. TUBE is brilliant red (53B); medium length and thickness; 24mm (15/16") long x 7mm (1/4") wide. STAMENS extend 12mm (1/2") beyond the corolla; dark red (53A) filaments, light tan (161C) anthers. PISTIL extends 6mm (1/4") beyond the corolla; red (46B) style, light orange (31C) stigma. BUD is ovate. FOLIAGE is dark green (137A) upper surface, medium green (147B) lower surface. Leaves are 91mm (3 9/16") long x 36mm (1 7/16") wide, lanceolate shaped, serrulated edges, acute tips and acute bases. Veins and stems are dark redish purple (59A), branches are reddish purple (58A). PARENTAGE: 'Alda Alders' x 'Wingrove's Mammoth'. Medium upright. Self branching. Makes good upright. Prefers overhead filtered light and warm climate. Best bloom and foliage colour in filtered light. Tested three years in Leopoldsburg, Belgium. Certificate N.B.F.K. at Meise. Distinguished by delicate bloom colour and bronze colour of leaves when young.
Busschodts 2002 BE AFS4981.

McGeez Princess Aba. Upright/Trailer. Double. COROLLA: three quarter flared; opens violet blue (92A) veined magenta (58B); matures light rose (58D) veined magenta (58B), edged violet blue (92A); 22mm (7/8") long x 20mm (3/4") wide. PETALOIDS: Same colour as corolla; 18mm (11/16") long x 11mm (7/16") wide. SEPALS: half up, tips reflexed up; red (53B) upper surface; red (53C) lower surface; 35mm (1 3/8") long x 16mm (5/8") wide. TUBE: red (53B); medium length & thickness; 10mm (3/8") long x 7mm (1/4") wide. STAMENS extend 20mm (3/4") beyond the corolla; magenta (58B) filaments; dark reddish purple (59A) anthers. PISTIL extends 40mm (1 9/16") beyond the corolla; dark reddish purple (60B) style; dark grayish purple (183A) stigma. BUD is ovate. FOLIAGE is dark green (137A) upper surface; medium green (138B) lower surface. Leaves are 48mm (1 7/8") long x 29mm (1 1/8") wide; cordate shaped, serrulate edges, acute tips, rounded bases. Veins are light green (138D), stems & branches are dark reddish purple (60A). PARENTAGE: sport of 'Dollar Princess'. Lax upright or stiff trailer. Makes good basket or upright. Prefers overhead filtered light or full sun. Cold weather hardy to -7° C (20° F). Best foliage colour in bright light. Tested 3 years in Woodburn, Oregon, USA. Distinguished by blossom colour, profuse blooms & plant hardiness.
Monnier 2009 USA AFS6984.

303

Mechtildis De Lechy. Upright/Trailer. Single. COROLLA is quarter flared with turned under toothed petal margins; opens dark purple (78A), dark rose (58C) base and midvein; matures magenta (67B), light rose (58D) base and midvein; 22mm (7/8") long x 22mm (7/8") wide. SEPALS are half down, tips recurved; red (45B) upper surface, red (52A) lower surface; 38mm (1 1/2") long x 11mm (7/16") wide. TUBE is dark red (47A), medium length and thickness; 18mm (11/16") long x 6mm (1/4") wide. STAMENS extend 13mm (1/2") beyond the corolla; magenta (63A) filaments, dark rose (58C) anthers. PISTIL extends 19mm (3/4") below the corolla; magenta (63A) style, light yellow (2C) stigma. BUD is elliptic, pointed. FOLIAGE is dark green (137A) upper surface, medium green (137C) lower surface. Leaves are 75mm (2 15/16") long x 35mm (1 3/8") wide, lanceolate shaped, serrated edges, acute tips and acute bases. Veins, stems and branches are reddish purple (58A). PARENTAGE: 'Braamt's Glorie' x unknown. Lax upright or stiff trailer. Self branching. Makes good basket. Prefers overhead filtered light. Best bloom and foliage colour in filtered light. Tested three years in Rummen, Belgium. Certificate N.B.F.K. at Meise. Distinguished by strong growth, profuse blooms.
Ector 2002 BE AFS4895.

Médard's Ardnas. Upright. Single. COROLLA: quarter flared, turned under smooth petal margins; opens reddish purple (67A); matures dark rose (67C); 12mm (1/2") long x 10mm (3/8") wide. SEPALS: horizontal; tips recurved; magenta (58B) upper surface; dark rose (55A) lower surface; 23mm (15/16") long x 8mm (5/16") wide. TUBE: magenta (58B); medium length & thickness; 17mm (11/16") long x 7mm (1/4") wide. STAMENS: extend 8mm (5/16") below corolla; dark rose (67C) filaments; pale lavender (65D) anthers. PISTIL: extends 22mm (7/8") below the corolla; magenta (67B) style; light pink (65B) stigma. BUD: oblong. FOLIAGE: medium green (138A) upper surface, medium green (138B) lower surface. Leaves are 47mm (1 7/8") long x 26mm (1") wide, ovate shaped, serrulated edges, acute tips and cordate bases. Light grayish red (182D) veins; light red purple (185D) stems; very dark reddish purple (186A) branches. PARENTAGE: 'Spike Jones' x unknown. Small upright. Makes good upright. Prefers overhead filtered light and cool climate. Best bloom and foliage colour in filtered light. Tested 3 years in St. Gilles

Waas, Belgium. Award at Meise, 5/7/03. Distinguished by bloom shape.
Van Vooren 2004 BE AFS5424.

Medard's Belijn. Trailer. Double. COROLLA: Quarter flared; opens reddish purple (70B), dark rose (54B); matures light reddish purple (72C); 18mm (11/16") long x 18mm (11/16") wide. SEPALS: horizontal, tips reflexed; dark rose (54A) upper surface; dark rose (54B) lower surface; 42mm (1 5/8") long x 14mm (9/16") wide. TUBE: dark rose (55A); medium length & thickness; 21mm (13/16") long x 5mm (3/16") wide. FOLIAGE is dark green (137A) upper surface; medium green (138B) lower surface. PARENTAGE: 'Oranje King' x 'Rolla'.
Van Vooren 2007 BE AFS6403.

Medard's Botsaert. Upright/Trailer. Double. COROLLA: 3 quarter flared; opens purple (77A) striped red (53D); matures dark reddish purple (72A) striped red (52A); 35mm (1 3/8") long x 22mm (7/8") wide. PETALOIDS: same colour as corolla; 27mm (1 1/16") long x 15mm (9/16") wide. SEPALS: fully up, tips recurved; red (53D) upper surface; dark rose (51A) lower surface; 43mm (1 11/16") long x 16mm (5/8") wide. TUBE: red (52A); medium length & thickness; 15mm (9/16") long x 7mm (1/4") wide. FOLIAGE is medium green (138A) upper surface; medium green (138B) lower surface. PARENTAGE: 'Sofie Michiels' x 'Jubelin'.
Van Vooren 2007 BE AFS6404.

Medard's Bruin. Upright/Trailer. Double. COROLLA: 3 quarter flared; opens rose (65A) & reddish purple (72B); matures pink (62A) & light purple (70C); 26mm (1") long x 17mm (5/8") wide. PETALOIDS: same colour as corolla; 17mm (5/8") long x 8mm (5/16") wide. SEPALS: horizontal, tips reflexed; pink (55C) tipped light yellowish green (150C) upper surface; pink (52D) tipped light yellowish green (150C) lower surface; 44mm (1 3/4") long x 17mm (5/8") wide. TUBE: pale pink (56B); medium length & thickness; 10mm (3/8") long x 6mm (1/4") wide. FOLIAGE is dark green (137A) upper surface; medium green (138B) lower surface. PARENTAGE: 'BreeVis Evelien' x 'Plumb Bob'.
Van Vooren 2007 BE AFS6417.

Medard's Cleenbejach. Trailer. Double. COROLLA: Half flared; opens reddish purple (67A), rose (54C) base; matures magenta (61C); 23mm (7/8") long x 17mm (5/8") wide.

SEPALS: horizontal, tips recurved, twisted left; pink (62C) tipped light green (142C) upper surface; rose (54C) tipped light green (142C) lower surface; 47mm (1 7/8") long x 12mm (7/16") wide. TUBE: pale pink (62D); short & thick; 12mm (7/16") long x 7mm (1/4") wide. FOLIAGE is medium green (137B) upper surface; medium green (138B) lower surface. PARENTAGE: 'Oranje King' x 'Veenlust'.
Van Vooren 2007 BE AFS6405.

Medard's Courtois. Upright/Trailer. Double. COROLLA: 3 quarter flared; opens purple (N82A) blotched pink (62C); matures reddish purple (N80B) blotched rose (65A); 19mm (3/4") long x 17mm (5/8") wide. SEPALS: horizontal, tips recurved; light pink (65C) tipped light apple green (144D) upper surface; pink (62C) light apple green (144D) lower surface; 42mm (1 5/8") long x 16mm (5/8") wide. TUBE: white (155B); medium length & thickness; 17mm (5/8") long x 5mm (3/16") wide. FOLIAGE is medium green (138A) upper surface; medium green (138B) lower surface. PARENTAGE: 'Bicentennial' x 'Marleen's Cyrano'.
Van Vooren 2007 BE AFS6406.

Medard's Cuwaert. Upright. Double. COROLLA: 3 quarter flared; opens purple (N81A); matures reddish purple (N74B); 19mm (3/4") long x 23mm (7/8") wide. PETALOIDS: same colour as corolla; 15mm (9/16") long x 12mm (7/16") wide. SEPALS: horizontal, tips reflexed; magenta (63B) upper surface; magenta (58B) lower surface; 38mm (1 1/2") long x 16mm (5/8") wide. TUBE: rose (61D); short & thick; 10mm (3/8") long x 7mm (1/4") wide. FOLIAGE is medium green (137A) upper surface; medium green (137C) lower surface. PARENTAGE: 'Howlet's Hardy' x 'Sofie Michiels'.
Van Vooren 2007 BE AFS6414.

Médard's Dradem. Upright/Trailer. Semi Double. COROLLA: half flared, turned under smooth petal margins; opens pale pink (62D); matures light pink (62B); 17mm (11/16") long x 14mm (9/16") wide. PETALOIDS: same colour as corolla; 10mm (3/8") long x 7mm (1/4") wide. SEPALS: half down; tips reflexed; rose (55B) striped light gray (156C) tipped yellowish green (144B) upper surface; white (155B) striped rose (55B) tipped yellowish green (144B) lower surface; 29mm (1 1/8") long x 14mm (9/16") wide. TUBE: rose (55B); short & thick; 15mm (9/16") long x 8mm (5/16") wide. STAMENS: extend 15mm (9/16") below corolla; dark

rose (58C) filaments; purple (83A) anthers. PISTIL: extends 23mm (15/16") below the corolla; light rose (58D) style; yellow (1B) stigma. BUD: oblong. FOLIAGE: dark green (137A) upper surface, medium green (137C) lower surface. Leaves are 42mm (1 11/16") long x 19mm (3/4") wide, ovate shaped, serrulated edges, acute tips and rounded bases. plum (184C) veins; plum (184B) stems; grayish red (181A) branches. PARENTAGE: 'Ann Adams' x unknown. Lax upright or stiff trailer. Makes good upright. Prefers overhead filtered light and cool climate. Best bloom and foliage colour in filtered light. Tested 4 years in St. Gilles Waas, Belgium. Award at Meise, 9/8/03. Distinguished by bloom colour and shape.
Van Vooren 2004 BE AFS5422.

Médard's Elise. Upright. Single. COROLLA: half flared, turned under wavy petal margins; opens light reddish purple (71B), light purple (74C) base; matures light reddish purple (72C); 26mm (1") long x 15mm (9/16") wide. SEPALS: horizontal; tips reflexed; pink (51D) tipped light apple green (145C) upper surface; rose (55B) tipped light apple green (145C) lower surface; 39mm (1 9/16") long x 12mm (1/2") wide. TUBE: light pink (38D); medium length & thickness; 15mm (9/16") long x 5mm (3/16") wide. STAMENS: extend 14mm (9/16") below corolla; reddish purple (71B) filaments; pale purple (74D) anthers. PISTIL: extends 3mm (1/8") below the corolla; pale purple (70D) style; pale lavender (69D) stigma. BUD: oblong. FOLIAGE: medium green (137B) upper surface, medium green (138B) lower surface. Leaves are 51mm (2") long x 23mm (15/16") wide, ovate shaped, serrulated edges, acute tips and rounded bases. Light green (138D) veins; medium green (138B) stems & branches. PARENTAGE: 'Drama Girl' x unknown. Small upright. Self branching. Makes good upright. Prefers overhead filtered light. Best bloom and foliage colour in filtered light. Tested 3 years in St. Gilles Waas, Belgium. Award at Meise, 9/8/03. Distinguished by bloom colour combination.
Van Vooren 2004 BE AFS5421.

Médard's Ettegroeg. Upright. Single. COROLLA: quarter flared, turned under smooth petal margins; opens dark rose (58C) & reddish purple (74B); matures reddish purple (74A); 17mm (11/16") long x 14mm (9/16") wide. SEPALS: half down; tips recurved; dark rose (58C) upper surface; magenta (58B) lower surface; 19mm (3/4") long x 7mm (1/4") wide. TUBE: light rose

(58D); short & thick; 10mm (3/8") long x 6mm (1/4") wide. STAMENS: extend 5mm (3/16") below corolla; magenta (63B) filaments; dark reddish purple (64A) anthers. PISTIL: extends 23mm (15/16") below the corolla; magenta (63B) style; pink (62C) stigma. BUD: oblong. FOLIAGE: medium green (138A) upper surface, light green (138C) lower surface. Leaves are 34mm (1 5/16") long x 20mm (13/16") wide, ovate shaped, serrulated edges, acute tips and rounded bases. Light red purple (185D) & medium green (139C) veins; light red purple (185D) stems; plum (185C) branches. PARENTAGE: 'Spike Jones' x unknown. Small upright. Self branching. Makes good upright. Prefers full sun and warm climate. Best bloom and foliage colour in bright light. Tested 3 years in St. Gilles Waas, Belgium. Award at Meise, 9/8/03. Distinguished by bloom shape.
Van Vooren 2004 BE AFS5423.

Medard's Evelin. Upright. Single. COROLLA: quarter flared, turned under wavy petal margins; opens light purple (80C); matures reddish purple (80B); 12mm (1/2") long, 17mm (11/16") wide. SEPALS: half down; tips reflexed; rose (55B) upper surface; dark rose (54B) lower surface; 21mm (13/16") long x 9mm (3/8") wide. TUBE: rose (54C); short, medium thickness; 6mm (1/4") long x 4mm (3/16") wide. STAMENS: do not extend below corolla; dark rose (54B) filaments; purple (80B) anthers. PISTIL: extends 8mm (5/16") below the corolla; reddish purple (74B) style; reddish purple (74A) stigma. BUD: oblong. FOLIAGE: medium green (139B) upper surface; medium green (139C) lower surface. Leaves are 30mm (1 3/16") long x 22mm (7/8") wide, ovate shaped, serrulated edges, acute tips and rounded bases. Light green (139D) veins; medium green (139C) stems; medium green/ light grayish red (139C/182C) branches. PARENTAGE: 'Spike Jones' x unknown. Tall upright. Self branching. Makes good upright. Prefers overhead filtered light, cool climate. Best bloom and foliage colour in bright light. Tested 3 years in St. Gilles Waas, Belgium. Award, Meise, 9/20/03. Distinguished by erect, continuous, profuse blooms.
Van Vooren 2004 BE AFS5622.

Medard's Grimbeert. Upright/Trailer. Double. COROLLA: 3 quarter flared; opens rose (55B) & magenta (71C); matures pale pink (56B) & dark rose (71D); 29mm (1 1/8") long x 25mm (1") wide. PETALOIDS: rose (48B) & reddish purple (64B); 17mm (5/8")

long x 8mm (5/16") wide. SEPALS: horizontal, tips reflexed; rose (55B) tipped light green (143C) upper surface; rose (52C) tipped light green (143C) lower surface; 35mm (1 3/8") long x 13mm (1/2") wide. TUBE: pale pink (56B); medium length & thickness; 20mm (3/4") long x 6mm (1/4") wide. FOLIAGE. PARENTAGE: 'Oranje King' x 'Rolla'.
Van Vooren 2007 BE AFS6415.

Medard's Hermeline. Trailer. Double. COROLLA: 3 quarter flared; opens pink (43D) & reddish purple (64B); matures pink (48C) & dark reddish purple (64A); 32mm (1 1/4") long x 19mm (3/4") wide. SEPALS: half up, tips recurved up; pink (55C) tipped light greenish yellow (151C) upper surface; pink (43D) tipped light greenish yellow (151C) lower surface; 37mm (1 7/16") long x 14mm (9/16") wide. TUBE: light pink (55D); medium length, thin; 15mm (9/16") long x 4mm (1/8") wide. FOLIAGE is dark green (136B) upper surface; medium green (138B) lower surface. PARENTAGE: 'Oranje King' x 'De Brouwer'.
Van Vooren 2007 BE 6407.

Médard's Hersinde. Upright. Single. COROLLA is quarter flared; opens light reddish purple (72C) edged dark reddish purple (72A); matures light purple (74C) edged light reddish purple (72C); 18mm (11/16") long x 12mm (1/2") wide. SEPALS are half down, tips reflexed; magenta (59D) upper surface; magenta (63B) lower surface; 21mm (13/16") long x 6mm (1/4") wide. TUBE is magenta (59D); 9mm (3/8") long x 5mm (3/16") wide. FOLIAGE: dark green (139A) upper surface; medium green (138B) lower surface. PARENTAGE: 'De Vondeling' x 'Happy'. Meise 9/17/05. Distinguished by bloom colour.
Van Vooren 2006 BE AFS6066.

Medard's Isegrim. Upright/Trailer. Double. COROLLA: 3 quarter flared; opens dark rose (67C), light rose (58D) base; matures magenta (71C), rose (68C) base; 31mm (1 1/4") long x 22mm (7/8") wide. PETALOIDS: same colour as corolla; 17mm (5/8") long x 8mm (5/16") wide. SEPALS: half up, tips recurved up, twisted left; pink (62C) tipped pale yellowish green (150D) upper surface; light rose (58D) tipped pale yellowish green (150D) lower surface; 42mm (1 5/8") long x 19mm (3/4") wide. TUBE: light pink (62B); medium length & thickness; 27mm (1 1/16") long x 7mm (1/4") wide. FOLIAGE is dark green (N138A) upper surface; medium green

(138B) lower surface. PARENTAGE: 'Bicentennial' x 'Brevis Evelien'. Van Vooren 2007 BE AFS6408.

Médard's Jannick. Upright. Double. COROLLA: three quarter flared, turned under wavy petal margins; opens reddish purple (70B) edged violet (82C), white (155C) base; matures dark reddish purple (70A) edged purple (82B); 17mm (11/16") long x 14mm (9/16") wide. PETALOIDS: reddish purple (155C) base; 11mm (7/16") long x 9mm (3/8") wide. SEPALS: half down; tips reflexed; white (155C) tipped light yellow green (150B) upper surface; rose (55B), white (155C) base, tipped light green (150B) lower surface; 36mm (1 7/16") long x 20mm (13/16") wide. TUBE: white (155C); medium length & thickness; 20mm (13/16") long x 5mm (3/16") wide. STAMENS: extend 6mm (1/4") below corolla; light purple (78A) filaments; pale purple (75C) anthers. PISTIL: extends 9mm (3/8") below the corolla; light purple (78D) style; pale purple (74D) stigma. BUD: oblong. FOLIAGE: medium green (137B) upper surface, medium green (138B) lower surface. Leaves are 49mm (1 15/16") long x 30mm (1 3/16") wide, ovate shaped, serrulated edges, acute tips and rounded bases. Light green (138C) veins; medium green (138B) stems; medium green (139C) branches. PARENTAGE: 'Drama Girl' x unknown. Small upright. Self branching. Makes good upright. Prefers overhead filtered light. Best bloom and foliage colour in filtered light. Tested 3 years in St. Gilles Waas, Belgium. Award at Meise, 9/8/03. Distinguished by bloom colour. Van Vooren 2004 BE AFS5418.

Médard's Jolein. Upright. Single. COROLLA is half flared with turned under smooth petal margins; opens purple (81A), pale pink (49D) base; matures purple (81A); 12mm (1/2") long x 9mm (3/8") wide. SEPALS are half up, tips recurved up; pink (55C), pale pink (55C) base, tipped light yellowish green (149C) upper surface; rose (65A), pale pink (55C) base, tipped light yellowish green (149C) lower surface; 19mm (3/4") long x 9mm (3/8") wide. TUBE is pale pink (49D); short & thick; 6mm (1/4") long x 5mm (3/16") wide. FOLIAGE: yellowish green (144B) & light yellow (8C) upper surface; yellowish green (145B) & light yellow (8C) lower surface. Leaves are 39mm (1 9/16") long x 23mm (15/16") wide, ovate shaped. PARENTAGE: 'Lambada' x unknown. Meise 8-14-04. Distinguished by colour combination.

Van Vooren 2005 BE AFS5718.

Médard's Karin. Upright. Semi Double. COROLLA: half flared, turned under wavy petal margins; opens reddish purple (71B); matures dark purple (77A); 19mm (3/4") long x 17mm (11/16") wide. SEPALS: horizontal; tips reflexed; white (155C) tipped light yellowish green (144B) upper surface; pink (52D) tipped light yellowish green (144B) lower surface; 24mm (15/16") long x 9mm (3/8") wide. TUBE: white (155C); medium length & thickness; 16mm (5/8") long x 6mm (1/4") wide. STAMENS: extend 11mm (7/16") below corolla; dark reddish purple (64A) filaments; light gray (156C) anthers. PISTIL: extends 26mm (1") below the corolla; rose (64D) style; white (155A) stigma. BUD: oblong. FOLIAGE: medium green (139B) upper surface, medium green (138B) lower surface. Leaves are 41mm (1 5/8") long x 23mm (15/16") wide, ovate shaped, serrulated edges, acute tips and rounded bases. Dark red purple (187D) veins; dark reddish purple (187B) stems; plum (183D) branches. PARENTAGE: 'Hawkshead' x unknown. Small upright. Self branching. Makes good upright or standard. Prefers overhead filtered light. Best bloom and foliage colour in filtered light. Tested 3 years in St. Gilles Waas, Belgium. Award at Meise, 9/8/03. Distinguished by bloom colour. Van Vooren 2004 BE AFS5419.

Médard's Katelijne. Upright. Single. COROLLA: quarter flared, turned under wavy petal margins; opens purple (71A), rose (68C) base; matures reddish purple (72B); 18mm (11/16") long x 14mm (9/16") wide. PETALOIDS: same colour as corolla; 12mm (1/2") long x 5mm (3/16"). SEPALS: half down; tips recurved; white (155B) tipped medium green (141C) upper surface; white (155C) tipped medium green (141C) lower surface; 29mm (1 1/8") long x 7mm (1/4") wide. TUBE: white (155B) striped medium green (141C); medium length & thickness; 12mm (1/2") long x 3mm (1/8") wide. STAMENS: extend 11mm (7/16") below corolla; magenta (63B) filaments; light gray (156B) anthers. PISTIL: extends 13mm (1/2") below the corolla; white (155C) style; pale yellow (1D) stigma. BUD: oblong. FOLIAGE: dark green (139A) upper surface, medium green (138B) lower surface. Leaves are 57mm (2 1/4") long x 17mm (11/16") wide, lanceolate shaped, serrulated edges, acute tips and rounded bases. Light green (138C) veins; medium green (137D) stems; medium green (137C) branches. PARENTAGE:

'Hawkshead' x unknown. Small upright. Self branching. Makes good upright. Prefers overhead filtered light and cool climate. Best bloom and foliage colour in filtered light. Tested 3 years in St. Gilles Waas, Belgium. Award at Meise, 9/8/03. Distinguished by bloom colour and shape.
Van Vooren 2004 BE AFS5420.

Médard's Kcinna. Upright. Single. COROLLA is quarter flared with turned under smooth petal margins; opens violet (77C), pale purple (76C) base; matures violet (76A), pale purple (80D) base; 21mm (13/16") long x 21mm (13/16") wide. PETALOIDS: Same colour as corolla; 11mm (7/16") long x 11mm (7/16") wide. SEPALS are horizontal, tips reflexed; white (155D), tipped light apple green (145B) upper surface; white (155D), tipped light apple green (144D) lower surface; 21mm (7/8") long x 9mm (3/8") wide. TUBE is white (155D); short & thick; 12mm (1/2") long x 6mm (1/4") wide. FOLIAGE: dark green (136B) upper surface; medium green (138B) lower surface. Leaves are 58mm (2 5/16") long x 30mm (1 3/16") wide, elliptic shaped. PARENTAGE: 'Nicky Veerman' x unknown. Meis 3-7-04. Distinguished by colour combination.
Van Vooren 2005 BE AFS5663.

Médard's Klingenaar. Trailer. Single. COROLLA is quarter flared with turned under smooth petal margins; opens reddish purple (67A), red (50A) base; matures magenta (61C); 27mm (1 1/16") long x 16mm (5/8") wide. PETALOIDS: reddish purple (72B), red (50A) base; 13mm (1/2") long x 9mm (3/8") wide. SEPALS are half down, tips reflexed; dark rose (51A) upper surface; red (50A) lower surface; 34mm (1 5/16") long x 10mm (3/8") wide. TUBE is dark rose (54B); long & thin; 35mm (1 3/8") long x 4mm (3/16") wide. FOLIAGE: dark green (136A) upper surface; medium green (138B) lower surface. Leaves are 52mm (2 1/16") long x 28mm (1 1/8") wide, ovate shaped. PARENTAGE: 'Pink Darling' x unknown. Meise 8-14-04. Distinguished by bloom colour & long thin TUBE.
Van Vooren 2005 BE AFS5827.

Médard's Klompenmaker. Upright. Single. COROLLA is three quarter flared with turned under wavy petal margins; opens reddish purple (74A); matures light purple (78B); 18mm (11/16") long x 20mm (13/16") wide. SEPALS are half up, tips recurved up; magenta (63A) upper surface; dark rose (64C) lower surface; 20mm (13/16") long x

9mm (3/8") wide. TUBE is magenta (63A); short & thick; 4mm (3/16") long x 4mm (3/16") wide. FOLIAGE: dark green (139A) upper surface; medium green (137C) lower surface. Leaves are 37mm (1 7/16") long x 17mm (11/16") wide, lanceolate shaped. PARENTAGE: 'Pink Fantasia' x unknown. Meise 8-14-04. Distinguished by colour & shape.
Van Vooren 2005 BE AFS5719.

Médard's Koning Nobel. Upright. Single. COROLLA is unflared; opens light reddish purple (72C); matures pale purple (74D); 9mm (5/16") long x 7mm (1/4") wide. SEPALS are full down, tips recurved; dark rose (58C) upper surface; magenta (63B) lower surface; 12mm (7/16") long x 6mm (1/4") wide. TUBE is magenta (61C); 6mm (1/4") long x 5mm (3/16") wide. FOLIAGE is dark green (136B) upper surface; medium green (138B) lower surface. PARENTAGE: 'Delta's Angelique' x 'Onbekend'. Meise 8/13/05. Distinguished by small, erect bloom.
Van Vooren 2006 BE AFS6016.

Médard's Krieke Putte. Upright. Single. COROLLA is quarter flared; opens light purple (78B); matures light purple (78D); 9mm (5/16") long x 7mm (1/4") wide. SEPALS are half down, tips reflexed; pale pink (55B), tipped light apple green (144D) upper surface; dark rose (55A), tipped light apple green (144D) lower surface; 12mm (7/16") long x 4mm (1/8") wide. TUBE is pink (55C); 5mm (3/16") long x 3.5mm (1/8") wide. FOLIAGE is dark green (139A) upper surface; medium green (138A) lower surface. PARENTAGE: 'De Vondeling' x 'Happy'. Meise 7/2/05. Distinguished by small erect blooms.
Van Vooren 2006 BE AFS6018.

Medard's Lamfroit. Upright/Trailer. Double. COROLLA: 3 quarter flared; opens dark rose (67C) & light reddish purple (72C); matures rose (68C) & magenta (68A); 29mm (1 1/8") long x 19mm (3/4") wide. PETALOIDS: same colour as corolla; 17mm (5/8") long x 12mm (7/16") wide. SEPALS: half down, tips recurved; light pink (65B) tipped light yellowish green (150C) upper surface; rose (65A) tipped light yellowish green (150C) lower surface; 62mm (2 7/16") long x 26mm (1") wide. TUBE: light pink (62B); medium length & thickness; 18mm (11/16") long x 7mm (1/4") wide. FOLIAGE is medium green (137B) upper surface; medium green (138B)

lower surface. PARENTAGE: 'Rohees Etamin' x 'Oranje King'.
Van Vooren 2007 BE AFS6416.

Médard's Malpertus. Trailer. Single. COROLLA is quarter flared; opens magenta (63B) with white (155D) base; matures light rose (63D); 16mm (5/8") long x 14mm (9/16") wide. SEPALS are half down, tips reflexed; pink (55C) with white (155D) base, tipped light apple green (145B) upper surface; light pink (55D) with white (155D) base, tipped light apple green (145B) lower surface; 21mm (13/16") long x 9mm (5/16") wide. TUBE is white (155D); 14mm (9/16") long x 10mm (3/8") wide. FOLIAGE is dark green (137A) upper surface; medium green (138B) lower surface. PARENTAGE: 'Rohee's Etamine' x 'Onbekend'. Meise 8/13/05. Distinguished by bloom colour, large leaves. Van Vooren 2006 BE AFS6017.

Médard's Reinaertsland. Upright. Single. COROLLA is quarter flared; opens red (52A); matures rose (51B); 18mm 1/16") long x 13mm (1/2") wide. SEPALS are horizontal, tips reflexed; pink (49A), tipped apple green (144C) upper surface; light rose (50C), tipped apple green (144C) lower surface; 23mm (7/8") long x 5mm (3/16") wide. TUBE is pink (51D); 18mm (11/16") long x 5mm (3/16") wide. FOLIAGE is dark green (139A) upper surface; medium green (138B) lower surface. PARENTAGE: 'Anita Taelens' x 'Onbekend'. Meise 7/2/05. Distinguished by bloom colour. Van Vooren 2006 BE AFS6019.

Médard's Reynaerdijn. Upright. Double. COROLLA: 3 quarter flared; opens light reddish purple (72C), light rose (58D) base; matures light purple (70C) & light pink (62B); 31mm (1 1/4") long x 22mm (7/8") wide. SEPALS: horizontal, tips recurved; pink (62A) upper surface; light rose (58D) lower surface; 32mm (1 1/4") long x 13mm (1/2") wide. TUBE: white (155C); medium length & thickness; 18mm (11/16") long x 5mm (3/16") wide. FOLIAGE is medium green (137B) upper surface; medium green (138B) lower surface. PARENTAGE: 'Howlet's Hardy' x 'Sofie Michiels'. Small upright. Van Vooren 2007 BE AFS6409.

Médard's Reynaert. Upright. Double. COROLLA: Half flared; opens reddish purple (61B) blotched rose (52C); matures magenta (59C); 35mm (1 3/8") long x 24mm (15/16") wide. PETALOIDS: same colour as corolla; 28mm (1 1/8") long x 15mm (9/16") wide.

SEPALS: half down, tips recurved; light pink (62B) tipped pale yellowish green (149D) upper surface; rose (52C) tipped pale yellowish green (149D) lower surface; 53mm (2 1/8") long x 14mm (9/16") wide. TUBE: pale pink (56D); medium length & thickness; 13mm (1/2") long x 6mm (1/4") wide. FOLIAGE is medium green (137B) upper surface; medium green (138B) lower surface. PARENTAGE: 'Oranje King' x 'Veenlust'. Van Vooren 2007 BE AFS6410.

Médard's Roede. Trailer. Double. COROLLA: Half flared; opens magenta (68A) blotched rose (52C); matures light reddish purple (73A) blotched rose (51B); 19mm (3/4") long x 17mm (5/8") wide. PETALOIDS: magenta (68A); 12mm (7/16") long x 9mm (5/16") wide. SEPALS: horizontal, tips recurved; pink (55C) upper surface; rose (52C) lower surface; 47mm (1 7/8") long x 20mm (3/4") wide. TUBE: pale pink (56D); medium length & thickness; 21mm (13/16") long x 5mm (3/16") wide. FOLIAGE is medium green (137B) upper surface; medium green (138B) lower surface. PARENTAGE: 'Bicentennial' x 'BreeVis Evelien'. Van Vooren 2007 BE AFS6411.

Médard's Tiebeert. Upright. Double. COROLLA: Half flared; opens white (155B); matures white (155B) striped pale rose (73D); 22mm (7/8") long x 26mm (1") wide. SEPALS: half down, tips recurved; white (155B) tipped apple green (144C) upper surface; pale rose (73D) tipped apple green (144C) lower surface; 40mm (1 9/16") long x 12mm (7/16") wide. TUBE: white (155C); short & thick; 9mm (5/16") long x 7mm (1/4") wide. FOLIAGE is medium green (137B) upper surface; medium green (138B) lower surface. PARENTAGE: 'Oranje King' x 'Veenlust'. Van Vooren 2007 BE AFS6412.

Médard's Tiecelijn. Trailer. Double. COROLLA: Half flared; opens dark reddish purple (64A), rose (52C) base; matures magenta (68A); 29mm (1 1/8") long x 21mm (13/16") wide. PETALOIDS: same colour as corolla; 22mm (7/8") long x 15mm (9/16") wide. SEPALS: half up, tips recurved up; dark rose (58C) upper surface; rose (52C) lower surface; 42mm (1 5/8") long x 18mm (11/16") wide. TUBE: pink (55C); medium length & thickness; 21mm (13/16") long x 7mm (1/4") wide. FOLIAGE is medium green (137C) upper surface; medium green (138B) lower surface. PARENTAGE: 'Bicentennial' x 'Veenlust'.

Van Vooren 2007 BE AFS6413.

Megan Burns. Upright. Double. COROLLA opens purple-violet (N81a), matures lighter (N82a); corolla is half to fully up. SEPALS red (N66b) on the upper and lower surfaces, matures to light red (58c); SEPALS are half to fully up with recurved tips. TUBE red. PARENTAGE 'Diana Princess of Wales' x 'Black to the Fuchsia'.
Nutt 2009 UK BFS0123.

Megan Vollebregt. Upright. Single. COROLLA: half flared, bell shaped; smooth petal margins; opens violet (76A); matures violet (76A); 25mm (1") long x 27mm (1 1/16") wide. SEPALS: half up, tips recurved up; red (52A) upper & lower surfaces; 30mm (1 3/16") long x 13mm (1/2") wide. TUBE: red (53C); short & thick; 9mm (5/16") long x 6mm (1/4") wide. STAMENS extend 2mm (1/16") beyond the corolla; reddish purple (61B) filaments & anthers. PISTIL extends 22mm (7/8") beyond the corolla; magenta (61C) style; pale tan (161D) stigma. BUD is pegtop shaped. FOLIAGE is dark green (147A) upper surface; medium green (147B) lower surface. Leaves are 58mm (2 5/16") long x 33mm (1 5/16") wide; elliptic shaped, serrulate edges, acute tips, rounded bases. Veins, stems & branches are light green. PARENTAGE: 'Ivana van Amsterdam' x 'Clarien®'. Medium upright. Self branching. Makes good upright. Prefers overhead filtered light. Best bloom & foliage colour in filtered light. Tested 3 years in Haarlem, The Netherlands. Nominated by NKvF as recommendable cultivar. Distinguished by bloom shape & colour.
van der Putten 2009 NL AFS7014.

Megeti. Upright. Single. COROLLA is half flared; opens light rose (68A) edged white (155D); matures rose (68C) edged white (155D); 18mm (11/16") long x 20mm (13/16") wide. SEPALS are half up, tips recurved up; reddish purple (61B) upper surface; magenta (58B) lower surface; 33mm (5/16") long x 11mm (7/16") wide. TUBE is magenta (58B); 22mm (7/8") long x 6mm (1/4") wide. FOLIAGE: medium green (139B) upper surface; medium green (138B) lower surface. PARENTAGE: 'Jenny Sorensen' x 'Swingtime'. Meise 9/17/05. Distinguished by bloom colour & white corolla edge.
Geerts L. 2006 BE AFS6065.

Mein Krummnussbaum. Upright. Single. COROLLA opens light red, matures to light reddish violet; corolla is three quarter flared.

SEPALS red on the upper and lower surfaces; sepals are fully up with recurved tips. TUBE red. PARENTAGE 'Maxim Pourple' x 'Royal Velvet'. Free flowering and self branching.
Nicola 2008 AT BFS0068.

Mein Winklarn. Upright. Double. COROLLA is full flared with smooth petal margins; opens & matures white (155B) veined red (52A); 30mm (1 3/16") long x 32mm (1 1/4") wide. SEPALS are horizontal, tips recurved; red (52A) upper & lower surfaces; 35mm (1 3/8") long x 14mm (9/16") wide. TUBE is red (52A); medium length & thickness; 15mm (9/16") long x 6mm (1/4") wide. FOLIAGE: dark green (137A) upper surface; medium green (137C) lower surface. Leaves are 50mm (2") long x 33mm (1 5/16") wide, ovate shaped. PARENTAGE: (seedling #7/1991) x (seedling #1A/1991). Distinguished by flower colour.
Gindl 2005 AT AFS5803.

Melchert. Upright. Single. COROLLA: half flared; opens purple (83B); matures dark reddish purple (72A); 19mm (3/4") long x 16mm (5/8") wide. SEPALS: horizontal, tips recurved; dark reddish purple (60A) upper surface; reddish purple (61B) lower surface; 24mm (15/16") long x 10mm (3/8") wide. TUBE: dark reddish purple (60A); 6mm (1/4") long x 5mm (3/16") wide. FOLIAGE is dark green (147A) upper surface; medium green (147B) lower surface. PARENTAGE: ('Sunangels Cheerio' x 'Hertogin van Brabant') x 'Josephine Margaretha'.
Krom 2008 NL AFS6945.

Menne Moat. Upright/Trailer. Single. COROLLA is quarter flared; opens purple (82A), light rose (73B) base; matures purple (81B), pale rose (73D) base; 19mm (3/4") long x 13mm (1/2") wide. SEPALS are half up, tips recurved up; light purple (75B) tipped yellowish green (144A) upper surface; light rose (73B) tipped yellowish green (144A) lower surface; 24mm (15/16") long x 7mm (1/4") wide. TUBE is rose (68B); 4mm (1/8") long x 4mm (1/8") wide. FOLIAGE: dark green (136A) upper surface; medium green (138A) lower surface. PARENTAGE: 'Rosea' x 'Bleu Rebel'. Meise 9/17/05. Distinguished by bloom colour.
Michiels 2006 BE AFS6073.

Meta Ermel. Trailer. Double. COROLLA: half flared, bell shaped, smooth petal margins; opens & matures white (155B); 20mm (3/4") long x 25mm (1") wide. SEPALS: fully up,

tips recurved; white (155D) upper surface; white (155D), rose (50C) base lower surface; 35mm (1 3/8") long x 14mm (9/16") wide. TUBE: white (155A); medium length & thickness; 13mm (1/2") long x 8mm (5/16") wide. STAMENS extend 20mm (3/4") beyond the corolla; rose (55B) filaments; brown (177B) anthers. PISTIL extends 35mm (1 3/8") beyond the corolla; white (155D) style; amber (162C) stigma. BUD: cordate. FOLIAGE: dark green (137A) upper surface; medium green (138A) lower surface. Leaves are 60mm (2 3/8") long x 30mm (1 3/16") wide; ovate shaped, serrate edges, acute tips, rounded bases. Veins are bright green, stems are red purple, branches are green & red purple. PARENTAGE: 'Katie Elisabeth' x 'Enid Carter'. Natural trailer. Makes good basket or standard. Prefers overhead filtered light. Best bloom & foliage colour in filtered light. Tested 5 years in South Germany. Distinguished by bloom shape & colour.
Dietrich 2009 DE AFS7115.

Meta Ermel. Trailer. Double. COROLLA white; and is half flared. SEPALS white on the upper and lower surfaces; sepals are fully up with recurved tips. TUBE white. PARENTAGE 'Katie Elizabeth' x 'Enid Carter'.
Dietrich 2008 DE BFS0087.

Michael Braham. Upright/Trailer. Single. COROLLA: quarter flared, bell shaped, turned under smooth petal margins; opens reddish purple (74B) veined red; matures reddish purple (66A) veined red; 10mm (3/8") long x 15mm (9/16") wide. SEPALS: fully up; tips recurved; red (52A) upper surface; red (44A) lower surface; 20mm(13/16") long x 9mm (3/8") wide. TUBE: red (44A); short & thick; 7mm (1/4") long x 5mm (3/16") wide. STAMENS: extend 15mm (9/16") below corolla; red (52A) filaments; white (155A) anthers. PISTIL: extends 30mm (1 3/16") below the corolla, red (55A) style; red (49A) stigma. BUD: small, oval. FOLIAGE: dark green (147A) upper surface, medium green (147B) lower surface. Leaves are 45mm (1 3/4") long x 30mm (1 3/16") wide, cordate shaped, serrulated edges, acute tips and cordate bases. Veins are green, red center; branches are red; stems are brown. PARENTAGE: 'Janeke Brinkman-Saletijn' x 'Mini Rose'. Lax upright or stiff trailer. Self branching. Makes good basket, standard or bonsai. Prefers overhead filtered light. Heat tolerant if shaded. Cold weather hardy to 32° F. Best bloom colour in bright light. Tested 4 years in Walthamstow, London, England. Distinguished by reddish

aubergine colour combination against dark foliage.
Allsop M. 2004 UK AFS5377.

Michael Wallis. Single. COROLLA salmon pik. SEPALS light coral.
Kimberley 2002 UK.

Michel Strogoff. Upright/Trailer. Single. COROLLA is unflared; opens & matures magenta (67B), lighter base; 23mm (7/8") long x 11mm (7/16") wide. SEPALS are horizontal, tips recurved; pale yellowish green (149D) tipped light yellowish green (149C) upper & lower surfaces; 32mm (1 1/4") long x 6mm (1/4") wide. TUBE is pale yellowish green (149D); 24mm (15/16") long x 5mm (3/16") wide. FOLIAGE: medium green (146A) upper surface; yellowish green (146B) lower surface. PARENTAGE: 'Prince of Orange' x 'Subliem'. Distinguished by bloom contrast & long SEPALS.
Massé 2006 FR AFS6241.

Michelle C. Struck. Upright/Trailer. Single. COROLLA is unflared with turned under smooth petal margins; opens reddish purple (59B); matures dark red (53A); 6mm (1/4") long x 7mm (1/4") wide. SEPALS are half down, tips recurved; rose (51B) upper surface; dark reddish purple (60B) lower surface; 12mm (1/2") long x 4mm (3/16") wide. TUBE is magenta (58B); medium length and thin; 18mm (11/16") long x 4mm (3/16") wide. STAMENS extend 3mm (1/8") beyond the corolla; reddish purple (61B) filaments, light grayish rose (181D) anthers. PISTIL extends 5mm (3/16") beyond the corolla; reddish purple (61B) style, pale yellow (18D) stigma. BUD is elliptic. FOLIAGE is medium green (137B) upper surface, medium green (139C) lower surface. Leaves are 60mm (2 3/8") long x 24mm (15/16") wide, lanceolate shaped, serrulated edges, acute tips and rounded bases. Veins are grayish red (181B), stems are plum (185B), branches are plum (183B). PARENTAGE: 'Rosea' x 'F. *fulgens* var *gesneriana*'. Lax upright or stiff trailer. Self branching. Makes good basket. Prefers full sun and warm climate. Best bloom and foliage colour in bright light. Tested four years in Naksov, Denmark. Distinguished by dark colour.
Struck 2002 DK AFS4952.

Michelle Coleman. Upright. Double. COROLLA is unflared, bell shaped, with smooth margins; opens dark reddish purple (61A) splashed reddish orange (43C),

311

matures magenta (57A) splashed rose (52C); 28mm (1 1/8") long x 26mm (1") wide. SEPALS are half up, tips recurved up; light rose (73B) upper surface, pink (43D) lower surface; 42mm (1 3/8") long x 18mm (11/16") wide. TUBE is white (155A), medium length and thickness; 14mm (9/16") long x 6mm (1/4") wide. STAMENS extend 17mm (11/16") below the corolla; dark rose (67C) filaments, reddish purple (67A) anthers. PISTIL extends 31mm (1 1/4") below the corolla; magenta (67B) style, pale lavender (65D) stigma. BUD is ovate. FOLIAGE is medium green (138A) upper surface, medium green (139C) lower surface. Leaves are 72mm (2 13/16") long x 38mm (1 1/2") wide, lanceolate shaped, serrulated edges, acute tips and rounded bases. Veins are green, stems and branches are red. PARENTAGE: 'Branksome Belle' x 'Ruth Graham'. Small upright. Makes good upright. Prefers overhead filtered light and cool climate. Best bloom colour in filtered light. Tested three years in Stockbridge, Hampshire, England. Distinguished by blossom colour.
Graham 2002 UK AFS4876.

Michelle de Bruijn. Upright/Trailer. Double. COROLLA: 3 quarter flared; opens violet (86B); matures purple (80A); 30mm (1 3/16") long x 24mm (15/16") wide. SEPALS: fully up, tips reflexed; light pink (62B) upper surface; rose (63C) lower surface; 60mm (2 3/8") long x 14mm (9/16") wide. TUBE: light pink (62B); medium length & thickness; 20mm (3/4") long x 6mm (1/4") wide. FOLIAGE is dark green (137A) upper surface; medium green (137D) lower surface. PARENTAGE: 'Rose Bradwardine' x 'Pinto The Blue'.
Scharf 2007 NL AFS6572.

Mieke. Upright. Semi Double. COROLLA is half flared with turned under smooth petal margins; opens dark reddish purple (64A); matures dark rose (64C); 27mm (1 1/16") long x 19mm (3/4") wide. PETALOIDS: dark reddish purple (61A); 16mm (5/8") long x 10mm (3/8") wide. SEPALS are horizontal, tips reflexed; dark reddish purple (64A) upper surface; reddish purple (71B) lower surface; 34mm (1 5/16") long x 16mm (5/8") wide. TUBE is reddish purple (64B); medium length & thickness; 16mm (5/8") long x 7mm (1/4") wide. FOLIAGE: dark green (139A) upper surface; medium green (138B) lower surface. Leaves are 88mm (3 7/16") long x 37mm (1 7/16") wide, elliptic shaped. PARENTAGE: 'Roesse Blacky' x 'Sofie

Michiels'. Meis 3-7-04. Distinguished by bluish purple bloom colour.
Michiels 2005 BE AFS5670.

Mieke Sarton. Upright. Single. COROLLA is full flared, bell shaped, with turned up petal margins; opens light orange (41C); matures orange (41B); 3mm (1/8") long x 3mm (1/8") wide. SEPALS are half up, tips recurved up; rose (54C) upper & lower surfaces; 3mm (1/8") long x 2mm (1/16") wide. TUBE is rose (54C); medium length & thickness; 7mm (1/4") long x 2mm (1/16") wide. FOLIAGE: dark green (147A) upper surface; light olive green (147C) lower surface. Leaves are 55mm (2 3/16") long x 23mm (15/16") wide, elliptic shaped. PARENTAGE: 'Jan Van Erp' x 'F. fulgens var. goselii'. Distinguished by small flowers and corolla colour.
de Keijzer 2005 NL AFS5788.

Mien Antonis. Upright/Trailer. Double. COROLLA: half flared, smooth petal margins; opens purple (77A); matures dark reddish purple (61A); 30mm (1 3/16") long x 21mm (13/16") wide. SEPALS: fully up; tips recurved; rose (65A) upper surface; magenta (63B) lower surface; 32mm (1 1/4") long x 12mm (1/2") wide. TUBE: light yellowish orange (19B); medium length & thickness; 17mm (11/16") long x 7mm (1/4") wide. STAMENS: extend 26mm (1") below corolla; magenta (61C) filaments; dark reddish purple (61A) anthers. PISTIL: extends 42mm (1 11/16") below the corolla; light rose (63D) style; light yellow (11C) stigma. BUD: ovate. FOLIAGE: dark green (137A) upper surface; medium green (138B) lower surface. Leaves are 66mm (2 5/8") long x 31mm (1 1/4") wide, cordate shaped, serrated edges, acute tips and rounded bases. Veins, stems & branches are red. PARENTAGE: {[('Bon Accord' x 'Bicentennial') x ('Vobeglo' x 'Dancing Flame')] x 'Rohees Alrami'} x 'Allure'. Lax upright or stiff trailer. Makes good stiff trailer. Prefers overhead filtered light and cool climate. Best bloom and foliage colour in filtered light. Tested 4 years in Duizel, The Netherlands. Distinguished by bloom colour & profuse flowering.
Tamerus 2003 NL AFS5297.

Mien de Jong. Trailer. Single. COROLLA: full flared; opens & matures purple (77A); 22mm (7/8") long x 30mm (1 3/16") wide. SEPALS: half up, tips reflexed up; red (46B) upper surface; red (46C) lower surface; 26mm (1") long x 16mm (5/8") wide. TUBE: red (46B); 12mm (7/16") long x 9mm (5/16") wide. FOLIAGE is dark green (137A) upper surface;

medium green (137C) lower surface. PARENTAGE: 'Roesse Carme' x 'Maxima's Baby'.
van Bree 2008 NL AFS6893.

Miet van Eijk. Trailer. Semi Double. COROLLA is half flared; opens reddish purple (61B); matures magenta (61C); 24mm (15/16") long x 25mm (1") wide. SEPALS are half up, tips reflexed up; magenta (58B) upper & lower surfaces; 27mm (1 1/16") long x 10mm (3/8") wide. TUBE is magenta (58B); 22mm (7/8") long x 6mm (1/4") wide. FOLIAGE: dark green (137A) upper surface; medium green (138B) lower surface. PARENTAGE: 'Roesse Lupus' x 'Sofie Michiels'. Distinguished by bloom colour.
Roes 2006 NL AFS6176.

Mike Wing Trailer. Double. COROLLA: three quarter flared, turned under wavy petal margins; opens rose (63C) & magenta (67B) edged reddish purple (70B); matures magenta (61C) edged magenta (63B); 22mm (7/8") long x 19mm (3/4") wide. SEPALS: half up, tips recurved up; twisted left to right; magenta (58B) upper surface; dark rose (51A) lower surface; 34mm (1 3/8") long x 16mm (5/8") wide. TUBE: rose (N57C); medium length & thickness; 20mm (3/4") long x 6mm (1/4") wide. STAMENS extend 13mm (1/2") beyond the corolla; magenta (61C) filaments; purple (71A) anthers. PISTIL extends 29mm (1 1/8") beyond the corolla; magenta (63B) style; light rose (68D) stigma. BUD: bulbous. FOLIAGE: dark green (136B) upper surface; medium green (137C) lower surface. Leaves are 66mm (2 5/8") long x 35mm (1 3/8") wide; ovate shaped, serrulate edges, acute tips, rounded bases. Veins are very dark reddish purple (186A), stems are light red purple (185D), branches are plum (184C). PARENTAGE: 'Manfried Kleinau' x 'First Lord'. Natural trailer. Self branching. Makes good basket. Prefers overhead filtered light, cool climate. Best bloom & foliage colour in filtered light. Tested 3 years in Koningshooikt, Belgium. Waanrode 8/9/08. Distinguished by bloom colour.
Michiels 2009 BE AFS7202.

Mikey's Reward. Trailer. Single. COROLLA: quarter flared, bell shaped, turned under smooth petal margins; opens rose (65A); matures light pink (65B); 20mm (13/16") long x 25mm (1") wide. SEPALS: half up; tips recurved up, half twist counterclockwise; pale lavender (65D) tipped green upper surface; rose (65A) tipped green lower surface; 30mm(1 3/16") long x 10mm (3/16")

wide. TUBE: yellowish white (158A) striped green; short & thick; 9mm (3/16") long x 6mm (1/4") wide. STAMENS: extend 15mm (9/16") below corolla; dark rose (55A) filaments, yellowish gray (160D) anthers. PISTIL: extends 20mm (13/16") below the corolla, pale pink (49D) style; grayish yellow (160A) stigma. BUD: medium, oval. FOLIAGE: dark green (147A) upper surface; medium green (147B) lower surface. Leaves are 70mm (2 3/4") long x 45mm (1 3/4") wide, cordate shaped, serrulated edges, acute tips and rounded bases. Veins & branches are green, stems are brown. PARENTAGE: 'Pink La Campanella' x 'Loveable Rascal'. Natural trailer. Self branching. Makes good basket or standard. Heat tolerant if shaded. Prefers warm climate. Cold weather hardy to 32° F. Best bloom colour in bright light. Tested 3 years in Walthamstow, London, England. Distinguished by luminous pink blooms.
Allsop M.R. 2003 UK AFS5152.

Milan Peeters. Upright/Trailer. Double. . COROLLA is three quarter flared with turned under wavy petal margins; opens dark purple (79A), reddish purple (61B) base; matures purple (71A); 28mm (1 1/8") long x 26mm (1") wide. PETALOIDS: dark purple (79B), reddish purple (61B) base; 14mm (9/16") long x 14mm (9/16") wide. SEPALS are horizontal, tips recurved; reddish purple (64B) upper surface; reddish purple (61B) lower surface; 44mm (1 3/4") long x 14mm (9/16") wide. TUBE is magenta (63A); medium length & thickness; 22mm (7/8") long x 7mm (1/4") wide. FOLIAGE: dark green (137A) upper surface; medium green (138B) lower surface. Leaves are 67mm (2 5/8") long x 32mm (1 1/4") wide, elliptic shaped. PARENTAGE: 'Roesse Blacky' x 'Heikantenaer'. Meise 8-14-04. Distinguished by flower shape.
Michiels 2005 BE AFS5737.

Mildred Wagg. Single. COROLLA white with a touch of pink. SEPALS pale pink.
Evans 2002 UK.

Millicent. Upright. Single. COROLLA is quarter flared, square shaped, with smooth petal margins; opens purple (88B), dark rose (58C) base; matures dark purple (78A); 20mm (13/16") long x 15mm (5/8") wide. SEPALS are half up, tips recurved up; pale pink (62D) flushed dark rose (58C) upper surface, dark rose (58C) lower surface; 30mm (13/16") long x 8mm (5/16") wide. TUBE is pale pink (62D) striped dark rose

(58C), medium length and thickness; 13-15mm (1/4"-5/8") long x 4-5mm (3/16") wide. STAMENS extend 20mm (13/16") beyond the corolla; magenta (58B) filaments and anthers. PISTIL extends 45mm (1 3/4") beyond the corolla; dark rose (64C) style; magenta (58B) stigma. BUD is slender, square, pointed. FOLIAGE is yellowish green (145A) upper and lower surfaces. Leaves are 70mm (2 3/4") long x 35mm (1 3/8") wide, elliptic shaped, serrulated edges, acute tips and acute bases. Veins, stems and branches are red. PARENTAGE: Sport of 'Genii'. Small upright. Self branching. Makes good upright. Prefers full sun. Best bloom and foliage colour in bright light. Tested five years in Staffordshire, England. Distinguished by blossom colour and foliage/blossom colour combination.
Horton 2002 UK AFS4933.

Minas Morgul. Trailer. Double. COROLLA: Quarter flared; opens dark purple (79B) spotted reddish purple (61B); matures dark reddish purple (72A); 30mm (1 3/16") long x 36mm (1 7/16") wide. SEPALS: fully up, tips recurved; reddish purple (61B) upper & lower surfaces; 50mm (2") long x 15mm (9/16") wide. TUBE: reddish purple (61B); medium length & thickness; 18mm (11/16") long x 9mm (5/16") wide. FOLIAGE is medium green (137B) upper surface; medium green (137D) lower surface. PARENTAGE: 'George Gloßner' x 'Rohees Queen'.
Burkhart 2007 DE AFS6495.

Miramere. Upright. Single. COROLLA: Full flared, saucer shaped; opens & matures light greenish white (157D), lightly veined red; 19mm (3/4") long x 43mm (1 11/16") wide. SEPALS: half up, tips recurved up; magenta (58B) tipped green upper & lower surfaces; 27mm (1 1/16") long x 9mm (5/16") wide. TUBE: magenta (58B); short & thick; 6mm (1/4") long x 5mm (3/16") wide. FOLIAGE is medium green (143A) upper surface; yellowish green (144B) lower surface. PARENTAGE: 'Love's Reward' x ('Brookwood Belle' x 'Swingtime').
Chapman 2007 UK AFS6713.

Mireille Koppens. Upright/Trailer. Double. COROLLA: half flared, smooth petal margins; opens magenta (68A); matures purple (77A); 18mm (11/16") long x 9mm (5/16") wide. SEPALS: half down, tips reflexed; pink (62D) upper surface; pink (62A) lower surface; 32mm (1 1/4") long x 16mm (5/8") wide. TUBE: white (155A); long & thin; 35mm (1 3/8") long x 3mm (1/8") wide. STAMENS

extend 10mm (3/8") beyond the corolla; rose (65A) filaments; light reddish purple (73A) anthers. PISTIL extends 24mm (15/16") beyond the corolla; white (155D) style & stigma. BUD: round, long TUBE. FOLIAGE: dark green (137A) upper surface; medium green (138A) lower surface. Leaves are 69mm (2 3/4") long x 39mm (1 1/2") wide; lanceolate shaped, serrulate edges, acute tips, acute bases. Veins, stems & branches are green. PARENTAGE: 'Roesse Alba' x 'Impala'. Lax upright or stiff trailer. Makes good upright or stiff trailer. Prefers overhead filtered light, cool climate. Best bloom colour in filtered light. Tested 3 years in Knegsel, The Netherlands. Distinguished by bloom colour.
Roes 2009 NL AFS7247.

Miriam Königs. Upright/Trailer. Double. COROLLA is quarter flared with turned under smooth petal margins; opens purple (77A), dark rose (58C) base; matures reddish purple (72B); 20mm (13/16") long x 23mm (15/16") wide. PETALOIDS: One per sepal, same colour as corolla; 12mm (1/2") x 4mm (3/16"). SEPALS are half down, tips recurved; pink (55C) tipped white (155A) upper surface, dark rose (55A) lower surface; 33mm (1 5/16") long x 10mm (3/8") wide. TUBE is dark rose (55A), medium length and thickness; 31mm (1 1/4") long x 4mm (3/16") wide, 6mm (1/4") at base. STAMENS extend 12mm (1/2") beyond the corolla; dark rose (58C) filaments, orangy brown (164A) anthers. PISTIL extends 30mm (1 3/16") below the corolla; light rose (58D) style, grayish yellow (161A) stigma. BUD is ovate. FOLIAGE is dark green (137A) upper surface, medium green (138A) lower surface. Leaves are 56mm (2 3/16") long x 25mm (1") wide, lanceolate shaped, serrulated edges, acute tips and rounded bases. Veins are light green (138C), stems and branches are light reddish violet (180A). PARENTAGE: 'Berba's Inge Mariel' x unknown. Lax upright or stiff trailer. Self branching. Makes good basket. Prefers overhead filtered light. Best bloom and foliage colour in filtered light. Tested three years in Rummen, Belgium. Certificate N.B.F.K. at Meise. Distinguished by bloom colour and shape.
Ector 2002 BE AFS4896.

Miss Vendée. Upright. Single. COROLLA: Quarter flared; opens reddish purple (71B); matures magenta (71C); 20mm (3/4") long x 17mm (5/8") wide. SEPALS: horizontal, tips recurved; light pink (49C) upper surface; pink (49A) lower surface; 22mm (7/8") long x

314

7mm (1/4") wide. TUBE: light pink (49C) streaked pink (48D); medium length & thickness; 13mm (1/2") long x 7-8mm (1/4"-5/16") wide. FOLIAGE is dark green (147A) upper surface; medium green (147B) lower surface. PARENTAGE: 'Prince of Orange' x 'Kathleen Muncaster'.
Massé 2007 FR AFS6485.

Misty Grey Lady. Trailer. Double. COROLLA is three quarter flared; opens violet (85B), pale lavender (69D) base; matures light purple (75B); 27mm (1 1/16") long x 22mm (7/8") wide. PETALOIDS: violet (85B); 11mm (7/16") long x 8mm (5/16") wide. SEPALS are horizontal, tips recurved; pale lavender (69D) tipped yellowish green (145A) upper surface; pale lavender (69B) tipped yellowish green (145A) lower surface; 43mm (1 11/16") long x 15mm (9/16") wide. TUBE is white (155D) & yellowish green (145A); 17mm (5/8") long x 5mm (3/16") wide. FOLIAGE: dark green (137A) upper surface; medium green (138B) lower surface. PARENTAGE: sport of 'Lady in Grey'. Meise 9/17/05. Distinguished by bloom colour.
Michiels 2006 BE AFS6068.

Mitchel van der Putten. Upright. Single. COROLLA: quarter flared, closed shaped; smooth petal margins; opens violet (75A); matures pale purple (75C); 25mm (1") long x 26mm (1") wide. SEPALS: half down, tips reflexed; pink (62A) upper surface; rose (61D) lower surface; 32mm (1 1/4") long x 15mm (9/16") wide. TUBE: white (155A); short, medium thickness; 7mm (1/4") long x 8mm (5/16") wide. STAMENS extend 0-6mm (0-1/4") beyond the corolla; pink (62A) filaments; magenta (63A) anthers. PISTIL extends 23mm (7/8") beyond the corolla; pale pink (62D) style; light yellow (4C) stigma. BUD is pegtop shaped. FOLIAGE is dark green (137A) upper surface; medium green (137C) lower surface. Leaves are 73mm (2 7/8") long x 39mm (1 1/2") wide; lanceolate shaped, serrulate edges, acute tips, rounded bases. Veins are medium green, stems & branches are reddish. PARENTAGE: 'Ivana van Amsterdam' x 'Shelford'. Tall upright. Self branching. Makes good upright. Prefers overhead filtered light. Best bloom & foliage colour in filtered light. Tested 3 years in Haarlem, The Netherlands. Nominated by NKvF as recommendable cultivar. Distinguished by bloom shape & colour.
van der Putten 2009 NL AFS7013.

Mitsike. Trailer. Double. COROLLA: half flared; opens white (155C) & violet (76A); matures pale purple (76C); 30mm (1 3/16") long x 24mm (15/16") wide. PETALOIDS: white (155C) & violet (76A); 15mm (9/16") long x 9mm (5/16") wide. SEPALS are horizontal, tips recurved, twisted left to right; white (155C) & light rose (63D) tipped light apple green (144D) upper surface; light pink (65C) tipped light apple green (144D) lower surface; 39mm (1 1/2") long x 13mm (1/2") wide. TUBE is white (155C); 14mm (9/16") long x 6mm (1/4") wide. FOLIAGE is dark green (139A) upper surface; medium green (138A) lower surface. PARENTAGE: 'Lavender Heaven' x 'Delta's Trick'. Waanrode 7/7/2007.
Michiels 2008 BE AFS6724.

Moe Katelijne. Upright/Trailer. Single. COROLLA: quarter flared, turned under wavy petal margins; opens purple (71A), matures reddish purple (72B); 13mm (1/2") long x 19mm (3/4") wide. SEPALS: half down; tips reflexed; dark reddish purple (60B) upper surface; reddish purple (61B) lower surface; 24mm (15/16") long x 9mm (3/8") wide. TUBE: reddish purple (58A); medium length & thickness; 24mm (15/16") long x 9mm (3/8") wide. STAMENS: do not extend below the corolla; reddish purple (61B) filaments, magenta (59D) anthers. PISTIL extends 4mm (3/16") below the corolla; magenta (61C) style, pink (62C) stigma. BUD: cordate. FOLIAGE: dark green (139A) upper surface, medium green (139C) lower surface. Leaves are 41mm (1 5/8") long x 24mm (15/16") wide, ovate shaped, serrulated edges, acute tips and rounded bases. Veins are dark reddish purple (187C), stems are are dark reddish purple (187B), branches very dark purple (187A). PARENTAGE: 'WALZ Harp' x 'Regal Robe'. Lax upright or stiff trailer. Self branching. Makes good upright. Prefers overhead filtered light. Best bloom and foliage colour in filtered light. Tested 3 years Scherpenheuvel, Belgium. NBFK certificate at Meise. Distinguished by bloom shape.
Antoon 2003 BE AFS5087.

Moeder Cent. Upright/Trailer. Single. COROLLA is half flared with turned under wavy petal margins; opens reddish purple (61B), dark rose (55A) base, edged dark purple (78A); matures light reddish purple (72C), reddish purple (61B) base; 14mm (9/16") long x 18mm (11/16") wide. SEPALS are horizontal, tips reflexed; light pink (49B), tipped light yellow green (150B) upper surface; dark rose (55A), tipped light yellow

315

green (150B) lower surface; 24mm (15/16")
long x 12mm (1/2") wide. TUBE is light pink
(49B); long & thin; 22mm (7/8") long x 3mm
(1/8") wide. FOLIAGE: dark green (137A)
upper surface; medium green (137C) lower
surface. Leaves are 68mm (2 11/16") long x
37mm (1 7/16") wide, ovate shaped.
PARENTAGE: 'WALZ Harp' x 'Blue Rebel'.
Meise 8-14-04. Distinguished by flower
colour combination.
Geerts L. 2005 BE AFS5726.

Moeke Turbo. Upright/Trailer. Single.
COROLLA is half flared; opens dark reddish
purple (64A); matures reddish purple (61B);
25mm (1") long x 22mm (7/8") wide. SEPALS
are horizontal, tips reflexed; magenta (63A)
upper surface, and red (52A) lower surface;
37mm (1 7/16") long x 9mm (5/16") wide.
TUBE is dark rose (58C); medium length &
thickness; 14mm (9/16") long x 6mm (1/4")
wide. FOLIAGE is dark green (137A) upper
surface; medium green (138B) lower surface.
PARENTAGE: 'Rohees New Millenium' x
'Onbekend'.
Willems 2007 BE AFS6422.

Moemoe Angele. Trailer. Double. COROLLA:
three quarter flared; opens purple (71A);
matures dark reddish purple (70A); 25mm
(1") long x 22mm (7/8") wide. PETALOIDS:
dark reddish purple (72A); 17mm (5/8") long
x 8mm (5/16") wide. SEPALS are fully up,
tips recurved; light purple (75B) upper
surface and rose (68B) lower surface; 30mm
(1 3/16") long x 9mm (5/16") wide. TUBE is
pale purple (75C); medium length &
thickness; 13mm (1/2") long x 5mm (3/16")
wide. FOLIAGE is dark green (136B) upper
surface; medium green (138B) lower surface.
PARENTAGE: 'Leon Pauwels' x 'Monique
Sleidernik'. Meise 9/16/2006: Outstanding.
Michiels 2007 BE AFS6528.

Moi Non Plus. Upright. Single. COROLLA:
unflared, compact, smooth petal margins;
opens purple (83A); matures dark reddish
purple (72A); 17mm (5/8") long x 10mm
(3/8") wide. SEPALS: half up, tips recurved
up; magenta (63A) upper & lower surfaces;
40mm (1 9/16") long x 8mm (5/16") wide.
TUBE: magenta (63A); short, medium
thickness; 12mm (7/16") long x 6mm (1/4")
wide. STAMENS extend 15mm (9/16")
beyond the corolla; magenta (63A) filaments;
purple (71A) anthers. PISTIL extends 34mm
(1 3/8") beyond the corolla; magenta (63A)
style; magenta (63B) stigma. BUD: elongated.
FOLIAGE: medium green (137B) upper
surface; yellowish green (146B) lower

surface. Leaves are 85mm (3 3/8") long x
35mm (1 3/8") wide; elliptic shaped, serrate
edges, acute tips, rounded bases. Veins are
red, stems are red, branches are reddish brown.
PARENTAGE: 'Earrebarre' x F. *regia ssp.
serrae hoya*. Medium upright. Makes good
upright or standard. Prefers full sun, warm
climate. Heat tolerant if shaded. Cold
weather hardy to -15° C (6° F). Best bloom &
foliage colour in bright light. Tested 6 years
in Bavaria, Southern Germany.
Distinguished by flower colour & shape.
Burkhart 2009 DE AFS7096.

Molenkerk. Upright. Semi Double.
COROLLA is quarter flared; opens white
(155A); matures white (155B); 25mm (1")
long x 29mm (1 1/8") wide. SEPALS are half
up, tips recurved up; rose (52C) upper &
lower surfaces; 44mm (1 3/4") long x 17mm
(11/16") wide. TUBE is rose (52B); 18mm
(11/16") long x 6mm (1/4") wide. FOLIAGE:
dark green (137A) upper surface; grayish
green (191A) lower surface. PARENTAGE:
('Prosperity' x 'Dollar Princess') x ('Prosperity'
x 'Dollar Princess'). Distinguished by
unusually large red & white flowers.
de Boer 2006 NL AFS5985.

Molly Chatfield. Upright. Single. COROLLA
white veined pink at base; corolla is half
flared. SEPALS white veined pink on the
upper and lower surfaces; sepals are half up
with recurved tips. TUBE white, veined pink.
PARENTAGE Seedling of 'Harry Gray'. This
cultivar has found to be hardy in Derbyshire
for the past 4years.
Chatfield 2008 UK BFS0090.

Monica Scott. Upright. Single. COROLLA
opens violet, lighter at base with red veining,
matures to violet pink; corolla is quarter
flared and is 15mm long x 26mm wide.
SEPALS neyron rose on the upper and lower
surfaces; sepals are horizontally held with
recurved tips and are 23mm long x 8mm
wide. TUBE neyron rose and is 6mm long x
5mm wide. PARENTAGE 'Breeders Delight' x
'Sophie Louise'.
Waving 2006 UK BFS0035.

Monica Vanbets. Upright/Trailer. Double.
COROLLA: three quarter flared, turned
under wavy petal margins; opens purple
(N78A) edged purple (79C); matures dark
rose (67C) edged reddish purple (70B); 21mm
(13/16") long x 21mm (13/16") wide.
PETALOIDS: Same colour as corolla; 11mm
(7/16") long x 8mm (5/16") wide. SEPALS:
horizontal, tips recurved, twisted left to right;

white (155C) tipped light apple green (145C) upper surface; pink (52D) tipped light apple green (145C) lower surface; 34mm (1 3/8") long x 16mm (5/8") wide. TUBE: white (155B); medium length & thickness; 15mm (9/16") long x 5mm (3/16") wide. STAMENS extend 4mm (1/8") beyond the corolla; magenta (63B) filaments; light reddish purple (73A) anthers. PISTIL extends 18mm (11/16") beyond the corolla; pink (62A) style; pale yellow (2D) stigma. BUD: globular. FOLIAGE: dark green (136B) upper surface; medium green (137C) lower surface. Leaves are 72mm (2 7/8") long x 31mm (1 1/4") wide; elliptic shaped, serrate edges, acute tips, rounded bases. Veins are dark reddish purple (187B), stems are dark red purple (187D), branches are plum (184B). PARENTAGE: 'Manfried Kleinau' x 'Jan Vander Kuylen'. Lax upright or stiff trailer. Self branching. Makes good basket. Prefers overhead filtered light, cool climate. Best bloom & foliage colour in filtered light. Tested 3 years in Koningshooikt, Belgium. Waanrode 9/20/08. Distinguished by bloom colour combination.
Michiels 2009 BE AFS7203.

Monika Wandeler. Upright. Single. COROLLA is quarter flared with turned under smooth petal margins; opens reddish purple (67A), white (155B) base; matures dark rose (67C); 26mm (1") long x 39 mm (1 9/16") wide. SEPALS are half up, tips recurved up; white (155B) tipped rose (52B) upper surface, white (155D) tipped rose (52B) lower surface; 32mm (1 1/4") long x 12mm (1/2") wide. TUBE is light yellow (4C), ovate shaped, medium length and thick; 13mm (1/2") long x 8mm (5/16") wide. STAMENS extend 12mm (1/2") beyond the corolla; dark rose (58C) filaments, dark reddish purple (59A) anthers. PISTIL extends 37mm (1 7/16") below the corolla; pink (62C) style, light yellow (1C) stigma. BUD is ovate, pointed. FOLIAGE is dark green (137A) upper surface, medium green (137D) lower surface. Leaves are 92mm (3 5/8") long x 48mm (1 7/8") wide, ovate shaped, serrulated edges, acute tips and rounded bases. Veins, stems and branches are medium green (139C). PARENTAGE: 'Margrit Willimann' x unknown. Medium upright. Self branching. Makes good basket or upright. Prefers overhead filtered light. Best bloom and foliage colour in filtered light. Tested three years in Rummen, Belgium. Certificate N.B.F.K. at Meise. Distinguished by rose sepal tips and colour contrast of blooms/leaves.

Ector 2002 BE AFS4897.

Monique Comperen. Upright. Double. COROLLA: three quarter flared, smooth petal margins; opens dark purple (79A); matures dark reddish purple (59A); 25mm (1") long x 28mm (1 1/8") wide. SEPALS: horizontal; tips reflexed; dark reddish purple (64A) upper surface; dark reddish purple (61A) lower surface; 34mm (1 5/16") long x 15mm (9/16") wide. TUBE: dark reddish purple (64A); medium length & thickness; 20mm (13/16") long x 8mm (5/16") wide. STAMENS: extend 35mm (1 3/8") below corolla; reddish purple (71B) filaments & anthers. PISTIL: extends 43mm (1 11/16") below the corolla; reddish purple (71B) style, magenta (61C) stigma. BUD: cordate. FOLIAGE: dark green (137A) upper surface; medium green (138B) lower surface. Leaves are 74mm (2 15/16") long x 40mm (1 9/16") wide, ovate shaped, serrulated edges, acute tips and rounded bases. Veins, stems & branches are red. PARENTAGE: 'Hertogen van Brabant' x 'Phenomenal'. Medium upright. Makes good upright or standard. Prefers overhead filtered light and cool climate. Best bloom and foliage colour in filtered light. Tested 4 years in Diessen, The Netherlands. Distinguished by bloom colour.
Comperen 2003 NL AFS5265.

Monique Diremszian. Upright. Single. COROLLA: quarter flared; smooth petal margins; opens & matures white (155C),veined rose (50B); 24mm (15/16") long x 19mm (3/4") wide. SEPALS: horizontal, tips recurved; red (45B) upper surface; red (45D) lower surface; 33mm (1 1/4") long x 9mm (5/16") wide. TUBE: red (45B); medium length & thickness; 18mm (11/16") long x 4mm (1/8") wide. STAMENS extend 6-9mm (1/4-5/16") beyond the corolla; red (45C) filaments; dark red (185A) anthers. PISTIL extends 28-32mm (1 1/8-1 1/4") beyond the corolla; rose (47C) style; light pink (49B) stigma. BUD is ovate. FOLIAGE is dark green (147A) upper surface; yellowish green (146B) lower surface. Leaves are 76 to 96mm (3 to 3 3/16") long x 33-52mm (1 1/4 to 2 1/16") wide; ovate shaped, serrulate edges, acute tips, rounded bases. Veins are yellowish green, stems & branches are light brown. PARENTAGE: 'Port Océane' x 'Nancy Lou'. Medium upright. Makes good upright or standard. Prefers overhead filtered light & cool climate. Cold weather hardy to -7° C (20° F). Tested 4 years in Pornic & Luçon, France. Distinguished by bloom colour & shape.

Massé 2009 FR AFS6994.

Monique Krekels. Upright/Trailer. Double. COROLLA: half flared, smooth petal margins; opens purple (77A); matures dark rose (64C); 28mm (1 1/8") long x 26mm (1") wide. SEPALS: fully up; tips recurved; magenta (58B) upper & lower surfaces;47mm (1 7/8") long x 17mm (11/16") wide. TUBE: magenta (58A); medium length & thickness; 16mm (5/8") long x 7mm (1/4") wide. STAMENS: extend 15mm (9/16") below corolla; reddish purple (60D) filaments, purple (77A) anthers. PISTIL: extends 28mm (1 1/8") below the corolla; light rose (58D) style; light yellow (4D) stigma. BUD: ovate. FOLIAGE: medium green (137B) upper surface; medium green (137B) lower surface. Leaves are 57mm (2 1/4") long x 32mm (1 1/4") wide, ovate shaped, serrulated edges, acute tips and obtuse bases. Veins, stems & branches are red. PARENTAGE: 'Bicentennial' x 'Parasol'. Lax upright or stiff trailer. Makes good stiff trailer. Prefers overhead filtered light and cool climate. Best bloom and foliage colour in filtered light. Tested 4 years in Reusel, The Netherlands. Distinguished by bloom colour. van Eijk 2003 NL AFS5254.

Monique Luijten. Upright/Trailer. Double. COROLLA: half flared, smooth petal margins; opens & matures white (155D); 24mm (15/16") long x 26mm (1") wide. SEPALS: horizontal, tips recurved; white (155D) upper & lower surfaces; 39mm (1 1/2") long x 20mm (3/4") wide. TUBE: white (155D); medium length & thickness; 26mm (1") long x 6mm (1/4") wide. STAMENS extend 10mm (3/8") beyond the corolla; rose (65A) filaments; dark reddish purple (59A) anthers. PISTIL extends 39mm (1 1/2") beyond the corolla; white (155A) style; pale yellow (2D) stigma. BUD is ovate, long TUBE. FOLIAGE is dark green (137A) upper surface; medium green (138B) lower surface. Leaves are 58mm (2 5/16") long x 32mm (1 1/4") wide; ovate shaped, serrulate edges, acute tips, obtuse bases. Veins, stems & branches are red. PARENTAGE: 'Sofie Michiels' x 'Silver Dawn'. Lax upright or stiff trailer. Makes good stiff trailer. Prefers overhead filtered light, cool climate. Best bloom colour in filtered light. Tested 3 years in Veldhoven, The Netherlands. Distinguished by bloom & foliage combination. Buiting 2009 NL AFS6935.

Monique Reemers. Upright. Semi Double. COROLLA: half flared; opens magenta (68A) & light reddish purple (73A); matures dark rose (64C); 21mm (13/16") long x 20mm (3/4") wide. SEPALS are horizontal, tips reflexed; dark rose (54A) upper surface; dark rose (55A) lower surface; 40mm (1 9/16") long x 17mm (5/8") wide. TUBE is pale pink (56D) striped dark rose (54A); square; 24mm (15/16") long x 11mm (7/16") wide. FOLIAGE is dark green (137A) upper surface; medium green (138B) lower surface. PARENTAGE: 'Walz Harp' x unknown. Waanrode 9/15/2007. Geerts L. 2008 BE AFS6728.

Monique Sleiderink. Upright/Trailer. Double. COROLLA is three quarter flared with smooth petal margins; opens purple (90B), matures violet (84A); 26mm (1") long x 30mm (1 3/16") wide. SEPALS are horizontal, tips recurved; reddish pink (62A) upper and lower surfaces; 47mm (1 7/8") long x 20mm (13/16") wide. TUBE is pale pink (62D), proportionately medium length and thickness; 18mm (11/16") long x 6mm (1/4") wide. STAMENS extend 14mm (9/16") below the corolla; violet (75A) filaments; magenta (63B) anthers. PISTIL extends 36mm (1 7/16") below the corolla; pale purple (75D) style; cream (11D) stigma. BUD is ovate. FOLIAGE is dark green (137A) on upper surface and medium green (138A) on lower surface. Leaves are 70mm (2 3/4") long x 32mm (1 1/4") wide, lanceolate shaped, smooth edges, acute tips and obtuse bases. Veins, stems and branches are green. PARENTAGE: ('Annabel' x 'Annabel') x 'Lechlade Rocket'. Lax upright or stiff trailer. Makes good stiff trailer. Prefers overhead filtered light and cool climate. Best bloom colour in filtered light. Tested four years in Knegsel, The Netherlands. Distinguished by bloom colour. Roes 2003 NL AFS5058.

Monrose. Upright. Single. COROLLA: unflared; smooth petal margins; opens red (44A) edged & blushed dark blue (95B); matures dark red (47A) edged & blushed dark blue (95B); 18mm (11/16") long x 18mm (11/16") wide. SEPALS: full down, tips reflexed; dark red (46A) upper & lower surfaces; 20mm (3/4") long x 8mm (5/16") wide. TUBE: dark red (46A); long, medium thickness; 58mm (2 5/16") long x 8mm (5/16") wide. STAMENS extend 7mm(1/4") beyond the corolla; red (44A) filaments; yellow orange (17B) anthers. PISTIL extends 20mm (3/4") beyond the corolla; pink (48C) style; dark red (46A) stigma. BUD: long, small, triphylla type. FOLIAGE: dark green (137A) upper surface; light olive green (148B) lower surface. Leaves are 80mm (3 3/16") long x 45mm (1 3/4") wide; pubescent on upper surface; ovate shaped, serrulate edges, acute tips, rounded bases. Veins, stems & branches are dark reddish purple (59A). PARENTAGE: 'Thalia' (Turner) x 'Goldings Perle'. Medium upright. Self branching. Makes good upright or standard. Prefers overhead filtered light. Best bloom & foliage colour in filtered light. Tested 3 years in Stadskanaal, The Netherlands. Distinguished by triphylla features with blue on the corolla. Koerts T. 2009 NL AFS7048.

Moppie. Upright. Single. COROLLA: quarter flared, rounded shape, turned under smooth petal margins; opens & matures orange (41B), lighter base; 14mm (9/16") long x 13mm (1/2") wide. SEPALS: half down; tips reflexed; cream (158D) tipped light apple green (144D) upper surface; cream (158D) lower surface; 20mm (13/16") long x 8mm (5/16") wide. TUBE: cream (158D); medium length, thick; 16mm (5/8") long x 8mm (5/16") wide. STAMENS: extend 7mm (1/4") below corolla; pale pink (56D) filaments; pale yellow (8D) anthers. PISTIL: extends 20mm (13/16") below the corolla; white (155D) style; yellowish white (4D) stigma. BUD: oblong. FOLIAGE: dark green (147A) upper surface; medium green (147B) lower surface. Leaves are 43mm (1 11/16") long x 40mm (1 9/16") wide, ovate shaped, serrulated edges, obtuse tips and cordate bases. Veins are light yellow green, stems & branches are reddish light yellow green. PARENTAGE: 'Eleanor Leytham' x unknown. Medium upright. Self branching. Makes good upright or standard. Prefers full sun. Best bloom and foliage colour in bright light. Tested 4 years in Wognum, The Netherlands. Distinguished by bloom colour.
Dekker 2003 NL AFS5355.

Morton Martianette. COROLLA pink. SEPALS pink. TUBE pink. PARENTAGE 'F. nana' x 'Lechlade Martianess'.
Muncaster 2005 UK.

Morton Splendide. Upright. Single. COROLLA bright orange. SEPALS red tipped green. TUBE dark red. PARENTAGE 'F. magdalenae' x 'F. Splendens'.
Muncaster 2006 UK.

Most Königin. Upright. Single. COROLLA: unflared, square shaped, smooth petal margins; opens & matures red (50A); 15mm (9/16") long, 15mm (9/16") wide. SEPALS: half down; tips reflexed; coral (39B), lighter

to the tips, tipped green, upper surface; coral (39B) creped lower surface; 22mm (7/8") long x 11mm (7/16") wide. TUBE: light pink (38D) striped coral (39D); medium length & thickness; 17mm (11/16") long x 8mm (5/16") wide. STAMENS: extend 3mm (1/8") below corolla; red (50A) filaments; dark reddish purple (60A) anthers. PISTIL: extends 20mm (13/16") below the corolla; pink (50D) style; yellow (12B) stigma. BUD: drop shaped. FOLIAGE: medium green (138A) upper surface; medium green (138B) lower surface. Leaves are 70mm (2 3/4") long x 44mm (1 3/4") wide, ovate shaped, serrulated edges, obtuse tips and rounded bases. Green veins & branches; grayed orange stems. PARENTAGE: 'Nici's Findling' x 'Golden Glow'. Medium upright. Self branching. Makes good upright. Heat tolerant if shaded. Best bloom and foliage colour in filtered light. Tested 5 years in Amstetten, Austria. Distinguished by bloom colour combination & shape. Note: The Amstetten area is well known for its apple plantations and cider. Many related events are held each year with the election of a "Mostkönigin" or "Cider Queen".
Gindl 2004 AT AFS5627.

Mostarichi. Upright. Single. COROLLA: unflared, smooth petal margins; opens & matures plum (184C); 30mm (1 3/16") long, 15mm (9/16") wide. SEPALS: half up; tips recurved up; rose (63C) upper surface; light rose (63D) lower surface; 50mm (2") long x 10mm (3/8") wide. TUBE: light rose (63D) striped magenta (63A); medium length & thickness; 40mm (1 9/16") long x 7mm (1/4") wide. STAMENS: extend 20mm (13/16") below corolla; reddish orange (43B) filaments; dark reddish purple (59A) anthers. PISTIL: does not extend below the corolla; light rose (43D) style; pale yellow (12D) stigma. BUD: longish. FOLIAGE: dark green (137A) upper surface; medium green (137C) lower surface. Leaves are 50mm (2") long x 15mm (9/16") wide, ovate shaped, serrated edges, acute tips and rounded bases. Green veins & branches; plum stems. PARENTAGE: 'Checkerboard' x 'Golden Glow'. Tall upright. Makes good standard. Prefers overhead filtered light. Best bloom and foliage colour in filtered light. Tested 3 years in Amstetten, Austria. Distinguished by bloom colour combination & shape.
Gindl 2004 AT AFS5628.

Mounts Bay. Upright/Trailer. Single. COROLLA: Quarter flared, bell shaped; opens pale purple (75C) streaked rose (68C);

matures light purple (75B); 50mm (2") long x 20mm (3/4") wide. SEPALS: half down, tips recurved; pale tan (162D) tipped yellowish green (149A) upper surface; rose (68C) tipped yellowish green(149A) lower surface; 25mm (1") long x 12mm (7/16") wide. TUBE: light greenish white (157C); short & thin; 8mm (5/16") long x 4mm (1/8") wide. FOLIAGE is medium green (147B) upper surface; dark green (139A) lower surface. PARENTAGE: 'Lady Patricia Mountbatten' x 'Nathan Brown'.
Negus 2007 UK AFS6502.

Mrs. Kathleen Bradshaw. Upright. Single. COROLLA opens purple, matures to reddish purple; corolla is half flared and is 20mm long x 22mm wide. SEPALS red on the upper and lower surfaces; sepals are fully recurved with recurved tips and are 30mm long x 13mm wide. TUBE red and is 13mm long x 7mm wide. PARENTAGE found seedling. This cultivar is found to be hardy in Mid Cheshire.
Bradshaw K. 2005 UK BFS0022.

Mrs. Savage. Upright/Trailer. Single. COROLLA is three quarter flared with wavy petal margins; opens and matures pale pink (62D) lightly veined pink (62A); 22mm (7/8") long x 40mm (1 9/16") wide. PETALOIDS are same colour as corolla; 13mm (1/2") long x 13mm (1/2") wide. SEPALS are half up, tips recurved up; pink (62A) tipped green upper and lower surfaces; 37mm (1 7/16") long x 18mm (11/16") wide. TUBE is pale pink (62D), medium length and thickness; 13mm (1/2") long x 7mm (1/4") wide. STAMENS extend 18mm (11/16") below the corolla; pink (62A) filaments, magenta (63B) anthers. PISTIL extends 26mm (1") below the corolla; pale pink (62D) style, white (155A) stigma. BUD is ovate. FOLIAGE is medium green (137A) upper surface, medium green (138B) lower surface. Leaves are 75mm (2 15/16") long x 40mm (1 9/16") wide, lanceolate shaped, serrated edges, acute tips and rounded bases. Veins are plum (185B), stems are plum (185C) and branches are plum (184B). PARENTAGE: "Found" seedling. Lax upright or stiff trailer. Makes good trellis. Prefers overhead filtered light. Heat tolerant if shaded. Best bloom colour in filtered light. Tested three years in Worthing, Sussex, England. Distinguished by blossom shape.
Hobbs 2002 UK AFS4844.

Murray's Mist. Upright. Double. COROLLA is compact, slightly flared, with smooth petal margins; opens light purple (70C) with fine

cerise lines, matures reddish purple (70B); 25mm (1") long x 32mm (1 1/4") wide. PETALOIDS are same colour as corolla; 10mm (3/8") long x 13mm (1/2") wide. SEPALS are fully up, tips recurved, twisted clockwise; magenta (57A) upper surface, magenta (57B) lower surface; 48mm (1 7/8") long x 19mm (3/4") wide. TUBE is light pink (65B) with magenta (57A) stripes, proportionately short and thick; 6mm (1/4") long x 3mm (1/8") wide. STAMENS extend 25mm (1") below the corolla; magenta (68A) filaments and brown (200C) anthers. PISTIL extends 38mm (1 1/2") below the corolla; rose (67D) style and brown (200C) stigma. BUD is ovate. FOLIAGE is medium green (139C) on upper and lower surfaces. Leaves are 83mm (3 1/4") long x 57mm (2 1/4") wide, ovate shaped, serrulated edges, acute tips and rounded bases. Veins are red in center, branching veins green; stems and branches are reddish brown. PARENTAGE: Sport of 'Brulingën'. Medium upright. Makes good upright or standard. Heat tolerant if shaded. Cold weather hardy to 30°F. Best bloom colour in filtered light. Tested four years in Poole, Dorset, England. Distinguished by profuse and compact blooms.
Swinbank 2002 UK AFS4808.

Murru's Pierre Marie. Upright. Double. COROLLA violet. SEPALS white. TUBE white.
Murru 2002.

Muskham Melody. Upright. Single. COROLLA opens mauve with white base, matures slightly darker mauve; corolla is three quarter flared. SEPALS light pink edges deeper tipped light green on the upper surface, mauve on the lower surface; sepals are fully up, edges curl upwards, slightly twisted with recurved tips. TUBE light pink. PARENATGE 'Lady Isobel Barnet' x 'Unknown'. This cultivar has proven to be hardy in Newark, Nottinghamshire for the past 8 years.
Raynor 2008 UK BFS0073.

My Belinda. Upright. Single. COROLLA pale lilac, lighter at base, veined rose; corolla is fully flared. SEPALS white, striped rose on the upper surface, rose on the lower surface, tipped green; SEPALS are fully up with recurved tips. TUBE white striped rose. PARENTAGE 'Adelaide Hoodless' x 'Texas Longhorn'.
Allen 2009 UK BFS0109.

My Birthstone. Trailer. Single. COROLLA is half flared, smooth petal margins; opens purple (81A), matures reddish purple (74A); 25mm (1") long x 14mm (9/16") wide. SEPALS are twisted, curled when mature; fully up; tips recurved; white (155A) tipped green upper surface and white (155A) striped light rose (58D) lower surface; 44mm (1 3/4") long x 9mm (3/8") wide. TUBE white (155A), medium length & thickness; 13mm (1/2") long x 7mm (1/4") wide. STAMENS extend 9mm (3/8") below the corolla; reddish purple (70B) filaments, purple (81A) anthers. PISTIL extends 32mm (1 1/4") below the corolla; white (155B) style & stigma. BUD is long & slender. FOLIAGE is orangish brown (174A) upper surface and orangy brown (174B) lower surface. Leaves are 70mm (2 3/4") long x 38mm (1 1/2") wide, ovate shaped, serrated edges, acute tips and rounded bases. Veins are yellow green, stems and branches are dark reddish purple (187B). PARENTAGE: 'Moonglow' x 'My Blue Heaven'. Natural trailer. Self branching. Makes good basket. Prefers overhead filtered light. Best bloom colour in filtered light. Tested 4 years in Kent, Washington, USA. Distinguished by sepal shape and sepal colour, resembling an amethyst gem.
Pearson 2003 USA AFS5068.

My Kath. Upright. Double. COROLLA opens voilet, matures to reddish purple; corolla has no flare and is 14mm x 14mm wide. SEPALS rosy red on the upper surface, rosy red on the lower surface; sepals are half up with recurved tips and are 24mm long x 8mm wide. TUBE rosy red and is 9mm long x 5mm wide. PARENTAGE 'Caradella' x Unknown.
Joiner C. 2007 UK BFS0043.

My Little Gem. Single. COROLLA dark aubergine. SEPALS red.
Reynolds G. 2007 UK.

My Little Ruby. Upright. Single. COROLLA pale peachy pink with bright pink edging. SEPALS peachy pink. TUBE peachy pink.
Reynolds G. 2009 UK.

My Little Star. Upright. Single. COROLLA opens and matures to white; corolla is none flared and is 16mm long x 9mm wide. SEPALS are pink on the upper surface, pale pink tipped green on the lower surface; sepals are half up with recurved tips and are 20mm long x 7mm wide. TUBE is lime green and is 5mm long x 4mm wide. PARENTAGE 'Twinny' x 'Sophie Louise'.

Reynolds G. 2004 UK BFS0009.

My Little Treasure. Single. COROLLA blue shading to white, maturing light mauve. SEPALS white. TUBE white.
Reynolds G. 2007 UK.

My Marion. Single. COROLLA red striped rose matures red orange striped dark red. SEPALS pink tipped green. TUBE pink.
Tibbatts 2006 UK.

My Pat. Trailer. Single. COROLLA pale blue maturing lilac. SEPALS pale pink. TUBE pale pink.
Chatters 2006 UK.

Myrtle. Upright. Single. COROLLA: half flared; opens purple (83B); matures red (43A); 15mm (9/16") long x 15mm (9/16") wide. SEPALS: half down, tips recurved; red (45C) upper & lower surfaces; 20mm (3/4") long x 10mm (3/8") wide. TUBE: red (45C); 10mm (3/8") long x 5mm (3/16") wide. FOLIAGE is medium green (138A) upper surface; medium green (138B) lower surface. PARENTAGE: 'Aloha' x 'Brookwood Belle'.
Smith R. 2008 UK AFS6820.

Mystical Rose. Upright. Single. COROLLA lavender. SEPALS pink.
Ainsworth 2004 UK.

Nana Christine Brown. Upright/Trailer. Single. COROLLA: three quarter flared, skirt-like, turned under smooth petal margins; opens dark purple (78A); matures dark reddish purple (72A) veined red; 20mm (13/16") long x 40mm (1 9/16") wide. SEPALS: half up; tips reflexed up; rose (63C) striped magenta (68A) upper surface; magenta (68A) tipped green lower surface; 35mm(1 3/8") long x 14mm (9/16") wide. TUBE: rose (63C); medium length & thick; 15mm (9/16") long x 8mm (5/16") wide. STAMENS: extend 15mm (9/16") below corolla; reddish purple (64B) filaments, purple (77A) anthers. PISTIL: extends 40mm (1 9/16") below the corolla, dark rose (67C) style; yellowish white (158A) stigma. BUD: medium, round. FOLIAGE: medium green (146A) upper surface; yellowish green (146B) lower surface. Leaves are 80mm (3 1/8") long x 50mm (2") wide, cordate shaped, serrulated edges, acute tips and cordate bases. Veins are green, stems are brown& branches are red. PARENTAGE: 'Rolt's Ruby' x 'Cheeky Chantelle'. Lax upright or stiff trailer. Self branching. Makes good basket or standard. Heat tolerant if shaded. Prefers warm

321

climate. Cold weather hardy to 32° F. Best bloom colour in bright light. Tested 5 years in Walthamstow, London, England. Distinguished by bloom shape and colour. Allsop M.R. 2003 UK AFS5155.

Naomi Eggli. Trailer. Single. COROLLA: quarter flared, turned under smooth petal margins; opens & matures dark purple (78A), dark rose (58C) at base; 21mm (13/16") long x 18mm (11/16") wide. SEPALS: fully up; tips recurved; white (155B) edged magenta (57A), tipped light yellow green (150A) upper surface; magenta (58B) lower surface; 36mm (1 7/16") long x 6mm (1/4") wide. TUBE: red (46B); medium length & thickness; 16mm (5/8") long x 4mm (3/16") wide. STAMENS: extend 11mm (7/16") below the corolla; reddish purple (61B) filaments, grayish yellow (161A) anthers. PISTIL extends 8mm (5/16") below the corolla; magenta (58B) style, orange (29A) stigma. BUD: elongated, pointed. FOLIAGE: dark green (137A) upper surface; medium green (138B) lower surface. Leaves are 40mm (1 9/16") long x 19mm (3/4") wide, elliptic shaped, smooth edges, acute tips and acute bases. Veins, stems & branches are dark reddish purple (59A). PARENTAGE: 'Rosea' x unknown. Natural trailer. Self branching. Makes good basket. Prefers overhead filtered light. Best bloom and foliage colour in filtered light. Tested 3 years in Rummen, Belgium. NBFK certificate at Meise. Distinguished by bloom colour. Ector 2003 BE AFS5116.

Natasha Lynn. Upright. Double. COROLLA opens violet blue suffused red/pink at base, matures to a pink shade of violet; corolla opens no flare, matures to quarter flared. SEPALS dark rose at base suffusing to white, tipped green on the upper surface, rose at base suffusing to white tipped green on the lower surface; SEPALS are half up with recurved tips. TUBE rose striped darker. PARENTAGE 'Lynne Patricia' x 'Lynne Patricia'.
Swaby 2009 UK BFS0125.

Naturpark Solktaler. Upright/trailer. Single. COROLLA bishop's violet (81b), veined pale currant red (46d). SEPALS pale currant red (46d), tipped green on the upper and lower surfaces; SEPALS are horizontally held with recurved tips. TUBE light currant red (46c). PARENTAGE 'Berba's Kirsten' x 'Bert's Whisky'.
Klemm 2009 AT BFS0131.

Nebe Mentha. Trailer. Single. COROLLA: quarter flared, turned under smooth petal margins; opens dark red (53A), reddish purple (58A) base; matures magenta (59C); 21mm (13/16") long x 19mm (3/4") wide. SEPALS: horizontal; tips recurved; red (53B) upper surface; dark red (53A) lower surface; 23mm (7/8") long x 10mm (3/8") wide. TUBE: red (53B); medium length & thickness; 14mm (9/16") long x 4mm (3/16") wide. STAMENS: extend 14mm (9/16") below corolla; magenta (61C) filaments; dark purple (79B) anthers. PISTIL: extends 17mm (11/16") below the corolla; magenta (61C) style; purple (71A) stigma. BUD: sack shaped. FOLIAGE: dark green (139A) upper surface, medium green (139C) lower surface. Leaves are 32mm (1 1/4") long x 19mm (3/4") wide, ovate shaped, serrulated edges, acute tips and rounded bases. Veins are light red purple (185D); stems are plum (185B); branches are very dark purple (187A). PARENTAGE: 'Bicentennial' x unknown. Natural trailer. Self branching. Makes good basket. Prefers overhead filtered light and cool climate. Best bloom and foliage colour in filtered light. Tested 3 years in Werm, Belgium. Award at Meise, 5/7/03. Distinguished by bloom shape.
Wagemans 2004 BE AFS5411.

Nectarine. Upright. Single. COROLLA is quarter flared, trumpet shaped, with wavy margins; opens peach (38B), matures pink (52D); 7mm (1/4") long x 8mm (5/16") wide. SEPALS are horizontal, tips recurved; rose (48B) upper surface, pink (52D) lower surface; 10mm (3/8") long x 5mm (3/16") wide. TUBE is rose (52B), dark base, long with medium thickness, trumpet shaped; 20mm (13/16") long x 7mm (1/4") wide. STAMENS extend 1mm (1/16") beyond the corolla; light pink (38C) filaments and cream (158C) anthers. PISTIL extends 4mm (3/16") below the corolla; pink (48C) style, light grayish rose (181D) stigma. BUD is long TUBEd, pear shaped. FOLIAGE is dark green (147A) tinted red upper surface, medium green (147B) tinted red lower surface. Leaves are 108mm (4 1/4") long x 54mm (2 1/8") wide, elliptic shaped, serrated edges, acute tips and acute bases. Veins, stems and branches are dark purple red. PARENTAGE: 'Panache' x 'Panache'. Medium upright. Self branching. Makes good upright. Prefers overhead filtered light. Heat tolerant if shaded. Best bloom colour in filtered light. Best foliage colour in bright light. Tested four years in Lisse, Holland. Distinguished by

branching panicles of erect flowers with unique shape and colour.
de Graaff 2002 NL AFS4882.

Nel Tamerus. Upright/Trailer. Semi Double. COROLLA is half flared with smooth petal margins; opens and matures light purple (75B); 17mm (11/16") long x 17mm (11/16") wide. SEPALS are horizontal, tips recurved; dark reddish purple (70A) upper surface; reddish purple (71B) lower surface; 22mm (7/8") long x 9mm (3/8") wide. TUBE is dark reddish purple (70A); medium length and thickness; 14mm (9/16") long x 5mm (3/16") thick. STAMENS extend 9mm (3/8") beyond the corolla; purple (77A) filaments, pale purple (75D) anthers. PISTIL extends 28mm (1 1/8") beyond the corolla; purple (77A) style, pale purple (75D) stigma. BUD is ovate, pointed. FOLIAGE is dark green (137A) upper surface, medium green (138B) lower surface. Leaves are 47mm (1 7/8") long x 28mm (1 1/8") wide, ovate shaped, serrated edges, acute tips and obtuse bases. Veins are green, stems and branches are red. PARENTAGE: ('Annabel' x 'Annabel') x 'Rohees Metalla'. Lax upright or stiff trailer. Makes good stiff trailer. Prefers overhead filtered light and cool climate. Best bloom colour in filtered light. Tested four years in Duizel, The Netherlands. Distinguished by bloom colour.
Tamerus 2002 NL AFS4997.

Nel van Hoof. Upright. Semi Double. COROLLA is three quarter flared with smooth petal margins; opens purple (71A) and matures dark reddish purple (60A); 23mm (15/16") long x 27mm (1 1/16") wide. SEPALS are half up, tips reflexed up; reddish purple (61B) upper and lower surfaces; 27mm (1 1/16) long x 15mm (5/8") wide. TUBE is reddish purple (61B), medium length and thickness; 12mm (1/2") long x 7mm (1/4") wide. STAMENS extend 11mm (7/16") below the corolla; light reddish purple (66C) filaments and dark reddish purple (60A) anthers. PISTIL extends 30mm (1 3/16") below the corolla; light reddish purple (66C) style and reddish purple (60D) stigma. BUD is round, pointed. FOLIAGE is dark green (137A) on upper surface and medium green (138A) on lower surface. Leaves are 60mm (2 3/8") long x 42mm (1 11/16") wide, ovate shaped, smooth edges, acute tips and rounded bases. Veins, stems and branches are green. PARENTAGE: [('Bon Accord' x 'Bicentennial') x ('Vobeglo' x 'Dancing Flame') x 'Rohees Alrami'] x 'Supersport'. Medium upright. Makes good standard. Prefers overhead filtered light and cool climate. Best bloom colour in filtered light. Tested four years in Duizel, The Netherlands. Distinguished by bloom colour.
Tamerus 2002 NL AFS4824.

Nelekes. Upright. Semi Double to Double. COROLLA: half flared; opens light purple (N78B); matures reddish purple (67A); 18mm (11/16") long x 15mm (9/16") wide. PETALOIDS: same colour as corolla; 9mm (5/16") long x 7mm (1/4") wide. SEPALS: horizontal, tips reflexed; pale violet (76D) tipped light green (138C) upper surface; pale purple (75C) tipped light green (138C) lower surface; 27mm (1 1/16") long x 14mm (9/16") wide. TUBE: white (155C) & light green (139D); short & thick; 9mm (5/16") long x 5mm (3/16") wide. FOLIAGE is dark green (136A) upper surface; medium green (138B) lower surface. PARENTAGE: 'Mieke' x 'Dorset Delight'.
Michiels 2007 BE AFS6328.

Nele-Mareike. Upright/Trailer. Double. COROLLA: fully flared; smooth petal margins, roundish shape; opens light purple (93B); matures purple (80A); 25mm (1") long x 30mm (1 3/16") wide. SEPALS: fully up, tips recurved; white (155D) tipped green (w/touch of red) upper & lower surfaces; 30mm (1 3/16") long x 18mm (11/16") wide. TUBE: white (155D); medium length & thickness; 20mm (3/4") long x 8mm (5/16") wide. STAMENS extend 2mm (1/16") beyond the corolla; dark rose (71D) filaments; tan (174C) anthers. PISTIL extends 22mm (7/8") beyond the corolla; white (155D) style; grayish yellow (161B) stigma. BUD is globular. FOLIAGE is medium green (138A) upper surface; medium green (138B) lower surface. Leaves are 65mm (2 9/16") long x 32mm (1 1/4") wide; ovate shaped, serrulate edges, acute tips, rounded bases. Veins are reddish/green, stems are grayed-orange, branches are green. PARENTAGE: 'Hula Girl' x 'Cliantha'. Lax upright or stiff trailer. Self branching. Makes good basket. Prefers overhead filtered light. Heat tolerant if shaded. Best bloom & foliage colour in filtered light. Tested 3 years in Graz, Austria. Distinguished by bloom shape & colour.
Strümper 2009 DE AFS7000.

Nelleke van Eekert. Trailer. Single. COROLLA is half flared with smooth petal margins; opens dark rose (51A); matures rose (51B); 25mm (1") long x 31mm (1 1/4") wide. SEPALS are fully up, tips recurved; rose (68C) tipped green upper & lower surfaces; 27mm (1 1/16") long x 11mm

(7/16") wide. TUBE is light rose (68D); medium length & thickness; 16mm (5/8") long x 8mm (3/16") wide. FOLIAGE: dark green (137A) upper surface; medium green (138B) lower surface. Leaves are 64mm (2 1/2") long x 37mm (1 7/16") wide, ovate shaped. PARENTAGE: 'Roesse Carme' x 'Leon Pauwels'. Distinguished by bloom colour.
van Eijk 2005 NL AFS5904.

Nellie Lamers. Trailer. Single. COROLLA: quarter flared, smooth petal margins; opens purple (71A); matures reddish purple (59B); 17mm (11/16") long 19mm (3/4") wide. SEPALS: fully up; tips reflexed; magenta (63B) upper surface; magenta (63A) lower surface; 26mm (1") long x 8mm (5/16") wide. TUBE: magenta (63B); medium length & thickness; 14mm (9/16") long x 4mm (3/16") wide. STAMENS: extend 11mm (7/16") below corolla; magenta (67B) filaments & anthers. PISTIL: extends 39mm (1 9/16") below the corolla; magenta (67B) style; rose (61D) stigma. BUD: ovate, curved, pointed. FOLIAGE: medium green (137B) upper surface; medium green (138B) lower surface. Leaves are 64mm (2 1/2") long x 32mm (1 1/4") wide, ovate shaped, serrulated edges, acute tips and rounded bases. Green veins, stems & branches. PARENTAGE: ('Sofie Michiels' x 'Rohees Metallah') x 'Willy Tamerus'. Natural trailer. Self branching. Makes good basket. Prefers overhead filtered light and cool climate. Best bloom and foliage colour in filtered light. Tested 4 years in Diessen, The Netherlands. Distinguished by bloom colour.
Comperen 2004 NL AFS5569.

Nelly van Heijst. Upright/Trailer. Double. COROLLA is three quarter flared with smooth petal margins; opens purple (77A), matures dark reddish purple (72A); 22mm (7/8") long x 22mm (7/8") wide. SEPALS are fully up, tips reflexed; pale lavender (65D) upper surface; pink (62A) lower surface; 21mm (13/16") long x 11mm (7/16") wide. TUBE is pale yellow (1D); medium length and thin; 21mm (13/16") long x 5mm (3/16") thick. STAMENS extend 21mm (13/16") beyond the corolla; reddish purple (70B) filaments, light purple (70C) anthers. PISTIL extends 29mm (1 1/8") beyond the corolla; reddish purple (70B) style, light yellow (3D) stigma. BUD is globular, pointed. FOLIAGE is dark green (139A) upper surface, medium green (138A) lower surface. Leaves are 75mm (2 15/16") long x 36mm (1 7/16") wide, lanceolate shaped, serrated edges, acute tips and rounded bases. Veins, stems and

branches are green. PARENTAGE: [('Bon Accord' x 'Bicentennial') x ('Vobeglo' x 'Dancing Flame') x 'Rohees Alrami'] x ('Annabel' x 'Annabel'). Lax upright or stiff trailer. Makes good stiff trailer. Prefers overhead filtered light and cool climate. Best bloom colour in filtered light. Tested four years in Duizel, The Netherlands. Distinguished by bloom and foliage combination.
Tamerus 2002 NL AFS5003.

Nephele. Upright. Single. COROLLA: half flared; smooth petal margins; opens rose (63C) edged reddish purple (64B); matures reddish purple (64B); 10mm (3/8") long x 12mm (7/16") wide. SEPALS: horizontal, tips recurved; rose (52B) tipped pale yellow green (149D) upper surface; rose (52C) lower surface; 17mm (5/8") long x 8mm (5/16") wide. TUBE: rose (52B); short & thick; 6mm (1/4") long x 5mm (3/16") wide. STAMENS extend 7mm (1/4") beyond the corolla; pale pink (56A) filaments & anthers. PISTIL extends 4mm (1/8") beyond the corolla; cream (158D) style; yellowish white (158A) stigma. BUD: pegtop shape. FOLIAGE: dark green (138A) upper surface; light green (138B) lower surface. Leaves are 55mm (2 3/16") long x 40mm (1 9/16") wide; elliptic shaped, serrate edges, acute tips, rounded bases. Veins are light green, stems & branches are medium green. PARENTAGE: ['Sparkling Whisper' x ('Playboy' x ?)] x 'Prince Syray'. Medium upright. Makes good upright or standard. Prefers overhead filtered light or full sun, warm climate. Heat tolerant if roots are shaded. Best bloom & foliage colour in bright light. Tested 5 years in Ohé en Laak, The Netherlands. Nominated by NKvF as recommendable cultivar. Distinguished by strong, radiant flowers.
de Cooker 2009 NL AFS7024.

Nestor-Berte Menten. Trailer. Double. COROLLA: three quarter flared; opens light reddish purple (73A); matures dark rose (64C); 25mm (1") long x 16mm (5/8") wide. PETALOIDS: light reddish purple (72C); 15 mm (9/16") long x 10 mm (3/8") wide. SEPALS are fully up, tips recurved, twisted left to right; white (155C) tipped light green (142B) upper surface and pale pink (56A) tipped light green (142B) lower surface; 34mm (1 3/8") long x 13mm (1/2") wide. TUBE is white (155C) striped light green (142B); medium length and thickness; 19mm (3/4") long x 5mm (3/16") wide. FOLIAGE is dark green (136B) upper surface; medium

324

green (138B) lower surface. PARENTAGE: 'Vreeni Schleeweiss' x 'Kiss'.
Michiels 2007 BE AFS6504.

Newmel. Single. COROLLA deep purple. SEPALS deep rose.
Evans 2003 UK.

Niagara Falls. Trailer. Double. COROLLA: half flared; opens purple (N82A) striped pale violet (76D); matures purple (N80A) striped pale purple (75C); 23mm (7/8") long x 16mm (5/8") wide. PETALOIDS: purple (N82B) striped pale violet (76D); 17 mm (5/8") long x 9 mm (5/16") wide. SEPALS are half up, tips recurved up; white (155C) tipped light apple green (145B) upper surface and pale lavender (69D) tipped light apple green (145B) lower surface; 43mm (1 11/16") long x 14mm (9/16") wide. TUBE is white (155B); medium length and thickness; 16mm (5/8") long x 6mm (1/4") wide. FOLIAGE is dark green (137A) upper surface; medium green (138B) lower surface. PARENTAGE: 'Waanrodes Silver Star' x 'Ina Frazer'.
Michiels 2007 BE AFS6505.

Nibelungenstadt Pochlarn. Upright/Trailer. Semi Double. COROLLA dark pink red; corolla is half flared. SEPALS light pink, tipped green on the upper and lower surfaces; sepals are fully up with recurved tips. TUBE light pink. PARENTAGE 'Königin der Nacht" x 'Zellertal'.
Nicola 2009 AT BFS0104.

Nicholas Parsons. Upright/Trailer. Double. COROLLA is three quarter flared with turned up smooth petal margins; opens dark purple (78A) flushed magenta (68A), white (155) streaks at base; matures light purple (78B); 42mm (1 11/16") long x 69mm (2 3/4") wide. SEPALS are horizontal, tips recurved; white (155) flushed rose (68B) upper surface, white (155), striped rose (68B) at tips lower surface; 61mm (2 7/16") long x 19mm (3/4") wide. TUBE is white (155); medium length and thickness; 15mm (5/8") long x 7mm (1/4") wide. STAMENS extend 6mm (1/4") below the corolla; rose (68B) filaments; light rose (68D) anthers. PISTIL extends 25mm (1") below the corolla; white (155) style; white (155D) stigma. BUD is extended pear shaped. FOLIAGE is dark green (139A) upper surface, medium green (137C) lower surface. Leaves are 93mm (3 11/16") long x 61mm (2 7/16") wide, ovate shaped, serrulated edges, acute tips and rounded bases. Veins, stems, branches are very pale green. PARENTAGE: 'Opalescent' x 'Deep Purple'. Lax upright or

stiff trailer. Self branching. Makes good basket, upright, standard or decorative. Prefers cool climate. Heat tolerant if shaded. Best bloom colour in filtered light. Tested three years in Gloucester, England. Distinguished by large SEPALS and flower/foliage combination.
Hickman 2002 UK AFS4852.

Nicki Fenwick-Raven. Upright. Single. Corolla opens white, matures to pink tinged red at edges; corolla is fully flared. Sepals are white on the upper and lower surfaces; matures to pink through to red; sepals are fully recurved with recurved tips. Tube is greenish white. This cultivar is an encliandra.
Morrison B.C. 2007 UK BFS0041.

Nico Bouwman. Upright. Single. COROLLA is quarter flared, bell shaped, with smooth petal margins; opens white (155A), blushed & edged red (50A); matures white (155A), edged dark orange (41A); 14mm (9/16") long x 14mm (9/16") wide. SEPALS are horizontal, tips reflexed; pale tan (159A) blushed pink (62A) upper surface; light pink (65C), tipped pale tan (159A) lower surface; 18mm (11/16") long x 10mm (3/8") wide. TUBE is pale yellow (158B); short, medium thickness; 8mm (5/16") long x 6mm (1/4") wide. FOLIAGE: dark green (137A) upper surface; medium green (138B) lower surface. Leaves are 50mm (2") long x 35mm (1 3/8") wide, ovate shaped. PARENTAGE: 'Eleanor Leytham' x 'Prince Syray'. Distinguished by bloom colour & small clusters of horizontally held flowers.
Koerts T. 2005 NL AFS5777.

Nico Gailliaert. Trailer. Double. COROLLA is half flared; opens dark reddish purple (72A) with white (155C) base; matures magenta (63A); 19mm (3/4") long x 16mm (5/8") wide. SEPALS are horizontal, tips recurved; white (155C), tipped light green (142A) upper surface; white (155C) and pale pink (56D), tipped light green (142A) lower surface; 37mm (1 7/16") long x 10mm (3/8") wide. TUBE is white (155C); 15mm (9/16") long x 5mm (3/16") wide. FOLIAGE is medium green (137B) upper surface; medium green (137C) lower surface. PARENTAGE: 'Sofie Michiels' x 'Diana Wills'. Meise 8/13/05. Distinguished by bloom colour.
Michiels 2006 BE AFS6032.

Nico Vollebregt. Upright/Trailer. Single. COROLLA: quarter flared; turned under smooth petal margins; opens & matures light

rose (58D); 15mm (9/16") long x 18mm (11/16") wide. SEPALS: half down; tips recurved; pale pink (56D),rose (52B) base, upper surface; pale pink (56D), rose (51B) base, lower surface; 38mm(1 1/2") long x 12mm (1/2") wide. TUBE: pale pink (56B); medium length & thickness; 16mm (5/8") long x 10mm (3/8") wide. STAMENS: extend 8mm (5/16") below corolla; rose (51B) filaments, light yellow (4C) anthers. PISTIL: extends 25mm (1") below the corolla, pale pink (56D) style, orange (39C) stigma. BUD: ovate, pointed. FOLIAGE: dark green (147A) upper surface; medium green (147B) lower surface. Leaves are 72mm (2 13/16") long x 37mm (1 7/16") wide, elliptic shaped, serrulated edges, acute tips and rounded bases. Veins are reddish to yellow green; stems & branches are reddish. PARENTAGE: 'Dutch Kingsize' x unknown. Lax upright or stiff trailer. Self branching. Makes good basket or upright. Prefers overhead filtered light and cool climate. Best bloom and foliage colour in filtered light. Tested 8 years in Noordwÿkerhout, Holland. Award of Merit, VKC, Aalsmeer. Distinguished by flower shape and colour.
Franck 2003 NL AFS5169.

Nicola Storey. Upright. Single. COROLLA is unflared, bell shaped with smooth petal margins; opens violet (83D); matures light purple (78B); 16mm (5/8") long x 14mm (9/16") wide. SEPALS are horizontal; tips recurved; violet (75D) upper surface and light rose (58D) lower surface; 35mm (1 3/8") long x 10mm (3/8") wide. TUBE is light greenish white (157D), short, medium thickness; 9mm (3/8") long x 6mm (1/4") wide. STAMENS extend 11mm (7/16") below the corolla; magenta (57C) filaments, light magenta (57D) anthers. PISTIL extends 22mm (7/8") below the corolla; light pink (65C) style and light rose (58D) stigma. BUD is angular and pointed. FOLIAGE is dark green (147A) upper surface and medium green (147B) lower surface. Leaves are 48mm (1 7/8") long x 32mm (1 1/4") wide, ovate shaped, smooth edges, acute tips and rounded bases. Veins and stems are green, branches are light green. PARENTAGE: 'Estelle Marie' x 'Joan Goy'. Small upright. Makes good upright. Cold weather hardy to 22⁰ F. Best bloom colour in bright light. Tested 12 years in Burstwick, East Yorkshire, England. Distinguished by horizontal flowers.
Storey 2003 UK AFS5065.

Nicolaas van Brederode. Upright/Trailer. Single. COROLLA: quarter flared, turned under wavy petal margins; opens dark reddish purple (61A); matures dark reddish purple (60C); 17mm (5/8") long x 19mm (3/4") wide. SEPALS: horizontal, tips reflexed; rose (55B) tipped light olive green (153D) upper surface; reddish purple (60D) tipped light olive green (153D) lower surface; 19mm (3/4") long x 7mm (1/4") wide. TUBE: red (53C); medium length & thickness; 9mm (5/16") long x 5mm (3/16") wide. STAMENS extend 11mm (7/16") beyond the corolla; purple (71A) filaments; dark purple (79A) anthers. PISTIL extends 19mm (3/4") beyond the corolla; purple (77A) style; pale purple (75D) stigma. BUD: elongated. FOLIAGE: dark green (137A) upper surface; medium green (138B) lower surface. Leaves are 59mm (2 3/8") long x 27mm (1 1/16") wide; elliptic shaped, serrulate edges, acute tips, rounded bases. Veins are dark grayish purple (184A), stems are plum (184B), branches are dark reddish purple (187C). PARENTAGE: 'Pink La Campanella' x 'Maxima'. Lax upright or stiff trailer. Self branching. Makes good basket. Prefers overhead filtered light, cool climate. Best bloom & foliage colour in filtered light. Tested 3 years in Opglabbeek, Belgium. Waanrode 8/9/08, awarded Outstanding. Distinguished by bloom colour.
Cuppens 2009 BE AFS7069.

Niederosterreich. Upright. Double. COROLLA light pink with pink veins; corolla is fully flared. SEPALS white overtoned pink on the upper and lower surfaces; sepals are horizontally held with yellowish green recurved tips. TUBE white overtoned pink. PARENTAGE 'Sweet Darling' x 'Nettala'.
Klemm 2008 AT BFS0083.

Niels. Trailer. Double. COROLLA: three quarter flared; opens pink (52D) and magenta (68A); matures pink (62C) and magenta (67B); 31mm (1 1/4") long x 27mm (1 1/16") wide. PETALOIDS: pink (52D) and magenta (68A); 23 mm (7/8") long x 11 mm (7/16") wide. SEPALS are half down, tips recurved ; pale pink (56D) tipped light apple green (144D) upper surface and light pink (65C) tipped light apple green (144D) lower surface; 41mm (1 5/8") long x 16mm (5/8") wide. TUBE is light green (145D) and white (155C); medium length, thin; 15mm (9/16") long x 5mm (3/16") wide. FOLIAGE is dark green (137A) upper surface; medium green (138B) lower surface. PARENTAGE: 'Leon Pauwels' x 'Oso Sweet'.
Michiels 2007 BE AFS6506.

Nifty Norman. Upright. Single. COROLLA opens coral pink, white at base, matures paler; corolla is three quarter flared and is 20mm long x 30mm wide. SEPALS white flushed light rose on the upper and lower surfaces; sepals are fully up with recurved tips and are 27mm long x 18mm wide. TUBE white flushed light rose and is 12mm long x 8mm wide. PARENTAGE 'My Mum' (AFS 2921) x 'Coachman'.
Rolt G. 2006 UK BFS0023.

Ninon Massé-Massebeuf. Upright/Trailer. Single. COROLLA is unflared; opens & matures reddish purple (66A); 16mm (5/8") long x 8mm (5/16") wide. SEPALS are half down, tips recurved; yellowish white (4D) tipped light yellowish green (149C) upper & lower surfaces; 24mm (15/16") long x 4mm (1/8") wide. TUBE is pale yellowish green (149D); 18mm (11/16") long x 3mm (1/8") wide. FOLIAGE: medium green (146A) upper surface; light olive green (147C) lower surface. PARENTAGE: 'Prince of Orange' x 'Subliem'. Distinguished by bloom colour.
Massé 2006 FR AFS6242.

Nirak. Upright. Semi Double to Double. COROLLA is half flared with turned under wavy petal margins; opens magenta (71C); matures reddish purple (72B); 19mm (3/4") long x 22mm (7/8") wide. SEPALS are horizontal, tips reflexed; light rose (50C) tipped light apple green (145C) upper surface; rose (51B) tipped light apple green (145C) lower surface; 26mm (1") long x 14mm (9/16") wide. TUBE is light pink (49B); long & thick; 31mm (1 1/4") long x 9mm (3/8") wide. FOLIAGE: dark green (139A) upper surface; medium green (138B) lower surface. Leaves are 103mm (4 1/16") long x 61mm (2 3/8") wide, ovate shaped. PARENTAGE: 'WALZ Harp' x 'Ting-a-Ling'. Meise 9-18-04. Distinguished by double coloured flower.
Geerts L. 2005 BE AFS5856.

No Frills. Upright. COROLLA: none. SEPALS: full down; tips recurved; red (46D) upper surface; red (45D) lower surface; 25mm (1") long x 7mm (1/4") wide. TUBE: red (45D); short & thin; 15mm(9/16") long x 6mm (1/4") wide. STAMENS: white (155B) filaments & anthers. PISTIL: dark red (46A) style, red (45D) stigma. BUD: torpedo shaped. FOLIAGE: dark green (137A) upper surface; medium green (137C) lower surface. Leaves are 25mm (1") long x 15mm (9/16") wide, ovate shaped, wavy edges, acute tips and rounded bases. Veins are light green,

stems & branches are grayish green (191B). PARENTAGE: found seedling. Small upright. Self branching. Makes good basket, miniature or bedding plant. Prefers full sun. Heat tolerant if shaded. Cold weather hardy to -10° C. Best bloom and foliage colour in filtered light. Tested 3 years in Blackpool, Northwest England. Distinguished by lack of a corolla, very small Stamens, profuse small blooms.
Cartmell 2003 UK AFS5203.

Nobla. Upright. Double. COROLLA is half flared with turned under wavy petal margins; opens light rose (73B); matures light rose (73C); 15mm (9/16") long x 22mm (7/8") wide. SEPALS are horizontal, tips reflexed; red (53B) upper surface; red (53C) lower surface; 27mm (1 1/16") long x 14mm (9/16") wide. TUBE is red (53B); medium length & thickness; 21mm (13/16") long x 6mm (1/4") wide. FOLIAGE: dark green (139A) upper surface; medium green (138B) lower surface. Leaves are 58mm (2 5/16") long x 30mm (1 3/16") wide, elliptic shaped. PARENTAGE: 'WALZ Harp' x 'Apache'. Meise 9-18-04. Distinguished by flower colour & shape.
Geerts L. 2005 BE AFS5855.

Novecento. Upright. Double. COROLLA: half flared, turned under; opens magenta (68A), edged light reddish purple (72C); matures magenta (63B) edged dark rose (67C); 20mm (3/4") long x 14mm (9/16") wide. PETALOIDS: magenta (68A); 12 mm (7/16") long x 9 mm (5/16") wide. SEPALS are half up, tips recurved up, twisted right; pink (55C) tipped apple green (144C) upper surface and pink (49A) tipped apple green (144C) lower surface; 39mm (1 1/2") long x 10mm (3/8") wide. TUBE is pale pink (56D) striped light green (141D); long & thin; 34mm (1 3/8") long x 6mm (1/4") wide. FOLIAGE is dark green (139A) upper surface; medium green (137B) lower surface. PARENTAGE: 'Vendelzwaaier' x 'Jackie Bull'.
Michiels 2007 BE AFS6509.

Nöel Lahaye. Upright/Trailer. Double. COROLLA: 3 quarter flared; opens purple (83C); matures dark purple (78A); 25mm (1") long x 26mm (1") wide. SEPALS: half up, tips recurved up; magenta (58B) upper & lower surfaces; 36mm (1 7/16") long x 15mm (9/16") wide. TUBE: magenta (58B); medium length & thickness; 14mm (9/16") long x 5mm (3/16") wide. FOLIAGE is dark green (137A) upper surface; medium green (137D)

327

lower surface. PARENTAGE: 'Rose Bradwardine' x 'Pinto The Blue'. Scharf 2007 NL AFS6573.

Noël van Steenberghe. Trailer. Double. COROLLA is half flared; opens light purple (78D) with pink (62C) base; matures violet (77B); 22mm (7/8") long x 18mm (11/16") wide. PETALOIDS are light purple (78D) with pink (62C) base; 15mm (9/16") long x 12mm (7/16") wide. SEPALS are half down, tips reflexed; pale pink (62D) with light green (142B) base, upper surface, and pink (62C) with light green (142B) base, lower surface; 41mm (1 5/8") long x 15mm (9/16") wide. TUBE is white (155C); 19mm (3/4") long x 9mm (5/16") wide. FOLIAGE is dark green (136A) upper surface; medium green (138B) lower surface. PARENTAGE: 'Sofie Michiels' x 'Weleveld'. Meise 8/13/05. Distinguished by bloom colour. Michiels 2006 BE AFS6023.

Noël vander Loo. Upright. Double. COROLLA is half flared with smooth petal margins; opens purple (83A); matures purple (71A); 28mm (1 1/8") long x 21mm (13/16") wide. SEPALS are horizontal, tips recurved; light reddish purple (72C) upper surface; dark reddish purple (64A) lower surface; 28mm (1 1/8") long x 9mm (3/8") wide. TUBE is light reddish purple (72C); medium length and thickness; 17mm (11/16") long x 6mm (1/4") thick. STAMENS extend 14mm (9/16") beyond the corolla; purple (71A) filaments, reddish purple (70B) anthers. PISTIL extends 34mm (1 3/8") beyond the corolla; purple (71A) style, light purple (70C) stigma. BUD is ovate, pointed. FOLIAGE is dark green (137A) upper surface, medium green (138B) lower surface. Leaves are 78mm (3 1/16") long x 41mm (1 5/8") wide, ovate shaped, serrulated edges, acute tips and obtuse bases. Veins, stems and branches are green. PARENTAGE: ('Annabel' x 'Annabel') x 'Rohees Metalla'. Small upright. Makes good standard. Prefers overhead filtered light and cool climate. Best bloom colour in filtered light. Tested four years in Duizel, The Netherlands. Distinguished by bloom and foliage combination. Tamerus 2002 NL AFS4985.

Noelsy. Upright. Single. COROLLA is half flared with turned under wavy petal margins; opens light purple (74C), magenta (63B) base; matures pale purple (74D), pale purple (73B) base; 27mm (1 1/16") long x 21mm (13/16") wide. SEPALS are half up, tips recurved up; magenta (63B) tipped light apple green (145B) upper surface; magenta (58B) tipped light apple green (145B) lower surface; 26mm (1") long x 9mm (3/8") wide. TUBE is rose (63C); medium length & thickness; 9mm (3/8") long x 6mm (1/4") wide. FOLIAGE: dark green (139A) upper surface; medium green (138B) lower surface. Leaves are 53mm (2 1/16") long x 22mm (7/8") wide, elliptic shaped. PARENTAGE: 'Pink Fantasia' x unknown. Meise 8-14-04. Distinguished by colour & shape. Van Vooren 2005 BE AFS5720.

Noortje. Trailer. Single. COROLLA: unflared, smooth petal margins; opens purple (80A), red (46C) base; matures purple (80A); 16mm (5/8") long 9mm (3/8") wide. SEPALS: half up; tips recurved up; red (46C) upper & lower surfaces; 31mm (1 1/4") long x 7mm (1/4") wide. TUBE: red (46B); short, medium thickness; 19mm (3/4") long x 9mm (3/8") wide. STAMENS: extend 2mm (1/16") below corolla; red (46C) filaments; red (46D) anthers. PISTIL: extends 28mm (1 1/8") below the corolla; red (46C) style; red (46D) stigma. BUD: round ball. FOLIAGE: dark green (147A) upper surface; dark green (147A) lower surface. Leaves are 41mm (1 5/8") long x 19mm (3/4") wide, lanceolate shaped, serrated edges, acute tips and rounded bases. Light green veins, green stems & dark red branches. PARENTAGE: 'Pink Bon Accord' x unknown. Natural trailer. Makes good basket, standard or bonsai. Prefers full sun, warm climate. Heat tolerant if shaded. Best bloom and foliage colour in bright light. Tested 3 years in Purmerend, The Netherlands. Award of Merit, VKC-KMTP Aalsmeer, 1995. Distinguished by flower colour combination. van der Made 2004 NL AFS5588.

Norbert Cornelis. Upright/Trailer. Double. COROLLA is three quarter flared with turned under smooth petal margins; opens light purple (74C), rose (68B) base; matures magenta (63B); 25mm (1") long x 22mm (7/8") wide. SEPALS are horizontal, tips recurved; white (155C), tipped light apple green (145C) upper surface; white (155D), tipped light apple green (145C) lower surface; 35mm (1 3/8") long x 13mm (1/2") wide. TUBE is white (155C); medium length & thickness; 21mm (13/16") long x 5mm (3/16") wide. FOLIAGE: dark green (137A) upper surface; medium green (138B) lower surface. Leaves are 69mm (2 3/4") long x 32mm (1 1/4") wide, ovate shaped. PARENTAGE: 'Sofie Michiels' x 'Annabelle

Stubbs'. Meise 8-14-04. Distinguished by small size & corolla/sepal contrast. Michiels 2005 BE AFS5745.

Norbury Smith. Upright. Single. COROLLA dark carmine; corolla is half flared. SEPALS waxy carmine on the upper and lower surfaces; SEPALS are half up with recurved tips. TUBE mixture of dark red and dark green. PARENTAGE found Seedling. Owen 2009 UK BFS0146.

Norman Welton. Upright. Single. COROLLA: quarter flared; opens & matures white (155A); 20mm (3/4") long x 18mm (11/16") wide. SEPALS: half up, tips reflexed up; white (155A) upper & lower surfaces; 8mm (5/16") long x 5mm (3/16") wide. TUBE: white (155A); 5mm (3/16") long x 8mm (5/16") wide. FOLIAGE is dark green (137A) upper surface; medium green (137D) lower surface. PARENTAGE: 'Border Reiver' x 'Sophie Louise'. Also registered with the BFS. Gordon 2008 UK AFS6737 BFS0061.

North Star. Upright. Single. COROLLA: quarter flared, bell shaped, smooth petal margins; opens & matures white (155A) veined pale pink (56A); 30mm (1 1/4") long 25mm (1") wide. SEPALS: half down; tips recurved; pale pink (56C) upper surface; pale pink (56B) lower surface; 44mm (1 3/4") long x 15mm (9/16") wide. TUBE: pale pink (56B); medium length & thin; 13mm (1/2") long x 5mm (3/16") wide. STAMENS: extend 10mm (3/8") below corolla; pale pink (55B) filaments; dark red (53A) anthers. PISTIL: extends 35mm (1 3/8") below the corolla; pale pink (56B) style; pale yellow (18D) stigma. BUD: oval, pointed. FOLIAGE: dark green (137A) upper surface; medium green (137C) lower surface. Leaves are 45mm (1 3/4") long x 25mm (1") wide, ovate shaped, serrated edges, acute tips and rounded bases. Medium green (139B) veins; plum (185B) stems; light gray (197D) branches. PARENTAGE: 'Richita' x seedling of 'Blue Ice' x 'Norah Henderson'. Small upright. Makes good upright or bush. Prefers full sun, cool climate. Best bloom and foliage colour in bright light. Tested 3 years in N.E. England. Distinguished by colour combination. Hall 2004 UK AFS5579.

Nouvelle Republique. Upright/Trailer. Single. COROLLA: Quarter flared; opens white (155B); matures pale pink (49D); 25mm (1") long x 20mm (3/4") wide. SEPALS: half up, tips recurved up; rose (63C) upper & lower surfaces; 30mm (1

3/16") long x 8mm (5/16") wide. TUBE: light pink (62B); medium length & thickness; 15mm (9/16") long x 6mm (1/4") wide. FOLIAGE is dark green (139A) upper surface; medium green (138A) lower surface. PARENTAGE: ('Nellie Nuttall' x 'Ting-a-Ling') x 'La Paloma'. Gaucher 2007 FR AFS6440.

Nuit Sans Lune. Upright/Trailer. Single. COROLLA: quarter flared; smooth petal margins; opens & matures dark purple (79B); 23mm (7/8") long x 18mm (11/16") wide. SEPALS: horizontal, tips recurved; dark reddish purple (64A) upper & lower surfaces; 31mm (1 1/4") long x 6mm (1/4") wide. TUBE: magenta (63A); longish, medium thickness; 23mm (7/8") long x 6mm (1/4") wide. STAMENS extend 19-23mm (3/4-7/8") beyond the corolla; reddish purple (72B) filaments; reddish purple (80A) anthers. PISTIL extends 42mm (1 5/8") beyond the corolla; light reddish purple (72C) style; purple (77A) stigma. BUD is ovate. FOLIAGE is medium green (147B) upper & lower surfaces. Leaves are 76mm-96(3-3 3/16") long x 33-52mm (1 5/16-2 1/16") wide; ovate shaped, serrulate edges, acute tips, rounded bases. Veins are yellowish green, stems are light brown, branches are light reddish brown. PARENTAGE: 'Richlieu' x 'Roes New Millenium'. Lax upright or stiff trailer. Makes good upright. Prefers overhead filtered light & cool climate. Heat tolerant if shaded. Tested 3 years in Pornic, France. Distinguished by dark colour of bloom. Massé 2009 FR AFS6995.

Ocean Sunset. Upright. Single. COROLLA is half flared with smooth petal margins; opens & matures red (45A) at tips, orange (41B) at center; 19mm (3/4") long x 22mm (7/8") wide. SEPALS are half down, tips reflexed; pink (48C) veined reddish orange (43B) upper surface, dark orange (40B) lower surface; 32mm (1 1/4") long x 11mm (7/16") wide. TUBE is light orange (31C) veined reddish orange (43B), short & thick; 16mm (5/8") long x 11mm (7/16") wide. STAMENS extend 35mm (1 3/8") beyond the corolla; rose (48C) filaments; dark red (46A) anthers. PISTIL extends 13mm (1/2") below the corolla; rose (47C) style; light tan (162A) stigma. BUD is long with blunt point. FOLIAGE is dark green (139A) upper surface, medium green (137C) lower surface. Leaves are 70mm (2 3/4") long x 57mm (2 1/4") wide, ovate shaped, serrated edges, obtuse tips and rounded bases. Veins, stems & branches are yellowish green (144B). PARENTAGE: ('Feather Duster'

x 'San Francisco') x 'Orange Drops'. Small upright. Self branching. Makes good basket or decorative. Prefers overhead filtered light & cool climate. Cold weather hardy to 30⁰ F. Best bloom & foliage colour in bright filtered light. Tested seven years in Fortuna, CA, USA. Distinguished by bloom colour combination & long blooming period.
McLaughlin 2004 USA AFS5366.

Oeterdal. Upright. Single. COROLLA is quarter flared; opens dark reddish purple (59A); matures reddish purple (60D); 15mm (9/16") long x 13mm (1/4") wide. SEPALS are half down, tips recurved; red (53B) upper surface; red (53C) lower surface; 23mm (7/8") long x 9mm (5/16") wide. TUBE is red (53C); 9mm (5/16") long x 5mm (3/16") wide. FOLIAGE: dark green (136A) upper surface; medium green (137B) lower surface. PARENTAGE: 'Ben's Ruby' x 'Onbekend'. Meise 8/13/05. Distinguished by bloom colour.
Baeten 2006 BE AFS6014.

Old Dick. Upright/Trailer. Single. COROLLA: half flared, bell shaped, turned under smooth petal margins; opens violet (83A), splashed reddish purple (63A); matures purple (71A) splashed magenta (57A); 30mm (1 3/16") long x 25mm (1") wide. PETALOIDS: reddish purple (61B) slightly edged white; 20mm (13/16") long x 15mm (9/16") wide. SEPALS: horizontal; tips recurved; magenta (57A), upper surface; reddish purple (61B) lower surface; 35mm(1 3/8") long x 12mm (1/2") wide. TUBE: magenta (57A); short & thick; 10mm (3/8") long x 7mm (1/4") wide. STAMENS: extend 15mm (9/16") below corolla; reddish purple (66A) filaments; reddish purple (70B) anthers. PISTIL: extends 45mm (1 3/4") below the corolla, reddish purple (66A) style; pink (36A) stigma. BUD: medium, round. FOLIAGE: dark green (147A) upper surface, medium green (147B) lower surface. Leaves are 55mm (2 3/16") long x 40mm (1 9/16") wide, cordate shaped, serrated edges, acute tips and rounded bases. Veins & stems are green; branches are brown. PARENTAGE: 'Cheeky Chantelle' x 'Delta's Night'. Lax upright or stiff trailer. Self branching. Makes good upright or standard. Prefers overhead filtered light and warm climate. Heat tolerant if shaded. Cold weather hardy to 32⁰ F. Best bloom colour in bright light. Tested 3 years in Walthamstow, London, England. Distinguished by purple splashed magenta colour in corolla.
Allsop M. 2004 UK AFS5380.

Olga Storey. Upright/Trailer. Semi Double. COROLLA: smooth petal margins; opens purple (81A); matures dark purple (78A); 30mm (1 3/16 ") long x 23mm (7/8 ") wide. SEPALS: horizontal, tips recurved; magenta (57B) upper surface; dark rose (58C) lower surface; 42mm (1 5/8") long x 10mm (3/8") wide. TUBE: magenta (57B); short, medium thickness; 10mm (3/8") long x 7mm (1/4") wide. STAMENS extend 15mm (9/16") beyond the corolla; magenta (57B) filaments; magenta (59C) anthers. PISTIL extends 26mm (1") beyond the corolla; magenta (57C) style; magenta (59C) stigma. BUD: round, long, slight twist. FOLIAGE: light apple green (144B) upper surface; yellowish green (145A) lower surface. Leaves are 67mm (2 5/8") long x 30mm (1 3/16") wide; cordate shaped, serrulate edges, acute tips, rounded bases. Veins, stems & branches are red. PARENTAGE: 'Annabel' x F. regia ssp. regia. Lax upright or stiff trailer. Self branching. Makes good basket or upright. Cold weather hardy to -3° C (26° F). Best bloom colour in bright light. Best foliage colour in filtered light. Tested 9 years in Burstwick, East Yorkshire, England. Distinguished by bloom & foliage colour combination.
Storey 2009 UK AFS7138.

Olivia Kate Hutchinson. Upright. Double. COROLLA is three quarter flared; opens white (155A) striped rose; matures white (155B) striped rose; 25mm (1") long x 13mm (1/2") wide. SEPALS are fully up, tips recurved; reddish purple (186B) upper & lower surfaces; 35mm (1 3/8") long x 10mm (3/8") wide. TUBE is dark reddish purple (187B); 40mm (1 9/16") long x 4mm (3/16") wide. FOLIAGE: dark green (138B) upper surface; medium green (138A) lower surface. PARENTAGE: Sport of 'Melting Moments'. Distinguished by corolla colour combination.
Fowler 2006 UK AFS5984.

Olivier Morice. Upright. Single. COROLLA: unflared, smooth petal margins; opens & matures pink (43D) edged reddish orange (43C); 11mm (7/16") long x 9mm (3/8") wide. SEPALS: horizontal; tips recurved; light pink (38C) from base to tip, long tips yellowish green (145A), upper & lower surfaces; 21mm (13/16") long x 5mm (3/16") wide. TUBE: light pink (38C); medium length & thickness; 19mm (3/4") long x 5mm (3/16") wide. STAMENS: extend 5 - 8mm (3/16–5/16") below corolla; light pink (38C) filaments, light tan (161C) anthers. PISTIL: extends 22mm (7/8") below the corolla, light pink (38D)

style, yellowish white (4D) stigma. BUD: Long, ovate. FOLIAGE: dark green (147A) upper surface; medium green (147B) lower surface. Leaves are 58mm (2 5/16") long x 37mm (1 7/16") wide, ovate shaped, serrulated edges, acute tips and rounded bases. Veins, stems & branches are yellowish green. PARENTAGE: 'Prince of Orange' x 'Small Pipes'. Small upright. Self branching. Makes good upright. Prefers overhead filtered light and cool climate. Best bloom and foliage colour in filtered light. Tested 3 years in Pornic, France. Distinguished by bloom colour.
Massé 2003 FR AFS5217.

Ons Jantje. Upright/Trailer. Double. COROLLA is three quarter flared; opens magenta (63B); matures dark rose (64C); 25mm (1") long x 23mm (7/8") wide. PETALOIDS: violet (85B); 19mm (3/4") long x 10mm (3/8") wide. SEPALS are half up, tips recurved up; dark rose (58C) upper surface; magenta (61C) lower surface; 32mm (1 1/4") long x 11mm (7/16") wide. TUBE is dark rose (58C); 20mm (13/16") long x 5mm (3/16") wide. FOLIAGE: dark green (136B) upper surface; medium green (138B) lower surface. PARENTAGE: 'Roesse Blacky' x 'Scarborough Jamboree'. Meise 9/17/05. Distinguished by bloom colour combination.
Michiels 2006 BE AFS6069.

Ons Jaspertje. Upright/Trailer. Double. COROLLA: half flared; opens pale purple (N81D), pale lavender (69D) base; matures light purple (N78D), pale purple (75C) base; 29mm (1 1/8") long x 13mm (1/2") wide. SEPALS: horizontal, tips reflexed; pale lavender (69B) tipped apple green (144C) upper surface; rose (68C) tipped apple green (144C) lower surface; 42mm (1 5/8") long x 13mm (1/2") wide. TUBE: white (155C); medium length & thickness; 22mm (7/8") long x 6mm (1/4") wide. FOLIAGE is dark green (137A) upper surface; medium green (138B) lower surface. PARENTAGE: 'Vreni Schleeweiss' x 'Kiss'.
Michiels 2007 BE AFS6329.

Onze Kameroad. Upright/Trailer. Single. COROLLA is quarter flared; opens pale violet (84D) striped magenta (63B); matures violet (76A) striped reddish purple (66B); 14mm (9/16") long x 12mm (1/2") wide. SEPALS are horizontal, tips recurved; magenta (63A) tipped olive green (152B) upper surface; magenta (63B) tipped olive green (152B) lower surface; 32mm (1 1/4") long x 7mm (1/4") wide. TUBE is magenta (63A); 5mm

(3/16") long x 3mm (1/8") wide. FOLIAGE: dark green (136B) upper surface; medium green (138A) lower surface. PARENTAGE: 'Tresko' x 'Canopy'. Meise 9/17/05. Distinguished by bloom colour.
Michiels 2006 BE AFS6072.

Orange Heart. Upright. Single. COROLLA is half flared with turned up petal margins; opens & matures orange (28A); 10mm (3/8") long x 5mm (3/16") wide. SEPALS are half down, tips recurved; red (45A) upper surface; grayish orange (164D) lower surface; 10mm (3/8") long x 3mm (1/8") wide. TUBE is red (45A); medium length & thickness; 10mm (3/8") long x 3mm (1/8") wide. FOLIAGE: dark green (137A) upper surface; grayish green (191A) lower surface. Leaves are 42mm (1 11/16") long x 18mm (11/16") wide, elliptic shaped. PARENTAGE: ('F. obconica' x 'F. cylindracea') x 'F. decussata'. Distinguished by dwarf growth & flower colour.
de Boer 2005 NL AFS5769.

Orange Ray. Upright. Single. COROLLA opens and matures orange; corolla is none flared and is 10-12mm long x 14mm wide SEPALS are pink fading to light pink with light green tips on the upper surface, orange pink on the lower surface; sepals are horizontally held with recurved tips and are 20mm long x 10mm wide TUBE is waxy pink and is 20mm long x 8mm wide. PARENTAGE 'Coachman' x Unknown. This cultivar requires minimum pinching to form a nice bush, performs well in a small pot and also makes a nice mini standard; if grown as a biennial plant it can be in flower by the end of April.
Skuse R. 2004 UK BFS0005.

Orange Star. COROLLA orange. SEPALS orange.
Robson 2002 UK.

Os Deurp. Upright/Trailer. Double. COROLLA: three quarter flared, turned under wavy petal margins; opens rose (63C), reddish purple (61B) & dark reddish purple (61A); matures light purple (70C), magenta (59C) & reddish purple (61B); 32mm (1 1/4") long x 24mm (15/16") wide. PETALOIDS: rose (63C) & dark reddish purple (61A); 14mm (9/16") long x 10mm (3/8") wide. SEPALS: horizontal, tips recurved, twisted left to right; light pink (55D) tipped pale yellow green (150D) upper surface; pink (55C) tipped pale yellow green (150D) lower surface; 58mm (2 5/16") long x 21mm

(13/16") wide. TUBE: rose (51C); medium length & thickness; 17mm (5/8") long x 5mm (3/16") wide. STAMENS extend 12mm (7/16") beyond the corolla; dark rose (64C) filaments; reddish purple (71B) anthers. PISTIL extends 19mm (3/4") beyond the corolla; rose (68B) style; pale yellow (1D) stigma. BUD: elongated. FOLIAGE: dark green (136B) upper surface; medium green (138B) lower surface. Leaves are 76mm (3") long x 44mm (1 3/4") wide; ovate shaped, serrate edges, acute tips, obtuse bases. Veins are very dark reddish purple (186A), stems are dark red purple (186D), branches are light red purple (185D) & light green (139D). PARENTAGE: 'Niagara Falls' x 'Rusty Olympic'. Lax upright or stiff trailer. Self branching. Makes good basket. Prefers overhead filtered light, cool climate. Best bloom & foliage colour in filtered light. Tested 3 years in Koningshooikt, Belgium. Waanrode 9/20/08, Outstanding. Distinguished by bloom & foliage colour. Michiels 2009 BE AFS7204.

Oskar Lehmeier. Upright/Trailer. Single. COROLLA: unflared, compact shape; opens purple (83A); matures purple (N79C); 15mm (9/16") long x 9mm (5/16") wide. SEPALS: half up, tips recurved up; magenta (63A) upper & lower surfaces; 40mm (1 9/16") long x 11mm (7/16") wide. TUBE: magenta (63A); 14mm (9/16") long x 8mm (5/16") wide. FOLIAGE is dark green (137A) upper surface; yellowish green (146B) lower surface. PARENTAGE: 'Robert Götz' x 'F. regia ssp serrae Hoya. Burkhart 2008 DE AFs6861.

Ossi. Upright/Trailer. Double. COROLLA: half flared; opens light reddish purple (73A); matures magenta (68A); 22mm (7/8") long x 16mm (5/8") wide. PETALOIDS: light reddish purple (73A); 17mm (5/8") long x 11mm (7/16") wide. SEPALS are horizontal, tips recurved; light pink (55D) tipped pale yellow green (150D) upper surface & rose (55B) tipped pale yellow green (150D) lower surface; 41mm (1 5/8") long x 14mm (9/16") wide. TUBE is white (155C) striped rose (55B); 26mm (1") long x 7mm (1/4") wide. FOLIAGE is dark green (136B) upper surface; medium green (138B) lower surface. PARENTAGE: 'Leen Vander Kuylen' x 'Charlotte Martens'. Meise 7/7/2007. Michiels 2008 BE AFS6725.

Otto Jerey. Upright/Trailer. Semi Double. COROLLA opens dark violet purple (93a), matures to dark violet (88a); corolla is three quarter flared. SEPALS light rhodamine purple (65d) on the upper and lower surfaces; SEPALS are half down with recurved tips. TUBE light rhodamine purple (65d). PARENTAGE 'Cliff's Own' x seedling of ('Cliff's Own' x 'Delta's Parade'). Klemm 2009 AT BFS0132.

Our Debbie. Upright. Single. COROLLA violet. SEPALS carmine. Evans 2004 UK.

Our Hilary. Upright. Single. COROLLA palest pink. SEPALS pale pink. TUBE pale pink. PARENTAGE 'Katrina Thompsen' x 'Alisha Jade'. Dodman 2008 UK BFS0042.

Our Kath. Upright. Single. COROLLA opens pale pink, edged darker pink; corolla is quarter flared and is 14mm long x 23mm wide. SEPALS pink, tipped green on the upper and lower surfaces; sepals are half up with recurved tips and are 27mm long x 10mm wide. TUBE pink and is 6mm long x 5mm wide. PARENTAGE 'Love's Reward' x 'Barbara Windsor'. This cultivar makes a good show plant, it's won best in show in 2006 at the Tee-side show 2006. This one is one for the show bench, makes a nice shaped bush. Riley 2007 UK BFS0028.

Our Kid. Upright. Single. COROLLA opens white; corolla is quarter flared and is 20mm long x 16mm wide. SEPALS blush-pink on the upper and lower surfaces; sepals are horizontally held with recurved tips and are 35mm long x 8mm wide. TUBE blush pink and is 10mm long x 7mm widef. PARENTAGE 'Sophie Louise' x 'Baby Bright'. Joiner 2006 UK BFS0033.

Our Nell. Upright. Double. COROLLA mauve splashed pink. SEPALS deep pink. Harris 2002 UK.

Our Pamela. Upright. Double. COROLLA bluish mauve rose pink fading magenta rose. SEPALS rose. TUBE rose red. Astle 2007 UK.

Our Shep. Semi Double. COROLLA violet mauve. SEPALS cream. Reynolds G. 2002 UK.

Our Spencer. Upright. Single. COROLLA white, slight flush rose vein; corolla is half flared. SEPALS white blushed rose; sepals are horizontally held with recurved green

tips.TUBE white, striped green.PARENTAGE Seedling from 'Katy Elizabeth Ann'. 3½" & 5" single pot classes at BFS Eastern Show 2008.
Dodman 2008 UK BFS0070.

Our William. Upright. Single. COROLLA is quarter flared, square shaped, with smooth turned under petal margins; opens dark reddish purple (61A); matures reddish purple (71B); 14mm (9/16") long x 15mm (5/8") wide. SEPALS are fully up, tips recurved; reddish purple (58A) tipped green upper surface, magenta (61C) lower surface; 25mm (1") long x 6mm (1/4") wide. TUBE is reddish purple (58A), short and thin; 10mm 3/8") long x 5mm (3/16") wide. STAMENS extend 5mm (3/16") below the corolla; rose (67A) filaments and light pink (36B) anthers. PISTIL extends 15mm (5/8") below the corolla; rose (67A) style and yellowish white (158A) stigma. BUD is small, elongated. FOLIAGE is dark green (147A) on upper surface and medium green (147B) on lower surface. Leaves are 85mm (3 3/8") long x 40mm (1 9/16") wide, cordate shaped, serrated edges, acute tips and acute bases. Veins are green; stems brown; branches are red. PARENTAGE: 'Janneke Brinkman-Saletijn' x 'Minirose'. Small upright. Self branching. Makes good upright. Prefers full sun and warm climate. Heat tolerant if shaded. Hardy to 32°F. Best bloom colour in bright light. Tested three years in Walthamstow, London, England. Distinguished by profuse blooms.
Allsop 2002 UK AFS4815.

Overvecht. Upright. Single. COROLLA is quarter flared, bell shaped, with wavy margins; opens violet (77C), matures light purple (74C); 5mm (3/16") long x 4mm (3/16") wide. SEPALS are full down, tips recurved; reddish purple (58A) upper surface, magenta (68A) lower surface; 6mm (1/4") long x 3mm (1/8") wide. TUBE is reddish purple (58A), long with medium thickness; 12mm (1/2") long x 4mm (3/16") wide. STAMENS are 2mm (1/16") inside the corolla; pale purple (75D) filaments and yellowish white (158A) anthers. PISTIL extends 1mm (1/16") below the corolla; magenta (67B) style, rose (68B) stigma. BUD is long TUBEd, ovate. FOLIAGE is dark green (147A) upper surface, medium green (147B) lower surface. Leaves are 44mm (1 3/4") long x 23mm (15/16") wide, elliptic shaped, serrulated edges, obtuse tips and acute bases. Veins, stems and branches are light yellow green. PARENTAGE: 'Panache' x

'Panache'. Medium upright. Horizontal grower (dwarf). Self branching. Makes good basket. Prefers overhead filtered light. Heat tolerant if shaded. Best bloom and foliage colour in filtered light. Tested four years in Lisse, Holland. Distinguished by branching panicles of erect flowers with unique shape and colour.
de Graaff 2002 NL AFS4883.

Pabbe's Bélle. Upright. Single. COROLLA: quarter flared, long bell shaped, turned up & toothed petal margins; opens violet (75A), light rose (73C) base, edged & veined magenta (71C); matures light rose (73C) edged reddish purple (74A); 20mm (13/16") long 16mm (5/8") wide. SEPALS: 1/4 twist to left; horizontal; tips reflexed; light pink (36C) upper surface; light pink (36C) blushed pink (55C) lower surface; 26mm (1") long x 8mm (5/16") wide. TUBE: cream (158B) shaded pink; medium length, thin; 16mm (5/8") long x 4mm (3/16") wide. STAMENS: extend 4mm (3/16") below corolla; pink (54D) filaments; reddish purple (67A) anthers. PISTIL: extends 10mm (3/8") below the corolla; light pink (36C) style; light yellow (11B) stigma. BUD: small, long, pointed. FOLIAGE: yellowish green (146B) upper surface; yellowish green (146C) lower surface. Leaves are 75mm (2 15/16") long x 24mm (15/16") wide, lanceolate shaped, serrated edges, acute tips and obtuse bases. Light green (146C) veins, stems & branches. PARENTAGE: 'Summerdaffodil' x 'Prince Syray'. Medium upright. Self branching. Makes good upright, standard, pyramid or pillar. Prefers overhead filtered light, warm climate. Heat tolerant if shaded. Best bloom colour in filtered light. Best foliage colour in bright light. Tested 3 years in Stadskanaal, The Netherlands. Distinguished by long bell shaped corolla and colour contrast in the flower.
Koerts T. 2004 NL AFS5589.

Pabbe's Dieverdoatsie. Upright/Trailer. Single. COROLLA is half flared with wavy petal margins; opens light reddish purple (66C), veined (red (45B), edged reddish purple (67A); matures light reddish purple (66C), edged reddish purple (67C); 12mm (1/2") long x 16mm (5/8") wide. SEPALS are half down, tips reflexed; red (55A) edged red (52A) upper surface; red (55A) lower surface; 30mm (1 3/16") long x 14mm (9/16") wide. TUBE is light reddish purple (66C), magenta (57B) base, striped magenta (57B); long & thin; 40mm (1 9/16") long x 5mm (3/16") wide. FOLIAGE: medium green (147B) upper surface; light olive green (147C) lower surface. Leaves are 70mm (2 3/4") long x 45mm (1 3/4") wide, cordate shaped. PARENTAGE: 'Obergartner Koch' x 'Torville and Dean'. Distinguished by blooms in triphylla clusters; flower/foliage colour. Koerts T. 2005 NL AFS5775.

Pabbe's Eelskemede. Upright/Trailer. Single. COROLLA: half flared, turned up petal margins; opens dark orange (33A); matures dark orange (40B); 22mm (7/8") long x 36mm (1 7/16") wide. SEPALS: half down; tips reflexed; orange (32A) tipped light green (138C) upper & lower surfaces; 14mm (9/16") long x 4mm (3/16") wide. TUBE: light orange (28C) blushed orange (32A); long & thin; 40mm(1 9/16") long x 4mm (3/16") wide. STAMENS: extend 3mm (1/8") below corolla; red (43A) filaments, light yellow (1C) anthers. PISTIL: extends 14mm (9/16") below the corolla, dark orange (33A) style & stigma. BUD: short, small. FOLIAGE: dark green (137A) upper surface; dark green (147A) lower surface. Leaves are 124mm (4 7/8") long x 32mm (1 1/4") wide, lanceoplate shaped, smooth edges, acute tips and obtuse bases. Veins, stems & branches are light green. PARENTAGE: 'F. dependens' x 'F. venusta'. Lax upright or stiff trailer. Makes good basket or upright. Prefers full sun, warm climate. Heat tolerant if shaded. Cold weather hardy to -6° C. Best bloom and foliage colour in filtered light. Tested 3 years in Stadskanaal, The Netherlands. Award of Merit, VKC/KMTP, The Netherlands. Distinguished by bright orange colour and flowering in panicles. Koerts T. 2003 NL AFS5183.

Pabbe's Fokse. Upright. Single. COROLLA is three quarter flared, bell shaped, with smooth petal margins; opens & matures reddish purple (59B); 12mm (1/2") long x 16mm (5/8") wide. SEPALS are half down, tips reflexed; magenta (63A), tipped green upper surface; reddish purple (64B), tipped green lower surface; 21mm (13/16") long x 9mm (3/8") wide. TUBE is magenta (58B); short, medium thickness; 12mm (1/2") long x 7mm (1/4") wide. FOLIAGE: dark green (147A) upper surface; medium green (147C) lower surface. Leaves are 68mm (2 11/16") long x 40mm (1 9/16") wide, cordate shaped. PARENTAGE: ('Bon Accord' x 'White Knight's Amethyst') x 'Prince Syray'. Distinguished by racemes of bloom & foliage colour combinations. Koerts T. 2005 NL AFS5772.

Pabbe's Glinne Riepe. Upright. Single. COROLLA: quarter flared, smooth petal margins; opens & matures bright orange (32A); 8mm (5/16") long 8mm (5/16") wide. SEPALS: half down; tips reflexed; red (45B) tipped green upper surface; orange (32B) lower surface; 14mm (9/16") long x 7mm (1/4") wide. TUBE: red (45B); long, medium thickness; 52mm (2 1/16") long x 4mm (3/16") wide at end to 8mm (5/16") wide at sepal. STAMENS: extend 3mm (1/8") below corolla; orange (32A) filaments; yellow (10B) anthers. PISTIL: extends 6mm (1/4") below the corolla; red (45B) style; pink (36A) stigma. BUD: long, triphylla type. FOLIAGE: dark green (147A) upper surface; dark reddish purple (187D) lower surface. Leaves are 88mm (3 7/16") long x 44mm (1 3/4") wide, cordate shaped, serrulated edges, acute tips and obtuse bases. Dark reddish purple (187C) veins, stems & branches. PARENTAGE: ('F. magdalenae' x 'F. fulgens rubra grandiflora') x 'Göttingen' . Medium upright. Self branching. Makes good upright, standard, pyramid or pillar. Prefers full sun, warm climate. Heat tolerant if shaded. Cold weather hardy to 6⁰ C. Best bloom and foliage colour in bright light. Tested 12 years in Stadskanaal, The Netherlands. Distinguished by bright flower colour combination against dark leaves. Koerts T. 2004 NL AFS5590.

Pabbe's Hozevörrel. Upright/Trailer. Single. COROLLA: quarter flared, square shaped, smooth petal margins; opens dark rose (54A); matures red (52A); 10mm (3/8") long x 10mm (3/8") wide. SEPALS: half down; tips recurved; light orange (49C) blushed dark rose (54A) upper surface; pale pink (36D) lower surface; 18mm (11/16") long x 6mm (1/4") wide. TUBE: dark rose (54A); long & thin; 35mm(1 3/8") long x 3mm (1/8") wide. STAMENS: do not extend below corolla; pale yellow (1D) filaments, greenish yellow (1B) anthers. PISTIL: extends 5mm (3/16") below the corolla, white (155D) style, white (155A) stigma. BUD: thin & short. FOLIAGE: dark green (147A) upper surface; light olive green (148B) lower surface. Leaves are 82mm (3 1/4") long x 44mm (1 3/4") wide, elliptic shaped, serrulated edges, acute tips and rounded bases. Veins & stems are red, branches are reddish brown. PARENTAGE: 'Thalia' x 'Other Fellow'. Lax upright or stiff trailer. Makes good basket. Prefers overhead filtered light, warm climate. Heat tolerant if shaded. Best bloom and foliage colour in filtered to limited light. Tested 4 years in Stadskanaal, The Netherlands. Award of

Merit, VKC/KMTP, The Netherlands (with praise). Distinguished by contrasting bloom colours.
Koerts T. 2003 NL AFS5185.

Pabbe's Juk. Upright. Single. COROLLA is half flared, bell shaped, with smooth petal margins; opens pink (62C) edged magenta (63B); matures pale pink (62D) edged magenta (63A); 12mm (1/2") long x 12mm (1/2") wide. SEPALS are half up, tips reflexed up; pale yellow (158B) blushed pink (37C), tipped green upper surface; cream (158C) blushed pink (37C) lower surface; 22mm (7/8") long x 12mm (1/2") wide. TUBE is light yellow (4C) blushed green; short, medium thickness; 16mm (5/8") long x 8mm (5/16") wide. FOLIAGE: dark green (147A) upper surface; medium green (147B) lower surface. Leaves are 55mm (2 3/16") long x 35mm (1 3/8") wide, cordate shaped. PARENTAGE: 'Eleanor Leytham' x 'Prince Syray'. Distinguished by racemes of flowers & flower colour.
Koerts T. 2005 NL AFS5774.

Pabbe's Kameleon. Upright. Double. COROLLA is quarter flared with smooth petal margins; four outside petals & four inside petals; opens light orange (41C) outside, dark reddish purple (61A) inside; matures red (44A); 18mm (11/16") long x 9mm (3/8") wide outside; 12mm (1/2") long x 15mm (9/16") wide inside. SEPALS are half down, tips recurved; peach (38B) tipped green upper surface; light orange (32C) tipped green lower surface; 24mm (15/16") long x 8mm (5/16") wide. TUBE is light tan (161C); short & thin; 12mm (1/2") long x 4mm (3/16") wide. FOLIAGE: medium green (138A) upper surface; light olive green (148C) lower surface. Leaves are 60mm (2 3/8") long x 45mm (1 3/4") wide, cordate shaped. PARENTAGE: 'Cambridge Louie' x 'Prince Syray'. Distinguished by racemes of flowers & flower colour combination.
Koerts T. 2005 NL AFS5773.

Pabbe's Katjewaai. Upright/Trailer. Single. COROLLA: quarter flared, bell shaped, smooth petal margins; opens light reddish purple (73A) veined magenta (67B); matures magenta (67B); 10mm (3/8") long 6mm (1/4") wide. SEPALS: horizontal; tips reflexed; dark rose (54A) tipped yellow (11B) upper surface; rose (55B) lower surface; 14mm (9/16") long x 3mm (1/8") wide. TUBE: rose (55B); long, thin; 20mm (13/16") long x 4mm (3/16") wide. STAMENS: extend 3mm (1/8") below corolla; dark rose (54A)

filaments; very pale orange (159B) anthers. PISTIL: extends 13mm (1/2") below the corolla; rose (54A) style; very pale orange (159B) stigma. BUD: long, pointed. FOLIAGE: yellowish green (146B) upper surface; light olive green (148C) lower surface. Leaves are 47mm (1 7/8") long x 34mm (1 5/16") wide, ovate shaped, wavy edges, acute tips and rounded bases. Yellowish green (146B) veins & stems; reddish brown branches. PARENTAGE: 'Panache' x 'Papy Rene' . Lax upright or stiff trailer. Makes good basket. Prefers overhead filtered light, warm climate. Heat tolerant if shaded. Best bloom and foliage colour in filtered light. Tested 12 years in Stadskanaal, The Netherlands. Distinguished by flowering in long racemes and flower colour.
Koerts T. 2004 NL AFS5591.

Pabbe's Kirrevaalk. Upright/Trailer. Single. COROLLA: full flared, saucer shaped, smooth petal margins; opens dark purple (79A); matures dark reddish purple (61A); 14mm (9/16") long 8mm (5/16") wide. SEPALS: horizontal; tips recurved; dark reddish purple (60A) upper & lower surfaces; 17mm (11/16") long x 8mm (5/16") wide. TUBE: dark reddish purple (60A); short, thick; 6mm (1/4") long x 6mm (1/4"). STAMENS: extend 5mm (3/16") below corolla; dark reddish purple (60A) filaments; purple (71A) anthers. PISTIL: extends 22mm (7/8") below the corolla; dark reddish purple (60A) style; orangish white (159C) stigma. BUD: round. FOLIAGE: dark green (147A) upper surface; yellowish green (146B) lower surface. Leaves are 38mm (1 1/2") long x 24mm (15/16") wide, cordate shaped, smooth edges, acute tips and rounded bases. Yellowish green (146B) veins, stems & branches. PARENTAGE: ('Bon Accord' x 'White Knight's Amethyst') x 'Prince Syray'. Lax upright or stiff trailer. Self branching. Makes good basket or standard. Prefers overhead filtered light, warm climate. Heat tolerant if shaded. Best bloom and foliage colour in bright light. Tested 3 years in Stadskanaal, The Netherlands. Distinguished by saucer shaped flowers in clusters of three.
Koerts T. 2004 NL AFS5592.

Pabbe's Koatsebaal. Upright. Single. COROLLA: half flared, bell shaped; turned under petal margins; opens purple (82A), rose (65A) base; matures magenta (68A), light reddish purple (73A) base; 13mm (1/2") long x 18mm (11/16") wide. SEPALS: half up, tips recurved up; greenish white (157B), pink (49A) base & blush, upper surface; light

greenish white (157C), pink (49A) base & blush, lower surface; 18mm (11/16") long x 8mm (5/16") wide. TUBE: light greenish white (157D) blushed pink (49A); short, medium thickness; 6mm (1/4") long x 6mm (1/4") wide. STAMENS extend 14mm (9/16") beyond the corolla; magenta (68A) filaments; pale pink (69A) anthers. PISTIL extends 22mm (7/8") beyond the corolla; pale lavender (69C) style; yellow (2C) stigma. BUD: globular. FOLIAGE: dark green (147A) upper surface; medium green (147B) lower surface. Leaves are 66mm (2 5/8") long x 44mm (1 3/4") wide; cordate shaped, serrate edges, acute tips, rounded bases. Veins, stems & branches are light olive green (147C). PARENTAGE: ('Toos' x 'Whiteknight's Amethyst') x 'Prince Syray'. Medium upright. Self branching. Makes good upright, standard or bonsai. Prefers overhead filtered light. Best bloom & foliage colour in filtered light. Tested 3 years in Stadskanaal, The Netherlands. Distinguished by flower colour combination & erect growth in panicles.
Koerts T. 2009 NL AFS7044.

Pabbe's Kopstubber. Upright. Double. COROLLA: half flared, rose shape, wavy petal margins; opens rose (68C) edged reddish purple (67A), blushed dark rose (67C); matures light rose (73C) edged reddish purple (74A); 10mm (3/8") long 20mm (13/16") wide. SEPALS: horizontal; tips reflexed; greenish white (157B), tipped light yellowish green (149B) upper surface; white (155A) blushed pale pink (69A) lower surface; 20mm (13/16") long x 8mm (5/16") wide. TUBE: greenish white (157B); short, thick; 7mm (1/4") long x 8mm (5/16") wide. STAMENS: extend 12mm (1/2") below corolla; rose (62C) filaments; magenta (63A) anthers. PISTIL: extends 26mm (1") below the corolla; white (155D) style; light yellowish green (154C) stigma. BUD: round, pointed. FOLIAGE: medium green (146A) upper surface; medium green (147B) lower surface. Leaves are 68mm (2 11/16") long x 47mm (1 7/8") wide, cordate shaped, serrated edges, acute tips and rounded bases. Yellowish green (146C) veins & stems; dark red purple (187D) branches. PARENTAGE: 'Cambridge Louie' x 'Prince Syray'. Medium upright. Self branching. Makes good upright, standard, pyramid or pillar. Prefers full sun, warm climate. Best bloom and foliage colour in bright light. Tested 3 years in Stadskanaal, The Netherlands. Distinguished by erect blooms in carrousel pattern on the end of short branches.
Koerts T. 2004 NL AFS5593.

Pabbe's Meroakel. Upright. Single. COROLLA: quarter flared, bell shape, smooth petal margins; opens reddish purple (67A); matures magenta (67B); 6mm (1/4") long, 9mm (3/8") wide. SEPALS: half down; tips reflexed; yellowish white (158A), tipped light yellowish green (149B) upper surface; pale yellow (158B) lower surface; 9mm (3/8") long x 4mm (3/16") wide. TUBE: yellowish white (158A); medium length, thin; 23mm (15/16") long x 4mm (3/16") wide. STAMENS: extend 2mm (1/16") below corolla; yellowish white (158A) filaments & anthers. PISTIL: does not extend below the corolla; pale yellow (158B) style; very pale orange (159B) stigma. BUD: long, white, erect. FOLIAGE: medium green (137C) upper surface; medium green (137C) lower surface. Leaves are 36mm (1 7/16") long x 22mm (7/8") wide, elliptic shaped, wavy edges, acute tips and rounded bases. Light green veins & stems; dark green branches. PARENTAGE: [('F. *magdalenae*' x 'F. *fulgens rubra grandiflora*') x 'Wendy van Wanten'] x 'Pupy René'. Medium upright. Makes good upright, pyramid or pillar. Prefers overhead filtered light, warm climate. Best bloom and foliage colour in filtered light. Tested 3 years in Stadskanaal, The Netherlands. Distinguished by erect long white blooms in racemes.
Koerts T. 2004 NL AFS5594.

Pabbe's Oelepetoet. Upright/Trailer. Single. COROLLA: quarter flared, bell shape, smooth petal margins; opens magenta (57B); matures reddish purple (67A); 13mm (1/2") long, 12mm (1/2") wide. SEPALS: horizontal; tips recurved; pink (37C) upper surface; dark rose (55A) lower surface; 22mm (7/8") long x 6mm (1/4") wide. TUBE: light pink (36B); short, thin; 10mm (3/8") long x 5mm (3/16") wide. STAMENS: extend 12mm (1/2") below corolla; dark rose (58C) filaments; dark reddish purple (61A) anthers. PISTIL: extends 32mm (1 1/4") below the corolla; rose (55B) style; light yellow (11C) stigma. BUD: long, pouch shaped. FOLIAGE: medium green (146A) upper surface; medium green (147B) lower surface. Leaves are 50mm (2") long x 28mm (1 1/8") wide, elliptic shaped, serrulated edges, acute tips and rounded bases. Green veins; brown stems; red brown branches. PARENTAGE: 'Nonchalance' x 'Prince Syray'. Lax upright or stiff trailer. Self branching. Makes good basket. Prefers overhead filtered light, warm climate. Heat tolerant if shaded. Best bloom and foliage colour in bright light. Tested 3 years in Stadskanaal, The Netherlands. Distinguished by erect blooms year round.

Koerts T. 2004 NL AFS5595.

Pabbe's Piebe. Upright. Single. COROLLA: quarter flared, bell shaped; smooth petal margins; opens red orange (42B); matures reddish orange (42A); 10mm (3/8") long x 10mm (3/8") wide. SEPALS: half down, tips reflexed; dark red (47A) upper surface; light orange (41C) lower surface; 18mm (11/16") long x 6mm (1/4") wide. TUBE: red (52A) striped dark red (47A); medium length, thin; 38mm (1 1/2") long x 5mm (3/16") wide. STAMENS do not extend beyond the corolla; light pink (49C) filaments; pale yellowish orange (20C) anthers. PISTIL extends 6mm (1/4") beyond the corolla; red orange (42C) style; light yellowish orange (19B) stigma. BUD: long sack, pointed. FOLIAGE: dark green (147A) upper surface; medium green (147B) lower surface. Leaves are 78mm (3 1/8") long x 42mm (1 5/8") wide; lanceolate shaped, serrate edges, acute tips, acute bases. Veins are green (137C), stems are green (137C) blushed dark grayish red (182A), branches are dark grayish red (182A). PARENTAGE: 'Thalia' (Turner) x 'Golding's Perle'. Tall upright. Makes good upright, standard, pyramid or pillar. Prefers full sun, warm climate. Best bloom & foliage colour in bright light. Tested 3 years in Stadskanaal, The Netherlands. Distinguished by flower colour combination.
Koerts T. 2009 NL AFS7042.

Pabbe's Plume. Upright. Single. COROLLA: Quarter flared; opens reddish purple (70B) edged purple (80A); matures magenta (63B) edged reddish purple (66A); 9mm (5/16") long x 18mm (11/16") wide. SEPALS: horizontal, tips reflexed; pale tan (159A) tipped green upper surface; rose (68C) lower surface; 24mm (15/16") long x 6mm (1/4") wide. TUBE: pale tan (159A) veined pink; medium length, thin; 10mm (3/8") long x 3mm (1/8") wide. FOLIAGE is olive green (148A) upper surface; yellowish green (146C) lower surface. PARENTAGE: ('Toos' x 'Prince Syray') x ('Toos' x 'Prince Syray').
Koerts T. 2007 NL AFS6450.

Pabbe's Poehaai. Upright. Single. COROLLA: unflared, smooth petal margins; opens dark purple (79A), purple (71A) base; matures dark purple (79A); 16mm (5/8") long, 14mm (9/16") wide. SEPALS: half up; tips reflexed up; dark red (53A) upper surface; dark reddish purple (60A) lower surface; 20mm (13/16") long x 8mm (5/16") wide. TUBE: dark reddish purple (59A); short, thin; 10mm (3/8") long x 5mm (3/16") wide. STAMENS:

extend 12mm (1/2") below corolla; purple (71A) filaments; dark purple (79A) anthers. PISTIL: extends 20mm(13/16") below the corolla; reddish purple (67A) style; magenta (67B) stigma. BUD: long, pointed. FOLIAGE: dark green (137A) upper surface; medium green (137D) lower surface. Leaves are 66mm (2 5/8") long x 35mm (1 3/8") wide, cordate shaped, smooth edges, acute tips and obtuse bases. Medium green (137D) veins & stems; red brown branches. PARENTAGE: ('Bon Accord' x 'White Knight's Amethyst') x 'Prince Syray'. Tall upright. Makes good upright, standard, pyramid or pillar. Prefers full sun, warm climate. Heat tolerant if shaded. Best bloom and foliage colour in bright light. Tested 3 years in Stadskanaal, The Netherlands. Distinguished by dark purple colour maturing to dark red in full sun.
Koerts T. 2004 NL AFS5596.

Pabbe's Proemke. Upright/Trailer. Semi Double. COROLLA: three quarter flared; smooth petal margins; opens reddish purple (72B); matures reddish purple (66B); 30mm (1 3/16") long x 24mm (15/16") wide. PETALOIDS: reddish purple (71B) edged purple (71A); 12mm (7/16") long x 12mm (7/16") wide. SEPALS: half down, tips reflexed; white (155C), reddish purple (58A) base, tipped light apple green (145B) upper surface; white (155D) tipped light apple green (145B) lower surface; 36mm (1 7/16") long x 16mm (5/8") wide. TUBE: white (155A) striped light gray green (193A), glowing light apple green (144D); short, medium thickness; 9mm (5/16") long x 7mm (1/4") wide. STAMENS extend 7mm (1/4") beyond the corolla; magenta (68A) filaments; reddish purple (71B) anthers. PISTIL extends 22mm (7/8") beyond the corolla; pale pink (69A) style; light yellow (3D) stigma. BUD: China lantern shape. FOLIAGE: dark green (137A) upper surface; medium green (147B) lower surface. Leaves are 68mm (2 11/16") long x 30mm (1 3/16") wide; ovate shaped, smooth edges, acute tips, rounded bases. Veins & stems are light green (147B), branches are dark grayish red (182A). PARENTAGE: 'Lyn Philip' x 'Bicentennial'. Lax upright or stiff trailer. Makes good basket or upright. Prefers overhead filtered light. Best bloom & foliage colour in filtered light. Tested 3 years in Stadskanaal, The Netherlands. Distinguished by flower colours.
Koerts T. 2009 NL AFS7041.

Pabbe's Scheertje. Upright/Trailer. Single. COROLLA: unflared, turned under petal margins; opens reddish purple (74B);

matures light reddish purple (73A); 16mm (5/8") long, 12mm (1/2") wide. SEPALS: half down; tips reflexed; very pale orange (159B), tipped green, upper surface; pink (62C) lower surface; 28mm (1 1/8") long x 9mm (3/8") wide. TUBE: pale tan (159A) striped dark rose (48A); long, thin; 34mm (1 5/16") long x 4mm (3/16") wide. STAMENS: extend 2mm (1/16") below corolla; pink (62C) filaments; very pale orange (159B) anthers. PISTIL: extends 8mm(5/16") below the corolla; pale tan (159A) style; light yellow (11C) stigma. BUD: long, thin. FOLIAGE: dark green (137A) upper surface; medium green (137C) lower surface. Leaves are 74mm (2 15/16") long x 34mm (1 3/8") wide, ovate shaped, serrated edges, acute tips and rounded bases. Plum (184B) veins & stems; brown branches. PARENTAGE: [('F. *magdalenae*' x 'F. *fulgens rubra grandiflora*') x 'Wendy van Wanten'] x [('Toos' x 'Prince Syray') x Bon Accord']. Lax upright or stiff trailer. Self branching. Makes good basket. Prefers full sun, warm climate. Best bloom colour in filtered light. Best foliage colour in bright light. Tested 2 years in Stadskanaal, The Netherlands. Distinguished by profuse flowering.
Koerts T. 2004 NL AFS5597.

Pabbe's Schim. Upright. Single. COROLLA: quarter flared, smooth petal margins; opens red (43A) edged red (44A); matures red (45A); 10mm (3/8") long, 8mm (5/16") wide. SEPALS: half down; tips reflexed; rose (48B) upper surface; reddish orange (42A), light orange (41C) base, lower surface; 20mm (13/16") long x 8mm (5/16") wide. TUBE: pink (48C) striped orange (40C); long, medium thickness; 36mm (1 7/16") long x 7mm (1/4") wide. STAMENS: extend 2mm (1/16") below corolla; orange (40C) filaments; light yellow (11C) anthers. PISTIL: extends 3mm(1/8") below the corolla; orange (40C) style; orangy red (44C) stigma. BUD: long, pointed. FOLIAGE: dark green (147A) upper surface; medium green (147B) lower surface. Leaves are 62mm (2 7/16") long x 38mm (1 1/2") wide, cordate shaped, wavy edges, acute tips and rounded bases. Grayish red (181A) veins, stems & branches. PARENTAGE: 'Thalia'(Turner, 1855) x 'Albert H'. Medium upright. Makes good upright, standard or pillar. Prefers full sun, warm climate. Cold hardy to 6⁰ C. Best bloom and foliage colour in bright light. Tested 3 years in Stadskanaal, The Netherlands. Distinguished by bright, fluorescent colours and long TUBEs.
Koerts T. 2004 NL AFS5598.

Pabbe's Siddeltop. Upright. Double. COROLLA: quarter flared, bell shaped, petals folded, smooth petal margins; opens dark purple (74A), violet (75A) at base; matures magenta (63B), magenta (57A) at base; 16mm (5/8") long x 24mm (15/16") wide. SEPALS: horizontal; tips recurved; cream (158C) veined pink (62C) upper surface; rose (64D) tipped yellowish green (144B) lower surface; 24mm (15/16") long x 10mm (3/8") wide. TUBE: cream (158C) flushed pink (62C); short & thick; 20mm(13/16") long x 10mm (3/8") wide. STAMENS: extend 3mm (1/8") below corolla; magenta (63B) filaments, light yellow (2C) anthers. PISTIL: extends 2mm (1/16") below the corolla, cream (158C) style, light yellow (2C) stigma. BUD: thin & short. FOLIAGE: dark green (137A) upper surface; medium green (137C) lower surface. Leaves are 70mm (2 3/4") long x 50mm (2") wide, cordate shaped, wavy edges, acute tips and rounded bases. Veins & stems are red, branches are reddish brown. PARENTAGE: 'Thalia' x ('F. *crassistipula* x 'F. *fulgens grandiflora*'). Tall upright. Self branching. Makes good upright, standard, pyramid or pillar. Prefers overhead filtered light, warm climate. Heat tolerant if shaded. Best bloom and foliage colour in filtered light. Tested 3 years in Stadskanaal, The Netherlands. Award of Merit, VKC/KMTP, The Netherlands. Distinguished by flower shape (short & thick) and colour combination.
Koerts T. 2003 NL AFS5186.

Pabbe's Siepeltrien. Upright. Single. COROLLA: unflared, smooth petal margins; opens & matures rose (68C) edged magenta (68A); 9mm (3/8") long, 12mm (1/2") wide. SEPALS: half down; tips reflexed; pale pink (36D), tipped green (142A), orangish white (159C) base, upper surface; very pale orange (159B), edged dark rose (54B), lower surface; 16mm (5/8") long x 7mm (1/4") wide. TUBE: orangish white (159C) blushed dark rose (54B); medium length & thickness; 17mm (11/16") long x 7mm (1/4") wide. STAMENS: do not extend below corolla; orangish white (159C) filaments; yellow (10B) anthers. PISTIL: extends 16mm(5/8") below the corolla; rose (54C) style; light yellowish orange (19C) stigma. BUD: long, elliptic. FOLIAGE: dark green (137A) upper surface; medium green (137C) lower surface. Leaves are 82mm (3 1/4") long x 66mm (2 5/8") wide, cordate shaped, wavy edges, acute tips and rounded bases. Dark green veins, red (53B) stems & dark red (53A) branches. PARENTAGE: [('F. *magdalenae*' x 'F. *fulgens* *rubra grandiflora*'] x 'Wendy van Wanten'] x 'Lye's Unique'. Medium upright. Makes good upright, standard, pyramid, pillar decorative or trellis. Prefers overhead filtered light, warm climate. Best bloom and foliage colour in bright light. Tested 3 years in Stadskanaal, The Netherlands. Distinguished by colour combination. Koerts T. 2004 NL AFS5599.

Pabbe's Toesnust. Upright. Single. COROLLA: full flared, smooth petal margins; opens dark reddish purple (64A); matures reddish purple (74A); 22mm (7/8") long, 20mm (13/16") wide. SEPALS: horizontal; tips recurved; reddish purple (67A) upper surface; dark reddish purple (64A) lower surface; 34mm (1 5/16") long x 10mm (3/8") wide. TUBE: red (50A); short & thick; 8mm (5/16") long x 12mm (1/2") wide. STAMENS: extend 24mm (15/16") below corolla; reddish purple (67A) filaments; cream (158C) anthers. PISTIL: extends 48mm(1 7/8") below the corolla; dark reddish purple (64A) style & stigma. BUD: long sack. FOLIAGE: dark green (147A) upper surface; olive green (148A) lower surface. Leaves are 90mm (3 9/16") long x 42mm (1 11/16") wide, cordate shaped, serrulated edges, acute tips and rounded bases. Olive green veins, stems & branches. PARENTAGE: 'Bon Accord' x 'White Knight's Amethyst' x 'Impudence'. Small upright. Makes good upright or standard. Prefers overhead filtered light, full sun & warm climate. Best bloom and foliage colour in bright light. Tested 3 years in Stadskanaal, The Netherlands. Distinguished by bloom shape and colour. Koerts T. 2004 NL AFS5600.

Pabbe's Torreldoeve. Upright/Trailer. Single. COROLLA: quarter flared, smooth petal margins; opens purple (71A); matures reddish purple (71B); 12mm (1/2") long x 9mm (3/8") wide. SEPALS: half down; tips reflexed; magenta (71C) striped purple (71A), tipped yellow green (144A) upper surface; magenta (67B) lower surface; 18mm (11/16") long x 6mm (1/4") wide. TUBE: purple (71A) striped dark reddish purple (60A); long, medium thickness; 48mm(1 7/8") long; width is 6mm (1/4") top, 4mm (3/16") middle, 8mm (5/16") base. STAMENS: extend 3mm (1/8") below corolla; purple (71A) filaments, yellow (8B) anthers. PISTIL: extends 12mm (1/2") below the corolla, purple (71A) style & stigma. BUD: long, small. FOLIAGE: dark green (147A) upper surface; light olive green (147C) lower surface. Leaves are 126mm (4 15/16") long x

48mm (1 7/8") wide, lanceolate shaped, serrulated edges, acute tips and rounded bases. Veins & stems are light green, branches are dark green. PARENTAGE: 'F. *juntasensis*' x 'F. *denticulata*'. Lax upright or stiff trailer. Self branching. Makes good upright or standard. Prefers overhead filtered light, warm climate. Heat tolerant if shaded. Cold weather hardy to 6° C. Best bloom and foliage colour in filtered to limited light. Tested 4 years in Stadskanaal, The Netherlands. Award of Merit, VKC/KMTP, The Netherlands. Distinguished by bright orange colour and flowering in panicles. Koerts T. 2003 NL AFS5184.

Pabbe's Twin Sister. Upright. Single. COROLLA: quarter flared, bell shaped; smooth petal margins; opens dark orange (41A) edged red (45A); matures red (43A) edged red (45A); 14mm (9/16") long x 12mm (7/16") wide. SEPALS: half down, tips reflexed; red (46C) upper surface; dark orange (33A) lower surface; 24mm (15/16") long x 6mm (1/4") wide. TUBE: coral (39B) blushed red (46C); long & thin; 50mm (2") long x 5mm (3/16") wide. STAMENS do not extend beyond the corolla; light pink (38C) filaments; light yellow (11B) anthers. PISTIL extends 8mm (5/16") beyond the corolla; red (43A) style; yellow orange (16C) stigma. BUD: long triphylla type. FOLIAGE: dark green (147A), bronze shine, upper surface; light olive green (148B) lower surface. Leaves are 87mm (3 7/16") long x 44mm (1 3/4") wide; cordate shaped, serrulate edges, acute tips, obtuse bases. Veins, stems & branches are grayed orange (175A). PARENTAGE: 'Thalia' (Turner) x 'Golding's Perle'. Tall upright. Self branching. Makes good upright, standard or pyramid. Prefers full sun, warm climate. Best bloom & foliage colour in bright light. Tested 3 years in Stadskanaal, The Netherlands. Distinguished by bronze green foliage & bright red triphylla shaped flowers. Koerts T. 2009 NL AFS7043.

Pabbe's Ukkepuk. Trailer. Single. COROLLA: quarter flared, bell shaped; smooth petal margins; opens light purple (78B) edged purple (77A); matures reddish purple (64B), pink (62C) base; 18mm (11/16") long x 18mm (11/16") wide. SEPALS: fully up, tips reflexed; rose (68C) blushed light reddish purple (73A) upper surface; pale pink (62D) tipped rose (68B) lower surface; 25mm (1") long x 8mm (5/16") wide. TUBE: light rose (68D) striped pink (62A); medium length & thickness; 11mm (7/16") long x 7mm (1/4") wide. STAMENS extend 2mm (1/16") beyond

the corolla; rose (68B) filaments; dark reddish purple (61A) anthers. PISTIL extends 35mm (1 3/8") beyond the corolla; pink (62A) style; yellow (10B) stigma. BUD: ovate. FOLIAGE: dark green (147A) upper surface; medium green (147C) lower surface. Leaves are 92mm (3 5/8") long x 35mm (1 3/8") wide; ovate shaped, serrulate edges, acute tips, rounded bases. Veins & stems are light green (139C), branches are plum (185C). PARENTAGE: 'Gerharda's Panache' x 'La Campanella'. Natural trailer. Makes good basket. Prefers overhead filtered light. Best bloom & foliage colour in filtered light. Tested 3 years in Stadskanaal, The Netherlands. Distinguished by wide panicles of flowers & flower colours.
Koerts T. 2009 NL AFS7040.

Pabbe's Wikwief. Upright. Single. COROLLA: unflared, rose shape, turned under petal margins; opens light pink (65B) edged pink (62A); matures magenta (63B); 6mm (1/4") long, 8mm (5/16") wide. SEPALS: full down; tips reflexed; rose (68C) tipped green upper & lower surfaces; 11mm (7/16") long x 5mm (3/16") wide. TUBE: rose (68C) striped & blushed magenta (63B); short & thick; 18mm (11/16") long x 8mm (5/16") wide. STAMENS: do not extend below corolla; cream (158C) filaments; grayish yellow (161A) anthers. PISTIL: extends 3mm(1/8") below the corolla; rose (68C) style; light yellow (11C) stigma. BUD: long, pointed. FOLIAGE: dark green (147A) upper surface; medium green (147B) lower surface. Leaves are 68mm (2 11/16") long x 36mm (1 7/16") wide, elliptic shaped, wavy edges, acute tips and rounded bases. Yellowish green (146C) veins & stems; red brown branches. PARENTAGE: [('F. *magdalenae*' x 'F. *fulgens rubra grandiflora*') x 'Wendy van Wanten'] x [('Toos' x 'Prince Syray') x Bon Accord']. Medium upright. Makes good upright, standard, pyramid or pillar. Prefers overhead filtered light, warm climate. Best bloom and foliage colour in filtered light. Tested 3 years in Stadskanaal, The Netherlands. Distinguished by bloom colour and erect blooms that form carrousels on the end of branches.
Koerts T. 2004 NL AFS5601.

Pagona Fuhrmann. Trailer. Double. COROLLA: 3 quarter flared; opens purple (N81B), violet (76B) base; matures reddish purple (N80B); 29mm (1 1/8") long x 13mm (1/2") wide. PETALOIDS: same colour as corolla; 13mm (1/2") long x 12mm (7/16") wide. SEPALS: horizontal, tips reflexed; rose (63C) tipped apple green (144C) upper surface; dark rose (58C) tipped apple green (144C) lower surface; 33mm (1 5/16") long x 15mm (9/16") wide. TUBE: rose (61D); medium length & thickness; 13mm (1/2") long x 6mm (1/4") wide. FOLIAGE is dark green (139A) upper surface; medium green (138A) lower surface. PARENTAGE: 'Stad Genk' x 'Rocket Fire'.
Michiels 2007 BE AFS6330.

Panhoven. Trailer. Double. COROLLA: half flared; opens light violet (84B) & violet (85B), pale violet (76D) base; matures violet (76A) & light violet (N82D); 29mm (1 1/8") long x 13mm (1/2") wide. PETALOIDS: pale violet (76D) & violet (85A); 14mm (9/16") long x 6mm (1/4") wide. SEPALS: half down, tips recurved; pale lavender (69C) tipped light apple green (145C) upper surface; dark rose (73C) tipped light apple green (145C) lower surface; 44mm (1 3/4") long x 17mm (5/8") wide. TUBE: pale lavender (69C) striped pale rose (73B); medium length & thickness; 17mm (5/8") long x 7mm (1/4") wide. FOLIAGE is dark green (136A) upper surface; medium green (138B) lower surface. PARENTAGE: 'Vreni Schleeweiss' x 'Futura'.
Michiels 2007 BE AFS6331.

Papa Schurli. Upright. Semi Double. COROLLA: unflared, smooth petal margins, small & longish shape; opens & matures dark purple (79A); 30mm (1 3/16") long x 20mm (3/4") wide. SEPALS: fully up, tips recurved; magenta (59C) upper & lower surfaces; 40mm (1 9/16") long x 5mm (3/16") wide. TUBE: magenta (59C); medium length & thickness; 17mm (5/8") long x 6mm (1/4") wide. STAMENS extend 10mm (3/8") beyond the corolla; magenta (59C) filaments; dark reddish purple (59A) anthers. PISTIL extends 12mm (7/16") beyond the corolla; magenta (59C) style & stigma. BUD: longish, pointed. FOLIAGE: dark green (137A) upper surface; medium green (137C) lower surface. Leaves are 100mm (4") long x 50mm (2") wide; ovate shaped, serrulate edges, acute tips, rounded bases. Veins are light green, stems are grayish brown, branches are green. PARENTAGE: 'Santa Cruz' x 'Rohees New Millenium'. Medium upright. Makes good upright. Prefers overhead filtered light. Heat tolerant if shaded. Best bloom & foliage colour in filtered light. Tested 4 years in Dorf Haag, Austria. Distinguished by very dark corolla colour. Note: "Shurli" is the nickname for "George" in Austria.
Gindl 2009 AT AFS7086.

340

Papy Claude. Upright/Trailer. Single. COROLLA: quarter flared, smooth petal margins; opens light purple (78B), magenta (63B) veins & base; matures light purple (78C); 30mm (1 3/16") long x 20mm (13/16") wide. SEPALS: horizontal; tips recurved; red (50A) upper & lower surfaces; 44mm (1 3/4") long x 10mm (3/8") wide. TUBE: red (50A); medium length & thickness; 15mm (9/16") long x 6mm (1/4") wide. STAMENS: extend 15-18mm (9/16-11/16") below corolla; rose (50B) filaments; rose (48B) anthers. PISTIL: extends 39mm (1 9/16") below the corolla; rose (50B) style; red (47B) stigma. BUD: long, ovate. FOLIAGE: dark green (147A) upper surface, medium green (147B) lower surface. Leaves are 60-95mm (2 3/8 - 3 3/4") long x 34-55mm (1 3/8 – 2 3/16") wide, ovate shaped, serrulated edges, acute tips and rounded bases. Yellowish green veins & stems; yellowish green/light brown branches. PARENTAGE: 'Henri Verdeur' x 'Speciosa'. Lax upright or stiff trailer. Self branching. Makes good upright. Prefers overhead filtered light and cool climate. Best bloom and foliage colour in filtered light. Tested 3 years in Pornic, France. Distinguished by large single flowers. Massé 2004 FR AFS5453.

Papy Raymond. Upright. Semi Double. COROLLA: half flared, petticoat shape; opens purple (80A); matures reddish purple (80B); 31mm (1 1/4") long x 25mm (1") wide. PETALOIDS: reddish purple (72B); 18mm (11/16") long x 14mm (9/16") wide. SEPALS: half up, tips recurved up; pale pink (56D), veined light pink (55D) upper surface; cream (158D) lower surface; 42mm (1 5/8") long x 16mm (5/8") wide. TUBE: cream (11D); 16mm (5/8") long x 8mm (5/16") wide. FOLIAGE is dark green (139A) upper surface; medium green (137C) lower surface. PARENTAGE: 'Showtime' x unknown. Simon 2008 AFS6841.

Pasodoble. Trailer. Double. COROLLA is half flared with wavy petal margins; opens rose (64D), matures rose (52C); 26mm (1") long x 32mm (1 1/4") wide. SEPALS are half up, tips recurved up; pale pink (56A) upper and lower surfaces; 36mm (1 7/16") long x 14mm (9/16") wide. TUBE is pale pink (56C); medium length and thickness; 16mm (5/8") long x 7mm (1/4") wide. STAMENS extend 7mm (1/4") beyond the corolla; pink (62C) filaments, light rose (50C) anthers. PISTIL extends 18mm (11/16") beyond the corolla; pale pink (62D) style, pale yellow green (154D) stigma. BUD is ovate, pointed.

FOLIAGE is dark green (147A) upper surface, medium green (147B) lower surface. Leaves are 65mm (2 9/16") long x 43mm (1 11/16") wide, ovate shaped, serrated edges, acute tips and rounded bases. Veins, stems and branches are reddish. PARENTAGE: Seedling of unknown Parentage. Natural trailer. Self branching. Makes good basket. Prefers overhead filtered light and cool climate. Best bloom colour in filtered light. Tested fifteen years in Wognum, The Netherlands. Distinguished by colour combination. Dekker 2002 NL AFS4948.

Pater Damiaan. Upright/Trailer. Double. COROLLA: three quarter flared, turned under wavy petal margins; opens reddish purple (72B) blotched rose (68C); matures dark reddish purple (64A) blotched rose (68B); 29mm (1 1/8") long x 24mm (15/16") wide. PETALOIDS: Same colour as corolla; 16mm (5/8") long x 11mm (7/16") wide. SEPALS: half up, tips recurved up; rose (55B) tipped pale yellow green (150D) upper surface; rose (N57C) tipped pale yellow green (150D) lower surface; 47mm (1 7/8") long x 18mm (11/16") wide. TUBE: white (155B); short & thick; 11mm (7/16") long x 7mm (1/4") wide. STAMENS extend 14mm (9/16") beyond the corolla; magenta (67B) filaments; purple (71A) anthers. PISTIL extends 32mm (1 1/4") beyond the corolla; rose (68B) style; pale yellow (1D) stigma. BUD: globular. FOLIAGE: dark green (137A) upper surface; medium green (137C) lower surface. Leaves are 70mm (2 3/4") long x 44mm (1 3/4") wide; ovate shaped, serrulate edges, acute tips, rounded bases. Veins are olive green (152B), stems are light grayish red (182C), branches are dark grayish red (182A) & light green (139D). PARENTAGE: 'Manfried Kleinau' x 'Dal's Conquest'. Lax upright or stiff trailer. Self branching. Makes good upright. Prefers overhead filtered light, cool climate. Best bloom & foliage colour in filtered light. Tested 3 years in Koningshooikt, Belgium. Waanrode 9/20/08. Distinguished by bloom colour combination. Michiels 2009 BE AFS7205.

Patricia Bervoets. Upright. Double. COROLLA is three quarter flared with turned under wavy petal margins; opens rose (68B) edged magenta (68A), white (155B) base; matures magenta (68A) rose (65A) base; 24mm (15/16") long x 36 mm (1 7/16") wide. PETALOIDS: Two per sepal, same colour as corolla; 13mm (1/2") x 9mm (3/8"). SEPALS are full down, tips recurved; white (155B) tipped light yellow green (150A) upper surface, white (155D) lower surface; 33mm (1 5/16") long x 18mm (11/16") wide. TUBE is white (155A), medium length and thickness; 17mm (11/16") long x 6mm (1/4") wide. STAMENS extend 17mm (11/16") beyond the corolla; white (155A) filaments, light greenish white (157C) anthers. PISTIL extends 32mm (1 1/4") below the corolla; white (155B) style, yellow (5A) stigma. BUD is round, pointed. FOLIAGE is dark green (139A) upper surface, medium green (137C) lower surface. Leaves are 80mm (3 3/16") long x 55mm (2 3/16") wide, ovate shaped, serrated edges, acute tips and rounded bases. Veins are light green (138C), stems and branches are brown (166A). PARENTAGE: 'Applause' x unknown. Medium upright. Self branching. Makes good basket or upright. Prefers overhead filtered light. Best bloom and foliage colour in filtered light. Tested three years in Rummen, Belgium. Certificate N.B.F.K. at Meise. Distinguished by bloom colour combination. Ector 2002 BE AFS4898.

Patricia Hodge. Trailer. Single. COROLLA: quarter flared, smooth petal margins; opens orange (41B); matures dark orange (41A); 20mm (3/4") long x 25mm (1") wide. SEPALS: horizontal, tips recurved; rose (48B) upper & lower surfaces; 38mm (1 1/2") long x 10mm (3/8") wide. TUBE: pink (48C); long, medium thickness; 14mm (9/16") long x 7mm (1/4") wide. STAMENS extend 13mm (1/2") beyond the corolla; magenta (63A) filaments; dark reddish purple (64A) anthers. PISTIL extends 25mm (1") beyond the corolla; light rose (63D) style; light yellow (10D) stigma. BUD: long, pointed. FOLIAGE: medium green (138A) upper surface; medium green (138B) lower surface. Leaves are 63mm (2 1/2") long x 39mm (1 1/2") wide; ovate shaped, serrate edges, acute tips, rounded bases. Veins are green, stems are light rose, branches are brown. PARENTAGE: 'Coachman' x 'Blaze Away'. Natural trailer. Self branching. Makes good basket. Prefers overhead filtered light. Heat tolerant if shaded. Best bloom colour in filtered light. Tested 4 years in Ormskirk, Lancashire, England. Distinguished by early & continuous flowering; flower colour & shape. Sinton 2009 UK AFS7092.

Patricia My Love. Upright. Semi Double. COROLLA: quarter flared, smooth petal margins; opens & matures pale pink (62D); 15mm (9/16") long x 15mm (9/16") wide. SEPALS: half down, tips recurved; pale pink (62D) upper & lower surfaces; 20mm (3/4") long x 10mm (3/8") wide. TUBE: greenish

white (157B); short, medium thickness; 10mm (3/8") long x 5mm (3/16") wide. STAMENS extend 10mm (3/8") beyond the corolla; rose (65A) filaments; reddish purple (74B) anthers. PISTIL extends 20mm (3/4") beyond the corolla; white (155A) style & stigma. BUD: ovate. FOLIAGE: medium green (137B) upper surface; medium green (137D) lower surface. Leaves are 40mm (1 9/16") long x 25mm (1") wide; cordate shaped, serrulate edges, obtuse tips, obtuse bases. Veins are green, stems are light brown, branches are light green. PARENTAGE: 'Snowbird' x 'Diana Princess of Wales'. Small upright. Self branching. Makes good upright. Prefers overhead filtered light. Best bloom colour in filtered light. Tested 3 years in Rayleigh, Essex, England. Distinguished by blossom colour & shape. Smith R. 2009 UK AFS7122.

Patrick Mioulane. Upright/Trailer. Single. COROLLA is quarter flared; opens and matures dark orange (41A); 14mm (9/16") long x 15mm (5/8") wide. SEPALS horizontal, tips recurved; pink (37D) tipped yellowish green upper and lower surfaces; 20mm (13/16") long x 6mm (1/4") wide. TUBE is pink (37C), medium length and thickness; 17mm (11/16") long x 6mm (1/4") wide. STAMENS extend 2 - 5mm (1/16" – 3/16") below the corolla; peach (38B) filaments and light yellow (4C) anthers. PISTIL extends 26mm (1") below the corolla; light pink (38C) style, light yellow (4C) stigma. BUD is ovate. FOLIAGE is medium green (146A) upper surface, yellowish green (146B) lower surface. Leaves are 90mm (3 9/16") long x 52mm (2 1/16") wide, ovate shaped, serrulated edges, rounded tips and acute bases. Veins and stems are yellowish green, branches are yellowish green and light brown. PARENTAGE: 'Speciosa' x 'Mrs. W. Rundle'. Lax upright or stiff trailer. Self branchingMakes good upright or standard. Prefers cool climate. Heat tolerant if shaded. Best bloom colour in limited light. Tested four years in Prefailles, France. Certificat de Merit du Comité de selection de la Societé Nationale d'Horticulture de France. Distinguished by bloom colour and profuse semi-terminal and terminal blooms. Boquien 2002 FR AFS4867.

Pat's Smile. Upright. Single. COROLLA: unflared, rectangular, turned under smooth petal margins; opens dark reddish purple (59A); matures dark reddish purple (61A); 15mm (9/16") long x 10mm (3/8") wide. SEPALS: horizontal; tips recurved; reddish

purple (61B) upper & lower surfaces; 30mm(1 3/16") long x 9mm (3/8") wide. TUBE: dark red (46A); long, medium thickness; 20mm (13/16") long x 6mm (1/4") wide. STAMENS: extend 10mm (3/8") below corolla; magenta (63A) filaments; dark reddish purple (59A) anthers. PISTIL: extends 25mm (1") below the corolla, magenta (63A) style; grayish yellow (160A) stigma. BUD: medium, elongated. FOLIAGE: medium green (146A) upper surface; yellowish green (146B) lower surface. Leaves are 60mm (2 3/8") long x 35mm (1 3/8") wide, cordate shaped, serrated edges, acute tips and rounded bases. Veins & branches are green, stems are brown. PARENTAGE: 'Janneke Brinkmann-Saletijn' x 'Orange Glow'. Medium upright. Self branching. Makes good upright or bedding plant. Heat tolerant if shaded. Prefers warm climate. Cold weather hardy to 28° F. Tested 3 years in Walthamstow, London, England. Distinguished by mass of flowers produced terminally.
Allsop M.R. 2003 UK AFS5146.

Paul. Upright. Single. COROLLA: unflared, smooth petal margins, compact; opens dark purple (79A); matures purple (N79C); 10mm (3/8") long x 6mm (1/4") wide. SEPALS: horizontal, tips recurved; dark reddish purple (60B) upper & lower surfaces; 20mm (3/4") long x 7mm (1/4") wide. TUBE: dark reddish purple (60B); medium length, thin; 10mm (3/8") long x 5mm (3/16") wide. STAMENS extend 10mm (3/8") beyond the corolla; dark reddish purple (60B) filaments; reddish purple (N66A) anthers. PISTIL extends 25mm (1") beyond the corolla; dark reddish purple (60B) style; dark purple (N79A) stigma. BUD: small, elongated. FOLIAGE: dark green (147A) upper surface; medium green (147B) lower surface. Leaves are 68mm (2 11/16") long x 36mm (1 7/16") wide; ovate shaped, serrulate edges, acute tips, obtuse bases. Veins & stems are red, branches are reddish maturing to light brown. PARENTAGE: 'Rosea' x 'Oscar Lehmeier'. Medium upright. Self branching. Makes good upright or standard. Prefers full sun, warm climate. Heat tolerant if shaded. Best bloom & foliage colour in bright light. Tested 3 years in Bavaria, Southern Germany. Distinguished by corolla colour & shape.
Burkhart 2009 DE AFS7108.

Paul Borremans. Upright/Trailer. Double. COROLLA: three quarter flared, turned under wavy petal margins; opens purple

(77A), purple (71A) base; matures dark reddish purple (70A); 27mm (1 1/16") long x 24mm (15/16") wide. SEPALS: fully up; tips recurved; dark reddish purple (64A) tipped yellowish green (145A) upper surface; magenta (71C) lower surface; 32mm (1 1/4") long x 17mm (11/16") wide. TUBE: dark reddish purple (60A); medium length & thickness; 15mm(9/16") long x 5mm (3/16") wide. STAMENS: extend 23mm (7/8") below corolla; light reddish purple (72C) filaments; purple (79C) anthers. PISTIL: extends 57mm (2 1/4") below the corolla, reddish purple (72B) style, yellowish white (4D) stigma. BUD: cordate. FOLIAGE: dark green (139A) upper surface; medium green (139C) lower surface. Leaves are 61mm (2 7/16") long x 30mm (1 3/16") wide, elliptic shaped, serrulated edges, acute tips and rounded bases. Veins are grayish red (182B), stems are plum (184C), branches are light red purple (185D). PARENTAGE: 'Rohees New Millennium' x 'Frank Saunders'. Lax upright or stiff trailer. Self branching. Makes good basket. Prefers overhead filtered light. Best bloom and foliage colour in filtered light. Tested 3 years in Koningshooikt, Belgium. NBFK Certificate at Meise. Distinguished by bloom colour and sepal shape.
Michiels 2003 BE AFS5194.

Paul Kennes. Upright. Double. COROLLA is three quarter flared with turned under smooth petal margins; opens purple (83A), reddish purple (71B) at base; matures purple (71A), reddish purple (59B) at base; 31mm (1 1/4") long x 32mm (1 1/4") wide. PETALOIDS are reddish purple (71B) tipped purple (71A); 18mm (11/16") long x 10mm (3/8") wide. SEPALS are horizontal, tips reflexed; reddish purple (64B) upper surface; magenta (63A) lower surface; 34mm (1 3/8") long x 20mm (13/16") wide. TUBE is reddish purple (61B); medium length and thickness; 21mm (13/16") long x 7mm (1/4") wide. STAMENS extend 17mm (11/16") beyond the corolla; dark reddish purple (61A) filaments, dark gray (202B) anthers. PISTIL extends 34mm (1 3/8") beyond the corolla; reddish purple (66B) style, yellow (10A) stigma. BUD is round. FOLIAGE is medium green (139B) upper surface, medium green (137C) lower surface. Leaves are 70mm (2 3/4") long x 31mm (1 1/4") wide, elliptic shaped, serrulated edges, acute tips and rounded bases. Veins are plum (184B), stems are light plum (184D), branches are plum (185B). PARENTAGE: 'Rohees New Millennium' x 'Orange King'. Medium upright. Self branching. Makes good upright. Prefers overhead filtered light and cool climate. Best bloom and foliage colour in filtered light. Tested three years in Koningshooikt, Belgium. Certificate N.B.F.K. at Meise. Distinguished by bloom colour. Michiels 2002 BE AFS4971.

Paul Meeus. Upright. Semi Double. COROLLA is half flared with smooth petal margins; opens & matures pale lavender (65D); 21mm (13/16") long x 22 mm (7/8") wide. SEPALS are fully up, tips reflexed; light pink (65C) upper surface; rose (65A) lower surface; 24mm (15/16") long x 8mm (5/16") wide. TUBE is light pink (65C), medium length & thickness; 9mm (3/8") long x 5mm (3/16") wide. FOLIAGE: medium green (137B) upper surface; medium green (138B) lower surface. Leaves are 67mm (2 5/8") long x 40mm (1 9/16") wide, ovate shaped. PARENTAGE: 'Indy van Roovert' x 'Delta's Wonder'. Distinguished by bloom colour. Comperen 2005 NL AFS5641.

Paul Und Carola. Trailer. Double. COROLLA: half flared; opens violet (84A), rose (61D) base; matures light purple (N80C); 21mm (13/16") long x 11mm (7/16") wide. PETALOIDS: same colour as corolla; 13mm (1/2") long x 9mm (5/16") wide. SEPALS: horizontal, tips reflexed; light rose (58D) & pink (62C) tipped light green (143C) upper surface; rose (61D) tipped light green (143C) lower surface; 30mm (1 3/16") long x 11mm (7/16") wide. TUBE: light rose (58D); long & thin; 17mm (5/8") long x 3mm (1/8") wide. FOLIAGE is medium green (138A) upper surface; medium green (138B) lower surface. PARENTAGE: 'Jef Vander Kuylen' x 'Hilda'. Michiels 2005 BE AFS6332.

Paul Van Gorp. Trailer. Double. COROLLA: three quarter flared; opens white (155C) striped rose (63C); matures white (155B) striped rose (68C); 34mm (1 3/8") long x 28mm (1 1/8") wide. SEPALS: half down, tips recurved; white (155C) striped light green (142B) upper surface; pale lavender (69C) tipped light green (142B) lower surface; 49mm (1 15/16") long x 14mm (9/16") wide. TUBE: white (155C) striped light green (142B); 14mm (9/16") long x 7mm (1/4") wide. FOLIAGE is dark green (136A) upper surface; medium green (139B) lower surface. PARENTAGE: 'Leen Vander Kuylen' x 'Kiss'. Michiels BE 2008 AFS6739.

Paul van Hassel. Upright/Trailer. Double. COROLLA: half flared, turned under wavy petal margins; opens reddish purple (61B) &

purple (71A) edged dark purple (79B); matures dark reddish purple (64A) edged purple (83A); 31mm (1 1/4") long x 26mm (1") wide. PETALOIDS: Same colour as corolla; 14mm (9/16") long x 12mm (7/16") wide. SEPALS: half down, tips recurved; reddish purple (64B) upper surface; reddish purple (61B) lower surface; 42mm (1 5/8") long x 14mm (9/16") wide. TUBE: dark reddish purple (60C); medium length & thickness; 14mm (9/16") long x 6mm (1/4") wide. STAMENS extend 18mm (11/16") beyond the corolla; purple (71A) filaments; purple (83A) anthers. PISTIL extends 32mm (1 1/4") beyond the corolla; dark reddish purple (72A) style; pale lavender (69D) stigma. BUD: bulbous. FOLIAGE: dark green (137A) upper surface; medium green (139C) lower surface. Leaves are 75mm (3") long x 32mm (1 1/4") wide; elliptic shaped, serrulate edges, acute tips, rounded bases. Veins are dark reddish purple (187B), stems are dark red purple (187D), branches are red purple (N77B). PARENTAGE: 'Manfried Kleinau' x 'Jubie-Lin'. Lax upright or stiff trailer. Self branching. Makes good basket or upright. Prefers overhead filtered light, cool climate. Best bloom & foliage colour in filtered light. Tested 3 years in Koningshooikt, Belgium. Waanrode 7/5/08. Distinguished by bloom colour combination. Michiels 2009 BE AFS7206.

Paula. Trailer. Single. COROLLA: full flared; opens violet (85A) & rose (65A); matures violet (84A) & rose (65A); 30mm (1 3/16") long x 30mm (1 3/16") wide. SEPALS: half up, tips recurved up; pale pink (62D) upper & lower surfaces; 50mm (2") long x 19mm (3/4") wide. TUBE: light pink (65B); medium length & thickness; 25mm (1") long x 8mm (5/16") wide. STAMENS extend 45mm (1 3/4") beyond the corolla; light rose (73B) filaments; reddish purple (78C) anthers. PISTIL extends 80mm (3 3/16") beyond the corolla; light rose (73C) style; pale orange (22C) stigma. BUD: ovate, curved tip. FOLIAGE: yellowish green (144A) upper surface; yellowish green (144A) lower surface. Leaves are 70mm (2 3/4") long x 45mm (1 3/4") wide; ovate shaped, smooth edges, obtuse tips, rounded bases. Veins are reddish purple (59B), stems & branches are dark reddish purple (59A). PARENTAGE: 'Pink Marshmallow' x 'Guurtje'. Natural trailer. Makes good basket or upright. Prefers overhead filtered light, cool climate. Best bloom & foliage colour in filtered light. Tested 8 years in Amsterdam, The Netherlands.

V.K.C Aalsmeer 10/28/2000. Distinguished by flower colour & shape. Krom 2009 NL AFS7060.

Paula Liebregts. Upright. Semi Double. COROLLA is full flared with smooth petal margins; opens violet (84A); matures dark reddish purple (72A); 39mm (1 9/16") long x 35mm (1 3/8") wide. SEPALS are fully up, tips recurved; magenta (58B) upper surface; dark rose (58C) lower surface; 37mm (1 7/16") long x 15mm (9/16") wide. TUBE is light magenta (58D); medium length & thickness; 15mm (9/16") long x 9mm (3/8") wide. FOLIAGE: dark green (137A) upper surface; medium green (138B) lower surface. Leaves are 58mm (2 5/16") long x 45mm (1 3/4") wide, ovate shaped. PARENTAGE: ['Rohees Rana' x ('Roesse Apus' x 'Roesse Apus')] x 'Yvette Klessens'. Distinguished by bloom shape.
Buiting 2005 NL AFS5874.

Paulette van Mandelbeek. Trailer. Double. COROLLA: half flared, turned under smooth petal margins; opens violet (84A), white (155B) base, veined dark rose (58C); matures purple (81B), light pink (65C) base, veined dark rose (58C); 16mm (5/8") long x 30mm (1 3/16") wide. SEPALS: horizontal; tips recurved; magenta (58B) tipped light yellow green (150B) upper surface; dark rose (58C) lower surface; 25mm (1") long x 12mm (1/2") wide. TUBE: dark rose (58C); short, medium thickness; 7mm(1/4") long x 4mm (3/16") wide. STAMENS: 12mm (1/2") below corolla; light rose (58D) filaments, reddish purple (58A) anthers. PISTIL: extends 22mm (7/8") below the corolla, light rose (63D) style, grayish yellow (161A) stigma. BUD: ovate. FOLIAGE: dark green (137A) upper surface; medium green (138A) lower surface. Leaves are 61mm (2 3/8") long x 34mm (1 5/16") wide, ovate shaped, smooth edges, acute tips and rounded bases. Veins, stems & branches are light reddish purple (59A). PARENTAGE: 'La Campanella' x unknown. Natural trailer. Self branching. Makes good basket. Prefers overhead filtered light. Best bloom and foliage colour in filtered light. Tested 3 years in Roeselare, Belgium. NBFK Certificate at Meise. Distinguished by bloom colour.
Vandewalle 2003 BE AFS5199.

Pauline Copple. Upright/Trailer. Semi Double. COROLLA pale lilac, veined pink; corolla is half flared. SEPALS dark pink on the upper and lower surfaces; sepals are half up with recurved tips. TUBE dark pink. PARENTAGE 'Swingtime' x 'Patio Princess'.

Norcross 2009 UK BFS0107.

Pavlovsk. Trailer. Single. COROLLA: quarter flared; opens white (155C) striped dark rose (58C); matures white (155B)) striped rose (61D); 36mm (1 7/16") long x 24mm (15/16") wide. SEPALS: fully up, tips recurved; reddish purple (58B) upper surface; magenta (61C) lower surface; 46mm (1 13/16") long x 11mm (7/16") wide. TUBE: magenta (63A); medium length & thickness; 16mm (5/8") long x 6mm (1/4") wide. FOLIAGE is dark green (139A) upper surface; medium green (138B) lower surface. PARENTAGE: 'Lavender Heaven' x 'Delta's Trick'. Meise 8/12/06, Outstanding.
Michiels 2007 BE AFS6358.

Pays De Retz. Upright. Single. COROLLA: quarter flared, smooth petal margins; opens & matures purple (81A); 25mm (1") long x 21mm (13/16") wide. SEPALS: horizontal; tips recurved, slightly twisted, margins up; pink (62A), tipped yellowish green (146E), upper & lower surfaces; 39mm (1 9/16") long x 12mm (1/2") wide. TUBE: pale pink (62D) striped light pink (62B); very short, medium thickness; spherical, 8mm (5/16") diameter. STAMENS: extend 2 - 4mm (1/16–3/16") below corolla; light reddish purple (73A) filaments, magenta (68A) anthers. PISTIL: extends 26mm (1 1/16") below the corolla, light rose (73B) style, light yellow (4B) stigma. BUD: ovate. FOLIAGE: medium green (146A) upper surface; yellowish green (146B) lower surface. Leaves are 53mm (2 1/8") long x 32mm (1 1/4") wide, ovate shaped, quasi-smooth to serrulated edges, acute tips and rounded bases. Veins, stems & branches are yellowish green. PARENTAGE: 'Philippe Boennec' x 'Mirobolant'. Medium upright. Makes good upright. Prefers overhead filtered light and cool climate. Best bloom and foliage colour in filtered light. Tested 3 years in Pornic, France. Distinguished by bloom shape and colour.
Massé 2003 FR AFS5219.

Peerke Heylen. Upright/Trailer. Double. COROLLA: half flared, smooth petal margins; opens dark purple (79A); matures purple (71A); 22mm (7/8") long x 24mm (15/16") wide. SEPALS: horizontal; tips recurved; light reddish purple (72C) upper & lower surfaces;32mm (1 1/4") long x 15mm (9/16") wide. TUBE: light reddish purple (72C); medium length & thickness; 22mm (7/8") long x 6mm (1/4") wide. STAMENS: extend 22mm (7/8") below corolla; purple (71A) filaments & anthers. PISTIL: extends 33mm

345

(1 5/16") below the corolla; reddish purple (71B) style; pale rose (73D) stigma. BUD: spherical. FOLIAGE: medium green (137B) upper surface; medium green (138B) lower surface. Leaves are 52mm (2 1/16") long x 40mm (1 9/16") wide, cordate shaped, serrulated edges, acute tips and obtuse bases. Veins, stems & branches are red. PARENTAGE: 'Bicentennial' x 'Rohees Queen'. Lax upright or stiff trailer. Makes good stiff trailer. Prefers overhead filtered light and cool climate. Best bloom and foliage colour in filtered light. Tested 4 years in Reusel, The Netherlands. Distinguished by bloom colour.
van Eijk 2003 NL AFS5255.

Pegasus. Trailer. Double. COROLLA: half flared, turned under; opens white (155C); matures white (155D); 20mm (3/4") long x 18mm (11/16") wide. PETALOIDS: white (155C); 11 mm (7/16") long x 8 mm (5/16") wide. SEPALS are horizontal, tips recurved, twisted left; white (155C) tipped light apple green (144D) upper and lower surfaces; 32mm (1 1/4") long x 11mm (7/16") wide. TUBE is white (155C) striped medium green (138B); medium length, thin; 20mm (3/4") long x 5mm (3/16") wide. FOLIAGE is dark green (137A) upper surface; medium green (138B) lower surface. PARENTAGE: 'Vreeni Schleeweiss' x 'Kiss'.
Michiels 2007 BE AFS6507.

Peggy Belle 'G'. Single. COROLLA medium pink. SEPALS medium pink. TUBE medium pink.
Kimberley 2004 UK.

Peggy Burford. Trailer. Single. COROLLA reddish orange. SEPALS reddish orange. TUBE reddish orange.
Kimberley 2004 UK.

Pepi Hartl. Upright. Single. COROLLA: unflared; long, slender, compact shape; opens dark purple (79A); matures reddish purple (59B); 18mm (11/16") long x 9mm (5/16") wide. SEPALS: full down, tips recurved; red (53B) upper surface; magenta (58B) lower surface; 25mm (1") long x 9mm (5/16") wide. TUBE: red (53B); 18mm (11/16") long x 5mm (3/16") wide. FOLIAGE is dark green (137A) upper surface; yellowish green (146B) lower surface. PARENTAGE: 'Rohees King' x 'F. regia ssp serrae Hoya.
Burkhart 2008 DE AFS6859.

Pepsy. Trailer. Single. COROLLA opens violet, matures to light purple; corolla is

quarter flared and is 20mm long x 19mm wide. SEPALS deep pink on the upper and lower surfaces; sepals are half up with recurved tips and are 20mm long x 6mm wide. TUBE deep pink and is 8mm long x 7mm wide. PARENTAGE 'Loves Reward' x 'seedling No 1020'. This cultivar good show plant, makes a very nice hanging pot.
Reiley B. 2007 UK BFS0045.

Percival's. Upright. Single. COROLLA: quarter flared, bell shaped; opens purple (89C); matures dark purple (78A); 20mm (3/4") long x 13mm (1/2") wide. SEPALS: half down, tips recurved; dark rose (58C) tipped green upper surface; light rose (58D) lower surface; 25mm (1") long x 13mm (1/2") wide. TUBE: cream (158D); 7mm (1/4") long x 5mm (3/16") wide. FOLIAGE is dark green (137A) upper surface; medium green (137D) lower surface. PARENTAGE: 'Julie Ann Goodwin' x 'Shellford'.
Goodwin 2008 UK AFS6940.

Peter Meredith. Upright. Single. COROLLA pale peachy pink bright pink picotee edging. SEPALS peachy pink. TUBE peachy pink.
Reynolds G. 2008 UK.

Peter Peeters. Upright/Trailer. Double. COROLLA is three quarter flared with turned under smooth petal margins; opens purple (77A), dark reddish purple (64A) base; matures purple (71A); 26mm (1") long x 29mm (1/8") wide. PETALOIDS: same colour as corolla; 14mm (9/16") long x 9mm (3/8") wide. SEPALS are horizontal, tips reflexed; dark reddish purple (64A) upper surface; reddish purple (61B) lower surface; 48mm (1 7/8") long x 21mm (13/16") wide. TUBE is magenta (63A); medium length & thick; 18mm (11/16") long x 10mm (3/8") wide. FOLIAGE: dark green (136B) upper surface; medium green (138C) lower surface. Leaves are 78mm (3 1/16") long x 35mm (1 3/8") wide, ovate shaped. PARENTAGE: 'Roesse Blacky' x 'Heikantenaer'. Meis 3-7-04 Approved with Excellence. Distinguished by purple bloom colour.
Michiels 2005 BE AFS5673.

Petit Frèr. Upright. Single. COROLLA is quarter flared with smooth petal margins; opens & matures reddish purple (67A); 21mm (13/16") long x 18mm (11/16") wide. SEPALS are horizontal, tips recurved; pale pink (69A) tipped yellowish green (154A) upper surface; light rose (73B) lower surface; 27mm (1 1/16") long x 7mm (1/4") wide. TUBE is cream (158D) & slightly light

greenish white (157D); very short & thick; 8mm (5/16") long x 8mm (5/16") wide. FOLIAGE: dark green (147A) upper surface; medium green (147B) lower surface. Leaves are 55mm (2 3/16") long x 31mm (1 1/4") wide, ovate shaped. PARENTAGE: 'Porte Océane' x 'F. boliviana alba'. Distinguished by very short TUBE & contrasting bloom colour.
Massé 2005 FR AFS5700.

Petra van Bergen. Trailer. Single. COROLLA: Half flared; opens light pink (65B); matures light pink (65C); 24mm (15/16") long x 27mm (1 1/16") wide. SEPALS: fully up, tips recurved; light rose (58B) upper surface; light rose (58C) lower surface; 19mm (3/4") long x 11mm (7/16") wide. TUBE: light rose (58D); medium length & thickness; 15mm (9/16") long x 6mm (1/4") wide. FOLIAGE is dark green (139A) upper surface; medium green (137B) lower surface. PARENTAGE: ('Swanley Gem' x 'Roesse Dione') x 'Silver Dawn'.
Roes 2007 NL AFS6699.

Pfarrer Raimund. Upright. Double. COROLLA is three quarter flared with smooth petal margins; opens light purple (87C), white (155B) base; matures violet (77C), white (155B) base; 25mm (1") long x 40mm (1 9/16") wide. SEPALS are fully up, tips recurved; white (155A) upper & lower surfaces; 50mm (2") long x 12mm (1/2") wide. TUBE is white (155A); medium length & thickness; 17mm (11/16") long x 7mm (1/4") wide. FOLIAGE: medium green (139B) upper surface; medium green (139C) lower surface. Leaves are 55mm (2 3/16") long x 35mm (1 3/8") wide, ovate shaped. PARENTAGE: 'Margaret Tebbit' x 'Fey'. Distinguished by pure white, lightly curled SEPALS & long white pistil.
Strümper 2005 DE AFS5859.

Philip Fortes. Upright/Trailer. Semi Double. COROLLA: half flared, turned under wavy petal margins; opens dark rose (54A) & violet (77C); matures dark rose (58C) & light purple (75B); 26mm (1") long x 24mm (15/16") wide. SEPALS: horizontal, tips recurved; pale pink (56A) tipped light green (145D) upper surface; rose (52C) tipped light green (145D) lower surface; 33mm (1 5/16") long x 14mm (9/16") wide. TUBE: light pink (55D); medium length & thickness; 14mm (9/16") long x 7mm (1/4") wide. STAMENS extend 18mm (11/16") beyond the corolla; magenta (63B) filaments; magenta (63A) anthers. PISTIL extends 32mm (1 1/4") beyond the

corolla; rose (68B) style; light yellow (2C) stigma. BUD: oblong. FOLIAGE: dark green (137A) upper surface; medium green (137D) lower surface. Leaves are 57mm (2 1/4") long x 24mm (15/16") wide; elliptic shaped, serrate edges, acute tips, rounded bases. Veins are dark red (185A), stems are plum (185B), branches are dark reddish purple (187C). PARENTAGE: 'Manfried Kleinau' x 'Jan Vander Kuylen'. Lax upright or stiff trailer. Self branching. Makes good basket. Prefers overhead filtered light, cool climate. Best bloom & foliage colour in filtered light. Tested 3 years in Koningshooikt, Belgium. Waanrode 7/5/08. Distinguished by bloom colour combination.
Michiels 2009 BE AFS7207.

Phil's Pill. Upright. Single. COROLLA opens pale beetroot, matures paler; corolla is quarter flared. SEPALS pale pink with aubergine on the upper and lower surfaces; SEPALS are half down with recurved tips. TUBE pale pink with aubergine. PARENTAGE 'Purperklokje' x 'Smouldering Fires'.
Horsham 2009 UK BFS0117.

Piannes Berg. Trailer. Double. COROLLA: half flared; opens pale purple (75C) base, tipped white (155C); matures rose (65A) base, tipped white (155D); 23mm (7/8") long x 16mm (5/8") wide. PETALOIDS: pale purple (75C) base, tipped white (155C); 10 mm (3/8") long x 8 mm (5/16") wide. SEPALS are half down, tips reflexed; pale lavender (69D) tipped light apple green (145B) upper surface and pale purple (75D) tipped light apple green (145B) lower surface; 38mm (1 1/2") long x 16mm (5/8") wide. TUBE is white (155C); medium length and thickness; 18mm (11/16") long x 7mm (1/4") wide. FOLIAGE. PARENTAGE: 'Godelieve Elli' x 'Jessie Pearson'.
Michiels 2007 BE AFS6508.

Pibiorix. Trailer. Single. COROLLA: quarter flared, turned under smooth petal margins; opens & matures dark rose (67C) edged reddish purple (72B), pale pink (62D) at base; 13mm (1/2") long x 13mm (1/2") wide. SEPALS: half up; tips recurved up; pale yellowish green (149D), tipped light green (142A) upper & lower surfaces; 23mm (15/16") long x 7mm (1/4") wide. TUBE: pale yellowish green (149D); medium length & thickness; 13mm (1/2") long x 5mm (3/16") wide. STAMENS: extend 11mm (7/16") below the corolla; pink (62A) filaments, light yellow (11B) anthers. PISTIL extends 11mm (7/16") below the corolla; white (155D) style, pale

yellow (2D) stigma. BUD: ovate, pointed. FOLIAGE: dark green (137A) upper surface, medium green (138A) lower surface. Leaves are 52mm (2") long x 29mm (1 1/8") wide, ovate shaped, serrated edges, acute tips and rounded bases. Veins light green (138D), stems & branches are light green (138C). PARENTAGE: 'Salmon Glow' x unknown. Natural trailer. Self branching. Makes good basket. Prefers full sun. Best bloom and foliage colour in bright light. Tested 3 years in Wellen, Belgium. NBFK certificate at Meise. Distinguished by bloom colour, profuse blooms.
Vanwalleghem 2003 BE AFS5091.

Piccola Lisa. Upright/Trailer. Single. COROLLA: unflared, square shape; opens light purple (78C); matures dark rose (71D); 23mm (7/8") long x 16mm (5/8") wide. SEPALS: horizontal, tips recurved; dark rose (55A) upper surface; rose (55B) lower surface; 37mm (1 7/16") long x 8mm (5/16") wide. TUBE: rose (54C); 13mm (1/2") long x 6mm (1/4") wide. FOLIAGE is dark green (137A) upper surface; medium green (138B) lower surface. PARENTAGE: 'Belle de Spa' x unknown.
Ricard 2008 BE AFS6848.

Piccolo Giacomo. Upright. Single. COROLLA: quarter flared, smooth petal margins; opens dark reddish purple (61A), matures reddish purple (58A); 19mm (3/4") long x 10mm (3/8") wide. SEPALS: half down; tips reflexed; dark rose (51A) upper & lower surfaces; 23mm (15/16") long x 9mm (3/8") wide. TUBE: dark rose (51A), medium length & thickness; 15mm (5/8") long x 7mm (1/4") wide. STAMENS: extend 17mm (11/16") below the corolla; magenta (58B) filaments, reddish purple (58A) anthers. PISTIL extends 33mm (1 5/16") below the corolla; dark rose (58C) style, peach (37B) stigma. BUD: rounded. FOLIAGE: medium green (146A) upper surface, medium green (147B) lower surface. Leaves are 65mm (2 9/16") long x 39mm (1 9/16") wide, ovate shaped, serrated edges, acute tips and rounded bases. Veins are dark reddish purple (60A), stems are reddish, branches are dark green. PARENTAGE: 'F. magellanica' x unknown. Small upright. Makes good upright, standard. Prefers full sun, warm climate. Best bloom and foliage colour in bright light. Tested 3 years in Como & Milano, Italy. Distinguished by blossom colour and dark reddish foliage in spring.
Ianne 2003 IT AFS5071.

Piero Bonati. Upright. Single. COROLLA: quarter flared, square shape; opens dark reddish purple (61A), red (53B) base; matures reddish purple (67A), red (53B) base; 11mm (7/16") long x 10mm (3/8") wide. SEPALS: horizontal, tips recurved; red (53C), lightly pubescent, upper surface; red (53D) lower surface; 25mm (1") long x 8mm (5/16") wide. TUBE: red (53C), lightly pubescent, square; 17mm (5/8") long x 6mm (1/4") wide. FOLIAGE is dark green (147A) upper surface; medium green (147B) lower surface. PARENTAGE: 'F. magellanica' x unknown.
Ianne 2008 IT AFS6947.

Piero's Jam. Upright. Single. COROLLA: unflared; opens purple (83A); matures purple (77A); 19mm (3/4") long x 16mm (5/8") wide. SEPALS: full down, tips recurved; red (53C) upper surface; dark rose (51A) lower surface; 23mm (7/8") long x 4mm (1/8") wide. TUBE: red (53D); 8mm (5/16") long x 3mm (1/8") wide. FOLIAGE is dark green (147A) upper surface; yellowish green (146B) lower surface. PARENTAGE: 'Dr. Foster' x unknown.
Ianne 2008 IT AFS6946.

Pierre Dubois. Upright. Single. COROLLA: Unflared; long, large petals; opens dark purple (79B); matures reddish purple (71B); 35mm (1 3/8") long x 18mm (11/16") wide. SEPALS: horizontal, tips recurved; red (45B) upper surface; red (46C) lower surface; 51mm (2") long x 11mm (7/16") wide. TUBE: red (45B); medium length & thickness; 18mm (11/16") long x 7mm (1/4") wide. FOLIAGE is dark green (147A) upper surface; medium green (147B) lower surface. PARENTAGE: 'Bon Roi Renté' x unknown.
Massé 2007 FR AFS6486.

Pierre En Joanna. Upright/Trailer. Semi Double. COROLLA: half flared; opens red (53D) & reddish purple (71B); matures reddish purple (64B); 25mm (1") long x 23mm (7/8") wide. SEPALS: horizontal, tips reflexed; red (53C) tipped olive green (152A) upper surface; red (47B) tipped olive green (152C) lower surface; 32mm (1 1/4") long x 12mm (7/16") wide. TUBE: red (53C); 30mm (1 3/16") long x 6mm (1/4") wide. FOLIAGE is medium green (137B) upper surface; medium green (138B) lower surface. PARENTAGE: 'WALZ Harp' x 'De Acht Zaligheden'.
Geerts J. 2008 BE AFS6764.

Piet de Jong. Upright/Trailer. Semi Double. COROLLA: three quarter flared; opens dark reddish purple (59A); matures dark reddish purple (60B); 36mm (1 7/16") long x 12mm (7/16") wide. SEPALS: fully up, tips recurved; light pink (65B) upper surface; rose (65A) lower surface; 24mm (15/16") long x 26mm (1") wide. TUBE: light pink (65B); 24mm (15/16") long x 7mm (1/4") wide. FOLIAGE is dark green (137A) upper surface; medium green (137C) lower surface. PARENTAGE: 'Roesse Lupus' x 'Silver Down'. van Bree 2008 NL AFS6890.

Piet den Breejen. Upright. Double. COROLLA: half flared; opens light pink (62B); matures rose (64D); 35mm (1 3/8") long x 31mm (1 1/4") wide. PETALOIDS: same colour as corolla; 33mm (1 5/16") long x 31mm (1 1/4") wide. SEPALS: horizontal, tips recurved; red (53D) upper surface; red (53C) lower surface; 56mm (2 1/4") long x 15mm (9/16") wide. TUBE: magenta (63B); 18mm (11/16") long x 7mm (1/4") wide. FOLIAGE is yellowish green (144B) upper surface; medium green (138B) lower surface. PARENTAGE: 'Gerwin van den Brink' x 'White King'. Nomination by NKVF as Recommendable Cultivar. van den Brink 2008 NL AFS6777.

Piet Driessen. Trailer. Double. COROLLA: three quarter flared, turned under wavy petal margins; opens dark rose (54A), purple (71A) & reddish purple (71B); matures rose (51B) & reddish purple (61B); 28mm (1 1/8") long x 18mm (11/16") wide. SEPALS: horizontal, tips recurved; pale pink (56A) upper surface; rose (52B) lower surface; 35mm (1 3/8") long x 16mm (5/8") wide. TUBE: dark rose (55A); medium length & thickness; 12mm (7/16") long x 6mm (1/4") wide. STAMENS extend 14mm (9/16") beyond the corolla; magenta (63A) filaments; purple (71A) anthers. PISTIL extends 21mm (13/16") beyond the corolla; rose (61D) style; pale lavender (65D) stigma. BUD: globular. FOLIAGE: dark green (137A) upper surface; medium green (138D) lower surface. Leaves are 58mm (2 5/16") long x 32mm (1 1/4") wide; ovate shaped, serrate edges, acute tips, rounded bases. Veins are very dark reddish purple (186A), stems are light red purple (185D), branches are plum (184C). PARENTAGE: 'Manfried Kleinau' x 'First Lord'. Natural trailer. Self branching. Makes good basket. Prefers overhead filtered light, cool climate. Best bloom & foliage colour in filtered light. Tested 3 years in Koningshooikt, Belgium. Waanrode 7/5/08. Distinguished by bloom colour.

Michiels 2007 BE AFS7208.

Piet Zijnen. Upright. Single. COROLLA: half flared, smooth petal margins; opens dark reddish purple (60A); matures red (53C); 18mm (11/16") long 24mm (15/16") wide. SEPALS: horizontal; tips recurved; red (52A) upper surface; red (50A) lower surface; 21mm (13/16") long x 9mm (3/8") wide. TUBE: red (52A); medium length & thickness; 15mm (9/16") long x 7mm (1/4") wide. STAMENS: extend 6mm (1/4") below corolla; rose (54C) filaments; dark rose (54B) anthers. PISTIL: extends 19mm (3/4") below the corolla; red (52A) style; light yellow (4C) stigma. BUD: ovate, pointed. FOLIAGE: dark green (137A) upper surface; medium green (138B) lower surface. Leaves are 64mm (2 1/2") long x 43mm (1 11/16") wide, ovate shaped, serrulated edges, obtuse tips and rounded bases. Green veins, stems & branches. PARENTAGE: 'Roesse Apus' x 'Willy Tamerus'. Medium upright. Makes good upright or standard. Prefers overhead filtered light and cool climate. Best bloom and foliage colour in filtered light. Tested 4 years in Diessen, The Netherlands. Distinguished by bloom colour.
Comperen 2004 NL AFS5568.

Pieter de Coninck. Trailer. Single. COROLLA: quarter flared; opens magenta (67B); matures dark rose (64C); 21mm (13/16") long x 21mm (13/16") wide. SEPALS: half down, tips recurved; rose (54C) tipped pale yellow green (150D) upper surface; pink (52D) tipped pale yellow green (150D) lower surface; 30mm (1 3/16") long x 11mm (7/16") wide. TUBE: dark rose (55A); 53mm (2 1/8") long x 7mm (1/4") wide. FOLIAGE is medium green (138A) upper surface; medium green (138B) lower surface. PARENTAGE: 'Lechlade Rocket' x 'Igloo Maid'.
Vandenbussche 2008 BE AFS6740.

Piggelmee. Upright. Single. COROLLA is unflared with turned under petal margins; opens & matures dark reddish purple (59A); 11mm (7/16") long x 7mm (1/4") wide. SEPALS are fully up, tips recurved; dark reddish purple (60C) upper surface; dark reddish purple (60A) lower surface; 19mm (3/4") long x 3mm (1/8") wide. TUBE is magenta (63A); medium length & thickness; 11mm (7/16") long x 3mm (1/8") wide. FOLIAGE: dark green (137A) upper surface; medium green (137B) lower surface. Leaves are 47mm (1 7/8") long x 17mm (11/16") wide, lanceolate shaped. PARENTAGE: 'Wout'

x 'Mantilla'. Distinguished by flower shape & colour.
Krom 2005 NL AFS5796.

Pijnwinning. Trailer. Double. COROLLA: half flared, turned under wavy petal margins; opens dark rose (58C) & dark rose (67C); matures magenta (63B) & dark reddish purple (72A); 19mm (3/4") long x 17mm (5/8") wide. PETALOIDS: Same colour as corolla; 14mm (9/16") long x 8mm (5/16") wide. SEPALS: horizontal; tips reflexed; pale pink (56C) tipped pale yellow green (150D) upper surface; pink (55C) tipped pale yellow green (150D) lower surface; 24mm (15/16") long x 11mm (7/16") wide. TUBE: white (155C); medium length & thickness; 11mm (7/16") long x 6mm (1/4") wide. STAMENS extend 12mm (7/16") beyond the corolla; rose (64D) filaments; purple (71A) anthers. PISTIL extends 19mm (3/4") beyond the corolla; light pink (65B) style; pale yellow (1D) stigma. BUD: globular. FOLIAGE: medium green (137C) upper surface; medium green (139C) lower surface. Leaves are 54mm (2 1/8") long x 32mm (1 1/4") wide; ovate shaped, serrulate edges, acute tips, rounded bases. Veins are plum (185B), stems are dark grayish purple (184A), branches are plum (184C) & light green (138C). PARENTAGE: 'Manfried Kleinau' x 'Baroncelli'. Natural trailer. Self branching. Makes good basket or upright. Prefers overhead filtered light, cool climate. Best bloom & foliage colour in filtered light. Tested 3 years in Koningshooikt, Belgium. Waanrode 7/5/08. Distinguished by bloom colour combination.
Michiels 2009 BE AFS7209.

Pink Cross. Upright. Single. COROLLA: half flared, smooth petal margins; opens purple (83A) striped magenta (63B); matures dark reddish purple (72A) striped magenta (63B); 25mm (1") long 32mm (1 1/4") wide. SEPALS: half up; tips recurved up; red (46C) upper & lower surfaces; 35mm (1 3/8") long x 10mm (3/8") wide. TUBE: red (46C); medium length & thickness; 10mm (3/8") long x 3mm (1/8") wide. STAMENS: extend 12mm (1/2") below corolla; magenta (63B) filaments & anthers. PISTIL: extends 32mm (1 1/4") below the corolla; magenta (63B) style & stigma. BUD: oval, pointed. FOLIAGE: dark green (137A) upper surface; medium green (139C) lower surface. Leaves are 63mm (2 1/2") long x 38mm (1 1/2") wide, ovate shaped, serrulated edges, acute tips and rounded bases. Green veins, stems & branches. PARENTAGE: 'Estelle Marie' x

'Lady Boothby'. Medium upright. Self branching. Makes good upright. Prefers overhead filtered light, cool climate. Best bloom and foliage colour in filtered light. Tested 3 years in Stoke-On-Trent, England. Distinguished by contrasting colour combination and resemblance to a pink cross when fully open.
Goodwin 2004 UK AFS5577.

Pink Lucy. Upright. Single. COROLLA: 3 quarter flared; opens orange (33C), matures dark orange red (34A); 3mm (1/8") long x 4mm (1/8") wide. SEPALS: half down, tips recurved; dark rose (58C) tipped light yellowish green (154C) upper surface; pale pink (62D) tipped white (155D) lower surface; 4mm (1/8") long x 2mm (1/16") wide. TUBE: dark rose (58C); long, medium thickness; 7mm (1/4") long x 3mm (1/8") wide. FOLIAGE is dark green (137A) upper surface; medium green (137D) lower surface. PARENTAGE: '*F. encliandra obcylin*' x unknown.
Nutt 2007 UK AFS6316.

Pink Poppet. Upright/Trailer. Double. COROLLA very pale pink with cerise veining. SEPALS pink. TUBE pink.
Chatters 2005 UK.

Pippa Penny. Upright. Single. COROLLA opens pale violet, matures to very pale pink violet; corolla is half flared. SEPALS white with hint of pink on the upper surface, white flushed pink on the lower surface; sepals are half up with green recurved tips. TUBE white tinged green. PARENTAGE ('Linda Grace' x 'Waveney Gem seedling') x 'Sophie Louise'.
Nicholls 2008 UK BFS0094.

Pleasures. Upright/Trailer. Single. COROLLA: quarter flared; compact; smooth petal margins; opens & matures violet (75A) edged darker; 13mm (1/2") long x 11mm (7/16") wide. SEPALS: horizontal; tips recurved; light rose (73C) upper surface; violet (75A) lower surface; 22mm(7/8") long x 4mm (3/16") wide. TUBE: light rose (73B); medium length & thin; 10mm (3/8") long x 3mm (1/8") wide. STAMENS: extend 6mm (1/4) below corolla; violet (75A) filaments, pink (62C) anthers. PISTIL: extends 12mm (1/2") below the corolla, light purple (75B) style, light rose (73C) stigma. BUD: thin, cylindrical, cordate tip. FOLIAGE: medium green (146A) upper surface; medium green (147B) lower surface. Leaves are 45mm (1 3/4") long x 23mm (15/16") wide, elliptic shaped, serrulated edges, acute tips and rounded bases. Veins are reddish & light

yellow green; stems & branches are red. PARENTAGE: 'Gerharda's Panache' x 'Major Heaphy'. Lax upright or stiff trailer. Self branching. Makes good basket. Prefers overhead filtered light and cool or warm climate. Best bloom and foliage colour in filtered light. Tested 4 years in Lisse, Holland. Distinguished by flowers held in horizontally spread multiple panicles.
de Graaff 2003 NL AFS5166.

Plessey Muskateer. Upright. Single. COROLLA is unflared, bell shaped, with smooth petal margins; opens reddish purple (74A); matures purple (83A); 25mm (1") long x 20 mm (13/16") wide. PETALOIDS: purple (74A) veined pink; 30mm (1 3/8") long x 23mm (15/1/16") wide. SEPALS are half down, tips recurved; red (52A) upper surface, dark rose (54B) lower surface; 45mm (1 3/4") long x 12mm (1/2") wide. TUBE is reddish orange (43E), short & thick; 10mm (3/8") long x 8mm (5/16") wide. FOLIAGE: medium green (143A) upper surface; light green (143B) lower surface. Leaves are 55mm (2 3/16") long x 21mm (13/16") wide, lanceolate shaped. PARENTAGE: 'Golden Penny' x unknown. Distinguished by vivid colouring.
Fraser 2005 UK AFS5648.

Pluisje. Upright. Single. COROLLA: unflared; closed shaped, smooth petal margins; opens reddish orange (43C) edged dark orange (41A); matures red orange (40A); 14mm (9/16") long x 10mm (3/8") wide. SEPALS: half down, tips reflexed; rose (51B) tipped light green (145D) upper surface; pink (52D) lower surface; 24mm (15/16") long x 7mm (1/4") wide. TUBE: pink (62C); medium length & thickness; 16mm (5/8") long x 8mm (5/16") wide. STAMENS extend 12mm (7/16") beyond the corolla; magenta (58B) filaments; reddish purple (58A) anthers. PISTIL extends 30mm (1 3/16") beyond the corolla; light rose (58D) style; pale yellow (1D) stigma. BUD: long. FOLIAGE: dark green (147A) upper surface; medium green (147B) lower surface. Leaves are 53mm (2 1/8") long x 36mm (1 7/16") wide; ovate shaped, serrulate edges, acute tips, rounded bases. Veins, stems & branches are red. PARENTAGE: 'Eleanor Leytham' x 'Mrs. Lovall Swisher'. Tall upright. Makes good upright or standard. Prefers full sun. Best bloom & foliage colour in bright light. Tested 6 years in Hulshorst, The Netherlands. Nominated by NKvF as recommendable cultivar. Distinguished by flower shape & profuse flowers.

van den Brink 2009 NL AFS7020.

Poetry. Upright/Trailer. Single. COROLLA: half flared, bell shape, toothed petal margins; opens light pink (62B); matures rose (64D); 9mm (3/8") long, 7mm (1/4") wide. SEPALS: half down; tips reflexed; magenta (63B) upper surface; light pink (62B) lower surface; 11mm (7/16") long x 5mm (3/16") wide. TUBE: light pink (62B); long, medium thickness; 25mm (1") long x 6mm (1/4") wide, tapered to 3mm (1/8") at base. STAMENS: do not extend below corolla; pale pink (62D) filaments; light yellow (11B) anthers. PISTIL: extends 4mm(3/16") below the corolla; pale pink (62D) style; light pink (62B) stigma. BUD: triphylla type. FOLIAGE: dark green (147A) upper surface; olive green (148A) lower surface. Leaves are 107mm (4 3/16") long x 26mm (1") wide, lanceolate shaped, serrulated edges, acute tips and acute bases. Red veins, stems & branches. PARENTAGE: 'Gerharda's Panache' x 'Göttingen'. Lax upright or stiff trailer. Makes good basket or upright. Prefers overhead filtered light. Heat tolerant if shaded. Best bloom and foliage colour in filtered light. Tested 5 years in Lisse, The Netherlands. Distinguished by flower/leaf shapes & colours; flowers in multiple racemes.
de Graaff 2004 NL AFS5605.

Poi Poi Mai Mai. Upright/Trailer. Single. COROLLA: quarter flared, bell shape; opens dark reddish purple (72A); matures magenta (71C); 18mm (11/16") long x 13mm (1/2") wide. SEPALS: horizontal, tips recurved; dark rose (58C) upper & lower surfaces; 30mm (1 3/16") long x 6mm (1/4") wide. TUBE: dark rose (58C); 25mm (1") long x 4mm (1/8") wide. FOLIAGE is medium green (137B) upper surface; olive green (147A) lower surface. PARENTAGE: 'Zulu King' x 'Oranje van Os'.
Ianne 2008 IT AFS6948.

Poljannie. Upright. Single. COROLLA light pink. SEPALS rose with green tip.
van de Pol 2002 NL.

Pöls. Upright/Trailer. Double. COROLLA: three quarter flared; smooth petal margins; opens & matures pink (55C); 35mm (1 3/8") long x 42mm (1 11/16") wide. SEPALS: half up; tips recurved up; red (52A); rose (52B) lower surface; 35mm(1 3/8") long x 15mm (9/16") wide. TUBE: red (52A); medium length & thickness; 20mm (13/16") long x 8mm (5/16") wide. STAMENS: extend 15mm (9/16) below corolla; pink (55C) filaments,

351

dark rose (180C) anthers. PISTIL: extends 20mm (13/16") below the corolla, rose (55B) style, rose (52B) stigma. BUD: tear drop shape. FOLIAGE: medium green (137B) upper surface; medium green (137D) lower surface. Leaves are 55mm (2 3/16") long x 48mm (1 7/8") wide, ovate shaped, serrated edges, acute tips and rounded bases. Veins are green, stems are brown, branches are green. PARENTAGE: 'Pink Galore' x unknown. Lax upright or stiff trailer. Self branching. Makes good basket. Prefers overhead filtered light. Best bloom and foliage colour in filtered light. Tested 4 years in Amstetten, Austria. Distinguished by attractive colour combination.
Gindl 2003 AT AFS5161.

Polskie Fuksji. Trailer. Double. COROLLA is three quarter flared with turned under smooth petal margins; opens dark purple (79B), purple (77A) base; matures purple (71A); 19mm (3/4") long x 22mm (7/8") wide. PETALOIDS: dark purple (79B); 12mm (1/2") long x 8mm (5/16") wide. SEPALS are horizontal, tips reflexed; dark reddish purple (64A) upper surface; dark reddish purple (60B) lower surface; 30mm (1 3/16") long x 17mm (11/16") wide. TUBE is dark reddish purple (61A); medium length & thickness; 21mm (13/16") long x 9mm (3/8") wide. FOLIAGE: medium green (139B) upper surface; medium green (139C) lower surface. Leaves are 74mm (2 15/16") long x 40mm (1 9/16") wide, ovate shaped. PARENTAGE: 'Roesse Blacky' x 'Pinto de Blue'. Meis 3-7-04. Distinguished by flower shape.
Note: This fuchsia is named after a Polish fuchsia society. The name is too long to be easily understood and has been abbreviated with the hybridizer's concurrence. The full name is 'Polskie Stowarzijszenie Milósnikow Fuksji'.
Michiels 2005 BE AFS5685.

Pornic Atlantique. Upright. Single. COROLLA is quarter flared with smooth petal margins; opens and matures orangy red(39A); 16mm (5/8") long x 15mm (5/8") wide. SEPALS are horizontal, tips recurved; pale pink (36D) upper and lower surfaces; 30mm (13/16") long x 6mm (1/4") wide. TUBE is pale pink (36D); medium length and thickness; 22mm (7/8") long x 6mm (1/4") thick. STAMENS extend 8 – 11mm (5/16 – 7/16") beyond the corolla; pink (48D) filaments, yellowish white (4D) anthers. PISTIL extends 32mm (1 1/4") beyond the corolla; light pink (38D) style, yellowish white (4D) stigma. BUD is ovate. FOLIAGE is dark green (137A) upper surface, light olive green (147C) lower surface. Leaves are 70mm (2 3/4") long x 36mm (1 7/16") wide, ovate shaped, serrulated edges, acute tips and rounded bases. Veins are yellowish green, stems are yellowish green and light brown, branches are light brown. PARENTAGE: 'Porte Océane' x 'Leonhart von Fuchs'. Small upright. Self branching. Makes good upright. Prefers overhead filtered light and cool climate. Best bloom colour in filtered light. Tested four years in Pornic, France. Distinguished by profuse terminal blooms.
Massé 2002 FR AFS5016.

Pornic Féérie. Upright. Semi Double. COROLLA is half flared with smooth petal margins; opens dark violet (87A), light purple (87E) base; matures violet (87B); 30mm (1 3/16") long x 35mm (1 3/8") wide. SEPALS are horizontal, tips recurved up; rose (55B) & pink (55C) tipped yellowish white (4D) upper surface; dark rose (55A) lower surface; 32mm (1 1/4") long x 12mm (1/2") wide. TUBE is pink (36A); medium length & thickness; 13mm (1/2") long x 5mm (3/16") wide. FOLIAGE: medium green (146A) upper surface; yellowish green (146B) lower surface. Leaves are 57mm (2 1/4") long x 33mm (1 5/16") wide, ovate shaped. PARENTAGE: 'Swingtime' x 'Bicentennial'. Distinguished by profuse blooms and bloom/foliage contrast.
Massé 2005 FR AFS5696.

Pornic Hélico. Upright/Trailer. Single. COROLLA: unflared; smooth petal margins; opens & matures violet (84A); 24mm (15/16") long x 7mm (1/4") wide. SEPALS: horizontal, tips recurved; red (52A) upper & lower surfaces; 55mm (2 3/16") long x 6mm (1/4") wide. TUBE: red (52A); medium length, thin; 18mm (11/16") long x 4mm (1/8") wide. STAMENS are not visible; PISTIL extends 26mm (1") beyond the corolla; rose (52B) style; red (53D) stigma. BUD is lanceolate. FOLIAGE is yellowish green (144A) upper surface; light olive green (148B) lower surface. Leaves are 40mm (1 9/16") long x 22mm (7/8") wide; ovate shaped, serrulate edges, obtuse tips, rounded bases. Veins, stems & branches are light brown. PARENTAGE: 'Nancy Lou' x 'Cordifolia'. Lax upright or stiff trailer. Makes good upright. Prefers overhead filtered light & cool climate. Tested 3 years in Pornic, France. Distinguished by exceptionally long SEPALS.
Massé 2009 FR AFS6996.

352

Pornic Junior. Upright. Single. COROLLA is unflared with smooth petal margins; opens purple (83B); matures purple (71A); 15mm (5/8") long x 10mm (3/8") wide. SEPALS are horizontal, tips recurved; red (45B) upper surface; dark rose (54B) lower surface; 24mm (15/16") long x 7mm (1/4") wide. TUBE is red (45B); bulbous, very short, medium thickness; 5mm (3/16") long x 6mm (1/4") thick. STAMENS extend 5 – 7mm (3/16 – 1/4") beyond the corolla; rose (68B) filaments, magenta (68A) anthers. PISTIL extends 18mm (11/16") beyond the corolla; magenta (63B) style, plum (185B) stigma. BUD is ovate. FOLIAGE is dark green (147A) upper surface, medium green (147B) lower surface. Leaves are 60mm (2 3/8") long x 27mm (1 1/16") wide, ovate to lanceolate shaped, serrulated edges, acute tips and acute bases. Veins are yellowish green and light brown, stems and branches are light brown. PARENTAGE: 'Thamar' x 'Nettala'. Small upright. Self branching. Makes good upright. Prefers overhead filtered light and cool climate. Best bloom colour in filtered light. Tested five years in Pornic, France. Distinguished by semi-erect, profuse little blooms.
Massé 2002 FR AFS5017.

Pornic Surprise. Upright. Single. COROLLA: unflared, smooth petal margins; opens dark rose (51A); matures rose (51B); 27mm (1 1/16") long x 10mm (3/8") wide. SEPALS: half down; tips recurved; yellowish white (4D), tipped yellowish green (145A-B), upper & lower surfaces; 26mm (1 1/16") long x 6mm (1/4") wide. TUBE: yellowish white (4D) (waxy), medium length & thickness; 15mm (9/16") long x 7mm (1/4") wide. STAMENS: extend 5 - 9mm (3/16–3/8") below corolla; rose (51C) filaments, pink (48C) anthers. PISTIL: extends 21mm (13/16") below the corolla, pink (51D) style, light yellow (4C) stigma. BUD: ovate. FOLIAGE: dark green (147A) upper surface; medium green (147B) lower surface. Leaves are 56mm (2 3/16") long x 30mm (1 3/16") wide, ovate shaped, serrulated edges, acute tips and rounded bases. Veins, stems & branches are yellowish green. PARENTAGE: 'Porte Océane' x 'Subliem'. Small upright. Makes good upright. Prefers overhead filtered light and cool climate. Best bloom and foliage colour in filtered light. Tested 3 years in Pornic, France. Distinguished by sepal colour.
Massé 2003 FR AFS5218.

Président Henri Mahu. Upright. Single. COROLLA: Half flared, petticoat shaped;

opens pale violet (85D); matures pale lavender (69C); 23mm (7/8") long x 28mm (1 1/8") wide. SEPALS: fully up, tips recurved; cream (11D) tipped green upper surface; greenish yellow (151A) lower surface; 24mm (15/16") long x 11mm (7/16") wide. TUBE: light. FOLIAGE is dark green (137A) upper surface; medium green (147B) lower surface. PARENTAGE: 'Li Belle Dama' x unknown.
Ricard 2007 BE AFS6441.

Président Herman Ferriére. Upright. Single. COROLLA: unflared, square shape, turned under smooth petal margins; opens purple (77A) veined red (46D); matures purple (71A); 19mm (3/4") long x 18mm (11/16") wide. SEPALS: half down, tips recurved; red (46D) upper surface; red (45D) lower surface; 28mm (1 1/8") long x 10mm (3/8") wide. TUBE: red (45D); medium length & thickness; 15mm (9/16") long x 9mm (5/16") wide. STAMENS extend 45mm (1 3/4") beyond the corolla; magenta (57B) filaments; reddish purple (58A) anthers. PISTIL extends 51mm (2") beyond the corolla; magenta (57C) style; pink (49A) stigma. BUD: ovate. FOLIAGE: dark green (137A) upper surface; yellowish green (146B) lower surface. Leaves are 40mm (1 9/16") long x 23mm (7/8") wide; lanceolate shaped, serrate edges, acute tips, rounded bases. Veins & stems are green, branches are red. PARENTAGE: 'Belle de Spa' x unknown. Small upright. Self branching. Makes good upright. Prefers overhead filtered light. Heat tolerant if shaded. Cold weather hardy. Best bloom & foliage colour in filtered light. Tested 8 years in Herstal, Belgium. Distinguished by blossom colour combination & profuse, continuous blooms.
Ricard 2009 BE AFS7121.

President Jim Muil. Upright/Trailer. Single. COROLLA: quarter flared, smooth petal margins; opens & matures pink (54D) edged dark rose (58C), light pink (55D) throat; 7mm (1/2") long x 7mm (1/2") wide. SEPALS: horizontal; tips recurved; white (155D) tipped light green (139D) upper & lower surfaces; 19mm (3/4") long x 7mm (1/4") wide. TUBE: white (155D); long & thin; 25mm(1") long x 10mm (3/8") wide. STAMENS: 12mm (1/2") below corolla; white (155D) filaments & anthers. PISTIL: extends 25mm (1") below the corolla, white (155D) style, white (155A) stigma. BUD: ovate, pointed. FOLIAGE: dark green (137A) upper & lower surfaces. Leaves are 38mm (1 1/2") long x 19mm (3/4") wide, cordate shaped, serrated edges, acute tips and cordate bases. Veins, stems & branches

are light green (138C). PARENTAGE: ('Gartenmeister Bonstedt' x 'Daisy Bell') x 'Bertha Gadsby'. Lax upright or stiff trailer. Makes good upright, standard, pillar or decorative. Prefers overhead filtered light. Heat tolerant if shaded. Best bloom and foliage colour in filtered light. Tested 10 years in East Yorkshire, England. Distinguished by continuous, heavy flowering.
Bielby/Oxtoby 2003 UK AFS5204.

Prestige. Trailer. Single. COROLLA: half flared, trumpet shape, toothed petal margins; opens & matures dark rose (55A); 11mm (7/16") long, 7mm (1/4") wide. SEPALS: horizontal; tips recurved; pink (51D), tipped greenish yellow (151A) upper surface; pale pink (56A), tipped greenish yellow (151A) lower surface; 19mm (3/4") long x 4mm (3/16") wide. TUBE: pink (50D); long, thin; 39mm (1 9/16") long x 6mm (1/4") wide. STAMENS: extend 3mm (1/8) below corolla; pink (48C) filaments; grayish yellow (161B) anthers. PISTIL: extends 2mm(1/16") below the corolla; pink (48D) style; light pink (49C) stigma. BUD: triphylla type. FOLIAGE: medium green (146A) upper surface; yellowish green (146B) lower surface. Leaves are 87mm (3 7/16") long x 31mm (1 1/4") wide, elliptic shaped, serrulated edges, acute tips and obtuse bases. Reddish yellow green veins; reddish stems & branches. PARENTAGE: 'Gerharda's Panache' x 'Insulinde'. Natural trailer. Self branching. Makes good basket. Prefers overhead filtered light. Heat tolerant if shaded. Best bloom and foliage colour in filtered light. Tested 5 years in Lisse, The Netherlands. Distinguished by long salmon rose flowers in terminal pendant racemes.
de Graaff 2004 NL AFS 5604.

Pretty Girl. Upright. Single. COROLLA: quarter flared, bell shaped; opens violet blue (91A); matures violet (75A); 20mm (3/4") long x 16mm (5/8") wide. SEPALS: horizontal, tips recurved; pink (62A) fading to white, tipped green upper & lower surfaces; 39mm (1 1/2") long x 13mm (1/2") wide. TUBE: light pink (62C); 10mm (3/8") long x 6mm (1/4") wide. FOLIAGE is medium green (137C) upper surface; medium green (138B) lower surface. PARENTAGE: 'Julie Ann Goodwin' x 'Shellford'.
Goodwin 2008 UK AFS6938.

Prickly Heat. Upright. Single. COROLLA: quarter flared, bell shaped; opens dark rose (54B) edged dark rose (51A); matures light pink (49B), edged red (52A); 18mm (11/16") long x 12mm (1/2") wide. SEPALS: horizontal; tips recurved; pink (49A) tipped green (146A) upper surface; pink (49A) tipped yellowish green (145A) lower surface; 27mm (1 1/16") long x 8mm (5/16") wide. TUBE: light pink (49B) flushed pink (49A); short & thin; 11mm(7/16") long x 3mm (1/8") wide. STAMENS: extend 13mm (1/2") below corolla; light pink (49B) filaments, dark rose (54B) anthers. PISTIL: extends 16mm (5/8") below the corolla, pink (49A) style, light yellow (11B) stigma. BUD: ovate. FOLIAGE: olive green (148A) upper surface; light olive green (147C) lower surface. Leaves are 56mm (2 3/16") long x 34mm (1 5/16") wide, ovate shaped, smooth edges, acute tips and rounded bases. Veins & stems are light green, branches are medium green. PARENTAGE: Sport of 'WALZ Jubelteen'. Medium upright. Self branching. Makes good upright, standard, pyramid or decorative. Prefers full sun, warm climate. Best bloom and foliage colour in filtered light. Tested 3 years in Stadskanaal, The Netherlands. Award of Merit as the 1000ste Dutch Cultivar, VKC/KMTP, The Netherlands. Distinguished by upright flowers and bright colour combination.
Koerts T. 2003 NL AFS5187.

Pride of Roualeyn. Upright. Double. COROLLA: full flared, smooth petal margins; opens dark reddish purple (59A); matures reddish purple (59B); 13mm (1/2") long x 25mm (1") wide. PETALOIDS: dark reddish purple (61B); 7mm (1/4") long x 7mm (1/4") wide. SEPALS: horizontal, tips recurved; dark reddish purple (61A) tipped green upper surface; reddish purple (61B) lower surface; 20mm (3/4") long x 12mm (7/16") wide. TUBE: reddish purple (61B); short, medium thickness; 13mm (1/2") long x 7mm (1/4") wide. STAMENS extend 4mm (1/8") beyond the corolla; magenta (59D) filaments; pale pink (62D) anthers. PISTIL extends 20mm (3/4") beyond the corolla; reddish purple (59B) style; pale pink (62D) stigma. BUD: round, pointed. FOLIAGE: medium green (137B) upper surface; medium green (137D) lower surface. Leaves are 45mm (1 3/4") long x 22mm (7/8") wide; ovate shaped, serrulate edges, acute tips, rounded bases. Veins are purple, stems are purple & green, branches are light brown. PARENTAGE: 'Dorothy Hanley' x 'Blaze Away'. Small upright. Self branching. Makes good upright or decorative. Prefers overhead filtered light, cool climate. Best bloom colour in filtered light. Tested 3 years in Ormskirk, Lancashire, England.

Distinguished by aubergine coloured profuse small double flowers blooming from every joint.
Sinton 2009 UK AFS7090.

Pride of Windsor. Upright. Single. Upright. COROLLA is unflared, bell shaped with turned under smooth petal margins; opens & matures reddish purple (70B) & light rose (73B) veined red (52A); 13mm (1/2") long x 14mm (9/16") wide. SEPALS are half down; tips recurved; red (52A) upper surface and red (52A) creped lower surface; 19mm (3/4") long x 8mm (5/16") wide. TUBE red (52A), medium length & thickness; 10mm (3/8") long x 7mm (1/4") wide. STAMENS extend 15mm (9/16") below the corolla; red (52A) filaments, blushed cream anthers. PISTIL extends 25mm (1") below the corolla; red (52A) style and blushed cream stigma. BUD is cordate. FOLIAGE is dark green (137A) upper surface and lighter green lower surface. Leaves are 45mm (1 3/4") long x 29mm (1 1/8") wide, ovate shaped, serrated edges, acute tips and rounded bases. Veins are green, stems are dark green, branches are brown. PARENTAGE: 'White Clove' x unknown. Small upright. Self branching. Makes good upright, standard, pyramid, pillar or bedding. Prefers full sun. Cold weather hardy to 32° F. Best bloom colour in bright light. Tested 10 years in Edenbridge, Kent, England. Distinguished by natural bush growth.
Holmes 2003 UK AFS5067.

Prince Charming. Upright. Single. COROLLA: quarter flared; opens & matures rose (50B); 20mm (3/4") long x 20mm (3/4") wide. SEPALS: half up, tips recurved up; pale pink (56A) upper & lower surfaces; 30mm (1 3/16") long x 15mm (9/16") wide. TUBE: light pink (55D); 15 mm (9/16") long x 10mm (3/8") wide. FOLIAGE is medium green (139B) upper surface; medium green (139C) lower surface. PARENTAGE: 'Hannah Louise' x 'Lye's Unique'.
Smith R. 2008 UK AFS6825.

Prince Zoulou. Upright. Single. COROLLA: Quarter flared; trilobed petal margins; opens & matures dark reddish purple (61A); 31mm (1 1/4") long x 25mm (1") wide. SEPALS: horizontal, tips recurved; red (53C) upper & lower surfaces; 48mm (1 7/8") long x 7mm (1/4") wide. TUBE: red (45D); short & thick; 12mm (7/16") long x 9mm (5/16") wide. FOLIAGE is dark green (147A) upper surface; medium green (147B) lower surface. PARENTAGE: 'Delta's Groom' x 'Eve Ruggiéri'.

Massé 2007 FR AFS6487.

Princess Kaja. Upright/Trailer. Double. COROLLA: half flared, turned under wavy petal margins; opens white (155C) & violet (76B); matures pale purple (76C); 33mm (1 5/16") long x 24mm (15/16") wide. PETALOIDS: Same colour as corolla; 18mm (11/16") long x 12mm (7/16") wide. SEPALS: horizontal, tips recurved, twisted left to right; white (155C) tipped pale yellow green (150D) upper surface; white (155C) & pink (55C) tipped pale yellow green (150D) lower surface; 44mm (1 3/4") long x 18mm (11/16") wide. TUBE: white (155B); medium length & thickness; 12mm (7/16") long x 8mm (5/16") wide. STAMENS extend 5mm (3/16") beyond the corolla; pink (62B) filaments; rose (68C) anthers. PISTIL extends 24mm (15/16") beyond the corolla; white (155C) style; pale yellow (1D) stigma. BUD: elongated. FOLIAGE: dark green (136B) upper surface; medium green (138B) lower surface. Leaves are 53mm (2 1/8") long x 30mm (1 3/16") wide; ovate shaped, serrulate edges, acute tips, rounded bases. Veins are magenta (59D), stems are magenta (59C), branches are magenta (59C) & light green (139D). PARENTAGE: 'Coen Bakker' x 'Lut'. Lax upright or stiff trailer. Self branching. Makes good basket or upright. Prefers overhead filtered light, cool climate. Best bloom & foliage colour in filtered light. Tested 3 years in Koningshooikt, Belgium. Waanrode 7/5/08. Distinguished by bloom colour & shape.
Michiels 2009 BE AFS7210.

Princess Leanne. Upright. Semi Double. COROLLA: half flared; opens violet (82C) with flash of white; matures violet (82C); 20mm (3/4") long x 20mm (3/4") wide. SEPALS: half down, tips reflexed; dark rose (55A) tipped light green (130C) upper & lower surfaces; 30mm (1 3/16") long x 15mm (9/16") wide. TUBE: pink (49A); 13mm (1/2") long x 8mm (5/16") wide. FOLIAGE is medium green (138A) upper surface; medium green (139B) lower surface. PARENTAGE: 'Lovely Charlotte' x 'Alison Patricia'.
Smith R. 2008 UK AFS6813.

Princess Melissa. Upright. Semi Double. COROLLA: half flared; opens & matures light purple (78B); 20mm (3/4") long x 20mm (3/4") wide. SEPALS: half up, tips reflexed up; dark rose (51A) upper surface; rose (51B) lower surface; 20mm (3/4") long x 10mm (3/8") wide. TUBE: dark rose (51A); 15mm (9/16") long x 8mm (5/16") wide. FOLIAGE is

355

dark green (147A) upper surface; medium green (147B) lower surface. PARENTAGE: 'Dollar Princess' x 'Lovely Les'. Smith R. 2008 UK AFS6821.

Princess Olga. Upright. Double. COROLLA opens light mauve with orange patches, matures to deep pink; corolla is half flared. SEPALS ivory pink on the upper surface, matt pink on the lower surface; sepals are half down with recurved tips. TUBE ivory pink. PARENTAGE 'Bill Stevens' x 'White King'. This cultivar is a very free, early and continuous flowering variety, capable of producing a strong standard also good as a bush or for hanging baskets, easy to propagate, survived 13 years over wintered in a greenhouse with only o fleece for protection, said to be worthy of the title of 'Princess'; named after Princess Olga Dolgorouky, a Russian Princess born in 1915, who later married Evan Morgan of Tredegar House. Elliot 2009 UK BFS0101.

Prinzessin Angela. Trailer. Single. COROLLA is quarter flared with smooth petal margins; opens white (155A) and matures white (155B); 26mm (1") long x 22mm (7/8") wide. SEPALS are half up, tips recurved up; white (155B) tipped green upper and lower surfaces; 50mm (2") long x 12mm (1/2") wide. TUBE is white (155A), proportionally medium length and thickness; 10mm (3/8") long x 7mm (1/4") wide. STAMENS extend 20mm (13/16") below the corolla; light reddish purple (73A) filaments and anthers. PISTIL extends 38mm (1 1/2") below the corolla; pale lavender (65D) style and light pink (65C) stigma. BUD is ovate, pointed. FOLIAGE is dark green (137A) on upper and medium green (137C) on lower surface. Leaves are 52mm (2 1/16") long x 22mm (7/8") wide, ovate shaped, serrated edges, acute tips and rounded bases. Veins and branches are green, stems are red. PARENTAGE: 'Wiebke' x 'Flying Cloud'. Natural trailer. Makes good basket. Prefers overhead filtered light. Best bloom colour in filtered light. Tested five years in Göttingen, Germany. Distinguished by bloom and foliage colour combination. Strümper 2002 DE AFS4805.

Prinzessin Laura. Upright. Single. COROLLA is three quarter flared, square shaped, with toothed petal margins; opens violet (86B) veined red, matures violet (87B) veined red; 20mm (13/16") long x 35mm (1 3/8") wide. SEPALS are horizontal, tips reflexed; red

(46C) upper surface, red (46D) lower surface; 28mm (1 1/8") long x 18mm (11/16") wide. TUBE is red (46C), short and thin; 10mm (3/8") long x 6mm (1/4") wide. STAMENS extend 10mm (3/8") beyond the corolla; red (46C) filaments and anthers. PISTIL extends 30mm (3/16") beyond the corolla; red (46C) style, orangy brown (174B) stigma. BUD is drop-shaped. FOLIAGE is medium green (138A) upper surface, light green (138C) lower surface. Leaves are 55mm (2 3/16") long x 35mm (1 3/8") wide, ovate shaped, serrated edges, acute tips and rounded bases. Veins are green, stems are brown, branches are reddish. PARENTAGE: 'Cymon' x 'Anka'. Medium upright. Makes good upright. Prefers full sun. Best bloom colour in bright light. Tested three years in Plettenberg, Germany. Distinguished by short, thin TUBE and large dominant SEPALS. Strümper 2002 DE AFS4946.

Professeur Frédéric Baud. Upright. Single. COROLLA is unflared with smooth petal margins; opens & matures dark reddish purple (61A); 23mm (15/16") long x 8mm (5/16") wide. SEPALS are half down, tips reflexed; bright red (45A) upper & lower surfaces; 43mm (1 11/16") long x 6mm (1/4") wide. TUBE is bright red (45A); long & thin; 17mm (11/16") long x 3mm (1/8") wide. FOLIAGE: dark green (147A) upper surface; medium green (147B) lower surface. Leaves are 57mm (2 1/4") long x 24mm (15/16") wide, lanceolate shaped. PARENTAGE: 'Lucifer' x unknown. Distinguished by extra long, bright flowers in clusters. Massé 2005 FR AFS5699.

Prutske van Donk. Upright. Single. COROLLA: quarter flared; opens dark rose (64C); matures magenta (63B); 14mm (9/16") long x 15mm (9/16") wide. SEPALS are half down, tips reflexed; dark rose (54B) upper surface; dark rose (55A) lower surface; 27mm (1 1/16") long x 11mm (7/16") wide. TUBE is rose (54C) striped dark rose (54A); 30mm (1 3/16") long x 9mm (5/16") wide. FOLIAGE is dark green (137A) upper surface; medium green (138B) lower surface. PARENTAGE: 'Lovely Fonske' x unknown. Waanrode 7/7/2007. Geerts L. 2008 BE AFS6734.

Que Du Bonheur. Trailer. Single. COROLLA: quarter flared; smooth petal margins; opens & matures magenta (67B); 21mm (13/16") long x 17mm (5/8") wide. SEPALS: horizontal, tips recurved; cream (159D)

tipped yellowish green upper surface; pink (50D) lower surface; 32mm (1 1/4") long x 6mm (1/4") wide. TUBE: white (155B); medium length, thin; 16mm (5/8") long x 4mm (1/8") wide. STAMENS extend 8-11mm (5/16-7/16") beyond the corolla; pink (62C) filaments; yellowish white (4D) anthers. PISTIL extends 20mm (3/4") beyond the corolla; pink (62C) style; yellowish white (4D) stigma. BUD is long, ovate. FOLIAGE is medium green (146A) upper surface; light olive green (148B) lower surface. Leaves are 70mm (2 3/4") long x 39mm (1 1/2") wide; ovate shaped, serrulate edges, acute tips, rounded bases. Veins, stems & branches are light yellowish green. PARENTAGE: 'Henri Massé' x 'La Campanella'. Natural trailer. Makes good basket. Prefers overhead filtered light & cool climate. Tested 4 years in Pornic, France. Distinguished by contrasting flower colours.
Massé 2009 FR AFS6997.

Queen Elizabeth II. COROLLA purple. SEPALS scarlet.
Tickner 2002 UK.

Queen of Spades. Upright/Trailer. Single. COROLLA: three quarter flared; trumpet shaped; turned up toothed petal margins; opens & matures dark reddish purple (61A); 13mm (1/2") long x 13mm (1/2") wide. SEPALS: horizontal; tips recurved; dark reddish purple (61A) upper surface; dark reddish purple (59A) lower surface; 18mm(11/16") long x 8mm (5/16") wide. TUBE: dark reddish purple (64A); long, medium thickness; 31mm (1 1/4") long x 13mm (1/2") wide. STAMENS: extend 1mm (1/16) below corolla; magenta (59C) filaments, magenta (59D) anthers. PISTIL: extends 12mm (1/2") below the corolla, light purple (75B) style, light rose (73C) stigma. BUD: cylindrical, cordate tip. FOLIAGE: dark green (147A) upper surface; medium green (147B) lower surface. Leaves are 69mm (2 3/4") long x 44mm (1 3/4") wide, ovate shaped, serrulated edges, acute tips and obtuse bases. Veins are reddish; stems & branches are light reddish purple. PARENTAGE: 'Gerharda's Panache' x 'War Pipes'. Lax upright or stiff trailer. Makes good basket. Prefers overhead filtered light and cool climate. Heat tolerant if shaded. Best bloom and foliage colour in filtered light. Tested 4 years in Lisse, Holland. Distinguished by dark purple flowers carried in terminal racemes.
de Graaff 2003 NL AFS5167.

Queen Of The May. Upright. Single. COROLLA plum purple. SEPALS pink tipped green.
Ainsworth 2002 UK.

Queen Of The Snow. Upright. Double. COROLLA white. SEPALS white. Ainsworth 2006 UK.

Quita. Upright. Single. COROLLA is half flared, bell shaped, with turned up petal margins; opens peach (38B); matures light coral (38A); 10mm (3/8") long x 5mm (3/16") wide. SEPALS are half down, tips recurved; rose (48B) upper surface; yellowish green (145A) lower surface; 11mm (7/16") long x 3mm (1/8") wide. TUBE is dark rose (48A); medium length & thickness; 18mm (11/16") long x 4mm (3/16") wide. FOLIAGE: dark green (147A) upper surface; medium green (147B) lower surface. Leaves are 48mm (1 7/8") long x 25mm (1") wide, ovate shaped. PARENTAGE: [('F. cylindracea' x 'F. obconica') x 'Ashley'] x 'F. splendens'. Distinguished by small, rose coloured flowers, always two on each leaf.
Dijkstra 2008 NL AFS5786.

Raffaelle Rubens. Upright/Trailer. Single. COROLLA is half flared with turned under wavy petal margins; opens reddish purple (74A), pale lavender (69C) base; matures light purple (78B), pale lavender (69C) base; 27mm (1 1/16") long x 19mm (3/4") wide. SEPALS are half down, tips reflexed; pink (52D), pink (50D) base, tipped yellowish green (145A) upper surface; dark rose (54A), tipped yellowish green (145A) lower surface; 21mm (13/16") long x 10mm (3/8") wide. TUBE is pink (50D); medium length & thickness; 11mm (7/16") long x 5mm (3/16") wide. FOLIAGE: dark green (136A) upper surface; medium green (138A) lower surface. Leaves are 50mm (2") long x 28mm (1 1/8") wide, ovate shaped. PARENTAGE: 'Querry' x unknown. Meise 8-14-04. Distinguished by unique bloom shape.
Willems 2005 BE AFS5722.

Ralph Storey. Upright. Single. COROLLA: unflared, smooth petal margins, bell shaped; opens purple (81A); matures reddish purple (74A); 17mm (5/8") long x 17mm (5/8") wide. SEPALS: half down, tips reflexed; dark rose (54B) mottled lighter rose, tipped green upper surface; pink (55C) lower surface; 21mm (13/16") long x 8mm (5/16") wide. TUBE: dark rose (55A); short, thin; 5mm (3/16") long x 5mm (3/16") wide. STAMENS extend 10mm (3/8") beyond the corolla;

magenta (67B) filaments; reddish purple (71B) anthers. PISTIL extends 20mm (3/4") beyond the corolla; dark rose (67C) style; rose (68C) stigma. BUD: small square, slight taper. FOLIAGE: medium green (146A) upper surface; yellowish green (146C) lower surface. Leaves are 32mm (1 1/4") long x 24mm (15/16") wide; cordate shaped, serrulate edges, acute tips, rounded bases. Veins, stems & branches are green. PARENTAGE: F. coccinea x 'Estelle Marie'. Small upright. Makes good upright. Prefers full sun. Cold weather hardy to -3° C (26° F). Best bloom & foliage colour in bright light. Tested 5 years in Burstwick, East Yorkshire, England. Distinguished by bloom colour, horizontally erect flowers.
Storey 2009 UK AFS7133.

Ram. Upright/Trailer. Single. COROLLA: Unflared; opens magenta (58B) & reddish purple (61B); matures magenta (58B); 22mm (7/8") long x 18mm (11/16") wide. SEPALS: half down, tips reflexed; rose (65A) tipped light apple green (145C) upper surface; light rose (58D) tipped light apple green (145C) lower surface; 34mm (1 3/8") long x 8mm (5/16") wide. TUBE: light pink (62C); long & thin; 24mm (15/16") long x 4mm (1/8") wide. FOLIAGE is dark green (136B) upper surface; medium green (138B) lower surface. PARENTAGE: 'Ghislane' x 'Bleu Rebell'.
Geerts L. 2007 BE AFS6383.

Raphael. Upright. Double. COROLLA baby pink. SEPALS pink tipped green.
Ainsworth 2002 UK.

Raspberry Ripple. Upright/Trailer. Double. COROLLA: three quarter flared; opens white (155A), heavy rose (52B) splashes from base; matures white (155B), heavy rose (52B) splashes from base; 31mm (1 1/4") long x 44mm (1 3/4") wide. SEPALS: half up, tips recurved up; red (53C) upper surface; rose (52B) lower surface; 37mm (1 7/16") long x 16mm (5/8") wide. TUBE: red (53C); 9 mm (5/16") long x 8mm (5/16") wide. FOLIAGE is medium green (137B) upper surface; medium green (147B) lower surface. PARENTAGE: ('Baby Bright' x 'Zulu King') seedling x 'Midnight Sun'. Also registered with the BFS.
Swaby 2009 UK AFS6828 BFS0048 (2007).

Raxkönigin. Upright. Double. COROLLA is half flared with smooth petal margins, very fluffy; opens and matures white (155D), strong veins of rose (55B); 35mm (1 3/8") long x 38mm (1 1/2") wide. PETALOIDS are rose (55B) to white, strong veins of rose

(55B); 20mm (13/16") x 10mm (3/8"). SEPALS are fully up, tips reflexed; dark rose (55A) upper surface; rose (55B) lower surface; 46mm (1 13/16") long x 22mm (7/8") wide. TUBE is rose (55B); medium length and thickness; 14mm (9/16") long x 8mm (5/16") thick. STAMENS extend 20mm (13/16") beyond the corolla; dark rose (54A) filaments, yellowish orange (22A) anthers. PISTIL extends 20mm (13/16") beyond the corolla; dark rose (54A) style, dark rose (55A) stigma. BUD is drop shaped. FOLIAGE is medium green (138A) upper surface, medium green (138B) lower surface. Leaves are 65mm (2 9/16") long x 40mm (1 9/16") wide, ovate shaped, smooth edges, acute tips and rounded bases. Veins and branches are green, stems are light brown. PARENTAGE: 'Pink Galore' x 'Dark Eyes'. Tall upright. Makes good upright or standard. Prefers overhead filtered light. Best bloom colour in filtered light. Tested four years in Amstetten, Austria. Distinguished by large flowers on a strong and tall plant.
Gindl 2002 AT AFS5052.

Raymond McGowan. Upright. Single. COROLLA is unflared with smooth petal margins; opens & matures red (46B-46C); 15mm (9/16") long x 10mm (3/8") wide. SEPALS are full down, tips recurved; rose (48B) & red (46C & D) upper & lower surfaces; 26mm (1") long x 5mm (3/16") wide. TUBE is rose (48B); medium length and thickness; 20mm (13/16") long x 6mm (1/4") wide. STAMENS extend 12mm (1/2") beyond the corolla; magenta (67B) filaments; cream & white anthers. PISTIL extends 45mm (1 3/4") below the corolla; dark rose (67C) style; white & cream stigma. BUD is cylindrical, pointed. FOLIAGE is dark green (147A) upper surface, light olive green (147C) lower surface. Leaves are 70mm (2 3/4") long x 42mm (1 11/16") wide, cordate shaped, serrated edges, acute tips and rounded bases. Veins are medium green (147B), stems & branches are dark reddish purple (59A). PARENTAGE: 'Checkerboard' x 'Coachman'. Small upright. Makes good upright, standard, pyramid, pillar or trellis. Prefers overhead filtered light. Heat tolerant if shaded. Best bloom colour in bright or filtered light. Tested ten years in Napa, CA, USA. Distinguished by strong growth, three buds per leaf axil.
McGowan T. 2004 USA AFS5364.

Razzmatazz. Upright. Semi Double. COROLLA blue lightens towards the base, matures to mauvish blue; corolla is half flared. SEPALS light pink on the upper and lower surfaces; SEPALS are half up with recurved tips. TUBE light pink. PARENTAGE 'Bealings' x 'General Monk'. Edmonds 2009 UK BFS0137.

Rebel Speed. Upright/Trailer. Semi Double. COROLLA: half flared, turned under wavy petal margins; opens magenta (63A); matures magenta (63B); 21mm (13/16") long x 16mm (5/8") wide. SEPALS: horizontal, tips reflexed; magenta (63B) upper surface; dark rose (58C) lower surface; 30mm (1 3/16") long x 14mm (9/16") wide. TUBE: rose (65A); short & thick; 12mm (7/16") long x 7mm (1/4") wide. STAMENS extend 15mm (9/16") beyond the corolla; reddish purple (61B) filaments; purple (71A) anthers. PISTIL extends 34mm (1 3/8") beyond the corolla; pink (62A) style; light rose (68D) stigma. BUD: bulbous. FOLIAGE: dark green (136B) upper surface; medium green (138B) lower surface. Leaves are 58mm (2 5/16") long x 34mm (1 3/8") wide; ovate shaped, serrate edges, acute tips, rounded bases. Veins are olive green (152D), stems are light grayish red (182C) & light green (139D), branches are light grayish red (182D) & light green (139D). PARENTAGE: 'Manfried Kleinau' x 'Coen Bakker'. Lax upright or stiff trailer. Self branching. Makes good basket. Prefers overhead filtered light, cool climate. Best bloom & foliage colour in filtered light. Tested 3 years in Koningshooikt, Belgium. Waanrode 8/9/08. Distinguished by bloom colour. Michiels 2009 BE AFS7211.

Red River. Upright. Single. COROLLA is quarter flared with slightly toothed petal margins; opens dark purple (86A); matures violet (86B); 10mm (3/8") long x 14mm (9/16") wide. SEPALS are half up, tips recurved up; magenta (67B) upper surface; reddish purple (71B) lower surface; 20mm (13/16") long x 5mm (3/16") wide. TUBE is magenta (67B); short & thin; 10mm (3/8") long x 4mm (3/16") wide. FOLIAGE: dark green (137A) upper surface; medium green (147B) lower surface. Leaves are 45mm (1 3/4") long x 25mm (1") wide, lanceolate shaped. PARENTAGE: 'Roseworthy' x 'Cornish Pixie'. Distinguished by intense blossom colours. Negus 2005 UK AFS5979.

Red Wings. Upright/Trailer. Single. COROLLA: three quarter flared; smooth petal margins; opens magenta (61C) edged dark reddish purple (61A); matures reddish purple (61B); 18mm (11/16") long x 18mm (11/16") wide. SEPALS: half up, tips recurved up; rose (41C) tipped yellowish green (145A) upper surface; rose (41C) lower surface; 24mm (15/16") long x 7mm (1/4") wide. TUBE: reddish orange (42A); short, medium thickness; 11mm (7/16") long x 5mm (3/16") wide. STAMENS extend 4 x 4mm (1/8") & 4 x 16mm(5/8") beyond the corolla; pale purple (70D) filaments; dark purple (79A) anthers. PISTIL extends 40mm (1 9/16") beyond the corolla; magenta (57A) style; dark rose (58C) stigma. BUD: pegtop shape. FOLIAGE: dark green (147A) upper surface; light olive green (148B) lower surface. Leaves are 48mm (1 7/8") long x 38mm (1 1/2") wide; cordate shaped, wavy edges, acute tips, rounded bases. Veins & stems are light green (146D), branches are dark red (185A). PARENTAGE: 'Nellie Nuttall' x 'Prince Syray'. Lax upright or stiff trailer. Self branching. Makes good basket or upright. Prefers full sun. Best bloom & foliage colour in bright light. Tested 3 years in Stadskanaal, The Netherlands. Distinguished by flower shape & colour. Koerts T. 2009 NL AFS7047.

Red Zulu King. Upright/Trailer. Single. COROLLA: unflared, smooth petal margins; opens dark purple (79A); matures purple (71A); 18mm (11/16") long, 15mm (9/16") wide. SEPALS: horizontal; tips recurved; red (53C), upper surface; magenta (57B) lower surface; 30mm (1 3/16") long x 5mm (3/16") wide. TUBE: red (53C); medium length, thin; 17mm (11/16") long x 5mm (3/16") wide. STAMENS: extend 13mm (1/2") below corolla; purple (71A) filaments; reddish purple (186B) anthers. PISTIL: extends 36mm (1 7/16") below the corolla; reddish purple (58A) style; reddish purple (59B) stigma. BUD: long TUBE, ovate, pointed. FOLIAGE: medium green (146A) upper surface; medium green (147B) lower surface. Leaves are 67mm (2 5/8") long x 28mm (1 1/8") wide, elliptic shaped, serrulated edges, acute tips and obtuse bases. Reddish veins; red stems & branches. PARENTAGE: sport of 'Zulu King'. Lax upright or stiff trailer. Self branching. Makes good upright. Prefers overhead filtered light, cool climate. Best bloom and foliage colour in filtered light. Tested 5 years in Lisse, The Netherlands. Distinguished by flower colour combination. de Graaff 2004 NL AFS5610.

Regio 29. Trailer. Double. COROLLA: half flared, turned under wavy petal margins; opens purple (77A); matures purple (N78A); 27mm (1 1/16") long x 18mm (11/16") wide.

SEPALS: half up, tips recurved up & horizontal, tips recurved; pale pink (56C) tipped pale yellow green (150D) upper surface; rose (N57C) tipped pale yellow green (150D) lower surface; 34mm (1 3/8") long x 14mm (9/16") wide. TUBE: pale pink (56D); medium length & thickness; 20mm (3/4") long x 7mm (1/4") wide. STAMENS extend 14mm (9/16") beyond the corolla; reddish purple (64B) filaments; purple (77A) anthers. PISTIL extends 23mm (7/8") beyond the corolla; magenta (67B) style; yellowish white (4D) stigma. BUD: globular. FOLIAGE: dark green (137A) upper surface; medium green (138B) lower surface. Leaves are 72mm (2 7/8") long x 42mm (1 5/8") wide; ovate shaped, serrate edges, acute tips, rounded bases. Veins are light olive green (147C), stems are medium green (138B), branches are light green (138D). PARENTAGE: 'Manfried Kleinau' x 'De Boerin'. Natural trailer. Self branching. Makes good basket. Prefers overhead filtered light, cool climate. Best bloom & foliage colour in filtered light. Tested 3 years in Koningshooikt, Belgium. Waanrode 8/9/08. Distinguished by bloom colour.
Michiels 2009 BE AFS7212.

Regnar Hansen. Upright/Trailer. Double. COROLLA: half flared, turned under wavy petal margins; opens magenta (63A) & purple (77A); matures magenta (63B), red (52A) & purple (71A); 29mm (1 1/8") long x 19mm (3/4") wide. PETALOIDS: magenta (63A) & purple (77A); 14mm (9/16") long x 9mm (5/16") wide. SEPALS: half down, tips recurved; red (53D) upper surface; rose (52B) lower surface; 48mm (1 7/8") long x 19mm (3/4") wide. TUBE: dark rose (51A); medium length & thickness; 18mm (11/16") long x 6mm (1/4") wide. STAMENS extend 18mm (11/16") beyond the corolla; dark reddish purple (60B) filaments; dark purple (N79A) anthers. PISTIL extends 34mm (1 3/8") beyond the corolla; magenta (61C) style; magenta (63B) stigma. BUD: bulbous. FOLIAGE: medium green (137B) upper surface; medium green (137D) lower surface. Leaves are 78mm (3 1/8") long x 35mm (1 3/8") wide; elliptic shaped, serrate edges, acute tips, rounded bases. Veins are reddish purple (186B), stems are very dark reddish purple (186A), branches are grayish red (182B) & light green (138C). PARENTAGE: 'Manfried Kleinau' x 'Jubie-Lin'. Lax upright or stiff trailer. Self branching. Makes good basket. Prefers overhead filtered light, cool climate. Best bloom & foliage colour in filtered light. Tested 3 years in

Koningshooikt, Belgium. Waanrode 8/9/08. Distinguished by bloom colour.
Michiels 2009 BE AFS7213.

Reinhold of Rautenberg. Upright/Trailer. Single. COROLLA: quarter flared; opens & matures red (45D); 13mm (1/2") long x 13mm (1/2") wide. PETALOIDS: red (45D); 13mm (1/2") long x 13mm (1/2") wide. SEPALS: half down, tips recurved; light pink (62C) tipped green upper surface; pink (49A) lower surface; 39mm (1 1/2") long x 9mm (5/16") wide. TUBE: orangy red (39A); medium length & thickness; 33mm (1 5/16") long x6mm (1/4") wide. FOLIAGE is medium green (139A) upper surface; medium green (137B) lower surface. PARENTAGE: 'F. splendens' x 'F. magellanica alba'.
Weber 2007 USA AFS6315.

Remember Eric. COROLLA pink edged deeper pink. SEPALS pale pink tipped green.
Johns 2002 UK.

Remember Tommy Struck. Upright. Semi Double. COROLLA: quarter flared; opens dark purple (79A), dark reddish purple (61A) base; matures purple (71A); 13mm (1/2") long x 14mm (9/16") wide. SEPALS: horizontal, tips reflexed; reddish purple (59B) upper surface; dark reddish purple (61A) lower surface; 17mm (5/8") long x 8mm (5/16") wide. TUBE: magenta (59C); short & thin; 11mm (7/16") long x 4mm (1/8") wide. FOLIAGE is dark green (136A) upper surface; medium green (137B) lower surface. PARENTAGE: 'Rosea' x 'Rohees New Millennium'.
Michiels 2007 BE AFS6359.

Remembering Claire. Trailer. Single. COROLLA: quarter flared, bell shaped; wavy petal margins; opens reddish purple (61B); matures reddish purple (71B); 24mm (15/16") long x 18mm (11/16") wide. SEPALS: half down, tips reflexed, light twisting of tip to left & right; light rose (68D) tipped light yellowish green (154B) upper surface; rose (68B) lower surface; 30mm (1 3/16") long x 9mm (5/16") wide. TUBE: light rose (68D); long & thin; 43mm (1 11/16") long x 5mm (3/16") wide. STAMENS do not extend beyond the corolla; magenta (67B) filaments; light yellow (2B) anthers. PISTIL extends 10mm (3/8") beyond the corolla; magenta (67B) style; light yellow (2B) stigma. BUD: long. FOLIAGE: medium green (137B) upper surface; medium green (137C) lower surface. Leaves are 75mm (3") long x 40mm (1 9/16") wide; elliptic shaped, serrate edges,

360

acute tips, rounded bases. Veins are gray green, stems & branches are reddish. PARENTAGE: {[(F. *juntasensis* x F. *inflata*) x F. *magdalenae*] x [('Checkerboard' x 'Machu Picchu') x ('Checkerboard' x 'Machu Picchu')]} x 'Wilson's Pearls'. Natural trailer. Makes good basket. Prefers overhead filtered light, cool climate. Heat tolerant if shaded. Best bloom & foliage colour in filtered light. Tested 4 years in Ohé en Laak, The Netherlands. Nominated by NKvF as recommendable cultivar. Distinguished by beautiful long thin TUBE.
de Cooker 2009 NL AFS7025.

Renate Schaller. Trailer. Semi Double. COROLLA: half flared, turned under wavy petal margins; opens violet (76A) striped light purple (70C); matures light reddish purple (72C) striped rose (68C); 33mm (1 5/16") long x 25mm (1") wide. PETALOIDS: Same colour as corolla; 22mm (7/8") long x 14mm (9/16") wide. SEPALS: horizontal, tips recurved, twisted left to right; pale pink (56D) tipped apple green (144C) upper surface; rose (55B) tipped apple green (144C) lower surface; 52mm (2 1/16") long x 14mm (9/16") wide. TUBE: white (155C) striped dark rose (54B); short & thick; 9mm (5/16") long x 5mm (3/16") wide. STAMENS extend 18mm (11/16") beyond the corolla; pink (62A) filaments; tan (174C) anthers. PISTIL extends 31mm (1 1/4") beyond the corolla; light pink (65C) style; pale lavender (69D) stigma. BUD: oblong, square. FOLIAGE: dark green (137A) upper surface; medium green (138B) lower surface. Leaves are 69mm (2 3/4") long x 33mm (1 5/16") wide; ovate shaped, serrulate edges, acute tips, rounded bases. Veins are grayish orange (179C), stems are dark rose (180C), branches are rose (180D) & light green (138C). PARENTAGE: 'Niagara Falls' x 'Alfred Fuhrmann'. Natural trailer. Self branching. Makes good basket. Prefers overhead filtered light, cool climate. Best bloom & foliage colour in filtered light. Tested 3 years in Koningshooikt, Belgium. Waanrode 8/9/08. Distinguished by bloom colour.
Michiels 2009 BE AFS7214.

Rene Dahlen. Trailer. Double. COROLLA: half flared; opens violet (85B), pale violet (85D) base; matures light violet (84B); 15mm (9/16") long x 14mm (9/16") wide. PETALOIDS: same colour as corolla; 11mm (7/16") long x 7mm (1/4") wide. SEPALS: horizontal, tips reflexed; white (155C) tipped light green (144B) upper surface; pale rose white (N155D) tipped light green (144B) lower

surface; 32mm (1 1/4") long x 12mm (7/16") wide. TUBE: white (155C) striped light green (138C); medium length & thickness; 18mm (11/16") long x 6mm (1/4") wide. FOLIAGE is medium green (137B) upper surface; medium green (138B) lower surface. PARENTAGE: 'Vreeni Schleeweis' x 'Kiss'.
Michiels 2007 BE AFS6333.

Rene van Eijk. Upright/Trailer. Double. COROLLA: quarter flared, smooth petal margins; opens magenta (63A); matures magenta (63B); 32mm (1 1/4") long x 30mm (1 3/16") wide. SEPALS: half up; tips reflexed up; white (155B) upper & lower surfaces; 52mm (2 1/16") long x 17mm (11/16") wide. TUBE: white (155B); medium length & thickness; 22mm (7/8") long x 6mm (1/4") wide. STAMENS: extend 12mm (1/2") below corolla; light rose (68D) filaments, dark reddish purple (60A) anthers. PISTIL: extends 26mm (1") below the corolla; light rose (68D) style, light yellow (4D) stigma. BUD: ovate. FOLIAGE: dark green (137A) upper surface; medium green (138A) lower surface. Leaves are 57mm (2 1/4") long x 28mm (1 1/8") wide, lanceolate shaped, serrulated edges, acute tips and obtuse bases. Veins, stems & branches are green. PARENTAGE: 'Sofie Michiels' x 'Veenlust'. Lax upright or stiff trailer. Makes good stiff trailer. Prefers overhead filtered light and cool climate. Best bloom and foliage colour in filtered light. Tested 4 years in Reusel, The Netherlands. Distinguished by bloom colour.
van Eijk 2003 NL AFS5257.

Renhoeks Lieke. Upright. Single. COROLLA: half flared, smooth petal margins; opens & matures white & pink (62A); 22mm (7/8") long x 22mm (7/8") wide. SEPALS: fully up; tips reflexed; reddish purple (67A) upper surface; dark rose (67C) lower surface; 32mm (1 1/4") long x 12mm (1/2") wide. TUBE: reddish purple (67A); medium length & thickness; 10mm (3/8") long x 5mm (3/16") wide. STAMENS: extend 16mm (5/8") below corolla; pink (62A) filaments & anthers. PISTIL: extends 44mm (1 3/4") below the corolla; light pink (62B) style, light rose (63D) stigma. BUD: long, ovate. FOLIAGE: dark green (137A) upper surface; medium green (138B) lower surface. Leaves are 48mm (1 7/8") long x 27mm (1 1/16") wide, ovate shaped, serrulated edges, acute tips and rounded bases. Veins, stems & branches are red. PARENTAGE: Sport of 'Leonora'. Medium upright. Makes good upright or standard. Prefers overhead filtered light and cool climate. Best bloom and foliage colour in filtered light. Tested 4 years in Leende, The Netherlands. Distinguished by bloom & foliage combination. Liebregts 2003 NL AFS5246.

Renhoeks Renske. Upright. Single. COROLLA is half flared; opens reddish purple (80B); matures light purple (80C); 17mm (5/8") long x 21mm (13/16") wide. SEPALS are half up, tips reflexed up; red (52A) upper & lower surfaces; 19mm (3/4") long x 11mm (7/16") wide. TUBE is red (52A); 4mm (1/8") long x 6mm (1/4") wide. FOLIAGE: dark green (137A) upper surface; medium green (138B) lower surface. PARENTAGE: 'Nici's Findling' x unknown. Distinguished by erect blooms & bloom colour.
Liebregts 2006 NL AFS6188.

Rens van Dommelen. Upright. Single. COROLLA: quarter flared, smooth petal margins; opens dark purple (79A); matures dark reddish purple (59A); 21mm (13/16") long x 18mm (11/16") wide. SEPALS: half up; tips recurved up; reddish purple (61B) upper surface; dark reddish purple (60C) lower surface; 24mm (15/16") long x 8mm (5/16") wide. TUBE: reddish purple (61B); medium length & thickness; 14mm (9/16") long x 7mm (1/4") wide. STAMENS: extend 15mm (9/16") below corolla; dark reddish purple (59A) filaments; dark purple (79A) anthers. PISTIL: extends 34mm (1 5/16") below the corolla; reddish purple (59B) style; light rose (63D) stigma. BUD: ovate. FOLIAGE: dark green (137A) upper surface; medium green (138B) lower surface. Leaves are 61mm (2 3/8") long x 25mm (1") wide, lanceolate shaped, serrulated edges, acute tips and obtuse bases. Veins, stems & branches are red. PARENTAGE: 'Rohees Metallah' x 'Belle de Spa'. Small upright. Makes good upright or standard. Prefers overhead filtered light and cool climate. Best bloom and foliage colour in filtered light. Tested 4 years in Diessen, The Netherlands. Distinguished by bloom colour.
Comperen 2003 NL AFS5280.

Restaurant De Kempen. Upright/Trailer. Single. COROLLA: half flared, turned under toothed petal margins; opens & matures light reddish purple (72C), light rose (73C) base; 19mm (3/4") long x 29mm (1/8") wide. SEPALS: half up; tips recurved up; pink (62A) upper surface; rose (65A) lower surface; 23mm (15/16") long x 11mm (7/16") wide. TUBE: pale pink (56D), dark green (140A) at top; long, medium thickness; 24mm (15/16")

long x 6mm (1/4") wide. STAMENS: extend 4mm (3/16") below corolla; magenta (63B) filaments; orangy brown (163A) anthers. PISTIL: extends 2mm (1/16") below the corolla; rose (63C) style; yellow (11A) stigma. BUD: round, ribbed. FOLIAGE: dark green (137A) upper surface, medium green (138B) lower surface. Leaves are 83mm (3 1/4") long x 38mm (1 1/2") wide, elliptic shaped, smooth edges, acute tips and rounded bases. Yellowish green (144B) veins & branches; brown (176B) stems. PARENTAGE: 'Alda Alders' x 'Party Frock'. Lax upright or stiff trailer. Self branching. Makes good basket or upright. Prefers full sun and warm climate. Best bloom and foliage colour in bright light. Tested 4 years in Leopoldsburg & Helchteren, Belgium. Distinguished by tolerance of sun exposure.
Busschodts 2004 BE AFS5438.

Rêve D'antan. Upright/Trailer. Single. COROLLA is unflared with smooth petal margins; opens & matures light reddish purple (73A); 19mm (3/4") long x 7mm (1/4") wide. SEPALS are half up, tips recurved up; light coral (38A) in sun, pale pink (36D) in shade, tipped yellowish white (4D) upper surface; pink (48D) lower surface; 26mm (1") long x 7mm (1/4") wide. TUBE is light coral (38A) in sun, pale pink (36D) in shade; medium length & thickness; 15mm (9/16") long x 4mm (3/16") wide. FOLIAGE: dark green (147A) upper surface; yellowish green (146C) lower surface. Leaves are 48mm (1 7/8") long x 18mm (11/16") wide, ovate to lanceolate shaped. PARENTAGE: 'Philippe Boënnec' x 'Mirobolant'. Distinguished by bloom colour.
Massé 2005 FR AFS5698.

Rhées Harmonie. Trailer. Semi Double. . COROLLA: half flared, petticoat shape; opens violet (90D); matures violet (86D); 25mm (1") long x 25mm (1") wide. PETALOIDS: same colour as corolla; 20mm (3/4") long x 15mm (9/16") wide. SEPALS: fully up, tips recurved; magenta (61C) upper surface; magenta (58B) lower surface; 41mm (1 5/8") long x 11mm (7/16") wide. TUBE: magenta (58B); 11mm (7/16") long x 7mm (1/4") wide. FOLIAGE is yellowish green (146B) upper surface; yellowish green (146C) lower surface. PARENTAGE: 'Rhées Symphonie' x unknown.
Ricard 2008 BE AFS6844.

Rhées Marina. Trailer. Single. COROLLA: quarter flared, square shape; opens red (53D); matures red (53C); 18mm (11/16")

long x 13mm (1/2") wide. SEPALS: full down, tips recurved; very pale orange (27D) tipped green upper surface; very pale orange (27D) lower surface; 35mm (1 3/8") long x 9mm (5/16") wide. TUBE: pale orange (27B); 22mm (7/8") long x 6mm (1/4") wide. FOLIAGE is medium green (146A) upper surface; yellowish green (146B) lower surface. PARENTAGE: 'Hidcote Beauty' x unknown.
Ricard 2008 BE AFS6847.

Rianne. Trailer. Double. COROLLA is three quarter flared with turned under wavy petal margins; opens & matures white (155C), dark rose (54A) base; 32mm (1 1/4") long x 36mm (1 7/16") wide. SEPALS are horizontal, tips reflexed; red (53D) upper surface; dark rose (51A) lower surface; 39mm (1 9/16") long x 16mm (5/8") wide. TUBE is reddish purple (61B); medium length & thickness; 14mm (9/16") long x 7mm (1/4") wide. FOLIAGE: medium green (137B) upper surface; medium green (138B) lower surface. Leaves are 68mm (2 11/16") long x 31mm (1 1/4") wide, elliptic shaped. PARENTAGE: 'Fort Bragg' x unknown. Meise 9-18-04. Distinguished by flower colour.
Dewez 2005 NL AFS5844.

Richard Branson. Upright/Trailer. Double. COROLLA is unflared, pointed plum shaped, with turned under petal margins; opens violet blue (92A); matures violet (76A) and violet (75A); 50mm (1") long x 40mm (1 9/16") wide. SEPALS are horizontal, tips recurved, half twisted sideways and up; light rose (73C) streaked light rose (73B) at joints upper surface, dark rose (58C) creped lower surface; 68mm (2 11/16") long x 19mm (3/4) wide. TUBE is light rose (73C) striped light rose (73B); short with medium thickness; 13mm (1/2") long x 8mm (5/16") wide. STAMENS extend 10mm (3/8") below the corolla; magenta (58B) filaments and anthers. PISTIL extends 30mm (1 3/16") below the corolla; white (155) style and stigma. BUD is long, pointed with flat base. FOLIAGE is dark green (137A) upper surface, medium green (137C) lower surface. Leaves are 63mm (2 1/2") long x 110mm (4 5/16") wide, ovate shaped, serrulated edges, acute tips and rounded bases. Veins are red at stalk, turning green, stems are pale green, branches are green tinged pink. PARENTAGE: 'Tuonela' x 'Flair'. Lax upright or stiff trailer. Makes good basket, upright, standard or pillar. Prefers cool climate. Heat tolerant if shaded. Best bloom colour in filtered light. Tested five years in Gloucester, England. Distinguished by unusual sepal formation and bloom colour.
Hickman 2002 UK AFS4864.

Richard Trevithick. Upright. Single. COROLLA is unflared with smooth petal margins; opens magenta (68A); matures dark rose (67C); 18mm (11/16") long x 15mm (9/16") wide. SEPALS are horizontal, tips reflexed; rose (65A) tipped light yellow green (150B) upper surface; light pink (65C) lower surface; 22mm (7/8") long x 7mm (1/4") wide. TUBE is light pink (65C); long & thin; 15mm (9/16") long x 5mm (3/16") wide. FOLIAGE: medium green (137C) upper surface; medium green (137D) lower surface. Leaves are 60mm (2 3/8") long x 38mm (1 1/2") wide, lanceolate shaped. PARENTAGE: 'Jonathan Negus' x 'Lizard Point'. Distinguished by colour combination.
Negus 2005 UK AFS5978.

Rico Neggers. Upright. Double. COROLLA: 3 quarter flared; opens light violet (84B), pale purple (75C) base; matures light violet (84C); 18mm (11/16") long x 16mm (5/8") wide. SEPALS: horizontal, tips recurved; white (155C) striped medium green (138B), tipped apple green (144C) upper surface; pale purple (75C) tipped apple green (144C) lower surface; 36mm (1 7/16") long x 16mm (5/8") wide. TUBE: white (155C) striped medium green (138B); medium length & thickness; 14mm (9/16") long x 6mm (1/4") wide. FOLIAGE is dark green (136A) upper surface; medium green (139C) lower surface. PARENTAGE: 'Vreni Schleeweiss' x 'Kiss'.
Michiels 2007 BE AFS6360.

Rie Comperen. Upright. Double. COROLLA: half flared, smooth petal margins; opens & matures white (155B); 20mm (13/16") long x 24mm (15/16") wide. SEPALS: half up; tips reflexed up; white (155A) upper surface; white (155C) lower surfaces; 20mm (13/16") long x 10mm (3/8") wide. TUBE: white (155A); short & thick; 6mm (1/4") long x 7mm (1/4") wide. STAMENS: extend 15mm (9/16") below corolla; pale purple (74D) filaments; dark reddish purple (61A) anthers. PISTIL: extends 26mm (1") below the corolla; white (155A) style; light yellow (11C) stigma. BUD: spherical. FOLIAGE: dark green (137A) upper surface; medium green (138A) lower surface. Leaves are 62mm (2 7/16") long x 27mm (1 1/16") wide, lanceolate shaped, serrulated edges, acute tips and rounded bases. Veins, stems & branches are green. PARENTAGE: 'Sofie Michiels' x 'Cameron Ryle'. Tall upright. Makes good miniature.

Prefers overhead filtered light and cool climate. Best bloom and foliage colour in filtered light. Tested 4 years in Diessen, The Netherlands. Distinguished by bloom & foliage combination.
Comperen 2003 NL AFS5279.

Riedlingen. Upright. Single. COROLLA dark pink red; corolla is quarter flared. SEPALS light pink on the upper and lower surfaces; SEPALS are half up with recurved tips.. TUBE light pink. PARENTAGE 'La Campanella' x 'Cara Mia'.
Nicola 2009 AT BFS0105.

Rien Que Toi. Upright. Single. COROLLA is quarter flared; opens & matures violet (77B), lighter base; 20mm (3/4") long x 22mm (7/8") wide. SEPALS are fully up, tips recurved; cream (159D) upper & lower surfaces; 32mm (1 1/4") long x 11mm (7/16") wide. TUBE is yellowish white (4D); 12mm (7/16") long x 7mm (1/4") wide. FOLIAGE: dark green (147A) upper surface; medium green (147B) lower surface. PARENTAGE: 'Gaulois Futé' x 'Joël Boquien'. Distinguished by colour & form of the flowers.
Massé 2006 FR AFS6244.

Rigolo. NO COROLLA. SEPALS: horizontal, tips recurved; red (47B) upper & lower surfaces; 29mm (1 1/8") long x 4mm (1/8") wide. TUBE: red (47B); medium length, thin; 14mm (9/16") long x 3mm (1/8") wide. FOLIAGE is medium green (146A) upper surface; yellowish green (146B) lower surface. PARENTAGE: 'Philippe Boënnec' x 'Eve Ruggiéri'.
Massé 2007 FR AFS6488.

Rik Knapen. Trailer. Single. COROLLA is half flared; opens purple (83A); matures dark reddish purple (64A); 26mm (1") long x 36mm (1 7/16") wide. SEPALS are horizontal, tips recurved; light pink (65C) upper surface; light pink (65B) lower surface; 34mm (1 3/8") long x 16mm (5/8") wide. TUBE is light pink (65C); 9mm (3/8") long x 7mm (1/4") wide. FOLIAGE: medium green (137B) upper surface; medium green (138B) lower surface. PARENTAGE: 'Sofie Michiels' x 'Mission Bells'. Distinguished by bloom colour & shape.
Roes 2006 NL AFS6167.

Rillaarse Glorie. Trailer. Semi Double. COROLLA: half flared; opens light rose (68D) & light reddish purple (72C); matures light pink (62C) & reddish purple (70B); 27mm (1 1/16") long x 25mm (1") wide. PETALOIDS: rose (48B), & light reddish purple (67B) base; 20mm (3/4") long x 12mm (7/16") wide. SEPALS: twisted left to right; horizontal, tips recurved; rose (61D) upper surface; light rose (58D) lower surface; 48mm (1 7/8") long x 13mm (1/2") wide. TUBE: pale pink (56A); 39mm (1 1/2") long x 7mm (1/4") wide. FOLIAGE is medium green (138A) upper surface; medium green (138B) lower surface. PARENTAGE: 'Quasar' x unknown.
Willems 2008 BE AFS6747.

Rillaarse Parel. Trailer. Double. COROLLA: three quarter flared, turned under wavy petal margins; opens violet (76A); matures purple (N78C); 31mm (1 1/4") long x 23mm (7/8") wide. PETALOIDS: violet (77B); 19mm (3/4") long x 12mm (7/16") wide. SEPALS: half up, tips recurved up, curled back tips; pink (62B) tipped pale yellow green (150D) upper surface; light rose (58D) tipped light yellow green (150D) lower surface; 50mm (2") long x 14mm (9/16") wide. TUBE: rose (61D); medium length & thickness; 24mm (15/16") long x 7mm (1/4") wide. STAMENS extend 17mm (5/8") beyond the corolla; reddish purple (67A) filaments; dark purple (79A) anthers. PISTIL extends 32mm (1 1/4") beyond the corolla; rose (68B) style; pale yellow (2D) stigma. BUD: cylindrical. FOLIAGE: dark green (137A) upper surface; medium green (138B) lower surface. Leaves are 87mm (3 7/16") long x 41mm (1 5/8") wide; ovate shaped, serrate edges, acute tips, rounded bases. Veins are light green (139D), stems are light red purple (185D), branches are dark grayish red (182A) & medium green (139C). PARENTAGE: 'Quasar' x unknown. Natural trailer. Self branching. Makes good basket. Prefers overhead filtered light, cool climate. Best bloom & foliage colour in filtered light. Tested 5 years in Rillaar, Belgium. Waanrode 8/9/08. Distinguished by bloom colour & curled back sepal tips.
Willems 1008 BE AFS7080.

Rinie Post. Upright. Single. COROLLA: quarter flared, ovate shape; opens light rose (58D); matures light magenta (57D); 11mm (7/16") long x 9mm (5/16") wide. SEPALS: horizontal, tips recurved; light rose (58D) upper surface; dark rose (58C) lower surface; 20 mm (3/4") long x 5mm (3/16") wide. TUBE: dark rose (58C); 9mm (5/16") long x 6mm (1/4") wide. FOLIAGE is dark green (137A) upper surface; medium green (137C) lower surface. PARENTAGE: ('Toos' x 'Whiteknight's Amethyst') x 'Prince Syray'.

Nomination by NKVF as Recommendable Cultivar.
van Aspert 2008 NL AFS6786.

Rise and Shine. Upright. Single. COROLLA is three quarter flared, with wavy petal margins; opens & matures white (155B) veined red (47B); 19mm (3/4") long x 16mm (5/8") wide. SEPALS are fully up, tips reflexed; red (45C) tipped yellowish green (144B) upper surface; red (46C) tipped apple green (144C) lower surface; 32mm (1 1/4") long x 10mm (3/8") wide. TUBE is red (45B); short, medium thickness; 10mm (3/8") long x 3mm (1/8") wide. FOLIAGE: dark green (147A) upper surface; light olive green (147C) lower surface. Leaves are 25mm (1") long x 12mm (1/2") wide, ovate shaped, smooth edges, acute tips and rounded bases. Veins, stems & branches are green. PARENTAGE: 'Caradella' x 'Katie Elizabeth Ann'. Distinguished by profuse, long lasting flowers.
Edmond 2005 UK AFS5818.

Rita Closset. Upright/Trailer. Semi Double. COROLLA is half flared with turned under smooth petal margins; opens purple (80A), rose (54C) at base; matures reddish purple (74A), light purple (70C) at base; 30mm (13/16") long x 24mm (15/16") wide. PETALOIDS: dark purple (78A), pink (52D) at base; 22mm (7/8") x 14mm (9/16"). SEPALS are horizontal, tips recurved; dark rose (55A) tipped yellowish green (145A), rose (55B) at base, upper surface; dark rose (55A), magenta (63B) at base, lower surface; 52mm (2 1/16") long x 12mm (1/2") wide. TUBE is pink (54D); medium length and thickness; 16mm (5/8") long x 10mm (3/8") thick. STAMENS do not extend beyond the corolla; dark rose (58C) filaments, magenta (58B) anthers. PISTIL extends 27mm (1 1/16") beyond the corolla; pink (62A) style, yellow (20B) stigma. BUD is ovate, pointed. FOLIAGE is dark green (137A) upper surface, medium green (147B) lower surface. Leaves are 56mm (2 3/16") long x 42mm (1 11/16") wide, cordate shaped, serrated edges, acute tips and cordate bases. Veins are plum (185B), stems are plum (183B), branches are plum (185B). PARENTAGE: 'Gay Fandango' x unknown. Lax upright or stiff trailer. Makes good basket. Prefers overhead filtered light. Best bloom and foliage colour in filtered light. Tested three years in Rummen, Belgium. Certificate N.B.F.K. at Meise. Distinguished by bloom colour.
Ector 2002 BE AFS5006.

Rita Depré. Upright/Trailer. Double. COROLLA: half flared, turned under wavy petal margins; opens dark reddish purple (72A) striped reddish purple (61B); matures reddish purple (67A); 22mm (7/8") long x 15mm (9/16") wide. PETALOIDS: Same colour as corolla; 13mm (1/2") long x 9mm (5/16") wide. SEPALS: half down, tips recurved; white (155C) tipped light yellowish green (150C) upper surface; pale pink (56C) tipped light yellowish green (150C) lower surface; 35mm (1 3/8") long x 13mm (1/2") wide. TUBE: white (155C); medium length & thickness; 15mm (9/16") long x 6mm (1/4") wide. STAMENS extend 13mm (1/2") beyond the corolla; magenta (61C) filaments; pale pink (62D) anthers. PISTIL extends 28mm (1 1/8") beyond the corolla; pale lavender (69D) style; pale yellow (1D) stigma. BUD: oblong. FOLIAGE: dark green (137A) upper surface; medium green (137D) lower surface. Leaves are 64mm (2 1/2") long x 37mm (1 7/16") wide; ovate shaped, serrate edges, acute tips, rounded bases. Veins are plum (185C), stems are light red purple (185D), branches are dark grayish red (182A) & medium green (138B). PARENTAGE: 'Coen Bakker' x 'Frans Vander Kuylen'. Lax upright or stiff trailer. Self branching. Makes good basket or upright. Prefers overhead filtered light, cool climate. Best bloom & foliage colour in filtered light. Tested 3 years in Koningshooikt, Belgium. Waanrode 8/9/08. Distinguished by bloom colour combination.
Michiels 2009 BE AFS7216.

Rita Hombourg. Upright/Trailer. Double. COROLLA: 3 quarter flared; opens white (155C), magenta (63B) base; matures white (155C) striped dark rose (64C); 14mm (9/16") long x 13mm (1/2") wide. PETALOIDS: same colour as corolla; 9mm (5/16") long x 7mm (1/4") wide. SEPALS: horizontal, tips reflexed; magenta (58B) upper surface; reddish purple (58A) lower surface; 26mm (1") long x 13mm (1/2") wide. TUBE: dark rose (58C); short & thick; 9mm (5/16") long x 7mm (1/4") wide. FOLIAGE is dark green (137A) upper surface; medium green (137D) lower surface. PARENTAGE: 'Falco' x 'Gladiator'.
Michiels 2007 BE AFS6334.

Rita Preston. Upright. Single. COROLLA: half flared, bell shaped, wavy petal margins; opens light purple (78C); matures light purple (78D); 19mm (3/4") long x 25mm (1") wide. SEPALS: half up; tips recurved up; white (155D) tipped green upper & lower surfaces; 25mm (1") long x 8mm (5/16")

wide. TUBE: light green (145D); medium length & thickness; 7mm (1/4") long x 8mm (5/16") wide. STAMENS: extend 22mm (7/8) below corolla; white (155B) filaments; brown (200B) anthers. PISTIL: extends 32mm (1 1/4") below the corolla; white (155A) style; grayish yellow (160B) stigma. BUD: ovate, long. FOLIAGE: dark green (137A) upper surface, medium green (138B) lower surface. Leaves are 60mm (2 3/8") long x 32mm (1 1/4") wide, lanceolate shaped, serrulated edges, acute tips and rounded bases. Light green (143B) veins & stems; medium green (143C) branches. PARENTAGE: 'Estelle Marie' x 'Carla Johnston'. Small upright. Makes good upright or standard. Prefers overhead filtered light and cool climate. Best bloom and foliage colour in filtered light. Tested 4 years in West Yorkshire, England. Distinguished by delicate colour.
Preston 2004 UK AFS5441.

Riverdancer Caitlin. Upright. Single. COROLLA: Fully flared, flat flare shaped, out-standing smooth petal margins; opens & matures pink (62A) & violet (75A); 48mm (1 7/8") long x 48mm (1 7/8") wide. SEPALS: horizontal, tips recurved; yellowish white (158A) splashed light coral (38A) upper & lower surfaces; 30mm (1 3/16") long x 10mm (3/8") wide. TUBE: yellowish white (158A); short & thin; 12mm (7/16") long x 4mm (1/8") wide. FOLIAGE is medium green (147B) upper surface; light olive green (147C) lower surface. PARENTAGE: ('Bon Accord' x 'White Knight's Amethyst) x 'Carla Johnston'.
Koerts T. 2007 NL AFS6447.

Riverdancer Liam. Upright. Single. COROLLA: Fully flared, flat flare shaped, out-standing smooth petal margins; opens & matures dark rose (51A) & dark orange (41A); 40mm (1 9/16") long x 40mm (1 9/16") wide. SEPALS: horizontal, tips reflexed; light coral (38A) upper & lower surfaces; 30mm (1 3/16") long x 9mm (5/16") wide. TUBE: light pink (38C) striped light reddish purple (66C); short, medium thickness; 7mm (1/4") long x 13mm (1/2") wide. FOLIAGE is dark green (137A) upper surface; medium green (137D) lower surface. PARENTAGE: ('Bon Accord' x 'White Knight's Amethyst) x 'Carla Johnston'.
Koerts T. 2007 NL AFS6446.

Riverdancer Lorcan. Upright. Single. COROLLA: Fully flared, flat flare shaped, out-standing turned up petal margins; opens & matures violet (76A), red (45A) base; violet (76A) stripe with light rose (73B) base &

edge; 38mm (1 1/2") long x 38mm (1 1/2") wide. SEPALS: horizontal, tips recurved; red (45A) upper & lower surfaces; 21mm (13/16") long x 14mm (9/16") wide. TUBE: red (45A); short, medium thickness; 6mm (1/4") long x 6mm (1/4") wide. FOLIAGE is dark green (147A) upper surface; medium green (147B) lower surface. PARENTAGE: ('Bon Accord' x 'White Knight's Amethyst) x 'Carla Johnston'.
Koerts T. 2007 NL AFS6448.

Riverside. Upright. Double. COROLLA pink splashed lavender. SEPALS cream blushed pink.
Harris 2002 UK.

Rob. Trailer. Semi Double. COROLLA: quarter flared, turned under smooth petal margins; opens light reddish purple (72C), light purple (70C) at base; matures reddish purple (70B); 17mm (11/16") long x 11mm (7/16") wide. SEPALS: half down; tips recurved; white (155C), rose (55B) at base, tipped greenish yellow (1B) upper surface; dark rose (58C) magenta (58B), tipped greenish yellow (1B) lower surface; 26mm (1") long x 11mm (7/16") wide. TUBE: white (155D); medium length & thickness; 22mm (7/8") long x 5mm (3/16") wide. STAMENS: do not extend below the corolla; dark rose (58C) filaments, pale yellow (1D) anthers. PISTIL extends 4mm (3/16") below the corolla; dark rose (58C) style, yellowish white (4D) stigma. BUD: long, pointed. FOLIAGE: medium green (137B) upper surface; medium green (138B) lower surface. Leaves are 65mm (2 9/16") long x 25mm (1") wide, elliptic shaped, serrulated edges, acute tips and rounded bases. Veins light red purple (185D), stems are plum (184C), branches are plum (185C). PARENTAGE: 'WALZ Harp' x 'La Bergère'. Natural trailer. Self branching. Makes good basket. Prefers overhead filtered light. Best bloom and foliage colour in filtered light. Tested 3 years in Koningshooikt, Belgium. NBFK certificate at Meise. Distinguished by bloom colour and shape.
Michiels 2003 BE AFS5103.

Rob Gasaway. Upright/Trailer. Single. COROLLA is half flared with smooth petal margins; opens dark purple (79B), matures purple (71A); 26mm (1 1/16") long x 21mm (13/16") wide. SEPALS are fully up, tips recurved; reddish purple (61B) upper surface and magenta (67B) lower surface; 25mm (1") long x 11mm (7/16") wide. TUBE is reddish purple (61B), medium length and thickness; 10mm (3/8") long x 6mm (1/4") wide.

STAMENS extend 30mm (1 3/16) below the corolla; dark purple (79B) filaments and anthers. PISTIL extends 36mm (1 7/16") below the corolla; dark rose (67C) style, light yellow (8C) stigma. BUD is ovate, pointed. FOLIAGE is dark green (137A) upper surface and medium green (138A) lower surface. Leaves are 48mm (1 7/8") long x 30mm (1 3/16") wide, ovate shaped, serrated edges, acute tips and rounded bases. Veins, stems and branches are red. PARENTAGE: {[('Vobeglo' x ('Foline' x 'Dancing Flame')] x ('Parasol' x 'Cameron Ryle)} x 'Rohees New Millennium'. Lax upright or stiff trailer. Makes good stiff trailer. Prefers overhead filtered light and cool climate. Best bloom colour in filtered light. Tested four years in Knegsel, The Netherlands. Distinguished by bloom colour.
Roes 2002 NL AFS4831.

Rob Knapen. Upright/Trailer. Double. COROLLA: Half flared; opens purple (89C); matures purple (77A); 21mm (13/16") long x 21mm (13/16") wide. SEPALS: half up, tips reflexed up; light pink (62B) upper surface; pink (62A) lower surface; 21mm (13/16") long x 12mm (7/16") wide. TUBE: light pink (62B); medium length & thickness; 12mm (7/16") long x 6mm (1/4") wide. FOLIAGE is dark green (137A) upper surface; medium green (138A) lower surface. PARENTAGE: 'Roesse Charon' x 'Roesse Blacky'.
Roes 2007 NL AFS6702.

Robbe Kennes. Trailer. Double. COROLLA: half flared; opens white (155C), striped pale pink (62D); matures white (155D); 24mm (15/16") long x 15mm (9/16") wide. PETALOIDS: white (155C); 12 mm (7/16") long x 8 mm (5/16") wide. SEPALS are half up, tips recurved up, twisted left to right; white (155C), edged pale pink (62D), tipped light apple green (145C) upper surface; pale pink (62D) tipped light apple green (145C) lower surface; 40mm (1 9/16") long x 11mm (7/16") wide. TUBE is white (155C); medium length and thickness; 17mm (5/8") long x 7mm (1/4") wide. FOLIAGE is medium green (137B) upper surface; medium green (138B) lower surface. PARENTAGE: 'Vreni Schleeweiss' x 'Futura'.
Michiels 2007 BE AFS6510.

Robert Götz. Upright. Double. COROLLA is three quarter flared; opens dark purple (79A); matures reddish purple (59B); 27mm (1 1/16") long x 46mm (1 13/16") wide. SEPALS are fully up, tips recurved; dark reddish purple (60A) upper & lower surfaces; 43mm (1 11/16") long x 16mm (5/8") wide. TUBE is dark reddish purple (60A); 17mm (5/8") long x 10mm (3/8") wide. FOLIAGE: dark green (137A) upper surface; medium green (137C) lower surface. PARENTAGE: 'Georg Glossner' x 'Rohees Queen'.
Burkhart 2006 DE AFS6047.

Robert H. Vitzthum. Upright/Trailer. Single to Semi Double. COROLLA is three quarter flared with turned under wavy petal margins; opens dark purple (79A), magenta (59B) base; matures magenta (59B); 21mm (13/16") long x 23mm (15/16") wide. SEPALS are horizontal, tips recurved; magenta (59B) upper surface; dark reddish purple (61A) lower surface; 29mm (1 1/8") long x 14mm (9/16") wide. TUBE is magenta (59C); short & thick; 11mm (7/16") long x 8mm (3/16") wide. FOLIAGE: dark green (136A) upper surface; medium green (137C) lower surface. Leaves are 59mm (2 5/16") long x 18mm (11/16") wide, elliptic shaped. PARENTAGE: 'Roesse Blacky' x 'Margaret Tebbit'. Meise 9-18-04, Outstanding. Distinguished by wide open flower shape.
Michiels 2005 BE AFS5849.

Robert Liebens. Trailer. Single. COROLLA is half flared with smooth petal margins; opens dark rose (54A); matures red (50A); 22mm (7/8") long x 27 mm (1 1/16") wide. SEPALS are half down, tips reflexed; dark rose (54B) upper surface; red (50A) lower surface; 23mm (15/16") long x 8mm (5/16") wide. TUBE is pink (54D), medium length & thickness; 18mm (11/16") long x 8mm (5/16") wide. FOLIAGE: dark green (137A) upper surface; medium green (138B) lower surface. Leaves are 47mm (1 7/8") long x 26mm (1") wide, ovate shaped. PARENTAGE: 'Roesse Carme' x 'Luuk van Riet'. Distinguished by bloom and foliage combination.
Comperen 2005 NL AFS5642.

Roberto Boreal. Upright. Single. COROLLA: quarter flared, turned up wavy petal margins; opens reddish purple (74A), matures reddish purple (67A); 12mm (1/2") long x 10mm (3/8") wide. SEPALS: half down; tips reflexed; dark rose (55A) & light pink (55D) upper surface, dark rose (55A) lower surface; 18mm (11/16") long x 5mm (3/16") wide. TUBE: dark rose (55A) with ribslong & thin; 16mm (5/8") long x 4mm (3/16") wide. STAMENS: extend 3 - 8mm (1/8 – 5/16") below the corolla; dark rose (58C) filaments, pale tan (159A) anthers. PISTIL extends 23mm (15/16") below the corolla; pink (55C) & white style, pale tan (159A) stigma. BUD: ovate. FOLIAGE: medium green (146A) upper surface, light olive green (148B) lower surface. Leaves are 60mm (2 3/8") long x 25mm (1") wide, lanceolate shaped, serrated edges, rounded tips and rounded bases. Veins & stems are reddish, branches are brown. PARENTAGE: 'F. *magellanica*' x unknown. Medium upright. Makes good upright. Prefers full sun and warm climate. Best bloom and foliage colour in bright light. Tested 3 years in Como, Italy. Distinguished by profuse blooms, bright colour and multiple flowers each node. Ianne 2003 IT AFS5075.

Robinson. Upright/Trailer. Single. COROLLA is quarter flared; opens & matures white (155A); 17mm (5/8") long x 20mm (3/4") wide. SEPALS are half up, tips reflexed up; rose (52C) upper surface; rose (52B) lower surface; 23mm (7/8") long x 11mm (7/16") wide. TUBE is rose (52C); 52mm (2 1/16") long x 9mm (3/8") wide. FOLIAGE: dark green (147A) upper surface; medium green (147B) lower surface. PARENTAGE: 'Paul Berry' x 'F. fulgens rubra grandiflora'. Distinguished by bloom shape & colour. Krom 2006 NL AFS6271.

Rococo. Trailer. Single. COROLLA is half flared; opens reddish purple (74A); matures purple (71A); 15mm (9/16") long x 17mm (5/8") wide. SEPALS are fully up, tips recurved in a complete vertical circle; reddish purple (70B) upper surface; light reddish purple (72C) lower surface; 32mm (1 1/4") long x 6mm (1/4") wide. TUBE is dark reddish purple (70A); 29mm (1 1/8") long x 4mm (1/8") wide. FOLIAGE: dark green (147A) upper surface; medium green (147B) lower surface. PARENTAGE: 'Gerharda's Panache' x 'Bourguignon'. Distinguished by aubergine coloured flowers in terminal sub racemes & by SEPALS forming a complete vertical circle. de Graaff H. 2006 NL AFS6247.

Roel van Dommelen. Upright/Trailer. Single. COROLLA: three quarter flared, smooth petal margins; opens purple (83A); matures purple (77A); 22mm (7/8") long x 27mm (1 1/16") wide. SEPALS: fully up; tips reflexed; red (46B) upper & lower surfaces; 26mm (1") long x 15mm (9/16") wide. TUBE: red (46B); medium length & thickness; 7mm (1/4") long x 7mm (1/4") wide. STAMENS: extend 20mm (13/16") below corolla; red (45A) filaments & anthers. PISTIL: extends 32mm (1 1/4") below the corolla; magenta

(63A) style & stigma. BUD: spherical, pointed. FOLIAGE: dark green (137A) upper surface; medium green (138B) lower surface. Leaves are 64mm (2 1/2") long x 36mm (1 7/16") wide, ovate shaped, serrulated edges, acute tips and rounded bases. Veins, stems & branches are red. PARENTAGE: 'Rohees Segin' x 'Maxima''. Lax upright or stiff trailer. Makes good stiff trailer. Prefers overhead filtered light and cool climate. Best bloom and foliage colour in filtered light. Tested 4 years in Diessen, The Netherlands. Distinguished by bloom colour. Comperen 2003 NL AFS5278.

Roesse Achernar. Upright. Single. COROLLA: full flared, smooth petal margins; opens purple (83B); matures reddish purple (71B); 25mm (1") long 29mm (1 1/8") wide. SEPALS: fully up; tips recurved; red (46B) upper surface; red (50A) lower surface; 24mm (15/16") long x 11mm (7/16") wide. TUBE: red (46B); short & thick; 7mm (1/4") long x 7mm (1/4") wide. STAMENS: extend 29mm (1 1/8") below corolla; magenta (58B) filaments; dark reddish purple (60B) anthers. PISTIL: extends 51mm (2") below the corolla; magenta (58B) style; light rose (68D) stigma. BUD: cordate, pointed. FOLIAGE: dark green (137A) upper surface; medium green (138B) lower surface. Leaves are 61mm (2 7/16") long x 32mm (1 1/4") wide, ovate shaped, serrulated edges, acute tips and rounded bases. Green veins, stems & branches. PARENTAGE: 'Swanley Gem' x 'Katrien Michiels'. Medium upright. Makes good upright or standard. Prefers overhead filtered light and cool climate. Best bloom and foliage colour in filtered light. Tested 4 years in Knegsel, The Netherlands. Distinguished by bloom shape and colour. Roes 2003 NL AFS5489.

Roesse Acrux. Upright/Trailer. Double. COROLLA is half flared with smooth petal margins; opens dark purple (86A); matures reddish purple (74A); 24mm (15/16") long x 20mm (13/16") wide. SEPALS are horizontal, tips recurved; pale yellow (158B) upper surface, cream (158C) lower surface; 27mm (1 1/16") long x 14mm (9/16") wide. TUBE is cream (158D); medium length and thickness; 19mm (3/4") long x 6mm (1/4") thick. STAMENS extend 22mm (7/8") beyond the corolla; reddish purple (64B) filaments and anthers. PISTIL extends 34mm (1 3/8") beyond the corolla; reddish purple (64B) style, pale pink (62D) stigma. BUD is elliptic, pointed. FOLIAGE is dark green (137A) upper surface, medium green (137C) lower surface.

Leaves are 72mm (2 13/16") long x 34mm (1 3/8") wide, ovate shaped, serrated edges, acute tips and rounded bases. Veins, stems and branches are red. PARENTAGE: ('Annabel' x 'Annabel') x 'Rohees New Millennium'. Lax upright or stiff trailer. Makes good stiff trailer. Prefers overhead filtered light and cool climate. Best bloom colour in filtered light. Tested four years in Knegsel, The Netherlands. Distinguished by bloom and foliage combination.
Roes 2002 NL AFS5034.

Roesse Acturus. Upright/Trailer. Double. COROLLA: three quarter flared, smooth petal margins; opens purple (82A); matures light purple (80C); 30mm (1 3/16") long x 32mm (1 1/4") wide. SEPALS: fully up; tips recurved; pale lavender (65D) upper surface; rose (65A) lower surface; 32mm (1 1/4") long x 15mm (9/16") wide. TUBE: pale lavender (65D); medium length & thickness; 24mm (15/16") long x 6mm (1/4") wide. STAMENS: extend 28mm (1 1/8") below corolla; light rose (73C) filaments; dark reddish purple (60A) anthers. PISTIL: extends 32mm (1 1/4") below the corolla; pale pink (62D) style; cream (11D) stigma. BUD: round. FOLIAGE: dark green (137A) upper surface; medium green (138B) lower surface. Leaves are 42mm (1 5/8") long x 26mm (1") wide, ovate shaped, serrulated edges, acute tips and rounded bases. Veins, stems & branches are red. PARENTAGE: 'Roesse Apus' x 'Madalyn Drago'. Lax upright or stiff trailer. Makes good stiff trailer. Prefers overhead filtered light and cool climate. Best bloom and foliage colour in filtered light. Tested 4 years in Knegsel, The Netherlands. Distinguished by bloom & foliage combination.
Roes 2003 NL AFS5336.

Roesse Acubens. Upright. Double. COROLLA: half flared, smooth petal margins; opens purple (71A); matures dark reddish purple (72A); 20mm (13/16") long x 22mm (7/8") wide. SEPALS: horizontal; tips recurved; rose (63C) upper surface; dark rose (58C) lower surface; 34mm (1 5/16") long x 16mm (5/8") wide. TUBE: rose (63C); medium length & thickness; 16mm (5/8") long x 8mm (5/16") wide. STAMENS: extend 12mm (1/2") below corolla; reddish purple (72B) filaments; purple (71A) anthers. PISTIL: extends 18mm (11/16") below the corolla; reddish purple (67A) style; dark rose (67C) stigma. BUD: round, pointed. FOLIAGE: medium green (138A) upper surface; medium green (138B) lower surface. Leaves are 74mm (2 15/16") long x 50mm

(2") wide, ovate shaped, serrulated edges, acute tips and rounded bases. Veins, stems & branches are green. PARENTAGE: 'Roesse Apus' x 'Rohees Izar'. Medium upright. Makes good upright or standard. Prefers overhead filtered light and cool climate. Best bloom and foliage colour in filtered light. Tested 4 years in Knegsel, The Netherlands. Distinguished by bloom colour.
Roes 2003 NL AFS5337.

Roesse Adrastea. Upright. Semi Double. COROLLA: quarter flared, smooth petal margins; opens reddish purple (61B); matures magenta (58B); 16mm (5/8") long 21mm (13/16") wide. SEPALS: fully up; tips reflexed; red (53C) upper surface; red (45C) lower surface; 17mm (11/16") long x 10mm (3/8") wide. TUBE: red (53C); short & thick; 12mm (1/2") long x 8mm (5/16") wide. STAMENS: extend 8mm (5/16") below corolla; pink (48C) filaments; reddish purple (61B) anthers. PISTIL: extends 12mm (1/2") below the corolla; pink (48C) style; light rose (68D) stigma. BUD: round, pointed. FOLIAGE: dark green (137A) upper surface; medium green (138A) lower surface. Leaves are 54mm (2 1/8") long x 42mm (1 5/8") wide, ovate shaped, serrulated edges, acute tips and obtuse bases. Red veins, stems & branches. PARENTAGE: 'Roesse Carme' x ('Roesse Apus' x 'Roesse Apus'). Medium upright. Makes good upright or standard. Prefers overhead filtered light and cool climate. Best bloom and foliage colour in filtered light. Tested 4 years in Knegsel, The Netherlands. Distinguished by bloom colour.
Roes 2004 NL AFS5480.

Roesse Agrippa. Upright/Trailer. Single. COROLLA: Half flared; opens violet (76B); matures pale violet (76D); 10mm (3/8") long x 12mm (7/16") wide. SEPALS: horizontal, tips recurved; rose (68B) upper surface; magenta (68A) lower surface; 24mm (15/16") long x 8mm (5/16") wide. TUBE: rose (68B); short & thin; 2mm (1/16") long x 4mm (1/8") wide. FOLIAGE is medium green (137B) upper surface; medium green (138A) lower surface. PARENTAGE: 'Reg Gubler' x 'Venus Victrix'.
Roes 2007 NL AFS6689.

Roesse Alba. Trailer. Double. COROLLA: three quarter flared; opens pale purple (76C); matures violet (75A); 24mm (15/16") long x 26mm (1") wide. SEPALS: horizontal, tips recurved; white (155D) upper & lower surfaces; 36mm (1 7/16") long x 12mm (7/16") wide. TUBE: white (155C); 18mm

(11/16") long x 10mm (3/8") wide. FOLIAGE is dark green (137A) upper surface; medium green (138A) lower surface. PARENTAGE: 'Sofie Michiels' x 'Silver Dawn'.
Roes 2008 NL AFS6900.

Roesse Albireo. Upright. Single. COROLLA: half flared, smooth petal margins; opens rose (68C); matures light rose (68D); 15mm (9/16") long 22mm (7/8") wide. SEPALS: half up; tips recurved up; pale pink (62D), tipped green, upper surface; light pink (62B), tipped green, lower surface; 16mm (5/8") long x 11mm (7/16") wide. TUBE: pale pink (62D); medium length & thickness; 12mm (1/2") long x 6mm (1/4") wide. STAMENS: extend 12mm (1/2") below corolla; rose (68C) filaments; dark reddish purple (60B) anthers. PISTIL: extends 16mm (5/8") below the corolla; rose (68C) style; pale pink (62D) stigma. BUD: short TUBE, round. FOLIAGE: dark green (137A) upper surface; medium green (138A) lower surface. Leaves are 52mm (2 1/16") long x 27mm (1 1/16") wide, ovate shaped, serrulated edges, obtuse tips and obtuse bases. Green veins, stems & branches. PARENTAGE: 'Roesse Carme' x 'Luuk van Riet'. Small upright. Makes good upright or standard. Prefers overhead filtered light and cool climate. Best bloom and foliage colour in filtered light. Tested 4 years in Knegsel, The Netherlands. Distinguished by bloom and foliage combination.
Roes 2004 NL AFS5490.

Roesse Alcyone. Upright/Trailer. Double. COROLLA: half flared, smooth petal margins; opens violet (92B); matures violet (76A); 14mm (9/16") long 23mm (15/16") wide. SEPALS: half up; tips recurved up; pale pink (62D), tipped green, upper surface; light pink (65B), tipped green, lower surface; 32mm (1 1/4") long x 12mm (1/2") wide. TUBE: pale pink (62D); medium length & thickness; 6mm (1/4") long x 6mm (1/4") wide. STAMENS: extend 9mm (3/8") below corolla; reddish purple (66C) filaments; reddish purple (58A) anthers. PISTIL: extends 18mm (11/16") below the corolla; rose (65A) style; light yellow (4C) stigma. BUD: cordate, pointed. FOLIAGE: dark green (137A) upper surface; medium green (137C) lower surface. Leaves are 62mm (2 7/16") long x 36mm (1 7/16") wide, ovate shaped, serrated edges, acute tips and cordate bases. Red veins, stems & branches. PARENTAGE: ('Cameron Ryle' x 'Parasol') x 'Corrie Spoelstra'. Lax upright or stiff trailer. Makes good stiff trailer. Prefers overhead filtered light and cool climate. Best bloom and foliage colour in

filtered light. Tested 4 years in Knegsel, The Netherlands. Distinguished by bloom colour.
Roes 2004 NL AFS5492.

Roesse Algenib. Trailer. Double. COROLLA: three quarter flared, smooth petal margins; opens dark reddish purple (59A); matures dark reddish purple (60C); 22mm (7/8") long x 20mm (13/16") wide. SEPALS: fully up; tips reflexed; light rose (73B) upper surface; light reddish purple (73A) lower surface; 26mm (1") long x 16mm (5/8") wide. TUBE: light rose (73C); medium length & thickness; 16mm (5/8") long x 6mm (1/4") wide. STAMENS: extend 16mm (5/8") below corolla; light pink (62B) filaments; reddish purple (60D) anthers. PISTIL: extends 28mm (1 1/8") below the corolla; light pink (62B) style; pale pink (62D) stigma. BUD: round. FOLIAGE: medium green (138A) upper surface; medium green (137D) lower surface. Leaves are 60mm (2 3/8") long x 31mm (1 1/4") wide, ovate shaped, serrulated edges, acute tips and rounded bases. Veins, stems & branches are green. PARENTAGE: 'Dorothy Oosting' x 'Allure'. Natural trailer. Makes good basket. Prefers overhead filtered light and cool climate. Best bloom and foliage colour in filtered light. Tested 4 years in Knegsel, The Netherlands. Distinguished by bloom colour.
Roes 2003 NL AFS5339.

Roesse Algieba. Trailer. Double. COROLLA: three quarter flared, smooth petal margins; opens light purple (86C); matures violet (84A); 30mm (1 3/16") long x 24mm (15/16") wide. SEPALS: half up; tips recurved up; pale lavender (69C) upper surface; pale pink (69A) lower surface; 34mm (1 5/16") long x 17mm (11/16") wide. TUBE: pale lavender (69C); medium length & thickness; 15mm (9/16") long x 7mm (1/4") wide. STAMENS: extend 17mm (11/16") below corolla; light reddish purple (73A) filaments; light rose (73C) anthers. PISTIL: extends 36mm (1 7/16") below the corolla; pale rose (73D) style; light yellow (11C) stigma. BUD: ovate, pointed. FOLIAGE: dark green (137A) upper surface; medium green (138A) lower surface. Leaves are 47mm (1 7/8") long x 36mm (1 7/16") wide, cordate shaped, serrulated edges, acute tips and rounded bases. Veins, stems & branches are green. PARENTAGE: 'Madalyn Drago' x ('Sofie Michiels' x 'Lechlade Rocket'). Natural trailer. Makes good basket. Prefers overhead filtered light and cool climate. Best bloom and foliage colour in filtered light. Tested 4 years in Knegsel, The Netherlands. Distinguished by bloom colour.

Roes 2003 NL AFS5338.

Roesse Algorab. Upright. Double. COROLLA is half flared with smooth petal margins; opens dark reddish purple (72A); matures reddish purple (72B); 26mm (1") long x 24mm (15/16") wide. SEPALS are half up, tips recurved up; light pink (65C) upper surface, light pink (65B) lower surface; 30mm (1 3/16") long x 12mm (1/2") wide. TUBE is light pink (65C); medium length and thickness; 14mm (9/16") long x 6mm (1/4") thick. STAMENS extend 17mm (11/16") beyond the corolla; purple (71A) filaments, light reddish purple (74C) anthers. PISTIL extends 29mm (1 1/8") beyond the corolla; purple (71A) style, pale lavender (65D) stigma. BUD is round. FOLIAGE is dark green (137A) upper surface, medium green (137C) lower surface. Leaves are 53mm (2 1/8") long x 30mm (1 3/16") wide, ovate shaped, serrated edges, acute tips and rounded bases. Veins, stems and branches are green. PARENTAGE: {[('Bon Accord' x 'Bicentennial') x ('Vobeglo' x 'Dancing Flame')] x 'Rohees Alrami'} x ('Annabel' x 'Annabel'). Small upright. Makes good standard. Prefers overhead filtered light and cool climate. Best bloom colour in filtered light. Tested four years in Knegsel, The Netherlands. Distinguished by bloom and foliage combination.
Roes 2002 NL AFS5028.

Roesse Alnilam. Upright. Single. COROLLA: three quarter flared, smooth petal margins; opens dark reddish purple (59A); matures magenta (59C); 18mm (11/16") long x 26mm (1") wide. SEPALS: fully up; tips recurved; magenta (61C) upper surface; reddish purple (61B) lower surface; 30mm (1 3/16") long x 16mm (5/8") wide. TUBE: magenta (61C); medium length & thickness; 17mm (11/16") long x 8mm (5/16") wide. STAMENS: extend 12mm (1/2") below corolla; dark reddish purple (59A) filaments & anthers. PISTIL: extends 28mm (13/16") below the corolla; reddish purple (61B) style; cream (11D) stigma. BUD: round. FOLIAGE: dark green (137A) upper surface; medium green (138A) lower surface. Leaves are 77mm (3 1/16") long x 47mm (1 7/8") wide, ovate shaped, serrated edges, acute tips and rounded bases. Veins, stems & branches are red. PARENTAGE: 'Roesse Apus' x 'Roesse Apus'. Medium upright. Makes good standard. Prefers overhead filtered light and cool climate. Best bloom and foliage colour in filtered light. Tested 4 years in Knegsel, The Netherlands. Distinguished by bloom colour.

Roes 2003 NL AFS5340.

Roesse Alshain. Upright. Single. COROLLA: three quarter flared, smooth petal margins; opens dark reddish purple (59A); matures reddish purple (59B); 16mm (5/8") long x 24mm (15/16") wide. SEPALS: half up; tips reflexed up; dark reddish purple (60B) upper surface; magenta (61C) lower surface; 21mm (13/16") long x 8mm (5/16") wide. TUBE: dark reddish purple (60B); medium length & thickness; 13mm (1/2") long x 7mm (1/4") wide. STAMENS: extend 17mm (11/16") below corolla; reddish purple (61B) filaments; dark reddish purple (61A) anthers. PISTIL: extends 24mm (15/16") below the corolla; magenta (61C) style; light yellow (11C) stigma. BUD: round. FOLIAGE: dark green (137A) upper surface; medium green (137C) lower surface. Leaves are 65mm (2 9/16") long x 31mm (1 1/4") wide, ovate shaped, serrated edges, acute tips and obtuse bases. Veins, stems & branches are green. PARENTAGE: 'Roesse Apus' x 'Orange Crush'. Medium upright. Makes good standard. Prefers overhead filtered light and cool climate. Best bloom and foliage colour in filtered light. Tested 4 years in Knegsel, The Netherlands. Distinguished by bloom colour.
Roes 2003 NL AFS5341.

Roesse Alsuhail. Upright/Trailer. Double. COROLLA: three quarter flared, smooth petal margins; opens dark orange (41A) & dark red (46A); matures orange (34C) & pink (53D); 26mm (1") long 26mm (1") wide. SEPALS: fully up; tips recurved; light rose (50C) upper surface; orange red (34B) lower surface; 28mm (1 1/8") long x 15mm (9/16") wide. TUBE: pink (50D); medium length & thickness; 12mm (1/2") long x 6mm (1/4") wide. STAMENS: extend 24mm (15/16") below corolla; red (47B) filaments; dark red (47A) anthers. PISTIL: extends 31mm (1 1/4") below the corolla; red (47B) style; light yellow (4C) stigma. BUD: cordate, pointed. FOLIAGE: dark green (137A) upper surface; medium green (138B) lower surface. Leaves are 71mm (2 13/16") long x 41mm (1 5/8") wide, ovate shaped, serrated edges, acute tips and obtuse bases. Red veins, stems & branches. PARENTAGE: 'Roesse Apus' x 'Bicentennial'. Lax upright or stiff trailer. Makes good stiff trailer. Prefers overhead filtered light and cool climate. Best bloom and foliage colour in filtered light. Tested 4 years in Knegsel, The Netherlands. Distinguished by bloom colour.
Roes 2004 NL AFS5488.

Roesse Alwaid. Upright/Trailer. Double. COROLLA: half flared, smooth petal margins; opens dark purple (86A); matures purple (80A); 26mm (1") long x 24mm (15/16") wide. SEPALS: fully up; tips recurved; pale yellow (2D) upper & lower surfaces; 27mm (1 1/16") long x 15mm (9/16") wide. TUBE: pale yellow (2D); long & thin; 25mm (1") long x 5mm (3/16") wide. STAMENS: extend 22mm (7/8") below corolla; light purple (74C) filaments; reddish purple (59B) anthers. PISTIL: extends 28mm (1 1/8") below the corolla; pale rose (73D) style; light yellow (6D) stigma. BUD: round, long TUBE. FOLIAGE: dark green (137A) upper surface; medium green (138A) lower surface. Leaves are 62mm (2 7/16") long x 30mm (1 3/16") wide, ovate shaped, serrulated edges, acute tips and rounded bases. Veins, stems & branches are red. PARENTAGE: 'Orangeblossom' x 'Sofie Michiels'. Lax upright or stiff trailer. Makes good stiff trailer. Prefers overhead filtered light and cool climate. Best bloom and foliage colour in filtered light. Tested 4 years in Knegsel, The Netherlands. Distinguished by bloom & foliage combination.
Roes 2003 NL AFS5342.

Roesse Amold. Upright/Trailer. Single. COROLLA: Three quarter flared; opens & matures dark reddish purple (60A); 20mm (3/4") long x 26mm (1") wide. SEPALS: fully up, tips recurved; white (155D) upper & lower surfaces; 23mm (7/8") long x 7mm (1/4") wide. TUBE: white (155D); medium length & thickness; 22mm (7/8") long x 6mm (1/4") wide. FOLIAGE is dark green (137A) upper surface; medium green (137C) lower surface. PARENTAGE: 'Roesse Lupus' x ('Luuk van Riet' x 'Roesse Betelgeuze').
Roes 2007 NL AFS6673.

Roesse Ananke. Upright/Trailer. Semi Double. COROLLA: full flared, smooth petal margins; opens purple (71A); matures reddish purple (67A); 27mm (1 1/16") long 30mm (1 3/16") wide. SEPALS: half up; tips recurved up; magenta (58B) upper & lower surfaces; 32mm (1 1/4") long x 14mm (9/16") wide. TUBE: magenta (58B); short & thick; 7mm (1/4") long x 7mm (1/4") wide. STAMENS: extend 27mm (1 1/16") below corolla; magenta (61C) filaments; dark reddish purple (64A) anthers. PISTIL: extends 48mm (1 7/8") below the corolla; magenta (61C) style; pink (62C) stigma. BUD: ovate, pointed. FOLIAGE: dark green (137A) upper surface; medium green (138B) lower surface. Leaves are 67mm (2 5/8") long x 27mm (1 1/16") wide, lanceolate shaped,

smooth edges, acute tips and rounded bases. Green veins, stems & branches. PARENTAGE: 'Roesse Dione' x 'Delta's Bride'. Lax upright or stiff trailer. Makes good stiff trailer. Prefers overhead filtered light and cool climate. Best bloom and foliage colour in filtered light. Tested 4 years in Knegsel, The Netherlands. Distinguished by bloom colour.
Roes 2004 NLA AFS5479.

Roesse Apollonius. Trailer. Single. COROLLA is half flared; opens dark reddish purple (60B); matures dark reddish purple (60C); 20mm (3/4") long x 20mm (3/4") wide. SEPALS are fully up, tips reflexed; magenta (61C) upper surface; magenta (63A) lower surface; 29mm (1 1/8") long x 14mm (9/16") wide. TUBE is magenta (61C); 17mm (5/8") long x 6mm (1/4") wide. FOLIAGE: dark green (137A) upper surface; medium green (138A) lower surface. PARENTAGE: 'Roesse Lupus' x 'Roesse Rhea'. Distinguished by bloom colour.
Roes 2006 NL AFS6179.

Roesse Apus. Upright. Semi Double. COROLLA: quarter flared, smooth petal margins; opens purple (71A); matures dark reddish purple (60B); 16mm (5/8") long x 20mm (13/16") wide. SEPALS: fully up; tips recurved; reddish purple (61B) upper surface; dark reddish purple (60C) lower surface; 27mm (1 1/16") long x 12mm (1/2") wide. TUBE: dark reddish purple (61A); medium length & thickness; 7mm (1/4") long x 5mm (3/16") wide. STAMENS: extend 14mm (9/16") below corolla; purple (71A) filaments; reddish purple (61B) anthers. PISTIL: extends 23mm (15/16") below the corolla; purple (71A) style; pale pink (62D) stigma. BUD: ovate. FOLIAGE: medium green (137C) upper surface; medium green (138B) lower surface. Leaves are 55mm (2 3/16") long x 40mm (1 9/16") wide, cordate shaped, serrulated edges, acute tips and rounded bases. Veins, stems & branches are red. PARENTAGE: [('Bon Accord' x 'Bicentennial') x ('Vobeglo' x 'Dancing Flame')] x 'Rohees Alrami'. Medium upright. Makes good standard. Prefers overhead filtered light and cool climate. Best bloom and foliage colour in filtered light. Tested 4 years in Knegsel, The Netherlands. Distinguished by bloom colour.
Roes 2003 NL AFS5321.

Roesse Aquila. Upright/Trailer. Semi Double. COROLLA is full flared with smooth petal margins; opens purple (79C); matures reddish purple (71B); 19mm (3/4") long x 31mm (1 1/4") wide. SEPALS are fully up,

tips recurved; red (45D) upper surface; red (46C) lower surface; 21mm (13/16") long x 14mm (9/16") wide. TUBE is red (45D); medium length & thickness; 14mm (9/16") long x 7mm (1/4") wide. FOLIAGE: dark green (137A) upper surface; medium green (138B) lower surface. Leaves are 67mm (2 5/8") long x 41mm (1 5/8") wide, ovate shaped. PARENTAGE: 'Maxima's Baby' x 'Roesse Menkhib'. Distinguished by bloom shape.
Roes 2005 NL AFS5940.

Roesse Ara. Upright. Single. COROLLA is half flared with smooth petal margins; opens reddish purple (67A); 17mm (11/16") long x 19mm (3/4") wide. SEPALS are half up, tips reflexed up; yellowish green (145A) upper surface; light apple green (145C) lower surface; 22mm (13/16") long x 11mm (7/16") wide. TUBE is yellowish green (145A); medium length & thickness; 15mm (9/16") long x 6mm (1/4") wide. FOLIAGE: medium green (138A) upper surface; medium green (137D) lower surface. Leaves are 76mm (3") long x 41mm (1 5/8") wide, ovate shaped. PARENTAGE: 'Lechlade Martianes' x 'Lechlade Martianes'. Distinguished by bloom colour.
Roes 2005 NL AFS5943.

Roesse Arabia. Upright. Single. COROLLA: quarter flared; opens dark reddish purple (59A); matures magenta (59C); 13mm (1/2") long x 22mm (7/8") wide. SEPALS: half up, tips recurved up; pink (62C) upper surface; pink (62A) lower surface; 25mm (1") long x 10mm (3/8") wide. TUBE: pink (62C); 9mm (5/16") long x 9mm (5/16") wide. FOLIAGE is dark green (137A) upper surface; medium green (138A) lower surface. PARENTAGE: 'Roesse Despina' x 'Luuk van Riet'.
Roes 2008 NL AFS6898.

Roesse Arago. Upright/Trailer. Double. COROLLA is three quarter flared; opens dark reddish purple (59A); matures magenta (59C); 14mm (9/16") long x 12mm (1/2") wide. SEPALS are half up, tips reflexed up; magenta (61C) upper surface; red (45B) lower surface; 20mm (3/4") long x 14mm (9/16") wide. TUBE is magenta (61C); 20mm (3/4") long x 4mm (1/8") wide. FOLIAGE: dark green (137A) upper surface; medium green (137C) lower surface. PARENTAGE: 'Rohees Rana' x 'Magda van Bets'. Distinguished by bloom colour.
Roes 2006 NL AFS6130.

Roesse Aries. Upright/Trailer. Double. COROLLA is half flared with smooth petal margins; opens dark reddish purple (64A); matures magenta (58B); 20mm (13/16") long x 16mm (5/8") wide. SEPALS are fully up, tips recurved; red (45C) upper & lower surfaces; 19mm (3/4") long x 12mm (1/2") wide. TUBE is red (45C); medium length & thickness; 16mm (5/8") long x 6mm (3/16") wide. FOLIAGE: dark green (139A) upper surface; medium green (137C) lower surface. Leaves are 64mm (2 1/2") long x 33mm (1 5/16") wide, ovate shaped. PARENTAGE: ['Sofie Michiels' x ('Roesse Apus' x 'Roesse Apus')] x 'Roesse Apus'. Distinguished by bloom colour.
Roes 2005 NL AFS5934.

Roesse Aristilius. Trailer. Single. COROLLA: Full flared; opens purple (71A) & pink (62C); matures reddish purple (72B) & pink (62C); 18mm (11/16") long x 20mm (3/4") wide. SEPALS: fully up tips recurved; magenta (63A) upper & lower surfaces; 31mm (1 1/4") long x 8mm (5/16") wide. TUBE: magenta (63A); medium length, thick; 12mm (7/16") long x 3mm (1/8") wide. FOLIAGE is dark green (137A) upper surface; medium green (137D) lower surface. PARENTAGE: 'Roesse Lupus' x 'Reg Gubler'.
Roes 2007 NL AFS6678.

Roesse Asterope. Upright/Trailer. Semi Double. COROLLA: quarter flared, smooth petal margins; opens dark reddish purple (61A) & pink (48C); matures red (53C) & rose (48B); 26mm (1") long x 27mm (1 1/16") wide. SEPALS: fully up; tips recurved; pink (55C) upper surface; rose (54C) lower surface; 34mm (1 5/16") long x 16mm (11/16") wide. TUBE: pink (55C); medium length & thickness; 7mm (1/4") long x 5mm (3/16") wide. STAMENS: extend 12mm (1/2") below corolla; magenta (61C) filaments; dark reddish purple (60A) anthers. PISTIL: extends 44mm (1 3/4") below the corolla; light orange (41D) style; light yellow (4C) stigma. BUD: round. FOLIAGE: dark green (137A) upper surface; medium green (138B) lower surface. Leaves are 55mm (2 3/16") long x 32mm (1 1/4") wide, ovate shaped, serrulated edges, acute tips and rounded bases. Veins, stems & branches are red. PARENTAGE: 'Roesse Apus' x 'Bicentennial'. Lax upright or stiff trailer. Makes good stiff trailer. Prefers overhead filtered light and cool climate. Best bloom and foliage colour in filtered light. Tested 4 years in Knegsel, The Netherlands. Distinguished by bloom colour.
Roes 2003 NL AFS5317.

Roesse Atlas. Upright. Single. COROLLA: half flared, smooth petal margins; opens dark reddish purple (60A); matures reddish purple (61B); 21mm (13/16") long 28mm (1 1/8") wide. SEPALS: fully up; tips recurved; red (53C) tipped green upper surface; red (53B) lower surface; 31mm (1 1/4") long x 12mm (1/2") wide. TUBE: red (53C); short & thick; 9mm (3/8") long x 9mm (3/8") wide. STAMENS: extend 10mm (3/8") below corolla; magenta (61C) filaments; reddish purple (59B) anthers. PISTIL: extends 18mm (11/16") below the corolla; magenta (61C) style & stigma. BUD: ovate, pointed. FOLIAGE: dark green (137A) upper surface; medium green (137C) lower surface. Leaves are 55mm (2 3/16") long x 34mm (1 5/16") wide, ovate shaped, serrulated edges, acute tips and obtuse bases. Red veins, stems & branches. PARENTAGE: 'Roesse Carme' x 'Shangri-La'. Medium upright. Makes good upright or standard. Prefers overhead filtered light and cool climate. Best bloom and foliage colour in filtered light. Tested 4 years in Knegsel, The Netherlands. Distinguished by bloom and foliage combination. Roes 2004 NL AFS5477.

Roesse Auriga. Upright/Trailer. Double. COROLLA is three quarter flared with smooth petal margins; opens purple (79C); matures purple (77A); 26mm (1") long x 22mm (7/8") wide. SEPALS are fully up, tips recurved; magenta (63A) upper surface; light rose (63D) lower surface; 40mm (1 9/16") long x 12mm (1/2") wide. TUBE is magenta (63A); medium length & thickness; 24mm (15/16") long x 7mm (1/4") wide. FOLIAGE: dark green (137A) upper surface; medium green (137C) lower surface. Leaves are 84mm (3 5/16") long x 39mm (1 9/16") wide, lanceolate shaped. PARENTAGE: ('Sofie Michiels' x 'Rohees New Millennium') x 'Impala'. Distinguished by bloom colour. Roes 2005 NL AFS5927.

Roesse Ausonia. Trailer. Single. COROLLA: full flared; opens dark reddish purple (64A); matures dark reddish purple (60C); 20mm (3/4") long x 24mm (15/16") wide. SEPALS: fully up, tips recurved; magenta (63B) upper surface; magenta (63A) lower surface; 20mm (3/4") long x 11mm (7/16") wide. TUBE: magenta (63B); 10mm (3/8") long x 7mm (1/4") wide. FOLIAGE is dark green (137A) upper surface; medium green (137C) lower surface. PARENTAGE: 'Roesse Lupus' x ('Roesse Dione' x 'Delta's Bride'). Roes 2008 NL AFS6901.

Roesse Babbage. Upright/Trailer. Double. COROLLA: Three quarter flared; opens dark red (53A); matures red (53C); 12mm (7/16") long x 14mm (9/16") wide. SEPALS: half up, tips reflexed up; light pink (49C) upper surface; rose (52C) lower surface; 18mm (11/16") long x 12mm (7/16") wide. TUBE: light pink (49C); long & thin; 29mm (1 1/8") long x 4mm (1/8") wide. FOLIAGE is dark green (137A) upper surface; medium green (138A) lower surface. PARENTAGE: 'Roesse Lupus' x 'Roesse Auriga'. Roes 2007 NL AFS6687.

Roesse Barrow. Upright. Double. COROLLA: Half flared; opens reddish purple (67A); matures magenta (58B); 18mm (11/16") long x 21mm (13/16") wide. SEPALS: fully up, tips recurved; light pink (55D) upper surface; rose (55B) lower surface; 34mm (1 3/8") long x 10mm (3/8") wide. TUBE: light pink (55D); medium length & thickness; 20mm (3/4") long x 6mm (1/4") wide. FOLIAGE is dark green (137A) upper surface; medium green (137C) lower surface. PARENTAGE: ('Swanley Gem' x 'Roesse Dione') x 'Silver Dawn'. Roes 2007 NL AFS6691.

Roesse Beid. Upright/Trailer. Double. COROLLA is three quarter flared with smooth petal margins; opens dark purple (79A); matures dark reddish purple (59A); 26mm (1") long x 19mm (3/4") wide. SEPALS are horizontal, tips recurved; reddish purple (67A) upper and lower surfaces, light pink (65B) lower surface; 27mm (1 1/16") long x 11mm (7/16") wide. TUBE is magenta (67B); medium length and thickness; 21mm (13/16") long x 6mm (1/4") thick. STAMENS extend 18mm (11/16") beyond the corolla; dark purple (79A) filaments and anthers. PISTIL extends 32mm (1 1/4") beyond the corolla; reddish purple (59B) style, light pink (65C) stigma. BUD is elliptic, pointed. FOLIAGE is medium green (137C) upper surface, medium green (138B) lower surface. Leaves are 72mm (2 13/16") long x 37mm (1 7/16") wide, ovate shaped, serrated edges, acute tips and obtuse bases. Veins, stems and branches are red. PARENTAGE: {[('Bon Accord' x 'Bicentennial') x ('Vobeglo' x 'Dancing Flame')] x 'Rohees Alrami'} x ('Hertogin van Brabant'). Lax upright or stiff trailer. Makes good stiff trailer. Prefers overhead filtered light and cool climate. Best bloom colour in filtered light. Tested four years in Knegsel, The Netherlands. Distinguished by bloom colour. Roes 2002 NL AFS5029.

Roesse Belinda. Trailer. Double. COROLLA is half flared; opens pale pink (69A); matures pale lavender (69C); 12mm (7/16") long x 21mm (13/16") wide. SEPALS are half up, tips reflexed up; white (155D) upper & lower surfaces; 26mm (1") long x 14mm (9/16") wide. TUBE is dark rose (58C); 21mm (13/16") long x 2mm (1/16") wide. FOLIAGE: dark green (137A) upper surface; light green (138C) lower surface. PARENTAGE: [('Cameron Ryle' x 'Parasol') x 'Allure'] x 'Roesse Betelgeuze'. Distinguished by bloom colour & very thin TUBE.
Roes 2006 NL AFS6157.

Roesse Bellatrix. Trailer. Double. COROLLA is three quarter flared with smooth petal margins; opens purple (83A); matures dark reddish purple (61A); 26mm (1") long x 26mm (1") wide. SEPALS are half up, tips recurved up; reddish purple (67A) upper and lower surfaces; 36mm (1 7/16") long x 15mm (5/8") wide. TUBE is reddish purple (67A); medium length and thickness; 16mm (5/8") long x 5mm (3/16") thick. STAMENS extend 24mm (15/16") beyond the corolla; reddish purple (71B) filaments, purple (71A) anthers. PISTIL extends 36mm (1 7/16") beyond the corolla; reddish purple (71B) style, light pink (65C) stigma. BUD is ovate, pointed. FOLIAGE is dark green (137A) upper surface, medium green (138A) lower surface. Leaves are 72mm (2 13/16") long x 32mm (1 1/4") wide, lanceolate shaped, serrated edges, acute tips and rounded bases. Veins, stems and branches are red. PARENTAGE: ('Annabel' x 'Annabel') x 'Rohees King'. Natural trailer. Makes good basket. Prefers overhead filtered light and cool climate. Best bloom colour in filtered light. Tested four years in Knegsel, The Netherlands. Distinguished by bloom colour.
Roes 2002 NL AFS5033.

Roesse Berosus. Trailer. Double. COROLLA is half flared; opens & matures white (155D); 17mm (5/8") long x 21mm (13/16") wide. SEPALS are horizontal, tips recurved; magenta (63A) upper & lower surfaces; 21mm (13/16") long x 9mm (3/8") wide. TUBE is rose (63C); 24mm (15/16") long x 3mm (1/8") wide. FOLIAGE: dark green (137A) upper surface; medium green (137C) lower surface. PARENTAGE: 'Roesse Tucana' x 'Swanley Gem'. Distinguished by bloom shape.
Roes 2006 NL AFS6142.

Roesse Bessel. Upright. Single. COROLLA is three quarter flared; opens magenta (63B);

matures rose (63C); 17mm (5/8") long x 24mm (15/16") wide. SEPALS are half up, tips recurved up; reddish purple (58A) upper & lower surfaces; 19mm (3/4") long x 11mm (7/16") wide. TUBE is reddish purple (58A); 8mm (5/16") long x 8mm (5/16") wide. FOLIAGE: dark green (137A) upper surface; medium green (138A) lower surface. PARENTAGE: 'Roesse Carme' x 'Maxima'. Distinguished by bloom colour.
Roes 2006 NL AFS6185.

Roesse Betelgeuze. Upright/Trailer. Double. COROLLA: half flared, smooth petal margins; opens pink (62C); matures pale pink (62D); 32mm (1 1/4") long 30mm (1 3/16") wide. SEPALS: half up; tips reflexed up; rose (65A) upper & lower surfaces; 34mm (1 5/16") long x 14mm (9/16") wide. TUBE: pale lavender (65D); medium length & thickness; 22mm (7/8") long x 6mm (1/4") wide. STAMENS: extend 19mm (3/4") below corolla; rose (63C) filaments; reddish purple (63B) anthers. PISTIL: extends 24mm (15/16") below the corolla; pale pink (62D) style & stigma. BUD: ovate, pointed. FOLIAGE: dark green (137A) upper surface; medium green (137C) lower surface. Leaves are 74mm (2 15/16") long x 36mm (1 7/16") wide, ovate shaped, serrated edges, acute tips and obtuse bases. Green veins; red stems & branches. PARENTAGE: 'Sofie Michiels' x 'Allure'. Lax upright or stiff trailer. Makes good stiff trailer. Prefers overhead filtered light and cool climate. Best bloom and foliage colour in filtered light. Tested 4 years in Knegsel, The Netherlands. Distinguished by bloom and foliage combination.
Roes 2004 NL AFS5487.

Roesse Bianca. Trailer. Double. COROLLA is three quarter flared; opens purple (83A); matures purple (71A); 16mm (5/8") long x 22mm (7/8") wide. SEPALS are half up, tips reflexed up; reddish purple (61B) upper surface; dark reddish purple (61A) lower surface; 21mm (13/16") long x 11mm (7/16") wide. TUBE is reddish purple (61B); 35mm (1 3/8") long x 4mm (1/8") wide. FOLIAGE: medium green (137B) upper surface; medium green (138B) lower surface. PARENTAGE: 'Roesse Tucana' x 'Maxima'. Distinguished by bloom colour & shape.
Roes 2006 NL AFS6162.

Roesse Bianchini. Upright/Trailer. Semi Double. COROLLA: Half flared; opens dark reddish purple (59A); matures reddish purple (58A); 16mm (5/8") long x 21mm (13/16") wide. SEPALS: fully up, tips reflexed; light rose (73C) upper surface; rose (68B) lower surface; 26mm (1") long x 6mm (1/4") wide. TUBE: light rose (73C); medium length & thickness; 19mm (3/4") long x 6mm (1/4") wide. FOLIAGE is dark green (137A) upper surface; medium green (137C) lower surface. PARENTAGE: 'Roesse Lupus' x 'Allure'. Roes 2007 NL AFS6686.

Roesse Blacky. Upright/Trailer. Semi Double. COROLLA is three quarter flared with smooth petal margins; opens dark purple (79A) and matures purple (77A); 30mm (1 3/16") long x 28mm (1 1/8") wide. SEPALS are half up, tips recurved up; dark reddish purple (64A) upper and lower surfaces; 28mm (1 1/8") long x 14mm (9/16") wide. TUBE is dark reddish purple (64A), proportionately medium length and thickness; 14mm (9/16") long x 6mm (1/4") wide. STAMENS extend 30mm (1 3/16") below the corolla; dark purple (79A) filaments and dark purple (79B) anthers. PISTIL extends 58mm (2 5/16") below the corolla; purple (71A) style and reddish purple (67A) stigma. BUD is ovate and pointed. FOLIAGE is dark green (139A) on upper surface and medium green (138B) on lower surface. Leaves are 62mm (2 7/16") long x 30mm (1 3/16) wide, ovate shaped, smooth edges, acute tips and rounded bases. Veins, stems and branches are red. PARENTAGE: ('Grus aus dem Bodenthal' x 'Rohees Alrami') x 'Stad Elburg'. Lax upright or stiff trailer. Makes good stiff trailer. Prefers overhead filtered light and warm climate. Best bloom colour in filtered light. Tested four years in Knegsel, The Netherlands. Distinguished by bloom colour which is suggestive of black. Roes 2002 NL AFS4797.

Roesse Bootes. Upright/Trailer. Double. COROLLA is three quarter flared with smooth petal margins; opens purple (71A); matures dark reddish purple (61A); 16mm (5/8") long x 21mm (13/16") wide. SEPALS are horizontal, tips recurved; pale pink (62D) upper surface; light reddish purple (72D) lower surface; 31mm (1 1/4") long x 16mm (5/8") wide. TUBE is light apple green (145B); medium length & thickness; 8mm (5/16") long x 6mm (1/4") wide. FOLIAGE: dark green (137A) upper surface; medium green (137D) lower surface. Leaves are 68mm (2 11/16") long x 36mm (1 7/16") wide, lanceolate shaped. PARENTAGE: 'Roesse Carme' x ('Swanley Gem' x 'Katrien Michiels'). Distinguished by bloom colour. Roes 2005 NL AFS5928.

Roesse Boscovich. Upright/Trailer. Single. COROLLA: Half flared; opens dark reddish purple (59A); matures reddish purple (58A); 16mm (5/8") long x 14mm (9/16") wide. SEPALS: half down, tips recurved; light rose (58D) upper & lower surfaces; 20mm (3/4") long x 9mm (5/16") wide. TUBE: pink (48D); medium length & thickness; 24mm (15/16") long x 5mm (3/16") wide. FOLIAGE is dark green (137A) upper surface; medium green (137D) lower surface. PARENTAGE: 'Roesse Lupus' x 'Roesse Apus'. Roes 2007 NL AFS6679.

Roesse Caelum. Upright. Single. COROLLA is half flared with smooth petal margins; opens reddish purple (58A); matures dark reddish purple (60A); 18mm (11/16") long x 22mm (7/8") wide. SEPALS are fully up, tips recurved; dark rose (58C) upper surface; magenta (58B) lower surface; 17mm (11/16") long x 8mm (5/16") wide. TUBE is dark rose (58C); medium length & thickness; 11mm (7/16") long x 7mm (1/4") wide. FOLIAGE: dark green (137A) upper surface; medium green (138A) lower surface. Leaves are 58mm (2 5/16") long x 42mm (1 5/8") wide, cordate shaped. PARENTAGE: ('Roesse Carme' x 'Roesse Apus') x 'Roesse Apus'. Distinguished by bloom colour. Roes 2005 NL AFS5958.

Roesse Calatea. Upright/Trailer. Double. COROLLA is half flared; opens purple (77A); matures dark reddish purple (61A); 15mm (9/16") long x 19mm (3/4") wide. SEPALS are fully up, tips reflexed; rose (63C) upper surface; magenta (68A) lower surface; 24mm (15/16") long x 14mm (9/16") wide. TUBE is rose (63C); 11mm (7/16") long x 9mm (3/8") wide. FOLIAGE: dark green (137A) upper surface; medium green (138A) lower surface. PARENTAGE: 'Roesse Carme' x 'Roesse Apus'. Distinguished by bloom & foliage combination. Roes 2006 NL AFS6138.

Roesse Callipus. Upright. Single. COROLLA: Half flared; opens dark red (53A); matures red (53C); 16mm (5/8") long x 17mm (5/8") wide. SEPALS: fully up, tips reflexed; red (46D) upper surface; red (46C) lower surface; 31mm (1 1/4") long x 7mm (1/4") wide. TUBE: red (46D); medium length & thickness; 20mm (3/4") long x 5mm (3/16") wide. FOLIAGE is medium green (137C) upper surface; medium green (138A) lower surface. PARENTAGE: 'Roesse Lupus' x 'Luuk van Riet'. Roes 2007 NL AFS6674.

Roesse Callisto. Upright/Trailer. Single. COROLLA is full flared; opens dark purple (86A); matures dark reddish purple (72A); 26mm (1") long x 27mm (1 1/16") wide. SEPALS are half up, tips recurved up; reddish purple (66A) upper & lower surfaces; 34mm (1 3/8") long x 12mm (7/16") wide. TUBE is reddish purple (66A); 3mm (1/8") long x 3mm (1/8") wide. FOLIAGE: medium green (137C) upper surface; medium green (138B) lower surface. PARENTAGE: 'Maxima' x 'Reg Gubler'. Distinguished by bloom shape & colour.
Roes 2006 NL AFS6160.

Roesse Calypso. Upright. Single. COROLLA: full flared, smooth petal margins; opens violet (86B); matures violet (84A); 30mm (1 3/16") long 32mm (1 1/4") wide. SEPALS: fully up; tips recurved; red (52A) upper surface; dark rose (54A) lower surface; 27mm (1 1/16") long x 14mm (9/16") wide. TUBE: red (52A); short & thick; 10mm (3/8") long x 8mm (5/16") wide. STAMENS: extend 34mm (1 3/8") below corolla; magenta (63B) filaments; magenta (68A) anthers. PISTIL: extends 42mm (1 11/16") below the corolla; rose (63C) style; rose (68C) stigma. BUD: ovate, pointed. FOLIAGE: dark green (137A) upper surface; medium green (137C) lower surface. Leaves are 64mm (2 1/2") long x 42mm (1 11/16") wide, ovate shaped, serrulated edges, acute tips and rounded bases. Red veins, stems & branches. PARENTAGE: [('Cameron Ryle' x 'Parasol') x 'Allure'] x ['Sophie Michiels' x 'Allure']. Medium upright. Makes good upright or standard. Prefers overhead filtered light and cool climate. Best bloom and foliage colour in filtered light. Tested 4 years in Knegsel, The Netherlands. Distinguished by bloom and foliage combination.
Roes 2004 NL AFS5469.

Roesse Cancer. Upright/Trailer. Single. COROLLA is three quarter flared with turned under petal margins; opens purple (71A); matures dark reddish purple (61A); 21mm (13/16") long x 34mm (1 5/16") wide. SEPALS are fully up, tips recurved; red (52A) upper & lower surfaces; 22mm (7/8") long x 10mm (3/8") wide. TUBE is red (52A); short & thick; 7mm (1/4") long x 7mm (1/4") wide. FOLIAGE: dark green (137A) upper surface; medium green (138A) lower surface. Leaves are 52mm (2 1/16") long x 27mm (1 1/16") wide, ovate shaped. PARENTAGE: 'Arjan Spoelstra' x 'Magda van Bets'. Distinguished by bloom colour & shape.
Roes 2005 NL AFS5965.

Roesse Caph. Trailer. Semi Double. COROLLA is half flared with smooth petal margins; opens dark reddish purple (72A); matures dark reddish purple (64A); 34mm (1 3/8") long x 28mm (1 1/8") wide. SEPALS are fully up, tips reflexed; rose (65A) upper surface, magenta (68A) lower surface; 37mm (1 7/16") long x 14mm (9/16") wide. TUBE is light pink (65B); medium length and thickness; 24mm (15/16") long x 5mm (3/16") thick. STAMENS extend 24mm (15/16") beyond the corolla; reddish purple (64B) filaments, dark reddish purple (70A) anthers. PISTIL extends 32mm (1 1/4") beyond the corolla; rose (64D) style, rose (68B) stigma. BUD is ovate, pointed. FOLIAGE is dark green (137A) upper surface, medium green (137C) lower surface. Leaves are 61mm (2 7/16") long x 27mm (1 1/16") wide, lanceolate shaped, serrated edges, acute tips and obtuse bases. Veins, stems and branches are green. PARENTAGE: {['Vobeglo' x ('Foline' x 'Dancing Flame')] x 'Bon Accord'} x 'Rohees Queen'. Natural trailer. Makes good basket. Prefers overhead filtered light and cool climate. Best bloom colour in filtered light. Tested four years in Knegsel, The Netherlands. Distinguished by bloom and foliage combination.
Roes 2002 NL AFS5026.

Roesse Carme. Upright. Single. COROLLA: half flared, smooth petal margins; opens reddish orange (42A); matures orangy red (44C); 15mm (9/16") long 22mm (7/8") wide. SEPALS: fully up; tips reflexed; rose (51C) upper surface; rose (51B) lower surface; 18mm (11/16") long x 10mm (3/8") wide. TUBE: rose (51C); short & thick; 12mm (1/2") long x 12mm (1/2") wide. STAMENS: extend 14mm (9/16") below corolla; rose (61D) filaments; magenta (63B) anthers. PISTIL: extends 23mm (15/16") below the corolla; rose (61D) style; yellowish white (4D) stigma. BUD: ovate, pointed. FOLIAGE: dark green (137A) upper surface; medium green (138B) lower surface. Leaves are 64mm (2 1/2") long x 46mm (1 13/16") wide, cordate shaped, serrulated edges, acute tips and obtuse bases. Red veins, stems & branches. PARENTAGE: 'WALZ Harp' x ('Cameron Ryle' x 'Parasol'). Medium upright. Makes good upright or standard. Prefers overhead filtered light and cool climate. Best bloom and foliage colour in filtered light. Tested 4 years in Knegsel, The Netherlands. Distinguished by bloom and foliage combination.
Roes 2004 NL AFS5473.

Roesse Cassini. Upright/Trailer. Semi Double. COROLLA: Half flared; opens purple (77A); matures dark reddish purple (72A); 20mm (3/4") long x 9mm (5/16") wide. SEPALS: horizontal, tips recurved; pale lavender (65D) upper surface; rose (65A) lower surface; 20mm (3/4") long x 9mm (5/16") wide. TUBE: pale lavender (65D); medium length & thickness; 22mm (7/8") long x 7mm (1/4") wide. FOLIAGE is dark green (137A) upper surface; medium green (137C) lower surface. PARENTAGE: 'Roesse Lupus' x 'Roesse Tucana'.
Roes 2007 NL AFS6676.

Roesse Celaeno. Upright. Double. COROLLA is three quarter flared with smooth petal margins; opens dark purple (79A); matures dark reddish purple (59A); 28mm (1 1/8") long x 27mm (1 1/16") wide. SEPALS are fully up, tips reflexed; reddish purple (67A) upper and lower surfaces; 36mm (1 7/16") long x 16mm (5/8") wide. TUBE is rose (67D); medium length and thickness; 16mm (5/8") long x 7mm (1/4") thick. STAMENS extend 23mm (15/16") beyond the corolla; dark reddish purple (64A) filaments and anthers. PISTIL extends 42mm (1 11/16") beyond the corolla; magenta (63A) style, light rose (63D) stigma. BUD is ovate, pointed. FOLIAGE is dark green (137A) upper surface, medium green (138B) lower surface. Leaves are 66mm (2 5/8") long x 37mm (1 7/16") wide, ovate shaped, serrated edges, acute tips and rounded bases. Veins, stems and branches are red. PARENTAGE: {[('Bon Accord' x 'Bicentennial') x ('Vobeglo' x 'Dancing Flame')] x 'Rohees Alrami'} x 'Rohees King'. Medium upright. Makes good standard. Prefers overhead filtered light and cool climate. Best bloom colour in filtered light. Tested four years in Knegsel, The Netherlands. Distinguished by erect bloom and bloom colour.
Roes 2002 NL AFS5040.

Roesse Cepheus. Trailer. Double. COROLLA is half flared with smooth petal margins; opens purple (83C); matures violet (84A); 19mm (3/4") long x 21mm (13/16") wide. SEPALS are half down, tips recurved; pale lavender (69B) upper surface; rose (68C) lower surface; 31mm (1 1/4") long x 16mm (5/8") wide. TUBE is pale lavender (69D); medium length & thickness; 22mm (7/8") long x 5mm (3/16") wide. FOLIAGE: dark green (137B) upper surface; medium green (138B) lower surface. Leaves are 61mm (2 3/8") long x 37mm (1 7/16") wide, ovate shaped. PARENTAGE: 'Roesse Elara' x ('Sofie Michiels' x 'Allure'). Distinguished by bloom & foliage combination.
Roes 2005 NL AFS5949.

Roesse Cetus. Upright/Trailer. Double. COROLLA is three quarter flared with smooth petal margins; opens reddish purple (64B), purple (83A) base; matures reddish purple (64B), purple (71A) base; 21mm (13/16") long x 30mm (1 3/16") wide. SEPALS are fully up, tips recurved; reddish purple (64B) upper surface; dark reddish purple (64A) lower surface; 30mm (1 3/16") long x 16mm (5/8") wide. TUBE is reddish purple (64B); medium length & thickness; 9mm (3/8") long x 6mm (1/4") wide. FOLIAGE: dark green (137A) upper surface; medium green (138A) lower surface. Leaves are 76mm (3") long x 44mm (1 3/4") wide, ovate shaped. PARENTAGE: 'Maxima's Baby' x 'Roesse Menkhib'. Distinguished by bloom colour.
Roes 2005 NL AFS5967.

Roesse Charon. Upright. Single. COROLLA is half flared; opens purple (71A); matures dark reddish purple (64A); 16mm (5/8") long x 19mm (3/4") wide. SEPALS are half up, tips recurved up; pink (62A) upper surface; magenta (63A) lower surface; 21mm (13/16") long x 9mm (3/8") wide. TUBE is pink (62A); 16mm (5/8") long x 6mm (1/4") wide. FOLIAGE: dark green (137A) upper surface; medium green (138B) lower surface. PARENTAGE: 'Roesse Lupus' x 'Magda van Bets'. Distinguished by bloom colour.
Roes 2006 NL AFS6151.

Roesse Cih. Trailer. Double. COROLLA is three quarter flared with smooth petal margins; opens dark purple (86A); matures purple (83B); 30mm (1 3/16") long x 28mm (1 1/8") wide. SEPALS are fully up, tips reflexed; light reddish purple (73A) upper surface, magenta (68A) lower surface; 46mm (1 13/16") long x 16mm (5/8") wide. TUBE is light reddish purple (73A); medium length and thickness; 17mm (11/16") long x 7mm (1/4") thick. STAMENS extend 17mm (11/16") beyond the corolla; dark reddish purple (59A) filaments and anthers. PISTIL extends 36mm (1 7/16") beyond the corolla; reddish purple (59B) style, rose (63C) stigma. BUD is ovate, pointed. FOLIAGE is medium green (137B) upper surface, medium green (138B) lower surface. Leaves are 56mm (2 3/16") long x 27mm (1 1/16") wide, elliptic shaped, serrated edges, acute tips and obtuse bases. Veins, stems and branches are green. PARENTAGE: 'Rohees New

378

Millennium' x 'Stad Elburg'. Natural trailer. Makes good basket. Prefers overhead filtered light and cool climate. Best bloom colour in filtered light. Tested four years in Knegsel, The Netherlands. Distinguished by bloom and foliage combination.
Roes 2002 NL AFS5035.

Roesse Circinus. Upright/Trailer. Single. COROLLA is full flared with smooth petal margins; opens dark reddish purple (70A); matures reddish purple (67A); 20mm (13/16") long x 24mm (15/16") wide. SEPALS are fully up, tips recurved; pink (62A) upper surface; magenta (58B) lower surface; 24mm (15/16") long x 11mm (7/16") wide. TUBE is light pink (62B); medium length & thickness; 16mm (5/8") long x 7mm (1/4") wide. FOLIAGE: medium green (137B) upper surface; medium green (138B) lower surface. Leaves are 80mm (3 1/8") long x 48mm (1 7/8") wide, ovate shaped. PARENTAGE: 'Maxima's Baby' x 'Roesse Menkhib'. Distinguished by bloom shape.
Roes 2005 NL AFS5939.

Roesse Columba. Upright/Trailer. Single. COROLLA is quarter flared with smooth petal margins; opens dark reddish purple (61A); matures dark reddish purple (60A); 14mm (9/16") long x 19mm (3/4") wide. SEPALS are half up, tips reflexed up; magenta (63A) tipped green upper surface; dark reddish purple (60B) lower surface; 26mm (1") long x 12mm (1/2") wide. TUBE is magenta (63A); medium length & thickness; 17mm (11/16") long x 7mm (1/4") wide. FOLIAGE: dark green (137A) upper surface; medium green (137D) lower surface. Leaves are 69mm (2 3/4") long x 41mm (1 5/8") wide, ovate shaped. PARENTAGE: 'Roesse Apus' x 'Lechlade Rocket'. Distinguished by bloom colour.
Roes 2005 NL AFS5946.

Roesse Condorcet. Upright/Trailer. Single. COROLLA is quarter flared; opens violet (76A); matures violet (76B); 16mm (5/8") long x 18mm (11/16") wide. SEPALS are full down, tips recurved; rose (68B) upper surface; magenta (68A) lower surface; 42mm (1 5/8") long x 10mm (3/8") wide. TUBE is rose (68B); 17mm (5/8") long x 5mm (3/16") wide. FOLIAGE: medium green (137B) upper surface; medium green (138B) lower surface. PARENTAGE: ('Sofie Michiels' x 'Venus Victrix') x 'Delta's Wonder'. Distinguished by bloom colour.
Roes 2006 NL AFS6147.

Roesse Conon. Upright. Single. COROLLA: Half flared; opens dark rose (51A); matures dark red (47A); 10mm (3/8") long x 19mm (3/4") wide. SEPALS: half up, tips reflexed up; pink (49A) upper surface; pink (43D) lower surface; 19mm (3/4") long x 10mm (3/8") wide. TUBE: pink (49A); medium length & thickness; 20mm (3/4") long x 6mm (1/4") wide. FOLIAGE is dark green (137A) upper surface; medium green (137C) lower surface. PARENTAGE: 'Roesse Lupus' x ('Luuk van Riet' x 'Roesse Parel').
Roes 2007 NL AFS6680.

Roesse Copernicus. Upright. Single. COROLLA: Quarter flared; opens dark reddish purple (60B); matures magenta (59D); 16mm (5/8") long x 21mm (13/16") wide. SEPALS: fully up, tips reflexed; white (155D) upper & lower surfaces; 24mm (15/16") long x 12mm (7/16") wide. TUBE: white (155D); medium length & thickness; 18mm (11/16") long x 5mm (3/16") wide. FOLIAGE is medium green (137B) upper surface; medium green (137C) lower surface. PARENTAGE: 'Roesse Lupus' x ('Sofie Michiels' x 'Roesse Apus').
Roes 2007 NL AFS6666.

Roesse Corcaroli. Upright. Single. COROLLA: full flared, smooth petal margins; opens dark reddish purple (59A); matures dark reddish purple (61A); 18mm (11/16") long 21mm (13/16") wide. SEPALS: fully up; tips recurved; dark reddish purple (60B) upper surface; dark reddish purple (60C) lower surface; 21mm (13/16") long x 12mm (1/2") wide. TUBE: dark reddish purple (60B); short & thick; 8mm (5/16") long x 7mm (1/4") wide. STAMENS: extend 20mm (13/16") below corolla; magenta (59C) filaments; dark reddish purple (59A) anthers. PISTIL: extends 36mm (1 7/16") below the corolla; magenta (59C) style; light yellow (4C) stigma. BUD: cordate, pointed. FOLIAGE: medium green (137B) upper surface; medium green (138A) lower surface. Leaves are 52mm (2 1/16") long x 37mm (1 7/16") wide, ovate shaped, smooth edges, acute tips and obtuse bases. Red veins, stems & branches. PARENTAGE: 'Rohees Rana' x ('Roesse Apus' x 'Roesse Apus'). Medium upright. Makes good upright or standard. Prefers overhead filtered light and cool climate. Best bloom and foliage colour in filtered light. Tested 4 years in Knegsel, The Netherlands. Distinguished by bloom colour and erect bloom.
Roes 2004 NL AFS5491.

Roesse Cordelia. Trailer. Double. COROLLA is half flared; opens & matures white (155D); 22mm (7/8") long x 24mm (15/16") wide. SEPALS are horizontal, tips recurved; red (52A) upper & lower surfaces; 24mm (15/16") long x 16mm (5/8") wide. TUBE is pink (51D); 36mm (1 7/16") long x 4mm (1/8") wide. FOLIAGE: medium green (137B) upper surface; medium green (138B) lower surface. PARENTAGE: [('Cameron Ryle' x 'Parasol') x 'Allure'] x 'Magda van Bets'. Distinguished by bloom shape.
Roes 2006 NL AFS6172.

Roesse Coxa. Upright. Semi Double. COROLLA is three quarter flared with smooth petal margins; opens purple (71A); matures reddish purple (59B); 30mm (1 3/16") long x 27mm (1 1/16") wide. SEPALS are fully up, tips recurved; dark reddish purple (61A) upper surface, reddish purple (61B) lower surface; 27mm (1 1/16") long x 15mm (5/8") wide. TUBE is dark reddish purple (61A); medium length and thickness; 23mm (15/16") long x 8mm (5/16") thick. STAMENS extend 28mm (1 1/8") beyond the corolla; dark reddish purple (64A) filaments, purple (71A) anthers. PISTIL extends 28mm (1 1/8") beyond the corolla; dark reddish purple (64A) style, pale rose (73D) stigma. BUD is ovate, pointed. FOLIAGE is dark green (137A) upper surface, medium green (137C) lower surface. Leaves are 84mm (3 5/16") long x 46mm (1 13/16") wide, ovate shaped, serrated edges, acute tips and rounded bases. Veins, stems and branches are red. PARENTAGE: {[('Bon Accord' x 'Bicentennial') x ('Vobeglo' x 'Dancing Flame')] x 'Rohees Alrami'} x 'Rohees King'. Medium upright. Makes good standard. Prefers overhead filtered light and cool climate. Best bloom colour in filtered light. Tested four years in Knegsel, The Netherlands. Distinguished by bloom and foliage combination.
Roes 2002 NL AFS5030.

Roesse Crater. Upright. Single. COROLLA is quarter flared with smooth petal margins; opens red (46B); matures red (45D); 13mm (1/2") long x 19mm (3/4") wide. SEPALS are half up, tips reflexed up; magenta (58B) upper surface; dark red (47A) lower surface; 24mm (15/16") long x 11mm (7/16") wide. TUBE is magenta (58B); medium length & thickness; 14mm (9/16") long x 6mm (1/4") wide. FOLIAGE: dark green (137A) upper surface; medium green (138A) lower surface. Leaves are 67mm (2 5/8") long x 37mm (1 7/16") wide, ovate shaped. PARENTAGE:

'Roesse Apus' x 'Lechlade Rocket'. Distinguished by bloom colour.
Roes 2005 NL AFS5945.

Roesse Cressida. Trailer. Double. COROLLA is half flared; opens purple (83B); matures purple (77A); 17mm (5/8") long x 23mm (7/8") wide. SEPALS are half up, tips recurved up; light rose (68D) upper surface; rose (68B) lower surface; 36mm (1 7/16") long x 12mm (7/16") wide. TUBE is white (155D); 36mm (1 7/16") long x 6mm (1/4") wide. FOLIAGE: dark green (137A) upper surface; medium green (138A) lower surface. PARENTAGE: 'Sofie Michiels' x 'Lye's Unique'. Distinguished by bloom colour & shape.
Roes 2006 NL AFS6163.

Roesse Crux. Upright/Trailer. Double. COROLLA is three quarter flared with turned under smooth petal margins; opens very dark purple (187A); matures dark reddish purple (59A); 18mm (11/16") long x 26mm (1") wide. SEPALS are fully up, tips recurved; magenta (63A) upper & lower surfaces; 28mm (1 1/8") long x 19mm (3/4") wide. TUBE is magenta (63A); medium length & thickness; 15mm (9/16") long x 6mm (1/4") wide. FOLIAGE: dark green (139A) upper surface; medium green (137D) lower surface. Leaves are 64mm (2 1/2") long x 37mm (1 7/16") wide, ovate shaped. PARENTAGE: 'Roesse Apus' x 'Roesse Menkhib'. Distinguished by bloom colour & shape.
Roes 2005 NL AFS5957.

Roesse Dabih. Upright. Single. COROLLA is half flared with smooth petal margins; opens light pink (63B); matures magenta (58B); 16mm (5/8") long x 21mm (13/16") wide. SEPALS are fully up, tips reflexed; light rose (73C) upper surface, pale pink (62D) lower surface; 20mm (13/16") long x 7mm (1/4") wide. TUBE is pale pink (62D); short and thick; 5mm (3/16") long x 6mm (1/4") thick. STAMENS extend 18mm (11/16") beyond the corolla; magenta (63B) filaments, dark reddish purple (59A) anthers. PISTIL extends 22mm (7/8") beyond the corolla; magenta (63B) style, light yellow (10D) stigma. BUD is ovate, pointed. FOLIAGE is dark green (137A) upper surface, medium green (138B) lower surface. Leaves are 62mm (2 7/16") long x 29mm (1 1/8") wide, ovate shaped, serrated edges, acute tips and obtuse bases. Veins, stems and branches are green. PARENTAGE: {['Vobeglo' x ('Foline' x 'Dancing Flame') x ('Vobeglo' x 'Dancing Flame')] x 'Rohees Alrami'} x ('Bon Accord' x 'Bicentennial').

Small upright. Makes good upright or standard. Prefers overhead filtered light and cool climate. Best bloom colour in filtered light. Tested four years in Knegsel, The Netherlands. Distinguished by profuse blooms.
Roes 2002 NL AFS5039.

Roesse Deliste. Upright/Trailer. Single. COROLLA: Half flared; opens dark reddish purple (64A); matures reddish purple (64B); 16mm (5/8") long x 20mm (3/4") wide. SEPALS: horizontal, tips recurved; pale lavender (69C) upper & lower surfaces; 37mm (1 7/16") long x 10mm (3/8") wide. TUBE: pale lavender (69C); medium length & thickness; 18mm (11/16") long x 4mm (1/8") wide. PARENTAGE: 'Roesse Lupus' x 'Sofie Michiels'.
Roes 2007 NL AFS6670.

Roesse Despina. Upright. Single. COROLLA is half flared; opens dark red (46A); matures red (45A); 16mm (5/8") long x 22mm (7/8") wide. SEPALS are horizontal, tips recurved; rose (68C) upper & lower surfaces; 21mm (13/16") long x 8mm (5/16") wide. TUBE is light rose (68D); 11mm (7/16") long x 9mm (3/8") wide. FOLIAGE: dark green (137A) upper surface; light green (138D) lower surface. PARENTAGE: 'Roesse Lupus' x 'Lye's Unique'. Distinguished by bloom colour.
Roes 2006 NL AFS6150.

Roesse Dione. Upright. Single. COROLLA: full flared, smooth petal margins; opens dark purple (79B); matures purple (71A); 22mm (7/8") long x 36mm (1 7/16") wide. SEPALS: half up; tips recurved up; magenta (61C) upper & lower surfaces; 34mm (1 5/16") long x 14mm (9/16") wide. TUBE: magenta (61C); medium length & thickness; 12mm (1/2") long x 8mm (5/16") wide. STAMENS: extend 27mm (1 1/16") below corolla; dark reddish purple (59A) filaments; dark purple (79B) anthers. PISTIL: extends 41mm (1 5/8") below the corolla; dark reddish purple (59A) style; pale purple (75C) stigma. BUD: round. FOLIAGE: dark green (137A) upper surface; medium green (138B) lower surface. Leaves are 81mm (3 3/16") long x 41mm (1 5/8") wide, ovate shaped, serrulated edges, acute tips and obtuse bases. Veins, stems & branches are red. PARENTAGE: 'Roesse Apus' x 'Rohees Princess'. Tall upright. Makes good standard. Prefers overhead filtered light and cool climate. Best bloom and foliage colour in filtered light. Tested 4 years in Knegsel, The Netherlands. Distinguished by bloom colour.

Roes 2003 NL AFS5316.

Roesse Draco. Trailer. Double. COROLLA is half flared with smooth petal margins; opens & matures white (155D); 17mm (11/16") long x 21mm (13/16") wide. SEPALS are half up, tips reflexed up; reddish purple (67A) upper & lower surfaces; 20mm (13/16") long x 19mm (3/4") wide. TUBE is pale lavender (69D); long & thin; 38mm (1 1/2") long x 4mm (3/16") wide. FOLIAGE: dark green (137A) upper surface; medium green (138A) lower surface. Leaves are 67mm (2 5/8") long x 31mm (1 1/4") wide, lanceolate shaped. PARENTAGE: ('Sofie Michiels' x 'Rohees New Millennium') x 'Magda Vanbets'. Distinguished by bloom shape.
Roes 2005 NL AFS5954.

Roesse Duck. Trailer. Single. COROLLA is quarter flared; opens purple (83B); matures reddish purple (72B); 6mm (1/4") long x 7mm (1/4") wide. SEPALS are half up, tips recurved up; rose (68C) upper & rose (68B) lower surface; 19mm (3/4") long x 5mm (3/16") wide. TUBE is rose (68C); 10mm (3/8") long x 3mm (1/8") wide. FOLIAGE: medium green (137B) upper surface; medium green (137B) lower surface. PARENTAGE: 'Rosea' x 'Luuk van Riet'. Distinguished by small flower.
Roes 2006 NL AFS6156.

Roesse Elara. Trailer. Double. COROLLA: quarter flared, smooth petal margins; opens dark purple (89A); matures dark red (72A); 19mm (3/4") long x 17mm (11/16") wide. SEPALS: horizontal; tips recurved; reddish purple (67A) upper & lower surfaces; 38mm (1 1/2") long x 17mm (11/16") wide. TUBE: reddish purple (67A); medium length & thickness; 26mm (1") long x 6mm (1/4") wide. STAMENS: extend 12mm (1/2") below corolla; dark reddish purple (64A) filaments; reddish purple (64B) anthers. PISTIL: extends 26mm (1") below the corolla; rose (64D) style; pale lavender (65D) stigma. BUD: round, long TUBE. FOLIAGE: medium green (137B) upper surface; medium green (137D) lower surface. Leaves are 56mm (2 3/16") long x 31mm (1 1/4") wide, cordate shaped, serrated edges, acute tips and obtuse bases. Veins & stems are red, branches are green. PARENTAGE: [('Cameron Ryle' x 'Parasol') x 'Allure'] x 'Allure'. Natural trailer. Makes good basket. Prefers overhead filtered light and cool climate. Best bloom and foliage colour in filtered light. Tested 4 years in Knegsel, The Netherlands. Distinguished by bloom & foliage combination.

Roes 2003 NL AFS5353.

Roesse Electra. Upright/Trailer. Double. COROLLA: quarter flared, smooth petal margins; opens purple (77A); matures dark reddish purple (61A); 20mm (13/16") long x 24mm (15/16") wide. SEPALS: fully up; tips recurved; rose (68B) upper surface; rose (68C) lower surface; 29mm (1 1/8") long x 14mm (9/16") wide. TUBE: rose (68B); medium length & thickness; 17mm (11/16") long x 6mm (1/4") wide. STAMENS: extend 12mm (1/2") below corolla; rose (68B) filaments; light pink (62B) anthers. PISTIL: extends 29mm (1 1/8") below the corolla; rose (68B) style; cream (11D) stigma. BUD: ovate. FOLIAGE: dark green (137A) upper surface; medium green (137C) lower surface. Leaves are 64mm (2 1/2") long x 36mm (1 7/16") wide, ovate shaped, serrulated edges, acute tips and obtuse bases. Veins, stems & branches are green. PARENTAGE: 'Sofie Michiels' x 'Roesse Apus'. Lax upright or stiff trailer. Makes good stiff trailer. Prefers overhead filtered light and cool climate. Best bloom and foliage colour in filtered light. Tested 4 years in Knegsel, The Netherlands. Distinguished by bloom colour.
Roes 2003 NL AFS5318.

Roesse Eri Dania. Upright/Trailer. Semi Double. COROLLA: half flared; opens dark reddish purple (59A); matures dark reddish purple (60A); 16mm (5/8") long x 14mm (9/16") wide. SEPALS: half up, tips reflexed up; light rose (63D) upper surface; magenta (63B) lower surface; 30mm (1 3/16") long x 14mm (9/16") wide. TUBE: magenta (63A); 30mm (1 3/16") long x 4mm (1/8") wide. FOLIAGE is medium green (137B) upper surface; medium green (138A) lower surface. PARENTAGE: 'Roesse Lupus' x 'Roesse Bianca'.
Roes 2008 NL AFS6902.

Roesse Eridanus. Upright. Single. COROLLA is half flared with smooth petal margins; opens light rose (73B); matures light pink (65C); 22mm (7/8") long x 33mm (1 5/16") wide. SEPALS are fully up, tips reflexed; light rose (68D) upper surface; pink (62A) lower surface; 19mm (3/4") long x 12mm (1/2") wide. TUBE is magenta (63B); short & thick; 8mm (5/16") long x 10mm (3/8") wide. FOLIAGE: dark green (137A) upper surface; medium green (138B) lower surface. Leaves are 50mm (2") long x 42mm (1 5/8") wide, ovate shaped. PARENTAGE: 'Roesse Carme' x 'Thea Kroese'. Distinguished by bloom colour.

Roes 2005 NL AFS5962.

Roesse Eudoxus. Upright/Trailer. Semi Double. COROLLA: Half flared; opens red (43A); matures red orange (42B); 15mm (9/16") long x 14mm (9/16") wide. SEPALS: horizontal, tips recurved; pink (62C) upper surface; pink (62A) lower surface; 22mm (7/8") long x 7mm (1/4") wide. TUBE: pink (62C); medium length & thickness; 20mm (3/4") long x 4mm (1/8") wide. FOLIAGE is dark green (137A) upper surface; medium green (137C) lower surface. PARENTAGE: 'Roesse Lupus' x 'Roesse Betelgeuze'.
Roes 2007 NL AFS6675.

Roesse Euler. Upright/Trailer. Single. COROLLA: Quarter flared; opens dark reddish purple (72A); matures reddish purple (71B); 17mm (5/8") long x 12mm (1/2") wide. SEPALS: fully up, tips reflexed; light purple (70C) upper surface; dark reddish purple (70A) lower surface; 22mm (7/8") long x 8mm (5/16") wide. TUBE: light purple (70C); medium length, thin; 20mm (3/4") long x 4mm (1/8") wide. FOLIAGE is dark green (137A) upper surface; medium green (137C) lower surface. PARENTAGE: 'Roesse Lupus' x 'Roesse Sinope'.
Roes 2007 NL AFS6695.

Roesse Formalhaut. Upright/Trailer. Single. COROLLA: full flared, smooth petal margins; opens purple (79C); matures purple (81B); 21mm (13/16") long 24mm (15/16") wide. SEPALS: fully up; tips recurved; orange (34C) upper surface; dark orange red (34A) lower surface; 26mm (1") long x 12mm (1/2") wide. TUBE: orange (34C); medium length & thickness; 12mm (1/2") long x 6mm (1/4") wide. STAMENS: extend 24mm (15/16") below corolla; magenta (68A) filaments; rose (68B) anthers. PISTIL: extends 32mm (1 1/4") below the corolla; rose (68B) style & stigma. BUD: elliptic, pointed. FOLIAGE: dark green (137A) upper surface; medium green (138A) lower surface. Leaves are 56mm (2 3/16") long x 27mm (1 1/16") wide, lanceolate shaped, serrulated edges, acute tips and obtuse bases. Red veins, stems & branches. PARENTAGE: 'Swanley Gem' x 'Monique Sleiderink'. Lax upright or stiff trailer. Makes good stiff trailer. Prefers overhead filtered light and cool climate. Best bloom and foliage colour in filtered light. Tested 4 years in Knegsel, The Netherlands. Distinguished by bloom colour.
Roes 2004 NL AFS5486.

Roesse Fornax. Upright/Trailer. Double. COROLLA is half flared with smooth petal margins; opens violet (84A); matures light violet (84B); 17mm (11/16") long x 14mm (9/16") wide. SEPALS are half up, tips reflexed up; white (155C) tipped green upper & lower surfaces; 27mm (1 1/16") long x 14mm (9/16") wide. TUBE is white (155C); medium length & thickness; 24mm (15/16") long x 7mm (1/4") wide. FOLIAGE: dark green (137A) upper surface; medium green (138A) lower surface. Leaves are 76mm (3") long x 29mm (1 1/8") wide, lanceolate shaped. PARENTAGE: ('Sofie Michiels' x 'Rohees New Millennium') x 'Magda Vanbets'. Distinguished by bloom colour.
Roes 2005 NL AFS5952.

Roesse Franklin. Upright/Trailer. Double. COROLLA is three quarter flared; opens purple (83A); matures purple (71A); 14mm (9/16") long x 16mm (5/8") wide. SEPALS are horizontal, tips recurved; white (155C) upper & lower surfaces; 26mm (1") long x 12mm (7/16") wide. TUBE is white (155B); 11mm (7/16") long x 5mm (3/16") wide. FOLIAGE: dark green (139A) upper surface; medium green (137C) lower surface. PARENTAGE: 'Roesse Tucana' x 'Roesse Parel'. Distinguished by bloom colour.
Roes 2006 NL AFS6145.

Roesse Gambart. Upright. Double. COROLLA: Half flared; opens pink (62A); matures light pink (62B); 12mm (7/16") long x 11mm (7/16") wide. SEPALS: half up, tips reflexed up; pale green (62D) tipped green upper & lower surfaces; 20mm (3/4") long x 11mm (7/16") wide. TUBE: pale pink (62D); long & thin; 26mm (1") long x 4mm (1/8") wide. FOLIAGE is dark green (137A) upper surface; medium green (137C) lower surface. PARENTAGE: 'Roesse Scutum' x 'Allure'.
Roes 2007 NL AFS6696.

Roesse Gauss. Upright/Trailer. Semi Double. COROLLA is three quarter flared; opens purple (83A); matures purple (71A); 22mm (7/8") long x 26mm (1") wide. SEPALS are half up, tips reflexed up; magenta (59C) upper & lower surfaces; 27mm (1 1/16") long x 12mm (7/16") wide. TUBE is magenta (59C); 7mm (1/4") long x 6mm (1/4") wide. FOLIAGE: dark green (137A) upper surface; medium green (137C) lower surface. PARENTAGE: 'Reg Gubler' x 'Maxima'. Distinguished by bloom & foliage combination.
Roes 2006 NL AFS6161.

Roesse Gemini. Upright. Double. COROLLA is half flared with smooth petal margins; opens dark red (46A); matures red (45B); 18mm (11/16") long x 16mm (5/8") wide. SEPALS are fully up, tips recurved; rose (48B) upper surface; orange (44D) lower surface; 24mm (15/16") long x 16mm (5/8") wide. TUBE is rose (48B); short & thick; 11mm (7/16") long x 10mm (3/8") wide. FOLIAGE: dark green (137A) upper surface; medium green (138A) lower surface. Leaves are 58mm (2 5/16") long x 44mm (1 3/4") wide, ovate shaped. PARENTAGE: 'Roesse Carme' x 'Roesse Apus'. Distinguished by bloom colour.
Roes 2005 NL AFS5929.

Roesse Geminus. Upright/Trailer. Single. COROLLA is half flared; opens light purple (78B); matures light purple (80C); 12mm (7/16") long x 16mm (5/8") wide. SEPALS are half up, tips recurved up; pale pink (62D) upper surface; pink (62C) lower surface; 20mm (3/4") long x 12mm (7/16") wide. TUBE is pale pink (62D); 6mm (1/4") long x 7mm (1/4") wide. FOLIAGE: dark green (139A) upper surface; medium green (137C) lower surface. PARENTAGE: 'Roesse Norma' x 'Roesse Octans'. Distinguished by bloom & foliage combination.
Roes 2006 NL AFS6144.

Roesse Gianfar. Upright/Trailer. Double. COROLLA is three quarter flared with smooth petal margins; opens purple (83A); matures purple (77A); 26mm (1") long x 28mm (1 1/8") wide. SEPALS are horizontal, tips recurved; magenta (67B) upper surface, reddish purple (67A) lower surface; 32mm (1 1/4") long x 20mm (13/16") wide. TUBE is magenta (67B); short and thick; 16mm (5/8") long x 9mm (3/8") thick. STAMENS extend 22mm (7/8") beyond the corolla; reddish purple (67A) filaments and anthers. PISTIL extends 28mm (1 1/8") beyond the corolla; reddish purple (67A) style, rose (68C) stigma. BUD is elliptic, pointed. FOLIAGE is dark green (137A) upper surface, medium green (138A) lower surface. Leaves are 67mm (2 5/8") long x 34mm (1 3/8") wide, elliptic shaped, serrated edges, acute tips and cordate bases. Veins, stems and branches are green. PARENTAGE: 'Rohees Queen' x 'Delta's Bride'. Lax upright or stiff trailer. Makes good stiff trailer. Prefers overhead filtered light and cool climate. Best bloom colour in filtered light. Tested four years in Knegsel, The Netherlands. Distinguished by large flower.
Roes 2002 NL AFS5041.

Roesse Gomeisa. Upright. Single. COROLLA: three quarter flared, smooth petal margins; opens rose (65A); matures light pink (65B); 27mm (1 1/16") long x 32mm (1 1/4") wide. SEPALS: fully up; tips reflexed; red (53D) upper surface; dark red (53A) lower surface; 32mm (1 1/4") long x 16mm (5/8") wide. TUBE: red (53D); medium length & thickness; 8mm (5/16") long x 6mm (1/4") wide. STAMENS: extend 12mm (1/2") below corolla; red (53D) filaments; dark red (53A) anthers. PISTIL: extends 28mm (1 1/8") below the corolla; red (53D) style; rose (51C) stigma. BUD: round. FOLIAGE: medium green (137C) upper surface; medium green (138B) lower surface. Leaves are 57mm (2 1/4") long x 42mm (1 5/8") wide, cordate shaped, serrulated edges, acute tips and rounded bases. Veins, stems & branches are red. PARENTAGE: 'Roesse Apus' x 'Roesse Apus'. Small upright. Makes good standard. Prefers overhead filtered light and cool climate. Best bloom and foliage colour in filtered light. Tested 4 years in Knegsel, The Netherlands. Distinguished by bloom & foliage combination.
Roes 2003 NL AFS5322.

Roesse Grafias. Upright. Semi Double. COROLLA is half flared with smooth petal margins; opens dark purple (79A); matures dark reddish purple (61A); 22mm (7/8") long x 25mm (1") wide. SEPALS are fully up, tips recurved; reddish purple (71B) upper surface; magenta (63A) lower surface; 22mm (7/8") long x 16mm (5/8") wide. TUBE is reddish purple (71B); medium length and thickness; 12mm (1/2") long x 6mm (1/4") thick. STAMENS extend 27mm (1 1/16") beyond the corolla; dark reddish purple (64A) filaments, dark purple (79A) anthers. PISTIL extends 42mm (1 11/16") beyond the corolla; dark reddish purple (64A) style, reddish purple (64B) stigma. BUD is ovate, pointed. FOLIAGE is medium green (137B) upper surface, medium green (138B) lower surface. Leaves are 62mm (2 7/16") long x 44mm (1 3/4") wide, ovate shaped, serrated edges, acute tips and obtuse bases. Veins, stems and branches are red. PARENTAGE: {[('Bon Accord' x 'Bicentennial) x ('Vobeglo' x 'Dancing Flame')] x 'Rohees Alrami'} x 'Hertogin van Brabant'. Tall upright. Makes good standard. Prefers overhead filtered light and cool climate. Best bloom colour in filtered light. Tested four years in Knegsel, The Netherlands. Distinguished by bloom colour.
Roes 2002 NL AFS5022.

Roesse Grus. Upright/Trailer. Double. COROLLA is three quarter flared with smooth petal margins; opens purple (83B); matures reddish purple (80B); 16mm (5/8") long x 19mm (3/4") wide. SEPALS are fully up, tips recurved; reddish purple (59B) upper surface; dark reddish purple (60B) lower surface; 27mm (1 1/16") long x 14mm (9/16") wide. TUBE is reddish purple (59B); medium length & thickness; 9mm (3/8") long x 7mm (3/16") wide. FOLIAGE: dark green (137A) upper surface; medium green (138A) lower surface. Leaves are 70mm (2 3/4") long x 35mm (1 3/8") wide, ovate shaped. PARENTAGE: 'Swanley Gem' x 'Roesse Svalocin'. Distinguished by bloom colour.
Roes 2005 NL AFS5933.

Roesse Hagni. Upright. Single. COROLLA: unflared; opens & matures dark reddish purple (59A); 16mm (5/8") long x 13mm (1/2") wide. SEPALS: fully up, tips recurved; light pink (65B) upper surface; rose (65A) lower surface; 24mm (15/16") long x 10mm (3/8") wide. TUBE: light pink (65B); 6mm (1/4") long x 6mm (1/4") wide. FOLIAGE is dark green (137A) upper surface; medium green (138A) lower surface. PARENTAGE: 'Roesse Despina' x 'Maxima's Girl'.
Roes 2008 NL AFS6912.

Roesse Haki. Upright. Single. COROLLA: full flared; opens magenta (59C); matures magenta (58B); 17mm (5/8") long x 21mm (13/16") wide. SEPALS: fully up, tips recurved; pink (62B) upper surface; dark rose (58C) lower surface; 25mm (1") long x 12mm (7/16") wide. TUBE: pink (62B); 10mm (3/8") long x 4mm (1/8") wide. FOLIAGE is dark green (137A) upper surface; medium green (137C) lower surface. PARENTAGE: 'Roesse Lupus' x 'Oranje van Os'.
Roes 2008 NL AFS6908.

Roesse Harpalus. Upright. Single. COROLLA: Full flared; opens dark purple (79B); matures dark purple (78A); 18mm (11/16") long x 24mm (15/16") wide. SEPALS: fully up, tips reflexed; light rose (68D) upper surface; rose (67D) lower surface; 17mm (5/8") long x 10mm (3/8") wide. TUBE: light rose (68D); medium length & thickness; 10mm (3/8") long x 8mm (5/16") wide. FOLIAGE is dark green (137A) upper surface; medium green (137C) lower surface. PARENTAGE: 'Roesse Lupus' x 'Roesse Franklin'.
Roes 2007 NL AFS6697.

Roesse Helicon. Upright/Trailer. Double. COROLLA: Half flared; opens reddish purple (59B); matures magenta (59C); 16mm (5/8") long x 21mm (13/16") wide. SEPALS: half up, tips recurved up; magenta (63A) upper surface; magenta (58B) lower surface; 26mm (1") long x 12mm (7/16") wide. TUBE: magenta (63A); medium length & thickness; 16mm (5/8") long x 5mm (3/16") wide. FOLIAGE is medium green (137C) upper surface; medium green (138B) lower surface. PARENTAGE: 'Roesse Lupus' x 'Rohees New Millennium'.
Roes 2007 NL AFS6688.

Roesse Helene. Upright/Trailer. Single. COROLLA is half flared; opens dark reddish purple (61A); matures dark reddish purple (60B); 20mm (3/4") long x 26mm (1") wide. SEPALS are fully up, tips recurved; magenta (67B) upper surface; reddish purple (67A) lower surface; 38mm (1 1/2") long x 10mm (3/8") wide. TUBE is pale lavender (65D); 26mm (1") long x 4mm (1/8") wide. FOLIAGE: medium green (137B) upper surface; medium green (138A) lower surface. PARENTAGE: 'Roesse Lupus' x 'Roesse Rhea'. Distinguished by bloom & foliage combination.
Roes 2006 NL AFS6170.

Roesse Hercules. Upright. Single. COROLLA is half flared; opens purple (71A); matures dark reddish purple (61A); 21mm (13/16") long x 24mm (15/16") wide. SEPALS are half up, tips reflexed up; dark rose (64C) upper surface; reddish purple (64B) lower surface; 29mm (1 1/8") long x 7mm (1/4") wide. TUBE is dark rose (64C); 24mm (15/16") long x 7mm (1/4") wide. FOLIAGE: dark green (137A) upper surface; medium green (138A) lower surface. PARENTAGE: 'Roesse Lupus' x 'Sofie Michiels'. Distinguished by bloom colour.
Roes 2006 NL AFS6183.

Roesse Herodotus. Upright/Trailer. Semi Double. COROLLA: Half flared; opens dark reddish purple (60A); matures dark reddish purple (60B); 26mm (1") long x 19mm (3/4") wide. SEPALS: half up, tips reflexed up; pink (62C) upper surface; pink (62A) lower surface; 46mm (1 13/16") long x 11mm (7/16") wide. TUBE: pink (62C); medium length & thickness; 16mm (5/8") long x 6mm (1/4") wide. FOLIAGE is dark green (137A) upper surface; medium green (138A) lower surface. PARENTAGE: 'Roesse Lupus' x 'Carla Knapen'.
Roes 2007 NL AFS6671.

Roesse Himalia. Trailer. Double. COROLLA: three quarter flared, smooth petal margins; opens dark reddish purple (72A); matures dark reddish purple (70A); 22mm (7/8") long x 26mm (1") wide. SEPALS: half up; tips recurved up; light reddish purple (72C) upper & lower surfaces; 32mm (1 1/4") long x 18mm (11/16") wide. TUBE: light rose (73C); medium length & thickness; 16mm (5/8") long x 6mm (1/4") wide. STAMENS: extend 17mm (11/16") below corolla; light reddish purple (72D) filaments; purple (71A) anthers. PISTIL: extends 34mm (1 5/16") below the corolla; light reddish purple (72C) style; cream (11D) stigma. BUD: round. FOLIAGE: medium green (137B) upper surface; medium green (138B) lower surface. Leaves are 86mm (3 3/8") long x 32mm (1 1/4") wide, lanceolate shaped, serrulated edges, acute tips and rounded bases. Veins, stems & branches are red. PARENTAGE: 'Roesse King' x 'Miniskirt'. Natural trailer. Makes good basket. Prefers overhead filtered light and cool climate. Best bloom and foliage colour in filtered light. Tested 4 years in Knegsel, The Netherlands. Distinguished by bloom colour.
Roes 2003 NL AFS5319.

Roesse Hydrus. Trailer. Double. COROLLA is half flared with smooth petal margins; opens dark reddish purple (72A); matures dark reddish purple (60A); 27mm (1 1/16") long x 32mm (1 1/4") wide. SEPALS are horizontal, tips recurved; dark rose (58C) upper surface; magenta (58B) lower surface; 28mm (1 1/8") long x 17mm (11/16") wide. TUBE is dark rose (58C); medium length & thickness; 15mm (9/16") long x 7mm (1/4") wide. FOLIAGE: dark green (139A) upper surface; medium green (138A) lower surface. Leaves are 60mm (2 3/8") long x 44mm (1 3/4") wide, cordate shaped. PARENTAGE: ['Sofie Michiels' x ('Roesse Apus' x 'Roesse Apus')] x 'Katrien Michiels'. Distinguished by bloom & foliage combination.
Roes 2005 NL AFS5935.

Roesse Hyginus. Upright/Trailer. Semi Double. COROLLA: Half flared; opens dark reddish purple (72A); matures reddish purple (72B); 22mm (7/8") long x 24mm (15/16") wide. SEPALS: horizontal, tips recurved; pink (62A) upper surface; magenta (68A) lower surface; 22mm (7/8") long x 9mm (5/16") wide. TUBE: pink (62A); medium length & thickness; 20mm (3/4") long x 7mm (1/4") wide. FOLIAGE is dark green (137A) upper surface; medium green (138A) lower surface.

PARENTAGE: ('Roesse Lupus' x 'Magda Vanbets') ('Roesse Rhea' x 'Lye's Unique'). Roes 2007 NL AFS6682.

Roesse Indus. Upright. Semi Double. COROLLA is half flared with smooth petal margins; opens purple (71A); matures dark rose (71D); 12mm (1/2") long x 14mm (9/16") wide. SEPALS are half up, tips reflexed up; rose (68B) tipped green upper surface; pale lavender (69C) tipped green lower surface; 26mm (1") long x 10mm (3/8") wide. TUBE is rose (68B); medium length & thickness; 12mm (1/2") long x 5mm (3/16") wide. FOLIAGE: dark green (137A) upper surface; medium green (138B) lower surface. Leaves are 72mm (2 13/16") long x 37mm (1 7/16") wide, lanceolate shaped. PARENTAGE: ['Roesse Carme' x ('Roesse Apus' x 'Roesse Apus')] x 'Roesse Apus'. Distinguished by bloom & foliage combination. Roes 2005 NL AFS5961.

Roesse Japetus. Trailer. Double. COROLLA is half flared; opens purple (77A); matures light purple (74C); 17mm (5/8") long x 24mm (15/16") wide. SEPALS are horizontal, tips recurved; pale purple (75D) upper surface; pale purple (75C) lower surface; 29mm (1 1/8") long x 12mm (7/16") wide. TUBE is pale purple (75D); 17mm (5/8") long x 6mm (1/4") wide. FOLIAGE: medium green (138A) upper surface; light green (138C) lower surface. PARENTAGE: [('Cameron Ryle' x 'Parasol') x 'Allure'] x 'Roesse Octans'. Distinguished by bloom & foliage combination. Roes 2006 NL AFS6173.

Roesse Juliet. Upright/Trailer. Single. COROLLA is quarter flared; opens dark orange red (34A); matures orange red (34B); 12mm (7/16") long x 14mm (9/16") wide. SEPALS are horizontal, tips recurved; pink (43D) upper & lower surfaces; 27mm (1 1/16") long x 8mm (5/16") wide. TUBE is pink (43D); 24mm (15/16") long x 6mm (1/4") wide. FOLIAGE: dark green (137A) upper surface; medium green (138A) lower surface. PARENTAGE: 'Roesse Lupus' x 'Lye's Unique'. Distinguished by bloom colour. Roes 2006 NL AFS6155.

Roesse Kepler. Upright/Trailer. Single. COROLLA: Half flared; opens reddish purple (61B); matures magenta (61C); 10mm (3/8") long x 14mm (9/16") wide. SEPALS: horizontal, tips recurved; pale lavender (65D) upper & lower surfaces; 24mm (15/16") long

x 9mm (5/16") wide. TUBE: pale lavender (65D); medium length & thickness; 25mm (1") long x 4mm (1/8") wide. Leaves are 51mm (2") long x 31mm (1 1/4") wide; ovate shaped, serrate edges, acute tips, rounded bases. Veins, stems & branches are green. PARENTAGE: 'Roesse Lupus' x 'Lye's Unique'. Roes 2007 NL AFS6694.

Roesse Kochap. Upright/Trailer. Semi Double. COROLLA is three quarter flared with smooth petal margins; opens dark purple (79A); matures dark reddish purple (61A); 28mm (1 1/8") long x 34mm (1 3/8") wide. SEPALS are fully up, tips recurved; reddish purple (67A) upper and lower surfaces; 30mm (1 3/16") long x 19mm (3/4") wide. TUBE is reddish purple (67A); medium length and thickness; 18mm (11/16") long x 7mm (1/4") thick. STAMENS extend 22mm (7/8") beyond the corolla; dark purple (79A) filaments, purple (71A) anthers. PISTIL extends 37mm (1 7/16") beyond the corolla; purple (71A) style, light rose (73C) stigma. BUD is round, pointed. FOLIAGE is medium green (137B) upper surface, medium green (138B) lower surface. Leaves are 67mm (2 5/8") long x 44mm (1 3/4") wide, ovate shaped, serrulated edges, acute tips and obtuse bases. Veins, stems and branches are red. PARENTAGE: {[('Bon Accord' x 'Bicentennial) x ('Vobeglo' x 'Dancing Flame')] x 'Rohees Alrami'} x 'Hertogin van Brabant'. Lax upright or stiff trailer. Makes good stiff trailer. Prefers overhead filtered light and cool climate. Best bloom colour in filtered light. Tested four years in Knegsel, The Netherlands. Distinguished by bloom colour. Roes 2002 NL AFS5024.

Roesse Kums. Upright/Trailer. Single. COROLLA is full flared with wavy petal margins; opens purple (90B); matures dark purple (78A); 30mm (1 3/16") long x 34mm (1 5/16") wide. SEPALS are fully up, tips recurved; magenta (58B) upper surface; dark rose (58C) lower surface; 31mm (1 1/4") long x 16mm (5/8") wide. TUBE is magenta (58B); medium length & thickness; 12mm (1/2") long x 7mm (1/4") wide. FOLIAGE: dark green (137A) upper surface; medium green (138A) lower surface. Leaves are 54mm (2 1/8") long x 39mm (1 9/16") wide, ovate shaped. PARENTAGE: 'Madalyn Drago' x 'Eisvogel'. Distinguished by bloom & foliage combination. Roes 2005 NL AFS5969.

Roesse Lacerta. Upright. Semi Double. COROLLA is half flared with smooth petal margins; opens dark reddish purple (59A); matures reddish purple (60D); 18mm (11/16") long x 21mm (13/16") wide. SEPALS are fully up, tips recurved; pink (62A) upper & lower surfaces; 22mm (7/8") long x 12mm (1/2") wide. TUBE is pink (62A); short & thick; 10mm (3/8") long x 10mm (3/8") wide. FOLIAGE: dark green (139A) upper surface; medium green (138A) lower surface. Leaves are 55mm (2 3/16") long x 36mm (1 7/16") wide, ovate shaped. PARENTAGE: ('Roesse Apus' x 'Roesse Apus') x 'Roesse Svalocin'. Distinguished by erect blooms & colour.
Roes 2005 NL AFS5930.

Roesse Lambert. Upright/Trailer. Double. COROLLA: Half flared; opens & matures dark orange red (34A) & orange (33B); 14mm (9/16") long x 31mm (1 1/4") wide. SEPALS: horizontal, tips recurved; pink (49A) tipped green upper surface; light rose (50C) tipped green lower surface; 34mm (1 3/8") long x 14mm (9/16") wide. TUBE: yellowish white (4D); medium length & thickness; 13mm (1/2") long x 7mm (1/4") wide. FOLIAGE is medium green (137B) upper surface; medium green (138B) lower surface. PARENTAGE: 'Roesse Betelgeuze' x ('Roesse Elana' x 'Magda Vanbets').
Roes 2007 NL AFS6685.

Roesse Landsberg. Upright/Trailer. Double. COROLLA: Half flared; opens violet (76A); matures light purple (75B); 19mm (3/4") long x 23mm (7/8") wide. SEPALS: half up, tips reflexed up; white (155D) upper & lower surfaces; 34mm (1 3/8") long x 17mm (5/8") wide. TUBE: white (155D); medium length & thickness; 16mm (5/8") long x 6mm (1/4") wide. FOLIAGE is medium green (137B) upper surface; medium green (138B) lower surface. PARENTAGE: 'Sofie Michiels' x 'Roesse Parel'.
Roes 2007 NL AFS6698.

Roesse Larissa. Upright. Double. COROLLA is three quarter flared; opens magenta (58B); matures dark rose (58C); 18mm (11/16") long x 21mm (13/16") wide. SEPALS are fully up, tips recurved; pale pink (62D) upper & lower surfaces; 26mm (1") long x 6mm (1/4") wide. TUBE is pale pink (62D); 20mm (3/4") long x 6mm (1/4") wide. FOLIAGE is dark green (137A) upper surface; medium green (137C) lower surface. PARENTAGE: ('Sofie Michiels' x 'Venus Victrix') x 'Rohees Rana'.

Distinguished by bloom & foliage combination.
Roes 2006 NL AFS6139.

Roesse Leda. Upright/Trailer. Double. COROLLA: three quarter flared, smooth petal margins; opens purple (77A); matures reddish purple (72B); 37mm (1 7/16") long x 26mm (1") wide. SEPALS: fully up; tips recurved; light pink (65B) upper surface; pink (62A) lower surface; 40mm (1 9/16") long x 16mm (5/8") wide. TUBE: light pink (65B); medium length & thickness; 16mm (5/8") long x 7mm (1/4") wide. STAMENS: extend 24mm (15/16") below corolla; pale purple (74D) filaments; magenta (63A) anthers. PISTIL: extends 26mm (1") below the corolla; pale rose (73D) style; pale lavender (65D) stigma. BUD: ovate. FOLIAGE: dark green (137A) upper surface; medium green (138BA) lower surface. Leaves are 57mm (2 1/4") long x 41mm (1 5/8") wide, cordate shaped, serrulated edges, acute tips and rounded bases. Veins, stems & branches are red. PARENTAGE: 'Monique Sleiderink' x 'Madalyn Drago'. Lax upright or stiff trailer. Makes good stiff trailer. Prefers overhead filtered light and cool climate. Best bloom and foliage colour in filtered light. Tested 4 years in Knegsel, The Netherlands. Distinguished by bloom & foliage combination.
Roes 2003 NL AFS5311.

Roesse Lepus. Trailer. Single. COROLLA is half flared with smooth petal margins; opens purple (90A); matures purple (88A); 24mm (15/16") long x 27mm (1 1/16") wide. SEPALS are half up, tips recurved up; magenta (58B) upper surface; dark rose (58C) lower surface; 28mm (1 1/8") long x 12mm (1/2") wide. TUBE is magenta (58B); short, medium thickness; 7mm (1/4") long x 7mm (1/4") wide. FOLIAGE: dark green (137A) upper surface; medium green (138A) lower surface. Leaves are 47mm (1 7/8") long x 28mm (1 1/8") wide, ovate shaped. PARENTAGE: 'Swanley Gem' x 'Roesse Blacky'. Distinguished by bloom colour.
Roes 2005 NL AFS5936.

Roesse Linne. Upright. Single. COROLLA: Half flared; opens & matures dark reddish purple (60A); 16mm (5/8") long x 14mm (9/16") wide. SEPALS: half up, tips reflexed up; light rose (63D) upper surface; magenta (63B) lower surface; 18mm (11/16") long x 9mm (5/16") wide. TUBE: light rose (63D); medium length, thick; 20mm (3/4") long x 10mm (3/8") wide. FOLIAGE is medium green (137B) upper surface; medium green (138B) lower surface. PARENTAGE: 'Roesse Lupus' x 'Lye's Unique'. Roes 2007 NL AFS6693.

Roesse Littrow. Upright. Single. COROLLA is half flared; opens red (45A); matures red (45C); 24mm (15/16") long x 27mm (1 1/16") wide. SEPALS are half up, tips recurved up; rose (51B) upper surface; dark rose (51A) lower surface; 27mm (1 1/16") long x 14mm (9/16") wide. TUBE is rose (51B); 13mm (1/2") long x 9mm (3/8") wide. FOLIAGE: dark green (137A) upper surface; medium green (137C) lower surface. PARENTAGE: 'Roesse Lupus' x 'Roesse Parel'. Distinguished by bloom & foliage combination. Roes 2006 NL AFS6135.

Roesse Lyra. Trailer. Semi Double. COROLLA is half flared with smooth petal margins; opens violet (82C); matures light reddish purple (73A); 17mm (11/16") long x 23mm (15/16") wide. SEPALS are horizontal, tips recurved; magenta (58B) upper surface; dark rose (58C) lower surface; 26mm (1") long x 11mm (7/16") wide. TUBE is magenta (58B); medium length & thickness; 15mm (9/16") long x 8mm (5/16") wide. FOLIAGE: dark green (137A) upper surface; medium green (137C) lower surface. Leaves are 66mm (2 5/8") long x 36mm (1 7/16") wide, ovate shaped. PARENTAGE: 'Roesse Carme' x 'Shangri-La'. Distinguished by bloom colour. Roes 2005 NL AFS5964.

Roesse Manillius. Upright/Trailer. Semi Double. COROLLA: Three quarter flared; opens dark reddish purple (59A); matures reddish purple (59B); 19mm (3/4") long x 24mm (15/16") wide. SEPALS: horizontal, tips recurved; pale lavender (65D) tipped green upper surface; light pink (65C) tipped green lower surface; 34mm (1 3/8") long x 12mm (7/16") wide. TUBE: pale lavender (65D); medium length & thickness; 20mm (3/4") long x 6mm (1/4") wide. FOLIAGE is dark green (137A) upper surface; medium green (138A) lower surface. PARENTAGE: 'Roesse Lupus' x 'Carla Knapen'. Roes 2007 NL AFS6681.

Roesse Marduk. Upright/Trailer. Double. COROLLA: three quarter flared; opens & matures red (46B); 16mm (5/8") long x 14mm (9/16") wide. SEPALS: half up, tips reflexed up; rose (68C) upper surface; dark rose (58C) lower surface; 26mm (1") long x 14mm (9/16") wide. TUBE: light green

(138C); 20mm (3/4") long x 5mm (3/16") wide. FOLIAGE is dark green (137A) upper surface; medium green (137C) lower surface. PARENTAGE: 'Roesse Lupus' x 'Roesse Mensa'. Roes 2008 NL AFS6906.

Roesse Marian. Upright/Trailer. Single. COROLLA: Three quarter flared; opens red (50A); matures rose (50B); 12mm (7/16") long x 14mm (9/16") wide. SEPALS: fully up, tips reflexed; light pink (49B) upper surface; pink (49A) lower surface; 12mm (7/16") long x 6mm (1/4") wide. TUBE: light pink (49B); long & thin; 26mm (1") long x 5mm (3/16") wide. FOLIAGE is dark green (137A) upper surface; medium green (137C) lower surface. PARENTAGE: 'Roesse Lupus' x ('Luuk van Riet' x 'Roesse Betelgeuze'). Roes 2007 NL AFS6683.

Roesse Markap. Upright/Trailer. Semi Double. COROLLA is half flared with smooth petal margins; opens dark reddish purple (79A); matures dark reddish purple (61A); 21mm (13/16") long x 18mm (11/16") wide. SEPALS are horizontal, tips reflexed; reddish purple (64B) upper surface, dark reddish purple (64A) lower surface; 27mm (1 1/16") long x 16mm (5/8") wide. TUBE is reddish purple (64B); medium length and thickness; 10mm (3/8") long x 6mm (1/4") thick. STAMENS extend 18mm (11/16") beyond the corolla; dark reddish purple (64A) filaments and anthers. PISTIL extends 39mm (1 9/16") beyond the corolla; dark reddish purple (64A) style, reddish purple (64C) stigma. BUD is ovate, pointed. FOLIAGE is dark green (137A) upper surface, medium green (138B) lower surface. Leaves are 63mm (2 1/2") long x 32mm (1 1/4") wide, elliptic shaped, smooth edges, acute tips and rounded bases. Veins, stems and branches are red. PARENTAGE: 'Rohees New Millennium' x 'Roesse Tricolour'. Lax upright or stiff trailer. Makes good stiff trailer. Prefers overhead filtered light and cool climate. Best bloom colour in filtered light. Tested four years in Knegsel, The Netherlands. Distinguished by bloom colour. Roes 2002 NL AFS5042.

Roesse Mason. Upright/Trailer. Single. COROLLA is half flared; opens dark reddish purple (59A); matures reddish purple (59B); 16mm (5/8") long x 21mm (13/16") wide. SEPALS are half down, tips reflexed; pale pink (62D) upper surface; pink (62C) lower surface; 26mm (1") long x 8mm (5/16") wide. TUBE is pale pink (62D); 22mm (7/8") long x 7mm (1/4") wide. FOLIAGE: dark green

(137A) upper surface; medium green (138A) lower surface. PARENTAGE: 'Roesse Lupus' x 'Lustre'. Distinguished by bloom colour. Roes 2006 NL AFS6133.

Roesse Matisse. Upright/Trailer. Semi Double. COROLLA: half flared; opens dark reddish purple (59A); matures dark reddish purple (60A); 16mm (5/8") long x 23mm (7/8") wide. SEPALS: horizontal, tips recurved; rose (64D) upper surface; dark rose (64C) lower surface; 22mm (7/8") long x 10mm (3/8") wide. TUBE: rose (64D); 37mm (1 7/16") long x 4mm (1/8") wide. FOLIAGE is dark green (137A) upper surface; medium green (137C) lower surface. PARENTAGE: 'Roesse Lupus' x 'Roesse Bianca'. Roes 2008 NL AFS6904.

Roesse Mayer. Upright. Single. COROLLA: Quarter flared; opens reddish purple (61B); matures magenta (61C); 14mm (9/16") long x 17mm (5/8") wide. SEPALS: horizontal, tips recurved; light rose (58D) upper surface; dark rose (58C) lower surface; 22mm (7/8") long x 9mm (5/16") wide. TUBE: light rose (58D); medium length, thick; 17mm (5/8") long x 8mm (5/16") wide. FOLIAGE is dark green (137A) upper surface; medium green (137C) lower surface. PARENTAGE: 'Roesse Lupus' x 'Roesse Rhea'. Roes 2007 NL AFS6677.

Roesse Menelau. Trailer. Single. COROLLA is three quarter flared; opens violet blue (92A); matures light purple (78B); 20mm (3/4") long x 18mm (11/16") wide. SEPALS are half up, tips recurved up; magenta (63A) upper & lower surfaces; 22mm (7/8") long x 11mm (7/16") wide. TUBE is magenta (63A); 16mm (5/8") long x 6mm (1/4") wide. FOLIAGE: dark green (137A) upper surface; medium green (138B) lower surface. PARENTAGE: 'Roesse Tucana' x 'Swanley Gem'. Distinguished by bloom colour. Roes 2006 NL AFS6184.

Roesse Menkhib. Upright/Trailer. Single. COROLLA: full flared, wavy petal margins; opens purple (88A); matures purple (80A); 30mm (1 3/16") long 32mm (1 1/4") wide. SEPALS: half up; tips recurved up; dark rose (58C) upper surface; dark reddish purple (58A) lower surface; 39mm (1 9/16") long x 14mm (9/16") wide. TUBE: light rose (58D); medium length & thickness; 14mm (9/16") long x 7mm (1/4") wide. STAMENS: extend 37mm (1 7/16") below corolla; dark reddish purple (60C) filaments; magenta (63B) anthers. PISTIL: extends 51mm (2") below

the corolla; dark reddish purple (60C) style; light yellow (4C) stigma. BUD: cordate, pointed. FOLIAGE: dark green (137A) upper surface; medium green (138A) lower surface. Leaves are 62mm (2 7/16") long x 40mm (1 9/16") wide, ovate shaped, serrated edges, acute tips and rounded bases. Red veins, stems & branches. PARENTAGE: 'Roesse Dione' x 'Delta's Bride'. Lax upright or stiff trailer. Makes good stiff trailer. Prefers overhead filtered light and cool climate. Best bloom and foliage colour in filtered light. Tested 4 years in Knegsel, The Netherlands. Distinguished by bloom shape and colour. Roes 2004 NL AFS5485.

Roesse Mensa. Trailer. Double. COROLLA is half flared with smooth petal margins; opens & matures white (155D); 19mm (3/4") long x 24mm (15/16") wide. SEPALS are half up, tips reflexed up; rose (61D) upper & lower surfaces; 24mm (15/16") long x 14mm (9/16") wide. TUBE is white (155D); long & thin; 30mm (1 3/16") long x 4mm (1/4") wide.. FOLIAGE: dark green (137A) upper surface; medium green (137C) lower surface. Leaves are 68mm (2 11/16") long x 26mm (1") wide, lanceolate shaped. PARENTAGE: ('Sofie Michiels' x 'Rohees New Millennium') x 'Magda Vanbets'. Distinguished by bloom shape. Roes 2005 NL AFS5953.

Roesse Messala. Upright. Single. COROLLA is half flared; opens red (46B); matures red (44A); 14mm (9/16") long x 19mm (3/4") wide. SEPALS are horizontal, tips recurved; peach (37B) upper surface; coral (37A) lower surface; 27mm (1 1/16") long x 8mm (5/16") wide. TUBE is peach (37B); 22mm (7/8") long x 8mm (5/16") wide. FOLIAGE: dark green (137A) upper surface; medium green (137C) lower surface. PARENTAGE: 'Roesse Lupus' x 'Lye's Unique'. Distinguished by bloom & foliage combination. Roes 2006 NL AFS6143.

Roesse Metis. Upright. Double. COROLLA: half flared, smooth petal margins; opens purple (71A); matures light reddish purple (72D); 27mm (1 1/16") long x 31mm (1 1/4") wide. SEPALS: half up; tips reflexed up; reddish purple (61B) upper surface; magenta (61C) lower surface; 27mm (1 1/16") long x 12mm (1/2") wide. TUBE: reddish purple (61B); medium length & thickness; 10mm (3/8") long x 7mm (1/4") wide. STAMENS: extend 26mm (1") below corolla; dark reddish purple (64A) filaments; dark reddish purple (59A) anthers. PISTIL: extends 34mm (1

5/16") below the corolla; dark reddish purple (64A) style; light yellow (11C) stigma. BUD: round, pointed. FOLIAGE: dark green (137A) upper surface; medium green (138A) lower surface. Leaves are 67mm (2 5/8") long x 48mm (1 7/8") wide, cordate shaped, serrulated edges, acute tips and obtuse bases. Veins, stems & branches are red. PARENTAGE: 'Roesse Apus' x 'Bicentennial'. Medium upright. Makes good standard. Prefers overhead filtered light and cool climate. Best bloom and foliage colour in filtered light. Tested 4 years in Knegsel, The Netherlands. Distinguished by bloom colour.
Roes 2003 NL AFS5310.

Roesse Meton. Trailer. Single. COROLLA: Half flared; opens violet blue (91A); matures violet (84A); 12mm (7/16") long x 14mm (9/16") wide. SEPALS: horizontal, tips recurved; pale pink (76D) upper & lower surfaces; 24mm (15/16") long x 10mm (3/8") wide. TUBE: pale violet (76D); long & thin; 24mm (15/16") long x 3mm (1/8") wide. FOLIAGE is dark green (137A) upper surface; medium green (138A) lower surface. PARENTAGE: 'Roesse Duck' x 'Sofie Michiels'.
Roes 2007 NL AFS6672.

Roesse Milton. Upright. Single. COROLLA: full flared; opens dark reddish purple (60A); matures magenta (58B); 24mm (15/16") long x 26mm (1") wide. SEPALS: fully up, tips recurved; pink (62A) upper & lower surfaces; 24mm (15/16") long x 16mm (5/8") wide. TUBE: pink (62A); 12mm (7/16") long x 10mm (3/8") wide. FOLIAGE is dark green (137A) upper surface; medium green (137C) lower surface. PARENTAGE: 'Roesse Charon' x 'Maxima's Girl'.
Roes 2008 NL AFS6905.

Roesse Mimas. Upright/Trailer. Single. COROLLA: full flared, smooth petal margins; opens purple (83A); matures purple (71A); 27mm (1 1/16") long 32mm (1 1/4") wide. SEPALS: fully up; tips recurved; dark reddish purple (59A) upper surface; dark reddish purple (61A) lower surface; 24mm (15/16") long x 12mm (1/2") wide. TUBE: dark reddish purple (59A); short & thick; 7mm (1/4") long x 7mm (1/4") wide. STAMENS: extend 32mm (1 1/4") below corolla; purple (71A) filaments; dark purple (79A) anthers. PISTIL: extends 51mm (2") below the corolla; reddish purple (71B) style; light purple (78D) stigma. BUD: round, pointed. FOLIAGE: dark green (139A) upper surface; medium green (137C) lower surface. Leaves are 62mm (2

7/16") long x 32mm (1 1/4") wide, ovate shaped, smooth edges, acute tips and obtuse bases. Red veins, stems & branches. PARENTAGE: 'Swanley Gem' x 'Katrien Michiels'. Lax upright or stiff trailer. Makes good stiff trailer. Prefers overhead filtered light and cool climate. Best bloom and foliage colour in filtered light. Tested 4 years in Knegsel, The Netherlands. Distinguished by bloom shape colour.
Roes 2004 NL AFS5476.

Roesse Minelauva. Upright/Trailer. Double. COROLLA: three quarter flared, smooth petal margins; opens dark reddish purple (59A); matures magenta (59C); 17mm (11/16") long 23mm (15/16") wide. SEPALS: half up; tips reflexed up; reddish purple (61B) upper & lower surfaces; 29mm (1 1/8") long x 16mm (5/8") wide. TUBE: magenta (61C); medium length & thickness; 18mm (11/16") long x 6mm (1/4") wide. STAMENS: extend 10mm (3/8") below corolla; reddish purple (61B) filaments; reddish purple (59B) anthers. PISTIL: extends 16mm (9/16") below the corolla; reddish purple (61B) style; light yellow (4C) stigma. BUD: long TUBE, round. FOLIAGE: medium green (137B) upper surface; medium green (137D) lower surface. Leaves are 57mm (2 1/4") long x 41mm (1 5/8") wide, ovate shaped, serrated edges, obtuse tips and cordate bases. Red veins, stems & branches. PARENTAGE: 'Orangeblossom' x ('Roesse Apus' x 'Roesse Apus'). Lax upright or stiff trailer. Makes good stiff trailer. Prefers overhead filtered light and cool climate. Best bloom and foliage colour in filtered light. Tested 4 years in Knegsel, The Netherlands. Distinguished by bloom colour.
Roes 2004 NL AFS5484.

Roesse Miram. Upright/Trailer. Semi Double. COROLLA is full flared with smooth petal margins; opens white (155A); matures white (155B); 22mm (7/8") long x 22mm (7/8") wide. SEPALS are fully up, tips reflexed; reddish purple (74B) upper and lower surfaces; 47mm (1 7/8") long x 16mm (5/8") wide. TUBE is reddish purple (74B); medium length and thickness; 11mm (7/16") long x 7mm (1/4") thick. STAMENS extend 42mm (1 11/16") beyond the corolla; reddish purple (74B) filaments and anthers. PISTIL extends 53mm (2 1/8") beyond the corolla; reddish purple (74B) style, pale rose (73D) stigma. BUD is ovate, pointed. FOLIAGE is dark green (137A) upper surface, medium green (138B) lower surface. Leaves are 52mm (2 1/16") long x 40mm (1 9/16") wide, ovate

shaped, smooth edges, acute tips and rounded bases. Veins, stems and branches are green. PARENTAGE: 'Rohees Queen' x 'Sleigh Bells'. Lax upright or stiff trailer. Makes good stiff trailer. Prefers overhead filtered light and cool climate. Best bloom colour in filtered light. Tested four years in Knegsel, The Netherlands. Distinguished by bloom shape.
Roes 2002 NL AFS5025.

Roesse Misam. Trailer. Double. COROLLA: three quarter flared, smooth petal margins; opens dark purple (79B); matures dark reddish purple (59A); 20mm (13/16") long x 22mm (7/8") wide. SEPALS: half up; tips reflexed up; reddish purple (67A) upper surface; reddish purple (61B) lower surface; 27mm (1 1/16") long x 12mm (1/2") wide. TUBE: reddish purple (67A); medium length & thickness; 22mm (7/8") long x 8mm (5/16") wide. STAMENS: extend 24mm (15/16") below corolla; reddish purple (59B) filaments; dark reddish purple (59A) anthers. PISTIL: extends 46mm (1 13/16") below the corolla; dark reddish purple (60C) style; pale pink (62D) stigma. BUD: ovate. FOLIAGE: medium green (138A) upper surface; medium green (138B) lower surface. Leaves are 62mm (2 7/16") long x 42mm (1 5/8") wide, ovate shaped, serrulated edges, acute tips and cordate bases. Veins, stems & branches are red. PARENTAGE: ('Roesse Apus' x 'Rohees Izar') x 'Rohees Markab'. Natural trailer. Makes good basket. Prefers overhead filtered light and cool climate. Best bloom and foliage colour in filtered light. Tested 4 years in Knegsel, The Netherlands. Distinguished by bloom colour.
Roes 2003 NL AFS5323.

Roesse Mizar. Trailer. Double. COROLLA: quarter flared, smooth petal margins; opens rose (65A); matures light pink (65B); 27mm (1 1/16") long x 20mm (13/16") wide. SEPALS: half up; tips recurved up; pale lavender (65D) upper surface; light pink (65B) lower surface; 46mm (1 13/16") long x 14mm (9/16") wide. TUBE: cream (158D); medium length & thickness; 17mm (11/16") long x 6mm (1/4") wide. STAMENS: extend 10mm (3/8") below corolla; dark rose (54C) filaments & anthers. PISTIL: extends 28mm (1 1/8") below the corolla; pink (62C) style & stigma. BUD: ovate, pointed. FOLIAGE: dark green (137A) upper surface; medium green (137C) lower surface. Leaves are 74mm (2 15/16") long x 41mm (1 5/8") wide, ovate shaped, serrated edges, acute tips and rounded bases. Veins, stems & branches are

red. PARENTAGE: 'Sofie Michiels' x 'Allure'. Natural trailer. Makes good basket. Prefers overhead filtered light and cool climate. Best bloom and foliage colour in filtered light. Tested 4 years in Knegsel, The Netherlands. Distinguished by bloom & foliage combination.
Roes 2003 NL AFS5325.

Roesse Mulipheim. Upright. Semi Double. COROLLA: half flared, smooth petal margins; opens dark reddish purple (61A); matures dark reddish purple (60B); 21mm (13/16") long 25mm (1") wide. SEPALS: half up; tips recurved up; dark reddish purple (60B) upper surface; dark reddish purple (60A) lower surface; 22mm (13/16") long x 11mm (7/16") wide. TUBE: dark reddish purple (60B); medium length & thickness; 10mm (3/8") long x 6mm (1/4") wide. STAMENS: extend 10mm (3/8") below corolla; dark reddish purple (61A) filaments & anthers. PISTIL: extends 19mm (3/4") below the corolla; dark reddish purple (61A) style; magenta (61C) stigma. BUD: round, pointed. FOLIAGE: medium green (137B) upper surface; medium green (138A) lower surface. Leaves are 61mm (2 3/8") long x 34mm (1 5/16") wide, ovate shaped, serrated edges, acute tips and rounded bases. Red veins, stems & branches. PARENTAGE: 'Rohees Rana' x ('Roesse Apus' x 'Roesse Apus'). Small upright. Makes good upright or standard. Prefers overhead filtered light and cool climate. Best bloom and foliage colour in filtered light. Tested 4 years in Knegsel, The Netherlands. Distinguished by bloom colour.
Roes 2004 NL AFS5493.

Roesse Naiad. Trailer. Double. COROLLA is half flared; opens & matures pale rose (73D); 30mm (1 3/16") long x 26mm (1") wide. SEPALS are half up, tips recurved up; magenta (58B) upper surface; magenta (63A) lower surface; 31mm (1 1/4") long x 12mm (7/16") wide. TUBE is magenta (58B); 26mm (1") long x 6mm (1/4") wide. FOLIAGE: dark green (137A) upper surface; medium green (138A) lower surface. PARENTAGE: 'Luuk van Riet' x 'Roesse Betelgeuze'. Distinguished by bloom colour.
Roes 2006 NL AFS6148.

Roesse Nash. Upright/Trailer. Double. COROLLA is three quarter flared with smooth petal margins; opens dark purple (79A); matures purple (71A); 27mm (1 1/16") long x 29mm (1 1/8") wide. SEPALS are fully up, tips recurved; dark reddish purple (64A) upper surface, reddish purple (64B) lower

surface; 47mm (1 7/8") long x 16mm (5/8") wide. TUBE is dark reddish purple (64A); medium length and thickness; 18mm (11/16") long x 8mm (5/16") thick. STAMENS extend 38mm (1 1/2") beyond the corolla; dark purple (79A) filaments and anthers. PISTIL extends 47mm (1 7/8") beyond the corolla; reddish purple (67A) style, pale lavender (65D) stigma. BUD is ovate, pointed. FOLIAGE is medium green (137B) upper surface, medium green (138B) lower surface. Leaves are 68mm (2 11/16") long x 28mm (1 1/8") wide, lanceolate shaped, serrated edges, acute tips and acute bases. Veins, stems and branches are green. PARENTAGE: 'Rohees New Millennium' x 'Rohees King'. Lax upright or stiff trailer. Makes good stiff trailer. Prefers overhead filtered light and cool climate. Best bloom colour in filtered light. Tested four years in Knegsel, The Netherlands. Distinguished by bloom colour.
Roes 2002 UK AFS5036.

Roesse Nath. Upright/Trailer. Double. COROLLA: full flared, smooth petal margins; opens magenta (67B); matures dark rose (67C); 26mm (1") long x 29mm (1 1/8") wide. SEPALS: fully up; tips recurved; pale lavender (69D) upper surface; pale lavender (69C) lower surface; 34mm (1 5/16") long x 11mm (7/16") wide. TUBE: pale lavender (69D); medium length & thickness; 7mm (1/4") long x 4mm (3/16") wide. STAMENS: extend 15mm (9/16") below corolla; rose (65A) filaments; pink (62C) anthers. PISTIL: extends 27mm (1 1/16") below the corolla; light pink (65B) style; light yellow (11C) stigma. BUD: ovate. FOLIAGE: medium green (137B) upper surface; medium green (138B) lower surface. Leaves are 60mm (2 3/8") long x 45mm (1 3/4") wide, ovate shaped, serrated edges, acute tips and obtuse bases. Veins, stems & branches are red. PARENTAGE: 'Roesse Apus' x 'Allure'. Lax upright or stiff trailer. Makes good stiff trailer. Prefers overhead filtered light and cool climate. Best bloom and foliage colour in filtered light. Tested 4 years in Knegsel, The Netherlands. Distinguished by bloom & foliage combination.
Roes 2003 NL AFS5320.

Roesse Neper. Trailer. Single. COROLLA is half flared; opens magenta (63A); matures purple (77A); 16mm (5/8") long x 18mm (11/16") wide. SEPALS are horizontal, tips recurved; pale pink (62D) tipped green upper & lower surfaces; 33mm (1 5/16") long x 7mm (1/4") wide. TUBE is pale pink (62D);

17mm (5/8") long x 3mm (1/8") wide. FOLIAGE: dark green (137A) upper surface; medium green (137D) lower surface. PARENTAGE: ('Sofie Michiels' x 'Venus Victrix') x 'Lye's Unique'. Distinguished by bloom & foliage combination.
Roes 2006 NL AFS6180.

Roesse Norma. Upright/Trailer. Double. COROLLA is half flared with smooth petal margins; opens rose (68B), purple (83B) base; matures pink (62A), purple (74B) base; 17mm (11/16") long x 24mm (15/16") wide. SEPALS are half up, tips reflexed up; pink (62C) tipped green upper surface; rose (68C) tipped green lower surface; 32mm (1 1/4") long x 14mm (9/16") wide. TUBE is pink (62C); medium length & thickness; 8mm (5/16") long x 5mm (3/16") wide. FOLIAGE: dark green (137A) upper surface; medium green (137C) lower surface. Leaves are 76mm (3") long x 34mm (1 5/16") wide, lanceolate shaped. PARENTAGE: 'Roesse Menkhib' x 'Roesse Pandora'. Distinguished by bloom colour.
Roes 2005 NL AFS5968.

Roesse Oberon. Upright. Single. COROLLA is quarter flared; opens red (53B); matures red (53C); 12mm (7/16") long x 14mm (9/16") wide. SEPALS are half down, tips recurved; rose (65A) upper & lower surfaces; 24mm (15/'16") long x 9mm (3/8") wide. TUBE is white (155A); 8mm (5/16") long x 8mm (5/16") wide. FOLIAGE: medium green (137B) upper surface; medium green (137D) lower surface. PARENTAGE: 'Roesse Lupus' x 'Lustre'. Distinguished by bloom colour.
Roes 2006 NL AFS6140.

Roesse Octans. Upright/Trailer. Single. COROLLA is full flared with wavy petal margins; opens violet (84A); matures violet (77B); 25mm (1") long x 30mm (1 3/16") wide. SEPALS are fully up, tips recurved; magenta (58B) upper & lower surfaces; 27mm (1 1/16") long x 14mm (9/16") wide. TUBE is magenta (58B); medium length & thickness; 14mm (9/16") long x 6mm (3/16") wide. FOLIAGE: dark green (137A) upper surface; medium green (138A) lower surface. Leaves are 67mm (2 5/8") long x 32mm (1 1/4") wide, lanceolate shaped. PARENTAGE: 'Swanley Gem' x 'Roesse Menkhib'. Distinguished by bloom shape.
Roes 2005 NL AFS5932.

Roesse Odin. Upright/Trailer. Double. COROLLA: three quarter flared; opens purple (77A); matures purple (71A); 20mm (3/4")

long x 17mm (5/8") wide. SEPALS: half up, tips reflexed up; white (155D) upper & lower surfaces; 26mm (1") long x 12mm (7/16") wide. TUBE: white (155D); 46mm (1 13/16") long x 5mm (3/16") wide. FOLIAGE is dark green (137A) upper surface; medium green (137C) lower surface. PARENTAGE: 'Roesse Charon' x 'Roesse Ophelia'.
Roes 2008 NL AFS6903.

Roesse Oersted. Upright. Single. COROLLA is half flared; opens dark reddish purple (70A); matures reddish purple (67A); 15mm (9/16") long x 21mm (13/16") wide. SEPALS are fully up, tips reflexed; rose (68C) upper & lower surfaces; 22mm (7/8") long x 7mm (1/4") wide. TUBE is rose (68C); 16mm (5/8") long x 6mm (1/4") wide. FOLIAGE: medium green (137B) upper surface; medium green (138B) lower surface. PARENTAGE: 'Roesse Lupus' x ('Swanley Gem' x 'Eisvogel'). Distinguished by bloom & foliage combination.
Roes 2006 NL AFS6171.

Roesse Ophelia. Upright/Trailer. Single. COROLLA is full flared; opens violet (90C); matures dark purple (78A); 24mm (15/16") long x 32mm (1 1/4") wide. SEPALS are fully up, tips recurved; magenta (58B) upper & lower surfaces; 31mm (1 1/4") long x 16mm (5/8") wide. TUBE is magenta (58B); 6mm (1/4") long x 6mm (1/4") wide. FOLIAGE: dark green (137A) upper surface; medium green (137C) lower surface. PARENTAGE: 'Reg Gubler' x 'Maxima's Baby'. Distinguished by bloom shape & colour.
Roes 2006 NL AFS6181.

Roesse Pallas. Upright/Trailer. Single. COROLLA: Half flared; opens dark reddish purple (60C); matures reddish purple (60D); 14mm (9/16") long x 17mm (5/8") wide. SEPALS: horizontal, tips recurved; dark rose (55A) upper & lower surfaces; 24mm (15/16") long x 9mm (5/16") wide. TUBE: dark rose (55A); medium length, thick; 24mm (15/16") long x 10mm (3/8") wide. FOLIAGE is dark green (137A) upper surface; medium green (138A) lower surface. PARENTAGE: 'Roesse Lupus' x 'Roesse Apus'.
Roes 2007 NL AFS6692.

Roesse Pandora. Upright/Trailer. Semi Double. COROLLA: three quarter flared, smooth petal margins; opens purple (90A); matures purple (88A); 16mm (5/8") long 24mm (15/16") wide. SEPALS: half up; tips recurved up; light rose (63D) upper surface;

magenta (63B) lower surface; 27mm (1 1/16") long x 12mm (1/2") wide. TUBE: light rose (63D); medium length & thickness; 5mm (3/16") long x 5mm (3/16") wide. STAMENS: extend 12mm (1/2") below corolla; dark rose (64C) filaments; reddish purple (64B) anthers. PISTIL: extends 26mm (1") below the corolla; dark rose (64C) style; rose (64D) stigma. BUD: ovate, pointed. FOLIAGE: dark green (137A) upper surface; medium green (138B) lower surface. Leaves are 57mm (2 1/4") long x 32mm (1 1/4") wide, ovate shaped, serrated edges, acute tips and cordate bases. Green veins, stems & branches. PARENTAGE: 'Roesse Dione' x 'Delta's Bride'. Lax upright or stiff trailer. Makes good stiff trailer. Prefers overhead filtered light and cool climate. Best bloom and foliage colour in filtered light. Tested 4 years in Knegsel, The Netherlands. Distinguished by bloom colour.
Roes 2004 NL AFS5471.

Roesse Pavo. Upright/Trailer. Single. COROLLA is full flared with wavy petal margins; opens dark purple (86A); matures dark purple (78A); 17mm (11/16") long x 22mm (7/8") wide. SEPALS are fully up, tips recurved; rose (52B) upper surface; red (50A) lower surface; 24mm (15/16") long x 9mm (3/8") wide. TUBE is rose (52B); short & thick; 2mm (1/16") long x 3mm (1/8") wide. FOLIAGE: dark green (137A) upper surface; medium green (138A) lower surface. Leaves are 52mm (2 1/16") long x 27mm (1 1/16") wide, lanceolate shaped. PARENTAGE: 'Swanley Gem' x 'Roesse Pandora'. Distinguished by bloom shape.
Roes 2005 NL AFS5938.

Roesse Peacock. Upright/Trailer. Double. COROLLA is three quarter flared with smooth petal margins; opens dark purple (79A); matures purple (71A); 34mm (1 3/8") long x 34mm (1 3/8") wide. SEPALS are fully up, tips recurved; reddish purple (71B) upper surface, magenta (71C) lower surface; 46mm (1 13/16") long x 16mm (5/8") wide. TUBE is reddish purple (71B); medium length and thickness; 11mm (7/16") long x 6mm (1/4") thick. STAMENS extend 24mm (15/16") beyond the corolla; dark purple (79A) filaments and anthers. PISTIL extends 48mm (1 7/8") beyond the corolla; purple (77A) style, magenta (71C) stigma. BUD is ovate, pointed. FOLIAGE is medium green (137B) upper surface, medium green (138B) lower surface. Leaves are 74mm (2 15/16") long x 41mm (1 5/8") wide, ovate shaped, serrulated edges, acute tips and obtuse bases. Veins, stems and branches are green. PARENTAGE: 'Rohees New Millennium' x 'Rohees Queen'. Lax upright or stiff trailer. Makes good stiff trailer. Prefers overhead filtered light and cool climate. Best bloom colour in filtered light. Tested four years in Knegsel, The Netherlands. Distinguished by bloom and foliage combination. Roes 2002 NL AFS5037.

Roesse Perseus. Upright/Trailer. Semi Double. COROLLA is quarter flared with smooth petal margins; opens red (45A); matures orangy red (44C); 19mm (3/4") long x 12mm (1/2") wide. SEPALS are fully up, tips recurved; pink (52D) upper surface; rose (52C) lower surface; 18mm (11/16") long x 12mm (1/2") wide. TUBE is pink (52D); short & thick; 12mm (1/2") long x 8mm (5/16") wide. FOLIAGE: dark green (137A) upper surface; medium green (138B) lower surface. Leaves are 52mm (2 1/16") long x 44mm (1 3/4") wide, ovate shaped. PARENTAGE: ('Roesse Apus' x 'Roesse Apus') x 'Marcel Michiels'. Distinguished by bloom colour. Roes 2005 NL AFS5950.

Roesse Pherkad. Upright. Double. COROLLA: quarter flared, smooth petal margins; opens red (53D); matures red (52A); 14mm (9/16") long x 22mm (7/8") wide. SEPALS: horizontal; tips reflexed; pale pink (62D) upper surface; light pink (62B) lower surface; 25mm (1") long x 12mm (1/2") wide. TUBE: light green (145D); short & thick; 7mm (1/4") long x 7mm (1/4") wide. STAMENS: extend 5mm (3/16") below corolla; red (53D) filaments & anthers. PISTIL: extends 14mm (9/16") below the corolla; pink (52D) style; pale yellow (5D) stigma. BUD: ovate. FOLIAGE: medium green (137B) upper surface; medium green (137D) lower surface. Leaves are 67mm (2 5/8") long x 47mm (1 7/8") wide, ovate shaped, serrulated edges, acute tips and obtuse bases. Veins, stems & branches are red. PARENTAGE: 'Roesse Apus' x 'Roesse Apus'. Medium upright. Makes good standard. Prefers overhead filtered light and cool climate. Best bloom and foliage colour in filtered light. Tested 4 years in Knegsel, The Netherlands. Distinguished by erect blooms. Roes 2003 NL AFS5352.

Roesse Phoebe. Upright. Single. COROLLA is three quarter flared; opens purple (71A); matures reddish purple (71B); 16mm (5/8") long x 12mm (7/16") wide. SEPALS are fully up, tips recurved; light rose (68D) upper surface; rose (68B) lower surface; 22mm

(7/8") long x 9mm (3/8") wide. TUBE is light rose (68D); 12mm (7/16") long x 7mm (1/4") wide. FOLIAGE: dark green (137A) upper surface; medium green (138B) lower surface. PARENTAGE: ('Sofie Michiels' x 'Venus Victrix') x ('Sofie Michiels' x 'Roesse Apus'). Distinguished by bloom shape. Roes 2006 NL AFS6153.

Roesse Picard. Trailer. Single. COROLLA is half flared; opens red (53B); matures light reddish orange (42D); matures red (45A) & light reddish orange (42D); 19mm (3/4") long x 19mm (3/4") wide. SEPALS are horizontal, tips recurved; pale pink (62D) upper surface; light pink (62B) lower surface; 30mm (1 1/4") long x 7mm (1/4") wide. TUBE is greenish yellow (1D); 21mm (13/16") long x 3mm (1/8") wide. FOLIAGE: dark green (137A) upper surface; medium green (138A) lower surface. PARENTAGE: 'Roesse Lupus' x 'Roesse Rhea'. Distinguished by bloom colour. Roes 2006 NL AFS6178.

Roesse Pictor. Upright/Trailer. Semi Double. COROLLA is quarter flared with smooth petal margins; opens dark red (46A); matures red (53C); 14mm (9/16") long x 19mm (3/4") wide. SEPALS are fully up, tips recurved; light pink (38D) upper surface; dark rose (51A) lower surface; 21mm (13/16") long x 13mm (1/2") wide. TUBE is light pink (38D); short & thick; 10mm (3/8") long x 10mm (3/8") wide. FOLIAGE: dark green (137A) upper surface; medium green (138A) lower surface. Leaves are 57mm (2 1/4") long x 36mm (1 7/16") wide, ovate shaped. PARENTAGE: 'Roesse Carme' x 'Impala'. Distinguished by bloom & foliage combination. Roes 2005 NL AFS5948.

Roesse Pinius. Upright. Single. COROLLA is three quarter flared; opens magenta (57B); matures light magenta (57D); 9mm (3/8") long x 11mm (7/16") wide. SEPALS are half up, tips reflexed up; light rose (68D) tipped green upper surface; rose (68B) tipped green lower surface; 19mm (3/4") long x 9mm (3/8") wide. TUBE is light rose (68D); 16mm (5/8") long x 7mm (1/4") wide. FOLIAGE: dark green (137A) upper surface; medium green (138A) lower surface. PARENTAGE: 'Sofie Michiels' x 'Magda van Bets'. Distinguished by erect blooms. Roes 2006 NL AFS6131.

Roesse Piscus. Upright/Trailer. Double. COROLLA is three quarter flared with

smooth petal margins; opens violet (77B); matures light violet (77D); 21mm (13/16") long x 27mm (1 1/16") wide. SEPALS are fully up, tips recurved; rose (68B) upper surface; magenta (58B) lower surface; 44mm (1 3/4") long x 16mm (5/8") wide. TUBE is rose (68B); medium length & thickness; 14mm (9/16") long x 9mm (3/8") wide. FOLIAGE: dark green (139A) upper surface; medium green (138A) lower surface. Leaves are 69mm (2 11/16") long x 40mm (1 9/16") wide, ovate shaped. PARENTAGE: 'Sofie Michiels' x 'Roesse Svalocin'. Distinguished by bloom colour.
Roes 2005 NL AFS5966.

Roesse Plana. Upright/Trailer. Single. COROLLA is half flared; opens dark reddish purple (59A); matures dark reddish purple (60A); 14mm (9/16") long x 14mm (9/16") wide. SEPALS are half up, tips reflexed up; rose (61D) upper & lower surfaces; 24mm (15/16") long x 5mm (3/16") wide. TUBE is rose (61D); 29mm (1 1/8") long x 9mm (3/8") wide. FOLIAGE: medium green (137B) upper surface; medium green (138B) lower surface. PARENTAGE: 'Roesse Lupus' x 'Lye's Unique'. Distinguished by bloom & foliage combination.
Roes 200 6NL AFS6132.

Roesse Plato. Upright/Trailer. Double. COROLLA: Three quarter flared; opens violet (85A); matures violet (76A); 20mm (3/4") long x 26mm (1") wide. SEPALS: half up, tips reflexed up; pale violet (76D) upper & lower surfaces; 41mm (1 5/8") long x 20mm (3/4") wide. TUBE: pale violet (76D); medium length & thickness; 16mm (5/8") long x 6mm (1/4") wide. FOLIAGE is dark green (139A) upper surface; medium green (138A) lower surface. PARENTAGE: 'Sofie Michiels' x 'Silver Dawn'.
Roes 2007 NL AFS6690.

Roesse Pleione. Trailer. Double. COROLLA is full flared with smooth petal margins; opens purple (88A); matures reddish purple (80B); 22mm (7/8") long x 20mm (13/16") wide. SEPALS are fully up, tips reflexed; pale lavender (69D) upper surface, pale pink (69A) lower surface; 32mm (1 1/4") long x 13mm (1/2") wide. TUBE is pale lavender (69D); medium length and thickness; 17mm (11/16") long x 6mm (1/4") thick. STAMENS extend 32mm (1 1/4") beyond the corolla; light reddish purple (73A) filaments, magenta (63A) anthers. PISTIL extends 47mm (1 7/8") beyond the corolla; pale lavender (65D) style and stigma. BUD is ovate, pointed. FOLIAGE is dark green (137A) upper surface, medium

green (138B) lower surface. Leaves are 62mm (2 7/16") long x 33mm (1 5/16") wide, ovate shaped, smooth edges, acute tips and obtuse bases. Veins, stems and branches are red. PARENTAGE: ('Cameron Ryle' x 'Parasol') x 'Allure'. Natural trailer. Makes good basket. Prefers overhead filtered light and cool climate. Best bloom colour in filtered light. Tested four years in Knegsel, The Netherlands. Distinguished by bloom and foliage combination.
Roes 2002 NL AFS5038.

Roesse Portia. Upright/Trailer. Semi Double. COROLLA is three quarter flared; opens dark reddish purple (72A); matures reddish purple (64B); 11mm (7/16") long x 20mm (3/4") wide. SEPALS are half up, tips recurved up; rose (68B) upper & lower surfaces; 20mm (3/4") long x 11mm (7/16") wide. TUBE is light rose (68D); 12mm (7/16") long x 7mm (1/4") wide. FOLIAGE: medium green (137C) upper surface; medium green (138B) lower surface. PARENTAGE: [('Cameron Ryle' x 'Parasol') x 'Allure'] x 'Magda van Bets'. Distinguished by bloom colour.
Roes 2006 NL AFS6154.

Roesse Procius. Trailer. Single. COROLLA is half flared; opens red (45C); matures red (53D); 20mm (3/4") long x 18mm (11/16") wide. SEPALS are horizontal, tips recurved; rose (63C) upper & lower surfaces; 37mm (1 7/16") long x 10mm (3/8") wide. TUBE is light rose (63D); 14mm (9/16") long x 7mm (1/4") wide. FOLIAGE: medium green (137B) upper surface; medium green (138B) lower surface. PARENTAGE: 'Luuk van Riet' x 'Lye's Unique'. Distinguished by bloom & foliage combination.
Roes 2006 NL AFS6146.

Roesse Procyon. Upright/Trailer. Double. COROLLA is three quarter flared with smooth petal margins; opens violet (84A); matures reddish purple (64B); 28mm (1 1/8") long x 34mm (1 3/8") wide. SEPALS are fully up, tips reflexed; rose (63B) upper and lower surfaces; 28mm (1 1/16") long x 16mm (5/8") wide. TUBE is rose (63B); medium length and thickness; 12mm (1/2") long x 7mm (1/4") thick. STAMENS extend 22mm (7/8") beyond the corolla; rose (64D) filaments, pink (62A) anthers. PISTIL extends 47mm (1 7/8") beyond the corolla; rose (64D) style, pink (62A) stigma. BUD is round, pointed. FOLIAGE is dark green (137A) upper surface, medium green (138B) lower surface. Leaves are 66mm (2 5/8") long x 40mm (1

9/16") wide, ovate shaped, serrated edges, acute tips and rounded bases. Veins are green, stems are red, branches are green. PARENTAGE: {[('Bon Accord' x 'Bicentennial') x ('Vobeglo' x 'Dancing Flame')] x 'Rohees Alrami'} x 'Rohees King'. Lax upright or stiff trailer. Makes good stiff trailer. Prefers overhead filtered light and cool climate. Best bloom colour in filtered light. Tested four years in Knegsel, The Netherlands. Distinguished by bloom colour.
Roes 2002 NL AFS5027.

Roesse Proteus. Upright. Double. COROLLA is three quarter flared; opens dark reddish purple (59A); matures dark reddish purple (60B); 16mm (5/8") long x 21mm (13/16") wide. SEPALS are half up, tips reflexed up; dark reddish purple (60C) upper surface; dark reddish purple (60B) lower surface; 21mm (13/16") long x 14mm (9/16") wide. TUBE is dark reddish purple (60C); 12mm (7/16") long x 5mm (3/16") wide. FOLIAGE: dark green (137A) upper surface; medium green (138B) lower surface. PARENTAGE: 'Roesse Lupus' x 'Roesse Pandora'. Distinguished by bloom colour.
Roes 2006 NL AFS6137.

Roesse Puppis. Upright. Semi Double. COROLLA is three quarter flared with smooth petal margins; opens purple (77A); matures purple (71A); 15mm (9/16") long x 20mm (13/16") wide. SEPALS are fully up, tips reflexed; dark rose (58C) upper surface; magenta (58B) lower surface; 21mm (13/16") long x 12mm (1/2") wide. TUBE is dark rose (58C); short & thick; 9mm (3/8") long x 9mm (3/8") wide. FOLIAGE: dark green (137A) upper surface; medium green (137D) lower surface. Leaves are 65mm (2 9/16") long x 39mm (1 9/16") wide, ovate shaped. PARENTAGE: ('Roesse Carme' x 'Roesse Apus') x 'Roesse Svalocin'. Distinguished by erect bloom.
Roes 2005 NL AFS5959.

Roesse Regulus. Upright/Trailer. Single. COROLLA is full flared with smooth petal margins; opens purple (71A); matures reddish purple (59B); 24mm (15/16") long x 30mm (1 3/16") wide. SEPALS are fully up, tips recurved; dark reddish purple (60B) upper surface; dark reddish purple (60A) lower surface; 24mm (15/16") long x 11mm (7/16") wide. TUBE is dark reddish purple (60B); medium length and thickness; 8mm (5/16") long x 4mm (3/16") thick. STAMENS extend 22mm (7/8") beyond the corolla; purple (71A) filaments and anthers. PISTIL

extends 34mm (1 3/8") beyond the corolla; reddish purple (59B) style and stigma. BUD is ovate, pointed. FOLIAGE is dark green (137A) upper surface, medium green (138A) lower surface. Leaves are 71mm (2 13/16") long x 37mm (1 7/16") wide, ovate shaped, serrated edges, acute tips and obtuse bases. Veins, stems and branches are red. PARENTAGE: {[('Bon Accord' x 'Bicentennial) x ('Vobeglo' x 'Dancing Flame')] x 'Rohees Alrami'} x 'Swanley Gem'. Lax upright or stiff trailer. Makes good stiff trailer. Prefers overhead filtered light and cool climate. Best bloom colour in filtered light. Tested four years in Knegsel, The Netherlands. Distinguished by bloom colour.
Roes 2002 NL AFS5021.

Roesse Reinhold. Upright/Trailer. Semi Double. COROLLA: Half flared; opens violet (75A); matures pale purple (75C); 18mm (11/16") long x 16mm (5/8") wide. SEPALS: half up, tips reflexed up; light pink (65C) upper surface; light pink (65B) lower surface; 36mm (1 7/16") long x 11mm (7/16") wide. TUBE: light pink (65C); medium length & thickness; 15mm (9/16") long x 5mm (3/16") wide. FOLIAGE is medium green (137B) upper surface; medium green (138A) lower surface. PARENTAGE: 'Roesse Duck' x 'Sofie Michiels'.
Roes 2007 NL AFS6667.

Roesse Rhea. Upright/Trailer. Double. COROLLA: quarter flared, smooth petal margins; opens pale purple (75D); matures pale lavender (65D); 20mm (13/16") long 22mm (7/8") wide. SEPALS: fully up; tips recurved; pale pink (69A) upper surface; light purple (70C) lower surface; 49mm (1 15/16") long x 15mm (9/16") wide. TUBE: pale lavender (69B); medium length & thickness; 25mm (1") long x 6mm (1/4") wide. STAMENS: extend 12mm (1/2") below corolla; purple (71A) filaments & anthers. PISTIL: extends 46mm (1 13/16") below the corolla; pale purple (70D) style; yellowish white (4D) stigma. BUD: ovate, long, pointed. FOLIAGE: medium green (137B) upper surface; medium green (138B) lower surface. Leaves are 80mm (3 1/8") long x 37mm (1 7/16") wide, ovate shaped, serrated edges, acute tips and obtuse bases. Red veins, stems & branches. PARENTAGE: [('Cameron Ryle' x 'Parasol') x 'Allure'] x 'Impala'. Lax upright or stiff trailer. Makes good stiff trailer. Prefers overhead filtered light and cool climate. Best bloom and foliage colour in filtered light. Tested 4 years in Knegsel, The Netherlands. Distinguished by bloom colour.

Roes 2004 NL AFS5474.

Roesse Rigel. Upright. Single. COROLLA is three quarter flared with smooth petal margins; opens purple (77A); matures dark reddish purple (61A); 32mm (1 1/4") long x 34mm (1 3/8") wide. SEPALS are fully up, tips recurved; rose (68B) upper surface; magenta (68A) lower surface; 32mm (1 1/4") long x 20mm (13/16") wide. TUBE is rose (68B); short, medium thickness; 6mm (1/4") long x 6mm (1/4") thick. STAMENS extend 22mm (7/8") beyond the corolla; purple (71A) filaments and anthers. PISTIL extends 27mm (1 1/16") beyond the corolla; magenta (63B) style, pale orange (23D) stigma. BUD is round, pointed. FOLIAGE is dark green (137A) upper surface, medium green (138A) lower surface. Leaves are 57mm (2 1/4") long x 34mm (1 3/8") wide, ovate shaped, smooth edges, acute tips and rounded bases. Veins, stems and branches are red. PARENTAGE: {[('Bon Accord' x 'Bicentennial) x ('Vobeglo' x 'Dancing Flame')] x 'Rohees Alrami'} x 'Roesse Blacky'. Medium upright. Makes good standard. Prefers overhead filtered light and cool climate. Best bloom colour in filtered light. Tested four years in Knegsel, The Netherlands. Distinguished by bloom colour. Roes 2002 NL AFS5023.

Roesse Ritter. Upright. Single. COROLLA is quarter flared; opens & matures dark reddish purple (60C); 6mm (1/4") long x 7mm (1/4") wide. SEPALS are horizontal, tips recurved; light rose (63D) upper surface; rose (63C) lower surface; 19mm (3/4") long x 7mm (1/4") wide. TUBE is white (155A); 7mm (1/4") long x 5mm (3/16") wide. FOLIAGE: medium green (137B) upper surface; medium green (138B) lower surface. PARENTAGE: 'Roesse Lupus' x 'Lye's Unique'. Distinguished by bloom colour & shape.
Roes 2006 NL AFS6165.

Roesse Rutilicus. Upright/Trailer. Semi Double. COROLLA: half flared, smooth petal margins; opens purple (71A); matures dark reddish purple (61A); 22mm (7/8") long 26mm (1") wide. SEPALS: half up; tips reflexed up; rose (68B) upper surface; dark rose (67C) lower surface; 36mm (1 7/16") long x 14mm (9/16") wide. TUBE: light rose (68D); medium length & thickness; 17mm (11/16") long x 9mm (3/8") wide. STAMENS: extend 12mm (1/2") below corolla; magenta (63B) filaments; dark reddish purple (60C) anthers. PISTIL: extends 34mm (1 5/16") below the corolla; reddish purple (64B) style;

yellowish white (4D) stigma. BUD: cordate, pointed. FOLIAGE: dark green (137A) upper surface; medium green (138B) lower surface. Leaves are 72mm (2 13/16") long x 47mm (1 7/8") wide, ovate shaped, serrulated edges, acute tips and obtuse bases. Green veins, stems & branches. PARENTAGE: ('Cameron Ryle' x 'Parasol') x 'Rohees Izar'. Lax upright or stiff trailer. Makes good stiff trailer. Prefers overhead filtered light and cool climate. Best bloom and foliage colour in filtered light. Tested 4 years in Knegsel, The Netherlands. Distinguished by bloom colour. Roes 2004 NL AFS5483.

Roesse Sabine. Upright. Single. COROLLA is quarter flared; opens dark reddish purple (64A); matures reddish purple (64B); 11mm (7/16") long x 11mm (7/16") wide. SEPALS are horizontal, tips recurved; dark rose (58C) upper surface; magenta (58B) lower surface; 19mm (3/4") long x 6mm (1/4") wide. TUBE is dark rose (58C); 16mm (5/8") long x 7mm (1/4") wide. FOLIAGE: medium green (137A) upper surface; medium green (138B) lower surface. PARENTAGE: 'Rosea' x 'Lye's Unique'. Distinguished by bloom & foliage combination.
Roes 2006 NL AFS6164.

Roesse Sadalsud. Upright/Trailer. Single. COROLLA: three quarter flared, smooth petal margins; opens violet (92B); matures violet (75A); 30mm (1 3/16") long x 32mm (1 1/4") wide. SEPALS: fully up; tips reflexed; rose (67D) upper surface; rose (68B) lower surface; 31mm (1 1/4") long x 17mm (11/16") wide. TUBE: rose (67D); short & thick; 8mm (5/16") long x 7mm (1/4") wide. STAMENS: extend 17mm (11/16") below corolla; magenta (67B) filaments & anthers. PISTIL: extends 38mm (1 1/2") below the corolla; light rose (68D) style; pale rose (73D) stigma. BUD: round, pointed. FOLIAGE: dark green (137A) upper surface; medium green (138A) lower surface. Leaves are 54mm (2 1/8") long x 37mm (1 7/16") wide, cordate shaped, serrulated edges, acute tips and rounded bases. Veins, stems & branches are red. PARENTAGE: 'Madalyn Drago' x ('Sofie Michiels' x 'Lechlade Rocket'). Lax upright or stiff trailer. Makes good stiff trailer. Prefers overhead filtered light and cool climate. Best bloom and foliage colour in filtered light. Tested 4 years in Knegsel, The Netherlands. Distinguished by bloom colour. Roes 2003 NL AFS5334.

Roesse Saiph. Upright. Single. COROLLA is full flared with smooth petal margins; opens

dark reddish purple (72A); matures reddish purple (64B); 28mm (1 1/8") long x 32mm (1 1/4") wide. SEPALS are fully up, tips recurved; pale pink (62D) upper surface; light rose (63D) lower surface; 37mm (1 7/16") long x 12mm (1/2") wide. TUBE is rose (63C); medium length and thickness; 7mm (1/4") long x 6mm (1/4") thick. STAMENS extend 27mm (1 1/16") beyond the corolla; magenta (58B) filaments, reddish purple (59B) anthers. PISTIL extends 34mm (1 3/8") beyond the corolla; light rose (58D) style, pale yellow (2D) stigma. BUD is ovate, pointed. FOLIAGE is dark green (137A) upper surface, medium green (138B) lower surface. Leaves are 61mm (2 7/16") long x 24mm (15/16") wide, lanceolate shaped, serrated edges, acute tips and acute bases. Veins, stems and branches are red. PARENTAGE: {[('Bon Accord' x 'Bicentennial') x ('Vobeglo' x 'Dancing Flame')] x 'Rohees Alrami'} x 'Rohees Princess'. Medium upright. Makes good standard. Prefers overhead filtered light and cool climate. Best bloom colour in filtered light. Tested four years in Knegsel, The Netherlands. Distinguished by bloom and foliage combination.
Roes 2002 NL AFS5020.

Roesse Sarin. Upright. Semi Double. COROLLA is half flared with smooth petal margins; opens dark purple (79A); matures dark reddish purple (59A); 22mm (7/8") long x 20mm (13/16") wide. SEPALS are fully up, tips recurved; reddish purple (61B) upper and lower surfaces; 29mm (1 1/8") long x 15mm (5/8") wide. TUBE is reddish purple (61B); medium length and thickness; 17mm (11/16") long x 6mm (1/4") thick. STAMENS extend 24mm (15/16") beyond the corolla; reddish purple (59B) filaments, dark purple (79A) anthers. PISTIL extends 42mm (1 11/16") beyond the corolla; reddish purple (59B) style, light rose (63D) stigma. BUD is elliptic, pointed. FOLIAGE is medium green (137B) upper surface, medium green (138B) lower surface. Leaves are 76mm (3") long x 41mm (1 5/8") wide, ovate shaped, serrated edges, acute tips and obtuse bases. Veins, stems and branches are red. PARENTAGE: {[('Bon Accord' x 'Bicentennial') x ('Vobeglo' x 'Dancing Flame')] x 'Rohees Alrami'} x 'Roesse Blacky'. Tall upright. Makes good standard. Prefers overhead filtered light and cool climate. Best bloom colour in filtered light. Tested four years in Knegsel, The Netherlands. Distinguished by bloom colour.
Roes 2002 NL AFS5032.

Roesse Sceptrum. Upright. Double. COROLLA: three quarter flared, smooth petal margins; opens purple (77A); matures reddish purple (64B); 30mm (1 3/16") long x 36mm (1 7/16") wide. SEPALS: half up; tips reflexed up; reddish purple (61B) upper surface; magenta (63B) lower surface; 34mm (1 5/16") long x 16mm (5/8") wide. TUBE: reddish purple (61B); short & thick; 14mm (9/16") long x 10mm (3/8") wide. STAMENS: extend 26mm (1") below corolla; reddish purple (64B) filaments; dark reddish purple (59A) anthers. PISTIL: extends 51mm (2") below the corolla; dark rose (64C) style; light yellow (4C) stigma. BUD: round, pointed. FOLIAGE: medium green (137B) upper surface; medium green (138B) lower surface. Leaves are 80mm (3 1/8") long x 41mm (1 5/8") wide, ovate shaped, serrulated edges, acute tips and rounded bases. Veins, stems & branches are red. PARENTAGE: 'Roesse Apus' x 'Miniskirt'. Medium upright. Makes good standard. Prefers overhead filtered light and cool climate. Best bloom and foliage colour in filtered light. Tested 4 years in Knegsel, The Netherlands. Distinguished by bloom colour.
Roes 2003 NL AFS5346.

Roesse Scheat. Upright/Trailer. Double. COROLLA: quarter flared, smooth petal margins; opens dark reddish purple (72A) & coral (39B); matures dark reddish purple (70A) & coral (39B); 32mm (1 1/4") long x 32mm (1 1/4") wide. SEPALS: fully up; tips recurved; pink (52D) upper surface; rose (52C) lower surface; 42mm (1 11/16") long x 16mm (5/8") wide. TUBE: pink (52D); medium length & thickness; 14mm (9/16") long x 8mm (5/16") wide. STAMENS: extend 7mm (1/4") below corolla; dark rose (51A) filaments; dark red (53A) anthers. PISTIL: extends 32mm (1 1/4") below the corolla; rose (47D) style; light yellow (11C) stigma. BUD: ovate. FOLIAGE: dark green (137A) upper surface; medium green (138B) lower surface. Leaves are 67mm (2 5/8") long x 40mm (1 9/16") wide, ovate shaped, serrulated edges, acute tips and rounded bases. Veins, stems & branches are red. PARENTAGE: 'Roesse Apus' x 'Bicentennial'. Lax upright or stiff trailer. Makes good stiff trailer. Prefers overhead filtered light and cool climate. Best bloom and foliage colour in filtered light. Tested 4 years in Knegsel, The Netherlands. Distinguished by bloom colour.
Roes 2003 NL AFS5324.

Roesse Schedir. Upright. Single. COROLLA: quarter flared, smooth petal margins; opens

dark reddish purple (61A); matures dark reddish purple (60B); 24mm (15/16") long x 22mm (7/8") wide. SEPALS: fully up; tips recurved; magenta (63B) upper surface; dark reddish purple (60B) lower surface; 21mm (13/16") long x 9mm (3/8") wide. TUBE: rose (63C); medium length & thickness; 17mm (11/16") long x 6mm (1/4") wide. STAMENS: extend 11mm (7/16") below corolla; pink (62A) filaments; dark reddish purple (60C) anthers. PISTIL: extends 14mm (9/16") below the corolla; pink (62A) style; cream (11D) stigma. BUD: ovate. FOLIAGE: dark green (137A) upper surface; medium green (137C) lower surface. Leaves are 52mm (2 1/16") long x 42mm (1 11/16") wide, ovate shaped, serrulated edges, acute tips and rounded bases. Veins, stems & branches are green. PARENTAGE: ('Vobeglo' x 'Dancing Flame') x ['Roesse Apus' x ('Foline' x 'Dancing Flame')]. Medium upright. Makes good standard. Prefers overhead filtered light and cool climate. Best bloom and foliage colour in filtered light. Tested 4 years in Knegsel, The Netherlands. Distinguished by bloom colour.
Roes 2003 NL AFS5344.

Roesse Scorpius. Upright/Trailer. Double. COROLLA is half flared with smooth petal margins; opens pale lavender (69C); matures pale lavender (69D); 18mm (11/16") long x 26mm (1") wide. SEPALS are half up, tips reflexed up; pale pink (36D) upper & lower surfaces; 27mm (1 1/16") long x 18mm (11/16") wide. TUBE is pale pink (36D); medium length & thickness; 26mm (1") long x 6mm (1/4") wide. FOLIAGE: medium green (137B) upper surface; medium green (138B) lower surface. Leaves are 62mm (2 7/16") long x 35mm (1 3/8") wide, ovate shaped. PARENTAGE: ('Sofie Michiels' x 'Rohees New Millennium') x 'Magda Vanbets'. Distinguished by bloom & foliage combination.
Roes 2005 NL AFS5955.

Roesse Scutum. Upright/Trailer. Double. COROLLA is three quarter flared with smooth petal margins; opens light purple (75B); matures pale purple (75D); 12mm (1/2") long x 21mm (13/16") wide. SEPALS are horizontal, tips recurved; dark rose (58C) upper surface; magenta (58B) lower surface; 27mm (1 1/16") long x 14mm (9/16") wide. TUBE is dark rose (58C); long & thin; 30mm (1 3/16") long x 4mm (3/16") wide. FOLIAGE: dark green (137A) upper surface; medium green (138B) lower surface. Leaves are 68mm (2 11/16") long x 33mm (1 5/16") wide, lanceolate shaped. PARENTAGE: ('Sofie

Michiels' x 'Rohees New Millennium') x 'Luuk van Riet'. Distinguished by bloom colour & shape.
Roes 2005 NL AFS5941.

Roesse Serpens. Upright. Single. COROLLA is half flared with wavy petal margins; opens dark reddish purple (72A); matures magenta (71C); 24mm (15/16") long x 32mm (1 1/4") wide. SEPALS are fully up, tips recurved; dark rose (58C) upper surface; magenta (58B) lower surface; 44mm (1 3/4") long x 18mm (11/16") wide. TUBE is dark rose (58C); medium length & thickness; 20mm (13/16") long x 7mm (1/4") wide. FOLIAGE: dark green (137A) upper surface; medium green (138A) lower surface. Leaves are 62mm (2 7/16") long x 40mm (1 9/16") wide, cordate shaped. PARENTAGE: 'WALZ Mandoline' x 'Roesse Menkhib'. Distinguished by bloom & foliage combination.
Roes 2005 NL AFS5963.

Roesse Sextans. Upright. Single. COROLLA is quarter flared with smooth petal margins; opens dark orange (33A); matures orange (33C); 18mm (11/16") long x 16mm (5/8") wide. SEPALS are horizontal, tips recurved; rose (51C) upper & lower surfaces; 16mm (5/8") long x 9mm (3/8") wide. TUBE is rose (51C); medium length & thickness; 9mm (3/8") long x 6mm (1/4") wide. FOLIAGE: dark green (137A) upper surface; medium green (137D) lower surface. Leaves are 48mm (1 7/8") long x 36mm (1 7/16") wide, ovate shaped. PARENTAGE: 'Roesse Apus' x ('Swanley Gem' x 'Eisvogel'). Distinguished by bloom & foliage combination.
Roes 2005 NL AFS5956.

Roesse Sham. Trailer. Double. COROLLA is three quarter flared with smooth petal margins; opens violet (76A); matures light purple (78B); 32mm (1 1/4") long x 21mm (13/16") wide. SEPALS are half up, tips recurved up; pale lavender (65D) upper surface, light pink (65B) lower surface; 42mm (1 11/16") long x 18mm (11/16") wide. TUBE is pale lavender (65D); medium length and thickness; 11mm (7/16") long x 6mm (1/4") thick. STAMENS extend 17mm (11/16") beyond the corolla; pink (62C) filaments, light rose (73B) anthers. PISTIL extends 41mm (1 5/8") beyond the corolla; pale pink (62D) style, pale lavender (65D) stigma. BUD is ovate, pointed. FOLIAGE is dark green (137A) upper surface, medium green (138B) lower surface. Leaves are70mm (2 3/4") long x 36mm (1 7/16") wide, ovate

shaped, serrated edges, acute tips and acute bases. Veins, stems and branches are green. PARENTAGE: {[('Bon Accord' x 'Bicentennial') x ('Vobeglo' x 'Dancing Flame')] x 'Rohees Alrami'} x 'Miniskirt'. Natural trailer. Makes good basket. Prefers overhead filtered light and cool climate. Best bloom colour in filtered light. Tested four years in Knegsel, The Netherlands. Distinguished by bloom and foliage combination.
Roes 2002 NL AFS5031.

Roesse Sharp. Upright/Trailer. Double. COROLLA: Three quarter flared; opens violet blue (91A); matures violet (85B); 20mm (3/4") long x 23mm (7/8") wide. SEPALS: half up, tips recurved up; white (155D) upper & lower surfaces; 31mm (1 1/4") long x 12mm (7/16") wide. TUBE: white (155D); medium length & thickness; 13mm (1/2") long x 6mm (1/4") wide. FOLIAGE is dark green (137A) upper surface; medium green (137C) lower surface. PARENTAGE: 'Sofie Michiels' x 'Roesse Ophelia'.
Roes 2007 NL AFS6684.

Roesse Shaula. Upright/Trailer. Double. COROLLA: half flared, smooth petal margins; opens dark reddish purple (59A); matures dark reddish purple (59B); 24mm (15/16") long x 24mm (15/16") wide. SEPALS: fully up; tips recurved; magenta (63A) upper & lower surfaces; 25mm (1") long x 15mm (9/16") wide. TUBE: magenta (63A); medium length & thickness; 17mm (11/16") long x 5mm (3/16") wide. STAMENS: extend 21mm (13/16") below corolla; reddish purple (59B) filaments; dark reddish purple (59A) anthers. PISTIL: extends 21mm (13/16") below the corolla; reddish purple (59B) style; pale pink (62D) stigma. BUD: round. FOLIAGE: dark green (137A) upper surface; medium green (137C) lower surface. Leaves are 82mm (3 1/4") long x 44mm (1 3/4") wide, ovate shaped, serrated edges, acute tips and obtuse bases. Veins, stems & branches are green. PARENTAGE: 'Roesse Apus' x 'Roesse Blacky'. Natural trailer. Makes good basket. Prefers overhead filtered light and cool climate. Best bloom and foliage colour in filtered light. Tested 4 years in Knegsel, The Netherlands. Distinguished by bloom & foliage combination.
Roes 2003 NL AFS5315.

Roesse Sheliak. Upright. Single. COROLLA: half flared, smooth petal margins; opens purple (71A); matures reddish purple (64B); 17mm (11/16") long x 21mm (13/16") wide. SEPALS: fully up; tips reflexed; rose (68B)

upper surface; magenta (68A) lower surface; 32mm (1 1/4") long x 12mm (1/2") wide. TUBE: pale yellow (1D); medium length & thickness; 12mm (1/2") long x 7mm (1/4") wide. STAMENS: extend 17mm (11/16") below corolla; magenta (68A) filaments; magenta (61C) anthers. PISTIL: extends 27mm (1 1/16") below the corolla; magenta (68A) style; white (155A) stigma. BUD: cordate. FOLIAGE: medium green (137C) upper surface; medium green (138B) lower surface. Leaves are 74mm (2 15/16") long x 38mm (1 1/2") wide, ovate shaped, serrated edges, acute tips and acute bases. Veins, stems & branches are green. PARENTAGE: 'Roesse Apus' x 'Orange Crush'. Medium upright. Makes good standard. Prefers overhead filtered light and cool climate. Best bloom and foliage colour in filtered light. Tested 4 years in Knegsel, The Netherlands. Distinguished by bloom colour.
Roes 2003 NL AFS5312.

Roesse Sheratan. Upright. Semi Double. COROLLA: half flared, smooth petal margins; opens purple (71A); matures reddish purple (64B); 20mm (13/16") long x 32mm (1 1/4") wide. SEPALS: half up; tips reflexed up; rose (65A) upper surface; pink (62A) lower surface; 34mm (1 5/16") long x 14mm (9/16") wide. TUBE: rose (65A); medium length & thickness; 12mm (1/2") long x 6mm (1/4") wide. STAMENS: extend 14mm (9/16") below corolla; dark reddish purple (64A) filaments; purple (71A) anthers. PISTIL: extends 26mm (1") below the corolla; dark reddish purple (64A) style; light yellow (11C) stigma. BUD: round, pointed. FOLIAGE: dark green (137A) upper surface; medium green (138A) lower surface. Leaves are 60mm (2 3/8") long x 41mm (1 5/8") wide, cordate shaped, serrulated edges, acute tips and cordate bases. Veins, stems & branches are red. PARENTAGE: 'Roesse Apus' x 'Bicentennial'. Medium upright. Makes good standard. Prefers overhead filtered light and cool climate. Best bloom and foliage colour in filtered light. Tested 4 years in Knegsel, The Netherlands. Distinguished by bloom & foliage combination.
Roes 2003 NL AFS5326.

Roesse Sinope. Trailer. Double. COROLLA: half flared, smooth petal margins; opens purple (83A); matures dark reddish purple (64A); 24mm (15/16") long 31mm (1 1/4") wide. SEPALS: half up; tips recurved up; pale rose (73D) upper surface; reddish purple (70B) lower surface; 48mm (1 7/8") long x 16mm (5/8") wide. TUBE: pale rose (73D);

long & thin; 42mm (1 5/8") long x 6mm (1/4") wide. STAMENS: extend 18mm (11/16") below corolla; dark reddish purple (64A) filaments; reddish purple (64B) anthers. PISTIL: extends 27mm (1 1/16") below the corolla; dark reddish purple (64A) style; yellowish white (4D) stigma. BUD: cordate, pointed. FOLIAGE: medium green (137B) upper surface; medium green (138B) lower surface. Leaves are 64mm (2 1/2") long x 26mm (1") wide, lanceolate shaped, serrulated edges, acute tips and acute bases. Red veins, stems & branches. PARENTAGE: Roesse Elara' x [('Cameron Ryle' x 'Parasol') x 'Allure']. Natural trailer. Self branching. Makes good basket. Prefers overhead filtered light and cool climate. Best bloom and foliage colour in filtered light. Tested 4 years in Knegsel, The Netherlands. Distinguished by bloom shape and colour.
Roes 2004 NL AFS5478.

Roesse Sirius. Upright/Trailer. Semi Double. COROLLA: three quarter flared, smooth petal margins; opens dark purple (79A); matures dark reddish purple (59A); 32mm (1 1/4") long x 38mm (1 1/2") wide. SEPALS: half up; tips reflexed up; magenta (63B) upper surface; magenta (63A) lower surface; 26mm (1") long x 12mm (1/2") wide. TUBE: magenta (63B); short & thick; 12mm (1/2") long x 8mm (5/16") wide. STAMENS: extend 17mm (11/16") below corolla; magenta (59C) filaments; light pink (62B) anthers. PISTIL: extends 28mm (1 1/8") below the corolla; magenta (59C) style & stigma. BUD: ovate, pointed. FOLIAGE: medium green (137B) upper surface; medium green (138A) lower surface. Leaves are 56mm (2 3/16") long x 32mm (1 1/4") wide, ovate shaped, serrulated edges, acute tips and rounded bases. Veins, stems & branches are red. PARENTAGE: 'Roesse Apus' x 'Rohees Princess'. Lax upright or stiff trailer. Makes good stiff trailer. Prefers overhead filtered light and cool climate. Best bloom and foliage colour in filtered light. Tested 4 years in Knegsel, The Netherlands. Distinguished by bloom colour.
Roes 2003 NL AFS5345.

Roesse Sirrah. Upright/Trailer. Double. COROLLA: three quarter flared, smooth petal margins; opens purple (83A); matures purple (71A); 26mm (1") long x 26mm (1") wide. SEPALS: fully up; tips reflexed; pale lavender (69C) upper surface; rose (65A) lower surface; 36mm (1 7/16") long x 12mm (1/2") wide. TUBE: pale pink (69A); medium length & thickness; 16mm (5/8") long x 7mm (1/4")

wide. STAMENS: extend 16mm (5/8") below corolla; magenta (71C) filaments; purple (83A) anthers. PISTIL: extends 23mm (15/16") below the corolla; magenta (71C) style; cream (11D) stigma. BUD: ovate, pointed. FOLIAGE: medium green (137B) upper surface; medium green (137B) lower surface. Leaves are 70mm (3 3/4") long x 36mm (1 7/16") wide, ovate shaped, serrulated edges, acute tips and rounded bases. Veins, stems & branches are green. PARENTAGE: 'Roesse Apus' x 'Swanley Gem'. Lax upright or stiff trailer. Makes good stiff trailer. Prefers overhead filtered light and cool climate. Best bloom and foliage colour in filtered light. Tested 4 years in Knegsel, The Netherlands. Distinguished by bloom colour.
Roes 2003 NL AFS5347.

Roesse Skat. Trailer. Double. COROLLA: three quarter flared, smooth petal margins; opens dark purple (79B); matures dark reddish purple (64A); 36mm (1 7/16") long x 36mm (1 7/16") wide. SEPALS: fully up; tips recurved; pale purple (75C) upper surface; light purple (74C) lower surface; 32mm (1 1/4") long x 15mm (9/16") wide. TUBE: pale purple (75D); medium length & thickness; 8mm (5/16") long x 6mm (1/4") wide. STAMENS: extend 29mm (1 1/8") below corolla; rose (64D) filaments; dark reddish purple (59A) anthers. PISTIL: extends 46mm (1 13/16") below the corolla; rose (64D) style; pale lavender (65D) stigma. BUD: round. FOLIAGE: medium green (137B) upper surface; medium green (138B) lower surface. Leaves are 66mm (2 5/8") long x 46mm (1 13/16") wide, cordate shaped, smooth edges, acute tips and obtuse bases. Veins, stems & branches are green. PARENTAGE: 'Roesse Apus' x ('Rohees Queen' x 'Sofie Michiels'). Natural trailer. Makes good basket. Prefers overhead filtered light and cool climate. Best bloom and foliage colour in filtered light. Tested 4 years in Knegsel, The Netherlands. Distinguished by bloom colour.
Roes 2003 NL AFS5348.

Roesse Spica. Upright/Trailer. Single. COROLLA: half flared, smooth petal margins; opens reddish purple (70B); matures magenta (63B); 28mm (1 1/8") long x 34mm (1 5/16") wide. SEPALS: fully up; tips recurved; pink (62C) upper surface; pink (62A) lower surface; 27mm (1 1/16") long x 17mm (11/16") wide. TUBE: pale yellow green (150D); medium length & thickness; 12mm (1/2") long x 7mm (1/4") wide. STAMENS: extend 14mm (9/16") below corolla; magenta (63B) filaments; magenta

(63A) anthers. PISTIL: extends 27mm (1 1/16") below the corolla; pink (62C) style; yellowish white (4D) stigma. BUD: round, pointed. FOLIAGE: dark green (137A) upper surface; medium green (137C) lower surface. Leaves are 67mm (2 5/8") long x 41mm (1 5/8") wide, ovate shaped, serrulated edges, acute tips and obtuse bases. Veins, stems & branches are red. PARENTAGE: 'Roesse Apus' x 'Miniskirt'. Lax upright or stiff trailer. Makes good upright or stiff trailer Prefers overhead filtered light and cool climate. Best bloom and foliage colour in filtered light. Tested 4 years in Knegsel, The Netherlands. Distinguished by bloom colour.
Roes 2003 NL AFS5349.

Roesse Stadius. Upright/Trailer. Single. COROLLA: Three quarter flared; opens violet (84A); matures violet (85A); 20mm (3/4") long x 26mm (1") wide. SEPALS: fully up, tips recurved; magenta (63B) upper & lower surfaces; 37mm (1 7/16") long x 10mm (3/8") wide. TUBE: Magenta (63B); medium length & thickness; 8mm (5/16") long x 4mm (1/8") wide. FOLIAGE is dark green (137A) upper surface; medium green (137C) lower surface. PARENTAGE: 'Reg Gubler' x 'Silver Dawn'
Roes 2007 NL AFS6669.

Roesse Subra. Upright/Trailer. Single. COROLLA: three quarter flared, smooth petal margins; opens violet (90C); matures light purple (78B); 32mm (1 1/4") long x 32mm (1 1/4") wide. SEPALS: half up; tips recurved up; magenta (58B) upper & lower surface; 32mm (1 1/4") long x 12mm (1/2") wide. TUBE: magenta (58B); medium length & thickness; 11mm (7/16") long x 6mm (1/4") wide. STAMENS: extend 21mm (13/16") below corolla; magenta (63B) filaments; magenta (63A) anthers. PISTIL: extends 43mm (1 11/16") below the corolla; rose (64D) style; cream (11D) stigma. BUD: cordate. FOLIAGE: dark green (137A) upper surface; medium green (138A) lower surface. Leaves are 67mm (2 5/8") long x 32mm (1 1/4") wide, lanceolate shaped, serrulated edges, acute tips and rounded bases. Veins, stems & branches are green. PARENTAGE: 'Swanley Gem' x 'Sofie Michiels'. Lax upright or stiff trailer. Makes good stiff trailer Prefers overhead filtered light and cool climate. Best bloom and foliage colour in filtered light. Tested 4 years in Knegsel, The Netherlands. Distinguished by bloom colour.
Roes 2003 NL AFS5350.

Roesse Sudri. Upright. Double. COROLLA: three quarter flared; opens & matures rose

(68B); 23mm (7/8") long x 24mm (15/16") wide. SEPALS: fully up, tips reflexed; magenta (58B) upper surface; purple (71A) lower surface; 25mm (1") long x 11mm (7/16") wide. TUBE: magenta (58B); 20mm (3/4") long x 8mm (5/16") wide. FOLIAGE is dark green (137A) upper surface; medium green (137B) lower surface. PARENTAGE: ('Cameron Ryle' x 'Parasol') x 'Maori Maid'.
Roes 2008 NL AFS6909.

Roesse Sulaphat. Upright. Semi Double. COROLLA: quarter flared, smooth petal margins; opens dark red (46A); matures red (45B); 17mm (11/16") long 17mm (11/16") wide. SEPALS: half up; tips reflexed; rose (52C) upper surface; rose (47D) lower surface; 21mm (13/16") long x 17mm (11/16") wide. TUBE: rose (52C); short & thick; 6mm (1/4") long x 6mm (1/4") wide. STAMENS: extend 17mm (11/16") below corolla; rose (68C) filaments & anthers. PISTIL: extends 31mm (1 1/4") below the corolla; rose (68C) style; light pink (65C) stigma. BUD: ovate, pointed. FOLIAGE: dark green (137A) upper surface; medium green (138B) lower surface. Leaves are 66mm (2 5/8") long x 42mm (1 11/16") wide, cordate shaped, serrulated edges, acute tips and rounded bases. Red veins, stems & branches. PARENTAGE: 'Roesse Apus' x 'Rohees Izar'. Medium upright. Makes good standard. Prefers overhead filtered light and cool climate. Best bloom and foliage colour in filtered light. Tested 4 years in Knegsel, The Netherlands. Distinguished by bloom and foliage combination.
Roes 2004 NL AFS5468.

Roesse Svalocin. Upright. Double. COROLLA: three quarter flared, smooth petal margins; opens purple (83A); matures violet (83D); 24mm (15/16") long 27mm (1 1/16") wide. SEPALS: half up; tips recurved up; reddish purple (74B) upper surface; reddish purple (74A) lower surface; 37mm (1 7/16") long x 15mm (9/16") wide. TUBE: reddish purple (74B); medium length & thickness; 17mm (11/16") long x 8mm (5/16") wide. STAMENS: extend 14mm (9/16") below corolla; purple (71A) filaments & anthers. PISTIL: extends 27mm (1 1/16") below the corolla; reddish purple (71B) style; magenta (71C) stigma. BUD: ovate, pointed. FOLIAGE: dark green (137A) upper surface; medium green (137D) lower surface. Leaves are 74mm (2 15/16") long x 42mm (1 5/8") wide, ovate shaped, serrulated edges, acute tips and rounded bases. Green veins, stems & branches. PARENTAGE: ('Roesse Apus' x

402

'Rohees Izar) x "Roesse Blacky'. Medium upright. Makes good upright or standard. Prefers overhead filtered light and cool climate. Best bloom and foliage colour in filtered light. Tested 4 years in Knegsel, The Netherlands. Distinguished by bloom colour. Roes 2004 NL AFS5482.

Roesse Tabit. Trailer. Double. COROLLA: three quarter flared, smooth petal margins; opens violet (90C); matures dark violet (87A); 18mm (11/16") long x 16mm (5/8") wide. SEPALS: half up; tips reflexed up; light greenish white (157D) upper & lower surfaces; 27mm (1 1/16") long x 14mm (9/16") wide. TUBE: rose (63C); medium length & thickness; 22mm (7/8") long x 7mm (1/4") wide. STAMENS: extend 12mm (1/2") below corolla; pink (62A) filaments & anthers. PISTIL: extends 22mm (7/8") below the corolla; pink (62C) style; light yellow (11C) stigma. BUD: round. FOLIAGE: dark green (137A) upper surface; medium green (138A) lower surface. Leaves are 60mm (2 3/8") long x 35mm (1 3/8") wide, ovate shaped, serrulated edges, acute tips and rounded bases. Veins, stems & branches are green. PARENTAGE: 'Rohees New Millennium' x 'Tatjana'. Natural trailer. Makes good basket. Prefers overhead filtered light and cool climate. Best bloom and foliage colour in filtered light. Tested 4 years in Knegsel, The Netherlands. Distinguished by bloom colour. Roes 2003 NL AFS5313.

Roesse Taygeta. Upright/Trailer. Double. COROLLA: quarter flared, smooth petal margins; opens light pink (65C); matures pale pink (62D); 20mm (13/16") long x 24mm (15/16") wide. SEPALS: fully up; tips recurved; pink (62C) upper surface; pink (62A) lower surface; 32mm (1 1/4") long x 15mm (9/16") wide. TUBE: pink (62A); medium length & thickness; 24mm (15/16) long x 4mm (3/16") wide. STAMENS: extend 12mm (1/2") below corolla; magenta (63B) filaments & anthers. PISTIL: extends 26mm (1") below the corolla; light rose (63D) style; pale pink (62D) stigma. BUD: round. FOLIAGE: medium green (137B) upper surface; medium green (138B) lower surface. Leaves are 70mm (2 3/4") long x 27mm (1 1/16") wide, lanceolate shaped, serrulated edges, acute tips and obtuse bases. Veins, stems & branches are green. PARENTAGE: [('Cameron Ryle' x 'Parasol') x 'Allure'] x 'Allure'. Lax upright or stiff trailer. Makes good stiff trailer. Prefers overhead filtered light and cool climate. Best bloom and foliage

colour in filtered light. Tested 4 years in Knegsel, The Netherlands. Distinguished by bloom & foliage combination. Roes 2003 NL AFS5327.

Roesse Telesto. Trailer. Semi Double. COROLLA: three quarter flared, smooth petal margins; opens light pink (65B); matures pale lavender (65D); 17mm (11/16") long 22mm (7/8") wide. SEPALS: half up; tips recurved up; white (155D) upper surface; light pink (65C) lower surface; 33mm (1 5/16") long x 16mm (5/8") wide. TUBE: white (155D); medium length & thickness; 12mm (1/2") long x 6mm (1/4") wide. STAMENS: extend 21mm (13/16") below corolla; rose (65A) filaments; magenta (63A) anthers. PISTIL: extends 36mm (1 7/16") below the corolla; light pink (65C) style; white (155D) stigma. BUD: ovate, pointed. FOLIAGE: dark green (137A) upper surface; medium green (138A) lower surface. Leaves are 51mm (2") long x 26mm (1") wide, ovate shaped, serrulated edges, acute tips and obtuse bases. Green veins, stems & branches. PARENTAGE: ('Cameron Ryle' x 'Parasol') x 'Loeky'. Natural trailer. Self branching. Makes good basket. Prefers overhead filtered light and cool climate. Best bloom and foliage colour in filtered light. Tested 4 years in Knegsel, The Netherlands. Distinguished by bloom and foliage combination. Roes 2003 NL AFS5470.

Roesse Tempe. Upright/Trailer. Single. COROLLA: unflared; opens light violet (84B); matures magenta (68A); 9mm (5/16") long x 6mm (1/4") wide. SEPALS: horizontal, tips reflexed; dark rose (58C) upper surface; magenta (58B) lower surface; 16mm (5/8") long x 4mm (1/8") wide. TUBE: dark rose (58C);; 10mm (3/8") long x 4mm (1/8") wide. FOLIAGE is medium green (137B) upper surface; light green (138C) lower surface. PARENTAGE: 'Roesse Duck' x 'Venus Victrix'. Roes 2008 NL AFS6911.

Roesse Tethys. Upright. Double. COROLLA: half flared, smooth petal margins; opens purple (83A); matures dark reddish purple (59A); 20mm (13/16") long 24mm (15/16") wide. SEPALS: fully up; tips recurved; dark reddish purple (60A) upper surface; dark reddish purple (60B) lower surface; 24mm (15/16") long x 12mm (1/2") wide. TUBE: dark reddish purple (60A); medium length & thickness; 16mm (5/8") long x 6mm (1/4") wide. STAMENS: extend 16mm (5/8") below corolla; dark reddish purple (60A) filaments;

403

dark reddish purple (60C) anthers. PISTIL: extends 18mm (11/16") below the corolla; dark reddish purple (60C) style; yellowish white (4D) stigma. BUD: round, pointed. FOLIAGE: dark green (137A) upper surface; medium green (138B) lower surface. Leaves are 52mm (2 1/16") long x 34mm (1 5/16") wide, ovate shaped, serrulated edges, acute tips and rounded bases. Red veins, stems & branches. PARENTAGE: 'Rohees Rana' x ('Roesse Apus' x 'Roesse Apus'). Small upright. Makes good upright or standard. Prefers overhead filtered light and cool climate. Best bloom and foliage colour in filtered light. Tested 4 years in Knegsel, The Netherlands. Distinguished by bloom colour. Roes 2004 NL AFS5475.

Roesse Thalassa. Upright/Trailer. Double. COROLLA is half flared; opens dark reddish purple (59A); matures reddish purple (59B); 19mm (3/4") long x 19mm (3/4") wide. SEPALS are fully up, tips reflexed; reddish purple (61B) upper & lower surfaces; 26mm (1") long x 12mm (7/16") wide. TUBE is reddish purple (61B); 22mm (7/8") long x 6mm (1/4") wide. FOLIAGE: medium green (137C) upper surface; medium green (138B) lower surface. PARENTAGE: 'Rohees Rana' x 'Magda van Bets'. Distinguished by bloom colour.
Roes 2006 NL AFS6149.

Roesse Tharsis. Upright/Trailer. Single. COROLLA: half flared; opens dark reddish purple (61B); matures magenta (61C); 20mm (3/4") long x 26mm (1") wide. SEPALS: half up, tips reflexed up; light green (145D) tipped green upper & lower surfaces; 39mm (1 1/2") long x 12mm (7/16") wide. TUBE: light green (145D); 17mm (5/8") long x 10mm (3/8") wide. FOLIAGE is dark green (137A) upper surface; medium green (138A) lower surface. PARENTAGE: 'Sofie Michiels' x 'Oranje van Os'.
Roes 2008 NL AFS6899.

Roesse Thebe. Upright. Semi Double. COROLLA: half flared, smooth petal margins; opens dark reddish purple (59A); matures dark reddish purple (61A); 18mm (11/16") long 21mm (13/16") wide. SEPALS: fully up; tips reflexed; dark reddish purple (60A) upper & lower surfaces; 24mm (15/16") long x 11mm (7/16") wide. TUBE: dark reddish purple (60A); medium length & thickness; 14mm (9/16") long x 6mm (1/4") wide. STAMENS: extend 12mm (1/2") below corolla; dark reddish purple (60C) filaments; reddish purple (59B) anthers. PISTIL:

extends 18mm (11/16") below the corolla; dark reddish purple (60C) style; light yellow (4C) stigma. BUD: round, pointed. FOLIAGE: dark green (137A) upper surface; medium green (138B) lower surface. Leaves are 56mm (2 3/16") long x 41mm (1 5/8") wide, cordate shaped, serrulated edges, acute tips and obtuse bases. Red veins, stems & branches. PARENTAGE: 'Roesse Rana' x ('Roesse Apus' x 'Roesse Apus'). Medium upright. Makes good upright or standard. Prefers overhead filtered light and cool climate. Best bloom and foliage colour in filtered light. Tested 4 years in Knegsel, The Netherlands. Distinguished by bloom colour.
Roes 2004 NL AFS5472.

Roesse Theemin. Trailer. Double. COROLLA: quarter flared, smooth petal margins; opens pale purple (75C); matures pale purple (75D); 20mm (13/16") long 18mm (11/16") wide. SEPALS: horizontal; tips reflexed; light pink (65C) upper surface; light pink (65B) lower surface; 41mm (1 5/8") long x 17mm (11/16") wide. TUBE: light pink (65C); long & thin; 26mm (1") long x 3mm (1/8") wide. STAMENS: extend 15mm (9/16") below corolla; rose (68B) filaments; dark reddish purple (72A) anthers. PISTIL: extends 27mm (1 1/16") below the corolla; light rose (68D) style; pale pink (62D) stigma. BUD: cordate, pointed. FOLIAGE: dark green (137A) upper surface; medium green (138A) lower surface. Leaves are 64mm (2 1/2") long x 32mm (1 1/4") wide, ovate shaped, serrated edges, acute tips and obtuse bases. Red veins, stems & branches. PARENTAGE: [('Cameron Ryle' x 'Parasol') x 'Allure'] x 'Allure'. Natural trailer. Makes good basket. Prefers overhead filtered light and cool climate. Best bloom and foliage colour in filtered light. Tested 4 years in Knegsel, The Netherlands. Distinguished by bloom shape and colour.
Roes 2004 NL AFS5481.

Roesse Thurban. Upright/Trailer. Semi Double. COROLLA: three quarter flared, smooth petal margins; opens violet (85A); matures light purple (78B); 30mm (1 3/16") long x 34mm (1 5/16") wide. SEPALS: fully up; tips recurved; pink (62C) upper & lower surfaces; 26mm (1") long x 11mm (7/16") wide. TUBE: pink (62C); medium length & thickness; 12mm (1/2) long x 5mm (3/16") wide. STAMENS: extend 21mm (13/16) below corolla; magenta (68A) filaments; rose (63C) anthers. PISTIL: extends 24mm (15/16") below the corolla; light rose (68D) style; cream (11D) stigma. BUD: ovate.

FOLIAGE: dark green (137A) upper surface; medium green (138A) lower surface. Leaves are 46mm (1 13/16") long x 30mm (1 3/16") wide, ovate shaped, serrulated edges, acute tips and rounded bases. Veins, stems & branches are green. PARENTAGE: 'Madalyn Drago' x ('Sofie Michiels' x 'Lechlade Rocket'). Lax upright or stiff trailer. Makes good stiff trailer. Prefers overhead filtered light and cool climate. Best bloom and foliage colour in filtered light. Tested 4 years in Knegsel, The Netherlands. Distinguished by bloom & foliage combination.
Roes 2003 NL AFS5328.

Roesse Titan. Upright. Semi Double. COROLLA: half flared, smooth petal margins; opens reddish purple (72B); matures magenta (67B); 24mm (15/16") long x 31mm (1 1/4") wide. SEPALS: fully up; tips recurved; light pink (65B) upper & lower surfaces; 36mm (1 7/16") long x 14mm (9/16") wide. TUBE: light pink (65B); medium length & thickness; 7mm (1/4") long x 7mm (1/4") wide. STAMENS: extend 18mm (11/16") below corolla; rose (67D) filaments; magenta (63A) anthers. PISTIL: extends 27mm (1 1/16") below the corolla; rose (67D) style; light rose (63D) stigma. BUD: round. FOLIAGE: medium green (137B) upper surface; medium green (138B) lower surface. Leaves are 87mm (3 7/16") long x 41mm (1 5/8") wide, ovate shaped, serrated edges, acute tips and rounded bases. Veins, stems & branches are red. PARENTAGE: 'Roesse Apus' x 'Eisvogel'. Medium upright. Makes good upright or standard. Prefers overhead filtered light and cool climate. Best bloom and foliage colour in filtered light. Tested 4 years in Knegsel, The Netherlands. Distinguished by erect blooms.
Roes 2003 NL AFS5343.

Roesse Titania. Upright/Trailer. Single. COROLLA is quarter flared; opens red (43A); matures reddish orange (43B); 14mm (9/16") long x 19mm (3/4") wide. SEPALS are half down, tips reflexed; pink (48C) upper surface; rose (48B) lower surface; 31mm (1 1/4") long x 9mm (3/8") wide. TUBE is pink (48C); 24mm (15/16") long x 7mm (1/4") wide. FOLIAGE: medium green (138A) upper surface; medium green (138B) lower surface. PARENTAGE: 'Roesse Lupus' x 'Lye's Unique'. Distinguished by bloom colour.
Roes 2006 NL AFS6159.

Roesse Toliman. Trailer. Double. COROLLA: half flared, smooth petal margins; opens purple (83B); matures purple (81A); 24mm

(15/16") long x 20mm (13/16") wide. SEPALS: half down; tips reflexed; magenta (63B) upper & lower surfaces; 30mm (1 3/16") long x 15mm (9/16") wide. TUBE: light pink (65B); long & thin; 24mm (15/16") long x 4mm (3/16") wide. STAMENS: extend 20mm (13/16) below corolla; dark purple (75C) filaments; dark rose (71D) anthers. PISTIL: extends 28mm (1 1/8") below the corolla; pale purple (75D) style & stigma. BUD: round, pointed. FOLIAGE: medium green (137B) upper surface; medium green (138A) lower surface. Leaves are 60mm (2 3/8") long x 38mm (1 1/2") wide, ovate shaped, serrulated edges, acute tips and rounded bases. Veins, stems & branches are green. PARENTAGE: [('Cameron Ryle' x 'Parasol') x 'Allure'] x 'Allure'. Natural trailer. Makes good basket. Prefers overhead filtered light and cool climate. Best bloom and foliage colour in filtered light. Tested 4 years in Knegsel, The Netherlands. Distinguished by bloom & foliage combination.
Roes 2003 NL AFS5329.

Roesse Trapez. Upright/Trailer. Double. COROLLA: three quarter flared, smooth petal margins; opens dark reddish purple (72A); matures dark reddish purple (64A); 31mm (1 1/4") long x 31mm (1 1/4") wide. SEPALS: fully up; tips recurved; magenta (61C) upper surface; reddish purple (61B) lower surface; 44mm (1 3/4") long x 11mm (7/16") wide. TUBE: magenta (61C); medium length & thickness; 26mm (1") long x 6mm (1/4") wide. STAMENS: extend 30mm (1 3/16) below corolla; rose (63C) filaments; reddish purple (59B) anthers. PISTIL: extends 68mm (2 11/16") below the corolla; magenta (63A) style; light yellow (11C) stigma. BUD: ovate, pointed. FOLIAGE: medium green (137B) upper surface; medium green (138A) lower surface. Leaves are 70mm (2 3/4") long x 49mm (1 15/16") wide, ovate shaped, serrated edges, acute tips and obtuse bases. Veins are green, stems & branches are red. PARENTAGE: 'Roesse Apus' x 'Allure'. Lax upright or stiff trailer. Makes good stiff trailer. Prefers overhead filtered light and cool climate. Best bloom and foliage colour in filtered light. Tested 4 years in Knegsel, The Netherlands. Distinguished by bloom colour.
Roes 2003 NL AFS5330.

Roesse Triton. Upright. Double. COROLLA is half flared; opens purple (77A); matures reddish purple (71B); 22mm (7/8") long x 23mm (7/8") wide. SEPALS are half up, tips recurved up; pink (62C) upper surface; rose (63C) lower surface; 37mm (1 7/'16") long x

405

11mm (7/16") wide. TUBE is pale pink (62D); 19mm (3/4") long x 6mm (1/4") wide. FOLIAGE: medium green (137B) upper surface; medium green (138B) lower surface. PARENTAGE: 'Roesse Lupus' x 'Sofia Michiels'. Distinguished by bloom & foliage combination.
Roes 2006 NL AFS6141.

Roesse Tucana. Trailer. Double. COROLLA is half flared with smooth petal margins; opens violet (85B); matures violet (75A); 24mm (15/16") long x 22mm (7/8") wide. SEPALS are fully up, tips recurved; white (155D) upper & lower surfaces; 32mm (1 1/4") long x 16mm (5/8") wide. TUBE is dark rose (58C); medium length & thin; 21mm (13/16") long x 4mm (3/16") wide. FOLIAGE: dark green (137A) upper surface; medium green (138B) lower surface. Leaves are 72mm (2 13/16") long x 28mm (1 1/8") wide, lanceolate shaped. PARENTAGE: ('Sofie Michiels' x 'Rohees New Millennium') x 'Magda Vanbets'. Distinguished by bloom colour.
Roes 2005 NL AFS5951.

Roesse Tureis. Upright/Trailer. Double. COROLLA: quarter flared, smooth petal margins; opens & matures pale pink (62D); 24mm (15/16") long x 22mm (7/8") wide. SEPALS: half down; tips recurved; pale lavender (65D) upper surface; light pink (65B) lower surface; 34mm (1 5/16") long x 16mm (5/8") wide. TUBE: pale yellow green (150D); long & thin; 39mm (1 9/16") long x 4mm (3/16") wide. STAMENS: extend 12mm (1/2") below corolla; light pink (62B) filaments; maggenta (63A) anthers. PISTIL: extends 34mm (1 5/16") below the corolla; pale pink (62B) style & stigma. BUD: cordate, long TUBE. FOLIAGE: dark green (137A) upper surface; medium green (138B) lower surface. Leaves are 74mm (2 15/16") long x 32mm (1 1/4") wide, ovate shaped, serrulated edges, acute tips and obtuse bases. Veins, stems & branches are green. PARENTAGE: 'Sofie Michiels' x 'Allure'. Lax upright or stiff trailer. Makes good stiff trailer. Prefers overhead filtered light and cool climate. Best bloom and foliage colour in filtered light. Tested 4 years in Knegsel, The Netherlands. Distinguished by bloom colour.
Roes 2003 NL AFS5331.

Roesse Utopia. Trailer. Single. COROLLA: three quarter flared; opens dark reddish purple (61A); matures dark reddish purple (60C); 20mm (3/4") long x 22mm (7/8") wide. SEPALS: fully up, tips reflexed; magenta

(63A) upper & lower surfaces; 26mm (1") long x 14mm (9/16") wide. TUBE: magenta (63A); 24mm (15/16") long x 5mm (3/16") wide. FOLIAGE is dark green (137A) upper surface; medium green (137C) lower surface. PARENTAGE: ('Parasol' x 'Cameron Ryle') x 'Mission Bells'.
Roes 2008 NL AFS6910.

Roesse Vega. Upright/Trailer. Semi Double. COROLLA: three quarter flared, smooth petal margins; opens dark purple (79A); matures dark reddish purple (59A); 22mm (7/8") long x 30mm (1 3/16") wide. SEPALS: fully up; tips recurved; dark reddish purple (64A) upper surface; reddish purple (64B) lower surface; 22mm (7/8") long x 11mm (7/16") wide. TUBE: dark reddish purple (64A); medium length & thickness; 10mm (3/8") long x 7mm (1/4") wide. STAMENS: extend 21mm (13/16") below corolla; dark purple (79A) filaments & anthers. PISTIL: extends 30mm (1 3/16") below the corolla; purple (71A) style; magenta (71C) stigma. BUD: round. FOLIAGE: medium green (137B) upper surface; medium green (137C) lower surface. Leaves are 74mm (2 15/16") long x 38mm (1 1/2") wide, ovate shaped, serrulated edges, acute tips and obtuse bases. Veins, stems & branches are red. PARENTAGE: ('Roesse Apus' x 'Roesse Apus') x 'Maxima'. Lax upright or stiff trailer. Makes good stiff trailer. Prefers overhead filtered light and cool climate. Best bloom and foliage colour in filtered light. Tested 4 years in Knegsel, The Netherlands. Distinguished by bloom colour.
Roes 2003 NL AFS5333.

Roesse Vela. Upright/Trailer. Semi Double. COROLLA is three quarter flared with smooth petal margins; opens violet (90C); matures violet (84A); 21mm (13/16") long x 27mm (1 1/16") wide. SEPALS are fully up, tips recurved; light pink (62B) upper surface; dark rose (58C) lower surface; 42mm (1 11/16") long x 11mm (7/16") wide. TUBE is light pink (62B); medium length & thickness; 14mm (9/16") long x 6mm (1/4") wide. FOLIAGE: dark green (137A) upper surface; medium green (138A) lower surface. Leaves are 62mm (2 7/16") long x 24mm (15/16") wide, lanceolate shaped. PARENTAGE: 'Roesse Menkhib' x 'Roesse Pandora'. Distinguished by bloom colour.
Roes 2005 NL AFS5947.

Roesse Virgo. Upright/Trailer. Double. COROLLA is half flared with smooth petal margins; opens violet (83D); matures purple

(77A); 25mm (1") long x 27mm (1 1/16") wide. SEPALS are fully up, tips recurved; pale lavender (65D) upper & lower surface; 30mm (1 3/16") long x 11mm (7/16") wide. TUBE is pale lavender (65D); medium length & thickness; 11mm (7/16") long x 6mm (1/4") wide. FOLIAGE: dark green (137A) upper surface; medium green (138B) lower surface. Leaves are 60mm (2 3/8") long x 36mm (1 7/16") wide, cordate shaped. PARENTAGE: 'Roesse Rhea' x 'Roesse Calypso'. Distinguished by bloom colour.
Roes 2005 NL AFS5960.

Roesse Vitruvius. Upright. Single. COROLLA is half flared; opens reddish purple (59B); matures dark reddish purple (60B); 19mm (3/4") long x 24mm (15/16") wide. SEPALS are horizontal, tips recurved; pink (62A) upper surface; magenta (63B) lower surface; 34mm (1 3/8") long x 11mm (7/16") wide. TUBE is pink (62A); 19mm (3/4") long x 6mm (1/4") wide. FOLIAGE: dark green (137A) upper surface; medium green (137D) lower surface. PARENTAGE: 'Roesse Lupus' x 'Lye's Unique'. Distinguished by bloom colour.
Roes 2006 NL AFS6134.

Roesse Volans. Upright/Trailer. Single. COROLLA is full flared with smooth petal margins; opens violet (85A); matures light purple (78B); 21mm (13/16") long x 24mm (15/16") wide. SEPALS are fully up, tips recurved; magenta (58B) upper & lower surfaces; 26mm (1") long x 14mm (9/16") wide. TUBE is magenta (58B); medium length & thickness; 9mm (3/8") long x 5mm (3/16") wide. FOLIAGE: medium green (137B) upper surface; medium green (138B) lower surface. Leaves are 46mm (1 13/16") long x 32mm (1 1/4") wide, ovate shaped. PARENTAGE: 'Swanley Gem' x 'Roesse Menkhib'. Distinguished by bloom shape.
Roes 2005 NL AFS5931.

Roesse Volund. Upright/Trailer. Single. COROLLA: three quarter flared; opens purple (71A); matures reddish purple (71B); 20mm (3/4") long x 24mm (15/16") wide. SEPALS: half up, tips reflexed up; magenta (61C) upper surface; dark rose (64C) lower surface; 24mm (15/16") long x 10mm (3/8") wide. TUBE: magenta (61C); 30mm (1 3/16") long x 3mm (1/8") wide. FOLIAGE is dark green (137A) upper surface; medium green (137C) lower surface. PARENTAGE: 'Roesse Lupus' x [('Cameron Ryle' x 'Parasol') x 'Allure'].
Roes 2008 NL AFS6907.

Roesse Zibai. Upright/Trailer. Double. COROLLA: three quarter flared, smooth petal margins; opens purple (83B); matures reddish purple (72B); 23mm (15/16") long x 20mm (13/16") wide. SEPALS: fully up; tips reflexed; dark rose (58C) upper surface; magenta (58B) lower surface; 29mm (1 1/8") long x 16mm (5/8") wide. TUBE: dark rose (58C); medium length & thickness; 12mm (1/2") long x 7mm (1/4") wide. STAMENS: extend 19mm (3/4") below corolla; magenta (63A) filaments & anthers. PISTIL: extends 27mm (1 1/16") below the corolla; rose (68B) style; cream (11D) stigma. BUD: ovate. FOLIAGE: dark green (137A) upper surface; medium green (137C) lower surface. Leaves are 61mm (2 3/8") long x 32mm (1 1/4") wide, ovate shaped, serrulated edges, acute tips and obtuse bases. Veins, stems & branches are red. PARENTAGE: 'Dorothy Oosting' x 'Allure'. Lax upright or stiff trailer. Makes good stiff trailer. Prefers overhead filtered light and cool climate. Best bloom and foliage colour in filtered light. Tested 4 years in Knegsel, The Netherlands. Distinguished by bloom & foliage combination.
Roes 2003 NL AFS5332.

Roesse Zosma. Upright/Trailer. Single. COROLLA: quarter flared, smooth petal margins; opens light pink (65B); matures pale lavender (65D); 32mm (1 1/4") long x 25mm (1") wide. SEPALS: fully up; tips reflexed; rose (65A) upper & lower surfaces; 38mm (1 1/2") long x 10mm (3/8") wide. TUBE: light pink (65C); medium length & thickness; 15mm (9/16") long x 7mm (1/4") wide. STAMENS: extend 20mm (13/16") below corolla; rose (68B) filaments; magenta (71C) anthers. PISTIL: extends 28mm (1 1/8") below the corolla; light rose (68D) style; rose (68B) stigma. BUD: cordate, narrow. FOLIAGE: dark green (137A) upper surface; medium green (137C) lower surface. Leaves are 65mm (2 9/16") long x 31mm (1 1/4") wide, ovate shaped, serrulated edges, acute tips and rounded bases. Veins, stems & branches are red. PARENTAGE: [('Cameron Ryle' x 'Parasol') x 'Allure'] x 'Allure'. Lax upright or stiff trailer. Makes good stiff trailer. Prefers overhead filtered light and cool climate. Best bloom and foliage colour in filtered light. Tested 4 years in Knegsel, The Netherlands. Distinguished by bloom & foliage combination.
Roes 2003 NL AFS5335.

Rogaland Fuchsialag. Trailer. Double. COROLLA: three quarter flared, turned under wavy petal margins; opens rose (55B) & dark rose (64C) edged reddish purple (70B); matures rose (63C) & reddish purple (61B) edged magenta (67B); 26mm (1") long x 19mm (3/4") wide. PETALOIDS: Same colour as corolla; 17mm (5/8") long x 14mm (9/16") wide. SEPALS: half up, tips recurved up, twisted left to right; pink (55C) tipped light yellowish green (150C) upper surface; rose (52B) tipped light yellowish green (150C) lower surface; 52mm (2 1/16") long x 19mm (3/4") wide. TUBE: rose (55B); medium length & thickness; 19mm (3/4") long x 7mm (1/4") wide. STAMENS extend 15mm (9/16") beyond the corolla; dark rose (64C) filaments; purple (71A) anthers. PISTIL extends 24mm (15/16") beyond the corolla; dark rose (58C) style; pale pink (62D) stigma. BUD: oblong, square. FOLIAGE: dark green (137A) upper surface; medium green (137D) lower surface. Leaves are 74mm (2 15/16") long x 35mm (1 3/8") wide; ovate shaped, smooth edges, acute tips, rounded bases. Veins are very dark reddish purple (186A), stems are plum (185C), branches are light plum (184D). PARENTAGE: 'Manfried Kleinau' x 'First Lord'. Natural trailer. Self branching. Makes good basket. Prefers overhead filtered light, cool climate. Best bloom & foliage colour in filtered light. Tested 3 years in Koningshooikt, Belgium. Waanrode 8/9/08, Outstanding. Distinguished by bloom colour combination. Michiels 2009 BE AFS7215.

Roger Vanholst. Upright/Trailer. Single. to Semi Double. COROLLA: quarter flared, turned under wavy petal margins; opens and matures dark purple (78A), light coral (38A) at base; 26mm (1") long x 24mm (15/16") wide. SEPALS: half down; tips recurved; pale pink (62D), dark rose (58C) at edge & base, tipped yellow green (145A) upper surface; pink (62A) lower surface; 44mm(1 3/4") long x 13mm (1/2") wide. TUBE: light pink (62B); medium length, thick; 29mm (1 1/8") long x 12mm (1/2") wide. STAMENS: do not extend below corolla; no filaments; yellow (4A) anthers. PISTIL extends 18mm (11/16") below the corolla; pale pink (4A) style, yellow (4A) stigma. BUD: ovate. FOLIAGE: dark green (137A) upper surface; medium green (138B) lower surface. Leaves are 85mm (3 3/8") long x 37mm (1 7/16") wide, lanceolate shaped, serrulated edges, acute tips and obtuse bases. Veins & stems are brown (166A), branches are light brown (199B). PARENTAGE: 'Alda Alders' x 'Wingrove's Mammoth'. Lax upright or stiff trailer. Self branching. Makes good basket. Prefers

overhead filtered light. Best bloom and foliage colour in filtered light. Tested 4 years in Leopoldsburg, Belgium. NBFK Certificate at Meise. Distinguished by bloom colour and shape.
Busschodts 2003 BE AFS5129.

Rojo. Upright/Trailer. Double. COROLLA: three quarter flared, turned under wavy petal margins; opens purple (77A); matures reddish purple (64B); 24mm (15/16") long x 19mm (3/4") wide. SEPALS: half up, tips recurved up & horizontal, tips recurved; rose (61D) tipped light yellowish green (150C) upper surface; magenta (61C) lower surface; 39mm (1 1/2") long x 17mm (5/8") wide. TUBE: pale pink (56A) striped light rose (58D); medium length, thick; 15mm (9/16") long x 8mm (5/16") wide. STAMENS extend 17mm (5/8") beyond the corolla; reddish purple (71B) filaments; purple (77A) anthers. PISTIL extends 23mm (7/8") beyond the corolla; dark rose (67C) style; light yellow (2C) stigma. BUD: elongated. FOLIAGE: medium green (137B) upper surface; medium green (138B) lower surface. Leaves are 68mm (2 11/16") long x 40mm (1 9/16") wide; ovate shaped, serrulate edges, obtuse tips, rounded bases. Veins are light grayish red (182D), stems are plum (185C), branches are light green (138C). PARENTAGE: 'Manfried Kleinau' x 'Frans Vander Kuylen'. Lax upright or stiff trailer. Self branching. Makes good basket or upright. Prefers overhead filtered light, cool climate. Best bloom & foliage colour in filtered light. Tested 3 years in Koningshooikt, Belgium. Waanrode 8/9/08. Distinguished by bloom colour. Michiels 2009 BE AFS7217.

Roland Schindela. Upright/Trailer. Single. COROLLA pale scarlet (43b); corolla is half flared. SEPALS dark baby pink (36a) tipped green on the upper and lower surfaces; SEPALS are horizontally held with recurved tips. TUBE dark baby pink (36a). PARENTAGE 'Delicate Blue' x 'Careless Whisper'.
Klemm 2009 AT BFS0133.

Rolanda Bierinckx. Upright. Single. COROLLA is quarter flared with turned under smooth petal margins; opens reddish purple (67A), matures magenta (67B); 17mm (11/16") long x 17mm (11/16") wide. SEPALS are half down, tips reflexed; rose (54C) upper surface, pink (55C) lower surface; 23mm (15/16") long x 8mm (5/16") wide. TUBE is rose (55B), medium length and thickness; 26mm (1") long x 6mm (1/4")

wide. STAMENS extend 5mm (3/16") beyond the corolla; rose (67D) filaments, yellow orange (16C) anthers. PISTIL extends 7mm (1/4") beyond the corolla; pale purple (70D) style; light yellow (11B) stigma. BUD is round, pointed. FOLIAGE is dark green (147A) upper surface, medium green (147B) lower surface. Leaves are 63mm (2 1/2") long x 18mm (11/16") wide, elliptic shaped, serrulated edges, acute tips and rounded bases. Veins are dark reddish purple (187C), stems dark reddish purple (187B), branches are dark reddish purple (187C). PARENTAGE: 'WALZ Harp' x 'Waternymph'. Medium upright, dwarf growth. Self branching. Makes good upright or standard. Prefers full sun, warm climate. Best bloom and foliage colour in bright light. Tested three years in Koningshooikt and Hoeselt, Belgium. Certificate N.B.F.K. at Meise. Distinguished by bloom shape and leaf colour.
Michiels 2002 BE AFS4931.

Rommelaar. Upright/Trailer. Semi Double. COROLLA: three quarter flared, turned under smooth petal margins; opens purple (88B) veined magenta (58B); matures purple (80A); 24mm (15/16") long x 20mm (13/16") wide. PETALOIDS: light purple (86C) edged magenta (58B); 17mm (11/16") long x 14mm (9/16") wide. SEPALS: half down; tips reflexed; reddish purple (58A) tipped light yellowish green (150C) upper surface; magenta (58B) lower surface; 32mm (1 1/4") long x 18mm (11/16") wide. TUBE: magenta (58B); medium length & thickness; 20mm (13/16") long x 6mm (1/4") wide. STAMENS: extend 13mm (1/2") below the corolla; magenta (61C) filaments, dark reddish purple (64A) anthers. PISTIL extends 32mm (1 1/4") below the corolla; magenta (58B) style, dark reddish purple (60C) stigma. BUD: rectangular, pointed. FOLIAGE: dark green (139A) upper surface; medium green (137B) lower surface. Leaves are 55mm (2 3/16") long x 32mm (1 1/4") wide, cordate shaped, serrated edges, acute tips and rounded bases. Veins are dark reddish purple (184A), stems are plum (183C), branches are dark reddish purple (187C). PARENTAGE: 'Allison Reynolds' x unknown. Lax upright or stiff trailer. Self branching. Makes good basket. Prefers overhead filtered light. Best bloom and foliage colour in filtered light. Tested 3 years in Rillaar, Belgium. NBFK certificate at Meise. Distinguished by bloom colour.
Willems 2003 BE AFS5097.

Ronald van Dommelen. Trailer. Single. COROLLA: quarter flared, smooth petal margins; opens dark reddish purple (59A); matures reddish purple (59B); 20mm (13/16") long x 22mm (7/8") wide. SEPALS: half up; tips reflexed up; dark reddish purple (60A) upper surface; dark reddish purple (61A) lower surface; 28mm (1 1/8") long x 5mm (3/16") wide. TUBE: dark reddish purple (60A); medium length & thickness; 14mm (9/16") long x 6mm (1/4") wide. STAMENS: extend 10mm (3/8") below corolla; dark reddish purple (61A) filaments; dark reddish purple (59A) anthers. PISTIL: extends 28mm (1 1/8") below the corolla; magenta (61C) style; light yellow (11C) stigma. BUD: ovate. FOLIAGE: dark green (137A) upper surface; medium green (137D) lower surface. Leaves are 50mm (2") long x 32mm (1 1/4") wide, cordate shaped, serrulated edges, acute tips and rounded bases. Veins, stems & branches are red. PARENTAGE: 'Rohees Metallah' x 'Belle de Spa'. Natural trailer. Makes good basket. Prefers overhead filtered light and cool climate. Best bloom and foliage colour in filtered light. Tested 4 years in Diessen, The Netherlands. Distinguished by bloom colour.
Comperen 2003 NL AFS5282.

Ronalds Regalia. Upright. Semi Double. COROLLA opens deep lilac flushed with deep rosy pink; corolla is three quarter flared. SEPALS deep rosy pink on the upper and lower surfaces; sepals are fully up with recurved tips. TUBE deep rosy pink. PARENTAGE 'Nellie Nuttal' x Unknown. This cultivar is ideal for growing as a standard.
Chatfield 2009 UK BFS0103.

Ronnie Barker. Upright. Double. COROLLA is three quarter flared with smooth petal margins; opens dark orange (41A) and matures dark orangy red (44B); 35mm (1 3/8") long x 45mm (1 3/4") wide. SEPALS are half up, tips recurved up; light orange (41D) upper surface, dark orange (44D) creped lower surface; 51mm (2") long x 16mm (5/8") wide. TUBE is light orange (41D); medium length and thickness; 23mm (15/16") long x 10mm (3/8") wide. STAMENS extend 35mm (1 3/8") below the corolla; pink (55C) filaments; dark orange (41A) anthers. PISTIL extends 45mm (1 3/4") below the corolla; pink (55C) style; white (155D) stigma. BUD is pear shaped. FOLIAGE is dark green (137A) upper surface, medium green (137D) lower surface. Leaves are 70mm (2 3/4") long x 43mm (1 11/16") wide, cordate shaped, serrated edges, obtuse tips and obtuse bases. Veins, stems, branches are light green. PARENTAGE: 'Cheers' x 'Hinnerike'. Medium upright. Self branching. Makes good upright, standard or decorative. Prefers cool climate. Heat tolerant if shaded. Best bloom colour in filtered light. Tested six years in Gloucester, England. Distinguished by bloom colour and flower/foliage combination. Hickman 2002 UK AFS4853.

Ronny. Upright. Single. COROLLA: half flared; opens light reddish purple (73A) edged white (155C); matures rose (65A) & white (155B); 18mm (11/16") long x 24mm (15/16") wide. SEPALS: horizontal, tips reflexed; dark rose (54A) tipped medium green (141D) upper surface; dark rose (51A) tipped medium green (141D) lower surface; 19mm (3/4") long x 12mm (7/16") wide. TUBE: pink (55C) striped dark rose (54B); 38mm (1 1/2") long x 5mm (3/16") wide. FOLIAGE is dark green (137A) upper surface; medium green (137D) lower surface. PARENTAGE: 'WALZ Harp' x unknown. Daems 2008 AFS6766.

Ronny Bogaert. Trailer. Double. COROLLA: three quarter flared; opens rose (68B) striped magenta (63B); matures dark rose (67C) & reddish purple (67A); 33mm (1 5/16") long x 30mm (1 3/16") wide. PETALOIDS: rose (68B); 20 mm (3/4") long x 15 mm (9/16") wide. SEPALS are horizontal, tips recurved, twisted left; light green (145D) tipped light apple green (144D) upper surface and pale yellow green (150D) tipped light apple green (144D) lower surface; 38mm (1 1/2") long x 11mm (7/16") wide. TUBE is white (155A); medium length & thickness; 22mm (7/8") long x 6mm (1/4") wide. FOLIAGE is dark green (137A) upper surface; medium green (138B) lower surface. PARENTAGE: 'Vreni Schleeweiss' x 'Kiss'. Michiels 2007 BE AFS6511.

Roselynne. Upright/Trailer. Single. COROLLA: half flared; opens & matures lavender (69D) streaked light reddish purple (72D), white (155A) base; 19mm (3/4") long x 22mm (7/8") wide. SEPALS: fully up, tips reflexed; light pink (65C) at base suffusing to white, tipped light green upper surface; pink (62A) lower surface; 19mm (3/4") long x 9mm (5/16") wide. TUBE: light pink (65C); 9 mm (5/16") long x 9mm (5/16") wide. FOLIAGE is medium green (137B) upper surface; medium green (147B) lower surface. PARENTAGE: 'London 2000' x 'Carla Johnson'. Als registered with the BFS. Swaby 2008 UK AFS6829 BFS0049(2007).

Rosemarie Bauer. Upright. Double. COROLLA: half flared, smooth petal margins, square shape; opens magenta (63A); matures magenta (63B); 35mm (1 3/8") long x 35mm (1 3/8") wide. PETALOIDS: magenta (63A), red (52A) at base; short & small. SEPALS: half up, tips recurved up; red (52A) upper surface; rose (52B) lower surface; 50mm (2") long x 15mm (9/16") wide. TUBE: red (52A); medium length & thickness; 20mm (3/4") long x 8mm (5/16") wide. STAMENS extend 20mm (3/4") beyond the corolla; red (52B) filaments; gray (195A) anthers. PISTIL extends 35mm (1 3/8") beyond the corolla; rose (52B) style; grayish (197B) stigma. BUD: drop shape. FOLIAGE: medium green (146A) upper surface; light olive green (147C) lower surface. Leaves are 110mm (4 3/8") long x 50mm (2") wide; lanceolate shaped, serrulate edges, acute tips, rounded bases. Veins are light green, stems are grayish brown, branches are grayish red. PARENTAGE: 'Chris Lohner' x 'Lunters Trots'. Medium upright. Makes good upright. Prefers overhead filtered light. Best bloom & foliage colour in filtered light. Tested 4 years in Dorf Haag, Austria. Distinguished by flower shape & colour. Gindl 2009 AT AFS7087.

Roseworthy. Upright. Single. COROLLA: half flared; opens violet (90C); matures lavender (91D); 22mm (7/8") long, 22mm (7/8") wide. PETALOIDS: lavender (91D); 10mm (3/8") long x 3mm (1/8") wide, folded. SEPALS: half up; tips reflexed up; red (52A) upper surface; pink (52D) lower surface; 25mm (1") long x 13mm (1/2") wide. TUBE: red (52A); short, thin; 10mm (3/8") long x 4mm (3/16") wide. STAMENS: do not extend below corolla; pale pink (62D) filaments; rose (52B) anthers. PISTIL: extends 10mm (3/8") below the corolla; rose (52C) style; pale pink (62D) stigma. BUD: round. FOLIAGE: dark green (147A) upper surface; yellowish green (146B) lower surface. Leaves are 55mm (2 3/16") long x 30mm (1 3/16") wide, lanceolate shaped, serrulated edges, acute tips and acute bases. Very dark reddish purple (186A) veins; brown (177A) stems; light plum (184D) branches. PARENTAGE: found seedling x 'Leana Dalton'. Small upright. Makes good standard. Prefers overhead filtered light. Heat tolerant if shaded. Best bloom and foliage colour in filtered light. Tested 7 years in West Cornwall, England. Distinguished by bloom colour combination. Negus 2004 UK AFS5631.

Rosey Blue. Upright. Single. COROLLA: half flared, smooth petal margins; opens purple (90A); matures dark purple (78A); 25mm (1") long 19mm (3/4") wide. SEPALS: fully up; tips recurved; dark rose (58C) upper surface; magenta (58B) lower surface; 25mm (1") long x 8mm (5/16") wide. TUBE: dark rose (58C); medium length & thickness; 10mm (3/8") long x 5mm (3/16") wide. STAMENS: extend 12mm (1/2") below corolla; dark rose (64C) filaments; white (155C) anthers. PISTIL: extends 19mm (3/4") below the corolla; white (155C) style & stigma. BUD: oval, pointed. FOLIAGE: medium green (137B) upper surface; medium green (137C) lower surface. Leaves are 50mm (2") long x 25mm (1") wide, elliptic shaped, serrulated edges, acute tips and rounded bases. Light green veins, stems & branches. PARENTAGE: 'Julie Ann Goodwin' x 'Patty Harding'. Small upright. Self branching. Makes good upright, pyramid or pillar. Prefers overhead filtered light, cool or warm climate. Best bloom and foliage colour in filtered light. Tested 3 years in Stoke-On-Trent, England. Distinguished by erect blossoms and striking purple colour. Goodwin 2004 UK AFS5576.

Rossi. Upright. Single. COROLLA: quarter flared, smooth petal margins; opens reddish purple (74A), matures reddish purple (66A); 11mm (7/16") long x 11mm (7/16") wide. SEPALS: half down; tips reflexed; red (52A) upper surface; rose (52B) lower surface; 18mm (11/16") long x 8mm (5/16") wide. TUBE: red (52A), medium length & thickness; 12mm (1/2") long x 8mm (5/16") wide. STAMENS: extend 10mm (3/8") below the corolla; red (50A) filaments, rose (52B) anthers. PISTIL extends 19mm (3/4") below the corolla; light rose (50C) style, pink (50D) stigma. BUD: rounded. FOLIAGE: dark green (147A) upper surface, medium green (147B) lower surface. Leaves are 50mm (2") long x 31mm (1 1/4") wide, ovate shaped, serrated edges, acute tips and rounded bases. Veins & stems are dark green (147A), branches are brown. PARENTAGE: 'Phyllis' x unknown. Medium upright. Self branching. Makes good upright or standard. Prefers full sun and warm climate. Best bloom and foliage colour in bright light. Tested 3 years in Como, Italy. Distinguished by continuous bloom. Ianne 2003 IT AFS5074.

Roswitha Sundl. Upright. Double. COROLLA white; COROLLA is half flared. SEPALS white on the upper and lower surfaces; SEPALS are fully up with recurved tips. TUBE white. PARENTAGE 'Waldis Aquamarin' x 'Gilda'

Dietrich 2009 DE BFS0112.

Roy's Pride. Trailer. Single. COROLLA: half flared, smooth petal margins; opens & matures rose (63C); 20mm (3/4") long x 8mm (5/16") wide. SEPALS: half down, tips recurved; pink (62A) streaked tipped green upper surface; light pink (38C) lower surface; 20mm (3/4") long x 8mm (5/16") wide. TUBE: light pink (55D); medium length & thickness; 15mm (9/16") long x 5mm (3/16") wide. STAMENS extend 10mm (3/8") beyond the corolla; light pink (55D) filaments & anthers. PISTIL extends 20mm (3/4") beyond the corolla; light pink (55D) style; white (155A) stigma. BUD: ovate. FOLIAGE: medium green (137B) upper surface; medium green (138A) lower surface. Leaves are 40mm (1 9/16") long x 18mm (11/16") wide; lanceolate shaped, serrulate edges, acute tips, acute bases. Veins are green, stems are light brown, branches are light green. PARENTAGE: 'Snowbird' x 'Dana Samantha'. Natural trailer. Makes good basket. Prefers overhead filtered light. Best bloom colour in filtered light. Tested 3 years in Rayleigh, Essex, England. Distinguished by blossom colour & shape.
Smith R. 2009 UK AFS7128.

Royal Academy. Upright. Double. COROLLA: Half flared; opens light purple (86C); matures dark violet (87A); 30mm (1 3/16") long x 55mm (2 3/16") wide. SEPALS: half down, tips recurved; pale pink (58B) upper surface; pale pink (58C) lower surface; 29mm (1 1/8") long x 14mm (9/16") wide. TUBE: Light rose (58D); short & thick; 9mm (5/16") long x 6mm (1/4") wide. FOLIAGE is yellowish green (146B) upper surface; yellowish green (145A) lower surface. PARENTAGE: 'Brookwood Belle' x 'Royal Velvet'.
Chapman 2007 UK AFS6718.

Royal Diamond. Trailer. Double. COROLLA: half flared, turned under wavy petal margins; opens white (155C) striped rose (155B); matures white (155B) striped pink (55C); 24mm (15/16") long x 19mm (3/4") wide. PETALOIDS: Same colour as corolla; 16mm (5/8") long x 12mm (7/16") wide. SEPALS: half down, tips reflexed; white (155B) tipped light apple green (145B) upper surface; pale pink (56D) tipped light apple green (145B) lower surface; 48mm (1 7/8") long x 13mm (1/2") wide. TUBE: rose (51B); medium length & thickness; 22mm (7/8") long x 6mm (1/4") wide. STAMENS extend 11mm (7/16") beyond the corolla; dark rose (58B) filaments; light purple (70C) anthers. PISTIL extends 19mm (3/4") beyond the corolla; pink (55C) style; light yellow (2C) stigma. BUD: oblong. FOLIAGE: dark green (137A) upper surface; medium green (138B) lower surface. Leaves are 70mm (2 3/4") long x 31mm (1 1/4") wide; elliptic shaped, serrate edges, acute tips, rounded bases. Veins are dark red (185A), stems are reddish purple (185B), branches are plum (184B). PARENTAGE: 'Niagara Falls' x 'Ronny Bogaert'. Natural trailer. Self branching. Makes good basket. Prefers overhead filtered light, cool climate. Best bloom & foliage colour in filtered light. Tested 3 years in Koningshooikt, Belgium. Waanrode 8/9/08, Outstanding. Distinguished by shades of white & pink combination. Michiels 2009 BE AFS7218.

Royal Parade. Upright. Double. COROLLA is quarter flared, barrel shaped, with smooth petal margins; opens violet (84A); matures reddish purple (74B); 19mm (3/4") long x 19mm (3/4") wide. SEPALS are fully up, tips recurved; pale pink (56D) aging to rose (52C) upper surface; light pink (55D) aging to pink (52D) lower surface; 25mm (1") long x 10mm (3/8") wide. TUBE is pale pink (56D) & pale pink (49D); short & thin; 7mm (1/4") long x 3mm (1/8") wide. FOLIAGE: light green (143C) aging to dark green (141B) upper surface; yellowish green (144B) aging to yellowish green (144A) lower surface. Leaves are 32mm (1 1/4") long x 19mm (3/4") wide, ovate shaped. PARENTAGE: [('Grange Farm' x seedling) x 'Brookwood Belle'] x (seedling x 'General Monk'). Distinguished by small double, bright coloured flowers & light coloured foliage. Edmond 2005 UK AFS5819.

Royer Commanderie. Trailer. Single. COROLLA: quarter flared; opens light purple (N78C); matures violet (76A); 21mm (13/16") long x 19mm (3/4") wide. SEPALS: horizontal, tips recurved, twisted left; white (155C) & pale lavender (69D) tipped light apple green (145C) upper surface; pale purple (75D) tipped light apple green (145C) lower surface; 28mm (1 1/8") long x 12mm (7/16") wide. TUBE: white (155C); 15mm (9/16") long x 6mm (1/4") wide. FOLIAGE is dark green (137A) upper surface; medium green (138B) lower surface. PARENTAGE: 'Pink La Campanella' x unknown. Cuppens 2008 BE AFS6753.

Royer Lies. Trailer. Single. COROLLA: quarter flared, turned under smooth petal margins; opens magenta (61C), white (155A)

at base; matures dark rose (58C), white (155C) at base; 14mm (9/16") long x 12mm (1/2") wide. SEPALS: fully up; tips recurved; white (155A) tipped light green (142A) upper surface; white (155D) lower surface; 24mm(15/16") long x 10mm (3/8") wide. TUBE: pale yellow (158B); medium length & thick; 16mm (5/8") long x 8mm (5/16") wide. STAMENS: extend 8mm (5/16") below the corolla; pink (62C) filaments, reddish purple (58A) anthers. PISTIL extends 18mm (11/16") below the corolla; white (155D) style, light yellow (2C) stigma. BUD: ovate, pointed. FOLIAGE: medium green (137B) upper surface; medium green (138B) lower surface. Leaves are 40mm (1 9/16") long x 32mm (1 1/4") wide, cordate shaped, serrulated edges, acute tips and cordate bases. Veins, stems & branches are light green (138D). PARENTAGE: 'Pink La Campanella' x unknown. Natural trailer. Self branching. Makes good basket. Prefers overhead filtered light. Best bloom and foliage colour in filtered light. Tested 3 years in Gruitrode, Belgium. NBFK Certificate of Merit at Meise. Distinguished by profuse blooms. Cuppens 2003 BE AFS5122.

Royer Likkepotje. Upright/Trailer. Single. COROLLA is three quarter flared with turned under wavy petal margins; opens pale lavender (69D); matures light magenta (57D); 2mm (1/16") long x 1.5mm (1/16") wide. SEPALS are horizontal, tips reflexed; magenta (61C) tipped medium green (141C) upper surface; magenta (58B) tipped medium green (141C) lower surface; 3mm (1/8") long x 1mm (1/16") wide. TUBE is magenta (61C); medium length & thin; 8mm (5/16") long x 2mm (1/16") wide. FOLIAGE: dark green (137A) upper surface; medium green (138B) lower surface. Leaves are 16mm (5/8") long x 7mm (1/4") wide, elliptic shaped. PARENTAGE: 'Royer Pinkje' x unknown. Meis 3-7-04. Distinguished by very small and beautiful flowers. Cuppens 2005 BE AFS5666.

Royer Mia. Upright/Trailer. Double. COROLLA: three quarter flared, turned under smooth petal margins; opens purple (88A), rose (68B) at base; matures purple (81B), white (155B) at base; 12mm (1/2") long x 28mm (1 1/8") wide. SEPALS: fully up; tips reflexed; white (155B), tipped light yellowish green (149B) upper surface; white (155B) flushed pink (62A) lower surface; 20mm(13/16") long x 13mm (1/2") wide. TUBE: pale yellow (1D); short, medium thickness; 7mm (1/4") long x 5mm (3/16") wide. STAMENS: extend 21mm (13/16") below corolla; magenta (63A) filaments; reddish purple (58A) anthers. PISTIL extends 27mm (1 1/16") below the corolla; white (155D) style, white (155A) stigma. BUD: cordate. FOLIAGE: dark green (137A) upper surface; medium green (138B) lower surface. Leaves are 37mm (1 7/16") long x 25mm (1") wide, cordate shaped, serrulated edges, acute tips and cordate bases. Veins & stems are reddish purple (58A), branches are brown (177A). PARENTAGE: 'Christina Becker' x unknown. Lax upright or stiff trailer. Self branching. Makes good basket. Prefers overhead filtered light. Best bloom and foliage colour in filtered light. Tested 3 years in Gruitrode, Belgium. NBFK Certificate at Meise. Distinguished by bloom colour. Cuppens 2003 BE AFS5131.

Royer Milena. Upright. Single. COROLLA is three quarter flared with turned under wavy petal margins; opens reddish purple (70B), rose (68C) base; matures magenta (68A); 16mm (5/8") long x 22mm (7/8") wide. SEPALS are horizontal, tips recurved; rose (55B), pink (55C) base, tipped light apple green (145B) upper surface; light pink (62B), tipped light apple green (145B) lower surface; 17mm (11/16") long x 11mm (7/16") wide. TUBE is pink (55C); short & thick; 5mm (3/16") long x 5mm (3/16") wide. FOLIAGE: dark green (139A) upper surface; medium green (137D) lower surface. Leaves are 49mm (1 15/16") long x 29mm (1 1/8") wide, ovate shaped. PARENTAGE: 'Christine Becker' x unknown. Meise 9-18-04. Distinguished by flower colour. Cuppens 2005 BE AFS5843.

Royer Nathy. Upright/Trailer. Single. COROLLA: quarter flared, turned under smooth petal margins; opens & matures magenta (63A), dark orange(33A) at base; 11mm (7/16") long x 14mm (9/16") wide. SEPALS: half down; tips reflexed; light pink (62B) tipped pale yellowish green (154D) upper surface; rose (52C) lower surface; 22mm(7/8") long x 7mm (1/4") wide. TUBE: pink (62A); medium length & thickness; 24mm (15/16") long x 5mm (3/16") wide. STAMENS: extend 6mm (1/4") below the corolla; dark rose (58C) filaments, yellow (5A) anthers. PISTIL extends 27mm (1 1/16") below the corolla; light rose (58D) style, yellow (13C) stigma. BUD: ovate, pointed. FOLIAGE: dark green (137A) upper surface; medium green (138B) lower surface. Leaves are 81mm (2 3/16") long x 50mm (2") wide,

ovate shaped, serrated edges, acute tips and rounded bases. Veins, stems & branches are brown (166A). PARENTAGE: 'Rosea' x unknown. Lax upright or stiff trailer. Makes good basket. Prefers overhead filtered light. Best bloom and foliage colour in filtered light. Tested 3 years in Gruitrode, Belgium. NBFK Certificate of Merit at Meise. Distinguished by profuse blooms. Cuppens 2003 BE AFS5123.

Royer Seda. Trailer. Semi Double. COROLLA: quarter flared, turned under smooth petal margins; opens & matures dark reddish purple (70A), dark rose (58C) at base; 24mm (15/16") long x 54mm (2 1/8") wide. PETALOIDS: 2 per sepal; same colour as corolla, 22mm (7/8") long x 9mm (3/8") wide. SEPALS: fully up; tips recurved; magenta (58B) tipped medium green (146A) upper surface; magenta (58B) lower surface; 44mm(1 3/4") long x 15mm (5/8") wide. TUBE: magenta (58B); medium length & thickness; 19mm (3/4") long x 6mm (1/4") wide. STAMENS: extend 24mm (15/16") below the corolla; reddish purple (61B) filaments, dark reddish purple (61A) anthers. PISTIL extends 59mm (2 5/16") below the corolla; magenta (61C) style, pale yellow (5D) stigma. BUD: ovate. FOLIAGE: dark green (137A) upper surface; medium green (137C) lower surface. Leaves are 73mm (2 7/8") long x 53mm (2 1/16") wide, cordate shaped, serrulated edges, acute tips and cordate bases. Veins are reddish purple (58A), stems & branches are dark reddish purple (59A). PARENTAGE: 'Clem's Tinneke' x unknown. Natural trailer. Self branching. Makes good basket. Prefers overhead filtered light. Best bloom and foliage colour in filtered light. Tested 3 years in Gruitrode, Belgium. NBFK Certificate of Merit at Meise. Distinguished by bloom colour and shape. Cuppens 2003 BE AFS5124.

Royer Setti. Upright/Trailer. Single. COROLLA is half flared with turned under smooth petal margins; opens white (155C), dark rose (54B) base; matures white (155A), rose (55B) base; 25mm (1") long x 17mm (11/16") wide. PETALOIDS: dark rose (54B); 13mm (1/2") long x 4mm (3/16") wide. SEPALS are horizontal, tips reflexed; white (155C), dark rose (54B) base, tipped yellowish green (146C) upper surface; white (155C), rose (55B) base, tipped yellowish green (146C) lower surface; 38mm (1 1/2") long x 13mm (1/2") wide. TUBE is dark rose (54B); medium length & thickness; 13mm (1/2") long x 7mm (1/4") wide. FOLIAGE:

dark green (139A) upper surface; medium green (138B) lower surface. Leaves are 61mm (2 3/8") long x 27mm (1 1/16") wide, elliptic shaped. PARENTAGE: 'White Galore' x unknown. Meis 3-7-04. Distinguished by bloom colour.
Cuppens 2005 BE AFS5667.

Royer Veronica. Trailer. Single. COROLLA: quarter flared; opens red (52A) & magenta (58B); matures magenta (61C); 21mm (13/16") long x 19mm (3/4") wide. SEPALS: horizontal, tips recurved; pink (51D) tipped apple green (144C) upper surface; pink (49A) tipped apple green (144C) lower surface; 32mm (1 1/4") long x 7mm (1/4") wide. TUBE: rose (51C); 28mm (1 1/8") long x 5mm (3/16") wide. FOLIAGE is medium green (137B) upper surface; medium green (138B) lower surface. PARENTAGE: 'Pink La Campanella' x unknown.
Cuppens 2008 BE AFS6754.

Rozentanz. Upright/Trailer. Double. COROLLA: half flared ; opens violet (77B), base magenta (63A); matures magenta (71C); 14mm (9/16") long x 11mm (7/16") wide. PETALOIDS: violet (76A); 12mm (7/16") long x 7mm (1/4") wide. SEPALS are half up, tips recurved up; white (155C) tipped light apple green (145B) upper surface; pink (62C) tipped light apple green (145B) lower surface; 33mm (1 5/16") long x 12mm (7/16") wide. TUBE is white (155C) and light green (142B); medium length & thickness; 12mm (7/16") long x 5mm (3/16") wide. FOLIAGE is dark green (136B) upper surface; medium green (138B) lower surface. PARENTAGE: 'De Brommel' x 'BreeVis Luna'.
Michiels 2007 BE AFS6512.

Rubinero. Upright. Double. COROLLA: 3 quarter flared; opens purple (79C), magenta (67B) base; matures purple (83B); 26mm (1") long x 17mm (5/8") wide. PETALOIDS: same colour as corolla; 16mm (5/8") long x 7mm (1/4") wide. SEPALS: horizontal, tips recurved; rose (68C) tipped light apple green (145B) upper surface; magenta (67B) tipped light apple green (145B) lower surface; 36mm (1 7/16") long x 11mm (7/16") wide. TUBE: magenta (61C); medium length & thickness; 14mm (9/16") long x 6mm (1/4") wide. FOLIAGE is dark green (137A) upper surface; medium green (138B) lower surface. PARENTAGE: 'Leon Pauwels' x 'Monique Sleiderink'.
Michiels 2007 BE AFS6335.

Rubinstein. Trailer. Double. COROLLA: half flared; opens magenta (61C), edged magenta (63B); matures dark rose (64C) edged violet (85A); 22mm (7/8") long x 20mm (3/4") wide. PETALOIDS: magenta (61C); 14mm (9/16") long x 9mm (5/16") wide. SEPALS are half down, tips recurved; light pink (65C) tipped light yellowish green (154C) upper surface; rose (68C) tipped light yellowish green (154C) lower surface; 33mm (1 5/16") long x 12mm (7/16") wide. TUBE is white (155C); medium length & thickness; 18mm (11/16") long x 6mm (1/4") wide. FOLIAGE is dark green (137A) upper surface; medium green (138B) lower surface. PARENTAGE: 'Vendelzwaaier' x 'Jackie Bull'.
Michiels 2007 BE AFS6513.

Ruby Feyen. Upright/Trailer. Double. COROLLA is half flared; opens violet (85A); matures violet (77B); 20mm (13/16") long x 24mm (15/16") wide. SEPALS are fully up, tips recurved; pale lavender (65D) upper surface; light pink (65B) lower surface; 20mm (13/16") long x 11mm (7/16") wide. TUBE is pale yellow (2D); 10mm (3/8") long x 4mm (3/16") wide. FOLIAGE: dark green (137A) upper surface; medium green (138A) lower surface. PARENTAGE: ('Roesse Apus' x 'Roesse Apus') x 'Yvette Klessens'. Distinguished by bloom colour.
Buiting 2006 NL AFS5981.

Rudi Hartl. Trailer. Double. COROLLA: half flared, turned under wavy petal margins; opens dark rose (54A); matures rose (51B); 24mm (15/16") long x 19mm (3/4") wide. PETALOIDS: Same colour as corolla; 13mm (1/2") long x 9mm (5/16") wide. SEPALS: horizontal, tips recurved; light pink (62C) upper surface; reddish orange (43C) lower surface; 32mm (1 1/4") long x 15mm (9/16") wide. TUBE: pink (62A); short & thick; 7mm (1/4") long x 7mm (1/4") wide. STAMENS extend 11mm (7/16") beyond the corolla; dark rose (51A) filaments; magenta (63B) anthers. PISTIL extends 16mm (5/8") beyond the corolla; rose (51B) style; pale yellow (1D) stigma. BUD: globular. FOLIAGE: dark green (136B) upper surface; medium green (138B) lower surface. Leaves are 52mm (2 1/16") long x 30mm (1 3/16") wide; elliptic shaped, serrate edges, acute tips, rounded bases. Veins are plum (185C), stems are reddish purple (186B), branches are dark grayish red (182A) & medium green (138B). PARENTAGE: 'Manfried Kleinau' x 'Malibu Mist'. Natural trailer. Self branching. Makes good basket. Prefers overhead filtered light, cool climate. Best bloom & foliage colour in filtered light. Tested 3 years in

Koningshooikt, Belgium. Waanrode 8/9/08. Distinguished by bloom colour. Michiels 2009 BE AFS7219.

Rune Peeters. Upright/Trailer. Single. COROLLA is half flared with turned under smooth petal margins; opens reddish purple (67A), dark rose (58C) base; matures reddish purple (61B), dark rose (58C) base; 24mm (15/16") long x 26mm (1") wide. SEPALS are horizontal, tips recurved; rose (55B) tipped light apple green (145B) upper surface; dark rose (58C) tipped light apple green (145B) lower surface; 27mm (1 1/16") long x 11mm (7/16") wide. TUBE is pale pink (56B); long, medium thickness; 22mm (7/8") long x 6mm (1/4") wide. FOLIAGE: dark green (136B) upper surface; medium green (138B) lower surface. Leaves are 61mm (2 3/8") long x 31mm (1 1/4") wide, ovate shaped. PARENTAGE: 'Sofie Michiels' x 'WALZ Harp'. Meise 8-14-04. Distinguished by flower colour combination. Michiels 2005 BE AFS5740.

Rune Spinnoy. Trailer. Double. COROLLA: three quarter flared; opens violet (77B) blotched pink (51D); matures magenta (67B); 24mm (15/16") long x 20mm (3/4") wide. PETALOIDS: violet (77B) blotched pink (51D); 10mm (3/8") long x 8mm (5/16") wide. SEPALS are horizontal, tips recurved; pink (62B) tipped apple green (144C) upper surface; rose (55B) tipped apple green (144C) lower surface; 28mm (1 1/8") long x 13mm (1/2") wide. TUBE is rose (55B); 10mm (3/8") long x 7mm (1/4") wide. FOLIAGE is dark green (136A) upper surface; medium green (137B) lower surface. PARENTAGE: 'Vendelzwaaier' x 'Jackie Bull'. Waanrode 7/7/2007. Michiels 2008 BE AFS6721.

Rune Verheyden. Trailer. Single. COROLLA is half flared with turned under smooth petal margins; opens magenta (63B), pink (48C) base; matures light reddish purple (66C); 27mm (1 1/16") long x 17mm (11/16") wide. SEPALS are half down, tips recurved; pink (51D) tipped light green (143C) upper surface; pink (48C) tipped light green (143C) lower surface; 34mm (1 5/16") long x 12mm (1/2") wide. TUBE is light pink (49B); long, medium thickness; 25mm (1") long x 6mm (1/4") wide. FOLIAGE: dark green (137A) upper surface; medium green (138B) lower surface. Leaves are 72mm (2 13/16") long x 33mm (1 5/16") wide, elliptic shaped. PARENTAGE: 'Sofie Michiels' x 'F. fulgens var. rubra grandiflora'. Meis 3-7-04.

Distinguished by rich blooming & rare colour combination. Michiels 2005 BE AFS5681

Rupelbelleke. Upright/Trailer. Double. COROLLA: half flared, turned under wavy petal margins; opens reddish purple (70B) edged light purple (N77D); matures magenta (63D) edged grayish red (182B); 24mm (15/16") long x 22mm (7/8") wide. PETALOIDS: coral (39B), reddish purple (70B) edged light purple (N77D) ; 17mm (5/8") long x 8mm (5/16") wide. SEPALS: horizontal, tips recurved, twisted left to right; pale pink (56D) tipped light yellowish green (150C) upper surface; rose (51B) tipped light yellowish green (150C) lower surface; 42mm (1 5/8") long x 19mm (3/4") wide. TUBE: pale pink (56D) striped pink (52D); medium length & thickness; 15mm (9/16") long x 7mm (1/4") wide. STAMENS extend 8mm (5/16") beyond the corolla; rose (68C) filaments; light reddish purple (73A) anthers. PISTIL extends 14mm (9/16") beyond the corolla; pale lavender (69B) style; light yellow (1C) stigma. BUD: acorn shape. FOLIAGE: dark green (136A) upper surface; medium green (138B) lower surface. Leaves are 92mm (3 5/8") long x 56mm (2 1/4") wide; ovate shaped, serrate edges, acute tips, rounded bases. Veins are dark reddish purple (60C), stems are magenta (58B), branches are red purple (N77B). PARENTAGE: 'Manfried Kleinau' x 'Ann-Elisabeth Fuhrmann'. Lax upright or stiff trailer. Self branching. Makes good basket or upright. Prefers overhead filtered light, cool climate. Best bloom & foliage colour in filtered light. Tested 3 years in Koningshooikt, Belgium. Waanrode. Distinguished by bloom colour. Michiels 2009 BE AFS7220.

Rupert. Upright. Single. COROLLA is unflared with smooth petal margins; opens & matures pale pink (56D); 22mm (7/8") long x 20mm (13/16") wide. SEPALS are horizontal, tips recurved; pink (51D) tipped green upper surface; rose (51B) tipped green lower surface; 33mm (1 5/16") long x 10mm (3/8") wide. TUBE is rose (51C); medium length & thickness; 12mm (1/2") long x 6mm (1/4") wide. FOLIAGE: medium green (138A) upper surface; medium green (138B) lower surface. Leaves are 40mm (1 9/16") long x 22mm (7/8") wide, ovate shaped. PARENTAGE: 'La Campanella' x 'Wilson's Pearls'. Distinguished by flower & foliage colour combination. Gindl 2005 AT AFS5802.

415

Rusty. Trailer. Double. COROLLA: half flared; opens magenta (71C) striped rose (65A); matures reddish purple (67A) striped light pink (62B); 27mm (1 1/16") long x 17mm (5/8") wide. PETALOIDS: magenta (71C) striped rose (65A); 19mm (3/4") long x 14mm (9/16") wide. SEPALS are half down, tips reflexed; white (155C) and pale lavender (69C) tipped light apple green (144D) upper surface and rose (65A) tipped light apple green (144D) lower surface; 36mm (1 7/16") long x 16mm (5/8") wide. TUBE is white (155C) striped medium green (141D); medium length & thickness; 20mm (3/4") long x 6mm (1/4") wide. FOLIAGE is dark green (136B) upper surface; medium green (138B) lower surface. PARENTAGE: 'Leon Pauwels' x 'Oso Sweet'.
Michiels 2007 BE AFS6514.

Ruth Soeborg. Upright/Trailer. Double. COROLLA: half flared, turned under wavy petal margins; opens magenta (59D) & purple (71A); matures rose (52A) dark reddish purple (59A); 19mm (3/4") long x 19mm (3/4") wide. PETALOIDS: Same colour as corolla ; 15mm (9/16") long x 13mm (1/2") wide. SEPALS: horizontal, tips recurved; white (155B) tipped light apple green (145B) upper surface; magenta (58B) tipped light apple green (145B) lower surface; 30mm (1 3/16") long x 14mm (9/16") wide. TUBE: white (155B) striped magenta (61C); medium length & thickness; 17mm (5/8") long x 6mm (1/4") wide. STAMENS extend 13mm (1/2") beyond the corolla; reddish purple (64B) filaments; purple (79C) anthers. PISTIL extends 28mm (1 1/8") beyond the corolla; reddish purple (61B) style; pale yellow (2D) stigma. BUD: bulbous. FOLIAGE: dark green (139A) upper surface; medium green (138B) lower surface. Leaves are 59mm (2 3/8") long x 37mm (1 7/16") wide; ovate shaped, serrate edges, acute tips, rounded bases. Veins are light green (139D), stems are medium green (139B) & light plum (184D), branches are light green (138C) & plum (185C). PARENTAGE: 'Manfried Kleinau' x 'Imperial Fantasy'. Lax upright or stiff trailer. Self branching. Makes good basket or upright. Prefers overhead filtered light, cool climate. Best bloom & foliage colour in filtered light. Tested 3 years in Koningshooikt, Belgium. Waanrode 7/5/08. Distinguished by bloom colour combination.
Michiels 2009 BE AFS7221.

Rÿs 2001. Upright. Single. COROLLA is half flared, square shaped, with smooth petal margins; opens and matures white (155A); 7mm (1/4") long x 4mm (3/16") wide. SEPALS are full down, tips recurved; light greenish white (157D) upper and lower surfaces; 8mm (5/16") long x 4mm (3/16") wide. TUBE is dark rose (55A), medium length and thickness; 14mm (9/16") long x 6mm (1/4") wide. STAMENS do not extend beyond the corolla; white (155B) filaments, pale yellow (1D) anthers. PISTIL extends 10mm (3/8") below the corolla; white (155B) style and stigma. BUD is elongated, boat shaped. FOLIAGE is dark green (147A) upper surface, olive green (148A) lower surface. Leaves are 41mm (1 5/8") long x 24mm (15/16") wide, ovate shaped, serrulated edges, acute tips and rounded bases. Veins are dark green, stems are reddish, branches are brown. PARENTAGE: 'F. obconica' x 'F. splendens'. Lax upright. Self branching. Makes good basket. Prefers full sun and cool or warm climate. Hardy to 40° F. Best bloom and foliage colour in bright light. Tested three years in Blesdÿke, Holland. Award of Merit, Aalsmeer, 2001. Distinguished by blossoms similar to 'F. splendens' with unusual colouring.
de Boer 2002 NL AFS4889.

Sabrina. Upright. Double. COROLLA is quarter flared with wavy petal margins; opens white (155C), matures white (155D) lightly veined pink; 32mm (1 1/4") long x 38mm (1 1/2") wide. SEPALS are horizontal, tips recurved; pink (62C) upper surface and light pink (62B) lower surface; 44mm (1 3/4) long x 12mm (1/2") wide. TUBE is white (155A) blushed pink, short with medium thickness; 8mm (5/16") long x 6mm (1/4") wide. STAMENS extend 19mm (3/4") below the corolla; light pink (62B) filaments and magenta (63A) anthers. PISTIL extends 32mm (1 1/4") below the corolla; light pink (62B) style and pale pink (62D) stigma. BUD is pointed. FOLIAGE is medium green (138B) upper surface and light green (138C) lower surface. Leaves are 63mm (2 1/2") long x 32mm (1 1/4") wide, ovate shaped, serrulated edges, acute tips and rounded bases. Veins are rose, stems are pink; branches are light brown. PARENTAGE: 'Sintons Standard' x 'Pattie Sue'. Small upright. Self branching. Makes good upright or standard. Prefers overhead filtered light. Best bloom colour in filtered light. Tested three years in Ormskirk, Lancashire, England. Distinguished by free flowering over a long period.
Sinton 2002 UK AFS4828.

Salluyts Patricia. Upright/Trailer. Single. COROLLA is quarter flared with turned under smooth petal margins; opens magenta (71C), dark rose (58C) at base; matures magenta (67B), magenta (58B) at base; 15mm (5/8") long x 21mm (13/16") wide. SEPALS are half down, tips reflexed; rose (50B), light green (145D) at top, tipped apple green (144C) upper surface; pink (48C), pale yellowish green (149D) at top, tipped apple green (144C) lower surface; 25mm (1") long x 11mm (7/16") wide. TUBE is pink (54D); long, medium thickness; 36mm (1 7/16") long x 7mm (1/4") wide. STAMENS do not extend beyond the corolla; light pink (55D) filaments, light yellow (2C) anthers. PISTIL does not extend beyond the corolla; pale pink (56B) style, light yellow (1C) stigma. BUD is ovate, pointed. FOLIAGE is dark green (137A) upper surface, medium green (138B) lower surface. Leaves are 70mm (2 3/4") long x 37mm (1 7/16") wide, ovate shaped, serrulated edges, acute tips and rounded bases. Veins are plum (185B), stems are very dark reddish purple (186A), branches are plum (185C). PARENTAGE: 'Nettala' x 'Blue Veil'.Lax upright or stiff trailer. Makes good basket or upright. Prefers overhead filtered light. Best bloom and foliage colour in filtered light. Tested three years in Itegem, Belgium. Certificate N.B.F.K. at Meise. Distinguished by bloom shape.
Geerts L. 2002 BE AFS4977.

Salut Bruno. Upright. Single. COROLLA is unflared with smooth petal margins; opens & matures light violet (84B); 18mm (11/16") long x 9mm (3/8") wide. SEPALS are fully up, tips recurved in a circle; rose (50B) upper & lower surfaces; 35mm (1 3/8") long x 8mm (3/16") wide. TUBE is rose (50B); medium length, thin; 15mm (9/16") long x 4mm (3/16") wide. FOLIAGE: dark green (147A) upper surface; medium green (147B) lower surface. Leaves are 65mm (2 9/16") long x 34mm (1 5/16") wide, ovate shaped. PARENTAGE: ('String of Pearls' x F. regia reitzii 4574') x 'René Massé. Distinguished by bloom form & colour.
Massé 2005 FR AFS5834.

Sam. Upright. Double. COROLLA is three quarter flared with turned under wavy petal margins; opens magenta (68A), magenta (58B) base; matures dark rose (64C), dark rose (58C) base; 27mm (1 1/16") long x 19mm (3/4") wide. PETALOIDS: Same colour as corolla; 17mm (11/16") long x 13mm (1/2") wide. SEPALS are half up, tips recurved up; white (155C), tipped apple green (144C) upper surface; white (155B), tipped apple green (144C) lower surface; 36mm (1 7/16") long x 14mm (9/16") wide. TUBE is white (155B); medium length & thickness; 15mm (9/16") long x 5mm (3/16") wide. FOLIAGE: dark green (136A) upper surface; medium green (138B) lower surface. Leaves are 98mm (3 7/8") long x 57mm (2 1/4") wide, ovate shaped. PARENTAGE: 'Sofie Michiels' x 'Diana Wills'. Meise 8-14-04. Distinguished by flower colour.
Michiels 2005 BE AFS5744.

Sam Sheppard. Upright. Single. COROLLA opens cobalt violet with violet vein and white base; corolla is half flared and is 25mm long x 45mm wide. SEPALS are pale green-cream on the upper surface, rose bengal on the lower surface; sepals are fully up with recurved tips that are slightly twisted and are 30mm long x 10mm wide. TUBE is cream in colour and is 6mm long x 3mm wide. PARENTAGE 'Border Queen' x 'Doris Joan'. This cultivar will produce a nice standard, and is named after the hybridist's grandson.
Sheppard 2005 UK BFS0011.

Samantha Hine. Upright/Trailer. Single. COROLLA: Quarter flared; opens dark purple (78A); matures magenta (71C); 20mm (3/4") long x 20mm (3/4") wide. SEPALS: horizontal, tips recurved; red (52A) upper & lower surfaces; 30mm (1 3/16") long x 15mm (9/16") wide. TUBE: red (52A); medium length & thickness; 20mm (3/4") long x 5mm (3/16") wide. FOLIAGE is medium green (146A) upper surface; yellowish green (146B) lower surface. PARENTAGE: 'Orange Crush' x unknown.
Bell 2007 UK AFS6398.

Samke. Trailer. Double. COROLLA is three quarter flared; opens reddish purple (67A); matures dark rose (67C); 17mm (5/8") long x 24mm (15/16") wide. SEPALS are half up, tips reflexed up; magenta (58B) upper & lower surfaces; 32mm (1 1/4") long x 14mm (9/16") wide. TUBE is magenta (58B); 16mm (5/8") long x 6mm (1/4") wide. FOLIAGE: dark green (137A) upper surface; medium green (138B) lower surface. PARENTAGE: 'Phyllis' x unknown. Distinguished by bloom & foliage combination.
van der Vorst 2006 NL AFS6186.

Samuel Dickerson. Upright. Single. COROLLA: unflared, smooth petal margins, bell shaped; opens dark reddish purple (59A); matures reddish purple (59B); 27mm (1 15/16") long x 20mm (3/4") wide.

417

SEPALS: half up, tips recurved up; dark reddish purple (60A) upper surface; dark reddish purple (60B) lower surface; 36mm (1 7/16") long x 5mm (3/16") wide. TUBE: dark reddish purple (60A); medium length & thickness; 12mm (7/16") long x 7mm (1/4") wide. STAMENS extend 35mm (1 3/8") beyond the corolla; purple (71A) filaments; reddish purple (59B) anthers. PISTIL extends 43mm (1 11/16") beyond the corolla; magenta (59C) style; dark reddish purple (64A) stigma. BUD: slim, pointed, slight twist. FOLIAGE: dark green (139A) upper surface; medium green (147B) lower surface. Leaves are 51mm (2") long x 22mm (7/8") wide; cordate shaped, serrulate edges, acute tips, rounded bases. Veins, stems & branches are red. PARENTAGE: ['Susan Storey' x ('Pink Fantasia' x 'Fuchsiade 88')] x 'Susan Storey'. Medium upright. Self branching. Makes good upright or standard. Prefers full sun. Cold weather hardy to -3° C (26° F). Best bloom & foliage colour in bright light. Tested 8 years in Gainsborough, Lincolnshire & Burstwick, East Yorkshire, England. Distinguished by bloom colour & shape.

Storey 2009 UK AFS7135.

Sandra Bider. Upright. Single. COROLLA: quarter flared, smooth petal margins; opens dark purple (79A) veined red (45B) at base; matures dark reddish purple (64A); 23mm (15/16") long x 20mm (13/16") wide. SEPALS: horizontal; tips recurved; red (45A-45B) upper surface; red (50A) lower surface; 30mm(3/16") long x 11mm (7/16") wide. TUBE: red (45A-45B); short, medium thickness; 9mm (3/8") long x 3-7mm (1/8-1/4") wide, middle swells to 4mm (3/16"). STAMENS: extend 33mm (1 5/16") below corolla; red (53B) filaments; dark reddish purple (59A) anthers. PISTIL: extends 20mm (13/16") below the corolla; red (53B) style, reddish purple (59B) stigma. BUD: rounded. FOLIAGE: dark green (137A) upper surface; medium green (147B) lower surface. Leaves are 95mm (3 3/4") long x 40mm (1 9/16") wide, lanceolate shaped, serrulated edges, acute tips and rounded bases. Veins & stems are reddish, branches are brown-green. PARENTAGE: 'F. alpestris' x unknown. Tall upright. Makes good upright or standard. Heat tolerant if shaded. Cold weather hardy to 32° F. Prefers overhead filtered light & cool climate. Best bloom and foliage colour in filtered light. Tested 15 years in Biella, Torino & Como, Italy. Distinguished by TUBE shape.

Bider Bomati 2003 IT AFS5137.

Sandra Foreman. Upright. Single. COROLLA is half flared with turned under petal margins; opens dark violet (87A), light pink at base; matures violet (87B), lighter at base; 18mm (11/16") long x 21mm (13/16") wide. SEPALS are half up, tips recurved up; pale pink (69A) tipped green upper surface, pale pink (62D) tipped green lower surface; 25mm (1") long x 12mm (1/2") wide. TUBE is pale pink (69A), short with medium thickness; 10mm (3/8") long x 7mm (1/4") wide. STAMENS extend 8mm (5/16") beyond the corolla; light pink (65B) filaments and anthers. PISTIL extends 20mm (13/16") beyond the corolla; pale lavender (69C) style, white (155A) stigma. BUD is elongated. FOLIAGE is medium green (137B) upper surface, medium green (138B) lower surface. Leaves are 50mm (2") long x 30mm (1 3/16") wide, ovate shaped, wavy edges, acute tips and cordate bases. Veins are light green, stems are dull red, branches are light green to dull red. PARENTAGE: 'London 2000' x 'Alipatti'. Small upright. Self branching. Makes good upright, standard or pillar. Prefers overhead filtered light. Best bloom colour in filtered light. Tested three years in Maidstone, Kent, England. Distinguished by profuse blooms and blossom colour.

Waving 2002 UK AFS4936.

Sandro Hit. Trailer. Single. COROLLA: half flared; opens dark rose (67C) and matures magenta (71C); 22mm (7/8") long x 19mm (3/4") wide. SEPALS are horizontal; tips recurved; white (155C) tipped light apple green (145B) upper surface; pale lavender (69B) tipped light apple green (145B) lower surface; 35mm (1 5/8") long x 12mm (7/16") wide. TUBE is white (155C); medium length & thickness; 18mm (11/16") long x 7mm (1/4") wide. FOLIAGE is dark green (137A) upper surface; medium green (138B) lower surface. PARENTAGE: 'Jef Vander Kuylen' x 'Chandlerii'.

Michiels 2007 BE AFS6515.

Sankt Wendel. Upright. Double. COROLLA violet, veined rose; corolla is half flared. SEPALS rose on the upper and lower surfaces; SEPALS are fully up with recurved tips. TUBE rose. PARENTAGE 'Waldis Helle Glocke' x 'Bahia'.

Dietrich 2009 DE BFS0111.

Santorini Sunset. Upright/Trailer. Double. COROLLA: half flared, turned under smooth petal margins; opens red (46C); matures red (45D); 22mm (7/8") long x 16mm (5/8") wide. PETALOIDS: Reddish Orange (42A); 12mm

418

(1/2") long x 8mm (5/16") wide. SEPALS: horizontal; tips recurved; rose (52C) tipped yellowish green (146C) upper surface; rose (47C) lower surface; 27mm (1 1/16") long x 12mm (1/2") wide. TUBE: rose (51C); short & thick; 24mm(15/16") long x 9mm (3/8") wide. STAMENS: extend 3mm (1/8") below corolla; dark rose (54A) filaments, coral (39B) anthers. PISTIL: extends 28mm (1 1/8") below the corolla, dark rose (55A) style, rose (52C) stigma. BUD: cordate. FOLIAGE: dark green (139A) upper surface; medium green (138B) lower surface. Leaves are 84mm (3 5/16") long x 43mm (1 11/16") wide, ovate shaped, serrated edges, acute tips and rounded bases. Veins are light plum (184D), stems are plum (184B), branches are plum (183B). PARENTAGE: 'WALZ Mandoline' x 'Lechlade Rocket'. Lax upright or stiff trailer. Makes good basket. Prefers overhead filtered light. Best bloom and foliage colour in filtered light. Tested 3 years in Koningshooikt, Belgium. NBFK Certificate at Meise. Distinguished by bloom colour. Michiels 2003 BE AFS5193.

Sarah Brightman. Upright/Trailer. Double. COROLLA is three quarter flared, flat shaped, with smooth turned under petal margins; opens purple (88A), white (155A) at base; matures dark violet (87A); 35mm (1 3/8") long x 60mm (2 3/8") wide. SEPALS are half up, tips recurved up; white (155A) upper surface, white (155A) suffused violet (76B) creped lower surface; 30mm (1 3/16") long x 17mm (11/16) wide. TUBE is white (155A); short with medium thickness; 17mm (11/16") long x 10mm (3/8") wide. STAMENS extend 15mm (5/8") below the corolla; light purple (75B) filaments; magenta (57A) anthers. PISTIL extends 50mm (2") below the corolla; white (155A) style and white (155D) stigma. BUD is acorn shaped. FOLIAGE is medium green (138A) upper surface, medium green (138B) lower surface. Leaves are 87mm (3 3/8") long x 33mm (1 5/16") wide, lanceolate shaped, serrulated edges, acute tips and rounded bases. Veins and stems are light green, branches are red. PARENTAGE: 'Masquerade' x 'Corsair'. Lax upright or stiff trailer. Self branching. Makes good basket, upright or standard. Prefers cool climate. Heat tolerant if shaded. Best bloom colour in filtered light. Tested six years in Gloucester, England. Distinguished by bloom colour contrast and shape. Hickman 2002 UK AFS4856.

Sarah Peters. Upright/Trailer. Semi Double. COROLLA: quarter flared, smooth petal margins, bell shaped; opens light pink (65B); matures pink (54D); 25mm (1") long x 19mm (3/4") wide. SEPALS: full down, tips recurved; rose (52B) upper & lower surfaces; 32mm (1 1/4") long x 19mm (3/4") wide. TUBE: light reddish purple (73A); medium length & thickness; 19mm (3/4") long. STAMENS extend 13mm (1/2") beyond the corolla; light coral (38A) filaments & anthers. PISTIL extends 44mm (1 3/4") beyond the corolla; light coral (38A) style; peach (38B) stigma. BUD is oval. FOLIAGE is dark green (137A) upper surface; dark green (141A) lower surface. Leaves are 25mm (1") long x 19mm (3/4") wide; ovate shaped, serrulate edges, acute tips, rounded bases. Veins are green; stems & branches are purple. PARENTAGE: found seedling. Lax upright or stiff trailer. Makes good upright. Prefers overhead filtered light. Cold weather hardy to -7° C (20° F). Best bloom colour in filtered light. Tested 3 years in Telford, Shropshire, UK. Distinguished by bloom colour & shape. Peters 2009 UK AFS6956.

Sarah Walton. COROLLA pink. SEPALS light rose pink tipped green. Norcross 2007 UK.

Sara-Jane Cox. Upright. Single. COROLLA is quarter flared with turned under petal margins; opens light purple (88C) with pink (62A) flecks, light pink (62B) in center area, veined reddish orange (42A) at base; matures with slightly shading; 16mm (5/8") long x 14mm (9/16") wide. SEPALS are half up, tips reflexed up; reddish orange (42A) upper surface, pinkish rose (50B) lower surface; 30mm (1 3/16") long x 13mm (1/2") wide. TUBE is red (50A); medium length and thickness; 12mm (1/2") long x 6mm (1/2") wide. STAMENS extend 15mm (5/8") below the corolla; pink (62A) filaments; magenta (63B) anthers. PISTIL extends 24mm (15/16") below the corolla; pink (62C) style and pale pink (62D) stigma. BUD is round, pointed. FOLIAGE is dark green (137A) upper surface, medium green (138B) lower surface. Leaves are 60mm (2 3/8") long x 32mm (1 1/4") wide, elliptic shaped, serrulated edges, acute tips and rounded bases. Veins are green, stems are pale red and branches are dark brownish red. PARENTAGE: 'Joan Gilbert' x 'Leonora'. Medium upright. Self branching. Short jointed. Makes good upright or standard. Heat tolerant if shaded. Best bloom colour in filtered light. Tested five years in Gloucester, England. Distinguished by changing petal colours from petal to petal. Hickman 2002 UK AFS4858.

Saskia vander Heijden. Upright/Trailer. Double. COROLLA: half flared, smooth petal margins; opens purple (71A); matures reddish purple (71B); 18mm (11/16") long x 16mm (5/8") wide. SEPALS: horizontal; tips recurved; pale lavender (69D) upper & lower surfaces; 31mm (1 1/4") long x 17mm (11/16") wide. TUBE: pale lavender (69D); long & thin; 22mm (7/8") long x 16mm (5/8") wide. STAMENS: extend 10mm (3/8") below corolla; dark rose (58C) filaments, magenta (58B) anthers. PISTIL: extends 38mm (1 1/2") below the corolla, pale lavender (65D) style, yellowish white (4D) stigma. BUD: spherical. FOLIAGE: medium green (137B) upper surface; medium green (137C) lower surface. Leaves are 48mm (1 7/8") long x 38mm (1 1/2") wide, cordate shaped, serrated edges, obtuse tips and cordate bases. Veins, stems & branches are red. PARENTAGE: 'Bicentennial' x 'Allure'. Lax upright or stiff trailer. Makes good stiff trailer. Prefers overhead filtered light and cool climate. Best bloom and foliage colour in filtered light. Tested 4 years in Knegsel, The Netherlands. Distinguished by blossom colour combination.
van Bree 2003 NL AFS5233.

Saucy Sandra. Upright/Trailer. Double. COROLLA: three quarter flared, turned up smooth petal margins; opens violet (85A), light violet (84C) near TUBE; matures violet (75A), pale purple (75D) near TUBE; 50mm (2") long x 35mm (1 3/8") wide. PETALOIDS: Same colour as corolla; 10mm (3/8") long x 8mm (5/16") wide. SEPALS: half up; tips recurved up; cream (158D) tipped green upper surface; cream (158D) flushed light pink (65B) lower surface; 50mm(2") long x 12mm (1/2") wide. TUBE: yellowish white (158A); medium length & thin; 15mm (9/16") long x 5mm (3/16") wide. STAMENS: extend 20mm (13/16") below corolla; light magenta (57D) filaments; light pink (36C) anthers. PISTIL: extends 30mm (1 3/16") below the corolla, pale pink (49D) style; yellowish white (158A) stigma. BUD: large, elongated. FOLIAGE: medium green (146A) upper surface, light yellowish green (146D) lower surface. Leaves are 60mm (2 3/8") long x 35mm (1 3/8") wide, cordate shaped, serrulated edges, acute tips and rounded bases. Veins & stems are green; branches are brown. PARENTAGE: 'Pink La Campanella' x 'Orange Glow'. Lax upright or stiff trailer. Self branching. Makes good basket or standard. Prefers overhead filtered light and warm climate. Heat tolerant if shaded. Cold weather hardy to 32⁰ F. Best

bloom colour in bright light. Tested 3 years in Walthamstow, London, England. Distinguished by profuse violet blooms set against light green foliage.
Allsop M. 2004 UK AFS5382.

Schapenkoppen. Upright. Double. COROLLA: half flared; opens pale lavender (69C) & white (155C); matures pale lavender (65D) & white (155C); 18mm (11/16") long x 16mm (5/8") wide. PETALOIDS: same colour as corolla; 12mm (7/16") long x 6mm (1/4") wide. SEPALS: horizontal, tips reflexed; white (155B) tipped yellowish green (145A) upper surface; white (155C) tipped yellowish green (145A) lower surface; 29mm (1 1/8") long x 13mm (1/2") wide. TUBE: white (155C); medium length & thickness; 17mm (5/8") long x 5mm (3/16") wide. FOLIAGE is dark green (139A) upper surface; medium green (137B) lower surface. PARENTAGE: 'Vreni Schleeweiss' x 'Kiss'.
Michiels 2007 BE AFS6336.

Schloss Hexenagger. Upright. Double. COROLLA: half flared, smooth petal margins; opens dark purple (N79A) blushed red (53B); matures dark purple (N79B); 26mm (1") long x 35mm (1 3/8") wide. SEPALS: fully up, tips recurved; red (53B) upper & lower surfaces; 38mm (1 1/2") long x 18mm (11/16") wide. TUBE: red (53C); long, medium thickness; 22mm (7/8") long x 7mm (1/4") wide. STAMENS extend 28mm (1 1/8") beyond the corolla; red (53B) filaments; dark purple (N79A) anthers. PISTIL extends 37mm (1 7/16") beyond the corolla; red (53B) style; pale pink (62D) stigma. BUD: globular. FOLIAGE: dark green (137A) upper surface; medium green (138B) lower surface. Leaves are 100mm (4") long x 46mm (1 13/16") wide; lanceolate shaped, serrulate edges, acute tips, rounded bases. Veins & stems are red, branches are reddish maturing to light brown. PARENTAGE: 'Rohees Rana' x 'Oscar Lehmeier'. Medium upright. Self branching. Makes good upright or standard. Prefers full sun, warm climate. Heat tolerant if shaded. Best bloom & foliage colour in bright light. Tested 3 years in Bavaria, Southern Germany. Distinguished by corolla colour & shape.
Burkhart 2009 DE AFS7111.

Schloss Riedegg. Upright. Double. COROLLA: full flared, smooth petal margins; opens purple (83C); matures purple (80A); 22mm (7/8") long, 42mm (1 5/8") wide. SEPALS: half up; tips recurved up; magenta (61C) upper & lower surfaces; 32mm (1 1/4")

420

long x 16mm (11/16") wide. TUBE: magenta (61C); short, medium thickness; 5mm (3/16") long x 3mm (1/8") wide. STAMENS: extend 10mm (3/8") below corolla; reddish purple (61B) filaments; dark reddish purple (61A) anthers. PISTIL: extends 30mm (1 3/16") below the corolla; rose (61D) style; light orange (23A) stigma. BUD: drop shaped. FOLIAGE: medium green (137B) upper surface; medium green (137D) lower surface. Leaves are 55mm (2 3/16") long x 36mm (1 7/16") wide, ovate shaped, serrulated edges, acute tips and rounded bases. Green veins, brown stems & red branches. PARENTAGE: 'Christina Becker' x 'Leineperle'. Medium upright. Self branching. Makes good upright. Prefers overhead filtered light. Heat tolerant if shaded. Best bloom and foliage colour in filtered light. Tested 5 years in Plettenberg, Germany. Silver medal, IGA Rosbock 2003. Distinguished by bloom shape & colour. Strümper 2004 DE AFS5624.

Schloss Wartenfels. Upright/Trailer. Double. COROLLA: 3 quarter flared; opens light rose (73B), light pink (65B) base; matures magenta (61C); 21mm (13/16") long x 15mm (9/16") wide. PETALOIDS: same colour as corolla; 12mm (7/16") long x 7mm (1/4") wide. SEPALS: horizontal, tips reflexed; light pink (65B) tipped light green (142B) upper surface; light rose (73B) tipped light green (142B) lower surface; 28mm (1 1/8") long x 12mm (7/16") wide. TUBE: pale lavender (69B); medium length & thickness; 17mm (5/8") long x 5mm (3/16") wide. FOLIAGE is dark green (137A) upper surface; medium green (138A) lower surface. PARENTAGE: 'Leen Vander Kuylen' x 'Charlott Martens'. Michiels 2007 BE AFS6337.

Schlosz Bentheim. Upright/Trailer. Double. COROLLA is three quarter flared with smooth petal margins; opens dark purple (79B) and matures purple (79C); 22mm (7/8") long x 16mm (5/8") wide. SEPALS are half up, tips recurved up; reddish purple (74A) upper surface, reddish purple (74B) lower surface; 32mm (1 1/4") long x 14mm (9/16") wide. TUBE is reddish purple (74A), proportionately medium length and thickness; 12mm (1/2") long x 5mm (3/16") wide. STAMENS extend 24mm (15/16") below the corolla; purple (77A) filaments and anthers. PISTIL extends 36mm (1 7/16") below the corolla; dark purple (78A) style and pale pink (62D) stigma. BUD is ovate and pointed. FOLIAGE is medium green (137B) on upper surface and medium green (138B) on lower surface. Leaves are 57mm (2 1/4") long x 30mm (1 3/16) wide, elliptic shaped, smooth edges, acute tips and rounded bases. Veins, stems and branches are red. PARENTAGE: ('Grus aus dem Bodenthal' x 'Rohees Alrami') x 'Rohees King'. Lax upright or stiff trailer. Makes good stiff trailer. Prefers overhead filtered light and warm climate. Best bloom colour in filtered light. Tested four years in Knegsel, The Netherlands. Distinguished by bloom colour. Roes 2002 NL AFS4798.

Schnedl's Pupperl. Upright. Semi Double. COROLLA is quarter flared; opens light purple (N80D); matures light rose (N74C); 22mm (7/8") long (becomes longer while maturing) x 26mm (1") wide. SEPALS are half down, tips recurved; cream (N155C) spotted & edged red (N57B) upper & lower surfaces; 45mm (1 3/4") long x 15mm (9/16") wide. TUBE is cream (N155C), striped red; 18mm (11/16") long x 10mm (3/8") wide. FOLIAGE: dark green (137A) upper surface; medium green (137D) lower surface. PARENTAGE: 'Carla Johnston' x 'Hans Schnedl'. Small upright. Self branching. Distinguished by bud form & thin red edge on SEPALS. Burkhart 2006 DE AFS6050.

Schone Hanaurin. Trailer. Double. COROLLA pink with a hint of orange. SEPALS creamy rose. TUBE creamy rose. Pfefferle 2002.

Schone Maid. Upright. Double. COROLLA white. SEPALS red. Bocker 2003 DE.

Schwabacher Gold. Upright. Single. COROLLA: unflared, compact, smooth petal margins; opens dark purple (79B); matures purple (N79C); 10mm (3/8") long x 7mm (1/4") wide. SEPALS: fully up, tips recurved; reddish purple (61B) upper & lower surfaces; 30mm (1 3/16") long x 7mm (1/4") wide. TUBE: reddish purple (61B); medium length & thickness; 13mm (1/2") long x 6mm (1/4") wide. STAMENS extend 18mm (11/16") beyond the corolla; reddish purple (61B) filaments; dark reddish purple (61A) anthers. PISTIL extends 42mm (1 5/8") beyond the corolla; dark reddish purple (61A) style & stigma. BUD: elongated. FOLIAGE: olive green (152C), matures to medium green (146A) upper surface; olive green (152B) lower surface (variegated yellowish orange in full sun). Leaves are 83mm (3 5/16") long x 38mm (1 1/2") wide; elliptic shaped, serrate edges, acute tips, rounded bases. Veins are

reddish purple & stems are dark reddish purple, branches are light brown. PARENTAGE: F. *glaziovana* x 'Oscar Lehmeier'. Medium upright. Self branching. Makes good upright or standard. Prefers full sun. Cold weather hardy to -15° C (6° F). Best bloom & foliage colour in bright light. Tested 5 years in Bavaria, Southern Germany. Distinguished by variegated foliage & contrasting bloom colour.
Burkhart 2009 DE AFS7098.

Schweizer Landfrauen. Upright/Trailer. Double. COROLLA: half flared; opens purple (77A), magenta (58B) base; matures dark reddish purple (72A); 17mm (5/8") long x 15mm (9/16") wide. PETALOIDS: purple (71A), magenta (58B) base; 8mm (5/16") long x 4mm (1/8") wide. SEPALS: horizontal, tips reflexed; magenta (63B) tipped yellowish green (146C) upper surface; magenta (58B) tipped yellowish green (146C) lower surface; 22mm (7/8") long x 12mm (7/16") wide. TUBE: magenta (61C); medium length & thickness; 12mm (7/16") long x 5mm (3/16") wide. FOLIAGE is dark green (137A) upper surface; medium green (138B) lower surface. PARENTAGE: 'De Brommel' x 'Ben's Ruby'.
Michiels 2007 BE AFS6338.

Sea Bird. Trailer. Single. COROLLA opens white, lightly flushed pink; corolla is half flared and is 25mm long x 25mm wide. SEPALS white flushed pink on the upper and lower surfaces; sepals are fully up with recurved tips and are 32mm long x 15mm wide. TUBE pink and is 9mm long x 5mm wide. PARENTAGE Seedling x Seedling (Descended from 'Whitehaven', 'Harry Gray' and 'Edna May'. This cultivar grown for its free flowering blooms, and their ability withstands hot weather without blooms loosing their colour.
Flemming B. 2007 UK BFS0051.

Selma Lavrijsen. Upright. Single. COROLLA is full flared with wavy petal margins; opens reddish purple (72B); matures reddish purple (74A); 26mm (1") long x 31mm (1 1/4") wide. SEPALS are fully up, tips recurved; red (46B) upper surface; red (46C) lower surface; 26mm (1") long x 11mm (7/16") wide. TUBE is red (46B); medium length & thickness; 10mm (3/8") long x 5mm (3/16") wide. FOLIAGE: dark green (137A) upper surface; medium green (137C) lower surface. Leaves are 62mm (2 7/16") long x 37mm (1 7/16") wide, ovate shaped. PARENTAGE: 'Swanley Gem' x ('Roesse Dione' x 'Delta's Bride'). Distinguished by bloom shape.

van Eijk 2005 NL AFS5901.

Sémiramis. Upright/Trailer. Single. COROLLA: quarter flared, smooth petal margins; opens & matures pale/light purple (75B/C); 17mm (11/16") long x 16mm (5/8") wide. SEPALS: half up; tips recurved up; rose (47C) upper & lower surfaces; 31mm (1 1/4") long x 7.5mm (5/16") wide. TUBE: rose (47D); short, medium thickness; 13mm (1/2") long x 3.5mm (1/8") wide. STAMENS: extend 2-8mm (1/16-5/16") below corolla; red (47B) filaments; dark red (47A) anthers. PISTIL: extends 18mm (11/16") below the corolla; red (47B) style; rose (47C) stigma. BUD: ovate/lanceolate. FOLIAGE: dark green (147A) upper surface, medium green (147B) lower surface. Leaves are 59mm (2 5/16") long x 27mm (1 1/16") wide, ovate/lanceolate shaped, serrulated edges, acute tips and rounded bases. Yellowish green veins; yellowish green/light brown stems & branches. PARENTAGE: ('String of Pearls' x 'F. *regia* subsp. *retzii*') x 'Dame Nature'. Lax upright or stiff trailer. Self branching. Makes good upright. Prefers overhead filtered light and cool climate. Best bloom and foliage colour in filtered light. Tested 3 years in Pornic, France. Distinguished by delicate bloom colour combination.
Massé 2004 FR AFS5454.

Senang. Upright. Single. COROLLA: quarter flared; separate petals; smooth petal margins; opens red (45D); matures red (45B) 10mm (3/8") long x 5mm (3/16") wide. SEPALS: horizontal; tips reflexed; red (53B) upper surface; red (45C) lower surface; 18mm (11/16") long x 5mm (3/16") wide. TUBE: dark red (53A); long & thin; 27mm (1 1/16") long x 4mm (3/16") wide. STAMENS: extend 2mm (1/16) below corolla; red (45D) filaments, grayish yellow (161A) anthers. PISTIL: extends 9mm (3/8") below the corolla, red (46D) style, dark reddish purple (60C) stigma. BUD: thin, long & cylindrical, cordate tip. FOLIAGE: dark green (147A) upper surface; medium green (147B) lower surface. Leaves are 116mm (4 9/16") long x 36mm (1 7/16") wide, elliptic shaped, serrulated edges, acute tips and acute bases. Veins are reddish; stems & branches are reddish purple. PARENTAGE: 'Insulinde' x 'Gerharda's Panache'. Upright. Makes good upright. Prefers full sun and cool or warm climate. Best bloom and foliage colour in bright light. Tested 5 years in Lisse, Holland. Distinguished by horizontally held flowers on long vertical racemes.

de Graaff 2003 NL AFS5165.

Senna Krekels. Upright/Trailer. Double. COROLLA: quarter flared, smooth petal margins; opens reddish purple (61B); matures magenta (59C); 22mm (7/8") long x 22mm (7/8") wide. SEPALS: half down; tips recurved; white (155B) upper surface; white (155C) lower surface; 46mm (1 13/16") long x 7mm (1/4") wide. TUBE: pale yellow (1D); medium length & thickness; 22mm (7/8") long x 6mm (1/4") wide. STAMENS: extend 15mm (9/16") below corolla; light pink (62B) filaments, light rose (73B) anthers. PISTIL: extends 24mm (15/16") below the corolla; pale pink (62D) style, light yellow (4C) stigma. BUD: ovate, pointed. FOLIAGE: dark green (137A) upper surface; medium green (138B) lower surface. Leaves are 62mm (2 7/16") long x 36mm (1 7/16") wide, ovate shaped, serrated edges, acute tips and obtuse bases. Veins, stems & branches are green. PARENTAGE: 'Sophie Michiels' x 'Veenlust'. Lax upright or stiff trailer. Makes good stiff trailer. Prefers overhead filtered light and cool climate. Best bloom and foliage colour in filtered light. Tested 4 years in Reusel, The Netherlands. Distinguished by bloom & foliage combination.
van Eijk 2003 NL AFS5249.

Seppe. Upright. Single. COROLLA: half flared, turned under wavy petal margins; opens dark purple (79A); matures dark purple (79B), purple (71A) at base; 23mm (15/16") long x 14mm (9/16") wide. PETALOIDS: same colour as corolla; 15mm (9/16") long x 12mm (1/2") wide. SEPALS: fully up; tips recurved; dark reddish purple (64A) upper surface; reddish purple (61B) lower surface; 21mm(13/16") long x 8mm (5/16") wide. TUBE: magenta (63B); long & thin; 22mm (7/8") long x 4mm (3/16") wide. STAMENS: do not extend below the corolla; reddish purple (61B) filaments, pale yellow (1D) anthers. PISTIL extends 7mm (1/4") below the corolla; reddish purple (61B) style, purple (71A) stigma. BUD: ovate. FOLIAGE: medium green (139B) upper surface; medium green (139C) lower surface. Leaves are 45mm (1 3/4") long x 25mm (1") wide, elliptic shaped, serrulated edges, acute tips and rounded bases. Veins are dark red purple (187D); stems are dark reddish purple (187B), branches are very dark purple (187A). PARENTAGE: 'WALZ Harp' x 'Rohees New Millennium'. Medium upright. Makes good upright. Prefers overhead filtered light. Best bloom and foliage colour in filtered light. Tested 3 years in Berlaar, Belgium. NBFK

certificate at Meise. Distinguished by bloom colour and shape.
Geerts J. 2003 BE AFS5120.

Serge Gerard. Upright. Double. COROLLA: Half flared; opens dark reddish purple (60A); matures dark red (53A); 21mm (13/16") long x 23mm (7/8") wide. SEPALS: half up, tips recurved up; rose (63C) upper surface; magenta (58B) lower surface; 24mm (15/16") long x 12mm (7/16") wide. TUBE: rose (63C); medium length & thickness; 17mm (5/8") long x 6mm (1/4") wide. FOLIAGE is dark green (137A) upper surface; medium green (137D) lower surface. PARENTAGE: 'Roesse Carme' x 'Lye's Unique'.
Decoster 2007 BE AFS6619.

Setpoint. Upright/Trailer. Single. COROLLA is half flared, trumpet shaped; opens & matures rose (55B); 7mm (1/4") long x 6mm (1/4") wide. SEPALS are horizontal, tips reflexed; light pink (55D) upper surface; pink (55C) lower surface; 13mm (1/2") long x 4mm (1/8") wide. TUBE is pink (62C), darker base; 31mm (1 1/4") long x 4mm (1/8") wide. FOLIAGE: dark green (147A) upper surface; light olive green (148B) lower surface. PARENTAGE: 'Gerharda's Panache' x 'Gerharda's Panache'. Distinguished by panicles of triphylla shaped rose blossoms.
de Graaff H. 2006 NL AFS6246.

Seyst '95'. Upright. Single. COROLLA: Half flared, cup shaped; opens & matures white (155A); 25mm (1") long x 30mm (1 3/16") wide. SEPALS: half up, tips recurved up; pale pink (56A) upper surface; pink (55C) to light pink (55D) lower surface; 25mm (1") long x 12mm (7/16") wide. TUBE: pink (52D); short, medium thickness; 10mm (3/8") long x 5mm (3/16") wide. FOLIAGE is dark green (147A) upper surface; medium green (147B) lower surface. PARENTAGE: 'Cristina Becker' x unknown.
Krom 2007 NL AFS6555.

Shannan So Special. Upright. Double. COROLLA is three quarter flared and ruffled with smooth turned under petal margins; opens reddish purple (74A) and light purple (74C); matures reddish purple (74A) edged pale purple (74D), splashes rose (68C) ; 40mm (1 9/16") long x 70mm (2 3/4") wide. PETALOIDS are same colour as corolla; 20mm (13/16") long x 20mm (13/16") wide. SEPALS are horizontal, tips recurved; pale pink (62D) tipped green upper surface, pink (62A) tipped green lower surface; 55mm (2 3/16") long x 20mm (13/16") wide. TUBE is

yellowish white (158A), long and thin; 30mm (1 3/16") long x 6mm (1/4") wide. STAMENS extend 20mm (13/16") below the corolla; dark rose (67C) filaments and yellowish white (158A) anthers. PISTIL extends 30mm (1 3/16") below the corolla; rose (65A) style and yellowish white (158A) stigma. BUD is large, elongated. FOLIAGE is medium green (146A) on upper surface and yellowish green (146B) on lower surface. Leaves are 75mm (2 15/16") long x 50mm (2") wide, cordate shaped, serrulated edges, acute tips and rounded bases. Veins are green, red thru center; stems brown; branches are red. PARENTAGE: 'Deep Purple' x 'Marcus Graham'. Small upright. Self branching. Makes good upright or standard. Prefers overhead filtered light and warm climate. Heat tolerant if shaded. Hardy to 32°F. Best bloom colour in bright light. Tested three years in Walthamstow, London, England. Distinguished by profuse blooms and bloom colour combination.
Allsop 2002 UK AFS4811.

Sharon Leslie. Upright. Single. COROLLA fluorescent pink. SEPALS bright pink.
Reynolds G. 2002 UK.

Sheila Mary Mason. COROLLA almost scarlet. SEPALS light pink tipped green. TUBE light pink.
Strickland T. 2006 UK.

Sheila Purdy. Upright. Single. COROLLA is quarter flared, bell shaped, with turned under petal margins; opens purple (77A), rose (68B) at base; matures reddish purple (74A), rose (68B) at base; 15mm (9/16") long x 15mm (9/16") wide. SEPALS are horizontal, tips recurved; pale pink (69A) tipped green upper surface, rose (68B) creped lower surface; 20mm (13/16") long x 7mm (1/4") wide. TUBE is pale pink (69A) overlaid red (53C), medium length and thickness; 12mm (1/2") long x 7mm (1/4") wide. STAMENS extend 10mm (3/8") beyond the corolla; rose (68B) filaments; cream overlaid rose (68B) anthers. PISTIL extends 20mm (13/16") below the corolla; rose (68B) style; cream stigma. BUD is cordate. FOLIAGE is dark green (147A) upper surface, lighter green lower surface. Leaves are 42mm (1 11/16") long x 25mm (1") wide, lanceolate shaped, serrated edges, acute tips and rounded bases. Veins are light green, stems are dull red, branches are light green maturing to dull red. PARENTAGE: 'Dot Woodage' x 'Our Topsy'. Small upright. Makes good pillar. Prefers full sun. Best

bloom colour in bright light. Tested three years in Edenbridge, Kent & southern England. Distinguished by bloom colour combination.
Holmes 2004 UK AFS5365.

Sheila's Love. Upright. Single. COROLLA rich violet. SEPALS white tipped green.
Kirby 2002 UK.

Sheila's Surprise. Upright/Trailer. Semi Double. COROLLA is three quarter flared, triangular shaped with smooth turned under petal margins; opens dark rose (51A), pink (52D) near TUBE; matures red (52A), pink (50D) near TUBE; 20mm (13/16") long x 45mm (1 3/4") wide. SEPALS are half up, tips recurved up; pink (50D) tipped green upper surface, pink (52D) tipped green lower surface; 30mm (1 3/16") long x 12mm (1/2") wide. TUBE is pink (50D), proportionately medium length and thick; 12mm (1/2") long x 8mm (5/16") wide. STAMENS extend 20mm (13/16") below the corolla; dark rose (54B) filaments and pink (54D) anthers. PISTIL extends 50mm (2") below the corolla; pale pink (56A) style and yellowish white (158A) stigma. BUD is medium, elongated. FOLIAGE is medium green (146A) on upper surface and yellowish green (146B) on lower surface. Leaves are 65mm (2 9/16") long x 35mm (1 3/8") wide, cordate shaped, serrulated edges, acute tips and rounded bases. Veins are green; stems brown; branches are red. PARENTAGE: 'Coachman' x 'Tantalizing Tracy'. Lax upright. Self branching. Makes good basket or standard. Prefers overhead filtered light and warm climate. Heat tolerant if shaded. Hardy to 32°F. Best bloom colour in bright light. Tested three years in Walthamstow, London, England. Distinguished by profuse, "skirt" shaped blooms.
Allsop 2002 UK AFS4809.

Shekirb. Upright. Double. COROLLA magenta rose. SEPALS white flushed pink.
Kirby 2003 UK.

Siem Liebregts. Trailer. Double. COROLLA: half flared, smooth petal margins; opens & matures white (155B); 30mm (1 3/16") long x 24mm (15/16") wide. SEPALS: horizontal; tips recurved; pale pink (62D) upper surface; pink (62C) lower surface; 45mm (1 3/4") long x 17mm (11/16") wide. TUBE: pale pink (62D); medium length & thickness; 12mm (1/2") long x 7mm (1/4") wide. STAMENS: extend 17mm (11/16") below corolla; pink (62A) filaments; pale pink (62D) anthers.

PISTIL: extends 26mm (1") below the corolla; magenta (63A) style, yellowish white (4D) stigma. BUD: ovate, pointed. FOLIAGE: medium green (137C) upper surface; medium green (138B) lower surface. Leaves are 57mm (2 1/4") long x 26mm (1") wide, ovate shaped, serrulated edges, acute tips and rounded bases. Veins, stems & branches are red. PARENTAGE: 'Grüss an Graz' x 'Hilchenbacher Grüss'. Natural trailer. Makes good basket. Prefers overhead filtered light and cool climate. Best bloom and foliage colour in filtered light. Tested 4 years in Göttingen, Germany. Distinguished by bloom & foliage combination.
Strümper 2003 DE AFS5243.

Silbernes Erzgebirge. Upright/Trailer. Double. COROLLA: quarter flared; opens dark reddish purple (72A); matures light reddish purple (72C); 28mm (1 1/8") long x 32mm (1 1/4") wide. SEPALS: horizontal, tips recurved; red (52A) upper & lower surfaces; 36mm (1 7/16") long x 16mm (5/8") wide. TUBE: red (52A); 20mm (3/4") long x 7mm (1/4") wide. FOLIAGE is dark green (137A) upper surface; medium green (137C) lower surface. PARENTAGE: 'Orwell' x 'Rohees New Millenium'.
Burkhart 2008 DE AFS6865.

Silvia van Heijst. Upright/Trailer. Double. COROLLA: three quarter flared, smooth petal margins; opens violet (85A); matures violet (84A); 29mm (1 1/8") long x 21mm (13/16") wide. SEPALS: half up; tips recurved up; white (155A) upper & lower surfaces; 34mm (1 5/16") long x 12mm (1/2") wide. TUBE: white (155A); medium length & thickness; 14mm (9/16") long x 5mm (3/16") wide. STAMENS: extend 21mm (13/16") below corolla; light reddish purple (73A) filaments & anthers. PISTIL: extends 29mm (1 1/8") below the corolla; white (155C) style; light yellow (4C) stigma. BUD: ovate. FOLIAGE: medium green (137D) upper surface; medium green (138B) lower surface. Leaves are 70mm (2 3/4") long x 36mm (1 7/16") wide, cordate shaped, serrated edges, acute tips and rounded bases. Veins, stems & branches are red. PARENTAGE: 'Sofie Michiels' x 'Cameron Ryle'. Lax upright or stiff trailer. Makes good stiff trailer. Prefers overhead filtered light and cool climate. Best bloom and foliage colour in filtered light. Tested 4 years in Duizel, The Netherlands. Distinguished by bloom & foliage combination.
Tamerus 2003 NL AFS5302.

Simmersier. Upright. Single. COROLLA is half flared with turned up petal margins; opens & matures orange (31B); 9mm (3/8") long x 7mm (1/4") wide. SEPALS are half down, tips reflexed; red (53B) upper surface; yellowish green (144B) lower surface; 10mm (3/8") long x 4mm (3/16") wide. TUBE is red (45B); medium length & thickness; 15mm (9/16") long x 5mm (3/16") wide. FOLIAGE: medium green (137B) upper surface; medium green (137D) lower surface. Leaves are 62mm (2 7/16") long x 35mm (1 3/8") wide, ovate shaped. PARENTAGE: [('F. michoacanensis' x 'F. obconica') x 'Ashley] x 'F. splendens'. Nomination by N.K.V.F. as recommendable cultivar. Distinguished by profuse, little bright coloured flowers.
Dijkstra 2005 NL AFS5785.

Simone Slegers. Upright/Trailer. Double. COROLLA: three quarter flared, smooth petal margins; opens purple (83A); matures dark reddish purple (61A); 30mm (1 3/16") long x 24mm (15/16") wide. SEPALS: horizontal; tips recurved; reddish purple (58A) upper surface; magenta (63A) lower surface; 32mm (1 1/4") long x 16mm (5/8") wide. TUBE: magenta (59D); medium length & thickness; 17mm (11/16") long x 7mm (1/4") wide. STAMENS: extend 36mm (1 7/16") below corolla; reddish purple (61B) filaments; purple (77A) anthers. PISTIL: extends 47mm (1 7/8") below the corolla; dark reddish purple (60A) style; pale pink (62D) stigma. BUD: cordate. FOLIAGE: medium green (138A) upper surface; medium green (138B) lower surface. Leaves are 62mm (2 7/16") long x 40mm (1 9/16") wide, cordate shaped, serrated edges, acute tips and rounded bases. Veins are green, stems are red, branches are green. PARENTAGE: 'Sofie Michiels' x 'Rohees Mintaka'. Lax upright or stiff trailer. Makes good stiff trailer. Prefers overhead filtered light and cool climate. Best bloom and foliage colour in filtered light. Tested 4 years in Duizel, The Netherlands. Distinguished by bloom colour.
Tamerus 2003 NL AFS5296.

Simonne Bosmans. Trailer. Double. COROLLA: half flared; opens light purple (70C), striped dark rose (67C) and matures magenta (68A); 20mm (3/4") long x 18mm (11/16") wide. PETALOIDS: magenta (71C), striped rose (52C); 13mm (1/2") long x 11mm (7/16") wide. SEPALS are half down, tips reflexed; rose (68C) tipped apple green (144A) upper surface; rose (52C) tipped apple green (144C) lower surface; 36mm (1 7/16") long x 12mm (7/16") wide. TUBE is pale lavender

(65D); long & thin; 26mm (1") long x 4mm (1/8") wide. FOLIAGE is dark green (136B) upper surface; medium green (138A) lower surface. PARENTAGE: 'Leon Pauwels' x 'Oso Sweet'.
Michiels 2007 BE AFS6516.

Simonne Gijsels. Upright/Trailer. Single. COROLLA is quarter flared with smooth petal margins; opens and matures reddish orange (43B); 19mm (3/4") long x 20mm (13/16") wide. SEPALS half down, tips recurved; pink (54D) upper surface, rose (54C) lower surface; 36mm (1 7/16") long x 9mm (3/8") wide. TUBE is pink (54D), long with medium thickness; 30mm (1 3/16") long x 5mm (3/16") wide. STAMENS extend 7mm (1/4") below the corolla; pink (52D) filaments and anthers. PISTIL extends 18mm (11/16") below the corolla; pink (52D) style, light yellow (4C) stigma. BUD is long, ovate. FOLIAGE is medium green (137B) upper surface, medium green (137C) lower surface. Leaves are 80mm (3 3/16") long x 50mm (2") wide, ovate shaped, serrated edges, acute tips and rounded bases. Veins, stems and branches are light green (150D). PARENTAGE: 'Geneviéve de Fontenay' x unknown. Lax upright or stiff trailer. Self branching. Makes good upright or standard. Prefers cool climate. Heat tolerant if shaded. Best bloom colour in limited light. Tested four years in Pornic, France. Distinguished by bloom colour and profuse blooms.
Massé 2002 FR AFS4868.

Sint Bartholomeus. Trailer. Double. COROLLA: quarter flared, turned under smooth petal margins; opens dark purple (78A), reddish purple (74B) at base; matures magenta (71C); 24mm (15/16") long x 45mm (1 3/4") wide. PETALOIDS: two per sepal; same colour as corolla, 22mm (7/8") long x 13mm (1/2") wide. SEPALS: half up; tips recurved up; magenta (58B) upper and lower surfaces; 33mm (1 5/16") long x 17mm (11/16") wide. TUBE: magenta (58B); medium length & thickness; 14mm (9/16") long x 8mm (5/16") wide. STAMENS: extend 22mm (7/8") below the corolla; magenta (58B) filaments, reddish purple (58A) anthers. PISTIL extends 34mm (1 5/16") below the corolla; light rose (58D) style, dark yellowish orange (14A) stigma. BUD: cordate. FOLIAGE: dark green (137A) upper surface; medium green (138B) lower surface. Leaves are 73mm (2 7/8") long x 55mm (2 3/16") wide, cordate shaped, serrulated edges, acute tips and cordate bases. Veins light green (138D), stems and branches are

orangy brown (174B). PARENTAGE: 'Rohees New Millennium' x 'Pinto de Blue'. Natural trailer. Self branching. Makes good basket. Prefers overhead filtered light. Best bloom and foliage colour in filtered light. Tested 3 years in Koningshooikt, Belgium. NBFK certificate at Meise. Distinguished by bloom colour.
Michiels 2003 BE AFS5104.

Sint Ferdinand. Upright/Trailer. Single. COROLLA: half flared, turned under smooth petal margins; opens reddish purple (72B), magenta (58B) at base; matures reddish purple (64B), light rose (58D) at base; 22mm (7/8") long x 30mm (1 3/16") wide. SEPALS: horizontal; tips recurved; light pink (49C) tipped apple green (144C) upper surface; rose (55B) tipped apple green (144C) lower surface; 37mm (1 7/16") long x 15mm (9/16") wide. TUBE: light pink (49C) & yellowish green (145A); medium length & thickness; 27mm (1 1/16") long x 5mm (3/16") wide. STAMENS: do not extend below the corolla; pale pink (62D) filaments, dark red (178B) anthers. PISTIL extends 8mm (5/16") below the corolla; pale pink (56B) style, light yellow (11C) stigma. BUD: bulbous. FOLIAGE: dark green (137A) upper surface; medium green (138B) lower surface. Leaves are 85mm (3 3/8") long x 40mm (1 9/16") wide, lanceoate shaped, serrulated edges, acute tips and rounded bases. Veins are dark reddish purple (187D), stems are very dark reddish purple (186A), branches are plum (184B). PARENTAGE: 'WALZ Harp' x 'Norfolk Ivory'. Lax upright or stiff trailer. Self branching. Makes good basket. Prefers overhead filtered light. Best bloom and foliage colour in filtered light. Tested 3 years in Koningshooikt, Belgium. NBFK certificate at Meise. Distinguished by bloom shape.
Michiels 2003 BE AFS5105.

Siobhon Evans. Upright. Double. COROLLA white splashed pink. SEPALS coral pink.
Evans 2004 UK.

Sir Steve Redgrave. Upright/Trailer. Double. COROLLA is quarter flared, rounded, with smooth turned under petal margins; opens and matures white (155), magenta (57C) at base, blotched red (45A); 30mm (1 3/16") long x 48mm (1 7/8") wide. SEPALS are horizontal, tips recurved; red (45A) upper surface, red (45A) creped lower surface; 47mm (1 7/8") long x 20mm (13/16") wide. TUBE is red (45A); short and thin; 10mm (3/8") long x 6mm (1/4") wide. STAMENS extend 23mm (15/16") below the

426

corolla; red (45A) filaments and anthers. PISTIL extends 25mm (1") below the corolla; red (45A) style and stigma. BUD is acorn shaped. FOLIAGE is medium green (137C) upper surface, medium green (138B) lower surface. Leaves are 73mm (2 7/8") long x 28mm (1 1/8") wide, ovate shaped, smooth edges, acute tips and rounded bases. Veins, stems and branches are red. PARENTAGE: 'Seventh Heaven' x 'Satellite'. Lax upright or stiff trailer. Makes good basket, upright or decorative. Prefers cool climate. Heat tolerant if shaded. Best bloom colour in filtered light. Tested five years in Gloucester, England. Distinguished by striking colour contrast in petals, varying on some blooms.
Hickman 2002 UK AFS4850.

Sir Thomas Allen. Single. COROLLA lavender blue. SEPALS creamy pink tipped green. TUBE creamy pink tipped green.
Waving 2004 UK.

Siuol. Upright. Single. COROLLA is half flared with turned under wavy petal margins; opens rose (68B), pink (62C) base; matures rose (68C), light pink (62B) base; 24mm (15/16") long x 17mm (11/16") wide. SEPALS are half up, tips recurved up; dark rose (51A) tipped light apple green (145B) upper surface; red (53D) tipped light apple green (145B) lower surface; 36mm (1 7/16") long x 9mm (3/8") wide. TUBE is rose (54C); long, medium thickness; 30mm (1 3/16") long x 6mm (1/4") wide. FOLIAGE is dark green (139A) upper surface; medium green (138B) lower surface. Leaves are 70mm (2 3/4") long x 37mm (1 7/16") wide, ovate shaped. PARENTAGE: 'Leverkusen' x unknown. Meise 8-14-04. Distinguished by flower shape.
Geerts L. 2005 BE AFS5832.

Sjaan En Piet. Upright/Trailer. Double. COROLLA: half flared; opens light violet (N87C), rose (65A) base; matures light purple (N78B); 22mm (7/8") long x 21mm (13/16") wide. PETALOIDS: violet (N87B), light pink (65B) base; 11mm (7/16") long x 9mm (5/16") wide. SEPALS: horizontal, tips reflexed; pale lavender (65D) tipped yellowish green (144B) upper surface; light pink (65D) tipped yellowish green (144B) lower surface; 48mm (1 7/8") long x 15mm (9/16") wide. TUBE: pale pink (62D); medium length & thickness; 12mm (7/16") long x 6mm (1/4") wide. FOLIAGE is dark green (136B) upper surface; medium green (138A) lower surface. PARENTAGE: 'Vreni Schleeweis' x 'Futura'.
Michiels 2007 BE AFS6339.

Sjan Schilders. Upright/Trailer. Double. COROLLA: three quarter flared, smooth petal margins; opens dark reddish purple (59A); matures magenta (59C); 26mm (1") long x 24mm (15/16") wide. SEPALS: fully up; tips recurved; rose (68B) upper surface; magenta (63A) lower surface; 44mm (1 3/4") long x 12mm (1/2") wide. TUBE: rose (68B); medium length & thickness; 20mm (13/16") long x 6mm (1/4") wide. STAMENS: extend 19mm (3/4") below corolla; dark reddish purple (60C) filaments; dark reddish purple (59A) anthers. PISTIL: extends 42mm (1 11/16") below the corolla; reddish purple (61B) style; pale yellow (5D) stigma. BUD: ovate. FOLIAGE: dark green (137A) upper surface; medium green (138B) lower surface. Leaves are 76mm (3") long x 35mm (1 3/8") wide, cordate shaped, serrated edges, acute tips and rounded bases. Veins are green, stems & branches are red. PARENTAGE: {[('Bon Accord' x 'Bicentennial') x ('Vobeglo' x 'Dancing Flame')] x 'Rohees Alrami'} x 'Allure'. Lax upright or stiff trailer. Makes good stiff trailer. Prefers overhead filtered light and cool climate. Best bloom and foliage colour in filtered light. Tested 4 years in Duizel, The Netherlands. Distinguished by bloom colour.
Tamerus 2003 NL AFS5298.

Sleedoorn. Trailer. Double. COROLLA: half flared; opens white (155C); matures white (155B) & pale pink (56D); 21mm (13/16") long x 19mm (3/4") wide. PETALOIDS: white (155C); 13mm (1/2") long x 9mm (5/16") wide. SEPALS: horizontal, tips reflexed; white (155B) tipped yellowish green (144B) upper & lower surfaces; 35mm (1 3/8") long x 14mm (9/16") wide. TUBE: white (155C) striped medium green (137D); medium length & thickness; 13mm (1/2") long x 4mm (1/8") wide. FOLIAGE is dark green (136B) upper surface; medium green (138A) lower surface. PARENTAGE: 'Vreni Schleeweis' x 'Kiss'.
Michiels 2007 BE AFS6340.

Smarty. Upright. Single. COROLLA is unflared, bell shaped, with smooth petal margins; opens violet (87B) veined rose (61D); matures light purple (78B) veined rose (61D); 25mm (1") long x 24 mm (15/16") wide. SEPALS are fully up, tips recurved; rose (61D) tipped light green (145D) upper & lower surfaces; 27mm (1 1/16") long x 10mm (3/8") wide. TUBE is rose (61D), short, medium thickness; 10mm (3/8") long x 7mm (1/4") wide. FOLIAGE: medium green (137C) upper surface; medium green (137D) lower surface. Leaves are 50mm (2") long x 20mm (13/16") wide, lanceolate shaped.

PARENTAGE: 'Richita' x seedling of 'Blue Ice' x 'Norah Henderson'. Distinguished by profuse flowering over long period.
Hall 2005 UK AFS5649.

Sneeuwwitje. Upright/Trailer. Double. COROLLA: Three quarter flared; opens & matures white (155D); 16mm (5/8") long x 21mm (13/16") wide. SEPALS: half up, tips reflexed up; white (155D) upper & lower surfaces; 36mm (1 7/16") long x 11mm (7/16") wide. TUBE: white (155D); medium length, thin; 16mm (5/8") long x 3mm (1/8") wide. FOLIAGE is medium green (137B) upper surface; medium green (137C) lower surface. PARENTAGE: 'Sofie Michiels' x 'Oranje van Os'.
Roes 2007 NL AFS6703.

Snow Pearls. Upright. Single. COROLLA: three quarter flared, smooth petal margins; opens & matures light pink (55D) edged pale purple (75C); 12mm (1/2") long 16mm (5/8") wide. SEPALS: half up; tips recurved up; white (155B) tipped green upper & lower surfaces; 22mm (7/8") long x 10mm (3/8") wide. TUBE: cream (158D); medium length & thickness; 7mm (1/4") long x 7mm (1/4") wide. STAMENS: extend 19mm (3/4") below corolla; light rose (73C) filaments; dark reddish purple (59A) anthers. PISTIL: extends 25mm (1") below the corolla; cream (158D) style & stigma. BUD: oval, pointed. FOLIAGE: dark green (147A) upper surface; medium green (138B) lower surface. Leaves are 44mm (1 3/4") long x 32mm (1 1/4") wide, ovate shaped, serrulated edges, acute tips and rounded bases. Green veins, stems & branches. PARENTAGE: 'Julie Ann Goodwin' x 'WALZ Jubleteen'. Small upright. Self branching. Makes good upright or pillar. Prefers overhead filtered light, cool climate. Best bloom and foliage colour in filtered light. Tested 3 years in Stoke-On-Trent, England. Distinguished by colour combination.
Goodwin 2004 UK AFS5578.

Sofie Michiels. Upright/Trailer. Double. COROLLA is three quarter flared with smooth petal margins; opens and matures white (155A); 18mm (11/16") long x 21mm (13/16") wide. SEPALS are fully up, tips reflexed; light pink (65C) upper and lower surfaces; 46mm (1 13/16") long x 18mm (11/16") wide. TUBE is dark pink (62C), proportionally long with medium thickness; 28mm (1 1/8") long x 8mm (5/16") wide. STAMENS extend 12mm (1/2") below the corolla; pink (55C) filaments and pink (49A) anthers. PISTIL extends 24mm (15/16")

below the corolla; pink (55C) style and light pink (49C) stigma. BUD is ovate and pointed. FOLIAGE is medium green (137B) on upper surface and medium green (138B) on lower surface. Leaves are 71mm (2 13/16") long x 28mm (1 1/8) wide, cordate shaped, serrated edges, acute tips and rounded bases. Veins, stems and branches are red. PARENTAGE: ('Annabel' x 'Annabel') x ['WALZ Mandoline' x ('Annabel' x 'Vrijheid')]. Lax upright or stiff trailer. Makes good stiff trailer. Prefers overhead filtered light and cool climate. Tested four years in Knegsel, The Netherlands. Distinguished by bloom and foliage combination.
Roes 2002 NL AFS4796.

Sofiedoria. Upright. Single to Semi Double. COROLLA: quarter flared, turned under smooth petal margins; opens violet (84A), white (155B) base; matures light purple (78B), white (155B) base; 15mm (9/16") long x 22mm (7/8") wide. SEPALS: fully up; tips recurved; white (155A) flushed rose (68B) tipped yellowish green (145A) upper surface; light rose (63D) lower surface; 35mm (1 3/8") long x 10mm (3/8") wide. TUBE: white (155A); medium length & thickness; 10mm(3/8") long x 4mm (3/16") wide. STAMENS: 12mm (1/2") below corolla; dark rose (58C) filaments, dark reddish purple (59A) anthers. PISTIL: extends 23mm (7/8") below the corolla, light rose (58D) style, light yellow (4B) stigma. BUD: elongated. FOLIAGE: dark green (137A) upper surface; medium green (137C) lower surface. Leaves are 57mm (2 1/4") long x 22mm (7/8") wide, lanceolate shaped, serrulated edges, acute tips and rounded bases. Veins & stems are medium green (138B), branches are olive green (152C). PARENTAGE: 'Rosea' x unknown. Medium upright. Makes good upright. Prefers overhead filtered light. Best bloom and foliage colour in filtered light. Tested 3 years in Halen, Belgium. NBFK Certificate at Meise. Distinguished by bloom shape and profuse blooms.
Custers 2003 BE AFS5200.

Softpink Jubelteen. Upright. Single. COROLLA is quarter flared with turned under smooth petal margins; opens and matures pale lavender (65D) edged rose (65A); 12mm (1/2") long x 15 mm (5/8") wide. SEPALS are half down, tips reflexed; white (155A) tipped light green (142A) upper surface, white (155C) flushed pink (62A) lower surface; 21mm (13/16") long x 11mm (7/16") wide. TUBE is light pink (38D), medium length and thickness; 11mm (7/16")

long x 5mm (3/16") wide. STAMENS extend 11mm (7/16") beyond the corolla; light coral (38A) filaments, light yellow (3C) anthers. PISTIL extends 20mm (13/16) beyond the corolla; white (155C) style; light yellow (2B) stigma. BUD is ovate. FOLIAGE is dark green (137A) upper surface, medium green (138B) lower surface. Leaves are 57mm (2 1/4") long x 37mm (1 7/16") wide, ovate shaped, serrulated edges, acute tips and cordate bases. Veins, stems and branches are light green (138D). PARENTAGE: Sport of 'WALZ Jubelteen'. Medium upright. Self branching. Makes good upright or standard. Prefers full sun. Best bloom and foliage colour in bright or filtered light. Tested three years in Koningshooikt and Hoeselt, Belgium. Certificate N.B.F.K. at Meise. Distinguished by profuse upstanding light coral rose blooms.
Michiels-Wagemans 2002 BE AFS4928.

Song of Stars. Upright/Trailer. Single. COROLLA is quarter flared with turned under wavy petal margins; opens rose (68B); matures light reddish purple (73A); 24mm (15/16") long x 11mm (7/16") wide. SEPALS are horizontal, tips recurved; light pink (49B), tipped light apple green (145C) upper surface; pink (51D), tipped light apple green (145C) lower surface; 27mm (1 1/16") long x 7mm (1/4") wide. TUBE is pale pink (49D); medium length & thickness; 11mm (7/16") long x 6mm (1/4") wide. FOLIAGE: dark green (137A) upper surface; medium green (138B) lower surface. Leaves are 33mm (1 5/16") long x 17mm (11/16") wide, ovate shaped. PARENTAGE: 'Querry' x unknown. Meise 8-14-04. Distinguished by bloom colour.
Willems 2005 BE AFS5723.

Song of Twins. Upright/Trailer. Single. COROLLA is quarter flared; opens light reddish purple (72D); matures magenta (71C); 22mm (7/8") long x 18mm (11/16") wide. SEPALS are horizontal, tips reflexed; pale pink (56B) tipped light yellow green (150A) upper surface; rose (54C) tipped light yellow green (150A) lower surface; 21mm (13/16") long x 7mm (1/4") wide. TUBE is pink (55C); long & thin; 32mm (1 1/4") long x 5mm (3/16") wide. FOLIAGE is dark green (137A) upper surface; medium green (138B) lower surface. PARENTAGE: 'Ernest Claes' x 'Onbekend'.
Willems 2007 BE AFS6425.

Southern Pride. Single. COROLLA pink. SEPALS orange.

Swinbank 2002 UK.

Souvenir of Holland. Upright. Single. COROLLA is quarter flared with turned up wavy margins; opens and matures dark orange red (34A); 12mm (1/2") long x 10mm (3/8") wide. SEPALS are fully up, tips recurved; peach (37B) upper surface, rose (48B) lower surface; 15mm (5/8") long x 4mm (3/16") wide. TUBE is peach (37B), short and thin; 14mm (9/16") long x 3mm (1/8") wide. STAMENS extend 1mm (1/16") beyond the corolla; rose (48B) filaments and grayish yellow (161A) anthers. PISTIL extends 9mm (3/8") below the corolla; pink (48C) style, pale tan (159A) stigma. BUD is long TUBEd with tear drop shape. FOLIAGE is dark green (147B) upper surface, medium green (147C) lower surface. Leaves are 53mm (2 1/8") long x 28mm (1 1/8") wide, ovate shaped, smooth edges, acute tips and rounded bases. Veins, stems and branches are reddish. PARENTAGE: 'Rosea' x 'F. *fulgens*'. Small upright. Self branching. Makes good basket or upright. Prefers full sun. Heat tolerant if shaded. Best bloom and foliage colour in filtered light. Tested thirteen years in Lisse, Holland. Distinguished by small orange flowers on plume-like inflorescences (a shoot bearing clusters of flowers).
de Graaff 2002 NL AFS4881.

Special Angel. Upright. Semi Double. COROLLA: quarter flared; opens violet (76A); matures light purple (78C); 25mm (1") long x 25mm (1") wide. SEPALS: half down, tips reflexed; pink (62A), streaked white, tipped green upper surface; pink (62A) tipped green lower surface; 35mm (1 3/8") long x 15mm (9/16") wide. TUBE: pale pink (56C);; 20mm (3/4") long x 8mm (5/16") wide. FOLIAGE is medium green (138A) upper surface; medium green (138B) lower surface. PARENTAGE: 'Snowbird' x 'Dana Samantha'.
Smith R. 2008 UK AFS6817.

St. Laurens. Trailer. Single. COROLLA is quarter flared with turned under wavy petal margins; opens dark reddish purple (72A); matures purple (71A); 19mm (3/4") long x 14mm (9/16") wide. PETALOIDS: Same colour as corolla; 12mm (1/2") long x 10mm (3/8") wide. SEPALS are half down, tips reflexed; magenta (61C) upper surface; red (53C) lower surface; 28mm (1 1/8") long x 11mm (7/16") wide. TUBE is magenta (58B); long & thin; 26mm (1") long x 4mm (3/16") wide. FOLIAGE: dark green (137A) upper surface; medium green (138B) lower surface.

429

Leaves are 62mm (2 7/16") long x 39mm (1 9/16") wide, ovate shaped. PARENTAGE: 'Pink Fantasia' x unknown. Meis 3-7-04. Distinguished by colour combination. Van Vooren 2005 BE AFS5664.

St. Leonhard. Upright. Double. COROLLA: three quarter flared, smooth petal margins; opens purple (83C); matures purple (81B); 30mm (1 3/16") long, 55mm (2 3/16") wide. SEPALS: half up; tips recurved up; light pink (62B) tipped green upper surface; pink (62A) lower surface; 40mm (1 9/16") long x 20mm (13/16") wide. TUBE: white (155B); short, medium thickness; 15mm (9/16") long x 6mm (1/4") wide. STAMENS: extend 20mm (13/16") below corolla; magenta (63B) filaments; dark reddish purple (60B) anthers. PISTIL: extends 45mm (1 3/4") below the corolla; light rose (63D) style; yellow (12A) stigma. BUD: drop shaped. FOLIAGE: medium green (138A) upper surface; medium green (138B) lower surface. Leaves are 110mm (4 5/16") long x 80mm (3 1/8") wide, ovate shaped, serrated edges, acute tips and rounded bases. Green veins & branches; brown stems. PARENTAGE: 'Deep Purple' x 'Stadt Langenlois'. Tall upright. Self branching. Makes good upright or standard. Heat tolerant if shaded. Best bloom and foliage colour in filtered light. Tested 3 years in Amstetten, Austria. Distinguished by bloom colour & shape. Gindl 2004 AT AFS5629.

Stad Genk. Trailer. Double. COROLLA is three quarter flared with turned under smooth petal margins; opens purple (81A), white (155B) base; matures dark rose (71D); 29mm (1 1/8") long x 25mm (1") wide. PETALOIDS: dark reddish purple (72A); 18mm (11/16") long x 11mm (7/16") wide. SEPALS are horizontal, tips recurved; light reddish purple (72D), white (155B) base, tipped light green (142C) upper surface; light rose (73C) tipped light green (142C) lower surface; 33mm (1 5/16") long x 17mm (11/16") wide. TUBE is white (155B); medium length & thickness; 22mm (7/8") long x 5mm (3/16") wide. FOLIAGE: dark green (136B) upper surface; medium green (138B) lower surface. Leaves are 61mm (2 3/8") long x 24mm (15/16") wide, elliptic shaped. PARENTAGE: 'Sofie Michiels' x 'Rohees Alioth'. Meis 3-7-04. Distinguished by colour combination. Michiels 2005 BE AFS5682.

Stad Tienen. Upright/Trailer. Double. COROLLA: half flared, turned under wavy petal margins; opens violet (N87B); matures

dark violet (N80A); 22mm (7/8") long x 20mm (3/4") wide. PETALOIDS: violet (N82B); 12mm (7/16") long x 6mm (1/4") wide. SEPALS: horizontal, tips recurved; white (155C) tipped apple green (144C) upper surface; white (155B) tipped apple green (144C) lower surface; 42mm (1 5/8") long x 17mm (5/8") wide. TUBE: white (155B); medium length & thickness; 18mm (11/16") long x 8mm (5/16") wide. STAMENS extend 8mm (5/16") beyond the corolla; rose (68B) filaments; light purple (70C) anthers. PISTIL extends 19mm (3/4") beyond the corolla; pale lavender (69D) style; pale yellow (2D) stigma. BUD: conical. FOLIAGE: dark green (137A) upper surface; medium green (138B) lower surface. Leaves are 60mm (2 3/8") long x 37mm (1 7/16") wide; ovate shaped, serrate edges, acute tips, rounded bases. Veins are olive green (153A), stems are reddish purple (186B), branches are light grayish red (182C) & light green (138C). PARENTAGE: 'Nestor-Berthe Menten' x 'Ons Jaspertje'. Lax upright or stiff trailer. Self branching. Makes good basket or upright. Prefers overhead filtered light, cool climate. Best bloom & foliage colour in filtered light. Tested 3 years in Koningshooikt, Belgium. Waanrode 7/5/08. Distinguished by bloom colour combination. Michiels 2009 BE AFS7222.

Stadt Hollabrunn. Upright. Double. COROLLA is three quarter flared with smooth petal margins; opens and matures white (155D); 30mm (1 3/16") long x 38mm (1 1/2") wide. SEPALS are fully up, tips reflexed; reddish purple (58A) tipped green upper and lower surfaces; 35mm (1 3/8") long x 18mm (11/16") wide. TUBE is magenta (58B); medium length and thickness; 12mm (1/2") long x 9mm (3/8") thick. STAMENS extend 7mm (1/2") beyond the corolla; magenta (58B) filaments, reddish purple (58A) anthers. PISTIL extends 25mm (1") beyond the corolla; light rose (58D) style, reddish purple (58A) stigma. BUD is drop shaped. FOLIAGE is medium green (146A) upper surface, yellowish green (146B) lower surface. Leaves are 55mm (2 3/16") long x 35mm (1 3/8") wide, ovate shaped, serrated edges, acute tips and rounded bases. Veins and branches are green, stems are red. PARENTAGE: 'Pink Marshmallow' x 'Annabel'. Tall upright. Makes good upright or standard. Prefers overhead filtered light. Best bloom colour in bright light. Tested three years in Amstetten, Austria. Distinguished by gracefully reflexed SEPALS and contrasting corolla/sepal colours.

430

Gindl 2002 AT AFS5054.

Stadt Langenlois. Upright. Double.
COROLLA is full flared with smooth petal margins, very fluffy; opens and matures white (155D) short veins of light rose (50C); 36mm (1 7/16") long x 43mm (1 11/16") wide. SEPALS are fully up, tips reflexed; rose (50B) tipped yellowish green (146C) upper surface; light rose (50C) creped lower surface; 28mm (1 1/8") long x 22mm (7/8") wide. TUBE is rose (50B) striped cream; medium length and thickness; 15mm (5/8") long x 7mm (1/4") thick. STAMENS extend 10mm (3/8") beyond the corolla; light rose (50C) filaments, light brownish orange (165C) anthers. PISTIL extends 20mm (13/16") beyond the corolla; pink (50D) style, red (50A) stigma. BUD is globular. FOLIAGE is dark green (147A) upper surface, light olive green (147C) lower surface. Leaves are 60mm (2 3/8") long x 42mm (1 11/16") wide, ovate shaped, serrulated edges, acute tips and rounded bases. Veins are green, stems are light brown (199B), branches are yellowish green (146B). PARENTAGE: 'Swingtime' x 'Annabel'. Tall upright. Self branching. Makes good upright or standard. Prefers overhead filtered light. Best bloom colour in bright light. Tested four years in Amstetten, Austria. Distinguished by bright, large flowers.
Gindl 2002 AT AFS5051.

Stadt Papenburg. Upright/Trailer. Double.
COROLLA: half flared, turned under wavy petal margins; opens purple (N79C); matures purple (71A); 22mm (7/8") long x 17mm (5/8") wide. PETALOIDS: violet (76B), dark purple (N79B) base; 13mm (1/2") long x 11mm (7/16") wide. SEPALS: half down, tips reflexed; light pink (65B) tipped light apple green (145C) upper surface; magenta (61C) tipped light apple green (145C) lower surface; 38mm (1 1/2") long x 22mm (7/8") wide. TUBE: rose (65A); medium length & thickness; 21mm (13/16") long x 6mm (1/4") wide. STAMENS extend 6mm (1/4") beyond the corolla; purple (77A) filaments; dark purple (86A) anthers. PISTIL extends 21mm (13/16") beyond the corolla; dark reddish purple (72A) style; pale yellow (2D) stigma. BUD: bulbous. FOLIAGE: dark green (136B) upper surface; medium green (137C) lower surface. Leaves are 78mm (3 1/8") long x 48mm (1 7/8") wide; ovate shaped, serrulate edges, acute tips, rounded bases. Veins are very dark reddish purple (186A), stems are reddish purple (186B), branches are reddish purple (186B) & light green (138C).

PARENTAGE: 'Manfried Kleinau' x 'First Lord'. Lax upright or stiff trailer. Self branching. Makes good basket or upright. Prefers overhead filtered light, cool climate. Best bloom & foliage colour in filtered light. Tested 3 years in Koningshooikt, Belgium. Waanrode 8/9/08, Outstanding. Distinguished by bloom colour combination.
Michiels 2009 BE AFS7223.

Stadt Reine. Trailer. Semi Double.
COROLLA is quarter flared with smooth petal margins; opens purple (71A) and matures dark reddish purple (72A); 14mm (9/16") long x 12mm (1/2") wide. SEPALS are fully up, tips reflexed; reddish purple (67A) upper and lower surfaces; 51mm (2") long x 9mm (3/8") wide. TUBE is reddish purple (67A), proportionately medium length and thickness; 25mm (1") long x 10mm (3/8") wide. STAMENS extend 27mm (1 1/16") below the corolla; purple (71A) filaments and dark reddish purple (60A) anthers. PISTIL extends 32mm (1 1/4") below the corolla; purple (71A) style and pale yellow (158B) stigma. BUD is long, narrow and pointed. FOLIAGE is dark green (137A) on upper surface and medium green (138B) on lower surface. Leaves are 74mm (2 15/16") long x 34mm (1 3/8) wide, lanceolate shaped, serrulated edges, acute tips and rounded bases. Veins, stems and branches are red. PARENTAGE: 'WALZ Mandolinel' x 'Rohees King'. Natural trailer. Makes good basket. Prefers overhead filtered light and cool climate. Best bloom colour in filtered light. Tested four years in Knegsel, The Netherlands. Distinguished by bloom and foliage combination.
Roes 2002 NL AFS4799.

Stadt Wien. Upright. Semi Double.
COROLLA white with red veins; corolla is three quarter flared and is 32mm long x 30mm wide. SEPALS red purple (57a); sepals are horizontally held with recurved tips and are 50mm long x 12mm wide. TUBE red purple (57a) and is 12mm long x 5mm wide. PARENTAGE 'Sweet Darling' x 'Nettala'. This cultivar is a self branching, free flowering upright.
Klemm 2008 AT BFS0058.

Stadt Willich. Trailer. Double. COROLLA is half flared; opens white (155C) striped light pink (49B); matures white (155B) striped pink (48D); 25mm (1") long x 22mm (7/8") wide. SEPALS are half down, tips recurved; white (155C), with light pink (49 B) base, tipped light green (142B) upper and lower

431

surfaces; 48mm (1 7/8") long x 16mm (5/8") wide. TUBE is white (155C); 12mm (7/16") long x 6mm (1/4") wide. FOLIAGE is dark green (137A) upper surface; medium green (138B) lower surface. PARENTAGE: 'Sofie Michiels' x 'White Queen'. Meise 8/13/05. Distinguished by bloom colour and leaf size. Michiels 2006 BE AFS6020.

Stan Janssens. Upright. Single. COROLLA: three quarter flared, turned under smooth petal margins; opens light magenta (66D), matures rose (68B); 18mm (11/16") long x 14mm (9/16") wide. SEPALS: horizontal; tips recurved; magenta (58B) upper surface; dark rose (58C) lower surface; 30mm (1 3/16") long x 14mm (9/16") wide. TUBE: red (53C); medium length, thick; 22mm (7/8") long x 8mm (5/16") wide. STAMENS: do not extend below the corolla; reddish purple (58A) filaments, dark tan (164B) anthers. PISTIL extends 4mm (3/16") below the corolla; magenta (57A) style, magenta (59D) stigma. BUD: cordate. FOLIAGE: dark green (139A) upper surface, medium green (138B) lower surface. Leaves are 68mm (2 11/16") long x 32mm (1 1/4") wide, ovate shaped, serrated edges, acute tips and rounded bases. Veins are dark grayish purple (183A), stems are plum (183B), branches are very dark purple (187A). PARENTAGE: found seedling. Medium upright. Self branching. Makes good upright. Prefers full sun. Best bloom and foliage colour in bright light. Tested 3 years Berchem, Belgium. NBFK certificate at Meise. Distinguished by bloom shape and colour. Janssens 2003 BE AFS5085.

Star Wars. Upright. Single. COROLLA is slightly flared with smooth petal margins; opens violet (90D) and matures violet (70B); 16mm (5/8") long x 12mm (1/2") wide. SEPALS are half up, tips recurved up; white (155B) tipped green upper surface and white (155B) lower surface; 32mm (1 1/4) long x 8mm (5/16") wide. TUBE is white (155B), medium length and thickness; 9mm (3/8") long x 8mm (5/16") wide. STAMENS extend 6mm (1/4") below the corolla; pale violet (76D) filaments and reddish purple (186B) anthers. PISTIL extends 32mm (1 1/4") below the corolla; white (155B) style and white (155A) stigma. BUD is long, pointed. FOLIAGE is medium green (137B) upper surface and medium green (137D) lower surface. Leaves are 38mm (1 1/2") long x 19mm (3/4") wide, elliptic shaped, serrulated edges, rounded tips and rounded bases. Veins are green, stems are green shaded purple and branches are brown.

PARENTAGE: 'Hawkshead' x 'Ann H. Tripp'. Lax upright. Self branching. Makes good upright. Prefers full sun. Hardy to 20º F. Best bloom colour in bright light. Tested three years in Ormskirk, Lancashire, England. Distinguished by continuous blooming on long arching branches. Sinton 2002 UK AFS4826.

Starlette. Upright/Trailer. Single. COROLLA: unflared; smooth petal margins; opens & matures red (52A); 17mm (5/8") long x 12mm (7/16") wide. SEPALS: horizontal, tips recurved; light pink (36C) tipped light yellowish green (149C) upper surface; pink (52D) lower surface; 23mm (7/8") long x 6mm (1/4") wide. TUBE: light pink (36C); medium length & thickness; 16mm (5/8") long x 4mm (1/8") wide. STAMENS extend 3-5mm (1/8-3/16") beyond the corolla; rose (52B) filaments; yellowish white (158A) anthers. PISTIL extends 18mm (11/16") beyond the corolla; pink (52D) style; pale yellow (158B) stigma. BUD is ovate. FOLIAGE is medium green (147B) upper surface; yellowish green (146C) lower surface. Leaves are 70mm (2 3/4") long x 39mm (1 1/2") wide; ovate shaped, serrulate edges, acute tips, rounded bases. Veins not visible, stems are yellowish green branches are yellowish green & light brown. PARENTAGE: 'Berba's Coronation' x 'Annabel'. Lax upright or stiff trailer. Makes good basket. Prefers overhead filtered light & cool climate. Tested 3 years in Pornic, France. Distinguished by contrasting flower colours.
Massé 2009 FR AFS6998.

Stefan. Upright/Trailer. Single. COROLLA is quarter flared with turned under wavy petal margins; opens dark red (46A), red (47B) at base; matures red (45B), red (46C) at base; 18mm (11/16") long x 14mm (9/16") wide. SEPALS are half down, tips reflexed; red orange (42B) tipped pale yellow (8D) upper surface; orange (40C) lower surface; 23mm (15/16") long x 12mm (1/2") wide. TUBE is light pink (49B); long, medium thickness; 36mm (1 7/16") long x 6mm (1/4") wide. STAMENS do not extend beyond the corolla; light yellow (4C) filaments, yellow (10B) anthers. PISTIL does not extend beyond the corolla; light rose (50C) style, cream (11D) stigma. BUD is round, pointed. FOLIAGE is dark green (137A) upper surface, medium green (139C) lower surface. Leaves are 45mm (1 3/4") long x 23mm (15/16") wide, ovate shaped, serrulated edges, acute tips and rounded bases. Veins are plum (184B), stems

are dark red purple (187D), branches are very dark purple (187A). PARENTAGE: 'WALZ Harp' x unknown. Lax upright or stiff trailer. Self branching. Makes good basket. Prefers full sun. Best bloom and foliage colour in bright light. Tested three years in Koningshooikt, Belgium. Certificate N.B.F.K. at Meise. Distinguished by bud shape, bloom colour and compact growth.
Michiels 2002 BE AFS4972.

Stefan's Anni. Upright. Single. COROLLA opens dark violet blue, matures to light blue violet; corolla is fully flared. SEPALS red on the upper and lower surfaces; SEPALS are half up with recurved tips. TUBE red. PARENTAGE 'Nancy Lou' x 'Mission Bells'.
Nicola 2009 AT BFS0119.

Stella Virginia Devair. Upright/Trailer. Double. COROLLA: three quarter flared, smooth petal margins; opens & matures white (155D); 21mm (13/16") long x 18mm (11/16") wide. SEPALS: horizontal, tips recurved; white (155D) upper & lower surfaces; 31mm (1 1/4") long x 17mm (5/8") wide. TUBE: white (155D); medium length & thickness; 26mm (1") long x 6mm (1/4") wide. STAMENS extend 16mm (5/8") beyond the corolla; rose (68C) filaments; magenta (67B) anthers. PISTIL extends 31mm (1 1/4") beyond the corolla; white (155D) style & stigma. BUD: round. FOLIAGE: dark green (137A) upper surface; medium green (138A) lower surface. Leaves are 63mm (2 1/2") long x 28mm (1 1/8") wide; lanceolate shaped, serrate edges, acute tips, obtuse bases. Veins & branches are green, stems are red. PARENTAGE: 'Roesse Alba' x 'Impala'. Lax upright or stiff trailer. Makes good upright or stiff trailer. Prefers overhead filtered light, cool climate. Best bloom colour in filtered light. Tested 3 years in Knegsel, The Netherlands. Distinguished by bloom & foliage combination.
Roes 2009 NL AFS7246.

Stephanie Wheat. Upright/Trailer. Single. COROLLA is quarter flared, bell shaped with smooth petal margins; opens purple (77A), matures reddish purple (66B); 15mm (5/8") long x 15mm (5/8") wide. SEPALS are horizontal, tips recurved; light rose (58D) flushed deep rose upper surface, magenta (58B) lower surface; 18mm (11/16") long x 7mm (1/4") wide. TUBE is pale pink (36D) with deeper stripes, medium length and thickness; 9mm (3/8") long x 7mm (1/4") wide. STAMENS extend 15mm (5/8") below the corolla; light rose (58D) filaments,

reddish purple (60D) anthers. PISTIL extends 25mm (1") below the corolla; pale pink (36D) style, amber (162C) stigma. BUD is boat shaped. FOLIAGE is dark green (137A) upper surface, medium green (147B) lower surface. Leaves are 45mm (1 3/4") long x 25mm (1") wide, ovate shaped, serrated edges, acute tips and rounded bases. Veins, stems and branches are light apple green (145B). PARENTAGE: 'Empress of Prussia' x 'Chillerton Beauty'. Lax upright or stiff trailer. Makes good basket, standard, pyramid, pillar or decorative. Prefers overhead filtered light and cool climate. Heat tolerant if shaded. Best bloom and foliage colour in filtered light. Tested three years in Leyland, Lancashire, England. Distinguished by dainty, profuse blooms which are held out slightly.
Reynolds 2002 UK AFS4870.

Sternen-Städtchen. Upright/Trailer. Single. COROLLA is half flared, star shaped, with smooth petal margins; opens magenta (71C); matures magenta (57C); 19mm (3/4") long x 35mm (1 3/8") wide. PETALOIDS are magenta (71C) with pink (71B) patches; 19mm (3/4") long x 20mm (13/16") wide. SEPALS are fully up, tips reflexed; pink (55C) tipped green upper surface; rose (52C) lower surface; 26mm (1") long x 12mm (1/2") wide. TUBE is light pink (49C); short and thick; 6mm (1/4") long x 9mm (3/8") wide. STAMENS extend 15mm (5/8") beyond the corolla; magenta (58B) filaments, reddish purple (59B) anthers. PISTIL extends 17mm (11/16") beyond the corolla; rose (68C) style, light yellowish orange (19B) stigma. BUD is oblong and thick. FOLIAGE is dark green (147A) upper surface, medium green (137C) lower surface. Leaves are 59mm (2 5/16") long x 33mm (1 5/16") wide, lanceolate shaped, serrated edges, acute tips and rounded bases. Veins are medium green (138B), stems and branches are light green (139D). PARENTAGE: 'Nici's Findling' x 'Love's Reward'. Small lax upright or stiff trailer. Makes good upright. Heat tolerant if shaded. Best bloom and foliage colour in bright light. Tested four years in Austria. Distinguished by colour combination.
Haubenhofer 2002 AT AFS4951.

Steven Barberien. Upright. Double. COROLLA: half flared, smooth petal margins; opens violet (84A); matures light purple (78C); 20mm (13/16") long 24mm (15/16") wide. SEPALS: horizontal; tips recurved; light purple (74C) upper surface; reddish purple (67A) lower surface; 34mm (1 5/16") long x

14mm (9/16") wide. TUBE: light purple (74C); medium length & thickness; 16mm (5/8") long x 7mm (1/4") wide. STAMENS: extend 11mm (7/16") below corolla; magenta (68A) filaments; rose (68C) anthers. PISTIL: extends 35mm (1 3/8") below the corolla; light reddish purple (66C) style; rose (68C) stigma. BUD: elliptic. FOLIAGE: medium green (137B) upper surface; medium green (138B) lower surface. Leaves are 56mm (2 3/16") long x 26mm (1") wide, lanceolate shaped, serrated edges, acute tips and rounded bases. Green veins, stems & branches. PARENTAGE: 'Sofie Michiels' x 'Judy Salome'. Medium upright. Makes good upright or standard. Prefers overhead filtered light and cool climate. Best bloom and foliage colour in filtered light. Tested 4 years in Diessen, The Netherlands. Distinguished by bloom colour.
Comperen 2004 NL AFS5567.

Steven van Ruysschenberg. Upright/Trailer. Single. COROLLA: half flared, turned under wavy petal margins; opens dark reddish purple (70A); matures reddish purple (64B); 19mm (3/4") long x 21mm (13/16") wide. SEPALS: half up & horizontal, tips recurved up; rose (63C) tipped light apple green (145C) upper surface; magenta (68A) tipped light apple green (145C) lower surface; 32mm (1 1/4") long x 10mm (3/8") wide. TUBE: reddish purple (61B); short & thick, square shape; 14mm (9/16") long x 11mm (7/16") wide. STAMENS extend 14mm (9/16") beyond the corolla; dark reddish purple (70A) filaments; dark purple (86A) anthers. PISTIL extends 32mm (1 1/4") beyond the corolla; purple (71A) style; light rose (68D) stigma. BUD: elongated. FOLIAGE: dark green (137A) upper surface; medium green (138B) lower surface. Leaves are 64mm (2 1/2") long x 37mm (1 7/16") wide; ovate shaped, serrate edges, acute tips, rounded bases. Veins are plum (184C), stems are plum (185C), branches are plum (185C) & light green (139D). PARENTAGE: 'Pink La Campanella' x 'Maxima'. Lax upright or stiff trailer. Self branching. Makes good basket. Prefers overhead filtered light, cool climate. Best bloom & foliage colour in filtered light. Tested 3 years in Opglabbeek, Belgium. Waanrode 9/20/08, awarded Outstanding. Distinguished by bloom colour.
Cuppens 2009 BE AFS7070.

Stier. Upright/Trailer. Single. COROLLA: 3 quarter flared; opens light pink (N78B), purple (65C) base; matures magenta (71C);

18mm (11/16") long x 18mm (11/16") wide. SEPALS: half up, tips reflexed up; white (155C) tipped apple green (144C) upper surface; light pink (65C) tipped apple green (144C) lower surface; 24mm (15/16") long x 13mm (1/2") wide. TUBE: white (155C) & medium green (135C); medium length & thickness; 13mm (1/2") long x 5mm (3/16") wide. FOLIAGE is dark green (136A) upper surface; medium green (138B) lower surface. PARENTAGE: 'Impudence' x 'Rohees New Millennium'.
Geerts L. 2007 BE AFS6380.

Stijn. Upright/Trailer. Double. COROLLA: half flared; opens light rose (71B), reddish purple (73B) base and matures reddish purple (64B); 22mm (7/8") long x 20mm (3/4") wide. PETALOIDS: reddish purple (71B), base light rose (73B); 14mm (9/16") long x 12mm (7/16") wide. SEPALS are half down, tips reflexed; light pink (65C) tipped apple green (144C) upper surface; rose (68B) tipped apple green (144C) lower surface; 25mm (1") long x 12mm (7/16") wide. TUBE is white (155C); medium length & thickness; 20mm (3/4") long x 5mm (3/16") wide. FOLIAGE is dark green (136B) upper surface; medium green (138A) lower surface. PARENTAGE: 'Rune Peeters' x 'Collingwood'.
Michiels 2007 BE AFS6517.

Stijnie van den Brink. Trailer. Double. COROLLA is quarter flared; opens white (155D); matures white (155D); 42mm (1 5/8") long x 31mm (1 1/4") wide. SEPALS are half down, tips recurved; magenta (63A) upper surface; magenta (63A) lower surface; 47mm (1 7/8") long x 15mm (9/16") wide. TUBE is rose (63C); 25mm (1") long x 7mm (1/4") wide. FOLIAGE is yellowish green (144A) upper surface; yellowish green (146C) lower surface. PARENTAGE: 'Gerwin van den Brink' x 'Martinus'. Nomination by NKVF as Recommendable Cultivar. Distinguished by bloom colour.
van den Brink 2006 NL AFS6257.

Stokie. Upright. Single. COROLLA is quarter flared; opens magenta (63A); matures magenta (63B); 19mm (3/4") long x 13mm (1/2") wide. SEPALS are horizontal, tips recurved; white (155D) upper & lower surface; 32mm (1 1/4") long x 13mm (1/2") wide. TUBE is white (155D); 13mm (1/2") long x 6mm (1/4") wide. FOLIAGE: medium green (137B) upper surface; medium green (138B) lower surface. PARENTAGE: 'Bon Accord' x 'Tidler'. Distinguished by profuse, small and erect blooms.

Goodwin 2006 UK AFS6042.

Storey Time. Upright. Double. COROLLA is quarter flared, very full, with wavy petal margins; opens purple (81A); matures reddish purple (79C) veined red; 18mm (11/16") long x 18mm (11/16") wide. SEPALS are half up, tips recurved up; magenta (57B) upper surface; magenta (58B) lower surface; 19mm (3/4") long x 20mm (13/16") wide. TUBE is magenta (57B); short, medium thickness; 7mm (1/4") long x 6mm (1/4") wide. FOLIAGE: medium green (137B) upper surface; medium green (138B) lower surface. Leaves are 50mm (2") long x 30mm (1 3/16") wide, cordate shaped. PARENTAGE: ('Pink Fantasia' x 'Estelle Marie') x 'Eileen Storey'. Distinguished by double flowers facing horizontal to upright. Storey 2005 UK AFS5687.

Straat Accra. Upright. Single. COROLLA: unflared, bell shape, smooth petal margins; opens & matures purple (82B); 22mm (7/8") long x 19mm (3/4") wide. SEPALS: fully up; tips reflexed; light purple (80C) upper & lower surfaces; 9mm (3/8") long x 4mm (3/16") wide. TUBE: pale purple (87D); medium length & thickness; 7mm (1/4") long x 4mm (3/16") wide. STAMENS: do not extend below corolla; pale purple (87D) filaments, white (155A) anthers. PISTIL: does not extend below the corolla, pale purple (87D) style & stigma. BUD: longish. FOLIAGE: dark green (147A) upper surface, grayish green (191A) lower surface. Leaves are 87mm (3 7/16") long x 41mm (1 5/8") wide, elliptic shaped, serrulated edges, acute tips and acute bases. Veins & stems are light green; branches are reddish. PARENTAGE: ('F. procumbens' x 'F. paniculata') x 'F. obconica'. Tall upright. Self branching. Makes good upright. Prefers full sun, cool or warm climate. Best bloom and foliage colour in bright light. Tested 4 years in Blesdijke, The Netherlands. Distinguished by colour and flowering in panicles at leaf nodes. de Boer 2004 NL AFS5405.

Straat Agulhas. Upright. Single. COROLLA is quarter flared with smooth petal margins; opens dark purple (79A), matures dark reddish purple (61A); 9mm (3/8") long x 5mm (3/16") wide. SEPALS are horizontal, tips recurved; light magenta (66D) upper surface, reddish purple (67A) lower surface; 25mm (1") long x 7mm (1/4") wide. TUBE is rose (51C), medium length and thickness; 16mm (5/8") long x 6mm (1/4") wide. STAMENS extend 18mm (11/16") beyond the

corolla; dark reddish purple (60A) filaments and anthers. PISTIL extends 30mm (1 3/16") below the corolla; dark reddish purple (60C) style, light pink (65C) stigma. BUD is ovate, pointed. FOLIAGE is dark green (147A) upper surface, light olive green (148B) lower surface. Leaves are 42mm (1 11/16") long x 21mm (13/16") wide, elliptic shaped, serrulated edges, acute tips and rounded bases. Veins and stems are light green, branches are brown. PARENTAGE: ['WALZ Polka' x ('F. denticulata' x 'F. decussata') x ('Whiteknight's Amethyst' x 'F. procumbens')] x 'F apetala'. Medium upright. Self branching. Makes good basket. Prefers full sun and cool or warm climate. Hardy to 40° F. Best bloom and foliage colour in bright light. Tested three years in Blesdÿke, Holland. Award of Merit, Aalsmeer, 2001 with praise from the jury. Distinguished by profuse blossoms of almost fluorescent colour. de Boer 2002 NL AFS4888.

Straat Bali. Upright. Single. COROLLA is half flared; opens & matures red (45C); 4mm (1/8") long x 3mm (1/8") wide. SEPALS are fully up, tips recurved; red (45D) upper & lower surfaces; 5mm (3/16") long x 2mm (1/16") wide. TUBE is red (45D); 5mm (3/16") long x 1mm (1/16") wide. FOLIAGE: medium green (147B) upper surface; light olive green (147C) lower surface. PARENTAGE: ('F. obconica' x 'F. cylindracea') x 'F. boliviana'. Distinguished by profuse upright panicles of red flowers. de Boer 2006 NL AFS6282.

Straat Flores. Upright. Single. COROLLA is three quarter flared; opens & matures light purple (75B); 7mm (1/4") long x 6mm (1/4") wide. SEPALS are fully up, tips recurved; light pink (65C) upper surface, light pink (65B) lower surface; 10mm (3/8") long x 3mm (1/8") wide. TUBE is light pink (65C); 9mm (3/8") long x 3mm (1/8") wide. FOLIAGE: dark green (137A) upper surface; medium green (147B) lower surface. PARENTAGE: ('Straat Futami' x 'Straat Futami') x 'F. boliviana'. Distinguished by profuse upstanding plumes of flowers. de Boer 2006 NL AFS6281.

Straat Fuknoka. Upright. Single. COROLLA is half flared with smooth petal margins; opens & matures rose (52B); 10mm (3/8") long x 10mm (3/8") wide. SEPALS are horizontal, tips reflexed; dark rose (51A) upper surface; rose (51B) lower surface; 19mm (3/4") long x 5mm (3/16") wide. TUBE is dark rose (51A); long, medium thickness; 24mm (15/16") long x 5mm (3/16") wide. FOLIAGE: medium green (146A) upper surface; plum (185C) lower surface. Leaves are 82mm (3 1/4") long x 47mm (1 7/8") wide, ovate shaped. PARENTAGE: ('Sparkling Whisper' x 'F. boliviana alba') x 'F. boliviana'. Distinguished by profuse paniculed flowers de Boer 2005 NL AFS5766.

Straat Futami. Upright. Single. COROLLA is three quarter flared with turned up petal margins; opens & matures white (155D); 12mm (1/2") long x 10mm (3/8") wide. SEPALS are half up, tips recurved up; dark reddish purple (64A) & magenta (63B) upper surface; yellowish gray (160D) lower surface; 15mm (9/16") long x 5mm (3/16") wide. TUBE is light reddish purple (66C); medium length & thickness; 11mm (7/16") long x 6mm (1/4") wide. S FOLIAGE: dark green (147A) upper surface; medium green (147B) lower surface. Leaves are 49mm (1 15/16") long x 36mm (1 7/16") wide, cordate shaped. PARENTAGE: 'Straat of Plenty' x 'Alaska'. Distinguished by resemblance to 'F. encliandra' but larger. de Boer 2005 NL AFS5652.

Straat Gibraltar. Upright. Single. COROLLA is half flared; opens & matures light pink (55D); 16mm (5/8") long x 14mm (9/16") wide. SEPALS are horizontal, tips reflexed; dark rose (54B) upper surface; rose (54C) lower surface; 19mm (3/4") long x 5mm (3/16") wide. TUBE is dark rose (56A); 19mm (3/4") long x 6mm (1/4") wide. FOLIAGE: medium green (137C) upper surface; light olive green (148B) lower surface. PARENTAGE: ('Straat Futami' x 'Straat Futami') x ('Straat Futami' x 'Straat Futami'). Distinguished by flower shape & colour. de Boer 2006 NL AFS6280.

Straat Kobe. Upright. Single. COROLLA: quarter flared, smooth petal margins; opens & matures coral (39B); 10mm (3/8") long x 7mm (1/4") wide. SEPALS: fully up; tips reflexed; yellowish green (145A) upper surface; yellowish green (145B) lower surface; 13mm (1/2") long x 4mm(3/16") wide. TUBE: peach (37B); long, medium thickness; 26mm (1") long x 5mm(3/16") wide. STAMENS: extend 1mm (1/16") below corolla; pale purple (75D) filaments, yellowish white (4D) anthers. PISTIL: extends 7mm (1/4") below the corolla; pale purple (75D) style, yellowish white (4D) stigma. BUD: triphylla type. FOLIAGE: dark green (147A) upper surface, grayish green (191A)

lower surface. Leaves are 82mm (3 1/4") long x 42mm (1 5/8") wide, ovate shaped, serrulated edges, acute tips and rounded bases. Veins are green; stems are reddish green; branches are brown. PARENTAGE: 'Sparkling Whisper' x 'F. boliviana var. alba'. Medium upright. Self branching. Makes good basket. Prefers overhead filtered light, cool or warm climate. Best bloom and foliage colour in filtered light. Tested 3 years in Blesdijke, The Netherlands. Distinguished by large flowers in panicles. de Boer 2004 NL AFS5406.

Straat La Plata. Upright. Single. COROLLA is half flared with smooth petal margins; opens & matures light reddish purple (73A); 10mm (3/8") long x 5mm (3/16") wide. SEPALS are horizontal, tips reflexed; pink (55C) upper surface; rose (67D) lower surface; 16mm (5/8") long x 5mm (3/16") wide. TUBE is light pink (49B); medium length & thickness; 21mm (13/16") long x 4mm (3/16") wide. FOLIAGE: dark green (147A) upper surface; medium green (147B) lower surface. Leaves are 90mm (3 9/16") long x 53mm (2 1/16") wide, ovate shaped. PARENTAGE: ('F. procumbens' x 'F. paniculata') x 'F. apetala'. Distinguished by masses of paniculed flowers. de Boer 2005 NL AFS5765.

Straat Lombok. Trailer. Single. COROLLA is quarter flared; opens & matures dark reddish purple (72A); 17mm (5/8") long x 16mm (5/8") wide. SEPALS are half down, tips recurved; reddish purple (71B) upper surface; light reddish purple (72C) lower surface; 25mm (1") long x 8mm (5/16") wide. TUBE is reddish purple (71B); 22mm (7/8") long x 6mm (1/4") wide. FOLIAGE: dark green (137A) upper surface; medium green (147B) lower surface. PARENTAGE: ('Rijs 2001' x 'F.juntasensis') x 'Straat la Plata'. Distinguished by large trailing plumes of flowers. de Boer 2006 NL AFS6279.

Straat Messina. Upright. Single. COROLLA is quarter flared; opens & matures pale rose (73D); 11mm (7/16") long x 7mm (1/4") wide. SEPALS are half down, tips recurved; magenta (63A) upper surface; pale pink (69A) lower surface; 15mm (9/16") long x 3mm (1/8") wide. TUBE is magenta (63A); 19mm (3/4") long x 4mm (1/8") wide. FOLIAGE: medium green (146A) upper surface; gray green (197B) lower surface. PARENTAGE: ('Sparkling Whisper' x 'F. boliviana') x 'F.

apetala'. Distinguished by paniculate flowering & unusual colours.
de Boer 2006 NL AFS6276.

Straat Moji. Trailer. Single. COROLLA: three quarter flared, smooth petal margins; opens & matures violet (75A); 6mm (1/4") long x 6mm (1/4") wide. SEPALS: half up; tips reflexed up; light pink (62B) upper & lower surfaces; 5mm (3/16") long x 2mm (1/16") wide. TUBE: light pink (65B); medium length & thickness; 6mm (1/4") long x 3mm(1/8") wide. STAMENS: do not extend below corolla; violet (75A) filaments & anthers. PISTIL: extends 3mm (1/8") below the corolla; violet (75A) style, light pink (65B) stigma. BUD: ovate, pointed. FOLIAGE: dark green (147A) upper surface, light olive green (148B) lower surface. Leaves are 37mm (1 7/16") long x 20mm (13/16") wide, elliptic shaped, serrulated edges, obtuse tips and obtuse bases. Veins are green; stems are reddish; branches are reddish. PARENTAGE: [('F. *procumbens*' x 'F. *paniculata*') x 'F. *obconica*'] x 'F. *perscandens*'. Natural trailer. Self branching. Makes good basket or miniature. Prefers overhead filtered light, cool or warm climate. Best bloom and foliage colour in filtered light. Tested 3 years in Blesdijke, The Netherlands. Distinguished by colour.
de Boer 2004 NL AFS5407.

Straat Nagasaki. Upright. Single. COROLLA: unflared, cylindrical shape, turned under petal margins; opens purple (82A); matures reddish purple (67A); 22mm (7/8") long x 19mm (3/4") wide. SEPALS: half down; tips recurved; red (52A) upper & lower surfaces; 49mm (1 15/16") long x 8mm(5/16") wide. TUBE: red (52B); medium length & thickness; 18mm (11/16") long x 8mm(5/16") wide. STAMENS: extend 12mm (1/2") below corolla; red (52A) filaments, rose (65A) anthers. PISTIL: extends 26mm (1") below the corolla, red (52A) style; rose (65A) stigma. BUD: longish. FOLIAGE: dark green (137A) upper surface, medium green (146A) lower surface. Leaves are 66mm (2 5/8") long x 40mm (1 9/16") wide, ovate shaped, serrulated edges, acute tips and rounded bases. Veins are light green, stems are reddish; branches are brown. PARENTAGE: Diana Wills' x [('F. *denticulata*' x 'F. *decussata*') x 'White Knight's Amethyst']. Tall upright. Self branching. Makes good upright. Prefers full sun, cool or warm climate. Cold weather hardy to 14° F. Best bloom and foliage colour in bright light. Tested 11 years in Blesdijke, The Netherlands. Distinguished by tolerance to severe frost and large flowers.

de Boer 2004 NL AFS5404.

Straat of Dover. Upright. Single. COROLLA is quarter flared with smooth, bell shaped petal margins; opens & matures light purple (75B); 6mm (1/4") long x 7mm (1/4") wide. SEPALS are fully up, tips recurved; pink (62C) upper surface; pale pink (62D) lower surface; 15mm (9/16") long x 4mm (3/16") wide. TUBE is pink (62C); medium length, thick; 15mm (9/16") long x 8mm (5/16") wide. FOLIAGE: dark green (137A) upper surface; gray green (191A) lower surface. Leaves are 108mm (4 1/4") long x 54mm (2 1/8") wide, elliptic shaped. PARENTAGE: 'Gerharda's Panache' x 'Straat Kobe'. Distinguished by upstanding panicles.
de Boer 2005 NL AFS5764.

Straat of England. Upright/trailer. Single. COROLLA is quarter flared with smooth petal margins; opens & matures rose (68B); 9mm (3/8") long x 6mm (1/4") wide. SEPALS are horizontal, tips reflexed; light rose (73B) upper surface; rose (68B) lower surface; 11mm (7/16") long x 4mm (3/16") wide. TUBE is light rose (73B); long & thick; 28mm (1 1/8") long x 7mm (1/4") wide. FOLIAGE: medium green (146A) upper surface; gray green (194A) lower surface. Leaves are 87mm (3 7/16") long x 40mm (1 9/16") wide, elliptic shaped. PARENTAGE: 'Gerharda's Panache' x ('Sparkling Whisper' x 'F. *boliviana* alba'). Distinguished by extremely large panicles.
de Boer 2005 NL AFS5763.

Straat of Plenty. Upright. Single. COROLLA: full flared; smooth petal margins; opens & matures pale pink (56C); 4mm (3/16") long x 3mm (1/8") wide. SEPALS: fully up; tips recurved; rose (63C) upper & lower surfaces; 6mm(1/4") long x 2mm (1/16") wide. TUBE: pale pink (56C); medium length & thickness; 19mm (3/4") long x 9mm (3/8") wide. STAMENS: do not extend below corolla; pale pink (56C) filaments & anthers. PISTIL: extends 4mm (3/16") below the corolla, pale pink (56C) style & stigma. BUD: longish. FOLIAGE: dark green (137A) upper surface; medium green (147B) lower surface. Leaves are 38mm (2 1/2") long x 18mm (11/16") wide, lanceolate shaped, serrulated edges, acute tips and obtuse bases. Veins are green; stems & branches are reddish. PARENTAGE: 'F. *obconica*' x [('F. *procumbens*' x 'F. *paniculata*') x 'Igloo Maid']. Medium upright. Makes good basket or upright. Prefers overhead filtered light and cool or warm climate. Cold weather hardy to 36° F. Best bloom colour in filtered light. Best foliage

colour in bright light. Tested 3 years in Blesdÿke, Holland. Award of Merit, VKC, Aalsmeer. Distinguished by panicles of blooms throughout the year.
de Boer 2003 NL AFS5171.

Straat Osaka. Upright. Single. COROLLA is half flared with turned up petal margins; opens & matures rose (65A); 8mm (5/16") long x 5mm (3/16") wide. SEPALS are half down, tips recurved; rose (64D) upper surface; light rose (63D) lower surface; 11mm (7/16") long x 3mm (1/8") wide. TUBE is rose (64D); long & thin; 16mm (5/8") long x 2mm (1/16") wide. FOLIAGE: medium green (147B) upper surface; gray green (195A) lower surface. Leaves are 62mm (2 7/16") long x 38mm (1 1/2") wide, ovate shaped. PARENTAGE: 'Straat Kobe' x 'F. apetala'. Distinguished by one big mass of upstanding panicles.
de Boer 2005 NL AFS5762.

Straat Red Sea. Upright. Single. COROLLA is half flared with smooth petal margins; opens & matures dark rose (48A); 9mm (3/8") long x 6mm (1/4") wide. SEPALS are horizontal, tips reflexed; rose (48B) upper surface; pink (48C) lower surface; 8mm (5/16") long x 4mm (3/16") wide. TUBE is rose (48B); medium length & thickness; 12mm (1/2") long x 3mm (1/8") wide. FOLIAGE: dark green (147A) upper surface; light olive green (148B) lower surface. Leaves are 105mm (4 1/8") long x 40mm (1 9/16") wide, elliptic shaped. PARENTAGE: ('Sparkling Whisper' x 'F. boliviana alba') x 'F. apetala'. Distinguished by profuse upstanding bundles of paniculed flowers.
de Boer 2005 NL AFS5768.

Straat Singapore. Upright. Single. COROLLA is quarter flared with smooth petal margins; opens & matures rose (51B); 7mm (1/4") long x 4mm (3/16") wide. SEPALS are horizontal, tips reflexed; dark rose (51A) upper surface; rose (51C) lower surface; 11mm (7/16") long x 3mm (1/8") wide. TUBE is dark rose (51A); medium length & thickness; 15mm (9/16") long x 3mm (1/8") wide. FOLIAGE: medium green (137C) upper surface; gray (195A) lower surface. Leaves are 57mm (2 1/4") long x 33mm (1 5/16") wide, ovate shaped. PARENTAGE: 'Straat Kobe' x 'F. apetala'. Distinguished by profuse upstanding paniculed flowers.
de Boer 2005 NL AFS5767.

Straat Sparks. Upright. Single. COROLLA: three quarter flared; opens & matures rose (65A); 3mm (1/8") long x 2mm (1/16") wide. SEPALS: half up, tips recurved up; reddish purple (67A) upper surface; light reddish purple (66C) lower surface; 7mm (1/4") long x 1mm (1/16") wide. TUBE: reddish purple (67A); 7mm (1/4") long x 1mm (1/16") wide. FOLIAGE is dark green (137A) upper surface; light olive green (148B) lower surface. PARENTAGE: 'Straat Flores' x 'Straat Flores'.
de Boer 2008 NL AFS6855.

Straat Taiwan. Trailer. Single. COROLLA: quarter flared; opens dark reddish purple (72A); matures reddish purple (71B); 6mm (1/4") long x 7mm (1/4") wide. SEPALS: half up, tips recurved; dark rose (71D) upper & lower surfaces; 11mm (7/16") long x 3mm (1/8") wide. TUBE: magenta (71C); 16mm (5/8") long x 3mm (1/8") wide. FOLIAGE is medium green (146A) upper surface; olive green (148A) lower surface. PARENTAGE: ('Straat of Plenty' x 'Alaska') x ('Rijs 2001' x 'F. juntasensis').
de Boer 2008 NL AFS6856.

Straat van Diemen. Upright. Single. COROLLA: half flared, smooth petal margins; opens & matures magenta (67B); 2.5mm (1/8") long x 1.5mm (1/16") wide. SEPALS: horizontal; tips reflexed; reddish purple (70B) upper & lower surfaces; 4mm (3/16") long x 1.5mm(1/16") wide. TUBE: dark reddish purple (70A); medium length & thickness; 4mm (3/16") long x 2mm(1/16") wide. STAMENS: do not extend below corolla; pale purple (70D) filaments, light yellow (4B) anthers. PISTIL: extends 15mm (9/16") below the corolla, pale pink (62D) style; pale pink (70D) stigma. BUD: longish. FOLIAGE: dark green (147A) upper surface, light olive green (148B) lower surface. Leaves are 55mm (2 3/16") long x 26mm (1") wide, elliptic shaped, serrulated edges, acute tips and acute bases. Veins are light green, stems are red; branches are reddish brown. PARENTAGE: 'F. obconica' x 'F. procumbens' x 'F. paniculata'. Medium upright. Self branching. Makes good upright. Prefers full sun, cool or warm climate. Best bloom and foliage colour in bright light. Tested 3 years in Blesdijke, The Netherlands. Distinguished by flowering in panicles from leaf nodes and stems.
de Boer 2004 NL AFS5403.

Straat Yucatan. Upright. Single. COROLLA: unflared, round shape; opens & matures reddish purple (74A); 6mm (1/4") long x 6mm (1/4") wide. SEPALS: horizontal, tips recurved; reddish purple (71B) upper

surface; light rose (73B) lower surface; 12mm (7/16") long x 6mm (1/4") wide. TUBE: reddish purple (71B); 18mm (11/16") long x 5mm (3/16") wide. FOLIAGE is medium green (146A) upper surface; gray (195A) lower surface. PARENTAGE: 'Straat Futami' x ('Rijs 2001' x 'F. *juntasensis*').
de Boer 2008 NL AFS6857.

Sue Joiner. Upright. Single. COROLLA opens white; corolla is half flared and is 12mm long x 15mm wide. SEPALS blush-pink, tipped green on the upper and lower surfaces; sepals are horizontally held with recurved tips and are 28mm long x 11mm wide. TUBE blush-pink and is 6mm long x 5mm wide. PARENTAGE 'Sophie Louise' x 'Baby Bright'.
Joiner 2006 UK BFS0036.

Sue Oram. Upright. Single. COROLLA opens pale purple (75a), veined pink (66b), matures slightly paler; corolla is quarter flared and is 35mm long x 32mm wide. SEPALS pink (66a) on the upper surface, pink (66b) on the lower surface; sepals are horizontally held with recurved tips and are 40mm long x 12mm wide. TUBE pink and is 10mm long x 7mm wide. PARENTAGE 'Susan Travis' x 'Beacon Rosa'. This cultivar is proven to be hardy in Norfolk and Suffolk.
Welch 2006 UK BFS0024.

Suffolk Splendour. Upright. Double. COROLLA: full flared, turned up petal margins, spherical shape; opens & matures bright white (N155B); 32mm (1 1/4") long x 58mm (2 5/16") wide. SEPALS: fully up, tips reflexed; magenta (58B) upper surface; magenta (N57A) lower surface; 45mm (1 6/10") long x 15mm (6/10") wide. TUBE: magenta (58B); medium length & thickness; 9mm (5/16") long x 6mm (1/4") wide. STAMENS extend 19mm (3/4") beyond the corolla; reddish purple (N66B) filaments; pink (50D) anthers. PISTIL extends 30mm (1 3/16") beyond the corolla; magenta (63B) style; cream (158D) stigma. BUD is spherical. FOLIAGE is medium green (137B) upper surface; yellowish green (146B) lower surface. Leaves are 57mm (2 1/4") long x 35mm (1 3/8") wide; ovate shaped, serrulate edges, acute tips, rounded bases. Veins are light red; stems & branches are muted red. PARENTAGE: 'Crinkley Bottom' x 'Dreamy Days'. Medium upright. Makes good basket or upright. Prefers overhead filtered light. Best bloom colour in filtered light. Tested 3 years in Norfolk, England. Distinguished by spherical corolla shape.

Welch 2009 UK AFS6951.

Sugar Plum Fairy. COROLLA plum. SEPALS red.
Robson 2002 UK.

Suhrental. Trailer. Single. COROLLA is three quarter flared with turned under smooth petal margins; opens dark reddish purple (59A); matures dark reddish purple (61A); 19mm (3/4") long x 21mm (13/16") wide. SEPALS are horizontal; tips reflexed; reddish purple (58A) upper surface; reddish purple (61B) lower surface; 32mm (1 1/4") long x 12mm (1/2") wide. TUBE is dark reddish purple (60C); medium length & thickness; 22mm (7/8") long x 6mm (1/4") wide. FOLIAGE: dark green (139A) upper surface; medium green (139B) lower surface. Leaves are 47mm (1 7/8") long x 30mm (1 3/16") wide, ovate shaped. PARENTAGE: 'Roesse Blacky' x 'Beacon Baby Rose'. Meis 3-7-04. Distinguished by colour fade aubergine to brown.
Michiels 2005 BE AFS5676.

Summer Bells. Upright. Single. COROLLA: quarter flared, turned under smooth petal margins; opens dark rose (54A), matures dark rose (58C); 22mm (7/8") long x 20mm (13/16") wide. SEPALS: horizontal; tips reflexed; light rose (50C) tipped yellowish green (145A) upper surface; rose (52C) tipped yellowish green (145A) lower surface; 30mm (1 3/16") long x 11mm (7/16") wide. TUBE: pink (49A); long, medium thickness; 38mm (1 1/2") long x 5mm (3/16") wide. STAMENS: extend 7mm (1/4") below the corolla; light pink (62B) filaments, light yellow (2C) anthers. PISTIL extends 9mm (3/8") below the corolla; pink (62C) style, light yellow (1C) stigma. BUD: elongated. FOLIAGE: dark green (136B) upper surface; medium green (137D) lower surface. Leaves are 65mm (2 9/16") long x 40mm (1 9/16") wide, ovate shaped, serrulated edges, acute tips and rounded bases. Veins are grayish red (181C), stems are grayish red (181C), branches are grayish red (182B). PARENTAGE: 'WALZ Harp' x 'Waternymph'. Medium upright. Makes good upright or standard. Prefers full sun. Best bloom and foliage colour in bright light. Tested 3 years in Koningshooikt, Belgium. NBFK certificate at Meise. Distinguished by bloom colour and shape.
Michiels 2003 BE AFS5106.

Sunlit. Upright/Trailer. Single. COROLLA is half flared, trumpet shaped; opens magenta (71C); matures magenta (67B); 22mm (7/8") long x 17mm (5/8") wide. SEPALS are horizontal, tips recurved; magenta (57C) tipped green upper surface; reddish purple (61B) lower surface; 28mm (1 1/8") long x 8mm (5/16") wide. TUBE is rose (58D); 15mm (9/16") long x 8mm (5/16") wide. FOLIAGE: medium green (147A) upper surface; medium green (147B) lower surface. PARENTAGE: 'Gerharda's Panache' x 'Contramine'. Distinguished by flowers horizontally placed in terminal sub racemes. de Graaff 2006 NL AFS6264.

Sunna. Upright. Single. COROLLA: quarter flared, bell shape; opens light yellowish orange (19C); matures pink (48D); 9mm (5/16") long x 5mm (3/16") wide. SEPALS: half down, tips reflexed; yellowish green (144A) upper surface; yellowish green (144B) lower surface; 10mm (3/8") long x 4mm (1/8") wide. TUBE: light rose (35D); 17mm (5/8") long x 7mm (1/4") wide. FOLIAGE is dark green (137A) upper surface; light green (137C) lower surface. PARENTAGE: [('F. michoanensis' x 'F. obconica') x 'F. splendens'] x 'F. splendens'. Nomination by NKVF as Recommendable Cultivar. Dijkstra 2008 NL AFS6802.

Susanne Buiting. Upright/Trailer. Double. COROLLA is full flared with smooth petal margins; opens reddish purple (72B); matures light reddish purple (72D); 25mm (1") long x 30mm (1 3/16") wide. SEPALS are half up, tips recurved up; dark rose (58C) upper & lower surfaces; 35mm (1 3/8") long x 12mm (1/2") wide. TUBE is dark rose (58C); short & thick; 10mm (3/8") long x 8mm (5/16") wide. FOLIAGE: medium green (137B) upper surface; medium green (138B) lower surface. Leaves are 47mm (1 7/8") long x 29mm (1 1/8") wide, ovate shaped. PARENTAGE: 'Rohees Rana' x ('Roesse Apus' x 'Roesse Apus') x 'Yvette Klessens'. Distinguished by bloom shape. Buiting 2005 NL AFS5867.

Susan Drew. Single. COROLLA deep purple. SEPALS deep red. Drew 2002 UK.

Susan Gasaway. Upright/Trailer. Single. COROLLA is quarter flared with smooth petal margins; opens dark purple (79A), matures dark reddish purple (59A); 21mm (13/16") long x 24mm (15/16") wide. SEPALS are fully up, tips recurved; dark reddish purple (60B) upper surface and reddish purple (61B) lower surface; 34mm (1 3/8") long x 18mm (11/16") wide. TUBE is dark reddish purple (60B), medium length and thickness; 14mm (9/16") long x 8mm (5/16") wide. STAMENS extend 34mm (1 3/8) below the corolla; reddish purple (59B) filaments, dark reddish purple (59A) anthers. PISTIL extends 46mm (1 13/16") below the corolla; reddish purple (59B) style, dark reddish purple (59A) stigma. BUD is ovate, pointed. FOLIAGE is medium green (137B) upper surface and medium green (138A) lower surface. Leaves are 56mm (2 3/16") long x 27mm (1 1/16") wide, ovate shaped, serrated edges, acute tips and rounded bases. Veins, stems and branches are red. PARENTAGE: [('Gruss aus dem Bodethal' x 'Rohees Alrami') x 'Stad Elburg'] x 'Stad Elburg'. Lax upright or stiff trailer. Makes good stiff trailer. Prefers overhead filtered light and cool climate. Best bloom colour in filtered light. Tested four years in Knegsel, The Netherlands. Distinguished by bloom colour and suggestive black corolla. Roes 2002 NL AFS4832.

Susanna D Dijkman. Trailer. Double. COROLLA rosy pink with a hint of mauve. SEPALS flesh pink. Beije 2004 NL.

Suzanna Buitenweg. Upright/trailer. Double. COROLLA: three quarter flared; turned under petal margins; opens dark purple (86A), violet (87B) base; matures dark purple (86A); 31mm (1 1/4") long x 23mm (7/8") wide. PETALOIDS: dark purple (86A) striped rose red; 37mm (1 7/16") long x 15mm (9/16") wide. SEPALS: half down, tips recurved & twisted; reddish purple (64B) edged dark reddish purple (64A) upper surface; reddish purple (64B) lower surface; 58mm (2 5/16") long x 13mm (1/2") wide. TUBE: magenta (58B) veined magenta (57A); medium length & thin; 15mm (9/16") long x 5mm (3/16") wide. STAMENS extend 14mm (9/16") beyond the corolla; reddish purple (67A) filaments; dark reddish purple (59A) anthers. PISTIL extends 36mm (1 7/16") beyond the corolla; dark reddish purple (64A) style; light tan (162B) stigma. FOLIAGE is dark green (147A) upper surface; medium green (147B) lower surface. Leaves are 68mm (2 11/16") long x 34mm (1 3/8") wide; lanceolate shaped, wavy edges, acute tips, rounded bases. Veins & branches are magenta, stems are purple. PARENTAGE: ('Schneckerl' x 'Annabel') x ('Rohees King' x 'S Wonderful'). Lax upright or stiff trailer. Self branching. Makes good basket or upright. Prefers overhead filtered light, warm climate. Best bloom & foliage colour in filtered light.

Tested 3 years in Hoogezand, The Netherlands. Nominated by NKvF as recommendable cultivar. Distinguished by petaloid shape (stands out from corolla). Scheper 2009 NL AFS7017.

Sweet Gilly. Double. COROLLA dark aubergine veined light aubergine. SEPALS aubergine.
Waving 2003 UK.

Sweet Remembrance. Upright/Trailer. Single. COROLLA is three quarter flared, saucer shaped; opens & matures dark rose (64C); 18mm (11/16") long x 19mm (3/4") wide. SEPALS are fully up, tips recurved; rose (54C) upper surface; dark rose (64C) lower surface; 19mm (3/4") long x 6mm (1/4") wide. TUBE is rose (54C); 16mm (5/8") long x 5mm (3/16") wide. FOLIAGE: yellowish green (146B) upper surface; light olive green (147C) lower surface. PARENTAGE: 'Gerharda's Panache' x 'Contramine'. Distinguished by flowers in terminal sub panicles; bloom shape. de Graaff H. 2006 NL AFS6262.

Sylvia Fuhrmann. Trailer. Double. COROLLA: three quarter flared, turned under wavy petal margins; opens violet (77B); matures magenta (63B); 22mm (7/8") long x 18mm (11/16") wide. PETALOIDS: Same colour as corolla; 8mm (5/16") long x 7mm (1/4") wide. SEPALS: horizontal, tips recurved; pale pink (56B) tipped apple green (144C) upper surface; rose (55B) tipped apple green (144C) lower surface; 31mm (1 1/4") long x 18mm (11/16") wide. TUBE: pale pink (56C); short, medium thickness; 11mm (7/16") long x 6mm (1/4") wide. STAMENS extend 9mm (5/16") beyond the corolla; rose (68C) filaments; magenta (58D) anthers. PISTIL extends 16mm (5/8") beyond the corolla; rose (68B) style; rose (63C) stigma. BUD: bulbous. FOLIAGE: dark green (137A) upper surface; medium green (139C) lower surface. Leaves are 48mm (1 7/8") long x 32mm (1 1/4") wide; ovate shaped, smooth edges, acute tips, rounded bases. Veins are dark green (141A), stems are plum (185B), branches are grayish red (182B) & medium green (139C). PARENTAGE: 'Manfried Kleinau' x 'Julia Dietrich'. Natural trailer. Self branching. Makes good basket. Prefers overhead filtered light, cool climate. Best bloom & foliage colour in filtered light. Tested 3 years in Koningshooikt, Belgium. Waanrode 8/9/08. Distinguished by bloom colour combination. Michiels 2009 BE AFS7224.

Sylvia Spin. Upright. Single. COROLLA: half flared; opens reddish purple (71B); matures dark rose (71D); 14mm (9/16") long x 26mm (1") wide. SEPALS: horizontal; tips recurved; rose (68B) upper & lower surfaces; 24mm (15/16") long x 12mm (7/16") wide. TUBE: magenta (68A); medium length & thickness; 14mm (9/16") long x 7mm (1/4") wide. FOLIAGE is dark green (139A) upper surface; medium green (137B) lower surface. PARENTAGE: 'Roesse Lupus' x 'Sofie Michiels'. Roes 2007 NL AFS6312.

Sylvie Morice. Upright/Trailer. Single. COROLLA: unflared; smooth petal margins, petals form 4 rollers; opens & matures red (53C); 21mm (13/16") long x 10mm (3/8") wide. SEPALS: horizontal, tips recurved; rose (47D) tipped yellowish green upper & lower surfaces; 31mm (1 1/4") long x 6mm (1/4") wide. TUBE: rose (47D); medium length & thickness; 17mm (5/8") long x 4mm (1/8") wide. STAMENS extend 5 &12mm (3/16 & 7/16") beyond the corolla; red (53D) filaments; dark red (53A) anthers. PISTIL extends 36mm (1 7/16") beyond the corolla; red (53D) style & stigma. BUD is long, ovate. FOLIAGE is medium green (146A) upper surface; light olive green (148B) lower surface. Leaves are 45mm (1 3/4") long x 22mm (7/8") wide; ovate shaped, serrulate edges, acute tips, rounded bases. Veins are yellowish green, stems & branches are light brown. PARENTAGE: 'Philippe Boënnec' x F. *regia reitzii* 4514. Lax upright or stiff trailer. Self branching. Makes good upright. Prefers overhead filtered light & cool climate. Tested 4 years in Pornic, France. Distinguished by shape of COROLLA petals. Massé 2009 FR AFS6999.

't Compostvrouwke. Trailer. Single. COROLLA is half flared; opens magenta (63A) with rose (52B) base; matures magenta (58B); 26mm (1") long x 24mm (15/16") wide. SEPALS are half down, tips reflexed; rose (55B) upper surface, and rose (52 B) lower surface; 33mm (1 5/16") long x 14mm (9/16") wide. TUBE is pink (54D); 21mm (13/16") long x 7mm (1/4") wide. FOLIAGE is dark green (139A) upper surface; medium green (137C) lower surface. PARENTAGE: 'Sofie Michiels' x 'WALZ Harp'. Meise 8/13/05. Distinguished by bloom colour. Michiels 2006 BE AFS6027.

't Heimenneke. Upright. Single. COROLLA is quarter flared; opens purple (71A) with dark reddish purple (60C) base; matures reddish

441

purple (70B); 14mm (9/16") long x 16mm (5/8") wide. SEPALS are half up; tips recurved up; reddish purple (61B) upper surface; dark reddish purple (60B) lower surface; 23mm (7/8") long x 8mm (5/16") wide. TUBE is dark reddish purple (60C); 8mm (5/16") long x 4mm (1/8") wide. FOLIAGE is dark green (137A) upper surface; medium green (138B) lower surface. PARENTAGE: 'Rosea' x 'Roesse Blacky'. Meise 8/13/05. Distinguished by bloom shape & colour.
Michiels 2006 BE AFS6307.

't Heivrouwke. Trailer. Double. COROLLA is half flared; opens dark purple (79A) with reddish purple (64B) base; matures purple (77A); 18mm (11/16") long x 16mm (5/8") wide. PETALOIDS are dark purple (79A) blotched magenta (67B) with reddish purple (64B) base; 12mm (7/16") long x11mm (7/16") wide. SEPALS are fully up, tips recurved; dark reddish purple (60A) upper surface; reddish purple (64B) lower surface; 30mm (1 3/16") long x 10mm (3/8") wide. TUBE is dark reddish purple (60B); 14mm (9/16") long x 4mm (1/8") wide. FOLIAGE is dark green (138A) upper surface; medium green (138B) lower surface. PARENTAGE: 'Rosea' x 'Roesse Blacky'. Meise 8/13/05. Distinguished by bloom colour.
Michiels 2006 BE AFS6033.

't Jonas Belleke. Upright. Single. COROLLA is quarter flared; opens purple (71A) with red (46B) base; matures dark reddish purple (70A); 16mm (5/8") long x 14mm (9/16") wide. SEPALS are half up, tips recurved up; red (53B) upper surface; red (46B) lower surface; 18mm (11/16") long x 6mm (1/4") wide. TUBE is red (53C); 11mm (7/16") long x 4mm (1/8") wide. FOLIAGE is dark green (136B) upper surface; medium green (137C) lower surface. PARENTAGE: 'Rosea' x 'Roesse Blacky'. Meise 8/13/05. Distinguished by bloom colour and shape.
Michiels 2006 BE AFS6037.

T.C. Grootenboer Droger. Trailer. Double. COROLLA: half flared; opens pale purple (75D), violet (76A) base; matures light purple (N81C); 23mm (7/8") long x 15mm (9/16") wide. PETALOIDS: same colour as corolla; 16mm (5/8") long x 9mm (5/16") wide. SEPALS: horizontal, tips reflexed; pale lavender (69D) tipped yellowish green (145A) upper surface; pale purple (79D) tipped yellowish green (145A) lower surface; 38mm (1 1/2") long x 13mm (7/16") wide. TUBE: white (155B); medium length & thickness;

17mm (5/8") long x 6mm (1/4") wide. FOLIAGE is dark green (139A) upper surface; medium green (138B) lower surface. PARENTAGE: 'Leen Vander Kuylen' x 'Kiss'.
Michiels 2007 BE AFS6325.

T.I.S. Herentals. Trailer. Single to Semi Double. COROLLA: half flared; opens magenta (58B) & magenta (63B), pale lavender (69B) base; matures magenta (63A) & magenta (67B); 28mm (1 1/8") long x 24mm (15/16") wide. SEPALS: horizontal, tips reflexed; pale lavender (69D) tipped light apple green (144D) upper surface; pale lavender (69B) tipped light apple green (144D) lower surface; 47mm (1 7/8") long x 18mm (11/16") wide. TUBE: pale pink (56C); long & thick; 25mm (1") long x 8mm (5/16") wide. FOLIAGE is dark green (136B) upper surface; medium green (138B) lower surface. PARENTAGE: 'Jef Vander Kuylen' x 'Chandlerii'.
Michiels 2007 BE AFS6326.

T.V.L. Upright/Trailer. Double. COROLLA: half flared, turned under wavy petal margins; opens rose (48B) & red purple (N79C); matures dark rose (58C) & red purple (N77B); 30mm (1 3/16") long x 24mm (15/16") wide. PETALOIDS: Same colour as corolla; 13mm (1/2") long x 7mm (1/4") wide. SEPALS: horizontal, tips recurved; pale pink (56C) tipped light apple green (144D) upper surface; pink (49A) tipped light apple green (144D) lower surface; 42mm (1 5/8") long x 16mm (5/8") wide. TUBE: white (155B) & pink (55C); medium length & thickness; 18mm (11/16") long x 6mm (1/4") wide. STAMENS extend 9mm (5/16") beyond the corolla; dark rose (67C) filaments; reddish purple (64B) anthers. PISTIL extends 12mm (7/16") beyond the corolla; rose (68C) style; pale rose (73D) stigma. BUD: globular. FOLIAGE: dark green (136B) upper surface; medium green (137D) lower surface. Leaves are 81mm (3 1/4") long x 51mm (2") wide; ovate shaped, serrate edges, acute tips, rounded bases. Veins are plum (185B), stems are dark red (185A), branches are plum (184C). PARENTAGE: 'Manfried Kleinau' x 'Cor Leeuwestijn'. Lax upright or stiff trailer. Self branching. Makes good basket. Prefers overhead filtered light, cool climate. Best bloom & foliage colour in filtered light. Tested 3 years in Koningshooikt, Belgium. Waanrode 7/5/08. Distinguished by bloom colour combination.
Michiels 2009 BE AFS7225.

Tamara Balyasnikova. Trailer. Double. COROLLA: half flared; opens reddish purple (64B), light reddish purple (73A) base; matures purple (77A); 27mm (1 1/16") long x 22mm (7/8") wide. PETALOIDS: same colour as corolla; 19mm (3/4") long x 14mm (9/16") wide. SEPALS: horizontal, tips reflexed; rose (65A) tipped yellowish green (144B) upper surface; light reddish purple (73A) tipped yellowish green (144B) lower surface; 31mm (1 1/4") long x 14mm (9/16") wide. TUBE: pink (62C); medium length & thickness; 21mm (13/16") long x 6mm (1/4") wide. FOLIAGE is dark green (136A) upper surface; medium green (138B) lower surface. PARENTAGE: 'Mieke' x 'Dorset Delight'. Michiels 2007 BE AFS6327.

Tamerus Bobolink. Upright/Trailer. Double. COROLLA: three quarter flared, smooth petal margins; opens purple (77A); matures dark reddish purple (61A); 21mm (13/16") long x 26mm (1") wide. SEPALS: fully up; tips reflexed; magenta (63B) upper surface; magenta (63A) lower surface; 24mm (15/16") long x 11mm (7/16") wide. TUBE: magenta (63B); medium length & thickness; 14mm (9/16") long x 5mm (3/16") wide. STAMENS: extend 14mm (9/16") below corolla; pink (62C) filaments; purple (77A) anthers. PISTIL: extends 25mm (1") below the corolla; rose (68B) style; light yellow (18C) stigma. BUD: round, pointed. FOLIAGE: medium green (137B) upper surface; medium green (137C) lower surface. Leaves are 67mm (2 5/8") long x 37mm (1 7/16") wide, cordate shaped, serrated edges, acute tips and rounded bases. Veins are green, stems & branches are red. PARENTAGE: {[('Bon Accord' x 'Bicentennial') x ('Vobeglo' x 'Dancing Flame')] x 'Rohees Alrami'} x 'Allure'. Lax upright or stiff trailer. Makes good stiff trailer. Prefers overhead filtered light and cool climate. Best bloom and foliage colour in filtered light. Tested 4 years in Duizel, The Netherlands. Distinguished by bloom & foliage combination. Tamerus 2003 NL AFS5309.

Tamerus Bobwhite. Upright/Trailer. Double. COROLLA: three quarter flared, smooth petal margins; opens & matures white (155B); 25mm (1") long x 17mm (11/16") wide. SEPALS: fully up; tips reflexed; pale yellow (2D) upper surface; white (155A) lower surface; 25mm (1") long x 11mm (7/16") wide. TUBE: pale yellow (2D); medium length & thin; 12mm (1/2") long x 4mm (3/16") wide. STAMENS: extend 27mm (1 1/16") below corolla; pink (62C) filaments; dark

reddish purple (64A) anthers. PISTIL: extends 34mm (1 5/16") below the corolla; white (155B) style; light yellow (8C) stigma. BUD: ovate. FOLIAGE: medium green (137B) upper surface; medium green (138B) lower surface. Leaves are 74mm (2 15/16") long x 27mm (1 1/16") wide, lanceolate shaped, serrated edges, acute tips and rounded bases. Veins, stems & branches are green. PARENTAGE: 'Sofie Michiels' x 'Cameron Ryle'. Lax upright or stiff trailer. Makes good stiff trailer. Prefers overhead filtered light and cool climate. Best bloom and foliage colour in filtered light. Tested 4 years in Duizel, The Netherlands. Distinguished by profuse flowering. Tamerus 2003 NL AFS5299.

Tamerus Dream. Trailer. Double. COROLLA is three quarter flared with smooth petal margins; opens purple (83B); matures dark reddish purple (61A); 34mm (1 3/8") long x 32mm (1 1/4") wide. SEPALS are half up, tips reflexed up; reddish purple (64B) upper surface; reddish purple (61B) lower surface; 36mm (1 7/16") long x 16mm (5/8") wide. TUBE is reddish purple (64B); medium length and thickness; 20mm (13/16") long x 7mm (1/4") thick. STAMENS extend 20mm (13/16") beyond the corolla; dark reddish purple (72A) filaments and anthers. PISTIL extends 28mm (1 1/8") beyond the corolla; reddish purple (71B) style, dark reddish purple (72A) stigma. BUD is ovate, pointed. FOLIAGE is medium green (137B) upper surface, medium green (138B) lower surface. Leaves are 52mm (2 1/16") long x 30mm (13/16") wide, ovate shaped, serrated edges, acute tips and rounded bases. Veins are green, stems and branches are red. PARENTAGE: 'Rohees Mintaka' x 'Gilian Althea'. Natural trailer. Makes good basket. Prefers overhead filtered light and cool climate. Best bloom colour in filtered light. Tested four years in Duizel, The Netherlands. Distinguished by bloom and foliage combination. Tamerus 2002 NL AFS4987.

Tamerus Elepadio. Upright/Trailer. Single. COROLLA: half flared, smooth petal margins; opens purple (71A); matures dark reddish purple (61A); 22mm (7/8") long x 27mm (1 1/16") wide. SEPALS: fully up; tips recurved; dark rose (64C) upper surface; reddish purple (67A) lower surface; 26mm (1") long x 9mm (3/8") wide. TUBE: rose (64D); medium length & thickness; 15mm (9/16") long x 7mm (1/4") wide. STAMENS: extend 19mm (3/4") below corolla; reddish purple (61B)

443

filaments; dark reddish purple (61A) anthers. PISTIL: extends 36mm (1 7/16") below the corolla; magenta (61C) style; light yellowish orange (19C) stigma. BUD: cordate. FOLIAGE: medium green (137B) upper surface; medium green (138B) lower surface. Leaves are 54mm (2 1/8") long x 30mm (1 3/16") wide, cordate shaped, serrated edges, acute tips and rounded bases. Veins, stems & branches are red. PARENTAGE: {[('Bon Accord' x 'Bicentennial') x ('Vobeglo' x 'Dancing Flame')] x 'Rohees Alrami'} x 'Hennie Bouwman'. Lax upright or stiff trailer. Makes good stiff trailer. Prefers overhead filtered light and cool climate. Best bloom and foliage colour in filtered light. Tested 4 years in Duizel, The Netherlands. Distinguished by bloom colour.
Tamerus 2003 NL AFS5303.

Tamerus Emoe. Upright. Double. COROLLA: three quarter flared, smooth petal margins; opens purple (77A); matures dark reddish purple (72A); 22mm (7/8") long x 20mm (13/16") wide. SEPALS: fully up; tips reflexed; rose (64D) upper surface; dark rose (64C) lower surface; 22mm (7/8") long x 12mm (1/2") wide. TUBE: rose (64D); medium length & thickness; 12mm (1/2") long x 6mm (1/4") wide. STAMENS: extend 20mm (13/16") below corolla; reddish purple (72B) filaments; purple (71A) anthers. PISTIL: extends 36mm (1 7/16") below the corolla; dark rose (71D) style; pale pink (62D) stigma. BUD: round. FOLIAGE: dark green (137A) upper surface; medium green (138B) lower surface. Leaves are 64mm (2 1/2") long x 37mm (1 7/16") wide, cordate shaped, serrated edges, acute tips and rounded bases. Veins, stems & branches are green. PARENTAGE: {[('Bon Accord' x 'Bicentennial') x ('Vobeglo' x 'Dancing Flame')] x 'Rohees Alrami'} x ('Sofie Michiels' x 'Lechlade Rocket'). Tall upright. Makes good upright or standard. Prefers overhead filtered light and cool climate. Best bloom and foliage colour in filtered light. Tested 4 years in Duizel, The Netherlands. Distinguished by bloom & foliage combination.
Tamerus 2003 NL AFS5306.

Tamerus Finschia. Upright/Trailer. Semi Double. COROLLA: quarter flared, smooth petal margins; opens purple (71A); matures reddish purple (71B); 20mm (13/16") long x 20mm (13/16") wide. SEPALS: fully up; tips reflexed; pink (62C) upper & lower surfaces; 26mm (1") long x 10mm (3/8") wide. TUBE: light yellow (10D); medium length & thickness; 24mm (15/16") long x 6mm (1/4")

wide. STAMENS: extend 15mm (9/16") below corolla; magenta (63B) filaments & anthers. PISTIL: extends 14mm (9/16") below the corolla; pink (62C) style; purple (71A) stigma. BUD: ovate, long. FOLIAGE: medium green (137D) upper surface; medium green (138B) lower surface. Leaves are 70mm (2 3/4") long x 36mm (1 7/16") wide, cordate shaped, serrated edges, acute tips and rounded bases. Veins, stems & branches are red. PARENTAGE: {[('Bon Accord' x 'Bicentennial') x ('Vobeglo' x 'Dancing Flame')] x 'Rohees Alrami'} x 'Anta Tamerus'. Lax upright or stiff trailer. Makes good stiff trailer. Prefers overhead filtered light and cool climate. Best bloom and foliage colour in filtered light. Tested 4 years in Duizel, The Netherlands. Distinguished by bloom & foliage combination.
Tamerus 2003 NL AFS5293.

Tamerus Fitis. Upright/Trailer. Double. COROLLA is half flared with smooth petal margins; opens dark purple (79A); matures dark reddish purple (60A); 23mm (15/16") long x 29mm (1 1/8") wide. SEPALS are half up, tips reflexed up; magenta (63A) upper surface; red (53C) lower surface; 27mm (1 1/16") long x 14mm (9/16") wide. TUBE is magenta (63A); medium length and thickness; 14mm (13/16") long x 7mm (1/4") thick. STAMENS extend 21mm (13/16") beyond the corolla; magenta (63B) filaments, light rose (63D) anthers. PISTIL extends 32mm (1 1/4") beyond the corolla; magenta (63B) style, rose (65A) stigma. BUD is round, pointed. FOLIAGE is dark green (137A) upper surface, medium green (138B) lower surface. Leaves are 55mm (2 3/16") long x 39mm (1 9/16") wide, ovate shaped, smooth edges, acute tips and obtuse bases. Veins, stems and branches are red. PARENTAGE: 'Rohees Mintaka' x 'Gilian Althea'. Lax upright or stiff trailer. Makes good stiff trailer. Prefers overhead filtered light and cool climate. Best bloom colour in filtered light. Tested four years in Duizel, The Netherlands. Distinguished by bloom colour.
Tamerus 2002 NL AFS4988.

Tamerus Goudhaan. Trailer. Single. COROLLA is quarter flared with smooth petal margins; opens purple (71A); matures reddish purple (61B); 18mm (11/16") long x 21mm (13/16") wide. SEPALS are half up, tips recurved up; dark rose (51A) upper surface; red (46C) lower surface; 33mm (1 5/16") long x 9mm (3/8") wide. TUBE is dark rose (51A); medium length and thin; 12mm (1/2") long x 4mm (3/16") thick. STAMENS extend 15mm (5/8") beyond the corolla; rose (61D) filaments, magenta (63B) anthers. PISTIL extends 31mm (1 1/4") beyond the corolla; rose (61D) style, light yellow (4C) stigma. BUD is ovate, pointed. FOLIAGE is medium green (137B) upper surface, medium green (138B) lower surface. Leaves are 58mm (2 5/16") long x 29mm (1 1/8") wide, ovate shaped, serrated edges, acute tips and obtuse bases. Veins are red, stems and branches are green. PARENTAGE: 'Rohees King' x 'Anta'. Natural trailer. Makes good basket. Prefers overhead filtered light and cool climate. Best bloom colour in filtered light. Tested four years in Duizel, The Netherlands. Distinguished by bloom colour. Tamerus 2002 NL AFS4989.

Tamerus Grandala. Upright/Trailer. Semi Double. COROLLA: half flared, smooth petal margins; opens dark reddish purple (59A); matures dark reddish purple (60A); 24mm (15/16") long x 24mm (15/16") wide. SEPALS: fully up; tips reflexed; magenta (63A) upper surface; dark reddish purple (60C) lower surface; 23mm (15/16") long x 10mm (3/8") wide. TUBE: magenta (63A); medium length & thickness; 15mm (9/16") long x 5mm (3/16") wide. STAMENS: extend 19mm (3/4") below corolla; dark reddish purple (64A) filaments; dark reddish purple (61A) anthers. PISTIL: extends 22mm (7/8") below the corolla; dark reddish purple (60C) style; light yellowish orange (19B) stigma. BUD: cordate. FOLIAGE: medium green (137B) upper surface; medium green (138B) lower surface. Leaves are 74mm (2 15/16") long x 42mm (1 11/16") wide, cordate shaped, serrated edges, acute tips and rounded bases. Veins & branches are green, stems are red. PARENTAGE: {[('Bon Accord' x 'Bicentennial') x ('Vobeglo' x 'Dancing Flame')] x 'Rohees Alrami'} x 'Veenlust'. Lax upright or stiff trailer. Makes good stiff trailer. Prefers overhead filtered light and cool climate. Best bloom and foliage colour in filtered light. Tested 4 years in Duizel, The Netherlands. Distinguished by bloom colour. Tamerus 2003 NL AFS5300.

Tamerus Hoatzin. Upright. Single. COROLLA: quarter flared, smooth petal margins; opens reddish purple (61B); matures reddish purple (66B); 18mm (11/16") long x 21mm (13/16") wide. SEPALS: fully up; tips reflexed; light reddish purple (66C) upper surface; dark rose (58C) lower surface; 21mm (13/16") long x 8mm (5/16") wide. TUBE: light reddish purple (66C); medium length & thickness; 7mm (1/4") long x 5mm (3/16") wide. STAMENS: extend 11mm (7/16") below corolla; dark rose (58C) filaments; dark reddish purple (60A) anthers. PISTIL: extends 14mm (9/16") below the corolla; pink (62A) style; very pale orange (27D) stigma. BUD: cordate. FOLIAGE: medium green (137C) upper surface; medium green (137D) lower surface. Leaves are 56mm (2 3/16") long x 35mm (1 3/8") wide, cordate shaped, serrated edges, acute tips and rounded bases. Veins, stems & branches are green. PARENTAGE: {[('Bon Accord' x 'Bicentennial') x ('Vobeglo' x 'Dancing Flame')] x 'Rohees Alrami'} x 'Northway'. Medium upright. Makes good upright. Prefers overhead filtered light and cool climate. Best bloom and foliage colour in filtered light. Tested 4 years in Duizel, The Netherlands. Distinguished by profuse flowering. Tamerus 2003 NL AFS5289.

Tamerus Hop. Upright. Single. COROLLA: half flared, smooth petal margins; opens reddish purple (67A); matures magenta (67B); 16mm (5/8") long x 26mm (1") wide. SEPALS: half up; tips reflexed up; light pink (62B) upper surface; pink (62A) lower surface; 21mm (13/16") long x 13mm (1/2") wide. TUBE: light pink (62B); short & thick; 7mm (1/4") long x 7mm (1/4") wide. STAMENS: extend 16mm (5/8") below corolla; magenta (58B) filaments; dark reddish purple (59A) anthers. PISTIL: extends 24mm (1 15/16") below the corolla; pink (62C) style; cream (11D) stigma. BUD: cordate. FOLIAGE: dark green (137A) upper surface; medium green (138A) lower surface. Leaves are 56mm (2 3/16") long x 34mm (1 5/16") wide, cordate shaped, serrated edges, acute tips and rounded bases. Veins, stems & branches are green. PARENTAGE: {[('Bon Accord' x 'Bicentennial') x ('Vobeglo' x 'Dancing Flame')] x 'Rohees Alrami'} x 'Northway'. Medium upright. Makes good upright or standard. Prefers overhead filtered light and cool climate. Best bloom and foliage colour in filtered light. Tested 4 years in Duizel, The Netherlands. Distinguished by profuse flowering. Tamerus 2003 NL AFS5291.

Tamerus Hylia. Upright. Double. COROLLA: half flared, smooth petal margins; opens purple (83A); matures reddish purple (59B); 22mm (7/8") long x 22mm (7/8") wide. SEPALS: fully up; tips recurved; rose (63C) upper surface; magenta (63A) lower surface; 22mm (7/8") long x 11mm (7/16") wide. TUBE: rose (63C); medium length &

445

thickness; 12mm (1/2") long x 6mm (1/4") wide. STAMENS: extend 19mm (3/4") below corolla; reddish purple (61B) filaments & anthers. PISTIL: extends 24mm (15/16") below the corolla; reddish purple (61B) style; light yellow (11C) stigma. BUD: cordate. FOLIAGE: dark green (137A) upper surface; medium green (138B) lower surface. Leaves are 74mm (2 15/16") long x 42mm (1 11/16") wide, cordate shaped, serrated edges, acute tips and rounded bases. Veins, stems & branches are red. PARENTAGE: {[('Bon Accord' x 'Bicentennial') x ('Vobeglo' x 'Dancing Flame')] x 'Rohees Alrami'} x 'Allure'. Medium upright. Makes good standard. Prefers overhead filtered light and cool climate. Best bloom and foliage colour in filtered light. Tested 4 years in Duizel, The Netherlands. Distinguished by bloom colour. Tamerus 2003 NL AFS5301.

Tamerus Koerol. Upright. Single. COROLLA: three quarter flared, smooth petal margins; opens dark reddish purple (59A); matures dark reddish purple (61A); 19mm (3/4") long x 26mm (1") wide. SEPALS: half up; tips reflexed up; magenta (61C) upper surface; reddish purple (61B) lower surface; 20mm (13/16") long x 9mm (3/8") wide. TUBE: magenta (61C); medium length & thickness; 9mm (3/8") long x 6mm (1/4") wide. STAMENS: extend 15mm (9/16") below corolla; magenta (63B) filaments & anthers. PISTIL: extends 18mm (11/16") below the corolla; magenta (63A) style; light yellow (5C) stigma. BUD: cordate. FOLIAGE: dark green (137A) upper surface; medium green (137C) lower surface. Leaves are 52mm (2 1/16") long x 39mm (1 9/16") wide, cordate shaped, serrated edges, acute tips and rounded bases. Veins, stems & branches are red. PARENTAGE: {[('Bon Accord' x 'Bicentennial') x ('Vobeglo' x 'Dancing Flame')] x 'Rohees Alrami'} x 'Northway'. Medium upright. Makes good upright or standard. Prefers overhead filtered light and cool climate. Best bloom and foliage colour in filtered light. Tested 4 years in Duizel, The Netherlands. Distinguished by bloom colour, profuse flowering. Tamerus 2003 NL AFS5292.

Tamerus Merel. Upright/Trailer. Double. COROLLA is three quarter flared with smooth petal margins; opens dark purple (79A); matures purple (83B); 30mm (1 3/16") long x 26mm (1") wide. SEPALS are fully up, tips recurved; dark reddish purple (60B) upper surface; magenta (58B) lower surface; 32mm (1 1/4") long x 12mm (1/2") wide.

TUBE is dark reddish purple (60B); medium length and thickness; 15mm (5/8") long x 6mm (1/4") thick. STAMENS extend 12mm (1/2") beyond the corolla; dark purple (79B) filaments, purple (77A) anthers. PISTIL extends 34mm (1 3/8") beyond the corolla; magenta (61C) style, reddish purple (70B) stigma. BUD is ovate, pointed. FOLIAGE is medium green (137C) upper surface, medium green (138B) lower surface. Leaves are 70mm (2 3/4") long x 36mm (1 7/16") wide, ovate shaped, serrated edges, acute tips and rounded bases. Veins, stems and branches are red. PARENTAGE: 'Rohees Mintaka' x 'Gilian Althea'. Lax upright or stiff trailer. Makes good stiff trailer. Prefers overhead filtered light and cool climate. Best bloom colour in filtered light. Tested four years in Duizel, The Netherlands. Distinguished by bloom colour. Tamerus 2002 NL AFS4990.

Tamerus Nandoe. Upright. Single. COROLLA is half flared, bell shaped with turned under petal margins; opens dark reddish purple (70A); matures reddish purple (71B); 13mm (1/2") long x 16mm (5/8") wide. SEPALS are half down, tips recurved; white (155D) upper & lower surfaces; 19mm (3/4") long x 9mm (3/8") wide. TUBE is white (155D); medium length & thickness; 8mm (5/16") long x 6mm (1/4") wide. FOLIAGE: medium green (146A) upper surface; yellowish green (146B) lower surface. Leaves are 60mm (2 3/8") long x 32mm (1 1/4") wide, elliptic shaped. PARENTAGE: 'Rohees King' x 'North Way'. Nomination by N.K.V.F. as recommendable cultivar. Distinguished by flower shape & colour. Tamerus 2005 NL AFS5801.

Tamerus Palila. Upright/Trailer. Double. COROLLA: half flared, smooth petal margins; opens purple (71A); matures dark reddish purple (64A); 30mm (1 3/16") long x 26mm (1") wide. SEPALS: fully up; tips recurved; magenta (68A) upper surface; magenta (63A) lower surface; 30mm (1 3/16") long x 14mm (9/16") wide. TUBE: magenta (68A); medium length & thickness; 12mm (1/2") long x 6mm (1/4") wide. STAMENS: extend 22mm (7/8") below corolla; dark reddish purple (64A) filaments; reddish purple (64B) anthers. PISTIL: extends 40mm (1 9/16") below the corolla; reddish purple (64B) style; cream (11D) stigma. BUD: ovate. FOLIAGE: medium green (137B) upper surface; medium green (138B) lower surface. Leaves are 67mm (2 5/8") long x 32mm (1 1/4") wide, lanceolate shaped, serrulated edges, acute tips and

obtuse bases. Veins, stems & branches are green. PARENTAGE: 'Sofie Michiels' x 'Rohees Mintake'. Lax upright or stiff trailer. Makes good stiff trailer. Prefers overhead filtered light and cool climate. Best bloom and foliage colour in filtered light. Tested 4 years in Duizel, The Netherlands. Distinguished by bloom colour.
Tamerus 2003 NL AFS5288.

Tamerus Spreeuw. Upright. Double. COROLLA is three quarter flared with smooth petal margins; opens purple (83A); matures dark reddish purple (61A); 35mm (1 3/8") long x 27mm (1 1/16") wide. SEPALS are half up, tips recurved up; magenta (63A) upper and lower surfaces; 36mm (1 7/16") long x 18mm (11/16") wide. TUBE is magenta (63A), medium length and thickness; 12mm (1/2") long x 6mm (1/4") wide. STAMENS extend 27mm (1 1/16") beyond the corolla; dark reddish purple (61A) filaments, dark reddish purple (72A) anthers. PISTIL extends 48mm (1 7/8") beyond the corolla; dark reddish purple (61A) style, dark reddish purple (72A) stigma. BUD is round, pointed. FOLIAGE is dark green (137A) upper surface, medium green (138A) lower surface. Leaves are 73mm (2 7/8") long x 38mm (1 1/2") wide, ovate shaped, serrated edges, acute tips and acute bases. Veins are green, stems and branches are red. PARENTAGE: 'Rohees Mintaka' x 'Gilian Althea'. Tall upright. Makes good standard. Prefers overhead filtered light and cool climate. Best bloom colour in filtered light. Tested four years in Duizel, The Netherlands. Distinguished by bloom colour.
Tamerus 2002 NL AFS4938.

Tamerus Tjiftaf. Upright/Trailer. Semi Double. COROLLA is three quarter flared with smooth petal margins; opens reddish purple (80B); matures purple (90B); 28mm (1 1/8") long x 30mm (1 3/16") wide. SEPALS are fully up, tips reflexed; red (45B) upper surface; red (43A) lower surface; 26mm (1") long x 12mm (1/2") wide. TUBE is red (45B); medium length and thickness; 15mm (5/8") long x 7mm (1/4") thick. STAMENS extend 15mm (5/8") beyond the corolla; red (45D) filaments, peach (38B) anthers. PISTIL extends 5mm (3/16") beyond the corolla; red (45D) style, peach (38B) stigma. BUD is round, pointed. FOLIAGE is medium green (137B) upper surface, medium green (139C) lower surface. Leaves are 50mm (2") long x 28mm (1 1/8") wide, ovate shaped, serrated edges, acute tips and rounded bases. Veins, stems and branches are red. PARENTAGE:

'Rohees Mintaka' x 'Gilian Althea'. Lax upright or stiff trailer. Makes good stiff trailer. Prefers overhead filtered light and cool climate. Best bloom colour in filtered light. Tested four years in Duizel, The Netherlands. Distinguished by bloom colour.
Tamerus 2002 NL AFS4991.

Tamerus Toekan. Upright. Double. COROLLA: three quarter flared, smooth petal margins; opens dark reddish purple (61A); matures reddish purple (61B); 27mm (1 1/16") long x 27mm (1 1/16") wide. SEPALS: half up; tips recurved up; light pink (49C) upper surface; light reddish purple (66C) lower surface; 32mm (1 1/4") long x 11mm (7/16") wide. TUBE: light pink (49C); medium length & thickness; 14mm (9/16") long x 9mm (3/8") wide. STAMENS: extend 26mm (1") below corolla; magenta (61C) filaments; dark reddish purple (60A) anthers. PISTIL: extends 28mm (1 1/8") below the corolla; pink (62C) style; light yellow (10D) stigma. BUD: cordate. FOLIAGE: medium green (137C) upper surface; medium green (138B) lower surface. Leaves are 56mm (2 3/16") long x 26mm (1") wide, cordate shaped, serrated edges, acute tips and rounded bases. Veins & stems are red, branches are green. PARENTAGE: {[('Bon Accord' x 'Bicentennial') x ('Vobeglo' x 'Dancing Flame')] x 'Rohees Alrami'} x 'Allure'. Medium upright. Makes good upright. Prefers overhead filtered light and cool climate. Best bloom and foliage colour in filtered light. Tested 4 years in Duizel, The Netherlands. Distinguished by bloom colour & profuse flowers.
Tamerus 2003 NL AFS5295.

Tamerus Toerako. Upright. Single. COROLLA: three quarter flared, smooth petal margins; opens reddish orange (42A); matures dark rose (51A); 16mm (5/8") long x 17mm (11/16") wide. SEPALS: half up; tips recurved up; light pink (49C) upper surface; pink (50D) lower surface; 27mm (1 1/16") long x 11mm (7/16") wide. TUBE: light pink (49C); medium length & thickness; 10mm (3/8") long x 6mm (1/4") wide. STAMENS: extend 17mm (11/16") below corolla; pink (52D) filaments; red (53C) anthers. PISTIL: extends 24mm (1 15/16") below the corolla; pink (48D) style; grayish yellow (160A) stigma. BUD: cordate. FOLIAGE: medium green (137C) upper surface; medium green (137D) lower surface. Leaves are 47mm (1 7/8") long x 31mm (1 1/4") wide, cordate shaped, serrated edges, acute tips and rounded bases. Veins & branches are green,

stems are red. PARENTAGE: {[('Bon Accord' x 'Bicentennial') x ('Vobeglo' x 'Dancing Flame')] x 'Rohees Alrami'} x 'Northway'. Medium upright. Makes good upright or standard. Prefers overhead filtered light and cool climate. Best bloom and foliage colour in filtered light. Tested 4 years in Duizel, The Netherlands. Distinguished by bloom colour & profuse flowering.
Tamerus 2003 NL AFS5290.

Tanja's Beauty Bells. Trailer. Single. COROLLA is quarter flared; opens light reddish purple (66C); matures light magenta (66D); 14mm (9/16") long x 17mm (5/8") wide. PETALOIDS: reddish purple (66B); 10mm (3/8") long x 6mm (1/4") wide. SEPALS are half down, tips recurved; pale pink (56B) tipped light yellow green (150B) upper surface; light pink (62B) tipped yellowish green (150B) lower surface; 23mm (7/8") long x 9mm (3/8") wide. TUBE is pale pink (56D); 23mm (7/8") long x 6mm (1/4") wide. FOLIAGE: dark green (139A) upper surface; medium green (137C) lower surface. PARENTAGE: 'Ghislane' x 'Onbekend'. Meise 9/17/05. Distinguished by bloom colour combination.
Van Walleghem 2006 BE AFS6078.

Tanja's Beauty Vanilla. Upright/Trailer. Double. COROLLA is half flared with turned under smooth petal margins; opens white (155C) flushed yellowish white (4D), pink (62A) veins at base; matures white (155A); 34mm (1 3/8") long x 36 mm (1 7/16") wide. PETALOIDS: Two per sepal, same colour as corolla; 24mm (15/16") x 12mm (1/2"). SEPALS are horizontal, tips recurved; white (155D) tipped yellowish green (145A), pink (62A) edge and base upper surface; white (155D) lower surface; 42mm (1 11/16") long x 18mm (11/16") wide. TUBE is white (155B) flushed pink (62A), medium length and thickness; 20mm (13/16") long x 6mm (1/4") wide. STAMENS extend 13mm (1/2") beyond the corolla; light pink (65B) filaments, orangy brown (164A) anthers. PISTIL extends 22mm (7/8") below the corolla; white (155B) style; yellowish white (158A) stigma. BUD is elliptic, pointed. FOLIAGE is dark green (137A) upper surface, medium green (137D) lower surface. Leaves are 61mm (2 7/16") long x 40mm (1 9/16") wide, ovate shaped, serrulated edges, acute tips and rounded bases. Veins and stems are light green (138C); branches are medium green (138B). PARENTAGE: 'Annabel' x unknown. Lax upright or stiff trailer. Makes good upright. Prefers overhead filtered light. Best bloom

and foliage colour in filtered light. Tested three years in Wellen, Belgium. Certificate N.B.F.K. at Meise. Distinguished by vanilla bloom colour.
Van Walleghem 2002 BE AFS4905.

Tanja's Blue Bells. Upright. Semi Double. COROLLA is quarter flared; opens purple (81B); matures violet (82C); 23mm (7/8") long x 21mm (13/16") wide. PETALOIDS: purple (81A); 17mm (5/8") long x 10mm (3/8") wide. SEPALS are half down, tips reflexed; reddish purple (64B) upper surface; magenta (61C) lower surface; 24mm (15/16") long x 9mm (3/8") wide. TUBE is light rose (63D); 12mm (1/2") long x 5mm (3/16") wide. FOLIAGE: dark green (139A) upper surface; medium green (138B) lower surface. PARENTAGE: 'Witte van Zichem' x 'Rohees New Millennium'. Meise 9/17/05. Distinguished by bloom colour.
Van Walleghem 2006 BE AFS6079.

Tanja's Fantasy. Upright. Double. COROLLA is half flared with turned under wavy petal margins; opens magenta (61C), pink (48C) base; matures light rose (59D), pink (48D) base; 21mm (13/16") long x 17mm (11/16") wide. PETALOIDS: reddish purple (64B), pink (48C) base; 13mm (1/2") long x 9mm (3/8") wide. SEPALS are twisted left, horizontal, tips recurved; rose (51C), tipped light apple green (145C) upper surface; pink (48C), tipped light apple green (145C) lower surface; 33mm (1 5/16") long x 12mm (1/2") wide. TUBE is pale pink (36D); medium length & thickness; 15mm (9/16") long x 7mm (1/4") wide. FOLIAGE: dark green (136B) upper surface; medium green (137D) lower surface. Leaves are 69mm (2 3/4") long x 42mm (1 11/16") wide, ovate shaped. PARENTAGE: 'Danny Kay' x 'Quasar'. Meise 8-19-04. Distinguished by bloom resemblance to a flamed crown.
Van Walleghem 2005 BE AFS5808.

Tanja's Favoriet. Upright/Trailer. Single. COROLLA is quarter flared with turned under wavy petal margins; opens reddish purple (61B); matures magenta (58B); 19mm (3/4") long x 17 mm (11/16") wide. SEPALS are horizontal, tips reflexed; pink (55C) tipped yellowish green (149A) upper surface; rose (55B) lower surface; 26mm (1") long x 9mm (3/8") wide. TUBE is pink (55C), long with medium thickness; 52mm (2 1/16") long x 5mm (3/16") wide. STAMENS do not extend beyond the corolla; no filaments, light yellow (2B) anthers. PISTIL does not extend below the corolla; light pink (55D) style; light

yellow (4C) stigma. BUD is ovate, long TUBE. FOLIAGE is dark green (137A) upper surface, medium green (138A) lower surface. Leaves are 96mm (3 13/16") long x 49mm (1 15/16") wide, elliptic shaped, serrated edges, acute tips and rounded bases. Veins, stems and branches are light green (139D). PARENTAGE: 'WALZ Harp' x unknown. Lax upright or stiff trailer. Makes good basket. Prefers overhead filtered light. Best bloom and foliage colour in filtered light. Tested three years in Wellen, Belgium. Certificate N.B.F.K. at Meise. Distinguished by long TUBE and no filaments.
Van Walleghem 2002 BE AFS4906.

Tanja's Pink Bells. Upright. Semi Double. COROLLA is quarter flared; opens light purple (75B); matures light rose (73B); 24mm (15/16") long x 17mm (5/8") wide. SEPALS are half down, tips recurved; light pink (65C) tipped light apple green (144D) upper surface; pink (62C) tipped light apple green (144D) lower surface; 28mm (1 1/8") long x 12mm (1/2") wide. TUBE is pale pink (62D); 17mm (5/8") long x 7mm (1/4") wide. FOLIAGE: medium green (137B) upper surface; medium green (138B) lower surface. PARENTAGE: 'Witte van Zichem' x 'Paulus'. Meise 9/17/05. Distinguished by bloom colour.
Van Walleghem 2006 BE AFS6080.

Tanja's Snowball. Upright. Single. COROLLA: half flared, turned under smooth petal margins; opens & matures white (155D) flushed pale rose (73D) at base; 38mm (1 1/2") long x 40mm (1 9/16") wide. PETALOIDS: two per sepal, same colour as corolla; 27mm (1 1/16") long x 18mm (11/16") wide. SEPALS: half up; tips recurved up; white (155A), tipped light apple green (145C) upper surface, white (155D) lower surface; 55mm (2 3/16") long x 17mm (11/16") wide. TUBE: white (155A); medium length & thickness; 20mm (13/16") long x 8mm (5/16") wide. STAMENS: extend 23mm (15/16") below the corolla; dark rose (55A) filaments, light yellow (2B) anthers. PISTIL extends 37mm (1 7/16") below the corolla; pink (55C) style, yellowish white (4D) stigma. BUD: ovate. FOLIAGE: dark green (137A) upper surface, medium green (138B) lower surface. Leaves are 58mm (2 5/16") long x 40mm (1 9/16") wide, ovate or cordate shaped, serrulated edges, acute tips and cordate bases. Veins & stems are light green (138D), branches are grayish red (182B). PARENTAGE: 'Annabel' x unknown. Medium upright. Makes good basket or upright.

Prefers overhead filtered light. Best bloom and foliage colour in filtered light. Tested 3 years in Wellen, Belgium. NBFK certificate at Meise. Distinguished by bloom shape.
Van Walleghem 2003 BE AFS5092.

Tanja's Sunshine. Upright. Single. COROLLA is half flared with turned under wavy petal margins; opens reddish purple (72B), light rose (50C) base; matures light reddish purple (72C), pink (48C) base; 13mm (1/2") long x 16mm (5/8") wide. SEPALS are horizontal, tips reflexed; white (155C), pale pink (49D) base, tipped light apple green (144D) upper surface; white (155A), pink (50D) base, tipped light apple green (144D) lower surface; 18mm (11/16") long x 10mm (3/8") wide. TUBE is pale pink (49D); short & thick; 7mm (1/4") long x 6mm (1/4") wide. FOLIAGE: medium green (138B) & light yellow (4C) upper surface; medium green (138B) & light yellow (2C) lower surface. Leaves are 24mm (15/16") long x 11mm (7/16") wide, elliptic shaped. PARENTAGE: 'Pink La Campanella' x unknown. Distinguished by dwarf growth & bloom colour.
Van Walleghem 2005 BE AFS5807.

Tanja's Swinging Bells. Upright/Trailer. Single. COROLLA is half flared with turned under wavy petal margins; opens dark reddish purple (72A), rose (67D) base; matures magenta (63A); 24mm (15/16") long x 27mm (1 1/16") wide. SEPALS are half down, tips recurved; dark rose (55A), tipped yellowish green (144B) upper surface; rose (52B), tipped yellowish green (144B) lower surface; 40mm (1 9/16") long x 14mm (9/16") wide. TUBE is light pink (49C); short & thick; 8mm (5/16") long x 6mm (1/4") wide. FOLIAGE: dark green (139A) upper surface; medium green (138B) lower surface. Leaves are 82mm (3 1/4") long x 45mm (1 3/4") wide, ovate shaped. PARENTAGE: 'Paulus' x 'Quasar'. Meise 8-19-04, Outstanding Award. Distinguished by bloom shape.
Van Walleghem 2005 BE AFS5809.

Tanja's Treasure. Upright. Single. COROLLA: quarter flared, turned under smooth petal margins; opens light reddish violet (180A), matures grayish orange (179B); 18mm (11/16") long x 21mm (13/16") wide. SEPALS: half down; tips reflexed; magenta (58B), tipped greenish yellow (151B) upper surface, orange (31A) lower surface; 35mm (1 3/8") long x 13mm (1/2") wide. TUBE: magenta (58B); long, medium thickness;

449

square shaped; 44mm (1 3/4") long x 8mm (5/16") wide. STAMENS: extend 3mm (1/8") below the corolla; coral (37A) filaments, yellow (4A) anthers. PISTIL extends 38mm (1 1/2") below the corolla; coral (39B) style, dark yellowish orange (14A) stigma. BUD: ovate, long TUBE. FOLIAGE: dark green (139A) upper surface, medium green (137C) lower surface. Leaves are 73mm (2 7/8") long x 47mm (1 7/8") wide, ovate shaped, serrulated edges, acute tips and rounded bases. Veins & stems are medium green (139C), branches are grayish orange (179B). PARENTAGE: 'WALZ Harp' x unknown. Medium upright. Makes good upright. Prefers full sun. Best bloom and foliage colour in bright light. Tested 3 years in Wellen, Belgium. NBFK certificate at Meise. Distinguished by long square TUBE, smoky petals.
Van Walleghem 2003 BE AFS5093.

Tante Nonneke. Upright/Trailer. Single. COROLLA is 3 quarter flared; opens reddish purple (72B) with pink (48D) base; matures magenta (58B with pink (49A) base; 21mm (13/16") long x 24mm (15/16") wide. SEPALS are horizontal, tips reflexed; pink (52D) tipped light yellowish green (150C) upper surface, and pink (48D) tipped light yellowish green (150C) lower surface; 32mm (1 1/4") long x 14mm (9/16") wide. TUBE is pale pink (56B); medium length & thickness; 20mm (3/4") long x 7mm (1/4") wide. FOLIAGE is dark green (139A) upper surface; medium green (138B) lower surface. PARENTAGE: found seedling.
Willems 2007 BE AFS6421.

Tasty Tracy. Upright/Trailer. Semi Double. COROLLA: half flared, turned under smooth petal margins; opens pale pink (56B) veined dark rose (51A); matures pale pink (56C) veined dark rose (51A); 14mm (9/16") long x 20mm (13/16") wide. SEPALS: half up; tips reflexed up; dark rose (51A) upper surface; rose (52B) lower surface; 32mm (1 1/4") long x 15mm (9/16") wide. TUBE: dark rose (51A); medium length & thickness; 12mm(1/2") long x 7mm (1/4") wide. STAMENS: extend 25mm (1") below corolla; dark rose (54A) filaments, dark red (53A) anthers. PISTIL: extends 50mm (2") below the corolla, dark rose (54A) style & stigma. BUD: round. FOLIAGE: medium green (137C) upper surface; medium green (138A) lower surface. Leaves are 50mm (2") long x 25mm (1") wide, lanceolate shaped, serrulated edges, acute tips and rounded bases. Veins are green, stems are red; branches are brown.

PARENTAGE: 'R.A.F.' x 'Carla Johnson'. Lax upright or stiff trailer. Self branching. Makes good basket. Prefers overhead filtered light. Heat tolerant if shaded. Cold weather hardy to 32° F. Best bloom and foliage colour in filtered light. Tested 4 years in Walthamstow, London, England. Distinguished by delicate colour of blooms and colour retention with age.
Allsop J. 2003 UK AFS5212.

Telesto. Upright. Double. COROLLA white veined red. SEPALS light carmine.
Ainsworth 2005 UK.

Tenue de Soirée. Upright/Trailer. Single. COROLLA: unflared, smooth petal margins; opens & matures dark rose (54A), white (155A) at base; 27mm (1 1/16") long x 17mm (11/16") wide. SEPALS: horizontal; tips recurved; white (155D) upper & lower surfaces; 43mm (1 11/16") long x 6.5mm (1/4") wide. TUBE: light greenish white (157D); long, thin; 22mm (7/8") long x 5mm (3/16") wide. STAMENS: extend 9-11mm (3/8-7/16") below corolla; pale pink (56A) filaments; light tan (161C) anthers. PISTIL: extends 29mm (1 1/8") below the corolla; pale pink (56D) style; yellowish white (4D) stigma. BUD: ovate, long. FOLIAGE: dark green (147A) upper surface, medium green (147B) lower surface. Leaves are 90mm (3 9/16") long x 39mm (1 9/16") wide, lanceolate shaped, serrated edges, acute tips and obtuse bases. Yellowish green veins; Yellowish green & light brown stems; light brown branches. PARENTAGE: 'Checkerboard' x 'René Massé'. Lax upright or stiff trailer. Makes good basket or upright. Prefers overhead filtered light and cool climate. Best bloom and foliage colour in filtered light. Tested 3 years in Pornic, France. Distinguished by semi-terminal blooming, long SEPALS.
Massé 2004 FR AFS5444.

Tessa Krekels. Upright/Trailer. Double. COROLLA: three quarter flared, smooth petal margins; opens reddish purple (67A); matures magenta (58B); 22mm (7/8") long x 22mm (7/8") wide. SEPALS: fully up; tips reflexed; white (155A) upper surface; white (155B) lower surface; 40mm (1 9/16") long x 22mm (7/8") wide. TUBE: pale yellow (1D); medium length & thickness; 12mm (1/2") long x 8mm (5/16") wide. STAMENS: extend 20mm (13/16") below corolla; pale pink (62D) filaments, reddish purple (67A) anthers. PISTIL: extends 32mm (1 1/4") below the corolla; white (155C) style,

450

yellowish white (4D) stigma. BUD: spherical. FOLIAGE: medium green (137B) upper surface; medium green (138B) lower surface. Leaves are 60mm (2 3/8") long x 48mm (1 7/8") wide, ovate shaped, serrated edges, acute tips and obtuse bases. Veins, stems & branches are green. PARENTAGE: 'Sophie Michiels' x 'Veenlust'. Lax upright or stiff trailer. Makes good stiff trailer. Prefers overhead filtered light and cool climate. Best bloom and foliage colour in filtered light. Tested 4 years in Reusel, The Netherlands. Distinguished by bloom colour. van Eijk 2003 NL AFS5250.

Teuntje. Upright/Trailer. Double. COROLLA: three quarter flared; opens magenta (63B) and matures magenta (68A); 26mm (1") long x 18mm (11/16") wide. PETALOIDS: magenta (63B); 16mm (5/8") long x 14mm (9/16") wide. SEPALS are half up, tips recurved up; white (155C) tipped light yellowish green (150C) upper surface; rose (55B) tipped light yellowish green (150C) lower surface; 42mm (1 5/8") long x 15mm (9/16") wide. TUBE is white (155C); medium length & thickness; 15mm (9/16") long x 6mm (1/4") wide. FOLIAGE is dark green (136B) upper surface; medium green (138A) lower surface. PARENTAGE: 'Leen Vander Kuylen' x 'Charlotte Martens'. Michiels 2007 BE AFS6518.

Thea Kroese. Upright/Trailer. Double. COROLLA: three quarter flared, smooth petal margins; opens violet (85A); matures violet (75A); 22mm (7/8") long x 22mm (7/8") wide. SEPALS: fully up; tips recurved; rose (65A) upper & lower surfaces; 31mm (1 1/4") long x 16mm (5/8") wide. TUBE: pale lavender (65D); medium length & thickness; 17mm (11/16") long x 6mm (1/4") wide. STAMENS: extend 18mm (11/16") below corolla; dark reddish purple (73A) filaments & anthers. PISTIL: extends 48mm (1 7/8") below the corolla; pale rose (73D) style; yellowish white (4D) stigma. BUD: ovate. FOLIAGE: dark green (139A) upper surface; medium green (137C) lower surface. Leaves are 72mm (2 13/16") long x 37mm (1 7/16") wide, ovate shaped, serrulated edges, acute tips and rounded bases. Veins, stems & branches are green. PARENTAGE: 'Sofie Michiels' x 'Lechlade Rocket'. Lax upright or stiff trailer. Makes good stiff trailer. Prefers overhead filtered light and cool climate. Best bloom and foliage colour in filtered light. Tested 4 years in Knegsel, The Netherlands. Distinguished by bloom colour. Roes 2003 NL AFS5354.

Thelma Vint. Upright. Single. COROLLA: quarter flared, smooth petal margins; opens dark violet (87A); matures reddish purple (66B); 17mm (5/8") long x 17mm (5/8") wide. SEPALS: horizontal, tips recurved; rose (68C) tipped green upper surface; rose (68B) tipped green lower surface; 21mm (13/16") long x 8mm (5/16") wide. TUBE: rose (68C) & green; short, thin; 4mm (1/8") long x 4mm (1/8") wide. STAMENS extend 14mm (9/16") beyond the corolla; rose (52C) filaments; red (46B) anthers. PISTIL extends 25mm (1") beyond the corolla; pink (62C) style; light pink (49B) stigma. BUD: square, pointed, slight twist. FOLIAGE: dark green (139A) upper surface; medium green (138B) lower surface. Leaves are 34mm (1 3/8") long x 9mm (5/16") wide; cordate shaped, serrulate edges, acute tips, rounded bases. Veins, stems & branches are green. PARENTAGE: 'Estelle Marie' x 'Pink Fantasia'. Small upright. Self branching. Makes good upright. Prefers full sun. Cold weather hardy to -3° C (26° F). Best bloom & foliage colour in bright light. Tested 6 years in Burstwick, East Yorkshire, England. Distinguished by bloom colour, horizontally erect flowers. Storey 2009 UK AFS7132.

Theo de Vroom. Upright/Trailer. Semi Double. COROLLA: three quarter flared; opens & matures light rose (73B); 20mm (3/4") long x 26mm (1") wide. SEPALS: half up, tips reflexed up; magenta (58B) upper & lower surfaces; 25mm (1") long x 13mm (1/21") wide. TUBE: magenta (58B); 12mm (7/16") long x 10mm (3/8") wide. FOLIAGE is medium green (137B) upper surface; medium green (137C) lower surface. PARENTAGE: 'Roesse Carme' x 'BreeVis Paradoxa'. van Bree 2008 NL AFS6892.

Theo Heinsbergen. Trailer. Single. COROLLA: 3 quarter flared; opens & matures dark red (46A); 20mm (3/4") long x 24mm (15/16") wide. SEPALS: fully up, tips reflexed; pink (43D) upper surface; orange (44D) lower surface; 30mm (1 3/16") long x 15mm (9/16") wide. TUBE: pink (43D); short & thick; 10mm (3/8") long x 9mm (3/8") wide. FOLIAGE is dark green (137A) upper surface; medium green (137D) lower surface. PARENTAGE: 'Roesse Lupus' x 'Hula Girl'. van Eijk 2007 NL AFS6569.

Theo Jeukens. Trailer. Single. COROLLA is half flared, bell shaped, with turned up petal margins; opens rose (68B); matures magenta (68A); 21mm (13/16") long x 14mm (9/16") wide. SEPALS are horizontal, tips recurved;

pink (55C) upper surface; rose (55B) lower surface; 29mm (1 1/8") long x 6mm (1/4") wide. TUBE is rose (55B); medium length & thickness; 21mm (13/16") long x 6mm (1/4") wide. FOLIAGE: medium green (146A) upper surface; yellowish green (146B) lower surface. Leaves are 93mm (3 11/16") long x 52mm (2 1/16") wide, elliptic shaped. PARENTAGE: 'Gerharda's Panache' x 'Fey'. Nomination by N.K.V.F. as recommendable cultivar. Distinguished by wide standing bell shaped flowers.
de Keijzer 2005 NL AFS5789.

Theo van Bree. Trailer. Single. COROLLA: half flared; opens & matures white (155D); 19mm (3/4") long x 24mm (15/16") wide. SEPALS: fully up, tips reflexed; light rose (68D) upper & lower surfaces; 40mm (1 9/16") long x 11mm (7/16") wide. TUBE: red (45B); 15mm (9/16") long x 5mm (3/16") wide. FOLIAGE is dark green (137A) upper surface; medium green (137C) lower surface. PARENTAGE: 'Roesse Carme' x 'Roesse Ophelia'.
van Bree 2008 NL AFS6891.

Thierry Guillet. Upright. Single. COROLLA is unflared with smooth petal margins; opens & matures violet (84A); 16mm (5/8") long x 9mm (3/8") wide. SEPALS are horizontal, tips recurved; red (45D) upper & lower surfaces; 20mm (13/16") long x 5mm (3/16") wide. TUBE is red (45D); short, medium thickness; 12mm (1/2") long x 4mm (3/16") wide. FOLIAGE: very dark green (>147A) upper surface; medium green (147B) lower surface. Leaves are 58mm (2 5/16") long x 18mm (11/16") wide, lanceolate shaped. PARENTAGE: ('Whiteknight's Pearl' x 'Fiona') x ('Whiteknight's Pearl' x 'Fiona'). Distinguished by hardiness and bloom/foliage contrast.
Massé 2005 FR AFS5697.

Thieu Knapen. Trailer. Double. COROLLA is three quarter flared; opens & matures white (155D); 18mm (11/16") long x 26mm (1") wide. SEPALS are horizontal, tips recurved; pale purple (75C) upper surface; light purple (75B) lower surface; 32mm (1 1/4") long x 16mm (5/8") wide. TUBE is white (155D); 29mm (1 1/8") long x 4mm (1/8") wide. FOLIAGE: medium green (137B) upper surface; medium green (138B) lower surface. PARENTAGE: 'Sofie Michiels' x 'Luuk van Riet'. Distinguished by bloom & foliage combination
Roes 2006 NL AFS6152.

Thieu Marjan. Trailer. Double. COROLLA is half flared with smooth petal margins; opens & matures pale lavender (65D); 19mm (3/4") long x 17mm (11/16") wide. SEPALS are half up, tips reflexed up; pale lavender (69C) tipped green upper surface; pale pink (69A) lower surface; 25mm (1") long x 20mm (13/16") wide. TUBE is pale lavender (69C); medium length & thickness; 19mm (3/4") long x 5mm (3/16") wide. FOLIAGE: dark green (137A) upper surface; medium green (137D) lower surface. Leaves are 65mm (2 9/16") long x 43mm (1 11/16") wide, cordate shaped. PARENTAGE: 'Sofie Michiels' x 'Brenda Krekels'. Distinguished by bloom & foliage combination.
van Eijk 2005 NL AFS5898.

Thomas. Upright. Semi Double. COROLLA is half flared with turned under smooth petal margins; opens reddish purple (74A), matures reddish purple (74B); 22mm (7/8") long x 20mm (13/16") wide. SEPALS are half down, tips reflexed; magenta (57A) upper surface, magenta (58B) lower surface; 28mm (1 1/8") long x 13mm (1/2") wide. TUBE is rose (64D), medium length and thickness; 20mm (13/16") long x 7mm (1/4") wide. STAMENS extend 4mm (3/16") beyond the corolla; rose (63C) filaments, pale orange (27B) anthers. PISTIL extends 7mm (1/4") beyond the corolla; magenta (61C) style; magenta (59D) stigma. BUD is round. FOLIAGE is dark green (137A) upper surface, medium green (138C) lower surface. Leaves are 72mm (2 13/16") long x 33mm (1 5/16") wide, ovate shaped, serrulated edges, acute tips and rounded bases. Veins are plum (185B), stems plum (184C), branches are plum (184B). PARENTAGE: 'WALZ Harp' x 'Carl Wallace'. Medium upright, dwarf growth. Self branching. Makes good trellis. Prefers overhead filtered light. Best bloom and foliage colour in filtered light. Tested three years in Koningshooikt and Hoeselt, Belgium. Certificate N.B.F.K. at Meise. Distinguished by Stamens and pistil shape.
Michiels 2002 BE AFS4932.

Thomas Berge. Upright. Single. COROLLA: Quarter flared, bell shaped; opens pale purple (75D) edged violet (75A); matures rose (68C) edged magenta (68A); 13mm (1/2") long x 14mm (9/16") wide. SEPALS: half down, tips reflexed; orangish white (159C), edged rose (68C), tipped green upper surface; rose (68C) tipped green lower surface; 28mm (1 1/8") long x 12mm (7/16") wide. TUBE: pale yellow (158B); short, medium thickness; 6mm (1/4") long x 4mm (1/8") wide.

FOLIAGE is medium green (147B) upper surface; medium green (138A) lower surface. PARENTAGE: 'Audrey Hatfield' x 'Prince Syray'.
Koerts T. 2007 NL AFS6454.

Thomas Fuhrman. Upright/Trailer. Double. COROLLA: half flared, turned under wavy petal margins; opens dark reddish purple (61A); matures dark reddish purple (60B); 25mm (1") long x 23mm (7/8") wide. PETALOIDS: Same colour as corolla; 15mm (9/16") long x 11mm (7/16") wide. SEPALS: horizontal, tips recurved; light pink (62C) tipped apple green (144C) upper surface; magenta (63B) tipped apple green (144C) lower surface; 34mm (1 3/8") long x 15mm (9/16") wide. TUBE: pale pink (62D); medium length & thickness; 17mm (5/8") long x 6mm (1/4") wide. STAMENS extend 18mm (11/16") beyond the corolla; reddish purple (70B) filaments; dark reddish purple (72A) anthers. PISTIL extends 27mm (1 1/16") beyond the corolla; dark rose (64C) style; yellowish white (4D) stigma. BUD: bulbous. FOLIAGE: dark green (137A) upper surface; medium green (139C) lower surface. Leaves are 58mm (2 5/16") long x 36mm (1 7/16") wide; ovate shaped, smooth edges, acute tips, rounded bases. Veins are plum (185B), stems are light red purple (185D), branches are light red purple (185D) & light green (138C). PARENTAGE: 'Manfried Kleinau' x 'Corsair'. Lax upright or stiff trailer. Self branching. Makes good upright. Prefers overhead filtered light, cool climate. Best bloom & foliage colour in filtered light. Tested 3 years in Koningshooikt, Belgium. Waanrode 7/5/08. Distinguished by bloom colour combination.
Michiels 2009 BE AFS7227.

Thomas Pips. Upright/Trailer. Single. COROLLA: half flared, turned under smooth petal margins; opens & matures magenta (63A) edged reddish purple (64B); 27mm (1 1/16") long x 42mm (1 11/16") wide. SEPALS: half up; tips reflexed up; dark rose (58C) tipped light apple green (144D) upper surface; dark rose (58C) lower surface; 35mm (1 3/8") long x 17mm (11/16") wide. TUBE: dark rose (58C); medium length & thickness; 14mm(9/16") long x 7mm (1/4") wide. STAMENS: 13mm (1/2") below corolla; magenta (58B) filaments, reddish purple (58A) anthers. PISTIL: extends 30mm (1 3/16") below the corolla, dark rose (58C) style, magenta (61C) stigma. BUD: round. FOLIAGE: dark green (137A) upper surface; medium green (137C) lower surface. Leaves

are 61mm (2 3/8") long x 35mm (1 3/8") wide, cordate shaped, serrulated edges, acute tips and cordate bases. Veins & stems are reddish purple (58A), branches are orangy brown (176A). PARENTAGE: 'Rosea' x 'Patatin-Pataton'. Lax upright or stiff trailer. Self branching. Makes good basket. Prefers overhead filtered light. Best bloom and foliage colour in filtered light. Tested 3 years in Rummen, Belgium. NBFK Certificate at Meise. Distinguished by strong growth, bloom colour and profuse blooms.
Ector 2003 BE AFS5201.

Thomas Ritchie. Upright. Single. COROLLA opens imperial purple (n78a), matures to a lighter purple (n78b); corolla is quater flared and is 22mm long x 24mm wide. SEPALS are light pink (73d) on the upper surface, darker pink (73c) on the lower surface; sepals are fully up with recurved tips and are 31mm long x 13mm wide. TUBE light pink (73d) and is 9mm long x 5mm wide. PARENTAGE 'London 2000' x 'Ken Shelton'.
Waving P. 2004 UK BFS0003.

Thomas Sattler. Upright/Trailer. Semi Double to Double. COROLLA: half flared, turned under wavy petal margins; opens magenta (63A) dark reddish purple (64A); matures magenta (61C) & dark reddish purple (61A); 28mm (1 1/8") long x 26mm (1") wide. SEPALS: horizontal, tips recurved; pale lavender (69B) tipped apple green (144C) upper surface; magenta (68A) tipped apple green (144C) lower surface; 38mm (1 1/2") long x 13mm (1/2") wide. TUBE: light pink (65C); short & thick; 11mm (7/16") long x 8mm (5/16") wide. STAMENS extend 21mm (13/16") beyond the corolla; reddish purple (61B) filaments; purple (71A) anthers. PISTIL extends 27mm (1 1/16") beyond the corolla; reddish purple (64B) style; yellowish white (4D) stigma. BUD: globular. FOLIAGE: dark green (137A) upper surface; medium green (138B) lower surface. Leaves are 68mm (2 11/16") long x 35mm (1 3/8") wide; ovate shaped, serrulate edges, acute tips, rounded bases. Veins are dark reddish purple (187B), stems are red purple (N186D), branches are red purple (N186D) & medium green (137D). PARENTAGE: 'Manfried Kleinau' x 'Beauty of Everbeur'. Lax upright or stiff trailer. Self branching. Makes good upright. Prefers overhead filtered light, cool climate. Best bloom & foliage colour in filtered light. Tested 3 years in Koningshooikt, Belgium. Waanrode 7/5/08. Distinguished by bloom colour.
Michiels 2009 BE AFS7228.

Tielko Koerts. Upright. Single. COROLLA: Quarter flared; opens & matures red (52A), pale pink (36D) base, rarely striped cream; 25mm (1") long x 23mm (7/8") wide. SEPALS: half down, tips recurved; light yellow (4C) tipped yellowish green (144B) upper & lower surfaces; 41mm (1 5/8") long x 8mm (5/16") wide. TUBE: light yellow (4C); medium length, thin; 12mm (7/16") long x 4mm (1/8") wide. FOLIAGE is medium green (147B) upper surface; yellowish green (146B) lower surface. PARENTAGE: 'Henri Massé' x 'F. *boliviana alba*'.
Massé 2007 FR AFS6489.

Tilly Tamerus. Trailer. Semi Double. COROLLA is quarter flared with smooth petal margins; opens purple (71A), matures dark reddish purple (59A); 20mm (13/16") long x 24mm (15/16") wide. SEPALS are fully up, tips recurved; magenta (63B) upper surface; magenta (63A) lower surface; 28mm (1 1/8") long x 11mm (7/16") wide. TUBE is magenta (63B); medium length and thickness; 17mm (11/16") long x 7mm (1/4") thick. STAMENS extend 15mm (5/8") beyond the corolla; purple (71A) filaments and anthers. PISTIL extends 27mm (1 1/16") beyond the corolla; magenta (67B) style, light yellow (3D) stigma. BUD is globular, pointed. FOLIAGE is dark green (137A) upper surface, medium green (138B) lower surface. Leaves are 55mm (2 3/16") long x 26mm (1") wide, elliptic shaped, serrated edges, acute tips and obtuse bases. Veins, stems and branches are red. PARENTAGE: ('Rohees King') x 'Anta'. Natural trailer. Makes good basket. Prefers overhead filtered light and cool climate. Best bloom colour in filtered light. Tested four years in Duizel, The Netherlands. Distinguished by bloom colour.
Tamerus 2002 NL AFS4998.

Timkesber. Trailer. Double. COROLLA: half flared; opens light purple (N78A); matures light purple (N78B); 25mm (1") long x 16mm (5/8") wide. PETALOIDS: light purple (N78B); 16mm (5/8") long x 11 mm (7/16") wide. SEPALS are horizontal, tips recurved, twisted left; white (155C) tipped light green (145D) upper surface; white (155D) tipped light green (145D) lower surface; 49mm (1 15/16") long x 12mm (7/16") wide. TUBE is pale pink (62D); medium length & thickness; 14mm (9/16") long x 6mm (1/4") wide. FOLIAGE is dark green (137A) upper surface; medium green (138B) lower surface. PARENTAGE: 'Waanrodes Silver Star' x 'Ine Frozer'.
Michiels 2007 BE AFS6519.

Tine Pardon. Upright/Trailer. Double. COROLLA: half flared, turned under wavy petal margins; opens dark reddish purple (71B); matures red (53C) & reddish purple (64B); 19mm (3/4") long x 17mm (5/8") wide. PETALOIDS: dark rose (67C); 11mm (7/16") long x 11mm (7/16") wide. SEPALS: horizontal, tips reflexed; light pink (55D) tipped light olive green (153C) upper surface; dark rose (154B) tipped light olive green (153C) lower surface; 31mm (1 1/4") long x 14mm (9/16") wide. TUBE: white (155B); short & thick; 12mm (7/16") long x 6mm (1/4") wide. STAMENS extend 14mm (9/16") beyond the corolla; rose (61D) filaments; purple (71A) anthers. PISTIL extends 18mm (11/16") beyond the corolla; dark rose (58C) style; light rose (63D) stigma. BUD: bulbous. FOLIAGE: dark green (136B) upper surface; medium green (138B) lower surface. Leaves are 68mm (2 11/16") long x 41mm (1 5/8") wide; ovate shaped, serrate edges, acute tips, rounded bases. Veins are greenish yellow (151A), stems are light plum (184D), branches are light plum (184D) & light green (138C). PARENTAGE: 'Manfried Kleinau' x 'Lenny-Erwin'. Lax upright or stiff trailer. Self branching. Makes good basket or upright. Prefers overhead filtered light, cool climate. Best bloom & foliage colour in filtered light. Tested 3 years in Koningshooikt, Belgium. Waanrode 7/5/08. Distinguished by bloom colour.
Michiels 2009 BE AFS7229.

Tiny Scharf. Trailer. Double. COROLLA is three quarter flared; opens & matures pale lavender (69C); 22mm (7/8") long x 24mm (15/16") wide. SEPALS are horizontal, tips recurved; pale lavender (69C) tipped green upper & lower surfaces; 42mm (1 5/8") long x 16mm (5/8") wide. TUBE is light apple green (145C); 14mm (9/16") long x 5mm (3/16") wide. FOLIAGE: medium green (137B) upper surface; medium green (137C) lower surface. PARENTAGE: 'Lady in Grey' x unknown. Distinguished by bloom colour.
Scharf 2006 NL AFS6187.

Tinytobes. Upright. Single. COROLLA opens porcelain blue, matures to a shade darker; corolla is three quarter flared and is 20mm long x 18mm wide. SEPALS pale pink on the upper surface, pale pink - white on the lower surface; sepals are half up with recurved tips and are 27mm long x 9mm wide. TUBE pale pink and is 7mm long x 5mm wide. PARENTAGE ((Helen Nicholls x Katrina Thompsen Seedling) x Sophie Louise) x

Sophie Louise. This cultivar is free flowering and bushy, it is easy to shape and has proven to be a good show plant.
Nicholls A. 2007 UK BFS0054.

Tjiluwah. Trailer. Single. COROLLA is half flared with smooth petal margins; opens & matures orange (33B); 10mm (3/8") long x 7 mm (1/4") wide. SEPALS are half down, tips recurved; red (46C) upper surface, grayish yellow (161A) lower surface; 15mm (9/16") long x 4mm (3/16") wide. TUBE is red (46C), medium length & thickness; 14mm (9/16") long x 5mm (3/16") wide. FOLIAGE: dark green (147A) upper surface; gray green (194A) lower surface. Leaves are 51mm (2") long x 29 mm (1 1/8") wide, elliptic shaped. PARENTAGE: 'Rÿs 2001' x 'F. decussata'. Natural trailer. Self branching. Distinguished by unique colour combination.
de Boer J. 2005 NL AFS5651.

Toby Foreman. Upright. Single. COROLLA opens white with slight red veining; corolla is quarter flared and is 20mm long x 16mm wide. SEPALS light red on the upper and lower surfaces; sepals are half up with recurved tips and are 26mm long x 8mm wide. TUBE light red and is 10mm long x 5mm wide. PARENTAGE 'Breeders Delight' x 'Shopie Louise'.
Waving 2006 UK BFS0034.

Tom En Tinneke. Upright. Single. COROLLA is half flared with turned under wavy petal margins; opens reddish purple (72B), rose (47C) base; matures reddish purple (71B), rose (50B) base; 29mm (1 1/8") long x 24mm (15/16") wide. SEPALS are horizontal, tips recurved; rose (51C) tipped light yellowish green (150C) upper surface; rose (52C) tipped light yellowish green (150C) lower surface; 37mm (1 7/16") long x 14mm (9/16") wide. TUBE is pink (50D); long & thick; 57mm (2 1/4") long x 7mm (1/4") wide. FOLIAGE: dark green (139A) upper surface; medium green (138B) lower surface. Leaves are 82mm (3 1/4") long x 49mm (1 15/16") wide, cordate shaped. PARENTAGE: 'WALZ Harp' x 'Ting -a -Ling'. Meise 8-14-04. Distinguished by flower colour & long TUBE.
Geerts L. 2005 BE AFS5728.

Tom Knapen. Upright/Trailer. Single. COROLLA is half flared; opens purple (71A); matures dark reddish purple (64A); 22mm (7/8") long x 30mm (3/16") wide. SEPALS are horizontal, tips recurved; rose (68C) upper surface; magenta (68A) lower surface; 28mm (1 1/8") long x 16mm (5/8") wide.

TUBE is light rose (68D); 20mm (3/4") long x 7mm (1/4") wide. FOLIAGE: dark green (137A) upper surface; medium green (138B) lower surface. PARENTAGE: 'Roesse Rhea' x 'Lye's Unique'. Distinguished by bloom colour.
Roes 2006 NL AFS6169.

Tom Tamerus. Upright/Trailer. Single. COROLLA is quarter flared with smooth petal margins; opens dark purple (79A); matures purple (77A); 27mm (1 1/16") long x 20mm (13/16") wide. SEPALS are half up, tips recurved up; magenta (57A) upper and lower surfaces; 34mm (1 3/8") long x 8mm (5/16") wide. TUBE is magenta (57A), medium length and thickness; 20mm (13/16") long x 6mm (1/4") wide. STAMENS extend 12mm (1/2") beyond the corolla; purple (71A) filaments, and anthers. PISTIL extends 42mm (1 11/16") beyond the corolla; dark rose (64C) style, pink (62C) stigma. BUD is ovate, pointed. FOLIAGE is medium green (138A) upper surface, medium green (138B) lower surface. Leaves are 52mm (2 1/16") long x 27mm (1 1/16") wide, ovate shaped, serrated edges, acute tips and obtuse bases. Veins, stems and branches are red. PARENTAGE: 'Rohees King' x 'Anta Tamerus'. Lax upright or stiff trailer. Makes good stiff trailer. Prefers overhead filtered light and cool climate. Best bloom colour in filtered light. Tested four years in Duizel, The Netherlands. Distinguished by bloom colour.
Tamerus A. 2002 NL AFS4939.

Tombi. Upright. Double. COROLLA pale lilac white. SEPALS white flushed pink.
Ainsworth 2005 UK.

Tommy Baker. Upright/Trailer. Double. COROLLA is half flared with smooth margins; opens magenta (63B) splashed light orange (29B), matures magenta (63A) splashed pale orange (29C); 24mm (15/16") long x 38mm (1 1/2") wide. SEPALS are horizontal, tips reflexed; pale pink (49D) upper surface, pink (49A) lower surface; 36mm (1 7/16") long x 17mm (11/16") wide. TUBE is light pink (49A), medium length and thickness; 23mm (15/16") long x 8mm (5/16") wide. STAMENS extend 23mm (15/16") below the corolla; magenta (57C) filaments and anthers. PISTIL extends 32mm (1 1/4") below the corolla; magenta (63B) style, white (155A) stigma. BUD is obtuse. FOLIAGE is dark green (137A) upper surface, medium green (138B) lower surface. Leaves are 58mm (2 5/16") long x 32mm (1 1/4") wide, cordate shaped, serrulated edges,

acute tips and cordate bases. Veins are green, stems and branches are red. PARENTAGE: 'Ruth Graham' x 'Annabel'. Lax upright or stiff trailer. Makes good basket. Prefers cool climate. Heat tolerant if shaded. Best bloom colour in filtered light. Tested three years in Stockbridge, Hampshire, England. Distinguished by blossom colour combination.
Graham 2002 UK AFS4877.

Tommy Struck. Trailer. Double. COROLLA is quarter flared; opens reddish purple (72B) with magenta (58B) base; matures magenta (71C); 10mm (3/8") long x 6mm (1/4") wide. PETALOIDS are reddish purple (72B) with magenta (58B) base; 8mm (5/16") long x 5mm (3/16") wide. SEPALS are half up, tips recurved up; red (53B) upper surface, and magenta (58B) lower surface; 20mm (3/4") long x 6mm (1/4") wide. TUBE is red (53C); 8mm (5/16") long x 3mm (1/8") wide. FOLIAGE is medium green (138A) upper surface; medium green (138B) lower surface. PARENTAGE: 'Rosea' x 'Katrien Micheils'. Meise 8/13/05. Distinguished by bloom shape & colour.
Michiels 2006 BE AFS6040.

Ton Comperen. Trailer. Double. COROLLA: three quarter flared, smooth petal margins; opens purple (83C); matures reddish purple (80B); 22mm (7/8") long x 18mm (11/16") wide. SEPALS: fully up; tips reflexed; light green (145D) upper & lower surfaces; 29mm (1 1/8") long x 11mm (7/16") wide. TUBE: light green (145D); medium length & thickness; 10mm (3/8") long x 5mm (3/16") wide. STAMENS: extend 17mm (11/16") below corolla; light rose (68D) filaments; light rose (73B) anthers. PISTIL: extends 48mm (1 7/8") below the corolla; white (155B) style; cream (11D) stigma. BUD: ovate. FOLIAGE: dark green (137B) upper surface; medium green (138B) lower surface. Leaves are 56mm (2 3/16") long x 23mm (15/16") wide, lanceolate shaped, serrated edges, acute tips and rounded bases. Veins, stems & branches are green. PARENTAGE: 'Sofie Michiels' x 'Cameron Ryle'. Natural trailer. Makes good basket. Prefers overhead filtered light and cool climate. Best bloom and foliage colour in filtered light. Tested 4 years in Diessen, The Netherlands. Distinguished by bloom colour.
Comperen 2003 NL AFS5285.

Tonnie Sanders. Upright/Trailer. Semi Double. COROLLA is three quarter flared with turned up smooth petal margins; opens reddish purple (64B); matures magenta (58B); 30mm (3/16") long x 35mm (1 3/8") wide. SEPALS are fully up, tips recurved; magenta (58B) upper & lower surfaces; 37mm (1 7/16") long x 10mm (3/8") wide. TUBE is magenta (58B); medium length & thickness; 14mm (9/16") long x 8mm (5/16") wide. FOLIAGE: medium green (137B) upper surface; medium green (138B) lower surface. Leaves are 60mm (2 3/8") long x 35mm (1 3/8") wide, ovate shaped. PARENTAGE: ('Roesse Apus' x 'Roesse Apus') x 'Yvette Klessens'. Distinguished by bloom colour & shape.
Buiting 2005 NL AFS5872.

Tony Allcock. Upright. Double. COROLLA is three quarter flared, square shaped, with smooth petal margins; opens reddish purple (67A) /dark purple (89A) /dark purple (86A) veined magenta (67B) at base; matures reddish purple (67A); 30mm (1 3/16") long x 70mm (2 3/4") wide. SEPALS are fully up, tips recurved; light purple (74C) upper surface, light purple (74C) creped lower surface; 45mm (1 3/4") long x 17mm (11/16) wide. TUBE is rose (68C); short with medium thickness; 12mm (1/2") long x 8mm (5/16") wide. STAMENS extend 22mm (7/8") below the corolla; magenta (67B) filaments; reddish purple (67A) anthers. PISTIL extends 49mm (1 15/16") below the corolla; magenta (67B) style and white (155A) stigma. BUD is round, pointed. FOLIAGE is dark green (139A) upper surface, medium green (137C) lower surface. Leaves are 73mm (2 7/8") long x 43mm (1 11/16") wide, ovate shaped, serrulated edges, acute tips and rounded bases. Veins are red, stems are pale green and branches are red. PARENTAGE: 'Satchmo' x 'Seventh Heaven'. Tall upright. Makes good upright, standard or pillar. Prefers cool climate. Heat tolerant if shaded. Best bloom colour in filtered light. Tested five years in Gloucester, England. Distinguished by many shades of bloom colour.
Hickman 2002 UK AFS4859.

Tony Lawson. Upright. Single. COROLLA opens deep blue, matures to cerise; corolla is quarter flared. SEPALS white tipped green on the upper and lower surfaces; SEPALS are half down with recurved tips. TUBE white. PARENTAGE Seedling No. 1044 ('Anna Louise' x 'Emma Margaret')' x 'Seedling No. 1011(No Name). Blooms are upward facing and free flowering.
Riley 2009 UK BFS0120.

Toon's Tuinklokje. Trailer. Single. COROLLA is quarter flared; opens violet

(85A) striped magenta (58B) with light pink (55D) base; matures violet (76A); 15mm (9/16") long x 13mm (1/2") wide. SEPALS are horizontal, tips reflexed; magenta (58B) upper surface; magenta (61C) lower surface; 21mm (13/16") long x 6mm (1/4") wide. TUBE is rose (54B); 6mm (1/4") long x 6mm (1/4") wide. FOLIAGE is medium green (137B) upper surface; medium green (138B) lower surface. PARENTAGE: 'Tresco' x 'Blue Elf'. Meise 8/13/05. Distinguished by bloom colour.
Michiels 2006 BE AFS6035.

Top Green. Upright. Single. COROLLA: quarter flared, smooth petal margins; opens reddish purple (58A), matures magenta (57A); 12mm (1/2") long x 9mm (3/8") wide. SEPALS: horizontal; yellowish green (144A) upper surface, dark rose (48A) lower surface; 15mm (9/16") long x 2mm (1/16") wide. TUBE: red (50A), long & thin; 18mm (11/16") long x 2mm (1/16") wide. STAMENS: extend 18 - 19mm (11/16 – 3/4") below the corolla; magenta (58B) filaments, light yellow (11B) anthers. PISTIL extends 23mm (7/8") below the corolla; magenta (58B) style, light yellow (11B) stigma. BUD: ovate. FOLIAGE: dark green (147A) upper surface, medium green (147B) lower surface. Leaves are 55mm (2 3/16") long x 20mm (13/16") wide, lanceolate shaped, serrulated edges, acute tips and rounded bases. Veins, stems, branches are reddish green. PARENTAGE: 'F. magellanica molinae' x 'F. fulgens'. Small upright. Makes good upright or miniature. Prefers full sun and warm climate. Best bloom and foliage colour in bright light. Tested 3 years in Como, Italy. Distinguished by perfectly horizontal SEPALS.
Ianne 2003 IT AFS5073.

Top Hat. Upright/Trailer. Semi Double. COROLLA: Quarter flared; opens violet (83D); matures light purple (N78D); 14mm (9/16") long x 17mm (5/8") wide. SEPALS: half down, tips recurved, twisted right; white (155C), light rose (73C) base, tipped light green (145D) upper surface; light pink (62B) tipped light green (145D) lower surface; 49mm (1 15/16") long x 11mm (7/16") wide. TUBE: pale pink (49D); medium length & thickness; 14mm (9/16") long x 5mm (3/16") wide. FOLIAGE is medium green (138A) upper surface; medium green (139C) lower surface. PARENTAGE: 'Cambridge Louis' x 'Onbekend'.
Van Vooren 2007 BE AFS6418.

Topless. Upright/Trailer. Single. COROLLA: half flared; opens red (47B); matures red (43A); 14mm (9/16") long x 20mm (3/4") wide. SEPALS: fully up, tips reflexed; reddish orange (43C) upper surface; rose (47D) lower surface; 22mm (7/8") long x 12mm (7/16") wide. TUBE: peach (38B); 19mm (3/4") long x 6mm (1/4") wide. FOLIAGE is dark green (147A) upper surface; medium green (147B) lower surface. PARENTAGE: 'Gerharda's Panache' x 'Marcus Graham'.
de Graaff 2008 NL AFS6804.

Toutânkhamon. Upright. Single. COROLLA: Quarter flared; opens & matures reddish purple (67A); 30mm (1 3/16") long x 27mm (1 1/16") wide. SEPALS: horizontal, tips recurved; pink (62A) & light pink (62B) upper surface; magenta (63B) lower surface; 40mm (1 9/16") long x 9mm (5/16") wide. TUBE: light pink (62B); short, medium thickness; 8mm (5/16") long x 6mm (1/4") wide. FOLIAGE is dark green (147A) upper surface; medium green (147B) lower surface. PARENTAGE: 'Joy Patmore' x 'René Massé'.
Massé 2007 FR AFS6490.

Town Crier. Upright. Single. COROLLA deep violet. SEPALS pink. TUBE pink. PARENTAGE Seedling From 'London 2000'.
Western 2006 UK.

Tränen Meiner Liebe. Upright. Single. COROLLA: unflared, compact, smooth petal margins; opens light magenta (N66D) veined reddish purple (N66A); matures light magenta (N66D); 18mm (11/16") long x 9mm (5/16") wide. SEPALS: half up, tips recurved up; red (46C) upper & lower surfaces; 35mm (1 3/8") long x 9mm (5/16") wide. TUBE: red (46C); medium length & thickness; 12mm (7/16") long x 5mm (3/16") wide. STAMENS extend 10mm (3/8") beyond the corolla; red (46C) filaments & anthers. PISTIL extends 26mm (1") beyond the corolla; red (46C) style; red (46D) stigma. BUD: elongated. FOLIAGE: dark green (137A) upper surface; medium green (137C) lower surface. Leaves are 90mm (3 9/16") long x 45mm (1 3/4") wide; elliptic shaped, serrate edges, acute tips, rounded bases. Veins & stems are dark red, branches are reddish brown. PARENTAGE: 'König Manasse' x 'Mantilla'. Medium upright. Self branching. Makes good upright or standard. Prefers full sun. Best bloom & foliage colour in bright light. Tested 4 years in Bavaria, Southern Germany. Distinguished by bright bloom colours.
Burkhart 2009 DE AFS7102.

Treasure Me. Upright. Semi Double. COROLLA: half flared; opens violet (76A); matures light purple (76B); 18mm (11/16") long x 18mm (11/16") wide. SEPALS: fully up, tips reflexed; pale pink (62D) tipped green upper surface; pink (62A) tipped green lower surface; 35mm (1 3/8") long x 15mm (9/16") wide. TUBE: pink (62B); 15mm (9/16") long x 5mm (3/16") wide. FOLIAGE is dark green (137A) upper surface; medium green (139C) lower surface. PARENTAGE: 'Rose Fantasia' x 'Ann Howard Tripp'. Smith R. 2008 UK AFS6815.

Trees Hofman. Trailer. Double. COROLLA: half flared, smooth petal margins; opens violet (91A); matures violet (84A); 20mm (13/16") long 22mm (7/8") wide. SEPALS: fully up; tips recurved; pale purple (75D) tipped green upper surface; light rose (73B) lower surface; 27mm (1 1/16") long x 12mm (1/2") wide. TUBE: pale purple (75D); medium length & thickness; 14mm (9/16") long x 7mm (1/4") wide. STAMENS: extend 9mm (3/8") below corolla; magenta (68A) filaments & anthers. PISTIL: extends 30mm (1 3/16") below the corolla; pale lavender (69B) style; light yellow (4C) stigma. BUD: small, ovate, pointed. FOLIAGE: dark green (137A) upper surface; medium green (138B) lower surface. Leaves are 54mm (2 1/8") long x 31mm (1 1/4") wide, ovate shaped, serrulated edges, acute tips and rounded bases. Green veins, stems & branches. PARENTAGE: ('Cameron Ryle' x 'Parasol') x 'Corrie Spoelstra'. Natural trailer. Self branching. Makes good bonsai. Prefers overhead filtered light and cool climate. Best bloom and foliage colour in filtered light. Tested 4 years in Knegsel, The Netherlands. Distinguished by bloom colour. Roes 2004 NL AFS5467.

Treeske Robeyns. Trailer. Single. COROLLA: unflared, turned under smooth petal margins; opens dark rose (64C) veined white (155C), matures magenta (63B) veined white (155B); 21mm (13/16") long x 14mm (9/16") wide. SEPALS: full down; tips reflexed; light greenish white (157C) tipped yellowish green (144B) upper surface; white (155C) tipped yellowish green (144B) lower surface; 22mm (7/8") long x 7mm (1/4") wide. TUBE: light greenish white (157D); medium length & thickness; 18mm (11/16") long x 6mm (1/4") wide. STAMENS: extend 12mm (1/2") below the corolla; light pink (55D) filaments, very dark purple (187A) anthers. PISTIL extends 19mm (3/4") below the corolla; pale pink (56D) style, light yellow (2C) stigma. BUD:

ovate. FOLIAGE: dark green (137A) upper surface; medium green (138B) lower surface. Leaves are 35mm (1 3/8") long x 26mm (1") wide, cordate shaped, serrulated edges, acute tips and cordate bases. Veins are grayish red (181C), stems are grayish red (181C), branches are grayish red (182B). PARENTAGE: found seedling. Natural trailer. Makes good basket. Prefers overhead filtered light. Best bloom and foliage colour in filtered light. Tested 3 years in Rillaar, Belgium. NBFK certificate at Meise. Distinguished by bloom colour. Willems 2003 BE AFS5107.

Trelawny. Upright/Trailer. Double. COROLLA is half flared with smooth petal margins; opens purple (83C), dark rose (58C) top; matures light purple (86C); 22mm (7/8") long x 30mm (1 3/16") wide. PETALOIDS are same colour as corolla; 15mm (5/8") long x 12mm (1/2") wide. SEPALS are half down, tips reflexed; magenta (58B) upper surface, dark rose (58C) lower surface; 38mm (1 1/2") long x 14mm (9/16") wide. TUBE is light rose (58D); long and thin, curved shape; 25mm (1") long. STAMENS extend 14mm (9/16") beyond the corolla; reddish purple (58A) filaments, dark reddish purple (77A) anthers. PISTIL extends 18mm (11/16") beyond the corolla; magenta (58B) style, cream (159D) stigma. BUD is ovate. FOLIAGE is medium green (146A) upper surface, yellowish green (146B) lower surface. Leaves are 55mm (2 3/16") long x 25mm (1") wide, lanceolate shaped, serrulated edges, acute tips and rounded bases. Veins are dark grayish red (182A), stems are plum (185B) and branches are gray green (194B). PARENTAGE: 'Carol Brown' x 'Lands End'. Lax upright or stiff trailer. Makes good stiff trailer. Prefers overhead filtered light. Heat tolerant if shaded. Best bloom colour in filtered light. Tested three years in Cornwall, England. Distinguished by long bent TUBE. Negus 2002 UK AFS5045.

Tristan. Upright. Single. COROLLA: Quarter flared; opens light purple (80C); matures light reddish purple (73A); 25mm (1") long x 18mm (11/16") wide. SEPALS: horizontal, tips recurved; rose (48B) tipped light green (143B) upper surface; pink (48C-D) lower surface; 37mm (1 7/16") long x 7mm (1/4") wide. TUBE: pink (48D) striped light apple green (144D); medium length & thickness; 16mm (5/8") long x 4-6mm (1/8"-1/4") wide. FOLIAGE is dark green (147A) upper surface; medium green (147B) lower surface. PARENTAGE: 'Porte Océane' x 'F. boliviana'.

458

Massé 2007 FR AFS6491.

Trudi-Werner. Upright/Trailer. Double. COROLLA: three quarter flared, turned under smooth petal margins; opens purple (88A), rose (55B) base; matures dark purple (78A), rose (55B) base; 24mm (15/16") long x 37mm (1 7/16") wide. PETALOIDS: 1/sepal, purple (88A) edged rose (55B), tipped white (155B); 17mm (11/16") long x 11mm (7/16") wide. SEPALS: half up; tips reflexed up; dark rose (58C) tipped light green (142A) upper surface; light rose (58D) lower surface; 30mm (1 3/16") long x 15mm (9/16") wide. TUBE: white (155A) flushed dark rose (58C); medium length & thickness; 19mm(3/4") long x 5mm (3/16") wide. STAMENS: 21mm (13/16") below corolla; magenta (58B) filaments, reddish purple (58A) anthers. PISTIL: extends 37mm (1 7/16") below the corolla, light rose (58D) style, orangy brown (164A) stigma. BUD: globular. FOLIAGE: medium green (137B) upper surface; medium green (137D) lower surface. Leaves are 62mm (2 7/16") long x 34mm (1 3/8") wide, ovate shaped, serrulated edges, acute tips and rounded bases. Veins are light green (138C), stems & branches are dark red (178A). PARENTAGE: 'Mariken' x 'Monika Wandeler'. Lax upright or stiff trailer. Makes good basket. Prefers overhead filtered light. Best bloom and foliage colour in filtered light. Tested 3 years in Rummen, Belgium. NBFK Certificate at Meise. Distinguished by square blooms; white tips in every corner. Ector 2003 BE AFS5202.

Truus Laureijs. Upright. Semi Double. COROLLA is half flared with smooth petal margins; opens purple (77A); matures purple (71A); 29mm (1 1/8") long x 31mm (1 1/4") wide. SEPALS are fully up, tips recurved; white (155B) upper surface; white (155D) lower surface; 37mm (1 7/16") long x 14mm (9/16") wide. TUBE is white (155A); medium length & thickness; 18mm (11/16") long x 7mm (1/4") wide. FOLIAGE: medium green (137B) upper surface; medium green (137D) lower surface. Leaves are 50mm (2") long x 27mm (1 1/16") wide, ovate shaped. PARENTAGE: 'Roesse Apus' x 'Van Eijk Triksie'. Distinguished by bloom & foliage combination. van Eijk 2005 NL AFS5905.

Tübingen 2001. Upright/Trailer. Double. COROLLA is three quarter flared with smooth petal margins; opens and matures white (155D); 24mm (15/16") long x 26mm (1") wide. SEPALS are half up, tips recurved up; yellowish green (144B) upper and lower surfaces; 28mm (1 1/8") long x 10mm (3/8") wide. TUBE is apple green (144C), medium length and thickness. STAMENS extend 10mm (3/8") beyond the corolla; white (155D) filaments, orangish brown (174A) anthers. PISTIL extends 10mm (3/8") beyond the corolla; white (155D) style, light tan (163C) stigma. BUD is longish and narrow. FOLIAGE is yellowish green (144A) upper surface, yellowish green (144B) lower surface. Leaves are 56mm (2 3/16") long x 25mm (1") wide, ovate shaped, serrulated edges, acute tips and rounded bases. Veins are green, stems and branches are yellowish green (144A). PARENTAGE: 'Annabel' x 'Annabel'. Lax upright or stiff trailer. Self branching. Makes good basket. Prefers overhead filtered light and cool climate. Best bloom colour in filtered light. Silver medal at the BUGA 2001 in Tübingen, Germany. Named to celebrate Leonard Füch's 500th birthday. Tested three years in Plettenberg, Germany. Distinguished by cool white-green appearance. Strümper 2002 DE AFS4943.

Turkish Delight. Upright. Single. COROLLA is half flared with smooth petal margins; opens purple (88A) and matures purple (81B); 25mm (1") long x 25mm (1") wide. SEPALS are fully up, tips recurved; rose (58D) upper surface and rose (61D) lower surface; 32mm (1 1/4) long x 12mm (1/2") wide. TUBE is light rose (58D) with darker stripes, short with medium thickness; 6mm (1/4") long x 6mm (1/4") wide. STAMENS extend 12mm (1/2") below the corolla; light rose (58D) filaments and reddish purple (58A) anthers. PISTIL extends 25mm (1") below the corolla; dark rose (58D) style and orangish white (159C) stigma. BUD is pointed. FOLIAGE is medium green (137A) upper surface and medium green (137D) lower surface. Leaves are 51mm (2") long x 32mm (1 1/4") wide, ovate shaped, serrulated edges, acute tips and rounded bases. Veins and stems are green, branches are brown. PARENTAGE: 'Bealings' x 'Purple Patch'. Small upright. Self branching. Makes good upright, standard or patio container plant. Prefers overhead filtered light. Best bloom colour in bright light. Tested five years in Ormskirk, Lancashire, England. Distinguished by flower shape and colour. Sinton 2002 UK AFS4827.

Tuur van Eijk. Upright/Trailer. Semi Double. COROLLA: half flared, smooth petal margins; opens purple (77A); matures

459

reddish purple (64B); 30mm (1 3/16") long 26mm (1") wide. SEPALS: horizontal; tips recurved; light pink (62B) upper surface; light magenta (58D) lower surface; 56mm (2 3/16") long x 10mm (3/8") wide. TUBE: light pink (62B); medium length & thickness; 25mm (1") long x 5mm (3/16") wide. STAMENS: extend 15mm (9/16") below corolla; magenta (63B) filaments; magenta (58B) anthers. PISTIL: extends 37mm (1 7/16") below the corolla; light rose (63D) style; yellowish white (4D) stigma. BUD: cordate, curved, pointed. FOLIAGE: dark green (137A) upper surface; medium green (138B) lower surface. Leaves are 57mm (2 1/4") long x 28mm (1 1/8") wide, ovate shaped, serrulated edges, acute tips and obtuse bases. Red veins, stems & branches. PARENTAGE: 'Bicentennial' x 'Parasol'. Lax upright or stiff trailer. Makes good stiff trailer. Prefers overhead filtered light and cool climate. Best bloom and foliage colour in filtered light. Tested 5 years in Reusel, The Netherlands. Distinguished by bloom colour. van Eijk 2004 NL AFS5494.

Tweeling. Upright/Trailer. Double. COROLLA: 3 quarter flared; opens dark purple (N78A), rose (61D) base; matures reddish purple (71B); 19mm (3/4") long x 22mm (7/8") wide. PETALOIDS: same colour as corolla; 11mm (7/16") long x 11mm (7/16") wide. SEPALS: horizontal, tips recurved; rose (61D) tipped apple green (144C) upper surface; dark rose (54B) tipped apple green (144C) lower surface; 32mm (1 1/4") long x 13mm (1/2") wide. TUBE: white (155A); long & thin; 30mm (1 3/16") long x 4mm (1/8") wide. FOLIAGE is dark green (136A) upper surface; medium green (138B) lower surface. PARENTAGE: 'WALZ Harp' x 'Bleu Veil'. Geerts L. 2007 BE AFS6379.

Twell's Klumpke. Upright. Double. COROLLA: quarter flared; rosette shaped, smooth petal margins; opens violet (77A); matures reddish purple (61A); 27mm (1 1/16") long x 29mm (1 1/8") wide. PETALOIDS: Same colour as corolla; 28mm (1 1/8") long x 28mm (1 1/8") wide. SEPALS: half up, tips recurved up; light reddish purple (73A) tipped light apple green (145C) upper surface; light reddish purple (73A) lower surface; 38mm (1 1/2") long x 14mm (9/16") wide. TUBE: pink (62C); medium length, thin; 14mm (9/16") long x 5mm (3/16") wide. STAMENS extend 29mm (1 1/8") beyond the corolla; purple (71A) filaments & anthers. PISTIL extends 31mm

(1 1/4") beyond the corolla; purple (71A) style; tan (165B) stigma. BUD: pegtop shape. FOLIAGE: dark green (137A) upper surface; medium green (137D) lower surface. Leaves are 72mm (2 7/8") long x 35mm (1 3/8") wide; elliptic shaped, serrate edges, acute tips, rounded bases. Veins are light green, stems & branches are red. PARENTAGE: 'Gerwin van den Brink' x 'White King'. Small upright. Makes good upright or standard. Prefers overhead filtered light, cool climate. Best foliage colour in filtered light. Tested 6 years in Hulshorst, The Netherlands. Nominated by NKvF as recommendable cultivar. Distinguished by flower colour & shape. van den Brink 2009 NL AFS7023.

Twente Salland. Upright. Semi Double. COROLLA is half flared with smooth petal margins; opens purple (71A) and matures dark reddish purple (61A); 26mm (1") long x 26mm (1") wide. SEPALS are half up, tips reflexed up; magenta (63A) upper and lower surfaces; 26mm (1") long x 12mm (1/2") wide. TUBE is magenta (63A), proportionately medium length and thickness; 12mm (1/2") long x 5mm (3/16") wide. STAMENS extend 22mm (7/8") below the corolla; purple (71A) filaments and magenta (59C) anthers. PISTIL extends 43mm (1 11/16") below the corolla; purple (71A) style and magenta (59C) stigma. BUD is round and pointed. FOLIAGE is medium green (137B) on upper surface and medium green (138A) on lower surface. Leaves are 54mm (2 1/8") long x 38mm (1 1/2) wide, ovate shaped, serrated edges, acute tips and rounded bases. Veins, stems and branches are red. PARENTAGE: [('Bon Accord' x 'Bicentennial') x 'Rohees Alrami'] x 'Hertogin van Brabant'. Medium upright. Makes good standard. Prefers overhead filtered light and warm climate. Best bloom colour in filtered light. Tested four years in Knegsel, The Netherlands. Distinguished by bloom colour. Roes 2002 NL AFS4800.

Twilight Time. Upright/Trailer. Double. COROLLA is quarter flared, dense petals, with smooth petal margins; opens pale violet (91C) veined rose (52C); matures rose (52C) to white; 32mm (1 1/4") long x 32mm (1 1/4") wide. PETALOIDS: Same colour as corolla; 25mm (1") long x 19mm (3/4") wide. SEPALS are full down, tips recurved; white, edged rose (51C) tipped medium green (138A) upper surface; rose (52C) at TUBE to white lower surface; 48mm (1 7/8") long x 25mm (1") wide. TUBE is white striped medium

green (138A); medium length & thickness; 8mm (5/16") long x 22mm (7/8") wide. STAMENS extend 19mm (3/4") beyond the corolla; rose (52B) filaments; violet (75A) anthers. PISTIL extends 38mm (1 1/2") below the corolla; rose (52C) style; white stigma. BUD is heart shaped. FOLIAGE is dark green (137A) upper surface, medium green (137C) lower surface. Leaves are 92mm (3 5/8") long x 57mm (2 1/4") wide, cordate shaped, serrated edges, acute tips and rounded bases. Veins are light green (142A), stems are red (46B) & branches are light green (124A). PARENTAGE: 'Blush of Dawn' x 'White King'. Small lax upright or stiff trailer. Makes good basket or upright. Prefers overhead filtered light & cool climate. Cold weather hardy to 32⁰ F. Best bloom & foliage colour in bright and filtered light. Tested six years in Fortuna, CA, USA. Distinguished by delicate blossom colours.
McLaughlin 2004 USA AFS5369.

Ulla Meisner. Trailer. Semi Double. COROLLA: quarter flared; opens pale purple (76C) & matures pale purple (N74D); 20mm (3/4") long x 17mm (5/8") wide. SEPALS are half down, tips reflexed; white (155C) tipped light apple green (145C) upper and lower surfaces; 37mm (1 7/16") long x 12mm (7/16") wide. TUBE is white (155C); 18mm (11/16") long x 5mm (3/16") wide. FOLIAGE is dark green (139A) upper surface; medium green (138B) lower surface. PARENTAGE: 'Lavender Heaven' x 'Delta's Trick'. Waanrode 7/7/2007.
Michiels 2008 BE AFS6722.

Unser Ahnatal. Upright. Single. COROLLA opens white, veined red; corolla is fully flared. SEPALS red on the upper and lower surfaces; sepals are horizontally held with recuved tips. TUBE red. PARENTAGE 'Pink Galore' x 'Königin der Nacht'. Free flowering.
Nicola 2008 AT BFS0069.

Untamed. Upright.Trailer. Single. COROLLA is quarter flared, bell shaped, with smooth petal margins; opens pink (52D) with light base, matures rose (52C); 9mm (3/8") long x 6mm (1/4") wide. SEPALS are half down, tips reflexed; magenta (57B-57C) upper surface, pink (62C) lower surface; 9mm (3/8") long x 5mm (3/16") wide. TUBE is magenta-light magenta (57B-57D) with dark base, long with medium thickness; 12mm (1/2") long x 5mm (3/16") wide. STAMENS extend 2mm (1/16") beyond the corolla; pale pink (56D) filaments and orangish white (159C) anthers. PISTIL extends 6mm (1/4") below the corolla; pale

pink (56B) style, light rose (58D) stigma. BUD is long TUBEd, ovate. FOLIAGE is dark green (147A) upper surface, medium green (146A) lower surface. Leaves are 45mm (1 3/4") long x 23mm (15/16") wide, elliptic shaped, smooth edges, acute tips and acute to obtuse bases. Veins are red tinted yellow green, stems and branches are reddish. PARENTAGE: 'Panache' x 'F. venusta'. Lax upright or stiff trailer. Self branching. Makes good basket. Prefers full sun. Heat tolerant if shaded. Best bloom and foliage colour in bright light. Tested five years in Lisse, Holland. Distinguished by small racemes (a shoot bearing clusters of flowers on short stalks) of erect flowers.
de Graaff 2002 NL AFS4885.

Upright Bob. Upright. Single. COROLLA: unflared, square shaped, turned under smooth petal margins; opens dark purple (78A); matures reddish purple (74A); 10mm (3/8") long x 8mm (5/16") wide. SEPALS: horizontal; tips recurved; dark rose (55A) tipped green upper surface; dark rose (54A) tipped green lower surface; 20mm(13/16") long x 5mm (3/16") wide. TUBE: rose (50B); short, medium thickness; 8mm (5/16") long x 4mm (3/16") wide. STAMENS: extend 8mm (5/16") below corolla; pink (54D) filaments, white (155A) anthers. PISTIL: extends 15mm (9/16") below the corolla, pale pink (36D) style; yellow white(158A) stigma. BUD: small, elongated. FOLIAGE: medium green (146A) upper surface; yellowish green (146B) lower surface. Leaves are 50mm (2") long x 30mm (1 3/16") wide, cordate shaped, serrated edges, acute tips and cordate bases. Veins are green, stems are brown, branches are red. PARENTAGE: 'Janneke Brinkmann-Saletijn' x 'Mini Rose'. Small upright. Self branching. Makes good upright, bonsai or bedding plant. Heat tolerant if shaded. Prefers warm climate. Cold weather hardy to 32° F. Best bloom colour in bright light. Tested 3 years in Walthamstow, London, England. Distinguished by profuse blooms.
Allsop M.R. 2003 UK AFS5151.

Uriel. Upright. Double. COROLLA lilac gray. SEPALS pink flushed red.
Ainsworth 2002 UK.

Urmond's Antje. Upright/Trailer. Double. COROLLA: half flared, turned under wavy petal margins; opens dark reddish purple (72A) & purple (77A) striped light reddish purple (72C); matures reddish purple (64B) & dark reddish purple (61A); 32mm (1 1/4") long x 20mm (3/4") wide. PETALOIDS:

461

purple (N78A) & purple (N81A); 22mm (7/8")
long x 20mm (3/4") wide. SEPALS: half up,
tips recurved up & horizontal, tips recurved;
light pink (65B) upper surface; rose (N57C)
lower surface; 45mm (1 3/4") long x 21mm
(13/16") wide. TUBE: white (155C) & rose
(65A); medium length & thick; 21mm
(13/16") long x 10mm (3/8") wide. STAMENS
extend 16mm (5/8") beyond the corolla; dark
reddish purple (72A) filaments; purple (83A)
anthers. PISTIL extends 34mm (1 3/8")
beyond the corolla; reddish purple (71B)
style; pale yellow (5D) stigma. BUD: oblong.
FOLIAGE: dark green (137A) upper surface;
medium green (137C) lower surface. Leaves
are 48mm (1 7/8") long x 27mm (1 1/16")
wide; ovate shaped, serrate edges, acute tips,
rounded bases. Veins are very dark reddish
purple (186A), stems are light red purple
(185D), branches are light red purple (185D)
& light green (138C). PARENTAGE: 'Manfried
Kleinau' x 'Frans Vander Kuylen'. Lax
upright or stiff trailer. Self branching. Makes
good basket. Prefers overhead filtered light,
cool climate. Best bloom & foliage colour in
filtered light. Tested 3 years in
Koningshooikt, Belgium. Waanrode 8/9/08.
Distinguished by bloom colour.
Michiels 2009 BE AFS7230.

Urmond's Chelke. Trailer. Semi Double.
COROLLA: half flared; opens violet (86D),
pale pink (56C) base; matures violet (84A),
pale violet (84D) base; 19mm (3/4") long x
16mm (5/8") wide. PETALOIDS: same colour
as corolla; 14mm (9/16") long x 12mm
(7/16") wide. SEPALS: horizontal, tips
reflexed; light rose (58D) tipped apple green
(144C) upper surface; dark rose (55A) tipped
apple green (144C) lower surface; 34mm (1
3/8") long x 10mm (3/8") wide. TUBE: rose
(54C); medium length & thickness; 16mm
(5/8") long x 5mm (3/16") wide. FOLIAGE is
dark green (139A) upper surface; medium
green (137C) lower surface. PARENTAGE:
'Lavender Heaven' x 'Delta's Trick'.
Michiels 2007 BE AFS6321.

Valerie Hobbs. Upright/Trailer. Semi
Double. COROLLA is half flared with smooth
petal margins; opens and matures white
(155A) veined reddish purple (66A); 25mm
(1") long x 30mm (1 3/16") wide. SEPALS are
fully up, tips recurved; reddish purple (66A)
upper surface, dark rose (58C) lower surface;
36mm (1 7/16") long x 12mm (1/2") wide.
TUBE is reddish purple (66A), medium
length and thin; 20mm (13/16") long x 8mm
(5/16") wide. STAMENS extend 25mm (1")
below the corolla; dark rose (58C) filaments,

reddish purple (59C) anthers. PISTIL extends
40mm (1 9/16") below the corolla; light rose
(58D) style and stigma. BUD is oval.
FOLIAGE is dark green (136B) upper surface,
medium green (137C) lower surface. Leaves
are 75mm (2 15/16") long x 44mm (1 3/4")
wide, cordate shaped, serrulated edges,
acute tips and cordate bases. Veins, stems
and branches are dark reddish purple (187B)
and green. PARENTAGE: "Found" seedling.
Lax upright or stiff trailer. Makes good
espalier or fan. Prefers overhead filtered
light. Heat tolerant if shaded. Best bloom
colour in filtered light. Tested three years in
Worthing, Sussex, England. Distinguished by
long bloom pedicels and graceful growth.
Hobbs 2002 UK AFS4847.

Valerie Tooke. Upright. Semi Double.
COROLLA is three quarter flared with
smooth petal margins; opens violet (76B)
lightly veined rose (61D), matures violet
(76B); 26mm (1") long x 44mm (1 3/4") wide.
PETALOIDS are same colour as corolla;
15mm (5/8") long x 15mm (5/8") wide.
SEPALS are horizontal, tips recurved; pink
(62A) upper surface, rose (61D) lower
surface; 32mm (1 1/4") long x 14mm (9/16")
wide. TUBE is pale pink (62D), short and
thick; 10mm (3/8") long x 8mm (5/16") wide.
STAMENS extend 25mm (1") below the
corolla; pink (62A) filaments and anthers.
PISTIL extends 30mm (1 3/16") below the
corolla; pink (62C) style; pale pink (36D)
stigma. BUD is oval. FOLIAGE is dark green
(139A) upper surface, medium green (138B)
lower surface. Leaves are 50mm (2") long x
24mm (15/16") wide, lanceolate shaped,
serrated edges, acute tips and rounded
bases. Veins are dark reddish purple (187C),
stems are plum (183D), branches are plum
(183C). PARENTAGE: "Found" seedling.
Small upright. Makes good upright. Prefers
overhead filtered light. Heat tolerant if
shaded. Best bloom colour in filtered light.
Tested three years in Worthing, Sussex,
England. Distinguished by profuse blooms.
Hobbs 2002 UK AFS4849.

Valoche. Upright. Single. COROLLA:
unflared; opens violet (83D); matures purple
(77B); 21mm (13/16") long x 21mm (13/16")
wide. SEPALS: horizontal, tips recurved;
magenta (58B) upper surface; dark rose
(58C) lower surface; 31mm (1 1/4") long x
9mm (5/16") wide. TUBE: magenta (58B);
11mm (7/16") long x 6mm (1/4") wide.
FOLIAGE is dark green (147A) upper surface;
olive green (148A) lower surface.
PARENTAGE: 'Régia' x unknown.

462

Ricard 2008 BE AFS6846.

Van Brissinchove. Upright/Trailer. Double. COROLLA: half flared, turned under wavy petal margins; opens dark reddish purple (72A) & purple (N81A); matures dark reddish purple (64A) & purple (77A) blotched dark rose (71D); 29mm (1 1/8") long x 18mm (11/16") wide. PETALOIDS: dark reddish purple (72A); 14mm (9/16") long x 10mm (3/8") wide. SEPALS: half up, tips recurved up & horizontal, tips recurved; pale purple (75D) & magenta (68A) tipped light green (142B) upper surface; dark rose (58C) tipped light green (142B) lower surface; 34mm (1 3/8") long x 17mm (5/8") wide. TUBE: pale lavender (69C); short, medium thickness; 13mm (1/2") long x 5mm (3/16") wide. STAMENS extend 15mm (9/16") beyond the corolla; light reddish purple (72C) filaments; purple (83A) anthers. PISTIL extends 24mm (15/16") beyond the corolla; reddish purple (72B) style; yellowish white (4D) stigma. BUD: oblong. FOLIAGE: dark green (137A) upper surface; medium green (138B) lower surface. Leaves are 61mm (2 7/16") long x 36mm (1 7/16") wide; ovate shaped, serrulate edges, acute tips, rounded bases. Veins are light grayish rose (181D), stems are plum (185C), branches are dark red purple (187D). PARENTAGE: 'Manfried Kleinau' x 'Beauty of Everreur'. Lax upright or stiff trailer. Self branching. Makes good basket. Prefers overhead filtered light, cool climate. Best bloom & foliage colour in filtered light. Tested 3 years in Koningshooikt, Belgium. Waanrode 7/5/08, Outstanding. Distinguished by bloom colour & shape. Michiels 2009 BE AFS7231.

van Eijk Aika. Upright/Trailer. Single. COROLLA is quarter flared with smooth petal margins; opens red (53B); matures red (53C); 17mm (11/16") long x 18mm (11/16") wide. SEPALS are fully up, tips recurved; pale pink (62D) tipped green upper surface; light pink (62B) tipped green lower surface; 24mm (15/16") long x 9mm (3/8") wide. TUBE is pale pink (62D); medium length & thickness; 9mm (3/8") long x 5mm (3/16") wide. FOLIAGE: dark green (137A) upper surface; medium green (138B) lower surface. Leaves are 61mm (2 3/8") long x 31mm (1 1/4") wide, ovate shaped. PARENTAGE: 'Roesse Carme' x 'Leon Pauwels'. Distinguished by bloom & foliage combination. van Eijk 2005 NL AFS5895.

van Eijk Bello. Upright. Double. COROLLA is half flared with smooth petal margins; opens magenta (71C); matures magenta (58B); 22mm (7/8") long x 22mm (7/8") wide. SEPALS are half up, tips recurved up; pale pink (62D) upper & lower surfaces; 34mm (1 5/16") long x 15mm (9/16") wide. TUBE is pale pink (62D); medium length & thickness; 12mm (1/2") long x 5mm (3/16") wide. FOLIAGE: medium green (137B) upper surface; medium green (138B) lower surface. Leaves are 62mm (2 7/16") long x 32mm (1 1/4") wide, ovate shaped. PARENTAGE: 'Sofie Michiels' x 'Bicentennial'. Distinguished by bloom colour. van Eijk 2005 NL AFS5892.

van Eijk Bente. Upright. Double. COROLLA is three quarter flared with smooth petal margins; opens dark purple (79A); matures purple (79C); 18mm (11/16") long x 21mm (13/16") wide. SEPALS are half up, tips reflexed up; dark red (46A) upper & lower surfaces; 21mm (13/16") long x 12mm (1/2") wide. TUBE is dark red (46A); medium length & thickness; 10mm (3/8") long x 6mm (1/4") wide. FOLIAGE: dark green (137A) upper surface; medium green (138A) lower surface. Leaves are 54mm (2 1/8") long x 29mm (1 1/8") wide, elliptic shaped. PARENTAGE: 'Swanley Gem' x ('Roesse Apus' x 'Roesse Apus). Distinguished by bloom colour. van Eijk 2005 NL AFS5894.

van Eijk Blekkie. Upright. Double. COROLLA: three quarter flared, smooth petal margins; opens violet (84A); matures violet (77B); 20mm (13/16") long 22mm (7/8") wide. SEPALS: half up; tips reflexed up; light rose (58D) upper surface; dark rose (58C) lower surface; 24mm (15/16") long x 15mm (9/16") wide. TUBE: light rose (58D); medium length & thickness; 8mm (5/16) long x 6mm (1/4") wide. STAMENS: extend 14mm (9/16") below corolla; dark rose (67C) filaments; rose (68C) anthers. PISTIL: extends 26mm (1") below the corolla; dark rose (67C) style; light rose (68D) stigma. BUD: round, pointed. FOLIAGE: dark green (139A) upper surface; medium green (138A) lower surface. Leaves are 37mm (1 7/16") long x 27mm (1 1/16") wide, cordate shaped, serrated edges, acute tips and obtuse bases. Green veins, stems & branches. PARENTAGE: ('Cameron Ryle' x 'Parasol') x 'Locky'. Medium upright. Makes good upright or standard. Prefers overhead filtered light and cool climate. Best bloom and foliage colour in filtered light. Tested 4 years in Reusel, The Netherlands. Distinguished by bloom and foliage combination. van Eijk 2004 NL AFS5498.

463

van Eijk Cindie. Trailer. Single. COROLLA: quarter flared, smooth petal margins; opens purple (71A); matures dark reddish purple (60B); 22mm (7/8") long 12mm (1/2") wide. SEPALS: half up; tips reflexed up; magenta (58B) upper & lower surfaces; 36mm (1 7/16") long x 8mm (5/16") wide. TUBE: magenta (58B); medium length & thickness; 16mm (5/8) long x 5mm (3/16") wide. STAMENS: extend 14mm (9/16") below corolla; dark reddish purple (60C) filaments; reddish purple (60D) anthers. PISTIL: extends 34mm (1 5/16") below the corolla; dark reddish purple (60C) style; pink (62C) stigma. BUD: elliptic, pointed. FOLIAGE: medium green (137B) upper surface; medium green (138A) lower surface. Leaves are 55mm (2 3/16") long x 23mm (15/16") wide, lanceolate shaped, serrulated edges, acute tips and rounded bases. Green veins, stems & branches. PARENTAGE: 'Roesse Apus' x 'Willy Tamerus'. Natural trailer. Self branching. Makes good basket. Prefers overhead filtered light and cool climate. Best bloom and foliage colour in filtered light. Tested 4 years in Reusel, The Netherlands. Distinguished by bloom colour.
van Eijk 2004 NL AFS5500.

van Eijk Cora. Upright/Trailer. Single. COROLLA: three quarter flared, smooth petal margins; opens dark reddish purple (72A); matures reddish purple (71B); 20mm (13/16") long 27mm (1 1/16") wide. SEPALS: half up; tips recurved up; magenta (58B) upper surface; red (52A) lower surface; 27mm (1 1/16") long x 16mm (5/8") wide. TUBE: magenta (58B); medium length & thickness; 16mm (5/8) long x 9mm (3/8") wide. STAMENS: extend 17mm (11/16") below corolla; magenta (63A) filaments; dark reddish purple (60B) anthers. PISTIL: extends 34mm (1 5/16") below the corolla; dark rose (58C) style; light rose (58D) stigma. BUD: round, pointed. FOLIAGE: dark green (137A) upper surface; medium green (138B) lower surface. Leaves are 54mm (2 1/8") long x 32mm (1 1/4") wide, ovate shaped, serrulated edges, acute tips and rounded bases. Red veins, stems & branches. PARENTAGE: 'Roesse Carme' x 'Madalyn Drago'. Lax upright or stiff trailer. Makes good stiff trailer. Prefers overhead filtered light and cool climate. Best bloom and foliage colour in filtered light. Tested 4 years in Reusel, The Netherlands. Distinguished by bloom and foliage combination.
van Eijk 2004 NL AFS5499.

van Eijk Dino. Upright. Semi Double. COROLLA is half flared; opens purple (83B); matures purple (71A); 16mm (5/8") long x 21mm (13/16") wide. SEPALS are fully up, tips recurved; magenta (68A) upper & lower surfaces; 16mm (5/8") long x 6mm (1/4") wide. TUBE is rose (68B); 9mm (3/8") long x 6mm (1/4") wide. FOLIAGE: dark green (137A) upper surface; medium green (138B) lower surface. PARENTAGE: ('Roesse Apus' x 'Roesse Apus') x 'Arian Spoelstra'. Distinguished by bloom & foliage combination.
van Eijk 2006 NL AFS6194.

van Eijk Dollie. Upright/Trailer. Semi Double. COROLLA: quarter flared, smooth petal margins; opens dark purple (79A); matures dark reddish purple (61A); 16mm (5/8") long 19mm (3/4") wide. SEPALS: half down; tips recurved; reddish purple (61B) upper surface; dark reddish purple (61A) lower surface; 33mm (1 5/16") long x 11mm (7/16") wide. TUBE: reddish purple (61B); medium length & thickness; 18mm (11/16") long x 10mm (3/8") wide. STAMENS: extend 9mm (3/8") below corolla; purple (71A) filaments & anthers. PISTIL: extends 23mm (15/16") below the corolla; magenta (71C) style; magenta (58B) stigma. BUD: elliptic, pointed. FOLIAGE: dark green (137A) upper surface; medium green (137C) lower surface. Leaves are 66mm (2 5/8") long x 35mm (1 3/8") wide, ovate shaped, serrated edges, acute tips and obtuse bases. Red veins, stems & branches. PARENTAGE: 'Swanley Gem' x 'Roesse Blacky'. Lax upright or stiff trailer. Makes good stiff trailer. Prefers overhead filtered light and cool climate. Best bloom and foliage colour in filtered light. Tested 4 years in Reusel, The Netherlands. Distinguished by bloom colour.
van Eijk 2004 NL AFS5495.

van Eijk Dorus. Upright/Trailer. Double. COROLLA is half flared; opens violet (90D); matures pale violet (84D); 18mm (11/16") long x 20mm (3/4") wide. SEPALS are half down, tips recurved; white (155D) upper & lower surfaces; 31mm (1 1/4") long x 17mm (5/8") wide. TUBE is white (155D); 14mm (9/16") long x 6mm (1/4") wide. FOLIAGE: medium green (138A) upper surface; medium green (137C) lower surface. PARENTAGE: 'Sam' x 'Leen van der Kuylen'. Distinguished by bloom colour.
van Eijk 2006 NL AFS6195.

van Eijk Elvie. Upright. Double. COROLLA is three quarter flared with smooth petal

margins; opens reddish purple (72B); matures light reddish purple (72D); 19mm (3/4") long x 24mm (15/16") wide. SEPALS are horizontal, tips recurved; light pink (62B) tipped green upper surface; pink (62A) lower surface; 26mm (1") long x 14mm (9/16") wide. TUBE is pale pink (62D); medium length & thickness; 12mm (1/2") long x 6mm (1/4") wide. FOLIAGE: medium green (137B) upper surface; medium green (138B) lower surface. Leaves are 74mm (2 15/16") long x 41mm (1 5/8") wide, ovate shaped. PARENTAGE: 'Sofie Michiels' x 'Brenda Krekels'. Distinguished by bloom & foliage combination.
van Eijk 2005 NL AFS5893.

van Eijk Falko. Upright/Trailer. Double. COROLLA: Half flared; opens violet (77B); matures violet (77C); 17mm (5/8") long x 21mm (13/16") wide. SEPALS: fully up, tips reflexed; pale lavender (65D) upper surface; light pink (65B) lower surface; 24mm (15/16") long x 15mm (9/16") wide. TUBE: pale lavender (65D); medium length & thickness; 10mm (3/8") long x 6mm (1/4") wide. FOLIAGE is medium green (137B) upper surface; medium green (138B) lower surface. PARENTAGE: 'Sam' x 'Baby van Eijk'.
van Eijk 2007 NL AFS6564.

van Eijk Fastor. Upright/Trailer. Double. COROLLA: Half flared; opens light purple (78B); matures violet (77B); 24mm (15/16") long x 21mm (13/16") wide. SEPALS: horizontal, tips recurved; pale pink (62D) tipped green upper & lower surfaces; 35mm (1 3/8") long x 16mm (5/8") wide. TUBE: pale pink (62D); medium length & thickness; 12mm (7/16") long x 7mm (1/4") wide. FOLIAGE is dark green (137A) upper surface; medium green (138B) lower surface. PARENTAGE: 'Sam' x 'Baby van Eijk'.
van Eijk 2007 NL AFS6559.

van Eijk Fedor. Upright/Trailer. Double. COROLLA: three-quarter flared; opens & matures purple (82A); 26mm (1") long x 22mm (7/8") wide. SEPALS are horizontal, tips recurved; pale lavender (65D) upper surface; pale pink (65B) lower surface; 46mm (1 13/16") long x 22mm (7/8") wide. TUBE is pale lavender (65D); 16mm (5/8") long x 6mm (1/4") wide. FOLIAGE is dark green (137A) upper surface; medium green (137C) lower surface. PARENTAGE: 'Sam' x 'Baby van Eijk'.
van Eijk 2008 NL AFS6881.

van Eijk Fiber. Upright. Semi Double. COROLLA; opens dark purple (79B); matures reddish purple (71B); 12mm (7/16") long x 16mm (5/8") wide. SEPALS are fully up, tips reflexed; rose (64D) upper surface; dark reddish purple (64A) lower surface; 25mm (1") long x 11mm (7/16") wide. TUBE is rose (64D); 15mm (9/16") long x 7mm (1/4") wide. FOLIAGE is medium green (137B) upper surface; medium green (138A) lower surface. PARENTAGE: ('Roesse Lupus' x 'Hula Girl') x 'Van Eijk Reina'.
van Eijk 2008 NL AFS6880.

van Eijk Figor. Upright/Trailer. Double. COROLLA: 3 quarter flared; opens purple (77A); matures dark reddish purple (70A); 12mm (7/16") long x 20mm (3/4") wide. SEPALS: fully up, tips reflexed; rose (63C) tipped green upper surface; magenta (63D) lower surface; 26mm (1") long x 14mm (9/16") wide. TUBE: rose (63C); medium length & thickness; 10mm (3/8") long x 5mm (3/16") wide. FOLIAGE is dark green (137A) upper surface; medium green (138A) lower surface. PARENTAGE: ('Rohees Rana' x 'Roesse Apus') x 'Corrie Spoelstra'.
van Eijk 2007 NL AFS6561.

van Eijk Floor. Upright/Trailer. Single. COROLLA: Half flared; opens & matures reddish orange (42A); 17mm (5/8") long x 15mm (9/16") wide. SEPALS: half up, tips recurved up; light coral (38A) tipped green upper & lower surfaces; 30mm (1 3/16") long x 10mm (3/8") wide. TUBE: light coral (38A); medium length & thickness; 17mm (5/8") long x 6mm (1/4") wide. FOLIAGE is dark green (137A) upper surface; medium green (137C) lower surface. PARENTAGE: 'Roesse Lupus' x 'Oranje van Os'.
van Eijk 2007 NL AFS6557.

van Eijk Flunk. Upright/Trailer. Semi Double. COROLLA: Half flared; opens dark reddish purple (64A); matures dark rose (64C); 16mm (5/8") long x 21mm (13/16") wide. SEPALS: horizontal, tips recurved; pale pink (62D) tipped green upper surface; light pink (62B) tipped green lower surface; 31mm (1 1/4") long x 12mm (7/16") wide. TUBE: pale pink (62D); medium length & thickness; 16mm (5/8") long x 6mm (1/4") wide. FOLIAGE is dark green (137A) upper surface; medium green (137D) lower surface. PARENTAGE: 'Miet van Eijk' x 'Sofie Michiels'.
van Eijk 2007 NL AFS6566.

van Eijk Fonzie. Trailer. Double. COROLLA: Half flared; opens dark reddish purple (64A); matures reddish purple (64B); 25mm (1") long x 27mm (1 1/16") wide. SEPALS: half up, tips recurved up; magenta (58B) upper surface; red (52A) lower surface; 31mm (1 1/4") long x 16mm (5/8") wide. TUBE: magenta (58B); medium length & thickness; 8mm (5/16") long x 7mm (1/4") wide. FOLIAGE is dark green (137A) upper surface; medium green (137C) lower surface. PARENTAGE: ('Roesse Apus' x 'Roesse Apus') 'Corrie Spoelstra'.
van Eijk 2007 NL AFS6558.

van Eijk Galan. Upright/Trailer. Double. COROLLA: Half flared; opens violet blue (92A); matures light violet (84A); 20mm (3/4") long x 24mm (15/16") wide. SEPALS: horizontal, tips recurved; light pink (65C) upper surface; rose (65A) lower surface; 29mm (1 1/8") long x 16mm (5/8") wide. TUBE: light pink (65C); medium length & thickness; 16mm (5/8") long x 7mm (1/4") wide. FOLIAGE is dark green (137A) upper surface; medium green (138A) lower surface. PARENTAGE: 'Reg Gubler' x 'Thea Kroese'.
van Eijk 2007 NL AFS6560.

van Eijk Giese. Upright/Trailer. Single. COROLLA: Fully flared; opens & matures dark reddish purple (60A); 24mm (15/16") long x 27mm (1 1/16") wide. SEPALS: half up, tips recurved up; pink (62C) upper & lower surfaces; 22mm (7/8") long x 11mm (7/16") wide. TUBE: pink (62C); medium length & thickness; 24mm (15/16") long x 7mm (1/4") wide. FOLIAGE is dark green (137A) upper surface; medium green (138A) lower surface. PARENTAGE: 'Roesse Lupus' x 'Oranje van Os'.
van Eijk 2007 NL AFS6565.

van Eijk Gomer. Upright/Trailer. Double. COROLLA: 3 quarter flared; opens purple (83B); matures purple (83C); 30mm (1 3/16") long x 25mm (1") wide. SEPALS: half up, tips reflexed up; dark rose (67C) upper surface; magenta (67B) lower surface; 44mm (1 3/4") long x 17mm (5/8") wide. TUBE: light pink (65C); medium length & thickness; 16mm (5/8") long x 7mm (1/4") wide. FOLIAGE is dark green (137A) upper surface; medium green (137C) lower surface. PARENTAGE: 'Sam' x 'Ingrid van Eijk'.
van Eijk 2007 NL AFS6563.

van Eijk Greg. Upright/Trailer. Double. COROLLA: 3 quarter flared; opens & matures magenta (59C); 20mm (3/4") long x 21mm (13/16") wide. SEPALS: horizontal, tips recurved; light pink (65B) upper surface; rose (65A) lower surface; 26mm (1") long x 13mm (1/2") wide. TUBE: light pink (65B); medium length & thickness; 14mm (9/16") long x 6mm (1/4") wide. FOLIAGE is dark green (137A) upper surface; medium green (138B) lower surface. PARENTAGE: 'Roesse Lupus' x 'Laura Krekels'.
van Eijk 2007 NL AFS6567.

van Eijk Gundor. Upright/Trailer. Double. COROLLA: 3 quarter flared; opens & matures dark reddish purple (61A); 20mm (3/4") long x 24mm (15/16") wide. SEPALS: fully up, tips reflexed; rose (68C) upper surface; light rose (73B) lower surface; 32mm (1 1/4") long x 16mm (5/8") wide. TUBE: rose (68C); medium length & thickness; 20mm (3/4") long x 9mm (5/16") wide. FOLIAGE is dark green (137A) upper surface; medium green (138B) lower surface. PARENTAGE: 'Roesse Lupus' x 'Hula Girl'.
van Eijk 2007 NL AFS6562.

van Eijk Harrie-Maria. Upright. Single. COROLLA is full flared with smooth petal margins; opens violet blue (91A); matures violet (75A); 19mm (3/4") long x 21mm (13/16") wide. SEPALS are half up, tips recurved up; magenta (58B) upper surface; light light rose (58D) lower surface; 24mm (15/16") long x 14mm (9/16") wide. TUBE is magenta (58B); medium length & thickness; 9mm (3/8") long x 4mm (3/16") wide. FOLIAGE: dark green (137A) upper surface; medium green (138A) lower surface. Leaves are 62mm (2 7/16") long x 27mm (1 1/16") wide, lanceolate shaped. PARENTAGE: 'Swanley Gem' x ('Sofie Michiels' x 'Sofie Michiels'). Distinguished by bloom colour.
van Eijk 2005 NL AFS5896.

van Eijk Hilke. Upright. Single. COROLLA is half flared; opens reddish purple (72B); matures light reddish purple (72C); 12mm (7/16") long x 19mm (3/4") wide. SEPALS are horizontal, tips recurved; magenta (61C) upper surface; reddish purple (61B) lower surface; 14mm (9/16") long x 7mm (1/4") wide. TUBE is magenta (61C); 9mm (3/8") long x 7mm (1/4") wide. FOLIAGE: dark green (137A) upper surface; medium green (138A) lower surface. PARENTAGE: 'Roesse Carme' x 'Roesse Svalocin'. Distinguished by bloom & foliage combination.
van Eijk 2006 NL AFS6190.

van Eijk Kellie. Upright/Trailer. Double. COROLLA: three-quarter flared; opens violet

(75A); matures light rose (73C); 15mm (9/16") long x 20mm (3/4") wide. SEPALS are half up, tips reflexed up; light rose (63D) tipped green upper surface; magenta (63B), tipped green lower surface; 21mm (13/16") long x 14mm (9/16") wide. TUBE is magenta (63A); 12mm (7/16") long x 10mm (3/8") wide. FOLIAGE is dark green (137A) upper surface; medium green (137C) lower surface. PARENTAGE: 'Van Eijk Shelty' x 'Van Eijk Fonzie'.
van Eijk 2008 NL AFS6877.

van Ejik Laika. Upright/Trailer. Single. COROLLA: three-quarter flared; opens violet (76A); matures pale purple (75C); 21mm (13/16") long x 11mm (7/16") wide. SEPALS are half up, tips reflexed up; light pink (65C) upper & lower surfaces; 26mm (1") long x 12mm (7/16") wide. TUBE is pale lavender (65D); 14mm (9/16") long x 9mm (5/16") wide. FOLIAGE is dark green (137A) upper surface; medium green (137C) lower surface. PARENTAGE: 'Van Eijk Shelty' x 'Van Eijk Fonzie'.
van Eijk 2008 NL AFS6878.

van Eijk Loekie. Upright/Trailer. Single. COROLLA is half flared with smooth petal margins; opens magenta (67B), reddish purple (67A) base; matures reddish purple (73A), light rose (73B) base; 15mm (9/16") long x 21mm (13/16") wide. SEPALS are fully up, tips recurved; rose (65A) tipped green upper & lower surfaces; 19mm (3/4") long x 11mm (7/16") wide. TUBE is rose (65A); medium length & thickness; 12mm (1/2) long x 6mm (1/4") wide. FOLIAGE: dark green (137A) upper surface; medium green (138B) lower surface. Leaves are 56mm (2 3/16") long x 34mm (1 5/16") wide, ovate shaped. PARENTAGE: 'Roesse Carme' x 'Centenary'. Distinguished by bloom colour.
van Eijk 2005 NL AFS5909.

van Eijk Lotje. Trailer. Double. COROLLA: three quarter flared, smooth petal margins; opens & matures white (155D); 22mm (7/8") long 24mm (15/16") wide. SEPALS: fully up; tips reflexed; white (155A), tipped green, upper surface; white (155D), tipped green, lower surface; 22mm (7/8") long x 14mm (9/16") wide. TUBE: white (155A); medium length & thickness; 7mm (1/4) long x 7mm (1/4") wide. STAMENS: extend 16mm (5/8") below corolla; pale pink (62D) filaments; pink (62A) anthers. PISTIL: extends 33mm (1 5/16") below the corolla; white (155D) style & stigma. BUD: round, pointed. FOLIAGE: medium green (137B) upper surface; medium

green (138B) lower surface. Leaves are 42mm (1 11/16") long x 26mm (1") wide, ovate shaped, serrulated edges, acute tips and rounded bases. Green veins, stems & branches. PARENTAGE: 'Sofie Michiels' x 'Demi van Roovert'. Natural trailer. Makes good basket. Prefers overhead filtered light and cool climate. Best bloom and foliage colour in filtered light. Tested 4 years in Reusel, The Netherlands. Distinguished by bloom and foliage combination.
van Eijk 2004 NL AFS5501.

van Eijk Nanna. Upright. Single. COROLLA is quarter flared; opens purple (82B); matures violet (82C); 26mm (1") long x 21mm (13/16") wide. SEPALS are fully up, tips recurved; pink (62C) upper surface; light pink (62B) lower surface; 26mm (1") long x 9mm (3/8") wide. TUBE is pink (62C); 7mm (1/4") long x 5mm (3/16") wide. FOLIAGE: dark green (137A) upper surface; medium green (138A) lower surface. PARENTAGE: ('Parasol' x 'Cameron Ryle') x 'Regent Gubler'. Distinguished by bloom & foliage combination.
van Eijk 2006 NL AFS6193.

van Ejik Nikki. Upright/Trailer. Single. COROLLA: three-quarter flared; opens purple (71A); matures reddish purple (67A); 20mm (3/4") long x 24mm (15/16") wide. SEPALS are fully up, tips recurved; light rose (58D) upper surface; dark rose (58C) lower surface; 26mm (1") long x 10mm (3/8") wide. TUBE is light rose (58D); 10mm (3/8") long x 6mm (1/4") wide. FOLIAGE is dark green (137A) upper surface; medium green (137C) lower surface. PARENTAGE: ('Roesse Lupus' x 'Hula Girl') x 'Thieu Marjan'.
van Eijk 2008 NL AFS6882.

van Eijk Peggie. Upright. Double. COROLLA is three quarter flared; opens dark red (46A); matures red (46C); 17mm (5/8") long x 19mm (3/4") wide. SEPALS are horizontal, tips recurved; red (45A) upper & lower surfaces; 17mm (5/8") long x 12mm (7/16") wide. TUBE is red (45A); 8mm (5/16") long x 6mm (1/4") wide. FOLIAGE: dark green (139A) upper surface; medium green (137C) lower surface. PARENTAGE: 'Cameron Ryle' x 'van Eijk Sasja'. Distinguished by bloom colour.
van Eijk 2006 NL AFS6189.

van Eijk Reina. Upright. Semi Double. COROLLA is three quarter flared; opens violet (87B); matures light purple (87C); 12mm (7/16") long x 17mm (5/8") wide.

SEPALS are fully up, tips recurved; dark rose (71D) upper surface; magenta (71C) lower surface; 18mm (11/16") long x 11mm (7/16") wide. TUBE is dark rose (71D); 10mm (3/8") long x 8mm (5/16") wide. FOLIAGE: medium green (137B) upper surface; light green (138C) lower surface. PARENTAGE: 'Roesse Carme' x 'Delta's Wonder'. Distinguished by bloom colour.
van Eijk 2006 NL AFS6191.

van Eijk Remko. Upright/Trailer. Double. COROLLA is half flared; opens red (46B); matures red (46C); 17mm (5/8") long x 24mm (15/16") wide. SEPALS are fully up, tips recurved; pink (62C) upper & lower surfaces; 23mm (7/8") long x 12mm (7/16") wide. TUBE is pink (62C); 9mm (3/8") long x 7mm (1/4") wide. FOLIAGE: dark green (139A) upper surface; medium green (137C) lower surface. PARENTAGE: 'Roesse Carme' x 'Laura Krekels'. Distinguished by bloom & foliage combination
van Eijk 2006 NL AFS6192.

van Eijk Sasja. Upright. Double. COROLLA: half flared, smooth petal margins; opens red (53B); matures red (46B); 12mm (1/2") long 11mm (7/16") wide. SEPALS: fully up; tips recurved; red (46B) upper & lower surfaces; 13mm (1/2") long x 7mm (1/2") wide. TUBE: red (46B); medium length & thickness; 10mm (3/8") long x 6mm (1/4") wide. STAMENS: extend 10mm (3/8") below corolla; rose (51B) filaments; dark rose (51A) anthers. PISTIL: extends 10mm (3/8") below the corolla; rose (51B) style; light yellow (4C) stigma. BUD: round, pointed. FOLIAGE: dark green (137A) upper surface; medium green (138A) lower surface. Leaves are 64mm (2 1/2") long x 41mm (1 5/8") wide, ovate shaped, serrated edges, acute tips and rounded bases. Red veins, stems & branches. PARENTAGE: 'Roesse Carme' x ('Roesse Apus' x 'Roesse Apus'). Medium upright. Makes good upright or standard. Prefers overhead filtered light and cool climate. Best bloom and foliage colour in filtered light. Tested 4 years in Reusel, The Netherlands. Distinguished by bloom colour.
van Eijk 2004 NL AFS5496.

van Eijk Sheltie. Upright/Trailer. Double. COROLLA: three quarter flared, smooth petal margins; opens & matures white (155D); 20mm (13/16") long 18mm (11/16") wide. SEPALS: half up; tips reflexed up; pale pink (62D) upper surface; light pink (62B) lower surface; 27mm (1 1/16") long x 17mm (11/16") wide. TUBE: pale pink (62D);

medium length & thickness; 14mm (9/16") long x 7mm (1/4") wide. STAMENS: extend 12mm (1/2") below corolla; magenta (63B) filaments; reddish purple (58A) anthers. PISTIL: extends 36mm (1 7/16") below the corolla; pale pink (62D) style; yellowish white (4D) stigma. BUD: round, pointed. FOLIAGE: dark green (137A) upper surface; medium green (138A) lower surface. Leaves are 66mm (2 5/8") long x 32mm (1 1/4") wide, ovate shaped, serrulated edges, acute tips and rounded bases. Green veins, stems & branches. PARENTAGE: 'Sofie Michiels' x 'Demi van Roovert'. Lax upright or stiff trailer. Makes good stiff trailer. Prefers overhead filtered light and cool climate. Best bloom and foliage colour in filtered light. Tested 4 years in Reusel, The Netherlands. Distinguished by bloom and foliage combination.
van Eijk 2004 NL AFS5502.

van Eijk Tamira. Upright. Double. COROLLA is half flared with smooth petal margins; opens light pink (62B), purple (77A) base; matures light pink (62B), light purple (78B) base; 17mm (11/16") long x 22mm (7/8") wide. SEPALS are half up, tips reflexed up; pale pink (62D) tipped green upper surface; pink (62C) tipped green lower surface; 27mm (1 1/16") long x 11mm (7/16") wide. TUBE is pale pink (62D); short & thick; 7mm (1/4) long x 5mm (3/16") wide. FOLIAGE: medium green (137B) upper surface; medium green (138B) lower surface. Leaves are 70mm (2 3/4") long x 42mm (1 5/8") wide, ovate shaped. PARENTAGE: 'Roesse Apus' x 'Jorma'. Distinguished by bloom colour.
van Eijk 2005 NL AFS5910.

van Eijk Teddie. Upright/Trailer. Single. COROLLA: half flared, smooth petal margins; opens dark red (53A); matures red (53C); 11mm (7/16") long 17mm (11/16") wide. SEPALS: half down; tips recurved; red (53D) upper surface; reddish orange (42A) lower surface; 21mm (13/16") long x 11mm (7/16") wide. TUBE: red (53D); medium length & thickness; 15mm (9/16) long x 5mm (3/16") wide. STAMENS: extend 10mm (3/8") below corolla; red (46C) filaments & anthers. PISTIL: extends 26mm (1") below the corolla; red (46C) style; yellow white (4D) stigma. BUD: short TUBE, ovate, pointed. FOLIAGE: dark green (137A) upper surface; medium green (138A) lower surface. Leaves are 50mm (2") long x 37mm (1 7/16") wide, ovate shaped, serrulated edges, acute tips and cordate bases. Green veins, stems &

branches. PARENTAGE: 'Orangeblossom' x ('Roesse Apus' x 'Roesse Apus'). Lax upright or stiff trailer. Makes good stiff trailer. Prefers overhead filtered light and cool climate. Best bloom and foliage colour in filtered light. Tested 4 years in Reusel, The Netherlands. Distinguished by bloom and foliage combination.
van Eijk 2004 NL AFS5497.

van Eijk Triksie. Upright/Trailer. Double. COROLLA: three quarter flared, smooth petal margins; opens violet (76A); matures light violet (84B); 22mm (7/8") long x 22mm (7/8") wide. SEPALS: half up; tips recurved up; white (155A) upper surface; white (155B) lower surface;37mm (1 7/16") long x 9mm (3/8") wide. TUBE: white (155A); medium length & thickness; 17mm (11/16") long x 5mm (3/16") wide. STAMENS: extend 15mm (9/16") below corolla; light pink (62B) filaments, rose (63C) anthers. PISTIL: extends 37mm (1 7/16") below the corolla; pale pink (62D) style & stigma. BUD: ovate. FOLIAGE: medium green (137B) upper surface; medium green (138B) lower surface. Leaves are 70mm (2 3/4") long x 42mm (1 5/8") wide, ovate shaped, serrulated edges, acute tips and obtuse bases. Veins, stems & branches are green. PARENTAGE: 'Sofie Michiels' x 'Veenlust'. Lax upright or stiff trailer. Makes good stiff trailer. Prefers overhead filtered light and cool climate. Best bloom and foliage colour in filtered light. Tested 4 years in Reusel, The Netherlands. Distinguished by bloom colour.
van Eijk 2003 NL AFS5256.

van Eijk Wessel. Upright/Trailer. Semi Double. COROLLA: three-quarter flared; opens & matures white (155D); 17mm (5/8") long x 14mm (9/16") wide. SEPALS are fully up, tips reflexed; pale lavender (65D),tipped green upper surface; light pink (65B), ,tipped green lower surface; 22mm (7/8") long x 12mm (7/16") wide. TUBE is pale lavender (65D); 16mm (5/8") long x 6mm (1/4") wide. FOLIAGE is dark green (137A) upper surface; medium green (137C) lower surface. PARENTAGE: ('Roesse Lupus' x 'Hula Girl') x 'Michelle de Bruin'.
van Eijk 2008 NL AFS6879.

VAN Parijs Emile. Upright/Trailer. Double. COROLLA is three quarter flared with turned under wavy petal margins; opens dark purple (79B), dark reddish purple (64A) base; matures purple (79C), dark reddish purple (61A) base; 22mm (7/8") long x 25mm (1") wide. PETALOIDS: dark purple (79B), dark

reddish purple (61A) base; 19mm (3/4") long x 15mm (9/16") wide. SEPALS are horizontal, tips reflexed; dark reddish purple (64A) upper surface; dark reddish purple (61A) lower surface; 42mm (1 11/16") long x 18mm (11/16") wide. TUBE is dark reddish purple (61A); short & thick; 12mm (1/2") long x 7mm (1/4") wide. FOLIAGE: dark green (137A) upper surface; medium green (138B) lower surface. Leaves are 74mm (2 15/16") long x 42mm (1 11/16") wide, ovate shaped. PARENTAGE: 'Roesse Blacky' x 'Winzerin'. Meise 9-18-04, Outstanding. Distinguished by flamed pink flower colour.
Michiels 2005 BE AFS5852.

Vancuyck David. Upright/Trailer. Double. COROLLA is three quarter flared opens purple (90B); matures light purple (81C); 27mm (1 1/16") long x 32mm (1 1/4") wide. SEPALS are fully up, tips recurved; dark rose (58C) upper surface; pink (62A) lower surface; 32mm (1 1/4") long x 18mm (11/16") wide. TUBE is dark rose (58C); 17mm (5/8") long x 9mm (3/8") wide. FOLIAGE: dark green (137A) upper surface; medium green (137C) lower surface. PARENTAGE: 'Regent Gubler' x 'Thea Kroese'. Distinguished by bloom colour.
Decoster 2006 BE AFS6081.

Vancuyck Gregory. Upright/Trailer. Single. COROLLA is half flared; opens & matures magenta (59C); 14mm (9/16") long x 18mm (11/16") wide. SEPALS are horizontal, tips recurved; rose (63C) upper surface; light rose (63D) lower surface; 21mm (13/16") long x 8mm (5/16") wide. TUBE is rose (63C); 21mm (13/16") long x 10mm (3/8") wide. FOLIAGE: dark green (137A) upper surface; medium green (137D) lower surface. PARENTAGE: 'Roesse Lupus' x 'Lye's Unique'. Distinguished by bloom colour & shape.
Decoster 2006 BE AFS6082.

Vancuyck Isabeau. Upright. Single. COROLLA is three quarter flared; opens & matures reddish orange (43B); 12mm (1/2") long x 16mm (5/8") wide. SEPALS are half down, tips recurved; light orange (39C) upper surface; coral (39B) lower surface; 19mm (3/4") long x 7mm (1/4") wide. TUBE is light orange (39C); 16mm (5/8") long x 8mm (5/16") wide. FOLIAGE: dark green (137A) upper surface; medium green (138A) lower surface. PARENTAGE: 'Roesse Lupus' x 'Lye's Unique'. Distinguished by bloom & foliage combination.
Decoster 2006 BE AFS6088.

Vancuyck Lucien. Upright/Trailer. Double. COROLLA is three quarter flared; opens violet (84A); matures violet (75A); 27mm (1 1/16") long x 29mm (1 1/8") wide. SEPALS are half up, tips recurved up; magenta (58B) upper & lower surfaces; 36mm (1 7/16") long x 16mm (5/8") wide. TUBE is magenta (58A); 10mm (3/8") long x 4mm (1/8") wide. FOLIAGE: dark green (139A) upper surface; medium green (138B) lower surface. PARENTAGE: 'Regent Gubler' x 'Thea Kroese'. Distinguished by bloom colour & shape.
Decoster 2006 BE AFS6085.

Vancuyck Véronique. Upright. Single. COROLLA is quarter flared; opens & matures red (45C); 10mm (3/8") long x 16mm (5/8") wide. SEPALS are half down, tips reflexed; rose (63C) upper & lower surfaces; 17mm (5/8") long x 7mm (1/4") wide. TUBE is rose (63C); 15mm (9/16") long x 8mm (5/16") wide. FOLIAGE: dark green (137A) upper surface; medium green (137C) lower surface. PARENTAGE: 'Roesse Lupus' x 'Lye's Unique'. Distinguished by bloom colour.
Decoster 2006 BE AFS6087.

Vanessa Wright. Upright. Single. COROLLA: unflared, bell shaped, held horizontal, smooth petal margins; opens purple (80A); matures reddish purple (74B); 17mm (5/8") long x 17mm (5/8") wide. SEPALS: horizontal, tips recurved; red (45B) upper surface; dark red (46D) lower surface; 22mm (7/8") long x 8mm (5/16") wide. TUBE: red (45B); short, medium thickness; 5mm (3/16") long x 5mm (3/16") wide. STAMENS extend 15mm (9/16") beyond the corolla; red (43A) filaments; reddish orange (43B) anthers. PISTIL extends 28mm (1 1/8") beyond the corolla; red (45C) style; red (45D) stigma. BUD: square, pointed. FOLIAGE: dark green (137A) upper surface; medium green (137D) lower surface. Leaves are 32mm (1 1/4") long x 26mm (1") wide; cordate shaped, serrulate edges, acute tips, rounded bases. Veins, stems & branches are green. PARENTAGE: 'Eileen Storey' x 'Pink Fantasia'. Small upright. Self branching. Makes good upright. Prefers full sun. Cold weather hardy to -3° C (26° F). Best bloom & foliage colour in bright light. Tested 6 years in Burstwick & West Newton, East Yorkshire, England. Distinguished by bloom colour, horizontally erect flowers.
Storey 2009 UK AFS7131.

Variegated Machu Picchu. Upright. Single. COROLLA is unflared, square shaped, smooth petal margins; opens and matures orangy red (39A); 15mm (9/16") long x 15mm (9/16") wide. SEPALS are horizontal; tips recurved; light rose (50C) to white (155A) tipped yellowish green (154B) upper & lower surfaces; 19mm (3/4") long x 6mm (1/4") wide. TUBE light rose (50C), medium length & thickness; 16mm (5/8") long x 6mm (1/4") wide. STAMENS extend 6mm (1/4") below the corolla; light rose (50C) filaments, white (155D) anthers. PISTIL extends 25mm (1") below the corolla; pink (50D) style, white (155D) stigma. BUD is ovate. FOLIAGE is yellowish green (144B) upper surface edged light apple green (144D), light olive green (147C) edged light green (147D) lower surface. Leaves are 70mm (2 3/4") long x 44mm (1 3/4") wide, cordate shaped, smooth edges, acute tips and rounded bases. Veins are yellowish green (144B), stems are light apple green (145C). PARENTAGE: Sport of 'Machu Picchu'. Small upright. Makes good basket or upright. Prefers full sun. Best bloom colour in bright light. Tested 3 years in Victoria, British Columbia, Canada. Distinguished by variegated foliage.
Willoughby 2003 CA AFS5070.

Variegated Wigan Peer. Upright. Double. COROLLA white; corolla is fully flared. SEPALS white blushed pink on the upper and lower surface; sepals are half up with reflexed tips. TUBE white blushed pink. PARENTAGE sport of 'Wigan Peer'.
Bolton 2008 UK BFS0093.

Veldhoven. Upright. Double. COROLLA is three quarter flared with smooth petal margins; opens dark reddish purple (70A); matures reddish purple (67A); 19mm (3/4") long x 17mm (11/16") wide. SEPALS are fully up, tips reflexed; light pink (65B) upper surface; rose (65A) lower surface; 27mm (1 1/16") long x 14mm (9/16") wide. TUBE is light pink (65B); medium length & thickness; 8mm (5/16") long x 5mm (3/16") wide. FOLIAGE: dark green (137A) upper surface; medium green (138A) lower surface. Leaves are 67mm (2 5/8") long x 41mm (1 5/8") wide, ovate shaped. PARENTAGE: ('Roesse Apus' x 'Roesse Apus') x 'Yvette Klessens'. Distinguished by bloom & foliage combination.
Buiting 2005 NL AFS5861.

Vendee Tourisme. Trailer. Single. COROLLA: three quarter flared, smooth petal margins; opens & matures reddish purple (70B), rose (63C) at base & splashes; 20mm (13/16") long x 28mm (1 1/8") wide.

SEPALS: half up; tips recurved up; light rose (73B) upper surface; light reddish purple (73A) lower surface; 41mm (1 5/8") long x 8mm (5/16") wide. TUBE: light rose (73B); short, medium thickness; 14mm (9/16") long x 6mm (1/4") wide. STAMENS: extend 15-20mm (9/16–13/16") below corolla; light reddish purple (66C) filaments, dark grayish red (182A) anthers. PISTIL: extends 28mm (1 1/8") below the corolla, reddish purple (66B) style & stigma. BUD: ovate. FOLIAGE: medium green (147B) upper surface; medium green (147C) lower surface. Leaves are 84mm (3 5/16") long x 50mm (2") wide, ovate shaped, serrulated edges, acute tips and rounded bases. Veins & stems are yellowish green, branches are light brown. PARENTAGE: 'Royal Velvet' x 'Strawberry Delight'. Natural trailer. Makes good basket. Prefers overhead filtered light and cool climate. Best bloom and foliage colour in filtered light. Tested 4 years in Luçon, France. Distinguished by corolla colour. Young foliage is bronzy.
Massé 2003 FR AFS5222.

Vendelzwaaier. Upright. Single to Semi Double. COROLLA is three quarter flared with turned under wavy petal margins; opens light reddish purple (73A), pink (55C) base; matures light reddish purple (66C), pink (50D) base; 19mm (3/4") long x 17mm (11/16") wide. SEPALS are half up, tips recurved up; light pink (55D), pale pink (36D) base, tipped yellowish green (145A) upper surface; light pink (55B), pale pink (36D) base, tipped yellowish green (145A) lower surface; 24mm (15/16") long x 10mm (3/8") wide. TUBE is pale pink (36D); short & thick; 11mm (7/16") long x 8mm (5/16") wide. FOLIAGE: dark green (136A) upper surface; medium green (138B) lower surface. Leaves are 78mm (3 1/16") long x 40mm (1 9/16") wide, ovate shaped. PARENTAGE: 'Sofie Michiels' x 'Braamst Glorie'. Meise 8-14-04. Distinguished by rich blooming period.
Michiels 2005 BE AFS5742.

Vendeta. COROLLA mandarin orange. SEPALS deep red with dark green tips.
Blaber 2002.

Venezia. Upright/Trailer. Single. COROLLA: unflared, TUBE shaped, wavy petal margins; opens reddish purple (74A), matures reddish purple (61B); 15mm (9/16") long x 9mm (3/8") wide. SEPALS: twisted to the left like screw blade, full down; tips recurved; rose (61D) upper surface, dark rose (58C) lower surface; 32mm (1 1/4") long x 5mm (3/16") wide. TUBE: magenta (58B), long & thin; 30mm (1 3/16") long x 5mm (3/16") wide. STAMENS: extend 10 - 15mm (3/8 – 9/16") below the corolla; magenta (58B) filaments, pale tan (159A) anthers. PISTIL extends 25mm (1") below the corolla; pink (62A) style, pale tan (159A) stigma. BUD: long, ovate. FOLIAGE: medium green (146A) upper surface, light olive green (148B) lower surface. Leaves are 52mm (2 1/16") long x 29mm (1 1/8") wide, ovate shaped, serrated edges, acute tips and rounded bases. Veins, stems, branches are reddish green. PARENTAGE: 'F. magellanica' x unknown. Lax upright or stiff trailer. Self branching. Makes good upright. Heat tolerant if shaded. Best bloom and foliage colour in filtered light. Tested 3 years in Como, Italy. Distinguished by twisted sepal, long pedicels.
Ianne 2003 IT AFS5072.

Vermeulen Rani. Upright. Single. COROLLA is half flared; opens red (43A); matures orangy red (44B); 16mm (5/8") long x 19mm (3/4") wide. SEPALS are horizontal, tips recurved; light rose (58D) upper surface; dark rose (58C) lower surface; 20mm (3/4") long x 9mm (3/8") wide. TUBE is light rose (58D); short & thick; 15mm (9/16") long x 12mm (1/2") wide. FOLIAGE: dark green (137A) upper surface; medium green (137C) lower surface. PARENTAGE: 'Roesse Lupus' x 'Lye's Unique'. Distinguished by bloom shape.
Decoster 2006 BE AFS6084.

Vickie Ann. Upright. Single. COROLLA is quarter flared; opens & matures reddish purple (66B); 12mm (7/16") long x 12mm (7/16") wide. SEPALS are half down, tips reflexed; light pink (62B) tipped brown (177D) upper surface; light pink (62B) tipped white (155A) lower surface; 12mm (7/16") long x 7mm (1/4") wide. TUBE is white (155A) striped brown (199A); 80mm (3 3/16") long x 9mm (3/8") wide. FOLIAGE: dark green (147A) upper surface; medium green (147B) lower surface. PARENTAGE: ('F. magdalenae' x 'F. fulgens var. rubra grandiflora') x 'Kobold'. Distinguished by TUBE colour & bud shape. Named after the wife or Rick Stevens who runs the web site www.findthatfuchsia.info.
Koerts T. 2006 NL AFS6302.

Vickie Marr. Upright. Single. COROLLA is quarter flared with smooth petal margins; opens reddish purple (72B); matures light reddish purple (72C); 20mm (13/16") long x

25mm (1") wide. SEPALS are horizontal, tips recurved; pale pink (62D) upper & lower surfaces; 35mm (1 3/8") long x 12mm (1/2") wide. TUBE is cream (158D) flushed red at base; medium length & thin; 16mm (5/8") long x 7mm (1/4") wide. FOLIAGE: dark green (137A) upper surface; medium green (138B) lower surface. Leaves are 60mm (2 3/8") long x 30mm (1 3/16") wide, cordate shaped. PARENTAGE: 'Duchess of Albany' x 'Hobson's Choice'. Distinguished by colour combination.
Gibson 2006 UK AFS5976.

Victoria Bell. Upright/Trailer. Double. COROLLA: 3 quarter flared, open, ballerina shaped; opens purple (80A); matures purple (71A); 25mm (1") long x 40mm (1 9/16") wide. SEPALS: horizontal, tips recurved; dark reddish purple (60A) upper & lower surfaces; 40mm (1 9/16") long x 18mm (11/16") wide. TUBE: dark reddish purple (60A); medium length & thickness; 18mm (11/16") long x 10mm (3/8") wide. FOLIAGE is medium green (137C) upper surface; medium green (138B) lower surface. PARENTAGE: 'Swingtime' x 'Millennium'.
Bell 2007 UK AFS6400.

Victorian Speed. Upright/Trailer. Double. COROLLA: half flared, turned under wavy petal margins; opens reddish purple (61B) & dark reddish purple (64A); matures dark reddish purple (60C); 23mm (7/8") long x 19mm (3/4") wide. PETALOIDS: Same colour as corolla; 15mm (9/16") long x 10mm (3/8") wide. SEPALS: half down, tips recurved; pink (55C) tipped pale yellow green (150D) upper surface; dark rose (54A) lower surface; 27mm (1 1/16") long x 15mm (9/16") wide. TUBE: pale pink (56A); medium length & thickness; 14mm (9/16") long x 7mm (1/4") wide. STAMENS extend 8mm (5/16") beyond the corolla; reddish purple (64B) filaments; dark purple (79A) anthers. PISTIL extends 11mm (7/16") beyond the corolla; magenta (67B) style; yellowish white (4D) stigma. BUD: bulbous. FOLIAGE: dark green (136B) upper surface; medium green (137C) lower surface. Leaves are 58mm (2 5/16") long x 32mm (1 1/4") wide; ovate shaped, smooth edges, acute tips, rounded bases. Veins are plum (185B), stems are red purple (N186D), branches are grayish red (182B) & light green (138C). PARENTAGE: 'Manfried Kleinau' x 'De Boerin'. Lax upright or stiff trailer. Self branching. Makes good basket or upright. Prefers overhead filtered light, cool climate. Best bloom & foliage colour in filtered light. Tested 3 years in

Koningshooikt, Belgium. Waanrode 8/9/08. Distinguished by bloom colour combination.
Michiels 2009 BE AFS7232.

Vier Deuken. Upright/Trailer. Semi Double. COROLLA: half flared, turned under wavy petal margins; opens reddish purple (71B), magenta (63A) base; matures reddish purple (64B); 19mm (3/4") long x 17mm (11/16") wide. PETALOIDS: Same colour as corolla; 15mm (9/16") long x 17mm (11/16") wide. SEPALS: fully up; tips reflexed; red (53C) upper surface; red (50A) lower surface; 32mm (1 1/4") long x 12mm (1/2") wide. TUBE: dark red (53A); short & thick; 12mm(1/2") long x 7mm (1/4") wide. STAMENS: extend 7mm (1/4") below corolla; magenta (57B) filaments, dark reddish purple (59A) anthers. PISTIL: extends 22mm (7/8") below the corolla, magenta (57B) style, reddish purple (58A) stigma. BUD: round. FOLIAGE: medium green (137B) upper surface; medium green (138B) lower surface. Leaves are 67mm (2 5/8") long x 29mm (1 1/8") wide, elliptic shaped, serrulated edges, acute tips and rounded bases. Veins are light plum (184D), stems are plum (184B), branches are light reddish purple (185D). PARENTAGE: 'WALZ Mandoline' x 'Rohees Mintaka'. Lax upright or stiff trailer. Self branching. Makes good basket. Prefers overhead filtered light. Best bloom and foliage colour in filtered light. Tested 3 years in Koningshooikt, Belgium. NBFK Certificate at Meise. Distinguished by dented TUBE on four sides.
Michiels 2003 BE AFS5192.

Vignero Louis. Upright/Trailer. Double. COROLLA is three quarter flared with turned under wavy petal margins; opens purple (77A), dark rose (64C) base; matures dark reddish purple (72A); 14mm (9/16") long x 16mm (5/8") wide. PETALOIDS: same colour as corolla; 12mm (1/2") long x 9mm (3/8") wide. SEPALS are horizontal, tips recurved; dark rose (64C) upper surface; magenta (71C) lower surface; 34mm (1 5/16") long x 15mm (9/16") wide. TUBE is reddish purple (61B); medium length & thickness; 23mm (15/16") long x 7mm (1/4") wide. FOLIAGE: dark green (136A) upper surface; medium green (138B) lower surface. Leaves are 52mm (2 1/16") long x 28mm (1 1/8") wide, ovate shaped. PARENTAGE: 'Roesse Blacky' x 'Diana Wills'. Meise 9-18-04. Distinguished by flower colour.
Michiels 2005 BE AFS5846.

Vikar Mraz. Upright/Trailer. Double. COROLLA is three quarter flared with smooth petal margins; opens and matures pale pink (56C) dark rose (54A) veins and base; 25mm (1") long x 40mm (1 9/16") wide. SEPALS are horizontal, tips reflexed; dark rose (54B) upper surface, dark rose (54A) lower surface; 38mm (1 1/2") long x 20mm (13/16") wide. TUBE is dark rose (54B), medium length and thickness. STAMENS extend 5mm (3/16") beyond the corolla; dark rose (54B) filaments, reddish purple (58A) anthers. PISTIL extends 23mm (15/16") beyond the corolla; pink (54D) style, light orange (25A) stigma. BUD is globular. FOLIAGE is dark green (147A) upper surface, light olive green (147C) lower surface. Leaves are 60mm (2 3/8") long x 40mm (1 9/16") wide, ovate shaped, serrated edges, acute tips and rounded bases. Veins are reddish, stems are brown (177B), branches are grayish red (181B). PARENTAGE: 'Fenja' x unknown. Lax upright or stiff trailer. Self branching. Makes good basket. Prefers overhead filtered light. Heat tolerant if shaded. Best bloom colour in filtered light. Bronze medal at the BUGA 2001 in Tübingen, Germany. Tested three years in Plettenberg, Germany. Distinguished by blossom colour combination. Strümper 2002 DE AFS4945.

Ville De Bourges. Upright. Single. COROLLA is unflared with smooth petal margins; opens red (44A); matures dark orange red (34A); 19mm (3/4") long x 7mm (1/4") wide. SEPALS are full down, tips recurved; rose (47D) upper surface; rose (48B) lower surface; 20mm (13/16") long x 8mm (5/16") wide. TUBE is rose (51B); long, medium thickness; 35mm (1 3/8") long x 6mm (1/4") wide. STAMENS extend 3mm (1/8") beyond the corolla; rose (51B) filaments, yellow white (158A) anthers. PISTIL extends 6mm (1/4") beyond the corolla; rose (51B) style, rose (51C) stigma. FOLIAGE is dark green (137A) upper surface, medium green (137C) lower surface. Leaves are 9mm (3/8") long x 5mm (3/16") wide, ovate shaped, acute tips and acute bases. Veins, stems and branches are dark red (53A). PARENTAGE: 'F. triphylla' x 'Noblesse'. Medium upright. Makes good upright or standard. Prefers overhead filtered light and warm climate. Heat tolerant if shaded. Cold weather hardy to 0⁰ F. Best bloom and foliage colour in filtered light. Tested four years in Central France. Distinguished by blossom colour. Gaucher 2002 FR AFS4953.

Ville de Richelieu. Trailer. Single. COROLLA is unflared with smooth petal margins; opens and matures dark red (53A); 19mm (3/4") long x 11mm (7/16") wide. SEPALS are half up, tips recurved up; pink (48C) upper surface; rose (48B) lower surface; 31mm (1 1/4") long x 8mm (5/16") wide. TUBE is dark rose (48A); medium length and thin; 18mm (11/16") long x 4mm (3/16") thick. STAMENS extend 0 – 2mm (1/16") beyond the corolla; pink (48D) filaments, grayish orange (179A) anthers. PISTIL extends 15mm (5/8") beyond the corolla; dark rose (48A) style, yellowish white (4D) stigma. BUD is ovate. FOLIAGE is dark green (137A) upper surface, medium green (147B) lower surface. Leaves are 67mm (2 5/8") long x 37mm (1 7/16") wide, ovate shaped, serrulated edges, acute tips and rounded bases. Veins, stems are yellowish green, branches are yellowish green and light brown. PARENTAGE: 'Prince of Orange' x 'F. fulgens'. Natural trailer. Makes good willowy standard. Prefers overhead filtered light and cool climate. Best bloom colour in filtered light. Tested three years in Pornic & Luçon, France. Distinguished by corolla colour. Massé 2002 FR AFS5018.

Ville de Rouen. Upright. Single. COROLLA is unflared with smooth petal margins; opens and matures violet (75A), clearer at base; 29mm (1 1/8") long x 19mm (3/4") wide. SEPALS are fully up, tips recurved; pale lavender (69B) tipped light green (143C) upper surface; pale rose (73D) lower surface; 39mm (1 9/16") long x 10mm (3/8") wide. TUBE is light apple green (144D); ultra short, bulbous, medium thickness; 3mm (1/8") long x 6mm (1/4") thick. STAMENS extend 0 – 6mm (1/4") beyond the corolla; pale purple (75D) filaments, pale tan (161D) anthers. PISTIL extends 18mm (11/16") beyond the corolla; pale purple (75D) style, light plum (184D) stigma. BUD is ovate. FOLIAGE is dark green (147A) upper surface, medium green (147B) lower surface. Leaves are 41mm (1 5/8") long x 32mm (1 1/4") wide, ovate shaped, quasi-smooth edges, acute tips and rounded bases. Veins, stems are yellowish green, branches are light brown. PARENTAGE: ('String of Pearls' x unknown) x 'Piet Heemskerk'. Small upright. Self branching. Makes good upright. Prefers overhead filtered light and cool climate. Best bloom colour in filtered light. Tested three years in Pornic, France. Distinguished by ultra short TUBE and corolla/sepal colour. Massé 2002 FR AFS5019.

Villy Hvid. Trailer. Double. COROLLA is half flared; opens reddish purple (72B) with rose (61D) base; matures reddish purple (74B); 19mm (3/4") long x 18mm (11/16") wide. PETALOIDS are reddish purple (72B) with rose (61D) base; 8mm (5/16") long x 6mm (1/4") wide. SEPALS are fully up, tips reflexed; magenta (63B) tipped medium green (138B) upper surface, and rose (61D) tipped medium green (138B) lower surface; 34mm (1 3/8") long x 12mm (7/16") wide. TUBE is reddish purple (61B); 16mm (5/8") long x 6mm (1/4") wide. FOLIAGE is dark green (137A) upper surface; medium green (138B) lower surface. PARENTAGE: 'Sofie Michiels' x 'Cosmopolitan'. Meise 8/13/05. Distinguished by bloom shape.
Michiels 2006 BE AFS6025.

Vintage Dovecourt. Trailer. Double. CORROLA dark aubergine. SEPALS light aubergine. TUBE light aubergine.
Goulding 2004 UK.

Violet Perfection. Upright. Double. COROLLA violet blue. SEPALS red.
Ainsworth 2005 UK.

Vissen. Upright. Single. COROLLA: quarter flared; opens dark rose (54A); matures dark rose (58C); 18mm (11/16") long x 21mm (13/16") wide. SEPALS are half down, tips reflexed; light pink (49C) tipped light yellowish green (154C) upper surface; pink (49A) tipped light yellowish green (154C) lower surface; 34mm (1 3/8") long x 9mm (15/16") wide. TUBE is rose (51B); 68mm (2 11/16") long x 6mm (1/4") wide. FOLIAGE is medium green (138A) upper surface; medium green (138B) lower surface. PARENTAGE: 'Walz Harp' x 'Walz Mandoline'. Waanrode 7/7//2007.
Geerts L. 2008 BE AFS6732.

Vitalo. Upright. Single. COROLLA is unflared with smooth petal margins, square shaped; opens magenta (N57C); matures magenta (N57A); 6mm (1/4") long x 6mm (1/4") wide. SEPALS are half up, tips reflexed up; red (53B) upper surface; red (53C) lower surface; 15mm (9/16") long x 4mm (3/16") wide. TUBE is red (53B); short & thin; 7mm (1/4") long x 3mm (1/8") wide. FOLIAGE: dark green (137A) upper surface; medium green (137C) lower surface. Leaves are 60mm (2 3/8") long x 23mm (15/16") wide, lanceolate shaped. PARENTAGE: 'F. lycioides' x 'F. regia reitzii'. Distinguished by bloom flower shape.
Paechnatz 2005 DE AFS5695.

Vlasberg 39. Upright. Double. COROLLA: 3 quarter flared; opens dark reddish purple (72A), dark reddish purple (70A) base; matures reddish purple (71B); 32mm (1 1/4") long x 20mm (3/4") wide. PETALOIDS: same colour as corolla; 13mm (1/2") long x 5mm (3/16") wide. SEPALS: horizontal, tips reflexed; dark rose (64C) tipped light green (142B) upper surface; magenta (67B) tipped light green (142B) lower surface; 37mm (1 7/16") long x 18mm (11/16") wide. TUBE: magenta (63B); medium length & thickness; 15mm (9/16") long x 7mm (1/4") wide. FOLIAGE is dark green (137A) upper surface; medium green (138B) lower surface. PARENTAGE: 'Stad Genk' x 'Rocket Fire'.
Michiels 2007 BE AFS6322.

Vlierbeekhof. Trailer. Double. COROLLA: half flared, turned under wavy petal margins; opens magenta (58B) & violet (N82B); matures light purple (N78B); 27mm (1 1/16") long x 16mm (5/8") wide. PETALOIDS: Same colour as corolla; 17mm (5/8") long x 8mm (5/16") wide. SEPALS: horizontal, tips recurved; magenta (61C) upper surface; magenta (58B) lower surface; 48mm (1 7/8") long x 16mm (5/8") wide. TUBE: reddish purple (60D); medium length & thickness; 17mm (5/8") long x 7mm (1/4") wide. STAMENS extend 12mm (7/16") beyond the corolla; magenta (58B) filaments; dark purple (79A) anthers. PISTIL extends 18mm (11/16") beyond the corolla; magenta (63B) style; pale lavender (65D) stigma. BUD: elongated. FOLIAGE: dark green (137A) upper surface; medium green (138B) lower surface. Leaves are 68mm (2 11/16") long x 44mm (1 3/4") wide; ovate shaped, serrulate edges, acute tips, rounded bases. Veins are dark reddish purple (187B), stems are dark red purple (187D), branches are pale purple (N186D). PARENTAGE: 'Coen Bakker' x 'Dark Eyes'. Natural trailer. Self branching. Makes good basket. Prefers overhead filtered light, cool climate. Best bloom & foliage colour in filtered light. Tested 3 years in Koningshooikt, Belgium. Waanrode 7/5/08. Distinguished by bloom colour & foliage combination.
Michiels 2009 BE AFS7233.

Volendam. Upright/Trailer. Single. COROLLA is quarter flared; opens red (53B); matures dark red (47A) & red (47B); 32mm (1 1/4") long x 28mm (1 1/8") wide. SEPALS are half down, tips recurved; red (47B) upper surface; reddish orange (43C) lower surface; 38mm (1 1/2") long x 14mm (9/16") wide. TUBE is pink (48D); 25mm (1") long x 8mm

(5/16") wide. FOLIAGE: dark green (147A) upper surface; medium green (147B) lower surface. PARENTAGE: 'Paulus' x unknown. Distinguished by bloom colour.
Krom 2006 NL AFS6273.

Vorarlberg. Trailer. Semi Double. COROLLA soft pink; corolla is three quarter flared. SEPALS shell pink on the upper surface, shell pink blushed deeper pink on the lower surface; sepals are horizontally held with yellowish green recurved tips. TUBE pale pink. PARENTAGE 'Carla Johnson' x 'Cliff's Own'.
Klemm 2008 AT BFS0079.

Vreni Schleeweiss. Upright/Trailer. Double. COROLLA is three quarter flared with turned under smooth petal margins; opens white (155C), pink (54D) base; matures white (155A); 24mm (15/16") long x 18 mm (11/16") wide. PETALOIDS: same colour as corolla; 14mm (9/16") long x 8mm (5/16") wide. SEPALS are horizontal, tips recurved; white (155C), light pink (56D) base, tipped light apple green (145C) upper surface; white (155C), pink (54D) base, tipped light apple green (145C) lower surface; 45mm (1 3/4") long x 18mm (11/16") wide. TUBE is pale pink (56D), medium length & thickness; 19mm (3/4") long x 6mm (1/4") wide. FOLIAGE: dark green (136A) upper surface; medium green (138B) lower surface. Leaves are 80mm (3 1/8") long x 43mm (1 11/16") wide, ovate shaped. PARENTAGE: 'Sofie Michiels' x 'Bianca'. Approved with excellence at Meise, 3-7-04. Distinguished by colour combination.
Michiels 2005 BE AFS5654.

VV De Pinmaekers. Trailer. Double. COROLLA: Half flared; opens & matures white (155D); 16mm (5/8") long x 11mm (7/16") wide. SEPALS: horizontal, tips recurved; dark rose (58C) upper surface; magenta (59D) lower surface; 24mm (15/16") long x 9mm (5/16") wide. TUBE: dark rose (58C); long & thin; 32mm (1 1/4") long x 3mm (1/8") wide. FOLIAGE is dark green (137A) upper surface; medium green (138B) lower surface. PARENTAGE: 'Kristel vander Velden' x 'Luuk van Riet'.
Roes 2007 NL AFS6700.

W. Grootenboer. Upright/Trailer. Double. COROLLA: half flared; opens reddish purple (71B), dark rose (55A) base; matures purple (71A), dark reddish purple (64A) base; 28mm (1 1/8") long x 32mm (1 1/4") wide. PETALOIDS: same colour as corolla; 18mm

(11/16") long x 8mm (5/16") wide. SEPALS: half up, tips recurved up; rose (63C) upper surface; dark rose (55A) lower surface; 30mm (1 3/16") long x 13mm (1/2") wide. TUBE: rose (55C); medium length & thickness; 9mm (5/16") long x 3mm (1/8") wide. FOLIAGE is dark green (136B) upper surface; medium green (138B) lower surface. PARENTAGE: 'Leon Pauwels' x 'Monique Sleiderlink'.
Michiels 2007 BE AFS6323.

Waanrode Bloemendorp. Upright/Trailer. Single. COROLLA is unflared with turned under wavy petal margins; opens red (50A) edged red (53B); matures red (53C); 16mm (5/8") long x 14mm (9/16") wide. SEPALS are horizontal, tips reflexed; light orange (41C), orange (41B) at base, tipped olive green (153D) upper surface; orange (32A), dark orange (33A) at base, tipped light olive green (153C) lower surface; 20mm (13/16") long x 9mm (3/8") wide. TUBE is rose (52C); medium length and thickness; 22mm (7/8") long x 8mm (5/16") wide. STAMENS do not extend beyond the corolla; magenta (58B) filaments, light yellow (11B) anthers. PISTIL does not extend beyond the corolla; dark rose (58C) style, very pale orange (159B) stigma. BUD is ovate, pointed. FOLIAGE is dark green (136B) upper surface, medium green (138B) lower surface. Leaves are 44mm (1 3/4") long x 27mm (1 1/16") wide, ovate shaped, serrulated edges, acute tips and rounded bases. Veins are very dark reddish purple (186A), stems are plum (185B), branches are plum (183C). PARENTAGE: 'WALZ Harp' x unknown. Lax upright or stiff trailer. Self branching. Makes good basket. Prefers full sun. Best bloom and foliage colour in bright light. Tested three years in Koningshooikt, Belgium. Certificate N.B.F.K. at Meise. Distinguished by bloom colour and stalked petals.
Michiels 2002 BE AFS4973.

Waanrodense Menners. Upright. Double. COROLLA: half flared; opens dark reddish purple (64A); matures reddish purple (71B); 23mm (7/8") long x 21mm (13/16") wide. PETALOIDS: dark reddish purple (64A); 15mm (9/16") long x 5mm (3/16") wide. SEPALS are horizontal, tips reflexed; rose (61D) upper surface and dark rose (58C) lower surface; 38mm (1 1/2") long x 12mm (7/16") wide. TUBE is dark rose (54B); medium length & thickness; 17mm (5/8") long x 6mm (1/4") wide. FOLIAGE is dark green (135A) upper surface; medium green (138A) lower surface. PARENTAGE: 'Polskie Fuksji' x 'Impudence'.

475

Waanrodes Silver Star. Upright. Double. COROLLA is three quarter flared with turned under wavy petal margins; opens white (155D), pink (62C) base; matures white (155B); 27mm (1 1/16") long x 24mm (15/16") wide. PETALOIDS: same colour as corolla; 16mm (5/8") long x 7mm (1/4") wide. SEPALS are turned left & right; horizontal, tips recurved; white (155C) tipped light yellowish green (150C) upper surface; pale lavender (69D) tipped light yellowish green (150C) lower surface; 44mm (1 3/4") long x 11mm (7/16") wide. TUBE is white (155B); medium length & thickness; 13mm (1/2") long x 6mm (1/4") wide. FOLIAGE: dark green (137A) upper surface; medium green (138B) lower surface. Leaves are 84mm (3 5/16") long x 44mm (1 3/4") wide, ovate shaped. PARENTAGE: 'Sofie Michiels' x 'White Queen'. Meise 8-14-04. Distinguished by flower colour & shape.
Michiels 2005 BE AFS5760.

Wachter Van Meise. Upright/Trailer. Single. COROLLA: half flared, turned under wavy petal margins; opens dark reddish purple (72A); matures dark reddish purple (70A); 31mm (1 1/4") long x 23mm (7/8") wide. SEPALS: horizontal, tips recurved, twisted left to right; white (155C) tipped light yellowish green (149C) upper surface; white (155B) tipped light yellowish green (149C) lower surface; 47mm (1 7/8") long x 10mm (3/8") wide. TUBE: white (155C); short & thick; 12mm (7/16") long x 9mm (7/16") wide. STAMENS extend 11mm (7/16") beyond the corolla; magenta (71C) filaments; dark reddish purple (64A) anthers. PISTIL extends 26mm (1") beyond the corolla; rose (65A) style; pink (37C) stigma. BUD: elongated. FOLIAGE: dark green (137A) upper surface; medium green (138B) lower surface. Leaves are 59mm (2 3/8") long x 36mm (1 7/16") wide; ovate shaped, serrate edges, acute tips, rounded bases. Veins are yellowish green (144B), stems are yellowish green (144B) & plum (185C), branches are light green (139D). PARENTAGE: 'Manfried Kleinau' x 'Beth Robley'. Lax upright or stiff trailer. Self branching. Makes good upright. Prefers overhead filtered light, cool climate. Best bloom & foliage colour in filtered light. Tested 3 years in Koningshooikt, Belgium. Waanrode 7/5/08. Distinguished by bloom colour.
Michiels 2009 BE AFS7234.

Wajang. Upright/Trailer. Single. COROLLA is half flared, trumpet shaped, with toothed petal margins; opens reddish purple (64B); matures magenta (63B); 8mm (5/16") long x 6mm (1/4") wide. SEPALS are horizontal, tips reflexed; yellowish green (146B) upper surface; yellowish green (144A) lower surface; 12mm (1/2") long x 5mm (3/16") wide. TUBE is dark rose (51A); long, medium thickness, flat like 'F. splendens'; 29mm (1 1/8") long x 9mm (3/8") wide. FOLIAGE: dark green (147A) upper surface; medium green (147B) lower surface. Leaves are 56mm (2 3/16") long x 28mm (1 1/8") wide, elliptic shaped. PARENTAGE: ['F. splendens' x ('First Success' x 'F. magdalenae')] x ['F. splendens' x ('First Success' x 'F. magdalenae')]. Distinguished by flowers similar to 'F splendens var. cordifolia' but with red purple corolla.
de Graaff 2005 NL AFS5820.

Waldi. Upright. Single. COROLLA is quarter flared; opens dark purple (N79A); matures dark reddish purple (61A); 24mm (15/16") long x 27mm (1 1/16") wide. SEPALS are half up, tips recurved up; pale lavender (69B) upper & lower surfaces; 50mm (2") long x 10mm (3/8") wide. TUBE is pale lavender (65D), blushed dark rose (67C); 19mm (3/4") long x 10mm (3/8") wide. FOLIAGE: medium green (137C) upper surface; medium green (138B) lower surface. PARENTAGE: 'Checkerboard' x 'Rohees Queen'. Distinguished by distinctive colour contrast between corolla & SEPALS.
Burkhart 2006 DE AFS6051.

Waldis Erika. Upright. Double. COROLLA: three quarter flared, bell shaped; opens & matures pale purple (75C) striped reddish purple (66A); 15mm (9/16") long x 30mm (1 3/16") wide. SEPALS: half up, tips recurved up; reddish purple (66A) upper & lower surfaces; 25mm (1") long x 12mm (7/16") wide. TUBE: light magenta (66C); medium length & thickness; 10mm (3/8") long x 6mm (1/4") wide. STAMENS extend 20mm (3/4") beyond the corolla; dark reddish purple (64A) filaments; brown (177A) anthers. PISTIL extends 25mm (1") beyond the corolla; dark rose (67C) style; brown (177A) stigma. BUD: cordate. FOLIAGE: dark green (137A) upper surface; medium green (137B) lower surface. Leaves are 45mm (1 3/4") long x 25mm (1") wide; ovate shaped, serrulate edges, acute tips, rounded bases. Veins are medium green, stems are red purple, branches are green & red purple. PARENTAGE: 'Waldis Laura' x 'Bahia'. Medium upright. Makes good upright, standard or pyramid. Prefers overhead filtered light. Best bloom & foliage colour in filtered light. Tested 5 years in South Germany. Distinguished by bloom shape & colour. Also registered with the BFS. Dietrich 2009 DE AFS7114 BFS0088.

Waldis Lea. Upright. Single. COROLLA is three quarter flared, plate shaped, with smooth petal margins; opens white (155B), magenta (71C) base; matures white (155B), edged magenta (71C); 28mm (1 1/8") long x 28mm (1 1/8") wide. SEPALS are fully up, tips recurved; magenta (71C) upper & lower surfaces; 42mm (1 11/16") long x 10mm (3/8") wide. TUBE is magenta (71C); medium length & thickness; 20mm (13/16") long x 7mm (1/4") wide. FOLIAGE: medium green (146A) upper surface; yellowish green (146C) lower surface. Leaves are 40mm (1 9/16") long x 30mm (1 3/16") wide, ovate shaped. PARENTAGE: 'Krönprinzessin' x 'Delta's Wonder'. Distinguished by contrast of nearly aubergine SEPALS & pure white corolla. Dietrich 2005 DE AFS5860.

Waldis Tamara. Upright. Single. COROLLA opens salmon, matures lighter; corolla is none flared. SEPALS creamy rose on the upper and lower surfaces tipped green; SEPALS are half up with recurved tips. TUBE creamy rose. PARENTAGE 'Waldis Billy' x 'Waldis Gitta'
Dietrich 2009 DE BFS0110.

Waldis Winnie. Upright. Double. COROLLA: half flared, bell shaped; opens purple (90B); matures purple (80A); 18mm (11/16") long x 35mm (1 3/8") wide. SEPALS: half up, tips recurved up; greenish white (157A) upper surface; white (155B) lower surface; 30mm (1 3/16") long x 17mm (5/8") wide. TUBE: light green (145D); medium length & thickness; 12mm (7/16") long x 9mm (5/16") wide. STAMENS extend 18mm (11/16") beyond the corolla; rose (63C) filaments; pink (62A) anthers. PISTIL extends 30mm (1 3/16") beyond the corolla; white (155D) style; light yellow (5C) stigma. BUD: cordate. FOLIAGE: medium green (137B) upper surface; medium green (138A) lower surface. Leaves are 40mm (1 9/16") long x 30mm (1 3/16") wide; ovate shaped, serrulate edges, acute tips, rounded bases. Veins, stems & branches are green. PARENTAGE: D96 (own seedling) x 'Irene L. Peartree'. Tall upright. Makes good upright, standard, pyramid, pillar or decorative. Prefers overhead filtered light. Best bloom & foliage colour in filtered light. Tested 7 years

in South Germany. Distinguished by bloom shape & colour. Also registered with the BFS. Dietrich 2009 DE AFS7116 BFS0089.

Walita. Upright/Trailer. Semi Double. COROLLA: three quarter flared, turned under wavy petal margins; opens light reddish purple (73A) striped light pink (49B) & rose (55B); matures rose (68B) & reddish purple (67A); 30mm (1 3/16") long x 26mm (1") wide. PETALOIDS: Same colour as corolla; 17mm (5/8") long x 9mm (5/16") wide. SEPALS: horizontal, tips recurved, twisted left to right; white (155C) tipped light apple green (145B) upper surface; white (155B) tipped light apple green (145B) lower surface; 39mm (1 1/2") long x 17mm (5/8") wide. TUBE: white (155C) & light green (139D); medium length & thickness; 17mm (5/8") long x 7mm (1/4") wide. STAMENS extend 12mm (7/16") beyond the corolla; rose (63C) filaments; magenta (68A) anthers. PISTIL extends 33mm (1 5/16") beyond the corolla; rose (65A) style; pale pink (62D) stigma. BUD: bulbous. FOLIAGE: dark green (137A) upper surface; medium green (137D) lower surface. Leaves are 54mm (2 7/8") long x 32mm (1 1/4") wide; ovate shaped, serrulate edges, acute tips, rounded bases. Veins are light red purple (185D), stems are reddish purple (186B), branches are plum (185B). PARENTAGE: 'Coen Bakker' x 'Cotta Fairy'. Lax upright or stiff trailer. Self branching. Makes good basket or upright. Prefers overhead filtered light, cool climate. Best bloom & foliage colour in filtered light. Tested 3 years in Koningshooikt, Belgium. Waanrode 7/5/08. Distinguished by bloom colour.
Michiels 2009 BE AFS7235.

Wallace. Upright. Double. COROLLA opens blue violet (n88a), matures to pink purple; corolla is half flared. SEPALS dark pink (61c) on the upper and lower surfaces; SEPALS are fully up with recurved tips. TUBE green. PARENTAGE 'Helen Nicholls' x 'Jolu'. Nicholls 2009 UK BFS0141.

Walter Osseman. Upright. Double. COROLLA is three quarter flared with turned under smooth petal margins; opens reddish purple (67A), rose (63C) base; matures reddish purple (64B), light rose (63D) base; 31mm (1 1/4") long x 28mm (1 1/8") wide. PETALOIDS: light reddish purple (66C), rose (63C)base; 15mm (9/16") long x 11mm (7/16") wide. SEPALS are half down, tips recurved; pink (62C), tipped yellowish green (144B) upper surface; dark rose (55A), tipped

yellowish green (144A) lower surface; 38mm (1 1/2") long x 13mm (1/2") wide. TUBE is pale pink (36D); medium length & thickness; 17mm (11/16") long x 4mm (3/16") wide. FOLIAGE: dark green (136A) upper surface; medium green (138B) lower surface. Leaves are 96mm (3 13/16") long x 45mm (1 3/4") wide, ovate shaped. PARENTAGE: 'Sofie Michiels' x 'Annabelle Stubbs'. Meise 8-14-04. Distinguished by unique colour with spots.
Michiels 2005 BE AFS5746.

Waltraud Lechner. Upright. Single. COROLLA phlox purple (75c) veined red; corolla is half flared. SEPALS dark magenta rose (57a) on the upper and lower surfaces; SEPALS are horizontally held with recurved tips. TUBE dark magenta rose (57a). PARENTAGE 'Cliff's Own' x 'Delta's Parade'.
Klemm 2009 AT BFS0134.

WALZ Bandola. Upright. Single. COROLLA is half flared with smooth petal margins; opens and matures pink (55C); 9mm (3/8") long x 8mm (5/16") wide. SEPALS are half down, tips reflexed; pink (50D) upper surface, pink (49A) lower surface; 11mm (7/16") long x 7mm (1/4") wide. TUBE is light pink (49C), medium length and thickness; 18mm (11/16") long x 8mm (5/16") wide. STAMENS do not extend below the corolla; cream (11D) filaments and anthers. PISTIL extends 5mm (3/16") below the corolla; pink (49A) style, cream (11D) stigma. BUD is ovate with long TUBE. FOLIAGE is dark green (141A) upper surface and medium green (138A) lower surface. Leaves are 58mm (2 5/16") long x 43mm (1 11/16") wide, cordate shaped, serrulated edges, acute tips and cordate bases. Veins, stems and branches are green. PARENTAGE: [('F. *magdalenae*' x 'F. *fulgens grandiflora*') x 'Wendy Van Wanten'] x 'Prince Syray'. Small upright. Makes good upright. Prefers overhead filtered light. Best bloom and foliage colour in bright light. Tested three years in Herpen, The Netherlands. Award of Merit, VKC, KMTP, The Netherlands. Distinguished by pink upright flower.
Waldenmaier 2002 NL AFS4835.

WALZ Bekken. Upright. Single. COROLLA: unflared; round shaped, smooth petal margins; opens & matures magenta (57C); 13mm (1/2") long x 16mm (5/8") wide. SEPALS: horizontal; tips recurved; red (52C) upper surface; red (52A) lower surface; 25mm(1") long x 12mm (1/2") wide. TUBE: red (53C); short & thick; 20mm(13/16") long

x 15mm (9/16") wide. STAMENS: do not extend below corolla; light pink (36C) filaments, pale yellow (8D) anthers. PISTIL: extends 10mm (3/8") below the corolla, light pink (36C) style, very pale orange (19D) stigma. BUD: ovate. FOLIAGE: dark green (147A) upper surface; medium green (147B) lower surface. Leaves are 90mm (3 9/16") long x 60mm (2 3/8") wide, ovate shaped, serrulated edges, acute tips and rounded bases. Veins, stems & branches are green. PARENTAGE: 'WALZ Trumpet' x 'Prince Syray'. Medium upright. Makes good upright. Heat tolerant if shaded. Best bloom and foliage colour in bright light. Tested 4 years in Herpen, The Netherlands. Award of Merit, VKC, The Netherlands. Distinguished by horizontal flower and short, very thick TUBE.
Waldenmaier 2003 NL AFS5174.

WALZ Blokfluit. Upright. Single. COROLLA: quarter flared; bell shaped, smooth petal margins; opens & matures reddish purple (67A); 21mm (13/16") long x 25mm (1") wide. SEPALS: horizontal; tips recurved; reddish orange (43C) upper & lower surfaces; 22mm (7/8") long x 12mm (1/2") wide. TUBE: rose (52C); long, medium thickness; 38mm(1 1/2") long x 8mm (5/16") wide. STAMENS: extend 5mm (3/16") below corolla; light pink (36C) filaments & anthers. PISTIL: extends 15mm (9/16") below the corolla, light pink (36C) style, light yellow (3C) stigma. BUD: long TUBE, ovate tip. FOLIAGE: dark green (147A) upper surface; medium green (147B) lower surface. Leaves are 85mm (3 3/8") long x 55mm (2 3/16") wide, ovate shaped, serrulated edges, acute tips and rounded bases. Veins, stems & branches are green. PARENTAGE: 'WALZ Harp' x 'Prince Syray'. Medium upright. Makes good upright or standard. Heat tolerant if shaded. Best bloom and foliage colour in bright light. Tested 4 years in Herpen, The Netherlands. Award of Merit, VKC, The Netherlands. Distinguished by long TUBE and flower colour combination.
Waldenmaier 2003 NL AFS5180.

WALZ Bombardon. Upright. Single. COROLLA: quarter flared; bell shaped, smooth petal margins; opens & matures reddish purple (74B); 17mm (11/16") long x 17mm (11/16") wide. SEPALS: full down; tips recurved; red (45A) upper & lower surfaces; 30mm(1 3/16") long x 12mm (1/2") wide. TUBE: red (45A); long, medium thickness; 45mm(1 3/4") long x 5mm (3/16") wide. STAMENS: do not extend below corolla; reddish purple (74B) filaments & anthers.

PISTIL: does not extend below the corolla, dark rose (55A) style, rose (52C) stigma. BUD: long TUBE, ovate tip. FOLIAGE: dark green (147A) upper surface; medium green (147B) lower surface. Leaves are 105mm (4 1/8") long x 65mm (2 9/16") wide, ovate shaped, serrulated edges, acute tips and rounded bases. Veins, stems & branches are green. PARENTAGE: 'WALZ Harp' x unknown. Tall upright. Makes good upright. Prefers overhead filtered light. Best bloom and foliage colour in bright light. Tested 4 years in Herpen, The Netherlands. Award of Merit, VKC, The Netherlands. Distinguished by long TUBE, fused stamen filaments and pistil style; corolla separated from sepal. Waldenmaier 2003 NL AFS5179.

WALZ Cello. Upright. Single. COROLLA is half flared, bell shaped with smooth petal margins; opens and matures dark rose (67C); 8mm (5/16") long x 7mm (1/4") wide. SEPALS are half down, tips reflexed; pink (62C) upper surface, light pink (62B) lower surface; 9mm (3/8") long x 6mm (1/4") wide. TUBE is pale pink (62D), medium length and thick; 9mm (3/8") long x 6mm (1/4") wide. STAMENS do not extend below the corolla; pale pink (62D) filaments and yellow (5B) anthers. PISTIL extends 3mm (1/8") below the corolla; pale pink (62D) style, pale yellow (2D) stigma. BUD is ovate with short TUBE. FOLIAGE is dark green (141A) upper surface and medium green (138A) lower surface. Leaves are 70mm (2 3/4") long x 58mm (2 5/16") wide, cordate shaped, serrulated edges, acute tips and rounded bases. Veins and stems are green, branches are green and red. PARENTAGE: [('F. *magdalenae*' x 'F. *fulgens grandiflora*') x 'Wendy Van Wanten'] x 'Prince Syray'. Tall upright. Makes good upright. Prefers overhead filtered light. Best bloom and foliage colour in bright light. Tested three years in Herpen, The Netherlands. Award of Merit, VKC, KMTP, The Netherlands. Distinguished by tall growth and upright flowers. Waldenmaier 2002 NL AFS4836.

WALZ Cocktail. Upright/Trailer. Double. COROLLA: quarter flared; ellipse shaped, smooth petal margins; opens & matures with 4 petals light coral (38A) & 4 petals reddish purple (66B); 22mm (7/8") long x 17mm (11/16") wide. SEPALS: fully up; tips recurved; pink (62C) upper surface; rose (68C) lower surface; 33mm(1 5/16") long x 5mm (3/16") wide. TUBE: peach (37B); medium length & thin; 15mm(9/16") long x 5mm (3/16") wide. STAMENS: extend 8mm

(5/16) below corolla; light pink (36C) filaments, pale yellow (8D) anthers. PISTIL: extends 25mm (1") below the corolla, light pink (36C) style, pale yellow (8D) stigma. BUD: ovate, long, thin. FOLIAGE: dark green (147A) upper surface; medium green (147B) lower surface. Leaves are 80mm (3 1/8") long x 50mm (2") wide, ovate shaped, serrulated edges, acute tips and rounded bases. Veins are green, stems are light red & branches are green and red. PARENTAGE: 'Toos' x 'Prince Syray'. Lax upright or stiff trailer. Makes good basket or upright. Prefers overhead filtered light. Best bloom and foliage colour in filtered light. Tested 4 years in Herpen, The Netherlands. Award of Merit, VKC, The Netherlands. Distinguished by two colours of petals in the corolla. Waldenmaier 2003 NL AFS5176.

WALZ Dreumes. Upright/Trailer. Single. COROLLA is quarter flared, bell shaped with smooth petal margins; opens and matures light purple (70C); 2mm (1/16") long x 2mm (1/16") wide. SEPALS are horizontal, tips recurved; reddish purple (70B) upper surface, light purple (70C) lower surface; 4mm (3/16") long x 1mm (1/16") wide. TUBE is pale purple (70D), short with medium thickness; 4mm (3/16") long x 2mm (1/16") wide. STAMENS do not extend below the corolla; light purple (75B) filaments and white (155D) anthers. PISTIL does not extend below the corolla; light purple (70C) style and stigma. BUD is ovate with short TUBE. FOLIAGE is dark green (135A) upper surface and medium green (137C) lower surface. Leaves are 57mm (2 1/4") long x 9mm (3/8") wide, lanceolate shaped, serrulated edges, acute tips and acute bases. Veins and stems are green, branches are red. PARENTAGE: 'F. *paniculata*' (UC-B48-801) x 'F. *paniculata*' (UC-B48-801). Lax upright or stiff trailer. Makes good basket or miniature. Prefers overhead filtered light. Best bloom and foliage colour in bright light. Tested four years in Herpen, The Netherlands. Award of Merit, VKC, KMTP, The Netherlands. Distinguished by miniature growth. Waldenmaier 2002 NL AFS4837.

WALZ Fonola. Upright. Single. COROLLA: quarter flared; smooth petal margins; opens light rose (58D); matures rose (61D); 12mm (1/2") long x 10mm (3/8") wide. SEPALS: half down; tips reflexed; pale pink (49D) upper surface; pink (48D) lower surface; 17mm(11/16") long x 8mm (5/16") wide. TUBE: very pale orange (19D); medium length & thickness; 17mm (11/16") long x

8mm (5/16") wide. STAMENS: do not extend below corolla; light pink (36C) filaments, pale yellow (8D) anthers. PISTIL: does not extend below the corolla, light pink (36C) style, pale yellow (8D) stigma. BUD: ovate, curved tip. FOLIAGE: dark green (147A) upper surface; medium green (147B) lower surface. Leaves are 70mm (2 3/4") long x 40mm (1 9/16") wide, ovate shaped, serrated edges, acute tips and rounded bases. Veins, stems & branches are green. PARENTAGE: ['F. magdalenae' x ('F. fulgens grandiflora' x 'Wendy van Wanten')] x 'Prince Syray'. Medium upright. Makes good upright. Heat tolerant if shaded. Best bloom and foliage colour in bright light. Tested 4 years in Herpen, The Netherlands. Award of Merit, VKC, The Netherlands. Distinguished by upright TUBE-flowers in new colour combination.
Waldenmaier 2003 NL AFS5172.

WALZ Gusla. Upright/Trailer. Single. COROLLA: quarter flared; bell shaped, smooth petal margins; opens & matures rose (55B); 22mm (7/8") long x 20mm (13/16") wide. SEPALS: full down; tips recurved; pink (55C) upper surface; rose (55B) lower surface; 34mm(1 3/8") long x 9mm (3/8") wide. TUBE: dark rose (55A); long, medium thickness; 25mm(1") long x 7mm (1/4") wide. STAMENS: extend 5mm (3/16") below corolla; rose (55B) filaments, yellow (8B) anthers. PISTIL: extends 15mm (9/16") below the corolla, rose (55B) style, light pink (49C) stigma. BUD: ovate. FOLIAGE: dark green (147A) upper surface; medium green (147B) lower surface. Leaves are 75mm (2 15/16") long x 35mm (1 3/8") wide, ovate shaped, serrulated edges, acute tips and rounded bases. Veins, stems & branches are green. PARENTAGE: ('F. magdalenae' x 'F. fulgens grandiflora') x 'WALZ Floreat'. Lax upright or stiff trailer. Makes good basket. Heat tolerant if shaded. Best bloom and foliage colour in bright light. Tested 6 years in Herpen, The Netherlands. Award of Merit, VKC, The Netherlands. Distinguished by flower colour and shape.
Waldenmaier 2003 NL AFS5173.

WALZ Klokkenspel. Upright. Single. COROLLA: quarter flared; bell shaped, smooth petal margins; opens & matures reddish purple (67A); 14mm (9/16") long x 14mm (9/16") wide. SEPALS: half down; tips reflexed; light orange (41C) upper surface; reddish orange (43C) lower surface; 18mm(11/16") long x 8mm (5/16") wide. TUBE: pink (43D); medium length & thick;

19mm(3/4") long x 8mm (5/16") wide. STAMENS: do not extend below corolla; light pink (36C) filaments, pale yellow (8D) anthers. PISTIL: extends 5mm (3/16") below the corolla, light pink (36C) style, pale yellow (8D) stigma. BUD: ovate. FOLIAGE: dark green (147A) upper surface; medium green (147B) lower surface. Leaves are 75mm (2 15/16") long x 50mm (2") wide, ovate shaped, serrulated edges, acute tips and rounded bases. Veins, stems & branches are green. PARENTAGE: [('F. magdalenae' x 'F. fulgens grandiflora') x 'Wendy van Wanten'] x 'Prince Syray'. Medium upright. Makes good pyramid or upright. Heat tolerant if shaded. Best bloom and foliage colour in bright light. Tested 4 years in Herpen, The Netherlands. Award of Merit, VKC, The Netherlands. Distinguished by horizontal flower and pyramidal flowering pattern.
Waldenmaier 2003 NL AFS5178.

WALZ Panfluit. Upright/Trailer. Single. COROLLA is quarter flared, bell shaped with smooth petal margins; opens and matures orange (32A); 8mm (5/16") long x 7mm (1/4") wide. SEPALS are full down, tips reflexed; orange (32A) upper and lower surfaces; 12mm (1/2") long x 6mm (1/4") wide. TUBE is orange (32A), long and thin; 47mm (1 7/8") long x 4mm (3/16") wide. STAMENS do not extend below the corolla; orange (32A) filaments and yellow (10C) anthers. PISTIL extends 3mm (1/8") below the corolla; orange (32A) style, orange (32B) stigma. BUD is ovate with very long TUBE. FOLIAGE is dark green (137A) upper surface and medium green (137C) lower surface. Leaves are 90mm (3 9/16") long x 33mm (1 5/16") wide, lanceolate shaped, serrulated edges, acute tips and acute bases. Veins, stems and branches are dark red. PARENTAGE: ('F. magdalenae' x 'F. fulgens grandiflora') x 'F. triphylla'. Lax upright or stiff trailer. Makes good basket. Heat tolerant if shaded. Best bloom and foliage colour in bright light. Tested four years in Herpen, The Netherlands. Award of Merit, VKC, KMTP, The Netherlands. Distinguished by orange colour.
Waldenmaier 2002 NL AFS4838.

WALZ Sitar. Upright. Single & Semi Double. COROLLA: quarter flared; cordate shaped, smooth petal margins; opens & matures reddish orange (43C); 15mm (9/16") long x 13mm (1/2") wide. SEPALS: horizontal; tips recurved; light greenish white (157D) upper & lower surfaces; 30mm(1 3/16") long x 10mm (3/8") wide. TUBE: pale pink (36D);

long, medium thickness; 35mm(1 3/8") long x 10mm (3/8") wide. STAMENS: do not extend below corolla; light pink (49C) filaments, pale yellow (8D) anthers. PISTIL: extends 30mm (13/16") below the corolla, light pink (36C) style, pale yellow (8D) stigma. BUD: ovate, long. FOLIAGE: dark green (147A) upper surface; medium green (147B) lower surface. Leaves are 70mm (2 3/4") long x 50mm (2") wide, ovate shaped, serrulated edges, acute tips and rounded bases. Veins are green, stems are red & branches are green and red. PARENTAGE: 'WALZ Trumpet' x 'Berba's Coronation'. Medium upright. Makes good upright. Prefers overhead filtered light. Best bloom and foliage colour in filtered light. Tested 3 years in Herpen, The Netherlands. Award of Merit, VKC, The Netherlands. Distinguished by flower colour.
Waldenmaier 2003 NL AFS5175.

WALZ Spinet. Upright. Single. COROLLA is quarter flared, bell shaped with smooth petal margins; opens and matures red (47B); 13mm (1/2") long x 12mm (1/2") wide. SEPALS are half down, tips recurved; pale pink (62D) upper and lower surfaces; 15mm (5/8") long x 7mm (1/4") wide. TUBE is pale pink (62D), medium length and thickness; 20mm (13/16") long x 8mm (5/16") wide. STAMENS extend 5mm (3/16") below the corolla; pink (62C) filaments and light yellow (3C) anthers. PISTIL extends 5mm (3/16") below the corolla; pink (62C) style, light yellow (3C) stigma. BUD is ovate with short TUBE. FOLIAGE is dark green (137A) upper surface and medium green (137C) lower surface. Leaves are 68mm (2 11/16") long x 43mm (1 11/16") wide, cordate shaped, serrulated edges, acute tips and rounded bases. Veins and stems are green; branches are green and red. PARENTAGE: [('F. *magdalenae*' x 'F. *fulgens grandiflora*') x 'Wendy Van Wanten'] x 'Prince Syray'. Tall upright. Makes good upright. Prefers overhead filtered light. Best bloom and foliage colour in bright light. Tested three years in Herpen, The Netherlands. Award of Merit, VKC, KMTP, The Netherlands. Distinguished by horizontal to upright flowers and light pink/red colour combination.
Waldenmaier 2002 NL AFS4839.

WALZ Trombone. Upright/Trailer. Double. COROLLA is quarter flared, bell shaped with smooth petal margins; opens and matures orangy red (44B); 19mm (3/4") long x 21mm (13/16") wide. SEPALS are fully up, tips recurved; peach (33D) upper and lower surfaces; 40mm (1 9/16") long x 14mm (9/16") wide. TUBE is light yellow (10D), medium length and thick; 16mm (5/8") long x 9mm (3/8") wide. STAMENS extend 5mm (3/16) below the corolla; light pink (65B) filaments, rose (65A) anthers. PISTIL extends 20mm (13/16") below the corolla; light pink (65B) style, light yellow (2C) stigma. BUD is ovate with short TUBE. FOLIAGE is medium green (138A) upper surface and medium green (138B) lower surface. Leaves are 82mm (3 1/4") long x 43mm (1 11/16") wide, elliptic shaped, serrulated edges, acute tips and obtuse bases. Veins, stems and branches are green. PARENTAGE: 'WALZ Triangel' x 'Prince Syray'. Lax upright or stiff trailer. Makes good basket. Prefers overhead filtered light. Best bloom and foliage colour in bright light. Tested three years in Herpen, The Netherlands. Award of Merit, VKC, KMTP, The Netherlands. Distinguished by orange double blossom.
Waldenmaier 2002 NL AFS4840.

WALZ Ukelele. Upright. Single. COROLLA: quarter flared; bell shaped, smooth petal margins; opens pink (36A); matures light pink (38C); 8mm (5/16") long x 10mm (3/8") wide. SEPALS: half down; tips reflexed; light pink (65C) upper surface; white (155D) lower surface; 19mm(3/4") long x 10mm (3/8") wide. TUBE: light yellow (10D) shade side, pink (43D) sun side; medium length & thick; 17mm(11/16") long x 10mm (3/8") wide. STAMENS: do not extend below corolla; pale yellow (8D) filaments & anthers. PISTIL: extends 15mm (9/16") below the corolla, light pink (36C) style, pale yellow (8D) stigma. BUD: rounded, pointed. FOLIAGE: dark green (147A) upper surface; medium green (147B) lower surface. Leaves are 55mm (2 3/16") long x 40mm (1 9/16") wide, ovate shaped, serrated edges, acute tips and rounded bases. Veins, stems & branches are green. PARENTAGE: [('F. *magdalenae*' x 'F. *fulgens grandiflora*') x 'Wendy van Wanten'] x ('Toos' x 'Prince Syray'). Small upright. Makes good basket or upright. Prefers overhead filtered light. Best bloom and foliage colour in filtered light. Tested 3 years in Herpen, The Netherlands. Award of Merit, VKC, The Netherlands. Distinguished by horizontal flower and unique colour combination.
Waldenmaier 2003 NL AFS5177.

Warkant. Upright. Double. COROLLA: half flared; opens violet (77C); matures reddish purple (70B); 22mm (7/8") long x 19mm (3/4") wide. PETALOIDS: violet (77B); 16mm

(5/8") long x 12mm (7/16") wide. SEPALS are horizontal, tips recurved; light pink (65B) tipped apple green (144C) upper surface and pink (55C) tipped apple green (144C) lower surface; 34mm (1 3/8") long x 14mm (9/16") wide. TUBE is white (155C) striped medium green (141D); short & thick; 17mm (5/8") long x 7mm (1/4") wide. FOLIAGE is dark green (136A) upper surface; medium green (138A) lower surface. PARENTAGE: 'Vendelzwaaier' x 'Jackie Bull'. Michiels 2007 BE AFS6521.

Warke. Trailer. Semi Double. COROLLA is quarter flared; opens reddish purple (64B) with dark red (53A) base; matures purple (71A) with reddish purple (61B) base; 18mm (11/16") long x 12mm (7/16") wide. SEPALS are horizontal, tips recurved; reddish purple (58A) upper surface; dark red (53A) lower surface; 31mm (1 1/4") long x 8mm (5/16") wide. TUBE is reddish purple (61B); 10mm (3/8") long x 4mm (1/8") wide. FOLIAGE is medium green (137B) upper surface; medium green (137D) lower surface. PARENTAGE: 'Rosea' x 'Katrien Michiels'. Meise 8/13/05. Distinguished by bloom colour.
Michiels 2006 BE AFS6034.

Warum Nicht. Trailer. Double. COROLLA: half flared; opens light purple (N78C) blotched pale lavender (69C) and matures dark purple (N78A) blotched light rose (73C); 25mm (1") long x 17mm (5/8") wide. PETALOIDS: violet (76A) blotched light purple (75B); 13mm (1/2") long x 10mm (3/8") wide. SEPALS are horizontal, tips reflexed; white (155C) tipped light apple green (145B) upper & lower surfaces; 42mm (1 5/8") long x 16mm (5/8") wide. TUBE is white (155D); medium length & thickness; 20mm (3/4") long x 6mm (1/4") wide. FOLIAGE is dark green (137A) upper surface; medium green (138B) lower surface. PARENTAGE: 'Waanrodes Silver Star' x 'Ine Frozer'.
Michiels 2007 BE AFS6522.

Wäserpeer. Upright. Double. COROLLA: half flared; opens white (155B), striped light reddish purple (73A); matures white (155B), striped rose (68C); 19mm (3/4") long x 17mm (5/8") wide. PETALOIDS: same colour as corolla; 14mm (9/16") long x 7mm (1/4") wide. SEPALS: half down, tips reflexed; pale lavender (69C) tipped pale green (N138D) upper surface; light rose (73C) tipped pale green (N138D) lower surface; 31mm (1 1/4") long x 11mm (7/16") wide. TUBE: white (155D); medium length & thickness; 18mm

(11/16") long x 6mm (1/4") wide. FOLIAGE is dark green (139A) upper surface; medium green (138B) lower surface. PARENTAGE: 'De Brommel' x 'Bon Bon'.
Michiels 2007 BE AFS6324.

Waterman. Upright/Trailer. Single. COROLLA: Half flared;; opens red (53C) & dark reddish purple (72A); matures reddish purple (61B); 23mm (7/8") long x 18mm (11/16") wide. SEPALS: horizontal, tips reflexed; magenta (58B) tipped pink (54D) upper surface; magenta (58B) tipped red (53C) lower surface; 20mm (3/4") long x 8mm (5/16") wide. TUBE: light pink (62C); long & thin; 24mm (15/16") long x 11mm (7/16") wide. FOLIAGE is dark green (139A) upper surface; medium green (138B) lower surface. PARENTAGE: 'Ghislane' x 'Rohees New Millennium'.
Geerts L. 2007 BE AFS6384.

Weegschaal. Upright. Semi Double. COROLLA: half flared; opens reddish purple (N74B) & rose (52C); matures reddish purple (67A); 28mm (1 1/8") long x 26mm (1") wide. SEPALS: half down, tips reflexed; pink (51D) tipped light apple green (144D) upper surface; rose (52C) tipped light apple green (144D) lower surface; 31mm (1 1/4") long x 15mm (9/16") wide. TUBE: light pink (49B); medium length & thick; 27mm (1 1/16") long x 7mm (1/4") wide. FOLIAGE is dark green (136A) upper surface; medium green (138B) lower surface. PARENTAGE: 'WALZ Harp' x 'Ting-a-Ling'.
Geerts L. 2007 BE AFS6378.

Weleveld. Upright/Trailer. Double. COROLLA is half flared with smooth petal margins; opens pale violet (76A) and matures violet (75B); 23mm (15/16") long x 20mm (13/16") wide. SEPALS are half up, tips reflexed up; pink (62C) upper surface and pink (62A) lower surface; 46mm (1 13/16") long x 12mm (1/2") wide. TUBE is pale pink (62D), proportionally medium length and thickness; 20mm (13/16") long x 8mm (5/16") wide. STAMENS extend 10mm (3/8") below the corolla; magenta (68A) filaments and reddish purple (67A) anthers. PISTIL extends 22mm (7/8") below the corolla; pale pink (69A) style and yellow (10C) stigma. BUD is ovate, pointed. FOLIAGE is medium green (139B) on upper and medium green (138B) on lower surface. Leaves are 68mm (2 11/16") long x 32mm (1 1/4") wide, lanceolate shaped, serrulated edges, acute tips and rounded bases. Veins, stems and branches are green. PARENTAGE: 'Cymon' x

'Wastl'. Lax upright or stiff trailer. Makes good stiff trailer. Prefers full sun and warm climate. Best bloom colour in bright light. Tested five years in Göttingen, Germany. Distinguished by bloom and foliage colour combination.
Strümper 2002 DE AFS4806.

Wendy De Bie. Upright/Trailer. Single. COROLLA is quarter flared with turned under toothed petal margins; opens violet (84A), light violet (84B) base; matures light purple (81C); 22mm (7/8") long x 19 mm (3/4") wide. SEPALS are half down, tips recurved; white (155C) tipped yellowish green (149B), pink (62A) base, upper surface; pink (62A) lower surface; 31mm (1/4") long x 10mm (3/8") wide. TUBE is white (155A) striped light pink (65B), medium length and thickness; 12mm (1/2") long x 6mm (1/4") wide. STAMENS do not extend beyond the corolla; magenta (68A) filaments, yellow (6A) anthers. PISTIL extends 15mm (5/8") below the corolla; rose (65A) style; dark yellowish orange (14A) stigma. BUD is ovate. FOLIAGE is medium green (137C) upper surface, medium green (138B) lower surface. Leaves are 75mm (2 15/16") long x 40mm (1 9/16") wide, ovate shaped, serrulated edges, acute tips and cordate bases. Veins, stems and branches are light green (138D). PARENTAGE: 'Alda Alders' x 'Evy Penders'. Lax upright or stiff trailer. Self branching. Makes good basket. Prefers overhead filtered light and cool climate. Best bloom and foliage colour in filtered light. Tested three years in Leopoldsburg, Belgium. Certificate N.B.F.K. at Meise. Distinguished by bloom colour and shape.
Busschodts 2002 BE AFS4915.

Wendy Hebdon. Upright/Trailer. Semi Double. COROLLA: quarter flared; bell shaped, fluted petals; opens & matures light coral (38A); 20mm (3/4") long x 35mm (1 3/8") wide. SEPALS: horizontal, tips recurved; peach (38B) upper surface; light pink (38C) lower surface; 35mm (1 3/8") long x 15mm (9/16") wide. TUBE: light pink (36B); 20mm (3/4") long x 8mm (5/16") wide. FOLIAGE is medium green (139B) upper surface; medium green (139C) lower surface. PARENTAGE: 'Pink Marshmallow' x 'F. fulgens'. Also registered with the BFS.
Bielby & Oxtoby 2008 UK AFS6738 BFS0063.

Werner Koch. Trailer. Double. COROLLA: three quarter flared, turned under wavy petal margins; opens dark reddish purple (64A)

blotched pink (49A); matures dark rose (51A) blotched pink (48D); 30mm (1 3/16") long x 26mm (1") wide. PETALOIDS: Same colour as corolla; 12mm (7/16") long x 10mm (3/8") wide. SEPALS: horizontal, tips reflexed; rose (55B) tipped light greenish yellow (151C) upper surface; dark rose (55A) tipped light greenish yellow (151C) lower surface; 28mm (1 1/8") long x 13mm (1/2") wide. TUBE: pink (55C); medium length & thickness; 16mm (5/8") long x 5mm (3/16") wide. STAMENS extend 12mm (7/16") beyond the corolla; light pink (62C) filaments; dark reddish purple (72A) anthers. PISTIL extends 19mm (3/4") beyond the corolla; rose (52C) style; pale yellow (1D) stigma. BUD: bulbous. FOLIAGE: dark green (136B) upper surface; medium green (137D) lower surface. Leaves are 62mm (2 7/16") long x 32mm (1 1/4") wide; elliptic shaped, serrate edges, acute tips, rounded bases. Veins are dark reddish purple (187B), stems are dark reddish purple (187C), branches are dark red (185A) & light gerrn (139D). PARENTAGE: 'Manfried Kleinau' x 'Impala'. Natural trailer. Self branching. Makes good basket. Prefers overhead filtered light, cool climate. Best bloom & foliage colour in filtered light. Tested 3 years in Koningshooikt, Belgium. Waanrode 8/9/08, Outstanding. Distinguished by bloom colour combination.
Michiels 2009 BE AFS7236.

Werner Maassen. Trailer. Double. COROLLA: half flared, turned under wavy petal margins; opens violet (76A) & violet (76B); matures violet (75A); 26mm (1") long x 18mm (11/16") wide. PETALOIDS: Same colour as corolla; 17mm (5/8") long x 10mm (3/8") wide. SEPALS: half up, tips recurved up & horizontal, tips recurved, twisted left to right; white (155C) tipped light apple green (145C) upper surface; white (155D) tipped light apple green (145C lower surface; 43mm (1 11/16") long x 13mm (1/2") wide. TUBE: white (155C); medium length & thickness; 19mm (3/4") long x 6mm (1/4") wide. STAMENS extend 12mm (7/16") beyond the corolla; light rose (73C) filaments; brown (177C) anthers. PISTIL extends 18mm (11/16") beyond the corolla; white (155C) style; white (155B) stigma. BUD: elongated. FOLIAGE: dark green (137A) upper surface; medium green (137D) lower surface. Leaves are 50mm (2") long x 23mm (7/8") wide; elliptic shaped, serrate edges, acute tips, rounded bases. Veins are light grayish red (182C), stems are light grayish red (182D), branches are grayish red (181C). PARENTAGE: 'Niagara Falls' x 'Lavender

Heaven'. Natural trailer. Self branching. Makes good basket. Prefers overhead filtered light, cool climate. Best bloom & foliage colour in filtered light. Tested 3 years in Koningshooikt, Belgium. Waanrode 8/9/08. Distinguished by profuse blooms & colour combination.
Michiels 2009 BE AFS7237.

Werner Van Dessel. Upright/Trailer. Double. COROLLA is three quarter flared with turned under wavy petal margins; opens magenta (58B), matures dark rose (58C); 36mm (1 7/16") long x 22 mm (7/8") wide. PETALOIDS: dark rose (67C); 16mm (5/8") x 14mm (9/16"). SEPALS are horizontal, tips reflexed; rose (55B) upper surface, rose (51B) lower surface; 36mm (1 7/16") long x 20mm (13/16") wide. TUBE is pink (50D), long with medium thickness; 34mm (1 3/8") long x 8mm (5/16") wide. STAMENS do not extend beyond the corolla; dark rose (58C) filaments, cream (11D) anthers. PISTIL extends 35mm (1 3/8") beyond the corolla; rose (61D) style; pale orange (27B) stigma. BUD is round. FOLIAGE is dark green (136B) upper surface, medium green (146A) lower surface. Leaves are 70mm (2 3/4") long x 34mm (1 3/8") wide, ovate shaped, serrulated edges, acute tips and rounded bases. Veins are dark red (185A), stems are plum (184B), branches are plum (183C). PARENTAGE: 'WALZ Harp' x 'Blue Veil'. Lax upright or stiff trailer. Self branching. Makes good basket. Prefers overhead filtered light. Best bloom and foliage colour in filtered light. Tested three years in Itegem, Belgium. Certificate N.B.F.K. at Meise. Distinguished by profuse blooms and bloom shape.
Geerts L. 2002 BE AFS4927.

Western Rose. Upright. Double. COROLLA light plum purple. SEPALS light rose.
Ainsworth 2005 UK.

Wia Buze. Upright/Trailer. Double. COROLLA: quarter flared; smooth petal margins; opens reddish purple (80B) edged purple (77A); matures rose (67B), rose (51C) base; 37mm (1 7/16") long x 44mm (1 3/4") wide. PETALOIDS: magenta (71C) striped pink (48C); 21mm (13/16") long x 12mm (7/16") wide. SEPALS: half down, tips recurved; light rose (73C) tipped light yellow (11C) upper surface; rose (52C) tipped light yellow (11C) lower surface; 46mm (1 13/16") long x 20mm (3/4") wide. TUBE: pale tan (159A), striped & blushed light rose (73C); long, medium thickness; 23mm (7/8") long x 6mm (1/4") wide. STAMENS extend 11mm

(7/16") beyond the corolla; magenta (68A) filaments; dark reddish purple (69A) anthers. PISTIL extends 18mm (11/16") beyond the corolla; pink (62A) style; yellowish white (4D) stigma. BUD is long, Chinese lamp shaped. FOLIAGE is dark green (137A) upper surface; medium green (137C) lower surface. Leaves are 72mm (2 7/8") long x 41mm (1 5/8") wide; cordate shaped, serrulate edges, acute tips, rounded bases. Veins & stems are reddish brown, branches are very dark purple (187A). PARENTAGE: 'Schneckerl' x 'Bicentennial'. Tall/lax upright or stiff trailer. Makes good upright, pyramid or trellis. Prefers overhead filtered light. Best bloom colour in filtered light. Best foliage colour in bright light. Tested 3 years in Hoogezand, The Netherlands. Nominated by NKvF as recommendable cultivar. Distinguished by steel blue & pink colour combination of flower.
Scheper 2009 NL AFS7015.

Widnes Wonder. Upright. Single. COROLLA opens dark violet, matures to purple pink; corolla is un-flared. SEPALS white flushed pink on the upper surface, pink on the lower surface; sepals are half up with recurved tips. TUBE white flushed pink.
Bright 2008 UK BFS0097.

Wilhelm Hensen. Upright/Trailer. Double. COROLLA: half flared, turned under wavy petal margins; opens rose (52C) & dark rose (64C); matures magenta (58B); 25mm (1") long x 22mm (7/8") wide. PETALOIDS: violet (75A); 15mm (9/16") long x 12mm (7/16") wide. SEPALS: half up, tips recurved up; dark rose (54B) upper surface; rose (52B) lower surface; 26mm (1") long x 18mm (11/16") wide. TUBE: pink (52D); short & thick; 10mm (3/8") long x 6mm (1/4") wide. STAMENS extend 12mm (7/16") beyond the corolla; dark reddish purple (60C) filaments; purple (71A) anthers. PISTIL extends 16mm (5/8") beyond the corolla; dark rose (58C) style; pale pink (62D) stigma. BUD: bulbous. FOLIAGE: dark green (137A) upper surface; medium green (138B) lower surface. Leaves are 52mm (2 1/16") long x 28mm (1 1/8") wide; ovate shaped, serrate edges, acute tips, rounded bases. Veins are dark reddish purple (N186D), stems are dark reddish purple (187B), branches are dark reddish purple (N186C). PARENTAGE: 'Manfried Kleinau' x 'Dal's Conquest'. Lax upright or stiff trailer. Self branching. Makes good basket or upright. Prefers overhead filtered light, cool climate. Best bloom & foliage colour in filtered light. Tested 3 years in

Koningshooikt, Belgium. Waanrode 8/9/08. Distinguished by bloom & foliage colour combination.
Michiels 2009 BE AFS7238.

Will van Brakel. Upright/Trailer. Double. COROLLA is three quarter flared with smooth petal margins; opens purple (83B) and matures violet (86B); 25mm (1") long x 30mm (1 3/16") wide. SEPALS are horizontal, tips recurved; magenta (67B) upper and lower surfaces; 52mm (2 1/16") long x 21mm (13/16") wide. TUBE is rose (67D), proportionately medium length and thickness; 12mm (1/2") long x 8mm (5/16") wide. STAMENS extend 16mm (5/8") below the corolla; purple (77A) filaments and anthers. PISTIL extends 28mm (1 1/8") below the corolla; reddish purple (64B) style and light light yellow (11C) stigma. BUD is ovate and pointed. FOLIAGE is medium green (137C) on upper surface and medium green (137D) on lower surface. Leaves are 92mm (3 5/8") long x 43mm (1 11/16") wide, ovate shaped, serrated edges, acute tips and obtuse bases. Veins, stems and branches are red. PARENTAGE: 'Rohees Queen' x 'Breevis Evelien'. Lax upright or stiff trailer. Makes good stiff trailer. Prefers overhead filtered light and cool climate. Best bloom colour in filtered light. Tested four years in Knegsel, The Netherlands. Distinguished by bloom colour.
van Bree 2002 NL AFS4802.

Willeke Smit. Trailer. Double. COROLLA: half flared, smooth petal margins; opens purple (71A); matures reddish purple (61B); 22mm (7/8") long x 28mm (1 1/8") wide. SEPALS: horizontal; tips recurved; light pink (65B) upper surface; rose (68B) lower surface; 34mm (1 5/16") long x 17mm (11/16") wide. TUBE: light pink (65B); medium length & thickness; 18mm (11/16") long x 5mm (3/16") wide. STAMENS: extend 16mm (5/8") below corolla; magenta (61C) filaments, dark reddish purple (61A) anthers. PISTIL: extends 32mm (1 1/4") below the corolla, pink (62A) style, yellowish white (4D) stigma. BUD: ovate. FOLIAGE: dark green (137A) upper surface; medium green (137B) lower surface. Leaves are 82mm (3 1/4") long x 36mm (1 7/16") wide, lanceolate shaped, serrulated edges, acute tips and rounded bases. Veins & stems are red, branches are green. PARENTAGE: 'Bicentennial' x ('Rohees King' x 'Miniskirt'). Natural trailer. Makes good basket. Prefers overhead filtered light and cool climate. Best bloom and foliage colour in filtered light. Tested 4 years in

Knegsel, The Netherlands. Distinguished by blossom colour.
van Bree 2003 NL AFS5234.

Willem. Upright. Double. COROLLA is half flared with turned under smooth petal margins; opens reddish purple (74B), magenta (57B) base; matures dark rose (64C); 23mm (15/16") long x 20mm (13/16") wide. PETALOIDS: magenta (57C), magenta (57B) base; 16mm (5/8") long x 12mm (1/2") wide. SEPALS are half down, tips recurved; white (155D), tipped light apple green (145B) upper surface; white (155D), tipped light apple green (145B) lower surface; 34mm (1 5/16") long x 16mm (5/8") wide. TUBE is white (155C); medium length & thickness; 12mm (1/2") long x 5mm (3/16") wide. FOLIAGE: dark green (136B) upper surface; medium green (138B) lower surface. Leaves are 76mm (3") long x 40mm (1 9/16") wide, ovate shaped. PARENTAGE: 'Sofie Michiels' x 'Diana Wills'. Meise 8-14-04. Distinguished by flower colour combination.
Michiels 2005 BE AFS5748.

Willem Laurune. Trailer. Double. COROLLA: half flared; opens reddish purple (70B), pale lavender (69D) base; matures reddish purple (72B); 20mm (3/4") long x 17mm (5/8") wide. PETALOIDS: same colour as corolla; 14mm (9/16") long x 8mm (5/16") wide. SEPALS: horizontal, tips reflexed; pale lavender (69D) tipped medium green (141D) upper surface; pale lavender (69B) tipped medium green (141D) lower surface; 31mm (1 1/4") long x 13mm (1/2") wide. TUBE: light green (138C); medium length, thin; 18mm (11/16") long x 4mm (1/8") wide. FOLIAGE is dark green (137A) upper surface; medium green (138B) lower surface. PARENTAGE: 'De Brommel' x 'Bon Bon'.
Michiels 2007 BE AFS6319.

Willicher-Schützenfest. Trailer. Double. COROLLA: full flared, turned under wavy petal margins; opens rose (61D) & dark reddish purple (72A); matures magenta (58B) & reddish purple (64B); 33mm (1 5/16") long x 25mm (1") wide. PETALOIDS: Same colour as corolla; 24mm (15/16") long x 12mm (7/16") wide. SEPALS: horizontal, tips recurved; magenta (58B) tipped yellowish green (144A) upper surface; dark rose (58C) tipped yellowish green (144A) lower surface; 41mm (1 5/8") long x 19mm (3/4") wide. TUBE: dark rose (54A); medium length & thickness ; 22mm (7/8") long x 6mm (1/4") wide. STAMENS extend 23mm (7/8") beyond the corolla; reddish purple (61B) filaments;

485

reddish purple (67A) anthers. PISTIL extends 31mm (1 1/4") beyond the corolla; magenta (63A) style; rose (61D) stigma. BUD: bulbous. FOLIAGE: medium green (137B) upper surface; medium green (138B) lower surface. Leaves are 69mm (2 3/4") long x 37mm (1 7/16") wide; ovate shaped, serrate edges, acute tips, rounded bases. Veins are dark red (185A), stems are plum (184C), branches are dark grayish red (182A). PARENTAGE: 'Manfried Kleinau' x Jubie-Lin'. Natural trailer. Self branching. Makes good basket. Prefers overhead filtered light, cool climate. Best bloom & foliage colour in filtered light. Tested 3 years in Koningshooikt, Belgium. Waanrode   8/9/08,   Outstanding. Distinguished by bloom colour.
Michiels 2009 BE AFS7239.

Willow Tinsdale. Upright. Single. COROLLA: Unflared; smooth petal margins with neat whorl; opens violet (90D); matures light purple (78B); 17mm (5/8") long x 16mm (5/8") wide. SEPALS: horizontal, tips recurved; dark rose (51A) upper surface; dark rose (54B) lower surface; 23mm (7/8") long x 8mm (5/16") wide. TUBE: pink (37D); medium length & thickness; 12mm (7/16") long x 5mm (3/16") wide. FOLIAGE is greenish yellow (151A) upper surface; light yellowish green (146D) lower surface. PARENTAGE: 'Annabel' x unknown.
Bell 2007 UK AFS6402.

Willy Bittner. Upright/Trailer. Double. COROLLA: three quarter flared, smooth petal margins; opens dark reddish purple (61A) blushed rose (52C); matures reddish purple (61B); 26mm (1") long x 38mm (1 1/2") wide. SEPALS: half down, tips recurved; rose (52C) upper & lower surfaces; 42mm (1 5/8") long x 14mm (9/16") wide. TUBE: pink (49A); medium length & thickness; 18mm (11/16") long x 8mm (5/16") wide. STAMENS extend 23mm (7/8") beyond the corolla; rose (52C) filaments; rose (52B) anthers. PISTIL extends 48mm (1 7/8") beyond the corolla; pink (52D) style; light yellow (8C) stigma. BUD: elongated. FOLIAGE: medium green (137B) upper surface; medium green (138B) lower surface. Leaves are 96mm (3 13/16") long x 59mm (2 3/8") wide; ovate shaped, serrulate edges, acute tips, rounded bases. Veins & stems are red, branches are reddish brown. PARENTAGE: 'Bobby Juliana' x 'Daniel Pfaller'. Lax upright or stiff trailer. Makes good basket, upright or standard. Prefers full sun, warm climate. Heat tolerant if shaded. Best bloom & foliage colour in bright light. Tested 4 years in Bavaria, Southern Germany. Distinguished by bloom colour & shape.
Burkhart 2009 DE AFS7105.

Willy Van Wieter. Upright/Trailer. Semi Double to Double. COROLLA: half flared, turned under wavy petal margins; opens light reddish purple (73A) & violet (76A); matures light reddish purple (72C) & reddish purple (71B); 22mm (7/8") long x 19mm (3/4") wide. PETALOIDS: Same colour as corolla; 12mm (7/16") long x 8mm (5/16") wide. SEPALS: horizontal, tips recurved; white (155C) tipped light apple green (145B) upper surface; pale pink (56D) tipped light apple green (145B) lower surface; 36mm (1 7/16") long x 13mm (1/2") wide. TUBE: white (155C); medium length & thickness; 12mm (7/16") long x 6mm (1/4") wide. STAMENS extend 11mm (7/16") beyond the corolla; light rose (73C) filaments; light orange (31C) anthers. PISTIL extends 19mm (3/4") beyond the corolla; light purple (75B) style; pale yellow (1D) stigma. BUD: elongated. FOLIAGE: dark green (137A) upper surface; medium green (138B) lower surface. Leaves are 62mm (2 7/16") long x 36mm (1 7/16") wide; ovate shaped, serrulate edges, acute tips, rounded bases. Veins are plum (185C), stems are light red purple (185D), branches are light red purple (185D) & light green (138C). PARENTAGE: 'Manfried Kleinau' x 'Joergenhahn'. Lax upright or stiff trailer. Self branching. Makes good basket or upright. Prefers overhead filtered light, cool climate. Best bloom & foliage colour in filtered light. Tested 3 years in Koningshooikt, Belgium. Waanrode 8/9/08. Distinguished by bloom colour combination.
Michiels 2009 BE AFS7240.

Wilma van Druten. Upright/Trailer. Single. COROLLA is quarter flared, bell shaped, with turned under petal margins; opens & matures red (46C); 15mm (9/16") long x 7mm (1/4") wide. SEPALS are fully up, tips recurved; light green (142B), striped reddish purple (61B), tipped light green (143B) upper surface; pale yellow (5D), striped reddish purple (61B), tipped light green (143B) lower surface; 20mm (13/16") long x 6mm (1/4") wide. TUBE is pink (52D), striped reddish purple (61B); long & thin; 32mm (1 1/4") long x 3mm (1/8") wide at base to 6mm (1/4"). FOLIAGE: dark green (147A) upper surface; medium green (147B) lower surface. Leaves are 61mm (2 3/8") long x 3mm (1/8") wide, cordate shaped. PARENTAGE: 'Fuji-

San' x 'Pink Cornet'. Distinguished by racemes of flowers all year.
Koerts T. 2005 NL AFS5771.

Wim Ten Hoff. Upright/Trailer. Double. COROLLA: three quarter flared; smooth petal margins; opens pale lavender (69C) veined light purple (70C); matures pale lavender (69D); 24mm (15/16") long x 26mm (1") wide. PETALOIDS: Same colour as corolla; 18mm (11/16") long x 18mm (11/16") wide. SEPALS: horizontal, tips reflexed; pale pink (69A) upper & lower surfaces; 38mm (1 1/2") long x 16mm (5/8") wide. TUBE: dark red (47A); short & thick; 9mm (5/16") long x 9mm (5/16") wide. STAMENS extend 18mm(11/16") beyond the corolla; pale pink (69A) filaments; dark reddish purple (72A) anthers. PISTIL extends 44mm (1 3/4") beyond the corolla; pale pink (69A) style; dark reddish purple (72A) stigma. BUD: pegtop shape. FOLIAGE: dark green (147A) upper surface; light olive green (147C) lower surface. Leaves are 58mm (2 5/16") long x 36mm (1 7/16") wide; cordate shaped, wavy edges, acute tips, rounded bases. Veins & stems are light green, branches are brownish red. PARENTAGE: 'Götz-vier' x 'Bella Rosella'. Lax upright or stiff trailer. Makes good basket or upright. Prefers overhead filtered light. Best bloom colour in filtered light. Tested 3 years in Stadskanaal, The Netherlands. Distinguished by flower colour.
Koerts T. 2009 NL AFS7049.

Wim vander Palen. Upright/Trailer. Double. COROLLA: half flared, smooth petal margins; opens pink (62A); matures light pink (62B); 24mm (15/16") long 37mm (1 7/16") wide. SEPALS: fully up; tips recurved; light rose (68D) upper surface; rose (68C) lower surface; 21mm (13/16") long x 12mm (1/2") wide. TUBE: light rose (68D); short & thick; 8mm (5/16) long x 6mm (1/4") wide. STAMENS: extend 26mm (1") below corolla; rose (68B) filaments; pink (62A) anthers. PISTIL: extends 24mm (15/16") below the corolla; rose (68C) style; light yellow (4C) stigma. BUD: round, pointed. FOLIAGE: dark green (137A) upper surface; medium green (138A) lower surface. Leaves are 50mm (2") long x 41mm (1 5/8") wide, cordate shaped, serrulated edges, acute tips and rounded bases. Red veins, stems & branches. PARENTAGE: 'Roesse Carme' x 'Corie Spoelstra'. Lax upright or stiff trailer. Makes good stiff trailer. Prefers overhead filtered light and cool climate. Best bloom and foliage colour in filtered light. Tested 4 years in

Reusel, The Netherlands. Distinguished by bloom colour.
van Eijk 2004 NL AFS5503.

Windsword. Upright. Semi Double. COROLLA plum. SEPALS red.
Ainsworth 2005 UK.

Winfried Pouw. Upright/Trailer. Single. COROLLA: full flare; opens purple (71A); matures dark reddish purple (60A); 31mm (1 1/4") long x 34mm (1 3/8") wide. SEPALS are fully up, tips recurved; dark reddish purple (70A) upper & lower surfaces; 32mm (1 1/4") long x 14mm (9/16") wide. TUBE is dark reddish purple (70A); 20mm (3/4") long x 7mm (1/4") wide. FOLIAGE is dark green (137A) upper surface & medium green (138A) lower surface. PARENTAGE: 'Roesse Lupus' x 'Mission Bells'.
Spoelstra 2008 NL AFS6875.

Wiske Reynders. Trailer. Single. COROLLA is unflared with turned under wavy petal margins; opens pink (62A) edged violet (76A); matures light purple (80C), dark rose (58C) base; 24mm (15/16") long x 14 mm (9/16") wide. SEPALS are full down, tips recurved; magenta (58B) tipped light yellow green (150A) upper surface; red (53D) lower surface; 40mm (1 9/16") long x 11mm (7/16") wide. TUBE is light yellow (4C), long with medium thickness; 29mm (1 1/8") long x 5mm (3/16") wide. STAMENS extend 10mm (3/8") beyond the corolla; magenta (58B) filaments, orangy brown (163A) anthers. PISTIL extends 19mm (3/4") below the corolla; dark rose (58C) style; yellow (4A) stigma. BUD is ovate. FOLIAGE is dark green (137A) upper surface, medium green (137C) lower surface. Leaves are 92mm (3 3/4") long x 38mm (1 1/2") wide, elliptic shaped, serrulated edges, acute tips and rounded bases. Veins, stems and branches are reddish purple (58A). PARENTAGE: 'Alda Alders' x unknown. Natural trailer. Self branching. Makes good basket. Prefers overhead filtered light and warm climate. Best bloom and foliage colour in filtered light. Tested three years in Leopoldsburg, Belgium. Certificate N.B.F.K. at Meise. Distinguished by profuse blooms, 3 per leaf.
Busschodts 2002 BE AFS4916.

Witchipoo. Upright. Single. COROLLA: half flared, bell shaped, turned under smooth petal margins; opens dark purple (79B); matures dark purple (78A); 30mm (1 3/16") long x 10mm (3/8") wide. SEPALS: half down; tips reflexed; pale rose (73D), rose

(68B) at base upper surface; reddish purple (67A) lower surface; 20mm(13/16") long x 25mm (1") wide. TUBE: pale rose (73D); long, medium thickness; 18mm (11/16") long x 8mm (5/16") wide. STAMENS: extend 20mm (13/16") below corolla; reddish purple (67A) filaments; dark rose (67C) anthers. PISTIL: extends 25mm (1") below the corolla, reddish purple (72B) style; pale tan (159A) stigma. BUD: medium, elongated. FOLIAGE: medium green (146A) upper surface; yellowish green (146B) lower surface. Leaves are 70mm (2 3/4") long x 35mm (1 3/8") wide, cordate shaped, serrulated edges, acute tips and rounded bases. Veins & branches are green, stems are brown. PARENTAGE: 'Delta's Ko' x 'Doctor Foster'. Medium upright. Self branching. Makes good upright or standard. Heat tolerant if shaded. Prefers warm climate. Cold weather hardy to 32° F. Tested 4 years in Walthamstow, London, England. Distinguished by bloom colour combination. Allsop M. 2004 UK AFS5375.

Witte Van Munster. Trailer. Single. COROLLA: opens violet (75A); matures light purple (N78C); 21mm (13/16") long x 15mm (9/16") wide. SEPALS: horizontal, tips reflexed; white (155B) tipped apple green (144C) upper surface; pale lavender (65D) tipped apple green (144C) lower surface; 29mm (1 1/8") long x 10mm (3/8") wide. TUBE: white (155C) striped light green (141D); short, thick; 13mm (1/2") long x 7mm (1/4") wide. FOLIAGE is dark green (136B) upper surface; medium green (138A) lower surface. PARENTAGE: 'Jef Vander Kuylen' x 'Chandlerii'. Michiels 2007 BE AFS6320.

Witte Van Zichem. Upright. Single. COROLLA: three quarter flared, turned under wavy petal margins; opens cream (158D), matures white (155D); 24mm (15/16") long x 50mm (2") wide. PETALOIDS: three per sepal, same colour as corolla; 15mm (9/16") long x 10mm (3/8") wide. SEPALS: half down; tips recurved; white (155A), rose (63C) edge & base, tipped light green (142B) upper surface, white (155A), rose (63C) at base lower surface; 32mm (1 1/4") long x 14mm (9/16") wide. TUBE: white (155A); medium length & thickness; 14mm (9/16") long x 7mm (1/4") wide. STAMENS: extend 15mm (9/16") below the corolla; rose (63C) filaments, dark reddish purple (64A) anthers. PISTIL extends 25mm (1") below the corolla; white (155A) style, pale orange (23D) stigma. BUD: ovate. FOLIAGE: dark green (137A) upper surface; young

leaves yellowish green (144A) maturing to medium green (138B) lower surface. Leaves are 45mm (1 3/4") long x 32mm (1 1/4") wide, ovate shaped, serrulated edges, acute tips and rounded bases. Veins are yellowish green (144A), stems & branches are light reddish violet (180A). PARENTAGE: 'Annabel' x unknown. Medium upright. Makes good upright. Prefers overhead filtered light. Best bloom and foliage colour in filtered light. Tested 3 years in Wellen, Belgium. NBFK certificate at Meise. Distinguished by profuse blooms and bloom colour. Vanwalleghem 2003 BE AFS5094.

Worthersee. Upright/Trailer. Double. COROLLA dark rosy purple (80a) with deep orchid pink (63d) at base and flaming; corolla is fully flared. SEPALS deep orchid pink (63d), tipped green on the upper and lower surfaces; SEPALS are horizontally held with reflexed tips. TUBE deep orchid pink (63d). PARENTAGE 'Bahia' x 'Coq au Vin'. Klemm 2009 AT BFS0135.

Wout Das. Trailer. Double. COROLLA: 3 quarter flared; opens purple (83B); matures purple (72A); 21mm (13/16") long x 20mm (3/4") wide. SEPALS: fully up, tips reflexed; rose (63C) upper surface; magenta (63B) lower surface; 46mm (1 13/16") long x 14mm (9/16") wide. TUBE: rose (63C); medium length & thickness; 16mm (5/8") long x 8mm (5/16") wide. FOLIAGE is dark green (137A) upper surface; medium green (138A) lower surface. PARENTAGE: 'Rose Bradwardine' x 'Pinto The Blue'. Scharf 2007 NL AFS6570.

Wout Zonneveld. Upright. Single. COROLLA: quarter flared, bell shaped; smooth petal margins; opens & matures rose (52C) edged dark rose (58C); 11mm (7/16") long x 10mm (3/8") wide. SEPALS: half down, tips reflexed; rose (68C) tipped dark rose (58C) upper surface; white (155A) lower surface; 20mm (3/4") long x 7mm (1/4") wide. TUBE: dark rose (58C); medium length, thick; 28mm (1 1/8") long x 8mm (5/16") wide. STAMENS do not extend beyond the corolla; white (155B) filaments; light yellow (4B) anthers. PISTIL extends 8mm (5/16") beyond the corolla; rose (61D) style; light yellow (4C) stigma. BUD: triphylla shape. FOLIAGE: dark green (147A) upper surface; medium green (147B) lower surface. Leaves are 71mm (2 13/16") long x 48mm (1 7/8") wide; ovate shaped, serrulate edges, acute tips, rounded bases. Veins & stems are light green, branches are light green & reddish on top.

PARENTAGE: 'Thalia' (Turner) x 'Golding's Perle'. Medium upright. Makes good upright or standard. Prefers full sun. Best bloom & foliage colour in bright light. Tested 3 years in Stadskanaal, The Netherlands. Distinguished by contrast of light coloured SEPALS with dark coloured tips.
Koerts T. 2009 NL AFS7054.

Wyndhurst. Upright. Single. COROLLA opens dark violet, streaked pink, matures to light purple pink; corolla is un-flared. SEPALS white flushed pink on the upper surface, pink on the lower surface; sepals are horizontally held with recurved tips. TUBE white tinged pink. PARENTAGE ('Linda Grace' x 'Waveney Gem seedling') x 'Sophie Louise'.
Nicholls 2008 UK BFS0095.

Xerxes. Upright. Single. COROLLA bright purple. SEPALS very pale pink.
Ainsworth 2006 UK.

Yasmin Hinton. Upright/Trailer. Double. COROLLA: three quarter flared, turned under smooth petal margins; opens red (53D) splashed orange (33B) & light coral (38A); matures red (53C) splashed orange (33B) & light pink (38D); 25mm (1") long x 50mm (2") wide. PETALOIDS: same colour as corolla; 18mm (11/16") long x 6mm (1/4") wide. SEPALS: fully up; tips recurved; half twist counterclockwise; light pink (49B) tipped green upper surface; pale pink (49D) tipped green lower surface; 40mm(1 9/16") long x 14mm (9/16") wide. TUBE: pale pink (56C); medium length & thick; 22mm (7/8") long x 8mm (5/16") wide. STAMENS: extend 20mm (13/16") below corolla; dark rose (54B) filaments, white (155A) anthers. PISTIL: extends 30mm (1 3/16") below the corolla, pink (55C) style; grayish yellow (160A) stigma. BUD: medium, elongated. FOLIAGE: medium green (146A) upper surface; yellowish green (146B) lower surface. Leaves are 60mm (2 3/8") long x 40mm (1 9/16") wide, cordate shaped, serrulated edges, acute tips and cordate bases. Veins are green, stems are brown, branches are red. PARENTAGE: 'Coachman' x 'Marcus Graham'. Lax upright or stiff trailer. Self branching. Makes good basket or standard. Heat tolerant if shaded. Prefers warm climate. Cold weather hardy to 32° F. Best bloom colour in bright light. Tested 3 years in Walthamstow, London, England. Distinguished by bloom colour combination and pink splashing on petals.
Allsop M.R. 2003 UK AFS5150.

Yellow Heart. Trailer. Single. COROLLA is quarter flared, square shaped, with wavy petal margins; opens light yellowish orange (19B); matures pale tan (159A); 15mm (9/16") long x 16 mm (5/8") wide. SEPALS are half down, tips reflexed; pink (49A) upper & lower surfaces; 27mm (1 1/16") long x 11mm (7/16") wide. TUBE is pink (49A), long, medium thickness; 43mm (1 11/16") long x 11mm (7/16") wide. FOLIAGE: dark green (147A) upper surface; medium green (147B) lower surface. Leaves are 68mm (2 11/16") long x 43 mm (1 11/16") wide, ovate shaped. PARENTAGE: ('F. apetala' x 'Alaska') x {'WALZ Polka' x [('F. denticulata' x 'F. decussata') x ('Whiteknight's Amethyst' x 'F. procumbens')]}. Natural trailer. Self branching. Distinguished by special colour combination.
de Boer J. 2005 NL AFS5650.

YMYR. Upright. Single. COROLLA lilac. SEPALS white.
Ainsworth 2005 UK.

Your Lovely. Upright/Trailer. Double. COROLLA: half flared, turned up petal margins; opens reddish purple (61B); matures magenta (61C); 35mm (1 3/8") long x 15mm (9/16") wide. SEPALS: half down, tips recurved; cream (158D) tipped green upper surface; pink (52D) streaked cream, tipped green lower surface; 40mm (1 9/16") long x 18mm (11/16") wide. TUBE: greenish white (157A); medium length & thickness; 18mm (11/16") long x 8mm (5/16") wide. STAMENS extend 18mm (11/16") beyond the corolla; magenta (63B) filaments; magenta (61C) anthers. PISTIL extends 30mm (1 3/16") beyond the corolla; pale pink (62D) style; cream (158D) stigma. BUD: ovate. FOLIAGE: medium green (139A) upper surface; medium green (138A) lower surface. Leaves are 90mm (3 9/16") long x 40mm (1 9/16") wide; lanceolate shaped, serrate edges, acute tips, acute bases. Veins are light green, stems are light brown, branches are reddish green. PARENTAGE: 'Princess Rebecca' x 'Lovely Charlotte'. Lax upright or stiff trailer. Makes good upright. Prefers overhead filtered light. Best bloom colour in filtered light. Tested 3 years in Rayleigh, Essex, England. Distinguished by blossom colour & shape.
Smith R. 2009 UK AFS7126.

You're Beautiful. Upright. Semi Double. COROLLA: Half flared, bell shaped; opens & matures pale pink (36D); 18mm (11/16") long x 25mm (1") wide. SEPALS: half up, tips

recurved up; rose (68C) tipped green upper & lower surfaces; 24mm (15/16") long x 12mm (7/16") wide. TUBE: light yellowish green (150C); medium length & thickness; 13mm (1/2") long x 5mm (3/16") wide. FOLIAGE is dark green (147A) upper surface; medium green (147B) lower surface. PARENTAGE: 'Swingtime' x 'Lovely Charlotte'.
Smith R. 2007 UK AFS6475.

You're Gorgeous. Upright/Trailer. Double. COROLLA: Quarter flared; opens white (155D); matures white (155D) veined pink; 25mm (1") long x 20mm (3/4") wide. SEPALS: half up, tips recurved up; magenta (63B) streaked & tipped green upper surface; magenta (63B) tipped green lower surface; 30mm (1 3/16") long x 24mm (15/16") wide. TUBE: medium green (135B); medium length & thickness; 12mm (7/16") long x 5mm (3/16") wide. FOLIAGE is medium green (137B) upper surface; medium green (138B) lower surface. PARENTAGE: 'Gemma Fisher' x 'Annabel Stubbs'.
Smith R. 2007 UK AFS6476.

Yvette Klessens. Trailer. Single. COROLLA: three quarter flared, smooth petal margins; opens violet (90C); matures light purple (78B); 25mm (1") long 32mm (1 1/4") wide. SEPALS: fully up; tips recurved; rose (68B) upper surface; pink (62A) lower surface; 42mm (1 5/8") long x 19mm (3/4") wide. TUBE: rose (68B); medium length & thickness; 9mm (3/8") long x 5mm (3/16") wide. STAMENS: extend 10mm (3/8") below corolla; magenta (68A) filaments; rose (63C) anthers. PISTIL: extends 41mm (1 5/8") below the corolla; rose (68B) style; pal;e rose (73D) stigma. BUD: ovate, pointed. FOLIAGE: dark green (137A) upper surface; medium green (138A) lower surface. Leaves are 65mm (2 9/16") long x 21mm (13/16") wide, lanceolate shaped, serrulated edges, acute tips and acute bases. Red veins, stems & branches. PARENTAGE: ('Cameron Ryle' x 'Parasol') x 'Loeky'. Natural trailer. Self branching. Makes good basket. Prefers overhead filtered light and cool climate. Best bloom and foliage colour in filtered light. Tested 4 years in Knegsel, The Netherlands. Distinguished by bloom colour.
Roes 2004 NL AFS5462.

Yvonne. Upright. Double. COROLLA opens aubergine flushed beetroot red at base, matures to beetroot red flushed pink at base; corolla is half flared. SEPALS waxy beetroot red on the upper and lower surfaces; sepals are half up with recurved tips. TUBE waxy

beetroot red. PARENTAGE 'Gerharda's Aubergine' x 'Unknown'. This cultivar has proven to be hardy in Derbyshire, UK.
Parkes 2008 UK BFS0065.

Yvonne Hasselerharm. Upright/Trailer. Double. COROLLA: 3 quarter flared; opens pink (62C); matures pale pink (62D); 22mm (7/8") long x 20mm (3/4") wide. SEPALS: horizontal; tips recurved; light pink (65B) upper surface; rose (65A) lower surface; 40mm (1 9/16") long x 14mm (9/16") wide. TUBE: light pink (65B); medium length & thickness; 17mm (5/8") long x 5mm (3/16") wide. FOLIAGE is dark green (137A) upper surface; medium green (138B) lower surface. PARENTAGE: ('Cameron Ryle' x 'Parasol') x 'Allure'.
Roes 2007 NL AFS6311.

Ywan Van Cortenbach. Trailer. Double. COROLLA: three quarter flared; opens dark rose (51A) & light purple (82D); matures rose (65A); 19mm (3/4") long x 25mm (1") wide. PETALOIDS: same colour as corolla; 16mm (5/8") long x 12mm (7/16") wide. SEPALS: horizontal, tips recurved; pale pink (56D) tipped light yellowish green (150C) upper surface; pale pink (62D) tipped light yellowish green (150C) lower surface; 32mm (1 1/4") long x 13mm (1/2") wide. TUBE: white (155B); 14mm (9/16") long x 5mm (3/16") wide. FOLIAGE is dark green (137A) upper surface; medium green (138B) lower surface. PARENTAGE: 'Pink La Campanella' x unknown.
Cuppens 2008 BE AFS6751.

Zaandijk. Upright. Single. COROLLA is three quarter flared with turned up petal margins; opens & matures white (155B); 23mm (15/16") long x 23mm (15/16") wide. SEPALS are horizontal, tips recurved; rose (55B) tipped pale yellow (158B) upper surface; rose (55B) tipped pale yellowish green (154D) lower surface; 28mm (1 1/8") long x 10mm (3/8") wide. TUBE is pink (54D) & rose (55B); medium length & thickness; 15mm (9/16") long x 8mm (5/16") wide. FOLIAGE: dark green (147A) upper surface; medium green (147B) lower surface. Leaves are 25mm (1") long x 17mm (11/16") wide, ovate shaped. PARENTAGE: 'Cor Bruÿn' x unknown. Distinguished by compact growth & flower colour.
Krom 2005 NL AFS5836.

Zachaaron. Upright/Trailer. Semi Double. COROLLA: Half flared; opens violet (N82C), light rose (73B) base; matures light purple

(N78C), light purple (N78C) base; 29mm (1 1/8") long x 26mm (1") wide. PETALOIDS: same colour as corolla; 20mm (3/4") long x 12mm (7/16") wide. SEPALS: fully up, tips recurved, turned left; pale purple (75D) tipped apple green (144C) upper surface; rose (68C) tipped apple green (144C) lower surface; 47mm (1 7/8") long x 13mm (1/2") wide. TUBE: white (155C); medium length & thickness; 19mm (3/4") long x 5mm (3/16") wide. FOLIAGE is dark green (137A) upper surface; medium green (137D) lower surface. PARENTAGE: 'Allison Reynolds' x 'Onbekend'.
Willems 2007 BE AFS6600.

Zannekin Nicolaas. Upright. Single. COROLLA: quarter flared; opens dark rose (54A); matures rose (52B); 17mm (5/8") long x 15mm (9/16") wide. SEPALS: half down, tips reflexed; red (53D) & dark rose (54B) tipped olive green (152D) upper surface; rose (52B) tipped olive green (152D) lower surface; 24mm (15/16") long x 8mm (5/16") wide. TUBE: dark rose (54A); 48mm (1 7/8") long x 7mm (1/4") wide. FOLIAGE is medium green (137B) upper surface; medium green (138B) lower surface. PARENTAGE: 'Lechlade Rocket' x 'Tubingen 2001'.
Vandenbussche 2008 BE AFS6736.

Zarte Versuchung. Upright. Single. COROLLA: quarter flared, toothed petal margins; opens pale lavender (69C) veined pink (62C); matures pale lavender (69B); 20mm (3/4") [maturing to 32mm (1 3/16)] long x 20mm (3/4") wide. SEPALS: horizontal, tips recurved; pink (62C), later pink (62A) upper surface; pale pink (62D) lower surface; 55mm (2 3/16") long x 10mm (3/8") wide. TUBE: cream (11D); medium length, thin; 16mm (5/8") long x 7mm (1/4") wide. STAMENS extend 10mm (3/8") beyond the corolla; rose (61D) filaments; magenta (61C) anthers. PISTIL extends 18mm (11/16") beyond the corolla; pink (62C) style; cream (11D) stigma. BUD: elongated. FOLIAGE: medium green (137C) upper surface; medium green (138B) lower surface. Leaves are 75mm (3") long x 43mm (1 11/16") wide; ovate shaped, serrate edges, acute tips, rounded bases. Veins are red progressing to light green, stems are red, branches are light brown. PARENTAGE: 'Grayrigg' x 'Carla Johnston'. Medium upright. Self branching. Makes good upright. Prefers overhead filtered light, warm climate. Heat tolerant if shaded. Best bloom & foliage colour in filtered light. Tested 4 years in Bavaria, Southern Germany. Distinguished

by beautiful lavender & pink colour combination.
Burkhart 2009 DE AFS7103.

Zenderen. Trailer. Double. COROLLA is half flared with smooth petal margins; opens magenta (58B) and matures rose (52B); 18mm (11/16") long x 20mm (13/16") wide. SEPALS are horizontal, tips recurved; rose (51C) upper surface, rose (52B) lower surface; 48mm (1 7/8") long x 17mm (11/16") wide. TUBE is red (51C), proportionately medium length and thickness; 27mm (1 1/16") long x 8mm (5/16") wide. STAMENS extend 10mm (3/8") below the corolla; rose (55B) filaments and light pink (49C) anthers. PISTIL extends 24mm (15/16") below the corolla; rose (55B) style and light pink (49C) stigma. BUD is long TUBEd, tear drop shaped and pointed. FOLIAGE is medium green (137B) on upper surface and medium green (138B) on lower surface. Leaves are 68mm (2 11/16") long x 29mm (1 1/8) wide, lanceolate shaped, serrated edges, acute tips and rounded bases. Veins, stems and branches are red. PARENTAGE: 'WALZ Mandoline' x ('Annabel' x 'Vrijheid'). Natural trailer. Makes good basket. Prefers overhead filtered light and cool climate. Best bloom colour in filtered light. Tested four years in Knegsel, The Netherlands. Distinguished by bloom and foliage combination.
Roes 2002 NL AFS4801.

Zifi. Upright. Single. COROLLA: quarter flared, smooth petal margins, petals curled; opens dark rose (55A); matures magenta (57B), dark rose (48D) at base; 12mm (1/2") long x 13mm (1/2") wide. SEPALS: half down; tips recurved up at tips; waxy pinkish white (155D) upper & lower surfaces; 15mm(9/16") long x 5mm (3/16") wide. TUBE: waxy white (155A); medium length, thin; 9mm (3/8") long x 4mm (3/16") wide. STAMENS: extend 8mm (5/16") below corolla; rose (52B) filaments; pale yellow (158B) anthers. PISTIL: extends 15mm (9/16") below the corolla; white (155D), pubescent style; pale yellow (1D) stigma, folding 90°. BUD: rounded. FOLIAGE: dark green (147A) upper surface; medium green (147B) lower surface. Leaves are 35mm (1 3/8") long x 21mm (13/16") wide, lanceolate shaped, serrated edges, acute tips and rounded bases. Veins & stems are green, branches are brownish. PARENTAGE: 'Flash' x unknown. Small upright. Makes good upright. Prefers overhead filtered light & cool climate. Best bloom and foliage colour in

filtered light. Tested 3 years in Torino & Como, Italy. Distinguished by small, waxy, profuse flowers.
Ianne 2003 IT AFS5138.

Zita. Upright. Semi Double. COROLLA is half flared with smooth petal margins, very fluffy; opens violet (86B); matures violet (86D); 17mm (11/16") long x 27mm (1 1/16") wide. SEPALS are half up, tips recurved up; red (45C) upper surface, red (45D) lower surface; 22mm (7/8") long x 14mm (9/16") wide. TUBE is red (45C); short, thick; 12mm (1/2") long x 8mm (5/16") thick. STAMENS extend 10mm (3/8") beyond the corolla; red (45A) filaments and anthers. PISTIL extends 30mm (1 3/16") beyond the corolla; red (45C) style, red (45A) stigma. BUD is drop shaped. FOLIAGE is dark green (137A) upper surface, medium green (137C) lower surface. Leaves are 55mm (2 3/16") long x 32mm (1 1/4") wide, cordate shaped, serrulated edges, acute tips and cordate bases. Veins are green, stems and branches are brown. PARENTAGE: 'La Campanella' x 93/075. Medium upright. Self branching. Makes good upright or standard. Prefers full sun. Best bloom colour in bright light. Tested eight years in Amstetten, Austria. Distinguished by small profuse flowers and flower/leaf contrast.
Gindl 2002 AT AFS5050.

Zoels Belleke. Upright/Trailer. Single. COROLLA is quarter flared; opens reddish purple (67A); matures reddish purple (61B); 17mm (5/8") long x 15mm (9/16") wide. SEPALS are half down, tips reflexed; dark rose (51A), tipped light greenish yellow (151C) upper surface; magenta (58B), tipped light greenish yellow (151C) lower surface; 19mm (3/4") long x 9mm (5/16") wide. TUBE is rose (54C); long & thick; 23mm (7/8") long x 7mm (1/4") wide. FOLIAGE is dark green (137A) upper surface; medium green (138B) lower surface. PARENTAGE: found seedling.
Hermans 2007 BE AFS6420.

Zoeteke Zoet 20. Trailer. Single to Semi Double. COROLLA: quarter flared; opens dark purple (N78A), light rose (73B) base; matures dark reddish purple (72A); 24mm (15/16") long x 19mm (3/4") wide. SEPALS: half down, tips reflexed; light rose (73B) tipped light yellowish green (150B) upper surface; dark rose (58C) tipped light yellowish green (150B) lower surface; 36mm (1 7/16") long x 11mm (7/16") wide. TUBE: pale pink (62D); long, medium thickness; 27mm (1 1/16") long x 5mm (3/16") wide.

FOLIAGE is dark green (137A) upper surface; medium green (137C) lower surface.
PARENTAGE: 'Rune Peeters' x 'Illusion'.
Michiels 2007 BE AFS6318.

Zus Liebregts. Upright/Trailer. Double. COROLLA is three quarter flared; opens violet (84A); matures light violet (84B); 18mm (11/16") long x 16mm (5/8") wide. SEPALS are half down, tips reflexed; pink (62C) tipped green upper surface; light pink (62B) tipped green lower surface; 26mm (1") long x 11mm (7/16") wide. TUBE is pink (62C); 21mm (13/16") long x 6mm (1/4") wide. FOLIAGE: dark green (137A) upper surface; medium green (138A) lower surface. PARENTAGE: 'Bicentennial' x 'Sofie Michiels'. Distinguished by bloom & foliage combination.
Buiting 2006 NL AFS6106.

ZYZZY. Upright. Double. COROLLA creamy white. SEPALS creamy white.
Ainsworth 2005 UK.

Country Codes:

AT	Austria
BE	Belgium
DE	Germany
FR	France
IT	Italy
NL	Netherlands
NZ	New Zealand
SA	South Africa
UK	United Kingdom
USA	United States of America

Sepal and Corolla types:

Sepal positions:

Fully Up

½ Up

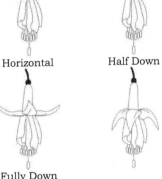

Horizontal

Half Down

Fully Down

Corolla Shapes:

No Flare

¼ Flared

½ Flared

¾ Flared

Fully Flared

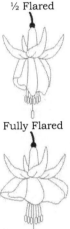

Sepal Tips:

Tips Recurved   Tips Reflexed

Further Reading:

Boullemier, Leo B. The Checklist of Species and Cultuvars of the Genus Fuchsia – Published 1985 and the revised edition published in 1991.

Ewart, Ron. Fuchsia Lexicon. Published 1982.

Goulding, Edwin. Fuchsias the Complete Guide. Published 1995.

Nijhuis, Miep. The Complete Handbook. Published 1994.

Penny, Jock. The World Book of Fuchsia Volume 1. Published 2002.

Penny, Jock. The World Book of Fuchsia Volume 2. Published 2003.

Fuchsias on the Internet:

www.findthatfuchsia.info – Lists over 12,000 fuchsias and hundred of Fuchsia photos.

www.fuchsiabooks.co.uk – Sells good quality second hand books on Fuchsias (all of the above books are available).

www.thebfs.org – Home of The British Fuchsia Society.

www.eurofuchsia.org – An association of European Fuchsia Societies.

www.americanfuchsiasociety.org – Home of the American Fuchsia Society.

www.fuchsiamagic.com – Has hundreds of high quality Fuchsia photos.

Thanks to:

Peter Swann – Front cover design, Sepals & Corolla drawings and for being a great neighbour. Peter has his own website at www.peterswann.co.uk

My wife Vickie Anne for putting up with me spending so much time working away on the computer and providing endless cups of coffee!

Finally, the British Fuchsia Society for helping with the joint venture into publishing this book.

Printed and Bound by Berforts Group, Stevenage Herts